EVIDENCE

NINTH EDITION

STEVEN L. EMANUEL

Founder & Editor-in-Chief, *Emanuel Law Outlines* and
Emanuel Bar Review
Harvard Law School, J.D. 1976
Member, NY, CT, MD and VA bars

The *Emanuel® Law Outlines* Series

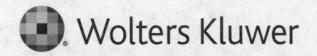 Wolters Kluwer

About Wolters Kluwer Legal & Regulatory U.S.

Wolters Kluwer Legal & Regulatory U.S. delivers expert content and solutions in the areas of law, corporate compliance, health compliance, reimbursement, and legal education. Its practical solutions help customers successfully navigate the demands of a changing environment to drive their daily activities, enhance decision quality and inspire confident outcomes.

Serving customers worldwide, its legal and regulatory portfolio includes products under the Aspen Publishers, CCH Incorporated, Kluwer Law International, ftwilliam.com and MediRegs names. They are regarded as exceptional and trusted resources for general legal and practice-specific knowledge, compliance and risk management, dynamic workflow solutions, and expert commentary.

Dedication

In memory of my father-in-law
Herman Mandel

Abbreviations Used in Text

B,M&G — Broun, Mosteller & Giannelli, *Evidence Cases and Materials* (7th Ed. 2007)

FRE — *Federal Rules of Evidence* (as restyled effective December 2011)

Graham — Michael Graham, *Federal Practice and Procedure*, Interim Edition (1992)

G&N — Green and Neeson, *Problems, Cases and Materials on Evidence* (2d Ed. 1994)

Imwinkelried — Edward Imwinkelried, *Evidentiary Foundations* (2d Ed. 1989)

L&S — Lempert & Saltzburg, *A Modern Approach to Evidence* (2d Ed. 1983)

Lilly — Graham Lilly, *An Introduction to the Law of Evidence* (2d Ed. 1987)

McC — Strong *et. al*, *McCormick on Evidence* (4th Ed. 1992)

M&K — Mueller & Kirkpatrick, *Evidence* (3d Ed. 2003) (textbook)

M&K (5th) -- Mueller & Kirkpatrick, *Evidence* (5th Ed. 2012) (textbook)

M&K (Csbk) — Mueller & Kirkpatrick, *Evidence Under the Rules* (7th Ed. 2011) (casebook)

S&R — Saltzburg and Redden, *Federal Rules of Evidence Manual* (4th Ed. 1986)

W&P — Waltz & Park, *Cases and Materials on Evidence* (8th Ed. 1995)

W,M,A&B — Weinstein, Mansfield, Adams & Berger, *Cases and Materials on Evidence* (8th Ed. 1988, with 1996 supplement)

W&B — Weinstein & Berger, *Weinstein's Evidence* (1986, with 1995 Supp.)

Wellborn (4th) — Wellborn, *Cases and Materials on The Rules of Evidence* (4th Ed. 2007)

ACKNOWLEDGMENTS

The diagrams on pages 183, 187, 188 and 189 of *Emanuel* on *Evidence* and the chart on page 572 were adapted in part from Lempert and Saltzburg, *A Modern Approach to Evidence*. Permission by West Publishing Co. to adapt them is gratefully acknowledged.

SUMMARY OF CONTENTS

TABLE OF CONTENTS

Chapter 1
BASIC CONCEPTS

Chapter 2
RELEVANCE

Chapter 3
CIRCUMSTANTIAL PROOF: SPECIAL PROBLEMS

Chapter 4
EXAMINATION AND
IMPEACHMENT OF WITNESSES

Chapter 5
HEARSAY

Chapter 6
EXCEPTIONS TO
THE HEARSAY RULE

Chapter 7
CONFRONTATION AND COMPULSORY PROCESS

Chapter 8
PRIVILEGES

Chapter 9
REAL AND DEMONSTRATIVE EVIDENCE, INCLUDING WRITINGS

Chapter 10

OPINIONS, EXPERTS, AND SCIENTIFIC EVIDENCE

Chapter 11
BURDENS OF PROOF, PRESUMPTIONS, AND OTHER PROCEDURAL ISSUES

Chapter 12
JUDICIAL NOTICE

CHECKLISTS

Preface

Thank you for buying this book.

This new edition covers all changes to the Federal Rules of Evidence since the prior edition, including those that became effective in December, 2017. It also features extensive coverage of major recent developments in (1) Confrontation Clause doctrine; and (2) the law (from both an FRE and a Sixth Amendment standpoint) regarding when a juror may "impeach" the verdict of a jury on which she served. The book covers all developments through November, 2017.

Here are some of this book's special features:

- **"Casebook Correlation Chart"** — This chart, located just after this Preface, correlates each section of my Outline with the pages covering the same topic in four of the leading Evidence casebooks.

- **"Capsule Summary"** — This is a 94-page summary of the key concepts of the law of Evidence, specially designed for use in the last week or so before your final exam.

- **"QuizYourself"** — Either at the end of the chapter, or after major sections of a chapter, are short-answer questions so that you can exercise your analytical muscles. There are 138 of these questions. They are for the most part selected and adapted from *Law in a Flash* on Evidence, which contains more than 500 flash cards and is available through your law school bookstore, or by going to **www.WKLegaledu.com**.

- **"Exam Tips"** — These alert you to the issues that repeatedly pop up on real-life Evidence exams and to the fact patterns commonly used to test those issues. My team and I created the Tips by looking at literally hundreds of multiple-choice and essay questions asked by law professors and bar examiners. You'd be surprised at how predictable the issues and fact-patterns chosen by profs really are!

- **"Multiple-Choice Q&As"** — These are 30 questions in an MBE-format, with extensive explanations of why each right answer is right and why each wrong answer is wrong. These are great for last-minute exam review.

- **"Checklists"** — Near the end of Chapters 3, 4 and 6, you'll find a 5- or 6-page table summarizing and illustrating the major components of the area covered by that chapter (Special Issues as to Circumstantial Evidence; Impeaching and Rehabilitating Witnesses; and Major Hearsay Exceptions and Exclusions, respectively). I've designed these for last-minute exam review and for open-book exams, to help you spot every issue.

I intend for you to use this book both throughout the semester and for exam preparation. Here are some suggestions about how to use it:[1]

1. During the semester, use the book in preparing each night for the next day's class. To do this, first

---

1. The suggestions below relate only to this book. I don't talk about taking or reviewing class notes, using hornbooks or other study aids, joining a study group, or anything else. This doesn't mean I don't think these other steps are important — it's just that in this Preface I've chosen to focus on how I think you can use this outline.

read your casebook. Then, use the *Casebook Correlation Chart* to get an idea of what part of the outline to read. Reading the outline will give you a sense of how the particular cases you've just read in your casebook fit into the overall structure of the subject. You may want to use a highlighter to mark key portions of the *Emanuel*.

2. If you make your own outline for the course, use the *Emanuel* to give you a structure, and to supply black letter principles. You may want to rely especially on the *Capsule Summary* for this purpose. You are hereby authorized to copy small portions of the *Emanuel* into your own outline, provided that your outline will be used only by you or your study group, and provided that you are the owner of the *Emanuel*.

3. When you first start studying for exams, read the *Capsule Summary* to get an overview. This will probably take you about one day.

4. Either during exam study or earlier in the semester, do some or all of the *Quiz Yourself* short-answer questions. You can find these quickly by looking for *Quiz Yourself* entries in the Table of Contents. When you do these questions: (1) record your short "answer" on the small blank line provided after the question, but also: (2) try to write out a "mini essay" on a separate piece of paper. Remember that the only way to get good at writing essays is to write essays.

5. Three or four days before the exam, review the *Exam Tips* that appear at the end of each chapter. You may want to combine this step with step **4**, so that you use the Tips to help you spot the issues in the short-answer questions. You'll also probably want to follow up from many of the Tips to the main outline's discussion of the topic.

6. The night before the exam: (1) do some *Quiz Yourself* questions, just to get your thinking and writing juices flowing; and (2) re-scan the *Exam Tips* (spending about 2-3 hours).

I would like to acknowledge the work done by Professor Joel Friedman of Tulane Law School, who prepared a prior edition of this book with me, and to whom I express my warmest thanks and gratitude. My deepest thanks also to my colleagues at Wolters Kluwer, Barbara Lasoff and Barbara Roth, who have helped greatly to assure the reliability and readability of this and my other books over many years.

Good luck in your Evidence course. If you'd like any other Wolters Kluwer publication, you can find it at your bookstore or at **www.WKLegaledu.com**. If you'd like to contact me, you can email me at **semanuel@westnet.com**.

Steve Emanuel
Larchmont, NY
December 4, 2017

1

CASEBOOK CORRELATION CHART

(**Note:** general sections of the outline are omitted from this chart. **NC** = not directly covered by this casebook.)

Emanuel's Evidence Outline *(by chapter heading)*	Fisher **Evidence** (3d Ed. 2013)	Leonard, Gold & Williams **Evidence, A Structured Approach** (4th Ed. 2016)	Mueller & Kirkpatrick **Evidence Under the Rules** (8th Ed. 2014)	Park & Friedman **Evidence Cases and Materials** (12th Ed. 2013)	Sklansky, **Evidence Cases, Commentary, & Problems** (4th Ed. 2016)
CHAPTER 2 **RELEVANCE**					
II. **Probative Value**	22-42	83-95	55-71	88-108	17-24
III. **Prejudice, Confusion, and Waste of Time**	42-65	95-110	71-84	88-108	24-40
CHAPTER 3 **CIRCUMSTANTIAL PROOF: SPECIAL PROBLEMS**					
II. **Character in Issue**	247-252	341-345	434-438	108-125	267, 279-280
IV. **Use of Circumstantial Character Evidence in Civil Cases**	245-247	NC	433-434, 436-438	150-155	279-280
V. **Other Crimes and Wrongs as Evidence, Especially in Criminal Cases**	145-152; 157-160	369-396	438-447	125-150	262-269, 280-300
VI. **Evidence of Criminal Defendant's Good Character**	234-243	345-355	425-427	111-119	267-268
VII. **Character of Victim, Especially in Cases of Assault, Murder, and Rape**	243-245; 318-361	358-364	427	162-171	309-327
VIII. **Methods of Proving Character: Reputation, Opinion, and Proof of Specific Acts**	245-247	338-341	427-433	121	269-280
IX. **Sexual Assault and Child Molestation — Special Rules for Other Crimes by the Defendant**	207-234	355-357	451-461	171-179	309; 327-336
X. **Habit and Custom**	252-256	396-398	461-466	155-162	300-308
XI. **Similar Happenings**	NC	398-401	NC	179-182	NC
XII. **Subsequent Remedial Measures**	96; 99-113	406-419	467-475	182-192	338-344
XIII. **Liability Insurance**	96; 126-137	440-443	484-485	NC	360-364
XIV. **Compromises, Offers to Plead Guilty and Offers to Pay Medical Expenses**	96; 113-126	420-440	475-483	192-195	345-360

CASEBOOK CORRELATION CHART (continued)

Emanuel's Evidence Outline *(by chapter heading)*	Fisher **Evidence** (3d Ed. 2013)	Leonard, Gold & Williams **Evidence, A Structured Approach** (4th Ed. 2016)	Mueller & Kirkpatrick **Evidence Under the Rules** (8th Ed. 2014)	Park & Friedman **Evidence Cases and Materials** (12th Ed. 2013)	Sklansky, **Evidence Cases, Commentary, & Problems** (4th Ed. 2016)
CHAPTER 4 **EXAMINATION AND IMPEACHMENT OF WITNESSES**					
I. Direct Examination	NC	447-453	517-524	12-31	366-377
II. Cross-examination	NC	447-453	524-532	31-40	366-377
III. Redirect and Recross	NC	11	NC	NC	9-10
IV. Refreshing Recollection and Other Techniques	NC	233-237	524	NC	164
V. Examination by Court	NC	NC	508; 645	NC	377-383
VII. Impeachment by Prior Criminal Convictions	260; 276-307	477-486	564-582	518-534	398-406
VIII. Impeachment by Prior Bad Acts	272-274	472-477	555-564	501-518	427-435
IX. Impeachment by Opinion and Reputation Regarding Character	258-259; 261-276	468-472	582-583	534-535	393-398
X. Impeachment by Prior Inconsistent Statements	NC	500-511	584-604	542-547	409-420
XI. Impeachment For Bias	260; 316-317	487-495	540-552	554-561	421-425
XII. Impeachment by Sensory or Mental Defects	NC	461-462	552-554	535-542	426-427
XIII. Impeachment by Contradiction	NC	495-500	604-618	494-501	427-435
XIV. Religious Beliefs	NC	486-487	634-635	NC	461
XV. Rehabilitating the Impeached Witness	307-311	511-519	619-634	547-554	435-456
XVI. Some Special Techniques for Developing or Evaluating Testimony	822-847	34-41	503-505	706-720	474-479
CHAPTER 5 **HEARSAY**					
I. The Definition of Hearsay	374-405	139-171	111-164	197-240	45-74

CASEBOOK CORRELATION CHART (continued)

Emanuel's Evidence Outline *(by chapter heading)*	Fisher **Evidence** (3d Ed. 2013)	Leonard, Gold & Williams **Evidence, A Structured Approach** (4th Ed. 2016)	Mueller & Kirkpatrick **Evidence Under the Rules** (8th Ed. 2014)	Park & Friedman **Evidence Cases and Materials** (12th Ed. 2013)	Sklansky, **Evidence Cases, Commentary, & Problems** (4th Ed. 2016)
CHAPTER 6 **EXCEPTIONS TO THE HEARSAY RULE**					
II. Admissions	406; 408-429	183-198	188-233	250-280	100-138
IV. Spontaneous, Excited, or Contemporaneous Utterances	406; 512-542	207-231	233-273	296-344	138-164
V. Past Recollection Recorded	406; 542-548	231-238	284-289	392-403	164-172
VI. Business Records	406; 548-562	239-245	289-302	404-430	172-185
VII. Public Records and Reports	406; 562-574	246-250	302-320	430-464	185-208
VIII. Miscellaneous Exceptions — Availability Immaterial	NC	294-295, 296-301	322-325	465-470	NC
IX. Unavailability Required — Generally	406; 474-475	251-255	325-335	NC	NC
X. Former Testimony	406; 474-488	255-262	336-345	344-354	208-220
XI. Dying Declarations	406; 497-504	262-266	346-348	369-377	220-227
XII. Declarations Against Interest	406; 488-497	266-277	348-361	355-368	227-232
XIII. Statements of Pedigree	NC	295-296	361-362	NC	NC
XIV. Forfeiture by Wrongdoing	406; 505-510	277-284	362-371	377-386	233-239
XV. Prior Statements of Available Witnesses	406; 430-474	198-205	166-188	386-391	93-100
XVI. The Residual ("Catch All") Exception	406; 575-585	284-294	371-381	471-476	239-244
CHAPTER 7 **CONFRONTATION AND COMPULSORY PROCESS**					
II.-V. Confrontation (all aspects)	586-717	302-326	233, 381-422, 530-532	240-250, 296-315, 378-386	74-92
VI. Compulsory Process	718-734	NC	795-796	NC	NC

CASEBOOK CORRELATION CHART (continued)

Emanuel's Evidence Outline (by chapter heading)	Fisher **Evidence** (3d Ed. 2013)	Leonard, Gold & Williams **Evidence, A Structured Approach** (4th Ed. 2016)	Mueller & Kirkpatrick **Evidence Under the Rules** (8th Ed. 2014)	Park & Friedman **Evidence Cases and Materials** (12th Ed. 2013)	Sklansky, **Evidence Cases, Commentary, & Problems** (4th Ed. 2016)
CHAPTER 8 **PRIVILEGES**					
II. The Attorney-Client Privilege	968-969, 975-1023	594-620	791-844	563-590; 636-640	622-669
III. Physician-Patient Privilege; Psychotherapist-Patient Privilege	934-944	620-631	844-857	590-608	677-679
IV. The Privilege Against Self-incrimination	1024-1042	252	875-894	NC	—
V. The Marital Privileges	1043-1066	638-645	857-875	608-615	669-677
VI. Miscellaneous Privileges	944-959; 960-968	632-638, 646-648	NC	615-635	677-679
CHAPTER 9 **REAL AND DEMONSTRATIVE EVIDENCE INCLUDING WRITINGS**					
II. Authentication	894-913	47-62	895-927	679-696	700-710
III. Other Foundation Requirements and Objections	NC	NC	895-896	NC	NC
IV. The "Best Evidence" Rule for Recorded Communications	913-929	63-69	929-951	669-679	710-724
V. Special Types of Real and Demonstrative Evidence	NC	11, 51-56	898-899, 920-925	NC	725-740
CHAPTER 10 **OPINIONS, EXPERTS, AND SCIENTIFIC EVIDENCE**					
I. First-hand Knowledge and Lay Opinions	735-748	534-542	637-645	783-791	491-502
II. Expert Witnesses — Generally	748-793	543-547	645-663	791-852	502-510
III. Experts, *Daubert* and Excluding Unreliable Testimony	793-822; 847-858; 876-893	547-566	663-691	852-877	510-534
IV. Scientific Evidence and Expertise — Particular Types	822-847; 858-876	110-122	691-712	877-970	569-618

CASEBOOK CORRELATION CHART (continued)

Emanuel's Evidence Outline *(by chapter heading)*	Fisher Evidence (3d Ed. 2013)	Leonard, Gold & Williams Evidence, A Structured Approach (4th Ed. 2016)	Mueller & Kirkpatrick Evidence Under the Rules (8th Ed. 2014)	Park & Friedman Evidence Cases and Materials (12th Ed. 2013)	Sklansky, Evidence Cases, Commentary, & Problems (4th Ed. 2016)
CHAPTER 11 **BURDENS OF PROOF, PRESUMPTIONS AND OTHER PROCEDURAL ISSUES**					
I. **Burdens of Proof**	NC	653-658	713-714, 734-739	745-781	741-765
II. **Presumptions**	NC	658-672	717-734	745-781	741-765
III. **Judge-Jury Allocation**	428-430	124-135	8-11	NC	12-16
IV. **Appeals and the "Harmless Error" Doctrine**	NC	18-23	44-50	NC	4, 74
CHAPTER 12 **JUDICIAL NOTICE**					
I. **Judicial Notice Generally**	NC	69-70	763-765	NC	765-766; 769-776
II. **Adjudicative Facts**	NC	70-74	765-774, 782-787	727-734	765-768
III. **Legislative Facts**	NC	75-78	777-780	734-739	765-774
IV. **Notice of Law**	NC	74-75	780-782	734-739	NC

CAPSULE SUMMARY

This Capsule Summary is intended for review at the end of the semester. Reading it is not a substitute for mastering the material in the main outline. Numbers in brackets refer to the pages in the main outline where the topic is discussed.

CHAPTERS 1 AND 2
BASIC CONCEPTS

I. FIRST PRINCIPLES

A. Roles of judge and jury: In cases tried to a jury, the judge and the jury divide the responsibility of dealing with the evidence [1]:

1. **Judge's role:** The role of the *judge* is to determine *whether the evidence is admissible*.

2. **Role of the jury:** Once the judge has decided to admit the evidence, the jury's role is to determine what *weight* the evidence should be given. For instance, it is up to the jury to judge the *credibility* of a witness, and the jury may choose to completely disregard admissible testimony because it believes the witness who is giving that testimony is mistaken or lying.

B. The Federal Rules: The *Federal Rules of Evidence* apply to *all trials in federal courts,* whether civil or criminal, and whether to a judge or a jury. See FRE 101. [1]

1. **Adoption by states:** The Federal Rules of Evidence have also been adopted, in one form or another, by *over four-fifths of the states*.

2. **2011 Restyling:** The language of the Federal Rules was extensively revised in 2011. This *"restyling"* project was done to make the rules more easily understood and to make style and terminology consistent. The restyling was not intended to change any actual evidence-ruling result.

II. ORGANIZATION OF THE TRIAL

A. Flow of the case: In the usual case, the plaintiff's case is presented first, followed by the defendant's. The typical case flows as follows [2]:

1. **Opening statement:** The plaintiff (or, in a criminal case, the prosecutor) makes his *opening statement* first. Then, the defendant may make his opening statement (though many courts allow him to reserve his opening statement until the end of the plaintiff/prosecutor's case).

2. **Plaintiff's case:** Then, the plaintiff (or prosecutor) puts on his *case in chief.* That is, he presents the witnesses, as well as documents and other tangible evidence, to establish the facts needed for him to prevail.

3. **Defendant's case:** After the plaintiff or prosecutor "rests" his case, it is the defendant's turn. The defendant presents witnesses and documents to disprove the elements of the plaintiff's case and/or to establish *affirmative defenses*.

4. **Plaintiff's rebuttal:** After the defendant rests, the plaintiff or prosecutor gets another turn at bat. This is called the plaintiff's *rebuttal* — the plaintiff may present additional witnesses, recall former witnesses, or present new exhibits, but *only to rebut the defendant's evidence*, not to buttress his own case in chief.

5. **Defendant's rejoinder:** Likewise, after the plaintiff's rebuttal, the defendant has a *rejoinder* — here, he may only rebut evidence brought out in the plaintiff's rebuttal.

6. **Closing arguments:** After both parties have presented all of their evidence, the two sides make *closing arguments*. Usually, the plaintiff (or prosecutor) goes first, the defendant goes second, and the plaintiff/prosecutor gets a last chance to rebut the defendant's closing remarks.

7. **Instructions:** Finally, the judge gives *instructions* to the jury, in which he explains to them the applicable law. In some jurisdictions, he may also comment upon, or summarize, the evidence.

B. **Examination of witnesses:** Here are the steps by which witnesses are examined. [3]

1. **Four stages:** The examination of a given witness proceeds through up to four stages:

a. **Direct:** First, the party who has called a witness engages in the *direct examination*.

b. **Cross-examination:** After the side that called the witness has finished the direct examination, the other side has the chance to *cross-examine* the witness.

c. **Re-direct:** The calling side then has an opportunity to conduct *re-direct* examination of the witness. Re-direct is generally limited to rebutting points made on cross-examination.

d. **Re-cross:** Finally, the cross-examining side gets a brief opportunity to conduct *re-cross*. This is limited to rebutting the effect of re-direct.

2. **Sequestration of witnesses:** If a witness were permitted to observe the testimony of other witnesses for the same side, he would be able to *tailor* his testimony (perhaps by *perjury*) so that it matched this other testimony. To prevent this, judges have, and often use, the power to *exclude all other witnesses* from the courtroom while one witness is testifying. This is known as the power to *"sequester"* witnesses. [3]

a. **Federal Rule:** The trial judge's right to sequester witnesses is codified in FRE 615, which says: "At a party's request, the court *must order witnesses excluded* so that they *cannot hear other witnesses' testimony.* Or the court may do so on its own."

i. **Mandatory at party's request:** So under FRE 615, *any party* has the *absolute right* to require the judge to exclude all witnesses (other than witnesses covered by certain exceptions, like a person who is a party) from hearing other witnesses' testimony. In other words, once a party makes the request for sequestration, the *judge does not have discretion to deny the request.*

III. COMPETENCY OF WITNESSES

A. **Meaning:** A witness is said to be *"competent"* if she possesses the qualifications necessary to give testimony. [7]

B. **Modern approach:** Witnesses are *presumed competent.*

1. **Federal Rules:** Under the Federal Rules, witnesses (other than the judge and the jury in the particular case) will be incompetent to testify *only for two reasons*:

   i. **Lack of personal knowledge:** First, as a general matter a witness may not testify to a matter unless she has ***personal knowledge*** of the matter. FRE 602. Thus if a witness describes a particular event, her testimony will be stricken if it turns out that she did not personally observe that event, and instead heard about it from someone else. [7]

   ii. **Oath:** Second, if the witness will not solemnly ***promise to tell the truth***, the court will not hear his testimony. FRE 603.

   a. **Mental incapacity or immaturity:** Thus under the federal approach, even a witness who is quite insane, or very young, will not be prevented from testifying if the trial judge is convinced that he has relevant first-hand knowledge and understands the obligation to tell the truth. Similarly, even if the witness was ***intoxicated*** or under the ***influence of drugs*** when he witnessed an event, he will be permitted, under the federal approach, to testify about it. [8]

IV. KINDS OF EVIDENCE

A. Direct versus circumstantial [12]

1. **Direct evidence:** Direct evidence is evidence which, if believed, automatically resolves the issue. (*Example:* W says, "I saw D strangle V." This is direct evidence on whether D strangled V.)

2. **Circumstantial:** Circumstantial evidence is evidence which, even if believed, does not resolve the issue unless ***additional reasoning*** is used. (*Example:* W says, "I saw D running from the place where V's body was found, and I found a stocking in D's pocket." This is only circumstantial evidence of whether D strangled V.)

3. **Probative value:** The probative value of direct evidence is not necessarily higher than circumstantial evidence, but it will sometimes be more readily admitted by the judge.

B. Testimonial versus real and demonstrative: [469]

1. **Testimonial:** Testimonial evidence arises when W makes assertions in court. The fact-finder must rely on W's interpretation of W's sensory data, W's memory, etc.

2. **Real and demonstrative:** Real evidence is a thing involved in the underlying event (e.g., a weapon, document, or other tangible item). Demonstrative evidence is a tangible item that illustrates some material proposition (e.g., a map, chart, summary). The fact-finder may interpret either real or demonstrative evidence by use of its own senses, without intervening sensing and interpreting by a witness.

V. CONDITIONS FOR ADMITTING EVIDENCE

A. Relevant: Only ***relevant*** evidence may be admitted. (FRE 402) [11-18]

1. **Definition:** Evidence is "relevant" if "(a) it has any tendency to make a fact more or less probable than it would be without the evidence; and (b) the fact is of consequence in determining the action." (FRE 401).

a. **"Brick is not wall":**   The piece of evidence need not make a material fact more probable than not; it must merely increase the probability (even by a small amount) that the material fact is so. "A brick is not a wall," and the piece of evidence merely has to be one brick in the wall establishing a particular fact.

2. **Exclusion:**   Even relevant evidence may be excluded if its *probative value* is *substantially outweighed* by the danger of: (1) *unfair prejudice*; (2) confusion of the issues; (3) misleading of the jury; or (4) considerations of undue delay, waste of time, or needless presentation of cumulative evidence. (FRE 403)

B. **Offering testimonial evidence**

1. **Lay (i.e., non-expert) witness:**

   a. W must take an *oath*, i.e., solemnly promise to testify truthfully. (FRE 603)

   b. W must testify from *personal knowledge*. (FRE 602)

   c. W must preferably state *facts* rather than *opinions*. But under FRE 701, W may give an opinion if it is: (1) rationally based on his own perceptions; (2) helpful to the fact-finder; and (3) not based on scientific, technical or other specialized knowledge.

   d. W must be *competent* (see *supra*, C-2).

2. **Experts:**   The same rules apply to *experts* as to lay witnesses, except:

   a. The expert may give an opinion if:

   ❏ the opinion relates to "scientific, technical or other *specialized knowledge*";

   ❏ the opinion will assist the trier to "*understand the evidence* or determine a fact in issue"; and

   ❏ the testimony is based on *sufficient facts or data* and is the product of "*reliable* principles and methods," and W has *applied* those principles and methods *reliably* to the *facts of the case*.

   FRE 702.

   b. The expert's opinion need not be based on his personal knowledge — it may be based on information supplied by others. At common law, this is usually done by the hypothetical question. Under Federal Rules, it may be done either by the hypothetical or by out-of-court statements made to the expert (even inadmissible evidence); FRE 703. Under FRE 705, facts relied on by the expert need not be disclosed except under cross-examination or as required by court.

   c. **Qualification:**   The expert may be qualified by reason of "knowledge, skill, experience, training, or otherwise" (FRE 702), so formal academic training is not necessary.

3. **Ultimate issues:**   At common law, opinions on "*ultimate*" issues are usually barred. But under FRE 704, even such opinions are allowed (except when they relate to the mental state of a criminal defendant).

C. **Offering real and demonstrative evidence:**   See p. 73 of this Capsule Summary.

D. **Making and responding to objections:**   [4-7]

1. **Making objections:**

a. **Not automatic:** Evidence will not be excluded unless the opponent makes an *objection.* FRE 103(a)(1).

b. **Timely:** The objection must be *timely* (usually before the witness can answer the question). FRE 103(a)(1).

c. **Specific:** The objection must be *specific* enough to explain to the trial judge and the appeals court the basis for it. *Id.*

d. **Taking of exceptions:** At common law, the opponent whose objection is denied must *"take exception"* in order to preserve the objection for appeal. In most states today, and under the Federal Rules, exceptions are no longer necessary.

2. **Responding to objection:** If the judge sustains objection, the proponent must usually make an *"offer of proof"* in order to preserve his right to argue on appeal that the evidence should have been admitted. That is, proponent must make it clear to the court (either by the lawyer's own explanation of what the evidence would be, or by questions and answers to the witness outside the jury's presence) what the evidence would be. FRE 103(a)(2).

CHAPTER 3

CIRCUMSTANTIAL PROOF: SPECIAL PROBLEMS

I. RELEVANT EVIDENCE SOMETIMES EXCLUDED

A. Possible exclusion: Normally, all relevant evidence is admissible. (FRE 402) But even relevant evidence may be excluded if its probative value is *"substantially outweighed"* by a danger of one or more of the following: *unfair prejudice,* confusing the issues, misleading the jury," etc. (FRE 403) Special rules govern certain types of circumstantial evidence which have been found over the years to be so misleading or so prejudicial that they should be categorically excluded without a case-by-case balancing of probative value against prejudice. [11, 15-18]

II. CHARACTER EVIDENCE

A. General rule: Evidence of person's character or character trait is, in general, *not admissible* to prove that "on a *particular occasion* the person *acted in accordance* with the character or trait." FRE 404(a)(1). (*Example:* In a civil suit from an auto accident, P cannot show that D has the general character trait of carelessness, or even that D is a generally careless driver, to suggest that D probably acted carelessly in the particular accident under litigation.) [22-24]

B. Character in issue: [24-25]

1. **Essential element:** A person's general character, or his particular character trait, is admissible if it is an *essential element* of the case. (*Example:* P says that D has libeled him by calling him a liar. D may introduce evidence of P's character for untruthfulness, since that character trait is an essential element of D's defense that his statement was true.)

a. **Illustrations:** True "character in issue" situations are rare. Civilly, *negligent entrustment* (D gave dangerous instrumentality, like a car, to one he should have known was of careless or otherwise bad character) and *defamation* (above example) are the most common.

Criminally, *entrapment* (prosecution rebuts by showing D was "predisposed" to commit the crime) is the only instance.

2. **Types of evidence:**   When character is directly in issue, all three types of character evidence (specific acts, W's opinion, or the subject's reputation) are admissible.

C. **Circumstantial evidence in civil cases:**   In civil cases, circumstantial evidence of character is generally inadmissible. [26-27]

1. **Quasi-criminal acts:**   A few courts allow one who is charged in a civil case with conduct that would also be a crime to rebut this charge by presenting circumstantial evidence of his good character. But most courts, and the Federal Rules, do not.

D. **Other-crimes (and "bad acts") evidence in criminal cases:**   [27-38]

1. **General rule:**   The prosecutor may *not* introduce evidence of *other crimes* committed by D for the purpose of proving that because D is a person of criminal character, he probably committed the crime with which he is charged. Nor may the prosecutor show D's prior *"bad acts"* that didn't lead to convictions for this purpose.

   a.   **FRE:** See FRE 404(b)(1): "Evidence of a *crime, wrong, or other act* is not admissible to *prove a person's character* in order to show that on *a particular occasion the person acted in accordance with the character.*"

2. **Proof of elements:**   But other crimes or bad acts by D may be admitted if this is done not to show D's general criminal disposition, but to establish circumstantially *some element of the crime charged.* See FRE 404(b) (other crimes, wrongs or acts "may be admissible for *another purpose*, such as *proving motive, opportunity, intent, preparation, plan, knowledge, identity, absence of mistake, or lack of accident.*"

   Here are some common elements that may be circumstantially proved by other crimes that D has committed:

   a.   **Signature:**   If the perpetrator's *identity* is in doubt, proof that D has committed prior crimes that are so similar in method that they constitute his *"signature,"* and thus identify him as the perpetrator of the crime charged, may be proved. This is often described as proof of *"modus operandi"* or "m.o." [31-33]

      Example: D is on trial for robbing a convenience store after midnight while wearing a mask similar to the very distinctive one worn in the movie "Clockwork Orange." The prosecution shows the jury a surveillance tape in which the masked robber can be seen wearing such a mask. D testifies that he wasn't the robber, and that the man in the tape must be someone else. The prosecution asks D, "Isn't it true that you were convicted two years ago of robbing another convenience store while wearing a 'Clockwork Orange' mask?" (It's true that D was so convicted.)

      The question is proper — the evidence of D's conviction is available not only to impeach him, but as substantive proof that he robbed the other store wearing such a mask. That's because the other crime is so similar to the present one that it tends to prove D's identity as the masked robber on the present occasion. Therefore, the evidence of the conviction is non-character other-crimes evidence offered for "another purpose, such as proving ... identity[.]" FRE 404(b).

   b.   **Intent:**   Other crimes may be used to prove that D had the particular *intent* required for the crime charged. Generally, this is done to rebut D's contention that he did the act charged *innocently* or *unknowingly*. (*Example:* D, a mail carrier, is charged with stealing a coin from the mails; the prosecution is allowed to show that D also unlawfully possessed credit cards taken from the mails, in order to rebut D's argument that the coin accidentally fell out of an envelope and he planned to return it. [33]

c. **Motive:** Other crimes may be used to establish the defendant's *motive* for the crime charged. (*Example:* D, a nurse, is charged with stealing Demerol from the hospital where she works. The prosecution may show that D is a Demerol addict, to show that she had a motive to steal the drug. [*U.S. v. Cunningham*]). [34]

d. **Identity:** Other crimes may be used to show that D was really the perpetrator, if he disputes this. For instance, the prosecution may be allowed to show that D committed other crimes, and that the other crimes and the crime charged are part of a *common plan or scheme*. (*Example:* D is charged with embezzling from his employer; he claims that someone else did the embezzling. The prosecution will be allowed to show that D embezzled from three prior employers, since this demonstrates that D was probably acting as part of a general scheme to steal from each of his employers.) [31, 35]

3. **Other aspects of other-crimes evidence:**

a. **No conviction:** The other crimes need not have led to a conviction. Many state courts require that the evidence of the defendant's guilt of the other crime be "clear and convincing" or "substantial." But in federal courts, it does not even have to be by a preponderance of the evidence. [37]

b. **Acquittal:** The fact that the defendant was *acquitted* of the other crime will be a factor in determining whether there is "substantial" evidence of his guilt (in courts requiring this). But most courts will probably not automatically exclude the evidence of the other crime merely because of the acquittal. (*Example:* D is charged with murdering her child. Evidence that four of her other children died of unnatural causes will probably be allowed because of its strong tendency to prove that the death currently charged was not accidental, even though D was acquitted of similar charges as to the first death, when no cumulative evidence was available.) [37]

c. **Balancing:** Even where other crimes by D circumstantially establish an element of the present charge, the judge must still balance probative value against prejudice, and must exclude if the latter substantially outweighs the former. (FRE 403) [38]

d. **Use by D:** It's ordinarily the prosecution that uses the proof of D's prior crime or bad act to show some element of the present crime. But *D*, too, may show someone's past crimes or bad acts, to suggest that *it's that other person*, not D, who did the present crime. [30]

E. **Evidence of criminal defendant's good character:** [40-42]

1. **Allowed:** Evidence by a criminal defendant that he has a *good character* — or a particular favorable character trait — is *allowed* by all courts, assuming that the trait is pertinent.

   Example: D is charged with murder. He will be allowed to show that he has the general character of being law-abiding. He will also be permitted to show the narrower trait of being peaceable, since that trait is relevant to the crime charged.

2. **Method of proof:**

    a. Common law: At common law, proof of good character must be made by ***reputation*** evidence only (not by the character witness's opinion, or by proof of specific acts showing good character).

    b. Federal: FRE 405(a) allows not only reputation evidence but also the character witness's own ***opinion*** as to D's good character. (But not even the Federal Rules allow proof of ***specific incidents*** showing D's good character.)

3. Relevance: The trait on which the defendant is offering good-character evidence is offered must be ***relevant (or "pertinent") to the crime charged***.

    Example: D is charged with beating V almost to death in a barroom brawl. D (without ever taking the stand) presents a witness, Wit, who expresses the opinion that D is a truthful person. Even though FRE 404(a)(1) allows an accused to offer favorable character evidence about himself, Wit's testimony would be excluded because it is not "pertinent" to any issue in the case. That is, to the extent that any character trait of D is an issue, it would be the trait of peaceableness, not truthfulness. [39]

4. Rebuttal by prosecution: If D puts on proof of his good character, the prosecution may ***rebut*** this evidence:

    a. Own witnesses: The prosecution may do this by putting on its own witnesses to say that D's character is bad.

    b. Cross-examination: The prosecution may cross-examine D's character witness to show that D's character is not really good. The prosecutor may even do this by asking the witness about ***specific instances*** of bad conduct by D, provided that: **(i)** the prosecutor has a ***good faith basis*** for believing that D really committed the specific bad act; and **(ii)** the specific bad act is ***relevant*** to the ***specific character trait*** testified to by the witness (so if W testified that D was honest, the prosecutor could not ask about specific bad acts showing D's character for violence). Even an arrest that did not lead to a conviction may be brought up in cross-examination, if relevant to the character trait in question.

    c. No extrinsic evidence: The prosecutor's ability to show specific bad acts is limited to cross-examination. He may not put on ***extrinsic evidence*** (e.g., ***other witnesses***) to prove that the specific acts took place, if the character witness denied that they did. Conversely, the defendant may not put on other witnesses to show that the specific act referred to by the prosecutor on cross-examination never took place.

F. Character of victim: [43-51]

1. V's violent character: The defendant in a homicide or assault case who claims that the victim was the first aggressor, may in all courts introduce evidence that the ***victim*** had a ***violent character.*** This is true even if D cannot show that he was aware of the victim's violent character at the time of the assault or murder. This character evidence must generally be in the form of reputation or opinion evidence; most states (and the Federal Rules) prohibit evidence of ***specific past acts*** of violence by the victim.

2. Federal Rules: FRE 404(a)(2)(B) allows the defendant to show not only proof of a murder or assault victim's violent character, but ***any*** "evidence of an alleged victim's ***pertinent trait***[.]" (But this is very limited in sexual assault cases, discussed below.)

3. Rebuttal by prosecution: Once the defendant introduces evidence of the victim's character for violence, the prosecution may then ***rebut*** this evidence by showing the victim's ***peaceable***

character. The Federal Rules expand this right of rebuttal; in a homicide case, if the defendant claims that the victim was the first aggressor (even though the defendant does not put in proof of the victim's general character for violence), the prosecution may put in evidence of the victim's peaceful character. FRE 404(a)(2)(C).

4. **Rape:** At common law, the defendant in a *rape or sexual assault* case could usually show the victim's character for *unchastity*, to show that the victim *consented* on this particular occasion. But nearly all states have now enacted *rape shield statutes* to restrict evidence of the victim's past sexual conduct.

    a. **FRE:** The FRE's rape shield provision, Rule 412, completely disallows reputation or opinion evidence concerning the victim's past sexual behavior. FRE 412 also prohibits evidence of specific acts concerning the victim's past sexual behavior in most situations; for instance, D is never allowed to offer evidence of V's past sexual behavior with *persons other than himself* if offered on the issue of whether there was consent.

        i. **Civil:** FRE 412 also applies to certain *civil* suits. For instance, if P sues for *sexual harassment*, D usually can't show that P was known to be promiscuous with others or dressed seductively, and thus indicated her willingness to accept sexual advances at work.

G. **Prosecution's evidence of criminal defendant's bad character:** If a criminal defendant uses FRE 404(a)(2)(B) to put on evidence of that V has a particular bad character trait, the prosecution is then automatically entitled to put on evidence that the *defendant has that same bad character trait.* See FRE 404(a)(2)(B)(ii).

1. **Evidence of D's violent character:** Most commonly, the way this happens is that D, charged with a crime of violence against V, uses FRE 404(a)(2) to put on evidence that *V had or has a violent character* (to show that V, not D, probably started the violence). The prosecution will then be entitled to show that *D, too, had a violent disposition.*

    a. **Not applicable if D uses source other than 404(a)(2):** But this special rule applies only where D's evidence about V's violent disposition is admitted under FRE *404(a)(2)(B),* not where D relies on *some other evidentiary theory* for the evidence of V's violent tendencies.

    Example: D is charged with murdering V by stabbing him during a barroom brawl. D defends on the grounds of self-defense, and shows that before the altercation, he knew that V had a reputation for often drawing a knife without warning. D testifies that this reputation was on his mind when he drew his own knife first. Since D is offering the evidence about V's violent reputation not under FRE 404(a)(2)(B) (i.e., not as a way of showing that V had a generally violent disposition, making it more likely that V started the fight), but rather as a way of supporting his self-defense claim (i.e., that he reasonably feared for his life), the prosecution will not be able to show that D, too, has a previously-demonstrated propensity for violence.

III. METHODS OF PROVING CHARACTER: REPUTATION, OPINION AND PROOF OF SPECIFIC ACTS

A. **FRE:** Whenever proof of a character trait *is* allowed, the FRE let that proof be by either *reputation* or *opinion* testimony. FRE 405(a).[48-53]

1. **D's good-character evidence:** So D in a criminal case can show his own good character by W's testimony that D has a good reputation for, say, honesty or non-violence, or by testimony that in W's opinion, D possesses these favorable character traits. (But D ***can't*** show ***specific instances*** of his own good character.) [51-52]

    a. **Rebuttal:** If D makes this showing (thus "opening the door"), the prosecution may ***rebut*** by reputation or opinion evidence of D's poor character. Also, the prosecution may use ***specific acts evidence*** during its ***cross*** of D's good-character witnesses. (*Example:* Prosecution can ask D's character witness, "Would it change your opinion of D's peaceful nature to know that he started three fights at the Tavern on the Green in the last year alone?") [48]

        i. **Good-faith basis for specific-act question:** Before the cross examiner asks about a specific act during cross, she must have a ***"good faith basis"*** for believing that the specific act really occurred. (*Example:* In above example, prosecutor must have a good-faith basis for believing that the barroom fights really occurred.) [51-53]

        ii. **No extrinsic acts:** Also, the prosecution can't use ***extrinsic evidence*** of the specific acts, merely ask the defense's witness about them. (*Example:* On the above barroom-fights Example, if D's witness W said, "I don't believe those fights ever happened, and if they did they weren't started by D," the prosecution can't prove otherwise.) [52]

2. **Character of victim:** Similarly, D can show the character of the victim by use of reputation or opinion evidence. (*Example:* In murder case where D claims self-defense, D can put on W to testify, "In my opinion, V was always the kind of guy who liked to start fights.") [48-50]

    a. **Rebuttal:** Again, the prosecution in rebuttal can not only use reputation or opinion, but can also refer to specific acts on cross.

3. **Proof for "other purposes":** Where a party (usually the prosecution) is using D's prior crimes or bad acts for some "other purpose" (e.g., identity, knowledge, etc.), this proof can be by "specific acts." (*Example:* If D is charged with robbing the 2nd Nat'l Bank with a blue ski mask and yellow raincoat, and D denies that he's the one who did it, prosecution can show that on June 21, D robbed the 1st Nat'l Bank wearing this distinctive garb, because it's so unusual as to amount to a "signature.") [50-51]

IV. PAST SEXUAL ASSAULT OR CHILD MOLESTATION BY D

A. **FRE allows:** Under FRE 413, if D is accused of a sexual assault, evidence that D has ***committed a sexual assault in the past*** is ***admissible***, and may be considered on any relevant matter. (*Example:* If D's charged with raping V, prosecution may show that 20 years ago, D raped someone else. Prosecution may also argue, "The fact that D raped before means he's extra likely to have committed the present rape.") [53-55]

1. **Child molestations; civil suits:** Similar rules (FRE 414 and 415) allow: (i) proof that D previously ***molested a child*** to be introduced in his present molestation trial, and (ii) proof of D's prior sexual assaults or child molestations to be introduced in ***civil*** proceedings where P claims D sexually assaulted or molested P.

V. HABIT AND CUSTOM

A. Generally allowable: Evidence of a person's *habit* is admissible in most courts (and the FRE) to show that he ***followed this habit on a particular occasion***. "Habits" are thus to be distinguished from "character traits" (generally disallowed as circumstantial evidence that the character trait was followed on a particular occasion). [59]

1. **Three factors:** There are three main factors courts look to in deciding whether something is a "habit" or merely a trait of character: [59]

    a. **Specificity:** The more *specific* the behavior, the more likely it is to be deemed a habit. (*Example:* If V is killed when his car is hit on the railroad tracks, his estate will be allowed to show that he had almost always stopped and looked before crossing those tracks every day — this conduct will be a "habit," because it is very specific. But V's general "carefulness" will be found to be a character trait, not a habit, and will thus not be admissible to show that he probably behaved carefully at the time of the fatal crossing.)

    b. **Regularity:** The more *"regular"* the behavior, the more likely to be a habit. "Regularity" means "ratio of reaction to situations." (So something that X does 95% of the time she's in a particular situation is more likely to be a habit than something X does 55% of the time in that situation.)

    c. **Unreflective behavior:** The more *"unreflective"* or *"semi-automatic"* the behavior, the more likely it is to be a habit. (*Examples:* Using a left-hand turn signal is probably a habit because it's semi-automatic; going to temple for the Sabbath each Friday night is probably not a habit, because it requires conscious thought and volition.)

B. Federal Rules: FRE 406 follows the majority rule, by providing that "Evidence of a person's habit or an organization's routine practice may be admitted to prove that on a particular occasion the person or organization acted in accordance with the habit or routine practice." [60]

C. Business practices: All courts allow evidence of the ***routine practice*** of an ***organization***, to show that that practice was followed on a particular occasion. (*Example:* A business may prove that a particular letter was mailed by showing that it was the organization's routine practice to mail all letters placed in any worker's "outgoing mail" box, and that the letter in question was placed in such a box.) [60]

VI. SIMILAR HAPPENINGS

A. General rule: Evidence that similar happenings have occurred in the past (offered to prove that the event in question really happened) is generally ***allowed***. However, the proponent must show that there is ***substantial similarity*** between the past similar happening and the event under litigation. [61-63]

1. **Accidents and injuries:** Thus evidence of past similar injuries or accidents will often be admitted to show that the same kind of mishap occurred in the present case, or to show that the defendant was negligent in not fixing the problem after the prior mishaps. But the plaintiff will have to show that the conditions were the same in the prior and present situations.

2. **Past safety:** Conversely, the defendant will usually be allowed to show due care or the absence of a defect, by showing that there have ***not*** been similar accidents in the past. However, D must show that: (1) ***conditions were the same*** in the past as when the accident occurred; and (2) had there been any injuries in the past, they would have been ***reported*** to D.

VII. SUBSEQUENT REMEDIAL MEASURES

A. General rule: Courts generally ***do not allow*** evidence that a party has merely taken ***subsequent remedial measures***, when offered to show that the party was negligent, or was conscious of being at fault. (*Example:* P trips on D's sidewalk; P may not show that just after the fall, D repaved the sidewalk and thus conceded the sidewalk's dangerousness.) [64-65]

   1. Federal Rules: FRE 407 follows this rule: subsequent remedial measures may not be admitted to prove negligence or culpable conduct in connection with an event.

B. Other purposes: But subsequent remedial measures may be shown to prove elements other than culpability or negligence. For instance, such measures may be used to rebut the defendant's claim that there was ***no safer way*** to handle the situation. Or, if the defendant claims that he ***did not own or control*** property involved in an accident, the fact that he subsequently repaired the property may be shown to rebut this assertion. [65-67]

C. Product liability: The FRE ***apply*** the no-subsequent-remedial-measures rule to ***product-liability*** cases, just as to negligence cases. FRE 407 says that subsequent-measures evidence is not admissible to prove "negligence; culpable conduct; a ***defect in a product or its design***; or a need for a ***warning or instruction***."

   Example: P, the owner of a single-engine plane made by D, crashes in the plane when it runs out of fuel because water has gotten into the fuel tanks. P sues D on a products liability defective-design theory. P's theory is that a defective design of the fuel tanks allowed condensation to form inside the tank. In support of this theory, P offers evidence that shortly after this and two other similar accidents, D redesigned the fuel tanks to make such condensation less likely. Under FRE 407, this evidence will not be admissible.

VIII. LIABILITY INSURANCE

A. General rule: Evidence that person carried or did not carry ***liability insurance*** is ***never*** admissible on the issue of whether he acted negligently. See FRE 411. (But evidence of the existence or non-existence of liability insurance is admissible for purposes other than proving negligence. For instance, the fact that W, a witness for D in a tort suit, works for D's liability insurance company, could be admitted to show bias on W's part.) [67-68]

IX. SETTLEMENTS AND PLEA BARGAINS

A. Settlements: The fact that a party has offered to ***settle*** a claim may ***not*** be admitted on the issue of the claim's validity. See FRE 408. [69-73]

   1. Collateral admissions of fact: ***Admissions of fact*** made during the course of settlement negotiations are generally admissible at common law, but not admissible under FRE 408. (*Example:* "I was drunk when I ran over you, so I'll pay you $5,000 in damages," would be admissible at common law to prove D's drunkenness, but not admissible under FRE 408.)

   2. Other purposes: But settlement offers may be admissible to prove issues other than liability. (*Example:* If W testifies on behalf of D in a civil suit, the fact that W received money from D in settlement for a related claim may be admitted to show that W is biased in favor of D and against P.)

B. Guilty pleas: [73-74]

1. **Defendant's offer to plead:** The fact that the defendant has offered to **plead guilty** (and the offer has been rejected by the prosecutor) may **not** be shown to prove that D is guilty or is conscious of his guilt. FRE 410(4) excludes not only the offer to plead guilty but any other **statement** made in the course of plea discussions with the prosecutor, from being used against the defendant.

2. **Withdrawn plea:** Similarly, the fact that D made a guilty plea and then later **withdrew it** may not be admitted against D in the ultimate trial.

3. **Later civil case:** The plea offer or withdrawn plea, and the accompanying factual admissions, are also not admissible in any **later civil case**. FRE 410(4).

C. **Offer to pay medical expenses:** The fact that a party has paid the **medical expenses** of an injured person is not admissible to show that party's liability for the accident that caused the injury. See FRE 409. But only the fact of payment, not related admissions of fact, are excluded. (*Example:* D says to P, "I'm paying your medical expenses because if I hadn't been drunk that night, I wouldn't have hit you." This may be admitted to show D's drunkenness but not to show that D paid the expenses.) [80]

CHAPTER 4
EXAMINATION AND IMPEACHMENT OF WITNESSES

I. FLOW OF EXAMINATION

A. **Four stages:** The examination of a witness goes through up to four stages: [3]

1. **Direct:** First, the party who called the witness engages in the **direct** examination.

2. **Cross:** After the calling side has finished the direct exam, the other side may **cross-examine** the witness.

3. **Re-direct:** The calling side then has the opportunity to conduct **re-direct** examination.

4. **Re-cross:** Finally, the cross-examining side gets a brief opportunity to conduct **re-cross**.

II. DIRECT EXAMINATION

A. **Leading questions:** Generally, the examiner **may not ask leading questions** on direct. [93-95]

1. **Definition:** A leading question is one that **suggests to the witness the answer desired by the questioner**. (*Example:* Auto negligence suit by P against D. Question by P's lawyer to P: "Was D driving faster than the speed limit at the time he hit you?" This is leading, since it suggests that the questioner desires a "yes" answer.)

2. **Hostile witness:** Leading questions are allowed on direct if the witness is **"hostile."** The **opposing party** will almost always be deemed hostile; so will a witness who is shown to be biased against the calling side, as well as a witness whose demeanor on the stand shows hostility to the calling side.

B. **Juror testimony and affidavits impeaching the verdict:** Unsuccessful litigants would often like to **impeach a jury verdict** by offering testimony by a juror as to **statements made or heard during the jury's deliberations** that indicate some mistake or impropriety associated with the verdict. But FRE 606(b)(1), like the common law, generally *prohibits* admission of *testimony (or affidavits) by a juror,* when used to *attack the validity of the verdict* reached by the jury on which that juror sat. [95]

1. **Three classes of prohibited testimony:** Under FRE 606(b)(1), there are *three classes* of testimony (or affidavits) by a juror that are *barred* by the Rule, assuming that the evidence is offered "during an inquiry into the validity of a verdict or indictment" [96]:

    [1] Testimony about "any *statement made* or *incident* that *occurred during the jury's deliberations*";

    [2] Testimony about "the *effect of anything* on that juror's or another juror's *vote*"; and

    [3] Testimony about "any juror's *mental processes concerning the verdict or indictment.*"

    Example: In a prosecution of D for burglary, Wit, called by the prosecution, testifies that before the trial started, Wit's and D's mutual friend X told Wit, "D confessed to me that he did the burglary." Immediately after Wit gives this testimony, the trial judge sustains a defense hearsay objection, and instructs the jury to disregard the testimony. The jury eventually votes to convict. D immediately moves for a new trial, claiming that the jury improperly considered Wit's hearsay testimony; in support, D offers an affidavit by Juror 1 that "At the start of deliberations, the foreperson told us that in her opinion the single most compelling evidence showing D's guilt was Wit's testimony that X told Wit that D had confessed."

    The trial judge may not hear Juror 1's testimony, because use of the testimony as part of this "inquiry into the validity of [the] verdict" would violate at least two of the three prohibitions in Rule 606(b)(1): it is about a "statement made ... during the jury's deliberations," and it is about "the effect of anything [namely, Wit's inadmissible testimony] on that juror's or another juror's vote." [96]

2. **Pre-deliberation events:** The Supreme Court has interpreted Rule 606(b)(1) so as to bar juror testimony even about events that occurred *prior to the start of deliberations.* This means that the Rule covers (i.e., excludes) testimony by one juror showing that another made a *false statement during voir dire* that *concealed the speaker's bias.* [*Warger v. Shauers*] [98]

3. **The exceptions to Rule 606(b)'s prohibition:** Rule 606(b)(2) contains three *exceptions* to the juror-secrecy provisions of 606(b)(1). Under 606(b)(2), a juror *may testify* about whether:

    (A) "*extraneous prejudicial information* was improperly brought to the jury's attention";

    (B) "an *outside influence* was improperly brought to bear on any juror"; or

    (C) "a *mistake* was made in *entering the verdict on the verdict form.*"

    a. **Case-specific information as meeting the "extraneous" exception:** The main type of juror testimony that is admissible under the *"extraneous prejudicial information" exception* (sub-paragraph (A) above) consists of testimony by one juror that another juror brought to the jury room *specific information about the case.* [100]

        Example: After a verdict for the prosecution, D brings a new-trial motion. In support of the motion, Juror 1 offers testimony that during deliberations Juror 2, referring to

Wit, who was D's sole alibi witness, said, "My brother-in-law works at the city jail, and he told me that just before our trial, Wit was jailed on a check-forging charge."

The judge *may* hear Juror 1's testimony, since it consists of specific information about the case, and such information constitutes "extraneous prejudicial information ... improperly brought to the jury's attention."

(1) Does not apply to "common knowledge": Courts interpreting the "extraneous information" exception have held that it applies *only* to *specific knowledge about the facts of the case,* not to *"common"* or *"regional"* knowledge that a juror would be expected to have. Information is "extraneous" (i.e., about the specific facts of the case) if and only if the information "derives from a source *'external' to the jury."* And, "external" matters "include *publicity and information related specifically to the case* that jurors are meant to decide."

By contrast, *"internal"* matters (not covered by the exception) "include *the general body of experiences that jurors are understood to bring with them to the jury room."* [*Warger v. Shauers, supra.*]

Example: At the start of a civil trial, juror Whipple says during voir dire that there is no reason she cannot be impartial in this type of case. The jury finds for D. P asks for a new trial, in support of which he offers an affidavit by a different juror. The affidavit says that Whipple's statements during deliberations show that she lied on *voir dire*, by concealing a strong pro-defendant bias. (According to the affidavit, Whipple said that (1) her daughter once caused a man's death in an auto accident, and (2) if the daughter had been sued, it would have "ruined her life.") The issue is whether the proposed juror affidavit falls within the "extraneous prejudicial information" exception, as P claims. The issue can be re-framed as being whether Whipple's daughter's accident, and the accident's role in giving Whipple an anti-defense bias, constitutes an "external" matter (covered by the extraneous-information exception) or an "internal" matter (not covered).

Held (by the U.S. Supreme Court): The bias here falls on the "internal" side of the external/internal line. That is, Whipple's daughter's accident may well have influenced Whipple's *general* views about negligence liability for car crashes, but it did not give either her or the rest of the jury any *specific knowledge* regarding D's collision with P. Therefore, the accident does not fall within the exception for "extraneous information," and Rule 606(b) requires that the affidavit be excluded from evidence. [*Warger v. Shauers* (2014)]. [102]

b. **"Outside influence" exception:** The second exception, given in sub-section (B) of Rule 606(b)(2) above, covers juror testimony about whether "an *outside influence* was improperly *brought to bear* on any juror[.]" [102]

i. **Interference by outsiders:** An important use of this provision is to allow testimony or affidavits by a juror that show efforts by *outsiders* to *interfere with deliberations,* such as by *bribery.* [102]

Example: D is charged with trying to bribe X, a public official, and is convicted. Seeking a new trial, D offers testimony by Juror 1 that during the course of the trial, Juror 1 witnessed Z (whom Juror 1 recognized as being X's political rival) hand a

$100 bill to Juror 2, and heard Z say to Juror 2, "So you'll vote to convict, right?" Since this proposed testimony is clearly "about whether an outside influence was improperly brought to bear on [a] juror," the testimony falls within the Rule 606(b)(2)(B) exception, preventing the testimony from being barred by Rule 606(b)(1). Thus the judge may hear Juror 1's testimony, and may use it as the basis for granting a new trial.

ii. **Doesn't cover substance abuse:** Testimony that one juror saw one or more other jurors *fall under the influence of drugs or alcohol* does *not* fall within the "outside influence" exception. [*Tanner v. U.S.*] [103]

Example: After the Ds are convicted of fraud, they move for a new trial. In support, they offer affidavits from two jurors describing how various jurors heavily abused multiple substances during the trial (e.g., that the affiant "observed one juror ingest cocaine five times and another juror ingest cocaine two or three times"). The trial judge holds that FRE 606(b) forbids consideration of this juror testimony, and denies the new-trial motion.

Held (by the Supreme Court), for the prosecution. Rule 606(b) prevented the trial judge from considering the affidavits and testimony offered here. The exception in Rule 606(b)(2)(B) for testimony about whether an "outside influence was improperly brought to bear on any juror" does *not* apply: "However severe their effect and improper their use, drugs or alcohol voluntarily ingested by a juror seems no more an 'outside influence' than a virus, poorly prepared food, or a lack of sleep[.]" [*Tanner v. U.S.*] [97]

c. **Use of non-juror evidence:** Note that Rule 606(b) does *not* prevent *non-juror* evidence offered to prove any of the matters covered by the Rule — it's *only* testimony (or affidavits) by a *juror* in the case, concerning something the juror heard, saw or learned during the trial, that is ever excluded under the Rule. [99]

i. **Non-juror evidence of falsehood on *voir dire*:** For instance, Rule 606(b) would not prevent the losing party from offering evidence by a *non-juror* that a juror told a material lie during *voir dire*. [100]

Example: Motor-vehicle accident suit, in which a jury that included Juror unanimously finds for D. Then, Juror's neighbor, Neigh, gives P's counsel an affidavit saying that before the case went to the jury, Juror told Neigh, "They asked me in *voir dire* whether I could be impartial in a negligence case, and I told them 'yes.' But as you know, my brother represents insurance companies who have to defend frivolous accident suits, so it would take a lot to persuade me to find for any plaintiff who brings an accident suit."

Since Neigh is not a juror in the case, Rule 606(b) doesn't apply, and the judge may consider Neigh's affidavit (and/or his live testimony) in deciding whether to grant P a new trial.

d. **Sixth Amendment as a limit on Rule 606(b):** Criminal defendants seeking, post-verdict, to introduce juror testimony blocked by Rule 606(b)(1) have sometimes claimed that the Rule violates their *Sixth Amendment right to an impartial jury.* But these attacks have *usually failed*, on the ground that even where 606(b)(1) blocks the use of one method for ensuring an impartial jury — post-verdict juror testimony about bias — *other methods* of detecting juror bias remain available.

However, in 2017 the Supreme Court for the first time recognized *one type* of juror bias as being so historically-systemic and corrosive that the application of Rule 606(b) to block juror testimony about the bias *will* be deemed a Sixth Amendment violation: clear indications of *racial or ethnic bias* on the part of a juror. [*Pena-Rodriguez v. Colorado*, (2017)] [103]

i. **Standard:** According to *Pena-Rodriguez, supra,* "[n]ot every *offhand comment* indicating *racial bias or hostility*" will justify the trial judge in disregarding Rule 606(b)'s no-impeachment rule. Rather, before the trial judge will be able (indeed, required) to ignore a state or federal jury-secrecy rule so that the judge becomes obligated by the Sixth Amendment to review a post-trial juror affidavit or testimony claiming another juror's racial/ethnic bias, two requirements must be satisfied:

❏ There must be evidence that the other juror "made statements exhibiting *overt racial bias* that *cast serious doubt* on the *fairness and impartiality* of the jury's deliberations and resulting verdict." Plus ...

❏ For a juror's statement showing overt bias to meet the above "serious doubt" standard, that statement "must tend to show that racial animus was a *significant motivating factor*" in that juror's vote to convict. [105]

Example: D, a Hispanic man, is charged in Colorado state court with attempting to sexually assault two teenage sisters he has encountered in a public bathroom. Each prospective member of the jury is asked standard questions to ensure impartiality. H.C. is among the jurors who answers that he can be impartial, and is seated. D is convicted of some of the charges. After the jury is discharged, two jurors tell D's counsel that during deliberations, H.C. made statements demonstrating anti-Hispanic bias against both D and his alibi witness. D's counsel then moves for a new trial, presenting affidavits from the two jurors detailing H.C.'s biased remarks (e.g., that he believed D was guilty because "Mexican men [have] a bravado that cause[s] them to believe they [can] do whatever they want[] with women"). The trial judge rejects the motion, saying that Colorado's version of FRE 606(b)(1) prevents the court from considering the affidavits.

Held (by the U.S. Supreme Court), the trial judge was wrong, and should have considered the affidavits. Racial/ethnic bias is so historically-systemic and corrosive that the application of juror-secrecy laws to block juror testimony about the bias *will* sometimes be deemed a violation of a criminal defendant's *Sixth Amendment right* to an impartial jury. The Sixth Amendment will be violated when there is "a showing that one or more jurors made statements exhibiting *overt racial bias* that *cast serious doubt on the fairness and impartiality* of the jury's deliberations and resulting verdict." And for this "serious doubt" standard to be met, the statement "must tend to show that racial animus was a *significant motivating factor* in the juror's *vote to convict.*" Here, both of these requirements were met by H.C.'s statement. Therefore, the trial judge was required to consider the affidavits in deciding the new-trial motion. [*Pena-Rodriguez v. Colorado*, (2017)] [103-106]

C
A
P
S
U
L
E

S
U
M
M
A
R
Y

ii. **Not applicable to civil cases:**   Since the Sixth Amendment applies only to *criminal* trials, *Pena-Rodriguez* does not require courts to disregard, in **civil cases,** a jurisdiction's rules that block juror testimony about another juror's statements indicating racial bias.

iii. **Applies to state and federal criminal trials:**   On the other hand, since *Pena-Rodriguez* is based on the Sixth Amendment, it applies to **both federal** and **state** criminal trials. So in *all* U.S. criminal trials, a defendant's Sixth Amendment right to an impartial jury means that evidence rules guarding the secrecy of jury deliberations must give way whenever there is a showing that a juror made a statement "exhibiting overt racial bias [casting] serious doubt on the fairness and impartiality" of a verdict against the defendant. [105]

iv. **Ethnicity as well as race:**   The rule announced in *Pena-Rodriguez* — that the Sixth Amendment requires that juror-secrecy rules be set aside to allow the court to consider jury testimony about overtly-biased juror statements — applies to indications of bias based not just on race but on **ethnicity** as well. (*Example:* In *Pena-Rodriguez* itself, the juror's remarks showed bias against "Mexicans," triggering D's Sixth Amendment right to have the jury-secrecy rules set aside.) [106]

(1) **Religious bias:** *Pena-Rodriguez* may well eventually be extended to hold that bias based on **religious** grounds is sufficiently suspect that this type of juror bias too, if overtly stated, justifies the same suspension of juror-secrecy rules.

Example: Following a verdict convicting D of aiding terrorism, Juror 1 signs an affidavit that during deliberations, Juror 2 said, "D is a Muslim, so even though he's a white native-born American who was born Catholic and didn't convert to Islam until last year, his current allegiance to Islam makes me think he's guilty."

A court might well hold that D's Sixth Amendment right to an impartial jury requires that the judge consider the affidavit on a new-trial motion, even though the juror bias involves religion rather than race or ethnicity. [106]

III. CROSS-EXAMINATION

A. **Leading questions:**   Leading questions are usually **permitted** during cross-examination. (FRE 611(c)) [106]

1. **Exception:**   But if the witness is biased in favor of the cross-examiner (e.g., one party is called by the other and then "cross"-examined by his own lawyer), leading questions are not allowed.

B. **Scope:**   The majority (and federal) rule is that cross is **limited** to the **matters testified to on the direct examination.** (FRE 611(b)) [107-108]

C. **Credibility:**   The witness's **credibility** may always be attacked on cross-examination. [107]

IV. RE-DIRECT AND RE-CROSS

A. **Re-direct:**   Re-direct is limited to those aspects of the witness's testimony that were **first brought out during cross**. [109]

B. **Re-cross:**   Similarly, re-cross is limited to matters newly brought up on the re-direct. [102]

V. REFRESHING RECOLLECTION AND OTHER TECHNIQUES

A. Refreshing recollection [113-117]

1. **General rule:** If the witness's memory on a subject is hazy, *any item* (picture, document, weapon, etc.) may be shown to the witness to refresh his recollection. This is the technique of *"present recollection refreshed."*

2. **Not necessarily admissible:** The item need *not* be *admissible*. For instance, it can consist of *inadmissible hearsay*. Furthermore, the item *does not become admissible* by virtue of being used for refreshment. [114]

   > **Example:** D is charged with bank robbery. The prosecution offers testimony by Officer, who investigated the crime. While testifying, Officer consults notes prepared by him during the course of his investigation. D's lawyer objects on the grounds that the notes haven't been introduced into evidence, that the notes *can't* be introduced because they are hearsay not within any exception, and that Officer should therefore be barred from testifying in reliance on their contents.
   >
   > As long as the court is satisfied that Officer is testifying from his own now-refreshed recollection, the fact that the notes haven't been introduced into evidence (and can't be, because of hearsay problems) is irrelevant. And once Officer has consulted the notes, they don't thereby become evidence.

3. **Abuse:** If the item shown to the witness is a *document*, and the trial judge concludes that the witness is really *reading the document on the stand* instead of testifying from his now-refreshed recollection, he may order the testimony stricken.

4. **Cross-examination:** The cross-examiner may *examine* the document or other item shown to the witness, and *use* any part of the document during cross-examination. Further, the cross-examiner may *introduce into evidence* any parts of the document that relate to the witness's testimony.

5. **Documents seen before trial:** If a document has been consulted by the witness *before he took the stand*, the Federal Rules give the trial court discretion to order that the document be shown to the other side, "if the court decides that *justice [so] requires*[.]" (FRE 612(a)(2))

B. Argumentative and misleading questions: A question will be stricken if it is either argumentative or misleading: [117]

1. **Argumentative:** An *argumentative* question is one which tries to get the witness to agree with counsel's interpretation of the evidence. It is more common on cross than on direct, and usually has an element of badgering the witness.

2. **Misleading:** A *misleading* question is one that assumes as true a fact that is either *not in evidence* or is in dispute. It usually has a "trick" aspect. (*Example:* "When did you stop beating your wife," will be misleading if there is no or disputed evidence of wife-beating, since any answer by W will be an implicit admission that he has beaten her.)

VI. EXAMINATION BY COURT

A. General rule: The trial judge may call his own witnesses, and may question any witness (whether called by the judge or by a party). (FRE 614(a) and (b)) [117]

VII. IMPEACHMENT — GENERALLY

A. Five types: There are five main ways of *impeaching* a witness, i.e., of destroying the witness's credibility: (1) by attacking W's general character (e.g., by showing past crimes, past bad acts, or bad reputation); (2) by showing a prior inconsistent statement by W; (3) by showing that W is biased; (4) by showing that W has a sensory or mental defect; and (5) by other evidence (e.g., a second witness's testimony) that contradicts W's testimony. [118]

B. Impeaching one's own witness: [119-120]

    1. Common law: At common law, *a party may not impeach his own witness*. That is, impeachment is generally *not allowed on direct examination*.

        a. Exceptions: But this common-law rule has several exceptions. Impeachment on direct is allowed if: (1) W's unfavorable testimony comes as a genuine surprise to the direct examiner (who may then show prior inconsistent statements by W); or (2) W is an adverse party or a hostile witness.

    2. Modern and Federal Rule: Many states, and the Federal Rules, have now completely *abandoned* the common law rule prohibiting impeachment of one's own witness. See, e.g., FRE 607 ("Any party, including the party that called the witness, may attack the witness's credibility.") Also, a criminal defendant may have the right under the Sixth Amendment's Confrontation Clause to impeach a witness he has called.

VIII. IMPEACHMENT BY PRIOR CRIMINAL CONVICTION

A. Common-law rule: At common law, two types of prior convictions may be used to impeach W's credibility: [120]

    1. *Any felony* conviction;

    2. A *misdemeanor* conviction, but only if the crime involved *dishonesty* or a *false statement*.

B. Federal Rule: The Federal Rules make it slightly harder to use prior convictions to impeach the witness. Under FRE 609(a): [121-129]

    1. *Crimen falsi:* If the crime included as an element *dishonesty or false statement* ("*crimen falsi*"), *it may always be used to impeach W,* regardless of whether it was a *misdemeanor or a felony*, and regardless of the *degree of prejudice* to W (who will usually be the defendant in a criminal proceeding). FRE 609(a)(2). [123-126]

        a. Judge has no discretion to exclude: Once it's established that the conviction is for a *crimen falsi*, the judge does *not* even have *discretion* to exclude it under FRE 403, which normally allows exclusion of evidence whose probative value is substantially outweighed by the danger of unfair prejudice. So no matter how prejudicial to the opponent the evidence is, and no matter how tiny its probative value, the judge must let it come in.

        b. Catalog of *crimen falsi*: Here is a partial catalog of crimes that *are* generally considered to be *crimen falsi* [123]:

            ❏ *Perjury* or *subornation of perjury*;

            ❏ *False statement*;

            ❏ *Criminal fraud*;

CAPSULE SUMMARY

❏ *Embezzlement*;

❏ Taking property by *false pretenses*;

❏ *Counterfeiting*;

❏ *Forgery*; and

❏ *Filing false tax returns*, or failing to file returns at all. (Not all courts agree on the latter.)

Example of *crimen falsi* analysis: D is charged with possession of marijuana, found on the front seat of a car in which D was a passenger when stopped. The prosecution calls the owner of the car, who testifies that the marijuana was not his. D's lawyer now asks the owner, "Isn't it true that three years ago, you were convicted of misdemeanor perjury charges?" The owner denies this, at which point D's lawyer offers into evidence proof of such a conviction.

The question and proof of conviction are admissible. That's because *perjury is always a crimen falsi*, i.e., a crime the conviction of which "required proving — or the witness's admitting — a dishonest act or false statement." (609(a)(2)). Therefore, the conviction is admissible (1) even though it was a misdemeanor rather than a felony (i.e., "regardless of the punishment," in the language of 609(a)(2)), and (2) regardless of the relationship between its prejudicial impact and its probative value.

c. **Not *crimen falsi*:** Other crimes just as clearly fall on the ***non*-*crimen falsi*** side of the line. These are crimes that are defined in such a way that deception is not one of the elements. Most crimes of *violence* (*murder*, *rape*, *assault and battery*, for instance), as well as a number of non-violent crimes (*drug offenses*; *prostitution*; driving while intoxicated; resisting arrest) are not *crimen falsi*, since dishonesty or false statement is not an element of those crimes. [124]

   i. **Other theft crimes:** *Theft crimes* other than false pretenses and embezzlement are ***not*** *crimen falsi*. So *shoplifting, robbery* and *receiving stolen goods* aren't *crimen falsi* under the FRE.

d. **Don't look to underlying facts:** Under FRE 609(a), the court may *not* treat a crime as *crimen falsi* **unless it is defined so as to require proof of dishonesty or false statement** -- it's not enough that the defendant *actually behaved in a deceitful way*.

Example: D sees V on the street, lures her into a secluded alleyway by falsely telling her he has a message for her from her husband, and then robs her. Since robbery is not defined to include dishonesty or false statement as an element of the crime, D's robbery conviction is not a *crimen falsi* under FRE 609(a) even though D committed this particular crime in a deceitful manner.

2. **Non-crimen-falsi felony used against criminal D:** If the crime was a *felony* not involving dishonesty or false statement, and the witness is the *defendant in a criminal case*, the crime may be used only "if the probative value of the evidence *outweighs* its prejudicial effect to [the] defendant." So criminal defendants get a slight degree of extra protection against having their non-*crimen-falsi* convictions used against them. [126-127]

   a. **Witnesses other than an accused:** By contrast, where the witness being impeached by a non-*crimen-falsi* felony conviction is *not* a criminal defendant (e.g., she's a prosecution witness, a witness for a criminal defendant, or any witness in a civil case), the witness gets *no special protection* against impeachment. Instead, FRE 403 applies, allowing a prior conviction to be excluded only if the person opposing its introduction bears the burden of showing that the conviction's probative value is "*substantially* outweighed by a danger of ... unfair prejudice[.]"

3. **Other misdemeanors:** If the crime was a *misdemeanor* not involving dishonesty or false statement, it may not be used for impeachment at all.

4. **Old convictions:** If *more than 10 years* have elapsed from both the conviction and the prison term for that conviction, the conviction may not be used for impeachment unless the court determines that there are "specific facts and circumstances" that make the probative value of the conviction substantially outweigh its prejudicial effect. FRE 609(b)(1). This makes it much harder to get more-than-10-year-old convictions into evidence. [128]

5. ***In limine* motions:** D may, before taking the stand, ask the trial court to rule *in limine* whether a particular conviction will be allowed to impeach him. If the ruling goes against D, D can then elect not to take the stand. (But if he doesn't take the stand, the *in limine* ruling will not be reviewed on appeal, at least in federal courts.) [128]

6. **Ineligible convictions:** Certain types of convictions are excluded by special rules: If W was *pardoned*, based on a finding of *innocence*, the conviction may never be used. (If the pardon was because W was rehabilitated, it may be used for impeachment only if W has been convicted of a subsequent felony.) A *"juvenile adjudication"* of D may not be used to impeach him. FRE 609(c), (d). [129]

IX. IMPEACHMENT BY PRIOR BAD ACTS

A. **Common law:** [130]

1. **Generally allowed:** Most common-law courts allow the cross-examiner to bring out the fact that the witness has committed *prior bad acts*, even though these have not led to a criminal conviction. (E.g., "Isn't it true that you lied on your job application by falsely stating that you had never used drugs?")

    a. **Questions about arrests:** Most courts say that the witness can't be asked whether he's been *arrested* for a particular act — the question must be, "Did you commit thus-and-such an act?" not "Did you get arrested for thus-and-such an act?"

2. **No extrinsic evidence:** The prior bad acts *must* be introduced solely through the cross-examination, *not* through *extrinsic evidence*. (*Example:* If W denies having lied on a job application, the cross-examiner cannot call a different witness to prove that the lie occurred.)

3. **Good-faith basis:** Before the prosecutor may ask a witness about a prior specific bad act, he must have a *good faith basis* for believing that the witness really committed the act.

B. **Federal Rule:** The Federal Rules basically follow the common-law approach to prior bad act impeachment. (FRE 608(b)) [130-135]

1. **Probative of truthfulness:** However, only prior bad acts that are *probative of truthfulness* may be asked about.

    Example: A prior act of lying on a job application or embezzling from an employer could be asked about, but the fact that W killed his wife and was never tried could not be, because this act does not make it more likely than it would otherwise be that W is now lying.

2. **No extrinsic evidence:** As at common law, any prior bad act must be shown only through cross-examination, not through extrinsic evidence.

3. **Discretion of court:** All questions about prior bad acts are in the ***discretion of the court***. The extent to which the questioner has a good faith basis for believing W really committed the act will, of course, be one factor the court normally considers.

X.   IMPEACHMENT BY OPINION AND REPUTATION REGARDING CHARACTER

A. **Common law:** [136-136]

1. **Allowed at common law:** Common law allows W1's credibility to be impeached by testimony from W2 that W1 has a ***bad reputation for truthfulness***.

2. **Opening issue:** As soon as a criminal defendant takes the stand, he opens himself up to this kind of evidence, even if he does not affirmatively state that he is a truthful person.

3. **Opinions:** W2 must say that W1 has a bad reputation for truthfulness; W2 may not state his own ***opinion*** that W1 is untruthful. Nor may W2 describe ***specific instances*** of conduct by W1 that led to his bad reputation for truthfulness.

4. **General bad character:** W2 must talk only about W1's reputation for truthfulness, not W1's reputation for general bad character.

B. **Federal Rules:** FRE 608(a) basically follows the common law, except that W2 may state his ***opinion*** that W1 is a liar (as well as stating that W1 has a reputation for being a liar). Here, too, no specific instances of untruthfulness by W1 are allowed. [136]

XI.   IMPEACHMENT BY PRIOR INCONSISTENT STATEMENT

A. **General rule:** W's credibility may generally be impeached by showing that he has made a ***prior inconsistent statement.*** [138]

B. **Foundation:** But before W's prior inconsistent statement may be admitted to impeach him, a ***foundation*** must be laid. [138-140]

1. **Common law:** At common law, the foundation requirement is rigid: W must first be told the substance of the alleged statement, the time, the place, and the person to whom it was made. He must then be given a chance to deny having made the statement, or to explain away the inconsistency. Only after all this may the prior inconsistent statement be introduced into evidence.

2. **Federal Rule:** The Federal Rules liberalize the foundation requirement: W must still be given a chance to explain or deny the prior inconsistent statement, but this opportunity does not have to be given to him until ***after*** the statement has been proved (e.g., by testimony from W2 that W1 made the prior inconsistent statement). For more about this, see Paragraph (C), "Extrinsic evidence," below.

3. **Writing:** If the prior inconsistent statement is ***written***, the common-law rule is that the writing must be shown to the witness before it is admitted. But FRE 613(a) relaxes this require-

ment, too: the examiner may first get W to deny having made the prior statement, and then admit it into evidence.

C. Extrinsic evidence: Special rules limit the questioner's ability to prove that W made a prior inconsistent statement by *"extrinsic"* evidence, i.e., by evidence other than W's admitting that he did so (e.g., testimony by W2 or admission of a copy of W's prior written statement). [140-142]

    1. Federal Rule: The Federal Rules make it easier than the common law did for a questioner to prove by extrinsic evidence that a witness made a prior inconsistent statement. But the FRE still impose important limits on this process. FRE 613(b) says that such extrinsic proof can only be made where *two requirements* are satisfied:

        [1] The witness who made the prior inconsistent statement must be *"given an opportunity to explain or deny"* it; and

        [2] The *opposite party* (the proponent of the testimony of the witness being impeached by the prior inconsistent statement) must be given "an *opportunity to examine* the witness [who made the inconsistent statement] about it."

    (But both of these requirements may be dispensed with "if "justice so requires.")

    These two requirements mean that, as a practical matter, *if the principal witness* (call her W1) *is to be impeached by a prior inconsistent statement*, the impeacher will have to be sure that *after the extrinsic evidence is presented, W1 remains physically available* to "explain or deny" it and to be interrogated about the statement by W1's proponent.

    Example: W testifies in an auto accident case, "D was travelling over 70 mph." W is excused by P, and leaves the country. D presents testimony by Officer that when Officer interviewed W two days after the accident, W said "D wasn't going more than 60 mph." Since W is no longer available to explain or deny making this statement, or to be interrogated about the alleged statement by P's counsel, FRE 613(b) prevents Officer's testimony. [142]

    a. No specific rule about extrinsic evidence on collateral matter: At common law, there was a *prohibition* on extrinsic proof of prior inconsistent statements dealing with *collateral matters* (i.e., matters that are not probative on a material issue in the case). The Federal Rules do not expressly say whether this collateral-matters rule is maintained. But the effective answer is *yes*: the trial judge has discretion, under FRE 403, to exclude evidence whose probative value is "substantially outweighed by a danger of ... confusing the issues, or undue delay [or] wasting time[,]" and extrinsic evidence of collateral matters will often *justify exclusion* under 403.

XII. IMPEACHMENT FOR BIAS

A. Generally allowed: All courts allow proof that the witness is *biased.* W may be shown to be biased in favor of a party (e.g., W and P are friends or relatives), or biased against a party (e.g., W and D were once involved in litigation). W's *interest in the outcome* may be also shown as a form of bias (e.g., if W is an expert, the fact that he is being paid a fee for his testimony is generally allowed as showing that he has an interest in having the case decided in favor of the party retaining him). [142-143]

B. Extrinsic evidence: Bias may be shown by use of ***extrinsic evidence***. However, most courts require a foundation before extrinsic evidence may be used for this purpose: the examiner must ask W about the alleged bias, and only if W denies it may the extrinsic evidence (e.g., testimony by another person that W is biased) be presented. [143]

XIII. IMPEACHMENT BY SENSORY OR MENTAL DEFECT

A. Generally allowed: W may be impeached by showing that his capacity to ***observe***, ***remember***, or ***narrate*** events correctly has been impaired. (*Example:* W may be shown to have such poor eyesight that he couldn't have seen what he claims to have seen.) [144-145]

B. Alcohol and drugs:

  1. Use during event: W may be impeached by showing that he was ***drunk*** or ***high on drugs*** at the time of the events he claims to have witnessed.

  2. Addiction: Courts are split on whether W may be shown to be a ***habitual*** or addicted user of alcohol and drugs — many courts will not allow this if there is no showing that W was drunk or high at the time of the events in question.

XIV. IMPEACHMENT BY CONTRADICTION; THE "COLLATERAL ISSUE" RULE

A. Showing of contradiction allowed: W1 may be impeached by presenting W2, who contradicts W1 on some point. (*Example:* W1 says that perpetrator of robbery had red hair; defense can put on W2 to testify that robber had brown hair — this not only is evidence of a material fact, but also impeaches W1.) [145-148]

B. Collateral issue rule: However, the right to put on a second witness to impeach the first by contradicting him, is limited by the ***"collateral issue"*** rule, at least at common law. By this rule, certain types of testimony by W2 are deemed to be of such collateral interest to the case that they will not be allowed if their sole purpose is to contradict W1. [148-152]

  1. Disallowed: Thus, W2 may not testify as to: (1) prior bad acts by W1 that did not lead to a conviction; (2) prior inconsistent statements made by W1 that do not relate to a material fact in the case; or (3) things said by W1 in his testimony which according to W2 are not true, unless these facts are material to the case.

  2. Allowed: On the other hand, testimony by W2 will not be deemed to be collateral, and will thus be allowed, as to the following subjects: (1) prior criminal convictions by W1; (2) W1's bad character for truthfulness; (3) W1's bias; or (4) W1's sensory or mental defect that prevents W1 from observing, remembering or narrating events correctly.

  3. Federal Rule: The Federal Rules do not contain any explicit "collateral issue" rule. However, the trial judge can apply the policies behind the rule by using FRE 403's balancing test (evidence excludable where its probative value is substantially outweighed by confusion, prejudice, or waste of time).

XV. RELIGIOUS BELIEFS

A. General rule: Most courts do not allow W to be impeached by a showing that he does not believe in God. Impeachment based on religious beliefs is also barred by FRE 610. [152]

XVI. REHABILITATING IMPEACHED WITNESS

A. **No bolstering:** A lawyer may not offer evidence *supporting his witness's credibility*, unless that credibility has first been *attacked* by the other side. This is known as the rule against *"bolstering one's witness"*. (*Example:* On direct, W tells a story favorable to P. P's lawyer will not be permitted to bring out on direct the fact that prior to the trial, W told the same story to the police — W's credibility has not yet been attacked, so it may not be bolstered by a showing that W made a prior consistent statement.) [153]

   1. **Prior identification:** However, the "no bolstering" rule does not apply where W has made a prior out-of-court *identification* — most courts allow this to be brought out as part of the direct examination of W.

   2. **Prompt complaint:** Similarly, in *rape* cases most courts allow the victim to in effect bolster her own testimony by stating that she made a *prompt complaint* to the police immediately following the crime.

B. **Rehabilitation:** Apart from these exceptions, W's credibility may be supported only to rehabilitate it, i.e., only to repair the damage done by the *other side's attack* on that credibility. [153]

   1. **Meet attack:** The rehabilitating evidence must *"meet the attack."* That is, it must support W's credibility in the same respect as that in which the credibility has been attacked by the other side. (*Example:* P attacks W as being biased because he is D's son. D may rehabilitate W's credibility by showing evidence of non-bias. But D may not rehabilitate W by showing W's good reputation for truthfulness, or W's prior out-of-court statements that are consistent with his trial testimony — D's attempts at rehabilitation do not respond directly to the charge of bias.)

   2. **Good character:** If W's credibility is attacked by evidence tending to show that he is generally untruthful, the proponent may show that W has a good character for truthfulness. Thus evidence of W's *good character for truthfulness* may be used to rebut evidence that: (1) W has a *bad reputation* for truthfulness; (2) that W2 has a *bad opinion* of W's truthfulness; (3) that W has been *convicted* of a crime; or (4) that W has committed a *prior bad act*; and perhaps (5) that W has been subjected to a slashing *cross-examination* by the opponent, implying or stating that W is a *liar*.

      a. **Attack on present testimony:** But if the attack on W has merely been to show that his testimony in the present case is inaccurate, W's credibility may not be rehabilitated by a showing of his general good character for truthfulness. Thus good character evidence will not be allowed to rebut evidence that: (1) W is *biased* because he is related to the other party; (2) W has given *erroneous testimony* in this case, perhaps through honest mistake.

      b. **Prior inconsistent statement:** If W has been attacked by a showing that he made a *prior inconsistent statement*, the courts are split. Most treat this as an implicit attack on W's general credibility, and thus allow him to be rehabilitated by a showing of good general character for truthfulness.

   3. **Prior consistent statement:** The fact that W has made a *prior consistent statement* (i.e., an out-of-court statement that matches his trial testimony) may be used only to rebut an express or implied charge that W's trial testimony is a *recent fabrication* or the product of *improper influence or motive*. This is the common-law rule, and is also carried out by FRE 801(d)(1)(B). [155-157]

    a. Attack on general character: Thus if W is attacked by showing his ***prior criminal convictions***, ***prior bad acts***, or his general ***bad reputation*** for veracity, his credibility may ***not*** be rehabilitated by a showing that he made prior consistent statements.

    b. Prior inconsistent statement: The opponent's showing that W has made a prior ***inconsistent*** statement will not, by itself, entitle the proponent to show that W has also made a prior consistent statement. The proponent must demonstrate that the adversary's use of the prior inconsistent statement amounts to an express or implied claim that W has recently made up his trial testimony, or is lying because of improper influence or ulterior motives. (Thus if the showing of the prior inconsistent statement can reasonably be interpreted as suggesting that W is merely honestly mistaken, W cannot be rehabilitated by the prior consistent statement.)

    c. Before motive arose: The proponent who wants to use a prior consistent statement must show that the prior statement was made ***before*** the alleged motive to fabricate or improper influence arose. This rule applies both at common-law and under FRE 801(d)(1)(B). [*Tome v. U.S.*]

XVII. SPECIAL TECHNIQUES FOR DEVELOPING OR EVALUATING TESTIMONY

A. Psychiatric testimony: The trial judge has discretion to allow psychiatric expert testimony to show that W's accuracy is doubtful because of some mental illness or defect. For instance, the judge might appoint a psychiatrist to give expert testimony as to whether V's mental illness may have caused her to imagine a rape, or to have falsified the surrounding details. But judges will generally order a party or witness to undergo psychiatric examination for purposes of evaluating credibility only if there are ***compelling reasons*** to do so. [168]

B. Hypnosis and truth serum: [168-169]

    1. Statement made under influence: Statements made under the influence of hypnosis or truth serum are almost always ***rejected***.

    2. Testimony at trial: Live testimony by W about an event, his recall of which has been refreshed through hypnosis or truth serum, is also usually ***rejected***. But a minority of courts allow hypnosis-influenced testimony if stringent safeguards have been followed (e.g., a video tape was made of the hypnosis session).

        a. Criminal defendant's right to testify: Where the hypnotized witness is a ***criminal defendant***, the court's right to reject hypnotically-refreshed testimony is limited by the defendant's constitutional right to ***testify in his own defense***. [*Rock v. Arkansas*]

C. Lie detectors: [170-171]

    1. General rule: Nearly all courts ***reject*** lie detector evidence when offered on the issue of whether the statements made by the subject during the test are true. (However, *Daubert v. Merrell Dow*, holding that scientifically valid techniques can't be excluded from federal trials just because they're not "generally accepted," may now be changing this blanket rule.)

    2. Stipulation: A substantial minority of courts allow lie detector results where both parties have ***stipulated*** before the test that the results may be admitted.

HEARSAY

I.   DEFINITION

A. Simple definition: Hearsay is *"a statement or assertive conduct that was made or occurred out of court and is offered in court to prove the truth of the matter asserted."* (*Example:* V says, "D tried to poison me last night." This is hearsay if offered to show that D really tried to kill V last night, since it is an out-of-court statement offered to prove the truth of the matter asserted.) [182]

   1. Writing: Hearsay may be *written* as well as oral. (*Example:* A letter written by V to her mother, "D tried to kill me last night," would be hearsay if offered to prove that D really did this, just as would V's oral statement to her mother to the same effect.)

B. Four dangers: The use of hearsay testimony presents four main dangers: (1) *ambiguity*; (2) *insincerity*; (3) *incorrect memory*; and (4) *inaccurate perception*. All of these relate to the fact that the person making the out-of-court statement (the declarant) is not available for cross-examination. [182, 183-184]

C. Triangle: In terms of a "testimonial triangle" (see Figure C-1 on next page), O's statement will only be hearsay if the trier of fact is asked to travel from point A to point B to point C (i.e., the fact-finder must be asked to determine that the declarant truly held the belief which his declaration suggests he held — point B — and also that declarant's belief accurately reflects reality — point C). [184]

   Example: O is prosecuted for robbery; he claims that he was captured and forced to take part in the robbery. He offers a note he wrote to his wife during the captivity, "If I don't take part in the robbery, they'll kill me." The fact-finder is asked to travel from point A to point B (i.e., to determine whether O really believed his statement), but not to travel from point B to point C (i.e., to determine whether O's belief accorded with reality). Since the fact-finder is not asked to travel all the way around the triangle, O's statement is not hearsay.

II.   SPECIAL ISSUES

A. "Out of court" statement: An out-of-court statement is any statement except one made "by a witness during the trial while testifying before the trier of fact." Therefore, the following will be out-of-court statements (and thus might be hearsay): [191]

   1. Any oral or written statement by someone other than the at-trial witness; and

   2. A prior statement by the at-trial witness, where the prior statement was not made in the present trial before the trier of fact. Therefore, W's prior statement made in a *deposition* or at an *earlier trial*, or even W's statement made in the judge's chambers during the present trial, are all "out of court" and so may be hearsay.

B. "Truth of matter asserted":   Here are some uses to which a statement may be put that do *not* constitute offering the statement for the "truth of the matter asserted": [191-196]

   1. Verbal acts: The statement is a "verbal act," i.e., an operative fact that gives rise to legal consequences. (*Example:* O says to W (a vice officer), "If you pay me $25 I will have sex

Figure C-1

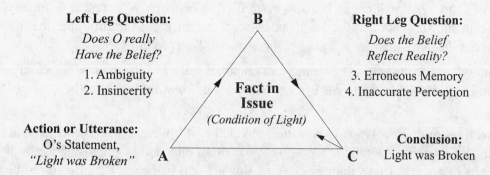

with you." If O is prosecuted for solicitation, her statement will not be hearsay because it is not offered to show its truth (that O would really have had sex with W had he paid her $25); rather, the crime of solicitation is defined so as to make an offer to have sex for money an act with legal consequences.)

    a. **Verbal parts of act:** Similarly, a *"verbal part of the act"*, i.e., words that accompany an ambiguous physical act, is not offered for truth and thus is not hearsay. (*Example:* O gives X money, saying, "This will repay you for the money you lent me last year." If offered by X in defense of a bribery charge, this will be non-hearsay because the words that accompanied the payment give the payment its particular legal effect — loan repayment.)

2. **Effect on hearer/reader:** A statement offered to show its effect on the *listener* or *reader* will generally not be hearsay. Thus if a statement is offered to show that the listener or reader was *put on notice*, had certain *knowledge*, had a certain *emotion*, or behaved *reasonably* or unreasonably, this will not be hearsay. (*Example:* Malpractice suit against D, a hospital, for having hired X as a doctor. P offers written statements by two other hospitals refusing to allow X on their staffs because he was incompetent. If P shows that D saw the letters before admitting X to the staff, this will not be hearsay — the letters are not being offered to prove the truth of the matters asserted (that X was really incompetent), merely to show that a reasonable person in D's position would have doubted X's competence.)

3. **Declarant's state of mind:** Statements introduced to show the *state of mind* of the *declarant* are not offered for the "truth of the matter asserted" and thus are not hearsay.

    a. **Knowledge:** Thus a statement offered to show the declarant's *knowledge* is not hearsay. (*Example:* D says to X, "I need to get my brakes checked because they haven't been working well." In a negligence suit by P against D, that statement is not hearsay, because it is not offered to show that the brakes really were defective, merely that D had knowledge that the brakes might be defective.)

    b. **Other mental state:** Statements offered to show the declarant's *sanity* or *emotion* (e.g., fear) are similarly not offered for truth and thus are not hearsay. (Also, there is an exception for "statements evidencing states of mind.")

4. **Reputation:** Statements about a person's *reputation* may not be hearsay. (*Example:* Libel action; W testifies at trial, "O told me that P has a reputation for thievery." If offered to show that O's statement caused this false reputation of P, this will not be hearsay — it is not offered to prove that P is really a thief, merely to prove that P has been given a false reputation for thievery.)

5. **Impeachment:** If W makes a statement at trial, use of a prior inconsistent statement made out of court by W will not be hearsay when used to *impeach* W's present testimony — what is being shown is not that the prior out-of-court statement was truthful, but that the conflict between the two statements raises questions about W's credibility.

C. **"Statement" and conduct:** The hearsay rule applies only to "statements." An oral or written assertion is obviously a statement. But certain types of *conduct* may also be statements: [196-200]

   1. **Assertive conduct:** *Assertive conduct* is treated as if it were a "statement," so that it can be hearsay. (*Example:* O pulls D's mug shot out of a collection of photos; since by this act O intends to assert, "That's the perpetrator," this act will be hearsay if offered on the issue of whether D was the perpetrator.) [197]

   2. **Silence:** A person's *silence* will be treated as a "statement," and thus possibly hearsay, only if it is *intended* by the person as an assertion.

      a. **Absence of complaints:** The fact that one or more people have *not made complaints* about a situation will *not* usually be treated as the equivalent of a statement by them that there is nothing to complain about. Therefore, absence of prior complaints can usually be admitted without hearsay problems.

      b. **Silence in face of accusation:** But a person's silence in the face of an *accusation against him*, where the silence is offered to show that the accusation was true, usually will be held to be intended as an assertion, and thus hearsay. (But the hearsay exception for admissions will usually apply anyway.) [197-198]

   3. **Non-assertive conduct:** Conduct that is *not intended as an assertion* will *never* be hearsay, under the modern and Federal Rules. (This reverses the earlier common-law rule of *Wright v. Doe*.) [199-200]

      a. **Non-assertive verbal conduct:** Even a verbal statement will not be hearsay if it is not intended as an assertion. (*Example:* D is charged with running a bookmaking operation out of his premises. W testifies that he answered D's phone, and the caller on the other end said, "Secretariat to place in the third." Caller's statement will not be hearsay, because even though it was verbal, the caller did not intend to assert, "I am talking to a betting parlor," or anything else.)

      b. **Non-verbal conduct:** Similarly, non-verbal conduct that is not intended as an assertion will not give rise to hearsay. (*Example:* O, while walking down the street, suddenly puts up his umbrella. If this act is introduced to show that it was raining, it will not be hearsay — O was not intending to assert to anyone, "It's raining.")

   4. **Assertions not offered to prove truth of matter asserted:** If an assertion is offered to prove another assertion that is *implied by* (or can be inferred from) the former, there is a hearsay problem only if the person making the assertion was *thinking about the proposition now sought to be proved*. (*Example:* O writes to T, "Cousin, the weather is wonderful in America and you would like it here." This assertion would not be hearsay if offered to establish that O thought T was sane, since it is unlikely that O was consciously thinking to himself when he wrote this letter, "T is sane." On the other hand, if O wrote to T, "As of your last letter, you

seemed to be of sound mind," this would be hearsay even if offered as circumstantial proof that at some later date, T was still sane — O was thinking about the very issue now sought to be proved, T's sanity.) [201-202]

D. Multiple hearsay: If one out-of-court declaration quotes or paraphrases another out-of-court declaration, there is a problem of **"multiple hearsay."** The evidence is inadmissible if **any** of the declarations is hearsay not falling within an exception. (*Example:* W, an investigator, writes a report saying, "D told me that at the time of the crash, he was travelling at 65 mph." If this report is offered by P to show that D was indeed travelling at 65 mph, there are two levels of hearsay: D's original oral statement and W's out-of-court written paraphrase of it. But each would probably fall within an exception — D's original statement as an admission, and W's report under the business records rule. Therefore, the report could come into evidence.) [204]

Chapter 6
HEARSAY EXCEPTIONS

I. ADMISSIONS

A. General rule: "Admissions" receive an exceptions from the hearsay rule. That is, **a party's words or acts may be offered as evidence against him,** even though these would be inadmissible hearsay if said or done by someone other than a party. (Under the Federal Rules, an admission is simply not hearsay at all. See FRE 801(d)(2). At common law, admissions are hearsay, but receive an exception.) [215-217]

    1. Distinguished from declaration against interest: Be sure to distinguish admissions from declarations against interest. Unlike a declaration against interest, an admission need not be against the declarant's interest at the time it is made; thus even a statement that seems neutral or self-serving at the time it is made may be introduced against the party who made it.

    2. Opinion: An admission is admissible even though it contains an **opinion** or a **conclusion of law**, and even though it is not based on the maker's **first-hand knowledge.** Thus it can be admitted more easily even than the same statement when made at trial.

B. Personal admissions: One type of admission is a **party's own statement**, offered against him ("personal admission"). [218-219]

    1. Pleadings: Statements a party makes in his **pleadings** are treated as personal admissions for most purposes, and are thus admissible.

    2. Conduct as admission: A party's conduct, even if it is intended as an assertion (and thus is hearsay under the modern rule) will be admissible under the exception for admissions. (*Example:* Proof of D's attempt to conceal V's body would be admissible as an admission by D of his guilt, even if the court decided that this was assertive conduct.)

C. Adoptive: Under common law and the Federal Rules, a party may be deemed to have **adopted** another person's statement, in which case the statement will be admissible as an admission by the former party. [219-222]

    1. "Real and knowing" test: If a party is claimed to have adopted another's statement and the adoption is merely **implied**, the test is: whether, taking into account all circumstances, the party's conduct or silence justifies the conclusion that he **knowingly agreed** with the other person's statement.

2. **Silence:** Often, the party's **silence** in the face of the other person's statement will, under the circumstances, indicate that the party agrees with the statement. If so, he will be held to have made an adoptive admission, which will thus be admissible. (*Example:* While D flashes a large wad of bills, X, his girlfriend, says to W, "D got that money as his piece of the National Bank job last week." D's silence in the face of this statement will probably be found by the court to show D's knowing agreement with X's statement, since otherwise, D would have denied the statement. Therefore, the statement will be admissible against D as an adoptive admission.)

    a. **Criminal cases:** In criminal cases, D's failure to respond to accusations made by the police while D is in **custody** will not be admissible against him as adoptive admissions, because this would violate the spirit of *Miranda*. But silence in the face of accusations made outside of police custody, or silence to accusations made by non-police, may be admitted against the criminal defendant under the adoptive-admission theory.

    b. **Writing:** A party's silence in the face of a **writing** will similarly be an adoptive admission, if the party can reasonably be expected to have objected were the writing untrue. (*Example:* D receives a bill from a creditor, reciting certain sums owed for specified work. If D does not respond, his silence in the face of the bill will be treated as an adoptive admission by him of the truth of the bill's contents.)

D. **Representative admission:** Even if a party did not make (or even learn of) another person's admission, that admission may be admissible against the party because he **authorized it** in some way. This is a "representative" or "vicarious" admission. [222-225]

1. **Explicit authorization:** This may occur because the party **explicitly** authorized another person to speak for him. (*Example:* Transport Co. authorizes any employee who is involved in an accident to make a statement to the police. A statement made by Employee arising out of such an accident will be admissible against Transport, because it was explicitly authorized.)

    a. **Statements to principal:** Even if the principal authorizes the agent only to make the report **to the principal,** the modern and federal approach is to treat this as an adoptive admission. Thus, an employee's accident investigation report, given only to the employee's boss, would nonetheless be admissible against the boss.

2. **Vicarious:** Even if an agent is not explicitly authorized to make statements, statements he makes arising from a **transaction within his authority** will, under the modern view, be deemed to be authorized admissions by the principal. These are called **"vicarious"** admissions.

    a. **Common law:** At common law, this was not so: only "authorized" admissions, not "vicarious" ones, would be admissible against the principal.

    b. **Modern and Federal Rule:** But the modern and Federal Rule recognizes vicarious admissions. See, e.g., FRE 801(d)(2)(D), admitting a statement offered against a party if made "by the party's **agent or employee** on a **matter within the scope of that relationship** and **while it existed**[.]"

    Example: Truck Driver makes an accident statement to the police. Even if Employer, the company for which Driver works, never authorized him to make accident reports, under the modern/federal rule Driver's statement will be admissible against Employer because it relates to matters — driving and accidents — that were within Driver's employment.

    i. How to prove: The proponent of the admission may *use the statement itself as one item of evidence* to show that the agent was acting within the scope of his agency or employment relationship when the declaration was made. But the statement *cannot be the sole item of evidence* demonstrating this point. FRE 801(d)2), last sent.

        Example: Same facts as above example. Suppose that in Driver's accident statement to the police, he says, "I was making a delivery for Employer at the time of the accident." When the trial judge determines whether Driver was acting on behalf of Employer at the time of the accident, the judge can consider, as one piece of evidence, the fact that in the statement at issue, Driver confirmed that he was acting on Employer's business. But there must be some additional evidence, beyond the statement, that Driver really was on company business at the time of the accident.

E. Co-conspirators: [225-228]

  1. General rule: There is an important hearsay exception for statements by *co-conspirators*: a statement by one co-conspirator is admissible against other members of the *same conspiracy*, so long as the statement is made: (1) *during the course* of the conspiracy; and (2) in *furtherance* of the conspiracy. (*Example:* A says to X, "Don't you want to join B and me in robbing the First National Bank next Thursday?" This statement may be used against B in a prosecution for the robbery of that bank that took place on that date, since the statement was made by a member of the same conspiracy, made while the conspiracy was taking place, and made for the purpose of furthering its aims by recruitment.) See FRE 801(d)(2)(E).

  2. "During course of": The requirement that the statement take place "during the course of" the conspiracy means that:

    a. After end: Statements made *after the conspiracy has ended* are admissible only against the declarant, not against the other members. Thus, if the conspiracy is broken up by the *arrest* of A and B (the only members of the conspiracy), anything B says to the police will not be admissible against A, since the arrest has terminated the conspiracy.

    b. Conspirator leaves: If A leaves the conspiracy, but B and C continue the conspiracy without him, statements made by B and C after A leaves may not be admitted against A. (But the converse is not true: statements made by A to the authorities after he has left the conspiracy might be admissible against B and C, since their conspiratorial activities are still continuing at the time of A's statement.)

    c. Statements before: Statements made by early conspirators *before* a later entry joins are admissible against the latter — when a conspirator enters an ongoing conspiracy, he is held to have adopted the earlier statements of fellow co-conspirators, so these are admissible against him.

  3. In furtherance: The "in furtherance" requirement means that a statement should be admitted against a co-conspirator only if it was made for the purpose of advancing the conspiracy's objectives.

    a. Weakly applied: But this requirement is often not taken seriously. Thus, confessions by a co-conspirator, narratives of past events, or statements by the declarant blaming a crime on his co-conspirators rather than himself, are all frequently admitted under the exception even though, strictly speaking, they don't seem to meet the "in furtherance" requirement since they don't advance the conspiracy's objectives.

4. **No need to charge conspiracy:** Statements by one co-conspirator against another may be admitted under the exception *even if no conspiracy crime is formally charged*.

5. **Procedure:** It is the judge who decides whether a conspiracy has been shown, so that the exception applies. He reaches this decision as follows:

   a. **Preponderance:** He need only find that a conspiracy exists by a *preponderance of the evidence*, not "beyond a reasonable doubt."

   b. **Statements:** In determining whether a conspiracy exists by a preponderance, he may *consider the alleged statement itself*.

      i. **May not be sole proof of conspiracy:** But the contents of the statement *may not be the sole proof* that the conspiracy existed (or that the defendant and the declarant were members). FRE 801(d)(2), final sent. In other words, there must be *some independent evidence* that the conspiracy existed.

II. AVAILABILITY IMMATERIAL — GENERALLY

A. **List of exceptions:** Four major hearsay exceptions apply even where the declarant is *available* to give courtroom testimony: [229]

   1. *Spontaneous, excited,* or *contemporaneous utterances* (including statements about *physical or mental condition*);

   2. *Past recollection recorded*;

   3. *Business records*; and

   4. *Public records* and *reports*.

III. SPONTANEOUS, EXCITED, OR CONTEMPORANEOUS UTTERANCES (INCLUDING STATEMENTS ABOUT THEN-EXISTING PHYSICAL OR MENTAL CONDITION)

A. **Statements of physical condition:** There is a hearsay exception for statements by a person about his then-existing *physical condition*. [230-232]

   1. **Statement to lay person:** If the statement is made to a lay person, it is covered by the exception only if it relates to the declarant's *present* bodily condition or symptoms. Usually, it will relate to pain. (*Example:* X says to W, "I'm feeling terrible chest pains." W can testify about this statement even if it is offered for the purpose of showing that X did indeed suffer chest pains.)

   2. **To treating doctor:** For statements made by a person about his bodily condition, when made to a *physician* who is *treating* him, the exception is broader:

      a. **Past symptoms:** The statement may be about *past* pain or past symptoms.

      b. **Cause:** The statement may include references to the *cause* of the bodily condition (though statements about whose *fault* the condition is will generally not be allowed; thus W's statement that he was hit by a car will qualify, but his statement that the car was driven through a red light would not).

c. Statement by friend or relative: A statement made *by a third person* (e.g., a friend or relative of the patient) is also covered, if made to help the patient get treatment.

d. Non-M.D.: Under FRE 803(4), statements made for purposes of getting medical treatment that are made to a *nurse*, ambulance driver, hospital admitting clerk, or other third person involved in the health-care process, are covered by the exception.

e. Non-treating physician: If the statement is made to a doctor who is not furnishing *treatment*, but who is consulted so that he can testify about the patient's condition at trial, the statement is covered by the federal exception (but not by the common-law exception).

B. Declaration of mental condition: There is a hearsay exception for statements by a person concerning his *present mental or emotional state*. [233-241]

1. State of mind directly in issue: The exception is often used where a declarant's state of mind is directly in issue. (*Example:* P sues D for alienating the affections of W, who is P's wife. W's statement to P, "I don't like you anymore," if offered to show that W does not like P anymore — an element of P's *prima facie* case — comes within the exception.)

a. Presently existing: The statement must relate to the declarant's *presently existing* state of mind. (*Example:* "I hate my husband," is acceptable to show the declarant now hates her husband. But, "Yesterday I was really furious at my husband," is not admissible, because it relates to a prior mental or emotional state, rather than the declarant's present one.)

b. Surrounding circumstances: If statement of present mental state includes a reference to surrounding circumstances, the entire statement will normally be admitted, but with a limiting instruction. (*Example:* "I hate my husband because he's an adulterer." The whole statement will be admitted under the exception, if offered to prove that the declarant hated her husband at the time of the statement; the jury will be instructed that it may not use the statement as proof that the husband was an adulterer.)

2. Proof of subsequent event: The exception also applies where a declaration of present mental state (especially present *intent*) is offered not because the mental state itself is in issue, but because that mental state is circumstantial evidence that a *subsequent event* actually took place. (*Example:* O says, "I plan to go to Crooked Creek." This statement of present intent is admissible to show that O probably subsequently went to Crooked Creek. *Mutual Life Ins. v. Hillmon.*) [236-238]

a. Intent coupled with recital of past acts: If the statement is mainly an expression of *intent to do a future act,* the fact that it contains a brief recital about some past, relevant, fact will not cause the statement to be excluded. This is especially true where the declarant explains a *past motive* for his contemplated action. (*Example:* O says to W, "D has asked for some bribe money. I'm going to send it to him in Bridgeport." Most courts would probably allow in the entire statement, since it is mainly a statement of intent offered to show that the intended act — delivering the money — eventually took place, and the reference to the past act is merely by way of explaining the intended act.)

b. Cooperation of other: If the statement of present intent concerns an act which requires the *cooperation* of a third person, most courts will allow the statement to be used as circumstantial evidence that the declarant did the contemplated act with the third person's cooperation. However, in this situation, courts usually require that there be *independent evidence* either that declarant really did the intended act, or that the third person actually participated. (*Example:* V says, "I'm going to buy drugs from D in the parking lot." This statement of present intent will be admissible to show that V probably did meet D in the parking lot, but only if there is some independent evidence — other than the statement — either that D really went to the parking lot or that V did. *U.S. v. Pheaster.*) [237-238]

3. **Statements of memory or belief:** The "state of mind" exception does *not* apply to statements of *memory* or belief about *past actions or events*, when offered to prove that the past action or event took place. Thus FRE 803(3) excludes "a statement of memory or belief to prove the fact remembered or believed. . . ." (*Example:* O says, "I believe that my husband has poisoned me." Even though this is a statement of present belief, it is not admissible under the "state of mind" exception to prove that the husband really did poison O, since it is offered to prove the fact believed. *Shepard v. U.S.*) [238-241]

   a. **Execution of will:** A declarant's statement relating to his *will* is covered by the "state of mind" exception, even though the statement may be one of memory or belief offered to prove the fact remembered or believed. See FRE 803(3), making the hearsay exception applicable to a statement of memory or belief that "relates to the validity or terms of the declarant's will." (*Example:* O says, "I changed my will yesterday to disinherit my no-good husband." If offered in a will contest to show that O intended to disinherit her husband, this statement will be admissible even though it is a statement of memory offered to prove the truth of the fact remembered.)

C. **Excited utterance:** There is a hearsay exception for certain statements made under the influence of a *startling event*; this is called the *"excited utterance"* exception. [242-244]

   1. **Requirements:** Under the Federal Rules and most courts, there are two requirements for the exception: (1) the statement must relate to a *startling event* or condition; and (2) the statement must have been made while the declarant was still *under the stress* of excitement caused by the event or condition. See FRE 803(2).

   2. **Time factor:** In determining whether the declarant was still under the influence of the startling event, the *time* that has passed between the event and the statement is of paramount importance. Usually, statements made during the exciting event or within half an hour afterward are admitted, statements made more than an hour later are not, and statements between a half hour and an hour are decided based on the surrounding circumstances.

   3. **Reflection:** Since the rationale behind the exception is that statements made by a declarant who does not have the *opportunity to reflect* should be admitted as unusually reliable, facts showing that the declarant really did reflect will cause the exception not to apply. Thus if the statement is very self-serving, or is in response to a detailed question, the court is likely to find that the declarant reflected (rather than speaking spontaneously), so that the exception should not apply.

   4. **Reference to startling event:** Some courts insist that the excited utterance explain or refer to the startling event. But this is not required by the Federal Rules or other courts. (*Example:* Truck Driver, after getting in an accident, says, "Hurry up, I've got to get to my next customer." If offered to prove that Driver was on business on behalf of his employer, some courts would reject the statement because it does not refer to the startling event — the accident — but the Federal Rules and other state courts would admit the statement anyway.)

D. **Present sense impression:** Many courts, and the Federal Rules, today recognize an exception for *"present sense impressions,"* even where the declarant is **not excited**. Thus FRE 803(1) gives an exception for a statement "describing or explaining an event or condition, made while or immediately after the declarant perceived it." (*Example:* O sees a car speed by in the opposite direction, and says, "If the driver keeps up that rate of speed, he'll surely crash." In courts recognizing the exception for present sense impressions, this statement would be admissible to show that the car was traveling fast. *Houston Oxygen Co. v. Davis.*) [244-245]

1. **Immediacy:** In contrast to the excited-utterance exception, the present-sense-impression exception applies only if *virtually no time passes* between the event being perceived and the declarant's statement about it.

2. **Must describe or explain:** The present sense impression must *describe or explain* the event that the declarant has perceived (in contrast to the usual rule for excited utterances).

IV. PAST RECOLLECTION RECORDED

A. **Four requirements:** A *written* record of an event, made shortly after the event has occurred, will be admissible under the hearsay exception for *"past recollection recorded,"* if four requirements are met (FRE 803(5)): [246]

1. **First-hand knowledge:** The memorandum must relate to matters of which the sponsoring witness once had *first-hand knowledge.* (*Example:* W writes down an inventory. If he says at trial that some of the information in the inventory was known only to his assistant who supplied the information, not to W, the memorandum will not be admissible under the past recollection recorded requirement unless the assistant is also available to testify.)

2. **Made when fresh in memory:** The record must have been made when the matter was *fresh in the witness's memory.* Under the Federal Rules, even a record made several days after the events in question might be held to satisfy this requirement if there was evidence that the person doing the recording would still have had a clear memory of it.

3. **Impaired recollection:** A sponsoring witness's memory of the event recorded must now be *impaired* — if he can clearly remember the events, he must testify from memory rather than have the document admitted. Under the Federal Rules, he must merely have *some* impairment of his memory (it must be the case that he "now cannot recall *well enough to testify fully and accurately,*" FRE 803(5)(A)), in contrast to the common law requirement that he lack *any* present memory of the event.

4. **Accurate when written:** The sponsoring witness at the trial must testify that the record was *accurate* when it was made. (But the sponsoring witness does not have to be the person who made the record; thus if X made the record, it may be sponsored by W, X's assistant, who can testify that after the record was made, W checked it and determined it to be accurate.)

   a. **Multi-party problem:** If A knows the facts and B records them, both A and B will probably have to testify at the trial for the record to be admissible: A will testify that the facts he told B were ones that he, A, knew to be accurate; then B will testify that he accurately recorded what A told him.

B. **Status as exhibit:** Under the Federal Rules, the record may merely be *read* to the jury; it cannot be taken into the jury room as an *exhibit*, unlike other forms of real or demonstrative evidence — the theory is that the record is in lieu of testimony, so it should not be given greater weight than testimony by being taken to the jury room. FRE 803(5), last sentence. But the record is *evidence.* (This makes the past recollection recorded different from a document used to jog the witness's

C
A
P
S
U
L
E

S
U
M
M
A
R
Y

memory under the present recollection refreshed exception — the latter is not evidence, but is merely an aid to stimulate testimony.) [248]

V. BUSINESS RECORDS

A. **General/Federal Rule:** Nearly all states recognize a hearsay exception for certain types of business records. The Federal provision (FRE 803(6)) is typical; the business record is admissible if: [249-250]

1. **Routine of business:** The record was made in the *routine of the business*;

2. **Knowledge:** The record was made by, or from information supplied by, a person with *personal knowledge* of the matter recorded and who is *working in the business*; and

3. **Timeliness:** The entry was made *"at or near the time"* of the matter recorded.

   Example: The shipping department of Store records every shipment sent out to a customer. Store's ledger showing a shipment made to D will be admissible under FRE 803(6) if Store establishes that: (1) it regularly kept a written record of every shipment that went out; (2) the person who wrote the ledger entries did so either from his personal knowledge that a given shipment had gone out, or by being told that this had happened by a person with such direct knowledge and a business duty to disclose that knowledge; and (3) the ledger entries were made shortly after each shipment actually went out.

B. **"Business" defined:** "Business" is defined broadly under modern statutes. Thus, FRE 803(6) applies to "organizations" (e.g., schools, churches, and hospitals), even though these are not necessarily profit-making entities. It also applies to any "occupation" or "calling." [250]

C. **Person supplying info:** The person who originally supplies the information that goes in to the record must satisfy two requirements: (1) he must have first-hand knowledge of the fact he reports; and (2) he must do his reporting *while working in the business*. The latter requirement means that if the source of the information is not an employee of the business that keeps the record, the exception may not apply — thus statements by *witnesses to an accident*, even if made to a police officer or other person with a business duty to compile a report, will *not* be admissible. *Johnson v. Lutz.* [250-252]

1. **Other exception covering source of info:** But if the third-party information (from a source who is not an employee of the business that keeps the record) falls within *some other hearsay exception*, then by a *two-step process* the *entire report* may nonetheless be admissible. [251]

   Example: P accuses her employer D, a business, of sexual harassment, because P's boss X made advances to her. D hires Security Co., a private-investigation firm, to investigate P's claim; D tells all its employees to cooperate with the investigation. Security Co. interviews W, who works for D; W tells Security Co., "Yes, I saw X make advances to P at the office." Security Co. prepares a report which repeats W's statement. At trial, P now seeks to introduce the report as evidence that W saw X make advances to P.

   The business-records exception won't by itself be enough to get the whole report into evidence, because W (the source of the information) didn't work for Security Co. (the business keeping the record, i.e., the report). But since W was an employee of D at the time he made the statement to Security Co., and did so as part of his job (which included cooperating with the investigation), W's statement will be admissible against D as an agent's admission, admissible against the principal. So the "outer layer" (the report) is admissible as a business record, and the "inner layer" (W's statement to Security Co.) is admissible as an admission by an agent. [Cf. *Norcon v. Kotowski*]

D. "Regular course of business": Although the proponent must show that the report was made in the "regular course of business," even reports of a sort that are rarely made may qualify. For instance, if a business makes a practice of making a record of any ***accident*** that occurs during the transaction of business, the "regular course of business" requirement will be satisfied even though accidents happen rarely. (But the rareness with which a certain type of record is kept may suggest that the particular record is untrustworthy, violating a different requirement, discussed below.) [251-253]

E. Opinion: The modern trend is to accept even ***opinions*** contained in the report, if these would be admissible when given as part of live testimony. Thus, if the person supplying the report or making the record is an expert, his statement (e.g., "Patient seems to be suffering from schizophrenia") will be admitted if he would be permitted to make the same statement at trial. FRE 803(6) even allows lay opinions to be admitted, assuming there is no grounds for doubting their trustworthiness. [253]

F. Untrustworthy: If the surrounding circumstances make the record seem ***untrustworthy***, the court should exclude it. For instance, if the facts indicate that the business that made record had a strong motive to create a ***self-serving*** record, the court may exclude it. (*Example:* After a train crash, Railroad conducts an internal investigation, and makes a report absolving the engineer. Railroad's strong incentive to cover-up so as to avoid liability may cause the court to exclude the report for untrustworthiness.) [254]

G. Absence of entry: If a regularly kept business record would otherwise qualify, it may usually be admitted to show that a particular entry is ***absent***, if such an entry would normally have been made had a particular event occurred. (*Example:* Merchant keeps regular records of every payment by a customer. If the issue is whether Customer has paid a particular bill, Merchant may admit its records to show that no indication that Customer paid this particular bill was ever placed on its records.) [254]

H. Oral reports: Most courts hold that the record must be ***in writing***. (*Example:* Foreman reports to Boss that Employee has hurt his hand on a machine. Even if making such an oral report is part of Foreman's job, Boss will not be permitted to testify that Foreman made the report, because the report was not in writing.) [255]

I. Proving the record: The business record is not "self admitting." Instead, a ***sponsoring witness*** must normally be called, who can testify that the requirements of the business-records statute were satisfied. Typically, this will be someone who knows enough about the record-keeping routine of the business to testify that the records were appropriately kept in the particular instance (even if this witness did not make or observe the particular entry in question). [255]

1. **Certification as alternative:** However, FRE 803(6) (together with FRE 902(11) gives an alternative method for a business record to be admitted, a method that does not need a "live" sponsoring witness. Instead, the proponent can supply a written ***"certification,"*** by a person who would be qualified to be a live sponsoring witness. As long as the certification document describes how the record meets the requirements for a business record, the hearsay rule does not bar the document, and no live sponsoring testimony is needed.

J. Special situations: Here are two recurring situations where the business records exception is often applied: [256-259]

1. **Hospital records:** *Hospital records* are often introduced to prove the truth of statements contained in them. Even statements contained in the record that are not declarations of symptoms (e.g., "Patient said he was hit by a truck") will be admitted if part of the record. But totally extraneous matter (e.g., "Patient says that the car that hit him ran a red light") will not be admitted.

   a. **Patient under no duty:** If the information comes from the patient, it will not normally satisfy the requirement that the person supplying the information must have been working for the business (in this case, for the hospital). However, the hospital record can usually be admitted for the limited purpose of showing that the patient made a particular statement; then, some other exception may apply to allow the patient's statement to be offered for the truth of the matter asserted. For instance, if the patient is the plaintiff, the defendant will be able to introduce the statement against him because it is an admission; similarly, if the patient is reporting his current symptoms or other bodily condition, the "statement of present physical condition" exception will apply.

2. **Computer print-out:** Computer print-outs will often be admissible to prove the truth of matters stated in the print-out. However, the proponent must show that: (1) the print-out comes from data that was entered into the system relatively promptly; and (2) the procedures by which the data was entered, the program written, the report prepared, etc., are all reasonably reliable.

VI. PUBLIC RECORDS AND REPORTS

A. **Common-law rule:** At common law, there is an exception for admission of a ***written report or record*** of a ***public official*** if: (1) the official has ***first-hand knowledge*** of the facts reported; and (2) the official had a ***duty*** to make the record or report. [259-260]

B. **Federal Rule:** The federal public records and reports exception is even broader. FRE 803(8) admits three different types of public records and reports: [260]

1. **Agency's own activities:** Subsection (A)(i) allows admission of a government agency's records of its ***own activities***, if offered to show that those activities occurred. (*Example:* P sues the FBI for invading his privacy; he could introduce the agency's own surveillance records to prove that the agency tapped his phone.) [261]

2. **Matters observed under duty:** Subsection (A)(ii) makes the written records of ***observations*** made by public officials admissible if: (1) the observation was made ***in the line of duty***; and (2) the official had a ***duty to report*** those observations. (*Example:* An IRS agent does a field audit of Smith's tax return at Smith's house. If Smith claims a deduction for "home office," and the agent finds no evidence of one, his written report to his superior can be introduced in a later civil suit on the issue of whether Smith had a home office. But the agent's observation that Smith possessed cocaine would not be admissible, since the agent had no duty to report non-tax related matters.) [261]

3. **Investigative reports:** Subsection (A)(iii) allows the admission of ***"factual findings"*** resulting from ***investigations***, except when used against a criminal defendant. (*Example:* Following an accident, the police send an accident investigator, who writes a report that concludes that the crash was caused when the vehicle traveling east-west went through a stop light. This report would be admissible in a civil suit arising out of the crash.) [261]

C. **Criminal cases:** Use of FRE 803(8) in criminal cases raises special issues: [262-265]

1. No use of (B) and (C):   Subsections (A)(ii) and (iii) may *not* be used against the ***defendant in a criminal case.*** Thus a police officer's written report stating that he has seen D commit a robbery, or a detective's report concluding that a previously unsolved crime has probably been committed by D, could not be admitted against D in his trial. (Probably each of these reports, however, could be used *by* D against the government in the criminal trial.)

2. "Law enforcement personnel":   Subsection (A)(ii) does not apply in criminal cases to matters "observed by ***law-enforcement personnel.***"

   a. Laboratory technicians: An important issue is whether ***laboratory technicians*** who work for law enforcement agencies doing substance analysis, are to be treated as "law enforcement personnel" whose out-of-court descriptions of tests they;ve made are therefore excluded.

      i. Not admissible: The answer is almost certainly *yes*, as the result of a comment the Supreme Court made in a 2009 state-law case, *Melendez-Diaz v. Massachusetts* (also discussed *infra*, p. C-55). The issue there was whether the defendant's ***Confrontation Clause rights*** were violated by the prosecution's introduction against him of a ***laboratory test report*** showing that the tested substance was cocaine; the prosecution did not make the writer of the report available for cross examination. In the course of deciding that the defendant's Confrontation Clause rights had been violated, the majority indicated that FRE 803(8)(B)'s ban on the hearsay use of "matters observed by police officers and other law enforcement personnel" will be read to apply to ***test reports prepared by technicians affiliated with law enforcement.***

3. Use of other exceptions: It is not clear whether a report that would otherwise come within subsection (A)(ii) or (iii), and that is excluded under those provisions because it is used against a criminal defendant, may nonetheless be admitted under ***some other*** exception, e.g., the business records exception.

   a. Minority view: Some courts have flatly rejected all such evidence. (*Example:* The prosecution offers a substance analysis report prepared by a chemist working for the government, to prove that substance taken from D was heroin. Even though this was a "regularly kept record" by an organization, and thus would otherwise have qualified under the business records exception, it was disallowed because it fell within the explicit exclusion of 803(8)(A)(ii). *U.S. v. Oates.*)

   b. Majority view: But probably the majority would allow a report of direct observations or investigations to be admitted against D at least where the maker of the report is ***produced in court and is subject to cross-examination.*** (*Example:* If the government chemist above were produced as a witness, a court would probably admit his report concluding that the substance taken from D was heroin.)

D. Other issues: Other issues arise in both a civil and criminal context: [265-268]

1. Evaluations: Subsection (A)(iii) refers to the "factual findings" in investigative reports. But so long as an investigative report includes factual findings, other ***"evaluative"*** parts of the report — ***opinions***, ***evaluations*** and ***conclusions*** — may ***also*** be admitted. [*Beech Aircraft Corp. v. Rainey*] (*Example:* The government, after investigating the crash of a Navy plane, produces a report containing numerous factual findings. The report then says that "the most probable cause of the accident was pilot error." This statement may be admitted, even though it is an "opinion" or "conclusion". *Beech Aircraft.*) [265-266]

2. **Multiple hearsay:** A government report must be carefully scrutinized for ***multiple hearsay*** problems. [267-268]

   a. **Report by one government agent to another:** If government employee A tells facts to employee B, who writes them up into a government report, A's statements will be admissible if A had a duty to give the report to B. (*Example:* Officer Jones witnesses a car accident, and later says to Officer Smith, "I saw the green Plymouth run a red light and cause the accident." Smith includes this statement in a report on the accident. The entire report, including Jones' quoted statement, will be admissible under 803(8)(A)(ii), because Jones had a duty to furnish the information to Smith, and Smith's report was otherwise covered as a "report of matters observed.")

   b. **Statement by one without duty to talk:** But if information is supplied by one who does ***not*** work for the government and does not have a duty to give the report, the resulting written report may not include the quoted statement, unless the quoted statement independently falls within some exception. (*Example:* Bystander tells Officer Jones, "I saw the blue car jump the light and cause the accident." Jones' report will be generally admissible as an investigative report under subsection (A)(iii), but Bystander's statement will have to be removed, because he did not observe the accident pursuant to any duty, or have any duty to make a report.)

3. **Trustworthiness:** If the "source of the information [or] other circumstances indicate a lack of ***trustworthiness***," the judge must keep the report out of evidence. FRE 803(8)(B). This is probably the case with respect to reports falling under any of the three subsections. (*Example:* Evidence that the public official who prepared a report had been bribed, or was motivated by ulterior motives, would cause it to be excluded for lack of trustworthiness.) [268]

VII. MISCELLANEOUS "AVAILABILITY IMMATERIAL" EXCEPTIONS

A. **Learned writings and commercial publications:** A learned writing (e.g., a ***scientific treatise*** or article) may be admitted for the truth of the matter asserted, under FRE 803(18). (The common law allowed such learned works to be used only for impeachment of the other side's expert witness.) [268-270]

   1. **Use on direct:** The application may come in as part of a party's ***direct*** case, if a favorable expert testifies that the treatise is authoritative.

   2. **Cross-examination:** The publication can be used as part of the ***cross-examination*** of the other side's expert, even if the expert refuses to admit that the publication is authoritative. (But the cross-examiner must establish the authoritativeness of the publication by some other means, such as another witness.)

   3. **Expert must be on the stand:** Whether it is introduced as part of the direct or cross-examination, the publication may only be introduced if there is an ***expert on the stand*** who can help the jury interpret its meaning.

   4. **Commercial publications:** The Federal Rules recognize a similar exception for ***commercial publications*** that are commonly relied upon by business people. See FRE 803(17), allowing admission of "market quotations, lists, directories, or other published compilations that are generally relied on by the public or by persons in particular occupations."

B. Ancient documents: [270-272]

1. **Common law:** The common law makes it easy to admit *"ancient documents."* A document will be presumed to be authentic if it is: (1) at least 30 years old; (2) unsuspicious in appearance; and (3) shown to have come from a place of custody natural for such a writing. However, in most courts this is merely a rule of authentication, not an exception to the hearsay rule, so the statements contained in it may not be shown for their truth. But some courts do treat it as a hearsay exception.

   a. **Ancient deeds:** *All* courts allow statements contained in an ancient *deed* to be shown for their truth. Thus a statement in a will, "O purchased this property from X in 1872," could everywhere be used to show that O really did purchase the property in 1872, if the above three requirements are satisfied.

2. **Federal Rules:** The Federal Rules explicitly make the ancient documents rule a hearsay exception. The document need merely have been in existence *20* years (not the 30 required at common law). The proponent must prove that the document is "authentic" (i.e., that it is at least 20 years old and meets the "no suspicion" and "likely place of custody" requirements). See FRE 901(b)(8).

   a. **Newer title documents:** A separate federal hearsay exception exists for less-than-20-year-old documents that relate to *title to property.* See FRE 803(15). (*Example:* A 10-year-old deed recites, "O sold this property to X in 2003." This will be admissible to prove that O did indeed sell the property to X in 2003.)

C. Reputation: There is a hearsay exception for several types of *reputation* evidence: [273-274]

1. **Birth, marriage, etc.:** There is an exception for a person's reputation within his family regarding some aspect of *birth*, *marriage*, or *relationship.* (*Example:* Reputation within the family that A is B's son, offered to prove that A really is B's son.) FRE 803(19) extends this to cover a reputation among one's *business* colleagues or one's reputation in a *community*, concerning some fact of the person's personal or family history.

2. **General historical facts:** There is an exception for proof of *facts of general history* and for proof of land boundaries. See FRE 803(20). (*Example:* To prove that there was an earthquake in San Francisco in 1906, a party could call a historian who would testify that in Northern California, it is commonly believed or remembered that there was an earthquake in that year.)

3. **Reputation for character:** There is an exception for proof that a person had a particular *reputation* for character. (*Example:* W may testify that P has a reputation in his hometown for being a liar, if offered by D to prove that P really is a liar and that therefore D did not commit libel by calling him one.)

D. Miscellaneous: [274-276]

1. **Vital statistics, marriage certificates:** Statements of fact contained in public records have an exception. (*Examples:* A report that X died on a certain day, offered to prove that fact. A statement in a marriage certificate that X married Y on a certain day, offered to prove that fact.)

2. **Absence of public record:** There is an exception for the fact that a certain record is *absent* from the public records, offered to prove that fact. (*Example:* Testimony that a search of the IRS's records does not disclose D's 1985 tax return, offered to prove that D did not file a return that year.)

3. **Previous felony conviction:**   Proof that X is guilty of a particular *crime* may be made by showing that X was convicted of that crime. (But the fact that X was convicted of a misdemeanor may not be used in a subsequent case to prove that he did the act charged.)

VIII.   UNAVAILABILITY REQUIRED — GENERALLY

A.   Five exceptions: Under the FRE, there are five hearsay exceptions that require that the declarant be unavailable to testify at trial: [277]

1. *Testimony* given in a *prior proceeding*;

2. Statements made while the declarant believed his death was impending so-called *"dying declarations"*);

3. Statements which were *against the declarant's interest* when made; and

4. Statements concerning either the declarant's or his relatives' *personal* or family history (so-called statements of "pedigree").

5. **Forfeiture by wrongdoing:** Statements offered against a party that has engaged in (or acquiesced in) *wrongdoing* that was intended to, and did, *procure the unavailability* of the declarant as a witness.

See FRE 804(b))

B.   Meaning of "unavailable":   [277-287]

1. **Federal:**   FRE 804(a) defines five situations in which the declarant will be deemed to be unavailable:

    a. He is *privileged* against testifying about the subject matter of his out-of-court statement;

    b. He *refuses* to testify despite a court order;

    c. He testifies that he *cannot remember* the statement's subject matter;

    d. He cannot be present to testify because of *death*, or physical or mental *illness*; or

    e. He is absent, and the proponent of his statement has been unable to procure his attendance (or his deposition) by *process* or other reasonable means (e.g., persuasion).

    f. **Proponent's fault:**   But none of the above reasons will make the declarant "unavailable" if his unavailability occurred because the *proponent "procured or wrongfully caused"* the declarant's unavailablity "in order to *prevent the declarant from attending or testifying."* FRE 804(a), last sentence.

2. **States follow:**   Most states recognize the first four exceptions. But with respect to the fifth, absence from the jurisdiction, most courts automatically treat the declarant as being "unavailable" if he is outside the jurisdiction — they don't require the proponent to make non-subpoena efforts (e.g., persuasion or the taking of a deposition) to procure his attendance or testimony.

3. **Constitutional problems:**   If the hearsay exception is one traditionally requiring unavailability, a criminal defendant's Sixth Amendment *Confrontation Clause* rights may be violated if the court admits the out-of-court statement without a showing that the declarant really was unavailable.

a. **"Unavailable" defined:** For this purpose, a witness will be deemed sufficiently "unavailable" (and the use of his out-of-court declaration will not violate his Sixth Amendment right) if the state shows:

    i.   that the witness is ***beyond that state's own process***; and

    ii.   that either the government made a ***good faith effort*** to get the witness to attend by means other than process, or such efforts would have been ***very unlikely to succeed***.

b. **D purposely causes unavailability to evade testimony:** But where the defendant *caused* the declarant's unavailability ***for the purpose of avoiding the declarant's trial testimony***, then the defendant will be deemed to have ***forfeited*** his right to invoke the Confrontation Clause. [*Giles v. California*]. [278]

IX. FORMER TESTIMONY

A. General rule: There is a hearsay exception for ***former testimony*** — that is, testimony given in an ***earlier proceeding*** — if the witness is unavailable for trial. FRE 804(b)(1), which basically follows the common law, imposes these requirements: [280]

1. **Hearing or deposition:** The testimony was given either at a ***hearing*** in the same or earlier action, or in a ***deposition*** in the same or different proceeding;

2. **Party present:** The party against whom the testimony is now offered was ***present*** at the earlier testimony (or, in a civil case, that party's "predecessor in interest" was present); and

3. **Opportunity to cross-examine:** The party against whom the testimony is offered had the ***opportunity*** and ***similar motive*** to develop the testimony. Usually, this opportunity will have been the chance to ***cross-examine***, but it may have been a chance to expand the testimony by ***direct*** or redirect examination.

    Example 1: P sues D for negligence. At a deposition in which D is present, P asks questions to X, a witness to the accident. Because D has had the chance to cross-examine X during the deposition, X's deposition answers may be introduced against D in the eventual suit, if X is unavailable to testify at trial (even if D did not use his right to cross-examine X at the deposition).

    Example 2: W gives testimony unfavorable to D before a grand jury while D is not present. At D's eventual criminal trial, this testimony cannot be introduced against D even if W is now unavailable, because D had no opportunity to cross-examine (but some courts might apply the residual or "catch all" exception, discussed below).

B. Meaning of "hearing" and "proceeding": "Hearing" and "proceeding" seem to include any official inquiry in which ***sworn testimony*** is taken. So a ***prior trial***, a ***preliminary hearing*** in a criminal case, a ***grand jury*** hearing, and a ***deposition***, all qualify. [281-282]

1. **Not covered:** But ***affidavits***, and ***statements*** (written or oral) made to ***law enforcement officials during investigations***, ***aren't*** covered because they're not truly hearings or proceedings.

C. Identity of issues: There must be enough overlap between the issues existing at the time of the prior hearing or deposition, and the issues existing at the present trial, that the above opportunity for cross-examination was a meaningful substitute for cross-examination in the present case. At common law, there must be "substantial identity" between issues; under the Federal Rules, the opponent must have had a ***"similar motive"*** in the earlier situation. [282-286]

1. **Different contexts:** This requirement can be satisfied even though the earlier and present proceedings are quite different contexts. (*Examples:* Testimony given at a ***preliminary hearing*** can be used at a later criminal trial, even though the issues are not absolutely "identical" in the two situations. Similarly, testimony given at a criminal trial can be admitted at a later civil proceeding, even though the issues and burdens of proof are not identical.)

D. **Identity of parties:** The ***proponent*** of the former testimony need ***not*** have been a party to the taking of the former testimony. Only the ***opponent*** must have been present. [287-289]

1. **Similar party in interest:** Furthermore, even if the opponent was not present, under the Federal Rule the testimony can be used so long as the present opponent's "predecessor in interest" was present, if the case is a civil case. This probably means merely that a person with a very similar motive must have been present. (But in criminal cases, there is no "predecessor in interest" provision. Thus a statement may not be offered against a criminal defendant who was not present, even if another person — e.g., a co-defendant — was present at the prior proceeding and had a highly similar motive to cross-examine.)

X. DYING DECLARATIONS

A. **General rule:** There is an exception for ***"dying declarations."*** The common law version is narrow: a declarant's statement, while believing that his death is imminent, concerning the cause or circumstances of his impending death, is admissible in a subsequent homicide prosecution concerning that death. FRE 804(b)(2) loosens several of these restrictions. [290]

B. **Requirements in detail:** [290-292]

1. **Awareness of imminent death:** The declarant must, at the time he made his statement, have been aware of his impending death. It is not enough that he knows he is seriously ill or wounded, or that he will probably die — at common law he must have ***lost all hope*** of recovery. (Under the Federal Rule, he must speak "while ***believing*** [his] ***death*** to be ***imminent***.")

2. **Actual death:** At common law, the declarant ***must in fact be dead*** by the time the evidence is offered. But this is not required under the Federal Rule (though the declarant must of course be unavailable, since this is one of the "unavailability required" exceptions).

3. **Homicide:** At common law, the declaration may be used ***only in a homicide case.*** Thus it may not be used in civil cases, or in criminal cases not charging homicide (e.g., a case in which D is charged with rape alone, even though V died after the rape). Under the Federal Rules, dying declarations are usable in civil suits and homicide cases, but not in non-homicide criminal cases.

4. **Declarant is victim:** At common law, declaration may be offered only in a trial for the killing of the ***declarant***, not the killing of someone else. (*Example:* D has probably murdered both H and W. He is prosecuted for the murder of H only. At common law, the prosecution cannot introduce W's dying declaration, "D did this to H and me.") The Federal Rules drop this requirement.

5. **Relating to circumstances of killing:** Both at common law and under the Federal Rules, the declaration must relate to the ***causes or circumstances of the killing***. (*Example:* Declarant, while dying, says, "X and I have been enemies for years." The exception probably does not apply, since it does not relate directly to the causes or circumstances of declarant's death. But, "X has been stalking me for two days," would satisfy this test.)

6. **For accused:** The statement may be admitted *on behalf of* the accused (though usually, it is admitted *against* him).

XI. DECLARATIONS AGAINST INTEREST

A. **Generally:** There is a hearsay exception for declarations which, at the time they are made, are *so against the declarant's interest that it is unlikely that they would have been made if they were not true*. [293]

1. **Common law:** At common law, there are three main requirements for the exception:

   a. The declaration must have been against the declarant's *pecuniary or* proprietary interest (not his penal interest) when made;

   b. The declarant must now be *unavailable*; and

   c. The declarant must have had first-hand knowledge of the facts asserted in the declaration.

2. **Federal Rule:** FRE 804(b)(3) follows this approach, except that declarations against *penal interest* are also admissible (except uncorroborated statements exculpating the accused).

B. **Meaning of "against interest":** [294-300]

1. **When made:** The declaration must have been made against the declarant's interest *at the time it was made.* The fact that later developments have turned what was an innocent-seeming statement into one that now harms some interest of the declarant is *not* enough to satisfy this requirement.

2. **Pecuniary interest:** At common law, only statements against the declarant's pecuniary or proprietary interest qualify.

   a. **Property:** Thus, a statement limiting the declarant's *property* rights, or a creditor's statement that a debt has been paid, will qualify. Modern cases also allow a statement subjecting the declarant to possible *tort liability* to qualify.

3. **Penal interest:**

   a. **Common law:** At common law, statements against the declarant's *penal* interest — that is, statements tending to subject him to *criminal* liability — do *not* qualify. (This is due mainly to fears that people will falsely confess, or falsely claim to have heard others confess, in order to exculpate the defendant.)

   b. **Federal approach:** The Federal Rules treat statements against penal interest as *qualifying.* However, a statement against penal interest that exposes the declarant to criminal liability (e.g., one that's offered to exculpate the accused by implicating the declarant instead as the purpetrator) is not admissible unless it is "supported by *corroborating circumstances* that clearly indicate its *trustworthiness*[.]" (*Example:* D is charged with burglary. W offers to testify that while in jail, he heard X, another inmate, confess to having done this burglary alone. Because both W and X are felons whose word is somewhat doubtful, this testimony will be allowed only if there is independent evidence that X may well have done the burglary — e.g., he was out of prison at the time, and is known to have performed other, similar burglaries.)

4. **Collateral statements:** If statement includes a disserving part but also a self-serving part, the court will try to excise the self-serving part. If the statement has both a disserving and a neutral part, the court will probably let in the whole statement. (*Example:* "It was Joe and I

that pulled off that bank job," will be admissible against Joe, even though the part of the statement referring to Joe was not directly against the declarant's interest.) [298-300]

    a. Neutral or self-serving statements not allowed as collateral: But a *neutral* or *self-serving* declaration *won't* be allowed in merely because it's part of the same broader statement that includes against-interest declarations — *each individual declaration* must be scrutinized to see if it's against interest. (*Example:* W, in custody for a particular crime, says, "I participated in a small way." W then goes on to describe D's participation in detail, and says that D was the ringleader. The description of D's participation won't be allowed in as against-interest, because that description isn't specifically against W's interest. [*Williamson v. U.S.*])

C. Constitutional issues: [300-302]

    1. Use by prosecution: When the prosecution tries to introduce a third party's declaration to inculpate the accused, the Sixth Amendment *Confrontation Clause* rights of the accused may help him keep the statement out. For instance, a statement exposing the declarant to criminal liability, given while the declarant is under *police interrogation* in connection with a criminal investigation, will always be excluded from being used against the accused, if the declarant doesn't take the stand (and undergo cross on behalf of the accused) at the accused's trial. [*Crawford v. Washington*] [299]

        Example: X is arrested on suspicion of burglary. While under interrogation, he confesses to the burglary, and says he did it with D. At D's burglary trial (X hasn't been tried yet), the prosecution puts X on the stand. X pleads the Fifth. The prosecution now offers X's confession, to show that D did the crime with X. Even though the confession was against X's interest, the Confrontation Clause prohibits its being used against D, because X is unavailable for cross on behalf of D.

    2. Use by accused: Where it is the accused who seeks to *exculpate* himself by use of third person's declaration against interest, the accused may be able to rely on the Due Process Clause and the Sixth Amendment right to compulsory process to get the statement into evidence. (*Example:* D tries to show that X has confessed to the crime that D is charged with. If there are some solid facts corroborating X's confession, and X is unavailable to testify, D probably has a due process or compulsory process right to have X's out-of-court confession introduced.)

XII. STATEMENTS OF PEDIGREE

A. General rule: There is a hearsay exception for statements of *"pedigree,"* i.e., statements about a person's birth, death, marriage, genealogy, or other fact of personal or family history. Here are the requirements at common law and under the Federal Rules: [302-303]

    1. Declarant unavailable: The declarant must be unavailable to testify;

    2. Person or relative: At common law, the declarant must be either the person whose history the statement concerns, or a *relative* of the person whom the statement concerns. Under FRE 804(b)(4), it will also suffice if the declarant is so "intimately associated" with the family of the person the statement concerns that "the declarant's information is likely to be accurate." (*Example:* O is the servant for X's family during X's entire lifetime. If O tells W, "X is the illegitimate son of Y," under the federal but not the common-law approach, W will be permitted to repeat the statement in court, even though O was not a member of the family.)

3. **Before controversy:** The statement must have been made before the *present controversy arose*, under the common-law approach. (But this requirement is completely dropped by the Federal Rules.)

4. **No motive to falsify:** The declarant must not have had any *apparent motive* to falsify.

XIII. FORFEITURE BY WRONGDOING

A. **The problem generally:** A criminal defendant will often have an incentive to attempt to keep a witness from testifying against him at trial. A defendant might do this by *intimidating* the witness, *bribing* him, or even *murdering* him. However, in many instances the witness will previously have made an out-of-court declaration (e.g., a statement to the police, "D did it.").

B. **FRE 804(b)(6)'s solution:** To remove the incentive for witness-tampering, FRE 804(b)(6) now gives a hearsay exception for "[a] statement offered against a party that *wrongfully caused* — or *acquiesced in wrongfully causing* — the *declarant's unavailability* as a witness, and did so *intending* that result." [304-306]

> **Example:** W is arrested at an airport when large quantities of cocaine are discovered on his person. While under arrest, he tells DEA agents, "I was doing this smuggling for D [a drug kingpin], who promised to pay me $1,000 when the drugs got through." D is then arrested and charged with conspiracy to import narcotics. D learns of W's statements, and wants to make sure that W does not testify at D's (or W's own) trial. D therefore tells W that if W testifies at D's trial he will be killed. W is frightened, and refuses to testify.
>
> Under 804(b)(6), the government will be able to introduce at D's trial W's original out-of-court statement to the agents that D was W's boss. This is true even though the statement does not fall under any other hearsay exception. D has, through his threats, "*wrongfully caused* ... [W's] *unavailability*" as a witness, and did so *intending* that result."

1. **Common scenarios:** The out-of-court statements to which 804(b)(6) is often applied include:

   ❑ Statements made by W while under *police interrogation* (as in the above example);

   ❑ Statements made by W in a *grand jury proceeding* or preliminary hearing;

   ❑ Statements made by W in *W's own criminal trial*, or in a criminal trial of some third person.

2. **No reliability requirement:** Rule 804(b)(6) does not contain any requirement that the out-of-court declaration be *reliable* in order to be admitted. This makes the exception much easier to use than, say, the residual exception of FRE 807 (which requires "circumstantial guarantees of trustworthiness" equal to those required by the standard 803 and 804 exceptions).

> **Example:** A suspect, "W," is being interrogated by the police for a particular robbery. W admits to some involvement, but says that the robbery was masterminded by someone else, D. W's statements implicating D are probably not especially trustworthy, given W's strong incentive to get rid of the blame by putting it on someone else. Therefore, W's statements are unlikely to make it into evidence under the residual exception.
>
> But now suppose that the prosecution can show that D threatened W so that W refused to testify at D's trial even under a grant of immunity. Here, W's prior statement under

police interrogation is exempt from the hearsay rule, no matter how untrustworthy the statement appears to be.

XIV. PRIOR STATEMENTS OF AVAILABLE WITNESS

A. Common-law rules: At common law, it is very difficult to make use of *prior statements* by a person who is a *witness* at the current trial: [306-307]

1. **Prior inconsistent statement:** The trial witness's prior *inconsistent* statement is inadmissible hearsay at common law. (However, the prior inconsistent statement may used to *impeach* the witness at the present trial.)

2. **Prior consistent statement:** Similarly, the trial witness's prior *consistent* statement is not substantively admissible at common law. (But if the witness is accused of having recently fabricated his trial testimony, or of having been improperly influenced or motivated, the prior consistent statement may be used for the non-substantive purpose of rehabilitating his credibility.)

3. **Prior identification:** Proof that the trial witness has previously made an *eyewitness identification* is technically hearsay, but many common-law courts allow it as substantive evidence if it seems to have probative value. (*Example:* D is charged with robbing V. Many common-law courts would allow trial testimony by W, a police officer, that shortly after the episode, V pointed to D in a police lineup and said, "That's the one who robbed me.")

B. Federal Rule on prior inconsistent statements: [308-308]

1. **General rule:** FRE 801(d)(1) makes certain prior *inconsistent* statements of the trial witness substantively admissible (i.e., not hearsay). If the defendant testifies at trial and is *subject to cross-examination* concerning his prior statement, that statement is admissible if it is "inconsistent with the declarant's [trial] testimony and was given *under penalty of perjury* [i.e., under oath] at a *trial, hearing,* or *other proceeding* or in a *deposition*[.]"

   a. **Proceeding:** In other words, only statements given under oath as part of a formal proceeding (generally a trial, preliminary hearing, or deposition) may be substantively introduced if the witness's trial testimony differs. An *informal oral* statement previously made by the witness will *not* be substantively admissible. (*Example:* In an accident case, W testifies at trial on behalf of P, "D went through the red light." D cannot introduce for substantive purposes a previous statement by W to her husband H, "The light was green when D went through it." But if W had made that same statement during the course of a deposition under oath, or during testimony at a prior trial, it could be substantively admitted in the present trial.)

2. **Cross-examination not required:** This Federal Rule allows the prior inconsistent statement into evidence even when there was *no cross-examination*, or even any *opportunity* for cross-examination. (*Example:* W testifies in favor of D at a criminal trial. The prosecution may substantively introduce W's prior inconsistent grand jury testimony, even though D and his lawyer were not present and had no opportunity to cross-examine W at that grand jury session — the theory is that D has the opportunity to cross-examine W *now*.)

C. Federal Rule on prior consistent statements: If the prior statement is *consistent* with the witness's trial testimony, it is substantively admissible, but only if it is "offered to rebut an express or implied charge that the declarant *recently fabricated it* or acted from a *recent improper influence* or motive in so testifying[.]" FRE 801(d)(1)(B). (*Example:* W, a witness to a robbery, testifies at trial that the robber was not D. The prosecutor asserts in cross-examination that D has recently intimidated W and gotten him to change his story. D's lawyer may substantively introduce a statement made long ago by W at a grand jury, in which W told the same story.) [312]

D. Federal Rule on prior identifications: A statement that "*identifies* a person as someone the declarant *perceived earlier*" is substantively admissible, if the declarant testifies at the trial and is available for cross-examination. FRE 801(d)(1)(C). [313-315]

    1. No oath or proceeding: Unlike a prior inconsistent statement, a statement of identification is substantively admissible under this provision even though it was *not made under oath* or at a formal *proceeding*. (*Example:* V, a robbery victim, is walking down the street the day after the robbery when she spots D. She says to H, who is with her, "That's the robber." H will be permitted to repeat this statement at D's trial, even though W's statement was not made under oath or at a proceeding.)

XV. RESIDUAL ("CATCH ALL") EXCEPTION

A. Federal Rule generally: Modern courts now tend to admit hearsay evidence that does not fall within any well-defined exclusion, if it is highly reliable and badly needed in the particular case. The Federal Rules codify this *residual* or *"catch all"* exception in FRE 807. FRE 807 imposes five requirements: [315-318]

    1. Circumstantial guarantees of trustworthiness: The statement must have *"circumstantial guarantees of trustworthiness"* that are *equivalent* to those inherent in the other, more specific, federal hearsay exceptions. (Factors the courts consider are summarized below.)

    2. Material fact: The statement must be offered as evidence of a *material fact*.

    3. More probative: The statement must be *"more probative"* on the point for which it is offered than any other evidence which is available through reasonable efforts. (*Example:* If the declarant can give equally probative live testimony, or if there is some other witness who can give the same evidence as that contained in the out-of-court declaration, the catch all exception does not apply.)

    4. Interests of justice: Use of the evidence must be consistent with "the purposes of [the Federal] Rules and the interests of justice."

    5. Notice: The proponent of the evidence must give the adversary *"reasonable notice* of the intent to offer the statement" so that the adversary has "a fair opportunity to meet [the statement]." The notice must include the "particulars" of the statement, including the declarant's name and address. (But federal courts often disregard the precise language of this requirement, and allow use of evidence without a pre-trial notice if the need for the evidence does not become apparent until the trial starts; the court will usually give a continuance to the opponent in order to let him prepare to meet the evidence.)

        Example 1: W has given detailed, credible, and important *grand jury testimony*, and is not available to testify at a civil trial. The residual exception will probably apply. (The "former testimony" exception of 804(b)(1) does not apply to this testimony, because the opponent did not have the opportunity to cross-examine.)

        Example 2: X took contemporaneous *hand-written notes* of an event he witnessed, but is not available to testify at a civil trial. If the notes seem to be reliable, and there is no equally probative or better testimony available, the notes will be admitted under the residual exception. (The document cannot constitute Past Recollection Recorded, under FRE 803(5), because the author is by hypothesis not available as a witness to authenticate it.)

Example 3: W, D's building superintendent, orally tells P not to use a particular safety measure because it will inconvenience W's pets. P is injured. W is not available as a trial witness, and P has no other way to rebut D's claim that P was contributorily negligent. Assuming that there is some corroboration of W's alleged statement (e.g., some independent proof that the safety measure would indeed have inconvenienced W's pets), the court will probably apply the residual exception.

B. Circumstantial guarantees of trustworthiness: In determining whether the statement has "equivalent circumstantial guarantees of trustworthiness" (requirement 1 above), the court is likely to consider these factors, among others: [318]

[1] Oath: Whether the declaration was *under oath.* (If so, it is more reliable.)

[2] Time lapse: How much *time elapsed* between the event and the statement. (The longer the time lapse, the less reliable the statement.)

[3] Motive: The declarant's *motive* for telling the truth. (The stronger the motive to tell the truth, the more reliable.) (*Example:* D1, who is been arrested on a criminal charge, tells a grand jury that the crime was committed by D2, and that D1 was just a bystander. Because D1 had a strong motive to exculpate himself by incriminating another, his statement will probably be viewed as unreliable.)

[4] First-hand knowledge: Whether the declarant had *first-hand knowledge* of what he said. (If he merely repeated what someone else said, this makes the statement less reliable.)

[5] Written vs. oral: Whether the statement is *written* or oral. (Written statements, whether written by the declarant or transcribed stenographically as in a confession to police, are presumed to be more reliable than oral statements.)

[6] Recanted statement: Whether the declarant has subsequently *recanted* his statement. (A statement that has subsequently been recanted is less reliable.)

C. "Near miss": When a particular fact pattern comes very close to matching the requirements for a recognized hearsay exception, but *just misses*, a few courts refuse to apply the residual exception. But most courts are willing to apply the residual exception in this *"near miss"* situation, if the other requirements are met. [319-320]

D. Grand jury testimony: Prior to 2004, the most common use of the residual exception was to allow *grand jury testimony* to be used against a *criminal defendant* when the testifier isn't available to testify at trial. But the 2004 decision in *Crawford v. Washington* means that because of the **Confrontation Clause** of the Sixth Amendment, grand jury testimony can't be used against a criminal defendant (other than the testifier, that is) unless the testifier takes the stand and is available for cross examination. [321]

Example: W witnesses a fatal shooting of V. W tells a grand jury looking into the shooting, "I saw the shooter, and it was D." At D's later trial, W can't be found (he's moved out of state, with no forwarding address). Since W is not available to be cross-examined by D's lawyer at trial, and since D didn't have the opportunity to cross-examine W at the time of the grand jury, W's grand-jury testimony can't be used against D on account of D's Sixth Amendment right to be confronted with witnesses against him. And that's true even if the trial court is convinced that the grand-jury testimony has circumstantial guarantees of trustworthiness, and that it meets all the other requirements for the residual exception.

CHAPTER 7

CONFRONTATION AND COMPULSORY PROCESS

I. INTRODUCTION

A. Confrontation Clause: The Confrontation Clause of the Sixth Amendment guarantees a criminal defendant the right "to be confronted with the witnesses against him." This Clause gives a criminal defendant the right to keep out of evidence certain out-of-court declarations, where the declarant is not available to be cross-examined in court. [361]

B. Compulsory process: The Sixth Amendment's Compulsory Process Clause gives the criminal defendant the right "to have compulsory process for obtaining Witnesses in his favor." This Clause may allow the defendant to *gain admission* of otherwise-inadmissible evidence. For instance, this Clause may give the defendant the right to introduce an out-of-court declaration (e.g., a confession to the crime by someone else) that would otherwise be excluded under traditional hearsay principles. [362]

II. CONFRONTATION CLAUSE

A. First thing to decide: When you analyze hearsay evidence used against a criminal defendant to see whether it violates the Confrontation Clause rights of the accused, you must first decide whether the out-of-court statement at issue is *"testimonial."* That's because the testimonial/non-testimonial distinction makes a huge difference in how or whether the Confrontation Clause applies. [*Crawford v. Washington*; *Davis v. Washington; Michigan v. Bryant*; *Ohio v. Clark*] [365-382]

1. Summary of rule: In brief, here's why the testimonial/non-testimonial distinction is key:

❏ an out-of-court *testimonial* statement by W *can't be admitted* in a criminal case against D unless W is *made available for cross-examination* at D's trial (or was subject to cross by D at the time W made the statement), but

❏ an out-of-court *non-testimonial* statement by W *can* be admitted against D *without any Confrontation Clause problem* even if W is never made available for cross by D.

2. What is "testimonial": Here's an overview of when a statement will be considered *"testimonial"*:

a. Rough definition: The rough meaning of "testimonial" is "bearing testimony." The idea is that the declarant has some idea that the statement will be or may be *used in a serious legal proceeding*, such as a *criminal investigation.* So a *casual offhand remark* to a friend or acquaintance who happens to be standing near the declarant would typically *not* be testimonial.

In the case of a *police interrogation,* a testimonial statement is one where "the primary purpose of the interrogation is to *establish or prove past events potentially relevant to later criminal prosecution."* [*Davis v. Washington*] [367]

b. **Listing of "testimonial" statements:** At a minimum, the following types of statements *will* be considered testimonial under *Crawford* and *Davis v. Washington*:

❏ *prior testimony* at a *preliminary hearing*;

❏ *prior testimony* before a *grand jury*;

❏ testimony at a *former trial* (whether of the present defendant or of someone else);

❏ an *affidavit* issued as part of a law-enforcement proceeding;

❏ statements made in *forensic laboratory reports* created to help solve or prosecute a crime;

❏ perhaps most significantly, *statements made during the course of police interrogations,* including interviews by police at *crime scenes,* as long as the focus of the interrogation is on *investigating a completed crime*, not on *managing an ongoing emergency.*

Example: The police get a report that a domestic disturbance is occurring at V's house. They show up, and determine that sometime previously, V may have been attacked by her husband D, but that there is no present danger. An officer asks V, "What happened?", and V answers, "My husband John attacked me." V's statement is "testimonial" (made as part of an investigation into a completed crime rather than in response to a present emergency); therefore, as we'll see below it can't be introduced against D unless V is available for cross-examination. [Cf. the "*Hammon*" fact pattern portion of *Davis v. Washington*]

c. **Presence of ongoing emergency:** The presence of an *ongoing emergency* makes it much more likely that a statement made during an interrogation will be found to be *non-testimonial.*

i. **Consider both declarant and interrogator:** What counts is the "primary purpose of the *interrogation*," and the statements and actions of *both* the declarant *and the interrogators* are to be considered in determining the "investigation's" purpose. So if the police interrogators believe they're dealing with an ongoing emergency, apparently that can be enough to override a lack of evidence about what the *declarant* intended. [374]

Example: Police, responding to a dispatch call, find V lying on the ground in great pain from a gunshot wound to the abdomen. The police ask V a number of questions, including "Who shot you?" and "Where did it happen?" V answers that "Rick shot me through the back door of his house," which is a few miles away. After about 10 minutes of such questioning by multiple officers, EMT workers arrive and take V to the hospital, where he dies. In prosecuting "Rick" (D), the government offers V's statement that D was the shooter. D's counsel objects that since V can't be cross-examined, use of his statement violates D's Confrontation Clause rights.

Held (by a 5-4 Supreme Court vote), the statement was properly admitted, because it was not testimonial. The issue is whether the primary purpose of "the interrogation" was testimonial, and that issue requires considering the intent of both the declarant and the interrogators. Here, V was in such pain that he probably had no primary intent of any sort. And the primary purpose of the police questioning was to "allow the police to '*assess the situation*, the *threat to their own safety*, and possible danger to the potential victim' ... and *to the public*[.]" Since the primary purpose was to deal with the ongoing emergency, the admission of V's statements did not violate D's Confrontation Clause rights. [*Michigan v. Bryant*] [371-377]

ii. Consider the level of formality: The degree of *formality* in the encounter is another significant factor in the emergency/non-emergency decision. The presence of formality suggests the *absence of an emergency*. By contrast, if the encounter is very *informal,* that's an indication that the interrogation is focused on *resolving an emergency*, not gathering facts to be used in a prosecution. [374]

Example: In *Bryant*, supra, the questioning occurred "in an *exposed, public area* ... and in a *disorganized fashion*," helping to make apparent that it was focused on an ongoing emergency. By contrast, the formal station-house interrogation in *Crawford* made that interrogation more likely to be found devoted to finding facts for an ultimate prosecution, not for dealing with any emergency. [375]

d. Lab reports by law-enforcement personnel: *Laboratory reports* by created by or for *law enforcement* personnel *are "testimonial."* Therefore, these reports cannot be introduced unless the *person who produced them is made available* for cross-examination at trial. [*Melendez-Diaz v. Massachusetts* (2009).] [382]

Example: D is charged with cocaine trafficking under state law. To prove that the substance seized by the police from D is cocaine, the prosecution offers into evidence (as allowed by an unusual state law) "certificates of analysis" stating that the tests conducted by the state police lab on the substance confirm that it's cocaine. The analysts who prepared the certificates sign them and have them notarized. The prosecution does not make the analysts themselves available at trial.

Held (5-4), the certificates *are "testimonial statements"* under *Crawford* and *Davis*. Therefore, the analysts who prepared them were "witnesses" for Confrontation Clause purposes. Since the prosecution did not produce the analysts for cross-examination at trial and didn't show that they were unavailable, admission of the certificates violated D's Confrontation Clause rights. [*Melendez-Diaz, supra*].

Note: For a discussion of *whose* testimony must be given live in the case of a laboratory report, see *infra*, p. C-57.

e. Non-testimonial statements: The following types of statements are probably *not* "testimonial," because the circumstances surrounding them don't suggest that the statement will be used in a later proceeding:

❏ statements by a *co-conspirator* during the course of the conspiracy, and in furtherance of it;

❏ *excited utterances,* spoken to a friend or relative who happens to be nearby, or spoken to a *911 operator* under emergency conditions;

Example: V phones a 911 line, and tells the operator, "My boyfriend is attacking me." The operator, in order to do a records search to find out whether the boyfriend is likely to be dangerous to police officers, asks, "What's your boyfriend's name?" V answers, "His name is John Smith." Because this statement, although made in response to official interrogation, was made under emergency circumstances (rather than as part of an investigation into a completed crime), it is non-testimonial (and therefore may be admitted against Simth in a criminal trial without Confrontation Clause review). [Cf. the "*Davis*" fact pattern of *Davis v. Washington*.]

❑ ***present sense impressions,*** spoken to a friend or relative who happens to be nearby;

❑ ***state-of-mind*** statements, spoken to a friend or relative who happens to be nearby.

❑ statements by an ***injured person*** to a ***health-care provider,*** if the speaker's main purpose is to ***get appropriate medical care.***

B. **Rule for testimonial statements:** If the statement ***is "testimonial,"*** *Crawford* imposes a bright-line rule: the statement ***may not be admitted against the accused unless the declarant is made available for cross-examination by the accused,*** either at the ***time of the statement, or at the time of the accused's trial.*** [390]

1. **Three important scenarios:** There are three especially important scenarios in which the bright-line rule of *Crawford* is likely to apply: (1) statements made ***during police interrogations;*** (2) ***grand jury testimony***; and (3) statements made in ***forensic or laboratory reports.***

   a. **Police interrogations:** The situation in which the *Crawford* rule probably applies most often is where W is ***interrogated by the police***, perhaps while under suspicion of some sort of criminality, and W implicates D. If W doesn't testify at D's trial, W's statement can't be used against D (unless somehow D had a prior opportunity to cross-examine W about the statement). [391]

   Example: X is questioned by the police about the fatal shooting of V. X says, "I didn't shoot V, but I did lend my gun to D knowing that D wanted to shoot V, and I then watched as D did the shooting." At D's murder trial, X pleads the Fifth Amendment. The prosecution then offers (as a declaration against interest) testimony by Ollie, the police detective who interviewed X, about what X said concerning the shooting. Because X's statement during interrogation is "testimonial," it can't come in against D unless X is made available for cross by D. Since X has pleaded the Fifth, he's deemed not available for cross. Therefore, the Confrontation Clause blocks X's statement from being used against D.

      i. **Crime-scene interview:** Statements made by W under police interrogation at a ***crime scene*** will be testimonial even if W is not under suspicion, as long as the police's focus is on asking the questions is to find out "what happened" (with a view towards "solving the case") rather than to deal with a present emergency.

      Example: In the domestic-disturbance Example on p. C-54 (V says that her husband D attacked her earlier), V's statement is testimonial, even though V was never under suspicion and even though the possible crime had occurred fairly recently. That's because the police were in an investigative "what happened?" mode rather than in a "solve the pending emergency" mode. Therefore, if V doesn't take the stand to testify in D's trial, an officer may not testify, "V told me that her husband attacked her." [Cf. the "*Hammon* portion" of *Davis v. Washington*]

   b. **Grand jury testimony:** Another important instance in which the rule of *Crawford* will lead to the declaration's being kept out is where the declaration is made in ***grand jury testimony***, and the declarant refuses to testify at D's later trial.

Example: Same basic fact pattern as above Example in which X says he lent his gun to D. Now, however, assume that X makes his statement — "I didn't shoot V, but I did lend my gun to D knowing that D wanted to shoot V, and I then watched as D did the shooting" — not to the police, but to a grand jury. This, too, is obviously a "testimonial" statement. And, of course, D's lawyer doesn't have the opportunity to cross-examine X about it in front of the grand jury (since lawyers for the suspect never get the right to cross-examine grand jury witnesses). Then, suppose the prosecution wants to use this against D at his trial, under the hearsay exception for declarations against the speaker's (X's) interest. If X pleads the Fifth at D's trial instead of repeating the remark, his grand jury testimony inculpating D can't be used against D.

c. **Who must testify (forensic report situation):** In the case of a declaration in a *forensic report* (e.g., a report of a laboratory test), obviously the live testimony of the person who did the test and wrote the report will suffice. But what if that person is not available? Can someone *other than the preparer* of the report — a *"surrogate witness"* — testify in court and meet the demands of the Confrontation Clause? The answer is *"no"* — someone who *worked on*, or at the very least *observed or reviewed* the test and the report — must testify. If the witness didn't observe or review the work or report, then her testimony won't suffice, even if she is familiar with the *general methods used* by the person who actually prepared the report. [*Bullcoming v. New Mexico* (2011)] [384]

Example: In a police lab, X uses a gas chromatograph to test D's blood sample for its blood alcohol level, then writes the result ("blood alcohol level = .11%") in a report, which he signs and certifies as true. At trial, because X has recently been put on unpaid leave, the prosecution offers the report into evidence, supported by testimony by Y, X's co-worker at the lab. Y testifies about how a gas chromatograph works, but says she didn't watch X do the test, and can't answer questions about whether he made any mistakes, or about why he was put on unpaid leave.

Held (by 5-4 vote in the Supreme Court), Y's testimony did not satisfy D's Confrontation Clause rights. Only X's testimony could have sufficed, because had X been present, D's counsel "could have asked questions designed to reveal whether incompetence, evasiveness, or dishonesty accounted for [X's] removal from his workstation." *Bullcoming, supra.* [384-386]

Note: Remember, in the three situations discussed above (statements made in response to police interrogation, statements made to a grand jury, and forensic reports created for use by the prosecution), the statement can pose a Confrontation Clause problem *only if it's "testimonial."* And the rules for deciding whether a statement is or isn't "testimonial" are the ones summarized in Par. (2) above on pp. C-53 - C-56.

C. **Rules for non-testimonial statements:** Next, let's look at the rules governing use of *"non-testimonial"* statements. The *Confrontation Clause plays no role where a non-testimonial statement is concerned.* Therefore, as a Confrontation Clause matter, a non-testimonial statement can come into evidence *no matter* whether it falls within a *firmly-rooted hearsay exception*, and no matter whether the circumstances surrounding its making suggest that it is reliable. [*Crawford v. Washington; Davis v. Washington*] [396]

Example: Suppose that X and W are old friends, who have committed various crimes together and who trust each other. One day, while the two are having a casual conversation, X says to W, "You know that murder of V last year — well, D and I were the doers."

(X is not intending to supply "evidence" against D – he's just gossiping.) Later, in a prosecution of D for the murder, the prosecution would like to offer W's testimony about what X told him. X refuses to repeat the remark at D's trial, pleading the Fifth Amendment.

The remark is *non-testimonial* (since X's primary purpose in making the remark was not to create evidence for a criminal prosecution of himself or D). Therefore, under *Crawford* and *Davis*, this non-testimonial declaration ***doesn't get Confrontation Clause analysis at all***, and there is no constitutional barrier to its use against D in the form of W's live testimony about what X said to him.

D. Interrogations by persons not working for law enforcement (*Ohio v. Clark*): As we saw above (pp. C-53 - C-57 *supra*), in situations involving a Confrontation Clause claim, the issue will *always* be, "Was the statement testimonial?" (since testimonial statements will generally be covered by the Clause, and non-testimonial statements will *never* be covered). In the usual scenario of statements made in response to an "interrogation," most often the statement will be in response to questions asked by ***law enforcement personnel.*** But let's now consider out-of-court statements made in response to questions asked by persons who are ***not*** working on behalf of law enforcement. We want to know, ***does the questioner's non-law-enforcement status automatically prevent the statement from being "testimonial"?***

The answer is: (1) the statement is ***not automatically*** rendered "non-testimonial" by virute of the fact that the questioner is not working for law enforcement; but (2) this fact certainly make it ***less likely*** that the declarant's ***"primary purpose"*** will be found to have been a testimonial one. See ***Ohio v. Clark*** (2015), discussed immediately below. [377]

1. Facts of *Ohio v. Clark*: In *Clark*, the declarant was a ***three-year-old boy,*** L.P., who told his ***preschool teachers*** that he had been abused by his mother's boyfriend, D. D was then charged with child abuse, and L.P. was found incompetent to testify. The trial judge allowed L.P.'s statement to his teachers into evidence over D's Confrontation Clause objection, and D was convicted.

2. Holding: The U.S. Supreme Court held for the prosecution. The Court held unanimously that L.P.'s statement was ***not testimonial***, thereby preventing the Confrontation Clause from applying, and making the statement admissible against the boyfriend. [378]

 a. Meaning of "testimonial: The Court said in *Clark* that "a statement ***cannot fall within the Confrontation Clause unless its primary purpose was testimonial.***" And a statement is testimonial only if "[c]onsidering all the relevant circumstances," the statement was "made with the ***primary purpose*** of ***creating evidence for [the defendant's] prosecution.***" [378]

 b. Application of rule here: Applying this definition to L.P.'s statement, the Court found that the statement was clearly ***non-testimonial***, because: [379]

  [1] The teachers were, of course, not law-enforcement officers. And when they asked L.P. how he had been hurt and by whom, they ***feared ongoing child-abuse*** — their main concern was that if they released L.P. to his guardian at the end of the day, they might be entrusting him to the very person who had abused him. Therefore, their main purpose was not helping to "uncover[] and prosecut[e] criminal behavior," the purpose required for a declaration to be "testimonial."

  (2) The declarant, L.P., was a ***very young child***. "Statements by very young children will

rarely, if ever, implicate the Confrontation Clause." To implicate the Clause, the statement must be "testimonial," and "it is extremely unlikely that a 3–year–old child in L.P.'s position would *intend his statements to be a substitute for trial testimony*" (the intent required for a statement to be testimonial). [379]

    c. **Conclusion:** Therefore, the Court held: (1) since L.P.'s statement to his teachers was not "testimonial," it couldn't trigger D's Confrontation Clause rights; and (2) the trial judge was thus correct to admit the statement against D.

E. **Consequences when Clause applies:** Once the statement in question is found to be "testimonial," so that a criminal defendant's Confrontation Clause rights are probably triggered, there are some issues about what the *consequences* of the Clause's application will be in the trial. Here's a brief discussion of a couple of those issues:

    1. **Mere unused "opportunity" to cross-examine:** What if the accused merely has an *"opportunity"* to conduct such a cross-examination of the declarant at the time of the declaration, and *does not take advantage* of that opportunity? Here, it is unclear whether the declaration can be used at the accused's later trial without Confrontation Clause problems, if the declarant is unavailable at that trial. We simply don't know the answer yet. [398]

    2. **What is "availability" for cross:** There are situations in which it's not perfectly clear whether the declarant (call him "W" for witness) is *"available"* for cross by the accused at trial. Here are some of the important availability scenarios [398-399]:

        a. **W not found, or doesn't come to court:** If W *cannot be located* for a subpoena, or *receives the subpoena but doesn't come to court*, W is clearly "unavailable." In that event, W's prior un-cross-examined testimonial statement can't be used against D. This is true even if the prosecution made all possible efforts to get W into court.

        b. **W pleads privilege:** If W takes the stand at D's trial, but then *refuses to testify* about the statement and instead *pleads a privilege* (e.g., the *Fifth Amendment*), W is unavailable.

        c. **W can't remember or is evasive:** But if W takes the stand, and purports to answer questions, the fact that W is *evasive*, or says he *can't remember*, probably does *not* prevent W from being considered "available" for cross by D. And that's probably true even if W seems to be *behaving in bad faith.*

F. **D's forfeiture of rights by making the witness unavailable:** Suppose the defendant *causes the declarant to be unavailable*, for instance by *killing* her. This will cause the defendant to be deemed to have *forfeited* his Confrontation Clause right, but *only if the defendant acted for the purpose of procuring the declarant's unavailability.* [*Giles v. California* (2008)] [399]

    1. **Ordinary murder case:** So in an ordinary murder case – ordinary in the sense that D killed V for some purpose *other than* preventing V from testifying against D – the fact that D killed V will *not* be deemed to be a forfeiture by D of his Confrontation Clause rights. Therefore, the prosecution will still be blocked by the Confrontation Clause from introducing testimonial-type statements made by V before the murder (e.g., a statement by V to police investigators about a threat of violence D made to V three months previously).

    2. **D acts to avoid V's testimony:** But if the prosecution can show that D procured the declarant's unavailability *for the purpose of avoiding the declarant's trial testimony* (e.g., by killing her), then D *will* be deemed to have forfeited his Confrontation Clause rights.

Example: D kills V to prevent V from testifying against him at an upcoming trial. V's prior statements about the crime are admissible notwithstanding D's Confrontation Clause rights.

G. Confession implicating someone else, used during joint trial: Special problems arise when *A* and *B* are tried together, and *A*'s confession implicating himself and *B* is sought to be used by the prosecution. If the same jury hears *A*'s confession implicating *B* (and *A* doesn't take the stand), then *B*'s Confrontation Clause rights are violated even if the prosecution only purports to be offering the confession against *A*. That's true even if the judge warns the jury not to consider *A*'s confession as evidence against *B*. [*Bruton v. U.S.*] [399]

1. **The "two jury" technique:** One way around this problem is to use *two juries* when co-conspirators are being tried. The trial court empanels a separate jury for each defendant. Then, D1 is allowed to withdraw his jury during presentation of evidence that D2 confessed and implicated D1. This saves the necessity of conducting two entirely separate trials.

III. COMPULSORY PROCESS

C
A
P
S
U
L
E

S
U
M
M
A
R
Y

A. Generally: The Compulsory Process Clause gives the defendant the right to obtain and present all evidence helpful to his defense. [403]

B. State rules restricting evidence: This means that a state evidence rule that restricts the defendant's ability to present exculpatory evidence may run afoul of his Compulsory Process rights. [403-404]

1. **Ban on accomplice's testimony:** For instance, a statute providing that if A and B are charged as co-participants, A may not testify in B's defense, violates B's compulsory process rights.

2. **Restrictive hearsay rule:** Similarly, a state hearsay rule that prevents D from showing that someone else has made an out-of-court declaration confessing to the crime, may violate D's compulsory process rights. However, this will only happen if D convinces the court that the third person's alleged out-of-court confession is somewhat *corroborated* by surrounding circumstances. Thus if D offers X's out-of-court confession, but the prosecution shows that X was in jail at the time of the crime, D has no compulsory process right to present that confession.

C. "Arbitrary or disproportionate" standard: Rules excluding particular types of evidence will not violate an accused's Compulsory Process rights "so long as they are *not 'arbitrary' or 'disproportionate* to the purposes they are designed to serve.'" (Furthermore, this "arbitrary or disproportionate" standard will be violated only if the exclusion of evidence infringes upon a "weighty interest" of the accused.) [*U.S. v. Scheffer*] [404]

Example: Rules prohibiting all parties (including criminal defendants) from introducing lie-detector evidence don't violate the accused's Compulsory Process rights. That's because polygraph evidence is of debatable reliability, so excluding it is not "arbitrary" or "disproportionate to the purpose" (ensuring reliability of evidence) that the rule of exclusion is designed to achieve. [*Scheffer*]

D. Equality principle: State rules that consistently *favor the prosecution* are especially likely to violate the Compulsory Process Clause. (*Example:* A state rule banning one accomplice from testifying on behalf of another, but not banning one accomplice from testifying against the other, favors the prosecution consistently, and therefore, violates the Compulsory Process Clause.) [404-405]

CHAPTER 8
PRIVILEGES

I. PRIVILEGES GENERALLY

A. **Not constitutionally based:** Most privileges are not constitutionally based. (The privilege against self-incrimination is the only exception.) Therefore, each state is free to establish whatever privileges it wishes and to define the contours of those privileges as it wishes. [413-415]

1. **Federal:** There were a number of specific proposed federal rules of privilege. But these were never enacted. Instead, FRE 501 is the only Federal Rule dealing with privileges. It provides that normally, "[t]he common law — as interpreted by United States courts in the light of reason and experience — governs a claim of privilege[.]" That is, normally federal judges will decide what privileges to recognize based on *prior federal case law* and the court's *own judgment.*

    a. **Diversity:** But in *diversity* cases, the existence and scope of a privilege will be decided by the law of the *state* whose substantive law is being followed.

2. **States:** The states vary greatly on what privileges they recognize. All recognize the husband-wife and attorney-client privileges, most by statute. All recognize a privilege for certain government information. Nearly all recognize some kind of physician-patient and clergyman-penitent privileges. Three other privileges are recognized only in a minority of states: journalist-source, parent-child, and accountant-client.

B. **Proceedings where applicable:** If a privilege not to disclose certain information exists, that privilege applies *regardless of the proceeding*. That is, it will apply to protect the holder against disclosure in a trial, administrative hearing, deposition, or any other proceeding. [414]

C. **Who may assert:** The privilege *belongs* to the *person whose interest or relationship is intended to be fostered* by that privilege. Therefore, he is the *only one* who may assert it. (*Examples:* The client is the one protected by the lawyer-client privilege, so it may be asserted only by him, or on his behalf, not by the lawyer on the lawyer's behalf. Similarly, the physician-patient privilege is meant to protect only the patient, so only he, not the doctor, may assert it.) [414]

D. **Third person learns:** Most privileges protect communications between two parties to a specified relationship. If a *third party* somehow learns of the conversation, the privilege may be found to have been *waived*. [414-415]

1. **Older, strict view:** The traditional view is very strict: if a third party somehow learns of the conversation, even if the original parties to it had no reason to anticipate this, the privilege will be held to be lost. (*Example:* Telephone operator eavesdrops on a phone conversation between lawyer and client; the privilege is held to lost, and the operator may testify as to what she heard.)

2. **Modern view:** But modern courts usually hold that the communication is protected even if intercepted, as long as the interception was not reasonably to be anticipated. (So the prior example would be decided differently today.) But if the party protected should reasonably

have anticipated the interception, he will not be protected. (*Example:* Patient or client discloses a confidence to his doctor or lawyer in a crowded elevator; the risk of it being overheard is so great that if it is overheard, the privilege will be held waived.)

II. THE ATTORNEY-CLIENT PRIVILEGE

A. **Generally:** The privilege is basically that a client has **right not to disclose** (and the right to prevent his lawyer from disclosing) **any confidential communication between the two of them relating to the professional relationship**. The key elements are: [416-433]

1. **Client:** The "client" can be a **corporation** as well as an individual.

2. **Belongs to client:** The privilege **belongs to the client**, not to the lawyer or any third persons. The lawyer may assert it, but only if he is acting on behalf of the client in doing so.

3. **Professional relationship:** The privilege applies only to communications made for the purpose of facilitating the rendition of **professional legal services**.

4. **Confidential:** The privilege applies only to communications which are intended to be **"confidential."**

5. **Fact of employment or client's identity:** The fact that the lawyer-client relationship **exists**, and the **identity** of the client, are normally **not** privileged. Only the substance of the confidences exchanged between them is generally privileged (though there are a couple of exceptions).

6. **Physical evidence:** Normally, the privilege does not permit the lawyer to conceal **physical evidence** or documents given to him by the client; the lawyer may not only have to turn over the physical evidence but describe how and where he got it.

7. **Crime or fraud exception:** The privilege does not apply where the confidence relates to the commission of a **future crime or fraud**.

B. **Professional relationship:** The privilege applies only in the context of a professional lawyer-client relationship. [418]

1. **No retainer:** The required relationship can exist even though the client does **not pay a fee.** (*Example:* Client receives a free initial consultation; the privilege applies even though, at the end of the consultation, either lawyer or client decides that the lawyer will not handle the case.)

2. **Non-legal advice:** But the mere fact that the person giving the advice is a lawyer is not enough — the relationship must involve the giving of legal advice. Thus, if the lawyer gives **business** advice, **friendly** advice, political advice, etc., the privilege does not apply.

3. **Reasonable belief:** So long as the client **reasonably believes** that the person he is talking to is a lawyer, the privilege applies even though the other person is in fact not a lawyer. Similarly, the privilege applies if the person is a lawyer who is not, and is known to the client not to be, admitted to practice in the state where the advice is given.

C. **Confidential communications:** Only **"confidential"** communications are protected. [418-422]

1. **Client-to-lawyer:** Disclosures by the **client to the lawyer** are protected if they are intended to be confidential.

    a. **Lawyer's observation:** However, if the lawyer makes an ***observation*** that third parties could also have made, this will not be a confidential communication. (*Example:* Lawyer observes scratch marks on Client's face, in a meeting that takes place right after Client's wife has been found stabbed to death. Since anyone could have made this observation, it is not privileged, and Lawyer can be forced to testify at Client's trial about the scratches.)

2. **Lawyer-to-client statements:** The privilege also applies to statements made ***by the lawyer*** to the client.

3. **Information involving third parties:**

    a. **Representative of lawyer:** If a ***third party*** is assisting the lawyer, he is treated as being a representative of the lawyer and communications involving him are treated the same way as if he were himself a lawyer. (*Example:* Lawyer retains Private Detective to help investigate the case; statements made by Client to Detective, Lawyer to Detective, Detective to Client, Detective to Lawyer, are all privileged.)

    b. **Not assisting lawyer:** But if a third person is ***not*** assisting the lawyer, there is ***no*** privilege for communications between that third person and the lawyer, even if these communications relate to the lawyer's providing of legal services. (*Example:* Lawyer interviews Witness; statements made by Witness that incriminate Client are not privileged, because Witness is not working on behalf of Lawyer. However, if the only reason Lawyer knew to interview Witness is because Client told him to do so, the privilege might apply to witness's statements.)

4. **Waiver:** The attorney-client privilege can be ***waived***. Most importantly, if the client ***voluntarily discloses*** the communication — or consents to its being disclosed by someone else, such as her attorney — the disclosure will normally act as a waiver. [420]

    a. **Presence of third persons:** One form of waiver-by-disclosure will occur when the client permits a ***third person to be present*** when the communication takes place, if that person's presence does not advance the legal representation.

       Example: If the communication takes place on a crowded elevator, where it is overheard by third persons, this setting will indicate that the client could not reasonably have expected confidentiality. Similarly, if the client, following the conference with the lawyer, tells a friend all about the conference, this is likely to be held to be an implied waiver of confidentiality.

    b. **Inadvertent disclosure:** Disclosures of privileged information sometimes occur ***inadvertently***. FRE 502 (added in 2008) says that for purposes of federal-court litigation, an inadvertent disclosure does ***not*** operate as a waiver as long as the privilege-holder (i) took ***reasonable steps*** to ***prevent*** the disclosure before it happened, and then (ii) ***promptly took reasonable steps*** to ***rectify*** the error after it occurred. Rule 502(b), (c).

5. **Underlying facts:** It is only the ***communication*** that is privileged, not the underlying fact communicated.

D. **Fact of employment; client's identity:** Generally, the ***fact*** that the attorney has been hired, and the ***identity*** of the client, are ***not*** privileged. (*Example:* At a grand jury investigating local cocaine trafficking, L, a well known specialist in defending high-level cocaine importers, may be required to say whether he is representing X, one such importer.) [422]

1. **Exceptions:** Some courts have recognized one or both of the following exceptions to this general rule of non-privilege:

    a. **Anonymous restitution:** Some courts allow Lawyer to make anonymous restitution on behalf of Client. (*Example:* Lawyer sends tax money to the IRS, without disclosing that it comes from Client — the purpose is to give Client a restitution defense if his taxes are ever audited. Some courts will allow Lawyer to refuse the IRS' demand to identify the Client.)

    b. **"Missing link":** Most courts will allow the lawyer to keep the client's identity secret where so much other information is already public that disclosure of the client's identity would have the effect of disclosing a privileged communication, or violating the client's self-incrimination privilege. (*Example:* X and Y are both suspected of murdering V. L represents X before a grand jury. A court might allow L to refuse to say whether Y is paying L's fee for representing X, on the theory that an affirmative answer might tend to incriminate Y.)

E. **Physical evidence:** If the client turns over to the lawyer *physical evidence*, the lawyer may generally not conceal this evidence or refuse to answer questions about whether he has it, on attorney-client privilege grounds. [422-426]

1. **No ongoing fraud:** The most important rule concerning this problem is that the attorney-client privilege does not apply where the lawyer's assistance is sought to enable the client to *commit a future crime or fraud*. Since all states prohibit the concealment or destruction of evidence in a pending proceeding, a lawyer who helps his client conceal or destroy evidence is a co-conspirator to a new crime, and the lawyer's assistance is thus not privileged. This is especially true where the evidence is contraband, stolen money, or a weapon or other instrument used to commit the crime.

2. **Destruction advice:** Similarly, the lawyer may not advise his client to destroy the evidence, and if he does so, the giving of that advice is not privileged.

3. **Lawyer's choices:** The lawyer may, however, simply return the evidence to the client with the advice not to conceal it; if the lawyer does this, he is probably privileged not to disclose the evidence's existence to the other side (usually the prosecution). Alternatively, he may take the evidence for a reasonable time for inspection or testing, and then return it to the client, without disclosing this fact to the other side. (But if the property is stolen, the lawyer must take steps to return it to his rightful owner. Similarly, if the lawyer believes that the client will destroy the evidence, he probably must turn it over to the other side, and is not privileged to keep silent about the evidence's existence.)

4. **Evidence of source:** If the other side (e.g., the prosecution) learns of particular physical evidence in the lawyer's possession, some courts hold that the lawyer is not privileged to refuse to say how he came into possession of it. (*Example:* D is charged with murdering and robbing V. From prison, D tells L to inspect D's garbage can; L does so, and finds V's wallet, which he takes with him and puts in his safe. At trial, many courts would require L to testify about how he came into possession of the wallet, since otherwise the prosecution is unfairly impeded in its efforts to tie the wallet to D.)

    a. **No custody:** But if the lawyer merely learns of an item's existence for his client, or inspects it and then gives it back to the client, the lawyer may not be required to say at trial how he learned about the item.

F. Corporations as clients: [426-428]

1. **Corporations have privilege:** A *corporation* may possess the attorney-client privilege just as an individual may.

2. **Who may communicate:** Only communications made "on behalf" of the corporation's business are covered. But probably no matter how low level an employee is, if he is really acting in what he reasonably perceives to be the corporation's interests, communications made between him and the corporation's lawyer will be privileged as to the corporation.

3. **Must concern employment:** The mere fact that one party to the communication is an employee is not sufficient — the communication must *relate to the employee's performance of corporate duties.* (*Example:* Driver, who works for Bus Co., happens to see an accident involving one of the company's buses while he is off duty. Statements about the accident by Driver to Bus Co.'s lawyer are not privileged, because they do not relate to anything that happened while Driver was performing his corporate duties.)

4. **Reports and routine communications:** The communication must be primarily for the purpose of obtaining legal services. Therefore, if the communication is a *routine report* generated in the ordinary course of the corporation's business, the privilege will not apply merely because the report happened to be received by one of the corporation's attorneys. (*Examples:* Accident reports, personnel records, and financial documents probably won't be privileged even if circulated to the company's attorneys, because none of these is typically created for the primary purpose of obtaining legal services.)

5. **Confidentiality:** The requirement of confidentiality means that only those communications that the corporation handles on a *"need to know"* basis will be privileged.

G. Exceptions: There are several situations where the privilege will be held not to apply even though the usual requirements are met: [428-431]

1. **Crime or fraud:** As noted above, a communication relating to the carrying out of a future *crime or wrong* is not privileged. (*Example:* Client says to Lawyer, "If X and I were to rob the First National Bank, and X were then to get caught and give a confession implicating me, could the police use this confession against me?" If the robbery is later committed, the statement may be used against Client, since even though he was seeking legal services, he was doing so with reference to a future crime.)

2. **Death of client:** In general, the privilege *survives* the *death* of the client. But there is a key exception: if the suit is a will contest or other case in which the issue is who receives the deceased client's property, the privilege does not apply. (*Example:* In will contest, Son may call Lawyer to testify about Lawyer's conversations with Testator, in which Testator said that he wanted to provide for Son in his will.)

3. **Attorney-client dispute:** The privilege does not apply to a *dispute between lawyer and client* concerning the services provided by lawyer. (*Examples:* The privilege does not apply if Lawyer sues Client for a fee, or if Client sues Lawyer for malpractice.)

4. **Joint clients:** The privilege may be inapplicable to a dispute between multiple clients who were originally on the same side of a transaction.

    a. **Same lawyer:** If two clients *retain a single lawyer*, and a dispute later breaks out between the two, the privilege does not apply. This is true regardless of whether the other client was privy to the communication in question. (*Example:* Driver is sued by Passenger for injuries from a car crash. Insurer, who insures Driver, hires Lawyer for the case. Driver makes confidential communications to Lawyer. Later, Driver and Insurer have a dispute about policy limits. In that dispute, Insurer may probably compel Lawyer to disclose otherwise-privileged statements between Driver and Lawyer.)

  b. Different lawyers: But if two clients retain *separate* lawyers, and both lawyers and both clients meet together and discuss common legal issues, the privilege applies even in the event of a later dispute between clients.

H. Work product immunity: Separately from the attorney-client privilege, the doctrine of *work product immunity* prevents an attorney from being required to disclose certain information that he obtains *while preparing for a lawsuit*. [431-432]

 1. Qualified protection: Generally, documents prepared in anticipation of litigation may be discovered by the other side only if the party seeking discovery shows that he has a *substantial need* for the materials, and that he cannot get the substantial equivalent by other means. This is a *"qualified"* immunity. Fed. R. Civ. Proc. 26(b)(3). (*Example:* Client fills out a questionnaire about the facts of his injuries, to help Lawyer prepare the case for trial. Even if the questionnaire is not covered by the attorney-client privilege — perhaps because Client has disclosed it to a journalist — Lawyer can refuse to release it in response to a discovery request by the other side.)

  a. Absolute immunity: Documents that show a lawyer's "mental impressions, conclusions, opinions, or legal theories" concerning litigation are probably *absolutely* privileged, in the sense that no showing of need by the other side will be sufficient to overcome the work product immunity.

III. PHYSICIAN-PATIENT PRIVILEGE

A. Generally: All but 10 states have a statutory physician-patient privilege. These statutes usually apply to: [433]

 1. a *confidential communication*;

 2. made to a *physician* (including psychiatrist);

 3. if made for the purpose of obtaining *treatment*, or diagnosis looking toward treatment.

B. Constitutional underpinning: Some aspects of the privilege may be constitutionally compelled. At least one state court (California) has held that the "confidentiality of the psychotherapeutic session" falls within one of the "zones of privacy" created by the U.S. Constitution (though California has held that its statute, with exceptions for the patient-litigant situation, see below, is constitutional). [433]

C. Relationships covered: All statutes that cover general physician-patient confidences also cover *psychotherapist*-patient confidences. In fact, virtually all states (even ones that don't cover physician-patient confidences) protect psychotherapist-patient confidences. [412, 416]

 1. Psychologist: Nearly all states cover *psychologists* (not just psychiatrists) within the psychotherapist-patient privilege.

 2. Consulted for litigation: Consultations that take place concerning *litigation* rather than for purposes of treatment or diagnosis are *not* covered. For instance, examination by or disclosures to a court-appointed physician, or an expert witness consulted so that he can testify at trial, are not covered.

D. Patient-litigant exception: Nearly all statutes have some kind of exception for the *"patient-litigant"* situation, under which a patient-litigant who puts his *medical condition in issue* is deemed to have in effect waived the privilege. (*Example:* Car collision case; P sues D for a broken leg. P's doctor and hospital records, including notations of disclosures made by P to the doctor, will be admissible, because P has placed the nature and extent of his injuries in issue by seeking damages for them.) [434-435]

IV. THE PRIVILEGE AGAINST SELF-INCRIMINATION

A. Generally: [437- 449]

1. Constitutional basis: The privilege derives from the U.S. Constitution. The Fifth Amendment provides that "no person . . . shall be compelled in any criminal case to be a witness against himself. . . ."

    a. Applicable to states: This provision is binding not only on the federal judicial system but also on the *states*, by operation of the Fourteenth Amendment's Due Process Clause.

    b. Two types: The privilege applies not only to criminal defendants, but also to any other person who is asked to give testimony that may incriminate him (e.g., witnesses in grand jury proceedings, congressional investigations, other people's criminal trials, etc.).

B. Requirements: The privilege applies only when four requirements are met: (1) it is asserted by an *individual*; (2) the communication sought is *testimonial*; (3) the communication is *compulsory*; and (4) the communication might *incriminate* the witness. [420-423]

1. Individuals: The requirement that the privilege be individual and "personal" means that:

    a. Another's privilege: A person may not assert *another's* privilege. (*Example:* D is on trial for robbery. The prosecution puts on testimony by X, an unindicted co-conspirator, in which X says that he and D did the robbery together. D may not exclude this testimony by claiming that it violates X's privilege — since it is X who is testifying, only he may assert or waive the privilege.)

    b. Business organization: *Business organizations* do *not* have the privilege. Thus, neither *corporations*, partnerships, nor labor unions may claim the privilege. (But a person doing business as a sole proprietorship may assert it — it is not the fact of doing business that removes the privilege, but rather the use of an "artificial organization.")

    c. Agent: An employee or other *agent* of a business organization will usually have to produce and identify the organization's books and records on request, even though those books and records (or the fact that the agent has them) might incriminate him. But he will usually not have to do anything more if this would incriminate him (e.g., he usually will not have to state the whereabouts of corporate records that he does not possess).

2. Testimonial: Only *"testimonial"* activity is covered. Thus, the suspect may be required to furnish a blood sample, fingerprints, handwriting samples, or even to speak so that his voice may be compared with a previously recorded conversation. Also, a suspect may be required to appear in a lineup for identification.

3. **"Compulsory":** A communication must be *"compulsory."* The main importance of this requirement is that if a person *voluntarily* puts the information in *written form*, the document is not privileged. (But the writer may have a privilege against *producing* the document for the government, as discussed below.)

4. **Incriminatory:** The response must have a *tendency to incriminate* the person. Thus if there are procedural reasons why no prosecution can take place (e.g., the statute of limitations has run, or the witness has been given immunity), the privilege does not apply. The fact that answering the question might subject the witness to ridicule or civil liability is not enough.

C. **Proceedings where applicable:** The privilege applies not only where asserted by a defendant in a criminal trial, but also by any witness in *any kind of proceeding.* Thus it may be asserted by witnesses to a grand jury investigation, to another person's criminal trial, to a civil proceeding, to pre-trial discovery proceedings (e.g., W's deposition is being taken), or to questioning by the police. [439-441]

D. **Procedure for invoking:** [441-442]

1. **Criminal defendant:** When the assertion is made by the defendant in a criminal trial, he may invoke the privilege merely by *declining to testify.* In that event, he does not have to take the stand at all, and cannot even be questioned.

2. **Non-defendant witness:** But if the privilege is being claimed by a *witness* (i.e., someone other than the defendant in a criminal trial), the procedure is different: the witness must *take the stand*, be sworn, listen to the question, and then assert the privilege. In this event, it is the judge who decides whether the response might be incriminatory; but the person seeking the testimony bears an extremely heavy burden of proving that the response *could not possibly* incriminate W, a showing that can only rarely be made.

E. **Waiver:** A person who takes the stand and gives some testimony may be held to have *waived* the privilege with respect to further questions: [443]

1. **Criminal defendant:** If a criminal defendant does take the stand, and testifies in his own defense, he has waived his privilege at least with respect to those questions that are *necessary for an effective cross-examination*. (*Example:* In a murder trial, D testifies that he was not anywhere near the scene of the crime. The prosecution would certainly be entitled to ask D where he was, and D could not assert the privilege in refusing to answer.)

2. **Witness:** Since an ordinary witness must take the stand and listen to each question, a witness who answers non-incriminating questions will not be held to have waived the privilege with respect to later, incriminating, questions. However, if W makes a general and incriminatory statement about a matter, he must then answer *follow-up questions eliciting the details*, at least where these details would not add significantly to the incrimination.

3. **Later proceedings:** If the defendant or witness does waive the privilege, this waiver is effective *throughout the current proceedings*, but not for subsequent proceedings. (*Example:* W's waiver during grand jury proceedings would not prevent him from asserting the privilege when called as a witness at a subsequent trial of X on an indictment returned by that same grand jury.)

F. **Documentary evidence:** When a document is subpoenaed by the government, the person receiving the subpoena may have a fifth amendment right not to comply: [443]

1. **Contents:** The *contents* of the subpoenaed document will practically never be protected by the Fifth Amendment: so long as the taxpayer was not originally compelled to create the document, its contents are not protected by the privilege.

2. **Act of producing:** But a person's act of *producing* the documents in response to a subpoena may implicitly incriminate him, in which case he probably has a Fifth Amendment privilege not to produce it. For instance, if there were no way that the government could obtain or authenticate a certain personal diary kept by D except through production of this diary by him, D might be allowed to plead the Fifth by arguing that his production would implicitly mean that he is stating: (1) that the diary exists; (2) that the diary was in his possession or control; and (3) that he believes that this is indeed the genuine diary the government is seeking. (But if the government can show that it has other ways of authenticating this diary, then the privilege will not apply.)

3. **"Required records" exception:** Even if a person is *compelled* to keep a certain type of record, he may not have a Fifth Amendment right to refuse to do so: the record keeper must turn the record over even though it might incriminate him, if: (1) the record is one that a party has customarily kept, (2) the law requiring the keeping of it is "essentially regulatory," and (3) the records are analogous to a "public document." This is the *"required records"* exception to the privilege against self-incrimination. (*Example:* Records of prices charged to customers, kept under a mandatory price control law, still have to be turned over because they are essentially regulatory.)

G. **Inference and comment:** When a criminal defendant pleads the Fifth, he gets two other procedural safeguards to extend the privilege's usefulness. [445-447]

1. **"No comment" rule:** First, neither the judge nor the prosecution may *comment adversely* on D's failure to testify (e.g., by saying, "If D is really innocent, why hasn't he taken the stand to tell you that?")

2. **Instruction:** Second, D has an affirmative right to have the judge *instruct the jury* that they are not to draw any adverse inference from his failure to testify.

3. **Prior silence:** If the criminal defendant has remained silent at *prior proceedings*, the judge and prosecutor may not comment if the silence was the result of clear exercise of a constitutional privilege:

   a. **Arrest:** Thus, if D was previously silent during *custodial police interrogation*, the prosecutor and judge may not comment on this fact at D's later criminal trial.

   b. **Pre-arrest silence:** But if D remained silent *before being arrested*, this fact may be comment on, since D was not exercising any formal Fifth Amendment privilege. (*Example:* D pleads self-defense to a murder charge. The prosecution may comment upon the fact that for the two weeks between the killing and D's arrest, he did not go to the police to tell them his story.)

4. **Civil suit:** If the suit is a *civil* one, either side may freely comment adversely on the other party's (or a witness's) failure to testify. (*Example:* P sues D for causing a car accident; D fails to take the stand because he is afraid that if he does so, the fact that he was drunk will come out, and he may be prosecuted. P may nonetheless say to the jury, "If D wasn't driving drunk, why doesn't he take the stand and tell you that?")

H. Immunity: If W is given *immunity* from prosecution, he may not assert the privilege (since he has received the same benefit — freedom from having his testimony used against him — that the privilege is designed to provide). [447-448]

1. **"Transactional" vs. "use" immunity:** There are two types of immunity: *"transactional"* and *"use."* Transactional protects the witness against any prosecution for the *transaction* about which he testifies. Use immunity is much narrower — it merely protects against the direct or indirect use of the *testimony* in a subsequent prosecution.

2. **Use immunity sufficient:** Use immunity is *sufficient* to nullify the witness's Fifth Amendment privilege. (But the prosecutor then bears a heavy burden of showing that he could not have used the testimony, even indirectly, in preparing for the subsequent case.)

3. **Defense witness immunity:** If a person could give testimony that a criminal defendant thinks would help exonerate him, but the witness refuses to testify without immunity, the defendant may attempt to have *"defense witness immunity"* conferred upon this witness. But the vast majority of courts have refused to grant such defense witness immunity.

V. THE MARITAL PRIVILEGES

A. Generally: [449-451]

1. **Two privileges:** In most states, two distinct privileges protect the marital relationship:

   a. **Adverse testimony:** The *adverse testimony* privilege (sometimes called "spousal immunity") gives a spouse *complete* protection from adverse testimony by the other spouse. (*Example:* H is on trial for murder; the adverse testimony privilege protects H from having W take the witness stand to testify against him, regardless of whether her testimony concerns anything he said.)

   b. **Confidential communication:** The *confidential communications* privilege is narrower: it protects only against the disclosure of confidential communications made by one spouse to the other during the marriage. (*Example:* H is on trial for murder. The confidential communications privilege protects H against having W disclose that H confessed to her, "I shot V," but does not protect him against having W describe to the jury how she witnessed H kill V.)

2. **Distinctions:** Here are some of the practical differences between the two privileges:

   a. **Before marriage, or after marriage ends:** The adverse testimony privilege applies only if the parties are still married at the time of the trial, but applies to statements made before the marriage took place. Conversely, the confidential communications privilege covers only statements made during the marriage, but applies even if the parties are no longer married by the time of the trial.

   b. **Civil vs. criminal:** The adverse testimony privilege is usually allowed only in criminal cases, but the confidential communications privilege is usually available in civil as well as criminal cases.

   c. **Acts:** The adverse testimony privilege prevents the non-party spouse from testifying even as to *acts* committed by the spouse, but the confidential communications privilege does not (since it covers only "communications").

3. State coverage: Only a slight majority of states recognize the adverse testimony privilege, but virtually all recognize the confidential communications privilege. In *federal* courts, *both* privileges are recognized.

B. Adverse testimony privilege: [450-452]

   1. Who holds: Courts disagree about who holds the adverse testimony privilege:

   a. Federal: In federal cases, the privilege belongs only to the *testifying spouse*, not the party spouse. Thus, D in a federal criminal trial may not block his spouse's testimony; only the witness-spouse may assert or waive the right.

   b. States: Of those states recognizing the adverse testimony privilege, a slight majority give the privilege to the party (i.e., the criminal defendant); the rest follow the federal approach of giving the privilege only to the witness-spouse.

   2. Criminal vs. civil: Most jurisdictions (including the federal courts) grant the adverse testimony privilege only in *criminal* cases.

   3. Special marriage: If D is worried about his girlfriend's being required to disclose something she has heard or seen, he may marry her the night before the trial, and thereby keep her off the stand using the adverse testimony privilege.

C. Confidential communications: Virtually every state recognizes the confidential communications privilege. [452-453]

   1. Federal: Federal courts apply this privilege on the basis of *general federal common law*, since there is no federal rule granting it.

   2. Who holds: In most states, *either spouse* may assert the privilege. (But a few states grant it only to the spouse who made the communication.)

   3. "Communication" required: Only "communications" are privileged. Strictly speaking, an "act" that is not intended to convey information is not covered. (But some states have held that if an act is done in front of the spouse only because the actor trusts the spouse, the privilege should apply. Thus if H allows W to see his recently-fired shotgun before putting it away, the court might hold that this was the equivalent of a "communication" since it would not have happened had H not trusted W.)

   4. Marital status: The parties to the communication must be married at the time of the communication. If so, the privilege applies even though they have gotten divorced by the time of the trial.

   5. Exceptions: Here are some common exceptions to the confidential communications privilege:

   a. Crime against other spouse: Prosecution for crimes *committed by one spouse against the other*, or against the *children* of either;

   b. Suit between spouses: Suits by *one spouse against the other* (e.g., a divorce suit);

   c. Facilitating crime: Communications made for the purpose of *planning or committing a crime*. (*Example:* H brings home loot from a robbery, and asks W to help him hide it. Since H is seeking W's help in committing an additional crime — possession of stolen goods — most courts would find the privilege inapplicable to H's request for assistance.)

VI. MISCELLANEOUS PRIVILEGES

A. **Priest-penitent:** Virtually all states recognize a privilege for *confidential communications* made to a *clergyman* in his profession capacity as *spiritual advisor.* [453]

B. **Journalist's source:** Most states now recognize a privilege for a journalist's sources: [454-455]

1. **Statutes:** A slight majority of states have enacted *"shield laws"* preventing a journalist from being compelled to testify about his confidential sources. All of these statutes at least protect the journalist from having to disclose the *identity* of his sources; some protect him against forced disclosure of his *notes and records* of information learned from the source.

2. **Constitutional argument:** Some state and lower-federal courts have recognized a *First Amendment* basis for the privilege in some situations. (*Example:* If the information being sought is not very central to the case of the litigant who is seeking it, or can be gotten from other sources, the court may find that the journalist has a constitutional right not to supply it.) But the Supreme Court has never found such a First Amendment privilege to exist, and in one major case, a four-justice plurality concluded that no such privilege exists. *Branzburg v. Hayes.*

3. **Conflict with defendant's rights:** If the journalist's statutory or constitutional privilege *conflicts* with a criminal defendant's Sixth Amendment right to *compulsory process* or *confrontation*, the journalist's privilege will probably have to give way. (*Example:* Reporter conducts a murder investigation, leading to charges against D; D's constitutional right to compulsory process outweighs Reporter's rights under the state shield provision, so Reporter is required to supply his notes on his investigation. *In re Farber.*)

C. **Government information:** The government may have a privilege not to disclose *information in its possession*: [455-458]

1. **Military or diplomatic secrets:** The government has an *absolute* privilege not to disclose *military* or *diplomatic* secrets. No matter how badly a litigant needs such information, the government is privileged not to disclose it.

2. **Other government information:** Other types of government information receive merely a *qualified* privilege. That is, the privilege applies only where the harm to the public welfare from disclosure outweighs the litigant's need for the information.

   a. **Internal deliberations and policy making:** Thus internal government opinions, deliberations, and recommendations about policies are qualifiedly privileged. (But factual reports are not.)

   b. **Law enforcement investigatory files:** Similarly, *investigatory files* compiled by a law enforcement agency are qualifiedly privileged. (*Example:* A criminal defendant has no general evidence-law right to force the government to turn over to him the files it has compiled in investigating and preparing the case against him, though criminal discovery rules may give him the right to certain items, such as witnesses' statements.)

3. **Informers:** The government has a special privilege to decline to disclose the *identity of informants* who have given information about crimes.

   a. **I.D. only:** Usually, the government informant privilege protects only the *identity* of the informant, not the substance of the *information* that he gives to the government (unless that information would effectively reveal the informant's identity).

b. Qualified: The privilege is only a *qualified* one. Thus if disclosure of the informant's I.D. is likely to materially help the criminal defendant in his defense, the government must disclose it or drop the case. Participants and eyewitnesses are usually held to be so central that their I.D.s must be disclosed; but a mere "tipster" is not, so his identity may usually be concealed. Anyone called as a *witness* by the prosecution must be identified.

4. Consequences of upholding claim: If the court upholds the government's claim of privilege, and the government is the plaintiff (as in a criminal prosecution or a civil suit brought by the government), the government must normally *choose* between releasing the information or *dropping the case*.

D. Trade secrets: Some courts recognize a qualified privilege for *trade secrets*; that is, special secrets which a business possesses that aid it in competing. (*Examples:* Information about a company's relative market position; secret information about a device or process; design information about a product.) If the judge does partly override the privilege because of a litigant's great need for the material, he may issue a *protective order* limiting the use to which the information may be put (e.g., by ordering that the litigant not disclose it to anyone else). [458]

REAL AND DEMONSTRATIVE EVIDENCE, INCLUDING WRITINGS

I. INTRODUCTION

A. "Real" vs. "demonstrative" evidence: [470-471]

1. "Real": "Real" evidence is a tangible object that *played some actual role* in the matter that gave rise to the litigation. (*Example:* A knife used in a fatal stabbing.)

2. "Demonstrative": Demonstrative evidence is tangible evidence that merely *illustrates* a matter of importance in the litigation. (*Examples:* Maps, diagrams, models, summaries, and other materials created especially for the litigation. For instance, if the prosecution cannot find actual knife used in stabbing, a newly-acquired knife believed to be similar to the one actually used may be presented as a model to help the jury understand.)

3. Significance of distinction: The foundation requirements needed to authenticate the two types of evidence are different. See below.

II. AUTHENTICATION

A. Generally: All real and demonstrative evidence must be *"authenticated"* before it is admitted. That is, it must be shown to be *"genuine."* This means that the object must be established to be *what its proponent claims it to be*. See FRE 901(a). [472]

1. Real evidence: If the object is real evidence, authentication usually means showing that the object is *the* object that was involved in the underlying event (e.g., the actual knife used in the stabbing).

2. Demonstrative: If the evidence is demonstrative, authentication usually means showing that the object *fairly represents or illustrates* what it is claimed to represent or illustrate (e.g., proof that a diagram offered in evidence really shows the position of the parties and witnesses at the time of the murder).

B. Methods of authentication: [473-477]

   1. Real evidence: For real evidence, authentication generally is done in one of two ways:

   a. Readily or uniquely identifiable: If the item is *readily* or *uniquely* identifiable, it can be authenticated by showing that this is the case, and that the object is therefore the one that played the actual role. (*Example:* "I found the knife at the stabbing, and marked it with my initials; the knife you have just shown me has my carved initials, so it must be the knife found at the murder scene.")

   b. Chain of custody: Otherwise, the item's *"chain of custody"* must be demonstrated. That is, every person who handled or possessed the object since it was first recognized as being relevant must explain what he did with it. (*Example:* Each person who handled the white powder taken from D must testify about how he got it, how he handled it during his custody, and whom he turned it over to.)

   2. Demonstrative evidence: If the evidence is demonstrative, authentication is done merely by showing that the object *fairly represents* some aspect of the case.

   3. Federal Rules: The Federal Rules have a simple, basic principle of authentication that applies to all evidence (real, demonstrative, writings, and intangibles): the proponent must come up with evidence *"sufficient to support a finding* that the item is *what the proponent claims it is."* FRE 901(a). (901(b) gives illustrations of proper authentication.)

   4. Judge's role: The judge does not have to decide whether the proffered item *is* what its proponent claims it to be (the jury does this). But the judge does have to decide whether there is *some evidence* from which a jury could reasonably find that the item is what it is claimed to be.

C. Authentication of writings and recordings: Special rules exist for authenticating *writings* and other recorded communications: [477-483]

   1. Authorship: Usually, authentication of a writing consists of showing *who its author is*.

   2. No presumption of authenticity: A writing or other communication (just like any non-assertive evidence like a knife) carries *no presumption of authenticity*. Instead, the proponent bears the *burden* of making an affirmative showing that the writing or communication is what it appears to be and what the proponent claims it to be. [477-478]

   a. Signature: Thus, a *writing's own statement* concerning its authorship (e.g., its *signature*) is *not* enough — the proponent must make some independent showing that the signature was made by the person who the proponent claims made it.

   3. Direct testimony: One way to authenticate a writing or communication is by *direct testimony* that the document is what its proponent claims. (*Example:* If proponent wants to show that X really signed the document, he may produce W to testify that W saw X sign it.)

   4. Distinctive characteristics: A writing's *distinctive characteristics*, or the *circumstances* surrounding it, may suffice for authentication. See FRE 901(b)(4). (*Example:* The fact that a diary contains the logo of D Corp.; its entries match testimony previously given by X (D Corp.'s employee); it was produced by D Corp. during discovery; and it is similar to other diaries previously authenticated, all suffices to authenticate the diary as having been kept by X.) [478]

5. **Signature or handwriting:** A document's author can be established by showing that it was signed or written in the hand of a particular person. Even if no witness is available who saw the person do the signing or writing, the document may be authenticated by a witness who can identify the *signature or handwriting* as belonging to a particular person. [478]

    a. **Expert:** If W, the person identifying the signature or handwriting, is a handwriting *expert*, he may base his testimony based solely on handwriting specimens from X that he examined in preparation for his trial testimony. (But expert testimony on handwriting or signature-matching must meet the FRE 702 / *Daubert* requirements for *scientific evidence*, designed to ensure that such evidence is scientifically reliable. [479])

    b. **Non-expert:** But if W, the authenticating witness, is *not* a handwriting expert, his testimony may not be based on comparisons and studies made directly for the litigation; instead, he must testify that he saw X's handwriting at some time before the litigation began, and that he recognizes the signature or handwriting in question to be that of X.

    c. **Exemplars:** Exemplars (specimens prepared by the person claimed to have written the document in question) may be shown to the jury, which is then invited to make its own conclusion about whether the exemplar and the questioned document were by the same person.

6. **Reply letters and telegrams:** A *letter or telegram* can sometimes be authenticated by the circumstantial fact that it appears to be a *reply* to a prior communication, and the prior communication is proved. (*Example:* P proves that he wrote a letter to D on Jan. 1; a letter purporting to have been written by D to P on Jan. 15, that alludes to the contents of the earlier P-D letter, is authenticated by these circumstantial facts as indeed being a D-P letter.) [479-479]

7. **Phone conversation:** When the contents of a *telephone conversation* are sought to be proved, the proponent must authenticate the conversation by *establishing the parties to it*. [479-482]

    a. **Outgoing calls:** For *outgoing* calls (calls made *by* the sponsoring witness), the proponent can authenticate the call by showing that: (1) W made a call to the *number assigned by the phone company* to a particular person; and (2) the *circumstances* show that the person who talked on the other end was in fact the person the caller was trying to reach. FRE 901(b)(6). [479-481]

        i. **Circumstances:** The "circumstances" showing that the person on the other end was the one the caller was trying to reach, include: (1) *self-identification* by the callee ("This is George you're speaking to"); or (2) the *caller's identification* of the callee's voice through prior familiarity.

        ii. **Call to business:** If the outgoing call is to a *business*, FRE 901(b)(6)(B) says that authentication can be made by showing that the call was made to the listed number for the business and that the conversation "related to *business* [of a sort that would be] *reasonably transacted over the telephone*."

    b. **Incoming calls:** Where the call is an *incoming* one (i.e., the sponsoring witness is the recipient), *self-authentication by the caller is not enough*. There must be some additional evidence that the caller is who he said he was. (*Example:* W wants to testify that she received a call from X. It's not enough for W to testify, "I received a call from someone who said he was X." But if W adds, "I recognized the voice as belonging to X, from prior conversations with him," that *would* be enough to authenticate the call as having been from X.) [481-482]

8. **Attesting witnesses:** If a document is *attested to* or subscribed to by witnesses (e.g., a will), special rules sometimes apply:

   a. **Common law:** At common law, at least one attesting witness must be called to testify (even if he does not authenticate the document) before non-attesting witnesses may authenticate it.

   b. **Federal Rule:** But FRE 903 drops this requirement (except where the relevant state law imposes it).

9. **Ancient documents:**

   a. **Common law:** At common law, a writing is automatically deemed authenticated as an *"ancient document"* if it: (1) is at least *30 years old*; (2) is *unsuspicious* in appearance; and (3) has been found in a place of custody *natural* for such a document.

   b. **Federal Rules:** FRE 901(b)(8) applies the same requirements as the common law (above) for ancient documents, except that: (1) the document needs to be only *20* years old; and (2) the rule covers not only "documents" but "data compilations" (e.g., a computer tape, and probably photos, X-rays, movies, and sound tapes as well).

   c. **No guarantee of admissibility:** But keep in mind that a document that satisfies these requirements for the "ancient document" rule of authentication merely overcomes the authentication hurdle. The document still has to survive other obstacles (e.g., it must be not hearsay or fall within some exception; but there is also an ancient document exception to the hearsay rule; see *supra*, p. C-43).

D. **Self-authentication:** A few types of documents are *"self-authenticating,"* because they are so likely to be what they seem, that no testimony or other evidence of their genuineness need be produced. [483]

1. **State provisions:** Under most state statutes, the following are self-authenticating: (1) deeds and other instruments that are *notarized*; (2) *certified* copies of *public records* (e.g., a certified copy of a death certificate); and (3) books of statutes which appear to be printed by a government body (e.g., a statute book appearing to be from a sister state or foreign country).

2. **Federal Rules:** FRE 902 recognizes the above three classes, and also adds: (1) all *official publications* (not just statutes); (2) *newspapers* or periodicals; and (3) *labels, signs,* or other inscriptions indicating "origin, ownership, or control" (e.g., a can of peas bearing the label "Green Giant Co." is self-authenticating as having been produced by Green Giant Co.).

E. **Ways to avoid:** Authentication is not necessary if: [487]

1. **Admission:** The proponent has served on the opponent a written *request for admission*, and the opponent has granted this.

2. **Stipulation:** The parties have jointly *stipulated* to the *genuineness* of a particular document or object.

III. THE "BEST EVIDENCE RULE" FOR RECORDED COMMUNICATIONS

A. **Generally:** [490-491]

1. **Text of rule:** The common-law Best Evidence Rule (B.E.R.) provides that *"in proving the terms of a writing, where the terms are material, the original writing must be produced unless it is shown to be unavailable for some reason other than the serious fault of the proponent."*

2. **Components:** The B.E.R. has three main components:

   a. **Original document:** The *original document* must be produced, rather than using a copy or oral testimony about the document;

   b. **Prove terms:** The Rule applies only where what is to be proved is the *terms* of a *writing* (or, under the modern approach, an equivalent recorded communication such as an audio tape of a conversation); and

   c. **Excuse:** The Rule does not apply if the original is *unavailable* because it has been destroyed, is in the possession of a third party, or cannot be conveniently obtained, and the unavailability is not due to the serious fault of the proponent.

3. **Not applicable to evidence generally:** The B.E.R. does *not apply to evidence generally*, only to writings (or equivalent recorded communications).

4. **Federal Rule:** FRE 1002 gives the federal version of the B.E.R.: "An *original writing, recording,* or *photograph* is required in order to *prove its content*[.]" The federal approach changes the common-law rule in two major ways:

   a. **Broadened coverage:** Not just writings, but also *recordings* and *photographs* are covered by the Federal Rule in contrast to the common-law rule. (*Examples:* An audio tape of a conversation, or a computer tape of data, would be covered under the federal approach, so that if these items are available, they must be introduced instead of using oral testimony to describe their contents.)

   b. **Duplicate:** But unlike the common law, the federal rules allow a *duplicate* (e.g., a photocopy) in lieu of the original unless the opponent raises a genuine question about authenticity or it would be unfair in the circumstances to allow the duplicate. FRE 1003.

B. **What is a "writing" or other recorded communication:** [491-492]

1. **Short inscription:** An object that contains a short *inscription* (e.g., a pocket watch with words of affection engraved on it) might be held to be a "writing" covered by the B.E.R., depending on the surrounding circumstances (e.g., how important its precise, rather than approximate, content is to the litigation).

2. **Photographic evidence:** Under the modern and federal approach, a *photograph* or X-ray will be covered by the rule, if offered to prove the contents of the item. (*Example:* P, to prove that she has been injured, wants to prove that her X-rays show a spinal injury; the X-rays themselves must be used if available, rather than a radiologist's testimony about what the X-rays show.)

3. **Sound recordings:** Similarly, if a party tries to prove the contents of a *sound recording*, he must do so by presenting the actual recording rather than an oral or written account of what it provides.

C. **Proving the contents:** The B.E.R. only applies where what is sought to be proved are the "terms" or "contents" of the writing. [492-494]

C
A
P
S
U
L
E

S
U
M
M
A
R
Y

1. **Existence, execution, etc.:** Thus if all that is proved is that a writing *exists*, was *executed*, or was *delivered*, the B.E.R. does not apply. (*Example:* Prosecution of D for kidnapping; a prosecution witness, W, mentions that a ransom note was received but does not testify about the note's contents. Since this proof that the ransom note was delivered does not constitute proof of its terms, the note need not be produced in evidence. But if W goes on to give the details of what the note said, the note would have to be produced if available.)

2. **Incidental record:** The fact that there happens to be a writing memorializing a transaction does not mean that the transaction can only be proved by the introduction of a writing. Here, the writing is treated as an *incidental by-product* of the transaction. (*Example:* The earnings of a business can be proved by oral testimony, rather than by submitting the books and records, because those books and records are merely an incidental memorializing of the earnings.)

   a. **Transcript:** A person's prior *testimony* can generally be proved by an oral account of a witness who heard the testimony, even if a *transcript* exists. The transcript is merely an incidental by-product of the testimony. (But a *confession* by a defendant to the crime charged must generally be proved by the transcript or recording.)

   b. **Photo:** If a photograph, X-ray, audio recording, video tape, etc., has been made of an object or event, live testimony about the object or event will generally be *allowed* in lieu of introducing the photograph, etc. (*Example:* W may testify to seeing D shoot V, even though there happens to be a home movie showing the shooting. The movie is an incidental memorial of the event, so the event can be proved without the movie.)

   c. **Contract:** But if a document truly *embodies* a transaction, the document comes within the B.E.R. and must be produced if available. (*Example:* If two parties to an agreement have signed a formal written *contract*, that contract must be produced at the litigation, even though the parties could have bound themselves orally to the same terms; the contract embodies their arrangement, rather than merely being an incidental by-product of it.)

D. Collateral writings: The *"collateral writings"* exception means that a document which has only a *tangential connection* to the litigation need not be produced, even though its contents are being proved. See FRE 1004(4) (original need not be produced if the writing, recording, etc., is "not closely related to a controlling issue"). [495]

E. Which is original: If one writing is derived from another, the earlier one is not necessarily the "writing itself" that must be produced. The proposition being proved may be such that the derivative writing is the one whose contents are being proved, in which case it is the original of that derivative writing that must be produced. (*Example:* D writes a handwritten letter to X possibly defaming P; D then hands the letter to his secretary, who retypes it and sends the typed version. At P's libel suit against D, it is the derivative typed version, not the handwritten version, which is the "original" that must be produced if available.) [495]

F. Reproductions: [495-496]

1. **Common law:** At common law, no subsequently-created copy was the equivalent of the original. Therefore, if the B.E.R. applied, no copy (e.g., a handwritten version) could suffice.

2. **Modern statutes:** But today, most states have a statute by which regularly-kept *photocopies* of business and public records are admissible even if the original is available. Such statutes override the B.E.R.

3. **Federal:** The Federal Rules have a broad copying provision: copies produced by *any reliable modern method* (including photocopying) are "duplicates" that are *presumptively admissible*. Such a duplicate is admissible even if the original is available, unless "a genuine question is raised about the original's authenticity or the circumstances make it unfair to admit the duplicate." FRE 1003; 1001(e). (*Examples:* Photocopies, mimeograph copies, carbon copies, images scanned into a computer and then printed out, copies of an original video or audio tape made by re-recording, etc., would all qualify as "duplicates" under the federal approach. But any copies produced *manually*, whether by typing or handwriting, are *not* "duplicates" and therefore may not be used if the original is available.)

G. **Excuses for non-production:** There are several types of *"excuses"* for non-production, which will allow the proponent to use derivative evidence (e.g., a manual copy or oral testimony) instead of the original: [496-497]

1. **Loss or destruction:** If the proponent can show that the original has been *destroyed* or *lost* he may use a copy (unless the loss or destruction is due to the proponent's *bad faith* or serious fault).

2. **Inconvenience:** In some courts, *extreme inconvenience* of producing the original will suffice.

3. **Possession by third person:** If the original is in the *possession of a third person*, and cannot be obtained by judicial efforts (e.g., a subpoena duces tecum), this will excuse non-production.

4. **Original in opponent's possession:** If the original is in the hands of the *opponent*, or under the latter's control, and the proponent has *notified him* to produce it at the trial but the adversary has failed to do so, the proponent may use a copy instead. See FRE 1004(3).

H. **Summaries:** If original writings are so *voluminous* that they cannot conveniently be introduced into evidence and examined in court, most courts permit a *summary* to be introduced instead. FRE 1006. [498]

1. **Sponsoring witness needed:** The summary must be *sponsored* by a *witness* (often an expert) who testifies that he has prepared or reviewed the underlying writings and the summary, and that the *summary accurately reflects the underlying documents.* [498]

2. **Documents become evidence:** When Rule 1006 is used, the *underlying documents become evidence*, even though they are not individually presented in court.

3. **Absence of entries:** Testimony that one or more items *have not been found* in voluminous records, despite a diligent search by a person with access to the records, does *not* qualify under FRE 1006's summary-of-voluminous-records exception. So such testimony will have to come in under the exception in 803(7) for absence of regularly-kept records (*supra*, p. C-39) or not at all.

I. **Admission by adversary:** An adversary's *admission* about the terms of a writing is sometimes usable in lieu of the writing itself, to prove the terms of the writing. [499]

1. **Written:** A *written* admission or an admission under *sworn testimony* is always usable to prove the terms of the writing. (*Example:* D writes to P, "Remember that I wrote you in December offering to buy your farm." This later letter is evidence that D made this statement in his December letter. Similarly, D's oral deposition testimony — "I wrote to P in December

asking to buy his farm" — would suffice to prove that the December letter contained such an offer.)

2. **Oral:**   But courts are more reluctant to allow an ***unsworn oral*** admission by a party to be used by the other party to prove the terms of a writing. Thus FRE 1007 does ***not*** allow such proof of an unsworn oral admission.

J. **Preferences among secondary evidence:**   If the original does not exist, courts are split as to whether the ***next best available*** evidence must be used. [499]

1. **Majority rule:**   Most American state courts ***do*** recognize "degrees of substantive evidence," and hold that where there is a choice between a written copy and oral testimony, the ***written copy must be used.***

2. **Minority/Federal Rule:**   A minority of states (but also the ***Federal Rules***) hold that "there are no degrees of substantive evidence." Thus under FRE 1004, even if handwritten notes or a typed copy of a writing exist, a party may instead prove the terms of the writing by oral testimony.

K. **Judge-jury allocation:**   The judge, not the jury, decides most questions relating to application of the B.E.R. Thus under FRE 1008, it is the judge who decides such questions as: (1) whether a particular item of evidence is an "original"; (2) whether the original has been lost or destroyed; and (3) whether the evidence relates to a "collateral matter." [500-501]

IV. SPECIAL TYPES OF REAL AND DEMONSTRATIVE EVIDENCE

A. **Pictorial evidence:**   [500-502]

1. **Authentication:**   There are now usually two ways to authenticate ***pictorial*** evidence (e.g., photographs, X-rays, movies, and video tapes):

    a. **Illustration of what W saw:**   First, the proponent puts on a sponsoring witness, W, who says that the picture illustrates what W saw. (*Example:* W testifies, "I observed the scene of the crime just as the police photographer was arriving, and this photograph accurately depicts the scene as it was at that moment.")

    b. **"Silent witness" method:**   Alternatively, most courts allow a photograph to be verified not by the testimony of any witness who actually witnessed the scene or event portrayed, but rather from testimony about the ***reliability of the process*** by which the photo was produced. This is often used for X-rays and automatic picture-taking devices. (*Example:* W, an engineer for a company that makes bank surveillance photographic equipment, testifies, "Our machine reliably creates a photo with an image of a person doing a transaction at the teller's window on one side, and the document presented by that person to the teller on the other side. Therefore, this piece of film accurately shows that the person pictured presented the check pictured.")

B. **Computer print-outs:**   [502]

1. **Authentication:**   If a computer print-out is offered as evidence of the facts contained in the print-out (e.g., financial or numerical facts), the print-out must be authenticated. This is usually done by a witness who testifies that the methods used to put data into the computer, to program it, and to produce a print-out of the data, were all reliable.

2. **Best Evidence Rule:** Generally, a computer print-out can be used to prove the facts represented in the print-out without B.E.R. problems (the opponent can claim that the print-out is merely a "duplicate" of the original pre-computer paper documents, but he would then have the burden of showing that the print-out is not an accurate reproduction of the original paper record).

C. **Maps, models, diagrams, etc.:** [502]

     1. **Evidentiary status:** Courts will treat maps, models, diagrams, etc., as being ***incorporated into the witness's testimony***, so that they become evidence for purposes of trial and appeal.

D. **Views:** The judge may permit the jury to journey outside the courtroom to visit and observe a particular place, if this would help them understand an event. The excursion is called a ***"view."*** [503-504]

     1. **Discretion:** The judge has ***broad discretion*** about whether to allow the jury to take a view.

     2. **Presence of judge:** In civil cases, the judge need normally ***not be present.*** In criminal cases, most states have statutes requiring the judge to be present at the view.

     3. **Defendant's right to be present:** A criminal defendant usually has a statutory right to be ***present*** at the view (and may have a constitutional Confrontation Clause right to be present).

     4. **Evidentiary status:** Courts are split as to whether the view is ***evidence***, or merely an aid to the understanding of the evidence.

E. **Experiments:** An ***experiment*** conducted by a party may sometimes be admitted. If the experiment takes place out of court, its admissibility will depend mostly on whether the conditions are sufficiently ***similar*** between the experiment and the event that it is attempting to explain. (*Example:* Where P complains that his crash was caused by a defective transmission in a car produced by D, an experiment to see if the transmission breaks in a different car will be allowed only if both the test car and the conditions are shown to be highly similar to the original conditions.) [497-498]

CHAPTER 10

OPINIONS, EXPERTS, AND SCIENTIFIC EVIDENCE

I. FIRST-HAND KNOWLEDGE AND LAY OPINIONS

A. **First-hand knowledge required:** An ordinary (non-expert) witness must limit his testimony to facts of which he has first-hand knowledge. [516-517]

     1. **Distinguished from hearsay:** You must distinguish the "first-hand knowledge" requirement from the hearsay rule. If W's statement on its face makes it clear that W is merely repeating what someone else said, the objection is to hearsay; if W purports to be stating matters which he personally observed, but he is actually repeating statements by others, the objection is to lack of first-hand knowledge.

     2. **Experts:** The rule requiring first-hand knowledge does not apply to experts. (See below.)

B. **Lay opinions:** [516-518]

1. **Traditional view:** The traditional view is that a non-expert witness must state only facts, not "opinions." (*Example:* If W observes D's driving behavior leading to a crash, W may not testify that D "drove very carelessly," but must instead give more specific testimony, e.g., D's estimated rate of speed, degree of attention, etc.)

   a. **Exception for short-hand renditions:** Even under the traditional view, W may give an "opinion" that is really a *"short-hand rendition."* That is, if W has perceived a number of small facts that cannot each be easily stated, he may summarize the collective facts with a "shorthand" formulation. (*Example:* W may testify that D was "mentally disturbed," even though this has a conclusory aspect.)

2. **Modern/federal approach:** But the modern/federal view is that lay opinions will be *allowed* if they have *value* to the fact-finder. See FRE 701, allowing non-expert opinions or inferences that are "(a) rationally based on the witness's perception; (b) helpful to clearly understanding the witness's testimony or to determining a fact in issue; and (c) not based on scientific, technical, or other specialized knowledge within the scope of Rule 702 [dealing with expert testimony]."

C. **Opinion on "ultimate issue":** Of those courts that allow lay opinions, a few bar opinions on "*ultimate* issues." But most today allow even opinions on ultimate issues. Thus FRE 704(a) allows opinions on ultimate issues except where the mental state of a criminal defendant is concerned. [519]

   1. **Exceptions:** But even the liberal federal approach excludes a few types of opinions on ultimate issues. For instance, a witness will not be permitted to express his opinion on a *question of law* (except foreign law), or an opinion on how the case should be decided.

II. EXPERT WITNESSES

A. **Requirements for allowing:** FRE 702 imposes *five requirements* that expert testimony must meet in order to be admissible [521-524] :

[1] It must be the case that "scientific, technical, or other *specialized knowledge*" will "*help the trier of fact to understand* the evidence or to determine a fact in issue";

[2] The witness must be *"qualified"* as an expert by "knowledge, skill, experience, training, or education";

[3] The testimony must be based on *"sufficient facts or data"*;

[4] The testimony must be the product of *"reliable principles and methods"*; and

[5] The witness must have *"reliably applied"* these principles and methods "to the *facts of the case*."

Let's quickly review each of these five requirements.

1. **Specialized knowledge will be helpful:** It must be the case that "scientific, technical, or other *specialized knowledge*" will "*help the trier of fact to understand* the evidence or to determine a fact in issue"

   a. **Ordinary evidence:** Therefore expert testimony will be most appropriate whether it involves the interpretation of facts of a sort that *lay persons are not usually called upon to evaluate.* So testimony about whether two bullets were fired from the same gun, or two

DNA samples are from the same person, would be suitable for expert testimony, since lay persons usually don't have to make such determinations in ordinary life. By contrast, since juries and ordinary people are often called upon to evaluate the reliability of an eye-witness identification, expert testimony purporting to tell the jury why such I.D.s are often unreliable will often be rejected as not satisfying this requirement of "helpfulness."

2. **Qualifications:** Next, the expert must be *"qualified."* That is, he must have knowledge or skill in a particular area that distinguishes him from an ordinary person.

   a. **Source of expertise:** This expertise may come from either *education* or *experience*.

   b. **Need for sub-specialist:** Generally, a specialist in a particular field will be treated as an expert even though he is not specialist in the particular *sub-field* or branch of that field. (*Example:* If a medical condition involves kidney failure, a general practitioner would probably be found a qualified expert, even though he is not a sub-specialist in nephrology.)

3. **Based on "sufficient facts or data":** The third requirement is that the testimony be *"based on sufficient facts or data."* This requirement, plus the two that follow, reflect an attempt by the Rule drafters to *keep out unreliable testimony*, sometimes called "junk science." We explore this factor more in "Basis for expert's opinion," *infra*.

4. **Product of "reliable principles and methods":** The fourth requirement in FRE 702 is that the testimony must be the *"product of reliable principles and methods."* In the case of "scientific" testimony, this requirement is essentially a requirement that the testimony be based on "good science."

   Example: Testimony based on astrology would probably be rejected, because the court would probably not be satisfied that it was based on "reliable principles and methods."

   a. **Applies to non-scientific testimony:** This requirement of reliable principles and methods applies not just to scientific testimony but to *other types of expert testimony based on technical knowledge.*

5. **Reliable application to the facts of case:** Finally, FRE 702 requires that the principles and methods referred to above be *"reliably applied ... to the facts of the case."* This is just common sense: the most reliable of "principles" and "methods" won't lead to useful testimony unless the witness shows that she is applying those principles and methods to the actual facts of the case.

   Example: Suppose that W, a prosecution DNA expert, offers to testify that under the principles of DNA comparison, a sample of blood purportedly found on the body of a murder victim, V, matched the blood of the defendant, D. If W (and other witnesses put on by the prosecution) cannot demonstrate that the sample tested by W in fact was found on V's body, W's testimony will be meaningless, and will be excluded.

B. **Basis for expert's opinion:** The expert's opinion may be based upon any of several sources of information, including: (1) the expert's *first-hand knowledge*; (2) the expert's observation of prior witnesses and other evidence at the trial itself; and (3) a hypothetical question asked by counsel to the expert. [524-527]

1. **Inadmissible evidence:** Today, the expert's opinion may be based on evidence that would otherwise be *inadmissible*. Under FRE 703, even inadmissible evidence may form the basis for the expert's opinion if "experts in the particular field would *reasonably rely on those*

kinds of facts or data in forming an opinion on the subject[.]" (*Example:* Driver tells an accident investigator that the accident occurred when his brakes failed. The investigator writes a report, which is read by Expert, an accident analysis specialist. Even though Driver's statements are probably otherwise-inadmissible hearsay, if experts in the field of accident analysis would rely on such hearsay statements, Expert's opinion may be based upon this statement.)

2. **Disclosure of basis to jury:** Some courts require the expert to ***state the facts or assumptions*** that he has based his opinion on, as part of his direct testimony. But most courts, and the Federal Rules, do not require this.

    a. **Inadmissible underlying facts:** Indeed, where the underlying facts or data are otherwise ***inadmissible*** (e.g., a report by another expert that is itself based on inadmissible hearsay), FRE 703 says that the expert (and the proponent of the expert's testimony) ***shall not disclose*** those facts or data unless the court affirmatively finds that their probative value outweighs their prejudicial effect.

    b. **Cross-examination:** However, the ***cross-examiner*** may require the expert to state the underlying facts or data on which he or she has relied. See FRE 705.

C. **The hypothetical question; basis for:** If the expert's underlying facts and assumptions come from a ***hypothetical question***, courts today are liberal about the source of these underlying facts and assumptions. Thus: (1) the underlying assumptions need not be supported by evidence in the record at the time of the question, or even by admissible evidence at all; (2) the assumptions may be based upon opinions by others, if an expert in that situation would rely on such an opinion. But there must be ***some basis*** for the assumptions in the hypothetical — if the assumptions are so far-fetched that no jury could possibly find them to be true, the hypothetical question will be stricken. [527-529]

D. **Some procedural aspects:** [529-531]

1. **Cross-examination by use of learned treatise:** All courts allow an expert to be cross-examined by use of a learned treatise that contains a differing view. (*Example:* "Isn't it true, Doctor, that according to Smith's Handbook of Pathology, lung cancer is sometimes caused by asbestos exposure or other factors, not always smoking as you have asserted?") Most courts today allow the use of the treatise as impeaching evidence even if the expert did not rely upon it in forming his opinion, so long as the expert concedes that the treatise is authoritative; the Federal Rules even allow the treatise to be used substantively, not just for impeachment.

2. **Court-appointed expert:** The Federal Rules allow the appointment of an expert ***by the court***, in which case each party may cross-examine the expert.

III. SPECIALIZED EVIDENCE — THE *DAUBERT* / FRE 702 STANDARD

A. **The requirement of reliability:** As we've just seen, in federal courts, when expert testimony based on "scientific, technical or other specialized knowledge" is to be introduced, the proponent must show that the test or principle is the ***"product of reliable principles and methods"*** that are "reliably applied ... to the facts of the case." (FRE 702). This language is essentially a codification of a major Supreme Court case, *Daubert v. Merrell Dow.* [531-537]

1. **Factors:** Under *Daubert* and FRE 702, the federal court should normally consider the following factors, among others, in deciding whether the test or principle is "the product of reliable

principles and methods." (A "yes" answer makes the test/principle more likely to be scientifically valid.)[1]

❑ whether it can be *reliably tested*;

❑ whether it's been *subjected to peer review* and/or *publication*;

❑ whether it's got a reasonably low *error rate*;

❑ whether there are *professional standards* controlling its operations;

❑ whether it's *"generally accepted"* in the field. (This used to be an absolute requirement for science in the federal courts, but *Daubert* makes it merely one factor.)

❑ whether it was developed for *purposes other than merely to produce evidence* for the present litigation.

2. **Non-scientific expert testimony:** *Daubert* itself (where the above factors were listed) dealt only with "scientific" testimony. But a post-*Daubert* Supreme Court case, *Kumho Tire*, says that the same principles apply to non-scientific testimony that relates to "technical" or other "specialized" knowledge. So *all expert testimony* must now satisfy these "reliability" factors. [537].

3. **State response:** State courts (even ones adopting the FRE) don't have to follow *Daubert* if they don't want to. Some already have. Others have rejected *Daubert* and continue to apply the older "generally accepted" standard. [535]

IV. PARTICULAR TYPES OF SCIENTIFIC EVIDENCE AND EXPERTISE

A. **Probabilities:** Courts increasingly accept *probability* evidence where it supplies a scientifically reliable way of estimating the probability that a disputed event occurred. (*Example:* In a paternity case, most courts will now accept the results of analysis of genetic markers, whereby an expert testifies that not only are D's genetic markers consistent with those of the child, but only, say, one adult American male out of 3,000 would have markers consistent with those of the child. Similarly, some courts would allow evidence in a rape case that only one in 10,000 males would have semen containing genetic markers consistent with the markers found in the semen in the victim, and that D's semen has such markers.) [539-543]

B. **Speed detection:** The results of *radar* and VASCAR are commonly admissible to prove the speed at which D's vehicle was traveling. But most courts require the prosecution to prove that the particular speed detection equipment in question was properly calibrated and properly used. [543]

C. **Voice prints:** Courts are almost evenly split as to the admissibility of *"voice print"* analysis, whereby the voice of an unidentified suspect on a taped telephone call is compared with a sample given by D after his arrest. [544]

---

1. These factors are not mentioned in FRE 702. But it's clear that the drafters of 702 intended that the factors mentioned in *Daubert* (and in later cases interpreting *Daubert*) be considered by courts in determining whether particular testimony meets the "reliable principles and methods" standard of 702.

D. Neutron activation analysis: Neutron activation analysis (NAA) is generally admitted as a method of identifying a small sample of material (e.g., whether a hair found near a crime scene belongs to D). [544]

E. Psychiatry and psychology: [544-546]

   1. Mental condition of criminal defendant: Courts generally allow a psychiatrist or psychologist to testify as an expert on the *mental condition* of a criminal defendant. However, courts try hard to keep the expert from crossing over into areas that are properly the province of law rather than medicine (e.g., whether the defendant knew right from wrong).

   a. FRE provision: Thus, FRE 704(b) provides that "[i]n a criminal case, an expert witness *must not state an opinion* about whether the defendant *did or did not have a mental state or condition* that constitutes an *element of the crime charged or of a defense*. Those matters are for the trier of fact alone." (*Example:* In a federal case in which D claims insanity, the defense psychiatrist would be permitted to say that D is a schizophrenic, but will probably not be permitted to say that this condition prevented D from appreciating the wrongfulness of his conduct, now the substantive federal insanity standard.)

   2. Reliability of evidence: Courts hesitate to allow expert psychiatric or psychological testimony concerning the reliability of other witnesses' testimony. Thus evidence that a particular eyewitness identification is likely to be unreliable for psychological reasons, or that a particular alleged victim is probably telling the truth because she shows the signs of Rape Trauma Syndrome, will be rejected by many courts.

CHAPTER 11

BURDENS OF PROOF, PRESUMPTIONS, AND OTHER PROCEDURAL ISSUES

I. BURDENS OF PROOF

A. Two burdens: There are two distinct burdens of proof, the burden of *production* and the burden of *persuasion.* [556-560]

   1. Burden of production: If P bears the burden of *production* with respect to issue A, P has the obligation to come forward with some evidence that A exists. This burden is sometimes also called the burden of "going forward."

   a. Consequence of failure to carry: If a party does not satisfy this burden of production, the court will decide the issue against him as a matter of law, and will not permit the jury to decide it.

   2. Burden of persuasion: If P has the burden of *persuasion* on issue A, this means that if at the close of the evidence the jury cannot decide whether A has been established with the relevant level of certainty (usually "preponderance of the evidence" in a civil case), the jury must find against P on issue A. This burden is also often called the *"risk of non-persuasion"* — if neither P nor D have persuaded the jury about whether A exists, to say that P bears the burden of persuasion or the risk of non-persuasion means that he is the one who will lose when the jury decides this issue.

3. **One shifts, other does not:** The burden of production as to issue A can, and often does, shift throughout the trial. (*Example:* Suppose P has the burden of showing that D received notice of a fact. If P comes up with evidence that D received notice — e.g., P's own testimony that he told the fact to D — the burden will shift to D to come up with evidence that he did not receive notice.) The burden of persuasion, by contrast, always remains on the party on whom it first rests.

B. Allocating the burdens in civil cases: [560-561]

1. **Factors:** In most issues in civil cases, both the burden of production and the burden of persuasion are on the *plaintiff.* (*Example:* In a negligence case, the plaintiff bears the burdens of production and persuasion with respect to showing D's negligence, P's harm, and the causal link between the two. But D bears both burdens with respect to contributory negligence, in most jurisdictions.) Courts consider a number of factors in determining where to place the burdens, including: (1) which party is trying to change the *status quo* (he is more likely to bear the burdens); (2) who is contending that the more unusual event has occurred (he is more likely to bear the burdens); and (3) which way do policy considerations cut (the court may allocate the burdens in a way that promotes some extra-judicial social policy).

2. **"Prima facie" case:** The collection of issues on which a civil plaintiff has the burden of *production* is sometimes called his *"prima facie case."* (*Example:* P has established a *prima facie* case for negligence if he has produced enough evidence of D's negligence, P's own harm, and a causal link between the two, to permit the case to go to the jury.)

C. Allocation in criminal cases: In criminal cases, the Due Process Clause of the U.S. Constitution places limits on the extent to which the burdens of proof may be placed on the defendant: [561-564]

1. **Element distinguished from affirmative defense:** The state is more limited in allocating the burdens as to an *"element"* of the offense than it is on allocating the burdens as to an *"affirmative defense."* An element of the crime is an aspect that is part of the basic definition of the crime; an affirmative defense is an aspect that is not part of the basic definition, but which the defendant is allowed to show as a mitigating or exculpating factor. (*Examples:* "Intent to kill" is an element of the crime of murder, but "self defense" is generally an affirmative defense.)

2. **General rules of allocation:**

    a. **Elements:** The *state* is constitutionally required to bear *both* the burdens of production and persuasion with respect to *all elements* of the crime.

    b. **Affirmative defense:** The *defendant* may constitutionally be required to bear both burdens with respect to affirmative defenses.

    c. **Overlap:** If the state defines an affirmative defense in a way that causes that defense to overlap almost completely with some element of the crime, the state must bear both burdens. (*Example:* Suppose the state makes "malice aforethought" an element of murder, and defines malice aforethought to include "any deliberate act committed by one person against another." If the state makes "heat of passion" an affirmative defense, the state, not D might have to bear the burden of proof and persuasion, because a court might hold that proof that D acted in the heat of passion is tantamount to proof that he did not act with malice aforethought.)

d. Allowable affirmative defenses: At least the following may be established as affirmative defenses on which D bears both burdens: ***insanity, self-defense,*** and ***extreme emotional disturbance.***

D. Satisfying the burden of production: [564-566]

   1. Civil case: In civil cases, on most issues (those as to which the persuasion burden follows the "preponderance of the evidence" standard), the party bearing the production burden must come forward with enough evidence *so that a reasonable jury could conclude, by a preponderance of the evidence, that the fact exists*.

      a. Judge decides: It is the judge, not the jury, who decides whether the party bearing the production burden has satisfied that burden. (*Example:* At the close of P's case, the judge decides whether P has come up with enough evidence of negligence that a reasonable jury could find that D was negligent by a preponderance of the evidence. The judge may find that P has done this even though the judge himself believes that it is less likely than not that D was negligent.)

      b. Cross-examination of adversary: If the burden of proof on issue A in a civil case is borne by P (as is usually the case), P will have to come up with a witness or real evidence tending to prove that A exists. It will not be enough that P conducts a withering cross-examination of a defense witness's denial of A. (But if it is D who bears the burden of proving A, his cross-examination of P and P's witnesses may be enough for him to avoid a directed verdict against him.)

   2. Criminal case: In a criminal case, the prosecution, to satisfy its burden of production on all elements of the case, must come forward with enough evidence on each element that a reasonable jury could find that the element was *proved beyond a reasonable doubt*. (In other words, the persuasion burden affects the production burden.)

E. Satisfying the burden of persuasion: [566-567]

   1. Civil cases: On most civil issues, the burden of persuasion must be satisfied by a showing that A exists *"by a preponderance of the evidence."* That is, the party bearing the burden must show that the existence of A is "more probable than not."

      a. Sheer statistics: Most courts refuse to find that this burden has been met by evidence that is ***purely statistical***. (*Example:* If P testifies that he was hit by a blue bus, and shows that 60% of all the blue buses in the town are owned by D, this will not be enough to meet P's persuasion burden.) Instead, the party bearing the persuasion burden must come up with some evidence that will lead the jury to have an *"actual belief"* (rather than a mere statistical estimate) in the truth of the fact in question.

   2. Criminal cases: In criminal cases, the prosecution's burden of persuasion on all elements of the crime means that these elements must be proved *"beyond a reasonable doubt."* This is required by the Due Process Clause. *In Re Winship.* (But issues other than elements of the crime may be decided according to a lesser standard. For instance, a confession usually only has to be shown to be voluntary by a preponderance of the evidence.)

II. PRESUMPTIONS

A. Generally: The term "presumption" refers to a relationship between a "basic" fact (B) and a "presumed" fact (P). When we say that fact P can be presumed from fact B, we mean that once B is established, P is established or at least rendered more likely. [567-570]

B. Effect of presumptions in civil cases: In civil cases, most courts hold that a presumption has one of two types of effects: (1) a *"bursting bubble"* effect; or (2) a so-called *"Morgan"* effect. [570-573]

1. **"Bursting bubble":** Most courts believe that a presumption should be given the following effect: if B is shown to exist, the burden of production (but not the burden of persuasion) should be shifted to the opponent of the presumption. This is called the *"bursting bubble"* approach, because once the opponent discharges his production burden by coming up with some evidence that the presumed fact does not exist, the presumption *disappears from the case*, and the jury decides the issue as if the presumption had never existed.

   Example: A presumption is established that where a letter has been properly addressed and mailed — the basic fact — the letter will be presumed to have been received by the addressee — the presumed fact. Suppose that P is the beneficiary of this presumption, and that P starts out bearing the burden of proving that D received the letter. If P shows that the letter was properly addressed and mailed, under the bursting bubble view D will have to come up with some evidence that he never received the letter, but once he does so, the presumption will not be mentioned to the jury, which will be told that P has the burden of persuading the jury that D received the letter.

2. **Morgan (minority) view:** A *minority* of courts follow the so-called *"Morgan"* view, that the presumption should not only shift the burden of production, but *also the burden of persuasion*, to the presumption's opponent. (*Example:* On the above letter scenario, once P showed that he properly addressed and mailed the letter, it would become up to D to not only come forward with evidence that he never received the letter, but also to persuade the jury by a preponderance of the evidence that he never received it.)

3. **Federal Rules:** The Federal Rules adopt the *majority, "bursting bubble"* view. Under FRE 301, "In a civil case ... the party against whom a presumption is directed has the burden of producing evidence to rebut the presumption. But this rule *does not shift the burden of persuasion,* which *remains on the party who had it originally.*"

   a. **Instructions to jury:** Under the majority/federal "bursting bubble" approach, the judge normally will *not mention* that the presumption exists (e.g., he will not say, "The law presumes that a properly addressed and mailed envelope was received by the addressee unless there is evidence to the contrary"). But the judge has discretion to tell the jury that it *may* presume P if B is shown.

4. **Conflicting presumptions:** If a case presents two *conflicting presumptions*, and neither is rebutted by the opponent, the court will generally apply the presumption that reflects the weightier social policy. If neither presumption reflects a social policy (both merely reflect an estimate of probabilities, or concerns for trial convenience), both presumptions will generally be held to have *dropped* from the case.

5. **Constitutional questions:** A civil presumption that is given either the "bursting bubble" or "Morgan" effect presents no significant constitutional issues. But a so-called *"irrebuttable presumption"* (which is really a substantive rule) must meet the same constitutional standard

as any other substantive rule of law — the legislature must have had a *rational reason* for linking the basic fact to the presumed fact.

C. **Effect in criminal cases:**   The constitutionality of a presumption in a *criminal case* depends on precisely the effect given to the presumption: [573]

1. **Permissive presumptions:**   A so-called *"permissive"* presumption (one in which the judge merely instructs the jury that it "may" infer the presumed fact if it finds the basic fact) will almost always be constitutional, so long as the fact finder could "rationally" have inferred the presumed fact from the basic fact, the presumption will be upheld. (*Example:* The jury is told that where a weapon is found in a car, the jury may infer that each person in the car possessed that weapon. Since the presumption was rational on these circumstances, it was constitutional even though it relieved the prosecution from showing that each D actually knew of or possessed a gun.)

2. **Mandatory:**   But a *"mandatory"* presumption is subjected to much more stringent constitutional scrutiny:

   a. **Shift of persuasion burden:**   If the presumption *shifts the burden of persuasion* to D, and the presumed fact is an *element of the crime*, the presumption will normally be *unconstitutional.* Such a presumption runs afoul of the rule that the prosecution must prove each element of the crime beyond a reasonable doubt. (*Example:* D, a dealer in second-hand goods, is charged with knowingly receiving stolen goods. The judge tells the jury that a dealer who buys goods that are in fact stolen, and who does not make reasonable inquiries about the seller's title to the goods, shall be presumed to have known they were stolen unless he shows that he didn't know this. Since this presumption has the effect of shifting to D the burden of showing that he did not know the goods were stolen — an element of the crime — it is unconstitutional.)

   b. **Possibly constitutional:**   But even a presumption that shifts the burden of persuasion on an element of the crime will be constitutional if the presumed fact flows from the basic fact beyond a reasonable doubt, and the basic fact is shown beyond a reasonable doubt. However, few if any presumptions can satisfy this stringent pair of requirements.

D. **Choice of law:**   In federal diversity cases, the court must apply the presumptions law of the state whose substantive law applies. (FRE 302). (*Example:* P sues D for negligence in a diversity suit in New Jersey federal court. If New Jersey law controls on the issue of negligence, then New Jersey law on the effect to be given to a presumption that one whose blood alcohol is more than .1% is legally drunk, must be applied by the federal court. Therefore, if New Jersey would apply a "Morgan" rather than "bursting bubble" approach to presumptions, the federal court must do the same.) [575]

III. JUDGE-JURY ALLOCATION

A. **Issues of law:**   Issues of *law* are always to be decided by the judge, not the jury. Therefore, when the admission of a particular piece of evidence turns on an issue of law, it is up to the judge to decide whether the item should be admitted. (*Example:* W refuses to disclose a statement she made to L, asserting the attorney-client privilege; L is a law school graduate but is not admitted to practice. It is the judge, not the jury, who will decide the legal issue of whether the privilege applies on these facts.) [577]

B. **Issues of fact:** If admissibility of evidence turns on an issue of *fact,* the division of labor

C
A
P
S
U
L
E

S
U
M
M
A
R
Y

between judge and jury depends on the nature of the objection: [577-580]

1. **Technical exclusionary rule:** If an objection to admissibility is based on a ***technical exclusionary rule*** (e.g., hearsay), any factual question needed to decide that objection belongs solely to the judge. Thus for factual issues in connection with a hearsay objection, an objection based on privilege, or most issues regarding the Best Evidence Rule, the judge decides.

   a. **Rules of evidence not binding:** Under FRE 104(a), when the judge makes such a finding he is ***not bound by the rules of evidence*** except those regarding privileges. (*Example:* In deciding whether V's out-of-court statement, "X shot me," qualifies as a "dying declaration" exception to the hearsay rule, the judge may consider other, inadmissible, hearsay declarations by V at about the same time that shed light on whether V knew he was dying.) The judge will normally decide such a factual issue by a ***preponderance of the evidence*** standard.

2. **Relevance:** If the objection is that the evidence is ***irrelevant***, the judge's role may be more limited:

   a. **Ordinary relevance problem:** Ordinarily, a relevance objection may be decided without any finding of fact — the judge merely has to decide whether, ***assuming*** the proffered fact is true, it makes some material fact more or less likely; this is purely a legal conclusion, so the judge handles it himself.

   b. **Conditional relevance:** In some cases, the proffered evidence is logically relevant only if some other fact exists. If fact B is relevant only if fact A exists, B is ***"conditionally relevant."*** It is the jury that will decide whether fact A exists, but the judge decides ***whether a reasonable jury could find that fact A (the preliminary fact) exists***.

   Example: P is injured when his tire blows out; D claims that he warned P of the problem. The preliminary fact is whether P heard the warning; the conditionally relevant fact is the warning's contents. The judge will decide whether a reasonable jury could find that P heard the warning; if he decides that the answer to this question is "yes," he will let the jury hear the warning's alleged contents, and it will be up to the jury to decide whether P really heard that warning and its contents.

      i. **Allowed subject to "connecting up":** The judge may allow the conditionally relevant fact into evidence ***prior*** to the showing of the preliminary fact; the conditionally relevant evidence is said to be admitted ***"subject to connecting up."***

      Example: In the tire blow-out example, D might be allowed to say what the warning's contents were, subject to subsequent proof by some other witness that P really heard the warning. If D does not come up with that later evidence, his testimony about the contents of the warning will be stricken.

C. **Limiting instructions:** If evidence is admitted that should properly be considered only on some issues, the judge will on request give a ***limiting instruction***, which tells the jury for what issues the evidence can and cannot be considered. [580]

D. **Non-jury trials:** [581]

1. **Same rules:** In general, ***all rules of evidence applicable to jury trials also apply to bench trials***. Thus if an item of evidence would be inadmissible in a jury trial, it is inadmissible in a bench trial.

2. **Practical relaxation:** On the other hand, appellate courts are generally less strict in review-

ing evidentiary rulings made in a bench trial than in a jury trial.

    a. "Sufficient competent evidence" rule: Thus even if the trial judge in a bench trial admits inadmissible evidence over objection, the appellate court will not reverse if there was also admissible evidence in the case *supporting* the findings. The trial judge is presumed to have disregarded the inadmissible and relied on the admissible evidence. (But if the trial judge in the bench trial erroneously *excludes* evidence, the appellate court will be strict, and will reverse if that exclusion is likely to have damaged the losing party. Therefore, judges in bench trials err on the side of admitting too much rather than too little.)

IV. APPEALS AND "HARMLESS ERROR"

A. "Harmless error": Appellate courts will only reverse if the error may have made a *difference to the outcome*. An error that is unlikely to have made a difference to the outcome is called *"harmless,"* and will not be grounds for reversal. See FRE 103(a) (error must affect a "substantial right" of a party). [582]

    1. Standards for determining: The test for determining whether an error is "harmless" varies depending on the context:

        a. Constitutional criminal issue: In a criminal case in which evidence is admitted in violation of the defendant's *constitutional* rights, the appellate court will find the error non-harmless unless it is convinced "beyond a reasonable doubt" that the error was harmless. (*Example:* A co-defendant's confession implicating D, given to the police while in custody, and admitted against D in violation of his Confrontation Clause rights, will almost never be found to be harmless beyond a reasonable doubt, and will thus generally be grounds for reversal.)

        b. Other errors: But in civil cases, and in criminal cases involving non-constitutional errors, the error will be ignored as harmless unless the appellate court believes it *"more probable than not"* that the error affected the outcome.

B. Sufficiency of evidence: If the appellate court needs to decide whether the evidence was *sufficient* to support the findings of fact, the standard will depend on whether the case is civil or criminal: [583]

    1. Civil: In civil cases, the sufficiency test mirrors the "preponderance of the evidence" standard used at the trial. (*Example:* If P wins, the appellate court will ask, "Could a reasonable jury have concluded that P proved all elements of his case by a preponderance of the evidence?")

    2. Criminal: In a criminal case where D is appealing, the appellate court will ask, "Could a reasonable jury have found, beyond a reasonable doubt, that D committed all elements of the crime?"

CHAPTER 12

JUDICIAL NOTICE

I. JUDICIAL NOTICE GENERALLY

A. Function: Under the doctrine of judicial notice, the *judge* can accept a fact as true even though no evidence to prove it has been offered. In a civil jury case, if the judge takes judicial notice of a fact he will instruct the jury that it must find that fact. [587]

B. Three types: The doctrine of judicial notice has evolved to recognize three distinct types of judicial notice: (1) *"adjudicative"* facts; (2) *"legislative"* facts; and (3) *law*. [588-589]

    1. Adjudicative facts: Adjudicative facts are those facts which relate to the ***particular event*** under litigation.

    2. Legislative facts: Legislative facts are more general facts that do not concern the immediate parties. (*Example:* A judge considering whether to impose an implied warranty of habitability for urban apartment buildings would take notice of legislative facts concerning the low bargaining power of urban tenants.)

    3. Law: Judicial notice of *"law"* relieves a party from having to formally plead and prove what the law is, in certain situations.

    4. Federal Rules: The only Federal Rule dealing with judicial notice, FRE 201, deals only with notice of adjudicative facts, not legislative facts or law.

II. ADJUDICATIVE FACTS

A. General rule: At common law, there are two different types of adjudicative facts which may be judicially noticed: (1) those that are "generally known"; and (2) those that are "capable of immediate and accurate verification." A fact will not be found to fall into either of these categories unless the court is convinced that it is virtually ***indisputable***. [589]

    1. "General knowledge": An instance of ***"general knowledge"*** in the community might be that a particular portion of Mission Street in San Francisco is a business district, or that traffic going towards Long Island beaches on Friday afternoon during the summertime is frequently very heavy.

        a. Judge's own knowledge: The fact that the ***judge himself*** knows a fact to be so does ***not*** entitle him to take judicial notice of it if it is not truly common knowledge.

    2. Immediate verification: Some of the kinds of facts that are capable of ***"immediate verification*** by consulting sources of ***indisputable accuracy"*** include: (1) facts of ***history and geography***; (2) ***scientific principles***, and the validity of certain types of scientific ***tests*** (e.g., the general reliability of radar for speed detection); and (3) a court's own record of things that have happened in the same or other suits in that court.

    3. Federal Rule: FRE 201 treats as being an adjudicative fact any fact that is "not subject to reasonable dispute" because it is either: (1) ***"generally known"*** within the "trial court's territorial jurisdiction" (typically, the state or portion of a state composing the "federal judicial district" in which the district judge sits); or (2) capable of being "accurately and readily determined" by the use of ***"sources whose accuracy cannot reasonably be questioned."*** (This basically matches the common-law approach.)

B. Jury's right to disregard: [591-592]

    1. Civil case: In civil cases, courts usually treat judicial notice as being ***conclusive*** on the issue. Therefore, the judge instructs the jury that it ***must*** treat the fact as being so. (FRE 201(f)).

    2. Criminal: But in criminal cases, courts usually hold that the notice fact is ***not conclusive*** on the jury — if it were, D's constitutional right to a jury trial might be impaired. (FRE 201(f)).

        a. On appeal: This means that if the prosecution has failed at trial to ask for judicial notice of a fact, the appeals court may not take notice of that fact.

C. **When taken:** Most courts hold that judicial notice of an appropriate adjudicative fact may be taken *at any time* during the proceeding. Thus notice may be taken before trial, or even on appeal (except in criminal cases). (See FRE 201(d).) [593]

III. LEGISLATIVE FACTS

A. **General rule:** A court may generally take notice of a *"legislative* fact" (i.e., a fact that does not pertain to the particular parties, but is more general) even though the fact is *not "indisputable."* [593]

1. **Standard:** Most jurisdictions allow the judge to take notice of a legislative fact so long as the judge *believes it to be true*, even though it is not indisputable.

2. **Examples:** (1) A fetus does not generally become viable until 28 weeks after conception (relevant to the constitutionality of state abortion rules); (2) Urban tenants have very little bargaining power (relevant to whether there should be an implied warranty of habitability of city apartments).

3. **Federal Rules silent:** The Federal Rules, and most state evidence statutes, are *silent* about whether and when judicial notice of legislative facts may be taken. This is simply an implicit part of the process of deciding cases.

B. **Binding on jury:** A judicially-noticed legislative fact will be *binding on the jury* even in a *criminal* case. (*Example:* The judge's decision that cocaine falls within the statutory ban on importing "cocoa leaves and any derivative thereof" is binding on the jury.) [594]

IV. NOTICE OF LAW

A. **Generally:** Judges may take judicial notice of some types of *law.* When they do so, the consequence is that a party need not plead the provisions of the law, and need not make a formal evidentiary showing that the law is such-and-such; also, the judge may do his own research into the law. [595-596]

B. **Domestic law:** A judge may always take judicial notice of *domestic* law. [595]

1. **State courts:** For a state court, "domestic" law is the *law of that state*, plus federal law. A state's own law is generally held to include *administrative regulations* (but usually not municipal ordinances, which must therefore be proved).

2. **Federal:** In federal courts, "domestic" law is usually held to include not only federal law, but also the law of *all states* if relevant.

C. **Laws of sister states:** At common law, one state may *not* take judicial notice of a *sister state's laws*; instead, the sister state's laws must be "proved" by submitting evidence as to what that sister state's law really is. (But most states have now adopted a uniform act that allows judicial notice of a sister state's laws.) [596]

D. **Law of other countries:** The law of *other countries* may not be judicially noticed, according to most states. Therefore, a party must generally plead and prove such law. [596]

1. **Federal Rules:** But this is not true in the federal courts: FRCP 44.1 allows the judge to conduct his own research on an issue of foreign law (though a party who intends to raise an issue concerning foreign law must nonetheless give notice of this fact in his pleadings).

CHAPTER 1

BASIC CONCEPTS

I. FIRST PRINCIPLES

A. Only admissible evidence usable: Probably the most basic rule of evidence law is that whether the case is tried to a judge or jury, the trier of fact must ***decide the case based solely on what is presented in court***. L&S, p. 4. This rule does not mean that the trier cannot use common sense, or general knowledge gained from experience (e.g., that it is usually hotter in the summer than in the winter). But it does mean that "no information pertaining to the parties or to the specific incident giving rise to the litigation may be considered by the decision maker unless the law permits the information to be received by a court." *Id.* The rules governing what may be received by the court constitute, of course, the law of evidence.

B. Roles of judge and jury: In cases tried to a jury, the judge and the jury divide the responsibility of dealing with the evidence:

1. **Judge's role:** The role of the ***judge*** is to determine ***whether the evidence is admissible***.

2. **Role of the jury:** Once the judge has decided to admit the evidence, the jury's role is to determine what ***weight*** the evidence should be given. The mere fact that the evidence has been admitted does not mean that the jury must attach any significant weight to it at all — for instance, it is up to the jury to judge the ***credibility*** of a witness, and the jury may choose to completely disregard quite admissible testimony because it believes the witness who is giving that testimony is mistaken or lying.

   a. **Jury assumed:** Throughout this book, we assume (unless otherwise noted) that the case is being decided by a jury. However, the rules of evidence are with very few exceptions exactly the same whether the case is tried to a jury or to a judge. For a discussion of the few differences, see *infra*, p. 581.

3. **Questions of fact:** Another way of looking at the roles of judge and jury is to say that the judge decides the ***law*** applicable to the case, and the jury decides the ***facts***. The admissibility of a given piece of evidence is simply one type of issue of law; the believability of that piece of evidence is one type of factual question.

   a. **Preliminary question of fact:** Occasionally, however, the admissibility of a given piece of evidence cannot be determined without first making a ***preliminary*** determination of fact. Depending on the situation, it may be the ***judge***, not the jury, who decides that preliminary factual issue. For a more complete discussion of preliminary questions of fact, see *infra*, p. 579.

C. The Federal Rules: In 1975, the ***Federal Rules of Evidence*** became effective, after having been enacted by Congress. These Rules apply to ***all trials in federal courts,*** whether civil or criminal, and whether to a judge or a jury. See FRE 101.

1. **Importance:** The Federal Rules are of increasingly great importance in the classroom, on bar examinations (e.g., the Multistate Bar Exam's Evidence questions test only the Federal Rules) and in practice. Therefore, we pay great attention to the Federal Rules in this

book. However, we also in most instances talk about the common-law approach that preceded adoption of the Federal Rules, and we sometimes talk about the statutory approach of particular states.

2. **Adoption by states:**   The Federal Rules of Evidence are so influential, and generally regarded as so well-drafted, that *over four-fifths of the states* have adopted them in one form or another. As of 2011, 43 states had codes based on the Federal Rules: Alabama, Alaska, Arizona, Arkansas, Colorado, Connecticut, Delaware, Florida, Hawaii, Idaho, Illinois, Indiana, Iowa, Kentucky, Louisiana, Maine, Maryland, Michigan, Minnesota, Mississippi, Montana, Nebraska, Nevada, New Hampshire, New Jersey, New Mexico, North Carolina, North Dakota, Ohio, Oklahoma, Oregon, Pennsylvania, Rhode Island, South Carolina, South Dakota, Tennessee, Texas, Utah, Vermont, Washington, West Virginia, Wisconsin, and Wyoming. Puerto Rico and the military have also adopted them. See M&K (7th) Csbk, p. 3.

3. **2011 Restyling:**   The language of the Federal Rules was extensively revised in 2011. This *"restyling"* project was done to make the rules "more easily understood and to make style and terminology consistent[.]" Advisory Committee's Note to 2011 Restyling. The restyling was not intended to change any actual evidence-ruling result. All rules quoted or cited in the book are the new restyled ones; you may therefore see differences between these and the rule language quoted in cases you read.

II. ORGANIZATION OF THE TRIAL

A. **Flow of the case:**   In the usual case, the plaintiff's case is presented first, followed by the defendant's. This is because the plaintiff generally has the burdens of proof (see *infra*, p. 560), and is given the compensating advantage of presenting his case first to the jury (as well as having the last word in closing argument). McC, p. 5. Thus, the typical case flows as follows:

1. **Opening statement:**   The plaintiff (or, in a criminal case, the prosecutor) makes his *opening statement* first. Then, the defendant may make his opening statement (though many courts allow him to reserve his opening statement until the end of the plaintiff/prosecutor's case).

2. **Plaintiff's case:**   Then, the plaintiff (or prosecutor) puts on his *case in chief.* That is, he presents the witnesses, as well as documents and other tangible evidence, to establish the facts needed for him to prevail.

3. **Defendant's case:**   After the plaintiff or prosecutor "rests" his case, it is the defendant's turn. The defendant presents witnesses and documents to disprove the elements of the plaintiff's case and/or to establish *affirmative defenses*.

4. **Plaintiff's rebuttal:**   After the defendant rests, the plaintiff or prosecutor gets another turn at bat. This is called the plaintiff's *rebuttal* — the plaintiff may present additional witnesses, recall former witnesses, or present new exhibits, but *only to rebut the defendant's evidence*, not to buttress his own case in chief.

5. **Defendant's rejoinder:** Likewise, after the plaintiff's rebuttal, the defendant has a *rejoinder* — here, he may only rebut evidence brought out in the plaintiff's rebuttal. McC, p. 6.

6. **Closing arguments:** After both parties have presented all of their evidence, the two sides make *closing arguments*. Usually, the plaintiff (or prosecutor) goes first, the defendant goes second, and the plaintiff/prosecutor gets a last chance to rebut the defendant's closing remarks. L&S, p. 83, n. 45.

7. **Instructions:** Finally, the judge gives *instructions* to the jury, in which he explains to them the applicable law. In some jurisdictions, he may also comment upon, or summarize, the evidence. See *infra*, p. 581.

B. **Examination of witnesses:** Let us focus now on the steps by which witnesses are examined.

1. **Four stages:** The examination of a given witness proceeds through up to four stages:

   a. **Direct:** First, the party who has called a witness engages in the *direct examination*. Generally, the direct examiner may *not* use *leading questions*, i.e., questions that suggest the desired answer. Instead, the direct examiner must let the witness give his own testimony, though the examiner may gently guide the path of the testimony. See *infra*, p. 93.

   b. **Cross-examination:** After the side that called the witness has finished the direct examination, the other side has the chance to *cross-examine* the witness. Here, because the witness may be expected to be hostile to the examiner, leading questions are permitted. See *infra*, p. 106.

   c. **Re-direct:** The calling side then has an opportunity to conduct *re-direct* examination of the witness. Re-direct is generally limited to rebutting points made on cross-examination. See *infra*, p. 109.

   d. **Re-cross:** Finally, the cross-examining side gets a brief opportunity to conduct *re-cross*. This is limited to rebutting the effect of re-direct.

2. **Sequestration of witnesses:** If a witness were permitted to observe the testimony of other witnesses for the same side, he would be able to tailor his testimony (perhaps by perjury) so that it matched this other testimony. To prevent this, nearly all courts have, and often use, the power to *exclude all other witnesses* from the courtroom while one witness is testifying.

   a. **Federal Rule:** The trial judge's right to sequester witnesses is codified in FRE 615, which begins: "At a party's request, the court must order witnesses excluded so that they cannot hear other witnesses' testimony. Or the court may do so on its own."

      i. **Exceptions:** The Federal Rules, like most state courts, recognize several exceptions to this principle of sequestration. Under FRE 615, the court may *not* order the sequestration of: "(a) party who is a natural person; (b) an officer or employee of a party that is not a natural person, after being designated as the party's representative by its attorney; (c) a person whose presence a party shows to be essential to presenting the party's claim or defense; or (d) a person authorized by statute to be present."

ii. **Investigating officer:** The most controversial issue is whether the *prosecution* may have the *law enforcement officer* who investigated the case present at the prosecutor's table, even though that officer will later be a witness. Most courts that have faced the issue have held that the investigating officer may remain present under exception (2) above, partly on the theory that this counter-balances an advantage held by the defense (since the defendant, as a natural person, may always be present to assist his attorney). L&S, p. 39, n. 19.

iii. **Mandatory at party's request:** Under FRE 615, *any party* has the *absolute right* to require the judge to exclude all witnesses (other than witnesses covered by the above exceptions) from hearing other witnesses' testimony. So once a party makes the request for sequestration, the *judge does not have discretion to deny the request.*

III.   MAKING AND RESPONDING TO OBJECTIONS

A. **Making objections:** When inadmissible evidence is offered, it is not the judge's responsibility to notice this and to exclude the evidence. Instead, our adversary system places *upon the other party* the responsibility of *objecting* to the evidence; only after a timely objection will the trial judge determine whether the evidence is admissible.

1. **Waiver:** A corollary of this rule is that where the non-offering party does not make a timely objection, he will normally be held to have *waived* any claim on appeal that the evidence was wrongfully admitted. (There is an exception, however, for "plain error," usually applicable in criminal cases. See *infra*, p. 583.)

B. **Time for objection:** The objection must be *timely.* If the question alone makes it clear that the answer would be inadmissible, the objection should come *before the witness answers.* "Counsel is not free to sit back, gambling that the witness will give a harmless or even a favorable answer, and then object when the answer proves to be damaging." K&W, p. 39.

1. **Answer shows inadmissibility:** Sometimes, however, it is not feasible to object before the answer. The inadmissibility may not become apparent until the answer is given (e.g., the witness gives an unresponsive and inadmissible answer that could not have been anticipated from the question). Or, the witness may simply answer so quickly that counsel does not have a reasonable opportunity to frame an objection beforehand. In these situations, an "after-objection" may be made following the witness's answer. The lawyer moves to have the witness's answer *stricken*, and to have the jury instructed that it should disregard this evidence. McC, p. 74.

C. **General vs. specific objections:** How *specific* must the objection be? Generally, the objection should be "sufficiently specific for the judge and opposing counsel to know which of the many rules of evidence is being invoked." Lilly, p. 473. Thus the general statement, "I object," will not be specific enough to tell the judge whether the objection is based on the theory that the answer would be irrelevant to the case, that it would be inadmissible hearsay, that it would violate a privilege, etc.

1. **Federal Rules:** The Federal Rules codify this requirement of specificity. FRE 103(a)(1) allows the appeals court to consider an evidentiary ruling only if the opponent made a timely objection that "states the *specific ground*, unless it was apparent from the context."

2. **Effect of specificity on appeal:** The handling of the ruling on appeal varies depending on whether the objection is specific or general:

   a. **General objection:** If the objection is *general*, here are the rules on appeal:

      i. **Objection overruled:** If the general objection was *overruled*, the objector will rarely win on appeal — "only if there is no purpose or theory of admissibility to support the trial judge's ruling will it be overturned." Lilly, p. 474.

      ii. **Objection sustained:** Conversely, if the general objection was *sustained*, the appellate court will *uphold* the ruling unless there is "no basis for it whatsoever." *Id.*

      iii. **Summary:** In other words, a trial judge's ruling on a general objection, whichever way the judge decides, will *rarely be reversed on appeal.*

   b. **Specific objection:** If the objection is *specific*, here is how it will be handled on appeal:

      i. **Correct ground cited:** If the objector has *correctly* pointed out a specific rule of exclusion to the judge, and the trial judge overrules the objection, the appellate court will reverse (unless it finds the error to have been "harmless"; see *infra*, p. 582).

      ii. **Wrong ground; objection overruled:** Suppose that the objector picks a specific ground that is *erroneous*, and the objection is overruled. Here, the objector will generally *lose* on appeal *even if there was a different specific ground which merited exclusion.* For instance, if a document is objected to on hearsay grounds and the objection is overruled, the objector will lose on appeal even if he convinces the appellate court that the document violated the Best Evidence rule. The rationale is that it is the party's duty to select the correct ground for objection, and all the trial judge can be expected to do is to rule correctly on that specific ground. Lilly, p. 475.

      iii. **Wrong ground; objection sustained:** The most difficult question arises when the specific ground cited in the objection is *erroneous*, but the trial judge erroneously *sustains* the objection even though there is a different, unnamed, valid ground for objection. Here, the courts are split — some sustain the trial judge's ruling on the grounds that the result was correct even though the reason was wrong; others reverse on the theory that the proponent, had he known of the valid ground, could have offered different evidence to support the point or otherwise cure the defect. The latter seems the better rule; see Lilly, p. 475. (Again, keep in mind that there will never be a reversal if the appellate court finds the error to have been "harmless.")

D. **Taking of "exceptions":** At common law, a party did not by the mere act of objecting preserve an objection for appeal — after the objection was overruled, the objecting counsel had to say, "I take *exception*," or similar words. Today, however, most states (as well as the federal courts) have dispensed with the need for taking an exception, so that a timely and specific objection is all that is needed to preserve the evidentiary issue for appeal. See, e.g., Fed. R. Civ. P. 46, dispensing with the need for exceptions. See also McC, p. 77.

E. Offer of proof: If the trial judge sustains an objection, the proponent of the evidence must normally make an *"offer of proof"* if he wishes to be able to contend on appeal that the exclusion was reversible error. This "offer of proof" must normally consist of two parts: (1) a description of the evidence being proposed; and (2) an explanation of how that evidence relates to the case, if its relevance is not clear from context. L&S, p. 54, n. 30.

> **Example:** P is suing D for battery. P's counsel calls W to the stand to ask about an altercation between D and X. During the testimony, the lawyer asks, "What did X say to you when you asked him why he was grimacing in pain?" D's counsel objects on hearsay grounds. P's counsel argues that a hearsay exception (for statement of present physical condition; see *infra*, p. 230) applies. The judge sustains the objection. To preserve his position on appeal, P's counsel should now make the following offer of proof: "Your Honor, if W were permitted to testify, he would state that X told him that he was grimacing in pain because he had just been struck in the face by D, for no apparent reason. This evidence is relevant because it shows that D has in the past made unprovoked attacks, and thus impeaches the testimony D has previously given in this trial in which he said that his attack upon my client was self-defense."

1. Rationale: The main rationale for the rule requiring an offer of proof is that only by such an offer can the *appellate court* be *completely informed* of what the offered evidence would have been and how it would have been significant to the trial; this in turn helps the appellate court decide not only the issue of admissibility but also the issue of whether the error, if there was one, was harmless. (The offer also gives the trial judge the chance to reassess his ruling sustaining the objection, and gives the opponent a chance to refine or withdraw his objection. Lilly, p. 470.)

2. Not needed on cross: Generally, an offer of proof is required only on direct examination, *not cross-examination*. K&W, p. 50. There are two common reasons for this limitation: (1) the cross-examiner will often not know what the witness would have testified to had the objection not been sustained; and (2) the likely answer of the witness will often be obvious to everyone, because the question was probably a "leading" one (permitted on cross-examination but not generally on direct; see *infra*, p. 93). L&S, p. 54, n. 30.

3. Question-and-answer form: Generally, the court will allow the offer of proof to be in the form of a statement by the proponent as to what the witness would say if permitted to testify, as in the above Example. (In this situation, the trial court is relying on the good faith of the proponent's counsel, since counsel could theoretically lie, and claim that the testimony would be more favorable than it would in fact be.) Alternatively, counsel may engage the witness in *question-and-answer* form, just as if the testimony were being admitted.

4. Presence of jury: Regardless of the form of the offer of proof, it will normally be made *outside the presence of the jury*, since if the jury hears the evidence, the whole point of a sustained objection will be lost.

5. **Federal Rules:** The Federal Rules codify the requirement of an offer of proof. Under FRE 103(a)(2), an appellate court will be permitted to consider a ruling excluding evidence only if "a *party informs the court* of [the evidence's] substance by an offer of proof, unless the substance was apparent from the context." FRE 103(c) allows the court to require that the proponent make the offer in question-and-answer form. FRE 103(d) requires, where practicable, that the offer of proof be made outside of the jury's hearing.

F. **The "plain error" and "harmless error" doctrines:** Not every error in the admission or exclusion of evidence will be grounds for reversal. Conversely, not every error to which no objection (or an incorrect objection) is made, will lead to affirmance. An error will not lead to reversal if it is *"harmless"*; conversely, an unobjected-to error may nonetheless lead to reversal if it is *"plain."* See *infra*, p. 582, for a discussion of these two concepts.

IV. COMPETENCY

A. **Meaning:** A witness is said to be *"competent"* if she possesses the qualifications necessary to give testimony. At common law, the competency of witnesses was an important topic, because there were a substantial number of ways in which a person could lose her competency. Today, nearly all of these have been eliminated.

B. **General common-law approach:** At common law, a witness would be found incompetent, and thus not permitted to give any testimony at all, if he occupied one of a number of statuses. Some of the types of persons automatically ruled incompetent were: (1) those who did not believe in a *supreme being* (i.e., agnostics and atheists); (2) convicted *felons*; (3) persons with an *interest* in the outcome of the litigation (e.g., *parties*); (4) *young children*; and (5) *insane* persons. Lilly, p. 85. The common law believed that all such people were either incapable of telling the truth or unwilling to do so.

C. **Modern approach:** Today, nearly all the automatic rules of incompetency have been *abolished* by statute. *Id.* For instance, no state now treats lack of belief in a supreme being as a disqualification. K&W, p. 714.

1. **Presumption of competence:** Instead, witnesses are presumed competent, and the common-law grounds for disqualification are today at most factors that go to the witness's *credibility*, not to whether he may give testimony at all. For instance, the fact that a witness has an interest in the outcome of the case can be used to *impeach* his credibility, even though it cannot be used to prevent him from testifying entirely; see *infra*, p. 143.

2. **Federal Rules:** The approach to competency of the Federal Rules is similar to that of most states.

   a. **Two reasons:** Under the Federal Rules, witnesses (other than the judge and the jury in the particular case) will be incompetent to testify *only for two reasons*:

      i. **Lack of personal knowledge:** First, a witness "may testify to a matter only if evidence is introduced sufficient to support a finding that the witness has *personal knowledge of the matter*." FRE 602. Thus if a witness describes a particular event, his testimony will be stricken if it turns out that he did not personally observe that event, and instead heard about it from someone else. This requirement of personal knowledge is discussed more extensively *infra*, p. 516.

    ii.   **Oath:**   Second, if the witness will not solemnly ***promise to tell the truth***, the court will not hear his testimony. FRE 603 requires that "Before testifying, a witness must give an ***oath*** or ***affirmation*** to testify truthfully. It must be in a form designed to impress that duty on the witness's conscience."

b.   **Mental incapacity or immaturity:**   Thus under the federal approach, even a witness who is quite insane, or very young, will not be prevented from testifying if the trial judge is convinced that he has relevant first-hand knowledge and understands the obligation to tell the truth. (Of course, the witness's mental impairment or extreme youth could be used to impeach his credibility, if there was evidence that the defect impaired the accuracy of his observation, recall or narration. See *infra*, p. 144.) Similarly, even if the witness was ***intoxicated*** or under the ***influence of drugs*** when he witnessed an event, he will be permitted, under the federal approach, to testify about it.

c.   **Diversity cases:**   However, federal courts may occasionally be required to follow the *state* rule on competency. The second sentence of FRE 601 provides, "[I]n a civil case, *state law* governs the witness's competency regarding a claim or defense for which *state law supplies the rule of decision*." This provision applies most frequently in *diversity* cases, as to which the federal court is required to follow state substantive principles; Congress decided to treat state rules of competency as if they were substantive provisions.

    Example: In a diversity action, P sues D's estate for breach of an oral contract. If the state whose substantive contract law applies to this case has a strict Dead Man's Statute (*infra*) preventing P from testifying about any transaction with the decedent, the federal court is required by FRE 601 to similarly disqualify P from testifying to that transaction.

3.   **Dead Man's Statutes:**   The one important rule of competency that survives from the common-law days relates to civil suits in which one of the parties is ***deceased***. When the states all abolished the rule that no one with an interest in the outcome of the suit could testify, most states enacted a small compromise, colloquially referred to as a ***Dead Man's Statute***. These statutes vary in their precise effect, but they all attempt to "***equalize the opportunities of proof*** in litigation involving a decedent and survivor where the subject matter of the suit is a transaction or event that occurred when both were living." Lilly, p. 88.

a.   **Extreme form:**   In their most extreme form, Dead Man's Statutes prevent the survivor from testifying *at all* about the transaction between him and the decedent. Under such a statute, if P claimed that D made an oral agreement with him, and D is dead, P will have to come up with some evidence other than his own testimony, or be thrown out of court; he will not be permitted to testify at the trial as to the alleged oral agreement.

b.   **More liberal:**   But an increasing number of states have enacted less Draconian Dead Man's Statutes. These typically permit the survivor to testify, but equalize his advantage by allowing the decedent's estate to introduce *hearsay statements made by the decedent* or other evidence that would otherwise be inadmissible. Lilly, p. 89.

c. **Federal Rules:** There is no federal Dead Man's Statute. That is, the Federal Rules do not directly limit a survivor's ability to testify against a decedent. However, as noted above, if the federal suit is brought in diversity, and the state whose substantive law applies has a Dead Man's Statute, the federal court is required by FRE 601 to honor the state Dead Man's Statute.

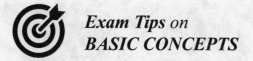

Exam Tips on
BASIC CONCEPTS

Of the topics covered in this chapter, *competency* is by far the most likely to be tested. Here's what to look for on this topic:

☞ In modern courts (federal and state), the only grounds for finding a witness, W, incompetent are that (1) W has *no personal knowledge* of the matter (FRE 602); or (2) W can't or won't take and understand the *oath* to tell the truth (FRE 603).

☞ Most frequently-tested: W is a *small child*, and the twin issues are: (1) does W *understand* what it means to promise to tell the truth?; and (2) does W have sufficient maturity to be capable of *receiving* and *reporting* correct *sensory impressions*? (*Example:* W was 4 at the time of the events and is now 5; he testifies that "People who don't tell the truth get spanked." W has probably demonstrated adequate knowledge of the need to tell the truth. Also, the judge will probably find that at 4, W was mature enough to observe and recall major events, such as the fact that D shot X with a rifle.)

☞ Also tested: W suffers from a *mental deficiency* (e.g., retardation or insanity). Typically, the court rules that this affects only the *weight* to be given to W's testimony, not its admissibility.

CHAPTER 2

RELEVANCE

ChapterScope

This chapter discusses the concept of relevance, which is the initial threshold which evidence must meet in order to be admitted. The key concepts in this chapter are:

- Evidence is *relevant* if "(a) it has any tendency to make a fact *more or less probable* than it would be without the evidence; and (b) the fact is *of consequence* in determining the action." FRE 401.

  - ❏ When evidence is relevant, the evidence is also said to have *"probative value"* on the issue to which it's addressed.

- An item of evidence can be either *"direct"* or *"circumstantial."*

  - ❏ *Direct* evidence is evidence that, if believed, proves the existence of a matter *without inferences*. Direct evidence always has probative value (though it's not admissible unless it concerns a material fact, i.e., an issue that matters in the litigation).

  - ❏ *Circumstantial* evidence is evidence that, even if believed, requires that *additional reasoning* be used to reach to proposition to which the evidence is directed.

I. RELEVANCE GENERALLY

- **A. All relevant evidence admitted:** The concept of "relevance" is the cornerstone of the law of admissibility of evidence. For instance, FRE 402 provides that, except as otherwise provided by the Rules or by other specific enactment, "[r]elevant evidence is admissible[.]" The Rule goes on to say that "[i]rrelevant evidence is not admissible."

- **B. Two aspects of relevance:** When we say that a piece of evidence is "relevant" to the case, we mean that there exist two distinct links between that piece of evidence and the case:

  - **1. Link One (probative relationship):** First, there must be a *"probative"* relationship between the piece of evidence and the factual proposition to which the evidence is addressed. That is, the evidence must make the factual proposition more (or less) likely than it would be without the evidence.

    Example: P is injured when he is hit by D's car. In a negligence suit against D, he offers testimony by W that she saw D driving at what she believed to be around 55 miles per hour. There is a link between W's testimony and a factual proposition asserted by P (that D was travelling at 55 miles per hour) — W's testimony makes it more likely that D was actually travelling at 55 mph than if W didn't so testify.

  - **2. Link Two (materiality):** Second, the evidence must be *material*. That is, there must be a link between the factual proposition which the evidence tends to establish, and the *substantive law*.

Example: On the facts of the above example, assume that the speed limit at the site of the accident was 35 mph. W's testimony satisfies this second link, because evidence that D was exceeding the speed limit by 20 mph affects a fundamental substantive law issue in the case, namely, whether D was negligent. If, on the other hand, the local speed limit was 55 mph, this link would not be present (though D's speed might relate to some other substantive law issue in the case).

    a. **Significance of substantive law:** This second type of link, that between the factual proposition sought to be established and the underlying substantive law, illustrates that there is ***no such thing as relevance "in the abstract."*** For any given proposition of fact which the evidence tends to establish, the evidence may be relevant to some claims or defenses, and not to others.

3. **Rule 401:** These two aspects of relevance are combined in FRE 401's definition of relevant evidence: "Evidence is relevant if: "(a) it has any tendency to make a fact ***more or less probable*** than it would be without the evidence; and (b) the fact is ***of consequence*** in determining the action."

The first link — a probative relationship between the evidence and the factual proposition — is indicated by the requirement that the existence of the fact be made "more or less probable." The second link — the requirement that the factual proposition be relevant to the substantive law — is indicated by the requirement that the fact be "of consequence in determining the action."

C. **"Direct" vs. "circumstantial" evidence:** Evidence is either ***"direct"*** or ***"circumstantial."***

1. **"Direct" evidence:** Direct evidence is "evidence which, if believed, ***resolves*** a matter in issue." McC, p. 339.

    Example: W testifies that she saw D strangle V with a stocking. W's testimony is direct evidence on the issue of whether D did in fact strangle V with a stocking, since if that testimony is believed, the issue is resolved.

2. **"Circumstantial" evidence:** Circumstantial evidence is evidence which, even if believed, does not resolve the matter at issue unless ***additional reasoning*** is used to reach the proposition to which the evidence is directed. *Id.*

    Example: Prosecution of D for strangling V. W, a policeman, testifies that shortly after hearing V's screams, he saw D running from the scene of the crime, and, after stopping D, found a stocking in D's pocket. While this testimony (if believed) is direct evidence on the issues of whether D was at the scene of the crime, was fleeing, and had a stocking in his pocket, it is merely circumstantial evidence as to whether D did the strangling. This is so because only by the application of additional reasoning ("A man seen fleeing from the scene of a strangling, who is found with a stocking in his pocket, is at least somewhat more likely to be guilty of the strangling than most other people are") does the evidence lead to the proposition to which it is addressed.

3. **Consequences of distinction:** The relevance of proffered evidence differs dramatically depending on whether the evidence is direct or circumstantial.

a. Direct evidence never irrelevant: When the evidence is *direct*, so long as it is offered to help establish a material issue (i.e., so long as Link 2, *supra*, p. 10, exists), *it can never be irrelevant*. *Id.*

b. Circumstantial evidence: By contrast, *circumstantial* evidence, even if offered to prove a material fact, will nonetheless be found to be irrelevant if the evidence has no *probative value*, i.e., it does not affect the probability of the proposition to which it was directed. (That is, Link 1, *supra*, p. 10, must exist as well as Link 2.)

II. PROBATIVE VALUE

A. The problem generally: As noted, evidence is relevant only if it has "probative value," that is, only if it affects the probability of the existence of a fact consequential to the action. Assessing the probative value of particular evidence is, therefore, a major part of what a judge must do in assessing relevance. (Also as noted, this is an issue that arises *only* in the case of circumstantial evidence, not direct evidence.)

B. Experience and logic, not law: The judge normally does not make this assessment of probative value by applying cut-and-dried legal principles. Rather, she applies her "own experience, ... general knowledge, and ... understanding of human conduct and motivation." McC, p. 340.

> **Example:** Suppose that D, after being charged with a crime, is caught attempting to flee the jurisdiction. If the prosecution offers evidence of the flight on the grounds that it tends to establish D's consciousness of his guilt, "the answer will not be found in a statistical table of the attempts at escape by those conscious of guilt as opposed to those not conscious of their guilt." *Id.* Instead, the judge will ask herself whether a reasonable juror could believe that the fact that D tried to escape makes it more probable than it would otherwise be that he was conscious of his guilt of the crime charged. *Id.* This inquiry is a matter of common sense, experience and logic, not the application of any legal principle.

1. Common patterns: Certain types of circumstantial evidence, however, are so frequently offered that a body of legal precedent has been built up concerning them. Indeed, the probative value of an escape attempt, offered to show consciousness of guilt, is probably one such type, so a judge might look to cases on this issue in making his decision. But the precise circumstances of the present case are always of ultimate significance in assessing probative value. For instance, if D in the above example had been charged with two unrelated crimes at the time he fled, and was only being tried for one of them, the probative value of his escape on the issue of his consciousness of guilt for the one crime at trial would be weaker than where only the one charge had been pending at the time of escape.

C. Chain of inference: In assessing probative value, the judge must determine what proposition the evidence is being offered to establish, and he must then follow the *"chain of inference"* between the evidence and that proposition. Sometimes this chain may be a complex and subtle one.

Example: Suppose the contested issue is whether D is the person who killed H, and the evidence is a love letter from D to W, H's wife. The "chain of inference" would be something like this: (1) A man who writes a love letter to a woman probably loves her ("probably" in the sense that he is more likely to love her than is a man who does not write a love letter); (2) A man who loves a woman probably wants her for himself alone; (3) A man who wants a woman for himself alone probably would like to get rid of her husband; (4) A man who wants to get rid of the husband of the woman he loves probably plans to do so; (5) A man who plans to get rid of someone probably does so, by killing him. W,M,A&B, p. 3.

1. **Evaluation:** Obviously, the more steps there are in the chain of inference, the less probative value the evidence has. Similarly, the less convincing any of the individual steps is, the less the probative value. K&W, p. 70.

    a. **"A brick is not a wall":** On the other hand, for an item of circumstantial evidence to have probative value as to a particular fact, *it is not necessary that the evidence render the fact more probable than not*. Rather, all that is required is that the evidence make the existence of the fact *more probable than it would be without the evidence*. As the idea has been most famously put, *"a brick is not a wall."* That is, if the particular fact in dispute is the wall, an item of evidence need merely be a valid brick in that wall. McC, p. 339. Or as the idea is sometimes put, "it is not to be supposed that every witness can make a home run." Adv. Comm. Note to FRE 401.

        Example: D is charged with murdering V. D claims self defense, and tries to prove that he had reason to fear V by testifying that he had been told that V had seriously injured or killed an old man. The prosecution offers the testimony of the doctor who treated the old man, that the old man died of natural causes and that there were no marks of violence. The defense argues that the doctor's testimony is irrelevant, since the issue is not whether the story of D's attacking the old man is true, but whether D had in fact heard the story.

        Held, the evidence was relevant to the truth of D's self-defense claim. The evidence showed that "somewhere between the fact and [D's] testimony there was a person who was not a true speaker." Since D could not or would not identify his informant, the doctor's testimony had a tendency to make D's claim of what he heard less likely to be true than it would be without the doctor's testimony. *Knapp v. State*, 79 N.E. 1076 (Ind. 1907).

    b. **Proposition can remain improbable:** Because all that is required is that the evidence make the disputed fact more probable than it would be without the evidence, it follows that evidence can have probative value even though, following receipt of the evidence, the proposition for which it is offered still seems quite improbable. McC, p. 339. Thus the common objection that the proposition sought to be proved "does not follow" from the evidence offered by the other side, makes no sense. *Id*.

        Example: Suppose that D is charged with murdering V. The state's first piece of evidence is that D was the beneficiary of an insurance policy on V's life. If this were the only piece of evidence in the case, it would be quite unlikely that D was the murderer: after all, an empirical study of murderers would undoubtedly show that less than half of all insured murder victims are murdered by their beneficiaries. But the evidence is nonetheless of probative value, because a reasonable juror could conclude that someone who stands to gain financially from another person's death is at least somewhat more likely to murder that other person than is one who does not stand to gain.

i. Almost always some probative value: In fact, very few pieces of circumstantial evidence are proffered that do not have at least *some* probative value. That is, almost every piece of evidence that is offered at least slightly increases the probability of the existence of the fact to which it is directed. Therefore, in point of fact, evidence should rarely be excluded for lack of probative value. On the other hand, evidence is very frequently excluded because its probative value is *outweighed* by prejudice, tendency to confuse, or other discretionary considerations. (These countervailing considerations are discussed extensively *infra*.) Even when a court states that it is excluding evidence for lack of probative value, it is probably doing so because the modest probative value is outweighed by one of these "counterweights." McC, p. 340. See, e.g., FRE 403, allowing such weighing and exclusion.

ii. Credibility not a factor: When the court measures probative value to determine whether it is outweighed by prejudicial effect, the court should *not* factor in doubts it may have about the *credibility* of the evidence. Rather, the test is what probative value the evidence would have *if believed*. The choice of whether to believe an item of evidence should be left to the jury.

III. PREJUDICE, CONFUSION, AND WASTE OF TIME

A. **"Counterweights" to relevance:** Even if evidence is relevant, the trial judge may exclude it on the basis of several largely discretionary countervailing considerations. FRE 403, for instance, allows the judge to exclude relevant evidence "if its probative value is *substantially outweighed* by a danger of one or more of the following: *unfair prejudice, confusing the issues, misleading the jury, undue delay*, wasting time, or needlessly presenting cumulative evidence."

These countervailing considerations can be thought of as falling into three main classes: (1) prejudice; (2) confusion; and (3) waste of time.

B. **Prejudice:** Relevant evidence may be excluded because its probative value is outweighed by the likelihood that it will cause "*unfair prejudice.*" The word "unfair" is an important aspect: any highly material evidence is likely to be prejudicial (in the sense of damaging) to the party not introducing it. "Unfair" prejudice means "an undue tendency to suggest decision on an *improper basis*, commonly, though not necessarily, an *emotional* one." Adv. Comm. Note to FRE 403.

1. **Comparison standard:** When a court is weighing an item's probative value against its prejudicial effect, the court should normally *compare* the proffered item against *other possible evidence on the same point.* If the alternative evidence has the same or nearly the same probative effect, and much less prejudicial value, the court should normally insist that the less-prejudicial item be used.

Example: D is charged with the crime of possession of a firearm while having a prior felony conviction, and also with the crime of assault with a deadly weapon. D offers to stipulate that he has a prior felony conviction. The trial judge instead allows the prosecution to read the prior judgment to the jury. Consequently, the jury learns that the prior conviction was for aggravated assault and that D was sentenced to five years imprisonment on it.

Held, the trial judge should have compared the probative value and prejudicial effect of reading the actual judgment to the jury, with the probative value and prejudicial effect of accepting D's stipulation. After such a comparison, the judge should have used the stipulation instead of the judgment. *Old Chief v. U.S.*, 519 U.S. 172 (1997) (discussed in more detail *infra*, p. 17).

2. **Gruesome photos:** One situation in which courts often exclude material on account of its prejudicial effect is where *gruesome photos* of human injuries, or of a corpse, are shown to the jury.

   a. **Photos of corpses:** Most commonly, the prosecution in a murder case seeks to admit gruesome *autopsy photographs*. Especially where the photos show not the body in the condition it was in immediately after the victim's death, but rather, "wounds" that are really the result of the autopsy itself, the trial judge is likely to exclude the photos. If the photos are *large*, and/or if they're in *color*, exclusion for prejudice is also more likely.

      i. **Allowed to show necessary detail:** But where the photos are necessary to convey to the jury the *details* of how the defendant brought about the victim's death, the fact that the photos are gruesome, colored, or greatly enlarged will *not* usually lead to exclusion. The question is always, are the photos more inflammatory than needed to show how the killing occurred? If not, then they're likely to be admitted despite their gruesome and prejudicial impact, on the grounds that that impact does not substantially outweigh probative value.

   b. **Photos of accident victim:** A similar problem arises when photos are introduced by the *plaintiff in a tort suit*, to show what the *injuries* he or she sustained looked like at the time. Here, courts generally allow the photos — however gruesome — so long as they're not distorted, since the precise nature of the injuries is highly relevant on the subject of damages (in contrast to the murder situation, where the nature of the injuries leading to death is not literally an element of the prosecution's case). M&K §4.10, pp. 176-77.

3. **Evidence of other crimes:** Another common situation in which evidence is excluded because of unfair prejudice is a showing that the defendant in a criminal case has in the *past* been *convicted of crimes* similar to the one with which he is now charged. The principal reason why such evidence is considered unfairly prejudicial is that it "may lead a juror to think that since the defendant already has a criminal record, an erroneous conviction would not be quite as serious as would otherwise be the case. A juror influenced in this fashion may be satisfied with a slightly less compelling demonstration of guilt than he should be." McC, p. 340.

Example: D is charged with the crime of possession of a firearm by one with a prior felony conviction, as well as the crime of assault with a dangerous weapon. D in fact has a prior felony conviction, for assault with a deadly weapon. At the present trial, D offers to stipulate that he has a prior felony conviction. However, the government declines the offer, and insists (with the judge's consent) on showing the jury the judgment in the prior case. The judgment mentions that the prior crime was an assault resulting in serious bodily injury, and that a five-year sentence was imposed. D is convicted, and argues on appeal that when the trial court admitted the prior judgment document, rather than the stipulation, the danger of unfair prejudice from this admission substantially outweighed the judgment's probative value, in violation of FRE 403.

Held, for D. When a court needs to decide under FRE 403 whether the prejudicial effect of an item of evidence substantially outweighs the item's probative value, probative value should be determined by comparing the *evidentiary alternatives* to the item. Here, the prior judgment was relevant only for purposes of satisfying a jurisdictional element (that D had a prior felony conviction). Therefore, the prior judgment had exactly the same probative value as D's proposed stipulation. On the other hand, the judgment itself — which revealed that the prior conviction was for serious bodily assault, just like the crime being charged in the present case — posed a large danger of prejudice to D, because of the risk that the jury would reason that since D committed serious assault before, he was probably guilty of the presently-charged assault as well. *Old Chief v. U.S.*, 519 U.S. 172 (1997).

a. **Special rule:** The problem of prior convictions is so serious, and recurs so often, that the Federal Rules have a special provision barring such evidence in most instances (including most instances where the evidence is used against a criminal defendant). The special rules governing this situation are discussed *infra*, p. 27. (These special procedures didn't apply in *Old Chief*, *supra*.)

b. **Other evidence of guilt:** Even where a prior conviction is not shown, evidence suggesting that the defendant is in fact guilty of past crimes may similarly be excluded on the grounds of unfair prejudice. See, e.g., *State v. Ball*, 339 S.W.2d 783 (Mo. 1960), in which the government in a robbery prosecution introduced evidence that several hundred dollars was found on D's person more than two weeks after the robbery, at a time when he was unlikely to have come by it honestly (since he was unemployed and only a few months out of jail). The evidence was ordered excluded as unfairly prejudicial on the theory that the jury may have inferred that D was guilty of a different robbery.

C. **Confusion:** Relevant evidence may be excluded if its probative value is outweighed by its tendency to *confuse* or *mislead* the jury, or unduly distract it from the main issues. McC, p. 340. For instance, evidence that the accused has committed past crimes may not only be prejudicial (as discussed above), but it may also distract the jury from the fact that there is only weak evidence that the accused was the person who did the act charged.

D. **Waste of time:** Evidence may also be excluded if it would be a *waste of time.* This is especially likely to be the case where the evidence is cumulative. For instance, in a case in which the accused is charged with having poisoned the decedent, presentation by either side of more than two or three witnesses all testifying as to the cause of death might be deemed to be needlessly cumulative and therefore excluded.

E. No "unfair surprise":   FRE 403 does *not* recognize "unfair *surprise*" as a ground for excluding otherwise relevant evidence. If the proposed evidence takes the other side by surprise, the appropriate remedy is a continuance. See Adv. Comm. Note to FRE 403.

F. Standard for appellate review: The exclusion of relevant evidence because its probative value is outweighed by the chance of prejudice, confusion, waste of time, etc., necessarily requires the trial court to perform a difficult balancing task. Appellate courts have generally given trial courts *wide discretion* in conducting this balancing — only where there is a *clear abuse of discretion* will the trial court's decision be overturned on appeal. The Federal Rules tip the scale in favor of the inclusion rather than exclusion of doubtful evidence, by allowing exclusion only where the probative value is "*substantially* outweighed" by the prejudice, confusion, etc.

Quiz Yourself on
RELEVANCE (ENTIRE CHAPTER)

1. A police detective finds a bloody brown left-hand glove, size 11 Isotoner, at a murder scene. A similar glove, but for a right hand, is later found at the residence of the victim's ex-husband, OJ. (No left glove is found at OJ's residence.) OJ is charged with the murder. The glove is offered as evidence that OJ is the murderer. Is the glove direct or circumstantial evidence? _____

2. To impeach Walt Dipsey's primary witness, the Evil Stepmother, Snow White plans to introduce testimony of seven diminutive witnesses in the neighborhood who will testify that the Evil Stepmother has a reputation for untruthfulness. On what basis can Dipsey exclude some of the witnesses? _____

Answers

1. It is *circumstantial* evidence, because it is *indirect,* and requires one or more *inferences* to establish the existence of a material fact — that OJ committed the crime. The inferences go like this: Where a glove is found at a crime scene, the person who dropped the glove is probably the criminal. If a glove found at a crime scene is an unusual one that is similar or identical to one known to have been possessed by X, then it's likely that X is the one who dropped it. Therefore, X is probably the criminal.

2. Dipsey can object on the grounds that the testimony is *cumulative* and will cause *undue delay and waste time.* Note, of course, that all the testimony is relevant, but its probative value is outweighed by the waste of time caused by its cumulative nature. See FRE 403.

Note that FRE 403 allows, in addition to exclusion for waste of time / needless cumulation, exclusion where the probative value is substantially outweighed by the danger of unfair prejudice, confusion of issues, or misleading the jury.

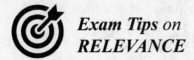

Exam Tips on RELEVANCE

No matter what the item of evidence being presented, you must first check to see whether it's *relevant*.

☛ **Makes more or less probable:** Remember that an item of evidence is relevant if it tends to "make the existence of any fact that is of consequence to the determination of the action more probable or less probable than it would be without the evidence." FRE 401.

☛ **Brick is not a wall:** In analyzing relevance, remember that *"a brick is not a wall"* (and feel free to quote this "rule"). In other words, if an item of evidence (call it *A*) is offered as tending to prove fact *X*, the fact that *X* is still less likely to be true than not true after proof of *A* does not block *A* from being relevant, as long as *X* is more likely to be true with *A* than without *A*. (*Example*: D, a black man, is charged with robbing a bank. The prosecution offers a surveillance tape of the robbery, which shows that the robber is black but which does not show enough detail to demonstrate that the robber is or is not D. The tape will be relevant, and admissible, because it tends to show that the robber was black, and this fact makes it more likely that the robber is D than would be the case if the tape was not in evidence — it doesn't matter that the tape is not by itself enough to make it more likely than not that D was the robber.)

☛ **Relatively rare:** Instances of evidence that is really *irrelevant* are relatively *rare*. On multiple choice questions, an answer like "The testimony is relevant, and thus admissible" is more likely to be correct than an answer like "The testimony is inadmissible because it's irrelevant."

☛ **Legal irrelevance:** The most common situation where the evidence is *irrelevant* involves *legal* irrelevance — if the item in question simply doesn't tie in with the *legal elements* for a claim or defense, it will be irrelevant. *Examples:*

❑ D is in a car accident, and is convicted of the criminal offense of operating an unregistered vehicle. In a later suit, the sole issue is whether D behaved negligently during the accident. The conviction will be irrelevant, because driving an unregistered vehicle doesn't make it more likely that D drove negligently.

❑ P sues solely for the wrongful death of her husband, H. P offers evidence that H suffered severe pain before dying. This evidence is irrelevant, because pain is not an element of damages in a wrongful death suit (though the pain would be relevant to a survival action brought by H's estate).

☛ **Probative value outweighed:** Also frequently tested: even where evidence is relevant, it's excludible if its probative value is *outweighed* by its tendency to cause *prejudice*, *confusion* or *waste of time*. (FRE 403) Prejudice is the most commonly tested aspect of this rule.

☞ **Graphic material:** Most common: *graphic*, visually shocking material. (*Example:* In a murder case, photos of V's body taken after autopsy, when V looked gorier than after the murder itself, might be excluded as likely to cause prejudice greater than the probative value, especially if pre-autopsy photos are available.) Remember that the prejudice/probative value balancing is largely within the judge's ***discretion***.

CHAPTER 3

CIRCUMSTANTIAL PROOF: SPECIAL PROBLEMS

ChapterScope

This chapter considers special problems that exist only with respect to circumstantial, as opposed to direct, evidence.

■ Most of the chapter deals with evidence of *"character."*

❏ **Core rule:** The core rule about character evidence is that in general, *evidence of a person's character* (or of a trait of character) is *not admissible to prove that the person acted in conformity with that character on a given occasion.* (*Example:* D can't be shown to be a habitual thief, to demonstrate that it's likely he stole on the occasion for which he's now being tried.)

❏ **Exceptions:** But there are some *exceptions* and *clarifications* to this rule. For instance:

❏ **Element of case:** A person's character (or, at least, a person's prior crimes and misdeeds) can be used to show not that he acted in conformity on the present occasion, but that *some element of the case is satisfied*. Thus a person's past actions can be used to show that he had certain knowledge, to show his identity as the person who committed a particular act, to show his motive, etc.

Example: If D is charged with defrauding an elderly homeowner in a siding scam, and he claims that he didn't intend to defraud, evidence that he defrauded others in the same way would probably be admissible to show intent or lack of mistake.

❏ **Proof of D's good character:** A *criminal defendant* may show evidence of a (good) pertinent trait of his own character. (*Example:* If D is charged with assault, he can show he's generally peaceful.) The prosecution may then *rebut* (but not initiate) by showing the defendant's *bad* character trait. FRE 404(a)(2)(A).

❏ **Victim's trait:** A criminal defendant may generally show evidence of a pertinent character trait of the *victim*. (But showing the sexual behavior of rape victims is severely restricted.)

■ **Habits:** Evidence of a person's *"habit"* is *admissible*.

■ **Remedial measures:** Evidence is *not* generally allowed that a person took *"subsequent remedial measures"* following a mishap, if offered to show that person's negligence or culpability.

■ **Insurance:** The fact that a person carried or did not carry *liability insurance* is not admissible on the issue of whether he acted negligently.

■ **Settlements:** The fact that a person has *offered to settle a claim* may not be admitted on the issue of the claim's validity.

❏ **Admissions of fact:** Collateral *"admissions of fact"* made during the course of settlement negotiations are also inadmissible, under the FRE.

■ **Medical expenses:** The fact that a party has paid, or offered to pay, the *medical expenses* of an injured person is *not admissible* to show that party's liability for the accident that caused the injury. (But related *admissions of fact are* admissible.)

I. CHARACTER EVIDENCE IN GENERAL

A. **Nature of the problem:** The fundamental problem of *"character evidence"* is this: To what extent may evidence of a person's character be used to show that in the particular instance in dispute, he acted in *conformity* with that character? The issue arises in many different contexts. Here are some illustrations:

> **Example 1:** D, a mail carrier, is charged with stealing from the mails. The prosecution wants to introduce evidence that D has been convicted in the past for stealing from the mail, as well as for embezzlement and robbery.

> **Example 2:** P and D are in a car collision, and P sues D for negligent driving. P offers to prove that D has been involved in numerous car accidents in the past, some of which involved D's being intoxicated or otherwise driving improperly.

> **Example 3:** D is charged with killing P in a fight. As part of D's claim of self-defense, D offers evidence to show that P had a reputation for violence, as well as evidence that he himself has always been a peaceful person.

1. **The problem:** In all of these instances, the offered evidence of "character" is probably at least loosely relevant. For instance, in Example 1, the fact that D has been convicted (or even merely charged with) larcenous offenses in the past probably makes it more likely that he is guilty of the present charged offense than if he had not been the subject of prior charges. Similarly, on the facts of Example 3, a jury could reasonably conclude that a person with a reputation for violence is more likely to have started a fight than a person without such a reputation.

2. **Countervailing considerations:** There are two major problems with this type of evidence, however:

   a. **Change:** First, we do not always act in conformity with our "character" — our moods change, and contexts change, and the notion of "character" is an imprecise one anyway. Therefore, a strong case can be made that the fact-finder should concentrate on evidence bearing directly on what happened in an episode in question, and less on evidence of the form "X is a ___-type of person; therefore, he probably acted in conformity with this character trait."

   b. **Prejudice:** Second, the risk of *unfair prejudice* is unusually great when character evidence is involved — the jury is especially likely to punish (or reward) X for being the "kind of person he is" rather than for what he did on the particular occasion in question.

      i. **Criminal cases:** This is particularly true in *criminal* cases where evidence of the defendant's bad character (e.g., evidence that he has committed other, similar crimes in the past) may induce the jury to convict him not because of evidence that he actually committed the deed in question, but because he is a "bad person."

3. **General rules:** In theory, the admissibility of character evidence could be left to trial judges to handle on a case-by-case balancing basis, whereby the evidence would only be admitted if its probative value was greater than its unfairly prejudicial effect. But this scheme would be the farthest thing from a "bright line" rule, and would be hard to administer. Instead, the courts have formulated specific rules, and exceptions, to deal with the major contexts in which character evidence is sought to be introduced.

   a. **General rule and exceptions:** As is discussed more extensively below, the general rule in most jurisdictions is that character evidence may not be admitted to show that a person acted in conformity with his character. However, there are a number of vital exceptions to this rule.

4. **Distinctions:** Two sets of distinctions should be kept in mind during the discussion which follows:

   a. **Character in issue:** First, situations in which character evidence is used as circumstantial evidence of conduct must be distinguished from those in which character is itself *in issue* in the case. In the character-as-circumstantial-evidence situation, the presumption is against the admissibility of the character evidence, because there is generally more direct evidence of the conduct in question. But where character is itself in issue (e.g., an action for defamation, in which the plaintiff complains that the defendant has said the plaintiff's character is bad, and the defendant raises the defense of truth), character evidence will be permitted since it is the *only* evidence available on a material issue. The "character in issue" problem is discussed *infra* at p. 24.

   b. **Types of circumstantial evidence:** The second distinction is that among the various types of circumstantial character evidence. There are three types, ranging from least to most specific: (1) evidence of a person's *reputation* for possessing a certain character trait; (2) the witness's own *opinion* as to whether a person has a particular character trait; and (3) evidence of particular *acts* showing that the person has a particular character trait.

      i. **Significance:** As we progress from the most general to the most specific of these kinds of evidence, the "pungency and persuasiveness" of the evidence increases. But so does its tendency to inspire undue prejudice, and to confuse and distract the jury from other issues. McC, p. 339.

      ii. **Traditional rule:** Therefore, the traditional rule has been that in those few instances where circumstantial evidence of character may be admitted, only the neutral and unexciting *reputation* evidence could be used. *Id.*

      iii. **Federal Rules:** The Federal Rules have made a major change in this traditional approach. Under FRE 405(a), *opinion*, as well as reputation, evidence may be admitted. (Evidence of specific acts may not be brought out in direct examination of the witness; but on cross-examination of a witness who has already given opinion or reputation testimony, "the court may allow an inquiry into relevant specific instances of the person's conduct.")

iv. **Character in issue:** Where a person's character is directly in issue (the situation discussed directly below), specific instances have almost always been permitted; FRE 405(b) continues this permissive rule. See *infra*, p. 50.

II. CHARACTER IN ISSUE

A. General rule: A person's general character, or a particular character trait that he has, may be an *essential element* of the case, in the sense that, under the substantive law, that character or trait determines the rights and liabilities of the parties. In such a situation, character evidence is *not only allowable, it is essential.*

> **Example:** D, a newspaper, prints an article calling P "the sort of man who would steal his mother's bones from the grave and sell them to buy flowers for a harlot." P sues D for libel. D may introduce evidence of P's despicable character, both to support the defense of truth and to minimize the damages (on the theory that P's reputation was already low and could not have been much damaged by the article). Since P's character is "in issue," the evidence about it is admissible. W&P, pp. 366-67.

B. Federal Rules: The FRE do not specifically state this principle that character is provable where directly in issue. But the language of FRE 404 indicates that this is true. FRE 404(a) states the general rule that "When evidence of a person's character or character trait is admissible, it may be proved by testimony about the person's reputation or by testimony in the form of an opinion." FRE 404(b) then says that "When a person's character or character trait is an *essential element of a charge, claim, or defense*, the character or trait may *also be proved* by relevant specific instances of the person's conduct." So the "may also be proved" language strongly implies that character as an essential element may be proved by all three methods: reputation, opinion and specific instances.

1. **Advisory Committe Notes:** Furthermore, the Advisory Committee Note to 404(a) says that where character is "an element of a crime, claim, or defense . . . *[n]o problem of the general relevancy of character evidence is involved*, and the present rule therefore has no provision on the subject." So the FRE clearly intend for such "character in issue" evidence to be freely admissible.

C. Rare: Situations in which character is truly in issue are relatively *rare*.

1. **Civil:** In the *civil* area, here are the principal ways character can be in issue:

   ❏ In a *tort* case, the essence of the claim may be that the defendant *entrusted some instrumentality* to a third person, and was negligent in doing so because the defendant knew or should have known that the third person had a poor character for care. Example 1 above (employment of drunk signalman by railroad) is an illustration. So would be a case against a car owner for negligently letting a friend drive drunk; the driver's character for drunkenness could be shown.

   ❏ In a *defamation* case, the plaintiff's character might be in issue in two different ways:

   (1) if the allegedly-defamatory statement is phrased in terms of P's character ("P is a crook"), D will be allowed to show that P indeed has the character trait (e.g., that P really *is* a crook);

(2) if P claims his reputation has been damaged, D is clearly entitled to show that P already had a poor reputation before the defamatory statement, and some courts — not very logically — let D show that P has a poor character to support an inference that P's reputation was poor (or that P's reputation *ought* to be poor). Example 2 above demonstrates both of these uses.

❑ In a ***wrongful death*** action, P's poor character may be proved, to show that her survivors haven't been financially or emotionally damaged very much. (For instance, evidence of the decedent's compulsive gambling would be relevant to his likely future earnings.)

See M&K §4.20, pp. 223-24.

2. Criminal: In ***criminal*** cases, the situations in which D's character is truly in issue are even rarer.

    a. Entrapment: The main situation is where D claims ***entrapment***. The prosecution is permitted to show that D was "predisposed" to commit the crime (in which case there's no entrapment). In a sense, D's predisposition to commit crimes like the one now charged is an aspect of his character. Clearly, evidence that D has committed similar crimes in the past is admissible to show his predisposition. M&K §4.20, p. 222-23.

D. Type of evidence: Most courts, and the Federal Rules, allow all three types of evidence of character when character is in issue. That is, the evidence may consist of: (1) ***specific acts*** to demonstrate character; (2) a witness's ***opinion*** of that character; or (3) evidence as to the subject's ***reputation*** for the character trait in issue.

1. Specific instances: Since FRE 405(a) ***always*** allows reputation and opinion evidence wherever character evidence is admissible at all, it is only proof of "***specific instances***" that needs a special provision to deal with the character-in-issue situation. As noted, 405(b) provides that "When a person's character or character trait is an essential element of a charge, claim, or defense, the character or trait may also be proved by ***relevant specific instances of the person's conduct***." See *infra*, p. 50.

III. CHARACTER AS CIRCUMSTANTIAL EVIDENCE — GENERALLY

A. General rule: We now turn to the use of character as ***circumstantial evidence*** of what a person did (or thought) on a particular occasion. The theory behind such evidence runs something like this: "Because X has the character trait of [honesty, trickery, intoxication, or whatever], during the episode in question he probably acted [honestly, trickily, drunkenly, or whatever]."

1. General rule of exclusion: As a general rule, ***such use of character evidence for circumstantial purposes is not admissible***.

    a. Federal rule: The Federal Rules ***follow*** this approach. FRE 404(a)(1) provides that "Evidence of a person's ***character or character trait*** is ***not admissible*** to prove that ***on a particular occasion*** the person ***acted in accordance with the character or trait***[,]" except under a few special circumstances.

Example: P brings a civil suit against D, alleging that D negligently drove his vehicle thereby injuring P. P offers evidence that D has been found to have driven negligently several times in the past, in suits by other accident victims. He also offers evidence that D has a reputation for being a careless driver, and offers the testimony of a witness who would express the opinion that D is a careless driver. All three of these types of evidence will be ruled inadmissible, because they are offered for the purpose of demonstrating that D is a careless driver who probably acted in conformity with this trait for carelessness during the accident involving P.

IV. USE OF CIRCUMSTANTIAL CHARACTER EVIDENCE IN CIVIL CASES

A. General rule: The general rule that circumstantial evidence of character is inadmissible, is applied in *civil* cases. The prior example is an illustration of this principle.

B. Character for care: The issue arises most frequently where a party in a case involving claims of negligence tries to prove that the other party had a character trait of *carelessness*, or that he himself had a trait of *carefulness*. Regardless of whether it is carelessness or carefulness that is sought to be proved, the virtually universal rule is that the evidence is *inadmissible*.

   1. Rationale: This rule of exclusion is based upon the theory that the probative value of such "character for care" evidence is nearly always outweighed by its tendency to arouse unfair prejudice and to distract or confuse the jury. The probative value of such evidence is questionable, principally because even generally careful or generally careless people act, in some instances, quite out of conformity with their usual character.

C. Quasi-criminal acts alleged: Suppose that one party to a civil suit charges the other with conduct that, in addition to being actionable, is *criminal*. As will be seen *infra*, p. 38, a criminal defendant receives the benefit of an exception to the no-character-evidence rule that permits him to introduce evidence of his own good character. Should a party to a civil suit who is charged with acts constituting crimes be given the benefit of a similar exception? The issue arises most frequently in tort cases for assault and/or battery, where the defendant wishes to show that the other party was the aggressor.

   1. Majority view: The majority view, implicitly adopted by the Federal Rules,[1] is that even in this "conduct constituting a crime" situation, rebuttal evidence of good character is *inadmissible*.

   Example: P, the beneficiary of an insurance policy on X's life, sues D, the insurance company, when D refuses to pay on the policy. The policy excludes coverage in cases where the decedent dies from his own criminal action. At trial, D shows that X was

---

1. FRE 404(a)(1) says that "Evidence of a person's character or character trait is not admissible to prove that on a particular occasion the person acted in accordance with the character or trait." FRE 404(a)(2), which gives the only exceptions to 404(a)(1)'s general no-character-evidence rule, says that the exceptions appy "in a criminal case." So by negative implication, the exceptions don't apply to a *quasi*-criminal case or act.

killed when he trespassed upon a cottage and was shot by a spring gun. P offers evidence that X was a peaceable and law abiding citizen.

Held, the evidence of X's character is inadmissible. "It is the generally accepted rule that in civil actions, even where fraud is imputed or dishonesty is charged, evidence of a party's good or bad character is incompetent in evidence unless it be made an issue by the pleadings or the proof." *Mutual Life Ins. Co. v. Kelly*, 197 N.E. 235 (Ohio 1934).

V. OTHER CRIMES AND WRONGS AS EVIDENCE, ESPECIALLY IN CRIMINAL CASES

A. General principle: A prosecutor would always love to be able to introduce evidence that the defendant has committed *other, similar crimes* (or other *"bad acts"*) in the past. The theory behind such evidence is that it shows that the defendant has a bad or criminal disposition, making it more likely that he committed the crime in question. But the universally-applied principle is that *such evidence of other crimes or bad acts is not admissible when offered for the purpose of suggesting that because the defendant is a person of criminal character, it is more probable that he committed the crime with which he is charged.* McC, p. 345.

> **Example:** D is charged with the murder of V. The prosecution shows that V and some others insulted D's wife, leading D to threaten to "bump them all off" if they didn't leave within five minutes. D then returned to his apartment, selected a gun from his weapons collection, went back out to the scene of the insult, and as part of an argument, shot V to death. At trial, the prosecution seeks to introduce into evidence the fact that, at the time of the encounter and of the subsequent arrest of D, D kept three pistols and a teargas gun in his apartment. (There is no claim that D had all of these weapons with him at the time of the shooting.)
>
> *Held* (on appeal), the weapons at the apartment should not have been admitted. They were introduced to persuade the jury that "here was a man of vicious and dangerous propensities, who because of those propensities was more likely to kill with deliberate and premeditated design than a man of irreproachable life and amiable manners." It is a fundamental principle that "character is never an issue in a criminal prosecution unless the defendant chooses to make it one. . . . In a very real sense a defendant starts his life afresh when he stands before a jury, a prisoner at the bar. . . ." *People v. Zackowitz*, 172 N.E. 466 (N.Y. 1930).

B. FRE 404: The Federal Rules embody this principle that prior crimes may not be introduced to show the defendant's character, thereby justifying the inference that he acted in conformity with that character on the present occasion. FRE 404(b)(1) does this, by saying that "Evidence of a *crime, wrong, or other act* is *not admissible* to prove a *person's character* in order to show that *on a particular occasion the person acted in accordance with the character.*"

1. **Use for other purposes:** But FRE 404(b) then goes on to set forth another principle shared with the common-law: other-crimes evidence *may* be introduced for *other purposes* than to show action in conformity with character. As 404(b)(2) puts it,

> "[Evidence of other crimes, wrongs or acts] may be admissible for *another purpose*, such

as proving *motive, opportunity, intent, preparation, plan, knowledge, identity, absence of mistake,* or *lack of accident.*"

These "other purposes" form the subject of most of the rest of our discussion of other-crimes evidence, from Paragraph (F) through (U) below.

C. Applies to other situations: Throughout this Section V, we speak of proving "prior crimes," and we assume as our situation that the prosecutor is trying to prove that the defendant committed these prior crimes. But the general rule against proving a person's "prior crimes" to show his propensity to do such things (embodied by FRE 404(a)) applies equally to a number of other situations.

1. **No conviction, or action not constituting a crime:** For instance, the prior act by the defendant need not be something for which he was convicted. Thus prior conduct by the defendant will come within 404(a)(1)'s ban even if: (1) it was an act that *never led to a criminal conviction*, but the act, if proven beyond a reasonable doubt, would have constituted a crime; or (2) it was a *morally-reprehensible* action that, even if proven beyond a reasonable doubt, would not have constituted a crime.

   Example 1 (unconvicted crime): D is charged with robbing a 7-11. FRE 404(a)(1) means, of course, that the prosecution can't introduce D's three prior *convictions* for robbing various commercial establishments, to show that D is a professional robber and that it's therefore more likely than it would otherwise be that D committed the robbery now charged. But 404(a)(1) *also* means that the prosecution can't show that D previously robbed a bank and was *never charged* (or that he was charged but never convicted), where this evidence is offered for the same "propensity to rob" purpose. Thus the prosecution couldn't put W on the stand to say, "D and I robbed the 1st National Bank a couple of years ago and got away with it," if the testimony is offered for this "propensity" purpose.

   Example 2 (bad act not amounting to a crime): D is charged with fraud, for having bilked an elderly widow out of her life's savings. The prosecutor wants to show that D owed money to various people, and failed to pay them back even though he had the funds to do so; the purpose of this evidence is to suggest that D behaves reprehensibly in money matters (making it more likely that he indeed bilked the widow). Even though the non-repayments aren't made crimes by the jurisdiction, 404(a)(1)'s ban on the use of character evidence to prove conduct on the present occasion applies, and the evidence won't be allowed. (This evidence might be usable for impeachment purposes, if D takes the stand; see the discussion of FRE 608(b), *infra*, p. 130.)

   Nonetheless, in our discussions in this Section V we use the short-hand "other-crimes evidence" to describe the type of evidence we're talking about.

2. **Use in civil cases:** Similarly, although the rule barring proof of other crimes to show propensity usually applies to criminal cases, it also applies to *civil suits*. Thus FRE 401(b)(1)'s ban is a general prohibition, that by implication applies to civil as well as criminal cases.

   Example: P, a bank, sues its former employee, D, contending that D has wrongfully taken funds from the bank. P seeks a money judgment for the missing funds. P will not be permitted to show that, say, D embezzled from a prior employer, if this evidence is offered for the purpose of showing that D has a propensity to embezzle from employers, making it more likely that he took the money on the present occasion. (But the evidence might be admissible to show a "common plan" on D's part, to embezzle from each of his employers in series; see *infra*, p. 31.)

3. **Use by defendant to show someone else did it:** The "no prior crimes to show propensity" rule also can occasionally apply to block proof offered *by* (rather than against) the defendant in a criminal case. For instance, suppose that D wants to show that someone else (let's call her "X") committed the crime for which D is now charged. D won't be able to put on evidence of past similar crimes by X to show that X may well have committed the present crime.

D. **Proof offered for purpose other than to show propensity:** Suppose that the prosecution offers evidence of the defendant's prior crimes *not* to show that he has a criminal disposition, but to show the existence of *some fact relevant to the crime*. For instance, the prosecution may be trying to establish circumstantially some *element of the crime* charged (e.g., D's intent). To put it another way, we're interested now in prior-crimes evidence offered for some *"other purpose"* than to show propensity.

1. **Admissible:** In this "other purpose" situation, the general rule of exclusion does *not* apply. So long as the probative value of the evidence outweighs its tendency to cause undue prejudice, confusion, etc., the evidence will be *admitted.*

   Example: On the facts of *Zackowitz, supra,* p. 27, suppose that the several weapons not used in the shooting had been brought by D to the scene of the crime and had been left there. If D had denied that he was the person who shot X, the weapons would have been admissible on the issue of *identity*. This would be the case even though proof that D had possessed the weapons would establish his guilt of another crime (illegal possession of weapons), and even though the fact-finder might infer from those weapons D's propensity for crime and violence. That is, so long as evidence of other crimes is relevant to *some issue* in the case (here, identity) it is admissible even though it may *also* show criminal disposition (again, assuming that its probative value is not outweighed by undue prejudice, confusion, etc.).

2. **Frequently litigated:** Every trial lawyer knows the general rule of "no other-crimes evidence to prove character and action in conformity therewith." Therefore, a litigator who wants to introduce other-crimes evidence will almost *always* try to convince the judge that the evidence is being offered for some "other purpose" than character-to-prove-action-in-conformity-therewith. (If the jury then happens to reason, "If he committed the other crime, he probably committed this one" — the forbidden inference — well then that's just too bad, the proponent will say to herself.)

   a. **Duty to distinguish:** Your job as law student is thus to *distinguish* the situations in which "other purposes" are truly being served, from those in which the forbidden action-in-conformity-with-character use is what the proponent is really trying to accomplish.

3. **No catalogue:** Some courts and statutes impose a list of particular elements (e.g., intent, motive, knowledge, identity, etc.) as to which other-crimes evidence is admissible; if the

evidence is not relevant to one of those enumerated elements, it is not admissible. But the majority rule, and that followed by the Federal Rules, is more inclusive.

a. **Federal Rule's formulation:** Thus, FRE 404(b)(2) enumerates some specific elements which may be proven by other-crimes evidence, but, by using the phrase "such as," does not foreclose the possibility of others:

> *"Permitted Uses; Notice in a Criminal Case.* [Evidence of a crime, wrong, or other act] may be admissible for another purpose, *such as* proving motive, opportunity, intent, preparation, plan, knowledge, identity, absence of mistake, or lack of accident."

The Advisory Committee's Note on this subdivision observes that "no mechanical solution is offered." Instead, the probative value of the evidence is to be weighed against the danger of undue prejudice "in view of the availability of other means of proof and other factors appropriate for making decisions of this kind under Rule 403."

  i. **Advance notice required:** Because other-crimes evidence may unfairly catch the defendant by surprise, FRE 404(b)(2) requires the prosecution in a criminal case to give the defendant *advance notice*, normally before the start of trial, of its intention to use the other-crimes evidence. (FRE 404(b)(2)(A) and (B).)

4. **Use by D:** Usually, it's the prosecution that wants to use 404(b)(2), to prove other crimes by the defendant, to show motive, identity, etc. But 404(b)(2) is not by its terms limited to use against defendants, and occasionally it is used *by* a defendant (so-called "*reverse 404(b) evidence*"). M&K §4.15, p. 198. For instance, the defendant may present 404(b)(2) evidence that some third person has committed prior crimes, in order to show that *the third person, not D, committed the present crime.* This happens most often where the evidence is *"modus operandi"* or "signature" evidence (see *infra*, p. 31), i.e., evidence that the prior crimes and the present crime are so similar in the way they were carried out that the person who did the prior crimes probably did the present one.

E. **Specific situations:** Paragraphs (F) through (U) below cover some of the special purposes for which other-crimes evidence has been admitted:

F. **Context:** Other-crimes evidence may be used to place the crime in *context*, by describing other events or conduct that were part of the *same transaction*.

> **Example:** Suppose that D is charged with murdering V, a policeman. The evidence shows that the murder occurred when V was trying to arrest D on a robbery charge. V's partner on the police force, W, testifies that while V and W were trying to arrest D, D not only shot V to death but also shot and wounded W. The "telling of the story" of the murder inevitably involves evidence of an additional crime by D — the attempted murder of W. Because this information is part of the overall context in which the murder took place, the other-crimes evidence is admissible. (Probably the evidence that D may have been guilty of robbery, the charge for which V and W were trying to arrest him, would also fall within the "same transaction" exception.)

G. **Larger plan:** Other-crimes evidence may be used to prove the existence "of a larger *plan, scheme,* or *conspiracy,* of which the crime on trial is a *part.*" McC, p. 345.

> **Example:** D is charged with stealing money from the person of V. The state shows that D came to V's place of business, put her hands all over him and propositioned him for sex, while picking his pocket. X and Y testify that in separate incidents, D came to their offices and picked their pockets in a similar way.
>
> *Held*, the evidence of the crimes upon X and Y was admissible because it showed that D's acts concerning V were part of a "common plan or scheme." *Jones v. State*, 376 S.W.2d 842 (Texas 1964).

1. **Why "common plan or scheme" is relevant:** The existence of a "common plan or scheme" is not itself generally an element of a crime (though it would be if the crime charged were that of conspiracy). However, the existence of a common plan or scheme in turn tends to show the defendant's intent, motive, identity, or other actual element of the crime charged. This illustrates the principle that for other crimes evidence to be admissible, it need not directly establish an element of the crime; all that is required is that it be reasonably strong circumstantial evidence of some element of the crime charged. Lilly, p. 149.

H. **Preparation:** Other-crimes evidence may be used to show ***preparation*** for the crime charged. Like "common plan or scheme," a showing of preparation is likely to reveal the defendant's state of mind — for instance, to show purposefulness and to negate the possibility of accident. It also increases the likelihood that the act prepared for in fact took place. Lilly, p. 157.

> **Example:** Recall *People v. Zackowitz* (*supra*, p. 27), in which D, after hearing his wife be insulted by V, went back to his apartment and selected a gun before returning to the scene and shooting V. If D argued self defense, or involuntary manslaughter of the "heat of passion" variety, evidence of D's deliberativeness in selecting an appropriate weapon would be admissible because it would negate these defenses.

I. **"Identity" by showing "signature":** Prior crimes may be used to show the ***"identity"*** of the present perpetrator (i.e., that it's D, not someone else for whom D has been mistaken). Thus FRE 404(b)(2) lists "identity" (together with "motive," "opportunity," etc.) as one of the "other purposes" for which other-crimes evidence may be introduced. Generally, when other crimes are offered to show "identity," the prosecution's theory is that the other crimes by the accused are ***so similar in method*** to the crime charged that all bear his ***"signature"*** (thus justifying the inference that if D committed the prior crimes, he also must have committed the present one).

1. **Requirements:** This kind of evidence of "signature" crimes is only admissible where two requirements are satisfied:

   a. **Denial by accused:** First, the accused must ***deny his participation*** in the crime charged. Thus if, in a murder case, D admits that he killed V by breaking his neck with a karate kick, and the only issue is D's state of mind, the prosecution may not use the "signature" rationale to show that D committed other killings with a neck-snapping karate kick (though these other killings may be admissible to negate, say, D's claim of self-defense).

b. Proof of identity: Second, the unique method involved in the other crime(s) (the "signature") must be *so very similar* to the method used in the crime charged that the court will find it "substantially probative of identity." Lilly, p. 159. "A mere showing that D has committed other crimes in the same class as the offense charged is insufficiently probative of identity to justify admission." *Id.*

Example: D is on trial for robbing a convenience store after midnight while wearing a mask similar to the very distinctive one worn in the movie "Clockwork Orange." The prosecution shows the jury a surveillance tape in which the masked robber can be seen wearing such a mask. D testifies that he wasn't the robber, and that the man in the tape must be someone else. The prosecution asks D, "Isn't it true that you were convicted two years ago of robbing another convenience store while wearing a 'Clockwork Orange' mask?" (It's true that D was so convicted.)

The question is proper — the evidence of D's conviction is available not only to impeach him, but as substantive proof that he robbed the other store wearing such a mask. The substantive admissibility results from the fact that the other crime tends to prove D's identity as the masked robber on the present occasion, and is thus non-character other-crimes evidence offered for "another purpose, such as proving ... identity[.]" FRE 404(b).

2. *Modus operandi:* A crude way to determine whether the precise method used in all of the crimes is so similar and so idiosyncratic that it amounts to a unique *"signature,"* is to ask whether the method can plausibly be described as what readers of detective fiction would call a *"modus operandi"* or "m.o." (Latin for "method of operation.") The similarity has to be so great that it's *extremely unlikely that two different criminals were involved*.

Example 1 (sufficiently similar): Recall the facts of *Jones v. State*, *supra*, p. 31, in which D was charged with entering V's place of business, sexually propositioning him while putting her hands on his body, and then pickpocketing him. Other business people who had different places of business were permitted to testify that D had picked their pockets by use of exactly the same ruse. The "signature" rationale could have been used to admit this evidence of other crimes, since the overall *modus operandi* used was so idiosyncratic that it strongly suggested that all of the crimes must have been by the same person (and the victims of the other crimes identified D as the perpetrator).

But the "signature" rationale would *not* have been usable had D conceded that she visited V, and the only dispute was whether she picked his pocket. That's because the first of the two requirements for a finding of signature — that D's participation in the present episode be disputed — would not be satisfied. (But the other crimes evidence would still have been admissible under the "common plan or scheme" exception, since it suggested that pickpocketing was the whole object of D's repeated office visits.)

Example 2 (not sufficiently similar): D is charged with distributing heroin and cocaine. The essence of the prosecution's case is testimony by an undercover officer, Alonzo, that he purchased a narcotics-filled balloon from D, while they were near the Three Kings Lounge. (D was not immediately arrested; instead, some time after the buy Alonzo picked D's photo out of police files as the seller, and only then was D arrested.) D claims mistaken identity, and offers the alibi defense that he was a few blocks away when the sale to Alonzo took place. The prosecution then offers testimony by two police officers that on one prior occasion, these officers saw D sell drugs near the Three Kings Lounge, and that on another occasion, they arrested him for drug possession (again, near the Three Kings), and found several heroin-filled balloons in his possession.

Held (on appeal), these other crimes by D were improperly admitted. Although the identity of the drug seller was at issue, the prior crimes were **not sufficiently similar** to the present crime to allow those prior crimes as evidence of D's identity as the present seller. Where the government's reasoning is that the prior crimes are so similar to the present crime that they must have been committed by the same person, there must be "such a high degree of similarity as to mark [the present crime] as the handiwork of the accused." This *"modus operandi"* method of showing identity requires that the method used be **uniquely different** from the standard practice. Here, it is so common for drug dealers to sell narcotics in balloons (because these can be quickly swallowed if arrest seems imminent) that the method used in the prior crimes was not sufficiently similar to the present crime. *U.S. v. Carrillo,* 981 F.2d 772 (5th Cir. 1993).

3. **Non-signature ways to prove D's "identity":** "Signature" or "m.o." is the most common, but **not the only**, rationale under which D's prior crimes may be introduced for purposes of showing his "identity." If some other rationale is being used to support the inference that the prior crimes establish D's identity as the present criminal, the proponent of the other-crimes evidence will usually **not** have to show that the prior and present crimes are so similar as to necessarily involve the same criminal. See W&G, §5246, p. 512.

   Example: Suppose that D is charged with selling drugs to X (a police informer) on June 1. X testifies at trial for the prosecution, and is asked by the prosecutor, "How do you know the one who sold you the drugs on June 1 was D?" X answers that he knows the one selling him the drugs on June 1 was D because on several previous occasions, he had bought drugs from D and had thus learned to recognize D's face. Here, the prior crimes are being introduced (properly) to show the present criminal's "identity," but the "signature/m.o." rationale isn't being used. Consequently, the prosecution will not have to prove that the similarities between the past and present drug sales were so great that both crimes must have been by the same person.

J. **Intent:** Other-crimes evidence may be used to show that the defendant acted *maliciously*, *deliberately*, or with the *specific intent* required for the crime.

   1. **Rebutting an innocent explanation:** Generally, the way other-crimes evidence becomes relevant to the defendant's mental state is that the defendant admits the act charged, but asserts an *innocent explanation* for that act; evidence of similar acts is admitted on the theory that "the oftener [sic] a like act has been done, the less probable it is that it could have been done innocently." 2 Wigmore §312.

   2. **Requirement of similarity:** For the defendant's guilty state of mind relative to the crime charged to be proved by the other crimes, there must be a substantial degree of *similarity* between the crime charged and the other crimes. For instance, the fact that D has commit-

ted many burglaries would not indicate the untruthfulness of his claim of self-defense in a murder case; but it might indicate the untruthfulness of his claim that, when he was arrested on a window ledge outside of V's apartment, he was there because he was fleeing from muggers in the street.

  3. Degree of similarity: Some courts have required a very high degree of similarity between the other crime and the act charged, in the sense that the "essential physical elements" of the two crimes must be alike. But the *majority* view now seems to be that the two must be alike *only in the sense that a guilty state of mind as to the other crime suggests a guilty state of mind as to the act charged.* See, e.g., *U.S. v. Beechum,* 582 F.2d 898 (5th Cir. 1978).

K. Sexual misconduct: The FRE, and some states, have special rules loosening the admissibility of evidence that the defendant has committed other crimes involving *sexual misconduct.* For instance, FRE 413 allows evidence of the defendant's past crimes of *sexual assault* to be introduced against him "on any matter to which it is relevant" — including as propensity evidence — if the present case is a prosecution for sexual assault. Similar rules apply to child molestation prosecutions (FRE 414) and civil suits involving sexual misconduct (FRE 415). These three rules are discussed extensively *infra,* p. 53.

L. Knowledge: Other-crimes evidence may be used to show, by similar acts, that the act in question "was *not performed inadvertently,* accidentally, involuntarily, or without guilty knowledge." McC, p. 346.

  1. Similar to intent: The line between other-crimes evidence used to prove intent (*supra,* p. 33) and other-crimes evidence used to prove knowledge is often a very blurry one. Where the other crimes are used to rebut the defendant's claim that he was unaware that a criminal act was taking place, the distinction is usually meaningless. But the exception is quite distinct in those situations where knowledge is *statutorily* made an *essential element* of the offense.

    Example: D is prosecuted for knowingly receiving stolen goods (blank video cassette tapes). D, who bought the tapes from one Wesby, claims that he did not know they were stolen. The prosecution offers evidence showing that on prior and subsequent occasions, D bought other stolen goods from Wesby, thus suggesting that D must have known that the tapes were stolen. This evidence of other possessions will be admitted, since it tends to prove knowledge, an element of the offense. See *Huddleston v. U.S.,* 485 U.S. 681 (1988), in which the Supreme Court affirmed D's conviction based in part on this evidence.

M. Motive: Other-crimes evidence may be used to establish *motive.* Since motive itself is never an essential element of a crime, the use of other-crimes evidence to establish motive is always part of a chain of reasoning. Thus the proof of motive may be probative either of conduct (did D commit the act charged? — if D had a motive to do so, it is more likely that he did the act than if he had no motive) or of intent (given that D did the act, did he do so intentionally, purposefully, maliciously, etc.?) The following example illustrates the first of these uses of motive proof.

Example: D, a hospital nurse, is charged with removing the painkiller Demerol from syringes, and replacing the Demerol with a saline solution. D is one of five nurses who, during the time of tampering, had access to the locked cabinet in which the syringes were kept. At D's trial, the judge allows the prosecution to place in evidence several of D's past acts, including the fact that: (1) D's nursing license was previously suspended because she stole Demerol; (2) she was addicted to Demerol; and (3) the suspension occurred in part because she falsified drug-test results to conceal her addiction.

Held, these past acts were properly admitted, because they tended to show that D had a motive for stealing the Demerol. These acts were not admitted to show that D had a "propensity" to steal Demerol. Rather, they were admitted to show that D, unlike the other nurses, had an incentive (a motive) to steal it so that she could gain a "free" supply to feed her addiction. *U.S. v. Cunningham*, 103 F.3d 553 (7th Cir. 1996).

N. Opportunity: Other-crimes evidence may be used to establish ***opportunity*** to commit the crime. Usually, this exception will be used to show that the defendant had access to the scene of the crime, or was present at the scene at the time of the crime. It may also apply where the other-crimes evidence shows that the defendant had special skills or abilities used in committing the crime charged.

Example: D is charged with car theft; the theft is said to have occurred on July 1, 2010. D defends on the grounds that he was in prison for the entire year 2010. The prosecution responds by showing that D was convicted of having escaped from prison on June 30, and offers trial testimony demonstrating that D was not recaptured until July 4. Although the prosecution's evidence consists of proof of other crimes (escape), it will be allowed, because it shows that D had the opportunity to commit the crime.

O. Identity: Other-crimes evidence may be used to prove ***identity***.

    1. Must be issue: This exception can only apply, of course, where the identity of the person who committed a particular act is truly ***in issue***. Thus if the defendant admits that it was he who performed certain conduct (e.g., a shooting), and the only issue is the defendant's state of mind, other-crimes evidence suggesting that the act charged must have been the work of the defendant will not be admissible because it would be irrelevant.

    2. Relation to other exceptions: Generally, the other-crimes evidence will be relevant to identity only indirectly, through one of the other exceptions. For instance, the other crime and the crime charged may both bear the same clear "signature," i.e., reflect the same unusual *modus operandi* (*supra*, p. 32). If there is evidence establishing that the person who committed the other crime was D, the other crime will suggest that the perpetrator of the crime charged was also D. Similarly, other-crimes evidence that shows a common plan or scheme (*supra*, p. 31) will tend to establish that the crime charged was done by the same person who carried out other parts of the common plan.

P. Conviction as predicate to present crime: Many jurisdictions now define particular crimes in such a way that a ***prior conviction*** of some sort is an ***element of the crime.*** When this happens, the prosecution is entitled to show the prior conviction as an element of the present crime.

Example: A federal statute makes it a crime for a person who has been convicted of a felony to be in possession of a firearm. In a prosecution for such a firearms-possession charge, the government is of course entitled to show that D was previously convicted of a felony.

1. **Weighing prejudice against probative value:** However, keep in mind that here (as in all other-crimes-evidence scenarios), the court must always weigh the danger of unfair prejudice against probative value, as required by FRE 403. Therefore, although the prosecution is entitled to show the prior crime, the precise pieces of evidence which it uses to make the showing may be limited by Rule 403. For instance, in *Old Chief v. U.S.*, 519 U.S. 172 (1997) (*supra*, p. 17), the Supreme Court held that the trial court should have accepted D's *stipulation* that he was convicted of a felony, rather than allowing the prosecution to show the jury the actual record of the prior conviction, with its detailed description of D's prior crime.

Q. **Impeachment:** Other-crimes evidence may be used to *impeach* an accused who takes the stand, by showing a prior conviction. In this situation, the evidence is being used not to prove directly that the defendant is guilty of the crime charged, but rather, to suggest that because he is a convicted criminal, his credibility as a witness is suspect. The use of criminal convictions to impeach an accused on the witness stand is discussed extensively *infra*, p. 120.

R. **Other exceptions:** Under the Federal Rules approach, as noted, a piece of other-crimes evidence does not have to fit into an enumerated "slot" to be admissible; the categories enumerated in FRE 404(b)(2) ("such as proving motive, opportunity, intent, preparation. . . .") are intended to be illustrative rather than exhaustive. The point is that the evidence must relate to some *particular element* of the crime charged, and must not be offered solely to suggest that because the accused had certain criminal traits, he probably acted in conformity with those traits on the occasion at issue.

S. **Other aspects:** Even where the other-crimes evidence is offered for one of the "other purposes" discussed above (and thus appears to be admissible), other issues may arise. Here are a few:

1. **Degree of certainty:** Must the other crime have led to a *conviction*, and thus have been proved beyond a reasonable doubt? The answer is *"no."*

   a. **Proof beyond a reasonable doubt not required:** Virtually no courts require that the defendant have been actually convicted of the other crime, or that the defendant's guilt in the prior crime be proven beyond a reasonable doubt in the present case.

   b. **Federal standard:** In fact, the Supreme Court has held that under the Federal Rules, evidence of the defendant's guilt in the other crime can be given to the jury even though that other crime has *not* been proved even by a *preponderance* of the evidence (let alone by "clear and convincing" evidence). In *Huddleston v. U.S.*, 485 U.S. 681 (1988), the Court held that all that what is now FRE 404(b)(2) requires is that the evidence of the other crime be strong enough that the jury could *"reasonably find"* that the other crime was committed by D.

      i. **Application to facts:** Thus in *Huddleston*, the evidence of the other crime (D's knowing purchase of stolen TV sets from X) was found to have been properly admitted on the issue of whether D knew that blank tapes he bought from X were stolen — the low price of the televisions, the large quantity D had for sale, and D's inability to produce a bill of sale, coupled with D's involvement in still other purchases of stolen goods from X, were enough to allow a reasonable jury to conclude that D knew the TV sets were stolen, and therefore, enough to let the jury consider this other-crimes evidence.

c. **Disapproved:** But many commentators and state courts have **criticized** *Huddleston*'s very low "jury could reasonably find that the other crime was committed" standard. Thus one authority says that "*Huddleston* seems wrong . . . to ignore the danger of allowing highly prejudicial evidence of defendant's alleged misconduct to come before the jury when the prosecutor has not even persuaded the trial court that such misconduct occurred." M&K §4.15, pp. 198.

d. **Acquittal:** Suppose the accused was tried and **acquitted** of the other crime. Should this acquittal by itself make the evidence of that crime inadmissible?

   i. **Pros and cons:**   There are strong arguments on either side of this question. Against admission, consider that admission causes the defendant, as a practical matter, to "defend against the same charge a second time . . . raising policy concerns that are related to those underlying collateral estoppel and the prohibition against double jeopardy. . . ." Lilly, p. 151. In favor of admission, acquittal means only that the finder of fact concluded that there was a *reasonable doubt* as to the existence of one or more essential elements of the offense; thus an acquittal is not inconsistent with the existence of "substantial" or even "clear and convincing" evidence of guilt.

   ii. **Split decisions:**   Paralleling these opposing arguments, courts are **split** on whether to allow other-crimes evidence where there was an acquittal. Probably a majority will **not automatically bar** the evidence in such cases. Lilly, p. 151.

   iii. **No constitutional problem:**   There is **no constitutional problem** with receiving other-crimes evidence where there was an acquittal. The Supreme Court has held that neither the Double Jeopardy Clause nor the Due Process Clause prevents the prosecution from putting on such evidence. *Dowling v. U.S.*, 493 U.S. 342 (1990).

2. **Subsequent acts:**   Thus far, we have assumed that the "other crimes" sought to be introduced are ones which occurred before the crime currently charged. While most of the time this will indeed be the case, it is not necessarily so: the same principles apply to determine the admissibility of criminal acts that took place *after* the acts charged.

   Example: D (Patty Hearst) is charged with participating in a bank robbery committed by a terrorist group. The prosecution anticipates that, since D was originally held for ransom by the group, she will assert the defense of duress. The prosecution, therefore, introduces evidence of other criminal acts committed by D *after the bank robbery,* to counteract the duress defense.

   Held, these subsequent crimes were properly admitted. *U.S. v. Hearst*, 563 F.2d 1331 (9th Cir. 1977).

3. **Balancing:**   Even where the other-crimes evidence bears directly on some element of the crime charged, it is not automatically admissible. The judge is still required to *balance* the probative value of that evidence against the disadvantages of allowing it. Under the Federal Rules, this is the same kind of balancing that is required for *any* relevant evidence pursuant to FRE 403.

    a. **Important factors:** But there are some *special factors* that courts normally consider in the other-crimes context. These include: (1) the *strength* of the other-crimes evidence; (2) the degree of *similarity* between the other crime and the crime charged; (3) the *interval of time* between the two crimes; (4) the strength of the prosecution's *need* for the evidence coupled with the availability of *alternative* evidence on the same issue; and (5) the extent to which the evidence will rouse the jury to *unfair prejudice.* See McC, p. 347.

4. **Procedure:**   Two *procedural* issues are specific to the problem of other-crimes evidence:

    a. **Notice:**   To what extent must the prosecutor give the defendant *advance notice* of its intent to use other-crimes evidence at the trial?

        i.   **Unfairness:** Absence of any advance notice can *unfairly surprise* the defendant. This is especially true where the other-crimes evidence relates not to prior convictions, or even prior prosecutions, but rather to episodes in which the defendant was *never prosecuted*. A defendant in a narcotics sale case, for instance, is quite unfairly surprised if the prosecution suddenly introduces evidence by an undercover agent that the agent saw the defendant on a prior occasion make a sale of narcotics but that no charges were ever filed.

        ii. **404(b) requires:**   For this reason, FRE 404(b)(2) requires that upon request by the accused, the prosecution must *warn* the defendant that such evidence may be coming. The prosecutor must:

            "(A) provide *reasonable notice* of the *general nature* of any such [other-crimes-or-wrongs] evidence that the prosecutor intends to offer at trial; and

            "(B) do so *before trial* — or during trial if the court, for good cause, excuses lack of pretrial notice."

    b. **Limiting instruction:**   Whenever other-crimes evidence is admitted, it is virtually never for the purpose of showing that the defendant has a propensity for criminal conduct and probably acted in conformity with that propensity. (See *supra*, p. 27.) Yet if the evidence is admitted for some other reason (i.e., it bears directly on some element of the crime), the jury may nonetheless *use it* for precisely the prohibited reason. How can such use be discouraged? Trial judges will often give a *"limiting instruction"* to the jury guiding them in the purpose for which the evidence may be used.

VI.   EVIDENCE OF CRIMINAL DEFENDANT'S GOOD CHARACTER

A. **General rule:**   Recall that as a general rule, evidence of a person's character is not admissible for the purpose of proving that he acted in conformance with that character. The rule against other-crimes evidence, discussed above, is one application of this general rule. It might, therefore, be supposed that a ***defendant*** in a criminal trial would not be permitted to give evidence of his ***good character*** for the purpose of showing that it is unlikely he committed the crime for which he is charged. However, in fact such evidence ***is allowed by all courts***.

> **Example:** D is charged with murdering a business rival. He calls a witness to testify that D has a well-established reputation in the community for being a peaceful and kind soul. Assuming that a proper foundation for the testimony is laid (i.e., that the witness discloses a basis for knowing about D's reputation in the community), all courts will accept the testimony.

1. **FRE follows the common-law:** The Federal Rules ***agree*** that the defendant in a criminal trial may present evidence of his good character in order to show that it's unlikely that he committed the crime with which he's now charged. After FRE 404(a)(1) states the general rule that "Evidence of a person's character or character trait is not admissible to prove that on a particular occasion the person acted in accordance with the character or trait," 404(a)(2) lists several exceptions applicable only to criminal cases, the first of which is that

   > "**(A)** a defendant may offer evidence of the defendant's pertinent trait, and if the evidence is admitted, the prosecutor may offer evidence to rebut it...."

2. **Relevance:** The admissibility of such character evidence is not restricted to "general character" (e.g., the trait of being law-abiding). It also applies to particular, possibly ***narrow***, character traits. However, the trait on which evidence is offered must be ***relevant (or "pertinent") to the crime charged***.

   > **Example 1:** D is charged with murder. He will be permitted to show that he has a reputation for being peaceable. But he will not be permitted to show that he has a reputation for being ***truthful***, since the trait of truthfulness is irrelevant to the issue of guilt or innocence of murder. Conversely, if D were charged with embezzlement, he would be permitted to show that he has a reputation for truthfulness, but not that he has one for peaceableness. McC, p. 347.

   > **Example 2:** D is charged with beating V almost to death in a barroom brawl. D (without ever taking the stand) presents a witness, Wit, who expresses the opinion that D is a truthful person. Even though FRE 404(a)(2)(A) allows an accused to offer favorable character evidence about himself, Wit's testimony would be excluded because it is not "pertinent" to any issue in the case. That is, to the extent that any character trait of D is an issue, it would be the trait of peaceableness, not truthfulness.

3. **"Mercy Rule":** The rule allowing the defendant to introduce evidence of his own good character is sometimes called the ***"Mercy Rule."***

B. Method of proof: The fact that the defendant may put on evidence of a favorable and relevant character trait does not mean that all types of evidence bearing on that trait are admissible.

1. **Reputation and opinion, not specific acts:** At common-law, ***only "reputation"*** evidence could be offered by the defendant to show his good character. FRE 405(a) allows, in addition to reputation evidence, ***opinion*** evidence on this issue. But virtually all courts agree

that the defendant may ***not*** show ***"specific instances"*** of his good character. The allowable methods of proof are discussed further *infra*, p. 48.

2. **Negative evidence:** Courts generally allow ***"negative"*** evidence, i.e., testimony that the character witness has ***not heard anything bad*** — or nothing bad concerning the trait in question — about the defendant. M&K §4.19, p. 215.

   a. **Claims that D doesn't do certain bad things:** Some courts go further, and allow what might be called "negative specific acts" evidence, in which the defendant or the character witness says that the defendant doesn't now (or hasn't ever) ***done a particular type of bad act.*** Thus a defendant will usually be permitted to testify, "I don't do drugs" or "I stay out of trouble with the law," even though this is in a sense "specific acts" evidence. *Id.* at 217-18. (But observe that if the defendant does this, he opens the door wide to specific-acts ***rebuttal*** evidence by the prosecution, as described below.)

C. **Rebuttal by prosecution:** The defendant's right to offer favorable character evidence sounds like a key advantage which would be frequently exercised. However, in order to keep this advantage from being unduly great, the prosecution is given two means of ***counteracting*** it: (1) if defense witnesses testify that the defendant's reputation is good, the prosecution may then put on witnesses who say it is ***bad***; and (2) the defense character witnesses may not only be cross-examined, but they may be asked about ***specific instances*** of bad conduct. L&S, p. 241. The second of these is by far the more important.

1. **Character "in issue":** Judges and lawyers sometimes say that the reason that the prosecution is permitted to introduce evidence of bad conduct in this situation is that the defendant, by putting on his character evidence, has "put his character in issue." However, this is a misleading expression — the defendant's character is not "in issue" in the sense that it now becomes an essential element of the crime. Instead, all the phrase "places his character in issue" means is that the prosecution is free to counter the defendant's good-character evidence with bad-character evidence.

2. **Cross-examination of defendant's witness:** The prosecution receives considerable leeway in ***cross-examining*** the defendant's character witness. Under FRE 405(a), "On cross-examination of the character witness, the court may allow an inquiry into relevant ***specific instances of the person's conduct.***" Cross-examination of defense character witnesses is discussed in detail *infra*, p. 52.

VII. CHARACTER OF VICTIM, ESPECIALLY IN CASES OF ASSAULT, MURDER, AND RAPE

A. **Problem generally:** The general rule forbidding character evidence to show that a person behaved in conformity with his character would prevent a criminal defendant from showing quite relevant evidence about the character of his ***victim***. Therefore, special rules have evolved to allow the defendant to introduce evidence about the character of his victim in two recurring situations:

   [1] Where a defendant charged with murder or assault claims ***self-defense***, and wants to show that the victim's propensity for violence makes it more likely that the victim, not

the defendant, was the first aggressor; and

[2] Where a defendant charged with rape wants to show the victim's *previous sexual history* or *sexual predisposition*, usually for the purpose of showing that her previous unchastity supports the defendant's defense of consent.

We consider each of these special situations in turn. As we'll see, the FRE allows the defendant in situation [1] to show the victim's relevant character, but does not allow him to do so in situation [2].

1. **FRE approach:** The FRE, like the common law, generally *allow* the defendant to introduce evidence about the victim's character, to show that the victim acted in conformity with that character on a particular occasion (the occasion of the crime for which the defendant is now being charged). FRE 404(a), after stating the general "no proof of character to prove action in accordance therewith" principle, lists several exceptions applicable only to criminal cases, two of which are that:

   "**(B)** subject to the limitations in Rule 412,[2] a defendant may offer evidence of an *alleged victim's pertinent trait*, and if the evidence is admitted, the *prosecutor* may:

      (i) offer evidence to rebut it; and

      (ii) offer evidence of the defendant's same trait; and

   (C) in a *homicide* case, the prosecutor may offer evidence of the *alleged victim's trait of peacefulness* to *rebut evidence that the victim was the first aggressor.*"

B. **Murder and assault victims:** The principal use of the rule allowing a defendant to show evidence of the victim's character is in homicide and battery/assault cases, in which the defendant claims self-defense and therefore claims that the *victim was the first aggressor*. In this situation, the FRE and virtually all jurisdictions *allow* the defendant to introduce evidence that the victim had a *violent character*. McC, p. 349.

   1. **Knowledge unnecessary:** This exception applies even where the defendant cannot show that he was *aware* of the victim's violent character.

      a. **Distinction:** However, before you ignore whether D was aware of V's violent character, be careful to verify that the victim's-character evidence is indeed really being offered to show that V was the first aggressor. Contrast the cases in which D is trying to show that V was the first aggressor (where D's awareness of V's character is irrelevant) with cases in which evidence of V's character is offered for the purpose of showing that D's *belief* that he needed to defend himself was a *reasonable one*. For instance, V's reputation for being "quick on the draw" would be admissible for the purpose of showing that D was reasonable in thinking that the situation was "kill or be killed," but only if D was aware of that reputation.

   2. **Rationale:** Allowing evidence of the victim's bad character does not suffer from one problem that evidence of the defendant's bad character suffers: *unfair prejudice against the defendant.* This helps explain why the former is admissible while the latter is, generally, not. However, victim character evidence does suffer a shortcoming from the stand-

---

2. FRE 412 is the federal "rape shield" provision; see *infra*, p. 45.

point of justice: the jury may conclude that, because the victim was a "bad person," he merely "got what he deserved," and the defendant should therefore be acquitted. McC, p. 349. Nonetheless, courts have universally concluded that when the identity of the first aggressor is in doubt, the advantages of evidence of the victim's bad character outweigh its disadvantages. *Id.*

3. **Federal Rules:** The Federal Rules embody this approach. In fact, they extend it to cover ***all*** pertinent traits of the victim, not just the trait of violence. FRE 404(a)(2)(B) says that despite the general no-character-evidence-to-prove-conduct rule, "a defendant may offer evidence of an ***alleged victim's pertinent trait***[.]"

   a. **Other contexts:** The overwhelming majority of uses of this sentence are in the contexts of murder and assault, where the defendant claims that the victim was the first aggressor. But uses of the rule in other contexts can be imagined. For instance, one writer has speculated that "a defendant accused of bribing a public official might show that the official in question had exhibited the trait of ***greed or abuse of power*** in order to advance a defense of extortion. Perhaps a person accused of 'joy riding' might be able to prove the owner's characteristic trait of ***generosity*** to support his claim that he was operating the car with the permission of the owner." 130 U. Pa. L. Rev. 845, 856.

   b. **Rape an exception:** But there is a critical exception to the broad coverage of FRE 404(a)(2)(B). Evidence of the sexual character of a ***rape victim*** (or a victim of some other type of sexual assault) is severely circumscribed by a special rule on that subject, FRE 412, discussed *infra*, p. 44.

   c. **Proof of specific acts:** Where the defendant is permitted to introduce proof of the victim's character, FRE 405(a) (as well as most non-FRE jurisdictions) requires that this proof normally be by ***reputation*** or ***opinion*** evidence, ***not*** proof of ***specific past acts or crimes*** by the victim. The allowable methods of proof are discussed further *infra,* p. 48.

4. **Rebuttal by prosecution:** Once the defense has introduced evidence of the victim's character for violence to support the assertion that the victim was the first aggressor, the prosecution then has the right to ***rebut*** this evidence by showing the victim's ***peaceable character***. The prosecution may do this by cross-examining the defendant's reputation (or, where allowed, opinion) witness. Alternatively, it may present its own witnesses who give reputation (or, where allowed, opinion) evidence that the victim was peaceable. Lilly, p. 139.

   a. **Defendant's indirect slur on victim:** Suppose the defendant does not expressly present evidence of the victim's aggressive character, but through the pleadings or the evidence, he attempts to prove that, at least on the occasion in question, the victim was the first aggressor. In this situation, the courts are split about whether the prosecutor may present rebuttal evidence. Traditionally, most courts have allowed defendants to plead self-defense and produce non-character evidence that the victim was the first aggressor, ***without opening the door*** to the prosecution evidence that the victim had a peaceable character. L&S, p. 238, n. 88.

      i. **Federal Rules approach:** The Federal Rules take an approach that, at least traditionally, has been the ***minority*** view. Under FRE 404(a)(2)(C), the general rule of exclusion does not apply to "evidence of the alleged victim's trait of *peacefulness* [offered by the prosecution] to rebut evidence that the victim was the *first aggressor.*"

(1) Rationale: The rationale for this rule is that in a homicide case, the victim is obviously not around to testify that the defendant was the aggressor; therefore, in the absence of other eyewitnesses, the only way that the prosecution can rebut the defendant's claim about who was the first aggressor is to show the victim's character for peaceableness.

Example: D is on trial for murdering V. D, taking the stand in his own defense, claims that V attacked him first. D does not try to show that V had a general character for violence; he merely asserts that on this particular occasion, V attacked first. FRE 404(a)(2)(C) gives the prosecution the right to show, by reputation or opinion testimony (see FRE 405(a)), that V was a peaceful person.

b. Prosecution evidence on defendant's character: Suppose that the defendant has argued the victim's violent character, either explicitly or implicitly (by claiming that the victim was the first aggressor). Has the defendant thereby opened the door to prosecution evidence showing that the *defendant* has a violent character?

i. FRE approach: The Federal Rules' answer to this question is *"yes."* FRE 404(a)(2)(B) says that "a defendant may offer evidence of an alleged *victim's pertinent trait*, and if the evidence is admitted, the prosecutor may: ... (ii) offer evidence of the *defendant's same trait*[.]"

(1) Rationale: The Advisory Committee Notes say that the provision's purpose is to make clear that "the accused cannot attack the alleged victim's character and yet *remain shielded* from the disclosure of equally relevant evidence concerning the same character trait of the accused." The comments make it clear that the main function of the provision is to deal with precisely the violent-victim/violent-defendant scenario.

Example: D is charged with murdering V in a barroom brawl. D claims self-defense, asserting that V attacked him first. To bolster this defense, D introduces evidence that V has a reputation for violence. FRE 404(a)(2)(B)(ii) says that D, by introducing V's violent disposition, has opened the door to similar reputation or opinion testimony about D's violent disposition. See Advisory Committee Notes to 2000 Amendment to Rule 404, 2nd Par., 2nd sentence, posing roughly this hypothetical and then saying that, "If the government has evidence that the accused has a violent character, but is not allowed to offer this evidence as part of its rebuttal, the jury has only part of the information it needs for an informed assessment of the probabilities as to who was the initial aggressor."

(2) Narrowly drafted: Notice that this aspect of 404(a)(2)(B)(ii) is very narrowly drafted — it applies only when the accused successfully offers evidence of the victim's character trait *under FRE 404(a)(2)(B),* not under some other rule. Suppose, for instance, that in the above example, D had taken the stand to testify that at the moment he used force in his own defense, he did so in part because he knew that V had a reputation for extreme violence. Here, D is not trying to get V's violent reputation into evidence under 404(a)(2)(B), but is instead trying to show the reasonableness of his own belief that self-defense was called for. Consequently 404(a)(2)(B)(ii) will not apply, and the prosecution does *not* get to show that D himself had a reputation for violence. See Advisory Committee Notes to 2000 Amendment to Rule 404, 4th Par., first two sentences.

C. Rape and other sexual assault: In cases of *rape* and other types of *sexual assault*, courts have, until recently, been quick to admit evidence of a victim's "character for *chastity*." In particular, they have traditionally given the defendant wide latitude to introduce evidence of the victim's *prior sexual activities* in cases where the defendant asserts that the woman *consented.*

1. **Rationale:** Allowing such evidence was usually justified on one or both of the following theories: (1) that a woman who has been "unchaste" is more likely to have in fact consented than one who is not; and (2) that where a woman had a *reputation* for unchastity (whether or not deserved) and that reputation was known to the defendant, this fact bears upon the credibility of his assertion that he believed (even if wrongly) that the woman was consenting.

2. **Disadvantages:** However, this traditional approach has the terrible effect of allowing the defendant to subject the victim to a great invasion of privacy and embarrassment — some victims have likened their role in the prosecution of their assailant to being raped a second time.

   Example: D is charged with the rape of V. The prosecution shows that D accosted V in the parking lot of a singles bar, spoke to her briefly, and forced her to have sex. At trial, D contends that V "led me on" during their initial conversation, and that he reasonably believed she was consenting to his advances. Under the traditional approach, D would be permitted to cross-examine V at trial, forcing her to disclose the names of any past lovers and the circumstances under which she met them; he could justify the relevance of this questioning on the grounds that if V had sex in the past with men who "picked her up" in places like singles bars, this makes it more likely that she consented, or seemed to consent, to D's advances. D might also be allowed to present the former lovers as witnesses, and to question them on the details of their affairs with V.

3. **"Rape shield" laws:** In recent years, nearly all jurisdictions have enacted some form of *"rape shield"* law. These laws attempt, in sharply differing ways, to channel or limit evidence about the victim's past sexual history. Some of the statutes merely set up special procedures, including notice and a preliminary screening by the judge, before such evidence can be used. Other statutes include substantive limits on the extent to which victims' past sexual behavior may be presented or explored at trial. The laws have withstood constitutional attack. McC, p. 350.

4. **The federal rape shield provision:** The Federal Rules of Evidence, as initially enacted, did not contain any special rape shield provision. Therefore, evidence of the victim's sexual history and reputation was governed by what is now FRE 404(a)(2)(B)'s right of the defendant to "offer evidence of an alleged victim's pertinent trait[.]" However, in 1978 a

special provision, FRE 412, was added governing specifically the "Relevance of Victim's Past Behavior" in rape cases; 412 has since then been amended.

a.   Text of 412: The substantive portions of FRE 412 read as follows:

> **"Rule 412.   Sex-Offense Cases: The Victim's Sexual Behavior or Predisposition**
>
> **(a) Prohibited Uses.** The following evidence is *not admissible* in a *civil or criminal proceeding* involving alleged *sexual misconduct*:
>
> **(1)** evidence offered to prove that a victim *engaged in other sexual behavior*; or
>
> **(2)** evidence offered to prove a *victim's sexual predisposition*.
>
> **(b) Exceptions.**
>
> **(1) Criminal Cases.** The court may admit the following evidence in a *criminal* case:
>
> (A) evidence of *specific instances of a victim's sexual behavior*, if offered to prove that *someone other than the defendant was the source of semen, injury, or other physical evidence*;
>
> (B) evidence of *specific instances of a victim's sexual behavior* with *respect to the person accused of the sexual misconduct*, if offered by the defendant to *prove consent* or if *offered by the prosecutor*; and
>
> (C) evidence whose exclusion would *violate the defendant's constitutional rights*.
>
> **(2) Civil Cases.** In a civil case, the court may admit evidence offered to prove a victim's sexual behavior or sexual predisposition if its *probative value substantially outweighs the danger of harm* to any victim and of unfair prejudice to any party. The court may admit evidence of a victim's *reputation* only if the *victim has placed it in controversy*."

b.   Protective: FRE 412 "is, from the victim's standpoint, one of the more protective of the rape shield laws that have been enacted." L&S, p. 637.

c.   Particular provisions: FRE 412 is long and complex. However, its key provisions can be summarized as follows:

d.   Reputation or opinion evidence: Evidence relating to the victim's *reputation* for past sexual behavior, and *opinion* testimony about that past behavior, is *generally excluded* in federal trials. That is, in those comparatively rare instances where, under other provisions of FRE 412, evidence concerning the victim's past sexual behavior is admissible, that evidence must always take the form of proof of *specific acts*. Thus FRE 412 carries out an exact reversal of the usual pattern of general character evidence under the Federal Rules, whereby *only* reputation and opinion testimony, not a showing of specific instances of conduct, may be used.

   i.   Criminal trials: In *criminal* trials, this "no opinion or reputation evidence" rule stems from a combination of 412(a)(1)'s general ban on proof of the victim's "other sexual behavior," 412(a)(2)'s ban on proof of the victim's "sexual predisposition," and 412(b)(1)'s provision of various exceptions allowing evidence of "specific instances" of behavior (but don't provide for reputation or opinion evidence).

ii. **Civil trials:** In *civil* trials, essentially the same principle applies. 412(b)(2) says that "The court may admit evidence of a victim's reputation *only* if the victim has *placed it in controversy.*"

Example: P, a woman, sues D, her employer, for sex discrimination. P alleges that D maintained a hostile workplace, in which male co-workers propositioned her and otherwise sexually harassed her. D defends on the grounds that P dressed in a provocative manner and otherwise "asked for" the sexually-oriented conduct she received. D will not be permitted to show, in furtherance of this defense, that P had a reputation (either in the workplace or elsewhere) for promiscuity. However, if P makes statements about her "good" sexual reputation (e.g., by saying, "I never gave them any reason to think I'd welcome their advances — all my friends know I don't sleep around"), then P would be found to have "placed [her reputation] in controversy," and D would be permitted to rebut her statement by showing that she has a reputation for *un*chastity.

(1) **Opinion:** FRE 412 doesn't specifically mention *opinion* evidence anywhere. But the implication of the rule is that such testimony will virtually never be allowable concerning the victim's sexual conduct or predisposition.

e. **Specific acts evidence:** *Specific acts* evidence concerning the victim's past sexual behavior is also *inadmissible* in criminal sexual-assault trials under FRE 412, unless it falls into one of three categories:

i. **Source of semen or injury:** The evidence concerns the victim's past sexual behavior with persons other than the accused, offered by the accused on the issue of whether the accused was *"the source of semen, injury* or other physical evidence"* (FRE 412(b)(1)(A));

ii. **Consent:** The evidence relates to the victim's past sexual behavior *with the accused*, and is offered by the defense on the issue of whether the victim *consented,* or is offered by the prosecution. (FRE 412(b)(1)(B)); or

iii. **Constitutional requirement:** The evidence is *constitutionally required* to be admitted. (FRE 412(b)(1)(C)).

f. **Exclusions:** Most significantly, FRE 412 *prevents the defendant from introducing evidence of the victim's past sexual behavior with persons other than himself, when offered on the issue of whether there was consent.* Thus on the facts of the example on p. 44 *supra*, D would not, in a federal trial, be permitted to ask questions about V's past relationships with others, or to put those others on the stand.

g. **Civil cases:** FRE 412 makes it slightly easier to introduce evidence about the victim's past sexual history in a *civil* case than in a criminal case. In civil cases "involving alleged sexual misconduct," 412(b)(2) provides that evidence proving the victim's sexual behavior or sexual predisposition is admissible if "its probative value *substantially outweighs* the danger of harm to any victim and of unfair prejudice to any party." So there's a "thumb on the scales": if the probative value just about equals the harm to the victim, the evidence can't come in.

i. Sexual harassment cases: *Sexual harassment* cases are the main area in which the civil-suit portions of 412 are likely to come into play. The example *supra*, p. 46, is the kind of situation Congress had in mind. On the facts of that example, D would probably not be allowed to demonstrate that "P asked for it" by showing that P had an affair with a particular co-worker — it's unlikely that the probative value of this information (which, after all, doesn't say much about how other co-workers did or should have assessed P's likely reaction to sexual advances) substantially outweighs its tendency to embarrass P.

h. Sexual predisposition: The rule also generally bars evidence of the victim's ***"sexual predisposition."*** The Advisory Committee Notes say that this will keep out evidence such as that relating to the victim's "***mode of dress, speech***, or ***life-style***."

Example: In a rape case where the defense is consent, D won't be able to show that V wore low-cut blouses or short skirts and that she thereby indicated her sexual availability.

i. Procedural rules: FRE 412, like most rape shield statutes, imposes strict rules governing the ***procedures*** that must be followed before a victim's past sexual behavior may be admitted in those circumstances where admission is substantively permitted. Highlights of the procedures include:

i. Notice: The accused gives ***prior notice*** of his intent to use such evidence. He must make a written motion saying that he wants to introduce such evidence and describing the evidence and its purpose. FRE 412(c)(1)(A). The motion must normally be filed at least 14 days before the trial date. 412(c)(1)(B).

ii. Hearing: The court then conducts a hearing in chambers to determine the admissibility of the evidence.

j. Possible constitutional problems: No one has so far successfully challenged any part of FRE 412 on constitutional grounds. However, a number of ***constitutional questions*** about the Rule arise.

i. Predisposition: For instance, even though the victim's ***"sexual predisposition"*** is always excluded by 412(a)(2), on occasion this predisposition may be so highly probative on the issue of consent that to exclude it would violate the defendant's due process rights.

Example: D is on trial for raping V. The prosecution claims that D met V on the street, had a drink with her, took her (with her consent) to her apartment, where he then had sex with her against her will. D offers testimony by V's girlfriend W, who would testify that 5 minutes before V met D, V said to W, "I'm horny; I'm ready to have sex with the first adult male I meet tonight." W's testimony would be barred by 412(a)(2) (since it's offered to prove the alleged victim's "sexual predisposition"). But excluding it would probably violate D's due process right to show highly probative evidence on the issue of consent. See Adv. Comm. Notes to 412, Subdiv. (b).

ii. Limits to clause: However, the "constitutional rights" clause of 412(b)(1)(C) has been read fairly ***tightly*** by courts. For instance, one authority writes that "where the circumstances of a rape suggest that there was a *very low probability of consent*, the Constitution should not be read so as to require the admission of sexual history evidence for whatever bearing it might have on that issue. Thus, if a woman is raped and beaten by a stranger in a parking lot and afterwards complains immediately to the police, evidence that the woman was promiscuous or, indeed, was a prostitute should not be admissible simply because the defendant has the gall to claim that the woman consented." L&S, p. 639.

VIII.   METHODS OF PROVING CHARACTER (FRE 405)

A. **FRE 405:** The Federal Rules systematize, and broaden, the *methods* by which character evidence may be proven when it is allowed at all. This is done by FRE 405, which reads as follows:

> "**Rule 405. Methods of Proving Character**
>
> **(a) By Reputation or Opinion.** When evidence of a person's *character or character trait* is admissible, it may be proved by *testimony about the person's reputation* or by *testimony in the form of an opinion*. On *cross-examination* of the character witness, the court *may allow an inquiry into relevant specific instances* of the person's conduct.
>
> **(b) By Specific Instances of Conduct.** When a person's character or character trait is an *essential element* of a charge, claim, or defense, the character or trait may also be proved by *relevant specific instances* of the person's conduct."

1. **Situations covered by 405(a):** 405(a), allowing reputation and opinion evidence, applies to *all* of the situations in which character evidence is allowed at all. This means that:

   a. **Character of accused:** Where the evidence shows the character of the *accused* (allowed under FRE 404(a)(2)(A)), *both reputation and opinion evidence are allowed*. So if D wants to show that he's got a *good character* (making it unlikely he committed the present crime), he can establish this by reputation evidence, opinion evidence, or both.

      i. **No proof of "specific acts" to support good character:**   But 405(a) does *not* allow the defense's character witness to give evidence of *specific incidents.* This happens by negative implication; 405(a) specifically allows reputation and opinion evidence, then goes on to say that "On cross-examination of the character witness, the court may allow an inquiry into relevant specific instances of the person's conduct. (Since the "good character" evidence happens on direct, the right to bring out specific instances on cross doesn't help the defendant here.) So there's no affirmative grant to the defendant of the right to use specific incidents to show his good conduct, and courts uniformly interpret this silence to mean that specific instances *aren't* allowable.

      ii. **Rebuttal by prosecution:** Once the defense has "opened the door" by showing evidence of the defendant's good character, the *prosecution* may *rebut* this evidence (see 404(a)(2)(B)(i)) by similarly using reputation or opinion evidence to show the defendant's bad character, or absence of good character. (Remember that the prosecution may not *initiate* the "bad character" evidence; see *supra*, p. 40.)

(1) Prosecution's use of specific acts: Furthermore, after the defense's door-opening, the court is likely to allow the prosecution's rebuttal to include use of *specific acts* evidence on *cross-examination* of the defense's character witness. This is authorized by the second sentence of 405(a): "On cross-examination of the character witness, the court may allow *an inquiry into relevant specific instances* of the person's conduct."

Example: Suppose that D is the defendant in a criminal case charging him with embezzling from his employer, First National Bank. D presents testimony by W, a character witness, who says, "In my opinion, D is a person of absolute honesty, whom I've never seen take money improperly or do anything else morally wrong." (This is opinion testimony, allowed under FRE 405(a).) Now, the prosecution may cross-examine W, and in doing so, the court may allow cross to include "an inquiry into relevant *specific instances* of [D's] conduct" (in the language of 405(a), second sentence). Thus the prosecutor would likely be permitted to ask W, "Would it change your opinion to know that D was charged with embezzling funds from Acme Tool & Die, where he worked before First National Bank?" (The court would probably insist that the prosecutor have a "good faith basis" for the question; see *infra*, p. 52.)

The prosecutor could also rebut W's testimony by calling a new witness (call her "X"), to testify that in X's opinion D is dishonest, or to testify that D's reputation is that of a dishonest person. (But the prosecutor *wouldn't* be able to have X testify as to specific bad acts by D [e.g., "D confessed to me that he embezzled from his prior job"], because specific instances may only be brought out on cross-examination of the defense's character witness, not by "extrinsic" evidence.)

2. **Character of victim:** Essentially the same rules apply to proving the character of the *victim*. Recall that in criminal cases, FRE 404(a)(2)(B) allows the defendant to "offer evidence of an alleged victim's pertinent trait," and allows the prosecutor to then respond with rebuttal evidence about the victim's trait. Also recall that in homicide cases, the prosecutor may "offer evidence of the alleged victim's trait of peacefulness to rebut evidence that the victim was the first aggressor." 404(a)(2)(C).

So when character evidence about the victim is allowed, it may be in the form of *reputation* or *opinion* evidence, but *not specific-acts* evidence.

Example: D is charged with murdering V. D claims self-defense (that V attacked D without provocation), and wants to offer evidence that V was the sort of person who frequently started fights. D will be allowed to offer testimony by W1 that "In my opinion, V was a violent person who frequently started fights" or "V had a reputation for being a violent trouble-maker, especially when he'd been drinking." (But W1 *won't* be allowed to present specific instances of V's violence, such as "I saw V start a fight with Z in a bar just a few days before D killed V.")

Once D offers this evidence (and in fact, once D offers *any* evidence that V started the fight, even if the evidence isn't "character" evidence at all), the prosecution will now be able to put on reputation or opinion evidence showing that V had a peaceful character (e.g., testimony by W2, "V was the most peaceful, unaggressive guy I ever saw"). But W2 won't be permitted to testify to specific acts of peacefulness by V (e.g., "I saw a tough guy challenge V to a fight in a bar last June, and V just walked away"). But the prosecution *could,* with court permission, cross-examine the defense's witness, W1, by using specific instances (e.g., "Would it change your opinion, W1, to learn that V was challenged to a bar-room fight by X last June, and V just walked away?").

Note: Where the crime charged is rape or sexual assault, FRE 412 places major limits on the defense's ability to introduce evidence about the victim's prior sexual conduct or sexual predisposition. See *supra*, p. 44.

3. **Proof for "other purposes" than conduct in conformity with character:**   Recall that under FRE 404(b)(2), evidence of a person's *other crimes, wrongs or acts* is not barred when offered for *"another purpose"* than to show character and action in conformity with that character. (Other possible purposes include proof of a larger plan, preparation, "signature," intent, etc.; see pp. 30-36.) Here, 404(b)(2) itself effectively gives a party the right to use "specific instances." The Rule does not use the phrase "specific instances" (as other Rules, such as 405(a) and (b), do). But 404(b)(2)'s statement that evidence of a crime, wrong, or other act "may be admissible for another purpose, such as proving motive, opportunity, intent," etc. seems to *mean* that the specifics of the other crime, wrong or act may be shown. So a considerable amount of specifics about the prior crime, wrong or act may be presented, and this may be done on direct (not just under cross of the other's party's witness).

   a. **Showing by prosecution:** Normally, it's the *prosecution* that will want to do this, to show D's prior crimes or wrongs as circumstantial proof of D's identity, motive, intent, etc.

      Example: D is charged with robbing a 7-11 while brandishing a sawed-off shotgun and while wearing a dark blue ski-mask. D claims that eyewitnesses have mistakenly identified him rather than the real robber. The prosecution would like to show that D has been convicted of robbing two other convenience stores nearby, each time using a sawed-off shotgun and wearing a dark blue ski-mask. Under 404(b)(2), the prosecution can make this showing for purposes of showing "identity" (on a *"modus operandi"* theory — see *supra*, p. 32). The prosecution will be able to make this proof by specific instances, and can do so with its own witnesses during its direct case. Thus the prosecution can call an eyewitness to one of the earlier robberies to testify, "I identified D as being the person who used the shotgun and wore the dark blue mask while robbing my Pick-and-Serve store."

   b. **Use by defense:** However, the *defense* may also show someone's prior crimes or wrongs as circumstantial evidence of some other relevant point. For instance, if D's defense is that he didn't commit the crime, X did, D will probably be permitted to show that X has committed other specifically-proved crimes that are so like the present crime as to justify the inference that the present crime bears X's signature.

4. **Essential element of charge, claim or defense:** Finally, where character is an *"essential element* of a charge, claim, or defense," proof of this element may be made not only by

reputation or opinion evidence but also by specific instances. See FRE 405(b) ("When a person's character or character trait is an essential element of a charge, claim, or defense, the character or trait may also be proved by relevant specific instances of the person's conduct"). So in those relatively rare cases where a person's character is truly in issue, specific instances may be used.

> **Example:** P brings a libel suit against D, claiming that D has ruined P's reputation for being a law-abiding citizen. D wants to show that P has committed prior crimes that have been well-publicized. D will be allowed to do this, by showing the details of the crimes, because P's character (in the sense of his reputation) is an essential element of D's defense to the libel charge.

B. Special problems of each type of evidence: Here is a brief discussion of the special problems posed by each of the three types of character evidence: reputation, opinion and specific-instances.

1. **Reputation:** Where the character evidence takes the form of *reputation* evidence (always allowed if character evidence is allowed at all), there are two main sub-issues that surface:

   a. **What community:** First, in *what community* must the reputation be shown to exist?

      i. **Traditional view:** Traditionally, the reputation had to be that of the person in the *community in which he lives*.

      ii. **Modern view:** But our society has become more mobile, and people frequently exist in *multiple* communities: the one in which they *reside*, the one in which they *work*, the one in which they pray, perhaps the one in which they frequently vacation, and maybe even some "virtual" ones (e.g., a discussion group in which they frequently participate on the Internet). In general, modern courts allow a character witness to testify as to the defendant's reputation in *any type of community with which he has a substantial connection*. M&K §4.19, p. 215.

         (1) **Temporal proximity:** However, the reputation must date from a *time reasonably close* to the date on which the conduct in question occurred. Also, if the person whose character is at issue is the accused, the reputation must probably be from *before* the charges against him were publicized. *Id.*

   b. **Must witness know defendant:** Second, must the character *personally know* the defendant (or whoever it is whose character is being vouched for)? The general answer is *"no"* — as long as the witness has sufficient familiarity with the defendant's reputation, the witness need not know the defendant personally. M&K §4.19, p. 215.

2. **Opinion:** *Opinion* evidence presents few problems. The main thing is that the witness must be shown to know the defendant sufficiently well that the witness's opinion about the defendant's character is worth listening to. M&K §4.19, p. 216.

3. **Specific instances:** *Specific-instances* evidence is, as we've seen, the most questionable of the three types.

   a. **General rule:** The general rule is that when a party offers character evidence about a person's character as part of the party's *direct* case, this evidence may *not* be in the form of specific instances of conduct. This is true where:

❏ D offers evidence of his own *good* character;

❏ The prosecution offers evidence of D's *bad* character, after D has opened the door by offering good-character evidence;

❏ Either D or the prosecution offers evidence of the *victim's* character.

b. Cross-examination: Thus the main use of specific-instances evidence is on *cross-examination of the other side's character witness:* the court may allow the examiner to make an "inquiry" into "relevant specific instances of conduct." (FRE 405(a), last sentence.) The main things to remember about the use of specific-instances evidence on cross are:

i. No extrinsic evidence: The questioner *can't* introduce *extrinsic* evidence of the specific instances — the examiner may only refer to the specific instances, as part of the question. Then, if the character witness denies that the event occurred (or denies that the event would affect the witness's opinion about the other person's character), the matter is at an end. M&K §4.19, p. 218.

Example: D, charged with murder, claims self-defense and offers W as a character witness. W says, "In my opinion, D is a peaceful man who's very unlikely to have been the aggressor." The prosecution can use specific instances on cross (e.g., "Would it change your opinion to know that D got in bar-room fights on three separate occasions in the past year?"). But it can't present extrinsic evidence of such fights (e.g., a new witness to say she observed such fights, or a conviction record).

(1) Defense can't disprove: Conversely, the *proponent* of the character witness may not introduce extrinsic evidence to prove that the specific acts referred to on cross *did not occur.* "Additional inquiry into this collateral subject is considered not worth the impairment of judicial expedition and efficiency." Lilly, p. 137. Thus in the above Example, once the prosecutor asked the question about bar-room fights, the defense wouldn't be permitted to put on a new witness (or documents) proving that the bar-room fights *didn't* occur. For this reason, the prosecutor's good faith (see immediately below) is doubly important in this situation. (See the discussion of the "collateral issue" rule *infra*, p. 148.)

ii. Good-faith basis: The examiner must have a *good-faith basis* for asking the specific-instance (or other) question on cross. For instance, on the facts of the above example, the prosecutor must have a good faith belief that D indeed got into three prior fights.

(1) *In camera* hearing: Courts frequently require that the questioner *demonstrate* the *underlying basis* for the specific-instances question *in camera* (i.e., outside the presence of the jury) before asking it. At the very least, the questioner should, before asking the question, put the judge on notice that the questioner is about to ask a specific-instances question. M&K §4.19, p. 219. If the questioner doesn't do this and the judge later concludes that there wasn't enough evidence that the prior act actually occurred, the result may be a mistrial or a reversal on appeal.

(2) Proof that act really took place: It's not clear *how much evidence* there must be that the specific bad act referred to on cross *actually took place*. One Supreme Court case holds that the mere fact that the defendant was *arrested* for a particular act is enough to allow the character witness to be asked about the arrest ("Are you aware that D was arrested for such-and-such an offense . . . ?") *Michelson v. U.S.*, 335 U.S. 469 (1948). But "the better view is to permit such questioning only where there are *additional facts demonstrating defendant's involvement in the underlying conduct.*" M&K §4.12, p. 190.

    iii. Relevance: The specific acts must be *relevant* to the *particular character trait* on which the witness is giving testimony. M&K §4.19, p. 219.

    Example: W testifies, on behalf of D, that D has a reputation for peaceableness. On cross-examination, the prosecution may not ask whether W has heard that D was once convicted of embezzlement, since embezzlement does not bear on the trait of peaceableness. L&S, p. 242.

  4. Form of question: Traditionally, the cross-examiner's question had to have a *form* that matched up closely with the form of the witness's direct testimony. Thus if the witness had given reputation evidence, the questions on cross had to be in a form precisely linked to reputation (i.e., the questioner had to ask, "Have you heard that D did thus-and-such?" rather than, say, "Would your testimony change if you were aware that D did thus-and-such?"). But the FRE, and most modern courts, *no longer place such limits* on the form of questions on cross; thus the second sentence of 405(a) allows inquiry into specific instances on cross without imposing any special requirements regarding the form of the question.

IX. SEXUAL ASSAULT AND CHILD MOLESTATION — BY THE DEFENDANT

  A. FRE 413-415 generally: Just as special rules exist for evidence of rape *victims'* past sexual conduct ("rape shield" rules), so special rules have sometimes been enacted to deal with evidence of the *defendant's* past sexual conduct. Most notably, FRE 413-415 make it dramatically easier for the prosecution in a sexual assault or child molestation case to show that the defendant has previously committed sexual assault or child molestation offenses, and for the plaintiff in a civil sex-offense case to do the same.

  1. Past sexual assaults: Thus FRE 413(a) says that "In a criminal case in which a defendant is accused of a *sexual assault*, the court *may admit* evidence that the defendant committed *any other sexual assault*. The evidence may be considered on *any matter to which it is relevant.*"

  2. Past child molestations: Similarly, FRE 414 applies the same rule for child molestation: in a present prosecution for child molestation, the prosecution may show that the defendant committed previous child molestations.

3. **Civil suits:** And if the present case is a civil suit, in which P is seeking damages on the grounds that D has committed sexual assault or child molestation against P, FRE 415 lets P introduce D's past crimes of sexual assault or child molestation.

B. **Practical impact:** The practical impact of FRE 413-415 is to completely revoke the "no showing of predisposition" rule as to sex offenses: the prosecution is expressly permitted to show past sex crimes, and to argue, "If he did it before, he did it now." Some examples of how 413-415 can work:

> **Example 1:** D is charged with raping V. The prosecution can present testimony by X that many years ago, D raped X, but that she never complained to authorities and D was never charged. FRE 413. This evidence can be used as substantive evidence that D raped V.

> **Example 2:** D is charged with molesting V, a 10-year-old boy. The prosecution can present evidence that D previously molested Y, a 6-year-old girl, and was arrested for it but never charged. Again, this can be used as substantive evidence that D committed the crime now charged. The evidence can probably be as informal and unreliable as a "rap sheet" showing the arrest. FRE 414.

> **Example 3:** P sues D for sexual battery, seeking damages for his having raped her. Again, P can show evidence that D raped others in the past, even though these other rapes were unreported or (probably) even if they resulted in an acquittal. FRE 415.

1. **Broadly drafted:** FRE 413-415 are extremely broadly drafted, to render admissible a wide range of evidence, for a wide range of purposes. Some illustrations of this breadth:

   a. **No conviction:** The prior offense doesn't have to have led to a *conviction*. Incidents that were *never reported to the police* may be introduced (by testimony of the victim, for instance), and apparently, incidents that ended in acquittal may also be proved.

   b. **Balancing:** The text of each rule says that the court "may admit" the prior-crimes evidence; it does not say that this evidence is *automatically* admissible. This indicates that the trial judge has *discretion to exclude the evidence*, perhaps under *FRE 403's balancing test.*

      i. **Courts say that 403 may be used:** So, for instance, if the evidence of whether the past sexual offense actually occurred is *"equivocal,"* or if the past acts *differ* from the charged act in major ways, the trial judge should *feel free* to keep out the evidence as insufficiently probative. *Johnson v. Elk Lake School Distr.*, 283 F.3d 138 (3d Cir. 2002).

   c. **Hearsay:** The "may admit" language of FRE 413-415 implies that the ordinary rules of evidence — the *hearsay* rule, most notably — *don't apply* to the other-crimes evidence. So probably, the prosecutor could put on testimony by W, "Y told me that 10 years ago, D raped her."

   d. **No time limit:** Rules 413-415 don't impose any *time limit* on the other-crimes evidence. So evidence from 30 years ago would be admissible, without any special judicial scrutiny. (Contrast this with FRE 609(b)(1), which says that for a more-than-10-year-old conviction to be introduced for impeachment, the conviction's probative value must be "supported by specific facts and circumstances," and that probative value must "substantially outweigh" the prejudicial effect. See *infra*, p. 128.)

2. **Criticisms:** FRE 413-415 have been widely criticized. The most common, and persuasive, criticism is that juries are likely to *"overvalue"* evidence that D has previously committed crimes similar to the one charged, and that this overvaluation problem is worst when the past crimes are the most repugnant.

   a. **Relief via Rule 403:** Courts can minimize these risks by using their power under *Rule 403* to disallow other-crimes evidence whose *probative value is substantially outweighed* by its tendency to be overweighted by the jury. Or, the judge can instruct the jury not to overstate the evidence's relevance.

Quiz Yourself on
CIRCUMSTANTIAL EVIDENCE (FROM BEG. OF CHAPTER TO THIS POINT)

3. Phil Zbiblenik, a carriage driver in Metropolis' Central Park, is sued for negligence when he falls asleep at the reins and his horse tramples the wedding reception of Mr. and Mrs. Amin Love. At the trial, the Loves seek to introduce evidence that on a previous occasion Phil had fallen asleep while working, disrupting a celebrity tennis tournament. The evidence is offered to show that it's likely Phil fell asleep again in the present situation. Is the evidence admissible, under the FRE? _____

4. Frank N. Stein is seeking sole custody of his son, Bier, from his former wife, Albertyne. Albertyne seeks to introduce character evidence showing that Frank conducts chemical experiments which would create an unhealthy atmosphere in which to raise a child. Stein's lawyer objects, saying that since Stein hasn't put his character at issue, the evidence shouldn't be admissible. How do you rule? _____

5. Sam Sleezeball is charged with selling obscene material. At trial, the prosecutor seeks to open his case by introducing testimony from Sam's neighbors that Sam is a trench-coat pervert who is frequently involved in shady enterprises. Sam objects. How do you rule? _____

6. Bouncer was charged with passing a bad check when he purchased an assault rifle while wearing a Bill Clinton mask. Bouncer claims he was out-of-state when the crime occurred. At trial, the prosecution attempts to introduce evidence that Bouncer had purchased two other assault rifles with bad checks while wearing a Bill Clinton mask. (Bouncer was never convicted for these other purchases.) Is this evidence admissible under the FRE? If so, for what purpose(s)? _____

7. Bart Egg, defendant in a criminal trial, wants to offer the testimony of Amy Ubble as to Bart's good reputation, to prove he didn't commit the crime in question. Bart's lawyer first shows that Amy is familiar with Bart's reputation. Then, when the lawyer asks what that reputation is, Amy hesitates, then says: "Well, I haven't heard anything bad about him." Is this "negative" reputation testimony admissible, under the FRE? _____

8. Killer Smith offers testimony at his murder trial that he has never started a fight in his whole life. The prosecutor then introduces testimony by Killer's lifelong friend that in the friend's opinion, Killer has always been hot-tempered and violent. Can Killer successfully object to the testimony? _____

9. David is on trial for the murder of Goliath. He claims self-defense and that Goliath was the first aggressor. May David introduce evidence of Goliath's violent nature to prove that Goliath was the

aggressor? _____

10. Otto Dingle is charged with raping Mata Hari. Dingle claims "consent" as a defense, and offers reputation evidence of Mata's renowned unchastity. The prosecutor objects, claiming that the victim's past behavior is inadmissible in rape cases. Under the FRE, how do you rule? _____

11. Psycho Bates, proprietor of the Bates Motel, is on trial for the murder of Wo Begonia, who had merely stopped at the motel to ask for directions. Betsy Boddie appears as a reputation witness for Bates, claiming his reputation in the community is "very good." On cross-examination, the prosecutor asks Betsy: "Have you heard about Mr. Bates stabbing Marion Crane to death in the shower in 1962?" Defense counsel objects to the question. How do you rule? _____

12. Jack T. Ripper is on trial for murdering Divine Brown, a prostitute. Ripper offers testimony by Hugh, who says that Ripper is known in the community as a non-violent, peaceful person. The prosecutor puts on a rebuttal witness, Elizabeth, who attempts to testify that if Ripper has a good reputation, the reputation is ill-deserved, because Ripper was previously convicted of mayhem. Ripper objects. How do you rule, under the FRE? _____

13. Duke is on trial for raping Gilda. The prosecution seeks to introduce testimony by Magdalena that 14 years ago, Duke raped her, an act for which he was never charged. Magdalena would testify that the rape took place when Duke, a stranger to her, attacked her in a parking lot. The rape of Gilda is alleged to have occurred following a date between the two. There are no meaningful similarities between the two crimes other than the fact was Duke was the alleged rapist. The prosecution's theory in seeking introduction of the Magdalena rape is that because Duke raped before, he's likely to have raped on the present occasion. Duke has not taken the stand as a witness. Is Magdalena's testimony admissible, under the FRE? _____

Answers

3. No. Here, Phil's negligence in disrupting the tennis tournament is offered as circumstantial evidence that he likely did the same thing again. The evidence won't be admissible, because it's circumstantial character evidence — a specific prior act offered to show Phil's general character for carelessness, to prove that Phil probably acted in conformity with that character on the present occasion. It is thus inadmissible under FRE 404(b) ("Evidence of a crime, wrong, or other act is not admissible to prove a person's character in order to show that on a particular occasion the person acted in accordance with the character.")

This evidence might be admissible to prove a common plan, motive, or lack of mistake, etc. FRE 404(b), 2nd sent. But none of these "other purposes" seems applicable here.

Note that the evidence here could not prove habit (admissible to show action in accordance therewith, under FRE 406), since habit is a regular response to a repeated situation, and a single instance can't show this.

4. Objection overruled. The general rule that character can't be proved to show action in conformity therewith doesn't apply where character is directly ***in issue*** in the case, in the sense that character is an ***element of a charge, claim or defense***. Stein's character is automatically "in issue" here, because it's an essential element of Stein's claim for sole custody – Stein's character goes to which parent will be a better guardian for the child. Consequently, under FRE 405(a) and (b), all three types of character evidence are admissible: reputation, opinion, and specific acts. (In common law jurisdictions, the modern trend is also to allow all three.)

5. **Objection sustained**. The testimony is inadmissible character evidence, because every indication is that it's being introduced solely to suggest that because Sam is a pervert, he's more likely to be guilty of the present offense than he would be if he weren't a pervert (i.e., that he's got the character trait of perversion, offered to show he probably acted in accordance with that trait on the present occasion). The prosecutor can only introduce character evidence to rebut character evidence introduced by Sam, or to impeach Sam's testimony. FRE 404(a)(2)(A) and (a)(3). Neither of these exceptions applies here: Sam hasn't introduced favorable evidence of his own character (we know this because the prosecution's just getting started), and Sam hasn't taken the stand so there's no testimony by him to impeach.

6. **The evidence would be admissible for the limited purpose of showing "identity," but not to show Bouncer's criminal predisposition.** FRE 404(b)(1) says that "Evidence of a crime, wrong, or other act is not admissible to prove a person's character in order to show that on a particular occasion the person acted in accordance with the character." So the prior purchases can't be used to show, in essence, that if Bouncer illegally bought guns in the past, he probably did so on the present occasion as well.

But 404(b)(2) goes on to say that other crimes or wrongs may be introduced for other limited purposes, one of which is to show *"identity."* Because Bouncer has put the identity of the purchaser in issue (rather than, for instance, admitting he made the purchase but claiming he didn't have the mental state for the crime), the prosecution will be allowed to show that the prior and present acts are so similar and so idiosyncratic that they bear Bouncer's unique "signature," thus establishing that he is the perpetrator.

NOTE: Under 404(b), other crimes or wrongs may be introduced for other limited purposes in addition to identity, including proof of motive, opportunity, preparation, plan, knowledge, or absence of mistake or accident.

7. **Yes**. Amy's testimony that she hasn't heard anything bad about Bart is admissible as favorable evidence of his reputation under the "Mercy Rule."

More precisely: FRE 404(a)(2)(A) applies the Mercy Rule, by which a criminal defendant can submit evidence of his good character, as circumstantial evidence that he probably didn't commit the crime. 405(a) allows character evidence, when admissible at all, to be in the form of reputation evidence. Courts construing this provision allow negative reputation evidence.

Note, however, that the prosecutor will then be free to *rebut* Amy's testimony with evidence of Bart's *bad* character. The prosecutor will also be able to question Amy about her knowledge of specific instances of bad conduct in Bart's past. FRE 405(a), last sent.

8. **No**. The prosecutor can introduce character evidence to rebut character evidence introduced by the accused. Under the FRE, this rebuttal evidence can be in the form of either reputation or opinion evidence. (At common law, only reputation, not opinion, evidence would be allowed.) FRE 404(a)(2)(A) and 405(a). Killer "opened the door" by introducing evidence that he never started a fight, so the prosecution can rebut by showing that Killer had a reputation for violence, or that in the witness's opinion Killer was violent.

9. **Yes**. FRE 404(a)(2)(B) says that "a defendant may offer evidence of an alleged victim's pertinent trait[.]" So by application of this rule, the accused may introduce pertinent character evidence of the victim's violent propensity, to prove that the victim was the aggressor. (The *quid pro quo* is that once the defendant does so, the prosecution may put on evidence that the victim was peaceful. FRE 404(a)(2)(B)(i).)

10. **Objection sustained**. Under FRE 412 (the federal "rape shield" statute), evidence offered to prove a victim's sexual predisposition is generally inadmissible in criminal cases. An exception exists for "evidence

of specific instances of a victim's sexual behavior with respect to the person accused of the sexual misconduct, if offered by the defendant to prove consent[.]" 412(b)(1)(B). However, this exception doesn't apply here, for two reasons: (1) Otto's proposed evidence does not relate to Mata's conduct with *him*; and (2) Otto's evidence is reputation evidence rather than specific-acts evidence. No other exception in FRE 412 applies, so the evidence is inadmissible.

11. **Objection overruled**. Under FRE 405(a), a reputation witness may be cross-examined about specific instances of conduct bearing on the reputation. (Theoretically, the rationale for this is that if the witness doesn't know about the specific instances – assuming they were commonly known – the witness's knowledge of the defendant's reputation is suspect. In reality, the questioner is trying to slip in the specific instance for its truth.)

Note that the question about specific instances must be asked in *good faith*. That is, the questioner must have a reasonable belief that the episode really occurred, and that a witness who knew the details of the defendant's reputation would have heard of it. Note, also, that a trial court could decide that the "specific acts" evidence here is substantially more prejudicial than it is probative; in that case, the judge could exclude it under FRE 403. However, courts will normally give the jury a limiting instruction on the evidence, and allow the question.

COMMON LAW RULE: At common law, the wording of such a question was crucial to its admissibility. It had to be in the format given: "Have you heard? . . ." not "Did you know? . . ." But the FRE don't recognize this distinction.

12. **Objection sustained**. Under the "Mercy Rule," the defendant in a criminal trial can offer pertinent character evidence, in the form of reputation or opinion testimony, to prove his innocence. After he does so, the prosecution can cross-examine the character witness, and in so doing can inquire into "relevant specific instances of the [target witness's] conduct" (FRE 405(a)). Thus the prosecutor could have asked Hugh on cross, "Didn't you hear that Ripper was once convicted of mayhem?"

Alternatively, once the accused uses the Mercy rule, the prosecution may put on substantive – i.e., direct rather than cross – rebuttal evidence. 404(a)(2)(A). But FRE 405(a) says that this evidence may be by *reputation* or *opinion* testimony; by negative implication, the rebuttal may *not* be by *specific instances* of conduct. (405(b) allows proof of specific instances of conduct on the issue of character, but only where character is an "essential element" of a charge, claim or defense, which is not the case here.) So it was improper for the prosecution to ask Elizabeth about specific instances of the accused's bad character, and Ripper's conviction for mayhem clearly falls into this category.

13. **Yes**, **probably**. If the matter had to be determined solely by reference to FRE 404(b)(1), the Magdalena rape would be inadmissible, because that provision says that "Evidence of a crime ... is not admissible to prove a person's character in order to show that on a particular occasion the person acted in accordance with the character."

However, Congress has made it dramatically *easier* for the prosecution to introduce evidence of the defendant's *prior sex crimes* for the purpose of showing that the defendant probably committed the sex crime for which he is now charged. FRE 413, in subsection (a), says that "In a criminal case in which a defendant is accused of a sexual assault, the court *may admit evidence that the defendant committed any other sexual assault*. The evidence *may be considered on any matter to which it is relevant*." So the fact that Duke previously raped Magdalena is admissible to show, in essence, "If he did it before, he probably did it again." However, the trial judge still has discretion to exclude the evidence under FRE 403, if she believes that the evidence's *probative value is substantially outweighed* by the possibility of *unfair prej-*

udice to the defendant. Such a finding could be based on the fact that the circumstances surrounding the two crimes (stranger rape vs. date rape) are quite different, and the fact that the prior crime took place a long time ago. But unless the judge makes this "substantially outweighed" finding (which she probably won't, given Congress' intent in enacting 413 to cover a broad range of prior sexual assault crimes), the evidence will be admissible.

X. HABIT AND CUSTOM

A. General rule allows: Evidence of a person's character, of course, is generally not admissible to show that he acted in accordance with that character on a particular occasion. Yet evidence of a person's *habit*, in most jurisdictions (and under the FRE), *is admissible* to show that he *followed his habit on a particular occasion.*

> **Example:** P, an auto mechanic, is injured while trying to warm up a can of refrigerant manufactured by D. At the trial of his products liability case, P asserts that he heated the refrigerant by surrounding it with warm tap water. D offers the testimony of W, who would testify that on prior occasions, he saw D use an immersion heating coil to heat the same kind of refrigerant, in violation of warnings on the label.
>
> *Held*, W's testimony should have been allowed. Evidence that P regularly serviced auto air-conditioning units by use of refrigerant, and that he routinely used a coil to heat the refrigerant, was sufficient to establish a habit on P's part. Such evidence of habit is admissible to prove conformity on a specific occasion, because "one who has demonstrated a consistent response under given circumstances is more likely to repeat that response when the circumstances arise again...." *Halloran v. Virginia Chemicals, Inc.*, 361 N.E.2d 991 (N.Y. 1977).

B. Distinction between habit and character: The distinction between "habit" and "character" is, in theory, not hard to draw: "Character" is a "generalized description of a person's disposition, or of the disposition in respect to a general trait, such as honesty, temperance, or peacefulness." McC, pp. 350-51. "Habit," by contrast, is "more specific. It denotes one's *regular response* to a *repeated situation*." McC, p. 351.

> **Example:** Evidence that X generally drives carefully goes to his "character," since it relates to a relatively general trait. Therefore, such evidence will normally be inadmissible. But evidence that every work day, X crosses a particular railroad, and that he always stops, looks both ways, and then proceeds, would be evidence of his "habit." Such evidence will, therefore, generally be admissible to prove that on the particular day in question (e.g., the day that X is hit by an oncoming train), X stopped and looked before crossing the tracks. Lilly, p. 146.

1. Three factors: There seem to be three main factors that courts consider when deciding whether something is a "habit" or merely a trait of character: (1) *specificity*; (2) *regularity*; and (3) degree of *reflection*.

a. Specificity: The more *specific* the behavior, the more likely it is to be deemed a habit rather than a character trait. The above example illustrates this factor — X's conduct crossing a particular railroad on his way to work is highly specific (and thus a habit), whereas his driving in a generally careful manner is not (and it's thus merely a character trait).

b. Regularity: Similarly, the more *"regular"* the behavior, the more likely it is to be a habit. This is probably the most important single factor. *Id.*

Example: Suppose D claims that it's his habit to drive to work via Main St., rather than via First Ave. If D uses the Main St. route, say, 95% of the time, that's quite regular, so his conduct will probably indeed be viewed as a habit. But if he only uses the Main St. route 55% of the time, that's much less regular, and therefore much less likely to qualify as a habit.

c. Unreflective behavior: Lastly, behavior is more likely to be a habit if it's *"unreflective"* or *"semi-automatic"* than if it's *volitional* and *conscious*.

Example 1 (semi-automatic): D claims that he always uses his turn signal when making a left-hand turn. Because a person's use of a turn signal is usually a semi-automatic act, i.e., one not requiring much conscious thought, it's likely to be considered a habit.

Example 2 (volitional): D asserts as an alibi defense that he has a "habit" of staying home on the Sabbath. Because this conduct involves a fairly high degree of conscious thought and volition, it probably *won't* be considered a habit. See *Levin v. U.S.*, 338 F.2d 265 (D.C. Cir. 1964).

See generally M&K §4.21, p. 226.

C. Federal Rule: FRE 406, in keeping with the rule of most states, allows *very liberal use of habit evidence.* The Rule provides that

> "Evidence of a *person's habit* or an *organization's routine practice* may be admitted to prove that *on a particular occasion* the person or organization *acted in accordance with the habit or routine practice.* The court may admit this evidence regardless of whether it is *corroborated* or whether there was an *eyewitness*."

1. No eyewitness requirement: Observe that this Rule expressly rejects any requirement that there be an eyewitness requirement (which some pre-FRE decisions required).

2. How proved: The Rule does not say anything about *how* the existence of a habit is to be proved. Proof will normally be made by the testimony of a witness who has observed the habit over a long enough time for him to be able to say that it is a routine, repeated practice. Lilly, p. 147. Sometimes, however, the opponent will have to prove a number of *separate instances* (perhaps by a number of different witnesses) which, when taken together, demonstrate the required regularity. *Id.* This method of proof by individual instances is generally acceptable, so long as there are a sufficient number of instances and they have enough in common with each other.

D. Business practice: All courts, even those that disallow or restrict habit evidence, freely allow evidence of the *routine practice* of an *organization*. This greater acceptance probably stems from the fact that "the need for regularity in business and organizational sanctions which may exist when custom is violated provide extra guarantees that the questioned activity followed the usual custom." L&S, p. 250.

Example: A party wishes to prove that a certain letter was mailed by X Corp., a business. The party need not produce testimony by the person who actually mailed the letter. It is sufficient that the party show that the letter was placed in an "out box" at X Corp., if X Corp.'s mail clerk testifies that it was part of his job to collect all letters in the out box and mail them every day. This would be sufficient proof that that particular letter was mailed, even if the mail clerk testified that he could not remember whether he mailed the letter in question. L&S, p. 250, n. 8.

1. **Need for testimony:** In many states, however, the routine business practice must be proven via the testimony of the individual whose behavior is in question (e.g., the mail clerk in the above example). In other jurisdictions, **anyone** who has knowledge of the custom may testify as to its existence. This liberal approach is implicitly followed in FRE 406.

XI. SIMILAR HAPPENINGS

A. **General problem:** A party will sometimes want to introduce evidence of an event that is **similar** to the event under litigation. Generally, the similar event will be one which took place prior to the event under litigation, but it may have taken place subsequently.

Example 1: P trips on a stairway in D's movie theater. She wishes to show that in the six months prior to her accident, two other people slipped and fell on the same stairway. She offers this evidence to prove that the carpet on the stairway was maintained in an unsafe condition, which D knew of or ought to have known of.

Example 2: P loses money on a stock touted to him by his broker, D. P claims that D knowingly made several specific misrepresentations about the stock. If D denies having made the statements to P, P would like to be able to show that D made the same statements to several others about the same stock at about the same time.

1. **Objections:** Yet there are several potential problems with such "similar happenings" evidence. In the stair-fall example, for instance, the earlier fall may have taken place under such different circumstances that it has no probative value on the fall under litigation; this would be the case, for instance, if the earlier fall were while the lights were dim and the later one while the lights were bright, or the earlier one was by a woman in high heels and the later by a child running in sneakers. Furthermore, the jury might overestimate the importance to be attached to the similar happening, or overestimate the similarity between the two events.

2. **General rule:** For these and other reasons, courts are generally **reluctant** to allow evidence of similar happenings. In most jurisdictions, there are no black letter rules governing when such evidence may be admitted. In general, such evidence is not flatly excluded, but the proponent must demonstrate that there is a **substantial similarity** between the collateral event offered as evidence and the event at issue in the case. L&S, p. 208.

Example: P falls while going down the stairs at D's theater. She produces evidence that the carpet on the stairs was loose because the tacks holding it to the floor had pulled out, and that the carpet slipped under her feet. D produces evidence that the carpet was securely fastened. P offers evidence that two or three weeks before her injury, two girls fell at the same spot, and that after they fell, the carpet was found to be loose because the tacks fastening it had been pulled out.

Held (on appeal), the evidence of the other falls should not have been admitted, because P did not show that on the earlier occasion, the tacks had been pulled out to the same distance, or that the carpet had the same degree of looseness, as during the time of P's accident. *Robitaille v. Netoco Comm. Theaters*, 25 N.E.2d 749 (Mass. 1940).

a. **FRE silent:** The Federal Rules do not specifically treat the admissibility of "similar happenings" evidence. However, FRE 402's general requirement that evidence be *relevant* means that federal courts can and should exclude prior episodes that are not sufficiently similar to the present episode. M&K §4.5, p. 165.

B. **Similar accidents and injuries:**   Probably the most common use of "similar happenings" evidence is in suits for personal injuries from *accidents or defective products*. As with "similar happenings" evidence generally, courts will *not exclude* the similar accident evidence automatically, but will closely *scrutinize* it. The plaintiff will have to show substantial similarity between the two accidents.

1. **Narrow element:** Furthermore, in negligence actions, the evidence will rarely be admitted for the broad purpose of showing that the defendant was negligent. Lilly, p. 169. Instead, the plaintiff will have to show *what particular element* of the case the other accident is being offered to prove. Possible elements that the accident may demonstrate include the following:

    a. **Defect:**   that a particular defect *existed*;

    b. **Causation:**   that a defect, whether or not disputed by the defendant, *caused* plaintiff's accident;

    c. **Risk:**   that the defendant's conduct created a substantial *risk*; or

    d. **Knowledge:**   that the defendant *knew*, or should have known, of the danger.

        i.   **Subsequent happenings:**   If the other event is *subsequent* to the event under litigation, it will not for that reason alone be made inadmissible on the first three of these elements. But it will be inadmissible on the last, knowledge — the fact that someone was injured after the plaintiff was, obviously cannot prove that the defendant knew or should have known of the danger at the time of plaintiff's injury. McC, p. 355.

2. **Evidence of past safety:**   A defendant will sometimes want to show that there have been *no accidents* of the kind suffered by the plaintiff. Logically, this kind of evidence should be admissible in courts allowing the plaintiff to introduce evidence of similar accidents. Most courts indeed *allow* such evidence of a safe history if the defendant shows that: (1) *conditions were the same* during the historical period as during the moment of plaintiff's injury; and (2) had there been any injuries, they would have been *reported* to the defendant.

Example: Let's return to the example of P falling on the carpeted stairway of D's theater. Assume that P does not have any evidence of other accidents. Most courts would allow D to introduce the fact that of the thousands or tens of thousands of customers who have gone up and down those stairs in the last year, none fell. However, this evidence would be admissible only if conditions had remained the same over the last year — if D had recarpeted the stairs just prior to P's injury, or relighted the premises, the situation might be deemed to be so different that the history of safety would be of too little probative value to be admitted. Also, D would have to show that in all likelihood, any injuries that did occur would have been reported to one of D's employees.

C. Other kinds of events: There are a number of other common settings in which similar-happenings evidence is sought to be admitted. Some of the common contexts are as follows:

1. Criminal allegations: When the plaintiff in a civil suit alleges that the defendant has committed conduct which amounts to a crime, evidence of *other acts by the defendant* are admissible on the same basis as they would be in a criminal trial of that defendant.

    a. Fraud: The most common illustration is a civil suit for *fraud*. Similar past acts by the defendant will be admissible to show the defendant's guilty knowledge, deceitful intent, or a broad plan or scheme, assuming that such element is a disputed issue in the civil case.

    Example: P, an investor, sues D, a new-issues stock broker, for fraud. P claims that D sold him stock in X Corp. by means of untrue statements, including that "the prospectus is out of date and should be disregarded" and that "the initial offering of the stock will be closed this weekend." D denies having made the representations. P offers the testimony of two witnesses that at about the same time D made essentially the same representations to them on the same stock.

    Held, all the claimed representations are so strikingly similar that they should be admitted to show a general plan or scheme by D. *Karsun v. Kelley*, 482 P.2d 533 (Or. 1971).

2. Prior claims by same plaintiff: A party (usually the defendant) will sometimes want to show that his adversary has previously raised *fraudulent claims* similar to the claim in the present action. If the proponent can show that these other claims were indeed fraudulent, and were similar to the present claim, most courts will accept the evidence.

3. Accident proneness: The defendant in a negligence action may try to show that the plaintiff is *"accident prone,"* either to suggest that the defendant was not negligent, or to show that there was contributory negligence by the plaintiff. Courts have generally *refused* to allow evidence of accident proneness on the issue of negligence.

    a. Rationale: One reason for this reluctance is that, as a purely statistical matter, *some* people simply will end up in markedly more accidents than others, even though they may be every bit as careful as their more fortunate peers. If 100 people in a village had 100 accidents, and the accidents "found their victim" in a totally random way, it would nonetheless probably turn out that some few unfortunates had two, three, even four accidents — that's simply the way the bell-shaped probability distribution works.

These unfortunates would be called "accident prone," yet only the laws of chance, not their own carelessness, would have been the cause. L&S, pp. 211-12, n. 41.

XII. SUBSEQUENT REMEDIAL MEASURES

A. **Problem generally:** After an accident, the owner of premises or property involved in it will often take *remedial measures*. For instance, when a pedestrian trips on a pothole in the sidewalk in front of a building, the building owner may have the pothole paved over. When suit is brought by the injured party, he will often want to introduce evidence of the subsequent repair, on the theory that that repair shows the defendant's consciousness of negligence or other fault. For instance, in the pothole situation, the plaintiff would be saying something like, "By paving over the pothole, Mr. Landowner, you acknowledge that prior to the repair the pothole made the sidewalk unsafe." Should such evidence of subsequent repairs be admissible?

1. **General rule:** Courts generally *do not allow* such evidence of subsequent repairs, when offered to the show the repairer's culpability.

2. **Rationale:** At first glance, this rule seems hard to understand. After all, the defendant's prompt repair does suggest that the defendant realized that prior to the accident, he had not been as careful as he might have been. Two reasons are usually given for the rule:

   a. **Little probative value:** First, such evidence is of relatively little probative value on the issue of negligence. "Certainly a conscientious individual, newly alerted to a dangerous condition, will do everything reasonable to remedy that condition regardless of his or her earlier care." L&S, p. 192.

   b. **Discouragement of repairs:** The second, and probably more important, reason for the general rule of exclusion is that if such evidence were allowed, it might have the effect of *discouraging repairs*. That is, a defendant might reason, "If I make this repair while suit is threatened or pending, the plaintiff will be able to use it against me. I'm better off not doing anything until the suit is resolved." This second rationale thus amounts to a rule of policy: For reasons having nothing to do with accuracy in the fact-finding process, the courts impose a rule of exclusion in the hopes that defendants will be encouraged to make things safer for the public in the future, or at least not discouraged from doing so.

3. **Remedial actions generally:** In any event, the law of exclusion is almost universally established (except in Maine, where it is abolished by statute).

   a. **Extension:** In fact, the rule has been extended beyond "repairs," and has been applied in the following situations:

      i. Installation of a new *safety device*;

      ii. Lowering of a speed limit or beefing up some other *safety rule*;

      iii. *Firing the employee* responsible for the accident.

   b. **"Subsequent remedial measures":** None of these actions is, strictly speaking, a "repair." For this reason, the rule is now stated as covering not just repairs, but *"subsequent remedial measures."*

4. **Federal Rule:** The Federal Rule on the subject, FRE 407, follows the common-law approach in general. However, it is broadly written to cover all types of remedial measures, when offered to prove all sorts of culpability-related facts:

> "When measures are taken that would have made an *earlier injury or harm less likely to occur*, evidence of the s*ubsequent measures* is *not admissible* to prove:

> - *negligence*;
> - *culpable conduct*;
> - a *defect* in a product or its design; or
> - a need for a *warning or instruction*."

(The Rule then makes it clear that it does not apply to evidence offered for purposes other than negligence or culpability — see immediately *infra*.)

B. **Permissible purposes:** The rule against subsequent-remedial-measures evidence applies *only* where the evidence is offered on the issue of *negligence or culpability*. If the evidence is relevant to *some other contested element* in the case, the exclusionary rule does not apply.

1. **Federal Rule:** FRE 407 expressly recognizes that the general rule of exclusion should not bar use for purposes other than the showing of negligence or culpable conduct. The second sentence of 407 states that the court may allow the evidence if it is offered "for *another purpose*, such as *impeachment* or — if disputed — proving *ownership*, *control*, or the *feasibility of precautionary measures*. This list is intended to be illustrative, *not exhaustive*.

2. **Typical issues:** Some of the more common issues as to which subsequent-measures evidence may be relevant and thus admissible, are as follows:

   a. **Feasibility:** The issue of *feasibility, but only if raised by the defendant.* Thus if the defendant claims that he was not negligent or culpable because *all feasible precautions were taken*, or claims that there was *no safer way to handle the situation,* evidence that the defendant implemented a safer way following the accident is uniformly *allowed*. Courts reason that: (1) the subsequent-remedial-measure evidence tends to be strongly *probative* on the issue of whether there was in fact a safer option open to the defendant; and (2) the defendant has made a voluntary decision to *"open the door"* to the subsequent-repair evidence by choosing to make an issue of feasibility.

      i. **"The measure wouldn't have helped":** Often, the defendant will put feasibility in issue by claiming that the remedial measure simply couldn't have been implemented. But sometimes, defendant's claim is that the measure could have been implemented, but that it *wouldn't have improved the safety of the situation*. Courts generally treat this "the measure wouldn't have helped" defense as putting feasibility in issue, and therefore let the plaintiff rebut with evidence that the defendant later used the very measures that she's claiming wouldn't have helped.

      ii. **Claim of "reasonably safe" doesn't place feasibility in issue:** But if all the defendant does is to claim that the existing design or arrangements were *"reasonably safe"* or "not defective," this limited claim does *not* put feasibility in issue. M&K §4.24, p. 238. (It's only where the defendant claims that "nothing more could have been done," "all reasonable precaution were taken," or the like, that the defendant will be found to have crossed over the line and put feasibility in issue.)

   iii. **Weighing of options:** Similarly, if all the defendant does is to contend that the method chosen seemed at the time to be *more practicable, or safer,* than some alternative method, the court will usually *not* allow the plaintiff to use a feasibility argument to introduce the fact that the defendant later chose to use the alternative method. Once again, the defendant will be found to have put feasibility in issue only by contending that an alternative was really *not practicable at all*, not by merely contending that the option used in the plaintiff's case was somewhat preferable.

b. **Ownership or control:**   Subsequent-measures evidence is also admissible on the issue of *ownership* or *control* of the property that caused the accident.

   Example: P, a pedestrian, is hit by a car driven by D. P brings a negligence action against D. D defends by showing that the car was not registered to him, and by claiming that the collision occurred because, unbeknownst to D, the brakes were faulty. P wants to introduce evidence that D had the brakes repaired after the collision.

   If P offers this evidence to prove directly that D was negligent in not inspecting the brakes beforehand, the evidence would be barred under the general rule of exclusion. But if P offers the subsequent repair to show that D had enough control over the vehicle to have it repaired (and thus had enough control to have had a duty to inspect the brakes before the accident), the evidence will be admitted. S&R, pp. 265-66.

c. **Impeachment:**   Lastly, subsequent-measures evidence is admissible to *impeach* an opposing witness.

   i. **Use to rebut claim of "there was no hazard":** One scenario in which the plaintiff will often be allowed to show subsequent measures to impeach is where the defendant claims that there was *no real hazard at all*. The plaintiff will then usually be allowed to show that the defendant's own later conduct — typically, the issuance of a *warning* — demonstrates an awareness that there really was a hazard. This constitutes "impeachment by contradiction" (see *infra*, p. 145).

      (1) **Overlap with other exceptions:** Often, the exception for impeachment will *overlap* with one of the other exceptions under which subsequent-measures evidence is allowed. For instance, if D testifies, "There's nothing more we could have done," evidence that D later "did more" (by using a better design, by placing warning signs, or whatever) will serve both to impeach D's testimony and to address the feasibility of alternatives after feasibility was placed in issue by D.

   ii. **Broad exception:** The impeachment exception is a *broad* one, broad enough so that a skilled plaintiff's lawyer will often be able to orchestrate events so as to get his evidence in under it. Typically, the defendant (or an employee of the defendant) will take the stand, and will testify, in essence, "We took reasonable safety precautions." The plaintiff's lawyer on cross, if she's clever, will then ask questions designed to explore safety measures that the defendant could have taken but didn't, and will then ask why. If the witness responds, in essence, that the measures would not have worked or weren't necessary, there's a good chance that the court will find that the witness may now be impeached by a showing that the measures were later used by the defendant (thus contradicting the testimony that they wouldn't have worked or weren't necessary).

3. **Must be controverted:**   For repair evidence to be admitted because it is relevant to a specific element other than negligence/culpability, that element must be ***disputed***. Thus evidence of a post-accident design improvement cannot be introduced to prove that that improved design is feasible, if the defendant concedes that such an improvement is feasible, and instead merely disputes the issue of negligence.

   a. **Strategy:**   If the defendant asserts that a particular issue (e.g., feasibility) is not in dispute, the trial judge may force the defendant to "put its money where its mouth is" by agreeing to a ***stipulation*** conceding that issue.

C. **Product liability:**   The most controversial issue concerning the repairs exclusion has historically involved suits brought in ***strict product liability***.

1. **The problem:**   In a strict product liability case, the negligence or culpability of the defendant is not, legally speaking, at issue — if a product is "dangerously defective," there is liability even though the manufacturer, at the time of manufacture, neither knew nor had reason to know of the defect. Since the rule barring admission of repair evidence applies only when the evidence is offered on the issue of negligence or culpability, arguably the rule should not apply in the product liability case.

2. **FRE now deny admission:**   But the FRE *apply* the no-subsequent-remedial-measures rule to product-liability cases, just as to negligence cases. FRE 407 now says that subsequent-measures evidence is not admissible to prove, among other things, "a ***defect in a product*** or its ***design***; or a need for a ***warning*** or ***instruction***."

   Example: P, the owner of a single-engine plane made by D, crashes in the plane when it runs out of fuel because water has gotten into the fuel tanks. P sues D on a products liability defective-design theory. P's theory is that a defective design of the fuel tanks allowed condensation to form inside the tank. In support of this theory, P offers evidence that shortly after this and two other similar accidents, D redesigned the fuel tanks to make such condensation less likely. Under FRE 407, this evidence will not be admissible.

   a. **Post-manufacture, pre-accident remedial measures:**   Since FRE 407 applies to product liability situations, an additional issue arises: does the rule apply where the subsequent remedial measure — typically a redesign or warning — occurs after the manufacture of the product that causes injury but ***before the accident*** under litigation? Rule 407 answers this question in the ***negative***: the exclusion of subsequent-measures evidence applies only to those measures that "would have made an ***earlier injury or harm*** less likely to occur[.]" (See first sentence of 407.)

XIII. LIABILITY INSURANCE

A. **General rule:**   Both the common law and the Federal Rules provide that evidence that a person carried or did not carry *liability insurance* is *not admissible* on the issue of whether he acted negligently. This rule bars such evidence when it is offered by a plaintiff to suggest that because the defendant was insured, the defendant was probably careless. Conversely, such evidence is barred when offered by the defendant to show that because he did not have adequate insurance, he had an incentive to be careful. S&R, p. 316.

1. **Federal Rule:** The Rule on the subject, FRE 411, codifies the common-law approach. The Rule provides that "Evidence that a person was or was not *insured against liability* is *not admissible to prove whether the person acted negligently or otherwise wrongfully*. But the court may admit this evidence for *another purpose*, such as proving a witness's bias or prejudice or proving agency, ownership, or control."

2. **Rationale:** As with several of the other rules of exclusion which we have considered above (e.g., the rule dealing with evidence of subsequent repairs), the rule barring liability insurance evidence has both a relevance and a prejudice rationale behind it:

    [1] The evidence is of relatively *little probative value*, because most people agree that "whether one has insurance coverage reveals little about the likelihood that he will act carelessly." McC p. 357.

    [2] A jury may well be *prejudiced* by information about insurance; it can be argued that "the mention of insurance *invites higher awards* than are justified, and conversely, the sympathy that the jury might feel for a defendant who must pay out of his own pocket could interfere with its evaluation of the evidence].]" *Id.*

3. **Other purpose:** Again as with other rules of exclusion, the rule does not apply where the evidence is offered for some *other purpose*. The possible purposes listed by FRE 411 are in fact the most commonly applicable ones, but the list is merely illustrative.

    a. **Insurance investigator:** A common way for the existence of insurance to come out in trial is if the defendant decides to put an insurance company *investigator* on the witness stand; in this situation, the plaintiff may inquire into the witness's relationship to the defendant both to show possible prejudice and as part of the general right to put a witness's testimony in context. (Of course, for this reason the defendant will often choose not to put an insurance company employee on the stand.) For instance, if the plaintiff gave his statement to a representative of the defendant's insurance company, the statement typically cannot be admitted into evidence without the testimony of the person who took it, and plaintiff's counsel will then be permitted to test the reliability of that person by inquiring on cross-examination into sources of possible bias.

    b. **Voir dire:** Also, most states allow questions during the *voir dire* of prospective jurors concerning a juror's employment by or interest in insurance companies. A juror who hears such questions being asked is likely to assume (not necessarily correctly) that the defendant has insurance. Such questions are proper even when the defendant is not insured, because if a juror has a bias in favor of or against insurance companies, this may influence his deliberation because of his mistaken belief that the defendant is covered by insurance.

XIV. COMPROMISES, OFFERS TO PLEAD GUILTY, AND OFFERS TO PAY MEDICAL EXPENSES

A. Compromises generally: Most lawsuits are settled before trial. Where a trial does take place, it has usually been preceded by attempts at settlement. The things that parties say during the course of settlement negotiations are often at least arguably relevant. Nonetheless, it has long been established that the fact that a party has ***offered to settle a claim*** may ***not be admitted*** on the issue of the claim's validity. McC, p. 466.

> **Example:** P, a pedestrian, is injured by a car driven by D. P sues for $10,000. D offers to settle the case for $5,000. P declines. At trial, P may not introduce D's settlement offer into evidence on the theory that it constitutes an admission by D of liability. Conversely, had P offered to take $5,000 in settlement and D had refused, D could not introduce P's offer to show that P had serious doubts about the merits of his claim.

1. Rationale: There are two reasons for this rule, which are similar to those we have seen for several of the other rules discussed in this chapter: (1) Settlement offers are of low probative value, since a litigant may be attempting to "buy peace" by settling, rather than expressing his real belief about the merits of his case; and (2) Admission of such information would give the parties a strong disincentive to pursue settlement negotiations.

B. Compromises — Federal Rules: The FRE follow the common-law approach of excluding settlement offers, and in fact broaden it. FRE 408 provides:

Rule 408. Compromise Offers and Negotiations

(a) Prohibited Uses. Evidence of the following is ***not admissible*** — on behalf of any party — either to ***prove or disprove the validity or amount of a disputed claim*** or to impeach by a prior inconsistent statement or a contradiction:

   (1) ***furnishing, promising, or offering*** — or ***accepting***, promising to accept, or offering to accept — a ***valuable consideration in compromising or attempting to compromise the claim***; and

   (2) ***conduct or a statement*** made ***during compromise negotiations about the claim*** — except when ***offered in a criminal case*** and when the negotiations related to a claim by a public office in the exercise of its regulatory, investigative, or enforcement authority.

(b) Exceptions. The court ***may admit*** this evidence for ***another purpose***, such as proving a ***witness's bias or prejudice***, negating a contention of undue delay, or proving an effort to obstruct a criminal investigation or prosecution.

1. Extension to cover collateral statements: So FRE 408 excludes settlement offers and acceptances of settlements offers, as the common law does. But 408 then goes beyond the common-law by also excluding ***collateral statements and admissions*** made in ***connection with*** settlement offers; see *infra*, p. 70.

C. Compromises — Actual dispute required: The rule of exclusion applies only where there is an ***actual dispute*** between the parties concerning either the validity of the claim or the amount at issue. See FRE 408(a), 1st sentence (rule of exclusion applies only to efforts to prove or dispute the validity or amount of "a ***disputed claim***.")

1. Agreement on liability: Thus if D agrees that P's claim has merit and both parties agree on the sum owed, their discussions will not be classified as "settlement discussions" merely because D admits liability or says he can't pay the full amount but will pay less.

D. Compromises — Must be intent to compromise: Conversely, FRE 408 requires a true compromise or attempted compromise — if all a party is doing is ***stating his position***, without "mak[ing] some ***movement*** away from the original boundaries of the dispute and towards the other's position," the rule of exclusion doesn't apply. That's because 408 applies only where the situation involves "***compromising or attempting to compromise***" the claim. M&K §4.25, p. 243.

> **Example:** P is injured by a steer that has escaped from D's truck. D contends that P was contributorily negligent in that P got too close to the steer while trying to "corner" it. In support of this defense, D offers a letter which P wrote to D before the trial began, in which P says that he "got out some 10 feet from the animal." P argues that the letter should be excluded because it was part of settlement negotiations, but the trial court admits it.
>
> *Held*, the trial court correctly admitted the letter, because it was not in fact part of settlement negotiations. The letter contained statements such as, "We don't intend to let you or that trucking company off . . . ," and demanded that D pay P's claim in full. The letter was thus "an attempt to inform [D] as to the facts of the incident," not a true offer of compromise as required by Rule 408. *Davidson v. Prince*, 813 P.2d 1225 (Ut. 1991).

E. Compromises — Collateral admissions: Exactly what is excluded under the rule? Clearly the offer itself. But what about collateral ***admissions of fact*** that are made during the course of settlement negotiations?

1. Common-law admits: The common-law rule is that such collateral factual admissions are ***generally admissible.***

> **Example:** P, a pedestrian, is run over by D and badly injured. P sues D; shortly thereafter, D says to P, "I'm so sorry about this — it's all my fault, because I was drunk that night. I'll pay you $5,000 to drop your action." P may not introduce the fact that D offered $5,000 to show that D believed he is liable. But she may, under the common-law rule, introduce D's admission to having been drunk, since that is an admission of fact.

a. Exceptions: There are two exceptions to the common-law rule on factual admissions. The factual admissions will be ***inadmissible*** if they are either:

i. ***Inextricably bound up*** with the settlement offer so that one cannot be introduced without the other; or

ii. ***Phrased in a hypothetical form*** (e.g., "Assuming for the moment that you may be able to prove that I was drunk that night, I'll offer you $5,000) or are preceded by the statement that the discussion is ***"without prejudice."***

2. Federal Rule: But the Federal Rules take a ***broader*** approach to exclusion with regard to collateral matters. FRE 408(a)(2) renders inadmissible any evidence of "***conduct or a statement made during compromise negotiations about the claim***[.]"

a. **Collateral statements also barred:** This sentence means that an admission of *fact* ("I was drunk that night"), if it occurs during the course of settlement negotiations, is *not admissible* even if it is quite separable from the settlement offer. This sentence reflects the desire of the rule's draftsmen to encourage free-wheeling settlement negotiations in which the parties simply do not have to worry that some of what they say may come back to hurt them.

b. **Later civil case brought by government:** But Rule 408 contains a special *exception* where the settlement discussions occur in a *civil suit brought by a governmental agency*: a collateral statement or conduct by the adverse private party *can* be introduced by the government in a *subsequent criminal case*. M&K §4.25, p. 246.

  i. **Rationale:** The theory behind this rule is that an individual who *speaks in front of governmental agents* should *anticipate* that such collateral statements could be admitted against him in a subsequent criminal action. ACN to Amended Rule 408.

  Example: The IRS brings a civil suit against D to recover income taxes. The parties conduct settlement negotiations. During these negotiations, D admits to the IRS auditor that he intentionally underreported his taxable income for the year in question. The parties settle. Then, the federal government brings criminal tax evasion charges against D. In this prosecution, the government tries to introduce evidence of D's admission.

  The evidence will be admissible, because FRE 408 allows admission, in a criminal case, of a private party's prior statement or conduct made during negotiations for settlement of a civil claim brought by a government agency.

  ii. **Applies only to proving statements or conduct:** But the special rule described above applies only to proof of prior *statements or conduct*, as distinguished from prior settlement offers. The fact that a party previously *offered to settle, or did settle*, a civil claim is made inadmissible by FRE 408 in any subsequent criminal case — and that's true whether the original civil suit in which the settlement discussions occurred was brought by a governmental agency or by a private party. M&K §4.25, p. 246.

c. **No ability to "immunize":** Suppose a party admits a certain fact during settlement negotiations. Under the Federal Rule, does this mean that the other party may not prove that fact by means independent of the settlement admission? The answer is *"no"* — the other party is still free to prove that fact by means other than the admission. Similarly, if a party gives a *document* to her adversary during settlement negotiations, the document is *not "immunized"* from admission — if the same document is or could be found through discovery or other techniques independent of the settlement negotiations, it may be admitted.

F. **Compromises — Other purposes:** Like most of the other rules of exclusion discussed in this chapter, the rule excluding settlement offers applies only where the evidence is offered in order to prove a core fact (here, the weakness of the opposing party's claim or defense) — it may be admitted for *other purposes*. FRE 408(b) mentions some of the possible other purposes: "proving a witness's **bias or prejudice**, negating a contention of **undue delay**, or proving an effort to **obstruct a criminal investigation** or prosecution."

1. **Impeachment use:** The most common situation in which the "other purpose" exception is sometimes deemed to apply occurs when what is at issue is a settlement between a party (usually the defendant) and a **third person** who is not a party to the present action, but who is a **witness**. Here, if the existence of the settlement is used to **impeach the credibility of the settling witness**, some courts will deem that to be "another purpose" and thus admissible.

    Example: P and W are both employees of D, a railroad. P is injured by one of D's trains while standing on a track, and claims that the train's engineer should have seen P and stopped the train. At the trial of P's suit against D, D calls W as a witness, and W gives testimony that is largely favorable to D. P's lawyer elicits from W in cross-examination that W was injured in the same collision as P. P then asks W, "Didn't you make a claim against D that D settled with you?" D objects on the ground that the answer would be inadmissible as evidence of settlement negotiations.

    Held, the question was proper. Proof of D's settlement with W was not offered for the purpose of showing the validity of W's (and by inference P's) claim. Rather, it was asked for the purpose of testing W's credibility as a witness (e.g., W may feel beholden to D, or he may have explicitly agreed to give favorable testimony in return for the settlement payment by D). *Joice v. Missouri-Kansas-Texas Ry.*, 189 S.W.2d 568 (Mo. 1945).

    a. **FRE 408(a) doesn't allow impeachment use:** But the Federal Rules of Evidence do **not** allow certain types of **impeachment use** of the settlement, or statements during settlement negotiations, as a result of a 2006 amendment. FRE 408(a) now says that neither settlement offers, nor conduct or statements made during settlement negotiations, may be admitted *"to impeach by a prior inconsistent statement or a contradiction[.]"*

        Example: So in the setting of *Joice, supra*, the FRE would still allow P to impeach W's credibility by showing W's settlement as a way of demonstrating his bias. (In other words, the result of Joice would be the same today.) But now, suppose that W had testified that D's engineer couldn't have known that there was anyone on the track, and P wanted to show on cross that W had asserted the contrary in W's own settlement negotiations with D.

        Under FRE 408(a), the court would not allow P to do this, since this would be "impeach[ment] by a prior inconsistent statement or a contradiction[.]" The Advisory Committee Note to the 2006 amendment to FRE 408(a) says that allowing statements made in settlement negotiations to be used for impeachment purposes "would tend to **swallow the exclusionary rule** and would impair the public policy of promoting settlements." (FRE 408's ban on impeachment use applies in the basic two-party situation as well as the three-party one.)

G. **Proof by party of her own settlement offer:** Usually, a party would like to show the *other party's* settlement offer or statement made during the settlement negotiations, and as we've seen nearly all courts disallow this. But what if a party wants to show that *she herself* made a settlement offer? Most courts, and the FRE, say that the usual rule applies here, too — in other words, the offering party **cannot unilaterally waive** the protection of the no-settlement-evidence rule as to the admissibility of **her own offer or statement.**

> **Example:** P sues D, a railroad, in federal district court on a diversity-based negligence claim arising out of a collision between D's train and P's car. D is afraid that the jury will think that D is heartless; therefore, it would like the jury to know that D made a real effort to settle P's claim for $100,000, and that P rejected this offer.
>
> Even though D is willing to waive the protection of FRE 408 so that it can introduce its own settlement offer into evidence (for the purpose of proving that it good-heartedly recognized its own potential liability), D cannot unilaterally carry out this waiver – P has the right to keep D from introducing D's own settlement offer. See ACN to the 2006 amendments to FRE 408 (saying that 408 excludes compromise evidence "even when a party seeks to admit its own settlement offer or [its own] statements made in settlement negotiations").

H. Compromises — Completed settlements: Suppose a settlement is not only attempted but **completed**, in the sense that the parties have signed a formal agreement. That agreement can be sued upon as a contract, and in the suit the agreement itself is always admissible. But suppose that defendant never pays the agreed-upon amount, and plaintiff instead reinstates his original claim (for more money than the amount called for in the settlement agreement). May either party introduce the settlement agreement to show that the other lacked confidence in its case?

> **Example:** D signs a settlement agreement in which he promises to pay $10,000 to P next June 15th. If June 15th comes and goes and D does not pay, P may well prefer to sue for $50,000 and use the agreement as an admission by D of liability, rather than having to go through all the trouble of suing just to collect the $10,000 called for in the agreement.

    1. Federal Rule: The Federal Rule **excludes** the completed settlement in this situation. See Advisory Committee's Note to FRE 408.

I. Guilty pleas: On the criminal side, the equivalent of the settlement is the **guilty plea**. The process of plea bargaining raises two major evidentiary questions: (1) If D offers to plead guilty, but the prosecution does not accept, may D's offer (or factual admissions accompanying it) be introduced against D at trial? and (2) If D actually enters a guilty plea as part of a plea bargain, but later withdraws the plea, may the fact of the initial plea be introduced against him at the trial? In general, the Federal Rules and most states are in accord that the answer to each of these questions is **"no."**

    1. Offer of plea: With respect to the defendant's offer to plead guilty, and any statements he makes in connection with that offer, FRE 410(a)(4) is in accord with the rule of most states. 410(a)(4) excludes from use against the defendant (either in the criminal trial on the very charge in question, or in **any other** criminal or civil proceeding) any "statement made during **plea discussions with an attorney for the prosecuting authority** if the discussions **did not result in a guilty plea** or they resulted in a **later-withdrawn guilty plea.**"

a. **Rationale:**   Once again, there is a two-fold rationale for the rule of exclusion: (1) an offer to plead guilty has relatively little probative value on the issue of guilt, since a defendant who fears conviction may find the lesser charge or lighter sentence offered to him to be attractive even though he is in fact innocent; and (2) because of the over-crowded criminal justice system, there is a strong public policy in favor of encouraging plea bargains.

b. **Factual admissions:**   Observe that the Federal Rule, like the rule in most states, protects the defendant from having the prosecution use against him either the fact of the guilty plea or any *factual admissions* made by him during the course of unsuccessful plea-bargaining negotiations.

   Example: D's lawyer says to the prosecutor, "My guy admits that he pulled the gun against the storekeeper that night, but will plead guilty to the lesser crime of burglary instead of robbery." The prosecutor refuses the offer, and goes to trial on robbery charges. The prosecutor won't be allowed to introduce either D's admission (an adoptive admission of his lawyer's statement — see *infra*, p. 219) about pulling the gun, or the offer to plead guilty to the burglary.

c. **Must be with prosecutor:**   Under FRE 410(a)(4), only statements made to "an *attorney for the prosecuting authority*" are covered. Therefore, if, say, an FBI agent, an IRS agent, or a police officer tells the defendant or his lawyer that he may be able to arrange leniency or a plea bargain, any resulting statement may be *used against the defendant*. (However, such statements may be inadmissible because of the *Miranda* rule's ban on unwarned statements made during custodial interrogation.)

d. *Nolo contendere:*   FRE 410, like the rule in most states, also excludes pleas of *nolo contendere*. See FRE 410(a)(2). In fact, the very purpose of entering a plea of *nolo contendere* is that it may not be admitted in any subsequent proceedings (e.g., civil ones alleging the same facts that gave rise to the criminal plea).

e. **Later civil proceedings:** Observe that FRE 410(a) makes the plea offer and any collateral statements equally inadmissible in any later *civil* proceeding.

   Example: D is charged with murdering V by shooting her. In plea negotiation sessions with the prosecutor, he offers to plead to manslaughter, and admits that he was the one who pulled the trigger (but claims self-defense). The prosecutor rejects the offer and goes to trial on the murder charges. D is acquitted. V's estate sues D civilly for wrongful death. The estate won't be allowed to introduce either D's offer to plead to manslaughter, nor his admission that he pulled the trigger.

2. **Withdrawn pleas:**   FRE 410(a)(4) makes it quite clear that the rule of exclusion applies to a plea of guilty that is entered and later *withdrawn*.

3. **Impeachment:**   If the *defendant* introduces into evidence a statement made during plea bargaining that he believes is exculpatory, the prosecution is then free to use other statements made during the same discussions to *impeach* him, "if in fairness [all] the statements *ought to be considered together*." FRE 410(b)(1). "The obvious purpose is to

Table 3-1

***CHECKLIST*: Special Issues as to Circumstantial Evidence**

Use this checklist to see whether your fact pattern triggers any of the special rules
regarding particular types of circumstantial evidence. A few rules are omitted (e.g.,
Guilty Pleas (FRE 410) and Similar Crimes in Child-Molestation Cases (FRE 414)).

Issue	Text of Rule; Note(s)	Examples
Character as Circumstantial Evidence: General "Acted in Accordance" Rule	"**(a) Character Evidence.** *(1) Prohibited Uses.* Evidence of a person's character or character trait is not admissible to prove that on a particular occasion the person ***acted in accordance*** with the character or trait." (FRE 404(a)(1))	Accident case. To prove that D probably drove negligently on the occasion in question, P calls W, D's acquaintance, who proposes to testify, "D has always been a very careless and distracted person, both when driving and when doing other tasks requiring concentration." *Inadmissible*, because it proves D's character trait of carelessness, offered to prove that on a particular occasion, D "***acted in accordance*** with" this trait of carelessness.
Character as Circumstantial Evidence: Special Rules in Criminal Cases -- Defendant's or Victim's Character	**In criminal cases:** **1. Defendant's character:** "(A) a ***defendant*** may offer evidence of the ***defendant's pertinent trait***, and if the evidence is admitted, the ***prosecutor*** may offer evidence to ***rebut*** it." (FRE 404(a)(2)(A)) **2. Victim's character:** "(B) subject to the limitations in Rule 412 [rape shield provision], a ***defendant*** may offer evidence of an ***alleged victim's pertinent trait***, and if the evidence is admitted, the ***prosecutor*** may: (i) offer evidence to ***rebut*** it; and (ii) offer evidence of the ***defendant's same trait***; and "(C) in a ***homicide*** case, the ***prosecutor*** may offer evidence of the ***alleged victim's trait of peacefulness*** to ***rebut*** evidence that the ***victim was the first aggressor***." **Note:** In both #1 and #2, the evidence must take the form of ***reputation*** or ***opinion*** testimony, ***not of specific instances*** of conduct illustrating the character or trait. (FRE 405(a))	**Example 1 (#1 at left) -- D's good character:** Murder case arising out of a bar fight. D raises defense of self-defense. D offers testimony by W, D's friend: "I've known D since we were both 5; he's a peaceable fellow who would never start a fight, in a bar or anywhere else." *Admissible*, to show D's relevant "pertinent trait" of character (peaceableness). **Example 2 (#1 at left) -- D's good character:** Same facts as Example 1. Now, W offers to testify, as first witness for D, "D is a completely honest person, who would never lie." *Inadmissible*, because not evidence of a pertinent trait (D's honesty is not relevant either to the charge, or to D's credibility since he hasn't yet been a witness). **Example 3 (#2(B) at left) -- V's bad character:** Same bar-fight case as Example 1. As D's first witness, W offers to testify, "V has a vicious temper, and has a reputation for starting a lot of bar fights." *Admissible*, as evidence of "an alleged victim's pertinent trait." **Example 4 (#2(B)(i) and (ii) at left) -- V's bad character:** Same bar fight as Examples 1 and 3. After W's testimony in Example 3, prosecution offers W2's testimony: "I know both D and V by reputation. D is known in the community as **(Cont. on next page)**

Table 3-1 (p. 2)

Issue	Text of Rule; Note(s)	Examples
Character as Circumstantial Evidence: Special Rules in Criminal Cases -- Defendant's or Victim's Character (cont.)	**(cont. from previous page)**	having a violent temper, but V is known for being very peaceable." *Admissible* as to both D and V: Since D introduced W's testimony, which was "evidence of an alleged victim's pertinent trait," prosecution can now "(i) offer evidence to rebut [that evidence]; and (ii) offer evidence of the defendant's same trait." **Example 5 (#2(C) at left) -- V's good character:** Murder case arising out of a bar fight. D raises defense of self-defense, by testifying on his own behalf that V started the fight. As prosecution's rebuttal witness, W offers to testify, "V is known in the community for being very peaceable." *Admissible*: in a homicide case, the prosecutor may "offer evidence of the alleged victim's trait of peacefulness to rebut evidence that the victim was the first aggressor." Note that this is so even though D did not offer any "character" evidence about either himself or V, but merely said that V started this particular fight.
Character as Circumstantial Evidence: Witness's Character	**In both criminal and civil cases:** **"(3) Exceptions for a Witness.** Evidence of a *witness's character* may be admitted under Rules 607, 608, and 609." (FRE 404(a)(3))	Accident case. W testifies for P, "I saw the accident, and it happened because D ran a red light." D calls W2 to testify, "W has a reputation for being a pathological liar." *Admissible* under FRE 608(a), as "testimony about the witness's reputation for having a character for ... untruthfulness."
Crimes or Other Bad Acts	"(1) Evidence of a crime, wrong, or other act is *not admissible* to prove a person's *character* in order to show that *on a particular occasion* the person *acted in accordance with the character*. (2) This evidence may be admissible for *another purpose*, such as proving motive, opportunity, intent, preparation, plan, knowledge, identity, absence of mistake, or lack of accident." (FRE 404(b))	**Example 1 (Clause (1) at left):** D is charged with robbing a 7/11 while wearing a mask. As part of its case in chief, prosecution offers evidence that twice before, D was charged with (but never convicted of) robbing a 7/11. Assume the basis for the evidence is to show that "D has robbed 7/11s in the past, so this makes it more likely than it would otherwise be that D is the masked robber this time." *Inadmissible* as "Evidence of a crime ... [offered] to prove [D's] character in order to show that on a particular occasion [D] acted in accordance with the character." **(Cont. on next page)**

Table 3-1 (p. 3)

Issue	Text of Rule; Note(s)	Examples
Crimes or Other Bad Acts (cont.)	**(Cont. from previous page)**	**Example 2 (Clause (2) at left):** D is charged with robbing a 7-Eleven. Security footage from the crime scene shows the robber wearing a distinctive Richard Nixon mask of a type not manufactured since 1978. In D's opening statement, counsel says that D denies being the robber. As part of its case in chief, prosecution offers evidence that last year, D was convicted of robbing a different 7-Eleven, and offers security footage from that crime showing the robber wearing a 1978 Richard Nixon mask. *Admissible:* This evidence is not being offered merely to "prove [D's] character in order to show that on a particular occasion [D] acted in accordance with the character." Instead, it's being offered "for ***another purpose***, such as ***proving ... identity***" (i.e., that it's D, not someone else, who's the robber here).
Character as Circumstantial Evidence: Victim's Sexual Behavior or Predisposition (Rape Shield provisions)	"**(a)** The following evidence is *not admissible* in a civil or criminal proceeding involving *alleged sexual misconduct:* (1) evidence offered to prove that a *victim engaged in other sexual behavior*; or (2) evidence offered to prove a *victim's sexual predisposition*." (FRE 412(a)). "**(b) Exceptions.** *(1) Criminal Cases.* The court may admit the following evidence in a criminal case: (A) evidence of specific instances of a victim's sexual behavior, if offered to prove that someone other than the defendant was the ***source of semen***, injury, or other physical evidence; (B) evidence of specific instances of a victim's sexual behavior ***with respect to the person accused*** of the sexual misconduct, if offered by the defendant to prove ***consent*** or if offered by the prosecutor; and (C) evidence whose exclusion would violate the defendant's ***constitutional rights***." [Exceptions for civil cases omitted for space reasons.]	**Example 1 (Clause (1)):** D is on trial for raping V at the end of their first date. D raises the defense of consent. D offers testimony by W, "I was V's roommate during the year in question. I know that she had sex with at least 3 men on the first date that year." *Inadmissible*, as "offered to prove that a victim engaged in other sexual behavior[.]" **Example 2 (Clause (2)):** D is on trial for raping V, a co-worker, at the end of their first date. D raises the defense of consent. D offers testimony by W, a co-worker of both, that V often wore low-cut blouses and short skirts to the office and told dirty jokes, suggesting that a reasonable person in D's position might have interpreted these acts as showing that D was predisposed to promiscuous behavior. *Inadmissible* as "evidence offered to prove a ***victim's sexual predisposition***" (which the ACN say includes evidence relating to a victim's "mode of dress, speech, or lifestyle.)" **Note:** Neither the evidence in Example 1 nor that in 2 would be covered by the exceptions in (b) at left.

Table 3-1 (p. 4)

Issue	Text of Rule; Note(s)	Examples
Character as Circumstantial Evidence: Defendant's Similar Crimes in Sexual-Assault Cases	**"Rule 413. Similar Crimes in Sexual-Assault Cases** **(a) Permitted Uses.** In a criminal case in which a defendant is *accused of a sexual assault*, the court may *admit* evidence that the defendant *committed any other sexual assault.* The evidence may be considered on *any matter to which it is relevant.*" **Note:** However, courts have interpreted this as not depriving the court of its right to exclude evidence under *FRE 403* where the evidence's "probative value is substantially outweighed by a danger of ... *unfair prejudice*[.]"	D is on trial for raping V at the end of their first date. D raises the defense of consent. The prosecution, in its case in chief, offers evidence that twice before, D was convicted of raping women on the first date, in trials where he claimed consent. *Admissible* on the issue of whether V consented, which is a "matter to which [the convictions are] relevant." And the fact patterns in the past and present cases are similar enough that the court would *not* find that the "probative value is substantially outweighed by a danger of ... unfair prejudice" under FRE 403.
Habit and Custom	**"Rule 406. Habit; Routine Practice** Evidence of a person's *habit* or an organization's *routine practice* may be admitted to prove that on a particular occasion the person or organization a*cted in accordance with the habit or routine practice.* The court may admit this evidence regardless of whether it is corroborated or whether there was an eyewitness."	Civil suit between P (insurance claimant) and D (insurer). Issue is whether D mailed a notice of cancellation to P by a certain deadline. D offers evidence that (1) its records show a notice was prepared 2 days before the deadline; and (2) it was the office's routine practice to mail all such notices the day they were completed. Admissible, as "an organization's routine practice ... to prove that on a particular occasion the ... organization acted in accordance with the ... routine practice." So no one from D needs to testify, "I know that I mailed the notice."
Similar Happenings	Not covered in the FRE. But may be admissible (after scrutiny) as generally relevant.	Slip-and-fall case, in which P claims that the sidewalk in front of D's premises was cracked and dangerous when P fell. P offers evidence of two other falls in the month before P fell. Probably *admissible*, as "similar happening" that's generally relevant, and not forbidden by any Rule.
Subsequent Remedial Measures	"When measures are taken that would have made an *earlier injury* or harm *less likely to occur*, evidence of the *subsequent measures* is *not admissible* to prove: *negligence*; culpable conduct; a defect in a product or its design; or a need for a warning or instruction. But the court may admit this evidence for *another purpose*, such as impeachment or — if disputed — proving ownership, control, or the feasibility of precautionary measures." (FRE 407).	Slip-and-fall case, in which P claims that the sidewalk in front of D's premises was cracked and dangerous when P fell. P offers evidence that 1 week after the accident, D had that patch of sidewalk repaved. *Inadmissible*, if offered to show D's prior negligence, or the need for a warning. But *admissible* for "another purpose," such as showing that D owned the property (if D claimed that someone else owned or controlled that portion of sidewalk).

Table 3-1 (p. 5)

Issue	Text of Rule; Note(s)	Examples
Liability Insurance	**"Rule 411. Liability Insurance** Evidence that a person was or was not *insured against liability* is *not admissible* to prove whether the person *acted negligently or otherwise wrongfully*. But the court may admit this evidence for *another purpose*, such as proving a witness's bias or prejudice or proving agency, ownership, or control."	**Example 1:** Car accident case, in which P, a pedestrian, is injured when a car driven by D hits him. P offers evidence that D was insured by a $10 MM auto liability policy. *Inadmissible* if offered to show that D was more likely to be careless because he knew that he probably wouldn't have to pay out-of-pocket for any injuries he caused while driving. **Example 2:** Same facts as above, but D defends on grounds that (1) he didn't own the car; (2) the accident was caused by bad brakes; and (3) he would have had no authority to get the brakes fixed even if he thought there was a problem with them. P offers evidence that the registered owner of the car was X (D's girlfriend) and that the policy named D as the daily user of the car. *Admissible* "for another purpose, such as proving ... control," i.e., to show that D probably had sufficient control over the car's use and maintenance that he had authority to get the brakes fixed.
Compromises (Settlements and Settlement Offers)	**"Rule 408. Compromise Offers and Negotiations** **(a) Prohibited Uses.** Evidence of the following is *not admissible* ... either to prove or disprove the *validity or amount* of a *disputed claim* or to *impeach* by a prior inconsistent statement or a contradiction: (1) furnishing, promising, or offering — or accepting, promising to accept, or offering to accept — a valuable consideration in *compromising or attempting to compromise the claim*; and (2) *conduct or a statement made during compromise negotiations about the claim* — except when offered in a criminal case and when the negotiations related to a claim by a public office in the exercise of its regulatory, investigative, or enforcement authority. **(b) Exceptions.** The court may admit this evidence for *another purpose*, such as proving a witness's bias or prejudice, negating a contention of undue delay, or proving an effort to obstruct a criminal investigation or prosecution."	**Example 1 (Clause a(1)):** Car accident case, in which a car driven by D hit a car driven by P. D defends on the grounds that he wasn't negligent. P offers her own testimony that right after P sued D, D called her and said, "I'll pay you $2,000, which is more than it'll cost to fix your car, as long as you agree to settle the case without reporting the accident to your insurance company." *Inadmissible* if offered for the likely purpose of showing that D must have thought he was liable, or he wouldn't have made such an offer, since that's evidence of "offering ... a valuable consideration in ... attempting to compromise [a] claim" in order to "prove ... the validity or amount of [the] disputed claim[.]" **Example 2 (Clause a(2)):** Same facts as above. P offers testimony that during the same post-suit conversation about settlement, D said, "I know it was my fault." *Inadmissible*, as "conduct or a statement made during compromise negotiations about [a disputed] claim," offered to show the claim's validity.

Table 3-1 (p. 6)

Issue	Text of Rule; Note(s)	Examples
Offers to Pay Medical Expenses	**"Rule 409. Offers to Pay Medical and Similar Expenses** Evidence of *furnishing, promising to pay, or offering to pay medical, hospital, or similar expenses* resulting from an *injury* is not admissible to prove *liability* for the injury." **Note:** Unlike the case of settlement offers, there's *no* provision excluding *collateral* "conduct or statements" made in connection with an offer to pay medical expenses.	**Example 1:** Car accident case, in which a car driven by D hit P, a pedestrian. D defends on the grounds that P jaywalked, making P, not D, the sole party at fault. P offers her own testimony that right after the accident, D stood over her fallen body and said, "Oh my God, I'm so sorry, I'll pay whatever medical expenses you have." *Inadmissible* if offered for the purpose (as seems likely) of proving that D made the offer and thus acknowledged that he was likely liable." **Example 2:** Same facts as above. Now, P offers to prove that after the accident, D said, "The accident was my fault, because I got distracted. I'll pay your medical expenses." The statement up to the word "distracted" can be admitted, because neither Rule 409 nor anything else excludes collateral statements made in connection with offers to pay medical expenses, even if the statement is offered to prove liability.

End of Table

prevent a defendant from taking advantage of FRE 410 by introducing a statement that is exculpatory only when taken out of context." L&S, p. 201.

J. Payment of medical expenses: The fact that a party has paid the *medical expenses* of an injured person is likewise excluded in nearly all states, when offered on the issue of the party's liability for the accident that caused the injury. FRE 409 follows this common-law approach: "Evidence of furnishing, promising to pay, or offering to pay *medical, hospital, or similar expenses resulting from an injury* is not admissible to *prove liability* for the injury."

1. Communications: But unlike the compromise and guilty plea contexts, in the medical-payment context only the *fact of the payment* is excluded. *Other admissions of fact* (e.g., "I'm paying your medical expenses because if I hadn't been drunk that night, I wouldn't have been driving on the shoulder and hit you") are *not excluded* either at common law or under FRE 409.

Quiz Yourself on
HABIT & CUSTOM; SIMILAR HAPPENINGS; SUBSEQUENT REMEDIAL MEASURES; LIABILITY INSURANCE; COMPROMISES; OFFERS TO PLEAD

GUILTY AND OFFERS TO PAY MEDICAL EXPENSES

14. Fast Freddie, proprietor of the Lots O' Lemons Car Lot, sells Sydney Suquer a used car. The car makes it two miles before the wheels fall off and the engine disappears in a cloud of black smoke. In a suit based on breach of warranty, Freddie denies giving warranties as a part of his sales. To prove that Freddie routinely gives warranties, Sydney seeks to introduce evidence of a prior customer who got a guarantee. Any objection? _____

15. Captain Hook loses his hand when it is sucked into the blade of his Mayhemart Food Processor, as he is feeding carrot sticks into the work-bowl as per the manufacturer's instructions. Hook sues Mayhemart for defective design. Mayhemart argues that there is nothing wrong with the design, and that Hook's accident was a bizarre aberration. In support of this argument, Mayhemart offers proof that 250,000 of the same model food processor were sold in the last two years, and the company has never received a complaint like Hook's. Under what circumstances, if any, will the evidence be admissible? _____

16. Captain Hook cuts off his hand on the drill with which he works. Hook brings a negligence action against his employer, Croc-O-Dial Metalworks. (There's no workers' compensation statute on the island where this happens.) Hook offers, as evidence of negligence, testimony that the day after the accident, Croc-O-Dial placed safety devices on the machines. Croc-O-Dial objects. How do you rule? _____

17. Batman finds that, every time he hits a pothole in the road, the ejector seat flips his passenger, the Boy Wonder, out of the Batmobile. Batman sues the manufacturer in strict liability for defective design of the seat. The manufacturer claims that the design was safe because the seat could not be made safer. Batman seeks to introduce evidence that, in the next model year, the manufacturer modified the ejector seat so it would only eject passengers when a secret button is pushed. Will this evidence be admissible to show the feasibility of safeguards? _____

18. Buddy Goode drives a truck for the Ashe Hauling Company. Buddy's vehicle sideswipes Molly Motorist, who suffers severe injuries. At Motorist's trial against Ashe, Ashe's President claims that Buddy is an independent contractor, and not an employee or agent of the company. Motorist's attorney then asks whether Buddy is covered by Ashe's liability insurance policy. Is there a basis to permit admission of the testimony over objection? _____

19. While Huey, Dewey and Louie are pheasant shooting from a boat in a lake, Donald carelessly drives his "Ski-doo" personal watercraft into them, injuring all three. All three sue Donald, but Huey and Dewey settle with him for a payment of a portion of the damages they were seeking. As part of the settlement, Huey and Dewey agree to testify against Louie in Louie's suit against Donald. When they so testify, can Louie introduce into evidence the fact that Donald settled with Huey and Dewey? _____

20. Stolitz Naya, engineer for the St. Petersburg Local, dozes off at the controls. He doesn't realize Anna Karenina has fallen in front of the train, and he runs her over, severing her legs. Anna lives — changing the course of Russian literature — and shortly after the accident, Naya calls her and says, "Gee, I'm sorry. I fell asleep at the wheel. It was all my fault. I'll pay your medical bills." Under the FRE, can (1) this statement (or any part) or (2) Naya's payment of Anna's medical bills, be admitted as evidence of liability at a subsequent trial? _____

―――――――――――

Answers

14. Yes. The only way the experience of prior customers would be relevant is to show Freddie had a "habit" of giving warranties. Evidence of a single prior guarantee is insufficient to demonstrate a person's habit or an organization's routine practice; to establish habit or routine practice, the behavior must be proven to be a *regular response to a repeated situation*. (If this *had* been enough to establish a habit, it would have been admissible. Under FRE 406, evidence of habit is admissible to prove that a person acted in accordance with that habit on a particular occasion. This is true regardless of whether there are eyewitnesses to the actual act, and whether or not there's corroboration of the existence of the habit.)

15. There is no blanket rule excluding this sort of "no prior accidents" evidence (which is the reverse of "similar happenings" evidence, also admissible subject to limits). However, the general requirement of relevance means that such "safety history" evidence will only be admissible if Mayhemart establishes that (1) the material circumstances of other customers' use were *substantially similar* and (2) Mayhemart probably *would have gotten complaints* if similar accidents had happened.

16. **Objection sustained**. Under FRE 407, evidence of subsequent remedial measures is inadmissible to prove negligence or culpable conduct. That's exactly what Hook is trying to do here. This rule is designed to encourage people to make things safer by not using this information against them to show negligence. (However, subsequent remedial measures are admissible for non-culpability purposes, such as proving ownership or control, or to rebut a claim of impossibility of precautions, etc. FRE 407.)

17. **Yes**. If the *feasibility* of safeguards is *disputed*, the fact that the safeguards whose feasibility was denied by the defendant were later implemented by him may be proved, notwithstanding the "no proof of subsequent remedial measures" rule. FRE 407. (The "yes" answers assumes that the technology used in the later model year was available at the time the seat in question was designed. If it wasn't, then the redesign doesn't bear on the feasibility of safeguards, and would be excluded.)

RELATED ISSUE: Suppose the manufacturer here hadn't argued that a safer design was impractical (merely that the design used was not unreasonably dangerous, the standard for strict product liability). Could Batman nonetheless have introduced the subsequent redesign to show that a safer seat was feasible, and thus by inference that the old design wasn't reasonably safe? Courts are split on this issue of whether the ban on subsequent remedial measures evidence applies to a showing of later design improvements when offered in a strict product liability case. Some hold that a strict liability case isn't about negligence or culpability, so the ban on subsequent remedial measures should not apply. Other courts (especially a lot of federal courts) hold that there is inevitably some element of culpability in an unsafe-design product liability case, and that the same policy reasons for barring remedial measures in negligence cases (don't discourage the taking of such measures by making them admissible) apply in strict liability cases.

18. **Yes**. Though evidence of liability insurance is inadmissible to prove Buddy's negligence, such evidence can be admitted to prove agency, ownership, control, or witness bias. FRE 411. Here, the fact that Buddy is covered by Ashe's liability policy tends to establish that Ashe controlled Buddy, and is therefore liable for Buddy's acts under respondeat superior.

19. **Yes**, but *only* for the purpose of demonstrating *bias* on the part of Huey and Dewey — *not* to prove Donald's *liability* for the accident. FRE 408. Remember that settlement offers, and completed settlements, are inadmissible to show the payor's liability. The reason is that settlements and settlement offers are of low probative value, since a litigant (here, Donald) may only be attempting to "buy peace" by settling.

20. (1) **Yes** and (2) **no**. Under FRE 409, the actual payment of medical bills, or an offer to pay, is not admissible to prove liability, due to the possibility that such payment may be prompted only by humanitarian motives. However, *admissions of fact* accompanying offers to pay medical bills are admissible. Thus, "Gee, I'm sorry. I fell asleep at the wheel. It was my fault," is admissible; "I'll pay your medical bills"

(and the fact that the bills were in fact paid) are not.

RELATED ISSUE: Assume that this had been a negotiation situation: "Gee, I'm sorry, I fell asleep at the wheel. It was all my fault. I'll pay you $5,000 to settle." Here, unlike the medical bills situation, the admission accompanying the settlement offer is *not* admissible under FRE 408; nor is the offer to settle or the settlement itself.

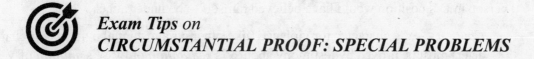

Exam Tips on
CIRCUMSTANTIAL PROOF: SPECIAL PROBLEMS

Of the topics in this chapter, the most-tested by far is character evidence; habit/custom, similar happenings, subsequent remedial measures, insurance and settlements are also tested with some frequency.

Character evidence

Here's what to focus on in connection with *character* evidence:

☛ **General rule:** The general rule, of course, is that a person's character is *inadmissible* to prove "action in accordance therewith," i.e., to prove that the person acted a certain way in accordance with his character on a particular occasion. (FRE 404(a)). (*Example:* P sues D civilly for negligently injuring P. P won't be allowed to show that D was a generally careless person, and D won't be allowed to show that D was a generally careful person.)

☛ **Character in issue:** Remember that the general rule applies only to *"circumstantial"* use of character evidence, i.e., X's character is used to prove that on a particular occasion, he probably acted in conformity with that character. In other words, if a person's character is itself directly *"in issue"* (i.e., his character is an element of a crime, claim or defense), the general "no character evidence" rule simply doesn't apply, and the evidence is admissible. However, there aren't many true instances of "character in issue."

   ☞ One context for testing this "character in issue" aspect is *defamation* — in a defamation action, P's character (or at least his reputation) will generally be in issue because it relates to damages. (*Example:* P, a religious leader, sues D, a newspaper, for claiming that P misused church funds. W, a former member of P's congregation, testifies that even before the article, members of the congregation rumored that P was misusing church funds. This testimony is admissible, because P's reputation is directly in issue — P's damages will be reduced or eliminated if it's shown that his reputation was damaged before the article appeared.)

   ☞ Similarly, it may occasionally be a direct issue whether someone *knew* that X possessed a certain character. (*Example:* C, a child, shoots P with an air rifle. P sues C's parents, the Ds, for negligently giving C the rifle. W, C's neighbor, testifies that C is a "vicious and malicious bully." This is admissible, as showing that the Ds should have known of C's dangerous tendencies and thus not given him the rifle.)

☛ **Victim's traits:** Whenever D in a criminal case is presenting evidence about the reputation or character of the *victim* (call the victim "V"), or about how V behaved in the particular episode, discuss whether this is allowed.

☞ The general rule is that D *may* offer such "victim's character" evidence. See FRE 404(a)(2) — a criminal defendant may offer "evidence of an alleged victim's pertinent trait."

☞ Most often, this is tested where D is claiming *self-defense* — V's reputation for unprovoked violence, or his violent character, *may* be used to establish that a reasonable person in D's position would have believed himself to be under attack.

Caution — V's character for violence (like other circumstantial evidence of character) must be proved by testimony about V's *reputation* or by W's *opinion* of V's character, *not by specific past acts* of violence by V. (FRE 405(a)). (*Example:* If D is charged with murdering V in a bar-room brawl, D's self-defense claim can be supported by W's testimony that V had a reputation for getting drunk and brawling, but not by evidence that on 3 particular occasions, V got into bar-room fights.)

☞ **Sexual behavior:** The other big "victim's character" area is the sexual behavior and reputation of a *rape* victim. Generally this evidence is *inadmissible*. The two main exceptions under the FRE: (i) V's past sexual history with persons other than D, if offered on the issue of whether D was the source of the injury or semen; and (ii) V's past sexual behavior with D, offered on the issue of whether V consented. (FRE 412(b)(1) and (2)).

☞ Most exam questions in this area arise where D claims that V *consented* (or that D reasonably believed that V consented). Here, D may put on evidence about V's past sexual conduct *with D* (e.g., D's lawyer may ask V, "Didn't you have consensual sex with D on previous occasions?" or "Didn't you sometimes play a game with D in which you pretended to resist but really were consenting?"), but *not* evidence about V's past conduct with *persons other than D* (e.g., D's lawyer may *not* ask V, "Didn't you have consensual sex with three other men to whom you weren't married, in the six months before this episode?")

☛ **Other crimes or bad acts by D:** Another big area for testing is D's *other crimes* or his *unconvicted bad acts.*

☞ **Generally inadmissible:** Remember that the general rule is that such evidence is *not* admissible to show that D's other crimes or bad acts make it more likely that he committed the particular crime with which he's now charged. (*Example:* If D is charged with armed robbery, the fact that D was previously convicted of embezzlement can't be used to show that "a thief's a thief," i.e., that D probably committed this theft as well.)

☞ **Exceptions:** However, most questions in this "other crimes and bad acts" area involve one of the many *exceptions* to the general rule. So before you conclude that the evidence is inadmissible because of the general rule, look hard to see if the fact pattern falls into one of these exceptions. Here are the most commonly tested exceptions:

☞ *Common plan and scheme.* (*Example:* D is arrested and charged with fraudulently using a credit card belonging to V. The prosecution wants to show that when arrested, D had in her possession 5 other credit cards in D's name, as well as 20 other credit cards and drivers licenses in the names of people other than D or V. This "unconvicted bad acts" evidence is admissible to show that the particular act charged is part of V's broader plan or scheme to fraudulently collect and use credit cards, thus making it more likely that D did the particular thing charged.)

☞ *"Signature" or modus operandi.* (*Example:* D is charged with illegally importing heroin in the false bottom of a brass statue. D claims that he bought the statue without knowing what was in it. The prosecution may show that D was convicted of smuggling cocaine in the false bottom of a brass statue 15 years before; this tends to show that D uses a particular MO, or method of operation. To put it another way, the "drugs in the brass statue" technique is so distinctive that it bears D's "signature.")

☞ *Identity.* (*Example:* D is charged with raping V. D's defense is that someone else must have committed the crime. The prosecution first puts on V's testimony that after the attack (in which the rapist wore a stocking mask), V told Detective that the rapist had a distinctive brown birthmark on his wrist. The prosecution then offers testimony by Detective that Detective listened to V's description, then consulted a police file of past sex offenders, and learned that one of them, D, had a brown birthmark on his wrist. Detective's testimony would probably be admissible as tending to establish D's identity as the rapist.)

☞ Also, remember that the other-crimes or bad-acts evidence *doesn't have to fit into a pre-defined slot* to be admissible; thus FRE 404(b) allows admission of other crimes or wrongs "for another purpose" and then lists (non-exhaustively) some specific exceptions like plan, identity, etc. So the real question to ask is, does the other-crime or bad-act evidence *tightly link* D to some element of the crime (in which case it's probably admissible)? Or does it have such a loose link to the crime charged that it merely suggests that because D has a certain character trait, he's more likely to have committed the crime charged (in which case it's probably inadmissible)?

☛ **Favorable evidence of D's character:** Remember that the *defendant* in a criminal case may offer evidence of a "pertinent trait" of his own character (FRE 404(a)(2)(A)) — i.e., *favorable character evidence*. (*Example:* D is charged with the crime of assaulting V, and pleads self-defense. He offers testimony by W that D has a reputation in the community as a peaceable, law-abiding citizen. This is admissible.)

Here are some special things to look out for in connection with defendant's favorable character evidence:

☞ Confirm that the case is a *criminal* case.

☞ Confirm that the evidence concerns a trait *pertinent* to the crime. (*Example:* D is charged with aggravated assault. He presents evidence of his good character for truth and veracity. This evidence will not be admissible, because D's truthfulness is not pertinent to this particular charge — it might be, however, if the charge were, say, embezzlement or fraud.)

☞ Make sure that the character evidence is in the form of *reputation* or *opinion* — proof of *specific acts* (i.e., D's "good" acts) is *not* permitted. FRE 405(a).

☞ Remember that once D presents proof of his good character, the **prosecution** is then allowed to **rebut** this character evidence. This rebuttal evidence may be by reputation opinion or specific acts (but extrinsic evidence of specific acts is not allowed). The rebuttal evidence may be either by questions to the defense's character witness or by rebuttal witnesses. (*Example:* D is charged with aggravated assault of V. He puts on W1, who testifies that D has a good reputation for non-violence. The prosecution may ask W1, "Didn't you witness a fight between D and X?" But the prosecution can't introduce extrinsic evidence of the fight, such as testimony by W2 or a document. The prosecution may also ask W1, "Didn't you tell Y that you thought D sometimes flies off the handle?" And, it may present W2 to testify that W2's opinion is that D is a violent person.)

Habit; Routine Business Practice

Remember that a person's *habit* can generally be used to show he acted in conformity with that habit on the particular occasion in question.

☛ The essence of a "habit" is that it is a *regular response* to a *repeated situation*. (*Example:* In an auto negligence case, the issue is whether D signalled before making a particular left turn. W, who was with D in the car that day but didn't watch, testifies that D drove with her on that same route every day, and at that particular turn, he almost always signalled. Admissible as habit evidence.)

☛ Before concluding that something is a "habit," check for 3 factors (if even one is absent, the evidence is probably not of a true "habit"):

    ☞ *Specificity:* The more specific the action, the more likely it is to be a habit rather than mere proof of a character trait. So beware of general descriptions of behavior (e.g., something that sounds like reputation evidence) — these are likely to flunk the specificity test, and be inadmissible character evidence. (*Example:* In an auto negligence case, P offers testimony that D had a reputation in the community for his dangerous driving, and was known as "Dare-Devil Dan." If offered to show that Dan had a habit of driving dangerously and thus probably did so on the particular occasion, it's inadmissible because it's too general.)

    ☞ *Regularity:* The habit must be regular. This has two sub-aspects.

        ☞ First, there must be a fair *number* of specific instances where the person adhered to the habit proved. (*Example:* The fact that P permitted insurance policies to lapse three times in her life is probably not sufficient evidence of habit to prove the same thing happened in the current situation.)

        ☞ Second, there must be sufficient *"uniformity of response,"* i.e., not very many instances where the situation arose and the habit was *not* followed. (*Example:* The fact that D breached seven contracts in 20 years in business probably won't establish a habit of breaching, if D had many dozens of contracts during that period.)

☞ *Unreflective behavior:* Finally, the behavior is more likely to be found to be habit if it's unreflective or semi-automatic, than where it's volitional and thought-out. (*Example:* Where D asserts an alibi defense that he was home on a particular day, evidence that it was the Sabbath, and that D had a habit of staying home to observe the Sabbath, probably won't be admitted, because D made a conscious choice each Sabbath to stay or not stay home. By contrast, signalling — or not signalling — before making a left turn meets the "semi-automatic" standard.)

   ☞ *Caution:* But unlike the first two factors, this one is not dispositive — if specificity and regularity are shown, the court may allow as habit evidence even action with a fair degree of volition to it (e.g., a doctor's habit of always informing his patients of the risks of a particular type of operation).

☛ Make sure the proof of the habit is in the proper form. Proof of *specific instances* known to the witness of the person's adherence to the habit is the best. (*Example:* "Most times when I walked with X, he jay-walked on that particular crossing.") Courts sometimes — but not generally — allow the witness's *opinion* that a person has a particular habit. Testimony that the person has a *reputation* for having a certain habit is virtually *never* allowed.

☛ Remember that evidence of the *routine practice* of an *organization* or institution is admissible to show that some event occurred. (*Example:* To prove that a notice of appeal was mailed on a particular day, the secretary to an attorney testifies that she, the secretary, personally enclosed the notice in a properly addressed envelope, sealed it, and placed it in the basket marked "Outgoing Mail" on that day at 2 p.m. She further testifies that, as a matter of office routine, the office mail clerk empties the basket every day at 4 p.m. and immediately takes the contents to the post office. This is sufficient to meet the requirements for proving the law firm's "routine practice," and thus to establish that the notice was probably mailed on the day in question.)

   ☞ Make sure the witness describes the routine business practice with *sufficient specificity*, and that the witness has *personal knowledge* of that practice. (*Example:* If in the above example, the testimony were merely that "We always mail notices out the day they're prepared, and I prepared this notice on May 1, so it must have gone out that day," the lack of detail about where the notices are put, who takes them to the post office and when, etc., would cause the court to deny admissibility.)

   ☞ The testimony need *not* be given by the *person who carries out* the business practice, as long as the witness has detailed personal knowledge of the practice. (*Example:* In the first, detailed example about mailing the notice, the fact that the secretary didn't personally empty the Outgoing box every day and take the contents to the post office didn't block admission, because she had first-hand knowledge of how this was done and who routinely did it.)

   ☞ Remember that a business custom can be used to prove the *non-occurrence* of an act. (*Example:* In a copyright infringement suit, a film company claims that its employees never read P's unsolicited manuscript. The company's mailroom clerk testifies that it was the invariable procedure of the company to have the mail room immediately return to the sender, unread, all unsolicited mailed scripts. This will be admissible to prove that the company never read the manuscript, whether or not it received it.)

Similar Accidents or other Happenings

Evidence that similar happenings occurred in the past, to show what happened on the present occasion, will often be admissible.

☛ **Substantial similarity:** "Similar happenings" evidence is most often tested in connection with *accidents* — the proponent typically wants to show that these other accidents shed light on what happened on the present occasion.

    ☞ Evidence that similar accidents or mishaps have happened in the past can be introduced on a number of different issues (e.g., Did the accident happen this time at all? Did D know of the risks? What caused the accident?). This evidence will generally be *admissible* if and only if there's a showing that the *circumstances* surrounding the other accidents and the present one are *substantially similar*.

    Example 1: P claims whiplash from an accident that occurred while P rode D's bus. P will be allowed to show that three other people on that bus suffered whiplash, because the others and P were obviously similarly situated.

    Example 2: Same basic facts. Now, P offers evidence that on other buses operated by D in the last year, there were two other accidents, in which three people suffered whiplash. Because there's probably no way to prove that the circumstances of these other accidents (e.g., the severity of the deceleration) matched those of the present accident, this "other accidents" evidence will be inadmissible.

    ☞ **Negative evidence:** Most often, D wants to use *"negative"* past-accidents evidence, by proving that because similar accidents involving D have not happened in the past, the present one either didn't happen at all, or wasn't caused by D's negligence. Again, this negative evidence will be allowed if and only if D shows the circumstances are substantially similar.

    Example: P falls in D's restaurant. P shows the floor was waxed 1/2 hour before the fall, and offers some evidence that excess wax remained on the tiles after this, making them too slippery. D offers testimony by W, its manager, that in the week before the accident, more than 10,000 people used the restaurant, and he neither saw nor heard about any other falls. This testimony is inadmissible, because there's no showing that the conditions were the same during the whole week as right before the accident (and, indeed, P's waxing evidence shows that conditions *weren't* the same).

        ☞ In this "negative" accident scenario, the proponent must also show that the witness is a person who would have *learned* of any such accidents. (*Example:* On the facts of the above restaurant example, the testimony could also be knocked out if there was no evidence that all falls would have been reported to W.)

☛ **Similar contracts:** Also, look for attempts to introduce evidence of similar *contracts,* offered to show the parties' intent in the present contract, or something else about the present contract.

    ☞ **Same parties:** Where the other contract involves the *same parties*, evidence about it will typically be admissible if and only if the contract's subject matter and surrounding circumstances are substantially *similar* to those of the present contract. (*Example:* D, a video store, orders blank cassette tapes from P. D refuses to accept delivery because the tapes are in paper boxes rather than clear plastic ones. D offers evidence that it placed three prior blank-tape orders from P, and that these orders all came in plastic. P shows that the present lot was sold at a special reduced price and the prior lots weren't. This change of circumstances will lead the court to find the past-contract evidence inadmissible.)

☞ **Contracts with third party:** Where the other contract is between one party to the litigation and a *third party*, it's much *less likely* to be admissible than where it involves both parties to the litigation. (*Example:* Same basic facts as prior example. Now, P offers evidence that in the prior four months, it had shipped paper-boxed videotapes to 20 other customers without objection. Assuming D didn't know about these other transactions, they won't be relevant to D's intent in entering the contract, so they'll be excluded.)

Subsequent Remedial Measures

Evidence that the defendant has taken subsequent remedial measures is *inadmissible* to prove D's *negligence*. (*Example:* After a truck operated by D is involved in an accident, D installs a "governor" to prevent it from going faster than 60 mph. If offered to show that the truck was driven too fast during the accident, the evidence is inadmissible.)

☛ **Other purposes:** But remember that subsequent-remedial-measure evidence is *admissible* if offered to prove something *other than negligence* (e.g., to prove ownership or control, or the feasibility of precautionary measures, or to impeach a witness).

☛ **Ownership central:** Most commonly-tested: repairs offered to proved *ownership or control* of the instrumentality. Look for a fact pattern where responsibility for the instrumentality is in dispute, yet the defendant fixes the item. (*Example:* P falls on pigeon droppings in an alley next to D's hotel; D claims it doesn't control the alley. P may show that since the accident, D has told its employees to regularly clean the alley.)

☞ **Owner-tenant disputes:** Ownership issues are especially likely where a *property owner* and the owner's *tenant* each claim the other was responsible. (*Example:* P falls in a hallway leading from a hotel to a restaurant. Evidence that the hotel owner replaced the floor covering will be admissible to show that it, not the restaurant, was responsible for maintaining the hallway.)

Insurance

Evidence that a party has liability insurance is inadmissible to show that he acted negligently or otherwise wrongfully. (FRE 411). (*Example:* P can't testify that after an accident, D said, "Don't worry, I have lots of insurance.")

☛ When the rule applies, it overcomes the more general rule allowing admissions to be admitted despite the hearsay rule. (So in the above example, it doesn't help P that D was making an implicit admission.)

☛ **Other purposes:** But again, remember that like remedial measures, the existence of insurance can be used to show something other than negligence, such as ownership or control of the insured instrumentality. (*Example:* After P is injured in a car accident, P sues D, who P believes is the owner of the car. D denies ownership. P offers an insurance policy on that car, written to cover D, and also offers testimony by an employee of Insurer that the policy was purchased by D. Admissible, because offered to show ownership, not negligence.)

☞   Similarly, existence of insurance can be admitted where it's part of a showing that the witness is *biased*. (*Example:* In an auto accident case, W, an investigator called to the stand by D, says that his investigation showed that P, not D, was at fault. P may show that W is likely to be biased because he was retained by D's insurance company.)

Settlements and Compromises; Offers to Pay Medical Bills; Guilty Pleas

Settlements: Evidence of an offer to *settle a claim* is inadmissible on the issue of the claim's validity.

☛ **Collateral admissions of fact:** Most frequently-tested: admissions *of fact* made in conjunction with settlement offers. Here, remember that such collateral admissions are usually admissible under the common-law, but not admissible under the FRE. (*Example:* D says to P, "Your claim seems high, but since I may have been a little negligent, I'll offer you $1,000." Both at common law and under the FRE, the fact of the offer must be excluded. But at common law, P could testify to the "I may have been a little negligent" part of D's statement. Under the FRE, the *entire statement* — including the collateral admission of fact — is inadmissible.)

Medical bills: Similarly, offers to pay, and payments, of a person's *medical bills* are inadmissible to prove the payor's liability. (*Example:* After D's car hits P, D offers to take P to the hospital and to pay the bill. This offer is not admissible to show that D was negligent or thought he was negligent.)

☛ But here, collateral admissions of fact are *admissible* (in contrast to the FRE's treatment of collateral admissions in conjunction with settlement offers). (*Example:* D tells P, "I'll pay your doctor bills because if I'd been driving on the right the accident wouldn't have happened." The offer to pay won't be admissible, but the statement about driving on the right will be, both at common law and under the FRE.)

Guilty pleas: Similarly, a person's offer (made to a prosecutor) to *plead guilty* to a criminal charge is inadmissible for any purpose if the plea never occurs. Likewise a person's actual *guilty plea,* if later withdrawn, is not admissible for any purpose. (*Example:* In a civil case, D takes the stand. To impeach him, P's lawyer asks, "Didn't you once plead guilty to violating Penal Law §234?" If D withdrew that guilty plea, the question is improper.)

☛ But under the FRE, the discussions must be with the prosecutor, not with other law enforcement personnel like police.

☛ Remember that *collateral admissions* ("Since I was the lookout during the robbery, I'll plead to a lesser charge") are also inadmissible if they occur during plea discussions.

CHAPTER 4

EXAMINATION AND IMPEACHMENT OF WITNESSES

ChapterScope

This chapter's main focus is on the *impeachment* of a witness's testimony. Other topics covered include the permissible and impermissible methods of questioning a witness, rehabilitating the impeached witness, and techniques for developing or evaluating testimony, such as the lie detector test. The most important concepts in this chapter are:

- **Leading questions:** Questions which *suggest to the witness the desired answer* — called *"leading questions"* — are permitted *only* on *cross-examination*, or on direct examination where the witness is *hostile*.

- **Scope-of-direct rule:** Most jurisdictions *limit cross-examination* to matters *testified to on direct examination*, plus matters involving the witness's *credibility.*

- **Refreshing recollection:** Any item may be *shown to a witness* for the purpose of jogging the witness's memory, but the item isn't admitted into evidence, because the testimony comes from the witness. This is called *"refreshing the witness's recollection."*

- *Impeachment* of an adverse witness or one's own witness may be accomplished through the introduction of the following:

  - ❏ **Prior criminal convictions:** If a prior crime is: (a) a *felony* or (b) a *misdemeanor involving dishonesty*, it is admissible to impeach. (If it's a felony not involving dishonesty, and the witness is the accused, the court must *balance* the probative value against the prejudicial effect before admitting it.)

  - ❏ **Prior bad acts:** A cross examiner may ask the witness about a prior *"bad act"* (typically, an act that didn't lead to a criminal conviction) by the witness, if: (a) the act is *probative* of truthfulness; and (b) the examiner has a *good-faith basis* for believing the witness committed the bad act. (But *"extrinsic,"* i.e., independent, evidence of the bad act is *not* allowed — it must be proved "from the mouth of the witness," i.e., through cross-examination, or not at all.)

  - ❏ **Character for truthfulness:** It may be shown that the witness has a poor *reputation* for truthfulness, or shown that another witness is of the *opinion* that the principal witness is untruthful.

  - ❏ **Prior inconsistent statements:** It may be shown that the witness has made a prior statement *inconsistent* with his trial testimony, but only if the witness is given the opportunity, at some point, to *explain or deny* the prior statement, and only if the statement relates to a material issue.

  - ❏ **Bias:** The witness may be shown to be *biased*, or to have a motive to lie. This may be shown on cross-examination, but may also be shown by *"extrinsic evidence"* (evidence that isn't from the witness's own mouth, such as a document or testimony by some other witness about the principal witness).

❑ **Sensory or mental defects:** Any defect the witness has in the capacity to *observe*, *remember* or *narrate* accurately may be shown for impeachment. (*Example:* An eyewitness's poor eyesight may be shown.)

❑ **Contradiction:** Another witness's statement (or physical evidence, like a document) that *contradicts* the principal witness's statement may be introduced, if it relates to a material (rather than "collateral") matter.

■ **No bolstering:** Generally, one who calls a witness may not introduce evidence *supporting* that witness's testimony, unless the witness has already been impeached by the other side.

❑ **Prior consistent statement:** Thus a party may only show that its witness has made a prior *consistent* statement if the other side has charged that the witness's trial testimony is the product of *improper influence or motive,* or is a recent *fabrication*. (Even then, the prior consistent statement must have been made *before* the alleged motive, influence or fabrication occurred.)

I.   DIRECT EXAMINATION

A. Definition of direct examination: When a lawyer calls a witness, the lawyer's questioning of that witness is called the *direct examination*. The direct examination is generally used to establish those facts that are *essential* to the claim or defense of the party calling that witness. For instance, in a negligence action, the plaintiff will need to show, by direct examination of his witnesses, that the defendant was negligent and caused injury to the plaintiff.

   1. Hope that witness is believed: Normally, the direct examiner hopes that the factfinder will *believe* the witness. (But there are exceptions; for instance, one party may call the other party as a witness, in which case the calling party hopes that the direct testimony by the witness-party will be disbelieved.)

B. Free narrative vs. specific questions: The direct examiner, in eliciting testimony from the witness, has two broad choices about how to question the witness: (1) to ask *specific questions* about the facts; or (2) to ask general questions eliciting a *narrative* from the witness. Each has its dangers and advantages.

   1. Specific questions: *Specific questions* about the facts have the advantage that they give the questioner tight control over how the witness testifies, so that the facts can be presented in the desired, and most comprehensible, order, and with the greatest clarity. The disadvantage is that very specific questions may, by their nature, suggest to the witness what answer is desired by the questioner, and thus be held to be *leading* (and therefore disallowed; see *infra*, p. 93).

   2. Narrative: Questions calling for a *narrative* (e.g., "Tell us, Mr. Plaintiff, what happened to you on the afternoon of June 13, 2009?") have the advantage that the witness is testifying completely in his own words, so that there is no danger that he is being "led." The main disadvantage is that the witness may blurt out inadmissible evidence (e.g., hearsay statements; see *infra*, p. 182), and the opposing lawyer will not have the ability to object to the question before the answer is given, as he could in the case of a more specific question.

(If this does happen, the court's only remedy is to order the inadmissible portion of the testimony stricken, and to attempt to explain to the witness what kinds of statements he should not make.)

3. **Neither required nor preferred:** Neither form of questioning is required or preferred as a matter of law. McC, p. 9. So long as the questions are not leading, and the statements are not inadmissible, the choice of whether to ask specific questions or merely request a narrative is entirely up to the direct examiner.

C. **Leading questions:** The most important rule concerning direct testimony is that, generally, the examiner *may not ask leading questions*.

1. **Definition of "leading":** A leading question is one that *suggests to the witness the answer desired by the questioner*. McC, p. 9.

> **Example:** D is charged with armed bank robbery. W, a teller, has just testified that D walked up to her and demanded money. The prosecutor then asks, "Did D point a gun at you?" This is a leading question, since it would suggest to a reasonable person in the witness's position the answer desired by the questioner (namely, "yes").

   a. **Re-phrasing:** A leading question can always be *rephrased* to make it non-leading. Thus, in the facts of the above example, the prosecutor could rephrase the question as follows: "What else, if anything, did the defendant say or do?" The court might also allow the prosecutor to ask a slightly more specific question: "What, if any, gestures did the defendant make?" On the other hand, probably any question calling the witness's attention to the fact that the defendant had or used a gun would be impermissibly leading.

2. **No mechanical formula:** There is no mechanical formula for determining whether a question is leading. The issue is always: Would a reasonable person in the witness's position understand what answer the questioner desired?

   a. **"Didn't" questions:** Questions beginning with "Didn't" will almost always be leading, since they almost always suggest that the questioner desires a "yes" answer. For instance, in a contract suit, where the plaintiff claims that the defendant refused to deliver, a question to the plaintiff, "Didn't the defendant then say that he wouldn't deliver the goods?" will certainly be leading. *Id.*

   b. **"Yes or no" questions:** Often, a question that lends itself to a simple "yes" or "no" answer will be leading. But this is not always the case. For instance, "Was the water hot?" will probably not be leading. *Id.*

   c. **Specific:** In general, the more *specific* the question, the more likely it is to be leading. Thus, "Did the defendant then punch you in the nose and stomp on you?" will almost certainly be leading, since the very specific facts contained in the question suggest to the witness that the questioner thinks that these things happened. Conversely, a question with almost no factual predicate (e.g., "What happened next?") will hardly ever be leading.

3. **Rationale for ban:** Why are leading questions prohibited on direct examination? A party who calls a witness will normally expect that that witness will give testimony favorable to

the calling party. Courts reasonably fear that such a "friendly" witness will tend to "adopt whatever words the lawyer puts in his mouth." L&S, p. 255. Our judicial system's ability to ascertain the truth depends on the factfinder's ability to judge the knowledge and credibility of each witness; therefore, it is important that the factfinder hear the story in the *words of the witness*, not the words of the calling lawyer.

4. **Exceptions:** There are several situations in which leading questions are *allowed* even on direct examination:

    a. **Unfriendly witness:** If the usual assumption that the witness is "friendly" to the party calling him is *incorrect*, leading questions may be asked. In this situation, there is little danger that the unfriendly witness will let the questioner put words in her mouth.

        i.   **Party:** Thus, the *opposing party* will almost always be deemed to be unfriendly and therefore open to leading questions. See, e.g., FRE 611(c), allowing leading questions to an "adverse party" in all situations.

        ii. **Witness identified with party:** Similarly, a witness who is biased in favor of an opposing party, or otherwise identified with that party, may be examined by leading questions. For instance, a *relative* of the opposing party (e.g., the son of the defendant, when being questioned on direct by the plaintiff) will normally be found to be a hostile witness.

        iii. **Other indications:** The witness's *demeanor* on the witness stand may similarly make it clear that he is "hostile" to the examiner, in which case leading questions may be used. For instance, the witness may claim that he cannot remember the transaction in question, under circumstances which lead the court to believe that the witness is being deliberately uncooperative rather than honestly forgetful. If so, leading questions may be used.

    b. **Other situations:** Apart from the "hostile witness" situation, leading questions may be used in a few other situations:

        i.   **Preliminary matters:** They may be used to develop *preliminary matters*, or matters that are not really in dispute. For instance, in our bank robbery example above, if neither side disputes that W, the teller, was on duty when a bank robbery took place (and the only question is whether D was the robber), the question, "Were you on duty at the Bank on the afternoon of August 12, 1987?" would be acceptable even though it is leading (it suggests that the questioner desires a "yes" answer).

        ii. **Suggestion of topic:** Similarly, a quite specific question will be allowed, if it merely suggests a *subject* rather than the desired answer. Thus in our bank robbery example above, the question, "Did you or anyone else make any attempt to summon the authorities while the robbery was in progress?" might well be allowed, despite its specificity, since it merely introduces a new topic (summoning of the authorities).

        iii. **Forgetful witness:** If the witness is *forgetful*, leading questions may sometimes be used to refresh his memory, by drawing his attention to the specific transaction.

Lilly, p. 95. Such "memory jogging" questions, however, will usually be allowed only briefly, and only if the judge is convinced that their effect is not to put the questioner's words into the witness's mouth. *Id.*

    iv. Less competent witness: The witness may have some kind of ***handicap*** that makes it difficult for him to respond to non-leading questions. This may be the case, for instance, if the witness is very ***young***, has trouble ***speaking English***, is unusually ***unintelligent***, or very ***timid***. McC, p. 10. In all of these situations, leading questions may be permitted. This is true even though the very disability may make it more, rather than less, likely that the witness will be very suggestible and thus will adopt the answer suggested by the leading question — in this situation, courts will usually hold that it is better to have possibly flawed testimony, subject to testing by cross-examination, than to have no testimony at all. *Id.*

  c. Reversals rare: In any event, the trial judge has ***wide discretion*** to determine what is or is not a leading question. No matter which way he decides, it will be ***very rare*** for him to be ***reversed*** on appeal. McC, p. 10.

    i. Unfair trial: Occasionally, however, the judge's rulings on the issue of leading questions will be so one-sided that they amount to the ***denial of a fair trial*** for one party. This is more likely to happen when the judge repeatedly ***allows*** what are obvious and intentional leading questions objected to by the other side.

D. Impeachment of own witness: Apart from the rule against leading questions, there is a second technique that is traditionally not permitted on direct examination: the direct examiner ***may not "impeach his own witness."*** That is, under the traditional rule, the direct examiner may not attempt to cast doubt on the accuracy or truthfulness of the witness he has called. This rule against impeaching one's own witness has been modified or abandoned in many jurisdictions, including the federal system; the rule is discussed more extensively *infra*, p. 119.

E. Juror testimony and affidavits impeaching the verdict: Unsuccessful litigants often attempt to ***impeach a jury verdict*** by offering testimony by a juror as to ***statements made or heard during the jury's deliberations.*** But both the common law and the FRE have long ***prohibited*** this type of impeachment. Thus FRE 606(b)(1), like the common law, generally prohibits admission of ***testimony (or affidavits) by a juror,*** when used to ***attack the validity of the verdict*** reached by the jury on which that juror sat.

  1. Text of Rule 606(b)(1): Here's the text of Rule 606:

    Rule 606. Juror's Competency as a Witness

    (a) At the Trial. [omitted]

    (b) During an Inquiry into the Validity of a Verdict or Indictment.

      (1) Prohibited Testimony or Other Evidence. During an inquiry into the validity of a verdict or indictment, a juror may not testify about ***any statement made or incident that occurred during the jury's deliberations;*** the ***effect of anything on that juror's or another juror's vote;*** or ***any juror's mental processes concerning the verdict or indictment.*** The court may not receive a juror's ***affidavit*** or ***evidence of a juror's statement*** on these matters.

      (2) Exceptions. A juror may testify about whether:

       (A) *extraneous prejudicial information* was improperly brought to the jury's attention;

       (B) an *outside influence* was improperly brought to bear on any juror; or

       (C) a *mistake* was made in *entering the verdict on the verdict form.*

2. Rationale: Rule 606(b) is designed to achieve several objectives:

    ❑ to promote the *finality* of jury verdicts;

    ❑ to maintain the *integrity* of the jury system;

    ❑ to *encourage frank jury deliberations*; and

    ❑ to protect jurors from *post-trial harassment by the losing party.*

M&K (5th), §6.10, p. 457.

3. Summary: Parsing the text of FRE 606(b)(1), there are *three classes* of testimony (or affidavits) by a juror that are barred by the Rule, assuming that the evidence is offered "during an inquiry into the validity of a verdict or indictment":[1]

[1] Testimony about "any *statement made* or *incident* that *occurred during the jury's deliberations*";

[2] Testimony about "the *effect of anything* on that juror's or another juror's *vote*";

[3] Testimony about "any juror's *mental processes concerning the verdict or indictment.*"

4. Examples of types of evidence that are barred: Here are some of the varieties of evidence that are *barred* by 606(b)(1):

    a. Reasons and evidence behind verdict: The Rule bars use of juror testimony or affidavits "as proof of the *evidence that counted most* or the *reasons behind the verdict.*" M&K (5th), §6.11, p. 460.

    Example: In a prosecution of D for burglary, the prosecution offers testimony by Wit that before the trial began, Wit's and D's mutual friend X told Wit, "D confessed to me that he did the burglary." The defense immediately raises a hearsay objection, and the trial judge sustains the objection, instructing the jury to disregard Wit's testimony. The jury convicts D. D moves for a new trial on the grounds that the jury improperly considered Wit's testimony. In support of the motion, the defense offers to put Juror 1 on the stand, who will testify that "At the start of deliberations, the foreperson told us that in her opinion the single most compelling evidence showing D's guilt was Wit's testimony that X told Wit that D had confessed."

    The trial judge may not hear Juror 1's testimony, because use of the testimony as part of this "inquiry into the validity of [the] verdict" would violate at least two of the three prohibitions in Rule 606(b)(1): it is about a "statement made ... during the jury's

---

1. The list assumes that none of the three 606(b)(2) exceptions applies; the exceptions are discussed *infra,* pp. 100- 103.

deliberations," and it is about "the effect of anything [namely, Wit's inadmissible testimony] on that juror's or another juror's vote."

b. Instructions: The Rule bars juror testimony "to show that certain *instructions* counted or would have counted if they had been given." M&K (5th), §6.11, p. 460.

c. Mistakes in reaching the verdict: The rule bars juror testimony that the jury used *improper methods* in reaching its verdict.

i. "Majority wins" agreement: For instance, a juror will not be permitted to testify, or say by affidavit, that the jurors agreed to *abide by the vote of a majority*. And the Rule bars testimony that one or more jurors "*gave in to pressure* from other jurors by casting votes against better judgment or conscience without being truly persuaded[.]" M&K (5th), §6.11, p. 462.

ii. Lack of attention, including due to substance abuse: Similarly, the Rule bars testimony by a juror that other jurors failed to *pay attention* during the trial, *slept*, or were under the influence of *drugs or alcohol*. As to the latter, the Supreme Court case set out in the following Example furnishes a dramatic illustration.

Example: After the Ds are convicted of fraud, they move for a new trial. In support, they offer affidavits from two jurors about substance abuse by various jurors during the trial. In one affidavit, juror Hardy says that "the jury was on one big party," that "seven of the jurors drank alcohol during the noon recess," that Hardy and three other jurors "smoked marijuana quite regularly during the trial," that Hardy "observed one juror ingest cocaine five times and another juror ingest cocaine two or three times," that one juror "sold a quarter pound of marijuana to another juror during the trial, and took marijuana, cocaine, and drug paraphernalia into the courthouse," that "some of the jurors were falling asleep during the trial," and that one of the jurors described himself to Hardy as "flying." The trial judge holds that FRE 606(b) forbids consideration of this juror testimony, and denies the new-trial motion.

Held (by the Supreme Court), for the prosecution. Rule 606(b) prevented the trial judge from considering the affidavits and testimony offered here. The legislative history of the rule shows that Congress considered and rejected a version of the Rule 606(b) that "would have allowed jurors to testify on juror conduct during deliberations, including juror intoxication." Furthermore, the exception in Rule 606(b)(2)(B) for testimony about whether an "outside influence was improperly brought to bear on any juror"[2] does not apply: "However severe their effect and improper their use, drugs or alcohol voluntarily ingested by a juror seems no more an 'outside influence' than a virus, poorly prepared food, or a lack of sleep[.]" *Tanner v. U.S.*, 483 U.S. 107 (1987).

d. Pre-verdict deliberations: If you looked just at the text of Rule 606(b)(1), you might get the impression that it applies *only* to juror testimony about things that happen *after the jury starts deliberating*. The reason you might get this impression is that the prohibition on juror testimony in (b)(1) mentions only testimony about "any state-

2. See *infra*, p. 102, for more about this exception.

ment made or incident that occurred ***during the jury's deliberations,***" or "the effect of anything on that juror's or another juror's ***vote,***" or "any juror's ***mental processes concerning the verdict*** or indictment" — all of these events seem to be ones that could not occur until after the trial proper has ended and deliberations have begun.

But the Supreme Court has *interpreted* 606(b)(1) *more broadly* than this, so as to also bar juror testimony about events that occurred ***prior to the start of deliberations.***

i.   **Conduct in *Tanner*:** Thus in *Tanner, supra*, Rule 606(b) was held to bar juror testimony about substance abuse that occurred during the trial itself (i.e., before deliberation began).

ii. **False statements on *voir dire* (*Warger v. Shauers*):** Even more dramatically, the Court has indicated that 606(b)(1) applies to bar testimony by one juror that another made false statements ***during the voir dire***, a process that obviously occurs not just before deliberations but even before the jury has been impaneled. The Court did so in ***Warger v. Shauers,*** 135 S.Ct. 521 (2014).

(1) ***Voir dire* in *Warger*:** In *Warger*, P, a motorcyclist, was hit from behind by a truck driven by D. P brought a negligence action against D, with the parties disagreeing about which of them was at fault. During *voir dire*, P's counsel asked each juror whether there was anything that would prevent that juror from being a fair and impartial juror on this kind of case. Regina Whipple, a prospective juror who was later selected as jury foreperson, answered "no."

(2) **Verdict and motion:** The jury returned a verdict for D. P immediately sought a new trial, based on an affidavit from a juror (not Whipple) saying that during deliberations, Whipple had mentioned a motor vehicle accident caused by Whipple's daughter, in which a man died; Whipple had then said that if her daughter had been sued, it would have ruined her life.[3] The trial court held that FRE 606(b) barred the use of the affidavit.

(3) **Supreme Court finds Rule applies:** The Supreme Court *agreed* with the trial court that Rule 606(b)(1) barred consideration of the affidavit. P had argued that 606(b)(1) applies only to juror testimony and affidavits that are focused on an error in the ***way the jury reached its verdict***; since the affidavit here said nothing about whether Whipple's false statements in *voir dire* affected how she or anyone else reached the verdict in favor of D, the affidavit was not covered by 606(b)(1), P asserted. But the Court *disagreed*: 606(b)(1) by its terms applies to "an inquiry into the ***validity of a verdict***," and the affidavit here was part of an attack by P on the verdict's validity, even though the attack did not focus on any error in the deliberation itself. Thus the affidavit

---

3. It's important to note that the first contact between the complaining juror and counsel for P was *not* initiated by counsel. Rather, it was the juror who approached P's counsel, soon after the verdict, with the story of what Whipple had said. So one of the objectives motivating Rule 606(b) — to ensure that, as the Court put it in *Tanner, supra*, "Jurors would [not] be harassed and beset by the defeated party in an effort to secure from them evidence of facts which might establish misconduct sufficient to set aside a verdict" — was not a factor on the facts of *Warger*.

had to be excluded under 606(b)(1) even though the statements in it did not relate specifically to the jury's deliberations.

(4) Implicitly covers pre-deliberative conduct: The Court's opinion in *Warger* did not *expressly* say that 606(b)(1) covers pre-deliberative conduct. But the Court clearly **assumed** that juror testimony about pre-deliberative statements and conduct must be covered as long as the testimony is offered to show that the verdict was invalid. *Warger* is thus consistent with *Tanner* (*supra*) on this point: both implicitly hold that juror testimony about events occurring before deliberations began (in *Tanner*, substance abuse by other jurors) will be covered by the Rule, as long as the testimony is offered to attack the verdict's validity.

iii. **No constitutional violation:** P in *Warger* made another argument: that if Rule 606(b) was interpreted to bar use of juror affidavits about falsehoods on *voir dire*, the interpretation would be a violation of the proponent's federal **constitutional right to an impartial jury.** But the Court quickly rejected this argument, saying that a party's federal-constitutional right to an impartial jury[4] remains protected, even though Rule 606(b) removes "one means of ensuring that jurors are unbiased." As the Court put it, "Even if jurors lie in *voir dire* in a way that conceals bias, juror impartiality is adequately assured by the parties' ability to **bring to the court's attention any evidence of bias before the verdict is rendered,**[5] and to **employ nonjuror evidence** even after the verdict is rendered."

(1) Racial bias: But the Court *has* recognized one situation in which Rule 606(b)'s bar to juror testimony demonstrating another juror's falsehood on *voir dire can* constitute a constitutional (Sixth Amendment) violation: cases in which the testimony would show that the latter juror lied to conceal her serious **racial bias**. See *Pena-Rodriguez v. Colorado*, 137 S.Ct. 855 (2017), discussed *infra*, p. 103.

e. **Use of non-juror evidence:** Note that Rule 606(b) does *not* prevent **non-juror** evidence offered to prove any of the matters covered by the Rule — it's *only* testimony (or affidavits) by a *juror* in the case, concerning something the juror heard, saw or learned during the trial, that is ever excluded under the Rule.

---

4. Since *Warger* was a *civil* case, the *Sixth Amendment's* right to an impartial jury did not apply. But P apparently argued that in civil cases, the Fourteenth Amendment's **Due Process Clause** confers a similar right to an impartial jury. The *Warger* majority agreed with this general assertion, saying that "The Constitution guarantees both criminal and civil litigants a right to an impartial jury." And the Court cited a case in support of this proposition: in *Ham v. South Carolina,* 409 U.S. 52 (1973), a civil case, the Court held that the trial judge's failure to grant a request by P, who was black, that jurors' racial attitudes be inquired into on *voir dire* violated P's due process rights. But as is discussed immediately below, the *Warger* Court found that P's constitutional right to an impartial jury was adequately protected despite the application of Rule 606(b).

5. Since Rule 606(b) by its text applies only to juror testimony that occurs "during an inquiry into the validity of a verdict," and since a verdict can't have "validity" before it's been rendered, the Rule does not bar juror testimony that is offered *before the jury reaches a verdict*. Therefore, if a juror (call her Juror 1) heard another juror (Juror 2) admit to having lied on *voir dire*, and Juror 1 went to the judge offering an affidavit or testimony to this effect before the jury handed down its verdict, it would not violate Rule 606(b)(1) for the judge to consider this evidence.

i. Non-juror evidence of falsehood on *voir dire*: For instance, Rule 606(b) would not prevent the losing party from offering non-juror evidence on the issue in *Warger*, that a juror knowingly lied on *voir dire*.

Example: Assume the same basic facts of *Warger*, that (1) prospective juror Whipple says in *voir dire* that she can be impartial; and (2) the jury (with Whipple as its foreperson) finds for D. Now, P's counsel moves for a new trial by offering an affidavit from Neigh, Whipple's next-door neighbor, saying that one evening soon after Whipple was elected foreperson, Whipple told Neigh, "I'm probably going vote for D, because my daughter once caused a car accident in which a man died, and if she had been sued, it would have ruined her life."

Nothing in Rule 606(b) prevents the trial judge from considering this affidavit (or live testimony by Neigh to the same effect). That's because 606(b) applies only to testimony by, or an affidavit by, a *juror in the case*, and Neigh is obviously not a juror. (Whether Neigh's testimony will *suffice* for a grant of a new trial is a separate issue, but neither Rule 606(b) nor any other rule of evidence prevents the judge from *considering* that testimony during a motion for a new trial.)

5. The exceptions to Rule 606(b)'s prohibition: Rule 606(b)(2) contains three *exceptions* to the juror-secrecy provisions of 606(b)(1). For convenience, here is the text of 606(b)(2) once again:

> **(2) Exceptions.** A juror *may testify* about whether:
>
> (A) *extraneous prejudicial information* was improperly brought to the jury's attention;
>
> (B) an *outside influence* was improperly brought to bear on any juror; or
>
> (C) a *mistake* was made in *entering the verdict on the verdict form.*

Let's focus now on the two most important of these exceptions, the one for "extraneous prejudicial information" (in sub-paragraph (a)) and the one for "outside influence" (in sub-paragraph (b)).[6]

a. "Extraneous prejudicial information": Rule 606(b)(2)(A) allows testimony by a juror that "*extraneous prejudicial information* was improperly brought to the jury's attention."

i. Some illustrations: Here are some illustrations of types of juror testimony that would be admissible under the "extraneous prejudicial information" exception:

❏ Proof that a juror brought to the jury room *specific personal information* about the case.

Example: After a verdict for the prosecution, D brings a new-trial motion, in support of which Juror 1 offers testimony that during deliberations Juror 2, referring to Wit, the defense's sole alibi witness, said, "My brother-in-law

---

6. The third exception, for a "mistake in entering the verdict," rarely applies, and is therefore not worth covering in any detail.

works at the city jail, and he told me that just before the trial, Wit was jailed on a check-forging charge."

The judge may hear Juror 1's testimony, since it concerns "extraneous prejudicial information ... improperly brought to the jury's attention."

❑ Proof that during the trial, a juror *acquired information* about the case from a *news-media source,* and discussed that information with other jurors during deliberations.

Example: P brings a personal-injury suit against D1 arising out of an accident at North Ave. and Main Street, involving cars driven by P, D1 and D2. (D2 is not a party.) The jury finds for D1. P moves for a new trial, offering testimony by Juror 1 that during deliberations, Juror 2 said, "I Googled this accident last night, and I saw that last year, P sued D2 for the same accident, and the jury there found for D2 on the grounds that the accident was caused by P."

The judge may hear Juror 1's testimony, since it concerns "extraneous prejudicial information ... improperly brought to the jury's attention."

❑ Proof that a juror conducted an *unauthorized experiment* or *view* inside or outside the jury room, and reported the results to the other jurors.

Example: See the "obscured stop sign" example ("Example 1 (covered by exception)") on p. 101 almost immediately below.

See generally M&K (5th), §6.12, pp. 465-66.

ii. **Does not apply to "common knowledge":** Courts interpreting the "extraneous information" exception have held that it applies *only* to *specific knowledge about the facts of the case,* not to *"common"* or *"regional"* knowledge that a juror would be expected to have. Here's how the Court put it in *Warger, supra*: Information is "extraneous" if (and only if) it "derives from a source *'external' to the jury"* (citing *Tanner, supra*, p. 97). And, *Warger* says, "External" matters "include *publicity and information related specifically to the case* that jurors are meant to decide." By contrast, *"internal"* matters (not covered by the exception) "include *the general body of experiences that jurors are understood to bring with them to the jury room."* See also M&K (5th), §6.12, p. 465.

Example 1 (covered by exception): The case is a negligence suit involving a two-car collision that happened six months before the trial. P testifies that D failed to stop at a stop sign at the intersection where the accident occurred. D, however, testifies that just before the collision, when his car was 10 yards from the intersection, his view of the stop sign was obscured by a dense grove of evergreens on his left, preventing his failure to stop from being his fault. There is no other testimony about the visibility of the stop sign. The case is given to the jury on a Friday. The following Monday during deliberations, Juror 1 tells the other jurors, "Yesterday, I visited the scene of the accident, and I can tell you that right now, there are no evergreen trees on the left near the intersection, so I think D was lying when he said there were." The jury finds for P. D moves for a new trial, offering the testimony of Juror 2 about what Juror 1 said.

The 606(b)(2)(A) exception for juror testimony about whether "extraneous prejudicial information was improperly brought to the jury's attention" *applies*. What Juror 1 learned from her unauthorized view of the scene is the sort of ***case-specific information*** — i.e., information not within the common or regional knowledge of the typical juror — that the exception is designed to cover. Therefore, the trial judge may (indeed should) hear Juror 2's testimony about what Juror 1 said, and if the judge believes that there is a substantial chance that the verdict was influenced by the improper view, she will grant a new trial.

Example 2: (not covered by exception): In a civil case, the issue is the proper amount of damages for pain and suffering to be awarded to P, who due to D's negligent driving has lost a leg from a point just above her knee. P testifies that she continues to suffer severe "phantom limb pain" from the missing lower leg. The case goes to the jury, which finds for P, and awards large damages for pain and suffering. D moves for a new trial, based on proposed testimony by Juror 1 that during the deliberations, Juror 2 told the other jurors, "My sister had to have her leg amputated below the knee, and she has had severe phantom limb pain ever since; so I can tell you that this sort of pain really exists, can be severe, and is worth a lot of money."

The trial judge will probably rule that Juror's 2 statement was *not* "extraneous prejudicial information," because phantom limb pain is a common enough phenomenon that such pain should be held to be general information (not covered by the 606(b)(2)(A) exception) rather than case-specific information (covered).

iii. **Found not to apply in *Warger*:** The distinction between general and case-specific information played a big role in *Warger, supra*, p. 98. P claimed that the proposed juror affidavit — saying that juror Whipple had made a statement during deliberations that showed she had lied on *voir dire* about her impartiality — fell within the "extraneous prejudicial information" exception. But the Court found that the exception did ***not*** apply. The Court made the distinction we're now discussing, between "external" matters (covered by the exception) and "internal" matters (not covered). The Court held that the affidavit here covered matters that ***"fall[] on the 'internal' side of the line."*** The opinion continued: "Whipple's daughter's accident may well have informed her ***general*** views about negligence liability for car crashes, but it did not provide either her or the rest of the jury with any ***specific knowledge*** regarding [D's] collision with [P]."

b. **"Outside influence":** The second exception given in Rule 606(b)(2) (in sub-section (B)) covers juror testimony about whether "an ***outside influence*** was improperly ***brought to bear*** on any juror[.]"

i. **Interference by outsiders:** An important use of this provision is to allow testimony or affidavits by a juror that "show efforts by ***outsiders*** to ***interfere with deliberations***," such as by ***bribery***. M&K (5th), §6.13, p. 468.

Example: D is charged with trying to bribe X, a public official, and is convicted. Seeking a new trial, D offers testimony by Juror 1 that during the course of the trial, Juror 1 witnessed Z (whom Juror 1 recognized as being X's political rival) hand a $100 bill to Juror 2, and heard Z say to Juror 2, "So you'll vote to convict, right?" Since this proposed testimony is clearly "about whether an outside influence was improperly brought to bear on [a] juror," the testimony falls within the Rule 606(b)(2)(B) exception, preventing the testimony from being barred by Rule 606(b). Thus the judge may hear Juror 1's testimony, and may use it as the basis for granting a new trial.

ii. **Doesn't cover substance abuse:** Testimony that one juror saw one or more other jurors *fall under the influence of drugs or alcohol* does *not* fall within the "outside influence" exception. Recall that in *Tanner v. U.S.* (*supra*, p. 97), the Supreme Court held that even extreme drug or alcohol use by a juror "seems *no more an 'outside influence' than a virus,* poorly prepared food, or a lack of sleep" (none of which would be considered to be an outside influence).

6. **Sixth Amendment as a limit on Rule 606(b) (*Pena-Rodriguez v. Colorado*):** Criminal defendants seeking, post-verdict, to introduce juror testimony blocked by Rule 606(b)(1) have sometimes claimed that the Rule violates their *Sixth Amendment right to an impartial jury.* As we've seen, these attacks have *usually failed*, on the ground that even where 606(b)(1) blocks the use of one method for ensuring an impartial jury — post-verdict juror testimony about bias — *other methods* of detecting juror bias remain available.

   However, in 2017 the Supreme Court for the first time recognized *one type* of juror bias as being so historically-systemic and corrosive that the application of Rule 606(b) to block juror testimony about the bias *will* be deemed a Sixth Amendment violation: clear indications of *racial or ethnic bias* on the part of a juror. The case was *Pena-Rodriguez v. Colorado*, 137 S.Ct. 855 (2017).

   a. **Facts of *Pena-Rodriguez*:** In *Pena-Rodriguez*, D, a Hispanic man, was charged in Colorado state court with attempting to sexually assault two teenage sisters in the bathroom of a racetrack. Each prospective member of the jury was asked standard questions to ensure that no juror was seated who could not be impartial; all jurors agreed that they could be fair and impartial. Following trial, D was acquitted of the felony attempted-sexual-assault charge, but convicted of lesser misdemeanor charges including unlawful sexual contact. After the jury was discharged, two jurors remained in the jury room and asked to speak to D's counsel in private. They told counsel that a third juror, H.C., had expressed, during deliberations, anti-Hispanic bias against both D and his alibi witness. The two jurors then signed affidavits attesting that H.C. had made the following statements, among others, to his fellow jurors:

   ❏ that H.C. believed D was guilty because, in H.C.'s experience as an ex-law enforcement officer, "Mexican men [have] a bravado that cause[s] them to believe they [can] do whatever they want[] with women";

   ❏ that H.C. thought D "did it because he's Mexican and Mexican men take whatever they want";

   ❏ that in H.C.'s experience, "nine times out of ten Mexican men [are] guilty of being aggressive towards women and young girls"; and

   ❏ that H.C. did not believe D's alibi witness, because the witness was "an illegal" (though the witness testified that he was a legal U.S. resident).

b. Affidavits rejected by trial court: D's counsel offered the two affidavits in support of a motion for a new trial. The trial court agreed that the affidavits showed H.C.'s apparent bias. But, the judge said, since the affidavits recounted statements made by H.C. during jury deliberations, Colorado's version of Rule 606(b)(1)[7] prevented the court from considering the affidavits.

c. Issue at U.S. Supreme Court: The U.S. Supreme Court granted certiorari on the question of "whether there is a *constitutional exception* to the no-impeachment rule for instances of *racial bias*."

d. Majority finds an exception: By a 5-3 vote,[8] the Court answered *"yes"* to this question. In an opinion by Kennedy, the majority said that "where a juror makes a *clear statement* that indicates he or she *relied on racial stereotypes or animus* to convict a criminal defendant, the *Sixth Amendment requires* that the no-impeachment rule *give way* in order to permit the trial court to *consider the evidence of the juror's statement* and any resulting denial of the jury trial guarantee."

    i. Rationale: Kennedy acknowledged that the Court had previously rejected — in contexts such as the substance abuse in *Tanner* (*supra*, p. 97) and the pro-defendant bias in *Warger* (*supra*, p. 98) — claims that Rule 606(b)(1)'s exclusion of one juror's testimony about another juror's bias or other misconduct during deliberations violated the U.S. Constitution. And he acknowledged that if such juror evidence of misconduct were generally allowed, the jury system would be "expose[d] to [such] unrelenting scrutiny" that the system might not survive. But, Kennedy said, *racial bias* is different from the types of bias and other wrongdoing that was at issue in these other cases. Kennedy listed two major ways in which racial bias in jury deliberations was a *special problem*:

        (1) "Unique historical and constitutional concerns": First, he said, racial bias "implicates *unique historical, constitutional, and institutional concerns.*" The Court had previously held, in the course of many decisions, that "discrimination on the basis of race, 'odious in all aspects, is *especially pernicious in the administration of justice.*'"

        (2) Other safeguards insufficient: Second, Kennedy said, in non-racial-bias cases like *Tanner* and *Warger*, the Court had emphasized that even without juror testimony about deliberations, the constitutional guarantee of an impartial jury is supported by *other forms of proof,* like non-juror evidence (e.g., questions during *voir dire*), as well as by juror evidence put forth before the verdict is rendered. But racial bias, Kennedy said, has special attributes that may prevent these other forms of evidence from being enough to ensure the constitutionally-required impartiality. For instance, pointed questions about racial prejudice during *voir dire* "could well *exacerbate whatever prejudice might exist* without substantially aiding in exposing it."

---

7. The Colorado version was essentially identical to the federal provision.

8. The case was decided after Justice Scalia's death, and before Justice Gorsuch was seated as his successor.

(3) Summary: In sum, Kennedy wrote, "A constitutional rule that racial bias in the justice system *must be addressed* — including, in some instances, after the verdict has been entered — is necessary to *prevent a systemic loss of confidence* in jury verdicts, a confidence that is a central premise of the Sixth Amendment trial right."

ii. **"Overt racial bias" casting "serious doubt on impartiality" is required:** But Kennedy made it clear that "[n]ot every *offhand comment* indicating *racial bias or hostility"* will justify the trial judge in disregarding Rule 606(b)'s no-impeachment rule. Rather, "there must be a showing that one or more jurors made statements exhibiting *overt racial bias* that *cast serious doubt on the fairness and impartiality* of the jury's deliberations and resulting verdict." And for this "serious doubt" standard to be met, the statement "must tend to show that racial animus was a *significant motivating factor* in the juror's *vote to convict."*

e. **Dissent:** Justice Alito *dissented*, in an opinion joined by Roberts and Thomas. Alito conceded that the majority's attempt to stamp out racial prejudice in jury deliberations was "well-intentioned." But he said that what he described as the majority's conclusion that "respecting the privacy of the jury room" in this case "violates the Constitution" was a *"startling development."* And he feared a slippery slope: "it is doubtful that there are *principled grounds* for preventing the *expansion* of today's holding."

i. **No reason for racial bias to be treated specially:** Alito argued that the "real thrust" of the majority opinion was that "the Constitution is *less tolerant of racial bias* than *other forms of juror misconduct*[.]" But he saw no basis for interpreting the Sixth Amendment this way: "Nothing in the text or history of the Amendment or in the inherent nature of the jury trial right suggests that the extent of the protection provided by the Amendment depends on the *nature of a jury's partiality or bias."*

f. **State and federal courts:** Note that since *Pena-Rodriguez* is based on the Sixth Amendment, it applies to *both federal* and *state* criminal trials. So in *all* U.S. criminal trials, a defendant's Sixth Amendment right to an impartial jury means that despite any rules guarding the secrecy of jury deliberations:

❑ The trial judge *must* receive evidence from a juror that another juror "made statements exhibiting *overt racial bias* that *cast serious doubt* on the *fairness and impartiality* of the jury's deliberations and resulting verdict." Furthermore ...

❑ For a juror's statement showing overt bias to meet the above "serious doubt" standard, that statement "must tend to show that racial animus was a *significant motivating factor"* in that juror's vote to convict.

g. **Not applicable to civil cases:** Since the Sixth Amendment applies only to *criminal* trials, *Pena-Rodriguez* does not require courts to disregard, in *civil cases,* a jurisdiction's rules that block juror testimony about another juror's statements indicating racial bias.

i. **Possible expansion:** However, it's quite possible that the Court will eventually conclude that overt and serious racial bias in *civil* cases so deeply impairs a litigant's Fourteenth Amendment right to *due process* that juror-secrecy rules like FRE 606(b)(1) must be disregarded, just as *Pena-Rodridguez* holds that the Sixth Amendment requires this step in criminal cases.

h. Covers "ethnic bias": The majority opinion in *Pena-Rodriguez* uses the phrase "racial bias" to denote the kind of bias to which the Court's new Sixth-Amendment-based rule applies. But the bias at issue in the case was of the sort that is usually referred to as *"ethnic"* bias, not racial bias — D was Hispanic, and the bias-riddled statements by juror H.C. referred to D as being a "Mexican man." But the majority opinion noted that both sides, in their briefs, used the term "race" to cover *both* racial and ethnicity bias, and the majority indicated that it, too, was using "race" to refer to both types. Therefore, the new rule announced in *Pena-Rodriguez* — that the Sixth Amendment requires that juror-secrecy rules be set aside to allow the court to consider jury testimony about overtly-biased juror statements — applies to indications of bias based not just on race but on *ethnicity* and *national origin.*

i. Religious bias: The *Pena-Rodriguez* majority may also eventually hold that bias based on *religious* grounds is sufficiently suspect that this type of juror bias too, if overtly stated, justifies the same suspension of juror-secrecy rules.

Example: Suppose that after D is convicted of terrorism, Juror 1 proposes to testify in support of D's new-trial motion, "Juror 2 told us during deliberations that 'Even though D is a native-born American of Irish ancestry, the fact that he converted to Islam five years ago makes me think, without more, that he's probably guilty of these charges'." This is testimony about religious bias, not ethnic or racial bias, but it might well be held to constitute such a dangerous denial of the Sixth Amendment right to an impartial jury as to justify the suspension of the juror-secrecy rules.

II. CROSS-EXAMINATION

A. Nature of cross-examination: After the party calling a witness has finished the direct examination, that party's adversary has the opportunity to *cross-examine* the witness. Cross-examination is usually thought to be indispensable to the truth-finding process. For instance, in some situations a criminal defendant's lack of opportunity to cross-examine a witness against him may be found to be a violation of the defendant's constitutional Confrontation Clause rights; see *infra*, p. 401. Similarly, lack of the opportunity to cross-examine is the main reason for the rule against hearsay (*infra*, p. 182), which prevents the use of out-of-court declarations to prove the truth of matters asserted therein.

B. Leading questions allowed: In contrast to direct examination, *leading questions* are usually *permitted* during cross-examination. McC, p. 32.

1. Rationale: Recall that the reason for not allowing leading questions on direct is that the witness is presumed to be friendly, and a friendly witness will all too readily acquiesce to the direct examiner's suggested answers. In cross-examination, by contrast, the witness will generally *not* be friendly, so there is little danger that the witness will adopt the questioner's suggested answers as his own.

2. **Federal Rules:** The Federal Rules follow the usual practice of allowing leading questions on cross-examination. FRE 611(c) provides that "ordinarily, the court should allow leading questions: (1) on cross-examination[.]"

3. **Exceptions:** But as in the direct examination context, the usual rule will be suspended if the typical relationship between questioner and witness is not present. Thus, if the witness is *biased in favor of the cross-examiner*, the trial judge has discretion to prevent leading questions. This will be true, for instance, if the witness is a *party* adverse to the side who called him. Thus if P calls D to the stand, not only will P's lawyer be allowed to use leading questions in the direct examination, but D's lawyer will *not* be allowed to use leading questions on the "cross" (since it is not really a "cross"-examination at all).

C. **Scope of cross:** Most jurisdictions impose *limits* on the *scope* of cross-examination.

1. **"Restrictive" majority rule:** Most states, and the Federal Rules, *limit the cross-examination to the matters testified to on the direct examination*. McC, p. 32. This is sometimes known as the *"scope of direct"* rule.

> **Example:** P, a passenger in a car, is injured in a collision with a truck owned by D and operated by D's employee, W. P calls W as a witness, and covers only two items on his direct examination (whether W was on company business at the time of the accident, and whether W can identify an accident report made by him to the authorities). On cross, D's lawyer elicits from W's entire version of the accident, none of which was touched on the direct exam by P.
>
> *Held*, the trial court erred in allowing this so-called "cross"-examination. In this jurisdiction, "cross-examination shall be limited to the subject-matter of the direct examination." Here, the trial judge's failure to follow this rule gave D "the distinct advantage of placing before the jury, at the outset of the trial, a version of the circumstances favorable to his contentions, proceeding from a witness called and in a sense vouched for by [P.]" *Finch v. Weiner*, 145 A. 31 (Conn. 1929).

   a. **FRE agree:** The Federal Rules implement the "scope of direct" rule, in FRE 611(b):

   > **"(b) Scope of Cross-Examination.** Cross-examination should *not go beyond the subject matter of the direct examination* and matters *affecting the witness's credibility*. The court *may allow* inquiry into additional matters as if on direct examination."

   b. **Credibility:** Even in jurisdictions following the restrictive majority rule, questions that are relevant to the witness's *credibility* are always regarded as within the proper scope of cross-examination. Thus FRE 611(b), quoted above, follows the majority rule by providing that "cross-examination should not go beyond the subject matter of the direct examination and matters *affecting the witness's credibility*."

   c. **Trial court's discretion:** The trial court generally has *discretion* to permit cross-examination on matters that are not literally within the scope of direct, so long as the discretion is not abused. Thus FRE 611(b) concludes by stating that the court "may allow inquiry into additional matters as if on direct examination."

   d. **Same transaction or statement:** Even in states following the majority "scope of direct" rule, the cross-examiner may bring out facts that relate to the *same transac-*

tion, *conversation*, or *statement* that was the subject of direct examination. McC, p. 33. For instance, suppose that on direct, P's lawyer asks W, "What did D say to you after the collision?" D's lawyer will be permitted to ask W on cross, "What did you say in return?" since W's response was part of the same conversation that was testified to on direct. As some courts put it, P, by his question on direct, has ***"opened the door"*** to the rest of the conversation.

e. **Tactics:** The majority "scope of direct" rule gives the direct examiner a substantial ability to ***control the facts*** and testimony brought out in his case.

> **Example:** In a negligence suit arising out of a car crash, P's lawyer wishes to withhold from the jury the fact that P was intoxicated while driving at the time of the accident. P does not testify, but his lawyer calls W, who was a passenger in the car, to testify that D went through a red light.
>
> So long as W confines his testimony solely to D's conduct, P's lawyer will probably be able to ensure that during P's case, the jury does not learn about P's intoxication. (Questions by D's lawyer on cross-examination of W concerning P's intoxication cannot be justified on credibility grounds so long as P never takes the witness stand.) P's lawyer cannot keep this information from the jury indefinitely — during D's case, D will be able to call W as a witness and ask whatever he wishes; furthermore, D will be able to call P and ask him about drunkenness. But the majority "scope of direct" rule does allow P's lawyer to see to it that this information does not come in until D's case, and that it does not come in from witnesses who have been called (and in a sense "vouched for") by P.

i. **Leading questions:** The "scope of direct" rule may also permit a direct examiner to deprive his adversary of the benefit of leading questions. Even if the trial judge permits the cross-examiner to go beyond the scope of direct, the trial judge has discretion to order the cross-examiner not to use ***leading questions*** to cover matters that go beyond the scope of direct.

D. Art of cross-examination: A real treatment of the "art of cross-examination" is beyond the scope of this outline, and is usually covered in trial advocacy courses. Here, however, briefly stated, are four cardinal rules of cross-examination:

1. **Preparation:** Even great "talent" at cross-examination is no substitute for ***preparation***. Most successful cross-examinations are less the product of talent than they are the fruits of extensive review of documents, depositions of hostile witnesses, interviews with favorable witnesses, and other forms of pre-trial preparation.

2. **Know the answer:** "Never ask a question to which you do not know the answer." While this is probably an overstatement, it reflects the well-established principle that the examiner must be at least reasonably confident that the question will produce a ***favorable response***.

> **Example:** D is arrested and charged with pick-pocketing. She tells her lawyer (librettist W.S. Gilbert, shortly before he teamed up with Sullivan) that she was on her way to church, with her hymn-book in her pocket, when she was arrested, and that the purse found on her must have been planted by some unknown evil person. Gilbert per-

forms the first cross-examination of his career, of the arresting policeman; he is determined to call attention to the hymn-book in D's pocket. The examination goes like this:

> *Gilbert:* You say you found the purse in her pocket, my man?
>
> *Constable:* Yes, sir.
>
> *Gilbert:* Did you find anything else?
>
> *Constable:* Yes, sir.
>
> *Gilbert:* What?
>
> *Constable:* Two other purses, a watch with the bow broken, three handkerchiefs, two silver pencil-cases, and a hymn-book.
>
> See K&W, p. 442.

3. **No broad questions or ones calling for explanation:** Control the witness with tightly-phrased, *narrow* questions. Don't give the witness a chance to expand or buttress his testimony by asking broad questions or questions that request an explanation.

> **Example:** D is charged with theft. D does not take the stand, but his lawyer shakes the testimony of the only eyewitness. D's lawyer then cross-examines the arresting policeman, bringing out the fact that D is a veteran and that D's wife is pregnant. He then asks one last question: "Having regard to this man's splendid record, how did you come to arrest him?"
>
> The policeman "drew a bundle of blue documents from the recesses of his uniform, and, moistening his tongue, read therefrom. [D's lawyer] learned in silent horror that the prisoner's record included nine previous convictions." Mathew, Forensic Fables by O (quoted in K&W, pp. 442-43).

4. **Make one or two big points:** End on a high note: try to make one or two big points, and don't dull them by also making a lot of insignificant points. When you make a big point, pass immediately on to another issue, so that the witness does not have a chance to recant or wriggle out of the trap. "When you have struck oil, stop boring." McC, p. 41.

See generally McC, pp. 40-41.

III. REDIRECT AND RECROSS

A. **Redirect:** After cross-examination, the party who called the witness has the opportunity to question him again, in what is called *redirect* examination.

1. **Scope:** The party who calls a witness is normally required to elicit on the original direct examination every part of the witness's story that is of interest to the calling party. Thus the redirect examination must normally be limited to aspects of the witness's testimony that were *first brought out during cross-examination.*

   a. **Drawing the sting:** As to these matters first revealed on cross, the redirect examiner's job is normally to *"draw the sting"* of the cross-examination by giving the witness an opportunity to explain or avoid the troublesome facts or statements that came out on cross. McC, p. 42.

Example: Let's return to our automobile collision example from p. 108. W (the passenger in a car driven by P) testifies on direct that D drove carelessly, but does not say anything about P's conduct. Assume that the jurisdiction allows wider cross-examination than would be permitted under the usual "scope of direct" rule, so that D's lawyer is permitted on cross to draw out the fact that W saw P have three beers just before the accident.

On redirect, P's lawyer would not be permitted to have W testify to any additional facts concerning D's carelessness, since that carelessness was the subject of the original direct exam. But he could ask W, "Did you notice any change in P's behavior after the three beers?" (hopefully the answer is "no") or "Did P's ability to drive seem to be impaired?" since the entire issue of P's intoxication did not come out until the cross-examination of W.

2. **Discretion of judge:** As with most issues regarding the order and scope of examination, the trial judge has *broad discretion* in what to allow on redirect. While he usually does not have discretion to allow entirely new matters to be brought out that could and should have been brought up on direct, he does generally have discretion to allow matters to be amplified that were first presented on direct. For instance, if the direct examiner can show that he honestly overlooked one aspect of an issue that was developed on direct, and that the aspect is very important, the trial judge may well allow redirect on this point (though the judge's refusal to allow it would not likely be grounds for reversal).

B. **Recross:** After redirect, the cross-examiner will have a limited opportunity to conduct *recross* examination. As with redirect, the recross may not cover subjects that were covered by the examiner in his previous questioning (in this case, the cross-examination) — only matters *newly brought up in the redirect* may be touched upon.

Quiz Yourself on
DIRECT EXAMINATION, CROSS-EXAMINATION, REDIRECT, AND RECROSS

21. Yakko and Wakko, brothers, serve on a jury in trial in which plaintiff Harvey Spacedout, a famous actor, asserts that defendant Juanna Starr, an aspiring actress, libeled him when she posted on Facebook, "Spacedout raped me in a supply closet at Actors Studio 15 years ago." The jury is sequestered throughout the proceedings, and told not to watch TV, use the Internet, or speak to anyone outside the jury about the case. After a week of deliberations, the jury returns a large verdict for plaintiff Spacedout. Starr immediately moves for a new trial, and seeks to have Yakko testify that one night during the deliberations, his sister Dot sent him and Wakko a text message containing a newspaper story about the case saying that Starr had been convicted of perjury in a different trial the previous year; Yakko will also testify that this information caused him and his brother to vote for Spacedout because they thought it showed that Starr was a habitual liar. (The newspaper story was in fact false, and the jury in the present trial was never presented with any evidence of prior perjury by Starr.) Spacedout argues that the judge's receipt of Yakko's testimony would violate the rule prohibiting a juror from attacking the verdict in this manner. May the judge hear Yakko's testimony? _____

22. Rodney Prince, a white male, is beaten by several Lalaland City police officers while Prince is taking part

in a street demonstration to protest police brutality. Prince brings a civil tort suit for his injuries against Bull O'Connor, the Lalaland Police Commissioner; the suit alleges that O'Connor facilitated the beating by instructing his troops, before the demonstration, to "feel free to give these rabble-rousers a police beating that'll show them who's boss." During jury selection, the judge asks all prospective jurors, "Is any member of your immediate family, including parents, siblings, children or grandchildren, a past or present employee of any police department?" A potential juror, Jerry, answers "no," and is seated on the jury. During a recess in the trial (before deliberations), Jerry and another juror, Joan, have lunch, during which Jerry says, "My daddy used to be Assistant Police Commissioner of Lalaland. Growing up in a law-enforcement household leads me to believe that if we let rabble-rousing demonstrators bring brutality claims against high-ranking police officials, we'll be opening the door to a massive increase in street crime. So I intend to vote in favor of the defense." The jury finds, by a vote of 11 to 1 (with Joan being the one pro-plaintiff vote) for the defendant, which is enough for a verdict. Joan seeks out the plaintiff's counsel after the trial, and offers to testify in a new-motion trial about what Jerry told her. May the judge hear Joan's testimony about what Jerry said? _____

23. Dwight, a 21-year-old black man, joins a street demonstration organized by the Black Lives Count movement, whose mission is to combat police brutality against black people. During the demonstration, Dwight gets into a fistfight with Oliver, a white on-duty police officer. Dwight is prosecuted under state law for assaulting Oliver, and for resisting Oliver's attempt to arrest him. At the beginning of Dwight's trial, the prospective jurors are told the basic facts of the case and the identities of the parties. The judge then asks each potential juror, "Is there anything about the parties, including their race, ethnicity or occupation, that would make you unable to be a fair and impartial judge in this case?" Jen answers, "no," and is seated. After the jury votes by 11-1 to convict (this type of not-quite-unanimous vote being sufficient for a conviction under state law), the one juror who voted to acquit, James, seeks out Dwight's counsel and offers to testify in support of Dwight's motion for a new trial. James' testimony would be as follows: "During deliberations, Jen said, 'Dwight is an angry young black male, and in my experience when young black men have a physical clash with the police, it's usually the black man's fault.' " James' proposed testimony continues, "Jen then made a couple of other anti-black remarks during deliberations, including, 'Even if all I knew was that Dwight was a black male protesting as part of Black Lives Count, that would be enough for me to convict, because I would feel sure that Dwight threw the first punch.' " The jurisdiction has a juror-secrecy law comparable to the one included in the Federal Rules of Evidence. May the judge hear James' testimony about what Jen said? _____

24. Macbeth is on trial for the murder of Duncan. Banquo is called as a witness for the prosecution, and testifies that he saw Macbeth leaving the castle shortly after midnight. It has already been established that the murder occurred at midnight, in the castle. Prosecutor asks, "Did you see anything else suspicious?" Banquo responds, "No, that's all I know." Prosecutor continues, "You're sure you didn't see anything else to suggest something strange had happened?" Banquo answers, "No." Prosecutor asks, "You didn't notice anything on Macbeth's hands?" In fact, Macbeth's hands were covered in blood, and Banquo had said so in his previous deposition. (a) What objection should the defense raise? _____ (b) Will that objection succeed? _____

Answer

21. **Yes.** It's true that FRE 606(b)(1) says that as a general principle, during an "inquiry into the validity of a verdict," a juror may not testify about various matters, including "[a] statement made or incident that occurred during the jury's deliberations[.]" But FRE 606(b)(2) specifies a couple of important exceptions

to this general ban. One of these is that "[a] juror *may* testify about whether: (A) ***extraneous prejudicial information*** was improperly brought to the jury's attention[.]" The newspaper story here, insofar as it revealed critical credibility information about a party that was never presented to the jury, is "extraneous prejudicial information" that was "improperly" brought to at least two jurors' attention. Therefore, the exception applies, and Yakko will be allowed to testify about his and his brother's receipt of the story even though the testimony is by a juror and offered as part of an attack on the verdict's validity.

22. **No.** FRE 606(b)(1) says, "During an ***inquiry into the validity of a verdict*** ... a juror may not testify about any statement made or incident that occurred during the jury's deliberations; the ***effect of anything on that juror's or another juror's vote;*** or any juror's ***mental processes concerning the verdict*** or indictment. The court may not receive a juror's affidavit or evidence of a juror's statement on these matters." Joan's proposed testimony would violate this rule. First, Joan's testimony is clearly being offered as part of an "inquiry into the validity of a verdict," so it meets the pre-condition for 606(b)(1)'s applicability. In addition, the testimony violates at least two of the three separate prohibitions in the Rule: (1) the testimony is "about ... the ***effect of anything on ... another juror's vote***;" and (2) it is also "about ... any juror's ***mental processes*** concerning the verdict[.]" The facts here make the situation comparable to the one in *Warger v. Shauers* (2014), a motor-vehicle-accident case where the Supreme Court held that Rule 606(b)(1) applied to prevent testimony by one juror (call her Juror 1) that another juror (Juror 2) had lied on *voir dire* by concealing Juror 2's daughter's experience in a similar accident matter that caused Juror 2 to develop a strong pro-defense bias.

Prince might plausibly argue that Joan's testimony should be covered Rule 606(b)(2)(A)'s exception allowing juror testimony that "extraneous prejudicial information was improperly brought to the jury's attention." Under this argument, Jerry's pro-police views, arising from his upbringing, should be considered "extraneous prejudicial information." But in *Warger, supra,* the Supreme Court rejected virtually the same argument, saying that a juror's "general views about negligence liability for car crashes" (there, a pro-defense bias) was not the sort of "specific knowledge" regarding the facts of the case that the (b)(2)(A) exception is meant to cover. It seems almost certain that here, *Warger* compels the conclusion that a juror's pro-defense bias arising out of the juror's law-enforcement background would, similarly, not be the sort of "specific knowledge" about the facts of the case that is required to trigger the "extraneous information" exception.

23. **Yes.** In a 2017 case, *Pena-Rodriguez v. Colorado,* the Supreme Court held that juror bias based on race or ethnicity is so different from other sorts of bias that, at least in criminal cases, the defendant's constitutional Sixth Amendment right to an impartial jury requires that rules of evidence protecting the secrecy of juror deliberations must "give way" to that Sixth Amendment right. More specifically, *Pena-Rodriguez* holds that in a criminal case, if a juror makes a ***"clear statement*** that indicates he or she ***relied on racial stereotypes or animus to convict,"*** the Sixth Amendment is triggered: that Amendment's guarantee of an "impartial jury" not only allows, but ***requires***, that any no-impeachment-by-jurors rule "give way in order to permit the trial court to consider the evidence of the juror's statement and any resulting denial of the jury trial guarantee." However, this Sixth Amendment rule applies only if there is "a showing that one or more jurors made statements exhibiting ***overt racial bias*** that ***cast serious doubt*** on the fairness and impartiality of the jury's deliberations and resulting verdict." And for this "serious doubt" standard to be met, the statement "must tend to show that racial animus was a ***significant motivating factor*** in the juror's vote to convict."

It's nearly certain that James' proposed testimony meets this standard, so that the judge may (indeed, must) hear the testimony. Jen's statement that "when young black men have a physical clash with the police, it's usually the black man's fault" certainly constitutes a "clear statement that indicates [the juror] relied on racial stereotypes or animus" (*Warger*). There is an additional issue as to whether Jen's statements satisfied *Warger*'s "serious doubt" test (under which the Sixth Amendment is triggered only if the juror's statements exhibiting overt racial bias were serious enough to "cast serious doubt on the fairness and impartiality of the jury's deliberations and resulting verdict"). But Jen's further statement, "Even if all I knew was that Dwight was a black male protesting as part of Black Lives Count, that would be enough for me to convict," almost certainly casts the required doubt on the fairness and impartiality of the resulting verdict. That's because Jen's bias seems every bit as serious, and as likely to influence the final verdict, as H.C.'s anti-Hispanic remark in *Warger*, that the defendant there "did it because he's Mexican and Mexican men take whatever they want." Therefore, Dwight's Sixth Amendment right to an impartial jury not only allows, but requires, the trial court to hear James' testimony about the statements Jen made during deliberations. And if (as seems likely), the trial judge agrees that the testimony casts serious doubt on whether Dwight received a fair trial from an impartial jury, the judge should grant Dwight's new-trial motion.

24. (a) **That the prosecutor is leading the witness**, i.e., suggesting the answer desired by the questioner.

(b) **No, probably.** It is true, as a general rule, that *leading questions are impermissible on direct examination*. However, there are exceptions. The facts here fit one of them: leading questions are permissible on direct examination when they serve to *jog the witness's memory about something he once knew*, rather than to supply the answer to him. This is especially true where, as here, the question merely clues the witness in to a particular *area* or *issue*, rather than supplying the specific substance of the answer – the Prosecutor may be suggesting that something was on Macbeth's hands, but isn't suggesting exactly what that something was. Also, the fact that Banquo is already on record as having remembered the answer in his deposition supplies an extra safeguard against the possibility that it's the Prosecutor, rather than Banquo, who is truly the one supplying the answer. (But if the prosecutor asked, "Did you see *blood* on Macbeth's hands?" this *would* be impermissible leading, because it would suggest the precise answer desired by the questioner, not merely the area to which the answer relates.)

IV. REFRESHING RECOLLECTION AND OTHER TECHNIQUES

A. **Refreshing the witness's recollection — generally:** Suppose that a witness's recollection of an event is hazy. It may be possible to *refresh* his recollection by showing him a statement, picture, or other item; the item triggers an association in the witness's mind, enabling him to recall the event more clearly.

   1. **Traditional rule:** Nearly all courts permit *any item* to be shown to the witness while he is on the stand, to refresh his recollection. This technique is usually called that of *"present recollection refreshed."*

      a. **Rationale:** The rationale for this liberal rule is that the item shown to the witness is *not evidence* at all. It is merely a *stimulus* to the witness's memory. After the witness's memory is refreshed, the evidence comes *from the witness*, not the document or other item shown to him.

      b. **Distinguished from "past recollection recorded":** This "present recollection refreshed" technique must be distinguished from the technique of "past recollection recorded," by which a witness is shown a writing that he has prepared or authenticated, and that was made shortly after an event. If the tests for past recollection recorded (see *infra*, p. 245) are satisfied, the writing *becomes evidence*, and can be used to prove the truth of the matters asserted in the writing, even if the witness testifies that he has no independent recollection of the events described.

2. **"Any item"**: As noted, courts allow a virtually infinite variety of items to be used to refresh the witness's testimony. "*Anything may be used* for this purpose — an object, a sound, a gesture, 'a song, a scent, a photograph, an allusion, even a past statement known to be false.' " M&K §6.66, p. 602.

    a. **No authenticity needed**: The examiner need *not* establish the authorship, time of making, or even correctness of the object. McC, p. 13. In other words, the rules requiring that items of evidence be *authenticated* (see *infra*, p. 472) do *not apply*.

    b. **Not necessarily admissible**: The item need *not* be *admissible*. For instance, it can consist of inadmissible hearsay. Nor does the item become admissible by virtue of being used for refreshment. (But the examiner's *adversary will* usually be entitled to have portions admitted that relate to the witness's testimony; see the discussion of FRE 612(b), *infra*, p. 116.)

        Example: D is charged with bank robbery. The prosecution offers testimony by Officer, who investigated the crime. While testifying, Officer consults notes prepared by him during the course of his investigation. D's lawyer objects on the grounds that the notes haven't been introduced into evidence, that the notes can't be introduced because they are hearsay not within any exception, and that Officer should therefore be barred from testifying in reliance on their contents.

        As long as the court is satisfied that D is testifying from his own now-refreshed recollection, the fact that the notes haven't been introduced into evidence (and can't be, because of hearsay problems) is irrelevant.

3. **Dangers:** Assume that the witness's memory of an event is hazy, that he is shown a document to refresh his recollection, and that he then proceeds to give refreshed testimony about the event. There is a danger that the witness's memory has not really been refreshed, and that he is instead simply reciting what the document says. This danger is increased by the rule, followed in many courts, that the witness may *repeatedly consult* the writing while testifying (see *infra*, p. 115). The danger is also magnified by the fact that the document need not be admissible; thus a witness who's really just reading a document that supposedly has refreshed his memory is in effect smuggling in essentially inadmissible material.

4. **Four limits:** To guard against abuse, most courts impose *four limits* on the use of the present-recollection-refreshed technique:

    a. **Memory exhausted:** First, the witness's memory must be, or at least seem to be, *exhausted* by regular direct and cross-examination before the examiner may attempt to refresh her memory.

    b. **Control of manner:** Second, the trial judge may *control the manner* in which the refreshment takes place. Some of the ways in which the judge may do this are by:

❏ requiring the questioner to show a ***good-faith factual basis*** for the refreshment;

Example: W can't remember whether he was at the Happy Acres Motel at any time in August, 2005, let alone what date. The examiner wants to ask, "Would it refresh your recollection to know that the records of the Motel show you stayed there on August 14?" The judge may require that before the examiner asks the question, he first satisfies the court that such a record actually exists.

❏ limiting the ***specificity*** with which the question is asked, so that not too much detail is exposed to the jury from the mouth of the examiner rather than the witness;

❏ requiring that the question be asked ***outside the presence of the jury***;

❏ making sure that the witness is ***in fact testifying from her own memory*** once refreshed, not, for example, merely ***reading*** from a document used for refreshment (see *infra*, p. 115).

c. **W says memory actually refreshed:** Third, the witness must ***say*** that her memory is ***in fact refreshed***. (Then, the testimony must seem to be truly refreshed — the witness can't merely be reading from the refreshing document; see *infra*.)

d. **Inspection:** Finally, the questioner's ***adversary*** is entitled to ***inspect*** the refreshing document. See *infra*, p. 116.

See generally M&K §6.66, pp. 605-07.

5. **Consulting document during testimony:** Some courts allow the witness to ***repeatedly consult*** the refreshing item while testifying. But this practice raises the danger that the witness is really just reading the (possibly inadmissible) document, not truly testifying from her own refreshed recollection. Except where the document contains precise numbers or dates, the better practice is ***not*** to allow such repeated consultation. M&K §6.66, p. 590. (If the document itself is important, it may be admissible under the exception for past recollection recorded; see *infra*, p. 245.)

Note: Other aspects of the "present recollection refreshed" technique are discussed in the treatment of hearsay, *infra*, p. 248.

6. **Federal Rules:** Perhaps surprisingly, the Federal Rules do ***not*** set forth anywhere the particular requirements for using the present recollection refreshed technique. The only specific mention of the technique is in FRE 612 (discussed *infra*, p. 116), which gives the adversary of an examiner using the technique the right to inspect, and in some instances introduce, the refreshing document.

a. **Judge's control over leading questions:** A second FRE provision indirectly influences how the recollection refreshed technique is used. FRE 611(c) says that ***leading questions*** should not normally be used on direct, but should ordinarily be usable on cross. (See *supra*, p. 106).) But the Rule implicitly gives the court ***discretion*** about whether to allow leading. Since the refreshing of a witness's recollection is a type of leading, 611(c) thus gives the trial judge authority to regulate the use of the refreshment technique. M&K §6.66, p.602.

B. **Refreshing recollection — Adversary's right to inspect document:** When an examiner uses a document to refresh a witness's recollection, it would clearly be unfair to prevent that examiner's adversary from seeing the document, or from using that document during the subsequent cross-examination of the witness. Therefore, virtually all jurisdictions give the non-calling party's lawyer some *access* to any document used to refresh the witness's recollection.

1. **FRE 612 — generally:** Under the Federal Rules, this access is conferred by FRE 612, which provides as follows:

> **"Rule 612. Writing Used to Refresh a Witness's Memory**
>
> **(a) Scope.** This rule gives an adverse party certain options when a witness uses a writing to *refresh memory*:
>
> > (1) *while testifying*; or
> >
> > (2) *before testifying*, if the court decides that *justice requires* the party to have those options.
>
> **(b) Adverse Party's Options; Deleting Unrelated Matter.** Unless 18 U.S.C. § 3500 provides otherwise in a criminal case, an adverse party is entitled to have the *writing produced* at the hearing, to *inspect* it, to *cross-examine* the witness about it, and to *introduce in evidence any portion* that relates to the witness's testimony. If the producing party claims that the writing includes unrelated matter, the court must examine the writing in camera, delete any unrelated portion, and order that the rest be delivered to the adverse party. Any portion deleted over objection must be preserved for the record.
>
> **(c) Failure to Produce or Deliver the Writing.** If a writing is not produced or is not delivered as ordered, the court may issue any appropriate order. But if the prosecution does not comply in a *criminal* case, the court must *strike the witness's testimony* or — if justice so requires — declare a mistrial."

2. **FRE 612 — Writing consulted during testimony:** So where the witness *consults* the refreshing document *during the course* of the witness's testimony, the non-calling party *automatically* gets three rights under FRE 612:

❑ the right to *inspect* the document;

❑ the right to *cross-examine* the witness *based on the document*; and

❑ the right to *introduce into evidence* the *portions* of the document that *relate to the testimony of the witness*.

a. **Admissibility:** The non-calling party's right to introduce portions of the document into evidence is *subject to other rules of evidence*. Most importantly, if, as will often be the case, the document is *hearsay* (i.e., it's being introduced to show the truth of the matters asserted in the document; see *infra*, p. 186), the document can come in only if it satisfies some hearsay exception. M&K, §6.68, p. 608.

3. **FRE 612 — Writing consulted before testimony:** But where the witness has merely consulted the document *before the witness gave testimony* — i.e., as part of *pretrial preparation* — the FRE do *not* give the opposing party any automatic right to inspect the document, to cross-examine based on it, or to introduce it. Instead, as FRE 612(a)(2) says, the opposing party gets these rights only "if the court decides that *justice requires* the party to have those options."

    a. Infrequent: In this pretrial-consultation situation, "disclosure is *not routine* but *unusual*, and many cases approve denial of disclosure." M&K §6.67, p. 606. The rationale is that a witness generally reviews a large number of documents before trial — many of them irrelevant to the witness's eventual testimony — and routine disclosure would invite "fishing expeditions" into the files of the calling party and her lawyer. *Id.*

C. Argumentative and misleading questions: We now treat briefly two other techniques for shaping a witness's testimony, both of which are *improper:* (1) *argumentative* questions; and (2) *misleading* questions.

    1. Argumentative: An *argumentative* question is one which is "designed to induce the witness to affirm counsel's interpretation of the evidence." Lilly, p. 97. Argumentative questions are disallowed because the interpretation of the evidence is to be done by the jury, not by the lawyer or the witness. *Id.*

        Example: In a prosecution against D for mayhem, D's lawyer asks W, "Isn't it a fact that [D's] mouth is so small that he could not reach up and get it wide enough open to get [Complainant's] ear in there?" *Held*, question is argumentative, since both mouth and ear were visible to jury. *White v. State*, 210 P. 313 (Ok. Cr. 1922).

        a. Cross-examination: Argumentative questions are heard more often on cross than on direct. On cross, trial judges have discretion, which they sometimes exercise, to allow a question that is, strictly speaking, argumentative. Lilly, p. 97.

    2. Misleading questions: A *misleading* question is one that assumes as true a fact that is either *not in evidence* or is *in dispute.* Most misleading questions have a "trick" aspect about them, since by answering the witness implicitly affirms the correctness of the assumption.

        Example: Lawyer to witness: "When did you stop beating your wife?" If there is no evidence that the witness ever beat his wife, or the evidence is in dispute, the question will be stricken as misleading, since any answer by the witness will be an implicit admission that he has beaten her.

V. EXAMINATION BY COURT

A. General rule: Virtually all states, and the Federal Rules, allow the trial judge to *call her own witnesses*, and to *question any witness* (whether called by the judge or by a party). L&S, p. 275. See FRE 614(a) and (b).

    1. Witness called by judge: If the judge calls a witness, either side may question the witness as if in *cross-examination*. Thus, each side may use leading questions.

    2. Judge's discretion: The decision whether to call a witness is generally left to the judge's *discretion.* One common situation for the discretion to be exercised arises in criminal cases in which the prosecution needs testimony from a particular witness, but does not want to call the witness itself, because either: (1) the witness will be uncooperative but not hostile (so that the prosecutor will not be allowed to use leading questions unless the court calls the witness); or (2) the prosecution does not wish to be seen to be vouching for or "sponsoring" the witness's testimony (perhaps because the witness is of clearly bad character, or has told inconsistent stories in the past), yet the prosecution needs the testimony. L&S, p. 275; McC, pp. 11-12.

3. **Questioning by judge:**   Most states do not permit the judge to *comment on the evidence* in jury trials. Therefore, although the trial judge has discretion to question the witnesses, he must be careful that his questioning does not seem so one-sided that it will seem to the jury to be an implied comment on the evidence. L&S, pp. 275-76. In the minority of states allowing the judge to comment on the evidence, and in bench trials, the judge can be much freer in his questioning of witnesses. *Id.*

VI. IMPEACHMENT — GENERALLY

A. **Meaning of "impeachment":**   In ordinary cross-examination, the questioner tries to show flaws in the witness's *testimony*. For instance, he may try to get the witness to change his story, or expose gaps in the account, or otherwise render the testimony less damaging. *Impeachment*, by contrast, is a technique to show *flaws in the witness*, rather than in the testimony. That is, the tool of impeachment is designed to destroy the witness's *credibility*. Thus whereas in the usual cross-examination the witness's honesty and ability are usually not questioned, in a successful impeachment these personal characteristics of the witness will be not only questioned but perhaps destroyed. L&S, p. 282.

B. **Five types:**   There are five common techniques for impeaching a witness, one of which has three sub-techniques:

1. **Character:**   The witness's general *character*, especially his character for *truthtelling*, may be attacked. This is usually done in one of three ways:

    a. **Convictions:**   By showing that he has previously been *convicted* of one or more *crimes*;

    b. **Bad acts:**   By showing that he has previously committed *bad acts* that have not led to a criminal conviction; or

    c. **Reputation:**   By showing that he has a *bad reputation* (usually a reputation for not telling the truth).

2. **Prior inconsistent statement:**   The witness's credibility may be attacked by showing that on a prior occasion, he has made a *statement* that is *inconsistent* with his present testimony.

3. **Bias:**   Credibility may be attacked by showing that the witness is *biased* in favor of or against one side, because of family relationship, financial interest, or other *ulterior motive.*

4. **Sensory or mental defect:**   Credibility may be weakened by a showing that the witness suffers from a *sensory* or *mental* defect (e.g., the witness is hard of hearing so he could not

have heard what he claims to have heard, or the witness is psychotic so his description of an event cannot be trusted).

5. **Contradiction:** Lastly, the witness may be impeached by the production of other evidence (e.g., testimony by a second witness) that statements made by the first witness are not correct. This is so-called "impeachment by contradiction."

We will be examining each of these types of impeachment in detail below.

C. **Impeaching one's own witness:** At common law, the rule has long been that *"a party may not impeach his own witness."* To put it another way, impeachment is generally *not allowed on direct examination*. L&S, p. 282.

1. **Rationale:** Several rationales have been asserted in support of this traditional rule. None is very convincing.

   a. **"Vouching" for one's witness:** The most commonly-cited rationale for the "no impeachment of own witness" is that by calling a witness, a party in a sense *"vouches for the credibility"* of that witness, and should therefore have no need to attack that credibility.

      i. **Criticism:** However, the assumption that a party vouches for the credibility of his witnesses is badly flawed. Usually, "the party has little or no choice of witnesses. The party calls only those who happened to have observed the particular facts in controversy." McC, pp. 50-51.

2. **Exceptions to common-law rule:** Because of the weakness of these rationales for the common-law prohibition on impeachment during direct, most of the courts still following the common law rule recognize several *exceptions* to it, which we won't go into here.

3. **Modern and Federal rule:** In recent years, many jurisdictions have wholly or partly *abandoned* the common law rule against impeachment on direct. See, e.g., Cal. Evid. Code §785 (complete abandonment of rule). Most dramatically, the Federal Rules *completely abandon the common-law rule.* FRE 607 provides that *"Any party*, including the party that *called the witness*, may *attack* the witness's credibility."

   a. **Constitutional requirement:** In some instances, it may even be *constitutionally required* that a party be permitted to impeach a witness that it has called. In a criminal case, if the defendant calls a witness and is then prevented from impeaching that witness, this may be a denial of the defendant's rights under the Constitution's *Confrontation Clause.*

      i. *Chambers:* For instance, in *Chambers v. Mississippi*, 410 U.S. 284 (1973) (discussed more extensively *infra*, p. 403), D, charged with murder, called one McDonald as a witness. McDonald had previously confessed in writing to the crime, and then recanted. When McDonald denied that his confession was valid, D wasn't permitted to grill him about the circumstances (since D had called him, and the grilling would amount to impeaching one's own witness). This, together with other errors, was enough to violate D's constitutional right to a fair trial, the Court held.

ii. **Limited right:** Courts have so far not accepted arguments by criminal defendants that the defendant is *always* constitutionally entitled to impeach his own witnesses. L&S, p. 283. But clearly there will be many situations, such as that in *Chambers*, where adherence to the strict common-law "no impeachment upon direct" rule will violate the Confrontation Clause. *Id.*

4. **Leading questions:** One way to impeach a witness is to ask him **leading questions** designed to test his credibility (e.g., "Isn't it true that you told a different story previously?") As we've just seen, some states, and the Federal Rules, now allow a party to impeach his own witness. Yet leading questions are not normally allowed on direct. How can these two rules be reconciled?

   a. **Hostility:** First, remember that where the witness is *hostile*, leading questions are normally allowed even on direct (see *supra*, p. 94).

   b. **Non-hostile:** Where, however, the witness is not truly hostile, but gives testimony that is **less favorable than expected**, it is not clear whether impeachment by leading questions should be allowed. Recall that FRE 611(c) provides that "leading questions should not be used on direct examination except as necessary to develop the witness's testimony." S&R (p. 565) suggest that in federal trials, any time a witness on direct gives unfavorable testimony (even if he is not truly "hostile"), FRE 611(c) should be interpreted to allow leading questions for purposes of impeachment.

VII. IMPEACHMENT BY PRIOR CRIMINAL CONVICTIONS

A. **Problem generally:** Of all the techniques of impeachment, probably the most controversial is that of showing that the witness has previously been **convicted of a crime**. The controversy is especially great when the issue is whether prior convictions can be used to impeach the credibility of the *accused* in a criminal case who takes the stand in his own defense. On the one hand, the fact that the witness has been convicted of a crime (especially a crime involving dishonesty) may be legitimately relevant to whether his present testimony is believable. But on the other hand, there is a danger that the factfinder will use the prior convictions not only for evaluating credibility, but also for impermissible substantive purposes. (Recall that use of prior crimes for the substantive purpose of showing that the defendant has a propensity to commit crimes, and therefore probably committed the presently-charged crime, is not allowed; see *supra*, p. 27.)

B. **Common law approach:** The common-law approach to this problem is, in general, that two types of prior convictions may be used to impeach the witness: (1) **any felony conviction**; or (2) a misdemeanor conviction, but only if the crime involved dishonesty or a **false statement**. L&S, p. 284. However, states following the general common-law approach vary widely in defining exactly what kinds of convictions can be used. McC, p. 55.

1. **Criminal defendant:** The common-law rule places a **criminal defendant** who has prior convictions in a terrible dilemma: if he takes the witness stand in his own defense, all of his prior felony convictions, and even misdemeanors that bear on veracity, can be disclosed to the jury. The jury may react not only by disbelieving the accused's testimony, but by further reasoning either that: (1) "If he did it before, he did it this time"; or (2) "If he

did it before, we'll all be better off if we get him off the streets whether or not he did it this time." Yet if the accused does *not* take the stand, the jury is likely to hold this silence against him (even if it is instructed not to do so by the trial judge); this is especially likely to be so where the facts are such that the defendant is the only one who can give a convincing explanation of why the defendant is innocent.

    a. Relevance to veracity: Furthermore, the common-law rule will often allow introduction of prior convictions that have ***practically nothing to do with the witness's veracity***. Since all felony convictions are usable under the common-law approach — regardless of whether they have anything to do with truthfulness — even a prior murder or child molestation conviction is usable. Yet the prejudicial effect of such a conviction is far greater than any relevance that that conviction may have to the issue of whether the witness is now telling the truth.

C. Federal Rules — Generally: The Federal Rules follow a ***middle approach*** between the widespread right to use prior convictions at common law, and the narrow admissibility urged by the common law rule's critics. The main parts of FRE 609 provide as follows:

> "Rule 609. Impeachment by Evidence of a Criminal Conviction
>
> **(a) In General.** The following rules apply to attacking a witness's character for truthfulness by evidence of a ***criminal conviction***:
>
>   (1) for a crime that, in the convicting jurisdiction, was punishable by death or by ***imprisonment for more than one year***, the evidence:
>
>   (A) ***must*** be admitted, subject to Rule 403, in a civil case or in a criminal case in which the ***witness is not a defendant***; and
>
>   (B) ***must*** be admitted in a ***criminal*** case in which the ***witness is a defendant***, if the ***probative value*** of the evidence ***outweighs*** its ***prejudicial effect*** to that defendant; and
>
>   (2) for any crime ***regardless of the punishment***, the evidence must be admitted if the ***court can readily determine*** that ***establishing the elements of the crime required proving*** — or the witness's ***admitting*** — a ***dishonest act or false statement.***
>
> **(b) Limit on Using the Evidence After 10 Years.** This subdivision (b) applies if ***more than 10 years have passed*** since the witness's conviction or release from confinement for it, whichever is later. Evidence of the conviction is admissible only if:
>
>   (1) its ***probative value***, supported by ***specific facts and circumstances***, ***substantially outweighs its prejudicial effect***; and
>
>   (2) the proponent gives an adverse party ***reasonable written notice*** of the intent to use it so that the party has a fair opportunity to contest its use."

1. How the Rule works: Here's a step-by-step description (a "verbal flow chart") of how to analyze impeachment material that constitutes evidence of either an unconvicted bad act or a crime:

    a. Step 1. Is the impeaching material evidence of either of the following types of criminal conviction: (1) conviction for a ***crime punishable by death or imprisonment in***

excess of one year; or (2) conviction for a crime that required the prosecution to prove *false statement or dishonesty* as an element (regardless of length of actual or possible sentence)?

If *"yes,"* go to Step 2.

If *"no,"* the material must come in (if at all) as an "unconvicted bad act" under FRE 608. See p. 129, *infra*.

b. Step 2. Is the material a conviction for a crime that required the prosecution to prove *dishonesty* or *false statement* as an element, i.e., a *"crimen falsi"*? (Examples of crimes that qualify: embezzlement, perjury, submitting false tax returns).) (Examples of crimes that don't qualify: robbery, assault, murder.)

If *"yes,"* go to Step 3.

If *"no,"* go to Step 4.

c. Step 3. [*crimen falsi*] Have *more than 10 years elapsed* since the date of conviction or of the release of W from confinement imposed for that conviction? (Choose the later date.) FRE 609(b).

If *"no,"* conviction is *admissible*. (FRE 609(a)(2)). Rule 403's balancing test does not apply, so no matter how little probative value the judge thinks the conviction has, and no matter how much prejudice it may cause, the judge *must* allow it to come in.

If *"yes,"* conviction is *inadmissible*, unless: (a) "its probative value, supported by specific facts and circumstances, substantially outweighs its prejudicial effect;" and (b) the proponent gives the adverse party *advance written notice*. FRE 609(b).

d. Step 4. [non-*crimen falsi*] Is the witness also the *accused* in a criminal case?

If *"no,"* go to Step 5.

If *"yes,"* go to Step 6.

e. Step 5. [W is not the accused] Is the conviction's *probative value* "*substantially outweighed*" by the danger of *unfair prejudice*, etc.? (Apply the balancing test of FRE 403.) FRE 609(a)(1)(A).

If *"yes,"* the conviction is inadmissible.

If *"no,"* the conviction is admissible. (But you must still apply the special 10-year rule, described in the "yes" part of Step 3 above. So for an old conviction, there will have to be "specific facts and circumstances" supporting the judge's conclusion that probative value substantially outweighs prejudice.)

f. Step 6. [W is the accused] Is the conviction's probative value "*outweighed*" (*not* "substantially outweighed") by its prejudicial effect?

If *"yes,"* the conviction is inadmissible.

If *"no,"* the conviction is admissible. (But you must still apply the special 10-year rule, described in the "yes" part of Step 3 above. So for an old conviction, there will have to be "specific facts and circumstances" supporting the judge's conclusion that probative value "substantially outweighs" prejudice.)

D. FRE 609 — "Falsehood or dishonesty" (*crimen falsi*) convictions: When you're analyzing the impeachment use of a conviction, the most important single issue is whether the conviction is for a crime defined so as to have required the prosecution to prove ***"dishonesty or false statement"*** (crimes that are often referred to by the Latin phrase ***"crimen falsi,"*** which means "crime of falsehood").

1. **Significance:** This issue makes a difference on two major points:

   a. **Can be misdemeanor:** First, the *crimen falsi* can be admitted ***even if it's only a misdemeanor*** (i.e., regardless of the punishment that was imposable, or actually imposed by the court). By contrast, the non-*crimen falsi* can ***only*** be admitted if it was for a ***felony***, i.e., "for a crime that, in the convicting jurisdiction, was punishable by death or by imprisonment for more than one year[.]" (FRE 609(a)(1)).

   b. **No balancing:** Second, the *crimen falsi* ***must*** be admitted by the trial court (as long as it's not too old; see FRE 609(b)), ***without any balancing of probative value against prejudice***. (See more about this *infra*, p. 125.) A non-*crimen falsi* can only be admitted if the judge conducts such a balancing, and concludes that the conviction's probative value "outweighs" its prejudicial effect (where the witness is an accused defendant) or "substantially outweighs" its prejudicial effect (where the witness is not an accused).

2. **Definition of *"crimen falsi"*:** So what crimes, then, are ones conviction of which require the prosecution to prove "dishonesty or false statement" as an element? The basic idea is that there must be an element of ***deceit*** or ***stealth***, not merely dishonesty in the broad sense of "crooked."

   a. **Conference Report:** The House Conference Report on FRE 609 says that the covered crimes are those involving "some element of ***deceit***, ***untruthfulness***, or ***falsification*** bearing upon the accused's ***propensity to testify truthfully***."

   b. **Catalog of *crimen falsi*:** Here is a partial catalog of crimes that ***are*** generally considered to be *crimen falsi*:

      ❑ ***Perjury*** or ***subornation of perjury***;

      ❑ ***False statement***;

      ❑ ***Criminal fraud***;

      ❑ ***Embezzlement***;

      ❑ Taking property by ***false pretenses***;

   Note: The above five crimes are specifically mentioned in the Conference Report for 609 as constituting *crimen falsi*.

      ❑ ***Counterfeiting***;

      ❑ ***Forgery***; and

      ❑ ***Filing false tax returns***, or failing to file returns at all. (Not all courts agree on the latter.)

      ❑ For ***theft crimes*** other than embezzlement and false pretenses, see the discussion below.

See generally M&K §6.32, p. 502.

> **Example:** D is charged with possession of marijuana, found on the front seat of the car in which D was a passenger when stopped. The prosecution calls the owner of the car, who testifies that the marijuana was not his. D's lawyer now asks the owner, "Isn't it true that three years ago, you were convicted of misdemeanor per-jury charges?" The owner denies this, whereupon D's lawyer offers into evidence proof of such a conviction.
>
> The question and proof of conviction are admissible. That's because *perjury is always a crimen falsi*, i.e., a crime the conviction of which "required proof or admission of an act of dishonesty or false statement by the witness" (609(a)(2)). Therefore, the conviction is admissible (1) even though it was a misdemeanor rather than a felony (i.e., "regardless of the punishment," in the language of 609(a)(2)), and (2) regardless of the relationship between its prejudicial impact and its probative value. (Note that 609(a)(2) says that the conviction "shall be admitted," and doesn't say, as the non-*crimen-falsi* language of 609(a)(1) does, that the judge should determine whether the probative value outweighs the preju-dicial effect.)

c. **Not *crimen falsi*:** Other crimes just as clearly fall on the **non**-*crimen falsi* side of the line. These are crimes that are defined in such a way that deception is not one of the elements. Most crimes of *violence* (*murder*, *rape*, *assault and battery*, for instance), as well as a number of non-violent crimes (*drug offenses*; *prostitution*; driving while intoxicated; resisting arrest) are not *crimen falsi,* since dishonesty or false statement is not an element of those crimes. As the ACN to the 2006 amendments to FRE 609 say, "[E]vidence that a witness was convicted for a crime of violence, such as murder, is not admissible under Rule 609(a)(2), even if the witness acted deceitfully in the course of committing the crime."

d. **Theft crimes:** The biggest controversy historically has concerned those crimes of *larceny* that are not defined so as to require false statement. Under the FRE, this con-troversy was put to rest in 2006. As a result of an amendment to Rule 609(a) in that year, *most theft crimes other than embezzlement and false pretenses will not be cri-men falsi,* because these crimes are not defined in such a way that "establishing the elements of the crime required proving — or the witness's admitting — a dishonest act or false statement" (as 609(a) now requires).

i. **Shoplifting, robbery and receiving stolen goods:** So, for instance, it is now pretty clear that crimes like *shoplifting, robbery* and *receiving stolen goods* are *not* crimen falsi. That's because an act of dishonesty or false statement is *not an element of the crime,* even though a *particular defendant* might have used dis-honesty or false statement in committing the particular crime.

> **Example:** D is charged with burglary. D raises an alibi defense, presenting W to testify that D was with W at W's house at the time of the burglary. The prosecution has examined W's criminal record, and has discovered that three years ago, W was convicted of minor state shoplifting charges, the maximum penalty for which was

nine months (though W was in fact only sentenced to 90 days in prison). A transcript of W's trial shows that X, a cashier for Store, testified on behalf of the prosecution that W took a watch from the display area of Store, put it on his wrist, and said to X, "Do you like the watch that my fiancée gave me last week?"

Here, it's clear that in committing the shoplifting, W behaved in a dishonest manner. But it's also clear that proof of W's dishonesty was not an "element of the crime" with which W was charged (since shoplifting can be and often is carried out without any deceit at all, as where D simply carries the goods out of the store hoping that no one will notice). Therefore, under the post-2006 version of FRE 609(a), the shoplifting charge was not a *crimen falsi* covered by 609(a)(2). Since the crime was not "punishable by ... imprisonment for more than one year," it's not admissible to impeach W under 609(a)(1) either. Therefore, it cannot be used to impeach W at all.

Note: This example reflects a significant change to 609(a)(2)'s operation. Before the 2006 amendment to FRE 609(a)(2), most courts had held that the court *could* treat an offense as a *crimen falsi* if the accused actually behaved in a deceitful or dishonest way in committing the crime (as in the shoplifting example above), even if the crime was defined in such a way that dishonesty and false statement were not elements of the crime.

3. **Looking to facts of particular crime:** Suppose that the elements of a crime are not defined so as to require proof of dishonesty or false statement, but that the witness happened to commit the crime by means of dishonesty or false statement; is the crime a *crimen falsi*? As FRE 609(a)(2) now reads, following a 2006 amendment, the answer is *no*. The above Example is one illustration of this principle. Another is given in the following Example.

   Example: Suppose D was previously convicted of misdemeanor charges of attempted sale of narcotics. The evidence at his earlier trial showed that he purported to be selling heroin, but that he in fact delivered a mixture of sugar and flour (but charged heroin prices for it). Now, after D takes the stand in his own defense, the prosecution wants to impeach D's credibility by showing this conviction. Under present FRE 609(a)(2), the prosecution won't be able to do this — since the attempted-sale-of-narcotics charge was defined in such a way that proof of dishonesty or false statement was not an element of the crime, the crime is not a *crimen falsi*.

4. **No discretion:** If the court does hold that the prior conviction is for a *crimen falsi*, the court has *no discretion* to exclude it, *no matter how prejudicial* to the defendant it may be. M&K, §6.32, n.1.

   a. **Effect of 1990 change:** Any doubt there might have been about whether the court has discretion to weigh prejudice against probative value for *crimen falsi* was removed by the 1990 amendments to Rule 609(a). Those amendments specifically added, for the non-*crimen falsi* felonies covered in 609(a)(1), a reference to Rule 403's prejudice-vs.-probative-value balancing test; the text of 609(a)(2), dealing with *crimen falsi*, was left without any such reference, and says simply that such convictions "must be admitted."

5. **Time limit:** The ***10-year "time limit"*** imposed by FRE 609(b) applies to *crimen falsi* convictions just as to non-*crimen falsi* ones. See *infra*, p. 128. So for convictions older than 10-years, the conviction will only come in if "its probative value, supported by specific facts and circumstances, substantially outweighs its prejudicial effect." In other words, for old felony convictions, it ***makes no difference*** whether the crime is a *crimen falsi* or not.

E. **FRE 609 — Felonies not involving dishonesty or false statement:** Where dishonesty or false statement was ***not*** an element of the crime, somewhat different rules apply:

1. **Must be felony:** First, the crime must be a ***felony***. So a misdemeanor not involving dishonesty or false statement can't be introduced at all, no matter how much probative value the judge may think it has.

2. **W is the accused:** The analysis of a non-*crimen falsi* felony varies depending on whether or not the witness is the ***accused*** in a criminal trial. Where W is the accused, she gets an ***extra measure of protection*** against the conviction's prejudicial effect: only if the court determines that ***"the probative value of the evidence [of the conviction] outweighs its prejudicial effect to the accused"*** may the court admit it. The key point is that the conviction gets excluded even if its prejudicial effect only ***slightly*** exceeds its probative value.

3. **W is not the accused:** By contrast, if W is ***not the accused***, the conviction will be blocked only if its prejudicial effect ***"substantially"*** exceeds its probative value. In this situation, covered by 609(a)(1)(A), Rule 403 (see *supra*, p. 15) is the only protection the witness and the proponent of the witness get against prejudice, and that Rule only kicks in where the prejudicial effect is "substantially" greater than the probative value. So the following types of witnesses ***don't*** get the same protection that the criminally-accused witness gets:

   a. **Prosecution witnesses:** Witnesses *for the prosecution* in a criminal case;

   b. **Defense witnesses:** Witnesses for a ***criminal defendant*** (other than the accused himself); and

   c. **Civil witnesses:** Witnesses for either the plaintiff or the defense in a ***civil*** case.

   Example: D is prosecuted for bank robbery. The prosecution offers testimony by W, an accomplice of D's in the crime, who has turned state's evidence. D's lawyer wishes to impeach W by showing that W was previously convicted of bank robbery, and is therefore not worthy of belief. The prosecution will be able to keep out this past felony conviction only if the prosecution can carry its burden under FRE 403 of showing that the probative value of the conviction is "substantially outweighed" by the danger of unfair prejudice to the prosecution, confusion of the issues, or one of the other items listed in FRE 403. The prosecution will probably not be able to bear this burden, in which case the prior conviction will be used for impeachment of W.

   Note: Observe that the witness can be impeached by a felony conviction that has ***nothing whatsoever to do with truthfulness.*** Thus in the above Example, even if W's conviction had been, say, for manslaughter — a crime having little if anything to do with W's propensity to tell the truth — the conviction would be admissible to impeach W.

It's true that the judge may exclude the conviction on the grounds that its prejudicial effect "substantially exceeds" its probative value under FRE 403, and that the judge in doing this balancing may take into account the low probative value of a manslaughter conviction on a witness's truth-telling propensity. But FRE 609 doesn't explicitly forbid use of a conviction having little bearing on truthfulness, and the 403 balancing is left to the judge's discretion (403 says that the judge "may," not "shall" or "must," exclude the evidence based on the balancing). Consequently, many convictions will be used for impeachment of non-accused witnesses where the conviction in reality says little about the witness's truthfulness.

4. **Balancing:** When a trial judge conducts the Rule 403 balancing of prejudice against probative value in deciding whether to allow impeachment use of a non-*crimen falsi* prior felony conviction, here are some of the ***factors*** that the judge is likely to consider:

   a. **Impeachment value:** The ***"impeachment value"*** of the prior crime. The more probative the prior crime is on the issue of whether the defendant-witness is now telling the truth, the more likely it is to be admitted. (So that heat-of-passion manslaughter, say, would be less likely to be admitted than shoplifting, since the former has no bearing whatsoever on veracity, whereas the latter's factor of stealth has a least a slight connection to truthtelling; see the Note above);

   b. **Recency:** The *recency* of the prior conviction. The older the conviction, the less relevant it is and thus the less likely to be admitted;

   c. **Similarity:** The *similarity* between the prior crime and the charged one. The more similar, the more prejudicial and thus, the less likely to be admitted.

      i. **Rationale:** If the prior offense is ***very similar*** or ***identical*** to the presently-charged offense, the jury is even more likely than usual to reason that "if he did it before, he'll do it again."

      ii. **Sanitizing:** Some courts have tried to deal with this "similarity" problem by allowing evidence of the prior similar events, but only in a ***"sanitized"*** version that does not identify the crime. Thus in an auto theft prosecution, a prior conviction for auto theft might be allowed for impeachment, but the prosecution might be permitted only to introduce the fact that the witness-defendant was previously convicted of "a felony involving theft."

   d. **Importance of defendant's testimony:** The ***importance*** of the defendant's ***testimony***. Thus if the witness is the accused himself, and he is the only witness who does or could testify for the defense, the prior conviction is less likely to be admitted than if the defendant's case is also buttressed by numerous other eyewitnesses, or if the witness is a non-party whose testimony is of somewhat peripheral importance to the calling party; and

   e. **Centrality of credibility issue:** The ***centrality*** of the ***credibility issue***. Thus if the case is likely to come down to a "swearing contest" between the defendant-witness and, say, a police officer, the prior conviction is less likely to be admitted than if the case turns mostly on non-credibility issues such as the results of scientific tests or the interpretation of documents.

F. **FRE 609 — Time limit:**   As noted, the *older* the conviction, the less probative value it has. FRE 609 contains a special provision making very old convictions hard to get into evidence: 609(b) provides that if more than *10 years* has elapsed from both the conviction and the end of the prison term for that conviction, the conviction is not admissible unless "its probative value, supported by *specific facts and circumstances*, *substantially outweighs* its prejudicial effect[.]"

1. **End of jail term is what counts:** Since people are ordinarily convicted before their jail term ends, this provision will normally kick in if, and only if, the person was *released from prison more than 10 years previously*.

2. **Significance:** The requirement of *specific facts and circumstances*, and the requirement that probative value *"substantially"* outweigh prejudice, make it *much harder* to get a 10-year-old conviction into evidence than a more recent one.

    a. **Distinctions wiped out:** Observe that when this "old convictions" provision applies, the standard for balancing prejudice against probative value applies exactly the same way whether or not the crime was a *crimen falsi*, and whether or not the witness is the accused.

3. **Advance notice required:** The last sentence of 609(b) imposes an additional, procedural, burden on the party that wants to use the more-than-10-year-old conviction for impeachment: that party must give *advance written notice* of its intent to use the conviction, so that the other party may have "a fair opportunity to contest its use."

G. **FRE 609 — Other issues:** Here are some other issues that can arise in connection with the impeachment use of convictions:

1. ***In limine* motions:**   Before a defendant who has prior convictions decides whether to testify, he will often want to know whether these convictions can be introduced against him. Therefore, he will often before taking the stand ask the trial judge for an *in limine* ruling, in which the judge specifies which, if any, of the prior convictions can be used against the defendant.

2. **Procedure:**   If use of the prior convictions is allowed, there are two main ways in which this evidence can be introduced. First, the opposing lawyer (usually the prosecutor) can ask the witness during cross-examination to admit the fact of the conviction. Alternatively, the cross-examiner may introduce a *certified copy* of the prior judgment. Lilly, p. 345.

3. **Permitted detail:** Courts disagree on what *details* about the previous conviction may be disclosed to the jury. The name of the crime and the date of the conviction are almost always allowed into evidence. Some, but not all, courts also allow the jury to learn the *sentence,* and some but not all allow the *place* to be mentioned. Most courts *disallow a detailed description* of the underlying acts; for instance, the court might allow disclosure that there was a conviction for assault, but not disclosure of the fact that the victim was the witness's wife. M&K, §6.34, pp. 517-518.

    a. **Right to explain:** Regardless of whether the details of the prior conviction are disclosed, the court will usually allow the impeached witness to give a short statement *explaining the circumstances* of the prior conviction (though this may be dangerous for the witness to do, since it may open the door to a rebuttal by the other side). L&S,

p. 291.

4. **State or federal:** The conviction need not be in the same jurisdiction as the present case. Thus a conviction from any state may be used in a federal trial, and vice versa. McC, p. 56.

5. **Juvenile adjudications:** At common law, evidence that the witness has been the subject of a *"juvenile adjudication"* (i.e., found to have committed an act which would have been a crime had the defendant been an adult), is generally *not admissible*. S&R, p. 525. But the Federal Rules change this slightly: FRE 609(d) makes evidence of a juvenile adjudication admissible, but only if "(1) [the evidence] is offered in a *criminal* case; (2) the adjudication was of a *witness other than the defendant*; (3) an adult's conviction for that offense would be admissible to attack the adult's credibility; and (4) admitting the evidence is *necessary to fairly determine* guilt or innocence."

   a. **Consequence:** This means that juvenile adjudications are *never admissible in civil cases*, and that an *accused who takes the stand* can *never be impeached by his own* juvenile adjudication.

6. **Appeals:** The fact that the prior conviction is being *appealed* does not make the conviction inadmissible, either at common law or under the Federal Rules. See FRE 609(e). But the pendency of the appeal is, under FRE 609(e), a fact that can be disclosed to the jury.

7. *Nolo contendere* **pleas:** It is not clear whether a conviction based upon a plea of *nolo contendere* is admissible. In federal cases, FRE 410(a)(2) makes pleas of *nolo contendere* inadmissible in later proceedings. However, since FRE 609 does not exclude convictions based on *nolo* pleas, it is probably the case that a conviction based on a *nolo* plea is admissible, even though the fact that the conviction came about by a *nolo* plea rather than by trial is not admissible. See McC, p. 57, urging this interpretation.

8. **Harmonizing convictions and bad-acts evidence under FRE 608:** The use of prior convictions for impeachment is fairly strictly — or at least precisely — controlled by FRE 609. FRE 608(b) (discussed more fully *infra*, p. 130), regulates the impeachment use of "*specific instances* of the conduct of a witness," and does so accordingly to a different — in some ways more limiting, in other ways less-restrictive — set of rules. Therefore, the question arises, if the fact of conviction can't be shown under FRE 609, can the underlying "bad acts" that gave rise to the conviction be shown provided that they meet the requirements of FRE 608(b)? The issue is discussed immediately below.

VIII. IMPEACHMENT BY PRIOR BAD ACTS

A. **Use of bad acts generally:** Just as a witness's prior criminal convictions may impeach his credibility, so may his past *misconduct* that has not led to a conviction. If it can be shown that the witness has lied on a job application, embezzled from an employer, evaded taxes, or done some other act that reflects poorly on his veracity, but that has not led to a criminal conviction, the witness will be shown to be less worthy of belief. Yet such prior misconduct by hypothesis has not been the subject of independent judicial proof "beyond a reasonable doubt," so in a sense it is more troubling to allow the witness to be impeached by such conduct than by a past conviction.

1. **Common-law view:** Most common law jurisdictions have adopted a compromise between freely allowing evidence of prior bad acts and completely excluding it. The majority rule at common law *allows* prior bad acts, but subject to limitations.

   a. **No extrinsic evidence:** The most important common-law limitation is that the questioner must introduce the prior bad act *solely through cross-examination* of the witness. For instance, he may ask the witness, "Isn't it true that you lied on your job application by falsely stating that you had never used drugs?" But if the witness denies the allegation, the examiner may *not* introduce *extrinsic evidence* to show that the witness is lying; thus, the questioner could not *put on a second witness* to testify that the first witness had indeed used drugs and lied on his job application. As the concept is often expressed, the examiner *must "take the witness's answer."* (But this restriction does not prevent the cross-examiner from hammering away at the witness, trying to overcome his denial of the allegation; it merely means that he may not introduce extrinsic evidence.)

   b. **Discretion of court:** Most courts allowing prior bad act impeachment give the trial court wide *discretion* about whether to allow or exclude such evidence. McC, p. 54. For instance, the trial judge may consider the degree of prejudice to the witness, the nearness or remoteness in time of the misconduct, and the relevance of the misconduct to the witness's truthfulness. *Id.*

   c. **Good faith basis:** The cross-examiner must have a *good faith basis* for asking about a particular prior bad act. Otherwise, an unscrupulous cross-examiner could convince the jury that the witness had committed a particular act even though there was no evidence that that act ever occurred at all.

B. **Federal Rules:** The Federal Rules follows the common-law approach in general. FRE 608(b) provides as follows:

   > "Rule 608. A Witness's Character for Truthfulness or Untruthfulness
   >
   > . . .
   >
   > **(b) Specific Instances of Conduct.** Except for a *criminal conviction under Rule 609*, *extrinsic evidence* is *not admissible* to prove *specific instances of a witness's conduct* in order to attack or support the witness's character for truthfulness. But the court may, on cross-examination, allow them to be *inquired into* if they are *probative of the character for truthfulness or untruthfulness* of:
   >
   >   (1) *the witness*; or
   >
   >   (2) *another witness* whose *character* the witness being cross-examined has *testified* about.
   >
   > By testifying on another matter, a witness does not waive any privilege against self-incrimination for testimony that relates only to the witness's character for truthfulness."

1. **Summary:** Thus FRE 608(b) incorporates several restrictions on the use of prior bad acts for impeachment:

   a. **No extrinsic evidence:** As at common law, the prior bad act may be proved *only through cross-examination,* not through the presentation of testimony by other witnesses or other *extrinsic evidence.* In other words, in federal courts (as at common law), the cross-examiner *must "take the witness's answer."*

b. Probative of truthfulness: Only those prior bad acts that are *"probative of the character for truthfulness or untruthfulness"* may be brought up.

Example 1: Prior acts of *violence*, unaccompanied by deceit, and not leading to conviction, will generally *not* be admissible, because they're not probative of a character for truthfulness. So the witness's prior act of, say, manslaughter or armed robbery not leading to conviction would not be admissible, because the fact that the witness had committed that deed does not make it more likely than it would otherwise be that he is now lying.

Example 2: In a civil car-accident case, P claims that D was speeding at the time of the accident. D, as a witness on direct in his own case, denies speeding. P's lawyer proposes to ask D on cross, "Isn't it true that you've gotten two speeding tickets in the last 3 years?" D's lawyer objects.

The question is not proper. The fact that D sped on two occasions *doesn't bear on his general character for truthfulness.* And it doesn't shed any real light on whether he's telling the truth on this particular occasion, since he could well have been driving within the speed limit this time even though he's sped in the past. (It's *really inadmissible character trait evidence*, implying, "He sped before, therefore he's probably lying when he says he didn't speed this time"; such evidence is inadmissible under FRE 404(a)(1) and (b)(1); see *supra*, pp. 25 and 27.)

    i. Contrast: Contrast this rule with the rules governing proof of prior *convictions* to impeach a witness's credibility, under FRE 609. A non-party witness's prior felony conviction may usually be automatically introduced to impeach him under 609(a)(1)(A) *even if the felony doesn't bear on truthfulness*; under 608(b)(1) and (2), the prior unconvicted bad act may come in only if it expressly bears on truthfulness. So in this sense a broader range of acts can come in if they resulted in convictions than if they didn't.

c. Discretion of the judge: The cross-examiner has no absolute right to bring up even those prior bad acts that clearly bear on truthfulness. All inquiry into "specific instances of the conduct of a witness" is left to the court's *discretion*, as indicated by 608(b)'s statement that "the court *may* [not "shall"], on cross-examination, allow [specific instances] to be inquired into if they are probative of the character for truthfulness or untruthfulness[.]" Typically, the court will weigh the probative value of the evidence against the prejudice that will result to the opposing party. The exercise of this discretion will rarely be reversed on appeal.

d. Applies to any witness: This principle that the cross-examiner may bring out unconvicted acts of the witness during cross *applies to any witness,* whether the witness is giving *substantive* testimony or merely *impeaching* another witness.

Example: The case involves a car accident, in which P asserts that D drove negligently. D takes the stand and testifies that he drove carefully on the occasion in question. P offers rebuttal testimony by W, D's neighbor, that D has a reputation in the neighborhood for being a liar. D's lawyer asks W on cross, "Isn't it true that when you were looking for a job last year, you falsified your resume?" (Assume that the lawyer has a good-faith basis for asking this.)

The questioning is *proper* (though whether to admit it is left to the discretion of the court). The fact that the examiner is asking about specific acts of misconduct doesn't matter, nor does the fact that W was called merely to give reputation or opinion testimony bearing on the truthfulness of another witness (D), rather than giving "occurrence" testimony.

2. **Self-incrimination:** The examiner's right to inquire about prior bad acts may run afoul of the witness's *privilege against self-incrimination* (see *infra*, p. 437).

   a. **The problem:** The problem is most likely to arise where the witness is the accused, who has taken the stand in his own defense. Normally, the accused or any other witness who voluntarily takes the stand and discloses part of a transaction is deemed to have waived the privilege against self-incrimination as to the rest of the transaction. See *infra*, p. 443.

   b. **No waiver:** But where the accused takes the stand in his own defense and speaks on direct only about the present crime, as a constitutional matter the accused does *not waive* his right to claim the privilege when asked about prior bad acts that have nothing directly to do with the present charged offense and are relevant only to credibility.

   c. **Federal Rule:** In part for this reason, the last sentence of FRE 608(b) provides that when a witness (whether an accused or not) testifies about some matter other than the prior bad act — such as an accused's testimony about the presently-charged crime — the witness "*does not waive* any privilege against self-incrimination for testimony that *relates only to the witness's character for truthfulness.*"

3. **Bad acts that are also crimes:** Suppose the prior bad act is something that is *also a crime*. How do 608(b) (allowing impeachment by questions about the witness's prior bad acts) and 609 (allowing impeachment by showing a prior conviction) interact?

   a. **Prior conviction:** Suppose the prior bad act actually led to the witness's criminal *conviction* for that act. A leading commentator says that "the better approach, and the one *supported by the trend* in the cases, would hold that FRE *609 provides the governing standard* whenever acts lead to conviction and that the cross-examiner must *proceed under that provision or not at all.*" M&K §6.34, p. 527.

      i. **Relevance:** The problem can arise where the prior act and conviction are very *old*, are for a juvenile offense, or are for a non-*crimen falsi* **misdemeanor** — in all of these situations, the special provisions of 609 may prevent the conviction, but the vaguer ones in 608(b) might not.

   Example: Suppose that W, a witness for D in D's criminal case, was previously convicted of shoplifting, for which the maximum sentence would have been 6 months (and that W actually served 5 months in prison). Recall (p. 124) that shoplifting is not a *crimen falsi*, because it is not defined in such a way that "dishonesty or false statement" is an element required for conviction. This conviction would therefore not be admissible to impeach W under Rule 609 (because it's not a felony, and thus doesn't come within 609(a)(1), and it's not a *crimen falsi*, and thus doesn't come within 609(a)(2)).

The prosecutor would like to ask W about the shoplifting incident as a prior bad act under FRE 608(b) ("Isn't it true that you committed shoplifting?"). In support of her right to ask the question, the prosecutor can point out that under 608(b), "the court may, on cross-examination, allow [specific instances of a witness's conduct] to be inquired into if they are probative of the character for truthfulness or untruthfulness of: (1) the witness[.]" This language seems to apply; shoplifting seems roughly probative on truthfulness, even if it doesn't exactly involve "dishonesty or false statement." Yet we have a much more specific rule — 609 — that won't let the conviction in. Should the court nonetheless allow the question about the bad act itself (without the fact of conviction) under 608(b)?

Most courts would likely hold that the prosecutor **cannot ask** the question, on the grounds that if a conviction resulted, FRE 609, not 608, applies. See the cases cited at M&K §6.34, p. 527, n. 7, including *U.S. v. Osazuwa*, 564 F.3d 1169 (9th Cir. 2009) (FRE 608(b) "permits impeachment only by specific acts that have *not* resulted in a criminal conviction"; impeaching use of criminal convictions "is treated exclusively under Rule 609.")

Note: Observe that exactly the same problem would arise if the conviction was older than 10 years (and thus couldn't meet the tough standard of 609(b)), or occurred when W was a juvenile (making it inadmissible under 609(d).).

Note: Also, don't forget that the examiner is ordinarily much more limited in ***how she can use*** a bad act under 608(b) than in how she can use a conviction under 609 — the "no proof by extrinsic evidence" rule applies to 608(b) but not to 609. So on the facts of the above Example, if the court *did* allow the prosecutor to ask W, "Didn't you commit shoplifting?" and W denied it, the prosecutor wouldn't be allowed to put the record of conviction in evidence.

b. **Prior act did not lead to conviction:** Now, suppose that the prior bad act ***never resulted in charges***, or resulted in charges that ended in W's ***acquittal***. Again, if the conviction would not have been admissible under 609 even had it occurred, should the court nonetheless allow the unconvicted bad act into evidence under 608(b)? If the conclusion given in the above Example for the conviction-occurred situation is correct (that the court should disallow the question under 608(b) if the conviction couldn't come in under 609), logically the same result should follow if there never was a conviction. So if, for instance, the bad act was a non-*crimen falsi* that could have led at most to a misdemeanor conviction, or if it occurred more than 10 years previously, the court should exercise its discretion to disallow the question about the bad act.

c. **Questions about arrests:** The questioner may *not* ask the witness questions about the witness's prior *arrests* on cross. Arrests, as well as the ***filing of charges*** or ***indictments***, are not proper subjects for impeachment, because they're frequently unreliable. So the cross-examiner must ask about the specific underlying act, not the fact of arrest or indictment. See *Michelson v. U.S.*, 335 U.S. 469 (1948) ("Arrest without more does not, in law any more than in reason, impeach the integrity or impair the credibility of a witness. It happens to the innocent as well as the guilty.") See also M&K, §6.25, p. 494.

Example: "Weren't you arrested for defrauding Annie Smith of her life savings?" is not proper. The questioner must ask, "Didn't you defraud Annie Smith of her life savings?"

Note: This same principle means that if the witness was eventually *convicted*, the question must be about the conviction, not the arrest or indictment leading up to the conviction. See *supra*, p. 133.

i.   **Impeachment by contradiction:** However, if the witness on direct happens to *deny* having been arrested, then the cross-examiner *will* be entitled to ask about the arrest — here, the impeachment is based on the *contradiction*, not the prior bad act (the arrest) itself. See *infra*, p. 145, for more about impeachment by contradiction. This may happen not only where the testimony on direct relates directly to arrests (e.g., "I've never been arrested" — which might be rebutted by a question on cross like, "Isn't it true that you were arrested for shoplifting at Wal-Mart last June?"), but also probably where the direct testimony relates more broadly to the witness's law-abiding nature (e.g., "I don't have a police record" or "I'm a law-abiding person.") M&K, §6.44, pp. 545.

4.   **Direct examination:**   FRE 608(b) on its face allows inquiry into prior bad acts only "on cross-examination." However, FRE 607 (allowing impeachment of a witness even on direct examination) probably means that 608(b) should be read to allow inquiry about prior bad acts on *direct examination* as well. See S&R, pp. 494-95, urging such an interpretation. This would mean that: (1) the direct examiner who is interrogating a *hostile witness* may impeach the witness's credibility by inquiring into prior bad acts; and (2) possibly, the direct examiner who is interrogating a friendly or neutral witness and who fears that his adversary will impeach by bringing up prior bad acts on cross, may *"draw the sting"* by bringing up these acts on direct. For more about drawing the sting in this manner, see *infra*, p. 157.

5.   **No use of extrinsic evidence:** Recall that Rule 608 bars the use of *"extrinsic evidence"* to prove specific bad acts by the witness. This is accomplished by the first sentence of 608(b), which provides that "Except for a criminal conviction under Rule 609, *extrinsic evidence is not admissible* to prove *specific instances of a witness's conduct* in order to attack or support the witness's character for truthfulness." This provision thus implements the common-law rule that the questioner must *"take the answer of the witness"* — if the witness denies having committed the bad act, the questioner may not use other methods to prove that the bad act took place.

a.   **Can't use second witness:** The rule against extrinsic bad-acts evidence means that if the principal witness (let's refer to her as W1) denies the bad act under questioning during cross, the attacker *can't call a second witness* (let's call him W2) to testify that W1 really did the bad act.

Example: Suppose D is charged with committing a robbery. He presents an alibi witness, W1, who says that she's D's girlfriend and that she was with D in D's apartment at the time the robbery was committed. The prosecutor, to impeach W1's credibility for truth-telling, asks her on cross, "Didn't you once defraud an old lady of her life's savings, by pretending to be an investment counselor?" W1 says, "No, that's not true." The prosecutor may ask a few follow-up questions (e.g., "Would it refresh your recollection if I told you that the woman in question was Annie Smith of 452 Mockingbird Lane, Chicago?") But if W1 sticks to her denial, the "no extrinsic evidence" rule kicks in: the prosecutor may not call W2, a police officer, to testify, "We conducted an investigation and concluded that W1 indeed defrauded poor Ms. Smith." Instead, the prosecutor must "take" W1's denial, and that's the end of the inquiry.

b. **Can't use document:** The rule against extrinsic bad-acts evidence also applies to a second type of extrinsic evidence: *documents*. The witness's bad act can't be proved by documents (or other physical evidence) any more than it can be proved by a second witness's testimony.

> **Example:** Same facts as above Example. Now, suppose that after W1 denies the fraud, the prosecutor seeks to introduce into evidence (while W1 is still on the stand) a letter from Mrs. Smith to the police, stating that W1 defrauded her of her life's savings. This letter will be inadmissible, under the "no extrinsic evidence" rule. M&K §6.42, p. 498. (On the other hand, if the prosecutor didn't seek to admit the letter, but brandished it during the cross, saying, "Would your answer be different if I told you I have here in my hand a letter from Mrs. Smith saying that you did defraud her?" the question would probably be proper, as staying within cross and not amounting to the use of extrinsic evidence.)

c. **Admitted for other purposes:** But it's only where the extrinsic evidence of prior bad acts is admitted for purposes of showing the witness's *bad character for truthfulness* that 608(b)'s rule against extrinsic evidence applies. There are many other reasons for which one might want to impeach a witness's testimony, and extrinsic evidence *is* allowed in support of some of these reasons. For instance, extrinsic evidence can be used to show that W1 should not be believed because: (1) W1 is *biased* for (or against) a party; (2) W1 has a *mental or sensory incapacity*; or (3) W1 has previously made a *statement inconsistent with W1's trial testimony*. M&K § 6.28, pp. 499-500. For more about these "extrinsic evidence permitted" situations, see *infra*, pp. 151-151.

6. **Good-faith basis:** The common-law rule that the attacker may be forced to show a *"good faith basis"* for the question about the bad act (see *supra*, p. 130) applies to questioning under the FRE as well. W&G, §6118, n. 19.

> **Example:** Same facts as the first Example on p. 134. Before the prosecutor asks W1, "Didn't you defraud an old woman . . . .," the prosecutor may be required to show, *in camera*, that she has a good faith basis for believing that the defrauding really took place. The showing the prosecutor should be required to make is "very close to probable cause." M&K §6.26, p. 495.

IX. IMPEACHMENT BY OPINION AND REPUTATION REGARDING CHARACTER

A. Issue generally: We turn now to the third and final way in which the witness's general character for veracity may be impeached. The two prior methods rely upon specific past acts by the witness to infer that he has a general character for lying, and is thus likely to be lying now. The final method of character impeachment is more direct: the opponent offers testimony from a second witness that the first witness has a ***bad character for truthfulness***.

1. **Distinguished from substantive evidence:** Recall that a party may not usually use character evidence to prove substantive elements of his case. For instance, the prosecution may not show that because the defendant has a character for drunken driving, he was probably driving while drunk in the present case. (See *supra*, p. 25.) Allowing the prosecution to show that because D has a general character for lying, he is probably lying in his present testimony, should logically be equally forbidden. L&S, p. 304. Such evidence is likely to be just as prejudicial to the witness as use of character as substantive evidence would be to the party against whom it is directed. Nonetheless, nearly all courts allow at least limited use of "character for truthfulness" evidence on impeachment.

B. Common-law rule: The general common-law approach allows some but not all types of proof that the witness has a bad character for truthfulness.

1. **Reputation:** Most importantly, most common-law jurisdictions allow a witness to impugn the truthfulness of the principal witness only by stating that the principal witness has a ***bad reputation*** for truthfulness. The second witness may ***not***, in most jurisdictions, recite his own ***opinion*** of the principal witness's veracity, nor may he recite ***specific instances*** of conduct by the principal witness leading to that witness's bad reputation for truthfulness. Lilly, p. 356. The rationale for this limitation is that it ***prevents delay***, and also minimizes prejudice.

2. **General character not allowed:** The vast majority of jurisdictions do ***not*** allow evidence of the witness's reputation for ***general*** good or bad "character," only evidence of his reputation for the particular trait of ***truthfulness***. McC, p. 59.

3. **Opinion:** As noted, most courts do not allow the second witness to state his personal ***opinion*** as to the principal witness's truthfulness. However, a growing ***minority*** of courts does allow such evidence.

4. **Opening the door:** The need to impeach the witness's character for truthfulness arises most often when the witness is the accused in a criminal case, who takes the stand in his own behalf. If the accused affirmatively states that he is a truthful person, it is easy to see why the prosecution should be able to impeach with witnesses who testify that the accused is a liar. But where the accused merely tells his side of the facts, and makes no assertion that he is a generally honest person, the defense has not really put the defendant's "character for truthfulness" in issue. Nonetheless, nearly all courts hold that ***merely by taking the stand***, the defendant has ***opened the door*** to evidence of his general character for untruthfulness.

C. Federal Rule: The Federal Rules follow the general common-law approach of allowing some types of evidence of the witness's character for truthfulness. FRE 608(a) provides as follows:

> **"(a) Reputation or Opinion Evidence.** A witness's credibility may be attacked or supported by testimony about the witness's **reputation** for having a character for truthfulness or untruthfulness, or by testimony in the form of an **opinion** about that character. But evidence of truthful character is admissible only after the witness's character for truthfulness has been attacked."

1. **Summary:** Only the first sentence of 608(a) is relevant to us now (since the second sentence relates to rehabilitation, and is discussed *infra*, p. 153). The first sentence directly or indirectly includes the following provisions:

   a. **Reputation:** As at common law, the second witness may recite that the first witness has a **bad reputation** for truthfulness.

   b. **Opinion:** Unlike most common-law jurisdictions, FRE 608(a) also allows the second witness to state his own **opinion** about the first witness's character for truthfulness.

   c. **Specific instances:** The second witness may **not**, on direct, refer to any **specific instances** of untruthful conduct by the first witness. This limitation comes from 608(b)'s ban on the use of "extrinsic evidence" to show "specific instances of a witness's conduct." Thus if D takes the stand to deny the crime, and the prosecution calls W to testify that W has a bad opinion of D's truthfulness, W may not recite the particular past lies by D that have led W to this unfavorable opinion of D's veracity. The rationale is that were the details of past lies allowed, these details would be unduly prejudicial to D, and a lot of trial time would be used up while D's counsel tried to show that D did not really lie on the prior occasions.

      i. **Cross-examination:** However, the ban on specific instances of past conduct does not apply to **cross-examination**. Thus, if W has testified on direct that he has a bad opinion of D's veracity, the defense counsel could, for instance, ask W, "Don't you remember when D was undercharged at the Bonanza Steakhouse restaurant, and he insisted on paying the proper amount?" See FRE 608(b)(2). However, past striking instances of truthfulness (unlike past instances of lying) are rare, so the right to use past instances of truthfulness on cross-examination is of little utility. L&S, p. 305.

   d. **General character:** As at common law, the second witness may testify only to the principal witness's character for **truthfulness**, not his character for other traits (e.g., physical aggressiveness), nor his "general" character.

X. IMPEACHMENT BY PRIOR INCONSISTENT STATEMENTS

A. **General principle:** Perhaps the most important technique for impeaching a witness is by showing that he has made a **prior inconsistent statement**. Evidence of prior inconsistent statements is impeaching in two ways: (1) it directly casts doubt on the truthfulness of the current statement; and (2) insofar as it suggests that the witness has told two stories, at least one of which must be incorrect, it suggests that the witness has a general tendency to lie, so that other aspects of his present testimony should be disbelieved.

1. **Relation to hearsay rule:**   Our present discussion concerns the use of prior inconsistent statements for impeachment only. Traditionally, impeachment use was the *only* use to which a prior inconsistent statement could usually be put, since the hearsay rule prevented use of the prior statement for substantive purposes. But the modern trend is to treat at least some types of prior inconsistent statements as not being barred by the hearsay rule, and thus as substantive proof of the matters contained therein. (For instance, FRE 801(d)(1) treats prior statements made in an earlier trial or proceeding, where the declarant spoke under oath and subject to perjury penalties, as not being hearsay. See *infra*, p. 307.) Our discussion of prior inconsistent statements here assumes that the statement is not admissible for substantive purposes, and is therefore admissible only for impeachment if at all.

B. **General rule:**   The general rule, both at common law and under the Federal Rules, is that when a witness testifies at trial, evidence of his prior inconsistent statement is *admissible* to impeach his credibility. L&S, p. 306.

1. **Limits:**   But there are two important rules that limit the use of prior inconsistent statements for impeachment:

    a. **Foundation:**   First, at common law (and to a lesser extent under the Federal Rules), a rigid *foundation* must be laid before the prior inconsistent statement may be introduced for impeachment. In brief, before the statement may be introduced, the witness must be given a chance to deny having made it or to explain away the inconsistency. See *infra*, p. 139, for a fuller discussion.

    b. **No extrinsic evidence on collateral matters:**   Second, if the prior statement involves only a *"collateral* matter," the statement may not be proven by *"extrinsic"* evidence (e.g., another witness's testimony that the first witness made the statement).

        Example: D is charged with robbing W by taking W's wallet. W testifies that the mugging occurred just after W left the Roxy theater where "Sound of Music" was being played. Defense counsel learns that shortly after the mugging, W told his friend X that the crime took place just after W had left the Sleazeball Cinema, where "I Was a Teenage Nymphomaniac" was playing.

        This prior inconsistent statement may be introduced to impeach W's testimony. However, defense counsel must first satisfy two common-law requirements: (1) He must ask W whether he made the earlier statement to X, and give W a chance to deny having made it or to explain away the inconsistency as to the movie seen; and (2) He may bring out the fact of the earlier statement in cross-examination, but since the inconsistency relates to a collateral matter (the movie W saw), he may not use extrinsic evidence (e.g., testimony by X that W really made the earlier statement to X) to prove the earlier statement — he must "take W's answer."

2. **Parties not covered:**   The rules governing prior inconsistent statements (i.e., the foundation requirement and the "no extrinsic evidence of collateral matters" rule) apply only where the *witness is not a party.* If the witness *is* a party, his prior inconsistent statement is substantively admissible as an *admission*, since admissions do not fall within the hearsay rule (see *infra*, p. 217). Therefore, the remainder of our discussion of prior inconsistent statements involves only prior statements by non-party witnesses. See, e.g., the last sen-

tence of FRE 613(b), making that Rule's foundation requirement inapplicable to admissions of a party-opponent.

C. Foundation requirement: Let's now examine more closely the requirement that before the prior inconsistent statement can be proved, preliminary questions must be asked to lay a ***foundation*** for it.

1. Common law: As noted, the common law imposed a very rigid foundation requirement. The witness must be told the substance of the alleged statement, the time, the place, and the person to whom it was made. McC, p. 48. This foundation gives the witness a chance to deny ever having made the statement, or to explain away the inconsistency. L&S, p. 306.

    a. Rationale: There seem to be two rationales for the common-law foundation requirement. First, there is the sense of ***fairness*** to the witness: the cross-examiner should not be allowed to plant a trap and "spring" the prior statement on the witness without any advance warning. Second, if the witness is not given a chance to explain or deny the prior statement, and extrinsic evidence of the prior statement is then presented (e.g., testimony by a person who heard the prior statement), time will be wasted, since the primary witness might have, if asked, been able to explain away the inconsistency.

2. Federal Rule: The common-law foundation requirement has been criticized as being unduly rigid; criticism has focussed on the requirement that the foundation be laid ***before*** the impeachment. For instance, suppose the cross-examiner does not learn of the prior inconsistent statement until the witness has not only left the stand but is now unavailable; the common-law rule prevents the prior statement from being shown. McC, p. 48. Furthermore, the foundation rule is a trap for the unwary, since in the heat of cross-examination it is easy to neglect to lay a sufficiently specific foundation.

Therefore, the Federal Rules have ***liberalized*** the foundation requirement by requiring the foundation, but allowing it to be made either before ***or after*** the impeachment. FRE 613(b) provides:

> **"(b) Extrinsic Evidence of a Prior Inconsistent Statement.** Extrinsic evidence of a witness's prior inconsistent statement is admissible only if the witness is given an ***opportunity to explain or deny*** the statement and an adverse party is given an ***opportunity to examine the witness about it***, or if ***justice so requires***. This subdivision (b) does not apply to an ***opposing party's statement*** under Rule 801(d)(2)."

    a. Summary: So under FRE 613(b), the attacking party can ***decline to mention*** any inconsistency while cross-examining W, ***wait until W leaves the stand***, and then put on extrinsic evidence of W's prior inconsistent statement (e.g., testimony by a second witness, X, that W previously told X a different story).

        i. Disclosure to opposing counsel: However, although the prior statement does not have to be shown to the witness — or its contents disclosed to him — FRE 613(a) says that "[T]he [attacking] party must, on request, show [the prior statement] or disclose its contents to an adverse party's attorney."

        Example: W is called by P in a car accident case, and testifies that "I saw the accident, and D was travelling 70 mph." D's lawyer knows that W previously signed an affidavit that D was traveling "no more than 60," and handed the affidavit to D's investigator. D's lawyer can ask W on cross, "Have you ever signed an affidavit that D was 'traveling no more than 60'?" If W says, "No I didn't," D can excuse the witness and introduce the affidavit later. D's counsel *does not have to disclose to the witness* at the time of the question that counsel has such an affidavit, or show W a copy. But if P's counsel asks for it, D's counsel must *show the affidavit* to him.

   b. Impeacher doesn't bear burden: The requirement in FRE 613(b) that the attacking party give the witness an "opportunity to explain or deny" the inconsistency does *not* mean that the attacker has to recall W to the stand to permit her to explain; instead, the *proponent* of W's testimony can be put to this burden of recalling W. The only real "bite" of 613(b) is that if W *becomes unavailable* after testifying (so that W now *can't* be recalled to explain or deny, or to be "interrogated" by W's proponent), the attacking party will lose the chance to use the extrinsic evidence, or have that evidence stricken after it's been used. For more about this, see *infra*, p. 142.

3. Writing: The common-law foundation requirement is especially strict where the prior inconsistent statement is *written*. Under the rule of *The Queen's [Caroline's] Case*, 129 Eng. Rep. 976 (1820), the beginning of the foundation for impeachment by a contradictory writing is that the writing must be *presented to the witness* for his examination. Lilly, p. 362.

   a. Criticism: This rule makes effective cross-examination of the witness much more difficult. First, the examiner loses the ability to trap a deceitful witness who would otherwise deny having made the prior inconsistent written statement. Second, the early disclosure to the witness gives him time to gather his thoughts, and perhaps make up an explanation of the inconsistency. *Id.*

   b. Modern and Federal Rule: Many modern courts, and the Federal Rules, abrogate the rule of *Queen's Case* for these reasons. *Id.* Thus FRE 613(a) provides that the prior written statement *need not be shown to the witness before or during examination* (though "the party must, on request, show ... its contents to an adverse party's attorney.")

D. Extrinsic evidence: Often, the prior inconsistent statement can be proved "out of the mouth" of the witness who made it. That is, after the witness testifies at trial to assertion *A*, the examiner can ask him, "Don't you remember saying not-*A* in a conversation with X on June 24, 2010?" If the witness admits having made the prior inconsistent statement, that is all that the cross-examiner needs. If the witness denies having made the earlier statement, however, the examiner will wish to prove the prior statement by *"extrinsic" evidence*, i.e., evidence other than the testimony of the witness who made the statement. If the prior statement was in writing, the writing itself would be extrinsic evidence. If the prior statement was oral, testimony by another witness who heard the statement would be extrinsic.

1. Limits: There are two important common-law rules limiting the use of extrinsic evidence to prove a prior inconsistent statement:

   a. Must be material: First, the inconsistency between the trial testimony and the prior statement must be *"material."* In other words, if the prior statement varies only slightly from the present testimony (so that it would ***not cast doubt*** on the truthfulness of the witness's present testimony), the prior statement cannot be proved by extrinsic evidence.

b. **No proof of collateral facts:**   Second, extrinsic proof of the prior inconsistent statement is not allowed if that statement involves only ***"collateral"*** matters. McC, p. 47. This means that the statement must deal with either: (1) facts relevant to the issues in the case; or (2) facts which are themselves provable by extrinsic evidence to discredit the witness.

   i. **Explanation:**   Category (2) above refers to facts which could be proved by extrinsic evidence ***even if there were no claim that the witness had contradicted himself***. Facts showing that the witness is ***biased***, and probably facts showing that the witness had no opportunity to know the facts that he testified to, fall within this category. L&S, p. 308.

   Example: D is charged with rape. W testifies that D was with W during the entire evening on which the rape allegedly took place, and that the rape did not take place. W testifies that she has no romantic involvement with D or any motive to lie on his behalf. On cross, the prosecutor asks W, "Isn't it true that before trial, you told X that you loved D and would lie to get him acquitted?" W denies having made this statement, and repeats that she has no reason to help D.

   The prosecutor will now be permitted to call X to testify that W did indeed tell him that she was in love with D and would lie for him. This is extrinsic proof of a prior inconsistent statement, and the subject of the statement is not directly relevant to the issues in the case. However, the prior statement shows bias, and a witness's bias may be shown even where the cross-examiner does not claim that the bias contradicts the witness's present testimony. Therefore, this statement falls into category (2) above. Similarly, the prosecutor would be permitted to introduce extrinsic evidence that W told X, "I was out of town on the night of the rape, so I don't know whether D did it or not."

2. **Federal Rule:**   As we noted previously (*supra*, p. 139), the Federal Rules make it easier than the common law did to prove that the witness made a prior inconsistent statement. But like the common law, the Federal Rules place some limits on the use of extrinsic evidence to prove a witness's prior inconsistent statement.

   a. **The "explain or deny" and "interrogate" rules:**   These rules limiting the questioner's ability to prove by extrinsic evidence that a witness (call her "W1") made a prior inconsistent statement are imposed by FRE 613(b). 613(b) says that such extrinsic proof can only be made where *two requirements* are satisfied:

   [1] The witness who made the prior inconsistent statement must be ***"given an opportunity to explain or deny"*** it; and

   [2] The ***opposite party*** (the proponent of the testimony of the witness being impeached by the prior inconsistent statement) must be given "an ***opportunity to interrogate*** the witness [who made the inconsistent statement] about it."

   (But both of these requirements may be dispensed with if "justice so requires.")

These two requirements mean that, as a practical matter, *if W1 is to be impeached by a prior inconsistent statement*, the impeacher will have to be sure that *after the extrinsic evidence is presented*, *W1 remains physically available* to "explain or deny" it and to be interrogated about the statement by W1's proponent.

Example: W testifies in an auto accident case, "D was travelling over 70 mph." W is excused by P, and leaves the country. D presents testimony by Officer that when Officer interviewed W two days after the accident, W said "D wasn't going more than 60 mph." Since W is no longer available to explain or deny making this statement, or to be interrogated about the alleged statement by P's counsel, FRE 613(b) prevents Officer's testimony.

i. **Exception to "explain or deny" and "interrogate" rules for hearsay declarants:** The "opportunity to explain or deny" rule does *not apply* when the prior inconsistent statement is *offered against a hearsay declarant*, rather than against a "live" witness. In other words, when FRE 613(b) says that "Extrinsic evidence of a witness's prior inconsistent statement is admissible only if the witness is given an opportunity to explain or deny the statement," the rule is referring only to a witness *at the trial*, not one who made an out-of-court statement being proved at trial.

Example: In an accident case, Pete claims that Dave was speeding at the time of the accident. Pete offers, as his first witness, Wanda, who testifies, "Right after the accident, I heard Fred say, 'Look at that idiot Dave — he was speeding and he just crashed.' " Dave's lawyer asks Wanda on cross, "Isn't it true that the day after Fred allegedly saw the accident, Fred told you, 'Dave wasn't really speeding, I just made that up'?" Pete objects on the grounds that Fred is not present, and therefore doesn't have an "opportunity to explain or deny" the statement.

The objection will be overruled. Fred is a hearsay declarant, not a live witness. Therefore, Dave was entitled to attempt to impeach Fred's credibility by asking questions of Wanda designed to expose Fred's inconsistent statement. FRE 613(b)'s "opportunity to explain or deny" rule does not apply when the prior inconsistent statement is offered against a *hearsay declarant* like Fred, only when the statement is offered to impeach a "live" witness.

b. **No specific rule about extrinsic evidence on collateral matter:** The Federal Rules do not expressly say whether the prohibition on extrinsic proof of prior inconsistent statements dealing with *collateral matters* is maintained or not. But the trial judge has discretion, under FRE 403, to exclude evidence whose probative value is "substantially outweighed by a danger of … confusing the issues, … undue delay, [or] wasting time," and extrinsic evidence of collateral matters will often justify exclusion under 403.

XI. IMPEACHMENT FOR BIAS

A. **Proof of bias generally:** All courts allow proof that the witness is *biased*.

B. Types of bias: A witness is biased whenever his emotions or feelings towards the parties or towards some aspect of the case make the witness ***desire one outcome rather than another.*** Here are some of the types of bias:

1. **Friendly feeling:** The witness may feel *friendly* to one of the parties. This may be due to a ***personal relationship*** between the two (e.g., a romantic or familial tie). Or, it may be because one employs or does business with the other. It may even be because the party has paid the witness money in ***settlement*** of a claim related to the transaction involved in the suit.

   Example: P and W are in a car driven by P, which collides with a car driven by D. In the P-D suit, W testifies that D was negligent and that P was careful. D may show that W is biased by showing that P paid W money to settle W's claims for injuries arising out of the accident. McC, p. 52.

2. **Hostility:** Conversely, the witness may be ***hostile*** to a party. Hostility may be evidenced by the fact that the witness and the party have argued in the past, or one has sued the other, or the witness has said nasty things about the party to others.

3. **Self-interest:** The witness may have an ***interest in the outcome***, apart from any feeling of favor or hostility to the parties.

   Example 1: If W is an expert witness, the fact that he is being paid for his testimony is usually allowed as evidence that he has an interest in having the case come out in favor of the party for whom he is testifying (even if the expert's receipt of payment for his time and testimony is completely proper). McC, p. 53.

   Example 2: In a criminal case, W's own legal status may be affected by the outcome. For instance, if W has pled guilty to some related event, has agreed to cooperate with the prosecution, and is awaiting sentencing, these facts may be shown to establish bias — it is plausible that W will get less jail time if his testimony aids in convicting the defendant.

4. **Membership in group:** Bias may even be shown by the fact that the witness belongs to a particular organization and subscribes to its beliefs. Thus, in *U.S. v. Abel*, 469 U.S. 45 (1984), the Supreme Court held that the prosecution was entitled to show that a defense witness, W, and D were both members of a secret prison organization which had a creed requiring members to lie to protect each other. "A witness's and a party's common membership in an organization, even without proof that the witness or party has personally adopted its tenets, is certainly probative of bias."

C. Foundation: The examiner may cross-examine the witness to show bias ***without laying any foundation.***

1. **Extrinsic evidence:** However, most jurisdictions do not allow a party to use ***extrinsic evidence*** to show a witness's bias (e.g., testimony by another witness as to the first witness's bias) unless a foundation has been laid. The questioner must first ***ask*** the principal witness about the alleged bias; only if he denies it may the extrinsic evidence be used, in courts following this majority approach. McC, p. 53.

2. **Federal Rules:**   The Federal Rules do not explicitly require a foundation before extrinsic evidence of bias may be introduced. (In fact, the Federal Rules do not explicitly mention bias as a form of impeachment at all.) However, FRE 611(a), by giving the federal judge control over the "mode and order of interrogating witnesses and presenting evidence so as to . . . avoid needless consumption of time," probably gives the federal judge *discretion* to require that a foundation be laid before the extrinsic evidence is introduced. W&B, Par. 607[03].

3. **Bias never collateral:**   Recall that extrinsic evidence of prior inconsistent statements may not be introduced if the statements relate to "collateral" matters. (See *supra*, p. 141.) A similar rule does *not* apply to extrinsic proof of bias. That is, *facts showing bias are not "collateral,"* and if the main witness denies being biased, the cross-examiner is not required to "take his answer" — he may instead call other witnesses to prove the facts suggesting bias. McC, p. 53.

D. **Confrontation Clause rights in criminal cases:**   In criminal cases, the defendant's right to show that a prosecution witness is biased will often be *constitutionally protected.* Thus in *Davis v. Alaska*, 415 U.S. 308 (1974), the Supreme Court held that the trial court's denial of cross-examination to show the witness's bias violated D's Confrontation Clause rights under the Sixth Amendment, as applied to the states through the Fourteenth Amendment.

1. **Sexual history of rape victim:**   Similarly, the trial judge's refusal to allow a *rape defendant* to cross-examine his victim to show bias arising from her sexual history, may represent a denial of the defendant's Confrontation Clause rights. Thus in *Olden v. Kentucky*, 488 U.S. 227 (1988), D, the rape defendant, tried to show that W, the victim, was living with her boyfriend at the time of the alleged rape, and that W falsely claimed to have been raped by D in order to convince the boyfriend that W had been faithful to him. The Supreme Court held that the trial judge's refusal to allow D to bring out these points during cross-examination of W violated D's Confrontation Clause rights.

XII.   IMPEACHMENT BY SENSORY OR MENTAL DEFECTS

A. **General rule:**   A witness can always be impeached by showing that his capacity to *observe, remember,* or *narrate events correctly* has been impaired. W&B, Par. 607[04].

1. **Sensory defect:**   Thus, a witness can be impeached by showing that he has a *sensory deficiency* that impaired his ability to observe the events in question.

> **Example:** W claims to have overheard, from 10 feet away, a whispered conversation in which D and X plotted a murder. D's lawyer can show that W was hard of hearing and could thus not have heard the conversation. Similarly, W's credibility could be attacked by showing that his vision was too poor to have seen an event that he claims to have seen.

2. **Mental defect:**   As a general rule, a *mental defect* that the witness has, that can be shown to have impaired his ability to *remember* events or to *narrate them* correctly, may also be shown for impeachment.

3. Drugs and alcohol: The most controversial issue concerning proof of sensory and mental incapacity involves evidence of *alcohol* or *drug addiction*.

    a. Proof of intoxication: All courts agree that the witness may be impeached by showing that he was *drunk* or *high on drugs* at the time of the events he purported to witness.

    b. Addiction: But there is no unanimity about whether the witness may be shown to be a *habitual*, i.e., addicted, user of alcohol and drugs. Probably most courts would not allow proof of alcoholism or drug addiction in the absence of proof that the witness was drunk or high on drugs at the time of the events in question. McC, p. 61.

B. Extrinsic evidence allowed: A witness's sensory or mental defect is *never* deemed to be of *"collateral"* importance. Therefore, the rule barring *extrinsic evidence* on a collateral issue (see *infra*, p. 148) does *not apply* to impeachment by sensory or mental defect.

    Example: Same facts as the prior example (W says he overheard a whispered conversation from 10 feet away). D would like to impeach W by showing W is hard of hearing. D can of course do this by cross-examination of W (e.g., "Isn't it true that you've been diagnosed as hard of hearing, and that a hearing aid has been prescribed for you that you never wear?") But D can also impeach W by extrinsic evidence, such as by putting on testimony by X, "I've known W to be hard of hearing for years, and if he wasn't wearing his hearing aid, there's no way he could have heard a whispered conversation from 10 feet away."

XIII. IMPEACHMENT BY CONTRADICTION; THE "COLLATERAL ISSUE" RULE

A. General theory of contradiction: The final method of impeachment is to *contradict* the witness in some way.

1. Several methods: There are four main ways in which a witness (let's refer to her as W1) may be impeached by contradiction:

    a. Cross-examination: First, the attacking party may use *cross-examination* to get W1 to concede that she was wrong in her direct testimony, or at least get her to hedge or retract what she previously stated unequivocally. The cross-examiner can often do this just by asking questions skillfully, without producing separate admissible evidence.

    Example: W1 is an alibi witness for D, who is on trial for robbing a 7-Eleven at 9:00 p.m. on the night of October 15. W1 testifies on direct, "D was with me in my apartment that night from 8 til 10." On cross, the prosecutor might ask W1, "Isn't it true that on the night of October 15, you were at your job as a waitress at the Hard Rock Café from 7 til 1 in the morning?" If W1 still denies this, the prosecutor might ask, "Would it change your recollection if I showed you your time card from the Café for the week that included that night?"

        These questions — at least if they're successful in getting W1 to change her story (and maybe even if W1 doesn't change the story but doesn't convincingly shoot down the prosecutor's attack either) — tend to impeach W1 by contradicting her direct testimony, even though the questions don't themselves present any new admissible evidence.

b. Use of other previously-introduced testimony: Second, the attacking party might use other ***previously-introduced testimony*** or physical evidence as a weapon during cross, to show that W1 has lied or is mistaken.

> **Example:** Same facts as above Example. The prosecutor asks W1, "How do you explain the fact that as Officer Jones testified this morning, when D was arrested, he told the police he was at his own apartment that night, not your apartment?"

c. W's own prior inconsistent statement: Third, the attacking party may show that W1 has ***previously made statements inconsistent with W1's trial testimony***. This "prior inconsistent statement" technique is so important that the FRE deal with it separately in FRE 613, and it's usually viewed as a separate means of impeachment, not a species of impeachment-by-contradiction. See *supra*, p. 137.

d. New evidence contradicting W1's story: Fourth and last, the attacking party may attack W1's credibility by ***introducing new evidence*** — either testimony by a ***second witness*** (call him W2) or ***physical*** evidence, such as a document — showing that W1's story is not correct. This will usually happen after W1 has left the stand (but in the case of documents or other physical evidence, might happen during the cross of W1).

> **Example:** Same facts as above two Examples. After W1 leaves the stand, the prosecutor calls W2, who testifies, "On the night of October 15, I was dancing with W1 at Studio 54 from 9 to midnight, so she couldn't have been home with D." Or, the prosecutor introduces into evidence (either during the cross of W1, or after she has left the stand) W1's time card showing she was at work at the Hard Rock Cafe that night from 7 til 1 AM.

> **Note:** By the way, one important feature of impeachment by contradiction, especially the third and fourth types, is that it may come ***out of the usual sequence***. Thus in the above Example of the fourth type, even though the prosecution has rested by the time W1 takes the stand as a defense witness, the prosecution would be permitted to rebut W1's testimony by calling W2. See M&K §6.43, p. 543.

See generally M&K §6.43, pp. 541-44.

2. Fourth way most significant: For purposes of analyzing the special problems of impeachment by contradiction (especially the "collateral issue" rule, discussed *infra*, p. 148), the most significant category is the ***fourth***, in which the attacker uses a ***new witness***, or introduces ***new physical evidence***, to contradict the principal witness's testimony.

B. Incomplete contradiction: Often, impeachment-by-contradiction will happen in a head-on manner: W1 says "A" and the contradictory evidence says "Not A". (The above alibi example fall into this category: either W1 was home with D during the time the crime took place, as she claims, or she wasn't home.) But equally often, the contradiction will be more subtle — W1's testimony is not flatly contradicted and made to look wholly false, but is instead shown to be ***incomplete***, or only ***partly true***.

Examples: In a criminal case, D might testify, or have a character witness testify, in a favorable way about D's *character*. The attacker (the prosecutor) might then try to contradict, but in a partial way. Thus D might testify, "I'm a law-abiding person," and the prosecution might show that D was arrested on one or more occasions. Or, in an embezzlement case, D might show that he was honest in specific previous jobs, and the prosecution might then show that in still other previous jobs (not the one in question) D was dishonest. See M&K § 6.44, p. 546.

1. **Same rules apply:** In general, the *same rules apply* to such "incompletely contradictory" evidence as to head-on contradictions. Thus the general rule allowing impeachment by contradiction applies, as does the "collateral evidence" rule. However, the more attenuated the contradiction, the more likely the court is to use its *discretion to exclude* the evidence, either under FRE 403 (where prejudicial impact substantially outweighs probative value; see *supra*, p. 15) or otherwise. See M&K, §6.45, pp. 549.

   Example: Suppose that in a criminal drug-possession case, D testifies, "I've basically kept out of trouble with the law." If the prosecution attempts contradiction-by-impeachment by showing that D has been arrested three times for drug possession, the court may well use her Rule 403 discretion to keep the "impeaching" evidence out, on the grounds that the similarity of the arrest charges to the present charge poses a large possibility of prejudice, and the evidence is of only weak probative value in terms of impeaching D's credibility.

C. **Rules of exclusion:** One problem with impeachment-by-contradiction evidence is that it's not always clear whether particular rules of *exclusion* apply. There are of course many specific rules of exclusion, rules that exclude a particular type of evidence on account of a particular policy determination. These rules are often unclear as to whether they apply to evidence that's offered not for substantive purposes, but merely to show that the principal witness lied or was mistaken on the point in question.

1. **Rule by rule analysis:** In general, this question must be answered separately for each rule of exclusion. Here are a few illustrations:

   a. **Clearly excluded:** Some exclusionary rules either expressly *apply* even to impeachment evidence, or are written in such a broad and unequivocal way that the court will probably conclude that the exclusion is to apply even to impeachment use.

      i. **Victim's sexual conduct:** The sexual history of a victim of rape or sexual assault probably falls into this "excluded even for impeachment" category.

         Example: D is charged with raping V, and defends on the grounds that D and V had just gotten back from a date, and D thought that V was consenting to his advances. V, testifying for the prosecution, says, "I was a virgin until that night, and there's no way I would have consented." The defense now offers testimony by X that X and V had slept together before the night in question, and that V was not a virgin even before she slept with X. FRE 412 (the federal "rape shield" provision, see *supra*, p. 45), would clearly bar substantive use of X's testimony.[9] So the question is, does FRE 412 also bar use of X's testimony to contradict something that V has voluntarily asserted?

There's a good chance that the court will look at the strong policies behind FRE 412 (to avoid trauma to the victim, from having her sex life dissected in open court), and conclude that the bar should apply even to contradiction evidence. In that event, X's testimony will be excluded even for impeachment use.

b.   **Clearly not excluded:** Conversely, some exclusionary rules clearly ***don't apply*** to impeachment evidence, either because the rule explicitly says that impeachment evidence isn't covered, or because the rule forbids some specified uses, and then says that evidence offered for "other purposes" isn't forbidden.

   i.   **Subsequent remedial measures:**   For instance, recall that FRE 407 forbids the introduction of ***"subsequent remedial measures"*** (see *supra*, p. 65). The rule is actually quite narrowly drawn: the subsequent-measures evidence is forbidden only where offered to prove "negligence; culpable conduct; [or] a defect in a product"; the last sentence goes on to say that the exclusion does not prevent admission "for another purpose, such as impeachment[.]"

   Example: P is injured from an assault by X, a stranger she lets into her motel room after he knocks. She sues D, the motel's operator, for failing to provide adequate security. D, in his direct testimony, asserts that the danger was "obvious," and that P was contributorily negligent, because had she looked out through the picture window in her room she would have seen that X looked menacing.

   FRE 407 will not prevent P from now offering evidence that after the incident, D installed peepholes in each door; this evidence is not being offered as substantive evidence to show D's negligence, but rather, to impeach D's testimony by showing that D did not treat the danger as having been obvious.

   ii.   **Character evidence:** Similarly, FRE 404 bans ***character evidence*** to prove "that on a particular occasion the person acted in accordance with the character or trait," but 404(b) allows character evidence for "another purpose." One such purpose can be impeachment by contradiction.

   Example: D, charged with drug-selling, says on direct, "I don't even do drugs, let alone sell them." The prosecution will probably be allowed to put on testimony by W that D sometimes takes drugs. This evidence is not being offered to show that because D takes drugs he's likely to have sold them on the present occasion (a use that would be forbidden by 404(a)(1); it's (theoretically) being offered merely to show that D lied when he said he doesn't take drugs (impeachment use, allowed under 404(b)(2)'s "admissible for another purpose" clause).

D. **"Collateral issue" rule:** When impeachment by contradiction is attempted, the most important (and frequently-applicable) rule is the so-called ***"collateral issue"*** rule, which might be better described as "the rule against ***extrinsic evidence on collateral issues***." The rule may be summarized as follows:

---

9. This assumes that excluding the evidence wouldn't violate D's constitutional rights, including the right of Confrontation. (FRE 412(b)(1)(C) allows "evidence the exclusion of which would violate the constitutional rights of the defendant.")

1. **Summary:** If Witness 1 makes an assertion of fact (let's call the assertion "*A*"), then testimony by Witness 2, whose sole purpose is to contradict Witness 1 by asserting not-*A*, will be allowed only if the *A*/not-*A* issue is either: (1) a ***material issue*** in the case; or (2) an issue as to which Witness 2 could assert not-*A* ***even if Witness 1 had never asserted A.***

   a. **Illustration of category (1):** The following Example shows how the collateral issue rule can operate to exclude evidence, as well as how the "material issue" exception (category (1) above) operates.

      Example: In an armed robbery prosecution of D, W1 testifies for the defense that she saw the robbery take place, and that the robber was not D. She also testifies that she remembers the episode vividly because she had just stopped to tie the laces on her running shoes when she saw the robbery. The prosecutor seeks to impeach W1 by putting on the testimony of W2 (a police officer), who says that when he arrived at the scene of the crime and questioned W1, he noticed that she was wearing high heels. This is impeachment by contradiction; most courts would probably hold that the contradiction deals solely with a "collateral issue" (shoes worn by W1), and is thus not allowed.

      Suppose, however, that W2 instead testifies that W1 picked D out of a police lineup shortly after the crime. This impeachment by contradiction would be *allowed* by all courts, because it is directly relevant to a material issue in the case (whether D was the robber).

   b. **Explanation of category (2):** Category (2) above means that if the extrinsic evidence could be used for impeachment ***even in the absence of contradiction,*** it may be used to show the contradiction. By this sub-rule, extrinsic evidence that the witness is ***biased***, has been ***convicted of a crime***, has a ***bad character for truthfulness***, or has a ***relevant sensory or mental defect***, may be used to contradict the witness's statement to the contrary, since such facts could be proved even if the witness did not otherwise assert. Application of the collateral issue rule to each of these categories is discussed further *infra*, p.150.

2. **Federal approach:** The Federal Rules do ***not*** contain any explicit "collateral issue" rule. However, the trial judge has general discretion under FRE 403 to exclude evidence whose probative value is substantially outweighed by "a danger of … confusing the issues … undue delay [or] wasting time[.]" This discretion allows the judge to keep out evidence that would, under the common-law approach, be banned as extrinsic evidence of a collateral issue.

   a. **Consequence:** Therefore in the cases and hypos below where we conclude that the collateral issue rule would (or wouldn't) apply, you can pretty much assume that the issue would come out the same way under the FRE as under the common-law.

3. **The *Oswalt* case as illustration:** To illustrate operation of the collateral issue rule, let's consider *State v. Oswalt*, 381 P.2d 617 (Wash. 1963).

   a. **Facts:** D was charged with a robbery that took place in Seattle on July 14, 1961. On behalf of D, W1 testified that he operated a restaurant in Portland, Oregon, that D was in the restaurant at such a time on July 14 that he could not have been in Seattle at the time of the robbery; and that D was in the restaurant every day for the two months prior to the robbery. To impeach W1 by contradiction, the prosecutor offered testimony by W2 (a police detective) who testified that D admitted to having been in Seattle on June 12. D never denied at trial having been in Seattle on June 12, so the only importance of whether he was in Seattle on that date was that if he was, W1's testimony on this point was incorrect and W1's credibility would be impeached.

b. **Holding:** The Washington Supreme Court held that W2's testimony should not have been allowed — the prosecutor was entitled to cross-examine W1 to try to show that he was wrong about D's June 12th location; but the prosecutor was not permitted to impeach W1 by the use of "extrinsic" evidence (i.e., testimony by another witness), since the issue was "collateral" to the main issues in the case.

c. **Application of test:** Analyzing *Oswalt* in terms of our test above, W2's testimony was properly rejected because: (1) it was offered solely to contradict the testimony of another witness; and (2) the issue to which it related (D's location more than a month before the robbery): (a) was not a material issue in the case (since his presence in either Seattle or Portland had no real probative value on whether he committed the robbery 32 days later); and (b) could not have been proved by W2's testimony in the absence of W1's testimony on that issue (e.g., it would not have impeached any other aspect of W1's testimony).

4. **Solely for contradiction:** The "collateral issue" rule does not mean that Witness 2 can never contradict Witness 1 on a collateral issue. It merely means that if *all* that Witness 2 does is to contradict Witness 1 on the collateral issue, Witness 2's testimony should not be allowed. Thus in *Oswalt*, had Witness 2 (the police detective) gotten on the stand to cover a *number of points* that were directly relevant to the facts in the case, he would have been allowed to state in passing that D had admitted to being in Seattle on June 12. L&S, p. 330.

5. **Rationale:** The rationale for the collateral issue rule is that it *saves time* and eliminates confusion. In *Oswalt*, for instance, had Witness 2's testimony been properly allowed, D would then have been entitled to produce two or three additional witnesses to prove that he had been in the Portland restaurant, not in Seattle, on June 12; the prosecution could have rebutted these witnesses, and so on. This would have led to a "trial within a trial," all for no purpose except to determine the credibility of Witness 1's testimony on other unrelated points.

6. **Various contexts for rule:** In prior sections of this chapter, we have already seen two instances of the collateral issue rule: (1) the ban on showing that the witness has made a *prior inconsistent statement* as to a collateral issue (*supra*, p. 141); and (2) the ban on using extrinsic evidence to show *prior bad acts* by the witness. Yet, the collateral issue rule is *not* applied to some types of impeachment evidence (e.g., proof of *bias*). Therefore, it's worth looking briefly at each of the major techniques for impeachment to see whether the collateral issue rule applies:

a. **Prior convictions:** Witness 1's *prior criminal convictions* are *never* deemed "collateral," so that they may always be proved by extrinsic evidence if they otherwise meet the tests described earlier in this book (*supra*, p. 120).

b. **Prior bad acts:**   In sharp contrast, Witness 1's ***prior bad acts*** that ***did not lead to a criminal conviction are*** deemed "collateral," and thus are not provable by testimony from Witness 2 or other extrinsic evidence. This is true even if Witness 1 has flatly denied the prior bad acts on the stand — since the prior bad acts could not be proved had Witness 1 been silent on the issue, the fact that Witness 2 would contradict him is deemed not to add enough impeachment value to justify Witness 2's testimony. This result is summed up in the phrase, noted above, that the cross-examiner "must take the witness's answer" as to prior bad acts.

c. **Bad character for truthfulness:**   Witness 1's ***bad character for truthfulness*** is ***not*** collateral, so it can be proved by testimony from Witness 2. Again, this is so regardless of whether Witness 1 has affirmatively asserted his good character for truthfulness. See *supra*, p. 137.

d. **Prior inconsistent statements:**   The fact that Witness 1 has made a ***prior statement*** inconsistent with his trial testimony ***is*** collateral, if the contradiction does not relate to a main issue in the case. In other words, if Witness 1 testifies to fact A on the stand, Witness 2 will not be allowed to testify that Witness 1 previously said not-A if A/not-A is not directly relevant to the case, any more than Witness 2 would be allowed to testify directly to not-A. To put it another way, what matters is the materiality of the A/not-A issue, and the fact that Witness 1 has made a prior inconsistent statement is irrelevant in this determination.

e. **Bias:**   The fact that Witness 1 is ***biased*** is ***never collateral***. Therefore, regardless of whether Witness 1 has testified to his own lack of bias, Witness 2 may testify that Witness 1 is biased.

f. **Sensory or mental defect:**   Witness 1's ***sensory or mental defects*** are ***not*** collateral. Therefore, if a particular sensory or mental defect could be brought out on cross-examination of Witness 1, that defect could also be brought out by later testimony from Witness 2.

g. **Contradiction of direct testimony about case:**   Finally, if Witness 1's testimony relates directly to the facts of the case (not to Witness 1's own qualifications or credibility), the collateral issue rule applies to contradictory testimony from Witness 2 — only if Witness 1's testimony relates to a fact that is important to the outcome of the case will Witness 2 be permitted to contradict the underlying fact. This category is where the *Oswalt* case fits.

h. **No explanation:**   In summary, the collateral issue applies to three categories of impeachment (prior bad acts, prior inconsistent statements, and direct contradiction of testimony about case) and does not apply in four other categories (prior convictions, bad character for truthfulness, bias, and sensory/mental defect). There is no convincing explanation for this split. Probably, however, it is fair to think of the latter four categories as usually involving types of impeachment evidence that are either more reliable and convincing, less prejudicial, or less time-wasting, than the former three categories. See Lilly, p. 373.

7. **Fact about which no honest mistake possible:**   Let us return now to one aspect of the use of contradiction relating to Witness 1's testimony about the case. Suppose Witness 1's

testimony does not relate to a fact that is material to the outcome, but does relate to a fact about which ***an honest witness would be very unlikely to be mistaken***. In this situation, the trial judge probably has discretion to allow contradictory evidence by Witness 2, even though the issue is, strictly speaking, "collateral." M&K §6.47, p. 559.

> **Example:** Return to our example of the witness to armed robbery (*supra*, p. 145), who claims that she tied her sneakers just before viewing the robbery. Whether Witness 1 tied her sneakers, or indeed whether she was wearing sneakers at all, is not strictly material to whether D did the robbery. However, a reasonable jury could conclude that if Witness 1 really saw the robbery, and had really stopped to tend to her shoes just before witnessing it, she could not have been innocently mistaken about whether she was wearing sneakers or high heels. Therefore, the judge should have discretion to allow Witness 2's testimony that Witness 1 was really wearing high heels.

8. **Impeachment by physical evidence:** Normally, the type of impeachment evidence to which the "collateral issue" rule applies will take the form of testimony by a second witness contradicting the first. Our witness-to-armed-robbery example just above falls into this category. But the collateral issue rule also bars use of ***physical evidence***, including ***documents***, to impeach by contradiction.

> **Example:** Recall the facts of *State v. Oswalt*, supra, p. 149. Suppose that to impeach W1, the prosecution supplied not the testimony of W2, but a credit card slip from June 12 at 1:00 PM with D's signature, showing that D was in Seattle at that moment. Again, assume that D never denied being in Seattle on June 12, so that the only effect of this physical evidence was to show that W1's testimony ("D was at my restaurant every day for two months prior to July 14") was wrong. The collateral issue rule, properly understood, should bar the prosecution from using the physical evidence to impeach W1 on this collateral issue, just as (the court held) it barred the use of W2's testimony. M&K, §6.27, p. 498.

9. **Not applicable to cross of principal witness:** The collateral issue rule applies only where a ***second witness***, or ***newly-introduced physical evidence***, is used to impeach the principal witness. The rule does ***not*** apply where the impeachment of the principal witness occurs ***during the cross-examination*** of that witness, and is carried out solely by the questions and the witness's answers (the type of impeachment listed as the first category on p. 145, *supra*). In other words, the rule is not truly a ban on "impeachment on collateral issues," it's only a ban on "***using extrinsic evidence*** to impeach on collateral issues."

XIV. RELIGIOUS BELIEFS

A. **Issue:** May the credibility of the witness be impeached by proof that he does not believe in a ***God*** who punishes untruths?

1. **Majority view:** The vast majority of courts do ***not*** allow impeachment of the witness's credibility for any reason relating to his religious beliefs.

2. Federal Rules: The Federal Rules explicitly adopt this majority view. FRE 610 provides that "Evidence of a witness's religious beliefs or opinions is ***not admissible to attack or support*** the witness's credibility."

XV. REHABILITATING THE IMPEACHED WITNESS

A. General rules: So far, we have talked about the ways in which a lawyer may impeach, or attack, the credibility of opposing witnesses. Now, we turn to how he may *support*, or *rehabilitate*, the credibility of his own witnesses.

1. No bolstering: A basic rule on which all courts agree is that a lawyer may ***not*** offer evidence ***supporting his witness's credibility***, unless that credibility has first been ***attacked*** by the other side. This is sometimes known as the ***rule against "bolstering" one's witness.*** See FRE 608(a), last sentence: "[E]vidence of truthful character is admissible only after the witness's character for truthfulness has been attacked."

> **Example:** In a civil suit, W testifies on behalf of P that D behaved negligently. On direct examination, P's lawyer will not be permitted to bolster W's credibility by showing that in a report to the police right after the accident, W told the same story as she is now telling in court. (But if D attacks W's credibility by asserting that she has recently concocted her trial testimony, P will be allowed to "rehabilitate" W by showing that right after the accident, she told the police the same story as she is now telling. Rehabilitation is discussed immediately below.)

2. Exceptions: There are two frequently-recognized *exceptions* to the rule against bolstering one's witness's credibility:

a. Prior identification: First, if the witness has made a ***prior out-of-court identification***, many courts will let that fact into evidence if the identifying witness is in court and available for cross-examination. Lilly, p. 374. (See *infra*, p. 312.) Sometimes this prior identification is substantive evidence (as under the Federal Rules), not merely bolstering of the witness's in-court testimony. In other courts, however, its function seems to be mainly to bolster the in-court identification.

b. Prompt complaint: Second, where the witness is a crime victim, many courts will allow evidence that he made a ***"fresh complaint"*** promptly following the crime, where the crime is one that is likely to be ***known only to the criminal and the victim.*** Lilly, p. 374. This rule is often applied to complaints by ***rape*** victims, and also sometimes to attempted bribery. *Id.*

B. Rehabilitation: Except in the two situations just described, a party may support the credibility of its witness only if that credibility has ***previously been attacked by the other side.*** This process of repairing the credibility of one's witness is usually called ***"rehabilitation."***

> **Example:** W testifies on behalf of D. P asserts, either on cross-examination of W or by separate direct evidence, that W has a romantic attachment to D and is therefore biased. D may now rehabilitate W's credibility by showing that W is not in fact romantically interested in D. This may be done either by W's own testimony or by

extrinsic evidence (e.g., testimony by W's best friend that W has never indicated any interest in D).

C. Must meet the attack: The basic rule of rehabilitation is that the rehabilitative evidence "must respond *as directly as possible* to the theory of the impeaching evidence." L&S, p. 333. Or, as McCormick puts it, "The wall, attacked at one point, may not be fortified at another and distinct point." McC, p. 64.

> **Example:** P attempts to show that W, a defense witness, is biased because he is D's son. D may rehabilitate W's credibility by showing that W is not D's son, or that although they are related, they do not especially like each other — the charge of bias is met with evidence of non-bias. But D may *not* rehabilitate W by showing that W has a good reputation for truthfulness, or that W has made prior out-of-court statements that are consistent with his trial testimony — these attempts to boost W's credibility do not respond directly to the charge of bias, and are thus excluded on grounds of relevance.

1. Two categories: Whether the rehabilitating evidence is sufficiently directly related to the impeaching evidence to justify admission, varies from court to court and depending on the particular facts. The most troublesome issues involve the use of two types of rehabilitative evidence: (1) evidence that the witness has a *good character* for truthfulness; and (2) evidence that the witness has made *prior statements* that are *consistent* with his trial testimony. Each of these techniques can be used to meet some, but not other, types of attacks.

2. Good character: Evidence that the witness has a *good character for truthfulness* is more likely to be accepted when the impeachment relates to the witness's general bad character for truthfulness, than when it merely casts doubt on the accuracy of his testimony in the present case.

    a. Attacks on general veracity: Thus if the witness is attacked by evidence that he has a *bad reputation* for truthfulness, that a second witness has a *bad opinion* of the first witness's truthfulness, that the witness has been *convicted of a crime*, or that he has committed a prior *bad act*, evidence of the principal witness's good reputation will be allowed. McC, p. 64. In all of these situations, the attack implies not only that the witness has given incorrect testimony in this case, but also that he is a generally unreliable person — therefore, evidence of good reputation is quite relevant to the attack. Similarly, the judge may allow good-reputation evidence if the witness has been attacked by a slashing cross-examination that implies or states that the witness is a liar. McC, p. 65.

    b. Attack on present testimony: Where, by contrast, the attack is merely on the witness's testimony *in the present case*, and does not assert that the witness is generally unreliable, evidence of good reputation will probably *not* be allowed. Evidence that W is biased because he is related to the other party, or evidence by X that W has given erroneous testimony, are attacks on W's present testimony alone, not his character — therefore, these attacks will have to be met not by evidence of W's good character, but rather by evidence that the particular testimony attacked is worthy of belief. McC, p. 65.

    c. Inconsistent statement: If the attack is by showing that W has made a *prior inconsistent statement*, the courts are split. Most treat this as an implicit attack on the witness's general credibility, and therefore allow it to be rebutted by a showing that the witness has a good character for truth. *Id.*

3. **Prior consistent statement:** The greatest confusion comes where a party tries to meet attacks on the credibility of its witness by showing that the witness has made *prior statements* that are *consistent* with the witness's trial testimony.

a. **Attack on general character:** If the attack is based upon the witness's *general character*, evidence of prior consistent statements is usually *not permitted*, again on the theory that it does not meet the attack. Thus, if W is attacked by showing his prior *criminal convictions*, *prior bad acts*, or his *bad reputation* for veracity, the fact that he has made prior consistent statements will be treated as irrelevant.

b. **Charge of recent fabrication or improper influence:** In fact, most courts allow prior consistent statements to be used *only* where there has been an *express or implied* charge that the witness's trial testimony is a *recent fabrication* or the product of *improper influence* or *motive*. L&S, p. 334. Unless one of these elements is present, no type of impeachment may be rebutted by prior consistent statements, according to most courts.

c. **Rebutting effect of prior inconsistent statement:** Most cases concerning prior consistent statements arise where the proponent of the witness is attempting to repair the damage done by a showing that the witness has made a *prior inconsistent statement*. Unless the proponent can demonstrate that his adversary's use of the prior inconsistent statement amounts to an express or implied claim that the witness has recently made up his trial testimony, or is lying because of improper influence or ulterior motives, the prior consistent statement will *not* be allowed.

   i. **Before motive:** Furthermore, the proponent who wants to use a prior consistent statement must, according to most courts, show that the prior statement was made *before* the alleged motive to fabricate or improper influence arose. Only in this situation does the fact of the prior consistent statement rebut the implication of deceit.

d. **Federal Rules:** The Federal Rules agree that if the use of a prior inconsistent statement amounts to a charge of recent fabrication or other wrongdoing by the witness, a prior consistent statement may be used to rehabilitate the witness. FRE 801(d)(1)(B) provides that where a witness testifies at trial and is available for cross-examination, his prior statement is admissible if it is "*consistent* with [his] testimony and is offered to (i) *rebut an express or implied charge* that [he] *recently fabricated it* or acted from a *recent improper influence or motive*[.]" In fact, if these conditions are met, the prior consistent statement may be used not only to rehabilitate the witness's credibility, but also as *substantive* evidence to prove the truth of the matters contained in the statement. In other words, in these circumstances, the prior consistent statement is *not hearsay* (see *infra*, p. 312).

   i. **Existence of motive to falsify:** Observe that FRE 801(d)(1)(B) does not explicitly repeat the common-law rule that the prior consistent statement must have been made *before* the witness had a motive to falsify. However, the Supreme Court has held that *such a requirement must be read into the Rule. Tome v. U.S.,* 115 S.Ct.

696 (1995). The Court reasoned that unless the prior consistent statement was made before the alleged fabrication, influence or motive came into being, introduction of that statement simply does not "rebut" the charge; therefore, the Court concluded, the drafters of 801(d)(1)(B) must have assumed that the common-law temporal requirement would continue to apply. The facts of *Tome* illustrate how the "before" requirement will operate in cases decided under 801(d)(1)(B).

Example: D is charged with sexually abusing A.T., his 4-year-old daughter. A.T. takes the stand and testifies about the abuse (though sometimes in an unclear manner). On cross, the defense suggests that A.T.'s allegations were concocted by her and her mother, so that custody of A.T. would be given to the mother rather than to D. (A custody battle had begun in 1989.) The prosecution then offers testimony by six witnesses (A.T.'s baby-sitter, A.T.'s mother, a social worker and three pediatricians), all of whom say that A.T. told them in 1990 that her father had abused her.

Held (by the Supreme Court, 6-3), the testimony by these six witnesses — who were repeating prior out-of-court consistent statements by A.T. to buttress her in-court testimony — should not have been admitted under FRE 801(d)(1)(B). The theory for admitting the prior consistent statements was that the prosecution was rebutting the defense's claim that A.T.'s testimony was falsified in order to fulfill A.T.'s wish to live with her mother. That motive, if it existed, already existed by the time A.T. made the out-of-court statements in 1990 that the six witnesses repeated on the stand. Therefore, the out-of-court statements did not truly "rebut" the charge of motive-to-fabricate, and should not have been admitted under FRE 801(d)(1)(B). The drafters of 801(d)(1)(B) meant the Rule to apply only to statements made *before* the alleged "recent fabrication or improper influence or motive" came into existence. *Tome v. U.S., supra.*

e. **Other contexts:** The use of prior consistent statements is ***not limited*** to rebutting a charge that the declarant's present testimony is a recent fabrication or is the product of a recent improper influence or motive (the situations covered by 801(d)(1)(B)(i), discussed in Par. (d) above). FRE 801(d)(1)(B)(ii)[10] says that where the declarant is testifying, her prior consistent statement is admissible "to rehabilitate the declarant's credibility as a witness when attacked ***on another ground***" (i.e., other than the recent-fabrication-or-improper-motive ground).

i. **Rebutting a charge of faulty memory:** For instance, the prior consistent statement may be introduced as substantive evidence to rebut a charge that the witness' present testimony ***results from a faulty memory,*** or to explain an ***apparent inconsistency*** in that present testimony. Adv. Comm. Note to 2014 Amendment to 801(d)(1)(B).

Example 1 (faulty memory): A civil case arises out of a two-vehicle accident that took place at an intersection six years previously. P, who is now 78 years old man, testifies, "When I drove through the intersection, the traffic light was green." On

---

10. Subsection (ii) was added to Rule 801(d)(1)(B) in 2014.

cross-examination, P agrees with D's lawyer that P's memory for events from six years ago is no longer as good as it might be.

This cross-examination testimony raises doubt about P's "credibility as a witness," stemming from an "attack on another ground" by D's counsel (i.e., a ground different from a charge of recent fabrication or recent improper motive, covered in 801(d)(1)(B)(i)). Therefore, 801(d)(1)(B)(ii) permits P's lawyer to rehabilitate P's credibility by introducing, for substantive purposes, the fact that when a police officer responded to the scene of the accident, P told the officer, "The light was green in my favor when I drove into the intersection."

Example 2 (inconsistency of testimony): Same basic facts as Example 1 above. Early in P's direct testimony, P says that D seemed to be traveling at about 20 mph when D went through the intersection while facing a red light. Later, under cross-examination, P concedes that D's speed through the intersection may have been only 15 mph, and that the light may not have turned red for D until D was halfway through the intersection.

P's lawyer will now be permitted to introduce, for substantive purposes, P's statement right after the accident to the police officer that "D was traveling 20 m.p.h. through the intersection several seconds after the light had already turned red against him." That is, the prior statement is being introduced to rehabilitate P's credibility by explaining P's apparently-internally-inconsistent testimony.

f. **Rationale for limits on use of prior consistent statement:** There is a simple reason why courts resist the use of the prior consistent statements except to repair attacks on the witness' credibility: general admissibility of such statements would offer parties a large incentive to *manufacture evidence*. If the witness were a party, he could through careful planning buttress his anticipated trial testimony by making numerous pre-trial statements consistent with what he expected to say at trial. And if the witness was a non-party, each party would have an incentive to pester him to make repeated prior statements consistent with the way that party hoped the witness would testify at trial. The rule restricting prior consistent statements to situations where they rebut an attack on credibility removes this incentive, since not until the adversary "opens the door" by making such an attack can the prior consistent statement be used.

D. **Anticipating impeachment ("drawing the sting"):** We've talked extensively about the general rule that rehabilitation may only occur after the witness has been impeached. There is one important quasi-exception to this rule: the calling party may *anticipate an attack*, and may *bring out the impeaching facts at the outset* in a way that attempts to minimize the impeaching impact. This is often called *"drawing the sting."* (So to the extent that the calling party's presentation of the impeaching material in a minimizing manner constitutes a kind of rehabilitation, it violates the general "no bolstering until attacked" rule.)

1. **Right to rebut if impeachment comes:** Then, if the anticipated impeachment does come from the other side, the proponent may perform a conventional rehabilitation (e.g., by use of a prior consistent statement), even though the impeachment material was first brought out by that same proponent.

Table 4-1

***CHECKLIST:* Impeaching and Rehabilitating Witnesses**
Use this checklist to figure out whether a particular technique of impeachment or
rehabilitation of a witness's credibility is acceptable. Examples assume (without
discussing) that Rule 403's balancing test is satisfied where it applies.

Name of Technique	Text of Rule; Note(s) on Application of Rule	Examples
W's Truthfulness: W's Criminal Convictions	General rule: "(a) The following rules apply to ***attacking a witness's character for truthfulness*** by evidence of a ***criminal conviction***: (1) for a crime that, in the convicting jurisdiction, was ***punishable by death or by imprisonment for more than one year*** [i.e., a ***felony***], the evidence: (A) ***must*** be admitted, subject to Rule 403, in a ***civil case*** or in a ***criminal case in which the witness is not a defendant***; and (B) ***must*** be admitted in a ***criminal case*** in which the witness is a ***defendant***, if the ***probative value*** of the evidence ***outweighs*** its prejudicial effect to that defendant; and (2) for any crime ***regardless of the punishment*** [i.e., felony or misdemeanor], the evidence ***must*** be admitted if the court can readily determine that establishing the elements of the crime required proving — or the witness's admitting — a ***dishonest act*** or ***false statement***." (FRE 609(a)).	**Example 1 (Clause 1 - felony; W <u>is not</u> a criminal defendant):** "Isn't it true that you were convicted of manslaughter in 2010?" *Admissible*, but only if Rule 403 is satisfied (i.e., probative value is not "*substantially* outweighed" by prejudice, confusion, etc.). **Note 1:** Crime doesn't have to bear on truthfulness. **Note 2:** Can't be used if conviction > 10 years old (unless probative value substantially outweighs prejudicial effect). **Example 2 (Clause 1 - felony; W <u>is</u> a criminal defendant):** Same manslaughter question as above. *Admissible*, but only if probative value outweighs prejudice to W (the defendant), which is a harder standard for prosecution to meet than in Example 1. (Same Note 1 & Note 2 as for Example 1.) **Example 3 (Clause 2 - *crimen falsi* misdemeanor or felony):** "Isn't it true that you were convicted of perjury?" [crime that required dishonest act or false statement]. *Admissible*, without regard to probative value/prejudice balancing, and regardless of whether length or even existence of prison sentence. (Same Note 2 as in Example 1.)
W's Truthfulness: Reputation or Opinion about W's truthfulness	"**(a)** *Reputation or Opinion Evidence.* A witness's credibility may be ***attacked or supported*** by testimony about the witness's ***reputation*** for having a ***character for truthfulness or untruthfulness***, or by testimony in the form of an ***opinion*** about that character. But evidence of ***truthful*** character is admissible only ***after*** the witness's character for truthfulness ***has been attacked***." (FRE 609(a))	**Example (negative reputation or opinion testimony):** After W1 has testified for P, D calls W2, who lives near W1. Q: "What's W1's reputation in the community for honesty?" A: "He's generally known as a pathological liar." Admissible, as "testimony about the witness's reputation for having a character for ... untruthfulness[.]" (Same result if W2 is asked W2's "opinion" about W1's honesty.)

Table 4-1 (p. 2)

Name of Technique	Text of Rule; Note(s) on Application of Rule	Examples
W's Truthfulness: Prior Bad Acts by W showing W's Untruthfulness	**"(b)** *Specific Instances of Conduct.* Except for a criminal conviction under Rule 609, *extrinsic evidence* is not admissible to prove *specific instances of a witness's conduct in order to attack* or support the witness's character for truthfulness. But the court may, on *cross*-examination, allow [specific instances] to be inquired into if they are *probative* of the *character for truthfulness or untruthfulness of*: (1) the witness; or (2) *another* witness whose character the witness being cross-examined has testified about." (FRE 608(a) and (b)) **Note:** The consensus is that if W's bad act led to a criminal conviction, the adversary *must proceed under FRE 609* (applying to impeachment by use of criminal convictions), or *not at all*. So suppose W's bad act led to a conviction that's more than 10 years old, and can't satisfy 609(b)'s standards for using old convictions; most courts would *not* let the attacker proceed under 608(b) (e.g., by asking about the underlying bad act on cross) even if 608(b) would otherwise apply.	**Example 1 (2d sentence of (b), covering specific instances on cross):** After W testifies for P, D's counsel asks on cross: "Isn't it true that when you applied for your present job, you lied when you said you'd never been arrested for any drug offense?" Court has discretion to allow, if judge believes that this specific instance is probative of W's character for untruthfulness (which judge *probably* will believe, assuming D's counsel has a good faith basis for the question). **Example 2 (1st sentence of (b), covering extrinsic evidence of specific instances):** After W1 testifies for P, D calls W2, and asks him, "Did you ever witness W1 behaving dishonestly?" W2 proposes to answer, "I saw W1 lie on a job application." The question and answer are inadmissible, because they call for *"extrinsic evidence,"* which "is not admissible to prove *specific instances of a* [target] *witness's conduct in order to attack* ... the witness's character for truthfulness." As the saying goes, D must "take [W1's] answer" (as in Example 1), rather than bringing in extrinisic evidence (W2's testimony, as in Example 2).
W's Prior Inconsistent Statements	**"Witness's Prior Statement: (a)** *Showing or Disclosing the Statement During Examination.* When examining a witness about the witness's *prior statement*, a party *need not show it or disclose its contents* to the witness. But the party must, on request, show it or disclose its contents *to an adverse party's attorney.* **(b)** *Extrinsic Evidence of a Prior Inconsistent Statement. Extrinsic evidence* of a witness's *prior inconsistent statement* is admissible only if the witness is *given an opportunity to explain or deny the statement* and an adverse party is given an *opportunity to examine the witness about it*, or if justice so requires. This subdivision (b) does not apply to an opposing party's statement under Rule 801(d)(2)." (FRE 613(a))	**Example 1 (Use during cross, as per Clause (a)):** Car accident. W, called by P, testifies that "D caused the accident by running a red light." D's counsel, L: Q: "Did you ever give anyone a different account of how the accident happened?" A: "No." Q: "Are you sure?" A: "Yes, I'm sure." Q: "I show you now a page from your deposition, where you say that you couldn't see whether D ran the red light or not." L's questioning is proper under 613(a) -- unlike at common law, L isn't required to show W the prior inconsistent statement before asking him about it (as long as L shows it to P's lawyer on request). **Example 2 (Extrinsic evidence, as per Clause (b)):** Same direct testimony by W for P as in Example 1 above. Now, instead **(Cont. on next page)**

Table 4-1 (p. 3)

Name of Technique	Text of Rule; Note(s) on Application of Rule	Examples
W's Prior Inconsistent Statements (cont.)	**Note:** If the attacker's extrinsic evidence of W's prior inconsistent statement involves an inconsistency on a ***"collateral"*** (not material) issue, then as a common-law matter the judge has discretion under FRE 403 to exclude the extrinsic evidence on the grounds that its probative value is substantially outweighed by its tendency to confuse the issues or waste time. Thus in Example 2 at right, if W had testified, "The accident happened at 3 PM," and the extrinsic evidence was W2's testimony that W had told W2, "The accident happened at 3:30 PM," the judge could exclude the extrinsic evidence if the precise time of the accident was not a material issue in the case.	of cross-examining W about any prior statement, L calls W2 (W's neighbor), who offers to testify that the day after the accident, W told W2, "I really didn't see whether D ran the red light or not." This testimony is admissible, but only on condition that (1) W "is ***given an opportunity to explain or deny the statement,***" and (2) P's lawyer is given a chance to ask W about the prior statement (e.g., whether she said it at all, how she explains the discrepancy, etc.). So if L has waited to introduce W2's testimony until after W has left the jurisdiction and can't be successfully re-subpoenaed, W2's testimony will be *inadmissible* under FRE 613(b).
W's Bias	No FRE on showing W's ***bias.*** By federal common law, bias is ***never "collateral,"*** and thus may always be ***shown by extrinsic evidence.***	Car accident. W, called by P, testifies that "D caused the accident by running a red light." D's lawyer, L, calls W2, who will testify that W used to date D, was jilted by him, and has a well-known grudge against him. Since this shows W's possible bias against D, it does not fall within the common-law "no extrinsic evidence of collateral matters" rule, and is *admissible.*
W's Sensory or Mental Defects	No FRE on showing W's ***sensory or mental defect.*** By federal common-law, sensory or mental defect is ***never "collateral,"*** and thus may always be ***shown by extrinsic evidence.***	Car accident. W, called by P, testifies that "D caused the accident by running a red light." D's lawyer, L, calls W2, W's optometrist, who will testify that even with glasses, W2 has extremely poor eyesight and couldn't accurately see an accident that took place 15 feet away. Since W2's testimony shows W's relevant sensory defect, it does not fall within the common-law "no extrinsic evidence of collateral matters" rule, and is *admissible.*
Contradicting W's Testimony; the "Collateral Issue" Rule	W's testimony can be ***contradicted*** by various means (apart from W's own prior inconsistent statement, discussed above), including (1) other previously-introduced testimony; or (2) newly-introduced testimony or physical evidence contradicting W's testimony. **(Cont. on next page)**	**Example 1 (contradiction by additional testimony):** Car accident. W, called by P, testifies that "D caused the accident by running a red light." D's lawyer, L, calls W2, who testifies that she, too, was at the accident scene, and that although W2 didn't see whether D ran the light, W2

Table 4-1 (p. 4)

Name of Technique	Text of Rule; Note(s) on Application of Rule	Examples
Contradicting W's Testimony; the "Collateral Issue" Rule (cont.)	There is no Federal Rule on how W's testimony can be contradicted (except for FRE 613's special rule on prior inconsistent statements of a witness). However, the common-law *"collateral issue"* rule will prevent use of *extrinsic evidence* to show a contradiction as to a collateral matter, as in Example 2 at right.	knows that W couldn't have seen it either, because W was talking to W2 and facing away from the accident scene when the accident occurred. W2's testimony is admissible; it's new evidence that attacks W's credibility by contradicting W's statement about what she witnessed. **Example 2 (collateral issue rule):** Same facts as Example 1. Now, however, W's testimony on direct includes the sentence, "After the accident, when D got out of the car, I noticed that he was wearing a red sweater." D's lawyer L calls W2, who testifies, "I was there, and D was wearing a green sweater at the time of the accident." Assuming (as seems likely) that the issue of D's sweater color doesn't matter to any issue in the case, W2's testimony should be excluded under federal common-law principles as "extrinsic evidence on a collateral issue" (a/k/a the "collateral issue rule").
Rehabilitating an Impeached Witness	**1.** General common-law *rule against "bolstering one's witness"* applies (i.e., proponent may not repair or support W's credibility before that credibility has been attacked by the other side). Last sentence of FRE 608(a) is to same effect: "But evidence of truthful character is admissible only after the witness's character for truthfulness has been attacked." **2.** Repair must *respond to the attack*. (Common-law rule, not mentioned in the FRE.) **(Cont. on next page)**	**Example 1 (#1 at left; no bolstering):** Accident case. P calls W, who testifies, "I saw D run the red light." P then calls W2, who wants to testify, "W has an excellent reputation for honesty, and it's my personal opinion, based on knowing her for years, that she would never lie." *Inadmissible*: Evidence of W's truthful character is admissible "only after the witness's character for truthfulness has been attacked" (608(a), last sentence), which hasn't happened yet. **Example 2 (#2 at left; repair must be responsive):** Same as Example 1 above. After W testifies for P on direct, "I saw D run the red light," D's lawyer, L, asks W on cross, "Don't you have very poor vision even when you're wearing glasses?" W agrees. P's lawyer then tries to repair the damage to W's credibility by showing that after the accident, W told the same story to an investigating officer. **(Cont. on next page)**

Table 4-1 (p. 5)

Name of Technique	Text of Rule; Note(s) on Application of Rule	Examples
Rehabilitating an Impeached Witness (cont.)	**3.** Once W's credibility has been *attacked*, *repair by reputation or opinion evidence* is *allowed*: "A witness's credibility may be ... *supported by testimony* about the witness's *reputation* for having a character for truthfulness ..., or by testimony in the form of an *opinion* about that character. But evidence of truthful character is admissible *only after the witness's character for truthfulness has been attacked*." (FRE 608(a)) **4.** *Prior consistent statement* may be used, but only to rebut charge of *recent fabrication or recent motive to falsify*. Such a statement is admissible, not just for credibility-repair but also *substantively*, if: "The declarant testifies and is subject to cross examination about a prior statement, and the statement: ... (B) is *consistent* with the declarant's testimony and is *offered to rebut an express or implied charge* that the declarant *recently fabricated it or acted from a recent improper influence or motive* in so testifying[.]" (FRE 801(d)(1)(B).)	*Inadmissible*: the attack is based on W's sensory defect, and the "repair" doesn't rebut the focus of the attack (i.e., doesn't show that the sensory defect wasn't a problem). **Example 3 (#3 at left; correct repair by reputation or opinion evidence):** Accident case. On direct, P calls W, who testifies, "I saw D run the red light." To rebut, D calls W2, who testifies (properly), "W's reputation in the community is for being a pathological liar." P then calls W3, who wants to testify, "W has an excellent reputation for honesty." *Admissible*: W's character for truthfulness has been attacked, so P (the proponent) is permitted to repair it by "testimony about the witness's reputation for having a character for truthfulness ... after the witness's character for truthfulness has been attacked." (FRE 609(a).) **Example 4 (#4 at left; correct use of prior consistent statement):** Accident case. On direct, P's lawyer calls W, who testifies, "I saw D run the red light." To rebut, D asks W on cross, "Isn't it true that P promised to pay you $500 out of any money she wins from D in this case?" P's lawyer now asks W on re-direct, "Isn't it true that right after the accident, before you could have talked to P about any deal to receive money, you told the police officer who came to the scene that you saw D run the red light?" *Admissible* (both as credibility repair and as substantive proof that D ran the light), since this prior consistent statement is "offered to rebut an express or implied charge that the declarant recently ... acted from a recent improper influence or motive in so testifying[.]" (FRE 801(d)(1)(B).)

End of Table

REFRESHING RECOLLECTION; IMPEACHMENT; REHABILITATION

25. George Washington, believing Benedict Arnold will be his best witness, calls Arnold to the stand. To Washington's surprise, Arnold testifies in a light highly unfavorable to Washington. Can Washington seek to minimize the damage to his case by impeaching Arnold's credibility? Answer with respect to both the FRE and the common law. _____

26. Yolanda Layr is a witness for the defendant in a civil case. The plaintiff seeks to impeach Yolanda by offering proof of her prior conviction for taking property by false pretenses, a misdemeanor. The defendant objects. What result? _____

27. Zoom Crashbang is a witness in a civil case. To impeach him, the adverse party offers evidence that Zoom has been convicted of vehicular homicide, a felony. Under the FRE, will this evidence be admitted to impeach Zoom? _____

28. Butch Cassidy gives up his life of crime and, after he's paid his debt to society, becomes an accountant. Twenty years after his last felony conviction, for larceny, and fifteen years after he was released from prison, he is called as an eyewitness in a civil automobile-collision case. Under the FRE, may he be impeached with evidence of the larceny conviction? _____

29. Lucius Lucullus appears as a witness for the defense in a negligence suit. On cross-examination, plaintiff, in order to impeach Lucullus, asks him: "You falsified your tax return two years ago, didn't you?" Defense objects, on the grounds that Lucullus was never charged with tax evasion. How do you rule? _____

30. Cock Robin is on trial for shooting Mr. Sparrow with his little bow and arrow. Big Bad Wolf is a witness for the prosecution. On cross-examination, defense counsel seeks to impeach him by asking: "Mr. Wolf, isn't it true that you terrorized the Three Little Pigs, threatened them, and obtained title to their brick house through lies and trickery?" Wolf denies it. He has never been convicted of a crime involving these acts. Later, during the defense case, Cock Robin's lawyer offers the testimony of Nice Lamb to the effect that he personally witnessed Wolf obtain title to the Pigs' house through threats and extortion. Under the FRE, is this evidence admissible to prove that Wolf's denial on cross was a lie? _____

31. McCoy is a witness in a case. To impeach him, Hatfield is called to the stand, and testifies: "I've known him for years, and I think he's a two-faced, lying swine who wouldn't know the truth if it hit him in the face." The opposition objects to this form of impeachment. Under the FRE, how do you rule? _____

32. The Three Bears sue Goldilocks for trespass. The Bears' lawyer calls Ranger Rick to the stand, and asks him if he saw Goldilocks at the Bears' house on the night in question. Ranger Rick answers: "I was there, and through the window I saw the defendant sleeping in the Mama Bear's bed." Goldilocks' lawyer can't shake Rick's statement during cross, and makes no reference to any previous statement made by Rick. Rick is dismissed from the stand, and moves out of the jurisdiction without leaving a forwarding address. Later, Goldilocks' lawyer attempts to enter into evidence Rick's sworn statement, taken at the time of the incident, saying he hadn't seen Goldilocks or anyone else at the house. The Bears' counsel objects, claiming a proper foundation for admitting Rick's prior statement is lacking. How do you rule? _____

33. Dr. Jekyll witnesses a hit-and-run car accident one evening. When the perpetrator is sued for negligence,

Dr. Jekyll is called as a witness by the victim. On cross-examination, he's asked, "Isn't it true that you have frequent blackouts in the evening, after which you can't remember anything?" Jekyll denies it. Counsel then seeks to offer a newspaper story about Dr. Jekyll's periodic transformation into Mr. Hyde. Opposing counsel objects, claiming extrinsic evidence is impermissible here, because Jekyll's blackouts are a "collateral matter." How do you rule? _____

34. Hamlet is on trial for the murder of Yorick. The prosecutor claims Hamlet had long been jealous of Yorick. Hamlet denies knowing Yorick at all. The prosecutor calls Horatio as a witness, who offers to testify: "Hamlet told me, 'Alas, poor Yorick — I knew him, Horatio.' " Admissible? _____

35. One of the King's Men is on trial for murdering Humpty Dumpty by pushing him off a wall. Wanda Wye testifies for the prosecution: "I saw the whole thing on my way to a Girl Scout Jamboree." The defense calls another witness, Wilfreda, who testifies that Wanda was *really* on her way to an assignation with her boyfriend. Upon objection, the defense claims the question is permissible because it reflects on Wanda's veracity. How do you rule? _____

36. Cy Witness sees Guy Fawkes set fire to the Houses of Parliament. In Fawkes' arson trial, the prosecution calls Cy as a witness, and he testifies as to what he saw. The defense does not cross-examine Cy. The prosecution then offers the testimony of Biggle Scoop, a newspaperman to whom Cy told the story at the time of the fire, to show Cy hasn't changed his story since the incident. Is Biggle's testimony admissible? _____

37. Uzi Submachine-Gun Kelly, mobster, is on trial for a gangland-style murder. Whitey Knuckles appears as a prosecution witness, testifying that he saw Kelly commit the murder. On cross-examination, Kelly's counsel asks Whitey, "Didn't you tell the police at the time of the murder that you didn't see Kelly anywhere near the scene of the crime?" Whitey admits that he did. On redirect, can Whitey explain that he made the earlier statement out of fear and that it was a lie? _____

38. Stepdad is charged with having sexually assaulted his 15-year-old step-daughter, Pamela, in May, 2012. Pamela testifies against Stepdad. On cross, Stepdad's lawyer asks Pamela, "Isn't it true that you hate Stepdad because you saw him hit your mother in April of 2012, and that you made up this whole story about rape and incest to get back at him?" Pamela denies this. The prosecutor, saying that he wants to rehabilitate Pamela's credibility, calls Psycho, the psychologist at Pamela's school. Psycho says that in June, 2012, Pamela told Psycho that Stepdad had sexually assaulted her the prior month. The defense objects. Result? _____

Answers

25. FRE: **Yes**. Under FRE 607, a party can impeach the credibility of a witness even if the witness was called by that party. COMMON LAW: **Yes**. Under the common-law rule, impeachment of one's own witness is generally not allowed; however, there are several exceptions, including where, as here, the party is honestly **surprised** by harmful testimony from his own witness.

26. **Objection overruled**, both under the FRE and under the majority common-law approach. Under FRE 609(a)(2), if a witness has been convicted of a crime for which **dishonesty or a false statement** was an element (**"crimen falsi"**), that conviction is admissible for impeachment purposes even if the offense was only a **misdemeanor**. The crime of taking property by false pretenses is defined in such a way as to require the prosecution to prove a false statement, so that the crime is a *crimen falsi*, and thus usable for impeachment.

Observe that Rule 609(a) makes an important distinction between *crimen falsi* and other crimes. Where the crime is not a *crimen falsi* (and thus admissible only if it's a felony, not a misdemeanor), 609(a)(1) makes admissibility "subject to Rule 403," so that the judge has discretion to exclude the conviction if she finds that the "***probative value*** is ***substantially outweighed*** by the danger of ... ***unfair prejudice***[.]" But 609(a)(2), dealing with *crimen falsi*, makes no reference to 403, and simply says that the evidence of the conviction "must" be admitted – so where, as here, false statement was an element of the crime (whether the crime was a misdemeanor or a felony), the judge ***must*** admit it for impeachment no matter how little its probative value or how great its prejudicial effect on the opponent.

Also, observe that misdemeanors that do *not* reflect on the witness's veracity are generally *inadmissible* to impeach.

27. **Yes, probably**, even though the material doesn't reflect on Zoom's truthfulness or honesty. FRE 609(a) distinguishes between felonies in which dishonesty/false statement was not necessarily an element (dealt with in subsection 1) and all crimes (felonies or misdemeanors) in which dishonesty/false statement was an element (dealt with in subsection 2). Vehicular homicide clearly falls in the first category. Subsection 1 says that such convictions "must be admitted, subject to Rule 403" if the witness is (as here) not the accused in a criminal case. So the judge *must* admit the conviction unless she in the exercise of her discretion finds that the test of Rule 403 (allowing exclusion of relevant evidence whose "probative value is substantially outweighed by the danger of unfair ... prejudice[.]") is satisfied.

Courts usually find that even a violent crime not defined so as to require proof of dishonesty or false statement nonetheless has some bearing on the perpetrator's credibility. The court here therefore probably won't find that the tough test of Rule 403 (i.e., the requirement that probative value be "substantially" outweighed by prejudice, etc.) is satisfied. (The court can probably take into account the facts of the ***particular crime*** on which Crashbag was convicted, not just the nature of vehicular homicide in general; so if Crashbag, for instance, left the scene of the accident, this additional element of dishonesty would make it less likely that the judge would find that the "substantially outweighed" test of Rule 403 was satisfied.)

28. **No, probably**. Under FRE 609(b), evidence of a conviction is normally inadmissible if a period of more than ten years has elapsed since the date of the conviction or of the witness's release from confinement due to the conviction, whichever occurred later. However, an ***exception*** to this general rule exists if ***both*** of the following conditions are satisfied:

1. The court decides that, "in the interests of justice . . . the ***probative value*** of the conviction supported by specific facts and circumstances **substantially outweighs** its ***prejudicial effect***." (609(b), 1st sent.); ***and***

2. The party trying to use the old conviction gives the adverse party "sufficient ***advance written notice*** of intent to use such evidence to provide the adverse party with a fair opportunity to contest the use of such evidence." (609(b)(1) and (2))

Even if the second requirement was satisfied here (we're not told), it's very unlikely that the court will find the first one to have been, since the conviction is much more than 10 years old, and there don't seem to be any "specific facts and circumstances" here giving it special probative value.

29. **Objection overruled**. The question is proper, because a witness can be impeached by inquiring, on cross-examination, about specific unconvicted bad acts, if these are "probative of the character for truthfulness or untruthfulness of: (1) the witness[.]" FRE 608(b)(1). Filing a false tax return is generally accepted as probative of truthfulness. (Note that under 608(b), the court "may" (not "must") allow such

questions about unconvicted bad acts; so the court has discretion as to whether to allow the question.)

IMPORTANT: Under the collateral issue rule, if the witness denies the unconvicted bad acts, they can't be proven via *extrinsic* impeachment (e.g., testimony by some other witness; introduction of an arrest warrant). FRE 608(b), 1st sent. The examiner must *"take the answer of the witness."*

30. **No**. Under FRE 608(b), *specific instances* of the conduct of a witness to attack or support credibility *may not be proven by extrinsic evidence*. Thus, unconvicted bad acts, when used to impeach the witness's general character for truthfulness, can be proven only by intrinsic evidence — that is, through the testimony (given under cross-examination) of the witness who purportedly committed the bad acts (here, Wolf). Once the witness denies the bad acts, the examiner must "take the answer of the witness."

31. **Objection overruled**. Under FRE 608(a), the credibility of a witness may be attacked by evidence in the form of *opinion* or *reputation*, so long as the evidence refers only to the witness's character for *truthfulness* or *untruthfulness*. The evidence here qualifies as opinion evidence. (Under the common law, the credibility of a witness can only be attacked by reputation evidence, not [as here] opinion evidence.)

Observe that Hatfield wouldn't be allowed to testify to *particular acts* of untruthfulness by McCoy; these would violate the rule against showing specific bad acts by extrinsic evidence. See FRE 608(b), 1st sent. Also, note that evidence of the witness's *truthfulness* (not, as here, *un*truthfulness) cannot be introduced by the proponent of the witness until the witness's character has been attacked.

32. **Objection sustained**. Under both the common law and FRE 613(b), when prior inconsistent statements are offered to impeach a witness, the witness must be given a chance to *explain or deny* the prior inconsistency. This provides the foundation for the introduction of the inconsistent statement. Since Rick is now unavailable to explain or deny the prior statement, the statement should be excluded.

Note that, under the common law, the rule of *Queen Caroline's Case* required that the witness be given a chance to explain or deny the prior statement *before* being questioned. However, the FRE and most modern courts do not require this – it's enough that the witness is given the chance to explain afterwards.

The party attacking Rick's credibility (Goldilocks) wasn't required to actually call Rick back to the stand to explain or deny; Goldilocks was entitled to thrust onto the party who wants to explain the inconsistent statement (the Bears) this burden of calling Rick back. However, the attacking party does bear the risk that the witness will have become unavailable by the time the other party learns of the inconsistent statement and wants to explain it. Goldilocks' lawyer should have used the inconsistent statement during the original cross-examination of Rick; having waited, the lawyer loses the right to admit the statement now that Rick is unavailable to explain or deny.

Observe that by 613(b), the court can dispense with the right to explain or deny if "justice so requires." However, in view of Goldilocks' lawyer's unused chance to bring out the prior statement during the original cross, the court is very unlikely to use this power here.

33. **Objection overruled**. The use of extrinsic evidence to impeach is always permissible when a witness's *perception*, *memory*, or *mental capacity* is questioned. Since a witness's ability to perceive and remember are always deemed material, the "collateral matters" rule doesn't apply. (The "collateral issue" rule forbids impeachment with extrinsic evidence only if the evidence is *solely* relevant for impeachment.)

34. **Yes, to impeach Hamlet**. Horatio's statement, of course, contradicts Hamlet's testimony. Impeachment by contradiction is allowed, as a general rule, only where the contradiction relates to a *material issue*. (If the contradiction doesn't relate to a material issue, it is inadmissible under the "collateral issue" rule.) This requirement is satisfied here, because the contradiction relates to Hamlet's acquaintance with

Yorick, and that acquaintance is a material issue in the case (the prosecution's claim of jealousy couldn't be true if Hamlet didn't even know Yorick). Note that no foundation is necessary prior to introducing such contradiction evidence.

35. Objection sustained. Under the *"collateral issue"* rule, extrinsic evidence can only be introduced to impeach a witness if it also bears on a *substantive* issue in the case (or if it proves something deemed important, like bias). Here, if the "boyfriend" testimony is true, it only proves Wanda is lying — it doesn't make any substantive fact at issue in the case either more or less probable. So the collateral issue rule applies, and the evidence is inadmissible.

COMPARE: Suppose the defense called Wilfreda to impeach Wanda as follows: "Everyone in town knows Wanda is a bald-faced liar!" Here, the testimony will be admissible, because witnesses may be impeached via extrinsic evidence in the form of poor *reputation* for honesty, under both FRE 608(a) and the common law. (In fact, under the FRE – but not the common law – extrinsic *"opinion"* evidence, e.g., Wilfreda's opinion that Wanda is generally dishonest, may be used as well.)

36. No. A witness's testimony can't be *"bolstered"* unless and until he's been impeached. (There are exceptions, such as a showing that the victim in a rape case made a timely complaint. But no exception applies here.) Since the defendant didn't cross-examine Cy at all, it certainly couldn't have impeached him.

37. Yes. On redirect, a witness may be *"rehabilitated,"* by being given the chance to explain facts brought out in cross-examination.

38. Objection sustained. It's true that when a witness has been impeached by a claim that she has been improperly influenced or motivated, or by a claim that her story is a recent fabrication, the witness may be rehabilitated by showing that she previously made a statement that is consistent with her present testimony. See FRE 801(d)(1)(B). But both at common law and under this provision of the FRE (as interpreted by the Supreme Court in *Tome v. U.S.*), the prior consistent statement must have been made *before* the improper motive, influence or fabrication came into existence. Since the alleged improper motive arose in April 2006 (when Stepdad supposedly hit Pamela's mother), and since the prior consistent statement was not made until after that episode, the statement doesn't qualify. Therefore, it can't be used for rehabilitation (and it's inadmissible hearsay).

XVI. SOME SPECIAL TECHNIQUES FOR DEVELOPING OR EVALUATING TESTIMONY

A. Scope: We conclude our treatment of the general rules on testimony by examining several scientific techniques that are arguably useful for developing or evaluating testimony: (1) the use of expert *psychiatric* testimony to help the jury evaluate the truthfulness of the witness; (2) the use of *hypnosis* and *truth serum* to help the witness remember facts; and (3) the use of the *lie detector* (polygraph) to evaluate the witness's truthfulness.

1. General view of courts: In general, courts take a dim view of these types of "scientific" assistance. Most courts regard them as interfering with the jury's right and duty to observe and judge the witness directly. However, a growing minority of courts do allow some of these kinds of evidence.

B. Psychiatric testimony: A party may wish to discredit an opposing witness by the use of *psychiatric expert testimony* to show that the witness's accuracy is doubtful because of some *mental illness* or *defect.* For instance, the defense in a criminal case might offer evidence by a psychiatrist that the prosecution's key witness is a paranoid schizophrenic who cannot distinguish fact from fantasy, and whose testimony therefore cannot be believed even if the witness himself believes it.

1. **Sexual assault cases:**   The issue of psychiatric expert testimony on credibility arises most frequently in *rape* and other sexual assault cases. Typically, the defendant argues that the alleged victim is making up or distorting the facts. The defendant asks the court to order the alleged victim to submit to examination by a court-appointed psychiatrist who will then give an opinion as to whether the alleged victim has any mental abnormality that should lead her testimony to be doubted.

   a. **Discretion:**   Generally, the trial court is given broad *discretion* to decide whether to appoint a psychiatrist in this situation, and whether to allow the jury to hear his resulting opinion. Usually, that discretion will be exercised only for *compelling reasons*. McC, p. 61.

C. Hypnosis and truth serum: Two techniques, *hypnosis* and *truth serum*, are sometimes used to help the witness remember the details of an event (especially a crime of which the witness was a victim). Such techniques raise two different types of admissibility questions: (1) whether the statement given under the influence of the hypnosis or truth serum may itself be admitted; and (2) whether a witness whose recollection has been sharpened by one of these techniques may then give live testimony at trial about the event in question. (During our discussion, we will refer to hypnosis only, but the same rules generally apply to truth serum.)

1. **Statement made under influence:**   Where admission is sought of the statement made under hypnosis, the vast majority of courts have *rejected* the statement. McC, p. 376. This is true whether the statement is offered as substantive evidence or for its bearing on the credibility of the witness's live testimony at trial. This rule stems both from fears of the technique's unreliability and also from hearsay problems (*infra*, p. 182).

2. **Testimony at trial:**   Where what is to be introduced is the witness's *live testimony* about an event, his recall of which has been refreshed through hypnosis, courts are split.

   a. **Complete exclusion:**   Many courts in this situation, too — perhaps still a majority — *exclude* the live testimony.

      i. **Rationale:**   This majority view stems mainly from judges' fear of the *unreliability* of testimony that derives from hypnosis or truth serum. The key danger is that of "confabulation," i.e., "pseudomemories where plausible fantasy has replaced gaps in recall." *State ex rel. Collins v. Superior Court*, 644 P.2d 1266 (Ariz. 1982). Furthermore, "because the person hypnotized is subjectively convinced of the veracity of the 'memory', this recall is not susceptible to attack by cross-examination." *State v. Mack*, 292 N.W.2d 764 (Minn. 1980).

   b. **Minority view:**   Other courts (probably still a minority but clearly increasing in number) *allow* at least some testimony influenced by prior hypnosis. These courts have generally imposed stringent *safeguards* to increase reliability and reduce the danger of suggestion. See, e.g., *State v. Hurd*, 432 A.2d 86 (N.J. 1981), requiring, *inter alia*, a written record of all information about the event given to the hypnotist before the session, a recording (preferably *videotape*) of all contacts between hypnotist and subject, and a limitation of attendance at the session to just hypnotist and subject.

c. **Pre-session recollections:** If the jurisdiction does not allow hypnotically-influenced testimony, or if it does allow it but the conditions have not been satisfied, it is not clear whether the witness will be found to be totally incompetent (*supra*, p. 7) to testify about the event. The issue is whether the witness may repeat those recollections he had *prior to the session*. Some courts hold that the witness's testimony must be completely excluded, because the session will inevitably increase the witness's confidence in his prior recollections, and therefore make it unfairly hard to cross-examine him. Other courts allow testimony limited to the pre-hypnotic recall. See, e.g., *State ex rel. Collins v. Superior Court*, *supra*, allowing testimony as to the pre-hypnotic recall, but only if there is a complete record made before the session showing the extent of the witness's pre-hypnotic recall.

d. **Leads:** Even if the state completely forbids testimony of witnesses who have been hypnotized about the event, hypnosis may be worthwhile. The hypnosis may generate *leads* which an investigator can then follow up on. These leads may in turn produce admissible evidence (e.g., other witnesses, forensic evidence, etc.). This hypnotically-derived evidence will presumably be admissible no matter how dim a view the jurisdiction takes of the reliability of hypnosis, since the derivative evidence will have to have its own foundation.

e. **Criminal defendant's right to testify:** Most hypnotized-witness cases have involved witnesses other than criminal defendants. Where the *criminal defendant* himself has been hypnotized, the trial court's ability to restrict hypnosis-influenced testimony may impair the defendant's *constitutional* right to *testify in his own defense*.

Example: D, while fighting with her husband, V, picks up a handgun. The gun goes off, shooting V in the chest. D is charged with manslaughter. D cannot remember all the details of the incident, and so undergoes hypnosis by a licensed neuropsychologist/ hypnotist. The hypnosis sessions are recorded on tape. During the sessions, D remembers that her finger was not on the trigger at any time during the fight, and that the gun went off when V grabbed D's arm. At trial, D offers testimony by a gun expert that the gun was defective and prone to fire if hit or dropped without the trigger's being pulled. D then offers her own hypnotically-refreshed testimony. The judge limits D's testimony to "matters remembered and stated to the examiner prior to being placed under hypnosis"; this ruling prevents D from testifying on the finger-on-the-trigger issue. D is convicted.

Held (by the Supreme Court), for D. D's constitutional right to testify in her own defense was violated by the trial judge's ruling. States have the broad right to restrict hypnotically-refreshed testimony by a non-criminal-defendant witness. Even where the testimony is by a criminal defendant, the states have some right to guard against unreliable hypnotic evidence. But the judge's ruling in this case — that all of D's testimony that D could not prove to be the product of pre-hypnosis memory must be excluded — went too far. For instance, testimony by D that was corroborated by other evidence should have been allowed. Since D's testimony that she did not pull the trigger was corroborated by the gun expert's testimony that the gun was defective and prone to fire if hit or dropped, D's testimony should have been allowed even though it was not remembered until hypnosis. *Rock v. Arkansas*, 483 U.S. 44 (1987).

D. Lie detector tests: The *lie detector* (polygraph) purports to determine whether the subject is lying by detecting changes in his physiological functions, such as pulse rate, blood pressure, and perspiration, on the theory that a person is more anxious when he is lying than when he is not, and these physiological reactions accompany anxiety. The polygraph is widely used in private industry to check employee honesty, and also widely used in the investigative stages of law enforcement (though generally only with the consent of the subject). Therefore, its proponents urge that it be accepted as *evidence* of the *credibility* of the subject. Its evidentiary use would be most applicable in criminal cases, where test results could be offered either by the defendant (to show that he is not lying when he denies involvement in the crime) or by the prosecution (to show that the story the defendant has been telling the police is a lie).

1. **General rule:** Except where both parties *stipulate* to allow the lie detector results in evidence, nearly all courts still *reject* polygraph evidence on the issue of whether the statements made by the subject during the test are true. As one authority writes, "In the early decades of the twenty-first century, polygraph results are excludable from evidence almost everywhere, and most jurisdictions bar comment on any refusal by a criminal defendant to take a polygraph test." M&K (5th), §7.20, p. 712.

2. **Rationale:** The traditional rule barring polygraph evidence on the issue of truth is supported by a number of rationales:

    a. **Unreliable:** Most importantly, the technique is of *questionable reliability*. Even its strongest advocates concede that it is wrong about 5% of the time and inconclusive another 10% of the time. L&S, p. 328. Opponents say the error rate is much higher. Also, accuracy depends upon a highly trained expert to administer and interpret the test, and many testers lack the necessary training.

        i. **Anxiety rather than guilt:** In particular, the test really measures only *anxiety*, not lying.

    b. **Seemingly scientific:** Conversely, the jury is likely to regard the results as *more scientific* than they are, and consequently to give them *too much weight*. McC, p. 375.

3. **Stipulation:** A substantial and growing minority of courts allow use of polygraph results where both parties have *stipulated* that the results may be admitted. McC, p. 374.

    a. **Before test:** Generally, the stipulation will be entered into before the test is administered, so that neither party knows for sure whether the results will be beneficial to him.

4. **Compulsory Process argument by defendants:** A criminal defendant has a constitutional right, under the *Compulsory Process clause* of the Sixth Amendment, to obtain and present *evidence helpful to his defense.* (See *infra*, p. 403.) Some defendants have therefore argued that the Compulsory Process clause entitles them, as a constitutional matter, to present evidence that they *passed a polygraph test.*

     a. Argument is rejected: However, the Supreme Court has ***rejected*** this argument. In *U.S. v. Scheffer*, 523 U.S. 303 (1998) (also discussed *infra*, p. 404), the Court held that rules excluding particular types of evidence from criminal trials do not violate the accused's right to present a defense so long as the rules are not "arbitrary" or "disproportionate to the purposes they are designed to serve." The Court noted that "the scientific community remains extremely polarized about the reliability of polygraph techniques." Therefore, the Court said, rules barring polygraph evidence — in this case, an outright ban on such evidence in military court-martial proceedings — are not arbitrary or disproportionate, because they are a "rational and proportional means of advancing the legitimate interest in barring unreliable evidence."

5. Expert testimony: When polygraph evidence is admitted, it is usually presented in the form of expert testimony by the examiner, who describes to the jury the questions and answers, interprets the technical test results, and gives his opinion as to the veracity of the subject.

6. Psychological Stress Evaluation: Nearly all courts have declined to admit the results of ***Psychological Stress Evaluation (PSE)*** tests. The PSE is a type of "voice stress analysis," which purportedly shows whether a person is lying by measuring stress in his voice. Most scientific literature has concluded that the PSE has no validity. McC, p. 374. Presumably any court that excludes lie detector evidence would exclude PSE results, and probably even some courts that allow lie detector evidence under certain conditions would exclude PSE results on the grounds that the latter are less reliable.

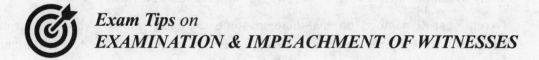

Exam Tips on
EXAMINATION & IMPEACHMENT OF WITNESSES

Of the topics in this chapter, two make up the overwhelming majority of test questions: cross-examination generally, and impeachment (with its counterpart, rehabilitation).

Direct Examination

Where your exam question involves ***direct*** examination, there's really only one rule that gets tested with any frequency: the examiner may not ask ***leading questions***. Remember that a leading question is one that suggests to the witness the answer desired by the questioner. (One common example: any question starting with "Didn't" or "Weren't.")

☛ But if the witness is "hostile," remember that leading questions are ***allowed***.

☛ **Juror's impeachment of own verdict:** Look out for scenarios in which the jury has rendered a verdict, and then one of the juror's offers to testify as to something that occurred during the trial and that ***casts doubt on the verdict's validity*** (i.e., ***"impeaches"*** the verdict).

   ☞ **General rule:** Remember the general rule (imposed by FRE 606(b)(1)): In the course of an "inquiry into the ***validity of a verdict,***" a juror may not testify about: (1) any "*statement made* or *incident that occurred* during the *jury's deliberations*"; or (2) the "*effect of anything*" on the *vote* of the testifying juror or any juror.

Example: D is on trial for violently resisting arrest, and is expected to claim that it was the arresting officer who committed any violence that occurred. During *voir dire*, a woman who will be seated as Juror 1 says that she does not have any law enforcement officers in her immediate family, and can be fair to a criminal defendant. The jury convicts D by a vote of 11 to 1 (sufficient for a conviction under state law), the dissenter being Juror 2. D's lawyer moves for a new trial, offering Juror 2's testimony that during deliberations, Juror 1 told the other jurors, "My husband is a police officer, and he says that when a defendant who resists arrest claims the police started the violence, 98% of the time the claim is baloney."

The judge may not hear Juror 2's testimony, since it violates the rules against (1) juror testimony about any "statement made ... during the jury's deliberations," and (2) juror testimony about the "effect of anything" (here, the husband's statement to Juror 1) on the vote of "any juror."

Note: But in a *criminal* trial, remember that the *Sixth Amendment* requires that FRE 606(b) or the equivalent be *ignored* if the testimony is about a juror's statement showing "*overt racial bias*" (or ethnic bias) that "cast[s] *serious doubt* on the *fairness and impartiality*" of the verdict, and if the bias seems to have been a "*significant motivating factor*" in that juror's vote to convict. (Cite to *Pena-Rodriguez v. Colorado* (2017).) So suppose, in the above Example, that the proposed testimony by Juror 2 was, "Juror 1 told the other jurors, 'D is black, and most blacks charged with resisting arrest started the violence themselves." D's Sixth Amendment right to an impartial jury would require the trial judge to hear Juror 2's testimony even though that testimony would be barred by FRE 606(b)(1) or the state-law equivalent.

☞ **Exceptions:** Remember, too, that there are some major *exceptions* to the rule barring consideration of a juror's testimony that would impeach the verdict. Most important: (1) testimony that "*extraneous prejudicial information*" was "improperly brought to the jury's attention"; and (2) testimony that "an *outside influence* was improperly brought to bear" on any juror".

Example of exception 1: In a civil suit involving an auto accident at the intersection of Main Street and West Avenue, after a verdict for P, Juror 2 testifies that Juror 1 said during deliberations, "I know from personal experience that there's a stop sign at that corner that D must have ignored." (There was no evidence introduced about whether there is or isn't a stop sign at that intersection.) The judge may hear Juror 2's testimony, since it's about "extraneous prejudicial information" improperly brought to the jury's attention.

Example of exception 2: After a jury civil verdict in favor of P in P's auto-accident suit against D, D moves for a new trial, and offers testimony by Juror 2 that "During the trial, I noticed that P's lawyer was having lunch with Juror 1, and I saw the lawyer hand a $100 bill to Juror 1." The judge may hear Juror 2's testimony, since it concerns "an outside influence" (the fact of the lunch, and the transfer of the money as a possible bribe) that was "improperly brought to bear" on a juror.

Cross-Examination

Here's what to look for when the exam question involves cross-examination:

☛ **Scope:** Look out for issues involving the proper *scope* of cross.

　☞ **Scope of direct:** The majority rule (followed by FRE 611(b)) is the *"scope of direct"* rule, i.e., cross is limited to the scope of the matters the witness testified to on her direct exam. (*Example:* In a car crash case, W testifies on behalf of P that D said to W after the accident, "I was speeding." W gives no other testimony on direct. D's lawyer asks W on cross, "You didn't see the accident, did you?" Strictly speaking, this violates the majority/FRE "scope of direct" rule and would be improper. However, most states give the trial judge discretion to allow the question.)

　☞ **Credibility:** Questions relevant to *credibility* are always within the scope of cross.

☛ **Leading:** Leading questions are permissible on cross.

☛ **Self-incrimination:** Also, look out for situations in which the witness under cross invokes the Fifth Amendment privilege against *self-incrimination*. Often-tested: when W takes the 5th, what should the trial judge do? Usual answer: strike W's direct testimony. (*Example:* In D's murder trial, W testifies on direct, "I saw D commit the murder." On cross, D's lawyer asks W, "Isn't it true that at the time in question, you were robbing a gas station 600 miles away?" If W takes the 5th, the trial judge should normally strike all W's direct testimony, because W's invocation of the 5th now prevents D from exercising his full 6th Amendment Confrontation Clause rights.)

Present Recollection Refreshed

Whenever a witness can't remember something, consider the possibility that the doctrine of "present recollection refreshed" may apply. Here are the aspects most often tested:

☛ Remember that the doctrine applies only when the witness *cannot remember* the answer without the document. (*Example:* If W gives an answer, but the questioner thinks this is the wrong answer, the doctrine doesn't apply.)

☛ *Any item* (a writing or thing) may be used. Most fact patterns involve a writing (e.g., a newspaper article; a letter written by or to W; company files).

　☞ The item *need not be admissible.* That's because the item is never being admitted into evidence, only the refreshed testimony becomes evidence. (*Example:* W observes an accident involving P and D. At trial, W — testifying on behalf of P — can't remember the details. P's lawyer shows W a report by a policeman, X, in which X says, "An unidentified witness says that D ran a red light." If W was that witness, W can now testify about the accident with his recollection refreshed, even though the report itself is inadmissible because of hearsay.)

　☞ Whether or not the witness's recollection is in fact refreshed by the item, check to see whether the item itself is admissible. Most common ways: *past recollection recorded* and *business record*.

☛ Remember that even if the doctrine applies, W's testimony must **still meet ordinary admissibility requirements.** (*Example:* W, listening to a police radio, hears a report about a red car speeding down a particular street. She makes a note of what she's heard. At trial, W can't remember the report, is shown her note, and then testifies to what she remembers the report saying. Even though showing W the note was a proper application of present recollection refreshed, her testimony is still inadmissible hearsay — it's not "immunized" from admissibility problems by virtue of having come from the properly-consulted document.)

☛ Frequently-tested: Does **opposing counsel** have the right to **see the item** and **use it for cross-examination** of the witness?

   ☞ If the item is shown to the witness **at trial**, all courts (and FRE 612) give the opposing party the **right** to inspect the item and use it for cross.

   ☞ But if the item is merely consulted by the witness **before** trial, most courts (and FRE 612) leave it up to the trial court's **discretion** whether to allow the opposing counsel to see the item and cross-examine W with reference to it.

Impeachment — Generally

When you conclude that a particular piece of evidence is inadmissible substantively, always check to see if it's admissible for **impeachment**. Evidence is being used for impeachment when it's used to **destroy a witness's credibility** (rather than to directly establish a fact at issue in the case).

☛ Types of evidence or questions likely to be impeaching: (1) attacks on W's **character**, especially **truthfulness**; (2) W's **prior inconsistent statement**; (3) W's **bias**; (4) W's **sensory or mental defect**; and (5) **contradiction** of W's testimony (e.g., by testimony of a different witness).

☛ Most commonly-tested: May a lawyer **impeach his own witness** (i.e., may impeachment be done on direct?)

   ☞ At common law: generally, no (but subject to exceptions, e.g. where W is hostile or Lawyer is surprised).

   ☞ Under FRE and many modern courts: **Yes**. (Thus FRE 607 completely revokes the "can't impeach your own witness" rule.)

      ☞ In multiple-choice exams where the FRE apply, a common **incorrect** "distractor" is "Inadmissible, because Lawyer can't impeach her own witness."

Impeachment By Prior Criminal Conviction or Prior Bad Acts

Impeachment by prior criminal convictions or prior bad acts are probably the most commonly-tested types of impeachment. The rules are detailed and non-obvious, so spend some time memorizing them. Here are the main things to watch for (discussion assumes the FRE, unless otherwise noted):

Prior convictions: Where the impeachment is by showing W's prior **criminal conviction**:

☛ **Dishonesty or false statement:** If the crime required the prosecution to prove **dishonesty** or *false statement* as an element (i.e., the crime was a *"crimen falsi"*), the evidence is always *admissible*. This is true both at common law and under FRE 609. And it's true even if the conviction was a *misdemeanor*, and whether W is or is not an "accused." (*Example:* Lawyer asks W, "Isn't it true that two years ago, you were convicted on misdemeanor charges of perjury?" Admissible.)

☞ Examples of *crimen falsi* under the FRE: perjury, criminal fraud, embezzlement, false pretenses, forgery, tax fraud (probably). Not covered: most crimes of violence; drug offenses; ordinary larceny (including shoplifting, but not embezzlement or false pretences), robbery, burglary.

☞ There's *no discretion* — the court can't conclude that the probative value is outweighed by the danger of unfair prejudice.

☛ **Felony not involving dishonesty; W not accused:** If the crime is a *felony for which proof of dishonesty or false statement was not an element*, and W is *not the accused*, the evidence is automatically *admissible*, unless the conviction's probative value is shown to be "*substantially outweighed* by the danger of unfair prejudice." (*Example:* W testifies as an alibi witness for D in a criminal case. Prosecution may ask W, "Isn't it true you were convicted of aggravated assault three years ago?" as long as this crime was punishable by at least one year in prison.)

☞ **Maximum punishment:** Remember that what counts is the maximum punishment *possible* in the state or federal system where the conviction occurred, not the punishment W actually received. (So even a sentence of probation would not make the conviction inadmissible if a 1-year sentence could have been given for the crime.)

☛ **Felony not involving dishonesty; W is accused:** If the crime is a *felony not involving dishonesty* as an element, and the witness *is* the *accused*, the judge may admit the evidence only if she determines that the probative value of admitting "outweighs" the conviction's prejudicial effect to the accused. (*Example:* In a criminal trial before a jury, D takes the stand, and says he didn't commit the crime. On cross, the prosecutor asks, "Weren't you convicted of burglary 6 years ago?" The question is proper if and only if the judge finds that the probative value of the evidence will outweigh the likely prejudicial effect on D.)

☞ Remember that D can only be impeached if he *takes the stand*. The fact pattern will sometimes try to distract you from this key point. (*Example:* In D's murder trial, Officer testifies that he previously arrested D several times for assault, and that D was convicted each time. The prosecutor then offers authenticated court records of the convictions. Neither Officer's testimony nor the court records are admissible for impeachment unless there's some indication in the question that D took the stand — without this, there's nothing to impeach.)

☛ **Non-dishonesty misdemeanor:** If the crime is a *misdemeanor not involving dishonesty*, it's *not admissible*, whether W is the accused or not.

☛ **Limits:** Don't forget some limits:

☞ **10-years:** Most important, the conviction is not admissible (whether it's a felony or a crimen falsi misdemeanor) if *more than 10 years* has elapsed since the conviction or release from confinement (whichever is later), unless the judge finds specific facts making the probative value substantially outweigh the prejudicial effect. Most often, this special showing won't be made (and the conviction will be excluded).

    ☞   **Rehabilitation:** Also, the conviction is not admissible if it's reversed on appeal, or, in most instances, if W was pardoned.

☛ **Procedures:** Usually, the impeachment will be by *questioning* of the witness ("Weren't you convicted . . . .") But it may also be by extrinsic evidence, i.e., by introducing a certified *copy of the judgment* of conviction.

Prior bad acts: Unconvicted *bad acts* that are probative of truthfulness are admissible at the discretion of the judge. FRE 608(b). Here's what to watch for:

☛ **Truthfulness:** The bad act must be of a sort that *bears on truthfulness*. (The definition is basically the same as for *crimen falsi* under FRE 609. So these don't qualify: most violent crimes; status crimes like drug-addiction; and theft crimes containing no element of false statement, like shoplifting and burglary.)

Bad acts that *do* meet the "bears on truthfulness" test: lying on an insurance policy; defrauding customers; committing perjury.

☛ **Good-faith basis:** The questioner must have a *"good-faith basis"* for believing that the witness committed the bad act.

☛ **No extrinsic evidence:** The bad acts must be proved only by *questioning the witness*, *not* by introducing *"extrinsic evidence."* This means that:

    ☞   A *second witness* can't be called to testify that the first witness committed the bad act; and

    ☞   *Documents* can't be introduced to show W's bad act, even during the cross-examination of W. (But a document can be referred to, as long as it's not introduced.) (*Example:* W can be asked, "Didn't you once file an insurance claim, in which you falsely said your car radio was stolen?" But the false claim form itself can't be introduced.)

    Note: The only way extrinsic evidence can be used to show W's character for truthfulness is by reputation or opinion testimony, not by "specific acts" testimony, which is what is being discussed here.

☛ **Bad act led to conviction:** If the bad act resulted in a conviction, the limits of the conviction rule probably must be adhered to even if only the bad act is inquired about. (*Example:* W probably can't be asked, "Did you commit perjury 12 years ago?" if W was in fact convicted and released from prison more than 10 years ago, making the conviction itself too old to introduce.)

Impeachment by Opinion and Reputation Testimony

Remember that the principal witness (W1) can be impeached by the testimony of a second, or "character" witness (W2), subject to these rules:

☛ **Reputation or opinion:** W2 must testify to W1's poor *reputation* for truthfulness, or testify that in W2's *opinion*, W1 is of untruthful character. (FRE 608(a)). In other words, W2 *can't* testify to *specific instances* in which W1 was untruthful. (*Example:* W2 can say, "I think, based on my past experience with him, that W1 often lies." But W2 can't continue on by saying, "For instance, I saw him lie about his income on a welfare application.")

☛ **Rehabilitation by specific instances:** But once W2 gives the reputation or opinion testimony about W1's poor reputation for truthfulness, the party who called W1 may at the court's discretion *rehabilitate* W1 by asking about specific instances of W1's truthfulness. (*Example:* To W2, "Didn't W1 tell you he'd been in jail, even though you had no other way to find this out?")

Impeachment by W's Prior Inconsistent Statement

Look for a witness testifying on the stand who is making a statement that is *inconsistent* with some *prior statement* made by that same witness. In general, the cross-examiner may impeach this witness by using the prior inconsistent statement.

☛ **Types of proof allowed:** Proof of the prior inconsistent statement may be by *either intrinsic* or *extrinsic* evidence.

Example of intrinsic proof: D testifies that a car belongs to him. L asks on cross, "When you were arrested, didn't you tell the officers that the car wasn't yours?" Proper.

Example of extrinsic proof: W1 is an alibi witness for D. W1 says, "On April 14, the evening of the crime, I had dinner with D." The prosecutor may put on W2, who testifies, "In May, W1 told me he hadn't seen D any time in April."

☛ **Extrinsic evidence:** Most test questions focus on the special rules for showing a prior inconsistent statement by extrinsic evidence:

   ☞ **Collateral matters rule:** Most courts don't allow extrinsic proof of prior incon. stmt. on a *collateral issue*, i.e., one that is not directly in issue in the case and that would not be directly provable apart from the inconsistency (as bias, say, would be). (*Example:* Same basic facts as prior example. In the course of his alibi testimony, W1 happens to mention, "On April 14, before I had dinner with D, I bought a gallon of milk from the 7-11." Prosecution puts on W2, who says, "W1 told me he never shops at 7-11 because it's a rip-off." Inadmissible, because its extrinsic evidence of prior incon. stmt., not relating to an issue in the case — whether W1 did or didn't shop at the 7-11 that day isn't a direct issue in the case.)

   ☞ **Foundation:** Under the modern/FRE approach, the extrinsic evidence (e.g., a writing) need *not* be shown to the witness, or summarized, before the inconsistency is revealed. (FRE 613(a). (*Example*: Civil suit involving auto accident. D tells an investigator, "I don't know whether I was speeding," and the investigator makes written notes of this statement. At trial, D says, "I definitely wasn't speeding." P's lawyer, L, can ask D the vague question, "Didn't you say at some other time that you didn't know you were speeding?" L need not first show the notes to D, or first warn D about the time and place of the prior statement — L can "spring" this on D by introducing the notes after D has denied making a prior incon. statement.)

   ☞ **Chance to explain or deny:** But remember that extrinsic evidence of the prior incon. stmt. is not admissible unless the witness is given a chance to *"explain or deny"* the statement, and the party who called that witness is given a chance to rehabilitate. (FRE

613(b)). This rule can be dispensed with if "the interests of justice otherwise require", and does not apply at all where the statement is made by a party-opponent.

☛ **Hearsay:** Don't get confused by a prior statement that seems to be *hearsay*. It's still admissible as a prior incon. stmt. if it's being used to impeach, not to prove its truth. (*Example:* In D's murder trial, W testifies for the prosecution that he, W, heard three gunshots immediately after hearing D shout, "I'll kill you!" D offers testimony of Police Officer, who testifies that when Officer interviewed W after the shooting, W said he hadn't heard any gunshots. Because Officer's testimony is being used to impeach W's credibility, not to prove whether D really heard gunshots, Officer's recounting of W's interview statement is not hearsay.)

☞ Also, examine the possibility that a prior inconsistent statement may be admissible **both substantively and as impeachment**. Two common situations where the the statement will be admissible for both purposes: (1) A party's *own prior statement* is being introduced by the other party (thus qualifying substantively as an *admission*); and (2) a person's prior statement was given **under oath** at a proceeding or deposition (thus qualifying substantively under FRE 801(d)(1)(A)'s "prior inconsistent statement" exception to the hearsay rule). (*Example* of (2): If W testifies at trial, his prior inconsistent statement at a grand jury proceeding may be admitted substantively.)

Impeachment by Showing Bias

Impeachment by showing W's *bias* is commonly-tested. *Examples:*

❑ An expert is asked, "How much are you getting paid to testify?";

❑ A witness for the defense is asked, "Isn't it true that the defendant bank in this case is your employer?";

❑ W testifies on D's behalf in a criminal case. Prosecution asks, "Isn't it true that you were also arrested for taking part in the same crime, and you're awaiting trial, so you have an incentive to help get D acquitted?"

☛ **Foundation:** Where the attacking party wants to use extrinsic evidence to show bias, focus on the possible need for a *"foundation,"* i.e., the need to give the witness who's being attacked the chance to explain before the extrinsic evidence is introduced.

☞ **Other requirements:** Many jurisdictions *require* such a foundation. (*Example:* In a civil suit between P and D, W testifies on behalf of P. D's lawyer puts on X, who says, "Two months ago, W told me that when this case came to trial, W was going to 'get' D good, because D blocked W from becoming a member of D's club." In some states, this testimony won't be allowed unless D's lawyer first asked W, "Did you ever tell X that you would try to 'get' D for keeping you out of his club?")

☞ **Federal courts:** Federal courts often require a foundation before the witness's own prior statement is introduced to show his bias, but not where some other kind of extrinsic evidence is used to show bias. (*Example:* On the facts of the above example, federal courts might require that D's lawyer first ask W about the prior statement to X. But the lawyer could introduce membership records showing that D kept W out of D's club, without first asking W about this, because here there's no prior statement by W being introduced.)

Impeachment by Showing W's Impairment

Remember that W can be impeached by showing an ***impairment*** of her capacity to ***observe, recall*** or ***narrate***. (*Example:* W says she was attacked by D in a parking lot at night. W says there were no artificial lights, but she could see D's face in the moonlight. D can call an expert witness to testify that there was no moonlight on the night of the attack; this shows impairment of W's ability to observe.)

Impeachment by Contradiction

Impeachment of W by ***contradiction*** occurs where evidence is offered that contradicts W's testimony in the case.

☛ Far and away the most frequently-tested aspect of impeachment-by-contradiction is the rule against impeachment on a ***"collateral matter."*** If W1 gives testimony (whether on direct or cross), the attacking party can't call W2 to contradict the truth of what W1 said if W2's evidence relates ***only to W1's credibility***.

Example 1: W1 testifies on P's behalf that a car accident was caused by D's negligence. D's lawyer, on cross, asks W1 "When you witnessed the accident, were you drunk?" W1 says, "No — in fact, I've never been drunk." D then calls W2, who testifies that 2 years before the accident, W2 saw W1 get drunk on New Year's Eve. Because this evidence bears only on W1's credibility (i.e., it doesn't bear directly on a substantive issue in the case), and because this evidence couldn't be admitted if W1 hadn't said he was never drunk (in other words, the evidence doesn't bear on some independently-provable item like W1's bias or general untruthfulness), it should be excluded as collateral.

Example 2: In a car crash civil case, P claims that D was negligent in speeding and in running a stop light. W1, an eyewitness to the crash, testifies on D's behalf; as part of his testimony, W1 mentions that D was wearing a green sweater at the time of the accident. P offers testimony by W2, who says only that on that day, D's sweater was blue. Because the sweater's color is not an issue in the case, and D wouldn't try to prove its color except to impeach W1, W2's testimony should be excluded as collateral. (If W1's mistake was so glaring that it couldn't be the result of honest and trivial error — for instance, if he said that D was wearing an orange hunting vest when he was in fact wearing a blue business suit — then W's contradictory testimony would probably *not* be collateral.)

☞ But where W2's testimony contradicting W1 *does* relate to a substantive issue in the case, or to some fact provable even if it didn't directly contradict W1 (e.g., it proves that W1 is biased, or habitually lies, or lacks capacity to observe or remember accurately), then it *won't* be excluded as collateral. (*Example:* W1, after giving testimony favorable to D, is asked, "Aren't you a personal friend of D?" W1 denies this. P may put on W2 to testify that W1 and D are in fact friends — this would be admissible to prove W1's bias even if W1 hadn't denied being D's friend.)

Rehabilitation

Once a witness's credibility has been attacked, it may be **rehabilitated** by the non-attacking party. This isn't a commonly-tested area. Just be on the lookout for two issues:

☛ First, the rehabilitating evidence must be sufficiently ***directly related*** to the impeaching evidence. (*Example:* P's expert witness, W1, is asked by D's lawyer on cross, "Doctor, how much are you being paid for testifying in this case?" W1 answers, "$500." P's lawyer then calls W2, who testifies solely that W1 has a good reputation for truth and veracity. This rehabilitating evidence is inadmissible, because it doesn't relate to W1's bias, and thus doesn't refute the impeaching evidence.)

☛ Second, a ***prior consistent statement*** can't be used to bolster a witness's credibility, unless the other side has first claimed that the testimony was a recent fabrication or the result of improper influence or motive.

Example (inadmissible): P sues D, a cosmetics company, for an infected leg that P testifies came from using D's hair remover product. D offers testimony by W1 that P received her injuries from falling on a pitchfork. P then offers testimony by W2, P's friend, who says that P often showed W2 her leg and said it had become infected from using the hair remover. Since D wasn't claiming that P recently fabricated her story or was improperly influenced by anyone, such as her lawyer, W2's testimony as to P's prior consistent statement is inadmissible for rehabilitation.

Example (admissible): Same facts, but now D's lawyer says to P on cross, "Isn't it true that you made up this "pitchfork" story 6 months after your injury, when you met your lawyer and decided to sue?" Now, since D has claimed that P's testimony is a recent fabrication, W2's testimony as to P's prior consistent statement is admissible to rehabilitate P's credibility, if the statement was made before D met with the lawyer.

CHAPTER 5

HEARSAY

ChapterScope

This chapter discusses the definition and the dangers of hearsay. The most important lesson from this chapter is how to distinguish between statements that are hearsay and those that are not.

- **Definition:** Hearsay is a ***statement or assertive conduct*** that was made or occurred ***out of court***, and that is offered in court to ***prove the truth of the matter asserted***.

  - ❏ **"Declarant":** The person who made the out-of-court statement is called the ***"declarant."***

  - ❏ **Documents:** Most hearsay consists of out-of-court statements made orally. But a ***document*** created out of court will also be hearsay if offered to prove the truth of a matter asserted in the document. (*Example:* A letter by X, in which X says, "D shot V," is hearsay if offered to show that D shot V.)

- **Rule:** Hearsay is ***not admissible***, unless it falls within some exception (covered in the next chapter) to the hearsay rule.

- **Nonhearsay:** Statements or conduct that are ***not*** offered to prove the truth of the matter they assert ***aren't*** hearsay. Most important:

  - ❏ **Verbal acts:** A statement which gives rise to ***legal consequences*** is not hearsay, when offered to show those legal consequences. (*Examples:* The words of an offer for a contract; words of defamation.)

  - ❏ **Effect on hearer or reader:** A statement offered to show that the listener ***knew or didn't know of something*** (not offered to show the truth of the thing known or not known) is not hearsay. (*Example:* D is being charged with a crime that requires that she knew fact *A*. Testimony that X told D *A*, offered to show that D knew *A*, is not hearsay.)

  - ❏ **Declarant's state of mind:** Similarly, a statement offered to show the ***declarant's state of mind*** (including ***knowledge*** and ***intent***) is nonhearsay. (*Example:* D is charged with statutory rape, in a jurisdiction where a reasonable mistake as to the victim's age is a defense. Victim's testimony, "Before we had sex, D told me, 'I know you're only 15' ," offered to prove D knew Victim was 15, is nonhearsay.)

  - ❏ **Nonassertive conduct:** Conduct that is ***not intended as an assertion*** is not hearsay. (*Example:* X opens an umbrella. Assume that X didn't intend to assert, "It's raining." To prove that it was raining, W may testify, "X opened his umbrella," and there's no hearsay violation.)

  - ❏ **Assertions and assertive conduct offered for different purpose:** Similarly, an assertion (or assertive conduct) offered to prove the ***truth of a matter other than the one asserted***, is not hearsay. (*Example:* X calls D's premises, and says, "I want to bet $10 on Cigar in the 4th race." This is an assertion, but it's not hearsay if offered to show that D's premises were used to take wagers.)

- **Multiple hearsay:** An out-of-court declaration that ***refers to another out-of-court statement*** poses the problem of "multiple hearsay." ***Each level*** of hearsay must be checked for admissibility (and if ***any*** level is hearsay not within an exception, the entire statement is ***excluded***). (*Example:* A police or business record quotes an oral statement of fact made by X. Even if the "business records" exception applies, the document is hearsay if X's statement is hearsay.)

I. INTRODUCTION

A. Nature of hearsay: The prohibition on the use of hearsay evidence is probably the single most important rule of evidence. It is not possible to give a statement of the rule that is both succinct and totally accurate. However, for the early part of our discussion of the topic, the following definition will be adequate:

1. **Basic definition:**   Hearsay is "a statement or assertive conduct which was made or occurred out of court and is offered in court to prove the truth of the facts asserted." L&S, p. 356. Evidence that falls into this hearsay category is simply ***inadmissible***. See FRE 802, setting out the general rule that "***Hearsay is not admissible***[.]"

    a. **More simplified version:**   The gist of the rule against hearsay can be stated even more simply: "The trier of fact may only be asked to believe those statements made by witnesses testifying at the trial." *Id.*, p. 347. In other words, the fact-finder may not be presented with out-of-court statements and asked to believe that the statements are true.

       Example: P sues D for negligence, claiming that D drove her car into the back of P's tractor. D argues that the cause of the accident was not her negligence, but P's contributory negligence in driving a tractor without a rear light. D calls as a witness the insurance adjuster who investigated the accident. The adjuster testifies that P's son told him that the rear light on the tractor had been out for some time before the accident occurred.

          Held, the adjuster's testimony was inadmissible hearsay, since it repeated an out-of-court statement (by P's son) that was offered to prove the truth of the matter asserted in the statement (that the light was indeed out). *Leake v. Hagert*, 175 N.W.2d 675 (N.D. 1970).

2. **Written hearsay:**   The non-lawyer generally thinks of hearsay as including only oral declarations made out of court. However, the rule in fact covers any kind of statement, whether oral or ***written***, so long as the statement is offered to show the truth of the matter asserted.

       Example: Same facts as above example, but the adjuster tells the jury that P's son wrote a written statement that the rear light was out; D then offers the statement into evidence. The statement would be inadmissible hearsay evidence if offered to prove that the light was out.

B. Truth of matter asserted: The key to the concept of hearsay is to remember that an out-of-court declaration is not, by itself, either hearsay or non-hearsay. The ***purpose for which the declaration is offered*** is dispositive: an out-of-court declaration may be offered into evidence for many purposes other than to prove the truth of the matter asserted in the declaration; in that event, there is no hearsay problem.

> **Example:** P, while shopping in a grocery store operated by D, slips on a puddle of ketchup. In defense of P's negligence suit against D, D claims that P failed to keep a proper lookout and failed to heed a warning from D's store manager. D offers the testimony of the store manager's wife (who happened to be in the store at the time) that just before the accident, her husband shouted to P, "Lady, please don't step in that ketchup."
>
> *Held*, the testimony is not hearsay. The manager's declaration is relevant to whether P was on notice of the dangerous condition, and is not being offered for the purpose of proving the truth of assertion (i.e., that there was ketchup on the floor). *Safeway Stores, Inc. v. Combs*, 273 F.2d 295 (5th Cir. 1960).

C. Dangers of hearsay: The use of hearsay testimony presents four main dangers: **(1)** *ambiguity*; **(2)** *insincerity*; **(3)** *incorrect memory*; and **(4)** *inaccurate perception*. All of these relate to the fact that the person making the out-of-court statement (the *declarant*, as he is usually called) is *not available for cross-examination*.

1. The four dangers: To understand the four dangers, it is worthwhile to use a triangle diagram first proposed by Professor Tribe. (See *Triangulating Hearsay*, 87 Harv. L. Rev. 957.) To make our use of the triangle technique concrete, assume that the facts are those of *Leake*, summarized in the Example on p. 182, *supra*, (out-of-court statement by O, "The tail light was broken before the accident"). We can represent the process by which the fact-finder can go from this out-of-court statement ("The tail light was broken") to the ultimate issue (Was the tail light broken?) by the following diagram:

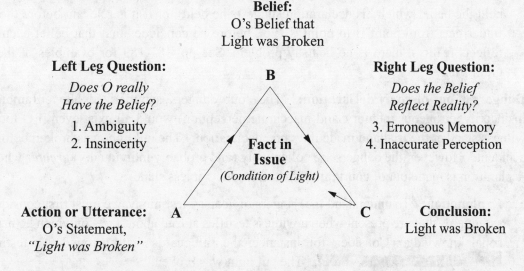

Figure 5-1
Adapted from L&S, p. 351

2. Trip around the triangle: In terms of the diagram, the fact-finder's process of inference goes as follows:

a. Step 1: We start at point A (O's out-of-court statement).

b. Step 2: We first want to get to point B (the conclusion that O really believed that the light was working). To do so, we must avoid two dangers:

    i. Ambiguity: The danger of ***ambiguity***. O may not really have meant to say that the light was broken. For instance, English might be a foreign language for him, and he really meant to say, "The tail light was on."

    ii. Insincerity: The danger of ***insincerity***. For instance, O may have known full well that the tail light was working, but because he hated his father, he lied to the insurance adjuster to get his father in trouble.

c. Step 3: Once we pass these dangers, we are at point B — that is, we're satisfied that O really believed that the light was broken. Now, we want to get to point C (the conclusion that the light was indeed broken). Here too, there are two principal dangers, problems which might prevent O's truly held belief from accurately representing reality:

    i. Erroneous memory: The risk of ***incorrect memory***. For instance, O might have honestly believed that the light was broken, but he might be forgetting that it was the family's other car that had a broken light.

    ii. Inaccurate perception: The danger of ***inaccurate perception***. For instance, O may have seen the car right before the accident, but because of weak eyesight or a blinding sun did not notice that it was really lit and working.

3. Significance of diagram: The triangle diagram is of value in two respects. First, it helps illustrate the four principal hearsay dangers. Second, it is a good tool for determining whether evidence is indeed hearsay. Techniques for using the diagram for this purpose will be developed more subsequently; for now, it is enough to note that evidence will be hearsay ***only if the trier of fact is asked to travel from point A to point B to point C*** in order to get to the fact to which the declaration is relevant. If the evidence is relevant before the trier of fact gets to point B (i.e., the point at which it is satisfied that the declarant truly held the belief which his declaration suggests he held), or if it is relevant before the fact-finder gets from point B to point C (i.e., before he concludes that that belief accurately reflects reality), there is no hearsay problem. See pp. 187-189 for examples of the diagram's use.

D. Dangers of out-of-court declaration: The four dangers summarized above (ambiguity, insincerity, erroneous memory, and inaccurate perception) would all exist even if O took the witness stand at the trial and made the same declaration, "The tail light was broken before the accident." However, the dangers are collectively (and probably individually) ***greater*** when the declaration is made out of court rather than from the witness stand.

1. Explanation: To understand the dangers of hearsay testimony, we must first consider the safeguards that are present when a witness testifies at trial about facts of which he has personal knowledge. Consider, for instance, the safeguards that surround O's testimony ***directly from the witness stand***, "The tail light was broken."

    a. Oath: First, O would be testifying ***under oath***. The oath "emphasizes the solemnity of the occasion and raises in potential liars the fear of perjury." L&S, p. 352.

b. Demeanor: Second, the jurors would be able to *observe O's demeanor* as he testifies. At least in theory, liars may appear shifty-eyed or nervous, or may squirm uncomfortably while telling their story.

   i. Criticism: However, there is little if any empirical evidence to support the view that observation of a witness's demeanor aids materially in determining whether she is telling the truth. *Id.*

c. Context: O will be making his statement in the *context of a larger story* (e.g., how he happened to notice that the tail light was broken; how he knows that it was still broken at the time of the accident, etc.). This context may help the jury evaluate the sincerity and accuracy of O's testimony.

d. Cross-examination: Most of all, O's testimony will be subject to *cross-examination* by the opposing lawyer. No technique known to jurisprudence is a better instrument for uncovering the truth.

2. **Hearsay contrasted:** Contrast this set of safeguards with the situation in which an out-of-court declaration is offered for the purpose of establishing the truth of the assertions made in that declaration. Where W testifies, "O said that the tail light was broken at the time of the accident," here's what the situation looks like:

a. No oath: O's statement is *not* made under *oath*, so at least to the extent that O was tempted to lie (and perhaps to the extent that he was merely being sloppy), his statement may be less accurate than had he been under oath.

b. Demeanor: The jury has *not* gotten a chance to *observe O's demeanor* while he made the remark.

c. Context: O is *not* telling his story as part of a *larger context* which the jury gets to hear. Probably the jury will get to hear only the one sentence that is most closely relevant ("The tail light was broken at the time of the accident"), and supporting clues to the accuracy or inaccuracy of O's statement will be lost.

d. Cross-examination: Most significantly, the adversary will have *no opportunity to cross-examine O, the absent declarant*. If O was telling an outright lie, there will be no opportunity for this lie to be exposed. Perhaps more importantly, if O was honestly mistaken, or his statement was slightly misleading or taken out of context, there will be no opportunity for the adversary to bring these facts to the jury's attention.

3. **Four dangers:** One way to assess the importance of cross-examination is to observe that where such examination is possible, all four of the potential dangers to the jury's correct evaluation of the factual assertion discussed above — ambiguity, *insincerity*, erroneous memory, and faulty perception — could be *exposed* by cross-examination, which by definition is not available in the hearsay situation. (Context, similarly, might help avoid each of these four dangers, but probably in a less direct way.)

a. Oath and demeanor: By contrast, oath and demeanor, even if present, would only help avoid the declarant's *insincerity*, not the other three potential dangers.

4. **Mistakes in transmittal:** Absence of oath, demeanor, context, and cross-examination all relate to the testimony of the out-of-court declarant. A *fifth difficulty* with hearsay testi-

mony relates to the testimony of the in-court witness who is repeating the out-of-court declaration. This is the danger of a ***mistake in transmittal***. While the usual safeguards (e.g., cross-examination) are available to make sure that the in-court witness is speaking accurately, these traditional safeguards are probably less effective where the in-court witness is repeating someone else's out-of-court statement than where more complex events are being described in court. L&S, p. 353.

> **Example:** Return to our example of the broken tail light (*supra*, p. 182). If W had actually witnessed the condition of the tail light, he would be telling a story that is somewhat complicated, with lots of surrounding detail and context. A small error in perception by W is unlikely to be conclusive. If, on the other hand, W is testifying about what O said, and W failed to hear the word "not" in O's statement, "The light was not broken at the time of the accident," the entire significance of O's statement will be distorted when W repeats it. Thus the risk of an inadvertent mistake in transmission by the in-court witness is probably greater when what is being described is someone else's statement rather than an actual event.

5. **Cross-examination:** Another reason why the in-court witness's testimony is less likely to be accurate when what is being recounted is someone else's statement rather than an actual event, is that ***cross-examination is less valuable.*** L&S, pp. 353-54.

> **Example:** Once again in our broken tail light example, consider the position of an adversary who wants to cross-examine W (the in-court witness). If W is describing the event itself as he witnessed it (e.g., his seeing the broken tail light), W will have to fit his story into a complicated fact pattern composed of evidence proved by other means (e.g., where W was on that day; what model the car was; what time the accident took place, etc.). If W's story doesn't fit, cross-examination can bring this fact out. If, by contrast, W is merely repeating O's statement, "The tail light was broken," W doesn't have to make the story fit with anything else; so cross-examination of W is largely useless as it relates to the underlying story — W can simply stubbornly repeat, "That's what O said." The lack of cross-examination is especially damaging where W is intentionally lying. *Id.*

II.   THE DEFINITION OF HEARSAY

A. **The problem generally:**   There is no single universally-accepted definition of hearsay. However, it is possible to state a common-law definition that squares with most decisions; after that, we will discuss the Federal Rule, which makes some modifications to the common-law one.

1. **Common-law definition:**   The best common-law definition of hearsay is probably the one with which we began this chapter: Hearsay is ***"a statement or assertive conduct which was made or occurred out of court and is offered in court to prove the truth of the facts asserted."*** M. Ladd, Cases on Evidence 384 (quoted in L&S, p. 356).

> **Note:** From here on, as a shorthand we'll generally use the word "statement" to include not only the term's conventional meaning of "declaration or remark," but also

to include nonverbal behavior that is intended as an assertion. (Such behavior is discussed *infra*, p. 196.)

    a. **Issues:** There are three types of issues raised by this common-law definition, each of which will be considered in turn below:

        i. **"Out of court":** What types of statements will be deemed to have occurred ***"out of court"***? See *infra*, p. 191.

        ii. **Truth:** When is a statement offered to prove "the ***truth*** of the facts asserted"? or, more precisely, what kinds of statements are ***not*** deemed to be offered for the truth of the facts asserted? See *infra*, p. 191.

        iii. **"Statement or assertive conduct":** What is included within the phrase "statement or assertive conduct"? More precisely, what is the difference between conduct that is ***"assertive"*** and that which is not? See *infra*, p. 199.

2. **Use of triangle:** The common-law definition can be tied into the testimonial triangle first presented on p. 183, *supra*, and reprinted in slightly different form here:

Figure 5-2

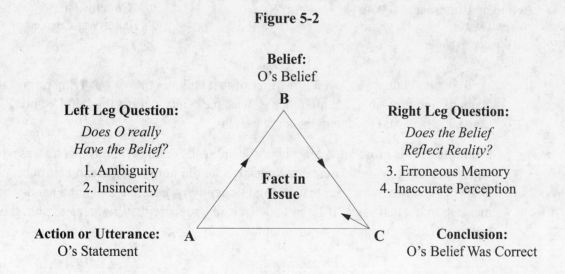

    a. **Must raise questions on both legs:** In the terms of this diagram, the statement of the out-of-court declarant (O) constitutes hearsay ***only if the inference that the proponent seeks to establish requires a "yes" answer to the questions raised by both legs.*** L&S, p. 359.

    Example 1: The issue is whether O is conscious after an accident. W testifies, "After the accident, I heard O say, 'I've been shot.'" The proponent of this testimony (the party who put W on the stand) is trying merely to establish that O was conscious. The inference which the proponent desires the trier of fact to make (that one who speaks must necessarily be conscious) can be reached by the factfinder without ever even getting to point B (that O believed his statement that he had been shot), let alone getting to point C (that O's belief that he had been shot was correct).

In diagrammatic terms, the trier of fact can go directly from point A to the center of the triangle, so neither the Left Leg questions nor the Right Leg questions require an affirmative answer:

Figure 5-3

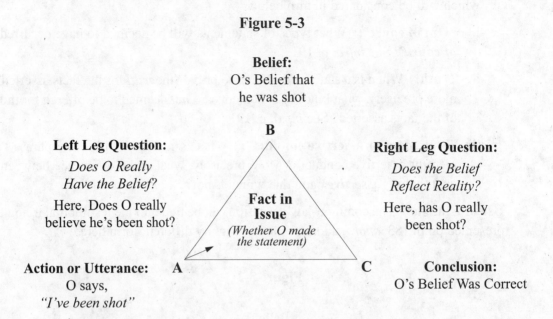

Belief:
O's Belief that
he was shot

Left Leg Question:
*Does O Really
Have the Belief?*
Here, Does O really
believe he's been shot?

Right Leg Question:
*Does the Belief
Reflect Reality?*
Here, has O really
been shot?

B

**Fact in
Issue**
*(Whether O made
the statement)*

Action or Utterance:
O says,
"I've been shot"   A

C

Conclusion:
O's Belief Was Correct

To put it another way, even if the trier of fact believes that O was lying or mistaken about having been shot, the inference is the same. Since neither the Left Leg nor Right Leg dangers exist, O's statement is not hearsay.

Example 2: O is prosecuted for robbery. He defends on the grounds that he was a hostage, and that he was threatened with death if he did not participate in the robbery. W, O's wife, testifies at the trial that during O's captivity, he smuggled out a hand-written message to her that said, "If I don't take part in a robbery they're going to pull, they'll kill me." This situation can be diagrammed as follows:

Figure 5-4

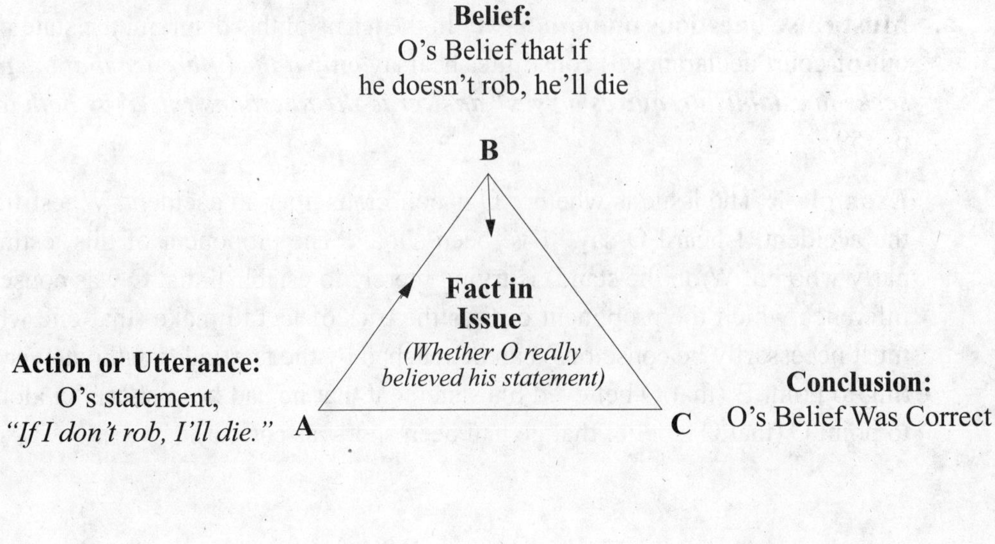

Belief:
O's Belief that if
he doesn't rob, he'll die

B

**Fact in
Issue**
*(Whether O really
believed his statement)*

Action or Utterance:
O's statement,
"If I don't rob, I'll die."   A

C

Conclusion:
O's Belief Was Correct

O, the proponent of this testimony, is merely trying to establish that O *believed* that he would be shot if he did not participate in the robbery, not that the captors would really have shot him. Therefore, to get to the desired inference, we have to travel the Left Leg ("Did O really believe that he would be shot?"), but not the Right Leg ("Was O's belief correct?"). Since the Right Leg question never arises, the statement is not hearsay.

Example 3: D is on trial for shooting O. In order to establish D's guilt, the prosecution offers the testimony of W, that when he found O lying in pool of blood, O said to him, "D shot me." Here is the appropriate diagram:

Figure 5-5

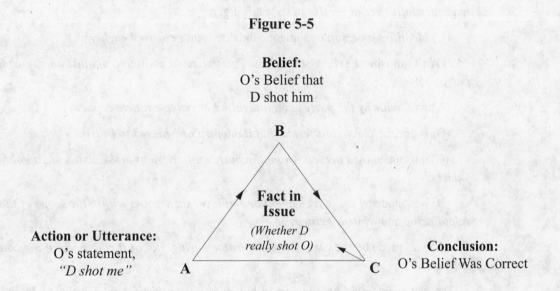

Because the prosecution is trying to use this testimony to directly establish D's guilt, it is asking the factfinder to make the following chain of inferences: because O said that D had shot him, O in fact believed that D shot him; a person who believes that another has shot him is probably correct in that belief. Thus to reach the inference that the prosecution desires it to reach, the trier of fact must travel to point B and then to point C, giving affirmative answers to both the Left Leg question and the Right Leg question. Therefore, the use of O's statement constitutes hearsay.

3. **Federal Rule:** The Federal Rule's definition of hearsay occurs in FRE 801. Since this provision is also in effect, in substantially identical form, in more than half the states, it is especially worthy of close scrutiny:

    [handwritten: FRE Def of Hearsay]

    "Rule 801. Definitions That Apply to This Article; Exclusions from Hearsay

    (a) Statement. "Statement" means a person's *oral assertion*, *written assertion*, or *non-verbal conduct*, if the person *intended it as an assertion*.

    (b) Declarant. "Declarant" means the *person* who *made the statement*.

    (c) Hearsay. "Hearsay" means a *statement* that:

    (1) the declarant *does not make while testifying at the current trial or hearing*; and

    (2) a party offers in evidence to *prove the truth of the matter asserted in the*

statement.

(d) Statements That Are Not Hearsay. A statement that meets the following conditions is *not hearsay*:

(1) A Declarant-Witness's Prior Statement. The declarant *testifies* and is *subject to cross-examination* about a prior statement, and the statement:

(A) is *inconsistent* with the declarant's testimony and was given *under penalty of perjury* at a *trial, hearing, or other proceeding* or in a *deposition*;

(B) is *consistent* with the declarant's testimony and is offered to *rebut an express or implied charge* that the declarant *recently fabricated it* or *acted from a recent improper influence or motive* in so testifying; or

(C) *identifies a person* as someone the declarant *perceived earlier.*

(2) An Opposing Party's Statement. The statement is offered *against an opposing party* and:

(A) was *made by the party* in an *individual or representative capacity*;

(B) is one the party *manifested that it adopted or believed to be true*;

(C) was made by *a person whom the party authorized* to *make a statement on the subject*;

(D) was made by the party's *agent or employee* on a matter *within the scope of that relationship* and *while it existed*; or

(E) was made by the party's *coconspirator during and in furtherance of the conspiracy.*

The statement *must be considered* but *does not by itself establish* the declarant's *authority* under (C); the *existence or scope of the relationship* under (D); or the *existence of the conspiracy* or participation in it under (E)."

a. **Difference from common-law rule:** The basic definition given in 801(c) is essentially identical to the common-law approach. To the extent that FRE 801 changes common-law principles, it does so through 801(a) and (d). These deviations will be considered in greater detail when the relevant common-law aspect is discussed. For now, here are the important departures:

i. **Non-assertive conduct:** Where non-verbal *conduct* that is *not intended as an assertion* is introduced to show a belief on the part of the actor, the traditional common-law approach was that this was hearsay. See the classic case of *Wright v. Doe d. Tatham*, discussed extensively *infra*, p. 199. FRE 801(a) by negative implication provides that non-verbal conduct that is not intended as an assertion will *not be hearsay.*

ii. **Prior inconsistent statements:** At common law, a witness's *prior inconsistent statement* is hearsay, and is therefore not admissible to prove the truth of the matter stated in the prior inconsistent statement (though it is admissible to impeach the witness's credibility). FRE 801(d)(1)(A) changes this by providing that the witness's prior inconsistent statement will not be hearsay, and is thus admissible for its truth, if the witness made it while testifying **under oath** in a previous **proceeding or deposition.** See the more detailed discussion *infra,* p. 309.

    iii. Prior consistent statement: At common law, a prior **consistent** statement by the witness is not admissible for its truth, although it is admissible for the limited purpose of rebutting the opposing party's claim that the witness was improperly influenced. FRE 801(d)(1)(B) makes such a statement non-hearsay (i.e., admissible for truth) where such a charge of recent fabrication or improper influence is made. (Observe that a consistent statement, unlike an inconsistent one, does not have to be made under an oath or in a proceeding.) See *infra,* p. 312.

    iv. Identification: Under the common-law definition, the fact that A has previously given an **eyewitness identification** of B is hearsay. FRE 801(d)(1)(C) makes such an identification non-hearsay, provided that the person who makes the identification is a witness at the trial. See *infra,* p. 313.

    v. Admissions: *Admissions* by a party-opponent are, at common law, treated as exceptions to the hearsay rule (which means that such admissions may be admitted for their truth). FRE 801(d)(2) makes such admissions non-hearsay rather than an exception to the hearsay rule. The distinction has little practical significance. S&R, p. 726. See *infra,* p. 217.

B. Statement made "out of court": What does it mean for a statement to be made *"out of court"*?

    1. Meaning: An "out-of-court" statement is any statement except one that is "made by witnesses during the trial while testifying before the trier of fact." L&S, p. 357. This means that the following statements will be deemed "out of court":

      a. Statement by non-witness: *any* oral or written statement by someone other than the at-trial witness; and

      b. Prior statements by witness: *prior statements* by the **at-trial witness**, where the prior statement was not made in the present trial before the trier of fact. Thus a witness's prior statement made in a **deposition** or in an **earlier trial**, or even when spoken in the judge's chambers during the present trial, are all "out of court," and so will constitute hearsay if the other aspects of the hearsay definition are met.

      Note: But don't forget that under FRE 801(d)(1), some prior statements by a witness that would be deemed "out of court" and thus hearsay under common-law rules, are treated as not being hearsay. See *infra,* p. 307.

C. "Truth of matter asserted": Most of the close questions involved in analyzing whether a statement is hearsay involve the requirement that the statement be "offered to prove the **truth of the matter asserted**" in the statement. Our discussion of this aspect of the definition will consist mainly of detailing the important uses of statements that are not for the truth of the matter asserted.

    1. Significance of assertions for truth: First, let's examine *why* only those statements offered to prove the truth of the matter asserted should fall within the hearsay rule. Recall the basic hearsay diagram (Figure 5-2, *supra,* p. 187). Only if the statement is offered to prove the truth of the matter asserted therein does the Right Leg question ("Does the declarant's belief reflect reality?") arise. Only then does the danger that the declarant mis-remembered the event, or inaccurately perceived it, matter.

a. Left Leg dangers: Of course, an out-of-court statement that is offered to prove that the declarant *believed* something, but not offered to prove that the belief was correct, would not satisfy the "truth of the matter asserted" requirement and would thus not be hearsay. Yet the use of such evidence at trial raises Left Leg dangers. (Remember that the Left Leg question is, "Did the declarant really have the belief that his statement suggests he did?") Thus the danger that the declarant's statement ambiguously reflected his belief, or that the declarant is lying, is present even though Right Leg questions are absent. Why, then, should the mere fact that the statement is not being introduced for its truth be enough to remove the statement from hearsay classification?

Example: D is charged with extorting money from O. A substantive element of the crime of extortion is that the victim must have believed that he would be harmed if he did not comply with the demand. The prosecution offers a statement made by O to his wife shortly after O paid money to D: "If I hadn't paid D, he would have shot off my kneecaps." Since the prosecution is not offering this statement for the truth of the matter asserted (that D would in fact have shot off O's kneecaps if he hadn't made the payment), the statement is not hearsay. Yet for the jury to reach the inference desired by the prosecutor (that O in fact believed that harm would befall him if he didn't pay up), the jury must answer the Left Leg question, "Did O really have the belief?" This inference in turn requires the jury to make a correct assessment that O was sincere in his statement. Yet O is not available for cross-examination, so his sincerity cannot be tested by this means. The situation thus seems to share the principal weakness of hearsay: the inability to test the out-of-court declaration by cross-examination.

i. Explanation: There is no totally convincing explanation of why a statement like the one in the above example should be treated as not hearsay. Two commentators give the following explanation: "Since the Right Leg problems are probably the most significant hearsay dangers, and since many hearsay exceptions are justified by only some support to one of the legs, it makes sense to classify statements used so as to eliminate the Right Leg dangers entirely as not hearsay." L&S, p. 358.

2. Approach: We now proceed to examine the various uses to which a statement may be put that do not constitute offering the statement for the truth of the matter asserted.

3. Verbal acts: A statement may be, by itself, an *operative fact* which gives rise to *legal consequences*. Such a statement, which is usually called a *"verbal act,"* is not offered for the truth of the matter asserted.

Example 1: D is prosecuted for running a brothel. W, a vice officer, testifies that while at the bar in D's establishment, he was propositioned by Pattie and Jean, who offered to have sex with him in return for money.

Held, the women's out-of-court statements (the offers to have sex for money) were not hearsay. These statements were "operative facts," since the mere fact that they were made is relevant to the charge, ***even if the statements were untrue*** (e.g., even if the women would not have performed sex for money). *Los Robles Motor Lodge, Inc.*

v. Dept. of Alcoholic Beverage Control, 246 Cal.App.2d 198 (Cal. Dist. Ct. App. 1966).

Example 2: D says to P, "You're a no-good thief who'd sell his mother for a dollar." P sues for slander, and testifies that D spoke these words. The speaking of the words was a "verbal act" which has legal effect (since it constitutes slander), ***regardless of the truth of the words spoken***. In fact, not only is P not offering the words to prove the truth of the matter asserted, he would be barred from recovery if the words *were* true.

Example 3: D says, "I'll sell you my house for $24,000." P says, "O.K., I accept." D refuses to perform, and P sues for breach of the oral contract. If P testifies that D spoke the words of the offer, this will not be hearsay — the words of the offer had an independent legal effect (they gave give rise to a power of acceptance in P) regardless of their "truth."

4. **Verbal parts of acts:** Closely related to "verbal acts" are situations in which a physical act is ambiguous, but words that accompany it resolve the ambiguity. In such situations, the accompanying words are called the ***"verbal part of the act,"*** and are not hearsay.

   Example: O hands money to X, a friend who happens to be mayor of the town in which they live. If the jury can't learn of the words that accompanied the transfer, it will not be clear whether the transfer was a loan, gift, or bribe. Therefore, O's statement to X at the time of the transfer, "This is to repay you for the money you lent me last year," will be non-hearsay, since it is the verbal part of the act of transferring the money.

   a. **Diagram:** Now let's analyze the "verbal part of the act" exception in terms of the triangles, Figures 5-3 and 5-4, *supra*, p. 188. In some situations, ***the mere utterance*** of the words (without regard to the declarant's intent) will be, under the applicable substantive law, enough to determine the nature of the act. In this situation, Figure 5-3 supplies the correct analysis. For instance, if, in the above example, X had been a bank teller rather than the mayor, applicable banking law would probably provide that O's payment should be treated as a loan repayment regardless of whether O secretly intended to be making a deposit to his own account — the mere speaking of the words gives rise to the legal effect.

   b. **Declarant's belief:** But in other situations, the applicable substantive law may make the declarant's ***belief*** the relevant question. For instance, if X is O's friend, and X claims that the money is a gift, O's accompanying statement will be looked at as evidence of O's underlying donative intent or lack of it. In this situation, the relevant diagram is Figure 3-4.

   c. **Significance:** It probably doesn't matter whether, in a particular case, the verbal part of an act is best analyzed under Figure 5-3 or Figure 5-4 — in either event, the verbal act should not be hearsay, since no complete trip around the triangle is required; that is, the truthfulness of the declarant's belief is irrelevant no matter which diagram is used. L&S, p. 360. But some authorities assert that the "verbal part of an act" exception only applies where the declarant's belief is irrelevant. See, e.g., McC, p. 430 (exception applies only where "under the substantive law the inquiry is directed only to objective manifestations rather than to the actual intent or other state of mind of the actor.") This limitation seems wrong, for the reason just stated.

5. **Effect on hearer or reader:**   If a statement is offered to show its *effect on the listener*, it will generally *not* be hearsay. This is so because the statement is not being offered to prove its truth, merely to prove the effect that that statement (whether true or false) had or should have had on the listener. This principle applies where the out-of-court declaration is offered to show that the listener (or reader) was *put on notice*, *had certain knowledge*, had a certain *emotion*, behaved reasonably or unreasonably, etc.

> **Example:** D, who is on trial for the murder of V, raises a self-defense claim. D presents W's testimony, "Just before the killing, I heard V say to D, 'I'm going to cut off your [expletive deleted] and shove it up your [expletive deleted.]'" This will not be hearsay. Why? The evidence is not being offered for the truth of the assertion (that V would really have done this to D), but rather to show that D probably had an actual, and reasonable, fear for his own safety. Cf. L&S, pp. 360-61.

   a. **Notice:**   Statements admitted to show the effect on the hearer are often admitted in negligence cases, where the issue is whether the hearer or reader was on *notice* of a dangerous condition.

   > **Example:** Slip-and-fall case, in which P fell on a piece of sidewalk that D, a property owner, was required to use reasonable care to maintain. P claims the sidewalk had a pothole that D knew of and should have fixed. P offers testimony by W that the day before P's accident, W heard X tell D, "You've got a pothole on your sidewalk." This is admissible for the non-hearsay purpose of showing that D was on notice of a potential problem. (It's not admissible for the hearsay purpose of showing that there actually was a pothole.)

   > **Note:** Of course, particular evidence may have both a hearsay and a non-hearsay purpose. The above example illustrates this. In this situation, all the objecting party can do is to ask for a *limiting instruction*, by which the jury is told to consider the evidence only for the non-hearsay purpose.

   b. **Emotion:**   Out-of-court statements may be introduced to show that they produced a certain *emotion* in the hearer or reader.

   > **Example:** P is injured when she slips in the lobby of D's hotel. She suffers a repeatedly collapsed lung, and sues for pain and suffering, including suffering from the fact that she is afraid to pursue many activities that she has formerly enjoyed. She testifies that X, her doctor, has "told me that I would have to live with myself and to be careful never to strain myself."

   > *Held*, the doctor's statement was not hearsay, because "it is well-settled that evidence of an out-of-court statement to show its effect upon the mental attitude of the person who hears it is properly admissible." The statement was not offered to show the accuracy of the doctor's diagnosis, but only to show the state of fear it introduced in P's mind. *194th St. Hotel Corp. v. Hopf*, 383 So.2d 739 (Fla.App. 1980).

   c. **Diagram:**   In all of the above situations involving a statement's effect on the listener or reader, the relevant diagram is Figure 5-3, *supra*, p. 188. That is, we never even reach the issue of the declarant's belief in the truth of his statement — all that matters is that the statement was made (and that the other party to it responded in a certain way). The situation is thus especially clearly non-hearsay, since neither Left Leg nor Right Leg problems arise.

d. Account of arresting officer: A more troubling situation arises when, in a criminal prosecution, the ***arresting officer describes how he came to make the arrest.*** The officer may recite all kinds of out-of-court declarations that he heard or read, and that led him to suspect D of the crime. (*Example:* "I kept D under surveillance because I'd been told that he was a drug smuggler.") Strictly speaking, this is not hearsay, because the prosecution is merely putting the arrest in context, a use to which the actual truth of the out-of-court declarations are irrelevant. But use of the statements may be very unfair to the defense, since the statements are likely to be used by the jury for purposes that are clearly hearsay (i.e., the jury is likely to assume that the statements implicating D in the crime and leading to his arrest are evidence of his guilt). Therefore, some courts have labelled it hearsay.

6. Declarant's state of mind: Statements introduced to show the ***state of mind*** of the ***declarant*** are, similarly, not barred by the hearsay rule. As with the statements discussed immediately above concerning the hearer's or reader's state of mind, a statement offered to show the declarant's state of mind is not offered to prove "the truth of the matter asserted," i.e., the truth of the declarant's statement.

a. Knowledge: Most frequently, such statements are introduced to show the declarant's ***knowledge*** of some matter, as manifested by his statement.

Example: P, a pedestrian, is hurt when D runs him over. P claims that D was negligent in not having his brakes checked after he knew that there was a problem. P introduces a statement made by D to X just before the accident: "I need to get my brakes checked; they don't seem to have been working too well recently."

Because the state of D's knowledge is in issue in the suit, D's statement to X will not be hearsay — it is offered to show the state of D's knowledge, not to show that the brakes were in fact defective at the time of the statement. (On the other hand, P will have to come up with some independent evidence that the brakes were in fact defective at the time of the accident in order to withstand a directed verdict motion by D. All of this ignores the exception to the hearsay rule for admissions by a party; see *infra*, p. 215.)

i. Knowledge relevant to other issue: In the above example, the issue of the declarant's knowledge was itself an issue in the case. In other situations, knowledge may not be an actual issue, but it may be a fact tending to resolve some other issue in the case. Here, too, the statement is not hearsay, because it merely shows something about the declarant's state of mind (the possession of knowledge), and is not offered for the purpose of proving the statement's truth.

Example: D is accused of having enticed O, a young girl, to come to his room and of then having sexually assaulted her. The prosecution seeks to introduce O's out-of-court statement describing the room and its contents, in order to show that O was in the room. Other evidence independently establishes that the room and its furnishings exactly match O's description of them.

   Held, O's out-of-court description is not hearsay, because it is not offered for the truth of the matter asserted (what the room really looked like), but rather to show that O knew what the room looked like, and therefore, by inference, that she must have been in it. *Bridges v. State*, 19 N.W.2d 529 (Wisc. 1945).

   b.   Other states of mind: Like knowledge, other states of mind of the declarant can be shown by her statement, without violating the hearsay rule.

   i.   Sanity: For instance, the declarant's *sanity* may be shown by his statements.

   ii.   Fear: Similarly, a declarant's statement may be used to show that he felt a certain *emotion*, such as *fear*.

   Example: In a custody fight between W and H for their daughter, Tracey, H tries to show that he should be given custody because W's paramour, Ray, is a violent criminal who has probably murdered H and W's other child, James. During the trial of Ray for this murder (which ended in a hung jury), Tracey was placed in a foster home. H now offers the testimony of the foster mother that when she told Tracey that her mother and Ray had gotten married, Tracey started crying and said, "He killed my brother and he'll kill my Mommie too." W objects to this statement as hearsay.

   Held, not hearsay. Tracey's out-of-court declaration was not admitted to prove the truth of the assertion she made (that Ray killed her brother), but "merely to indirectly and inferentially show [Tracey's] mental state . . . at the time[.]" *Betts v. Betts*, 473 P.2d 403 (Wash. 1970).

7.   Impeachment: When a witness tells a story at trial, the opposing lawyer will often confront him with a previous out-of-court statement, in which the witness told a different story. Such an *impeachment* use of an out-of-court statement is not hearsay, because the out-of-court statement is introduced not for the purpose of showing that it (rather than the in-court testimony) contains the truth, but rather, to suggest that a witness who changes his story is not credible. Impeachment of a witness by use of his prior inconsistent statements is discussed further, both *infra*, p. 308 and more generally *supra*, p. 137, as part of the treatment of cross-examination.

D.   Statements and conduct: Recall that a hearsay problem exists only where there has been an out-of-court *"statement."* (See *supra*, p. 186.) What is a "statement" for hearsay purposes?

1.   Open question: The most common type of "statement" for hearsay purposes is, in the words of FRE 801(a), a person's *"oral assertion* [or] *written assertion."* But more difficult problems are hinted at by the second part of FRE 801(a)'s definition: A statement can also consist of a person's *"nonverbal conduct*, if the person intended it as an assertion." There are several significant issues relating to the meaning of "statement":

   [1] What kind of *conduct* is likely to be "intended . . . as an *assertion*"?

   [2] When can *silence* constitute hearsay?

   [3] What is the proper treatment of *non-assertive conduct*? and

[4] What about intended assertions that *imply additional facts or assertions*?

We will treat each of these situations in some detail now.

2. **Assertive conduct:**   The most easily understood of these categories is *assertive conduct*. There are many illustrations of conduct that, although nonverbal, is nonetheless intended as an assertion. Such conduct is universally recognized as capable of being hearsay, since its use presents the same dangers as do the use of verbal assertions.

    > **Example:** O, a robbery victim, is hospitalized with her injuries. When she is shown a series of "mug shots" and asked whether she recognizes any of them as being the perpetrator, she pulls D's photo out of the stack and hands it to the detective. If the detective testifies in court that O picked out the photo of D, this will clearly be hearsay even though O made no verbal statement. O's picking out of the photo and handing it to the detective was intended by her to be the equivalent of an assertion, "This is the photo of the man who robbed me." The same hearsay dangers (e.g., that O's memory or perception are flawed, or that she is insincere) are present whether O picks out the photo silently, or points to it saying, "That's the one."

3. **Silence:**   A person's *silence* may in some situations lead to the reasonable inference that a particular fact, X, is true. Usually the inference goes like this: If X were not the case, the person would have said something; therefore, by the person's silence we may deduce that X is so. In this situation, is evidence of the person's silence, when offered to prove X, barred by the hearsay rule? The issue arises most frequently in two contexts: (1) the *absence of complaints* by others to prove that a danger or defect did not exist; and (2) silence by a person *accused* of something, to prove that the person was guilty. In each context, the courts are split.

    a. **Absence of complaints:**   Suppose that P claims to have been injured by some defect or danger caused by D. This might be allegedly poisonous food served by D to P; a slippery floor in D's store fallen on by P; or any other situation in which D's negligence or sale of a defective product is claimed to have caused injury to P. D will frequently try to make at trial the argument familiar to every disgruntled consumer: "We've never had any complaints about this from anybody else." Most courts will *allow* the absence of complaints into evidence.

        Example: P is a passenger on a train operated by D railroad. The car she is riding in is detached and stands for four hours in a railroad yard awaiting a connection. P, who suffers from a circulatory ailment, claims that during this wait the car became too cold for her, and that she suffered injury. D offers the testimony of the porter in P's car that none of the eleven other passengers in that car at the time complained about the cold.

        Held, the porter's testimony should have been admitted. If these other passengers had been cold, at least one of them would probably have complained to the porter; since all faced the same temperature conditions as P, it was reasonable to assume that neither they nor she actually suffered from cold. *Silver v. New York Central R.R.*, 105 N.E.2d 923 (Mass. 1952).

        i. **Hearsay argument:**   Notwithstanding the result in *Silver*, the plaintiff who wants to keep out evidence of others' silence can make a plausible-sounding hearsay argument. He can point out that the others' silence is the functional equivalent of their statement, "Everything is O.K." Since the defendant is offering the evidence of silence precisely to prove that everything was indeed O.K., this use of silence is for proof of the truth of the matter asserted, and is thus arguably hearsay.

    ii. No assertion intended: However, most modern courts (as well as the Federal Rules — see FRE 801(a)) treat a person's non-verbal conduct as being a "statement" only if it was *intended* by the person as an *assertion*. It is doubtful whether a person who remains silent because he does not suffer a particular ill consequence is intending to assert, "Everything's O.K." The other passengers in *Silver*, for instance, were almost certainly not reciting to themselves, or intending to say to the porter, "I'm not feeling cold" — it's unlikely that they focused on the issue of whether they were cold at all. Therefore, they don't seem to have intended to make any assertion, and under the modern (and Federal Rule) approach *their silence should not be treated as hearsay.* Thus the result in *Silver* would be followed by most courts today. McC, p. 437.

  b. Silence in face of accusation: A more troublesome situation is posed by a person's silence in the face of an *accusation against him*, where that silence is later offered to prove that the accusation was true.

    Example: W, a police officer, sees D smoking a cigarette that, in W's judgement, looks and smells like marijuana. As W approaches, D throws the cigarette in the street. W picks up the cigarette, determines that it seems to be marijuana, and says, "This is pot that you were just smoking, isn't it?" D remains silent. At trial, W testifies to these facts, including the fact of D's silence at the accusation. Putting aside any issue as to whether this testimony violates D's *Miranda* rights, can D keep the fact of his silence out of evidence on the grounds of hearsay? The correct result is not clear.

    i. Countervailing arguments: On these facts, D can argue that the prosecution's very theory for wanting to introduce the evidence is the following syllogism: An innocent person in D's situation would have protested his innocence; therefore, D's silence proves that he believed he was guilty, and that belief means that he was indeed guilty. Thus, D can argue, the prosecution is claiming that D's silence amounts to an assertion of his guilt, used to prove the truth of the matter asserted (the guilt). Furthermore, D can argue, the basic hearsay dangers are present; most spectacularly, there is an extreme risk of *ambiguity*, since D's silence may have nothing to do with consciousness of guilt — for instance, he may just have been applying a reasonable or unreasonable personal policy that it is never wise to speak to the cops.

    ii. Favoring admission: But the prosecution here can argue that D, by his silence, has not intended to assert anything at all. His silence is being offered not as a statement, but merely as non-assertive conduct that is circumstantial evidence of guilt.

    iii. Probable result: Most courts in this situation have held that the person objecting to the evidence has the better of the arguments, and have therefore treated the evidence as *hearsay*. L&S, p. 365. But this is usually an empty victory — even if the silence is hearsay, one of the exceptions to the hearsay rule will usually be available; most commonly, the exception for ***admissions*** by a party (*infra*, p. 215) will apply. This would be the result, for instance, on the facts of our marijuana example.

4. Non-assertive conduct: We've already suggested that the modern view is that nonverbal conduct will not be treated as a "statement" unless it was intended by the actor as an assertion. However, this was not the traditional rule; in fact, the contrary rule — that nonverbal conduct implying a fact is hearsay if offered to prove that fact, even if no assertion was intended — was established in perhaps the most famous evidence case of all time, ***Wright v. Doe d. Tatham***, 112 Eng. Rep. 488 (House of Lords 1837).

   a. *Wright v. Doe:* Because of *Wright v. Doe*'s historical importance (and the fascinating intellectual issue it presents), we consider it in detail:

   i. Facts of *Wright*: A testator, John Marsden, left his estate to his steward, one Wright. Tatham, Marsden's legal heir, contested the will, claiming that Marsden was mentally incompetent when he wrote it. In support of the will, Wright offered in evidence several letters that had been written to the testator by persons no longer living. The theory behind this offer was that the tone of the letters suggested that the authors thought they were corresponding with a man of ordinary intelligence and sanity; from their belief in Marsden's mental competence, it could be inferred that he was in fact competent when he wrote the will.

   ii. Holding: In an initial trial, the letters were admitted and the will sustained; in a retrial after appeal, the letters were excluded and the will was voided. The litigation was finally ended by the House of Lords, which ruled the letters ***inadmissible***, on the theory that they amounted to a ***hearsay declaration of Marsden's sanity***, offered to prove that sanity.

   iii. Parke's summary: The rationale for this result was explained by Baron Parke: "[P]roof of a particular fact, which is not of itself a matter in issue, but which is relevant only as implying a statement or opinion of a third person on the matter in issue, is inadmissible in all cases where such a statement or opinion not on oath would be of itself inadmissible. . . . The letters, which are offered only to prove the competence of the testator . . . were properly rejected, as the mere statement or opinion of the writer would certainly have been inadmissible."

   iv. Analogue: Baron Parke provided a number of hypothetical examples illustrating the Lords' view that a statement implied by conduct should be treated the same as an actual statement for hearsay purposes. For instance, he suggested, consider the conduct of a sea captain who examines every part of his vessel, and then loads it with his family for a trip. If this conduct is offered to prove that the vessel was seaworthy at the start of the voyage, it should be excluded on hearsay grounds. The proponent of the evidence is asking the fact-finder to reason as follows: (a) The fact that the captain boarded the ship with his family indicates that he believed the vessel was seaworthy; and (b) When a captain, after inspection, believes that a vessel is seaworthy, it probably is. In the view of Parke (and the House of Lords), this evidence is functionally no different from the captain's out-of-court statement, made immediately after his inspection, "This vessel seems to be seaworthy" — clearly inadmissible hearsay.

b. State of the law: In the years after *Wright*, most American courts faced with the issue of "statements implied from conduct" failed even to notice that there was a potential hearsay problem. Of those that did notice the problem, probably most agreed with the conclusion in *Wright* that such evidence is hearsay. L&S, p. 367.

c. Modern view: But there has clearly been a shift, begun even before the enactment of the Federal Rules. Modern courts have tended to attach great importance to the fact that in the "statement implied from conduct" situation, there is a key difference from the explicit verbal assertion of a fact: In the implied statement situation, there is ***no intent*** to make an assertion.

    i. Federal Rules: Thus the Federal Rules, in FRE 801(a), limit the meaning of "statement" to "a person's oral ***assertion***, written ***assertion***, or nonverbal conduct, if the person ***intended it as an assertion***." In other words, only "assertions" can be statements, and thus hearsay.

    ii. How *Wright* would come out under Federal Rules: The facts of *Wright* do not seem to fall within FRE 801(a). The Federal Rules do not define "assertion," but one court has held that the term means "a forceful or positive declaration." *U.S. v. Zenni*, 492 F.Supp. 464 (E.D.Ky. 1980), discussed *infra*, p. 200. The letters in *Wright* were clearly verbal, but they were not "assertions" under this definition, at least not assertions of the matter whose truth was to be proven, i.e., the testator's sanity. (One of the letters urges the testator to have his attorney meet with the writer's attorney to discuss some business matters; others invite him to come to certain meetings to discuss public business; a letter from a cousin who had emigrated to America discusses conditions there. McC, p. 433.) In none of these letters did the writer make a "forceful or positive declaration" of the testator's sanity. Nor was the "nonverbal conduct" of any of them (e.g., the mere act of writing the letter, without reference to its contents) intended by them as an assertion of Marsden's sanity. So it seems pretty clear that under the Federal Rules, the letters would have been ***admitted***, and Wright would have probably won his case.

d. Illustration of modern approach: The operation of the Federal Rules' modern approach to non-assertive conduct is illustrated by the following example.

Example: Government agents search D's premises, under a search warrant which allows them to search for evidence of bookmaking activity. While there, the agents answer D's telephone several times. The unknown callers attempt to place bets on various sports events. At D's trial, the prosecution attempts to introduce evidence of these calls to show that the callers believed that the premises were used in betting operations, and thereby prove that the premises were in fact so used. D contends that the calls are hearsay when used for this purpose.

Held, the evidence is admissible. Under FRE 801(a), verbal or nonverbal conduct is a "statement" only if it is intended as an "assertion." "Assertion" is not defined in the Rules, but "has the connotation of a forceful or positive declaration." Consequently, "the effect of the definition of 'statement' is to exclude from the operation of the hearsay rule all evidence of conduct, verbal or nonverbal, not intended as an assertion. The key to the definition is that nothing is an assertion unless intended to be one." (Quoting the Advisory Committee Note to FRE 801.) The utterances of the bettors telephoning in their bets were "nonassertive verbal conduct," offered as relevant for any proposition that could be inferred from them, i.e., that bets could be placed at the premises. "The language is not an assertion on its face, and it is obvious these persons did not intend to make an assertion about the fact sought to be proved or anything else." Since FRE 801(a) "removes implied assertions from the definition of 'statement' and consequently from the operation of the hearsay rule," the offered evidence, as an implied assertion, is excluded from operation of the hearsay rule and is admissible. *U.S. v. Zenni*, 492 F.Supp. 464 (E.D.Ky. 1980).

   i. Clarification: When FRE 801(a) applies to nonverbal conduct, its application is quite clear — evidence of such conduct can never be barred by the hearsay rule, except in those relatively rare instances (e.g., pointing a suspect out from a lineup) where the conduct is intended as an assertion. But where what is involved is an oral or written *utterance*, 801(a) is trickier. The utterance can fall within the hearsay rule only if it is an "assertion." The Federal Rules don't define "assertion," but the *Zenni* court seems correct in defining this to mean "a forceful or positive declaration." Putting it another way, an utterance must, in order to be an assertion, be offered with the ***intent to state that some factual proposition is true.*** The bettors who were placing their bets were not intending to make a factual statement about whether the premises were to be used for betting, so their words were not an "assertion."

E. Assertions not offered to prove truth of matter asserted: Our discussion of the "implied assertion" problem and *Wright v. Tatham* has focused on nonassertive conduct. A similar problem is faced when an ***assertion*** (or assertive conduct) is offered to prove not the truth of what is asserted, but the truth of some factual proposition that is ***inferred from the matter directly asserted.***

   Example: *Wright v. Tatham* itself actually falls into this category of "assertions inferred from other assertions." The letters to the testator were, at least to some extent, clearly assertive — the letter from the cousin in America, for instance, clearly contained positive declarations about the status of life in America. Yet, the letter from the cousin was not offered to prove conditions in America; it was offered to prove a proposition that could be inferred from the assertion, namely, that the writer thought the recipient was sane.

1. "Two-step inference": This class of situations is sometimes said to involve the problem of the *"two-step inference"*: to analyze what's going on, we need to perform a two-step, by jumping from the matter directly asserted (e.g., in *Wright v. Tatham*, "The weather's drier here in America") to a second proposition, where the second proposition (e.g., that the letter-writer thinks the recipient is sane) is what the proponent is trying to prove.

2. Treatment: The modern view is to treat "assertions inferred from other assertions" the same way as "assertions inferred from nonassertive conduct." That is, ***assertions inferred from other assertions are not barred by the hearsay rule.*** FRE 801 seems to carry this out by its definition of "hearsay" in subsection (c) — hearsay is a statement "a party offers in evidence to prove the truth of the ***matter asserted in the statement***." The Advisory Committee's Note to 801(a), after describing the reasons for not including nonassertive conduct within the definition of hearsay, goes on to say that "similar considerations govern nonassertive verbal conduct and verbal conduct which is assertive but offered as a basis for inferring ***something other than the matter asserted***, also excluded from the definition of hearsay by the language of subdivision (c)." Again, this language seems to means that two-step inferences aren't intended by the drafters to be hearsay.

a. **Difficulty:** However, where an utterance that is intended to be an assertion is used to infer some other assertion, ***a significant hearsay danger*** is present that is not present in the case of nonassertive conduct that is used to imply an assertion: the danger of ***insincerity*** by the speaker.

   Example: When a person raises his umbrella and carries it over his head (nonassertive nonverbal conduct), the use of this fact to show that it was probably raining does not involve any danger of that person's insincerity — he is not trying to communicate anything, so there is no danger of lies. Compare this with the cousin writing from America in *Wright v. Tatham*; if he says, "You would love it in America, cousin, because the weather is drier and warmer than in England," he is making an assertion. Use of this statement to prove that he thought the recipient was sane runs the traditional hearsay risk of declarant's insincerity — the letter writer may be ***lying*** for some reason we don't know anything about (e.g., to induce his cousin to come to America).

b. **Balancing:** However, on balance, the risk of insincerity in this "utterance implying some other fact" context is usually thought to be relatively small.

c. **L&S summary:** L&S, p. 369, suggest that the test should be as follows: "An out-of-court statement, offered not for its literal truth but for the truth of some proposition therein implied, should be considered hearsay so long as the validity of the desired implication depends on the existence and accuracy of a belief arguably implied by the intended statement." This test seems to be the equivalent of asking, "At the time he made his declaration, was the declarant thinking about the proposition that his statement is now being used to prove?" If the answer is "yes," the statement can be hearsay; if "no," the statement cannot be.

3. **Circumstantial evidence:** Two-step problems frequently arise where the proponent presents an out-of-court assertion on the way to trying to present ***circumstantial evidence*** about the ***nature of a place or item***, the existence of a ***relationship*** between people, the nature of an ***activity***, and the like. Generally, courts ***ignore the hearsay problem*** in this situation.

a. **"Mechanical traces":** One common instance of this problem has been called the ***"mechanical trace"*** situation: the ***presence of an item*** (containing an assertion) on or in a person, thing or premises can support an inference about the person, thing or premises.

   Example: A suitcase that is seized and found to contain narcotics bears the name tag "John Jones." Suppose the tag on the suitcase is introduced by the prosecution to support merely the inference that Jones has something to do with the narcotics (not that he's necessarily their owner). There's nonetheless at least a potential hearsay danger: we have to believe that the assertion on the tag (an assertion that "this suitcase belongs to John Jones") is true, before we can get to the ultimate inferred fact (that Jones also has something to do with the suitcase's contents). There's a risk that the declarant (the person who wrote out the tag and put it on the suitcase) is being insincere; perhaps someone's trying to frame John Jones, for instance. Yet many — though not all — courts would accept this as non-hearsay under FRE 801, on the theory that the tag is not being introduced to show its literal truth (suitcase ownership), but merely some inferred fact (when a person owns a suitcase, he probably has some involvement with the contents of that suitcase). See generally, Graham, §6706, pp. 412-13.

Other Examples:

❏ *Automobile license plates* (e.g., W testifies in at a grand jury, "I saw that the getaway car had license plate 'ABC123', " offered at trial to prove that the person to whom that plate is registered was somehow involved with the crime and the getaway);

❏ *Postmarks on envelopes* (e.g., envelope with postmark saying "Missoula," found in D's apartment, offered to show that D was acquainted with someone from Missoula);

❏ *Receipts from commercial transactions* (e.g., hotel receipt, offered to show that person whose name is on receipt stayed at that hotel on the night stated on the receipt).

In all of these situations, probably most courts would *allow* the evidence as non-hearsay, because it's being offered not principally to prove that the assertion on the physical document is correct (e.g., not offered to show that postmarked letter was in fact sent from Missoula), but to prove some further inference (e.g., that a person receiving a letter postmarked "Missoula" probably knows someone in Missoula).

b. **Character of premises:** Similarly, two-step-inference problems arise where a document found at a premises is offered to prove, circumstantially, the *character or use of the premises*. This happens most often in cases involving drugs, gambling or prostitution. Again, most courts, especially those applying the FRE, *allow* the evidence as non-hearsay where what's being proved is not the literal truth of the document, but some *inference* from the existence and location of the document.

Example: D, whose name is Suarez, is charged with distributing cocaine. In an apartment rented to "Rick Suarez" and known to have been frequented by D, the police find a "pay/owe sheet"; this sheet is offered by the prosecution. The sheet appears to record payments and debts from drug transactions, but no one testifies about who wrote it or precisely what each item means. The prosecution's purpose in offering the sheet is to establish that an apartment associated with D was used for transactions involving narcotics. D asserts that the sheet is inadmissible hearsay.

Held, the sheet is not hearsay. It's not being offered to show its literal truth — that so-and-so owes such-and-such amount for drugs. Instead, it's being offered merely to show the ***character of the premises*** in which it was found. Therefore, it's not hearsay under FRE 801. (Nor was the government required to prove the identity of the author — the authentication requirement (see *infra*, p. 477) was satisfied by proof that the document was found in an apartment associated with D.) *U.S. v. Jaramillo-Suarez*, 950 F.2d 1378 (9th Cir. 1991).

F.   Other hearsay problems: We turn now to several miscellaneous problems that arise in attempting to define hearsay.

1.   **Lack of first-hand knowledge:**   The rule against hearsay is sometimes confused with the rule disallowing testimony of facts not based upon the witness's ***first-hand knowledge*** (discussed *infra*, p. 515). The policy behind the two rules is similar, but they apply in differing circumstances.

> **Example:** Suppose that the witness, W, says, "The car that hit P was a red Volvo." If from other testimony by W it is clear that W was not present during the accident, the proper objection is, "The witness is not testifying from personal knowledge," not an objection based on hearsay. This is true even if the factfinder can reasonably infer that W has received his information from something that P told him.
>
> Now, assume that W testifies, "P told me that the car that hit him was a red Volvo." Here, the correct objection is hearsay — W is certainly testifying to something within his own first-hand experience (since he personally experienced P's declaration), but his testimony is the recitation of someone else's out-of-court declaration, offered to prove the truth of that declaration.

   a.   **Resemblance:**   Observe that the two rules are supported by comparable rationales. Each stems from the belief that the search for truth requires cross-examination of the person with the most direct knowledge of the fact offered as proof.

   b.   **Confusion:**   Courts, however, have not always carefully distinguished between the two types of objections. When the witness's statement literally sounds as if it comes from the witness's own knowledge, but it is clear from context that the statement is really based upon a declaration made to the witness by an out-of-court declarant, a hearsay objection is not unreasonable — it is an objection against hearsay from an anonymous informant, and the courts have sometimes so treated it.

2.   **"Not offered in presence of party":**   A lawyer will sometimes object to an out-of-court statement on the grounds that it was ***"not made in the presence of the party against whom it is offered."*** This is, as a general rule, ***not a valid objection***; rather, it is a "remarkably persistent bit of courthouse folklore." McC, p. 439.

   a.   **Significance:**   There are only a few situations in which the presence of the party against whom the statement is offered makes a difference. One is where a statement spoken in a party's presence is relied on to charge him with ***notice*** of some fact mentioned in the statement. (See *supra*, p. 194.) Another is where the party's silent failure to deny a statement (usually an accusation against him) is introduced to show that the party ***acquiesced*** in the statement. (*Supra*, p. 197.) *Id.*

3.   **Multiple hearsay:**   An out-of-court declaration may quote or paraphrase another out-of-court declaration. If each of the declarations is offered to prove the truth of the matter

asserted, the situation will amount to ***"double hearsay"*** or "hearsay on hearsay." (Indeed, three or more declarations, each referring to one of the others, may be involved. This is usually called ***"multiple hearsay."***)

a. **Rule:** In this double or multiple hearsay situation, the rule is the obvious one: The evidence will be inadmissible if ***any*** of the declarations are hearsay that does not fall within an exception. If both or all are covered by an exception, the package is admissible.

b. **Written report of oral statement:** The problem most frequently arises where a party wants to admit a ***written report*** of someone's ***oral out-of-court statement.***

Example: In a negligence suit arising out of a car accident, P seeks to introduce a report written by W, an employee of D's insurance company. In the report, W states, "D told me that at the time of the collision, he was traveling at 65 miles per hour." P offers the report to show that D was speeding and therefore negligent.

The proper analysis is as follows: First, we look at the report to see if it is hearsay. It is hearsay because it is an out-of-court declaration by W, offered for its truth (namely, what D told W). If there is no applicable exception, we need look no further — the report is not admissible. Here, however, the report would probably be admissible under the business records exception. (See *infra*, p. 249.) We now look at the incorporated statement, i.e., D's statement to W. This is hearsay since it, too, is being offered for its truth, namely, that D was speeding. Again, if there is no applicable exception, the whole report must be excluded. But the exception for admissions by a party would probably apply. Assuming that each statement falls within some exception to the hearsay rule, the report will be admitted. See L&S, p. 370.

c. **Federal Rule:** FRE 805 follows the approach outlined above: "Hearsay included within hearsay is not excluded under the hearsay rule if each part of the combined statements conforms with an exception to the hearsay rule provided in these rules."

4. **"Statements" by machines or animals:** The hearsay rule applies only to out-of-court declarations that are ***made by human beings.*** This proposition sounds self-evident, but it is not as obvious as it seems. A number of cases have involved out-of-court "statements" made by ***machines*** or ***animals***, in which serious hearsay objections were raised; however, the courts have all but universally rejected such arguments.

a. **Machines:** The "hearsay by machine" objection can be raised whenever a party seeks to introduce in court a ***measurement*** or other reading given by a machine. In such a situation, it can be plausibly argued that the machine has "spoken," and that that "statement" constitutes an out-of-court "declaration," offered for the truth of the matter asserted. But, as noted, such efforts have almost always failed.

Example: D is charged with speeding (40 mph in a 30 mph zone). W, the arresting police officer, testifies that he knew D was speeding because he used an electric timer. The timer is a specialized device that includes two tubes placed on the street, one at the start of a 132-foot zone and the other at its end; the device measures the time that a car takes to get from one tube to the other, and then indicates on a clock face how many miles per hour the car must have been going. D objects on the grounds of hearsay, claiming that in effect the readings of the timer were an out-of-court declaration.

Held, there is no hearsay. "Evidence is called hearsay when its probative force depends . . . on the competency and credibility of some person other than the witness by whom it is sought to be produced. . . . [Here,] the evidence as to the results obtained by the witness is not dependent on the perception, memory, and sincerity of an absent declarant." If D's objection had merit, evidence of measurements made by the use of scientific instruments would never be admissible; for instance, a doctor would not be permitted to testify as to the results heard through a stethoscope. *City of Webster Groves v. Quick*, 323 S.W.2d 386 (St. Louis Ct. App., Mo. 1959).

i.   **Rationale:** As the *Webster Groves* case indicates, "declarations" that emanate from a machine are not regarded as the kind of "statement" to which the hearsay rule applies. This is an entirely sensible result — the principal hearsay dangers relate to problems of memory, perception, and sincerity on the part of the absent declarant, and it is not reasonable to ascribe these peculiarly human frailties to a machine. In any event, the purpose of the hearsay rule is to bring the out-of-court declarant into court where he can repeat the same factual assertion and be cross-examined about it. One cannot bring the machine into court and cross-examine it (although one can demonstrate it; see *infra*, p. 504).

ii. **Foundation for evidence:** On the other hand, a machine may emit *incorrect information*, either because it is fed incorrect data (analogous to problems of perception) or because it processes the data in a flawed manner (analogous to faulty memory or insincerity). Therefore, evidence about data produced from a machine will only be accepted if a proper foundation (see *infra*, p. 472) is laid for it; this foundation must include information by which the court can conclude that the machine was accurate. Thus in the *Webster Groves* electric timer situation (or its more modern equivalent, radar detection), the prosecution will bear the burden of demonstrating that the device was of a sort that is scientifically accepted as accurate; that the device was properly calibrated and maintained; that the person using it was properly trained, etc.

b. **Retrieval by machine:** A different problem is presented where a machine is used not to "create" a factual proposition (as in *Webster Groves*) but rather to *retrieve* or compile *human statements*. In this situation, any proponent of the evidence must overcome two obstacles: (1) he must show that the machine functioned properly in its retrieval or compilation; and (2) he must show that the original statements that were compiled or retrieved fall within some hearsay exception, if they are offered to prove the truth of what they assert. See L&S, p. 371.

Example: D is charged with spying for the Russians. The prosecution introduces computer printouts, which are claimed to be the decoded form of coded messages sent by and to D and his alleged spy masters. (E.g., from KGB headquarters to head of KGB Chicago station: "We have recruited D and he will be giving you reports of U.S. missile silos via dead drop.") First, the prosecution will have to show that the computers were functioning accurately when they intercepted and decoded these messages. Second, the prosecution will have to show that the statements themselves fall within some exception to the hearsay rule, since they are being offered for the truth of the matter asserted (e.g., that D has indeed been recruited).

c. **Animals:** Occasionally, a party will attempt to introduce evidence that an *animal* has behaved in a certain way, in an attempt to prove some factual proposition that may be deduced from the animal's behavior. Courts have taken the position that an animal's behavior is never the sort of "statement" that the hearsay rule applies to, and that there is thus no hearsay problem.

Example: V is found dead in her isolated rural cottage. A scrap of clothing is found at the scene which is shown by forensic evidence to have probably been left by the murderer. Soon after the body is discovered, a trained bloodhound sniffs the clothing, and then heads off on a long trail culminating at the cottage of D, miles away. When D comes to the door, the dog barks furiously while sniffing at him. At D's murder trial, the prosecution, after producing evidence to demonstrate the dog's great training and expertise in pursuing criminals by scent, offers evidence of the dog's conduct to prove that D must have been present at V's cottage at around the time of the murder. A hearsay objection by D will almost certainly be unsuccessful, since the dog's conduct will not be treated as the sort of "statement" to which the hearsay rule applies.

i. **Criticism:** Zoological evidence, however, suggests that certain animals can make "statements" about past events, can fail to remember those events accurately, and perhaps more amazingly, can intentionally deceive. See, e.g., "Conversations with a Gorilla," 154 Natl. Geographic 438 (1978) (partially reproduced in K&W, pp. 121-23), recounting sign-language lies by the "talking" gorilla Koko. Evidence of a sign-language "statement" by a chimpanzee or gorilla, offered for the truth of the proposition stated, may thus reflect classical hearsay dangers and should be treated as presenting a hearsay problem.

Quiz Yourself on
HEARSAY

✓ 39. Evan Keel, a passenger on the last flight of the Hindenberg, is tried for negligence in lighting a cigarette that ignited the blimp. Keel's defense is that the "No Smoking/Fasten Seat Belts" sign was off when he lit up. The prosecution offers testimony by Walter Resc, a rescue worker, who will testify that when the fiery blimp touched down, Joe Surv (who survived the accident but later died of an unrelated illness) said to Resc, "The No Smoking light was on when Keel lit up." Hearsay? _____Yes_____

40. The Indians who own Manhattan Island renege on their offer to sell the island to Peter Minuit. Minuit sues, claiming they had an oral contract for the sale. To prove they had a contract, Peter offers the testimony of Clyde Tory: "I heard Chief Broken Arrow tell Minuit, 'It's decided, then. Manhattan is yours for $24 and a baseball stadium in Cleveland.' " The Indians' lawyer objects on hearsay grounds. Assuming that oral contracts for the sale of land are valid, is the statement hearsay? _____NO_____

41. Charles Foster Kane is arrested for possession of cocaine, which the prosecution asserts was contained in a "snowy" paperweight on Kane's desk. The prosecutor offers as evidence a lab report stating, "The 'snow' in the subject paperweight is 95% pure cocaine hydrochloride." Is the report hearsay? _____Yes_____

42. Rasputin, the Mad Monk, enters Czar Nicholas' study and tells him, "I am having an affair with your wife." The Czar pulls a pearl-handled pistol from his desk and shoots the Mad Monk. At the Czar's trial for murder, Rasputin's statement is offered by the Czar to prove that the killing was provoked. Is it hearsay?   **NO**

43. Bob Caulfield dies. In his will, he leaves his entire estate to one of his sons, D.B., and nothing to his other son, Holden. Holden contests the will, claiming undue influence by D.B. D.B. wants to rebut by proving that he had always been his father's favorite, long before the alleged undue influence. He offers the testimony of his father's lifelong friend, Spike, who will testify: "Bob told me fifteen years ago that 'D.B. is the finest child in my family.' " Is the statement hearsay?   **NO**

44. Elmer Fudd is on trial for the attempted murder of Daffy Duck. Fudd pleads insanity. Bugs Bunny, a prosecution witness, testifies that Elmer is perfectly normal. To impeach Bugs, Elmer has Sylvester the Cat testify that, the day after the incident, Bugs told Sylvester: "That Elmer Fudd is a real looney tune." Is Sylvester's testimony hearsay?   **No**

45. Gerhardt Werbezirk, world expert on fire protection, designs the sprinkler and fire protection system at the Koko-nut Grove nightclub. Later, he takes his family to the club. A week later, a horrible fire occurs at the nightclub, killing Paul. Paul's estate sues the club's owner. The owner attempts to introduce the Werbezirk's family outing as evidence that: (1) Werbezirk must have believed the system he designed was safe (or he wouldn't have taken his family there); and (2) if he believed it was safe, it probably *was* safe. Under the FRE, will Werbezirk's conduct be considered hearsay?   **No**

46. The Gingerbread Boy runs away and the Fox eats him. At Fox's murder trial, Mugwump, a witness, testifies: "When they were searching for Gingerbread Boy, Aardvark told me Fox said he'd eaten the Gingerbread Boy." The statement is offered by the prosecution to prove that Fox ate the Gingerbread Boy. Is Mugwump's testimony admissible under the rule making admissions by a party-opponent non-hearsay?   **No**

47. Sniffo is a bloodhound who searches out drugs for the FBI. His "beat" is the airport. While patrolling luggage, Sniffo indicates to his handler, Kay Nyne, that there are drugs in a suitcase. When the suitcase's owner, Maryjane Paraphernalia, is tried on drug charges, Kay testifies for the prosecution: "Sniffo indicated there were drugs in the suitcase." Hearsay?   **No**

Answers

39. Yes. *Hearsay is an out-of-court statement offered to prove the truth of the matter asserted.* FRE 801(c). The statement here is Surv's: "The light was on." It was made outside of court, and it's being offered to prove the truth of its assertion, namely, that the "No Smoking/Fasten Seat Belts" light was lit. Thus, it's hearsay. (Note that if the statement were offered for some other reason than to prove the truth of the matter asserted, for instance, to prove Surv's *belief* that the light was on, not to prove that in fact the light was on, then the statement would be admissible as non-hearsay.) Remember that just because the statement is hearsay, this doesn't necessarily mean it's inadmissible; it may be admissible under an *exception* to the hearsay rule. However, there's no exception that seems to apply here.

40. No, because the words aren't being offered to show the factual truth of any matter asserted in them. (Indeed, there really *is* no matter here whose truth is being asserted.) Tory's testimony is being offered to show that an oral contract was in fact formed, and to show the terms of that contract. The words of an oral contract are *legally operative facts* (or *"verbal acts"*), since they have a legal significance independent of their substantive content. Where legally operative facts are offered for their legal significance, they're not hearsay.

41. Yes. Since the lab report is an out-of-court statement being offered to prove that the snow is cocaine, it's hearsay. A statement need not be spoken to be hearsay; a ***document*** offered to prove the truth of an assertion in its contents can also be hearsay. The "statement" here is the lab report's sentence, "The 'snow' in the . . . paperweight is . . . cocaine." Since the statement is being offered to show that the snow *is* cocaine, it's hearsay. Of course, even though a statement is hearsay, it isn't necessarily inadmissible — the one here, for instance, might be (though probably isn't) admissible under the "public records" exception, FRE 803(8).

42. No. Hearsay is an out-of-court statement offered to prove the truth of the matter asserted. FRE 801(c). The assertion here is Rasputin's: "I am having an affair with your wife." However, it's not hearsay because it is not being offered for the truth of its assertion (that the Czarina and Rasputin were in fact having an affair), but only to show the statement's ***effect on the listener***, the Czar (that the statement so enraged him that he shot Rasputin).

43. No. It's being offered as ***circumstantial evidence of the declarant's (Bob's) state of mind***, not to prove that D.B. is in fact the finest child in the family. It's therefore not hearsay.

44. No. Hearsay is an out-of-court statement offered to prove the truth of the matter asserted. FRE 801(c). The out-of-court statement by Bugs, "That Elmer Fudd is a real looney tune," is being offered to ***impeach*** Bugs's current testimony, not to establish the truth of its assertion—namely, that Elmer was insane. Prior inconsistent statements, when used for impeachment purposes, are by universal understanding excluded from the definition of hearsay. (The same is true of prior consistent statements used to rehabilitate the witness.)

45. ***No, because the conduct was non-assertive.*** Under FRE 801(c), non-assertive conduct — that is, conduct not intended as communication — is not considered hearsay (because it's not a "statement," under 801(a), and only statements can be hearsay). The rationale is that non-assertive conduct is less subject to fabrication than assertive conduct and is therefore more reliable than assertive conduct. Here, for instance, Werbezirk is unlikely to have made the club visit to fool someone into thinking that the club was safe.

NOTE: Non-assertive conduct does not mean nonverbal conduct, since nonverbal conduct can be intended to communicate, e.g., a nod of the head. FRE 801(a).

COMMON LAW RULE: At common law, non-assertive conduct *was* considered hearsay if offered as an implied assertion of the actor's beliefs and of the consequent truth of those beliefs.

46. No. The statement is ***"multiple hearsay,"*** or "hearsay on hearsay," i.e., an out-of-court declaration which quotes or paraphrases another out-of-court declaration. Under FRE 805, hearsay included within hearsay is not excluded under the hearsay rule provided that ***each part*** of the combined statement satisfies an exception to the hearsay rule.

The principal out-of-court declarant here is Aardvark, whose statement is "Fox said he'd eaten the Gingerbread Boy." That statement is offered to prove that Fox ate the Gingerbread boy (so it's hearsay), and it doesn't fit an exception. The fact that Aardvark's statement subsumes an additional statement (Fox's statement that he did the eating), and the fact that that additional statement is non-hearsay because it's an admission, doesn't save the overall package from inadmissibility.

47. No. "Statements" from non-human sources, such as ***animals*** and ***machines***, aren't considered hearsay. (See, e.g., FRE 801(c), giving hearsay status only to "statements," and 801(a), defining "statement" to include nonverbal conduct only if the conduct is by "a person.")

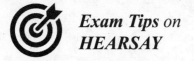

Exam Tips on HEARSAY

Hearsay typically accounts for 30-40% of a typical Evidence exam, so you need to be on the lookout for it in every fact pattern, whether essay or multiple choice.

Memorize every word of the classic definition: *"Hearsay is a statement or assertive conduct that was made or occurred out of court, and is offered in court to prove the truth of the facts asserted."* In an essay, begin your answer by quoting this verbatim, then show how it does or doesn't apply to the facts of the question.

Here's what to look for in analyzing a hearsay question (exceptions to the hearsay rule are covered in the next chapter):

☛ Look for a *statement*.

   ☞   A statement may be *oral* or *written*.

   ☞   Even things that don't sound at all "testimonial" may be statements, and thus hearsay. (*Example:* P tells the court that a bottle's label bore the words, "Contains sodium chloride." The label has since been destroyed. The label's contents are probably a "statement," so if P is offering those words in order to prove that that's what the bottle contained, this is probably hearsay.)

   ☞   Where what happened out-of-court is *non-verbal conduct*, consider whether the person who did it intended it as an *assertion* — if it was, it can be hearsay; if it wasn't, it can't be hearsay.

   Example: D is on trial for burglarizing W and W's wife Helen. W testifies that a week after the crime, W and Helen were in a park, when Helen saw D and shouted, "You're the one who burglarized my house!" W further testifies that D immediately ran away. If D's flight is found to be the equivalent of saying "I did it and don't want to be caught," W's statement about the flight would be hearsay. Probably, however, the court will find that D's flight was not intended by D as an assertion of any factual matter; in that case, W's testimony about the flight would not be hearsay.

     ☞ *Animals* and *machines* don't make statements. (*Example:* W, a DEA agent, testifies for the prosecution that a dog sniffed D's luggage and then started barking in a way he was trained to do if he found drugs. The barking isn't a statement, and therefore can't be hearsay. Same result if W testifies that a drug-testing machine beeped in a way that signifies "I've found drugs.")

☛ Check whether the statement is being offered to prove the *truth of the matters asserted therein*. If not, the statement isn't hearsay. Most frequently-tested aspects:

   ☞   **Verbal acts:** The statement may be an *operative fact* that gives rise to *legal conse-*

quences. If so, check whether the statement is being offered because of these consequences, not to prove the truth of the matter asserted. Some examples:

☞ ***Defamation*** suits. (*Example:* P sues D for defamation, claiming that D said, "P is a crook," during a TV interview. P puts on W, a video engineer who taped the interview, who testifies, "I heard D say 'P is a crook' during the interview." Since D's making of the statement has legal significance aside from its truth — P can't recover unless he shows D made the statement — D's statement is a "verbal act" that's not hearsay.)

☞ ***Breach of contract*** suits. (*Example:* W testifies that he heard P say to D, "I'll paint your portrait for $5,000," and that he heard D respond, "OK, I'll come to your studio tomorrow." Neither of these out-of-court statements — P's and D's — is hearsay, because the statements are being offered to show their independent legal significance, as offer and acceptance, respectively, not to show the truth of any matter asserted therein.)

☞ Suit where giving of a ***gift*** is at issue. (*Example:* The administrator of X's estate sues D, an orderly in the hospital where X died, seeking the return of a watch which the orderly allegedly took. D testifies, "X said to me, 'This watch is a gift to you.' " D's testimony is not hearsay, because X's statement, coupled with the delivery of the watch, had the independent legal effect of completing the gift of the watch.)

☞ **State of mind:** Statements which are not offered for their truth, but to show the ***state of mind*** either of the ***declarant*** or of a ***listener***. Look for patterns where ***knowledge, belief*** or ***intent*** is at issue. Some contexts:

☞ To show the intent of a party to ***contract*** negotiations. (*Example:* P, a Japanese exporter, contracts to deliver china dishes to D, an American importer. The writing does not specify the material to be used in the dishes. D refuses the goods, on the grounds that they are plastic, and the parties intended porcelain. At trial on the suit for breach, D offers the testimony of a translator, W, who says, "I translated during the negotiations between P and D. In response to a question by D, P told me in Japanese, 'The dishes will be genuine porcelain,' and that's what I told D in English." W's testimony is not hearsay, because P's statement went to D's understanding of what the contract called for — it's not being offered for the purpose of establishing the truth of P's statement.)

☞ To show the state of mind of a ***criminal defendant***.

Example 1: D, a labor union president, is charged with violating a state law making it a felony for a union official to knowingly misappropriate union funds. The charge is that D authorized a large raise for himself. D offers testimony by his predecessor as president, W, who says, "Before the raise, D asked me if he could lawfully take a raise and I told him he could if he honestly believed it was reasonable and necessary." W's testimony isn't hearsay because it's being offered to prove that D believed the union rules permitted him to act as he did, not to prove that he was in fact allowed to raise his own salary.

Example 2: D, a policeman, is accused of attempting to kill his wife by shooting her with a Sureshot 202 pistol from a distance of 1/4 mile. D maintains that the shot was an accident, and that the Sureshot is not accurate at more than 1/8 mile. The prosecution calls D's former classmate from the police academy, who testifies, "In pistol class, attended by D and myself at the academy, the instructor said the Sureshot 202 is accurate up to 1/2 a mile." Admissible, because it's offered to show that D believed the pistol would be accurate, not to prove that the pistol really *was* accurate at that range.

☞ To show a witness's **bias**. (*Example:* W1 says that D drove through a red light before hitting P. D puts on W2, who says, "Before trial, W1 told me, 'D blackballed me from becoming a member of the club he belongs to.' " Admissible, because it shows bias by W1 against D, and is not being offered to show that D really blackballed W1.)

☛ **Witness repeats own out-of-court statement:** Remember that there can be hearsay even where the witness is testifying to his or her *own* out-of-court statement. As long as the out-of-court statement is being offered for the truth of the matter asserted, the fact that the in-court witness and the out-of-court declarant are the same is irrelevant. (*Example:* In a civil car-crash suit, D says on the stand, "After the accident, I told the police officer who came to the scene that the light was green when I drove through the intersection." This is hearsay, if as seems probable it's being offered to show that the light really *was* green.)

☛ Once you've determined that a particular bit of evidence is hearsay, of course consider whether it's admissible as an exception. But ***don't skip the first step*** — the fact that something would fall within an exception even if it were hearsay should never prevent you from first carefully analyzing whether it really *is* hearsay.

CHAPTER 6

EXCEPTIONS TO THE HEARSAY RULE

ChapterScope

Correctly classifying a statement as hearsay/non-hearsay is only half the battle. The other half is determining whether some *exception* to the hearsay rule applies. (Much more than half of all hearsay statements that you'll encounter in class and on exams will turn out to fall within some exception or other.) Here are the key exceptions:

- ■ **Admissions:** A statement made by a *party to the litigation*, when offered *against that party*, falls within the exception for *"admissions."* (Under the FRE, admissions are technically non-hearsay rather than an exception, but the distinction doesn't really matter.)

    - ❑ **Adoptive admission:** An admission may take the form of an express or implied *adoption of someone else's statement*.

        - ❑ Often, this occurs when the declarant remains *silent in the face of an accusation* — if a reasonable person would have denied the statement, it may be admitted against the declarant as an adoptive admission.

    - ❑ **Representative admissions:** The declarant may be deemed to have adopted someone else's statement by the doctrine of *"representative"* or "vicarious" admissions.

        - ❑ **Employer-employee:** Thus an *employer* will be deemed to have adopted an *employee's statement*, if the statement is made during the course of the employment, and it relates to the employee's duties.

        - ❑ **Co-conspirators:** Similarly, one *conspirator's* statements will be admissible against other conspirators, if the statement was made *during and in furtherance of the conspiracy*.

- ■ **Statements about physical condition:** There are two distinct exceptions: (1) The declarant's statement about his *past or present physical condition*, made to obtain *medical diagnosis or treatment*; and (2) The declarant's statement of *present* (not past) physical condition, made to a *layperson*.

- ■ **Statements about mental state:** Statements by a declarant about his *present mental state*, when that state is in issue. This exception includes statements about the declarant's intent to *do something in the future* (when offered to show that the intent existed, and also when offered to show that the declarant later *acted in accordance with that intent)*.

- ■ **Excited utterances:** A statement made while the declarant is under the influence of a *startling event*, if the statement relates to that event.

- ■ **Present sense impressions:** A statement *describing or explaining an event*, while the declarant is *perceiving the event* (or immediately thereafter).

- ■ **Past recollection recorded:** A written *record of an event,* made *shortly after* the event, if: (1) someone (not necessarily the record-writer) had *first-hand knowledge* of the event; (2) the record was made when the matter was *fresh* in the source's memory; and (3) the sponsoring witness's *memory* of the event recorded is now (at trial) *impaired*.

- **Business records:** Entries made in the *routine of a business* by, or from information from, a person with personal knowledge of the matter recorded, if the entries were made *near the time the matter recorded occurred*.

  ❑ **Absence of entry:** Most courts allow the *absence* of an entry as evidence of the *non-occurrence* of an event.

- **Public records:** Three types of *"public records"* are given an exception:

  ❑ an agency's records of its *own activities*, offered to show those activities occurred;

  ❑ records of *observations* made by public officials, where the observation was made in the *line of duty*, and the official had a *duty to report it*; and

  ❑ *factual findings* resulting from *investigations* by a public body (*except* when used against a *criminal defendant*).

- The following exceptions require that the declarant be *"unavailable"* to testify at trial:

  ❑ **Former testimony:** The transcript of a previous *hearing* or *deposition*, if (1) the party against whom the transcript is now offered was *present* at the earlier testimony; and (2) that party had an *opportunity* and *similar motive* to *cross-examine* the declarant during the earlier testimony.

  ❑ **Dying declaration:** A declarant's statement concerning the *cause or circumstances of her impending death*, if made when the declarant *believed* her death was *imminent*. (Under the FRE, the case must be either a murder prosecution or a civil case, but the death need not have actually occurred.)

  ❑ **Declarations against interest:** Statements that were *against the declarant's interest* at the time they were *made*. (Under the FRE, the statement can be against either the declarant's *financial* interest or her *"penal"* interest.)

    ❑ Under the FRE, a statement *exculpating* the accused is admissible only if clearly *"corroborated."*

- **Prior statements of available witnesses:** If the declarant is testifying at trial, her *prior statements* are substantively (i.e., not just for impeachment) admissible as follows:

  ❑ **Prior inconsistent statement:** A prior *inconsistent* statement by the witness is admissible, if it was given *under oath* at a *trial*, *hearing* or *deposition*.

  ❑ **Prior consistent statement:** A prior *consistent* statement by the witness is admissible if and only if it is "offered to *rebut* an express or implied charge against [the witness] of *recent fabrication* or *improper influence or motive*."

  ❑ **Prior identification:** A statement of *"identification"* of a person (made after the declarant "perceived" the person) is admissible as long as the declarant testifies at trial, whether or not the identification was made under oath or at a formal proceeding.

- **Catchall exception:** A *"residual"* or *"catchall"* exception exists (under the FRE). The main requirement for the catchall is that the statement have "circumstantial *guarantees* of *trustwor-*

thiness" equivalent to those of the specific exceptions.

I. INTRODUCTION

A. Significance: The rules about hearsay might be better thought of not as a rule of exclusion coupled with exceptions, but rather as a general rule allowing hearsay, coupled with a narrow exception excluding it. As one commentator has put it, "In the sea of admitted hearsay, the rule excluding hearsay is a small and lonely island." Weinstein, 46 IOWA L. REV. 331, 346 (quoted in L&S, p. 381). In this chapter, we examine the large number of exceptions to the rule against hearsay, exceptions which cumulatively apply more often than not in real-life situations.

B. Availability of declarant: In considering the various exceptions to the rule against hearsay, one distinction should be constantly kept in mind: Some exceptions apply only where the ***declarant is unavailable*** to give testimony at the trial; others apply regardless of whether the declarant is available.

    1. Rationale: In the case of the exceptions for which unavailability is required, the theory is that live testimony by the declarant is ***preferable***, so that he can be cross-examined under oath; however, if his live testimony is not available, the judgment is made that the fact-finding process will be more accurate with the less-than-perfect out-of-court evidence than without it. In the case of the exceptions for which the declarant's availability is irrelevant, the theory is that the out-of-court declaration is, because of the circumstances, at least as accurate as in-court testimony would be.

C. Confrontation Clause of Constitution: A second distinction to keep in mind is that between the common-law rule against hearsay and the ***Confrontation Clause*** of the Sixth Amendment to the U.S. Constitution. That Clause provides that "in all criminal prosecutions, the accused shall enjoy the right . . . to be confronted with the witnesses against him." To the extent that a particular hearsay exception permits an out-of-court declaration to be used against a defendant in a criminal prosecution, there is a risk that the Clause is violated. In general, however, the use of declarations falling within well-established common-law hearsay exceptions has been held not to violate the Confrontation Clause, or the related Due Process Clause. The entire issue of these constitutional guarantees and their relation to the hearsay rule is discussed extensively in a separate chapter beginning *infra*, p. 361.

II. ADMISSIONS

A. Neither category: Our discussion of hearsay exceptions will first consider those in which the declarant's availability is immaterial, then those where it is a requirement. First, however, we consider a subject that does not fall neatly into either category: ***admissions made by a party-opponent***.

    1. Reasons for separate treatment: There are two reasons for treating admissions separately.

a. **Not more reliable:**   First, all other exceptions to the hearsay rule are based on the theory that they involve special circumstances which furnish *special guarantees of trustworthiness* not present in the usual hearsay situation. (For instance, a "dying declaration," see *infra*, p. 290, is thought to be more reliable because a person who knows he is dying has no motive to lie.) An admission by a party, by contrast, has *no* special circumstantial guarantees of reliability. McC, p. 448.

b. **Arguably not hearsay:**   Second, it's not really clear that admissions should be viewed as an "exception" to the hearsay rule. Things a party says could be more properly viewed as part of the context of the litigation rather than as an out-of-court declaration, just the way statements made in pleadings would not be thought of as hearsay. In fact, FRE 801(d)(2) treats admissions by party-opponents as not being hearsay at all, rather than as falling within an exception to the hearsay rule.

B. General rule: The general rule regarding admissions is this: *A party's words or acts may be offered as evidence against him*. Thus the rule allowing admissions of a "party-opponent" is a rule of evidence echoing the police interrogator's warning, "Anything you say may be used against you." McC, p. 447.

1. **Exception or outside of scope:**   Authorities differ on whether the rule allowing admissions should be arrived at by treating admissions as being non-hearsay, or rather by treating them as an exception to the rule barring hearsay. FRE 801(d)(2) treats admissions as being *non-hearsay*.

2. **Rationale:**   The rationale for the rule allowing admissions is not obvious. As noted above, admissions do not by their surrounding circumstances carry any special guarantees of trustworthiness, as all other traditional hearsay exceptions do. It has been suggested that the rule stems from "the adversary theory of litigation. A party can hardly object that he had *no opportunity to cross-examine himself* or that he is unworthy of credence save when speaking under sanction of an oath." Morgan, quoted in McC, p. 449. This theory — tied to the notion that people should take responsibility for their own words and acts — probably supplies the best rationale. L&S, p. 384.

3. **Distinguish from declaration against interest:**   An admission by a party-opponent must be distinguished from a *declaration against interest* (discussed *infra*, p. 293). An admission will usually be against the declarant's interest at the time it is made, but this is *not a requirement* — even statements that seem neutral or self-serving at the time they are made may be introduced against the party who made them. Thus to speak of the admissibility of "admissions against interest," as many courts do, is inaccurate.

a. **Other distinctions:**   Apart from the fact that admissions need not have been against interest when made, there are two other important distinctions between admissions and declarations against interest: (1) The declaration-against-interest exception applies only when the declarant is *unavailable* as a trial witness, whereas the admission by a party or a party's representative is admissible even where he is available to be a witness at trial; and (2) admissions must be made by a party (or his representative), and must be admitted *against*, not for him, whereas the declaration-against-interest exception applies to statements offered in evidence by the party who made them as well as statements made by third persons. McC, p. 449.

4. **Not binding:**   Once an out-of-court admission by a party is entered in evidence against him, may he offer evidence which ***contradicts*** his own out-of-court statement? The answer is universally ***"yes."*** That is, out-of-court admissions are different from "judicial" admissions (e.g., admissions made in the pleadings of a case), which may not be contradicted by the party who made them. L&S, p. 385.

5. **Can be opinion or conclusion:**   All other hearsay exceptions merely remove the hearsay obstacle; they do not overcome any non-hearsay related deficiency in the evidence. But the rule allowing admissions is different: The rules barring admissibility of ***opinions*** and of ***conclusions of law*** do ***not*** apply to an admission used against the party who made it. McC, p. 450.

> **Example:** After an auto accident, D tells a police officer, "The accident was my fault." Even though a lay witness's in-court expression of an opinion is normally not admissible (see *infra*, p. 516), this out-of-court expression of an opinion will be admissible against D. Of course, D is always free to take the stand to explain why his opinion is mistaken, taken out of context, etc. The same rule of admissibility would apply where D expressed a conclusion of law (e.g., "P will probably be able to sue my rear end off.")

   a. **First-hand knowledge not required:**   Similarly, the usual rule that a witness may speak only of facts of which he has ***first-hand knowledge*** (*infra*, p. 516) does ***not*** apply to out-of-court admissions used against the party who made them.

   > **Example:** Sophie is a wolf owned and raised by D (a wildlife research center). While she is in a fenced-in yard of the Center's Education Director, Mr. Poos, she is found licking the face of P, a 3-year-old boy who had climbed over the fence, and who is lying on his back screaming. P has lacerations of the face, chest, stomach, and legs. P's parents bring suit against D on the theory that Sophie attacked P. At trial, P introduces a note written right after the incident by Mr. Poos to the President of the Center, which says, "Sophie bit a child that came in our backyard," and also offers to prove that Mr. Poos later orally told the President, "Sophie bit a child." The trial judge refuses to admit the evidence, on the grounds that Mr. Poos did not have any personal knowledge of the facts. The jury finds for the defense.
   >
   > *Held* (on appeal), Mr. Poos' written and oral statements should have been admitted. FRE 801(d)(2)(D) prevents from being hearsay a statement offered against a party (here, the Center) that is "a statement by [the party's] agent or servant concerning a matter within the scope of [the] agency or employment, made during the existence of the relationship." Nothing in this Rule requires that the statement be based upon facts personally known to the agent. Nor does anything else in the Federal Rules require an implied condition of personal knowledge. New trial ordered. *Mahlandt v. Wild Canid Survival & Research Center, Inc.*, 588 F.2d 626 (8th Cir. 1978).

6. **Federal Rule:**   As noted, the Federal Rules treat admissions as non-hearsay rather than as exceptions to the rule barring hearsay. FRE 801(d)(2) treats five different kinds of admissions by a party as non-hearsay; our detailed discussion below will be similarly organized into these five categories. The full text of 801(d)(2) is as follows:

> **"(d) Statements That Are Not Hearsay.** A statement that meets the following condi-

tions is ***not hearsay***: ...

(2) An Opposing Party's Statement. The statement is offered ***against an opposing party*** and:

(A) was ***made by the party*** in an ***individual or representative capacity***;

(B) is one the party ***manifested that it adopted or believed to be true***;

(C) was made by ***a person whom the party authorized*** to ***make a statement on the subject***;

(D) was made by the party's ***agent or employee*** on a matter ***within the scope of that relationship*** and ***while it existed***; or

(E) was made by the party's ***coconspirator during and in furtherance of the conspiracy***.

The statement ***must be considered*** but ***does not by itself establish*** the declarant's ***authority*** under (C); the ***existence or scope of the relationship*** under (D); or the ***existence of the conspiracy*** or participation in it under (E)."

a. **Significance:** The Federal Rule essentially codifies the common law. While most common-law courts have treated admissions as being exceptions to the hearsay rule rather than non-hearsay, the Federal Rules' treatment of admissions as non-hearsay makes very little practical difference.

C. **Personal admissions:** The clearest kind of admission is that defined by FRE 801(d)(2)(A): a ***party's own statement***, offered against him.

Example: D is charged with murdering his wife by stabbing her. At the beginning of their investigation, police believe that the stabbing took place at 7:00 p.m. D tells them, "I left the house at 6:45 p.m." It later turns out that the murder probably took place at 6:30. The prosecution may introduce D's statement against him (assuming that there are no *Miranda* problems), since it is an admission. This is so even though the statement is not a "declaration against interest," since at the time he made it, D believed the statement was exculpatory.

1. **Representative capacity:** Observe that under the federal approach, the statement is admissible against its maker, regardless of whether the statement was made in an ***individual*** or ***representative*** capacity, and regardless of in which capacity suit is brought. For instance, if a trustee gossips to a friend about some property in the trust (a statement made in the trustee's individual rather than representative capacity), it may be used by the other side in a suit involving the trust, where the trustee is sued in his representative rather than individual capacity. L&S, p. 386.

2. **Pleadings:** The statements a party makes in his ***pleadings*** are treated as admissions for most purposes, and thus may be admitted as evidence against him. A number of situations can arise:

a. **Civil pleadings, same case:** The simplest case is where a party makes statements in his pleadings in a civil case, and the status of those statements in that same case is at issue. These statement are "judicial admissions," and their maker cannot controvert them except by amending his pleadings. If he does amend them, his adversary may use the original pleadings as evidence. L&S, p. 387.

b. Subsequent case: Statements made by a litigant in one case may be introduced against him in *subsequent cases*, under the "admissions" rationale.

c. Guilty pleas: A *guilty plea* that is *not withdrawn* is generally *admissible* as an admission. In the case for which the plea was entered, the plea is of course a judicial admission. But the plea is also generally admissible in later civil or criminal cases.

   i. Minor offense: However, a guilty plea to a *minor offense* will usually *not* be admissible. For instance, a guilty plea to a traffic offense will generally not be admissible in a later civil suit arising out of the same incident, on the theory that the plea may have been entered simply because the cost of litigating the traffic offense was greater than the cost of paying the ticket. L&S, p. 387.

   ii. Withdrawn guilty plea: Suppose that the defendant in a criminal case enters a guilty plea, and then is allowed to *withdraw* that plea. May the fact that he initially made the plea be introduced against him as an admission, either in the same criminal case or in a later civil or criminal one? As a matter of evidentiary logic, the plea is an admission, and should be admissible under the rule allowing admissions. But as a matter of policy, FRE 410 flatly excludes, from any civil or criminal proceeding, "a guilty plea that was later withdrawn."

3. Admissions in criminal cases: Admissions by a *criminal defendant* are admissible against him, so long as no specific constitutional guarantee (e.g., the *Miranda* rule) is infringed. That is, an admission by a criminal defendant falls within the general rule that admissions are admissible against the party who made them.

   a. Possible unfairness: Observe that this application of the general rule may be unfair, and may even threaten constitutional freedoms. For instance, suppose that a police officer in a drug prosecution testifies that he spotted a vial of crack near D's feet, and that, before he arrested D, D admitted that the vial was his. Suppose further that the police officer's testimony is false, and that D never said anything. Because this alleged admission is admissible against D, D is under great pressure to take the stand to deny having made the admission. Once he takes the stand, he will open himself up to cross-examination on all manner of things that he might prefer to avoid (e.g., what he was doing in the presence of other known drug users at the time of his arrest). D's practical ability to assert his privilege against self-incrimination is thus impaired. L&S, p. 387. Nonetheless, courts unanimously agree that the "admission" is admissible against D.

D. Adoptive admissions: Subsection (B) of FRE 801(d)(2) codifies the common-law notion of an "*adoptive* admission." Under subsection (B), a statement is not hearsay if it is offered against a party, and "the party *manifested that it adopted* or *believed* [the statement] *to be true*[.]"

1. Test for adoption: Occasionally, *A* will adopt *B*'s statement explicitly: "What *B* has just said is correct." This kind of express adoption clearly is sufficient to have *B*'s statement entered in evidence, and presents no special problems. However, most issues in the area of adoptive admissions involve *implied* adoptions: *A* is present while *B* makes a statement, and *A* either then takes an action which arguably amounts to an adoption of *B*'s statement, or remains silent in circumstances in which, arguably, the silence means acquiescence. In all "implied adoption" situations, the test is ***whether, taking into account all circumstances, A's conduct or silence justifies the conclusion that he knowingly agreed with B's statement.***

> **Example:** D is charged with bank robbery. W testifies that: prior to the robbery, D told him he was going to rob a bank; three weeks after the robbery, he saw D with money and diamond rings; and in the presence of D, D's girlfriend said, regarding D's sudden affluence, "That ain't nothin', you should have seen the money we had in the hotel room." The prosecution offers the girlfriend's out-of-court statement as an admission by D, on the theory that D, by remaining silent when the statement was made, adopted it.

> *Held*, admissible. "Under the total circumstances, we believe that probable human behavior would have been for [D] promptly to deny his girlfriend's statement if it had not been true — particularly when it was said to a person to whom he had previously related a plan to rob a bank." In some circumstances, a person's silence in the face of an inculpatory statement might not amount to an adoption (e.g., if D was in custody and knew that anything he said might be held against him); but here, no such reasoning was at all likely to have been in D's mind. *U.S. v. Hoosier*, 542 F.2d 687 (6th Cir. 1976).

2. **Real acquiescence:** The court will thus look to all the circumstances to determine whether the party's conduct or silence manifested a ***real and knowing agreement*** with the other person's statement.

   a. **Insurance claims:** The issue frequently arises where a claimant under a life insurance policy submits a ***death certificate***, and that certificate lists a ***cause of death*** that turns out to be one not covered by the policy. Can the insurance company introduce the death certificate on the theory that its contents were "adopted" by the claimant, or must the insurer put the maker of the death certificate on the stand? Many courts permit the insurer to introduce the death certificate on an adoption theory.

      i. **Criticism:** But this will often be unfair and unrealistic, since the claimant was typically trying to show merely *that* the insurer died, not *how* he died. (Indeed, it probably never occurred to the claimant that by attaching the death certificate, he might be deemed to have "adopted" the statements in that certificate.)

      ii. **Factors:** A claimant's odds of keeping the certificate out of evidence improve if either (a) the insurance company required the death certificate as part of the claims process; or (b) a representative of the insurance company assisted the claimant in filing the claim papers. L&S, p. 388.

3. **Silence:** The most difficult problems in connection with adoptive admissions are those in which the party remains ***silent*** in the face of the statement. All courts agree that the mere fact that the party remained silent does ***not*** by itself amount to an adoption. But there is no agreement about what else must be shown, and in any event the entire factual setting must be considered. As with adoption by conduct, the issue is always "whether a reasonable person would have denied under the circumstances[.]" McC, pp. 461-62.

a. **Special factors:** Here are some of the particular factors which courts have required before silence will be taken to be acquiescence to another's statement:

[1] The statement must have been *heard* by the party claimed to have acquiesced;

[2] It must have been *understood* by him;

[3] The subject matter must have been *within his knowledge*;

[4] Impediments to a response must not have been present (e.g., confusion or injury after an accident); and (most generally and most importantly)

[5] "The statement itself must be *such as would, if untrue, call for a denial under the circumstances.*"

McC, p. 461.

b. **Incentive to manufacture evidence:** Observe that the adoption-by-silence doctrine may furnish the other party with a strong incentive to *"manufacture" evidence*. For instance, suppose cars driven by P and D collide, and P, a lawyer knowledgeable in the rules of evidence, keeps his wits about him immediately after the accident. He has a strong incentive to say to D, "You ran the stop sign and this accident is your fault." P knows that if D remains silent, his (P's) statement can come into evidence as an adoption by D. And the statement is equally admissible whether it is true or totally fabricated by P.

c. **Criminal cases:** The problems with adoption by silence, especially the manufacture-of-evidence problem, are at their greatest in *criminal* cases. The adoption theory gives the police every incentive to make (possibly false) accusations against and to the accused, and then to argue that his silence constituted an adoption.

   i. *Miranda:* If the accusation comes at a time when the accused is *in custody*, the accused's silence *cannot be treated as an adoption* by him of the charges. The Supreme Court has so held in *Doyle v. Ohio*, 426 U.S. 610 (1976). In this situation, treating the silence as an adoptive admission would virtually nullify that part of the *Miranda* warnings informing the suspect that he has the right to remain silent.

   ii. **Other contexts:** But in non-custodial contexts, the accused's failure to respond to police accusations may be treated as an adoptive admission without violating the constitution. For instance, in *Jenkins v. Anderson*, 447 U.S. 231 (1980), D claimed self-defense at his murder trial, but the prosecution brought out the fact that he did not report the death to anyone for two weeks after it occurred, and suggested that if it had really been self-defense, D would have spoken out. The Supreme Court held that use of D's silence to impeach him in this way would not violate his privilege against self-incrimination. This suggests that at least where no governmental action induces the defendant to remain silent, his silence in the face of accusations may constitutionally be admitted under the adoption-by-silence rationale.

d. **Letter or other writing:** Suppose that the statement as to which acquiescence is urged is not an oral declaration, but rather a *letter* or other *written* communication.

Will the letter be admitted on the theory that the recipient's silence constituted an admission by adoption?

    i. **General rule:** In general, courts are less quick to recognize an admission by adoption where the statement is written than where it is oral. Nonetheless, the modern trend seems to be that the failure to reply to a letter (or the failure to contradict certain statements in the letter if there is a response) is ***admissible*** as evidence under the adoption-by-admission rationale. McC, p. 462. Admissibility is made more likely by the fact that either (a) the recipient wrote back, but did not deny the statement; or (b) the parties were in some business or other relationship such that the recipient would be unlikely to remain silent in the face of an incorrect statement.

    ii. **Bill or statement:** The most common illustration of (b) above is where the writing is a ***bill or statement*** of indebtedness sent to a customer. The customer's ***failure to question the bill*** is always ***admissible*** as evidence of an admission of its correctness. *Id.*

4. **Who makes decision on adoption, judge or jury:** *Who* should make the decision whether a person adopted another's statement: the ***judge*** or the ***jury***? Courts and commentators ***disagree***:

    a. **Judge decides:** Some say the ***judge*** should fully resolve the issue (and thus either exclude the statement completely as not being adopted, or admit it unconditionally as a party's adoptive admission). On this approach, the judge is deciding the question as a "preliminary question of fact" under FRE 104(a) (see *infra*, p. 577).

    b. **Jury decides:** Others say that the judge should merely ***"screen"*** the evidence, by deciding whether a ***reasonable jury could possibly find*** that the adoption occurred. If the answer is "yes," then the judge finds the evidence to be "conditionally relevant" (FRE 104(b); see *infra*, p. 579), and leaves the final decision to the jury: the jury will use the statement substantively if and only if it finds that the adoption in fact occurred. If the judge's answer is "no" (i.e., no reasonable jury could find adoption), then the judge never lets the jury consider the statement at all.

    c. **In favor of having judge decide:** At least where the adoption is alleged to have occurred by ***silence***, the better rule seems to be to have the ***judge*** decide this question, as a preliminary question of fact under FRE 104(a). The reason is that if the jury is permitted to decide the admissibility issue, the danger of prejudice to the party alleged to have adopted another's statement is too great: the jury is unlikely to be able to ignore the statement even if it finds that no adoption really occurred. M&K §8.29, p. 811.

E. **Representative admissions:** We now turn to three kinds of admissions that can be thought of as ***"representative"*** or ***"vicarious"*** ones. That is, the admission is made by a person other than the party against whom it is sought to be introduced, but it is usable against that party because it was in some way ***authorized*** by him. These three categories of authorized admissions correspond to subsections (C), (D), and (E) of FRE 801(d)(2); the first two have to do with express or implied agency; the third has to do with the specific problem of statements by a co-conspirator.

1. **Explicitly authorized admission:** The easiest of the three categories is that represented by subsection (C) of FRE 801(d)(2): A statement may be offered against a party if it "was made by a ***person whom the party authorized to make a statement on the subject***[.]" Thus subsection (C) applies in the situation where the party has ***expressly agreed*** that his agent may make a statement on the particular subject. Thus if *A* says, "On this subject, refer all questions to my associate, *B*," anything *B* says on the subject will be admissible against *A* as if it were said by *A*.

   a. **Corporations:** The most common application of this rule of express authority is where the party is a ***corporation*** that has designated one of its employees to speak for it on a certain matter. Thus if X Corp.'s plant explodes, and X appoints Employee to furnish the police with details about what caused the accident, anything Employee says will be admissible against X.

   b. **Statements to principal:** The rule allowing into evidence expressly authorized admissions clearly applies where the agent is authorized to speak to third persons and does so. The more interesting question is, what happens if the principal only authorizes the agent to speak ***to the principal***? The issue arises in the case of internal reviews, inspections, and other investigations undertaken at the request of a corporation, where the corporation intends that outsiders not see or hear the results. The courts are split.

      i. **Inadmissible:** The majority ***common-law*** approach is that such "for in house use only" statements are ***protected*** against disclosure at trial. L&S, p. 389. Courts following this approach have often relied on the substantive law of agency, under which the doctrine of *respondeat superior* (employer is responsible for acts of employee) does not apply to transactions between the agent and the principal.

         Example: P is crushed by a truck owned by D (a trucking corporation), and driven by Employee, who works for D. After the accident, Employee gives a report about it to a vice president of D.

         Held, this report is not admissible against D. Unless a principal intends his agent's report to be made to others, the fact that it is authorized to be made to the principal himself is not enough to make it admissible against the principal at trial. Here, there was nothing to indicate that D authorized Employee to release the report to the world. *Big Mack Trucking Co., Inc. v. Dickerson*, 497 S.W.2d 283 (Tex. 1973).

      ii. **Admissible:** The ***modern trend***, however, seems to be to treat such communications to the principal as being ***admissible*** against him. One of the reasons is that considerations of ***reliability*** favor admissibility. "Intra-organization reports are generally made as a basis for some action, and when this is so, they share the reliability of business records." McC, p. 456. Furthermore, those who prepare such reports usually have an insider's access to information, so the reports are likely to be accurate. L&S, p. 390.

      iii. **Federal Rules:** The ***Federal Rules*** follow the modern approach, and allow reports from agent to principal to be ***admitted*** against the principal. While FRE 801(d)(2)(C) does not make this clear, the Advisory Committee's Note states:

"The question arises whether only statements to third persons should be so regarded [as admissions], to the exclusion of statements by the agent to the principal. The rule is phrased broadly so as to encompass both." So under the FRE, the report in *Big Mack Trucking Co.*, *supra*, would have been admissible against D.

  iv. **Books and records:** Under the modern and Federal approaches, a party's ordinary **books and records**, prepared by employees for the company's internal use alone, will be admissible as admissions. Advisory Committee's Note to FRE 801.

2. **Vicarious admissions by agents:** Now suppose that the agent is *not* explicitly authorized to speak on a particular matter, but that the matter arises out of a *transaction* that is *within the agent's authority.* The question is: Does the fact that the agent had authority to engage in the transaction also mean that he will be deemed to be authorized to speak about it, so that admissions he makes will be admissible against the principal? In general, the answer is: (a) under the traditional common law approach, *"no"*; and (b) under the modern and Federal Rules approach, *"yes."*

   a. **General common-law approach:** There is *no concept at common law of "vicarious" admissions*, only "authorized" admissions. The common law approach is based on the formalistic theory that speaking is like any other act, and only *authorized* acts are binding against the principal.

   b. **Modern and Federal Rules:** But the traditional rule seems to be giving way to a modern rule embodied by FRE 801(d)(2)(D). 801(d)(2)(D) admits a statement offered against a party if it was made "by the party's agent or employee on a *matter within the scope of that relationship* and *while it existed*[.]"

   Example: T, a truck driver, works for D, a corporate employer. T has a driving accident while on the job, injuring P. T tells a police officer right after the accident, "Gee, I got distracted and ran a red light." P sues D and offers the officer's testimony about what T said. Under the modern and federal rule, the driving of the truck was "a matter within the scope of [T's] agency or employment." Therefore, T's statement concerning his driving is admissible against D. (Even if D can show that it expressly prohibited its drivers from making statements about any accidents they were involved in, this won't block admission against D, as it would have at common law.)

   i. **Rationale:** The modern rule (admitting statements relating to matters that the agent was authorized to handle) can be justified on the grounds of *reliability*. For instance, the agent is typically well-informed about the transactions he is commenting on, since they occur within his work for the employer. Also, while the employment continues the worker is not likely to make the statements unless they are true. McC, p. 455.

   c. **Showing fact of agency:** How can the proponent of an agent's admission *prove* that there was an agency relationship (a showing required under either the common law or modern approach)? Under the FRE, this showing *cannot be made solely by means of the contents of the statement itself,* though the statement's contents may be considered as one piece of evidence. See FRE 801(d)(2), final sentence ("The statement must be considered but *does not by itself establish* the declarant's authority under (C) [or] the existence or scope of the relationship under (D)[.]")

Example: Suppose that in the above example, after T (the truck driver) had the accident while on business for his employer D, he said to the police officer, "I was driving on business for D when I ran a red light and crashed." In deciding as a preliminary matter whether T's statement was "made by [D's] agent or employee on a matter within the scope of that relationship and while it existed," (the FRE test), the court may not decide the matter solely based on the contents of the statement (i.e., solely based on T's statement that he was on business for D when the crash occurred).

So there will have to be *some other evidence* that T was indeed on business for D (e.g., employment records, or the testimony of T on the stand). But the contents of the statement must be considered by the court as one item of evidence on the issue.

3. **Other exceptions:** Whether in a common-law or modern/federal jurisdiction, an admission by an employee may come in under some *other exception* to the hearsay rule even if the authorized or vicarious admissions rules fail to apply. Always consider, for instance, the *excited utterances* exception (*infra*, p. 242): thus in our truck driving example, suppose there wasn't enough evidence that T was really on duty for D when the accident occurred. P might successfully argue that T's statement to the police immediately after the accident was an excited utterance.

F. **Co-conspirators:** We turn now to special problems that are posed by admissions involving *conspiracies*.

1. **General rule on co-conspirators:** Courts have long recognized a special *conspiracy exception* to the hearsay rule: *statements made by one co-conspirator are admissible against other co-conspirators, so long as the statement was made during the course of the conspiracy and in furtherance of it.*

    Example: A and B are charged with robbing, and conspiring to rob, the First National Bank. The prosecution charges that A aided in all the master planning and got a share of the proceeds, and that B actually pulled the robbery. The prosecution calls as a witness W, a friend of A, who testifies, "B tried to recruit me to join in the robbery by telling me 'A's in this with me, and we're gonna make a million bucks.'" If this testimony is introduced to prove the truth of B's statement (i.e., that A really was part of the conspiracy), it will be hearsay.

    But W's testimony will nonetheless be *admissible*, because it falls within the co-conspirator exception to the hearsay rule. This is so because the statement was: (1) made by a co-conspirator (B); (2) made during the course of the conspiracy; and (3) made in furtherance of the objectives of the conspiracy (since recruitment of W would have added to the conspiracy's chances of success).

2. **Need for exception:** Before we look at the intricacies of co-conspirator statements exception, first observe that in many instances there will not really be a hearsay problem at all. This is because, as a matter of *substantive law*, in a conspiracy prosecution *all conspirators are liable for the acts of any of them.* Thus if A and B are shown to have conspired to rob a bank, A is liable for the actual robbery even if only B walked into the bank lobby and carried away the money. This rule of mutual liability for actions applies to "verbal acts" just as much as it does to physical acts. Statements made by one conspirator in

furtherance of the conspiracy are thus admissible against all conspirators *if conspiracy is charged*, since the statement is part of the illegal plan of action.

   a. **Hearsay problem:**   Sometimes, however, a statement by one co-conspirator will, if admitted against another conspirator, involve clear hearsay problems. This is most dramatically the case if the prosecution has *not charged conspiracy*, but is only prosecuting for the substantive crimes committed (e.g., bank robbery). In this situation, the statement is not admissible as part of any substantive crime, so it is likely to be relevant only insofar as it proves the truth of the matter asserted; in this instance, it is hearsay, and must therefore fall within some exception.

   Example: Again return to A, B, and their bank robbery. Assume that the prosecution has not charged conspiracy to rob, only the actual robbery. Now, B's recruitment statement to W ("A's in this with me") is not admissible as a substantive act in furtherance of any crime, since it is not part of the completed crime of bank robbery. It is only relevant for the truth of the matter asserted (that A was an accomplice to the robbery), so if it does not fall within some exception to the hearsay rule it will be excluded.

3. **FRE's requirements for exception:**   FRE 801(d)(2)(E) codifies the common-law requirements for the exception: a statement falls within the exception (or, in the approach of FRE 801, is non-hearsay) if it is offered against a party and "was made *by the party's coconspirator during and in furtherance of the conspiracy.*"

   a. **Three requirements:**   There are thus *three requirements* that must be made for the statement to be admissible:

   [1] it must be by a member of the *same conspiracy* of which the party against whom it is admitted (typically the defendant in a criminal action) is a member;

   [2] it must have been made while the conspiracy was *still in force*; and

   [3] it must have been made in order to *further the aims* of the conspiracy.

   The first of these requirements poses little problem (except for issues of proof and procedure, which are discussed below). We concentrate on the second and third.

4. **"During course of":**   The requirement that the statement have taken place *"during the course of"* the conspiracy has several implications:

   a. **Termination:**   Statements made *after the conspiracy has ended* are admissible only against the declarant, not against the other members of the conspiracy.

   i.   **Arrest:**   Thus if the conspiracy has been broken up by the *arrest* of one or more of its key members, anything the arrestees say to the police will not be admissible against the others. (But the prosecution may be able to argue successfully that the conspiracy continued after the arrest of some members. If so, statements by the arrestees would be admissible against the other members who continued with the conspiracy.)

   ii. **Achieving goal:**   Similarly, the conspiracy will be treated as ending when it *reaches its goal*, and statements made after that time will not be admissible.

Example: A and B conspire to rob the First National Bank. They carry out the robbery successfully, and split the proceeds. One year later, B mentions to X, whom he thinks is his friend, "A and I were the ones who pulled off the First National Bank job last year." This statement will not fall within the conspirator-statement exception to the hearsay rule, and may thus be introduced only against B, not against A, because it took place after the conspiracy was over.

    iii. Concealment: Some prosecutors have tried to argue that after the first phase of the conspiracy (the carrying out of the crime and splitting of the loot), there comes into existence a second phase: a conspiracy to *conceal* the crime. Therefore, so the argument goes, any statements made before the crime is solved are made during the course of the conspiracy, and are thus admissible against the non-declarant conspirators. However, courts have generally *rejected* such arguments. L&S, p. 398.

  b. Conspirator leaves: A conspirator may of course leave the conspiracy while it goes on. As noted, statements made by him to the authorities probably satisfy the "in the course of" requirement if the conspiracy goes on without him. But the *converse* is *not true*: if A leaves the conspiracy, statements made thereafter by the continuing conspirators, B and C, will *not* be admissible against A. L&S, p. 398.

  c. Statements before: Now consider the situation in which A and B begin a conspiracy, and make statements after the conspiracy has begun, but *before C has joined*. Are these statements admissible against C? The answer is *"yes."* "When a conspirator enters an ongoing conspiracy, he is held implicitly to have adopted the earlier statements of fellow co-conspirators, so these statements may be introduced as admissions against him." *Id.*

    i. Criticism: This may make sense where the statements concern matters that C reasonably should have anticipated at the time he joined (e.g., statements about the basic aim of the conspiracy). But the basic rule extends even to statements that C had no reason to expect to have been made, and in this context the rule seems wooden and unfair.

5. "In furtherance" requirement: The *"in furtherance"* requirement means that a statement should be admitted against a co-conspirator only if it was made for the purpose of *advancing the conspiracy's objectives.*

  a. Implications: If the "in furtherance" requirement is taken seriously, it renders inadmissible against a co-conspirator the following kinds of statements: (1) *confessions*, whether to authorities or to one the declarant thinks is a friend; (2) *narratives* of *past events*; and (3) *finger-pointing* by the declarant against a co-conspirator.

  b. Ignored: But *most courts have not taken the "in furtherance" requirement very seriously*. Confessions, narratives, and finger-pointing are all frequently allowed even though a strict construction of "in furtherance" would dictate their exclusion. L&S, p. 394.

6. No need to charge conspiracy: Statements by one co-conspirator against another may be admitted *even if no conspiracy crime is charged*.

Example: The prosecution believes that A and B worked together to carry out the robbery of the First National Bank. But since only B went into the bank and carried away the money, the prosecution decides to charge only B, and to charge him only with robbery, not conspiracy to rob. If the judge makes a preliminary finding (discussed *infra*) that A and B conspired together to carry out the robbery, A's statements incriminating B will be admissible against B for the truth of what those statements assert, even though no conspiracy is charged and A is not even a defendant.

a. **Previously-acquitted co-conspirator:** Even statements by a *previously acquitted* co-conspirator may be introduced if the requirements of the conspirator exception are otherwise satisfied. S&R, p. 736.

7. **Procedure:** As the previous paragraphs make clear, a proponent (typically the prosecution) who seeks to use one conspirator's statement against another, must establish that there was a conspiracy of which both the declarant and the other party were members, that the statement took place during the course of that conspiracy, and that the statement was in furtherance of the conspiracy. *Who is to decide* whether these factual requirements have been met? And *by what standard* should this issue be decided? These questions have over the years caused much disagreement among courts.

a. **Federal rule:** In the federal courts, a combination of a Supreme Court case and a 1997 amendment to FRE 801 have set a standard that seems to include the following rules:

i. **Judge:** Existence of the conspiracy, and satisfaction of the other factual requirements, is to be decided *by the judge*. He must find that these requirements are satisfied *by a preponderance of the evidence*. *Bourjaily v. U.S.*, 483 U.S. 171 (1987).

ii. **How he finds:** The judge can use any of three ways of ascertaining enough facts to make this judgment:

[1] He can conduct a *"mini trial"* outside of the presence of the jury to decide whether it is more likely than not that the defendant and the declarant were co-conspirators;

[2] By the time the statement is offered, there may already be *enough proof in the record* to justify the judge in finding that the conspiracy exists; or

[3] The judge can admit the statement *subject to "connecting up,"* i.e., subject to the later introduction of evidence sufficient to allow the judge to find it more likely than not that the conspiracy existed.

The third approach is dangerous for the prosecution, since if the later evidence never develops, the statement may be so damaging that a *mistrial* will have to be declared. However, in complicated cases involving many alleged conspirators and many crimes, this "subject to connecting up" approach is often the only practical way of trying the case. L&S, pp. 396-97.

iii. **Independent evidence:** The most interesting issue is: In deciding whether it is more likely than not that a conspiracy existed, may the judge *take into account the very statement whose admissibility is in issue*? FRE 801(d)(2) answers this question *"yes,"* though it makes clear that the statement cannot be enough by itself to establish the conspiracy. FRE 801(d)(2) says that "The statement *must be considered but does not by itself establish* the ... existence of the conspiracy or participation in it under (E)."

(1) Codification and extension of *Bourjaily*: The Advisory Committee Notes to this section (as amended in 1997) say that this amendment essentially codifies the Supreme Court's holding in *Bourjaily v. U.S.*, 483 U.S. 171 (1987) that the court may consider the alleged statement as one of the factors in determining whether the conspiracy existed. (Other aspects of *Bourjaily* are discussed *infra*, p. 578.) But the Notes observe that the amended Rule goes further, answering a question left open by the *Bourjaily* court: May the court find that the conspiracy existed based *only* on the statement? The Rule answers this question in the *negative*, by saying that "[t]he contents of the statement . . . are *not alone sufficient* to establish . . . the existence of the conspiracy and the participation therein of the defendant. . . ."

III. AVAILABILITY IMMATERIAL — GENERALLY

A. **Rationale:** We turn now to a group of exceptions to the hearsay rule that are *not conditioned upon the declarant's unavailability at trial*. The rationale behind applying these exceptions even where the declarant is available at trial is that these exceptions arise in situations "where courts have felt that a witness's account of an out-of-court statement was likely to be as probative of the issue in question as the declarant's courtroom testimony, or where the difficulty of proving unavailability or subpoenaing available witnesses was likely to outweigh the incremental benefits of courtroom testimony." L&S, p. 407.

B. **Partial list of exceptions:** Here, then, are the major exceptions that will apply even where the declarant is available to give courtroom testimony:

[1] *Spontaneous, excited,* or *contemporaneous* utterances (including statements about then-existing *physical* or *mental condition*);

[2] *Past recollection recorded*;

[3] *Business records*; and

[4] *Public records* and *reports*.

IV. SPONTANEOUS, EXCITED, OR CONTEMPORANEOUS UTTERANCES (INCLUDING STATEMENTS ABOUT THEN-EXISTING PHYSICAL OR MENTAL CONDITION)

A. **General principle:** Our first "availability of declarant immaterial" exception to the hearsay rule is really a collection of related exceptions. What they have in common is the element of *"contemporaneity"* — they are statements, usually (but not necessarily) oral, that concern something that is happening *at that moment*. Thus statements about one's present physical condition, statements about one's present mental state, as well as statements made under great excitement, all share this element of contemporaneity; so also do statements concerning "present sense impressions" (recognized under a modern exception). The sole exception to the contemporaneity requirement is that a person's statement to a physician concerning his medical condition or symptoms, if made in order to obtain ***diagnosis*** or ***treatment***, may relate to past symptoms or causes.

1. **"Res gestae":** Some courts have traditionally lumped these various situations together under the phrase ***"res gestae."*** McC, p. 471. However, this term is vague and unhelpful, and we'll avoid it.

B. **Statements of physical condition:** A well-recognized exception has evolved for statements by a person about his ***physical condition***. Most commonly, the exception is used to admit a person's statement about ***pain*** he is feeling, as proof that he really did feel the pain. Because the precise scope of the exception depends on whether the statement is made to a layperson or to a doctor, we consider each of these situations in turn.

1. **Statements to laypersons:** If the statement is made to a ***layperson***, it will come under the exception only if it relates to the declarant's ***present*** bodily condition or symptoms.

    Example: X says to W, "I'm feeling terrible chest pains." Even though W is not a doctor, X's statement falls within the bodily-condition exception to the hearsay rule. Therefore, either party would be permitted to prove at trial that X actually had chest pains by putting on W's testimony that X made the statement.

    If, on the other hand, X said, "I had terrible chest pains yesterday," the exception would not apply if W were a layperson, and not a physician. See L&S, p. 420.

    a. **Spontaneity:** The statement must also be ***spontaneous***. The requirement of spontaneity is mainly an attempt to prevent the ***manufacture of evidence***. In most states (and under the Federal Rules), the mere fact that the statement refers to the declarant's present condition will generally be sufficient to meet the requirement of spontaneity, unless there are particular reasons to suspect that the evidence is manufactured.

        Example: X is in a car accident, in which his car is hit by a Rolls Royce driven by a famous and wealthy woman, D. X does not consult a doctor, but within earshot of witnesses, says, shortly after the accident, "Oh, my neck. I think I have whiplash. Maybe I can sue." A trial judge might well hold that these surrounding circumstances indicate that this statement was a self-serving attempt to manufacture evidence; if so, the judge would exclude it on the grounds that it lacked "spontaneity."

    b. **Federal Rules:** The Federal Rules handle statements of bodily condition made to non-doctors as part of a more general provision dealing with the declarant's ***then existing mental, emotional, or physical condition***. FRE 803(3) creates an exception for "a statement of the declarant's ***then-existing state*** of ... ***physical condition*** (such as ... ***pain***, or ***bodily health***)[.]"

        i. **Spontaneity:** Observe that the requirement that the condition presently exist is explicit; however, the requirement of ***spontaneity*** is merely ***implied*** from the fact that the rule is "a specialized application of the broader rule recognizing a hearsay exception for statements describing a present sense impression, the cornerstone of which is spontaneity." McC, p. 480.

c. **Statements not about pain:** As noted, statements allowed under this rule will generally be ones about pain. A statement by the declarant to a non-doctor that purports to identify the precise medical condition will probably be excluded on grounds that it is an uninformed opinion (*infra*, p. 516) or made without firsthand knowledge (*infra*, p. 516).

    Example: X says to W (a friend who is not a doctor), "My leg must be broken." The judge will probably exclude the evidence on opinion or lack-of-firsthand-knowledge grounds. L&S, p. 420.

2. **Statements to a treating physician:** When a person goes to a doctor for treatment, he knows that any statement he makes about his condition will be relied upon by the doctor. Therefore, courts have long believed, statements made about a bodily condition, *made to a physician* in connection with *treatment*, carry this special guarantee of reliability. Therefore, courts have been more willing to accept such statements into evidence than in the case of statements made to non-doctors.

    a. **Recognized by FRE:** The FRE recognize this exception for statements made to get medical diagnosis or treatment. This is done by FRE 803(4), giving an exception for:

      "**Statement Made for Medical Diagnosis or Treatment.** A statement that:

        (A) is *made for*--and is reasonably *pertinent to--medical diagnosis or treatment*; and

        (B) describes *medical history*; past or present *symptoms* or sensations; their *inception*; or their *general cause*."

    b. **Past symptom:** Notice that under the FRE, the statement need not be in connection with a *present* bodily condition. Statements about *past* pain, past symptoms, or even past events that have given rise to pain or symptoms, are all admissible, if made to a physician in connection with treatment.

    c. **Self-serving statements:** The presumption of reliability is so strong that even statements that, if made to non-doctors would be rejected as clearly *self-serving*, will be admitted, as long as made in connection with procuring treatment. L&S, p. 421.

    d. **Causation:** Even statements that relate to the *cause* of the pain, symptoms, or other condition will be admitted, if they seem reasonably related to treatment. Notice that FRE 803(4) covers "A statement that: (A) is made for — and is reasonably pertinent to — medical diagnosis or treatment; and (B) describes ... past or present symptoms ... or their *general cause*."

    Example: D is charged with assault with intent to rape. The victim is a 9-year old girl, Lucy. The prosecution offers statements made by Lucy to Dr. Hopkins, the physician who treated her after the incident. Under the doctor's questioning, Lucy told him that she had been dragged into the bushes, that her clothes, jeans, and underwear were removed, and that the man had tried to force something into her vagina, which hurt. Dr. Hopkins repeats these statements at trial, and D objects on hearsay grounds.

    Held, these statements are admissible under FRE 803(4)'s exception to the hearsay rule. The statements related to (in terms of the later-amended text of 803(4)) the "cause or external source" of a medical condition, and were "reasonably pertinent to diagnosis or treatment." For statements regarding causation to be "reasonably pertinent to diagnosis or treatment," two tests must be satisfied: (1) the declarant's motive must be consistent with the purpose of the rule, which is to allow statements motivated by the patient's desire to obtain treatment; and (2) the information must be reasonable for the physician to rely upon in diagnosis or treatment. Here, both tests are satisfied. Even Dr. Hopkins' question, "Did the man take your clothes off" was one to which Lucy responded only because she was seeking treatment. (Importantly, the doctor's questions all related to *what* happened, not *who* did it.) All information was reasonably relied upon by the doctor in his examination and treatment; for instance, the information permitted him to pinpoint certain areas of the body and eliminate others. *U.S. v. Iron Shell*, 633 F.2d 77 (8th Cir. 1980).

    i.   **Statements of fault or identity:**   The Federal Rules go farther than the common law in allowing statements about causation to come in under the exception for statements made to a doctor relating to treatment or diagnosis. But the requirement that the causal statements be "reasonably pertinent" to diagnosis and treatment has some bite. For instance, the Advisory Committee's Note to FRE 803(4) states that statements about ***fault*** will ordinarily not qualify; for instance, a patient's statement that he was struck by an automobile would qualify but not his statement that the car was driven through a red light. *Id.* Similarly, a patient's statement that he was shot would be admissible, but a statement that he was shot by a white man would not be.

3. **Statements by third persons:** Normally, the statement will be one made by the patient. But FRE 803(4) does not require this. Therefore, the statement may be one made by a ***third person***, so long as the statement is made for the purpose of getting treatment or diagnosis for the patient. Thus a statement made by a ***friend or relative*** of the patient is covered (e.g., "He was hit from the rear by a speeding bicycle"), as is a statement made by a ***Good Samaritan*** (e.g., "I was just passing by when I saw him get hit by a speeding bicycle.") M&K §8.42, p. 871. Application of the exception to this third-party-statement situation is most likely where the patient herself is ***unconscious*** from the episode giving rise to the medical treatment.

4. **Statements to third persons:**   Suppose the statement is made "for purposes of" getting medical treatment, but is made not to a doctor, but rather to a ***nurse***, ambulance driver, hospital admitting clerk, or other person involved in the health care process. FRE 803(4)(A) would allow such statements to be admitted, since that rule applies wherever the statement "is made for — and is reasonably pertinent to — medical diagnosis or treatment." not merely where the statement is made to a physician. Indeed, the Advisory Committee's Note to 803(4) provides that "statements to hospital attendants, ambulance drivers, or even members of the family might be included."

5. **Physician who does not treat but testifies:**   So far, our discussion of statements to physicians has assumed that the physician is giving treatment to the declarant. Often, however, a physician is consulted not because he will be treating the patient, but rather because he will be asked to form an opinion about the patient's condition as to which he can ***testify***

at trial. Such an examination will often take place after litigation has commenced, or when it is contemplated.

   a. **Common-law approach:** In this situation, the declarant's incentive to tell the truth is obviously less than in the consultation-for-treatment situation, since the physician will not be rendering care based upon the declarant's statements. For this reason, most common-law courts *refuse* to apply the exception in this situation.

   b. **Federal rule:** FRE 803(4) makes no distinction at all between physicians consulted for treatment and those consulted for testimony only. As the Advisory Committee's Note to 803(4) makes clear, the Rule's reference to "medical diagnosis or treatment" covers statements made to a physician whose examination is made *solely in order to enable him to testify at trial.*

      i. **Rationale:** The drafters' rationale for this broadening of the rule is that the traditional rule on expert testimony, by which an expert is permitted to state the basis for his opinion, generally causes the evidence to come before the jury anyway.

C. **Statements about the declarant's mental state:** A declarant will often make statements that explicitly concern his own *mental* or *emotional* state. For instance, she may say, "I hate my husband." We'll address two conceptually distinct situations involving declarations of mental state:

   [1] Such statements when offered to prove *the very mental state asserted*, because that mental state is *directly at issue* in the litigation (e.g., "I hate my husband," where the declarant's emotions concerning her husband are directly at issue, as in a contest concerning the declarant's will);

   [2] Such statements when the mental or emotional state referred to in the statement is *not* directly in issue, but is *circumstantial evidence* of some other fact in issue; typically, the other fact will be a past or future *act by the declarant*.

   1. **State of mind directly in issue:** The declarant's state of mind will often be *directly in issue* in the litigation.

      a. **Illustrations:** The declarant's state of mind will often be in issue in a criminal case where the declarant is the defendant (for instance, the intent to kill X, or the intent to rob a store). The declarant's statement of emotional suffering may be at issue in the computation of damages in a suit by the declarant for intentional infliction of emotional distress. Or, the validity of a document asserted to establish a trust or a will may depend on the author's state of mind.

      b. **Not necessarily hearsay:** Before we examine the exception to the hearsay rule for statements of present mental state, it's important to realize that often, the declarant's statement will *not* be hearsay at all. This is because the statement will often merely be *circumstantial evidence* of the declarant's state of mind (in which case it will not be offered to prove the truth of the matter asserted), rather than a direct assertion of the declarant's state of mind offered to prove the matter asserted (that state of mind).

      Example 1: Declarant says, "My husband, Norman, is a two-timing adulterous S.O.B." Shortly after making this statement, she executes a new will, disinheriting

Norman. After she dies, Norman contests the will. Declarant's feelings about him at the time of the will are directly in issue, since the validity of the will depends in part on whether it accurately reflected her emotions. But her statement is not, strictly speaking, hearsay, since it is not offered to prove the truth of the matter asserted (that Norman was an adulterer); rather, it is offered as circumstantial evidence that Declarant did not like Norman. Thus a careful court should not even reach the question of whether a hearsay exception applies. Indeed, at least one of the principal reasons for the hearsay rule — avoiding problems of misperception — does not exist here, since the validity of the will simply does not depend at all on whether Declarant correctly or incorrectly perceived Norman's fidelity.

Example 2: Contrast the above example with one in which Declarant says, "I really hate my husband, Norman, because he's a two-timing adulterer." Here, the statement directly asserts the mental state (hatred of Norman) that is at issue in the suit. Therefore, the hearsay rule applies unless there is an applicable exception. This is true even though this remark also includes a statement that would not be hearsay (an assertion of Norman's adultery). In any event, the distinction is unlikely to make a difference, since the exception for statements of present mental state or emotion would apply here. (But procedural rules governing the handling of hearsay exceptions might make the distinction significant in a few instances.)

c. **General rule:** In any event, there is a general exception to the hearsay rule, both at common law and under the Federal Rules, for statements of the declarant's ***presently existing state of mind***. FRE 803(3)'s formulation gives the exception for "[a] statement of the declarant's ***then-existing state of mind*** (such as motive, intent, or plan) or emotional [or] sensory … condition (such as mental feeling ...)." The Federal Rule is essentially a restatement of common-law rules.

Example: P, the husband of W, sues D for D's alienation of W's affections. As part of P's case, P repeats in court W's earlier statements that D could give W a better time than P could, and that W now dislikes P.

Held, these statements are admissible. "[W]hen the intention, feelings, or other mental state of a certain person at a particular time . . . is material to the issues under trial, evidence of such person's declarations at the time indicative of his then mental state, even though hearsay, is competent as within an exception to the hearsay rule." Since the statements were admissible under this exception, they were not rendered inadmissible by the fact that they also contained other information that might otherwise have been inadmissible (such as W's statements that D took her for automobile rides and dinners, and gave her flowers). *Adkins v. Brett*, 193 P. 251 (Cal. 1920).

d. **Present state:** The most important thing to remember about the exception for statements of mental state is that it applies ***only*** to statements about the declarant's ***then existing*** mental state.

Example: Declarant says, "I hate my husband, Norman." The exception to the hearsay rule would apply, since this is a statement of Declarant's mental state ***existing at the time of the statement***. If, however, Declarant said, "Yesterday after I had a big fight with Norman, my hatred of him grew to new heights," the exception would not apply, because Declarant is speaking of a past mental state, not a present one.

    i.   **Rationale:**   Like statements of present physical condition, statements of present mental condition are considered more trustworthy because they are probably ***spontaneous*** and because the declarant usually has no motive for insincerity. As Justice Gray said in the famous case of *Mutual Life Insurance Co. v. Hillmon* (*infra*, p. 236), the exception makes sense because even if the declarant were to testify at trial, "his own memory of his state of mind at a former time is no more likely to be clear and true than a bystander's recollection of what he then said[.]"

e.   **Present state as bearing on past or future state:**   So long as the declarant's statement concerns a present mental state, the hearsay exception applies even though the ultimate mental state at issue in the case is one that ***pre-dates*** or ***post-dates*** the statement. In the following examples, admissibility of the statement turns on ***relevance***, not hearsay.

Example 1: On Monday, Declarant takes her will out of her safe deposit box and rips it up; the issue is whether this was done with an intent to revoke. On Tuesday, she says, "I don't want my husband Norman to get a cent." This statement is admissible under the exception for present declarations of present mental state, since the statement refers to her feelings at the very moment she made the declaration.

    In determining whether the exception to the hearsay rule applies, it would not matter that the ultimate mental state in issue (Declarant's feelings about Norman on Monday) relates to Monday and the declaration was made on Tuesday. The judge might conclude that Declarant's Tuesday feelings are not relevant to how she felt on Monday — this would depend on the particular facts of the case (e.g., if other evidence showed that Declarant discovered Norman's infidelity on Tuesday morning, the court might conclude that the Tuesday declaration was not logically probative of her Monday feelings). But the exclusion would be for lack of relevance, not hearsay.

Example 2: Similarly, a relevance, not hearsay, problem is raised where a declaration about a present mental state is used as circumstantial proof of a ***later*** mental state. Thus, if Declarant said on Tuesday, "I hate Norman and don't want him to receive a cent," and ripped up the will on *Wednesday*, the hearsay exception would apply and again the question would be one of relevance — are Declarant's Tuesday feelings probative of how she felt on Wednesday? See L&S, p. 423.

f.   **Surrounding circumstances:**   Declarations concerning state of mind often also include ***other assertions.*** Commonly, for instance, the declarant will go on to say that the defendant's actions caused the declarant's state of mind. If one of the issues in the case is whether the defendant's actions did indeed cause the declarant's state of mind, then the declaration is hearsay as to this issue. The court will normally deal with this problem by ***allowing*** in the entire statement, but then instructing the jury that it is to consider the statement only on the issue of the declarant's state of mind, not on the issue of whether this state of mind was caused by the defendant's acts. McC, p. 481. If the risk of prejudice is too great because the jury will probably be unable to heed this instruction, and there is other evidence of the declarant's state of mind, the judge has discretion to exclude the statement. *Id.*

2. **Proof of subsequent act:** We now turn to a quite different aspect of statements regarding mental condition: a proponent of the out-of-court declaration may be introducing it not to prove the mental state because the mental state is an issue in the case, but rather, to prove that a subsequent *act* took place, where the act is at issue. Most commonly, this will happen because the proponent wants to show that the declarant had the *intent* (mental state) to *take a certain action*, in order to prove that the declarant *did in fact eventually take that action*, where whether that act took place is an issue in the case.

   a. **General rule:** It is now generally accepted that the exception *applies* in this situation. "[O]ut-of-court statements which tend to prove a plan, design, or intention of the declarant are admissible . . . to prove that the plan, design, or intention of the declarant was carried out by the declarant." McC, p. 482.

   b. **Limitation:** Of course, considerations of *relevance* must always be satisfied, as with any other declaration of mental state. A's statement that he plans to kill B tomorrow might be held by the trial judge to be probative of whether A did in fact kill B the very next day; the same statement would probably be held to be irrelevant to whether B's unexplained death three years later was caused by A — the remoteness in time is simply too great.

   c. **Sufficient reliability:** Observe that the case for recognizing an exception in this situation is less strong than where the statement about mental condition is offered only to prove that the mental condition actually existed. There is a high likelihood that when a person says, with apparent sincerity, "I have the following mental condition," the person really has that condition. It is much less certain that when the person says, "I plan to take the following action," the act will actually occur — plans change, circumstances change, etc. Nonetheless, courts have concluded that such statements of intent are sufficiently reliable indicators of whether the intended act took place that the hearsay exception should be applied to them.

   d. **The *Hillmon* case:** The classic case illustrating this rule, indeed one of the classic cases in all of evidence law, is *Mutual Life Ins. Co. v. Hillmon*, 145 U.S. 285 (1892).

      i. **Facts:** The plaintiff in *Hillmon*, Sallie Hillmon, sued two insurance companies to recover on policies on the life of her husband, John Hillmon. She claimed that a body found in Crooked Creek, Colorado, was that of her husband. The defendants claimed that the body was that of one Walters. To support their defense, the defendants tried to introduce letters written by Walters to his sister and fiancee, in which he said that he planned to accompany Hillmon on a trip to Colorado.

      ii. **Holding:** The U.S. Supreme Court held that the letters should have been admitted. There was an issue in the case as to whether Walters went with Hillmon to Colorado. The letters were not directly evidence of whether Walters went on the trip. But the letters were the best available proof of his intention to go, and to go with Hillmon; that intention in turn "made it more probable both that he did go and that he went with Hillmon, than if there had been no proof of such intention."

    iii. Rationale: The Supreme Court's reasoning and the result in *Hillmon* make sense, in terms of our triangular technique for assessing hearsay dangers. (See *supra*, p. 187.) When Walters' statement of intent is allowed to give rise to the inference that he took the act he intended to take, there is no Right Leg danger — we're not worried that the declarant, Walters, misremembered his own intentions, or inaccurately perceived them. L&S, p. 428. It's true that the chain of inference between his having the intent and his taking the trip is not necessarily a strong one — circumstances may have changed, or he may simply have changed his mind. But these are issues of relevance, not hearsay. For instance, cross-examination of Walters at the time he wrote the letters would have revealed little about his intentions — it would almost certainly not have shown that he misremembered or misperceived them.

3. Cooperation of other: The most difficult issue involving declarations of intent arises when the stated intent is to do an act that requires the ***cooperation of another person***. That is, the declarant says, "I plan to do such-and-such with X." Most of the time, the proponent of this evidence is trying to prove that X did something with the declarant, not that the declarant did something with X.

    a. *Hillmon case:* The Supreme Court's opinion in *Hillmon*, *supra*, p. 236, almost — but not quite — deals with this problem. Recall that the declarant was Walters, and his out-of-court declarations amounted to the statement, "I plan to go to Colorado with Hillmon." Clearly, he could not have carried out this intent without Hillmon's cooperation. The Supreme Court held that his statement could be introduced as circumstantial evidence not only that he went, but that he went *with Hillmon*.

    b. Modern view: Most modern courts have followed the Supreme Court's apparent lead in *Hillmon*, and "allow a statement of an intention to engage in some action with another to support the inference that that action ***was done with the other*** and, since the two are not separable, to support the inference that the other did the action with the declarant." L&S, p. 429.

    c. Declarant is murder victim: The most fascinating cases raising this problem are those in which a murder victim tells friends beforehand, "I'm going to do such-and-such with X," and is never seen again; when X is charged with the crime, can the victim's statement be introduced as evidence to show that the victim and X were together, giving X the opportunity to commit the murder? At least one court, in the famous case set out in the following example, has ***allowed*** the statement into evidence.

    Example: Larry Adell, a sixteen-year-old boy, leaves a group of his high school friends in a restaurant, telling them that he plans to meet a man named Angelo in the parking lot, and that Angelo is supposed to give him a pound of free marijuana. Larry never returns to his friends, and is never seen again. At D's trial for kidnapping, the prosecution introduces other evidence to show that D was the man Larry knew as Angelo; it then seeks to introduce Larry's declaration to his friends about the rendezvous. (The FRE have been promulgated but not yet enacted as of the trial date; therefore, the trial court is to apply common-law evidence rules.)

Held (on appeal to the Ninth Circuit), the statement is admissible. The prevailing common-law rule is that such statements of intent of the declarant to do something with a third person are admissible. This is indicated by the Advisory Committee's Note to new FRE 803(3), which states that "[T]he rule of [*Hillmon*] allowing evidence of intention as tending to prove the doing of the act intended, is, of course, left undisturbed." (It is true that the Notes of the House Committee on the Judiciary concerning FRE 803(3) would exclude this evidence; those Notes say, "However, the Committee intends that the Rule be construed to limit the doctrine of [*Hillmon*] so as to render statements of intent by a declarant admissible only to prove his future conduct, not the future conduct of another person." However, this merely means that the new FRE, when effective, will take a narrower view than the common law did.) *U.S. v. Pheaster*, 544 F.2d 353 (9th Cir. 1976).

d. **Other evidence that declarant did act:**   Observe that this problem of using the declarant's statement of intent to prove a third party's action arises in two conceptually distinct situations: in one, there is no evidence that the declarant ever carried out the act he said he intended to commit; in the other, there is evidence that the declarant carried out, or attempted to carry out, the act, and the only question is whether he did it **with the third person**. In the former situation, the chain of inference is quite weak — the declarant may have been lying, he may have been mistaken about X's intent and learned later of his mistake before he acted, or other events may have occurred to prevent X from ever carrying out his part of their shared conduct. In the latter situation, by contrast, the fact that the declarant actually carried out his part of the shared action furnishes greater assurance of reliability.

  i. **Corroboration required:**   Most courts will, therefore, allow the declarant's statement to serve as evidence that X cooperated in the activity only if there is **independent, corroborative evidence** either that the **declarant actually participated** in the activity, or that *X* actually participated. M&K §8.39, pp. 825-26. Thus in *Pheaster*, there was no question but that Larry walked into the parking lot in pursuit of some kind of rendezvous; the only question was whether Angelo met him there. By contrast, if Larry had told his friends *the day before* that he planned to meet Angelo the next night in the restaurant parking lot, and there was no independent evidence that Larry or Angelo ever went to the parking lot, the court probably would *not* have allowed the statement to be introduced for the purpose of proving that Angelo met Larry in the parking lot.

4. **Proof of prior acts:**   Now, let us consider the converse problem: To what extent may a person's statement about his mental condition, memory, or belief be used as circumstantial evidence of something that happened *before* the statement? Whereas courts have been quite willing, as we've seen, to allow statements of intent to prove that the intended act later occurred, they have been very **unwilling** to allow statements of mental condition (especially statements of **memory** or **belief**) as circumstantial evidence that a **prior event** caused the mental state. The reason, in brief, is that allowing such evidence would **virtually abolish the hearsay rule.**

a. **The *Shepard* case:**   Here, too, there is a classic Supreme Court case on point: **Shepard v. U.S.**, 290 U.S. 96 (1933).

i. **Facts:** Dr. Shepard was charged with the murder by poison of his wife. In the absence of Dr. Shepard, Mrs. Shepard, then ill in bed, asked her nurse to bring the bottle of liquor from which she had drunk just before collapsing. She then asked the nurse whether there was enough left to test for poison, and said that the smell and taste were strange; she added, *"Dr. Shepard has poisoned me."* At the murder trial, the nurse repeated these statements to the jury.

ii. **Result:** The Supreme Court (in an opinion by Justice Cardozo) held that the statement, "Dr. Shepard has poisoned me," was admitted in violation of the hearsay rule.

iii. **Not dying declaration:** The trial court had admitted the testimony under the "dying declaration" exception (*infra*, p. 290). However, the Supreme Court rejected this rationale, on the grounds that there was no showing of the declarant's consciousness of impending death or her abandonment of hope, as required for that exception.

iv. **Not state of mind:** On appeal, the government argued that the statement was admissible under the "state of mind" exception, on the theory that there was evidence that Mrs. Shepard had thought of suicide, and the statement was relevant to whether she was indeed of a suicidal mind. The Court first rejected this argument on the narrow grounds that this was not the purpose for which the prosecution had really offered the testimony, and that a trial judge's decision to admit testimony for an illegitimate purpose (the dying declaration purpose) should not be sustained because the appellate court finds some other purpose, not even articulated at trial, that might sustain it.

v. **Not usable to prove past act by another:** But the Court also rejected the government's attempt to apply the "state of mind" exception for a much more fundamental reason, the one for which the case is remembered. The government would indeed have had the right to introduce Mrs. Shepard's declarations "to prove her present thoughts and feelings, or even her thoughts and feelings in times past." Here, however, the declarations were used "as proof of an *act* committed by someone else, as evidence that [declarant] was dying of poison given by her husband."

vi. **Might not be backwards-pointing:** The Court contrasted this situation with that in *Hillmon* (*supra*, p. 236). *Hillmon* involved a statement of intention used to prove that the intended act was *subsequently* accomplished. But in the *Shepard* court's view, "The ruling in [*Hillmon*] marks the high water line beyond which the courts have been unwilling to go. . . . Declarations of intention, casting light upon the future, have been sharply distinguished from declarations of memory, pointing backwards to the past." The testimony here *"faced backward and not forward,"* at least in its "most obvious implications." Furthermore, it "spoke to a past act, and more than that, to an act by someone not the speaker." The small tendency it might have had to establish the declarant's own present state of mind was clearly drowned by "the reverberating clang of those accusatory words."

vii. **Rationale:** The Court explained why the distinction between future-pointing statements (allowed under *Hillmon*) and past-pointing statements (disallowed under *Shepard*) was so significant: "***There would be an end***, or nearly that, ***to the rule against hearsay*** if the distinction were ignored."

b. **Modern rule:** The view of the *Shepard* court has essentially prevailed in every jurisdiction. The rule may be capsulized as follows: The "state of mind" exception to the hearsay rule does not apply to statements of *memory* or *belief* about *past actions or events*. This is true whether the past action was by the declarant ("I believe I went to the store yesterday") or by another ("I believe that Dr. Shepard has poisoned me.") Observe that not only would allowing such statements swallow up the hearsay rule, such statements also suffer from all of the standard hearsay dangers — both the Left Leg and Right Leg dangers (*supra*, p. 187).

   i. **Illustration from *Shepard*:** Thus on the facts of *Shepard*, the Left Leg dangers are clear: Mrs. Shepard may have been insincere (she may have committed suicide, and knowingly tried to get her husband blamed); also, her statement may have been ambiguous and been misheard by the nurse (e.g., she may have said, "Is it possible that Dr. Shepard has poisoned me?") Furthermore, the Right Leg dangers are equally present: Mrs. Shepard may have suffered from an erroneous memory of what had happened (e.g., she really put the poison in the liquor herself, and forgot that she had done so, in a paranoid delusion) or from inaccurate perception (e.g., she didn't notice that it was really the nurse who put poison in the bottle).

   ii. **Federal Rule:** The Federal Rules follow *Shepard* in not allowing statements of memory or belief to prove previous acts. FRE 803(3), after establishing the general hearsay exception for statements of the declarant's "then existing state of mind, emotion," etc., excludes "a statement of *memory or belief to prove the fact remembered or believed*[.]" (There is a special exception for statements regarding the declarant's will; see *infra*, p. 241.)

c. **Fear of another:** In one situation, a *minority* of courts have allowed into evidence the declarant's statement of memory or belief where that statement's principal tendency is to show another's action: where the declarant expresses *fear* of another, and the statement expressly or implicitly blames the fear on the other's acts.

   Example: V says (out of court), "I'm afraid that D will kill me." If V is later found dead, and D is charged with killing him, a few courts might allow the declaration. However, in most such cases the victim's state of mind is not directly in issue, and therefore most courts will not allow declarations concerning a victim's fear of the defendant, since the jury will probably view the declarations as direct evidence of the defendant's guilt. McC, p. 486.

   i. **Other purposes:** However, the generally-accepted rule that the victim's declarations of fear of the defendant do not fall within the state of mind exception applies only where the victim's statement is used as evidence that the defendant committed an act which caused the fear. In several other situations, the victim's declaration of fear of the defendant will be admitted, because that state of mind is directly relevant to *some other issue* in the case. This would be true, for instance, if: (1) The defendant claims *self-defense* as the justification for killing the victim; the victim's declaration that he fears the defendant will be admitted to rebut the defense, since it makes it less likely that the victim was the initial aggressor. (2) The defendant defends on the grounds that the victim committed ***suicide***; the victim's statements of fear of the defendant will be admitted to rebut a suicidal bent. (3) The defendant claims that the decedent died ***accidentally*** (e.g., he claims that the victim picked up the defendant's gun and was accidentally killed). Here, a statement by the victim that he was afraid of the defendant (or, for that matter, that he was afraid of guns) would be admitted to rebut defendant's defense. See *U.S. v. Brown*, 490 F.2d 758 (D.C. Cir. 1973), listing these situations.

d. Intent coupled with recital of past acts: Sometimes, a statement of intent to commit an act (admissible under the *Hillmon* rationale to prove that the act probably occurred) is ***coupled*** with a reference to the declarant's recollection of some ***past act*** by himself or by a third person. The latter reference, if standing alone, would of course not be admissible, under *Shepard*. But where the ***main thrust*** of the statement is the future-looking part, many courts will allow the ***entire statement*** to come in.

i. Statements explaining motive: The whole statement is especially likely to be allowed in where the reference to the remembered fact or belief is an explanation of ***why*** the future act is intended.

Example: D, a union official, is charged with taking an illegal payoff from a corporation, X Corp. The payoff is charged to have taken place on Aug. 15, 1999. At that time, Z was the President of X Corp. and W was the Chairman. Z is now dead. At trial, the prosecution wishes to put on testimony by W that on the morning of Aug. 15, 1999, Z said to W, "D has asked for a $10,000 payoff. I'll be meeting with him tonight in New York to give it to him."

A court might well allow this entire statement into evidence, on the following syllogism: (1) The statement that Z would be meeting with D that night is admissible under the *Hillmon* rationale, to show that the meeting probably took place; (2) the forward-looking piece (meeting will take place) is the main thrust; (3) the entire statement (including *why* the meeting is to take place) should be admitted to set the forward-looking part in context and explain it.

e. Execution of will: There is one very well-recognized exception to the ban on "memory or belief" statements: A person's statements relating to his own ***will*** are generally allowed, even if they are statements of memory or belief offered to prove the fact remembered or believed. This special exception exists not because this kind of out-of-court declaration is believed inherently more trustworthy, but simply because there is often a ***great need*** for it — no one else can know the decedent's wishes as well as the decedent, and he is of course not available.

i. Scope: Generally, this special exception applies to the testator's statements that he has or has not made a will, that his will is intended to reach a certain result, or that he has or has not revoked a will. McC, p. 485.

ii. Federal formulation: This special exception is carried over into the Federal Rules. FRE 803(3), after excluding statements of "memory or belief to prove the fact remembered or believed," carves out a special exception where the statement of memory or belief "relates to the validity or terms of the declarant's will."

D. Excited utterances: All courts recognize a hearsay exception for certain statements made under the influence of a ***startling event***. This is usually called the ***"excited utterances"*** exception.

1. **Federal codification:**   The common-law formulation of this exception has been codified in FRE 803(2): The exception applies to "A statement relating to a ***startling event*** or condition, made while the declarant was under the ***stress of excitement*** that it caused."

   a. **Two requirements:**   There are thus two independent requirements that must be satisfied in order for the excited utterances exception to apply:

      i. **Startling event:**   The event giving rise to the statement must be ***sufficiently startling*** to eliminate the declarant's capacity to reflect before speaking; and

      ii. **Still under effect:**   The statement must be made while the declarant is ***still under the influence*** of the startling event. See L&S, p. 418.

2. **Rationale:**   The main rationale for the exception is that where the event is so startling that the declarant's ***reflective capacity is eliminated***, the declaration is unlikely to be ***motivated by self-interest or otherwise insincere***. Therefore, the statement is likely to be accurate, or so the theory says.

   Example: V, immediately after being brutally assaulted and raped, calls out to a passerby, "Help. D did this to me." Given the stress on V at the moment, it's very unlikely that she has had the time or ability to cook up a false story about who her assailant is.

   a. **Mistake of perception:**   However, the increase in sincerity due to the startling occurrence is partially offset by a probable increase in ***errors of perception*** due to the startling event. "[E]xcitement tends to distort perception and may cloud memory. There is reason to believe that excited utterances are, on balance, less reliable than much of the hearsay we refuse to admit." L&S, p. 417. Nonetheless, the exception is firmly grounded and unlikely eliminated.

3. **Sufficiently startling:**   The requirement that the event be ***sufficiently startling*** to still reflective capacity, rarely causes problems. Physical violence is not required — even seeing a photograph in a newspaper may suffice. McC, p. 476. The basic issue is whether the event is sufficiently startling that the court believes that a normal person would probably have spoken before thinking.

   a. **Independent proof:**   Courts are split about whether the existence of the startling event can be proved by the statement alone, or whether ***independent evidence*** of the event must be presented. Most courts allow the statement to be used for this purpose. L&S, p. 418.

4. **Time factor:**   Most litigation has involved the second requirement, that the statement be made while the declarant is ***still under the influence*** of the startling event. In making this determination, courts look to all of the surrounding circumstances, including evidence that this particular declarant was in fact still under the event's sway (e.g., she was suffering from clinical shock). However, in making this determination, the courts have attached exceptional importance to the ***amount of time that passed*** between the event and the declaration.

a. **Rule of thumb:** One authority asserts that most cases fall within the following rule of thumb: "Statements made during the exciting event or within *half an hour* afterward are usually admitted, statements made an hour or more after the event are usually excluded, while statements made within thirty minutes to an hour of the event are dealt with . . . by a close look at the surrounding circumstances." L&S, p. 418.

b. **Shock or memory loss:** Occasionally the event may produce shock, memory loss, coma, or some other medical condition that *delays the time for reflection* far beyond what it would normally be. In this event, courts will generally apply the excited utterance exception despite the long time interval.

c. **Presence of reflection:** Even where the time interval is short, a court may find that the surrounding circumstances indicate that the declarant *did* have time to reflect, so that the exception should not apply.

   i. **Self-serving nature:** For instance, if the statement is clearly *self-serving* (e.g., "The accident wasn't my fault, because I carefully stopped at the stop sign. . . ."), the court will probably find that the required interference with reflective capacity did not exist. McC, p. 477.

   ii. **Questions:** If the statement is made *in response to a detailed question*, this will be evidence that there was not the required absence of reflection. However, a statement that comes in response to a simple "What happened?" will probably not be disqualified. L&S, pp. 418-19.

5. **Reference to exciting event:** Must the declaration *explain* or *refer to* the startling event? Or is it enough that the declaration is made while still under the influence of the event, and relates to it in some way? The courts are split.

   a. **Federal rule:** Under FRE 803(2), whose approach is also followed by many state courts, the declaration need *not* explain or refer to the startling event — it is sufficient that the excited utterance is one "*relating to* a startling event or condition."

   b. **Contrary rule:** But other state courts insist that the excited utterance explain or refer to the startling event. McC, p. 476.

   c. **Statements of agency:** The issue is most likely to arise where the declarant, while still under the influence of the startling event, makes a statement regarding his *employment* or other agency. Courts following the federal approach will allow the statement under the excited utterances exception; those following the opposite rule will not.

   Example: Declarant, a truck driver, gets in an accident. Immediately following the accident, he shouts, "Hurry up, I've got to call on a customer, and I want to get home." The statement is offered to prove that Declarant was really going to call on a customer (and therefore, by inference, that he was on business at the time of the accident so that his employer is liable). The statement does not explain or directly refer to the accident. Therefore, some state courts would exclude it; but the Federal Rules would allow it, since it "relates to" the accident.

    d. Distinguished from present sense impression rule: Observe that the Federal Rule on this point is quite different from the Federal Rule in the case of a statement of "present sense impression" under FRE 803(1) (*infra*, p. 244) — the statement of present sense impression must be one "***describing*** or ***explaining*** an event or condition."

    6. Rape cases: A separate common-law exception to the hearsay rule has developed in ***sexual assault*** cases, under which the prosecution may prove that the victim made a ***prompt complaint***. McC, p. 478. Today, such a declaration of complaint is more likely to be admitted under the excited utterances exception — whereas the special sexual assault complaint exception usually allows only the fact of complaint to be admitted, the excited utterances exception will allow the content of the declaration (especially any statement about the identity of the assailant) to be admitted. The Federal Rules make no special provision for declarations of complaint in sexual assault cases, so the excited utterances exception is typically the only way to get into evidence the contents of the victim's complaint. *Id.*

E. Present sense impressions: Recall that the exception for excited utterances has been criticized on the grounds that the startling event makes errors more, rather than less, likely. Consequently, it can be argued that a spontaneous statement by one who has witnessed an event should be admitted more readily if the speaker was ***unexcited*** than if he was excited. This reasoning was generally rejected traditionally, but in the last few decades, more and more courts have subscribed to it. Today, many if not most courts (and the Federal Rules) recognize a separate hearsay exception for what might be termed "***present sense impressions***."

    1. Federal formulation: The formulation of FRE 803(1) is typical of this trend: an exception is recognized for a statement "***describing*** or ***explaining*** an ***event or condition***, made ***while or immediately after*** the declarant ***perceived it***.

    2. *Houston Oxygen* case: The case with which the present sense impression exception is often associated is *Houston Oxygen Co. v. Davis*, 161 S.W.2d 474 (Tex.App. 1942).

        a. Facts: In *Houston Oxygen*, Mrs. Cooper and Mr. Sanders were riding together on the highway when a car containing P passed them. The defendants offered Mr. Sanders' testimony that as P's car passed by, Mrs. Cooper said that the people in P's car "must have been drunk, that we would find them somewhere on the road wrecked if they keep that rate of speed up."

        b. Holding: The declaration could not come in under the excited utterance exception, because there was no evidence that Mrs. Cooper was so startled by the event that she was incapable of reflection. Nonetheless, the court admitted the statement.

            i. Rationale: It did so on the theory that the statement was "sufficiently spontaneous to save it from the suspicion of being manufactured evidence. There was no time for a calculated statement." Since the statement was a report of an event at the moment the event was witnessed, there was no danger of any defect from memory. Furthermore, the statement was made to another (Mr. Sanders) who had an equal opportunity to observe the event and thus to correct any misstatement. In summary, the circumstances gave the statement a high degree of reliability. This was true even though the statement was made considerably before the principal event being litigated; (P's car did not crash until 4 miles later up the road).

3. **Immediacy:** In contrast to the excited-utterances exception, for the present-sense-impression exception *no material time may pass* between the event being perceived and the declarant's statement about it. FRE 803(1)'s requirement — that the statement take place "*while or immediately after* the declarant perceived" the event — is typical.

4. **Description:** Whereas the excited utterance need not describe the exciting event (it must merely take place under the influence of that event), the present sense impression must *describe* or *explain* the event that the declarant has perceived.

5. **Perception**: The declarant must be a "percipient witness" to the event. That is, he must have *perceived the event*, rather than have learned about it from some other means (e.g., reading the newspaper).

6. **Opinions allowed:** A declaration may be admitted under the exception even if it expresses an *opinion*, so long as it is an attempt to explain something that the declarant is perceiving.

7. **No corroboration required:** Although the listener (who will repeat the statement in court) will generally be present at the event and be able to corroborate the declaration, there is *no requirement* that there be *corroboration* of the statement.

8. **"*Res gestae*" label:** Recall (*supra*, p. 230) that the label *"res gestae"* is often applied to a variety of spontaneous or excited statements. This is especially likely to be the case in the present sense impression context — many courts have simply used the *res gestae* label instead of making it clear that the present sense impression exception is being applied. The better practice is to avoid the *res gestae* terminology entirely.

V.   PAST RECOLLECTION RECORDED

A. **The rule generally:** Sometimes a person makes a written record of an event, shortly after the event has occurred. Time passes, the writer's memory of the event dims, and then a trial occurs at which the event is in issue. The witness cannot testify satisfactorily about the event, because by hypothesis he has forgotten some of the details. The written account of the event cannot be offered as evidence for the truth of the facts recited in the document, unless there is an exception to the hearsay rule — for the writing is an out-of-court declaration offered for the truth of what it asserts. The rule permitting introduction of *"past recollection recorded"* provides such an exception, if certain requirements are satisfied whose effect is to increase the reliability of the document.

1. **Typical applications:** Here are some situations in which the writing might be admissible as a past recollection recorded:

   a. W takes an inventory for the business which employs him, and writes down the inventory on a slip of paper;

   b. W is an insurance company accident investigator, who investigates a car accident and writes down information about the damage, location of the vehicles, etc.;

   c. W is a police officer who interviews a witness after a crime, and makes notes about the witness's statement;

d. W is the admitting nurse at a hospital, who makes notes about the patient's symptoms and the patient's comments regarding pain.

2. Relation to business records exception: Observe that some of these types of documents might be alternatively admissible under the "business records" (or more generally, "regularly kept records") exception, *infra*, p. 249. However, the business records exception applies whether or not the person who made the entry is available to testify; the past recollection recorded exception applies only where the person who made the entry (or at least some person who approved the entry at the time it was made) is available to testify about the making of the entry.

3. FRE 803(5) recognizes a hearsay exception for: The Federal Rules follow the general outlines of the common-law exception. FRE 803(5), entitled "Recorded Recollection," provides a hearsay exception for:

"A record that:

(A) is on a matter the witness *once knew about but now cannot recall* well enough to testify fully and accurately;

(B) was *made or adopted by the witness* when the matter was *fresh in the witness's memory*; and

(C) *accurately reflects* the witness's knowledge.

If admitted, the record may be *read into evidence* but may be received as an *exhibit only if offered by an adverse party.*"

B. Requirements for the rule: There are four essential requirements which must be satisfied before a memorandum or record may be admitted under the past recollection recorded exception. These requirements exist in more or less the same form in most common-law jurisdictions as well as under the Federal Rules:

1. First-hand knowledge: The memorandum must relate to something of which the witness once had *first-hand knowledge*.

Example: W writes down the details of an inventory. If he testifies at trial that he had first-hand knowledge of the inventory details at the time he made the record, this requirement will be satisfied. If, however, he says on the stand that some of the information was supplied by his assistant (and the assistant is not available to testify that he, too, wrote or approved the record), the inventory records will not be admissible. McC, p. 492.

2. Made when fresh in memory: The record must have been made when the matter was *fresh in the witness's memory*.

a. Common law: The traditional common-law rule was that the record had to be made "at or near the time" of the events recorded.

b. Modern/federal: But the modern trend is somewhat more liberal. Thus FRE 803(5)(B) requires merely that the record have been made "when the matter was fresh in the witness's memory." Under the modern/federal approach, a record made several days after the events in question would still have a reasonable chance of being found to meet this requirement.

3. **Impaired recollection:** Both traditional and modern cases have nearly always required that the witness have suffered at least some *impairment* of his memory of the events recorded. That is, if the witness's memory at the time of trial is perfectly clear about the events, the earlier record may not be introduced — a key part of the rationale for the past recollection recorded exception is that it applies only where, in a sense, the witness's memory is partly "unavailable." However, courts have, over the years, differed as to how complete the impairment of the witness's memory must be.

    a. **Traditional approach:** The traditional common-law approach was that the witness who made the record must testify at trial that he *lacks all present memory* of the event, and thus cannot testify concerning it at all. McC, p. 493.

    b. **Federal and modern rule:** The Federal Rules approach, shared by most modern courts, is that the witness must suffer *some impairment* of his memory of the events, but this impairment need not be total. FRE 803(5)'s formulation is that it must be the case that the witness "*now cannot recall* [the matter] well enough to *testify fully and accurately*[.]"

        i. **Rationale:** The reason most courts require a substantial impairment of memory is that they are afraid that otherwise, there would be an increase in the use of statements that are prepared for the express purpose of being used in litigation; such statements might be drafted or influenced by interested parties or lawyers. Lilly, p. 262.

    c. **No impairment needed:** A very few courts have abandoned the requirement of memory impairment entirely, on the theory that the written record, since it was made so much closer to the time of the events, is inherently more reliable than the witness's testimony at the time of trial could possibly be. L&S, p. 437.

4. **Accuracy when written:** The witness at trial must testify as to the *accuracy* of the record when made. As FRE 803(5) puts it, the record must "accurately reflect[] the witness's knowledge." "What this means in practice is that the witness must testify either that he *remembers making an accurate recording* of the event in question although he no longer remembers the facts recorded, or, if the witness has entirely forgotten the situation in which the recording was made, that he is *confident he would not have written* or adopted some description of the facts unless that description *truly described* his observations at the time." L&S, p. 437.

    a. **Adopted by witness:** It is *not* required that the witness at trial be the person who *made* the record. All that is required is that the witness have *approved* or adopted the record, after it was made, as being an accurate reflection of his knowledge.

        Example: W, a forensic pathologist, performs an autopsy. He dictates the results of the autopsy to an assistant, who carefully makes notes of what W says. So long as W looks over the notes and approves them shortly after they are made, only W's testimony (and not that of the assistant) is needed at trial in order for the notes to come in under past recollection recorded.

    b. **Multi-party problem:** Now suppose that, as in the above example, W describes to X facts of which W has first-hand knowledge, X puts them into a record, but W does *not* check the record for accuracy. W's testimony will not, in most courts and under the Federal Rules, be sufficient by itself — W cannot testify that the document "accurately reflects [his] knowledge." In this situation, both W and X must testify at trial: W would testify that his oral statements to X correctly reflected the facts as he, W, then knew them; X would then testify that he accurately recorded what W told him. Together, the two witnesses would be found to have met the requirements of FRE 803(5). McC, pp. 493-94; L&S, p. 438.

C. Other considerations: Here are some miscellaneous aspects of the past recollection recorded exception:

1. **Non-writings:** Normally, the "record" will be a writing. However, this is not a formal requirement. Thus if W makes a ***tape recording*** of facts known to him (e.g., a tape dictated by a pathologist during an autopsy), the tape recording is probably admissible under the exception, assuming all the above requirements are met. McC, p. 492.

2. **Best Evidence rule:** The Best Evidence rule (see *infra*, p. 490), which applies to any written document, means that the record introduced must be the ***original***, unless the proponent can show that the original is unavailable through no fault of his own. L&S, p. 438. Thus if the record is, say, a police officer's notes on an accident investigation, the original notes, rather than a typed transcript of them, must be introduced at trial.

3. **Not always admissible as evidence:** All courts allow the record, if it meets the requirements for the exception, to be ***read out loud*** to the jury and into evidence. However, courts disagree about whether the memorandum or record itself should become an ***exhibit*** in evidence.

   a. **Don't allow:** Most courts, and the Federal Rules, take the view that the record is essentially ***testimony***; since transcripts of live witness's testimony are not exhibits intended to be taken into the jury room, these courts feel that the past recollection recorded should not be given better status, and therefore possibly greater probative value in the jury's eyes. Thus FRE 803(5) provides that "If admitted, the record may be read into evidence but may be ***received as an exhibit only if offered by an adverse party.***"

4. **Distinguished from present recollection refreshed:** Be sure to distinguish the exception for past recollection recorded from the doctrine called *"present recollection refreshed,"* whereby a witness on the stand who has trouble remembering an event may be given a writing, a picture, or some other document to aid his recollection. See *supra*, p. 113.

   a. **Not hearsay:** Strictly speaking, the use of the *present recollection refreshed* technique is ***not an exception*** to the hearsay rule at all — since the only thing that goes into evidence is the witness's present testimony, and not the document, there is simply no out-of-court declaration. The past recollection recorded doctrine, by contrast, is a true hearsay exception, subject to very technical rules as we've seen.

VI. BUSINESS RECORDS

A. Problem generally: Business enterprises keep records in the ordinary course of their business. For instance, a business typically keeps accounts that show who owes it money. If such a routine business record is offered as evidence, and offered to show the truth of the matter asserted in the document, a hearsay problem is presented.

   1. Illustration: For instance, suppose that P, a merchant, is suing D, a customer, for an unpaid balance. If P presents its ledger book to show that goods were sold to D on a certain date for a certain amount, and never paid for, the use of the document is hearsay — it is used to show that the matter asserted in the document (that D received the goods and never paid for them) is true. Yet there may be no other evidence available to P — the clerk who actually handed the goods to D may no longer be available; the clerk who made the notation in the records was not necessarily the one who delivered the goods; still another person may have been in charge of processing payments, and could thus give only a partial picture of the transaction, etc.

   2. Need for rule: In short, the complexities of modern business transactions mean that an enterprise's records, kept in the ordinary course of business, are often the best evidence of events that happen during the course of business. For this reason, a special hearsay exception for *"business records"* (or, somewhat more generally, *"regularly kept records"*) has arisen.

B. Federal Rule: FRE 803(6) is more or less representative of the way most states handle business records, except that on most controversial issues, it tends to be more liberal (i.e., to include more). 803(6) gives a hearsay exception, without regard to availability of the recorder, for:

> **"Records of a Regularly Conducted Activity.** A record of an act, event, condition, opinion, or diagnosis if:
>
> (A) the record was made *at or near the time by* — or *from information transmitted by* — *someone with knowledge*;
>
> (B) the record was *kept in the course of a regularly conducted activity* of a *business, organization, occupation, or calling*, whether or not for *profit*;
>
> (C) making the record was a *regular practice of that activity*;
>
> (D) all these conditions are shown by the *testimony of the custodian or another qualified witness*, or by a *certification* that complies with Rule 902(11) or (12) or with a statute permitting certification; and
>
> (E) the opponent does not show that the source of information or the method or circumstances of preparation indicate a *lack of trustworthiness*."

   a. Summary of requirements: Observe that FRE 803(6), like most modern-day statutes, imposes three major requirements before the record may be introduced:

   i. Regular entries: The entries must be made in the *routine* of a *business* or organization ("kept in the course of a regularly conducted activity of a business...", and "making the record was a regular practice of that activity");

       ii. Knowledge: The record must have been made by, or from information from, a person with ***personal knowledge*** of the matter recorded;

       iii. Timeliness: The entries must have been made ***"at or near the time"*** of the matter recorded.

C. Definition of a "business": Originally, the regularly-kept records exception only applied to a ***"business,"*** and the term "business" was construed quite literally. Today, most statutes are far broader. Thus FRE 803(6) applies to any record kept by a ***"business, organization, occupation, or calling,*** whether or not for ***profit."*** So ***schools***, ***churches***, and ***hospitals*** would be covered. S&R, p. 831.

D. Person who originally supplies information: The FRE and similar state rules pay special attention to the person who ***originally supplies*** the information that goes into the record. In most jurisdictions, this person must satisfy two requirements: (1) he must have ***first-hand knowledge*** of the fact he reports; and (2) he must do his reporting ***while working in the business.***

    1. First-hand information: Courts have generally insisted that the original source of the information be one with ***first-hand knowledge*** of the matter. Observe that this original source need not be the person who is actually making the entry. Thus FRE 803(6) merely requires that the record be "made … by — or from information transmitted by — someone with knowledge[.]" For instance, if a messenger for a retail store reports to the clerk that he has dropped off a shipment at X Corp., the fact that the clerk who records that information lacks personal knowledge is irrelevant, since the source of the information is one who has first-hand information (the messenger).

    2. Requirement of business duty: Suppose the person who supplies information from his own knowledge is ***not acting on behalf of the business*** that is making the record. Is the requirement of a "regularly kept business record" satisfied? Most courts that have considered the question have said, ***"no."*** The classic case on this issue is ***Johnson v. Lutz***, 170 N.E. 517 (N.Y. 1930).

       a. Facts: *Johnson v. Lutz* involved an accident report prepared by a policeman based on information supplied to him by people present at the scene of the accident.

       b. Holding: The New York Court of Appeals refused to apply its recently-enacted business records statute to this situation. The court pointed out that the statute was enacted to avoid the need for having every member of a business who had participated in the preparation of a given record testify. "It was not intended to permit the receipt in evidence of entries based upon voluntary hearsay statements made by third parties not engaged in the business or under any duty in relation thereto."

       c. Rationale: This rationale and result have seemed reasonable to most courts and commentators who have considered the problem. A person who works for the business that is making the record, or has some other relation of duty to that business, may make mistakes, but his conduct is subject to safeguards: a person's employment in a business makes it likely that he is operating in a well-established routine shared by other employees, and that he will be subject to punishment by superiors if he makes a mistake. L&S, p. 442. There are no such safeguards, however, in the case of information supplied by a third person who does not work for the business that is keeping the record.

Example: If X, a bystander at the accident, says, "Y caused the accident by going through a red light," there is no special reason to believe that X's statement is correct, merely because it ends up in a police officer's report. X's statement would not be admissible if another bystander heard it, and repeated it in court; why should X's out-of-court statement come into evidence merely because it happens to be transcribed by a policeman? *Id.*

d. **Two-step admission:** Most courts would, however, allow a report to be introduced for the *limited purpose* of proving that the statement was made. If some *other exception* to the hearsay rule would apply directly to the statement made by the person not acting on behalf of the business that is keeping the record, the record and the statement it includes can therefore both come into evidence.

Example: P works for D, a company. After P is fired by D, she sues it, alleging that her superior, Posehn, sexually harassed her by propositioning her to have sex in return for better work assignments. At trial, P offers an investigative report prepared for D by Purcell Security. D had hired Purcell to perform an investigation into the validity of P's allegations. The investigator, Ford (a Purcell employee), writes in the report that he interviewed two supervisory employees of D, Stampley and Coyle, and that they both told him that Posehn frequently attempted to have sex with females under his supervision. P offers the report under the business-records exception. D objects, contending that Stampley and Coyle were not employees of Purcell (the company making the business record), so that the business records exception should not apply to their statements. The trial judge overrules D's objection, and allows the report in evidence

Held, for P: the report was properly admitted. It's true that if the *only* exception available was the business records exception, Stampley's and Coyle's statements would not be admissible, because they were not acting on behalf of the business that was making the record (Purcell). However, P has offered an "alternative argument" governing these two statements, based on the fact that Stampley and Coyle were employees of D at the time they made the statement: as supervisors for D, Stampley's and Coyle's jobs required them to be concerned about allegations of sexual harassment, so that the statements by these two were made within the scope of their job. Therefore, the statements were statements by an agent of a party-opponent (D), concerning a matter within the scope of the agency or employment, and were thus admissible against D under the state equivalent of FRE 801(d)(2)(D). Consequently, both the report, and the statements by Stampley and Coyle contained in the report, were properly admitted. *Norcon, Inc. v. Kotowski*, 971 P.2d 158 (Alaska 1999).

E. **Made in "regular course of business":** The business records exception was originally designed to cover records made during the everyday routine of a business, and integrally related to its operations. Where the record is of a sort that the business prepares only *rarely*, and does not relate to its day-to-day operations, does the exception nonetheless apply? The issue usually arises in the case of *accident reports* prepared by a business.

1. ***Palmer*:** The leading case, the Supreme Court case of ***Palmer v. Hoffman***, 318 U.S. 109 (1943), suggests that the exception does ***not*** apply to such non-routine records. But more recent cases have limited *Palmer* fairly narrowly to its facts.

    a. **Facts:** In *Palmer*, the plaintiffs were the spouse and estate of a person killed in a rail-road grade crossing accident. The defendant railroad company tried to introduce a statement made after the accident by the train's engineer, in an interview conducted by a railroad supervisor and a member of the state Public Utilities Commission at the rail-road's office. The then-applicable federal business records statute required that the record have been made "in the regular course of [the] business."

    b. **Holding:** The Supreme Court concluded that the accident report did not qualify under the statute, since it was not in the "regular course" of the railroad's business. Unlike, say, payroll or accounts receivable records, the accident reports "are calculated for use essentially in the court, not in the business. Their primary utility is in litigating, not in railroading."

    c. **Criticism:** The Court's reasoning in *Palmer* can be criticized. The railroad made a routine of investigating *every* accident in which it was involved; indeed, it probably could not have continued successfully in business without doing so.

        i. **Self-serving nature:** However, the Court was clearly correct that this kind of report is fundamentally different from, say, a payroll account. This report was made ***only once litigation had become likely***, and the railroad (as well as the engineer who was making the statement) had a strong incentive to take a ***self-serving*** position, an incentive which is not present in the payroll records situation. Yet at the same time, the Court did not want to base the result directly on the self-serving nature of the record; otherwise, it might have had a problem admitting, say, accounts receivable records, where the business keeping the record has at least an arguable incentive to overstate the money owed to it.

2. **Modern view:** In interpreting modern statutes, courts have followed the precise result in *Palmer*, but have limited that case somewhat narrowly to its facts.

    a. **Rareness not dispositive:** Thus the mere fact that the type of record in question is kept rarely rather than in the business's everyday routine, is ***not*** in most courts sufficient to take the record out of the relevant statute or court rule. "Most courts feel that an activity may be in the regular course of business without being so frequent as to be routine." L&S, p. 443.

    b. **Self-serving motive:** But most courts will ***exclude*** the record where they sense a strong motive on the part of the business or the employee-declarant to behave in a ***self-serving*** manner. This is especially likely in the case of accident reports or other documents prepared in anticipation of litigation. Thus most courts today would reach the same result on the facts of *Palmer* itself.

    c. **Federal Rule:** The Federal Rules are in agreement with this general modern approach. Thus FRE 803(6)(C) requires merely that it must have been the case that "making the record was a regular practice of that activity[.]" There is no requirement that the making of such records be frequent or routine. But 803(6)(E) specifies that the exception does not apply if the person opposing the record shows that "the source of information or the method or circumstances of preparation *indicate a lack of trustworthiness.*" Thus in a *Palmer*-like situation, where the record is an accident report prepared by a defendant's employee in anticipation of litigation, the trial judge would likely conclude that the plaintiffs, by pointing out that the employee had an incentive to protect his employer from liability when he made the accident report, had borne their burdening of showing the report's probable "lack of trustworthiness," making the report inadmissible under FRE 803(6)(E).

3. **Police reports and records:** Where an accident or crime report is maintained by the *police*, the record may qualify under the business records exception — modern statutes may well include police operations (e.g., their activities are a "regularly conducted activity of a business [or] organization" under FRE 803(6)(B), and it would be the "regular practice of that activity" to make accident or crime reports under 803(6)(C)). However, a separate exception exists in most jurisdictions for *public* records and reports, and the rules for that exception may be different.

   a. **Issue:** Therefore, a question arises about the treatment of a police or other government report that would not be admissible for a particular use under the public records exception, but would be admissible under the business records exception. The most interesting version of this question is whether a police report or other government record that would not be admissible against a criminal defendant under FRE 803(8)(A)(ii) may nonetheless be admitted under the general business records exception of 803(6). Courts have split on this matter; the issue is discussed more extensively *infra*, p. 263.

F. **Opinions:** Sometimes the business record will contain an *opinion*. Courts and statutes vary substantially as to when a record containing an opinion may be introduced for the truth of that opinion.

1. **Speculative opinion:** In general, "the more speculative the opinion, the greater the probability of exclusion." L&S, p. 443.

2. **Lay opinions:** Where the opinion is a *"lay"* (as opposed to "expert") opinion, it will usually be *excluded.* If the lay opinion were given from the witness stand, it would probably be excluded under the general rule prohibiting such lay opinion testimony (see *infra*, p. 516). Most courts will not permit such otherwise inadmissible testimony to come in in the form of a business record.

3. **Expert testimony:** Most cases involve *expert* opinions contained in the business record. The most common situation involves *hospital records*, where the physician or nurse has written an opinion about the nature of the patient's ailment, its cause, or its prognosis. Courts vary significantly in their treatment of such opinions; the issue is discussed in detail *infra*, p. 256.

4. **Federal Rules:** FRE 803(6) rejects the tendency of some courts to exclude opinions contained in business records. 803(6) expressly allows a record of an "act, event, condition, *opinion*, or diagnosis[.]" However, the court will usually be at least as strict as it would be were the opinion given in courtroom testimony; thus if the opinion is unduly speculative, the court has discretion to exclude it.

a. **Basis for opinion not disclosed:**   Furthermore, the court may decide to keep out opinion evidence that does not disclose the factual basis for the opinions — if the opinion were given in courtroom testimony, the expert could be examined about the basis for it; with a mere physical record restating the opinion, no such examination is possible, and the court may therefore conclude that the evidence is not sufficiently trustworthy. In reaching such a decision, the court can rely on 803(6)(E)'s special provision excluding a record when the opponent shows that "the source of information or the method or circumstances of preparation indicate a lack of trustworthiness."

G. **Trustworthiness:**   As noted just above, even where the formal conditions for the business records exception are satisfied, the court may still exclude evidence that it finds to be unduly self-serving or otherwise ***untrustworthy.*** Most statutes and rules contain an implied or explicit exception similar to that of FRE 803(6)(E), which requires the exclusion of evidence if the opponent bears the burden of showing that "the source of information or the method or circumstances of preparation indicate a lack of trustworthiness."

> **Example:** P, who has been injured in the course of his employment, makes a worker's compensation claim. For purposes of this claim, he is examined by several doctors, some retained by the insurance company and some retained by P. P then brings a civil action arising out of the same accident. He wishes to introduce the reports prepared by each of these doctors, instead of calling them to give trial testimony.
>
> *Held,* the reports of the physicians retained by D may be admitted, but those prepared by P's treating physicians may not be. Even though all reports were made in anticipation of litigation, the trustworthiness of the reports prepared by D's physicians is enhanced by the fact that they are being offered by a party adverse to the one on whose behalf the reports were made. The reports by P's physicians, on the other hand, are "self-serving with no added degree of trustworthiness." *Yates v. Bair Transport, Inc.,* 249 F.Supp. 681 (S.D.N.Y. 1965) (a pre-FRE case).

H. **Absence of entry:**   Suppose that a regularly kept business record ***fails*** to contain a record of a particular event, and the circumstances are such that had that event taken place, the records would probably have reflected it. May the absence of an entry be introduced as evidence that the event did ***not occur***?

1. **General rule:**   Most courts ***allow*** the absence of the entry as evidence of the non-occurrence of the event. McC, p. 498.

> **Example:** P, a merchant, routinely records receipt of payments from customers against outstanding invoices. P sues D for failure to pay an invoice. D defends on the grounds that it paid the invoice. Most courts would allow P to introduce its receivables records, which do not show any payment by D, as evidence that there was no payment by D.

2. **Federal Rule:**   The Federal Rules agree with this principle. In fact, they contain a special provision governing it. FRE 803(7) provides a special hearsay exception for:

> **"Absence of a Record of a Regularly Conducted Activity.** Evidence that a matter is ***not included*** in a record described in paragraph [803(6)] if:
>
> (A) the evidence is admitted to prove that the matter ***did not occur or exist***;

(B) a record was regularly kept for a matter of that kind; and

(C) the opponent does not show that the possible source of the information or other circumstances *indicate a lack of trustworthiness.*"

a. May not be hearsay: Most of the time, absence of an entry would not, under the Federal Rules, be hearsay at all. Recall (*supra*, p. 200), that under the Federal Rules, conduct can only be hearsay if it is assertive. A business person's failure to record a transaction will generally not be assertive — that is, the record keeper is not intending to express to the world the fact that no transaction took place; the occasion to record the transaction simply never occurs. It is only in the rare instance where failure to make a notation is intended as a declaration that nothing has happened that FRE 803(7) is ever really necessary. The Advisory Committee's Notes to FRE 803(7) explain that this generally-unnecessary exception exists only to set to rest any possible doubts about the admissibility of such evidence.

I. Oral reports: Suppose that a business person, in the regular course of the business, makes an *oral* report to a co-worker, rather than making a written record. Can this oral report be introduced into evidence (by being recounted by the co-worker who heard it) under the business records exception? Most courts hold that oral reports *cannot* fall within the exception; but a few courts have allowed them under an analogy to the business records exception.

> **Example:** Foreman reports to Boss that Employee has hurt his hand on a machine. It is Foreman's duty to report, orally, all on-the-job accidents to Boss. Most courts would not allow the business records exception to be used to allow Boss to testify at trial about the contents of the report given by Foreman; a few courts might allow it on this ground, however. The courts that excluded it might nonetheless allow it under the "residual" hearsay exception (see *infra*, p. 315). McC, p. 498.

1. Federal Rules: The Federal Rules are silent about whether an oral report can ever come within the business records exception. But FRE 803(6)'s requirement of a "record," when taken together with 803(6)(B)'s requirement that the record be "kept," probably means that oral reports cannot qualify. McC, p. 498.

J. Proving the record: We turn now to the issue: How does a party "prove" a business record?

1. Not self-proving: Business records are not "self-proving." That is, for a business record to fall within the exception, witnesses must testify that it meets the requirements of the exception.

2. Who must be called: It is *not* necessary, under modern statutes, to call as a witness *each person who participated in the making* of the record. For instance, if A reported facts known to him to B, and B wrote them in the business' records, it is not necessary that both A and B testify about the making of the records. All that is required is that there be a witness who knows enough about a particular record-keeping process to be able to testify that: (1) it was the business' regular practice to make such a record; (2) the particular record in question was made in the regular course of business on the personal knowledge of the recorder or someone reporting to him; (3) the person with the first-hand knowledge was acting in the regular course of the business; and (4) the entries were made at or near the time of the transaction. McC, p. 502. Typically, that witness will be "a person in authority in the ***record-keeping department*** of the business." *Id.*

a. Certification as alternative: In fact, under FRE 803(6)(D) a business record can come into evidence based on a ***"certification"*** alone, ***without any testimony by a foundation witness.*** 803(6)(D) says that a record of a regularly-conducted activity (i.e., a business record) can avoid the hearsay rule based either upon "the testimony of the custodian or another qualified witness" *or* upon "***certification*** that complies with Rule 902(11) or (12) or with a statute permitting certification[.]"

    i. Nature of certification: The most important of these three methods of certification is Rule 902(11), a provision covering "certified domestic records of a regularly conducted activity." 902(11) says that a record of a regularly conducted activity is ***self-authenticating*** if accompanied by a ***written declaration*** by the record's custodian or other qualified person, stating that the record meets the requirements for the business-records exception (i.e., stating that the record "meets the requirements of Rule 803(6)(A)-(C)[.]")

K. Special situations: We conclude our discussion of the business record exception by examining two special contexts that have raised special problems: (1) hospital records; and (2) computer printouts.

1. Hospital records: *Hospital records* are often introduced to prove the truth of statements contained in them.

a. General rule: Generally speaking, a hospital record will almost always be found to be one regularly made during the course of an ongoing business activity. Therefore, the requirements of the business records exception will generally be found to be satisfied. McC, p. 502. However, two special kinds of problems can be presented by such records, which may lead to certain statements contained in the record being excluded.

b. Factual statements unrelated to treatment or diagnosis: First, when the patient gives the history of his ailment, and this history is recorded, it may contain a variety of statements. Those statements that are ***relevant*** to ***treatment*** or ***diagnosis*** (e.g., "I was a hit by a car" or "I was hit in the head with a baseball bat") will be treated as having been recorded within the "regular course" of the hospital's business, since the business of a hospital is the giving of treatment and diagnosis. If, on the other hand, statements are recorded that are totally unrelated to any conceivable treatment or diagnosis, the recording of these statements will not be treated as falling within the hospital's regular course of business, and that aspect of the record will not be admissible under the business records exception. McC, p. 503.

Example: P is injured by being hit by D's car. At trial, P offers part of his hospital record. D then attempts to introduce a different part of the hospital record, which recites that P told a doctor at the hospital that "[P] was crossing the street and an automobile ran into another automobile that was at a standstill, causing this car (standstill) to run into him."

Held, this part of the hospital record is inadmissible. Only acts or occurrences cited in a hospital record that are "germane to diagnosis or treatment" are admissible under the business records exception. It might have been useful to the doctor to know that P had been struck by *an* automobile. "However, whether the patient was hit by car A or car B, by car A under its own power or propelled forward by car B, or whether the injuries were caused by the negligence of the defendant or of another, cannot possibly bear on diagnosis or aid in determining treatment." *Williams v. Alexander*, 129 N.E.2d 417 (N.Y. 1955).

But a dissenting judge pointed out that P had already put the hospital record in evidence. Therefore, this dissenting judge argued, P had "vouched for" the authenticity of the record, and it should have been treated as satisfying the requirement of being made in the regular course of the hospital's business. The underlying statement by P, in turn, should have been admissible under the "admission" exception. (See *supra*, p. 215.)

    i.   **Second-level problem:** If the statements recorded do not relate to diagnosis and treatment (as the majority in *Williams* found that that statement did not), the record is not admissible even for the limited purpose of proving that the statement was made, let alone to prove the truth of the statement. M, p. 883. If the recorded statement does relate to treatment and diagnosis, the business records exception allows the record to be admitted for the limited purpose of proving that the statement was made. But normally, the business records exception does not by itself allow the record to be used as evidence of the ***truth*** of the statement, because of the generally-accepted rule of *Johnson v. Lutz*, *supra*, p. 250 — since the statement about symptoms, causation, etc., is usually made by the ***patient***, and since the patient has ***no duty to the hospital*** to relate the information, the patient is not acting in the course of the hospital's business. Therefore, the situation is like that of the bystander/informant in *Johnson*, and the admission of the record is ***not evidence of the truth of the patient's statement.*** *Id.*

    ii.   **Other exception:** However, often some ***other exception*** will make the patient's statement admissible notwithstanding the hearsay rule. For instance, if the patient is the plaintiff and the statement is offered by the defendant, the exception for admissions (*supra*, p. 215) will be enough to make the statement evidence of the truth of the matter asserted. Thus in *Williams*, if the majority had accepted the notion that P's statements were germane to treatment or diagnosis, not only would the overall record have been able to come into evidence, but the particular statement would then have been admissible against P as an admission.

  c. **Expert opinions:** The second problem presented by hospital records is that they will often contain ***opinions*** by physicians, concerning causation, prognosis, etc. The physician, if he were giving that same opinion in live testimony at trial, would normally be qualified to do so as an expert. (See *infra*, p. 520.) Yet courts are somewhat more reluctant to allow such opinions to come in via the hospital record, because the physician is not available to explain the basis for his opinion, or to be cross-examined about it.

    i.   **General rule:** Therefore, courts tend to be somewhat stricter about receiving such opinions in records than they would be about receiving the opinion in live testimony. "The more speculative the opinion, the greater the probability of exclusion." L&S, p. 443.

    ii. Objective criteria: Thus where the patient's symptoms are reasonably ***objective***, and the diagnosis or prognosis is reasonably cut-and-dried (e.g., a fractured elbow or appendicitis), nearly all courts would allow the attending physician's notation of diagnosis and prognosis into evidence. But where the appropriate diagnosis is, on the facts, much less certain, courts may exclude the record containing the opinion, even where they would accept that same opinion from that same physician at trial.

    Example: Suppose the hospital record contains the following notation written by the physician: "Diagnosis: substantial lung damage resulting from black lung disease due to working in a poorly ventilated coal mine." L&S, p. 444, suggests that "most courts would admit the entry to show lung damage, some would admit it to show black lung disease, but few, if any, would admit it to show that the disease was caused by poor working conditions."

    iii. Causation and prognosis: Courts are more willing to admit medical opinions that relate to precise diagnosis of a medical condition, than opinions regarding ***etiology*** (i.e., what caused the illness), or ***prognosis*** (i.e., prospects for recovery). L&S, p. 443.

2. Computer print-outs: Many if not most business records today are kept ***on computer*** rather than on paper. If a party wishes to prove that a fact is as recorded on a computer maintained by the party, this will generally have to be done by presenting a computer ***print-out***. Since the print-out is not a primary record, but merely a collection or arrangement of "real" data stored in the computer, use of print-outs under the business records exception poses special problems.

    a. Generally applicable: In general, courts have held that the business records exception ***applies*** to computer print-outs, so long as a proper foundation is laid.

    b. Time of entry: Recall that the business records exception requires that the record have been prepared "at or near the time" of the event being recorded. When a computer print-out is presented as evidence, when should the record be deemed to have been "made"? If the relevant time is when the ***print-out*** was prepared, this will generally be after litigation has begun, and long after the event being recorded. Therefore, the print-out would only rarely satisfy the rule. However, courts that have considered the issue have generally concluded that the requirement of timeliness means only that the data must have been ***entered*** into the computer at or near the time of the event.

    c. Trustworthiness: Recall (*supra*, p. 252) that the business records exception will not apply where the judge concludes that the record is ***untrustworthy***. The proponent's need to make an affirmative showing of trustworthiness is stronger in the case of computerized records than for hard-copy records — the degree of reliability of a written record will often be evident from an inspection of the record itself, whereas a computer print-out may appear to be quite meticulous and accurate, yet be based upon some hidden flaw in the procedures used to prepare it. Therefore, the witness who vouches for a computer print-out must generally testify as to the following:

    i. Equipment: At least a general description of the equipment;

ii. **Programming:** How the computer has been programmed, and how errors in programming are detected and corrected;

iii. **Data entry:** How the data is *entered* into the computer;

iv. **Controls:** What controls are used to *detect errors* at any stage in the procedure, especially errors in data entry and errors in the preparation of the final print-out; and

v. **Security:** Ways that unauthorized *access* to the programs and data files is prevented.

See McC, p. 505.

VII. PUBLIC RECORDS AND REPORTS

A. **Exception generally:** There is a common-law hearsay exception for *public records* and *reports* that is similar to the exception for business records. This exception, as codified in most states and in the Federal Rules, is an extremely important one because of the wide variety of material that it allows into evidence in both civil and criminal trials.

B. **Common-law rule:** The common-law form of the rule allows the admission of a *written report or record* of a *public official* if: (1) the official (or perhaps his subordinate) had *firsthand knowledge* of the facts reported; and (2) the official had a *duty* to make the record or report. McC, p. 507.

1. **Rationale:** The rationale for the exception is similar to that for the business records exception: An official who has knowledge of the facts, and a duty to report them, is likely to produce a reliable record.

2. **Self-authenticating:** Many government records and reports could qualify under the business records exception (*supra*, p. 249) as well as under the public records exception. But there is a key difference between these two exceptions that usually leads the proponent to use the public records exception: Whereas the business records exception applies only where a person with relevant knowledge of the record keeping system testifies at trial, the public records exception can be used *without any testimony at all*, if a certification procedure is used.

   a. **Certification:** If each time a public record were offered in evidence, testimony from the official in charge of the records was required, many officials would do little but give testimony. Similarly, if the *original* record were required (as is the case for most other kinds of documents; see *infra*, p. 490) filing problems would be unmanageable. Therefore, all states have established, by statute or court rule, *certification* procedures to deal with these two problems. Typically, the official in charge of a particular department makes a copy of a given public record, and attaches his certificate that the copy is a true copy of the original. This copy can then be entered into evidence, *without any testimony*. See, e.g., FRE 902(4) and 1005; see also *infra*, p. 483.

3. **Not necessarily open to public:** The common-law exception is generally held to apply even to those records and reports which are *not* otherwise *open to the public*. McC, p.

508. For instance, a state or federal Freedom of Information Act provision could be used to obtain otherwise secret government records, which could then be introduced under the public records exception.

4. **Evaluative reports:**   Most courts have limited the common law rule to reports that are essentially *factual* in nature. Thus *evaluative* reports have not usually been allowed under the exception; for instance, if a police report contained a notation by the reporting officer, "Accident seems to have been caused by Smith's careless driving," most courts would not allow it into evidence under the exception. (But cases under the Federal Rules have been more liberal on this issue; see *infra*, p. 265.)

C. **Federal Rule:**   The principal Federal Rule governing public records and reports, FRE 803(8), has been extraordinarily influential. That rule provides a hearsay exception for:

> "A *record or statement of a public office* if:
>
>   (A) it sets out:
>
>   (i) the *office's activities*;
>
>   (ii) a *matter observed while under a legal duty to report*, but *not including, in a criminal case*, a *matter observed by law-enforcement personnel*; <u>or</u>
>
>   (iii) in a *civil case* or *against the government in a criminal case*, *factual findings from a legally authorized investigation*; and
>
>   (B) *neither the source of information nor other circumstances indicate a lack of trustworthiness*."

1. **Focus:**   Because of the importance of 803(8), our remaining discussion of the public records exception focuses on the Federal Rules' treatment. Many states have a nearly identical provision; but other states may have statutes, especially ones adopted before the enactment of the Federal Rules, that are quite different on key issues (e.g., the admissibility of investigative reports).

2. **Uses of Rule:**   Because government today is so active, and performs investigations in so many situations, in a high proportion of litigations there will be a relevant government report or record. Here are some ways government reports may be relevant:

   a. **Accident:**   In a vehicular accident, there will usually be a *police report*;

   b. **Antitrust:**   In a civil antitrust case, there may well be industry market-share studies prepared by the Justice Department's Antitrust Division;

   c. **Plane crash:**   In a suit arising out of an airplane crash, an *FAA report* on the causes of the crash will be highly relevant;

   d. **Job discrimination:**   In a suit by an employee against an employer for *job discrimination* based on sex or race, various federal or state agencies may have already investigated and made a report.

   See generally, L&S, p. 447.

D. **Three categories:**   As is obvious from the text of FRE 803(8), it divides public records and reports into three categories:

1. **Activities of the office:** The first, subsection (A)(i) (covering the "office's activities"), covers reports that are also covered under the traditional common-law approach. An agency's records of its ***own activities*** can be used to show that those activities occurred.

> **Example:** Following an airplane crash, the FAA sends an inspector to the crash scene, who attempts to determine the cause of the crash. Under subsection (A)(i), the FAA's records may be used to show that the investigation took place (but not to show what the results of it were — that would have to come in under subsection (A)(iii) if at all).

2. **Matters observed under duty:** Subsection (A)(ii) (covering "a ***matter observed*** while under a legal duty to report, but not including, in a criminal case, a matter observed by law-enforcement personnel) also goes no further than the common-law exception. The written records of ***observations*** made by public officials are admissible if: (1) the observations were made in the ***line of duty***; and (2) the official had a ***duty to report*** those observations.

> **Example:** Suppose an IRS auditor goes to the Smith household to conduct a field audit of the Smith's tax return. Mr. Smith claims a business deduction for "an office at home." The auditor finds no evidence of such an office, and says so in his report. In a subsequent civil suit between Mr. Smith and his business partner, Mr. Jones, either side could, under FRE 803(8)(A)(ii), use the report as proof of the fact that Mr. Smith did not maintain an office at home.
>
> Now, however, assume that the auditor also noticed that Mr. Smith possessed cocaine, and put this fact into his report. Since the auditor had no duty to report non-tax-related matters, this aspect of the report could not be introduced in the later civil suit.

   a. **Oral reports:** Suppose, in the above example, the IRS auditor made an ***oral*** report to his supervisor about Mr. Smith's lack of a home office. By the literal language of FRE 803(8), the hearsay exception extends to "statements," and it could be argued that the supervisor may testify about what the auditor told her. However, everything in the legislative history of FRE 803(8) suggests that Congress had in mind only written records, and a court would probably reject this attempt to use the rule to get oral statements into evidence. L&S, p. 448. (But if the ***supervisor*** made notes of the auditor's statements, those notes would be admissible under FRE 803(8)(A)(ii). *Id.*)

   b. **Criminal cases:** Subsection (A)(ii) by its terms does not apply in ***criminal cases*** to "a matter observed by law enforcement personnel[.]" It is clear that such police reports cannot be used ***against*** the criminal defendant; it is not so clear whether they may be used ***by*** the criminal defendant. The matter is discussed more extensively *infra*, p. 262.

3. **Investigative reports:** The last category in FRE 803(8), covered by subsection (A)(iii), applies only in civil cases and against the government in criminal cases; it allows admission of "factual findings from a legally authorized investigation[.]" In other words, it involves ***investigative reports***.

   a. **Evaluative:** Subsection (A)(iii) allows into evidence only ***"factual findings"*** that result from investigation. However, most courts have viewed this requirement that the findings be "factual" somewhat liberally, and have accepted reports that include a substantial *"evaluative"* component. How evaluative a report may be and still be accepted as "factual" for purposes of subsection (A)(iii) is discussed more extensively *infra*, p. 265.

b. **No use against criminal defendant:** By the express terms of subsection (A)(iii), investigative reports may ***not*** be used ***against*** a criminal defendant. The purpose of this restriction is to prevent the prosecution from basing its case upon police reports and other inculpatory documents; law enforcement officials must give ***personal testimony*** at trial, rather than hiding behind the written report.

Example: Police Officer, investigating the murder of V, writes a report in which she concludes, "For all these reasons, this killing was certainly committed by D." Regardless of whether Police Officer is available to testify at the murder trial of D, the report will not be usable by the prosecution. Rather, Police Officer must give live testimony regarding the reasons why she believes the murder was done by D.

E. **Criminal cases:** Many of the issues involving FRE 803(8) have arisen in the context of ***criminal prosecutions***, especially situations in which the prosecution desires to use the exception to admit evidence against the accused. Our discussion below applies to all three subsections of 803(8), unless otherwise noted.

1. **Federal language:** Both subsection (A)(ii) and (A)(iii), by their literal language, prevent the prosecution from using materials against the accused in a criminal case. Thus if a police officer happened to see D commit a crime, and put his observations into a required daily activity report, this report would not be admissible against D in a criminal prosecution under subsection (A)(ii). Similarly, if a police officer did not witness the crime, but conducted an after-the-fact investigation of the crime, his investigative report would not be admissible against D under subsection (A)(iii).

2. **Accused's use of subsection (A)(ii):** Subsection (A)(ii), by its literal language, excludes from the coverage of that section "in a criminal case, a matter observed by law-enforcement personnel." Thus the section does not merely exclude ***prosecution*** use of such materials in a criminal case, but ostensibly also ***defense*** use of such matters.

a. **Liberal interpretation:** Observe that this phrasing is quite different from that of subsection of (A)(iii), where investigative reports are usable "against the government in a criminal case." The only reason why subsection (A)(ii) is drafted differently (and probably more clumsily) is that the language was hastily added on the floor of the House of Representatives, which was afraid that otherwise criminal defendants might be tried on the basis of police reports. Therefore, at least some of the courts that have interpreted subsection (A)(ii) have concluded that the section ***bars only the government, not the accused,*** from using such evidence.

3. **"Other law enforcement personnel":** Subsection (A)(ii) does not apply to matters observed by "law-enforcement personnel." It is not clear what types of individuals, apart from police officers, are included in this phrase "law enforcement personnel." For instance, are ***laboratory technicians*** who work for law enforcement agencies doing substance analysis, to be treated as "law-enforcement personnel" whose accounts of tests they make are therefore excluded?

a. **Not admissible:** The answer is almost certainly *yes*, as the result of a comment the Supreme Court made in a 2009 state-law case. In that case, *Melendez-Diaz v. Massachusetts*, 129 S.Ct. 2527 (2009) (discussed *infra*, p. 382), the issue was whether the defendant's Confrontation Clause rights were violated by the prosecution's introduction against him of a laboratory test report showing that the tested substance was cocaine; the prosecution did not make the writer of the report available for cross examination. In the course of deciding that the defendant's Confrontation Clause rights had been violated, the five-justice majority said that such lab reports, "like police reports generated by law-enforcement officials," *do not qualify as business or public records.* The majority then cited 803(8). So unless the Supreme Court changes its view, 803(8)(A)(ii)'s ban on the hearsay use of "a matter observed by law enforcement personnel" will be read to apply to *test reports prepared by technicians affiliated with law enforcement.*

4. **Routine observations:** Does subsection (A)(ii)'s exclusion of "in a criminal case [a report of] a matter observed by law-enforcement personnel" apply to *routine* police records? Or does it apply only to reports of episodes that are by their very nature confrontational, as when a police officer witnesses what he realizes at the time is a crime? The courts that have considered the question have generally answered that *routine*, non-adversarial observations that happen to be incorporated in police records are *not excluded* from criminal trials. McC, p. 509.

   Example: The Ds, who are involved on the Catholic side of the conflict in Northern Ireland, are charged with federal weapons violations. The prosecution seeks to introduce routine Irish police records of serial numbers and weapons receipts, showing that certain weapons were found in Northern Ireland after a certain date.

   Held, these records were admissible under what is now FRE 803(8)(A)(ii), because the exclusionary language in that subsection covers only "police officers' reports of their contemporaneous observations of crime," not routine bureaucratic observations of events that were not in themselves criminal acts. *U.S. v. Grady*, 544 F.2d 598 (2d Cir. 1976).

5. **Use of "business records" or other rules:** Reports by the police of matters they have observed, or investigations they have conducted, will often appear to qualify under *other* hearsay exceptions apart from FRE 803(8). For instance, a laboratory report might appear to qualify as a *business record* under 803(6), and a police officer's contemporaneous notes of a crime he has witnessed will often appear to meet the requirements for past recollection recorded under FRE 803(5). The issue arises, therefore: Does the fact that a police report offered against the defendant in a criminal case is excluded from 803(8)(A)(ii) or (iii) also mean that these other exceptions may not be used? The issue is probably the most important one that has arisen in the public records area. Courts are split, but the trend seems to be in favor of *allowing the use of other exceptions,* at least if the person who made the report is available for cross-examination at trial. McC, p. 510.

a. **General principle:** In general, hearsay exceptions *stand alone* — the fact that one exception is unavailable (even expressly made inapplicable) in a given situation does not mean that some other exception cannot be used. Thus if this general principle were to control, a police report would be allowed to come in under the business record exception, the past recollection recorded exception, or perhaps even FRE 807's residual exception (see *infra*, p. 316).

b. ***Oates* case excludes:**   Nonetheless, the first major case to consider the issue concluded unequivocally, and broadly, that "police and evaluative reports not satisfying the standards of [what is now FRE 803(8)(A)(ii) and (iii)] may not qualify for admission under FRE 803(6) or any of the other exceptions to the hearsay rule." ***U.S. v. Oates***, 560 F.2d 45 (2d Cir. 1977).

   i.   Facts: D was charged with heroin distribution. The prosecution offered as evidence a laboratory report prepared by a chemist who was a full-time employee of the United States Customs Service, reporting that analysis showed that the substance seized was indeed heroin. The government claimed that the chemist who prepared the report was "unavailable" (though it did not explain why, or appear to make any major attempt to produce him); instead it put on the stand another chemist from the Department who explained the steps that the Department customarily goes through in performing a heroin test.

   ii.   Result: The Second Circuit Court of Appeals held that the report should ***not*** have been admitted.

   iii.   Covered by (A)(ii) and (iii):   First, the court concluded that the report was covered by the general provisions of what is now 803(8)(A)(ii) and (iii). It then found that under these two subsections, the report would be inadmissible, because of the exclusion for use against criminal defendants. This exclusion was quite clear in the case of (iii); it was probable in the case of (ii), since, in the court's view, "law enforcement personnel" included full-time Customs Service Chemists. (See *supra*, p. 262.) Therefore, the issue became: Is a report that is expressly excluded from admission by 803(8) nonetheless admissible under some other hearsay exception, in this case the business records exception of 803(6)?

   iv.   Excluded: The court then concluded that "it was the clear intention of Congress to make evaluative and law enforcement reports ***absolutely inadmissible*** against defendants in criminal cases." Therefore, even though the report might seem to be admissible under the literal language of 803(6)'s business records exception, "803(6) must be read in conjunction with FRE [803(8)(A)(ii) and (iii).] ... The prosecution's utilization of any hearsay exception to achieve admission of evaluative and law enforcement reports would serve to deprive the accused of the opportunity to confront his accusers as effectively as would reliance on a 'public records' exception. Thus, there being no apparent reason why Congress would tolerate the admission of evaluative and law enforcement reports by use of some other exception to the hearsay rule ... it simply makes no sense to surmise that Congress ever intended that these records could be admissible against a defendant in a criminal case under *any* of the Federal Rules of Evidence's exceptions to the hearsay rule. ..."

   v.   Narrower ground rejected: The court also observed that there was reason to doubt the trustworthiness of the particular report at issue, because of crossed-out notations and other reasons. But the court explicitly declined to rely on 803(6)'s exclusion on account of factors indicating "lack of trustworthiness."

c. Subsequent cases: The *Oates* court seemed to be saying that so long as a document is an "evaluative [or] law enforcement report," it is ***automatically*** absolutely inadmissible against a criminal defendant no matter what other hearsay exceptions it seems to fall under. If this is what the court meant, most subsequent decisions from other courts have ***not agreed***. Many have adopted the following modification: "The limitations of [FRE 803(8)(A)(ii) and (iii)] will not be extended to ***other hearsay exceptions*** if the maker is ***produced in court as a witness***, subject to cross-examination, since the essential purpose of the Congress was simply to avoid uncross-examined evidence." McC, p. 510. Thus under the view of most courts other than the Second Circuit, if the chemist who prepared the report in *Oates* were placed on the stand, the report itself could be introduced in evidence against the accused.

  i. Use of present recollection recorded: This non-*Oates* view means that although the evidence can't automatically come in under the ***business records*** or ***catchall*** (since these don't require the maker's presence in court), the evidence can come in under the ***past recollection recorded exception*** where applicable, since that exception requires the supplier of the information to testify and be available for cross-examination. M&K (5th), §8.50, p. 913.

F. Other issues: Other issues under 803(8) arise in all contexts, not just in the context of a criminal case where the prosecution tries to use the evidence.

1. "Factual" versus "evaluative": Subsection (A)(iii), which applies to investigative reports, by its terms applies only to ***"factual findings"*** resulting from the investigation. The interpretation of the phrase "factual findings" has been the subject of much dispute; are ***"opinions,"*** ***"evaluations,"*** and ***"conclusions"*** contained in an investigative report admissible?

  a. Admission allowed: The Supreme Court finally answered ***"yes"*** to this question in *Beech Aircraft Corp. v. Rainey*, 488 U.S. 153 (1988). So long as the investigative report is based on factual statements, ***the conclusions or opinions stated in it are admissible***, along with the other portions of the report.

  Example: The Ps die when the Navy plane they are piloting suddenly loses altitude, crashes and burns. The Ps sue D, the plane's manufacturer. The defense offers into evidence an investigative report prepared by the Navy, which includes sections called "findings of fact" and "opinions." In the "opinions" section, the report contains a statement that "the most probable cause of the accident was the pilots [sic] failure to maintain proper interval." Over the Ps' objections, this "opinion" is allowed into evidence. The jury returns a verdict for the Ds.

  Held (by the U.S. Supreme Court), the trial judge properly allowed the "opinions" portion of the report into evidence. Nothing in the legislative history of FRE 803 suggests that the drafters meant to distinguish between "facts" and "opinions" contained in investigative reports. Also, there is great analytical difficulty in drawing a line between fact and opinion. Therefore, portions of investigatory reports otherwise admissible under [what is today Rule 803(8)(A)(iii)] are not inadmissible merely because they state a conclusion or opinion. "As long as the conclusion is based on a factual investigation and satisfies the Rule's trustworthiness requirement, it should be admissible along with other portions of the report." *Beech Aircraft Corp. v. Rainey*, *supra*.

    b. **Legal conclusions not allowed:** However, courts will generally not allow that portion of a report to be admitted that includes a ***"legal"*** conclusion. For instance, in a tort case, a report concluding that the defendant was "negligent" should probably not be admitted (or at least, that conclusion should be excised), since this is clearly a conclusion of law. (But a portion of the report concluding that the defendant was driving faster than the speed limit would probably be admitted; this may be a "conclusion" based upon other facts such as skid marks, but it would not be a conclusion of law. W&B, Par. 803(8)[03].)

2. **Trustworthiness in (a)(iii) cases:** Recall that 803(8)(B) prohibits admission of a report that would otherwise be admissible unless "neither the source of information nor other circumstances indicate a ***lack of trustworthiness.***" This exception is discussed more extensively *infra*, p. 268. However, it is quite clear that it not only applies, but is very important, in subsection (A)(iii) cases.

    a. **Factors:** In fact, the Advisory Committee's Note to subsection 803(8) lists several factors which should be taken into account in determining whether an evaluative report is sufficiently trustworthy to be admissible:

        i. The ***timeliness*** of the investigation;

        ii. The "special ***skill*** or ***experience*** of the official";

        iii. Whether a ***hearing was held*** and the level at which it was conducted; and

        iv. Possible ***"motivation problems"*** (e.g., the incentive that the railroad and its engineer had in *Palmer v. Hoffman*, *supra*, p. 252, when they gave statements about the railroad accident that were then contained in the government report on the accident).

    b. ***Baker*** **case:** These factors were applied, and found to establish trustworthiness, in *Baker v. Elcona Homes Corp.*, 588 F.2d 551 (6th Cir. 1978).

        i. **Facts:** *Baker* involved the investigative report prepared by an Ohio State Highway Patrolman after a car accident. The report contained two items whose admissibility was questioned: (1) a transcription of a statement made by D to the police officer; and (2) the officer's notation that "apparently [the Ps' car] entered the intersection against their red light."

        ii. **Factors considered:** The court began by concluding that the report should be admitted, if at all, under 803(8) (rather than as a recorded recollection under 803(5), because that rule does not allow the document to be admitted as an exhibit unless offered by an adverse party, and the report was in fact offered as an exhibit by its proponent, D). The court then concluded that the report's contents constituted "factual findings" even though they were in some sense evaluative. Finally, the court applied the Advisory Committee's factors for measuring trustworthiness, listed above.

iii. Conclusion: The court concluded that the report should be admitted: first, it was timely because the officer arrived at the scene of the accident soon after it occurred; second, the officer was highly experienced in accident reconstruction; the third requirement (hearing) was irrelevant; and finally, there was no sign of any lack of objectivity by the officer, who had no apparent motive to favor one side over the other. Therefore, the report had sufficient indicia of trustworthiness to be admissible.

3. **Multiple hearsay:** As was the case with the business records exception, public records may raise problems of ***multiple hearsay***. This problem will arise any time the report ***quotes statements made by others.*** This can be the case either in a subsection (A)(ii) "report of matters observed" situation or in a subsection (A)(iii) investigative report context. Three distinct situations must be analyzed:

   a. **Report by one government agent to another:** First, there may be two government agents involved, one who has knowledge of the facts and a duty to report them, and the other who makes up the report. In this situation, by analogy to the business records exception (*supra*, p. 249), it is clear that if the report quotes the first agent's statements, the quoted statements may come in as evidence of the truth of the matters they assert. L&S, p. 450.

   Example: Police Officer Jones witnesses a car accident. He goes back to the station house and says to Officer Smith, "I saw the green Plymouth go through a light and cause an accident." Smith records this statement in a report he compiles on the accident. Almost certainly, the entire report, including the quoted statement by Jones, will be admissible under 803(8)(A)(ii), in a civil case concerning the accident.

   b. **Statements by those without duty to talk:** The quoted statements may, by contrast, be ones made by third persons who had ***no duty*** to talk to the government. Unless these statements themselves fall under some other hearsay exception (e.g., they are made by a party and are offered against that party), they will ***not*** be admissible even though the report as a whole may fall within 803(8). In that event, the report will be entered, but with the quoted statements excised. L&S, p. 450.

   Example 1: On the facts of the above example, assume that Officer Jones also took down a statement by Brown, a passer-by. If the final report prepared by Smith says, "Brown said that the car driven by D ran a red light," this statement will be excluded, because it is hearsay that does not fall within any independent exception.

   Example 2: In the *Baker* case, *supra*, p. 266, D's statement to the police officer was not automatically admissible even though the report itself was, since D had no duty to make the report of the accident. However, because the cross-examination of D at trial suggested that D had changed his story, D's statement to the police officer was admissible on behalf of D under 801(d)(1)(B), which allows a witness's prior statement to be admitted if it is "consistent with the declarant's testimony and is offered to rebut an express or implied charge that the declarant recently fabricated it or acted from a recent improper influence or motive in so testifying[.]"

c. **Reports based on statements:** Finally, it may happen that the report makes findings based on hearsay statements made by others, but the report does not quote those statements. When this happens, the report is not automatically rendered inadmissible because of this hearsay basis. Thus in the above example, if Jones' report merely stated his conclusion that the accident had been caused by D's car going through a red light, it would not be rendered inadmissible because it was based on statements from third parties with no duty to speak to the police, which statements would have been inadmissible hearsay had they been quoted in the report.

i. **Untrustworthy:** However, the extent to which investigative findings in a report are based on inadmissible hearsay is a factor that the court should consider in determining whether the report should be excluded because "the source of information [or] other circumstances indicate a lack of *trustworthiness*" (the last phrase of 803(8)(B)). Thus a report that is based entirely on such inadmissible hearsay is far more likely to be excluded on grounds of untrustworthiness than one which is based upon a small amount of hearsay but mostly upon, say, scientific testing, observation by law enforcement officials, or other sources that would themselves be admissible. L&S, p. 450.

4. **Trustworthiness in (A)(i) and (A)(ii) cases:** Notice that 803(8)(B) (requiring exclusion unless "neither the source of information nor other circumstances indicate a lack of trustworthiness") *applies to all three subsections* of 803(8)(A). Thus if a building inspector writes a report stating that he has inspected premises at 1865 Palmer Avenue and found them to be in good repair (a report that would normally be admissible under 803(8)(A)(ii)), the judge could and should use the proviso to exclude the report if other evidence is presented that the building inspector was bribed by the property owner to prepare a favorable report.

VIII. MISCELLANEOUS EXCEPTIONS — AVAILABILITY IMMATERIAL

A. **In general:** We cover now the remaining "declarant's availability immaterial" exceptions to the hearsay rule.

B. **Learned writings and commercial publications:** Suppose that a party wants to prove a proposition of science, medicine, or other fact by showing that the authoritative professional *treatises* on the subject say that that fact is so. Such proof would clearly present a hearsay problem — the out-of-court treatise writer's assertion of fact would be used to show the truth of that fact. Yet, a treatise, professional journal, or other learned writing is free from at least some of the traditional hearsay problems — for instance, "the treatise is written primarily and impartially for professionals, subject to scrutiny and exposure for inaccuracy, with the reputation of the writer at stake." Advisory Committee Note to FRE 803(18). Yet, the most fundamental hearsay problem — that the writer/declarant is *not available for cross-examination* — remains in full force. Furthermore, there is an additional problem — a work prepared for a professional may well be misunderstood and misused by a lay juror.

1. **Common law:** For these reasons, the vast majority of common-law courts have *refused to allow* learned writings to be introduced as *substantive evidence*.

   a. **Cross-examination:** However, the common-law approach permitted at least some use of learned treatises as part of the *cross-examination* of an *expert witness*. But under the common-law approach, even though the treatise could be used on cross-examination, it was used only to undermine the witness's competency or dispute the accuracy of his conclusions; it could not be used for substantive evidence.

2. **Federal Rules:** The Federal Rules go *markedly further* than the common law in allowing use of learned writings. Indeed, this is one of the most important changes made by the Federal Rules. FRE 803(18) provides a hearsay exception for:

   "A statement contained in a *treatise, periodical,* or *pamphlet* if:

   (A) the statement is *called to the attention of an expert witness on cross-examination* or *relied on by the expert on direct examination*; and

   (B) the publication is *established as a reliable authority* by the *expert's admission or testimony*, by *another expert's testimony*, or by *judicial notice*.

   If admitted, the statement may be *read into evidence but not received as an exhibit*."

   a. **Aspects of the Federal Rule:** Let's look at some of the key aspects of this broadened rule:

   b. **Use upon direct:** The writing can come in on *direct examination*. That is, if the party can find a favorable expert who will testify that the treatise is authoritative, parts of the treatise can be read into the record as part of that party's direct case. S&R, p. 840.

   c. **Use on cross-examination:** The treatise can be used on cross-examination even if the expert being cross-examined not only has not relied on the treatise, but *refuses to recognize its authoritativeness.* The cross-examiner must still establish the authoritative standing of the treatise in some way (e.g., by some other expert, or perhaps even by judicial notice).

   d. **Use for truth:** In sharp contrast to the common-law approach, any statements read in from a treatise that has been "qualified" in this manner can come in *for their truth*, not merely for impeachment purposes.

   e. **Expert must be on the stand:** At the time the treatise is read into evidence, an expert *must be on the stand*. Because a treatise written for professionals might be misunderstood or misused by a lay jury, the expert's presence is needed to "interpret" it before the lay jury relies on it. S&R, p. 840.

      i. **Use in cross-examination:** This "interpretation" may (and often will) be by a *hostile* expert under cross-examination. Thus, suppose P brings a medical malpractice action, and is cross-examining D's expert witness, W, by use of a treatise favorable to P. The "interpretation" of the treatise may consist of W's saying why the treatise does not help P's case. W may point out that the treatise is out of date, that it doesn't say what P says it says, or that it is too general and fails to deal with the particularities of P's situation under litigation.

f.   Not admitted as exhibit: Even if all of the requirements are met, the treatise ***may not*** be admitted as an ***exhibit***. The jury has to be content with hearing the appropriate portions read to it (and "interpreted" by the expert who is on the stand at the time). This safeguard, too, prevents the jury from misunderstanding and misusing a work written for professionals. (Observe that this no-exhibits policy is similar to that for past recollection recorded, *supra*, p. 248.)

g.   Other types of materials: The classic use of FRE 803(18) is for a scientific or medical book. But the rule is written more broadly. It applies to any "treatise, periodical, or pamphlet," regardless of subject matter, as long as it is a "publication" that has been "established as a reliable authority." This language is broad enough to include "standards and manuals published by government agencies and industry and professional organizations." McC, p. 534.

Example: P is injured by a power saw, and sues on a product liability claim based upon defective design. He should be able to use FRE 803(18) to put into evidence Underwriters Laboratory Standards, and to show that the saw in question did not satisfy those standards. (Remember that he would have to have an expert on the stand while doing so. He might, for instance, call the chief engineer of D, and ask him whether Underwriters Laboratory Standards are recognized in the power saw industry as being a measure of the safeness of a saw.)

3.   Commercial publications: Related to "learned writings" are certain ***commercial publications*** that are commonly relied upon by business people. The impartiality and, in general, reliability of such publications has led to a separate Federal Rule giving them, too, an exception from the hearsay rule.

a.   Text of Rule: FRE 803(17) gives a hearsay exception for "***[m]arket quotations, lists, directories,*** or ***other compilations*** that are ***generally relied on by the public or by persons in particular occupations.***"

b.   Reliability: The proponent of the list or other compilation bears the burden of showing that it is indeed generally reliable.

C.   Ancient documents and documents relating to property: We now consider two closely-related exceptions, one for "ancient documents" and one for documents relating to property.

1.   Ancient documents: A special rule has evolved to allow the admission of ***"ancient"*** documents.

a.   Common-law approach: At common law, there has existed for a long time a rule of ***authentication*** governing ancient documents, whereby a document could be deemed to be authentic, and thus admissible, if it satisfies these requirements: (1) it is ***at least 30 years old***; (2) it is ***unsuspicious*** in appearance; and (3) its proponent proves that it was produced from a ***place of custody natural*** for such a writing. McC, p. 537.

b.   Federal Rules allow: The Federal Rules explicitly recognize a ***hearsay exception*** for ancient documents, but the FRE no longer set a certain number of years as the minimum age for the exception. FRE 803(16) (entitled "Statements in Ancient Documents") gives a hearsay exception for: "A statement in a document that was ***prepared***

before January 1, 1998, and whose ***authenticity is established***." (Proving authenticity is discussed in sub-paragraph (iii) below.)

i. **Rationale:** The FRE's exception for ancient documents can be justified on two grounds: (1) Since a document is required, there is at least the somewhat greater assurance of reliability that comes from a written, rather than oral, out-of-court declaration; and (2) The requirement of a creation-date earlier than Jan. 1, 1998 makes it very likely that the writing predates the present controversy, thus removing a motive for the writer to have lied.

ii. **Choice of January 1, 1998:** The requirement that the document have been prepared ***before January 1, 1998*** was the result of a change made to FRE 803(16) in late 2017. Prior to the change, 803(16) did not specify a date before which the document had to have been created; instead the rule had a moving target, by which the document had to be "at least 20 years old" at the time it was offered for the hearsay purpose. But the Advisory Committee on the FRE feared that the sharp post-1998 increase in the amount of ***"electronically stored information" ("ESI")*** might cause misuse of the ancient-documents exception. The Committee said that the "exponential development and growth" of ESI would create a "possible open door for ***large amounts of unreliable ESI,"*** given that no showing of reliability has to be made for a document that meets the ancient-documents exception. See Adv. Comm. Note to the 2017 version of Rule 803(16).

Example: Imagine that Charles, the CEO of D, a prescription drug manufacturer, has just been told orally in late 1999 by the company's chief scientist, Sy, that the company's anti-nausea drug Bendicta appears to greatly increase the risk of uterine cancer many years after the drug has been taken. Sy then emails Charles a computer-generated document listing 10 reports of uterine cancer from early users of the drug. Fearing future product liability suits against D, Charles makes an altered copy of the document (we'll call it the "Phony Document"), in which he changes the 10 reported incidents to a single incident, and stores the altered copy in place of the original in D's computer files. Charles also prints out a hardcopy of the Phony Document, makes some hand-written annotations on it (which he dates "Dec. 15, 1999"), and puts that hardcopy in a physical folder. In 2021, a group of Bendicta customers who took the drug in 2000 and who much later developed uterine cancer sue D on a product liability theory. D defends on the grounds that in 2000 it didn't know, and couldn't have known, about this elevated cancer risk, and offers the hardcopy version of the Phony Copy as proof. Since the Copy is being offered to prove the truth of the matter asserted in it (that there has only been one reported cancer incident), the Copy will have to qualify for a hearsay exception. D relies on FRE 803(16)'s ancient-document exception.

Under the pre-2017 version of 803(16), the hardcopy version of the Phony Copy would likely *qualify* for the ancient-document exception, since the document is "at least 20 years old." But under 803(16) as amended in 2017, the document will *not* qualify for the exception, since it was not "prepared before January 1, 1998."

(1) Effect: So now, no document, no matter how old, can be admitted under FRE 803(16)'s ancient documents exception, if the document was produced after January 1, 1998, i.e., after the onset of what the Rules drafters have determined to be the era of massive ESI. And this limitation applies even if the document is a *hard copy*, and even if there's *no indication* that the document *ever existed in electronically-stored form*. (Thus in the above example, even if the Phony Copy was completely handwritten and asserted by D never to have resided on any computer system, the Copy would still be inadmissible.)

iii. Proving authenticity: To authenticate a document (or "data compilation") as "ancient," FRE 901(b)(8) allows the proponent to do this by producing evidence that the document:

"**(A)** is in a condition that *creates no suspicion* about its authenticity;

(B) was *in a place* where, if authentic, it would *likely be*; and

(C) is *at least 20 years old* when offered."[1]

c. Newspaper reports: Reports in *newspaper articles* will sometimes be admissible under the ancient documents exception. For instance, a contemporaneous newspaper report might be used to show that a particular building was destroyed by fire in 1930.

i. First-hand knowledge: However, the requirement, discussed above, that the out-of-court declarant (here, the newspaper reporter) have had *first-hand knowledge* may disqualify some articles — the issue is probably whether the reporter himself observed the event (in which case the article is admissible) rather than merely interviewed others about it (in which case it is inadmissible). See McC, p. 537.

2. Newer title documents: The Federal Rules also contain a narrower exception for certain documents relating to *property titles.* This is done by FRE 803(15), which gives a hearsay exception for:

"A statement contained in a document that purports to establish or affect an *interest in property* if the matter stated was *relevant to the document's purpose* — unless later dealings with the property are inconsistent with the truth of the statement or the purport of the document."

a. Relation to common-law rule: This Rule does not break very much new ground, since nearly all common-law courts allowed a hearsay exception for recitals in deeds. The Rule does expand the common-law approach in two respects: (1) It applies no matter how recently-created the document is; and (2) It applies to any document "pur-

---

1. Note that FRE 901(b)(8)'s method of authentication specifies "at least 20 years old when offered," rather than the "prepared before January 1, 1998" formulation applicable to the 803(16) ancient-documents hearsay exception. Therefore, if a document (hardcopy or electronic) is shown to be at least 20 years old at the time of trial and meets the other two requirements of 901(b)(8), the document will be treated as authenticated, even if it was prepared after January 1, 1998. But if the post-January-1-1998 document is offered for what would be a hearsay purpose, the proponent will not be able to rely on the 803(16) ancient documents hearsay exception, and will have to satisfy some other hearsay exception (e.g., FRE 803(6)'s business-records exception or FRE 807's residual exception). See the Bendicta example on p. 271. Cf. Adv. Comm. Notes to 2017 Amendment to FRE 803(16).

porting to establish or affect an interest in property," thus making it applicable not only to wills and deeds, but also probably to contracts to sell real estate, as well as to contracts and bills of sale affecting **personal property** (e.g., a bill of sale for a piece of jewelry). W&B, Par. 803(15)[01].

D. Reputation: There is a cluster of situations in which evidence of **reputation** may be admitted even though it is technically hearsay.

1. Personal or family history: For instance, a person's reputation within his **family**, regarding some aspect of his **birth**, **marriage**, blood relationship, etc., has always been given a hearsay exception at common law.

> **Example:** If the issue is whether X is the son of Y, X could put on the stand Z, an acknowledged son of Y, who would be permitted to testify, "It was commonly understood in the family that X was Y's son."

a. Liberalization: The Federal Rules expand this exception for reputation regarding personal or family history. FRE 803(19) goes beyond the common-law exception — which in most instances was limited to reputation within the family — and extends it to cover reputation "among a person's **associates**" (e.g., his business colleagues), and also his reputation **"in the community."** It covers reputation as to the person's "birth, adoption, legitimacy, ancestry, marriage, divorce, death, relationship by blood, adoption, or marriage, or similar facts of **personal or family history**."

b. Family records exception: A related common-law exception allows the use of **contemporaneous family records** (e.g., entries in a family Bible) to prove such facts of personal or family history. FRE 803(13) carries forward this exception as well.

> **Example:** If the issue is whether X is Y's son, a family genealogy could be introduced to prove that fact under 803(13), provided that the entry in the chart was made soon after the alleged birth of X to Y.

2. Boundaries and general historical facts: Both at common law and under the Federal Rules, there is an exception for proof of **land boundaries** and for **facts of "general history."**

a. Federal Rules: Thus, FRE 803(20) gives a hearsay exception for "[a] reputation in a community — arising before the controversy — concerning **boundaries of land** in the community or customs that affect the land, or concerning **general historical events** important to that community, state, or nation."

> **Example:** Suppose P is trying to prove that a particular building was destroyed in the San Francisco Earthquake of 1906. He could call W, a historian, who could testify that within northern California, an earthquake has a reputation for having occurred in San Francisco in 1906, and for having destroyed all buildings within a certain area. (Observe that this fact could also be proved, perhaps more conveniently, by use of newspaper accounts through the "ancient documents" exception of FRE 803(16), or by the doctrine of judicial notice, covered *infra*, p. 587.)

3. **Reputation for character:**   Similarly, there is a hearsay exception for reputation concerning a person's *character*. Thus FRE 803(21) gives an exception for "[a] reputation among a person's associates or in the community concerning the person's character."

    a. **Caution:**   But this exception merely removes the hearsay problem. There remain some important restrictions on the use of character evidence generally (e.g., that a person's character is generally not admissible "to prove that on a particular occasion the person acted in accordance with the character[.]" FRE 404(a)(1)). See the discussion of character evidence generally *supra*, p. 22.

E. **Miscellaneous public and quasi-public records:**   A last category of hearsay exceptions relates to certain public and quasi-public records that don't quite fall within the conventional "public records" exception (see *supra*, p. 259).

1. **Vital statistics:**   There is an exception for *vital statistics*, such as official records of *births*, *deaths*, or *marriages*.

    a. **Regular public records rule not applicable:**   At first glance, it might seem that the regular *public records* rule (*supra*, p. 259) would apply to cover such vital statistics, and that the special exception is not necessary. However, recall that the general public records exception only applies where the out-of-court declarant had an *official duty* to make the report in question. In many instances, the person who reports the event to the keeper of the public records (e.g., a person reporting the death of a spouse) is not really acting under any official duty to make the report. Therefore, the special exception for vital statistics has arisen. See FRE 803(9), providing a hearsay exception for "[a] record of a birth, death, or marriage, if reported to a public office in accordance with a legal duty."

    b. **Cause of death:**   Most applications of this exception are cut and dried. But what if a *death certificate* (which is clearly admissible to show the fact of death under this exception) also recites the *cause* of death? In such situations, the person filling out the death certificate — usually the treating physician — may not have had personal knowledge of all the facts that went into the determination of cause of death. For instance, the physician's conclusion that the decedent died of suicide may have been influenced by the decedent's spouse's declaration, "He had been depressed lately," a fact of which the physician has no first-hand knowledge. Nonetheless, most courts would allow the physician's statement on the death certificate as to the cause of death — "suicide on account of depression" — to be admitted under the vital statistics exception. See generally W&B, Par. 803(9)[01].

2. **Marriage certificates:**   Statements of fact contained in a *marriage certificate* are given an exception. See FRE 803(12). Where the marriage is performed by a public official (e.g., a judge), no special exception is needed for the official's certificate that the marriage was performed, since the general "public records" exception covers this situation. But when the marriage certificate is signed by a *clergyman* or other private citizen, the certificate would not be admissible without this special exception.

3. **Vital statistics kept by religious organizations:**   Various facts of personal or family history, when contained in the records of a *religious organization*, are given an exception. See FRE 803(11), covering statements of "birth, legitimacy, ancestry, marriage, divorce,

death, relationship by blood or marriage, or similar facts of personal or family history, contained in a regularly kept record of a religious organization."

    a. Rationale: The business records exception might seem to cover such religious records. However, remember that that exception applies only where the person supplying the information was acting in the course of the business or other regular activity. Since the religious organization's records are often based on information supplied by an "amateur" (e.g., a parent reporting the birth of a child), the business records exception does not apply, and this special exception is needed.

4. Absence of public record: Sometimes a party may wish to prove that there is *no* entry in the public records about a certain event, or that a particular document or filing does not exist in the public records. Just as there is an exception allowing proof of the absence of a particular business record (see *supra*, p. 254), so there is an exception to prove *lack of a public record.* See FRE 803(10).

    a. Certificate or testimony: The absence of a particular public record can be proved in either of two ways, under FRE 803(10): (1) by a *certificate* by the keeper of the records in question, that diligent search has failed to find the record; or (2) by testimony of the record keeper to that effect.

    Example: In a prosecution of D for failure to file tax returns, the IRS could prove failure to file either by a certificate from a person who works in the relevant IRS records center that a search of the Service's records failed to disclose the relevant return, or by live testimony of that custodian that the return could not be found.

5. Previous felony convictions: Often a party will wish to show that another party has received a prior *conviction* for a crime. If the previous conviction is sought to be introduced as evidence that the convicted person committed the crime in question, this is technically hearsay. (That is, the out-of-court declarant — the judge or jury in the earlier action — is saying, "D committed the crime," and this statement is offered to prove that D did in fact commit the crime.)

    a. Traditional view: Traditionally, therefore, courts have been unwilling to allow prior convictions into evidence. McC, p. 511.

    b. Modern and federal view: However, a criminal conviction is accompanied by such safeguards that it is an unusually reliable piece of hearsay. Therefore, a special modern exception has evolved: prior *felony convictions* are generally admissible to prove any fact essential to the conviction. See, e.g., FRE 803(22).

        i. Use in subsequent civil case: This exception is most often used where the plaintiff in a *civil suit* wants to use the prior criminal conviction of the defendant or of a third person to prove some fact that is relevant to the civil case.

        Example: Suppose that D, a psychiatrist, is sued in a negligence action by the Ps, whose daughter was murdered by X, a patient of D who D knew had murderous tendencies. To prove that X killed their daughter, the Ps need merely prove that X was convicted of the murder — they don't have to relitigate the issue of whether X really did it.

ii. **Conviction of third person not usable in criminal case:**   Where the current proceeding is a *criminal* trial, it would probably be unconstitutional for the government to use a *third person's conviction* as part of its case in chief. Therefore, FRE 803(22)(D) disallows such a use.

    Example: D is charged with possession of stolen stamps. The prosecution cannot prove that the stamps were stolen by introducing the fact that the thieves (persons other than D) were convicted of the theft. Such use would violate D's constitutional right to confront the witnesses against him, since an essential element of his guilt — that the stamps were stolen — would have been established in a prior proceeding in which he was not represented and did not have the ability to question the witnesses. See *Kirby v. U.S.*, 174 U.S. 47 (1899).

iii. **Minor crimes:**   Most courts do *not* allow a *misdemeanor* conviction to be used in a subsequent proceeding. This restriction is based on the theory that, when faced with a minor conviction, the defendant may have found it more sensible to pay a fine rather than litigate the charges, even though he was in fact innocent. Thus a driver's conviction on a minor traffic charge (e.g., speeding) will usually not be admissible in a subsequent civil case to show that he did the act charged. FRE 803(22)(B) follows this policy, by allowing proof of convictions only where the crime was "punishable by death or by imprisonment for more than a year" (the traditional felony standard).

iv. **Prior civil judgments:**   The exception for prior judgments applies only to prior *criminal* convictions. A prior judgment in a *civil* case is not covered, either under modern state-law approaches or the Federal Rules. McC, p. 512. (However, general civil procedure principles of *res judicata* or collateral estoppel may cause the prior civil judgment to be dispositive, even though not formally admissible into evidence.)

v. **Acquittal:**   Only convictions are covered. Judgments of *acquittal* are not excepted from the hearsay rule. *Id.*

IX. UNAVAILABILITY REQUIRED — GENERALLY

A. **Introduction:**   All of the hearsay exceptions discussed so far apply regardless of whether the declarant is available to testify at the current trial. We turn now to the second major grouping of hearsay exceptions, those which apply only where the declarant is *unavailable* to testify at the current proceeding.

1. **Theoretically less reliable:**   These "declarant's unavailability required" exceptions would seem to cover evidence that is, on the whole, *less reliable* than the previously-considered exceptions, which apply regardless of whether the declarant is available.

2. **Not necessarily so:**   However, this lesser reliability often reflects only theory, not reality. For instance, it seems probable that former testimony (admissible only if the declarant is unavailable; see *infra*, p. 280) is generally much more reliable than excited utterances (admissible regardless of whether the declarant is available; see *supra*, p. 242). See L&S,

pp. 469-70. The breakdown between these two broad categories probably reflects historical accident more than sound policy.

3. **Five main exceptions:** Under the FRE (see FRE 804(b)), there are five basic exceptions that fall into this unavailability-required category:

    a. **Former testimony:** *Testimony given in a prior proceeding*;

    b. **Dying declaration:** Statements made while the declarant believed his *death was impending* (so-called *dying declarations*);

    c. **Statements against interest:** Statements which were *against the declarant's interest* when made;

    d. **Pedigree:** Statements concerning either the declarant's or his relative's *personal or family history* (so-called statements of *"pedigree"*); and

    e. **Forfeiture by wrongdoing:** Statements offered against a party that has engaged in (or acquiesced in) *wrongdoing* that was intended to, and did, *procure the unavailability* of the declarant as a witness.

B. Meaning of "unavailable": To determine whether one of these exceptions applies, it is first necessary to determine whether the declarant is "unavailable."

1. **The Federal Rule:** The Federal Rules reflect general state policies on when the declarant should be deemed to be "unavailable." FRE 804(a) defines "unavailability as a witness" to include situations in which the declarant:

    "(1) is exempted from testifying about the subject matter of the declarant's statement because the court rules that a *privilege* applies;

    (2) *refuses to testify* about the subject matter despite a court order to do so;

    (3) testifies to *not remembering* the subject matter;

    (4) cannot be present or testify at the trial or hearing because of *death* or a then-existing *infirmity, physical illness, or mental illness*; or

    (5) is *absent* from the trial or hearing and the statement's proponent has not been able, by *process or other reasonable means*, to procure:

       (A) the declarant's *attendance*, in the case of a hearsay exception under Rule 804(b)(1) or (6); or

       (B) the declarant's *attendance or testimony*, in the case of a hearsay exception under Rule 804(b)(2), (3), or (4).

    But this subdivision (a) *does not apply* if the statement's proponent *procured or wrongfully caused* the declarant's unavailability as a witness *in order to prevent the declarant from attending or testifying."*

2. **States generally follow:** The first four of these are pretty cut-and-dried, and nearly all states recognize these same ways of being "unavailable."

    a. **Absence:** But where the asserted unavailability of the declarant stems from his *absence* from the jurisdiction, the Federal Rule is more strict than that of most states. In most state courts, the declarant's mere absence from the state will be enough to render him "unavailable," since that absence will make him not reachable by *process*. L&S, p. 471. But under the Federal Rules, it is not enough to show that the declarant is beyond the reach of process; the person offering the out-of-court declaration must show that it was also not possible to procure the witness's attendance by *other means* (e.g., persuasion). In fact, for the exceptions given in FRE 804(b)(2), (3), and (4) (dying declarations, statements against interest, and statements of pedigree), the person offering the out-of-court declaration in a federal trial must *also* show that attempts to take the declarant's *deposition* were unsuccessful.

3. **Constitutional problems:** In civil cases, and in criminal cases where the declaration at issue is sought to be introduced by the defense, the issue of unavailability has no constitutional dimensions. But where, in a criminal case, the *prosecution* seeks to introduce an out-of-court declaration for which the declarant's unavailability is required, the Constitution's *Confrontation Clause* comes into play. That is, the defendant's right to cross-examine the witnesses against him may be violated by the use of an out-of-court declaration, unless the declarant is "unavailable" measured by a constitutional standard.

    a. **Absence from state not sufficient:** For example, the mere fact that the declarant is out of the state and cannot be compelled by process to testify, will generally *not* be sufficient to satisfy the Confrontation Clause — the state must show that attendance could not be procured by means other than process (e.g., persuasion). See, e.g., *Barber v. Page*, 390 U.S. 719 (1968) (where declarant was in federal prison in another state, he wasn't unavailable, because the federal prison system had a policy of allowing prisoners to testify in out-of-state state-court proceedings).

       i. **Degree of effort:** But, two later Supreme Court cases seem to have weakened this constitutional requirement of *Barber v. Page* that good faith efforts to procure the declarant's attendance must be shown. Thus in *Mancusi v. Stubbs*, 408 U.S. 204 (1972), the Court found that the prior witness, Holm, was unavailable for Confrontation Clause purposes, where he was living in Sweden at the time of the trial.

       ii. **"Good faith effort" found:** Similarly, the witness was held "unavailable" for Confrontation Clause purposes, in *Ohio v. Roberts*, 448 U.S. 56 (1980). The government had issued five separate subpoenas to the witness in care of her mother, and showed that the mother did not know of the witness's whereabouts. However, the government did not contact a social worker who the mother said might know the daughter's address. On the entire set of facts, the Court concluded that the prosecution "did not breach its duty of good-faith effort. . . . The great improbability that [contacting the social worker] would have resulted in locating the witness, and would have led to her production at trial, neutralizes any intimation that a concept of reasonableness required [this step]."

    b. **Unavailability caused by defendant:** What happens if the declarant's unavailability was *caused by the defendant* (e.g., D *killed* the declarant)? Does the fact that the defendant caused the unavailability somehow deprive the defendant of the right to assert the Confrontation Clause? The answer is, in brief, "*yes, but only sometimes.*"

       i. **D purposely causes unavailability to evade testimony:** Where the defendant caused the declarant's unavailability *for the purpose of avoiding the declarant's* *trial testimony*, then the defendant will be deemed to have *forfeited* his right to invoke the Confrontation Clause. See *Giles v. California*, discussed below.

Example: D knows that his ex-wife, V, is about to testify against him in his upcoming trial for the robbery of First Bank. He shoots her in the chest for the purpose of preventing her from so testifying. At V's robbery trial, the prosecution offers a statement made by V to robbery investigators three months prior to the murder, in which V tells the investigators, "I know D committed the robbery because I saw him come home that day with piles of cash wrapped in First Bank wrappers." (Assume that some unusual state-law exception to the hearsay rule permits this statement to be introduced.) D argues that the use of V's out-of-court statement against him will violate his Confrontation Clause rights, because V's statement was "testimonial" in nature, and V is not available to be cross-examined.

Because D procured V's unavailability for the purpose of keeping her from testifying, D will be deemed to have forfeited his Confrontation Clause rights. Therefore, the state is free to admit the statement against D, at least as far as federal constitutional principles are concerned. Cf. *Giles v. California*, immediately *infra*.

ii. **D did not act with purpose to avoid testimony:** But where D causes the declarant to be unavailable for some purpose *other* than preventing the declarant's trial testimony, D's act does *not* constitute a forfeiture of his Confrontation Clause rights. And that's true even if D *murdered* the declarant.

Example: D is charged with shooting his girlfriend V to death. D claims self-defense. The prosecution offers statements made by V to a police officer several weeks before the shooting, in which she said that D was jealous of her, choked her, and threatened to kill her if he found her cheating on him. The court admits the statement under a state statutory exception to the hearsay rule permitting certain out-of-court statements describing threats of physical injury. On appeal, D claims that the admission of V's statements to the officer violated his Confrontation Clause rights under *Crawford*. The prosecution defends by asserting that since D is the one who rendered V unavailable by killing her, he has forfeited his Confrontation Clause rights.

Held (by the U.S. Supreme Court), if D did not act for the purpose of making V unavailable to testify, then he will *not* be deemed to have forfeited his Confrontation Clause rights even though he did in fact make her unavailable by killing her. Since cases from the pre-Constitution era did not automatically allow out-of-court statements by murder victims to be used against the murder defendant, this proves that the mere fact that the defendant made the victim unavailable by killing him was not enough to forfeit the common-law right of confrontation. And since the scope of the common-law confrontation right as it existed prior to the 1789 adoption of the Constitution defines the scope of the Confrontation Clause, that Clause, too, doesn't provide for forfeiture on account of murders done for reasons other than preventing the declarant's testimony. *Giles v. California*, 128 S.Ct. 2678 (2008).

c. **Summary:** In summary, the following are the main things that can be said about when a witness will be deemed sufficiently "unavailable" that use of his out-of-court declaration will not violate a criminal defendant's Confrontation Clause rights:

❏ The state must show that the witness is ***beyond that state's own process***; and must also show either that (a) it made a ***good-faith effort*** to procure the witness's presence by means other than process, or (b) such efforts would have been ***very unlikely to succeed.***

❏ Furthermore, if the defendant ***intentionally made the witness unavailable*** (e.g., by killing him) for the ***purpose of preventing the witness from testifying***, then the defendant has automatically ***forfeited*** his Confrontation Clause rights. See *Giles v. California, supra.*

X. FORMER TESTIMONY

A. **In general:** There is a long-established exception for ***former testimony*** — that is, testimony given in an earlier proceeding — if the witness is unavailable for trial.

1. **Federal Rule:** The Federal Rules follow the common law, by and large. FRE 804(b)(1) provides a hearsay exception, if the declarant is unavailable as a witness, for:

"Testimony that:

(A) was given as a witness at ***a trial, hearing, or lawful deposition***, whether given during the ***current*** proceeding or a ***different*** one; and

(B) is now offered ***against a party who had*** — or, in a ***civil*** case, whose ***predecessor in interest had*** — an ***opportunity and similar motive to develop it*** by direct, cross-, or redirect examination."

2. **Rationale:** There is a very strong rationale in favor of allowing a hearsay exception for former testimony. "Cross-examination, oath, the solemnity of the occasion, and in the case of transcribed testimony the accuracy of reproduction of the words spoken, all combine to give former testimony a high degree of credibility." McC, p. 515.

a. **Not just for transcripts:** However, observe that the exception is ***not limited*** to ***transcripts*** of the prior hearing. For instance, a ***first-hand observer*** may ***orally recount*** the testimony, either from unaided memory or by refreshing his recollection by use of the transcript. McC, pp. 520-21. In this situation, the accuracy of the evidence — in the sense of avoiding errors in transmission — is not especially high. In the overwhelming majority of former testimony situations, however, a transcript will be used.

3. **Requirements summarized:** So under FRE 804(b)(1), here are the four requirements that the proponent must satisfy before the former testimony is admissible:

❏ The ***declarant*** must be ***unavailable***.

❏ The former testimony must have been made either in: (i) a ***"hearing"*** (e.g., a trial, a preliminary hearing, a grand jury proceeding, etc.) or (ii) a ***deposition***. Furthermore, the "hearing" or deposition must have occurred during a ***"proceeding."*** (But the testimony need not have been made in the same action.)

❑ The party *against whom* the prior testimony is now offered (or, in a civil case, that party's "predecessor in interest") must have had an *opportunity to examine* (usually cross-examine) the declarant in the prior proceeding or deposition.

❑ The party *against whom* the prior testimony is now offered (or, in a civil case, that party's "predecessor in interest") must have had a *similar motive* to develop the testimony in the prior proceeding by direct, cross or redirect examination. (So there must be *substantial overlap* in the *issue* that was *at stake* when the prior testimony was given and the issue at stake now.)

B. Meaning of "hearing" and "proceeding": As noted, the former testimony must have occurred at either a *"hearing"* or in a deposition, and the hearing or deposition must have taken place during a *"proceeding."* The term "deposition" is self-explanatory. But the terms "hearing" and "proceeding" are not.

1. **Broadly defined:** The terms "hearing" and "proceeding" seem to be interpreted broadly: "hearing" seems to include any setting in which *sworn testimony by a witness* is taken, and "proceeding" seems to include "any *official inquiry* conducted in a manner authorized by law whether *judicial*, *administrative*, *legislative*, *investigative*, or inquisitorial." M&K §8.68, p. 912.

2. **What's covered:** So testimony probably meets the "hearing" and "proceeding" requirements if it occurs during any of the following types of events:

   ❑ a *prior trial* (whether civil or criminal);

   ❑ a *preliminary hearing* in a criminal case;

   ❑ a *grand jury investigation*;

   ❑ a *suppression hearing* in a criminal case;

   ❑ plus, of course, as specifically mentioned in 804(b)(1), a *deposition*.

3. **What's not covered:** But two important situations in which a person "tells a story" are *not covered*:

   ❑ *Affidavits* aren't covered, even where they're prepared for use in a trial or other proceeding. This is so because the affidavit isn't given "at" a hearing (and also probably because it doesn't include "testimony," insofar as that term is usually understood to mean spoken statements). M&K, § 8.68, pp. 912-13.

   ❑ *Statements made to police or other law enforcement officials* during investigations aren't covered, because such investigations aren't "proceedings." *Id.*

4. **Under oath:** For a statement to qualify as admissible former testimony, it must be made *under oath*. This requirement isn't specifically stated in FRE 804(b)(1) itself, but the Advisory Committee Notes to that section say that "both oath and opportunity to cross-examine [are] present in fact" when former testimony is used. Court decisions have agreed that the testimony must be under oath (usually by concluding that "testimony" *means* statements given under oath).

C. Opportunity for cross-examination: A key requirement for the former testimony exception is that the party against whom the evidence is now offered must have had a reasonable opportunity to *cross-examine* the declarant at the time of the former testimony.

> **Example:** X is arrested in connection with a robbery. At a preliminary hearing on the charges, X gives testimony implicating D, who so far has not been suspected and who is not present at the hearing. At a subsequent prosecution of D for the crime, the state will not be permitted to introduce X's preliminary hearing testimony (even if X is now unavailable), because D had no opportunity to cross-examine X at that hearing. (In this prosecution-witness context, the requirement of cross-examination is imposed not only by general evidence principles, but also by the Constitution's Confrontation Clause.)

1. **Actual examination not required:**   There is no requirement that the party against whom the evidence is now offered have *actually* cross-examined the declarant at the earlier proceeding. All that is required is that the opponent have had a reasonable *opportunity* to do so.

    > **Example:** Suppose that, on the facts of the above example, D and X had been arrested together, and both were present (with D represented by counsel) at the same preliminary hearing. If D's counsel was given the opportunity to cross-examine X at the hearing, and chose not to do so, lack of cross-examination will not furnish a reason for D to keep X's hearing testimony out of D's eventual trial.

2. **Direct examination:**   Suppose the party opposing the former testimony at trial had the opportunity to do *direct* (rather than cross) examination at the prior proceeding. Such an opportunity is virtually always held to be the equivalent of an opportunity to cross-examine, so the requirement of cross-examination is satisfied.

    > **Example:** At Trial 1 of a negligence action between P and D, P calls X, a witness who ends up giving testimony unfavorable to P. After a mistrial, Trial 2 is held, and X is no longer available as a witness. If D offers X's former testimony, P cannot claim that he lacked the opportunity to cross-examine X at Trial 1 — P's opportunity to do a *direct* examination of X is the equivalent of cross-examination (even though local trial rules might have substantially impaired P's right to attack the credibility of his own witness, or even though, from a tactical perspective, P's decision not to attack his witness's credibility was reasonable). See L&S, p. 475.

D. "Similar motive" to cross-examine: An additional — and very major — requirement for use of prior testimony is that the party against whom the prior testimony is now offered (or, in a civil case, that party's "predecessor in interest"; see *infra*, p. 287) must have had a *"similar motive"* to develop the testimony in the prior proceeding by direct, cross or redirect examination.

1. **Common-law approach:** At common-law, most courts did not impose a "similar motive" requirement. Instead, they imposed a requirement that the *"same issue"* (or at least *"substantially* the same issue") be involved in the two situations. This requirement was imposed for the same purpose as the FRE's "similar motive" rule: to make sure that the other party (the one against whom the prior testimony is now offered) had at least a

roughly-equivalent incentive to cross-examine the witness at the prior proceeding. McC, p. 446.

2. **Rationale for "similar motive" rule:** *Why* does FRE 804(b)(1) require a "similar motive"? The basic idea is that only where a similar motive existed can we be assured that the former testimony is a ***reasonable substitute for the unavailable live testimony***. The single most important factor making testimony reliable is that the adverse party cross-examined (or had the opportunity to cross-examine) the witness on the prior occasion; yet if the adverse party had no incentive to cross-examine — for instance, because the ***issues were different***, or the ***stakes were very different*** — we don't have the requisite assurance that equivalent cross-examination was, or at least reasonably could and should have been, performed.

> **Example:** Paul's and David's cars collide in what seems to be a small fender-bender. Paul's car has some damage, and David's none; neither party seems to be physically injured. In a small-claims suit brought immediately by Paul against David for $200 in repair costs, Paul presents testimony by Walter, Paul's passenger (and brother), who says, "The accident was David's fault, because David went through a red light." David does not defend the suit, because he's out of town on business and thinks that too little's at stake to rush back to defend. Two weeks later, David realizes that he suffered whiplash in the collision; he ends up with serious and permanent injuries, and now sues Paul for $300,000. Meanwhile, Walter dies.
>
> The issue is, can Walter's testimony at the first trial (assuming that it was given under oath and properly recorded by a court stenographer, even though given in small-claims court) be used by Paul against David in David's suit? The "similar motive" requirement suggests that the answer is ***"no"*** — because so little was at stake in the first suit, and so much in the second suit, we can't really say that David had a "similar motive" to vigorously cross-examine Walter at the first suit as he would have now. Thus as a matter of fairness, as well as truth-seeking, we shouldn't make an exception to the hearsay rule for Walter's prior testimony — it's better to do entirely without any testimony from Walter than to allow this untested (and, now, untestable) testimony.

3. **Same issues, same stakes and same parties:** There seem to be three components that typically go into whether the "same motive" requirement is satisfied: similarity of ***issues***, similarity of ***stakes***, and similarity of ***parties***. If all three components are similar or identical between the prior proceeding and the present one, then the "similar motive" requirement will almost certainly be found to be satisfied; if one or more are not satisfied, then the party opposing the evidence now will have at least a colorable chance of establishing that the "similar motive" rule is not fulfilled.

   a. **Similarity of issues:** Similar motive is much more likely to be satisfied where the prior and present proceedings involve the ***same (or a very similar) issue(s)***. What counts here is not whether *all* the issues are the same between the two proceedings, but whether the issue to which the particular prior piece of testimony now sought to be used ***related*** is the same as the issue on which the proponent now seeks to introduce the testimony.

    b. **Similarity of stakes:** Similarly, if the *stakes* are much smaller during the first proceeding than at the present trial, the opponent of the prior testimony has a good chance of convincing the court that the prior testimony should be excluded because of a lack of "similar motive."

        i. **Preliminary proceedings, grand juries, etc.:** This "smaller stakes" issue is raised particularly sharply by prior testimony that occurs during a *preliminary stage* of an investigation or proceeding. Thus where a witness testifies at a *grand jury*, the prosecutor may not have much incentive to do a searching cross-examination; similarly, where a pro-prosecution witness testifies at a *preliminary hearing* in a criminal matter, the defense may have little incentive to cross-examine now. Nonetheless, in these two contexts, courts generally give the "I lacked incentive" argument short shrift, and tend to *allow* the former testimony. See *infra*.

    c. **Same parties:** Finally, where the *parties* are different, this can make it less likely that the present opponent of the testimony will be found to have a "similar motive." Observe that this situation can only arise in a civil case (where the issue is whether the present opponent's "predecessor in interest" had the same motive); in a criminal case, the party — typically the defendant — *must be the same* in the two proceedings. See *infra*, p. 287, for more about the "different parties" problem.

  4. **Specific contexts:** Now, let's take a brief look at how the "similar motive" issue tends to be decided in a variety of special contexts.

    a. **Grand jury testimony:** Where the prior testimony occurs in front of a *grand jury*, the prosecution can never use the testimony at the later trial (because grand juries operate in secret, and hear only one witness at a time; therefore, the defendant could never have had the opportunity to cross-examine a witness at the grand jury). Consequently, the only way former grand jury testimony might be used is if it's the *defense* that wants to use exculpatory testimony by a witness, and the prosecution resists on the grounds that it didn't have the requisite "similar motive" during the grand jury proceedings.

        i. ***Salerno* case:** A Supreme Court case, ***U.S. v. Salerno***, 112 S.Ct. 2503 (U.S. 1992), makes it clear that the "similar motive" requirement will be strictly *enforced* in this grand-jury-testimony scenario, even though this may deprive the defendant of valuable evidence that he may have no other way to get. In *Salerno*, the Court rejected the defendants' suggestion that the requirement that the prosecution be shown to have a similar motive not be strictly enforced on account of "adversarial fairness."

            (1) **Facts:** The facts of *Salerno* show how the "similar motive" requirement can deprive the defendant of valuable, and irreplaceable, evidence. A key issue there was whether the Ds (alleged to be organized crime figures) helped maintain a "Club" of concrete companies who controlled the local cement industry. Two witnesses, DeMatteis and Bruno (neither of whom ever became a defendant) were given use immunity in front of the grand jury, and each testified in detail that he never participated in any Club. The prosecutor clearly did at least some cross-examination of each, suggesting that their story was not believable. At the Ds' trial, the prosecution refused a defense request to again give DeMatteis and Bruno use immunity; the two took the Fifth Amendment (thus making them "unavailable"; see *supra*, p. 277), and the Ds then sought to use the two witnesses' grand jury testimony — which of course tended to exculpate the Ds as well — instead of live testimony.

(2) **Holding:** The Supreme Court, as noted, held that the "similar motive" requirement must be strictly enforced in this grand jury scenario. Therefore, unless the Ds could establish that the prosecution had a motive when it cross-examined DeMatteis and Bruno in front of the grand jury substantially similar to the motive it would have were it cross-examining them now at trial, the grand jury testimony couldn't come in. The Supreme Court declined to decide whether the requisite "similar motive" was present, and instead remanded on this point. (The Second Circuit finally concluded on remand that the government did not have the requisite similar motive. *U.S. v. DiNapoli*, 8 F.3d 909 (2d Cir. en banc 1993).)

ii. **Summary:** The defense will generally have a *hard time* persuading the court that the prosecution had a similar motive at the grand jury as at the ultimate trial.

b. **Criminal followed by civil trial:** Depending on the facts, the "similar motive" requirement may be met where the former testimony occurs at a *criminal trial* and is then sought to be introduced at a later *civil* trial. Typically, the way this happens is that W testifies against D in the civil suit, then becomes unavailable by the time a later civil suit by the victim (or the victim's family) comes to trial against D, and the plaintiff wants to use this testimony.

Example: O.J. Simpson is tried for murdering his wife Nicole and Ron Goldman. Limo driver Alan Parks testifies for the prosecution that O.J. wasn't home at 10:40 PM (near the estimated time of the crime), but was home at 10:50. O.J. is acquitted. Now, let's assume that Parks leaves the country and his whereabouts are unknown. Ron Goldman's parents bring a wrongful death action against O.J. The Goldmans will almost certainly be *allowed* to use Park's trial testimony in their civil suit, because O.J. will be found to have had substantially the same motive(s) (to either discredit Parks' testimony or to minimize its significance on the issue of whether O.J. did the killing) in cross-examining Parks during the criminal trial as he would have had if Parks were testifying now at the civil trial.

i. **Criminal followed by civil trial, but criminal D tries to use:** In the above example, it's the civil *plaintiff* who is now trying to use the former testimony against a person who was the defendant both in the original criminal trial and in the present civil proceeding. But suppose that in same criminal-trial-followed-by-civil-trial context, it's the *defendant* in the civil action (who was also the defendant in the criminal trial) who now wants to use the former testimony in the civil action. In this case, the former-testimony exception *can't possibly apply.* That's because a civil defendant against whom the prior testimony is now being offered cannot possibly have had the opportunity or motive to cross-examine the testifier at the prior criminal trial. In a criminal trial, *no private party* other than the defendant himself would ever have the opportunity or motive to cross-examine a witness.

(1) Use of grand jury testimony: Similarly, if the first proceeding was a ***grand jury hearing***, no private party, even a suspect on whom the proceeding is focusing, would ever have the opportunity to cross-examine a witness. Therefore, former grand jury testimony can never be used under the exception against a later private party who wasn't the grand jury witness.

ii. **Other configurations:** Although the configuration in our O.J. Simpson example (same person is defendant in both actions, and he's resisting re-use of the evidence) is the most common, other configurations may also lead to a conclusion that the person opposing the evidence had a similar motive in both trials. Thus one who was a defendant the first time might be a plaintiff the second time, and be trying to keep out evidence. The question is always the same: did the person now opposing the evidence have similar incentives to cross-examine the testimony during the first action?

Example: P1 and P2, business partners, bring a civil action against D, an insurance company, to recover on two fire insurance policies. At the trial, D seeks to introduce a transcript of testimony from an earlier criminal prosecution against P1, in which two witnesses, W1 and W2, testified that P1 had helped them burn down the premises. The Ps argue that there is no "identity of issues" between the earlier criminal case and the later civil one.

Held, for D. The main issue on which the Ws' testimony was relevant is the same in both actions: whether P1 was responsible for the burning of the building. This satisfies the requirement of "identity of issues," since P1 had the same motive and interest in cross-examining in the earlier criminal proceeding as P1 and P2 have in the subsequent civil one. (Also, there is sufficient "identity of parties," see *infra*, since P1 was a party to both proceedings and has a common interest with P2, sufficient to overcome the fact that P2 was not a party to the earlier criminal case.) *Travelers Fire Insurance Co. v. Wright*, 322 P.2d 417 (Okla. 1958).

c. **Depositions:** One last situation in which the "similar motive" issue frequently has to be addressed is that of ***deposition*** testimony. The problem occurs more often in civil cases than in criminal ones (since depositions get taken in criminal cases only in unusual circumstances).

i. **Deponent likely to become unavailable:** Where it's evident at the time of deposition that the deponent is ***likely*** to become unavailable (e.g., she's dying), then it's sensible to say that the opponent has a "similar motive" — the opponent is on notice that the deposition will be offered at trial if the deponent indeed becomes unavailable, so the opponent has every incentive to cross-examine vigorously because there'll be no second chance. (In any event, as described in the next paragraph, the Federal Rules of Civil Procedure make the deposition available, without the need for considering the "similar motive" issue.)

ii. **Deponent not likely to become unavailable:** But where, at the time of the deposition, there's ***no strong indication of coming unavailability***, this logic does not hold; as in the preliminary hearing situation, the opposing lawyer can plausibly reason, "I don't want to cross-examine too vigorously now, because I don't want to tip my hand, and there's nothing to be gained by doing a bang-up job — let's save the real carve-up job for the trial." However, the Federal Rules of *Civil Procedure* (Rule 32(a)) make the deposition *admissible* at a trial of the *same action*, if the deponent is unavailable at trial, *regardless of whether the opponent had the "same motive."* So FRE 804(b)(1)'s "similar motive" requirement never even kicks in, and the deposition will be automatically admissible. M&K §8.68, p. 916. "The message is that parties should fully examine witnesses in depositions or assume the risk that the deposition will be later admissible." *Id.* at 917.

E. Identity of parties: The last important requirement for the former testimony exception is that there must be an *"identity of parties"* as between the two proceedings.

1. **Applies only to opponent:** In modern cases, it is never required that *both* parties be the same in the two actions. All that is required is that the party *against* whom the former testimony is offered must have been a party to the prior proceeding. (Earlier common-law decisions required that both parties be the same; this requirement of "mutuality" has been abandoned in Evidence, just as it has been abandoned in the analogous Civil Procedure area of collateral estoppel. See Emanuel on *Civil Procedure*.)

   Example: Byars (driving a truck for Mattress Co.) collides with Martin (driving his own car); Gaines, who is working on the highway near the point of impact, is injured, and Martin is killed. In Trial 1, Martin's administrator sues Mattress, and Byars gives testimony. Byars then dies. In Trial 2, Gaines sues Martin's estate, and seeks to use Byars' testimony from Trial 1. Martin's estate claims that the requisite "identity of parties" is lacking, because Gaines was not a party to Trial 1.

   Held, for Gaines. Gaines' absence from Trial 1 is irrelevant. All that matters is that Martin (the party against whom the testimony is now offered) was a party to the first action, since his presence assured that he had the opportunity to cross-examine Byars in the first action. The requirement that there be "identity of issues" is but a means of assuring that there was an adequate opportunity for cross-examination by the party now opposing the evidence. *Gaines v. Thomas*, 128 S.E.2d 692 (S.C. 1962).

2. **FRE approach:** The Federal Rules provide, with a relatively minor exception, that *the party against whom the former testimony is offered must have been present in the earlier proceeding.*

   a. **Text of Rule:** FRE 804(b)(1)(B) says that the former testimony is admissible if it is "now offered *against a party* who had — or, in a *civil case*, whose *predecessor in interest had* — an *opportunity and similar motive* to develop it by direct, cross-, or redirect examination."

   b. **Summary:** So for former testimony to be admissible under FRE 804(b)(1), one of the following must be true: (1) The *party against whom the former testimony is now offered* must have had an opportunity (and similar motive) to cross-examine in the earlier proceeding; *or* (2) In *civil cases only*, the present opponent's *"predecessor in interest"* must have had such an opportunity.

c. ***Lloyd* case:**   What type of person will be deemed to be a "predecessor in interest," thus triggering the alternative in situation (2) above? The term seems to be interpreted quite loosely. Thus the leading case on this issue has held, in effect, that all the "predecessor in interest" requirement in FRE 804(b)(1) means is a person with a "***like motive*** to develop the same testimony about the same material facts[.]" *Lloyd v. American Export Lines, Inc.*, 580 F.2d 1179 (3d. Cir. 1978).

   i.   **Facts:**   In *Lloyd*, two members of a ship's crew (Lloyd and Alvarez) got into a fight. In Proceeding 1, the Coast Guard held a hearing to determine whether Lloyd's merchant mariner's document should have been suspended. Lloyd and Alvarez testified at this hearing, and each was represented by counsel. Proceeding 2 was a suit by Alvarez against the shipowner. The Shipowner tried to introduce the testimony of Lloyd (now unavailable) from the Coast Guard hearing, but Alvarez argued that he had had no opportunity to examine Lloyd at the first hearing (which was true), and that the Coast Guard was not a "predecessor in interest" to Alvarez.

   ii.   **Result:**   The former testimony was held ***admissible*** on appeal. "There was a sufficient community of interest shared by the Coast Guard in its hearing and Alvarez in the subsequent civil trial to satisfy Rule 804(b)(1)." The "nucleus of operative facts" — the conduct of Lloyd and Alvarez on the ship — was the same in the two proceedings, and the Coast Guard officer had the same motive — to establish Lloyd's wrongdoing — as Alvarez had in the later trial. Therefore, the Coast Guard was Alvarez's predecessor in interest because it had a "like motive to develop the testimony about the same material facts. . . ." (A concurring opinion pointed out that Rule 804(b)(1) has a separate requirement that there have been a "similar motive" to cross-examine in the two situations; given this "similar motive" requirement, the majority's interpretation of "predecessor in interest" to require merely a similar motive "eliminates the predecessor in interest requirement entirely.")

d.   **Present status of Rule in civil cases:**   Thus if the *Lloyd* approach is followed in civil cases, the "predecessor in interest" requirement virtually disappears, and it is sufficient that there was a different party in the earlier proceeding who had the same motive to cross-examine as the party who now opposes the former testimony. Most courts have apparently followed the *Lloyd* court's approach of interpreting "predecessor in interest" very loosely. W&B, Par. 804(b)(1)[04].

e.   **Rule in criminal cases:**   In ***criminal*** cases, by contrast, the "same parties" requirement is ***strictly construed***. FRE 804(b)(1)(B) has no exception for a "predecessor in interest" in this situation — if the defendant was not an actual party to the earlier proceeding, the presence of a person with even an extremely similar motive to cross-examine will not be sufficient to allow the testimony to be used against the defendant at trial.

Example: D1 and D2 are suspected of armed robbery. At D1's trial, W gives testimony implicating both D1 and D2. D1 vociferously cross-examines W, in a way designed to show that W is lying (and in a way that, if successful, will exculpate both

D1 and D2). At D2's later trial, W is unavailable. The prosecution will not be permitted to offer against D2 the transcript of W's prior testimony at D1's trial, because D2 was not a party to that trial. This is true even though D1 had every opportunity and motive to cross-examine in a manner similar to that which would be expected from D2 at the latter's trial. This rule safeguards D2's Confrontation Clause rights, since otherwise he would be deprived of the ability to confront W, a witness against him.

i. **Defense witness; prior trial was criminal:**   Observe that FRE 804(b)(1)(B)'s treatment of criminal cases requires that the party against whom the testimony is offered have been an actual party to the proceeding, without respect to whether that party is the defendant or the prosecutor. The above example shows why this is constitutionally required where the prior testimony is offered against the defendant. However, the Rule seems literally to mean that if the testimony is now offered against the ***prosecution***, and the earlier suit was also a criminal case against the same defendant, the ***same prosecuting body*** must have been involved in the first suit. Many commentators feel that such a result would probably be so unfair as to violate the defendant's due process rights, and "quite likely it was not intended by the Congress." McC, p. 517.

    Example: In Trial 1, D is prosecuted by the state for murdering X. He presents testimony of W, who is extensively cross-examined by the state prosecutor. In Trial 2, D is prosecuted by the federal government for violating X's civil rights, based upon the same alleged facts. W has since died, and D offers a transcript of his testimony from the prior state action. A literal reading of FRE 804(b)(1)(B) would indicate that the federal prosecutor can keep this evidence out, since the party against whom it is offered (the U.S. government) was not a party to the earlier action, and since there is no provision for a "predecessor in interest" in criminal cases. However, such a result would probably violate D's due process rights, so the former testimony would probably be allowed. *Id.*

ii. **Defense witness; prior trial was civil:** The prosecution in the second trial has a somewhat better chance of keeping out the testimony from the prior trial if the prior trial was a ***civil action*** — it's probably harder for the defendant to argue that, say, a private plaintiff was the present prosecutor's "predecessor in interest" than where both trials were criminal.

    Example: Suppose that in the above example, Trial 1 was a civil wrongful death suit by X's estate against D, in which W (now dead) testified on D's behalf. Now, in Trial 2 (as in the prior example, a federal civil rights criminal prosecution), the federal prosecutor has a respectable chance of keeping out W's former testimony. The prosecutor can argue that even if a state prosecutor might have been a "predecessor in interest" to the federal prosecutor, a private plaintiff in the estate's position — perhaps one who was not well-prepared, and certainly one who didn't need to prove anything beyond a reasonable doubt (as the federal prosecutor here needs to do) — is not. Allowing D to use W's testimony seems to ignore the "natural meaning" of Congress' language. M&K §8.69, p. 958.

XI. DYING DECLARATIONS

A. General rule: As long as there has been a hearsay rule, there has been an exception for *dying declarations*.

   1. Statement of rule: The common-law form of this rule is fairly narrow: *a declarant's statement, while believing that his death is imminent, concerning the cause or circumstances of his impending death, is admissible in a subsequent homicide prosecution concerning that death.*

   2. Rationale: The rationale for this exception is more religious and psychological than it is legal — it stems from the belief that "the dying declarant, knowing that he is about to die, would be unwilling to go to his Maker with a lie on his lips." 6 How. L.J. 109, 111.

      a. Criticism: In earlier times, this was probably a reasonable assumption, since most people feared Hell. Today, fear of God and fear of Hell are probably less prevalent, so there is less reason to believe that the exception produces reliable evidence. Furthermore, "the desire for revenge or self-exoneration or to protect one's loved ones may continue until the moment of death. [Also] the declarant's physical and mental condition at the time he is awaiting death may have impaired his faculties of perception, memory and communication and may contribute to the unreliability of the statements." W&B, Par. 804(b)(2)[01].

      b. Limitations: Because of these doubts about the real reliability of dying declaration evidence, both the common law and the Federal Rules have restricted such evidence to a fairly small set of circumstances, discussed below.

   3. Federal Rule: The Federal Rules provide the dying declaration exception in FRE 804(b)(2):

      "The following are not excluded by the rule against hearsay if the declarant is unavailable as a witness: … *(2) Statement Under the Belief of Imminent Death.* In a *prosecution for homicide* or in a *civil case*, a statement that the declarant, while *believing the declarant's death to be imminent*, made *about its cause or circumstances*."

B. Requirements: We now consider in detail the requirements for application of the dying declaration exception. At common law, there are five such requirements. As we discuss each, we will also cover the handling of that requirement under the Federal Rules (which relax several of them).

   1. Awareness of imminent death: The declarant must, at the time he made his statement, have been *aware of his impending death*. It is not enough that he believed that he would probably die — "he must have lost all hope of recovery." McC, pp. 523-24.

      a. How proven: There are a number of ways of showing that the declarant had the requisite awareness of his impending death. His own statements may demonstrate this knowledge (e.g., "I'm a goner"). His *wounds may be so severe* that he must have known that he was about to die. (But if there is no showing that the victim knew how severe his wounds were, their severity will not be enough.) Finally, statements made *to* the victim by others, especially doctors, can be evidence of the declarant's awareness of impending death.

b. Federal Rules: The Federal Rules continue the "awareness of impending death" requirement: FRE 804(b)(2) requires that the declarant have made the statement "while *believing* [his] *death to be imminent*[.]"

2. **Actual death required:** At common law, the declarant *must in fact be dead* at the time the evidence is offered. That is, no matter how certain the declarant was that he would die, if he makes a miraculous recovery and is alive at the time of trial (even if unable to testify), the common-law exception does not apply. McC, p. 524.

   a. Temporary recovery: On the other hand, it is *not* required that the declarant have died immediately or even soon after the declaration. "Periods even extending into months have been held not too long." McC, p. 524.

   b. Federal Rule: The Federal Rules *completely remove* the requirement that death have actually ensued. FRE 804(b)(2) is one of the "declarant unavailable" exceptions, but it will suffice if the declarant is unavailable for some reason other than death (e.g., disability or forgetfulness).

3. **Homicide:** At common law, dying declarations may be used *only in homicide cases*. That is, they may *not* be used in *civil* cases. Nor may they be used in other kinds of criminal actions, even where the victim has died from the episode (e.g., a prosecution for rape where the woman has in fact died).

   a. Rationale: The only rationale for this strange limitation is that dying declarations are really not such reliable evidence after all, so their use should be curtailed. But it is hard to see why such declarations are more reliable in a murder prosecution (where the defendant's life may well be at stake) than in, say, a robbery prosecution.

   b. Federal Rules: The Federal Rules relax the "homicide only" requirement somewhat. Such declarations are usable in *civil suits*. But they remain unusable in *non-homicide criminal cases*.

4. **Declarant must be victim:** The most bizarre of all the common-law requirements is that the declaration may be offered only in a trial for the homicide of the *declarant*, not the homicide of someone else.

   Example: There is evidence that D has murdered both H and W. He is prosecuted for the murder of H only, because the evidence is strongest as to this crime. At common law, the prosecution will not be permitted to introduce W's dying declaration, "It's D who has done this to H and me." McC, p. 525.

   a. Federal Rules: This silly requirement has been dropped from the Federal Rules.

5. **Must relate to circumstances of killing:** Finally, the declaration must relate to the *causes or circumstances* of the killing.

   Example: Suppose that Declarant, in anticipation of his death, says, "X and I have been deadly enemies for the last 10 years." This statement will probably not be admissible, because it does not relate directly to the causes or circumstances of Declarant's death. But if Declarant had said, "X has been stalking me for two days," this statement would probably be allowed into evidence.

    a. **Federal Rules:** The Federal Rules continue this requirement: 804(b)(2) requires that the declaration be one that the declarant "while believing [his] death to be imminent, made ***about its cause or circumstances***."

C. **Miscellaneous:** Here are some miscellaneous aspects of the dying declaration doctrine:

  1. **Usable on accused's behalf:** Such declarations may be admitted ***on behalf of the defendant***, even though most of the time they are admitted against him. McC, p. 525.

  2. **First-hand knowledge:** As with other out-of-court declarations, the dying declaration will be admissible only if it appears to come from the declarant's ***first-hand knowledge***.

      Example: Declarant says, "X shot me." If the other evidence shows that Declarant was shot in the back, and that he could not have had the opportunity to see that it was indeed X who was shooting him, the declaration will not be admitted. W&B, Par. 804(b)(2)[01]. This is true even though Declarant may have had other reasons to suspect that X was out to get him — the whole point is to exclude statements of suspicion, and to limit admissibility to statements that are unusually reliable because they come from the declarant's direct observation.

  3. **Opinions:** Suppose the declaration includes an element of the declarant's ***opinion***. A witness on the stand (other than an expert) will not usually be permitted to give an opinion. (See *infra*, p. 516.) However, the rule against opinion testimony is not strictly applied in the case of dying declarations. Thus a court will probably admit the declaration, "He shot me without cause." But if the judge finds that the opinion or speculation portion of the statement outweighs its factual portion, he can exclude the evidence on the grounds that it is prejudicial or not helpful. (Federal Rule 701, relating generally to lay opinion testimony, seems to apply to the dying declaration situation. See Advisory Committee's Note to 804(b)(2).)

  4. **Preliminary fact questions:** Observe that before a declaration can be found to be an admissible "dying declaration," some preliminary questions of fact must be answered. In particular, it must be determined whether the declarant was indeed aware of his impending death. Who should decide this question, the judge or the jury? This issue is part of the broader issue of who should decide factual issues in connection with "conditional relevance," and is discussed further *infra*, p. 579.

    a. **Resolution:** In brief, the answer is that in most state courts (and under the Federal Rules), the ***judge*** makes a ***preliminary factual determination***: if he decides that there is enough evidence that the requisite awareness of death existed that a jury could reasonably find that there was such awareness, he will let the jury hear the declaration (even though he may personally believe that it is less likely than not that there was such awareness). It will then be up to the jury to determine what weight is to be given to this evidence, and they may (but probably need not) consider whether, in their opinion, the declarant was really aware that he was dying. See FRE 104(b): "When the relevancy of evidence depends upon the fulfillment of a condition of fact, the court shall admit it upon, or subject to, the introduction of evidence sufficient to support a finding of the fulfillment of the condition."

XII. DECLARATIONS AGAINST INTEREST

A. Generally: There is a hearsay exception for declarations which, at the time they are made, are *so against the declarant's interest that it is unlikely they would have been made if they were not true*. At common law, the exception applies solely to statements against the declarant's financial interest; some states, and the Federal Rules, have expanded the exception to cover statements against penal interest.

1. **Summary of requirements:**   The exception has only three requirements, in most jurisdictions:

   [1] the declaration must be against the declarant's *pecuniary or proprietary interest* when made;

   [2] the declarant must be *unavailable*; and

   [3] as with virtually all other hearsay exceptions, the declarant must have had *first-hand knowledge* of the facts asserted in the declaration.

   (Some states add a fourth requirement, that the declarant have had no probable motive to falsify. When this requirement is imposed, it is generally of importance as to statements that are partly disserving and partly self-serving. See *infra*, p. 298.)

   Example: P, an employer, sues D, its insurer, on a policy of fidelity insurance protecting P from wrongdoing by its employees. P seeks to introduce written and signed confessions by several employees admitting that they have misappropriated P's funds.

   Held, the confessions are admissible as third-party declarations against interest. "The courts have reasoned that a person does not make statements against his own pecuniary interest unless they are true and have thus considered such statements trustworthy, even though there is no opportunity to confront the witness or to cross-examine him." Here, all requirements are met: (1) the employees could not be found by the sheriff, so they are unavailable; (2) they had first-hand knowledge of their own wrongdoing; (3) the confessions were against their pecuniary interest (since the confessions could be used to support a civil suit against them, in addition to criminal liability); and (4) they had no probable motive to falsify the facts in their confessions. *McKelvey Co. v. General Casualty Co. of America*, 142 N.E.2d 854 (Ohio 1957).

2. **Distinguished from admissions:**   It is important to distinguish a declaration against interest from an *admission* (see *supra*, p. 215). The exception for admissions applies only where the declarant is a party, and his opponent is offering the statement. An admission does not have to meet any of the requirements that are applied to declarations against interest: (1) the party need not be unavailable; (2) the declaration need not have been against the party's interest when made; and (3) the party need not have had first-hand knowledge.

   a. **Strategy:**   Therefore, if you represent a party and want to get a declaration by the opposing party into evidence, you should treat it as an admission, not a declaration against interest.

   b. **Practical use:**   Conversely, the practical use of the declaration-against-interest exception is where the declarant is *not a party*. Lilly, p. 297.

3. **Rationale:** As noted, the theory behind the exception is that a person will usually not make a statement against his own interest unless the statement is true. However, this rationale is not convincing in all cases: "Persons will lie despite the consequences to themselves to exculpate those they love or fear, to inculpate those they hate or fear, or because they are congenital liars. Others will not realize that they are making an admission against themselves, or will make ambivalent statements susceptible of differing interpretations." W&B, Par. 804(b)(3)[01]. It is for these reasons that there is a requirement of declarant unavailability — the evidence is better than no evidence at all, but not as good as having the declarant himself on the stand. These doubts are also the reason why, until recent years, declarations against penal interest (discussed *infra*, p. 295) were not covered by the rule.

4. **Federal Rule:** The Federal Rules apply the declaration-against-interest exception in more or less its common law form. FRE 804(b)(3) provides an exception, if the declarant is unavailable, for:

   "A statement that:

   (A) a *reasonable person in the declarant's position* would have made *only if the person believed it to be true because*, when made, it was so *contrary to the declarant's proprietary or pecuniary interest* or had so *great a tendency to invalidate the declarant's claim against someone else* or to *expose the declarant to civil or criminal liability*; and

   (B) is *supported by corroborating circumstances* that *clearly indicate its trustworthiness*, if it is offered in a *criminal* case as one that tends to *expose the declarant to criminal liability.*"

   a. **Covers penal interest:** The principal difference between this Federal Rule and the common-law rule is that the Federal Rule covers *statements against penal interest.*

B. **Meaning of "against interest":** Most of the tough questions regarding the declaration-against-interest exception relate to whether the declaration really is *against the declarant's interest.*

1. **When made:** The declaration must have been against the declarant's interest *at the time it was made*. The fact that later developments have turned what was an innocent-seeming statement into one that now harms some interest of the declarant, is *not* enough to satisfy the requirement.

   a. **Rationale:** The rationale behind the exception is that a person will not speak against his own interest unless he is telling the truth, so this rationale would not apply where the statement was not against interest at the time it was made.

2. **Pecuniary interest:** As noted, the common-law version of the exception requires that the statement have been against the declarant's *pecuniary* or *proprietary* interest. Statements that would subject the declarant to criminal liability, or to social scorn, but not affect his financial well-being, have traditionally not been covered by the rule. Thus declarations against interest have tended to have a business or financial flavor.

   a. **Property:** For instance, the declarant's statement may concern his *property*, and may have the effect of limiting his property rights in some way.

Example: D is charged with taking V's car for a joyride. D offers testimony by W that two days before the ride, V said to W, "I let D use my car whenever he wants." Because V's statement was against his pecuniary interest at the time it was made — it indicated that he had voluntarily curtailed his right to be the exclusive user of the car — D will be able to offer the statement as a declaration against interest.

b. Debts: Similarly, statements by ***creditors*** about debts owed to them will often be against interest. For instance, a creditor's declaration that a debt has been all or partly paid will be treated as being against his interest, since it extinguishes his right to sue on the debt.

    i. Receipt: Observe that the out-of-court "declaration" may be ***written*** as well as oral. Thus, a ***receipt*** signed by the creditor acknowledging payment will be admissible to show that the debt was paid.

c. Tort liability: Modern decisions also generally treat a statement that may give rise to, or extinguish, ***tort liability*** as being against interest.

Example: P, a driver, has a collision with a car driven by D. After the collision, D's wife, W (who was a passenger in D's car) says to P, "It was my fault — I distracted my husband." P sues D for negligence. Under the modern view, P will be permitted to repeat W's statement in court. This is so because W's statement is a declaration against interest, in that it exposed W to tort liability.

3. Against penal interest: At common law, statements against the declarant's ***penal*** interest — that is, statements exposing him to criminal liability — do ***not*** fall within the declaration-against-interest exception.

    a. Rationale: This limitation stems mostly from the ***fear of false evidence.*** There are several related dangers:

        i. False confessions: Many crimes, especially well-publicized ones, attract a substantial number of ***false confessions***. Thus suppose that D is charged with a murder, and that he offers testimony by W, that W has heard X confess to the murder. Even though W's testimony may be absolutely accurate — in the sense that he did indeed hear X confess to the crime — the underlying assertion (that X, not D, is guilty) may well be incorrect. Furthermore, it will waste a lot of prosecution and juror time if every false confession has to be admitted into evidence and then demonstrated to be false. See L&S, p. 490.

        ii. False testimony: Conversely, there is a great risk that the witness will ***falsely testify*** that he has heard another person confess. For instance, suppose again that D is charged with murder, and that D's good friend (and sometime partner in crime), W, wants to help D out. W could falsely testify that he heard X confess to the crime. Especially where X is no longer available (a requirement for the declaration-against-interest exception), it may be hard for the prosecution to prove that W is lying.

    b. Countervailing view: However, there is also a strong countervailing argument. Judicial refusal to allow evidence of out-of-court confessions by now-unavailable witnesses may cause an innocent person to be convicted.

Example: Suppose D is charged with robbing a 7-11 store on Dec. 12, 2011. D offers testimony by a police officer, W, that on Feb. 15, 2012, when W was interrogating X about another crime, X said, "I committed that 7-11 robbery last Dec. 12." (X has since died.) If D is not permitted to introduce this testimony, there is a substantial risk that D may be convicted of a crime he didn't commit.

c. **The federal and modern approach:**   Some states (though probably still a minority) have broadened the declaration-against-interest exception to cover declarations against penal interest. The Federal Rules have also done so — indeed, this is the most important change from common law to Federal Rules in the area of declarations against interest.

   i. **Corroborating circumstances:**   However, the Federal Rules have steered a *middle path* between keeping such evidence out entirely and letting it in wholesale: the last sentence of FRE 804(b)(3)(B) states that a statement must be "supported by *corroborating circumstances that clearly indicate its trustworthiness*, if it is offered in a *criminal case* as one that tends to *expose the declarant to criminal liability.*"

   ii. **Exculpatory statements:**   A common use of declarations against penal interest is the use by the accused of a statement by a third person (often a confession) *exculpating* the accused. In this common situation, FRE 804(b)(3)(B)'s corroboration requirement comes into play, and has significant bite.

   iii. **Blame-shifting statements:** Another common use of declarations against penal interest is the *prosecution's* use of one suspect's confession against a second suspect, where the confession implicates both. Although 804(b)(3)(B) does not impose an explicit requirement of corroboration in this prosecution-use scenario, courts are very skeptical of the confession and frequently exclude it as unreliable. This is especially true where there's evidence that the confessor is trying to *curry favor* with authorities, or trying to *shift most of the blame* onto the other suspect (the person against whom the confession is now sought to be used). See *infra*, p. 298; see also the facts of *Williamson v. U.S., infra,* p. 298, for a situation presenting these dangers.

d. **Meaning of "corroboration":**   There is no hard-and-fast standard as to what constitutes adequate *corroboration* (required for statements exculpating the defendant under FRE 804(b)(3)(B)). Here are some of the factors the courts look at:

   i. **Motive:**   Whether the declarant had an apparent *motive* to lie. For instance, if Declarant is shown to have been a friend of D, and was conveniently out of the jurisdiction or on his deathbed at the time he confessed to the crime with which D is now charged, Declarant's clear motive to falsify will probably be a strong non-corroborating factor.

   ii. **General character:**   The general *character* of the declarant. Thus if Declarant is a convicted criminal (especially a perjurer), his confession will be much less likely to be admitted.

iii. **Persons hearing statements:** Whether *more than one person* heard the statements. The more people who testify to having heard the out-of-court declaration, the more likely it is that the declaration was at least made (though this does not increase at all the likelihood that the declaration, when made, was truthful).

iv. **Spontaneous:** Whether the declaration was made *spontaneously* (if so, it is more likely to be received).

v. **Other:** The *timing* of the declaration, and the *relationship* between the declarant and the witness.

vi. **External connections:** Whether there is *other evidence* linking the declarant to the crime.

See *State v. Parris*, 633 P.2d 914 (Wash. 1981), applying factors i-v and concluding that corroboration was present.

Example: Suppose that D is charged with a robbery, and presents W, who testifies that shortly after the robbery, X told him, "It wasn't D who did it, it was me." If there is independent evidence that X could not have committed the crime because he was in prison at the time, the confession will be excluded. If, however, there is evidence that X was near the scene of the crime and had some motive or background connecting him to it, this will probably be enough. W&B, Par. 804(b)(3)[03]. "The court should only ask for sufficient corroboration to 'clearly' permit a reasonable man to believe that the statement *might have been made in good faith* and that it *could be true*." *Id.*

e. **Statements inculpating the accused:** The modern (and federal) tendency to allow statements against penal interest is not, by its terms, limited to statements introduced by the accused. That is, the *prosecution* may theoretically introduce an out-of-court declaration, made against the declarant's penal interest, that has the effect of *inculpating* the accused.

Example: D is charged with selling heroin. The prosecution offers testimony by W, an undercover narcotics officer, that he gave Declarant $100, that he (W) saw Declarant go to D's car and exchange something with him, and that when Declarant came back, W asked him whether he would get the drugs and Declarant responded, "Yes, I think so. There won't be any problem." The prosecution argues that Declarant's statement, taken in light of the surrounding circumstances, was against his penal interest, so the declaration-against-interest exception should apply.

Held, the exception applies, and the statement may be used against D. Declarant's statements "clearly indicated his involvement in an illicit drug transaction and 'strengthen the impression that he had an insider's knowledge of the crimes.' " At the time, Declarant did not know he was dealing with an undercover agent, and a reasonable person in his position would not have made the statements unless he believed them to be true. (Also, there was sufficient corroboration of the statement's reliability.) *State v. Parris*, 633 P.2d 914 (Wash. 1981).

i. **Need for corroboration:** Observe that FRE 804(b)(3)(B) does *not* explicitly impose a requirement that there be *corroboration* where the statement is used to *inculpate* (rather than *exculpate*) the accused. The draftsmen seem to have been mostly worried about false *exculpations* used by the accused, and seem to have ignored the possibility that a prosecutor might use an uncorroborated statement against the accused. Nonetheless, a number of courts have imposed a requirement of corroboration in this inculpatory situation as well. W&B, Par. 804(b)(3)[03]. *Parris*, *supra*, is one such decision.

f. Self-serving statements: Courts are especially reluctant to use the declaration-against-interest exception to admit statements that, although self-inculpatory, have a ***self-serving aspect*** to them. Thus statements that serve to ***shift some of the blame*** from the declarant (e.g., "Sure I was smuggling cocaine, but I was just the little fish — Smith was the ringleader who organized everything") will usually be excluded even if there is some corroboration. (See *Williamson v. U.S., infra.*) Similarly, statements given in circumstances suggesting that the declarant had an incentive to ***curry favor with the authorities*** (e.g., statements made while the declarant is in custody, under circumstances indicating that she is hoping to ***get a lighter sentence*** for herself by supplying evidence about others) are likely to be excluded.

4. Collateral statements: Perhaps the toughest issue concerning declarations against interest arises where a statement includes a ***part*** that is clearly against the declarant's interest and ***another part*** that is either ***"neutral"*** (in the sense that it doesn't affect the declarant's interest one way or the other) or ***self-serving.*** For purposes of this discussion, we'll refer to the non-self-inculpatory portion(s) (whether they're "neutral" or self-serving) as ***"collateral"*** statements.

a. Collateral statements not admissible under the FRE: For cases decided under the Federal Rules, the Supreme Court has laid down a bright-line rule: the "collateral" statements are simply ***not admissible*** under 804(b)(3). In ***Williamson v. U.S.***, 114 S.Ct. 2431 (1994), the Court held (by a 6-3 vote on this point) that "The most faithful reading of Rule 804(b)(3) is that it ***does not allow admission of non-self-inculpatory statements, even if they are made within a broader narrative that is generally self-inculpatory.***"

i. Rationale: The Court in *Williamson* reasoned that the fact that the collateral statement is made in close proximity to the self-inculpatory statement ***does not increase the former's likelihood of being true***. For instance, "The fact that a person is making a broadly self-inculpatory confession does not make more credible the confession's non-self-inculpatory parts. One of the most effective ways to lie is to mix falsehood with truth, especially truth that seems particularly persuasive because of its self-inculpatory nature. . . . The fact that a statement is self-inculpatory does make it more reliable; but the fact that a statement is collateral to a self-inculpatory statement says nothing at all about the collateral statement's reliability."

ii. Application to facts of *Williamson*: The facts of *Williamson* demonstrate how the Court's "no collateral statements" rule will cut off a large part of the uses of declarations against penal interest when used against an accused. Harris was stopped on the highway and found with 19 kilos of cocaine in two suitcases in his trunk. During two in-custody interrogations, he said that he knew the suitcases contained cocaine, that he was transporting the cocaine on behalf of D, and that D was travelling in another car ahead of him and saw the police stop Harris. (There was evidence that Harris was trying to minimize his own role and to characterize D as being the ringleader. There was also evidence that the interrogating officer promised to try to get Harris credit from the prosecutor for cooperating.) At D's trial, the officer who interrogated Harris was permitted to repeat Harris' entire confession, on the theory that it was all one "statement" that was against Harris' penal interest. But the Supreme Court ruled that only those individual declarations that were specifically against Harris' interest could be admitted. (The Court remanded for a determination of which individual statements were in fact against Harris' interest.)

    iii. The "curry favor" problem: Observe that the facts in *Williamson* posed the "curry favor" problem especially starkly. There was ample evidence that much of what Harris said — including most if not all of the parts that implicated D — may have been said for the purpose of *minimizing* Harris' problems by making D out to be the "big fish." After all, Harris didn't walk into the police station to confess spontaneously; he was already caught red-handed with the drugs, and statements conceding that he was part of a cocaine smuggling operation didn't really worsen his own legal position. Even the three Justices who disagreed with the majority's blanket rule that collateral statements could never be admitted under the declaration-against-interest exception agreed that such "blame-shifting" statements should not be admissible as declarations against interest.

b. State courts: State courts, of course, are not bound by *Williamson*. But most state decisions on the collateral-statement issue seem to follow at least the general theme of *Williamson*, if not the blanket rule that no collateral statement can be admitted. Thus most state courts won't allow into evidence a collateral portion that is ***self-serving*** (either because it shifts the blame to someone else, typically the person against whom the statement is now sought to be used, or because it seems to be motivated by the declarant's desire to get a lighter sentence), no matter how self-inculpatory other parts of the statement are. Thus statements made by declarants who are ***in custody*** are typically closely scrutinized, with the collateral parts usually excised. See M&K §8.75, p. 943.

    i. No self-serving motive: But where the collateral part is truly neutral rather than self-serving, state courts may allow it in, if its context indicates that it's fairly tightly related to the against-interest part.

    Example: Declarant tells a friend, "It was Joe and I that pulled off the First National Bank job the other day." Since the thrust of Declarant's statement is inculpatory to him, and since the other part (inculpating Joe) does not serve any apparent interest of Declarant, the whole statement may well be admitted against Joe.

c. For "testimonial" statements, a Confrontation Clause problem: Where the declaration against interest can be said to be ***"testimonial"*** in nature, the court will usually never even have get to the issue of whether collateral statements are admissible, because the ***entire statement*** is likely to be ***inadmissible*** for ***constitutional reasons***. In a 2004 decision, *Crawford v. Washington* (discussed extensively *infra*, pp. 301 and 364), the Supreme Court held that declarations against interest that are "testimonial," when used against an accused, violate the accused's Sixth Amendment Confrontation Clause rights, unless the declarant is available for cross-examination either at the time of the declaration or at the accused's later trial.

    i.   **Application to *Williamson*:**   Indeed, the scenario at issue in *Williamson* — where one suspect, under police interrogation, implicates another suspect while minimizing his own culpability — is precisely the sort of scenario that most concerned the *Crawford* Court. So on the facts of *Williamson* itself, it's quite clear that under *Crawford*, unless Harris took the stand at D's trial and underwent cross-examination by D's lawyer, no part of Harris's confession — even those parts that were specifically against Harris' interest — could be admitted against D, for Confrontation Clause reasons.

5. Factual background: In determining whether a statement was against the declarant's interest when made, the ***factual background***, and the proposition for which the declaration is now offered, will be relevant.

    a.   **Inferences:**   Thus, a statement may be against the declarant's interest when used to support one inference, but not against his interest when used to support a different inference.

    Example: Declarant writes on his tax return that he earned $10,000 in 1986. If this statement is used to show that Declarant earned at least $10,000, it is against interest (since Declarant had financial incentives to minimize the amount of income he reported). However, if it is used to show that he earned no more than $10,000, it should not be admitted (because of the same incentive). L&S, p. 488.

    b.   **Ignorance:**   If there is evidence that the declarant ***did not realize***, at the time he made his declaration, that it was against his interest, it should probably be excluded (since lack of awareness of the danger removes the guarantee of reliability that is the whole basis for the exception).

    c.   **Reasonable person:**   Keep in mind that, under the Federal Rules, a ***"reasonable person"*** standard applies on the question of whether the statement was against interest: FRE 804(b)(3)(A) requires that the statement have been so far contrary to the declarant's interest that "a reasonable person in the declarant's position would have made [the statement] only if the person believed it to be true[.]" However, the "reasonable" person is one having the ***degree of awareness*** that the declarant had. Therefore, if a reasonable person in declarant's position would not have realized, say, that the statement could expose himself to criminal liability, the statement would not be admissible.

C. Constitutional issues: When declarations against interest are sought to be introduced in criminal cases, various ***constitutional issues*** can arise. These vary, depending on whether the evidence is sought to be introduced by the accused or the prosecution.

1. **Use by prosecution:** Where the *prosecution* seeks to introduce a third-party declaration to inculpate the accused, the Confrontation Clause of the Sixth Amendment may help the accused keep the statement out.

    a. **"Testimonial" statement, such as statements made in custody:** The Confrontation Clause will give the accused the greatest help where declarant was in *custody* at the time he made the statement, or was otherwise responding to *police interrogation*. In this situation, a recent Supreme Court decision, *Crawford v. Washington*, 124 S.Ct. 1354 (2004), says that because the declaration is "testimonial," it *cannot be admitted against the accused unless the declarant is available to be cross-examined about it*. See further discussion of *Crawford infra*, p. 364.

        Example: Suppose that after V is shot to death, W and his brother D fall under suspicion for the crime, and are both interrogated by the police. W tells the police, "I was there, and I gave my brother D my gun. But it was D who shot V." Assume that only D is tried for the murder. W refuses to take the stand to answer questions about the shooting, pleading the Fifth Amendment. The prosecution offers to read to the jury W's original statement implicating D; the prosecution argues that since the statement implicates W as an accomplice, it satisfies the requirements for a declaration against penal interest.

        After *Crawford*, W's out-of-court statement to the police is almost certainly *inadmissible* on account of the Confrontation Clause. Because the statement was made as a result of police interrogation, it is deemed "testimonial" under *Crawford*. Since D has not had a chance to cross-examine W about the statement either at the time it was made or now at D's trial, *Crawford* says that the Confrontation Clause dictates its exclusion. And that is true regardless of how much other evidence there is corroborating the statement's reliability.

2. **Use by accused:** Where it is the *accused* who seeks to *exculpate* himself by use of a third person's declaration against interest, the accused may be able to make an argument based upon the *Due Process Clause,* and possibly on the Sixth Amendment's right to *compulsory process*.

    Example: Consider the hypothetical on p. 296 (D is charged with robbing a 7-11, and X has made an out-of-court statement confessing to the same crime). D could make a strong argument that depriving him of the right to prove that X confessed to the crime violates D's due process rights.

    a. *Chambers* **case:** The due process and compulsory process arguments are supported by a Supreme Court case, *Chambers v. Mississippi*, 410 U.S. 284 (1973). In *Chambers*, D sought to cross-examine one McDonald, who had, on previous occasions, admitted the crime for which D was on trial. (McDonald had later repudiated these confessions.) The state denied D both the right to cross-examine McDonald (because of a "voucher" rule that would not apply in federal courts; see *infra*, pp. 403-404) and the right to prove that McDonald had made the out-of-court confessions (finding the confessions to be hearsay). The Supreme Court held that D's due process rights were violated by this combination of factors.

    i. **Significance:** In *Chambers* itself, McDonald was "available," so the declaration-against-interest exception would not have applied. But if McDonald had been unavailable, it seems clear that either the Due Process or the Compulsory Process clauses, or both, would have required that D be given the ability to prove McDonald's prior confessions, at least if there was some evidence corroborating those confessions. W&B, Par. 804(b)(3)[03].

XIII. STATEMENTS OF PEDIGREE

    A. **In general:** There has always been a hearsay exception for statements of "pedigree," i.e., statements about a person's ***birth***, ***death***, ***marriage***, ***genealogy***, or other facts of personal or family history.

        1. **Requirements:** At common law, there are four requirements which must be met before such a statement of personal or family history may be admitted:

        [1] The declarant must be ***unavailable***;

        [2] The declarant must be either the person whose history the statement concerns, or a ***relative*** of the person whom the statement concerns;

        [3] The statement must have been made ***before the present controversy arose***; and

        [4] The declarant must not have had any apparent ***motive*** to falsify.

        McC, p. 536.

        Example: P, claiming to be Declarant's son, contests Declarant's will. P offers into evidence his own testimony that before Declarant died, Declarant told him, "You are my illegitimate son." P's testimony will be admissible at common law, because: Declarant is unavailable; Declarant is a close relative of the person whom the declaration concerns (i.e., P); the statement was made before the controversy (the will contest) began; and Declarant had no apparent motive to make a false statement. (It is irrelevant that *P* may have a motive to falsely quote Declarant's statement.)

        Note: It is ***not*** required that the declarant have had ***personal knowledge*** of the facts stated, because such knowledge is often too hard to come by (e.g., a person's statement about his own year of birth, something that he could not know first-hand).

        2. **Federal Rule:** The Federal Rules generally follow the common-law approach, but with a couple of liberalizations. FRE 804(b)(4) provides a hearsay exception for "statements of personal or family history":

        "A statement about:

        (A) the ***declarant's own birth***, adoption, legitimacy, ancestry, marriage, divorce, relationship by blood, adoption, or marriage, or similar facts of personal or family history, even though the declarant had no way of acquiring personal knowledge about that fact; or

        (B) ***another person*** concerning any of these facts, as well as death, if the declarant was ***related to the person by blood, adoption, or marriage*** or was so ***intimately associated*** with the person's family that the declarant's information is ***likely to be accurate***."

a. **Changes:** The main changes from the common law made by FRE 804(b)(4) are that: (1) the declaration need not have been made prior to the arising of the controversy; and (2) the declaration need not have been made by a relative of the person whom it concerns. These changes are discussed in more detail below.

B. **Family relationship:** As noted, most common-law jurisdictions require that the declarant have been a *relative* of the person whom the declaration concerns.

1. **Minority view:** But some states allow declarations by *intimate associates* of the person or family whom the statement concerns. (*Example*: A statement about X's parentage made by a longtime servant of X's family who was present at X's birth.)

2. **Federal Rule:** As noted, part (B) of FRE 804(b)(4) embodies this liberal rule, allowing the declaration if the declarant is a non-relative who is "so intimately associated with the person's family that the declarant's information is *likely to be accurate*."

C. **Before controversy:** The common law required that the declaration have been made not only before the present litigation, but even before the *"controversy" arose*. This requirement is summed up in the Latin words *ante litem motam*. This was a way of assuring the reliability of the declaration.

1. **Federal Rule:** The Federal Rule totally *drops* this requirement — the declaration may *even have been made after the litigation itself began.* (However, remember that the trial judge always has discretion under FRE 403 to reject evidence that is unfairly prejudicial or misleading.)

a. **Rationale:** The theory behind the federal approach is that the fact that the statement was made after the controversy or litigation arose is a factor that the jury will take into consideration when it decides what *weight* it will give to the declaration.

b. **Criticism:** L&S criticize this rule as going too far, insofar as it allows declarations even by one who is himself involved in the controversy. They advocate "a compromise admitting statements whenever made, so long as the declarant is not shown to be involved in the controversy. . . ." L&S, p. 496.

D. **Relation to reputation evidence:** Observe that there may be overlap between the pedigree exception and evidence relating to *reputation* concerning a matter of personal or family history. See *supra*, p. 273, including discussion of FRE 803(19) ("reputation concerning personal or family history"). However, the two are not identical: reputation evidence requires at least moderately widespread knowledge of the fact reputed (as opposed to statements of pedigree, as to which only the declarant needs to have had the knowledge). Conversely, however, reputation evidence of pedigree is admissible even if the declarant is available, whereas the statement-of-pedigree exception requires that the declarant be unavailable.

1. **Family documents:** Also, when the need to prove a fact of pedigree arises, don't overlook the *"family records"* exception (see *supra*, p. 273, and FRE 803(13)), by which statements of pedigree contained in family Bibles, genealogies, and the like can be introduced.

XIV. FORFEITURE BY WRONGDOING

A. The problem generally: Criminal defendants often try to keep out from trial the testimony of unfavorable witnesses. A defendant might do this by ***intimidating*** the witness, ***bribing*** him, or even ***murdering*** him. However, in many instances the witness will previously have made an out-of-court declaration (e.g., a statement to the police, "D did it.") Yet this out-of-court statement will frequently be hearsay not within any of the classic exceptions.

B. FRE 804(b)(6)'s solution: To discourage such witness-interference, FRE 804(b) was amended in 1997 by the addition of a new provision, 804(b)(6), that kicks in if the witness-tampering has been successful. That provision makes the witness's earlier out-of-court statement admissible notwithstanding the hearsay problem. 804(b)(6) gives a hearsay exception for "[a] statement offered against a party that ***wrongfully caused*** — or ***acquiesced*** in wrongfully causing — the ***declarant's unavailability*** as a witness, and did so ***intending that result***."

> **Example:** W is arrested at an airport when large quantities of cocaine are discovered on his person. While under arrest, he tells DEA agents, "I was doing this smuggling for D [a drug kingpin], who promised to pay me $1,000 when the drugs got through." D is then arrested and charged with conspiracy to import narcotics. D learns of W's statements, and wants to make sure that W does not testify at D's (or W's own) trial. D therefore sends an emissary to W in prison, and has the emissary tell W that if W testifies at D's trial he will be killed. W immediately tells the DEA agents that he was wrong about who his boss was, and that he will not testify at D's trial even if given immunity.
>
> On these facts, under 804(b)(6) the government will be able to introduce W's original out-of-court statement to the agents that D was W's boss. This is true even though the statement does not fall under any other hearsay exception. The statement is being offered against a party (D) who "wrongfully caused — or acquiesced in wrongfully causing — the declarant's [W's] unavailability as a witness, and did so intending that result." Cf. *U.S. v. Aguiar*, 975 F.2d 45 (2d Cir. 1992) (decided before the adoption of 804(b)(6), but allowing introduction of the statement on the theory that D's wrongdoing should constitute a waiver of his hearsay objection).

1. **Common scenarios:** The "forfeiture by wrongdoing" exception is used most commonly against ***criminal defendants*** who attempt to ***intimidate*** or otherwise ***remove witnesses*** against them. The out-of-court statements to which 804(b)(6) is often applied include:

   ❏ Statements made by W while under ***police interrogation*** (as in the above example);

   ❏ Statements made by W in a ***grand jury proceeding*** or preliminary hearing;

   ❏ Statements made by W in ***W's own criminal trial***, or in a criminal trial of some third person. (The former-testimony exception does not apply here because in such a situation, D, the present defendant, would typically not have had "an opportunity and similar motive to develop the testimony" by direct or cross examination, as required by Rule 804(b)(1)(B).)

2. **No reliability requirement:** Observe that Rule 804(b)(6) does not contain any requirement that the out-of-court declaration be ***reliable*** in order to be admitted. So a litigant who

intentionally commits wrongdoing in order to make a witness unavailable faces a very severe penalty.

a. **Contrast with residual exception:** Contrast this no-reliability-required rule with the rule applicable to FRE 807's *residual* exception. Under 807(a)(1), a declaration that does not fall within a specific hearsay exception can be admitted by meeting certain requirements, but only if it possesses "equivalent circumstantial guarantees of *trustworthiness*."

Example: Consider the common scenario of a suspect (call him "W") being interrogated by the police. W admits to some involvement, but says that most of the culpable conduct was committed by someone else ("D"). W's statements implicating D probably do not have very large "circumstantial guarantees of trustworthiness," given W's strong incentive to get rid of the blame by putting it on someone else. Therefore, W's statements are unlikely to make it into evidence under the FRE 807 residual exception. But if D gets caught, say, murdering or intimidating W so W's testimony at trial is not available, then under FRE 804(b)(6) W's prior statement made under interrogation *must* be admitted by the court, no matter how untrustworthy the statement appears to be.

3. **Acquiescence in another's wrongdoing:** Notice that the forfeiture-by-wrongdoing provision applies not only where the party actual commits the wrongdoing, but also where she merely *"acquiesces"* in the wrongdoing of another.

Example: Suppose that D1 and D2 are both charged with conspiracy to distribute narcotics, and are expected to be tried jointly. Both defendants know that another member of their conspiracy, W, has given statements implicated both of them to the police. D2 proposes to have W murdered so that W cannot testify at D1's and D2's trial. D1 knows that D2 is planning this murder, but does not try to dissuade D2 from following through. D2's accomplice then murders W. Even though D1 has not directly engaged in the murder (and would not have accomplice liability under substantive-law principles), D1 has probably "acquiesced" in the murder by not objecting. If so, W's out-of-court statements to the police will be admissible against D1, as well as against D2, under FRE 804(b)(6).

4. **Preponderance standard used:** The proponent of the out-of-court declaration only needs to show by a *preponderance of the evidence* (not, say, beyond a reasonable doubt) that the party against whom the declaration would be used has intentionally committed the wrongdoing that made the declarant unavailable. See Adv. Comm. Notes to 1997 Amendment to Rule 804(b)(6).

5. **Constitutional rule:** By the way, FRE 804(b)(6)'s idea that a person who brings about the witness's unavailability for the purpose of preventing the witness's trial testimony should forfeit any hearsay objection is echoed in federal *constitutional* law. A criminal defendant normally has a right under the Sixth Amendment's *Confrontation Clause* (see *infra*, p. 362) to prevent the prosecution from using testimonial-type out-of-court declarations against him if the declarant is not made available for cross examination at the trial. But if the defendant rendered the declarant unavailable (e.g., by killing him) for the purpose of avoiding the declarant's trial testimony, the defendant will be deemed to have for-

feited his Confrontation Clause rights. See *Giles v. California*, 128 S.Ct. 2678 (2008) (discussed *supra*, p. 279).

XV. PRIOR STATEMENTS OF AVAILABLE WITNESSES

A. **In general:** We turn now to a special problem: the admissibility of *prior statements* made outside of a courtroom by a person who is, or is available to be, a witness at the current trial.

1. **Not necessarily exception:** Although some types of "extrajudicial statements by available witnesses" have always been admissible, and under the Federal Rules even more kinds are, such statements do not necessarily, strictly speaking, constitute an "exception" to the hearsay rule. For instance, the Federal Rules treat those prior statements by available witnesses that are admissible as being *simply not hearsay at all*, rather than as falling within an exception to the hearsay rule. Nonetheless, we treat this problem in the present chapter on exceptions to the hearsay rule.

2. **Three different problems:** The problem of "prior statements by a witness" really breaks down into three distinct problems: (1) Can prior *inconsistent* statements by the witness be admitted as substantive evidence? (2) Can prior *consistent* statements by him be admitted substantively? and (3) Can a prior out-of-court *identification* by the witness be admitted substantively? Our discussion below will take each of these cases in turn.

3. **Common-law rules in brief:** The common law rules on the subject, in brief, are as follows:

    a. **Prior inconsistent statement:** A prior *inconsistent* statement by the witness is *inadmissible hearsay*. The reason is that the hearsay rule covers any statement offered for its truth other than one made from the witness stand *in the present proceeding*.

        i. **Impeachment use:** The prior inconsistent statement may be used to *impeach* the witness at the present trial. But it may not be offered *substantively*, i.e., to prove the truth of the matter asserted.

        Example: P brings a negligence action against D, alleging that D drove his car through a red light and hit P, a pedestrian. P's back was turned at the time, and the only witness other than D was W. At trial, D offers W's live testimony, "The light was green when D went through it." P offers to testify, "Right after D hit me, W rushed up and said, 'I saw D go through the intersection while the light was red.'"

        At common law, W's prior inconsistent out-of-court statement (that the light was red) may be offered *only for purposes of impeaching W's credibility*, not as substantive evidence. Allowing the prior inconsistent statement as substantive evidence would mean that an out-of-court declaration is being offered for the truth of the matter asserted (that the light was red), and that's hearsay at common law. Therefore, unless P has some other evidence of D's negligence, P will lose because the judge will have to take the case away from the jury by awarding a directed verdict for D.

    b. **Prior consistent statement:** Similarly, a witness's prior *consistent* statement is, at common law, not substantively admissible.

i. Rebut charge of recent fabrication: Again, use for non-substantive purposes is sometimes allowed. Most importantly, if the opponent claims that the witness has *recently fabricated* his trial testimony, or that the witness has been *improperly influenced* or *motivated*, the party offering that witness may show prior consistent statements by the witness, to rebut these charges. Again, as in the case of use of a prior inconsistent statement for impeachment purposes, the prior consistent statement is being used not to show the truth of the matter asserted (which would be a violation of the hearsay rule), but merely to support the credibility of the witness.

Example: As in the prior example, P asserts that D went through a red light. D offers W's testimony at trial, "The light was green when D went through it." P produces evidence suggesting that D has bribed W to change his story so that it is favorable to D. To rebut this charge of improper influence, all common-law courts agree that D may now testify that, at the time of the accident, W said to him, "The light was red." McC, p. 65. But D's testimony goes only to W's credibility, and is not substantive evidence.

ii. Fresh complaint: Also, in a few circumstances the fact that there has been a *"fresh complaint"* has special probative value. In criminal cases where the wrong-doing is likely to be known only to the criminal and the victim — *rape* and *bribery* for instance — the court will usually allow the fact that the victim made a prompt complaint as substantive evidence that the crime occurred, even though this complaint is an out-of-court declaration offered to prove the truth of the matter asserted, and is consistent with the victim's at-trial testimony. Lilly, p. 206.

c. Prior identification: Proof that a witness has previously made an *eyewitness identification* is technically hearsay, but many (perhaps most) common-law courts allow the prior I.D. as substantive evidence if the circumstances make it appear to have probative value. McC, p. 440.

Example: D is charged with robbing V. The prosecution offers testimony by W, a police officer, that shortly after the episode, V pointed to D in a police lineup and said, "That's the one who robbed me." Although V's declaration is technically hearsay — it is an out-of-court, uncross-examined statement offered to prove the truth of the matter asserted (that it really was D who robbed V) — many, if not most, common-law courts will allow it into evidence.

4. Federal Rules: The Federal Rules make some important modifications to these common-law rules, usually in the direction of increased admissibility. FRE 801 provides:

"(d) Statements That Are Not Hearsay. A statement that meets the following conditions is not hearsay:

(1) A Declarant-Witness's Prior Statement. The declarant *testifies* and is *subject to cross-examination about a prior statement*, and the *statement*:

(A) is *inconsistent* with the declarant's testimony and was *given under penalty of perjury at a trial, hearing, or other proceeding or in a deposition*;

(B) is *consistent* with the declarant's testimony and is offered to *rebut an express or implied charge that the declarant recently fabricated it* or acted from a *recent*

> *improper influence or motive in so testifying*; or

> **(C)** *identifies* a person as someone the declarant *perceived earlier.*"

- a. **Modifications:** The Federal Rule broadens the common law in several very important ways:

- b. **Inconsistent statement:** In the case of prior *inconsistent* statements, the Federal Rule: (1) allows *substantive* use (not just impeachment use) of (2) a previous statement made *under oath* at a "*proceeding*" or in a *deposition*.

   Example: Same facts as the example on p. 306, *supra*. W's prior inconsistent statement, "The light was red," will be admissible for its truth under the Federal Rules if it was made under oath at a prior trial, hearing (e.g., a preliminary hearing in a criminal negligence case against D), or even in a deposition. It will not be substantively admissible — any more than it would have been at common law — if it was merely an unsworn statement, say, to a casual bystander or a police officer investigating the accident.

- c. **Prior consistent statement:** With respect to prior *consistent* statements, the Federal Rule follows the common-law principle of allowing admission to rebut a charge that the witness has *recently fabricated* his story, or has been *improperly influenced* or *motivated.* But the Federal Rule makes one big change from the common law: if the "rebuttal of accusation" requirement is satisfied, the prior consistent statement is *substantively admissible*, i.e., admissible to show the truth of the prior consistent statement.

- d. **Identification:** With respect to prior *identifications*, the Federal Rule mirrors the approach of many common-law courts, by allowing the identification. Observe that, unlike a prior inconsistent statement offered under 801(d)(1)(A), an identification under 801(d)(1)(C) need not have been made under oath, and need not have been made in a proceeding.

   Example: Return to the example on p. 307, *supra*. V's statement in the lineup, "That's the man who robbed me," will be admissible as substantive evidence that it was indeed D who did the robbery, even though V did not make this statement under oath, and even though an informal police lineup would probably not be a "proceeding" as used in 801(d)(1)(A).

B. Prior inconsistent statements: We turn now to a detailed consideration of prior inconsistent statements, the category of prior-witness-statement law that is the most difficult.

1. **In favor of admitting:** Courts that would change the common-law rule against the substantive admission of prior inconsistent statements make the following arguments:

- a. **Hearsay dangers absent:** Generally, the classic dangers of hearsay are *absent* in this situation.

- b. **Cross-examination:** In particular, the witness is *now present to be cross-examined*. There is thus full opportunity to test the accuracy of his prior statement.

- c. **Oath:** The fact that the prior statement was not given *under oath* is of limited significance, since the oath is no longer as significant a guarantee of trustworthiness as it used to be, and since most of the other hearsay exceptions (e.g., dying declarations) are not given under oath.

d. Demeanor: The fact that the declarant's ***demeanor*** at the time he made the statement cannot be witnessed by the trier of fact is also largely irrelevant, since his present demeanor can be viewed.

e. Recency: The earlier statement is likely to be ***more reliable,*** because it was given ***earlier***, before the declarant's memory had a chance to fade. This is especially true of statements made immediately after the events in question.

f. Improper influence: Finally, a statement made shortly after the events in question is likely to be more reliable because it is less likely that the witness has been ***"gotten to,"*** i.e., bribed or intimidated into changing his story.

2. In favor of exclusion: Yet, those who would maintain the common-law rule, and exclude prior inconsistent statements as substantive evidence, have their own quite strong set of arguments:

a. Hearsay dangers: Nearly all of the protections of the hearsay rule are absent under the broad no-exclusion-of-prior-inconsistent-statements approach, since the prior statement is: (1) not under oath; (2) not in the presence of the trier of fact; and (3) not subject to cross-examination.

b. Cross-examination: In particular, the absence of cross-examination ***at the time of the statement*** is critically important, and later cross-examination is no substitute. "The chief merit of cross-examination is not that at some future time it gives the party opponent the right to dissect adverse testimony. Its principal virtue is the immediate application of the testing process. ***Its strokes fall while the iron is hot***. False testimony is apt to harden and become unyielding to the blows of truth in proportion as the witness has opportunity for reconsideration and influence by the suggestions of others. . . ." *State v. Saporen*, 285 N.W. 898 (Minn. 1939).

3. Federal Rules compromise: In part because of the arguments listed above in favor of exclusion, the drafters of the Federal Rules refused to provide a blanket hearsay exception for prior inconsistent statements. Instead, they pursued a ***compromise*** approach, which allows the prior statement in as substantive evidence only in those situations where there is some ***extra guarantee of reliability.***

a. Oath and proceeding: In particular, the prior statement must have been given "***under penalty of perjury***" (i.e., under oath), and must have occurred at a "***trial***, ***hearing***, or other ***proceeding***, or in a ***deposition***. . . ." FRE 801(d)(1)(A). The theory behind the compromise is that the solemnity of the oath, when coupled with the regularity inherent in a "proceeding" (especially the probable preparation of a transcript) reduces the danger that the declarant lied, or that the purported statement was never made.

b. Cross-examination not required: Observe, however, that the Federal Rule allows the prior inconsistent statement into evidence even where there was ***no cross-examination***, or even any ***opportunity*** for cross-examination. For instance, a witness's prior ***grand jury testimony*** is admissible against the accused if the witness tells a different story at trial, even though the accused not only did not have the opportunity for cross-examination at the grand jury, but did not even have the right to be present (or the right to object to leading questions by the prosecutor).

i.   **Confrontation Clause issue:**   However, the ***Confrontation Clause*** of the Sixth Amendment may separately pose an issue where the prior inconsistent statement is offered against a criminal defendant. According to *Crawford v. Washington,* 124 S.Ct. 1354 (2004), the Confrontation Clause means that any out-of-court ***"testimonial"*** statement can be admitted against an accused only if the maker of the statement is ***available for cross-examination*** either at the time the statement was made or at the accused's trial. (See *infra*, p. 364.) Where the accused did not have the opportunity to cross-examine the maker of the prior statement at the time the statement was made, some forms of present testimony might be held to be effectively uncross-examinable, in which case *Crawford* would dictate that the prior statement be kept out.

Example: Suppose that W testifies a grand jury hearing, "I saw D commit the crime." Then, at D's trial, in response to a question on direct from the prosecution, W unexpectedly says, "I don't remember whether I saw D commit the crime or not, and I don't remember telling the grand jury that I did see him." It's true that D's lawyer can in theory cross-examine W about her testimony before the grand jury (e.g., "Isn't it true that you told the grand jury that you saw me commit the crime?") But this is not very effective cross-examination — instead of minimizing the perceived value of W's testimony before the grand jury, this cross tends to maximize it, leaving the jury with the belief that W may well have seen D commit the crime.

Therefore, a court might hold that W is effectively unavailable for cross-examination about his statement to the grand jury, and that use of that statement against D therefore violates D's Confrontation Clause rights as interpreted by *Crawford*. (But other, pre-*Crawford* Supreme Court opinions suggest that in this situation, the Supreme Court would hold that W *is* "available for cross-examination" about her statement even though she is repudiating its accuracy. See M&K (Csbk), pp. 165-66.)

4.   **Special contexts:**   Let us now review several special contexts, and see how the common law and Federal Rules would apply to them:

5.   **Statement remembered but repudiated:**   First, suppose the witness concedes having made the prior statement, but says it was wrong, and tells a different story now. (This is Scenario B above.)

a.   **Common law:**   At common law, the statement is ***inadmissible*** as substantive evidence.

b.   **Federal:**   Under the Federal Rules, as long as the prior statement was made under oath in a "proceeding," it is substantively admissible, because it is clearly "inconsistent" with the witness's present testimony.

6. **Prior statement denied:** Suppose that the witness denies ever having made the prior statement, but there is independent evidence that the statement was made, and the witness now tells a story which is inconsistent with the prior purported statement.

   a. **Common-law rule:** Again, at common law, the statement will be excluded as substantive evidence.

   b. **Federal Rule:** Under the Federal Rules, this scenario will generally arise only under circumstances making the prior statement *inadmissible*:

      i. **Transcript:** If the statement was made under oath and in a trial, hearing, "other proceeding," or deposition, it will be admissible under the Federal Rules. However, if it was made in such a proceeding, there will normally be a *transcript* available. If there is a transcript, it is very unlikely that the witness will continue to deny having made the statement. Therefore, the whole scenario is unlikely to arise.

      ii. **Unrecorded oral statement:** If, on the other hand, the statement was merely an informal one made to, say, a bystander or a police officer, and was not made under oath or in a "proceeding" (so that there is no transcript available), the statement will not be admissible under the Federal Rules.

   c. **Use in state court:** Suppose that a state court, not bound by the Federal Rules, decides to admit the prior statement in this situation against a criminal defendant. Can the defendant argue that his constitutional rights under the Sixth Amendment's Confrontation Clause have been violated? Probably not; see *Nelson v. O'Neil*, 402 U.S. 622 (1971).

7. **Prior statement adopted but underlying facts not remembered:** Suppose now that W admits making the prior statement, but claims that he does not now remember the underlying facts. That is, W says at trial, "Yes, I told the Grand Jury that I saw D shoot V, but now I don't remember whether that's what I really saw."

   a. **Common law:** Again, at common law, the prior statement is simply not substantively admissible.

   b. **Federal Rules:** Under the Federal Rules, the result would depend on whether the judge believes that W is being *truthful* in his assertion that he cannot remember.

      i. **Truthful:** If the judge believes W is telling the truth about not being able to remember, then his prior statement is *not inconsistent* with his present testimony. Accordingly, the prior statement should not be found to be within FRE 801(d)(1)(A). W&B, Par. 801(d)(1)(A)[04].

      ii. **Not truthful:** If, however, the judge concludes that W is now lying about not being able to remember, then the prior statement should probably be viewed as inconsistent, and would be *admissible.* (But even then, the judge could keep it out under FRE 403, if he felt that the lack of a real opportunity to cross-examine the witness made the statement unfairly prejudicial or confusing.)

   c. **Constitutional issue:** The above situation — W admits making the statement but claims not to remember the underlying facts now — was the setting of a major Supreme Court Confrontation Clause case, in which the Court held that D's right to confront the witnesses against him was ***not violated***. See *California v. Green*, 399 U.S. 149 (1970). Under *Green*, if the trial judge finds that the witness who asserts lack of memory of the underlying facts is lying, the prior statement is probably not only an admissible prior inconsistent statement under the Federal Rules, but also one whose admission does not violate D's confrontation rights, so long as the jury had the opportunity to observe the demeanor of W.[2]

8. **Prior statement eventually adopted by witness:** Finally, suppose that the witness testifies in a manner that is inconsistent with the prior statement, is shown that statement, and then agrees that the prior statement is correct. (E.g., "Oh yes, I see that I was correct when I originally told the Grand Jury that I saw D shoot V.")

   a. **Common law:** Here, even at common law, the prior statement is ***admissible***. This is because it has now been adopted as ***present testimony*** — it has been repeated by the witness in court under oath, is subject to cross-examination, and the witness's demeanor while repeating it can be observed. W&B, Par. 801(d)(1)(A)[02].

   b. **Abuse:** However, there is a possible abuse. The witness's trial testimony might have been almost completely consistent with the prior statement, yet the person presenting that witness could seize upon the small deviations to claim that the prior statement is inconsistent and may now be admitted. This would lead to a "bolstering" of the witness by use of what is really a prior ***consistent*** statement. Since prior consistent statements are not normally admissible, the trial judge should not allow small variations to turn a statement into an admissible "inconsistent" one. *Id.*

C. **Prior consistent statements:** We now turn to prior ***consistent*** statements, i.e., those statements which match what the witness is now saying at trial.

1. **Common-law view:** In general, the common law treats such consistent statements as ***inadmissible hearsay.*** However, as noted, if the opponent has claimed that the witness has been "gotten to," i.e., persuaded to change his story because of improper influence, the common law allows the proponent to show that the witness told the same story earlier. However, this exception only goes to credibility, and the prior statement is not treated as substantive evidence. McC, p. 439.

2. **Federal Rule:** The Federal Rules allow substantive use of the prior consistent statement if "offered: (i) to rebut an express or implied charge that the declarant recently fabricated it or acted from a recent improper influence or motive in so testifying[.]" FRE 801(d)(1)(B). However, it is hard to see why this exception is even needed — if the prior statement is really consistent with what the witness is saying at trial, there already *is* substantive evidence on the point in question, so the only effect of the prior statement would be as to the witness's credibility. L&S, p. 516.

---

2. It is possible, but not likely, that *Crawford v. Washington, infra*, p. 364, may change this. *Crawford* says that the Confrontation Clause means that any out-of-court "testimonial" statement can be admitted against an accused only if the maker of the statement is available for cross-examination either at the time the statement was made or at the accused's trial. But there's no strong reason to believe that *Crawford* will cause the Supreme Court to reevaluate its ruling in *Green* that a witness who asserts lack of memory of the underlying facts is nonetheless "available" for cross-examination about her prior statement.

a. Statement must be made pre-motive: In any event, recall that the prior consistent statement, to be admissible under 801(d)(1)(B), must have been made *before* the "recent fabrication or improper influence or motive" came into existence. See *Tome v. U.S.*, *supra*, p. 155.

D. Prior identification: A *statement of identification* made by the witness on a prior occasion is theoretically hearsay. That is, if W says in court, "I picked D out of the lineup and told the police that that was who robbed me," W's statement at the time of the lineup is being used for the truth of the matter asserted (that it was D who did the robbery).

1. Common-law exception: Nonetheless, most states, either by statute or by case law, *allow* such prior statements of identification, if the identifier is *available for cross-examination at trial.* Similarly, W2 will be permitted in these states to testify that W1 previously made a statement of identification to him, if W1 testifies and is available to be cross-examined.

2. Federal Rules: The Federal Rules contain a similar exception for prior identifications. FRE 801(d)(1)(C) treats as non-hearsay a statement that "identifies a person as someone the declarant perceived earlier," if the declarant testifies at the trial and is available for cross-examination.

a. No oath or proceeding: Under the Federal Rules, prior identifications are easier to get into evidence than are prior inconsistent or consistent statements.

i. Compare with inconsistent statement: The prior ID need not have been made under oath, and need not have been part of a "proceeding," in contrast to a prior inconsistent statement.

ii. Compare with consistent statement: Furthermore, the prior ID is easier to get into evidence than any other prior *consistent* statement: unlike the prior consistent statement, the prior ID is admissible even though it is completely consistent with the at-trial testimony of the identifier, whose veracity has not been attacked.

b. Ability to cross-examine: Statements of identification, like prior inconsistent and consistent statements, are only allowed if the declarant "testifies and is subject to cross-examination about a prior statement].]" (First sentence of 801(d)(1).) Thus a major part of the rationale for allowing such prior statements of identification is that the opponent has the opportunity to test the accuracy of the prior identification by *questioning the declarant at the trial.* However, the Supreme Court has interpreted the requirement that the declarant be "subject to cross-examination" in such a loose way that much of the protection given by this requirement of cross-examination will in some cases be illusory. In *U.S. v. Owens*, 484 U.S. 554 (1988), the Court held that so long as the opponent has the ability to ask questions to the declarant about his prior identification, the prior identification qualifies as non-hearsay under 801(d)(1)(C) even though declarant admits to having a *total lack of memory* about the event that gave rise to the identification.

i. Facts: In *Owens*, declarant was a corrections officer who was beaten and almost killed by an inmate. During one of declarant's few days of lucidity following the attack, he told an FBI agent visiting his hospital room that the assailant had been

D. By the time of D's trial, declarant could no longer say that D was his assailant, but he testified that he remembered having identified D during the previous interview. Declarant could not explain why he had previously identified D, and admitted that he did not actually see D attack him.

ii.   **Holding:**   A majority of the Court held that declarant was "subject to cross-examination concerning the statement" despite this memory loss. Since declarant was placed on the stand, under oath, and responded to questions about his prior statement as well as he could, this was all that Rule 801(d)(1) required. (But two dissenters pointed out that declarant was clearly "unavailable as a witness" under FRE 804(a)(3), applicable when the witness "testifies to not remembering the subject matter[.]" The dissenters thought it absurd to hold that a witness who is "unavailable" under one Rule could be meaningfully cross-examined under another.)

(1)   **Effect of *Crawford*:**   It's possible that *Crawford v. Washington, infra*, p. 364, will end up changing the *Owens* holding that a witness who can't remember the facts surrounding the prior identification is nonetheless "subject to cross-examination." *Crawford* says that the Sixth Amendment's Confrontation Clause means that any out-of-court "testimonial" statement can be admitted against an accused only if the maker of the statement is available for cross-examination either at the time the statement was made or at the accused's trial. So it's possible that *Crawford* will eventually be interpreted to mean that (1) an out-of-court identification made to police is a "testimonial" statement;[3] and (2) if the identifier can't independently remember making the identification, or the facts surrounding the identification, the identifier is not "subject to cross-examination concerning the statement," at least for Confrontation Clause purposes if not for purposes of satisfying FRE 801(d)(1). However, the best guess is that holding (2) in this interpretation of *Crawford* will ***not*** come about, i.e., that nothing in *Crawford* will change *Owens'* ruling that an identifier who takes the stand but who cannot remember the circumstances surrounding the identification is nonetheless "subject to cross-examination."

c.   **Bias or suggestion:**   FRE 801(d)(1)(C) does not contain an explicit requirement that the identification have been "fair," i.e., not the product of unfair ***bias or suggestion***. For instance, suppose that W tells the police that his assailant is a black male around thirty years old, and the police then give him a four-man lineup in which D (whom W identifies) is the only black male between the ages of twenty and forty in the group. By its literal terms, 801(d)(1)(C) would allow W's identification into evidence.

---

3. In fact, the post-*Crawford* case of *Davis v. Washington* (*infra*, p. 367), makes it almost certain that this sort of out-of-court identification made to the police ***will be a testimonial statement***, as long as the statement is made during a post-crime investigatory phase rather than during police attempts to deal with a current emergency. The corrections officer's hospital-bed statement in *Owens* seems even more clearly testimonial than Ms. Hammon's post-assault statement to the crime-scene investigator in the Hammon part of *Davis*, which the Court found to be testimonial (p. 370) on the grounds that the "purpose of the interrogation [was] to establish or prove past events potentially relevant to later criminal prosecution."

i. Constitutional problem: However, use of such out-of-court identifications against a criminal defendant may pose **constitutional** problems. For instance, the holding of a **lineup** by the police will generally violate the defendant's Sixth Amendment **right to counsel** if the defendant is not given the right to have a lawyer present. Similarly, unduly suggestive identification procedures — such as the facts in the prior paragraph — would probably violate the defendant's **due process** rights.

XVI. THE RESIDUAL ("CATCH ALL") EXCEPTION

A. Generally: Suppose a piece of hearsay evidence does not fall neatly within any of the special exceptions cataloged above. If the facts surrounding it convince the court that the evidence is highly reliable and badly needed, must it nonetheless be excluded? Both common-law jurisdictions and statutory approaches (including the Federal Rules) seem to be increasingly willing to receive such evidence under a *"residual"* or "catch all" exception to the hearsay rule.

1. Broad approach: In its broadest form, the residual hearsay exception might be phrased this way: "If a particular item of hearsay evidence has circumstantial guarantees of trustworthiness equivalent to the guarantees which attach to the recognized exceptions, that item of evidence should be admitted whether or not it meets the requirements of an established hearsay exception [so long as there is little or no non-hearsay evidence that bears on the issue]." L&S, p. 499.

Example: The tower of the Dallas County Courthouse, in Selma, Alabama, collapses in 1957. P (the County) claims that the collapse was due to the tower's being struck by lightning several days before (in which case insurance would cover the loss). D (the insurance company) contends that the collapse was due to structural weakness and deterioration (not covered). Investigation of the debris shows the presence of charcoal and charred timbers. D, in order to show that this charring may not have been due to lightning, offers an unsigned article from the local newspaper, dated in 1901, describing a fire in the courthouse while it was under construction.

Held, the newspaper article is admissible, even though it is hearsay and falls within no recognized exception. (It does not satisfy the "ancient documents" exception because the declarant's identity is unknown, and there is no proof that he had first-hand knowledge of the matter asserted.) Two requirements must be met for hearsay evidence to be admitted: (1) necessity, and (2) trustworthiness. Requirement (1) is satisfied because, 58 years after the fact, it is very improbable that any eyewitness can be found to give accurate testimony, from first-hand knowledge, about whether the 1901 fire really occurred. Requirement (2) is satisfied because "it is inconceivable to us that a newspaper reporter in a small town would report that there was a fire in the dome of the new courthouse — if there had been no fire." Thus, even though the article does not fall within any "readily identifiable and happily tagged species of hearsay exception," it will be admitted because it is "necessary and trustworthy, relevant and material. . . ." *Dallas County v. Commercial Union Assurance Co.*, 286 F.2d 388 (5th Cir. 1961).

B. Federal Rules: The Federal Rules codify the residual or "catch all" exception, to pick up needed, trustworthy evidence that happens not to fall within any of the recognized exceptions.

1. **Text of Federal Rule:** The Federal Rule that provides a residual exception is FRE 807. Rule 807 gives a hearsay exception as follows:

    "Rule 807. Residual Exception

    (a) In General. Under the following circumstances, a hearsay statement is *not excluded* by the rule against hearsay even if the statement is *not specifically covered by a hearsay exception* in Rule 803 or 804:

      (1) the statement has *equivalent circumstantial guarantees of trustworthiness*;

      (2) it is offered as *evidence of a material fact*;

      (3) it is *more probative* on the point for which it is offered than *any other evidence that the proponent can obtain through reasonable efforts*; and

      (4) admitting it will *best serve the purposes of these rules* and the *interests of justice*.

    (b) Notice. The statement is admissible only if, before the trial or hearing, the proponent gives an adverse party *reasonable notice* of the intent to offer the statement and its *particulars*, including the declarant's name and address, so that the party has a fair opportunity to meet it."

2. **Five requirements:** Taking apart the language of 807, we see that there are five distinct requirements that must be met before the evidence may be admitted:

    ❏ **Circumstantial guarantees of trustworthiness:**   Most important, the statement must have *"circumstantial guarantees of trustworthiness"* that are "equivalent" to those inherent in the Rule 803 and 804(b) exceptions. (This all-important element is examined in detail *infra*, p. 318.)

    ❏ **Material fact:**   The statement must be "offered as evidence of a material fact."

    ❏ **More probative:**   The statement must be "*more probative on the point* for which it is offered than any other evidence that the proponent can obtain through reasonable efforts[.]" This is the other requirement that has some "bite" — if there is some other witness (or indeed, the declarant himself) who can give live testimony at the trial that is of equal probative value, the residual exception does not apply.

        ❏ **Unavailability:**   For this reason, most of the time the residual exception has been successfully invoked only where the declarant is *unavailable*, since if he were available, his at-trial testimony would normally be more probative.

    ❏ **Interests of justice:**   Use of the evidence must "*best serv*e the purposes of these rules and the *interests of justice*."

    ❏ **Notice:**   The person offering the evidence must before the trial or hearing give to any adverse party *"reasonable notice"* of the offering party's intent to offer the statement "so that the [adverse] party has a fair opportunity to meet [the statement]." The notice must include the *particulars* of the statement, including the declarant's name and address. This notice requirement, which is of considerable importance, is discussed *infra*, p. 320.

a. **Illustration:** The case set forth in the following Example illustrates the operation of the federal residual exception.

Example: D is charged with the murder of V, an 11-month-old girl who died while being babysat for by D. (D picked V up at V's house at 10:20 AM on Jan. 22, and at 11:14 AM that day called 911 to report that V was not breathing; V died the next day.) The prosecution's theory is that V died of "shaken baby syndome" caused by D. Forensinc evidence includes a contusion on the left side of V's skull. D is convicted, and seeks a new trial.

At the new trial, D proposes to introduce testimony by three women (none of whom knew D at the time of all events in question), each of whom will say that a few weeks after V's death, V's mother Tessia told the three of them that shortly before D picked V up on Jan. 22, while Tessia was dressing V, V fell and hit her head on a coffee table. These three potential witnesses each submit an affidavit recounting Tessia's statement to them; the affidavits are dated nearly three years after the statement by Tessia that the affidavits recount. The trial court grants D a new trial on account of this potential evidence, and rules that the three women's testimony about what Tessia told them can come in at the new trial under Iowa's catchall (identical to the federal version). The prosecution appeals this evidentiary decision, arguing that the testimony is not trustworthy, in part because of the nearly-three-year gap between the statements by Tessia and the making of the affidavits.

Held (on appeal), for D: the witnesses' testimony about what Tessia said is admissible under the catchall. The requisite "equivalent circumstantial guarantees of trustworthiness" are supported by a number of factors, including that: the witnesses reporting the statement are credible; the statement was made shortly after the incident so that the declarant could be expected to remember the events she was describing; the declarant had firsthand knowledge of the event she was describing; the statement was in response to an open-ended question, not the result of interrogation by D or by one acting on her behalf; the statement was made to more than one person; and the statement was corroborated by objective medical evidence (the contusion on the left side of V's head). The fact that there was a nearly-three-year gap between the statement and the affidavits about it goes to weight, not admissibility. *State v. Weaver*, 554 N.W.2d 240 (Iowa 1996).

Note: At the retrial in *Weaver*, the three women gave their testimony. Tessia testified that nothing unusual had happened to V on the morning in question, and that she had never made the "V fell and hit her head" statement to the three women. D was acquitted. Cf. M&K (Csbk), pp. 352-353. So there's good reason to believe that the availability of the catchall for the testimony here made the difference between the earlier conviction and the subsequent acquittal.

3. **How used:** Here are some contexts in which the federal residual exception has been applied:

a. **Grand jury testimony:** To allow use of ***grand jury testimony*** against the defendant, where the witness is not available to testify at trial. (The "former testimony" exception of 804(b)(1) does not apply to such testimony, because the opponent — the defendant — did not have the opportunity to cross-examine.)

b. Notes by observer: To admit *handwritten notes* taken by an observer of an event, where the observer is not available to testify at trial. (Such a document cannot constitute Past Recollection Recorded, under FRE 803(5), because the author is, by hypothesis, not present as a witness to authenticate it.) See *Turbyfill v. International Harvester Co.*, *infra*, p. 320.

c. Oral statement: To admit an *oral statement* by the declarant, where the declarant is now unavailable (or denies having made the statement), the evidence is badly needed, and there are circumstantial guarantees of reliability. (See, e.g., *State v. Weaver*, *supra*, where Tessia denied having made her "V fell and hit her head" declaration.)

4. Grand jury testimony: Much of the controversy concerning the use of the Federal Rules' residual exception has concerned the use of *grand jury testimony* in circumstances where the grand jury witness is unavailable at trial. Most, but not all, federal courts have been reasonably *receptive* to the use of the residual exception in this situation. The grand-jury-testimony situation is discussed in detail *infra*, p. 320.

C. Circumstantial guarantees of trustworthiness: The most important issue that arises in most residual exception cases is whether the statement has *"circumstantial guarantees of trustworthiness"* equivalent to those inhering in the specific exceptions (Rules 803(1)-(23), and 804(b)(1)-(4)).

1. "Average" of other exceptions: The requirement of "equivalent" circumstantial guarantees means guarantees equivalent to those inhering in the other, enumerated, exceptions. But there is tremendous variation in trustworthiness among the exceptions — for instance, an excited utterance (FRE 803(2)) is much less likely to be reliable than, say, former testimony subjected to cross-examination when given (FRE 804(b)(1)). Therefore, the question becomes: Should the standard for "equivalent trustworthiness" be that of the highest, lowest, or average other exception? "When the question has been asked, the answer seems to have been, 'not necessarily the highest.'" McC, p. 538. Most courts have implicitly assumed some sort of *"average." Id.*

2. Factors bearing on declarant: How should the court go about determining whether there are "equivalent circumstantial guarantees of trustworthiness"? The strongest case can be made for looking at factors that bore upon the *declarant at the time he made the statement*, since these are the kinds of indicia of reliability that common-law courts use to derive the recognized hearsay exceptions. Such factors would include:

a. Oath: Whether the statement was *under oath.* (So sworn grand jury testimony would be more reliable than, say, an unsworn statement to a police officer.)

b. Time lapse: The *length of time* that elapsed between the event and the statement (the longer the time gap, the less reliable).

c. Motive for truth: The declarant's *motive* for telling the truth. (So a co-defendant who is in custody at the time he implicates D will be viewed as having a motive to lie, since he may well believe that falsely implicating another may get him a lighter sentence.)

    d. First-hand knowledge: Whether the declarant had ***first-hand knowledge,*** or was merely repeating what someone else said. (Thus in *Weaver, supra,* the court stressed that Tessia, the declarant, was describing an event — V's hitting her head — that Tessia had personally witnessed.)

    e. Written vs. oral: Whether the statement is ***written*** or oral. (Written, whether written out by the declarant or transcribed stenographically as in a confession to police, is presumed to be more reliable than oral.)

    See generally W&B, Par. 803(24)[01]; McC, p. 539.

3. Corroboration by other evidence: The major controversy is whether reliability can be demonstrated by the fact that the statement is ***corroborated*** by ***other evidence in the case.***

    a. Against corroboration: Some courts and commentators have argued that the other, corroborating, evidence in the case should be treated as ***irrelevant*** for this purpose. They point out that Congress intended the residual exception to be applied in a manner analogous to the other hearsay exceptions. Yet the other hearsay exceptions ***never*** look at the presence of other corroborating evidence in the case; they focus solely on whether, looking at the circumstances of the declaration itself, the evidence is likely to be reliable. L&S, p. 503.

    b. In favor of corroboration: Other courts and commentators have argued, in contrast, that consistency with the other evidence in the case is indeed a good way of measuring the reliability of a particular statement. A strong match-up between the statement and the other evidence at least indicates that the declarant had first-hand knowledge of the facts, and was not engaging in wholesale lying.

    c. *Idaho v. Wright* probably knocks out use of corroboration: However, the Supreme Court's decision in *Idaho v. Wright,* 497 U.S. 805 (1990), makes it appear that, in federal courts, the statement's consistency with other evidence may ***not count*** when the trial judge looks for the requisite "circumstantial guarantees of trustworthiness." In *Wright,* the Court held that when the issue is whether the admission of hearsay not falling into a traditional exception would violate the defendant's *Confrontation Clause* rights, the hearsay's consistency with other evidence doesn't count for purposes of determining whether the hearsay contains the requisite "particular guarantees of trustworthiness." Lower courts and commentators interpreting *Wright* often concluded that the same is true in applying the catchall. (*Wright*'s Confrontation Clause analysis is apparently overruled by *Davis v. Washington, infra,* p. 367, but *Wright* likely still has significance for how the existence of "circumstantial guarantees of trustworthiness" is to be interpreted under FRE 807(a)(1)).

      i. Significance: If this view of *Wright* is correct, the trial must consider principally the facts ***surrounding the hearsay declaration itself*** — *not* the extent to which the hearsay matches other evidence — in deciding whether the required "equivalent circumstantial guarantees of trustworthiness" exist.

D. "Near-miss" problem: Suppose a particular fact pattern comes very close to matching the requirements for a recognized hearsay exception. Should the residual exception be available used in this kind of ***"near miss"*** situation?

1. **Policy decision:** Against such use, it can be argued that when Congress created the relevant narrow exception, it was making an explicit policy determination that unless the requirements were satisfied, the evidence should not be admitted.

2. **Contrary view, usually followed:** But most courts have *not agreed.* M&K, §8.81, pp. 1005-06. Indeed, the residual exception has probably been *used in "near miss" situations more often than for truly unanticipated novel fact patterns.*

   > **Example:** P, shopping on D's used car lot, is interested in a truck. P, together with Anderson (D's mechanic) try to start the engine; because one of P's companions is trying to pour gas into the carburetor at the time, the gas can catches fire and P is badly burned. At trial, D offers a handwritten, unsworn memo written by Anderson at the request of his supervisor three hours after the accident. (Anderson has died before trial.)
   >
   > *Held*, the handwritten statement is admissible under the FRE's residual exception (now FRE 807). Had Anderson been available at trial, the handwritten account would have been admissible under FRE 803(5)'s exception for past recollection recorded. This shows that such almost-contemporaneous written accounts are recognized by the Federal Rules as having circumstantial guarantees of trustworthiness. *Turbyfill v. International Harvester Co.*, 486 F.Supp. 232 (E.D.Mich. 1981).

3. **Grand jury testimony:** The use of *grand jury testimony* where the witness is unavailable is an important "near miss" situation. See the more extensive discussion of grand jury testimony and the catchall *infra*, in Par. (F).

E. **Notice:** The biggest innovation in the Federal Rules' residual exception is the requirement of *advance notice* that the residual exception will be used. FRE 807(b) makes the statement inadmissible unless "*before the trial or hearing*, the proponent gives an adverse party reasonable notice of the intent to offer the statement and its particulars … so that the party has a fair opportunity to meet it."

   1. **Some discretion given:** This language seems, on its face, to allow very little judicial discretion. For instance, it does not seem to contemplate that a notice given *after* commencement of the trial will ever be sufficient. But most courts have been willing to allow notice to be given after the trial starts, if it is only then that the need to use the exception becomes clear; the court will then often give a *continuance* to allow the opponent time to combat the testimony.

F. **Grand jury testimony used against criminal defendant:** Perhaps the most important and frequent use of the catchall has historically been to allow use of *grand jury testimony, against a criminal defendant,* given by a witness who is now unavailable to testify at trial. (Observe that such testimony can never be used under the "former testimony" exception of 804(b)(1), because the defendant wasn't present at the grand jury, and thus couldn't cross-examine the witness.)

   1. **How issue arises:** The issue is especially likely to arise where the grand jury witness either: (1) has been murdered prior to the trial (as not infrequently occurs in drug and organized crime cases); or (2) refuses to testify at trial, either by explicitly relying on his privi-

lege against self-incrimination or by merely being uncooperative (perhaps because he is in fear of the defendant).

2. **Effect of *Crawford***: But the 2004 decision in ***Crawford v. Washington*** (*infra*, p. 364) means that because of the ***Confrontation Clause*** of the Sixth Amendment, grand jury testimony ***can't be used against a criminal defendant in the very situation to which the catchall might otherwise apply:*** where the witness is ***now unavailable*** to testify at the trial of the person who is implicated by the witness's grand jury testimony. Under *Crawford*, an out-of-court "testimonial" declaration (and all grand jury testimony is "testimonial") may not be admitted against an accused unless the witness was made available for cross-examination by the accused either at the time of the declaration (which can't happen in the case of grand jury testimony) or at the accused's trial.

> **Example:** W witnesses a fatal shooting of V. W tells a grand jury looking into the shooting, "I saw the shooter, and it was D." At D's later trial, W can't be found (he's moved out of stand, with no forwarding address.) Since W is not available to be cross-examined by D's lawyer at trial, and since D didn't have the opportunity to cross-examine W at the time of the grand jury, W's grand-jury testimony can't be used against D on account of D's Sixth Amendment right to be confronted with witnesses against him. And that's true even if the trial court is convinced that the grand-jury testimony has circumstantial guarantees of trustworthiness, as well as meeting all the other requirements for the residual exception.

G. **Child-abuse victims:** Another common use of the catchall is to allow use of out-of-court statements by children who appear to be victims or sexual or physical ***abuse***. Typically, the child makes an out-of-court statement naming her abuser and supplying other details about the abuse; the prosecution then seeks to use the statement in the abuser's criminal trial. Sometimes the child also testifies at trial; often, however, the child is too traumatized to testify at trial, making the out-of-court statement even more important as evidence.

1. **Case-by-case adjudication:** Here, as in the grand-jury-testimony situation, courts have historically generally been ***willing*** to allow out-of-court statements that they find to be trustworthy. M&K, §8.83, p. 1009. The gauging of trustworthiness is done by looking at the facts of the particular out-of-court declaration.

    a. **Effect of *Crawford* and *Davis***: It is not clear what effect *Crawford v. Washington* (*infra*, p. 365), and *Davis v. Washington* (*infra*, p. 367) will have in this child-abuse scenario. A child victim's statement to non-law enforcement personnel (e.g., a pediatrician or E.R. doctor) might in some circumstances be held to be "testimonial," in which case it would trigger *Crawford's* rule that if the declarant isn't produced at trial, the out-of-court testimonial declaration cannot be admitted. *Crawford* and *Davis* don't squarely say whether or when statements made in response to questions by non-law-enforcement personnel will be deemed to be testimonial. But *Davis* emphasizes that even an informal questioning session will be testimonial if it is concerned with determining "what happened" rather than dealing with a pending emergency. So at least where the child victim's statement to, say, a doctor is focused not on obtaining treatment but on documenting events for possible use in the criminal justice process, the victim's statements ought to be deemed testimonial and thus inadmissible under the Confrontation Clause unless the victim takes the stand.

Quiz Yourself on

EXCEPTIONS TO THE HEARSAY RULE *(ENTIRE CHAPTER)*

48. Claudius stops for a cigarette while hiking on Mount Vesuvius. He flicks his ash into the crater, which ignites, the volcano explodes, and the city of Pompeii is history. Claudius is arrested on criminal negligence charges and pleads guilty. Subsequently, survivors of the disaster file civil negligence suits against him. Can they introduce the prior guilty plea as an admission by a party-opponent? _____

49. Wimp sues Atlas for battery, claiming that Atlas kicked sand in his face, permanently damaging his eyesight. At trial, Atlas offers into evidence Wimp's application for Bungling Brothers Clown College, submitted two weeks after the incident, to which Wimp attached a certificate from his optometrist, Dr. Convex Kincaid. The certificate states that Wimp's eyesight is perfect (a requirement for Clown College). Does the certificate satisfy an exception to the hearsay rule? _____

50. Des Pirado is a passenger on an Acme Airways flight that crashes in the Andes, injuring Des. In his suit against the company, Des offers as evidence the exclamation of the pilot, I.M. Dian, just before the plane crashed: "Holy Cow! I knew they shouldn't have glued the tail on! We should have taken another plane!" Des claims this statement is an admission by a party-opponent. Acme objects, claiming that the making of such a statement is outside the scope of the pilot's duties, so that the statement is inadmissible. Under the FRE, how do you rule? _____

51. Oink, Grunt and Slop — the Three Little Pigs — are going home from a wild party. (They're friends but have no other relationship.) Oink is driving when the car hits and injures B. B. Wolf, a pedestrian crossing the street at a crosswalk. Murray the Cop arrives five minutes later. Wolf subsequently sues Oink for negligence, claiming Oink was driving while intoxicated. Wolf offers the testimony of Murray the Cop: "At the scene, while everyone else was out of earshot, Grunt told me: 'We were on our way home from a party, where we were all drinking like there was no tomorrow.'" Oink objects. Will Murray's testimony be admissible? _____

52. Three months after Moe, Larry and Curly rob the Bucks Bank, Curly is stopped on the highway and ticketed for speeding. When the patrolman approaches the car, Curly blurts out, "The Bucks Bank job was Moe and Larry's idea." At Moe and Larry's trial, the state seeks to introduce the patrolman's testimony as to Curly's statement. Under the FRE, is the statement admissible as an admission by a party-opponent? _____

53. Little Bobo decides to play a trick on Isaac Newton. Bobo climbs a tree and, when Newton sits down in its shade, Bobo drops an apple on his head. Newton comments, "Ouch! I think my skull is fractured!" At Bobo's trial on battery charges, Newton's comment is offered to prove Newton was in pain. Bobo objects, on hearsay grounds. How do you rule, under the FRE? _____

54. Mary arrives in an ambulance at the hospital's emergency room, and is brought in in a wheel chair. The ER physician, Dr. Welby, asks her what happened. She says, "I was riding the escalator at Macy's, when I caught my heel in a hole in the metal, and fell. I think my ankle's broken." (The ankle indeed turns out to be broken.) At Mary's negligence trial against Macy's for improperly maintaining the escalator, Macy's claims that Mary must have fallen outside the store. Mary offers Dr. Welby to repeat what she told him about what caused her injury, to prove that she really did fall on the escalator at Macy's. Is his testimony admissible under the "medical treatment or diagnosis" exception of the FRE? _____

55. As proof that MacArthur returned to Corregidor in the Philippines, his statement "I shall return" is offered

57. Joe Phlebitz tells Mrs. O'Leary, "I'm planning to give you my cow next week." The Great Chicago Fire takes place two weeks later, and the cow caused it. In a lawsuit for negligence, Mrs. O'Leary denies ownership of the errant cow. The "udder" party offers Phlebitz' statement as proof that Phlebitz probably indeed gave Mrs. O'Leary the cow. O'Leary objects, claiming the statement is inadmissible hearsay. Will the statement be admissible under the "present state of mind" exception to the hearsay rule under the FRE? _____

58. Dr. Bovary is charged with the murder of his wife, Emma. At his murder trial, the Bovarys' maid, Felicity, offers to testify that on the day of her death, Emma told Felicity: "I'm frightened, because Dr. Bovary has threatened to kill me." This statement is offered as evidence that Dr. Bovary killed Emma. Is Felicity's testimony admissible, over objection, under the "present state of mind" hearsay exception? _____

59. At trial, Fred testifies, "Romulus told me that he and Remus were about to set out to found Rome." This testimony is offered to prove that Remus subsequently took off to found Rome. (There's no other evidence about whether Romulus ever left, or about whether Remus joined him.) Is Fred's testimony admissible under the "then existing state of mind" exception to the hearsay rule, under the FRE? _____

60. Tom-Tom the Piper's Son is on trial for larceny, for stealing a pig. Tom-Tom defends on grounds that he didn't realize the pig wasn't his. His friend, Fred-Fred, testifies: "He told me the day afterwards, 'You know, I took the wrong pig. I thought it was mine.'" The prosecution objects. Under the FRE, will the statement be admissible under the "state of mind" hearsay exception? _____

61. During Cinderella's magic night on the town, the Fairy Godmother turns a pumpkin into a coach. The pumpkin's owner, Frank, files suit against Fairy Godmother. As proof that the event took place, Frank offers the testimony of Furd, a bystander, who testifies: "I heard someone shout 'Holy Cow! She's turning that pumpkin into a coach!'" Furd admits that he never knew who made the statement. The defense objects on hearsay grounds to the admission of the statement. Under what hearsay exception, if any, is the statement admissible? _____

62. Francis Bacon is in court claiming he wrote the plays ascribed to Shakespeare. (He asserts that before he could publish them, Shakespeare stole the manuscripts and published them under his own name.) Bacon offers the testimony of Shakespeare's friend, Fred, that, while Fred and Shakespeare were at a tavern, a glass fell on Shakespeare's head and shattered. Dazed and excited, Shakespeare shouted: "Bacon wrote the plays!" Shakespeare objects. Bacon claims the statement is admissible under the excited utterance exception to the hearsay rule. Is he right? _____

6 Frasier and Niles are chatting on their front porch one day, when they see Sam Malone zoom by in his Corvette, through a red light, and into the side of another car. Frasier looks on calmly, and comments, "There goes Sam Malone, watching the women instead of the road again." At a subsequent trial concerning the accident, Frasier's statement is offered into evidence to prove Sam wasn't paying attention to the road. Is the statement admissible under the FRE, notwithstanding that Frasier was unexcited when he made it? _____

. Bush, an avid quail hunter, is out hunting one day. Unfortunately, one of his shots hits Clinton, playing golf on a neighboring course with his friend Al. Clinton sues Bush for battery. By the time the case gets to trial, Clinton's witness, Al, can't remember what happened. While Al is on the witness stand, he is handed some notes he took at the time of the incident. However, he still can't remember anything. If Al testifies that the notes were correct when made, under what hearsay exception, if any, can they now be read into the record? _____

65. Peter Pan gives John, Wendy and Michael fairy dust to help them fly. He is arrested on narcotics charges. Wendy is called as a witness at trial. She can't remember exactly what happened, but, when she is shown some notes she made at the time of the incident, she is able to remember the events perfectly without further reference to the notes. Are the notes admissible under the "recorded recollection" exception to the hearsay rule? _____

66. Sisko, captain of the tugboat U.S.S. Defiant, is injured when a large cruise ship under the command of Captain Picard rams him in Subic Bay. Sisko sues Picard for negligence. The incident is alleged to have happened on May 1. Picard's defense is that he wasn't even in Subic Bay at the time. At trial, Sisko seeks to introduce a sworn affidavit by Captain Janeway, another captain who happens to be currently lost at sea. In the affidavit, Janeway states that to her knowledge, Picard takes his ship to Subic Bay every May 1, and has done so for 50 years. Is the affidavit admissible over a hearsay objection? _____

67. Jed works for the Quo Vadis Railroad Company. One of his duties is to prepare a report on any accident in which a Q.V. train is involved. (These reports are mainly used by the railroad to defend against claims by shippers whose merchandise is damaged.) When the Venus de Milo is first sculpted, it is crated and transported on the Quo Vadis, where it suffers damage. The incident is described in Jed's accident report: "Statue was improperly packaged by owner. Fell out of box, onto tracks, and wham! Next car of train sheared its arms clean off." Venus' owner sues Q.V. for negligence. The railroad seeks to introduce Jed's report into evidence, in support of the railroad's defense that the accident was caused by the owner's negligence in packing the statue. Assume that both sides' lawyers litigate the evidentiary issues thoroughly. (a) What hearsay exception is the railroad's best chance for getting the report into evidence? _____ (b) What's the likely outcome of the railroad's attempt in (a)? _____

68. Jessie Hahn sues the No-Tell Motel for injuries she claims she incurred lying on a faulty mattress. Jessie offers as evidence the emergency room records of the hospital that treated her at the time. The records are regularly and scrupulously kept by personnel who attend to the patients and who must maintain such records. The records include Jessie' statement: "The mattress at the No-Tell was faulty." Is the statement admissible to show that the mattress was in fact faulty? _____

69. OK Simpleton is charged with murdering his wife. A police incident report prepared during the investigation the day the body was found contains the following statement: "Footprints that appear to be from two different pair of shoes seem to be leading away from body; these prints look like they were left after the murder." The signature on the report is illegible, and the prosecution and police department say they don't know who prepared it. Since Simpleton is charged with having committed the murder alone, he seeks to introduce the report to establish that there must have been two murderers. (a) Under what hearsay exception, if any, is the report most likely to be admitted? _____ (b) If your answer to (a) names an exception, will the report in fact be admitted under the exception you cite? _____

70. Unem Ployd brings a civil suit against Ma Belle Corp., alleging that Ma Belle refused to hire Ployd and that the refusal was based on illegal racial discrimination. In its defense, Ma Belle seeks to introduce a report by the state Equal Employment Opportunity Commission, which recently conducted a review of Ma Belle's hiring practices, and concluded that Ma Belle did not practice racial discrimination in hiring. Are the report and this conclusion admissible under the FRE's "public records and reports" exception, to prove that Ma Belle generally doesn't discriminate? _____

71. The Black Knight keeps a fire-breathing dragon as a pet. One night it gets loose, sneezes, and starts the Great Fire of London. The Lord Mayor of London, while sitting at his desk working on official business, looks out the window and is a witness to the whole incident. Although it's not his job to worry about reporting or recording the causes of natural disasters, he takes notes on what he sees. At a subsequent trial, the Lord Mayor's notes are offered under the FRE's "official records and reports" exception to the hearsay rule. Admissible? _____

72. George Washington is on trial for having chopped down a cherry tree. The prosecution seeks to admit against George a police "incident" report prepared by Officer Madison of the Mt. Vernon police force. The report says, in part, "At 2200 hours, I observed a person who looked like Geo. Washington — had ill-fitting teeth and a white wig — chop down a cherry tree. Suspect ran away before I could apprehend him." Madison is not available to testify at the trial (he moved away and can't be found), which is why the prosecution wants to use the report instead. The report bears Madison's signature, and the legend "Mt. Vernon Police Department - Incident Report" at the top. Each officer on the Mt. Vernon force is required to write up reports of any criminal activity observed by the officer while on duty. Can the report be admitted against George as a "public record or report," under the FRE? _____

73. A civil suit involves the issue of whether defendant, a cigarette company, knew in 1954 that cigarettes could cause cancer. Plaintiff offers a letter found under the following circumstances: Nicco Tine, the president of defendant, died in 1962. In his safe deposit box was found a carbon copy of a letter purporting to have been written by Tine to his son in 1953, in which he says, "Tommy, the scientists at the company have just finished experiments showing that smoking probably can cause lung cancer." The box was not discovered and opened until 2017. No other evidence has been offered proving that Tine actually wrote this letter. What hearsay exception, if any, allows the introduction of the letter into evidence for the purpose of proving that the scientists did the experiments referred to in the letter? _____

74. J. Needlepoint Morgan fraudulently convinces Commodore Peterbilt to sell all of his shares in International Bubble Makers to Morgan for 10¢ a share, a small fraction of their value. At trial, Peterbilt seeks to introduce a copy of the *Wall Street Journal* as evidence of the market price of the stock on the date of the sale. Can Morgan successfully object on the grounds that the newspaper's republication of the stock prices is hearsay? _____

75. Ralph dies, covered by an insurance policy that pays double in the event of an accidental death. The insurance company refuses to make the double payment, contending that Ralph died of natural causes. Ralph's widow, Alice, sues the insurer. At trial, the insurer attempts to introduce Ralph's death certificate, which was filled out and signed by Ralph's doctor, in which the cause of death is listed as "brain tumor." The certificate is offered to prove that Ralph indeed died of a brain tumor. Under the FRE, is the certificate admissible? _____

76. Burke is arrested on murder charges. Burke and his attorney, Nick Rofelia, attend a preliminary examination in the murder case. At that examination, Hare, who's the defendant in a separate prosecution for concealing the bodies of Burke's victims, is a prosecution witness. At Burke's trial Hare refuses to testify (fearing the effect his testimony would have on his concealment case), even when ordered to do so by the trial judge. The prosecutor now offers a transcript of Hare's preliminary examination testimony as substantive evidence. Under what FRE hearsay exception, if any, is the transcript admissible, and why? _____

77. Clouseau sues Kato for battery. Previously, Kato was tried and convicted on criminal battery charges arising from the same incident (Clouseau was the complainant). At the criminal trial, Dreyfus, a witness, had testified that he saw Kato attack Clouseau without provocation. Kato cross-examined Dreyfus at the criminal trial. Under the FRE, in the current civil trial, will Dreyfus' testimony be admissible, over Kato's objection? _____

78. Goldilocks is arrested for breaking and entering the Three Bears' house. Mama Bear suffers a complete nervous breakdown after the crime, and can't testify. Instead, a sworn affidavit as to her recollection of the facts, given to the police immediately after the break-in, is offered under the "former testimony" exception to the hearsay rule. Might it qualify, under the FRE? _____

79. Sleeping Beauty appears as a witness at a trial on behalf of plaintiff. Defense counsel doesn't cross-examine her, although given the chance to do so. She subsequently pricks her finger with a needle and falls asleep for 100 years, making her unavailable to testify in a subsequent trial where the parties and issues are substantially identical. When her recorded testimony is offered under the "former testimony" exception to the hearsay rule, defense counsel objects on the grounds that Sleeping Beauty wasn't cross-examined at the first trial. How do you rule? _____

80. The French Maid rushes into the Master's study, only to find him on the carpet, bleeding profusely, with a sharpened umbrella through his chest. She rushes to him, props him up, and he mumbles feebly: "The butler did it." He slumps over and dies. At the butler's murder trial, the prosecutor offers the French Maid's testimony as to the Master's statement, to prove the butler did it. Butler objects on hearsay grounds: "Everyone always says I did it." How do you rule, under the FRE? _____

81. Brutus and friends attack Julius Caesar on the steps of the Capital. As Brutus stabs him, Caesar, believing himself mortally wounded, looks up, and exclaims, "Et tu, Brute?" Caesar unexpectedly survives, changing the course of history. At Brutus' attempted murder trial, Caesar is one of the spectators. A bystander at the stabbing, Innocente Witnius, is testifying, and says: "I heard Caesar say, 'Et tu, Brute?'" On objection, is the statement admissible as a "dying declaration" under the FRE? _____

82. Rosebud Rosenbluhm suffers smoke inhalation when she is watching a play at the Iroquois Theatre and the theatre catches fire. Firefighters carry Rosebud outside, where she sees Iva Match, who set the fire. With her last ounce of energy, Rosebud points at Iva, and screams, "That's her! I saw her pour gasoline on the curtain and set it afire! She killed me!" Rosebud then wilts and dies. The prosecutor charges Iva with arson, but not with the homicide of Rosebud. Under the FRE, can Rosebud's statement be used as a "dying declaration" against Iva at trial, over Iva's hearsay objection? _____

83. King Khufu, owner of the greatest of the Pyramids, dies. In his will, he leaves the Pyramid, "Man's greatest architectural achievement, mine and mine alone, to my son, Bhufu." Khufu's second wife, Joanne, contests the will, claiming that the Pyramid was always community property and therefore now passes to her, not Bhufu. She offers as evidence the testimony of a neighbor, Cal: "Before Khufu died, he told me he realized the pyramid was community property." Under what hearsay exception, if any, will Khufu's statement to Cal be admissible? _____

84. Scrooge McDukk, a fabulously wealthy man, is prosecuted for income tax evasion. McDukk is elderly and has had several heart operations. At trial, the defense offers the testimony of Launchpad McQuakk, who will testify: "McDukk's cousin, Donald Dukk, told me that he himself prepared Scrooge's tax return, that he, Donald, knew he had put some questionable deductions into the return, and that the old man knew nothing about any wrongdoing." The defense offers nothing further about the circumstances surrounding Dukk's statement. The prosecutor objects. Is the statement admissible as a "declaration against interest" under the FRE? _____

85. Bert Littlefish is stopped by police for a traffic violation, and turns out to have 19 kilos of cocaine in his car. While interrogated by Otto, one of the arresting officers, Bert gives a 10-minute account of his involvement with the drugs, in which he claims, basically, that he was just a courier for the drugs, and that the real mastermind was Ernie Kingfish. Bert says Ernie arranged for the drugs to be smuggled in and delivered to Bert, and would have picked them up from Bert and re-sold them if Bert had not been arrested. At Ernie's federal smuggling trial, Bert refuses to repeat this story, even though given immunity. The prosecution seeks to have Otto recount all of Bert's statement to Otto, including those parts that implicate Ernie while not specifically implicating Bert (e.g., "Ernie was the mastermind, who arranged for the drugs to be smuggled in.") Can Otto so testify, under the FRE? _____

86. Homer Simpson's will provides that, if his son Bart reaches age 30 while Homer is still alive, Homer's estate is to go to his daughter Lisa and, if Bart doesn't reach 30 before Homer's death, then the estate is to go to Homer's other daughter, Maggie. When Homer dies, Bart has been dead for three years, but his birth certificate can't be found so it's hard to prove how old he was at his death. In the lawsuit that ensues to determine who is entitled to Homer's estate, Lisa offers the testimony of Molly Burns-Simpson, Bart's widow. She would testify that she lived with Bart during the last year of his life, during which he told her he was 33. Maggie Simpson objects on hearsay grounds. Under what hearsay exception, if any, is Molly's statement admissible? _____

87. Spartacus sues the Cisalpine Gaul Tavern under a Dramshop Act, for injuries he received when Crassus ran over him while he was crossing the street. (Spartacus claims the Cisalpine Gaul let Crassus drink too much.) The tavern calls Crassus as a witness, and expects him to testify that he was sober when he left the Tavern. In fact, on direct testimony, Crassus says he may have had a few too many at the tavern, after all. Can the tavern now introduce a statement from Crassus' pre-trial deposition, in which he claimed he left the bar sober, as substantive evidence that he was in fact sober? _____

88. The Joker successfully pulls off a bank job by super-gluing the bank manager's hands to a wall so the police can't be alerted. At Joker's trial, in order to prove that Joker committed the heist, the manager testifies that he picked Joker out from a valid line-up as the super-gluer. Is the manager's testimony hearsay under the FRE? _____

89. Charlotte Corday stabs Jean Paul Marat to death in his bathtub. Marat's maid, Fifi, sees Corday enter and leave the bathroom. The police ask Fifi to draw a picture of the woman she saw, and she does so. The picture bears a striking resemblance to Corday. Fifi dies of a heart attack the next day, and Corday is arrested the following week. At Corday's murder trial, Fifi's drawing is offered as evidence against her. On objection, the prosecution claims the picture is non-hearsay because it's a prior identification. Under the FRE, how do you rule? _____

90. Snow White is found dead in the forest, and the medical examiner concludes that she suffered head injuries when she hit her head on a rock after falling or being pushed. A grand jury is duly convened to investigate the death. Grumpy is called as a witness. (There is evidence that Grumpy desperately loved Snow White, and there's no evidence he had anything to do with her death.) Grumpy testifies, under oath, "I saw Sneezy kill Snow White — he sneezed right in her face, and she fell down and hit her head on a big rock. It looked to me like he did it on purpose." The prosecutor questions Grumpy briefly about his statement, and Grumpy supplies details in a convincing way. Sneezy is then put on trial for manslaughter. Grumpy refuses to testify at Sneezy's trial even after being granted immunity and threatened with contempt. (There's some evidence he's afraid of what Sneezy will do to him if he testifies.) There is no other evidence pointing unequivocally to Sneezy as the culprit. Putting aside any constitutional issues, under what hearsay exception, if any, can the transcript of Grumpy's grand jury testimony be introduced against

Sneezy? _____

Answers

48. Yes. A guilty plea is admissible as an admission, because a plea is considered a "statement" by a party. Note, however, that the plea is not necessarily conclusive — Claudius can explain the circumstances of the guilty plea, and thus affect the weight the jury places on it.

49. Yes, as an *adoptive admission* by Wimp. Wimp adopted the statement in the certificate when he attached it to his application. Adoptive admissions are admissible (against the party who did the adopting) on the same basis as regular admissions. FRE 801(d)(2)(B).

50. Objection overruled. The statement is admissible against Acme, since Dian is an employee, and an agent, of Acme Airways, and the statement was made in the scope of the agency (his duties as a pilot). Under the FRE, any statement an agent makes *during the existence of the agency*, on a *subject* that's *within the scope of the agency*, is admissible against the principal as an admission. FRE 801(d)(2)(D). There's *no* requirement that the principal have *authorized* the statement. (Note that the agency must be established by independent evidence; the out-of-court statements can't be the sole basis for the authority.)

51. No. The statement is hearsay, and no exception applies. Hearsay is an out-of-court statement offered to prove the truth of the matter asserted. FRE 801(c). Here, the out-of-court statement by Grunt is being offered for the truth of its assertion, namely, that Oink had been drinking prior to driving home. The statement can't be admitted as an admission under FRE 801(d)(2), because Grunt *wasn't authorized to speak for Oink*, nor was he Oink's agent, partner, or coconspirator, nor did Oink adopt Grunt's statement. Nor does the hearsay exception for *declarations against interest* (FRE 804(b)(3)) apply: the statement wasn't against *Grunt's* interest when made (even though it was against Oink's); also, there's no indication Grunt is unavailable as a witness.

52. No. FRE 801(d)(2)(E) treats as non-hearsay, when used against a party, a statement by a *co-conspirator* of that party, but only if the statement "was made by the party's coconspirator during and in furtherance of the conspiracy." The statement here, though made by a co-conspirator of the defendants, was made three months after the robbery and had nothing to do with completing or furthering the robbery. Therefore, it doesn't qualify under 801(d)(2)(E), and is thus inadmissible hearsay.

53. Objection overruled. The statement is admissible under the "statement of then-existing *mental, emotional, or physical condition*" hearsay exception of FRE 803(3). In fact, 803(3) specifically says, parenthetically, that a statement about the declarant's then-existing "pain or bodily health" is covered. So the statement, "Ouch! I think my skull is fractured!" can be offered to prove that Newton was in pain due to what he believed to be a skull fracture. (However, 803(3) *won't* support using the statement to prove that Newton's skull actually *was* fractured, because 803(3) doesn't allow a statement of "belief" to be used to prove the truth of the fact believed. But the exceptions for present-sense-impression [803(1)] and excited utterance [803(2)] *would* be usable to introduce the statement to show an actual fracture.)

54. Yes, probably. FRE 803(4) gives a hearsay exception for statements "made for — and *reasonably pertinent to — medical diagnosis or treatment*," and extends the exception to cover statements about the "inception or ... general cause" of "past or present symptoms[.]" Mary's statement about the cause — that her foot got caught in a hole in the step of an escalator — was probably "reasonably pertinent" to Dr. Welby's attempts to diagnose and treat her. However, it's possible that a court might take a narrow view of "reasonably pertinent," and hold that her identification of the particular place (Macy's) was not reasonably pertinent. At the very least, her statement that the accident occurred on an escalator would seem to be pertinent (and thus admissible) even if the part about Macy's isn't.

55. **The "statement of present state of mind" exception**. FRE 803(3) allows evidence of "the declarant's then-existing state of mind (such as ... intent, or plan...)." The rule doesn't expressly say whether the statement of intent can be admitted to show that the declarant *carried out* his intent. But courts interpreting the provision have generally held that a statement about what the declarant plans to do is admissible not only to prove that the declarant had that intent, but also to prove that he probably followed through on that intent.

56. **No, because it can't be offered to prove the crate was leaking**. It's hearsay, because it's an out-of-court statement offered to prove the truth of its assertion. FRE 801(c). The declarant is Mutt: "Look, Jeff, I think. . . ." It's being offered to prove the truth of its assertion, that the crate was leaking.

The most likely hearsay exception it could fit is the "present state of mind" exception, FRE 803(3). However, that exception specifically *excludes* "a statement of . . . *belief* to *prove the fact . . . believed*" (except in connection with wills). Since the statement is being offered to prove the fact believed (that the crate was leaking), the exclusion applies. Therefore, the statement can't come in for the purpose for which it's being offered.

57. **Yes**. Under FRE 803(3), the statement is admissible as a declaration of the speaker's "then-existing state of mind." Courts interpreting 803(3) allow statements of intent to show not only that the intent existed, but also to show that the speaker probably *acted in accordance* with the intent. The out-of-court statement: "I'm planning to give you my cow" is being offered to show that Phlebitz followed through with his intention, so the statement falls within the "present state of mind" exception.

58. **No**. The main problem is that the statement describes not only the speaker's present state of mind (fear of Dr. Bovary), but also what a *person other than the speaker* (Dr. Bovary) *did to induce that state of mind* (threaten to kill). Courts generally do not allow the "present state of mind" exception to be used for the purpose of proving what someone other than the speaker did to induce the declarant's state of mind. The main reason for this is that there is an extreme risk of prejudice, substantially outweighing any probative value the statement might have.

Observe that the facts here are a variation on the famous case of *Shepard v. U.S.* ("Dr. Shepard has poisoned me," offered to show that the Dr. in fact poisoned her.) There, the Supreme Court disallowed the use of the "state of mind" exception to prove the fact believed. Here, we're dealing not with proof of the fact believed, but proof of what another did to induce the declarant's state of mind; however, similar issues — risk of prejudice, and desire not to let the "state of mind" exception swallow up the entire hearsay rule — apply to both situations.

Note, also, that this is a "*multiple hearsay*" problem: Felicity is repeating in-court what Emma said about what Dr. Bovary said ("I'll kill you.") Multiple hearsay isn't admissible unless *each level is independently admissible*. FRE 805. Here, Dr. Bovary's statement is probably admissible as a statement of his intent, offered to show that the speaker later acted in accord with that intent (so that if Emma had survived, she'd be allowed to testify at trial to Dr. Bovary's threat). But, for the reasons given above, the second level — Emma's out-of-court repetition of Dr. Bovary's threat — doesn't fall within the "present state of mind" (or any other) exception, so the entire "package" must be excluded.

59. **Unclear, but probably not**. It's true that the FRE contain an exception (803(3)) for statements of present state of mind, and that a statement of intent may be introduced to prove that the *declarant* followed through on his own expressed intent. But courts interpreting 803(3) are split as to whether and when *A*'s

statement of intent to do something together with B can be used to prove that <u>B</u> did the thing. Most courts seem to hold that, at most, this use can only be made if there is some **corroborating evidence** that B joined with A. Since there's no corroboration here that Remus ever joined, most courts would probably hold 803(3) inapplicable.

60. No. The "state of mind" exception (FRE 803(3)) is, more precisely, an exception for statements about the declarant's "**then-existing**" state of mind. Here, the problem is that Tom-Tom's statement describes his state of mind at an **earlier time** (when he took the pig), not his state of mind at the time he was speaking. So the exception simply doesn't apply.

A different way of looking at the problem would be to argue that Tom-Tom's statement was a statement about his present memory (equivalent to "I now remember that at the time I took the pig, I thought it was mine.") But this view, too, runs into difficulties: FRE 803(3) specifically says that **a statement of memory or belief is not admissible to prove the fact remembered or believed** (except in connection with wills). Since Tom-Tom's statement, on this view, is an attempt to prove the fact remembered (not the fact that the pig really was Tom-Tom's, but the fact that at the moment of taking, Tom-Tom's mental state was "intent-to-take-his-own-property"), it falls within this bar.

RELATED ISSUE: Suppose Fred instead testified: "Just before he took the pig, Tom-Tom told me, 'I'm taking this pig because it's mine.' " The statement *would* fit the "then-existing state of mind" exception of FRE 803(3), and would be admissible to show Tom's lack of intent to deprive another of his property.

61. The "excited utterance" exception: the statement was made under the stress of excitement, due to a startling event, and it concerns the event. See FRE 803(2). The declarant of an excited utterance can be a **bystander** (rather than a person actually involved in the event), and **needn't be identified** by the person giving the in-court testimony about what the declarant said.

62. No. The statement isn't an excited utterance, since an excited utterance must **relate to the startling event that prompted it** in order to be admissible. Shakespeare's statement didn't have anything to do with the glass's falling on his head; therefore, it can't be an excited utterance. FRE 803(2).

RELATED ISSUE: Note that the statement *is* admissible as an **admission** against a party-opponent (non-hearsay under FRE 801(d)(2), and an exception to the hearsay rule under the common law).

63. Yes. Although the statement is hearsay — it's an out-of-court statement offered to prove its truth, namely, that Sam wasn't watching the road — it's admissible as a **present sense impression** under FRE 803(1). Unlike the excited utterance exception, the present sense impression exception **doesn't require that the declarant be under the stress of excitement** when he makes the statement. Note that, as with all exceptions under FRE 803, Frasier's **availability** to testify is **immaterial**.

RELATED ISSUE: If Frasier's statement had been made while he was stressed or excited ("Oh, my God, he's not watching where he's going! He's going to hit that parked car!"), it would be admissible as an "excited utterance" under FRE 803(2). (It would probably also satisfy the present-sense-impression requirements of 803(1).)

64. The "recorded recollection" exception (colloquially, **"past recollection recorded"**), under FRE 803(5). The notes satisfy all the prerequisites for admissibility under FRE 803(5): (1) they were made by Al at the time of the accident, when the shooting was still fresh in his mind; (2) Al had first-hand knowledge of the shooting, since he was there; (3) Al's memory of the event is impaired, and can't be refreshed; and (4) Al has verified that the notes were true when made. Therefore, as long as they're properly authenticated, the notes are admissible into evidence.

RELATED ISSUE: If *someone other than Al* had made the notes, and right after the accident Al read them and stated (or, probably, even thought), "Yes, that's what happened," then the notes would still be admissible; under the FRE, as long as Al *adopted* the written notes when made, they are just as admissible as if he had made them himself.

65. **No**. Under FRE 803(5), if a witness's present recollection is *revived* by her reference to the notes and the notes are no longer needed, they are not admissible under the "recorded recollection" exception to the hearsay rule. One of the prerequisites for admissibility under the past recollection recorded exception is that the witness's present recollection continues to be at least partially impaired; if the witness's present recollection has been revived, then that recollection is no longer impaired, and the notes are therefore inadmissible under the exception.

66. **No**. The affidavit is hearsay, since it's an out-of-court statement being offered for the truth of the matter asserted, namely, that Picard has a habit of taking his ship to Subic Bay every May 1. Affidavits, unlike deposition transcripts (see FRE 804(b)(1)), are not admissible *even if the affiant is unavailable*. Since neither the affidavit nor the statement in it falls within any hearsay exception, the affidavit is inadmissible.

Observe that although hearsay problems usually arise in the form of live trial testimony by a witness about what someone said out-of-court, a hearsay problem can also be presented where, as here, someone tries to introduce a *document* that contains a statement offered for the truth of the statement.

RELATED ISSUE: If Janeway were *testifying at trial*, she'd be allowed to testify about what Picard did every May 1, because evidence that someone had a particular habit is admissible to show that he acted in accord with that habit on the occasion in question. See FRE 406.

67. **(a) The business records exception**, FRE 803(6).

(b) Probably not. First, to qualify under the b.r. exception the report must be kept as part of the "regular practice" of a business activity. Some courts (though probably not a majority) read "regular practice" to mean "routine" or "related to the main function of the business"; these courts conclude that accident reports (especially ones made in anticipation of litigation) don't qualify. That is, to these courts Q.V.'s main function is transporting goods, and accident reports don't relate closely to that function.

An even bigger problem is that 803(6)(E) mandates exclusion if the opponent "show[s] that the source of information or the method or circumstances of preparation indicate a *lack of trustworthiness*." Since Jed knows that the main use of his reports is to help Q.V. defend against claims, Venus will be able to show that Jed has a strong interest to write up the reports so as to blame the customer rather than the railroad. Therefore, a court would probably conclude that in the circumstances here, Venus (the party opposing admission of the report) has borne its burden under 803(6)(E) of demonstrating that under the circumstances, the report is likely to be self-serving and thus untrustworthy.

68. **No, probably**. This is a case of "hearsay on hearsay," where there's a hearsay statement (Jessie's statement) inside another hearsay statement (the emergency room records). Thus, *both* hearsay statements must be admissible under exceptions to the hearsay rule, or neither will be admitted. FRE 805.

The emergency room records are probably admissible as a business record under the FRE 803(6). However, Jessie's statement is probably *inadmissible hearsay*. It's being offered for the truth of the matter asserted (that the mattress was faulty); however, it's probably not admissible as a statement for purposes of medical diagnosis or treatment under the FRE 803(4) exception, since it probably wasn't reasonably pertinent to her treatment. Nor does it fall within any other exception. Therefore, the entire hearsay on hearsay is *inadmissible*.

69. (a) FRE 803(8)'s "**public records**" **exception**.

(b) Yes. The report can come in either under 803(8)(A)(ii) (for "a matter observed while under a legal duty to report") or 803(8)(A)(iii) (for "factual findings from a legally authorized investigation") It's true that (A)(ii) contains the words "but not including, in a criminal case, a matter observed by law enforcement personnel." But this language has widely been interpreted to ban only use *against* criminal defendants, not *by* them.

Nor does it matter that it's unknown who wrote the report. Nothing in the public records exception (or, for that matter, in many of the other exceptions, such as the "excited utterance" exception) requires that the identity of the declarant be known. If the report is a public record — and that's clear from the facts here — details of precisely how it was made are immaterial, as long as the circumstances don't affect the report's trustworthiness (which they don't seem to do here).

70. Yes. The report and its conclusion are admissible under FRE 803(8)(A)(iii), which gives a hearsay exception "in a civil case or against the government in a criminal case," for "factual findings from a legally authorized ***investigation***." The report here is certainly an "investigation." An interesting aspect of 803(8)(C) is that it has been interpreted by the U.S. Supreme Court (*Beech Aircraft v. Rainey*, 1988) to allow introduction of ***interpretations*** and ***conclusions*** in reports, not just narrow factual findings. So the broad conclusion here — no racial discrimination — is admissible.

RELATED ISSUE 1: The text of FRE 803(8) doesn't say whether the report has to be based on the government author's ***first-hand knowledge***. The general Adv. Comm. Notes to 803 say that "neither this rule nor Rule 804 dispenses with the requirement of firsthand knowledge." But most courts interpreting 803(8) in particular have concluded that as long as the report seems trustworthy, the fact that the report is based in part on statements by third parties rather than entirely on the first-hand knowledge of the government author is ***irrelevant***.

RELATED ISSUE 2: Suppose the report ***quoted statements by individuals*** (e.g., "Joe Smith, who works for Ma Belle, told the investigator, 'I've never seen racial discrimination at the company.' ") Such statements by non-government third-parties are ***not*** admissible under 803(8)(A)(iii) to prove what the statements assert; only findings and conclusions *by* the government workers who prepared the report, not statements made *to* the preparers, fall within the exception.

71. No, because the notes weren't made by an official who was ***under a duty to report*** the event. The relevant Rule (FRE 803(8)(A)(ii)) allows admission of "a matter observed while under a legal duty to report[.]" The facts tell us that it's ***not*** the mayor's job to report on, or record, events like this, so the "legal duty to report" condition isn't satisfied.

RELATED ISSUE: If necessary, the notes could be used by the Lord Mayor to *refresh* his memory while on the stand. If that didn't work, they might then be admissible as a "recorded recollection" under FRE 803(5), if it was shown that the notes were made when the events were fresh in his memory.

72. No. The report would have to come in, if at all, under FRE 803(8)(A)(ii), covering reports of "a matter observed while under a legal duty to report[.]" But the problem is that (A)(ii) contains a special (and very important) exclusion: it ***excludes*** "in a ***criminal case*** a matter observed by ***law enforcement personnel***." It was precisely to prevent police reports from being used against criminal defendants that the exclusion was adopted.

RELATED ISSUE: Suppose the prosecution tried to get the report in as a "***business record***" under FRE 803(6) (and suppose the report met all the requirements for business records, e.g., made by a person with knowledge, kept in the course of a regularly conducted business activity, etc.). Does the fact that the report is specifically excluded under 803(8) mean that it can't come in under 803(6) either? Most courts have concluded that the answer is "*yes*" — that Congress, in prohibiting use of law enforcement reports against criminal defendants in 803(8)(A)(ii), meant to keep them out for purposes of all other hearsay exclusions (such as the business records and "catchall" exceptions). See, e.g., *U.S. v. Oates* (2d Cir. 1977). (But a court might allow the report to be used as *past recollection recorded* if Madison took the stand but couldn't remember the incident.)

73. **The "ancient documents" exception**. FRE 803(16) provides a hearsay exception for "A statement in a document that was prepared before January 1, 1998, and whose authenticity is established." So the letter qualifies as long as its authenticity is established. FRE 901(b)(8) specifies that an ancient document can be authenticated by "evidence that it: (A) is in a condition that creates no suspicion about its authenticity; (B) was in a place where, if authentic, it would likely be; and (C) is at least 20 years old when offered."

Here, there's nothing to create suspicion that the document may be invalid; a safe deposit box is a logical place for a person's important correspondence to be; and the date on the letter (plus the length of time since the last opening of the box) indicates that the document is at least 20 years old. So the letter's authenticity will probably be found to be established even without testimony that Tine wrote it, and the 803(16) hearsay exception will apply so that statements in the letter can come in.

74. **No**. It's true that normally, newspaper articles, if introduced to prove the truth of statements contained in them, are hearsay (and usually not within any exception). But a newspaper's stock-price listings fall within FRE 803(17)'s exception for "market quotations, lists, directories, or other compilations that are generally relied on by the public or by persons in particular occupations.

75. **Yes, it's admissible under FRE 803(9), the *"public records of vital statistics"* provision**. That provision grants a hearsay exception for "A record of a ***birth, death,*** or ***marriage***, if reported to a public office in accordance with a legal duty." Since doctors are everywhere required to fill out a death certificate giving a cause of death for one who dies while under the doctor's care, the certificate here was "reported to a public office in accordance with a legal duty." The fact that the doctor was ***not himself a public official*** (thus preventing the certificate from being a "record of a public office" as required by the basic public-records exception, FRE 803(8)) is ***irrelevant***. (Indeed, it's precisely to reach records of vital statistics reported by non-public persons that FRE 803(9) exists.)

76. **It's admissible under the *"former testimony"* exception** given in FRE 804(b)(1). All four requirements for this exception are satisfied, because: (1) Hare is ***"unavailable"*** (see below for why), (2) his former testimony was made at a "hearing" (since a preliminary hearing is a form of hearing); (3) Burke had an ***opportunity*** to ***cross-examine*** Hare at the preliminary exam (every defendant has such a right), and (4) Burke had a ***"similar motive"*** to cross-examine Hare at the preliminary exam as at the trial (since the same facts and issues were involved). Note that the witness's ***refusal to testify*** at the present trial (after being ordered to do so) is sufficient to make him "unavailable"; see FRE 804(a)(2). (At common law, simple refusal *wouldn't* suffice.)

77. **Not unless Dreyfus is *unavailable* to testify** (something the facts do not suggest to be so). Under FRE 804(b)(1), former testimony cannot be introduced unless the declarant is unavailable to testify. If Dreyfus *were* unavailable, the testimony would qualify because: there is a substantial identity of parties and issues, the former testimony was at a "hearing," and the party against whom the testimony is now sought to be used (Kato) had an opportunity and similar incentive to cross-examine the witness.

78. **No**. Under FRE 804(b)(1), to qualify for the former testimony exception, the testimony must have been

given in a "*hearing,*" trial or legal deposition, and the party against whom the evidence is now offered must have had a chance to examine (usually cross-examine) the witness. Here, Mama was not testifying at a "hearing," trial or deposition, and Goldilocks had no opportunity to cross-examine her. (So affidavits will *never* qualify; nor will testimony at coroner's inquests, nor *grand jury* testimony offered against a criminal defendant.)

79. **Objection overruled.**   Under the former testimony exception to the hearsay rule, it doesn't matter whether the witness was *actually* cross-examined at the first trial, as long as the party against whom the evidence is now sought to be used had an *opportunity and similar incentive to do so.*   All the other requirements of the exception are apparently fulfilled — it is former testimony, at a "hearing," and the declarant is unavailable — so the testimony will be admissible.

80. **Objection overruled.**   Master's statement is an out-of-court statement that is being offered to prove the truth of the matter asserted — that the butler "did it." So it's hearsay. However, the statement qualifies as a *dying declaration*. FRE 804(b)(2) gives an exception for: "In a prosecution for *homicide* or in a *civil* case, a statement that the declarant, *while believing the declarant's death to be imminent*, made *about its cause or circumstances.*"

Here, we have: (1) a homicide prosecution; (2) a statement made at a time when the declarant (Master) believed he was about to die; (3) explaining the cause of the impending death (action by the butler); and (4) declarant now unavailable (required for all FRE 804 exceptions), so all requirements are met.

81. **No.**   Under the FRE (and the common law, as well), the statement doesn't fit the dying declaration exception, because *Caesar is available to testify*.   The out-of-court statement here, "Et tu, Brute?" is being offered to prove the truth of its assertion — that Brutus did it.   The statement doesn't fit the "dying declaration" exception of FRE 804(b)(2), because that exception requires that the declarant be unavailable to testify at trial. (Normally, of course, the declarant will be dead, and thus indisputably unavailable; but a declarant who recovers and is unavailable for some other reason can nonetheless qualify, under the FRE.) (Recall that at common law, the declarant must *actually have died* in order for the statement to fit the dying declaration exception.)

82. **No.**   Dying declarations are only admissible, under FRE 804(b)(2), "in a prosecution for *homicide* or in a civil case." (But if Iva were being prosecuted for *killing* Rosebud, Rosebud's statement *would* qualify as a dying declaration under FRE 804(b)(2), because Rosebud is unavailable, she believed she was about to die, and the statement concerned her personal knowledge as to the circumstances of her death.)

NOTE: Under the traditional common law rule, the dying declaration exception could *only* be utilized in homicide cases; the FRE allow the exception in civil cases as well.

83. **As a "statement against interest"** (also colloquially called a "declaration against interest") (FRE 804(b)(3)). The statement qualifies, because it was *against the declarant's proprietary interest when made* (Khufu was admitting the Pyramid wasn't solely his), *made knowingly and willingly* and with *no motive to lie,* and Khufu is now *unavailable* as a witness.   Therefore, it's admissible, even though it's hearsay.

84. **No, probably.**   Although the FRE allow declarations against penal interest within the hearsay exception, there's a proviso: if, as here, the statement is offered in a criminal case and tends to expose the declarant to criminal liability, it's not admissible unless it's *"supported by corroborating circumstances that clearly indicate its trustworthiness*[.]" FRE 804(b)(3)(B). This requirement is especially focused at situations in which the statement exculpates an accused. Its rationale is that declarants who are friends or rel-

atives of an accused are likely to have an incentive to try to shield the accused from liability, and thus may not be trustworthy; therefore, we need extra guarantees of reliability in this situation. There do not seem to be any such corroborating circumstances present here.

85. **No, for two distinct reasons**. The first issue, of course, is whether these statements implicating Ernie can come in as declarations against interest. The particular statements that the prosecution seeks to introduce were not themselves specifically against Bert's interest (since they shifted blame to Ernie, and didn't further implicate Bert beyond the extent to which he was already implicated by virtue of having gotten caught red-handed with the 19 kilos). These statements were, however, *"collateral"* to the explicitly self-inculpatory ones; that is, they were part of the same overall narrative, and concerned the same overall events. The Supreme Court has held that, in federal courts interpreting FRE 804(b)(3), a non-self-inculpatory statement **cannot be admitted as a declaration against interest** merely by virtue of the fact that the statement is "collateral to" (i.e., related to) a declaration that is self-inculpatory; only if the **particular declaration in question** is against the declarant's interest can it come in. See *Williamson v. U.S.* (U.S. 1994), a case whose facts are similar to those of this question. So only those individual declarations by Bert that specifically inculpate him can be admitted against Ernie under 804(b)(3). (*State* courts construing provisions similar to 804(b)(3) are not bound by the *Williamson* decision, which affects only the FRE *per se*.)

A second problem with allowing Otto to recount Bert's statement is that this would violate Ernie's rights under the **Confrontation Clause** of the Sixth Amendment to the federal constitution. According to *Crawford v. Washington* (U.S. 2004), any out-of-court *"testimonial"* statement can be admitted against an accused only if the maker of the statement is available for cross-examination either at the time the statement was made or at the accused's trial. (See *infra*, p. 364.) *Crawford* makes it clear that statements given in response to a police interrogation that's not focused on an ongoing emergency are "testimonial" for this purpose, so Bert's statements while under interrogation by Otto are testimonial. The facts tell us that Bert has refused to repeat his story inculpating Ernie at Ernie's trial, so Bert is not "available for cross-examination" about the story. Consequently, Bert's entire story — even the parts that *do* specifically implicate Bert — may not be admitted against Ernie on account of the Confrontation Clause.

86. **It's admissible under the FRE's "reputation/family history" hearsay exception**. Under FRE 804(b)(4)(A), an unavailable declarant's statement about his *own* birth or similar fact of personal or family history is admissible, "even though the declarant had no way of acquiring personal knowledge about that fact[.]" Since Bart is dead, and thus unavailable, his statement about his age falls under the exception. (804(b)(4)(_B_), which applies to statements about a person made by a relative or intimate associate, would similarly apply, if Molly testified, "Bart's mother, Marge, told me just before Bart's death that Bart was 33." Marge would, however, have to be unavailable.)

RELATED ISSUE: Suppose Molly's testimony was, "I lived with Bart, and although he never told me his age, at his death he was **reputed** by his family to have been 33." This, too, would be admissible; FRE 803(19) gives a hearsay exception for "a reputation among a person's family ... or among a person's associates or in the community ... concerning the person's birth, adoption, legitimacy, ancestry, marriage, divorce, death, relationship by blood, adoption, or marriage, or similar facts of personal or family history." (Note that for this "reputation" exception, *neither* the person whom the reputation concerns, nor any person whose statements were the source of the witness's knowledge of the reputation, need be unavailable.)

87. **Yes**. The tavern can use the deposition as substantive evidence under FRE 801(d)(1)(A), which defines as non-hearsay a **prior inconsistent statement** given **under penalty of perjury** (i.e., under oath) at a **trial**,

hearing or other proceeding, or in a *deposition*, if the declarant is *available to testify* and be *cross-examined*. Since the deposition testimony isn't hearsay, it's substantively admissible (to prove the truth of the matter asserted in it). (Note that the tavern could also use the deposition testimony to *impeach* Crassus; when a prior inconsistent statement is used to impeach a witness, the statement is never considered hearsay, because it's offered to prove that the witness is not credible because he's changed his story, not offered to prove the truth of the matter asserted in the prior inconsistent statement.)

88. **No, since it's a *prior identification*.** Under FRE 801(d)(1)(C), *an out-of-court statement identifying a person, made after the declarant has perceived him or her and where the declarant is presently testifying and available for cross-examination, is specifically excluded as non-hearsay.* (The same rule applies at common law.)

89. **Objection sustained.** The picture is not admissible as a prior identification, since Fifi *isn't presently testifying* and *isn't available for cross-examination*; under FRE 801(d)(1)(C), these two requirements are *prerequisites* for a prior identification's admissibility. Without them, the prior identification is hearsay. (That is, it's the equivalent of Fifi's saying out of court, "The person who stabbed Marat looked like this. . . .") (Note that although the picture's hearsay, it may still be admissible under the *present sense impression* exception to the hearsay rule, assuming the picture was drawn immediately after Fifi saw Corday entering and leaving the bathroom.)

Anyway, there's probably a second difficulty with admitting the picture. According to *Crawford v. Washington* (U.S. 2004), the Sixth Amendment's **Confrontation Clause** means that any out-of-court *"testimonial"* statement can be admitted against an accused only if the maker of the statement is *available for cross-examination* either at the time the statement was made or at the accused's trial. (See *infra*, p. 364.) Responses to a police interrogation whose purpose is to build a case for prosecutors are considered testimonial. Therefore, the drawing is probably "testimonial," since the picture is the equivalent of Fifi's telling the police, under interrogation, "The stabber looked like this." Since Fifi was never subjected to cross-examination by Corday (and obviously won't be now at Corday's trial, since Fifi's dead), *Crawford* should block the use of the picture on Confrontation Clause grounds).

90. **The "residual" or "catchall" exception** of FRE 807. The testimony can't come in under the former-testimony exception of 804(b)(1), because the party against whom it's now offered (Sneezy) didn't have an opportunity to cross-examine Grumpy (one witness never has an opportunity to cross-examine another at a grand jury).

Under the residual exception of 807, hearsay can come in even though it doesn't meet a specific exception, if: (1) the statement has *"circumstantial guarantees of trustworthiness"* that are "equivalent" to those inherent in the specific exceptions; (2) the statement is offered as evidence of a *"material fact"*; (3) the statement is *"more probative* on the point for which it is offered than *any other evidence* that the proponent can obtain through reasonable efforts"; (4) use of the evidence is consistent with "the interests of justice"; and (5) the proponent gives *advance notice* of his intention to offer the statement.

Here, (2) through (4) seem satisfied, given the absence of any other evidence and the centrality of the issue to which the testimony relates. (5) can be satisfied as long as the prosecutor gives Sneezy advance notice (enough in advance to give Sneezy a "fair opportunity to meet" the evidence"). The real issues are: (a) does the statement have the requisite "circumstantial guarantees of trustworthiness"?; and (b) can the residual or catchall exception be applied to situations that "just miss" qualifying for a specific exception?

As to issue (a), probably the requisite circumstantial guarantees of trustworthiness are satisfied. Grumpy had no apparent motive to lie (for instance, he was not himself a suspect). Also, he was testifying about matters that he claimed to have himself witnessed (not merely repeating something someone else told him, for instance). Additionally, he was testifying under oath. (Lastly, the fact that Grumpy's unavailability seems to be due to intimidation by Sneezy would also weigh in favor of admitting the transcript.) As to issue (b), most courts are willing to apply the residual exception even where the facts "just miss" qualifying for a specific exception (here, the exception for former testimony). A few courts, however, might hold that Congress carefully considered the grand jury situation when it codified the former-testimony exception, and made a clear policy decision — which a court considering the residual exception shouldn't overturn — that former testimony shouldn't be usable against one who had no opportunity to cross-examine the witness at the time the testimony was given.

Notice that the question tells you to ignore any constitutional issues. That's because *Crawford v. Washington, infra*, p. 364, would probably make Grumpy's grand jury testimony inadmissible as a violation of Sneezy's Sixth Amendment **Confrontation Clause** rights. *Crawford* says that any out-of-court **"testimonial"** statement can be admitted against an accused only if the maker of the statement is available for cross-examination either at the time the statement was made or at the accused's trial. (See *infra*, p. 364.) It's perfectly clear that statements made to a grand jury are "testimonial" for this purpose, and also clear that (1) Grumpy wasn't available for cross-examination by Sneezy at the grand jury; and (2) Grumpy's refusal to testify at Sneezy's trial means that Grumpy is "unavailable for cross-examination" at trial, as *Crawford* uses that term. Therefore, even if the requirements of the catchall are satisfied, the statement can't come in because of *Crawford*.

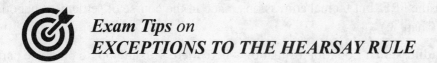

Exam Tips on
EXCEPTIONS TO THE HEARSAY RULE

Once you've concluded that something is hearsay, you'll of course need to determine whether it falls within one of the many exceptions to the hearsay rule. The substantial majority of test items that are hearsay will turn out to fall within an exception, and of those that don't, most will raise an issue about whether they fall within an exception.

THE "DECLARANT'S AVAILABILITY IRRELEVANT" EXCEPTIONS

Admissions by a Party-Opponent

The "admissions" exception is probably the most frequently-tested of all hearsay exceptions. Here's what to look for:

☛ **Party:** Most obviously, remember that the exception only applies where the out-of-court statement is made by a *party* to the present proceeding.

    ☞ *Common trap:* The statement is made by a **bystander witness** or a non-party **passenger** in a car. Even if this person is *closely linked to a party*, her statement regarding the accident is still not an admission as long as there's no principal-agent relationship between the declarant and the party against whom the statement is now sought to be used.

    Example: A car driven by Driver, and in which Passenger, Driver's friend, is riding, hits Pedestrian. Shortly after, Passenger tells Officer, "We were returning from a party, at which Driver was drinking." In Pedestrian's suit against Driver, Passenger's statement to Officer is not admissible against Driver as an admission, because Passenger isn't a party, and there's no relationship (e.g., principal and agent) by which Passenger's statement could be attributed to Driver. In fact, the statement doesn't fall within any exception, and is thus inadmissible hearsay. (But if the statement had been made by Driver, not Passenger, it would be admissible against him as an admission.)

Similar issue: Often, the declarant will be so ***closely aligned*** in interest with a party that you might be duped into thinking the declarant is a party — but the requirement that declarant be a party is very ***tightly construed***. (*Example:* The administrator of X's estate sues Orderly, an orderly in the hospital where X died, seeking the return of a watch which Orderly allegedly took. Orderly wants to testify that X told him, "Take this watch; it's a gift from me to you." This statement is not an admission, because it was made by X, and X is not a party, only his estate is.)

☞ **Against party:** Also, make sure the statement is being offered ***against***, not for, the party who made it.

☞ Remember that for admissions, there is ***no*** requirement that the party who made the statement be ***unavailable*** to testify.

☞ **Combinations:** Heavily-tested area: admissions ***combined*** with statements containing facts about insurance, offers to settle, or offers to pay medical bills. (Here, you just have to memorize the rules. For instance, factual admissions made while offering to pay medical bills are admissible under the FRE, but factual admissions made in the course of settlement negotiations aren't. See Chap. 3.)

☞ **Representative admissions:** Look for a situation where there's an attempt to bind one party with an admission ***made by another person***.

  ☞ **Vicarious admission:** Commonly, a party tries to use an ***employee's*** statement ***against the employer***, arguing that the employer is vicariously responsible for the statement. Two main tricks to watch out for (especially under FRE 801(d)(2)(D)):

    ☞ **Timing:** First, make sure the statement was made at a ***time when the employment relationship existed***. (*Example:* P is injured when a plane he's flying in, owned and operated by D airline, crashes. P offers the testimony of Investigator, who says, "I interviewed Walter after the crash. Walter was a mechanic for D at the time of the crash. Walter told me that before the crash, he told the president of D that the plane had cracks, but the president ignored him. Immediately after the crash, Walter was fired; he told me that this had happened as part of a cover-up by D." Walter's entire out-of-court statement is not admissible against D as a vicarious admission, because when it was made, Walter was no longer an employee of D.)

    ☞ **Scope:** Second, make sure that that statement concerns a matter ***within the scope of the employment relationship***. Commonly-tested: An employee is involved in a car accident, and statements made by him are sought to be attributed to the employer.

Example (within relationship): An accident occurs when a delivery van driver is en route making a delivery for his employer; the driver's statement about the accident to a witness is admissible against the employer.

Example (not within relationship): In a drug case against D, Officer testifies that D tried to buy drugs from Officer. W, D's girlfriend, testifies for D, "Once Officer arrested me for prostitution, and told me he'd let me off if I bribed him. I said I wouldn't, and he said he'd get me and my friends." This isn't admissible against the government as a vicarious admission, because Officer's solicitation of bribes, and threat of revenge, probably weren't within the scope of his employment relationship. [However, it would be admissible to *impeach* Officer by showing bias, subject perhaps to the need to lay a foundation by first questioning Officer about the episode. See Chap. 4.]

☞ Note that the statement of the employee may not be used to establish the employer-employee relationship. This must be proven *independently*.

☞ Also, note that at common-law, the employee must be shown to have been *authorized* by the employer to *make the statement* (it's not enough that the statement was about a matter falling within the scope of employment). But under FRE 801(d)(2)(D), this requirement is *dropped* — as long as the matter is within the scope of employment, the employee *doesn't need to have been authorized to speak about it*.

☞ **Adoptive admission:** If a party hears or sees another person's statement, and by her words or actions indicates that she "accepts" or "adopts" that statement, the statement is binding on the party as an admission.

☞ Most frequently-tested: an *implied* admission. Here, *A* claims that *B*'s *silence* in the face of a statement made by someone other than *B* amounts to an adoption by B of the statement. The test is, would a reasonable person in B's position have denied the statement had it not been true?

☞ Examples where silence is unreasonable (so adoption applies):

A is accused of murder or some other heinous crime;
A is accused of mislabelling his products;
A is told, "You know that's your signature" while being shown a contract.

In all 3 of the above examples, the statement will be admissible against *A* as an adoptive admission.

☞ **Co-conspirator's statement:** Where an out-of-court statement is made by one conspirator implicating another, the statement can often be introduced against the latter. Check that the statement was made: (1) while the conspiracy was *still in force*, and (2) in *furtherance* of that conspiracy. (FRE 801(d)(2)(E)).

☞ Most frequently-tested: the "in furtherance" requirement, when applied to *confessions*, *narratives of past events*, and *finger-pointing* by the declarant against one who ends up being the defendant. If the court applies the "in furtherance" requirement strictly, to mean "in an attempt to advance the conspiracy's objectives," all of these kinds of statements *won't* be admissible. (But a lot of courts don't apply the requirement very strictly.) (*Example:* After a burglary, the police catch X in a chase. X says, "You never would have caught me if D hadn't been so slow in finishing the job." This statement would probably be found not to have been made in furtherance of the conspiracy, and would thus not be usable as an admission against D at D's criminal trial for the burglary.)

☞ Keep in mind that the same out-of-court statement may sometimes be admissible *both* as a *prior inconsistent statement* for impeachment purposes, and as an admission for substantive purposes. This is likely to be true wherever a party makes an out-of-court statement that contradicts his trial testimony. (*Example:* P and D have a car accident. P hires an undercover investigator, W, who engages D in what seems to be a random conversation in a bar. D tells W, "I had a six-pack before the accident, but the police never tested me." At trial, D testifies on direct that he drove carefully and in full possession of his faculties, and on cross denies having ever said otherwise in any conversation in a bar. As part of P's case, W's testimony about what D told him in the bar will be admissible both as a prior inconsistent statement to impeach D, and substantively as an admission against a party-opponent.)

☞ **Distinction:** Keep straight the differences between an admission and a *declaration against interest*: a declaration against interest must be against the declarant's interest *at the time it was made* (an admission doesn't have to be); applies only when the declarant is *unavailable* (no such rule applies to admissions); and may be offered into evidence *by the party who made it* (whereas the admission may be used only *against* the party who made it).

☞ Quick rule of thumb: If used *against* the party who made it, always treat the statement as an admission. If used *by* the party who made it, or if *made by a non-party*, the statement can't be an admission, and will have to be a declaration against interest (if anything).

☞ When you're writing about the FRE, note in your answer that the admission is *nonhearsay* (not "hearsay subject to an exception," as at common law). This makes no practical difference, but it tends to show your grasp of fine distinctions.

Statements about a Person's Physical Condition

Look for a person's statement about her *physical condition*.

☞ **Treatment or diagnosis:** If the statement is made for purposes of obtaining *medical diagnosis or treatment*, then it's admissible if told to a physician, nurse, ambulance driver, hospital check-in clerk, etc. (FRE 803(4)). (*Example:* P is injured in a car crash with D, taken to the hospital, and then complains of severe pain. P dies from the injuries. The statement is admissible at trial against D to prove damages.)

☞ Remember that in this "diagnosis or treatment" situation, the statement can be about *either past or present* physical sensation. (*Example:* P says to Doctor, "Before the accident, I had no pain, and was able to hold a full-time job doing heavy lifting." As long as this statement related to P's attempt to get treatment or diagnosis, Doctor can repeat the statement at P's trial, even though the statement, when made, related to P's past rather than present physical condition.)

☞   Even if the doctor is consulted only in ***anticipation of litigation*** (e.g., to get the doctor to testify as an expert witness for the plaintiff), the person's statements can come in, as long as they're relevant to "diagnosis."

☞   Commonly-tested: the ***cause*** of the injury is included in the statement. If (and only if) it's ***pertinent to the diagnosis***, then it's admissible. (*Examples:* (1) Patient tells Doctor, "When I was hit by the car, my elbow hit the ground hard and I heard a sharp crack"; statement admissible. (2) Hospital record reads, "Patient says ladder collapsed and Patient fell." Record probably admissible to prove cause of accident. (3) Patient tells Doctor, "I was on my bicycle and D ran a stop light and knocked me to the ground." Part about the stop light inadmissible, because not reasonably pertinent to the diagnosis; rest of statement probably admissible.)

☞   Check to make sure the statement is made ***to*** the doctor, not ***by*** the doctor. (*Example:* Civil suit involving injuries from car crash. P is examined by MD. MD signs an affidavit saying that P is suffering from back spasms. The affidavit will not be admissible under the "statement of physical condition" exception, because it's MD's statement about what he found, not a repeating of P's statement about his physical condition.)

☞   Statement can be made by ***one other than the patient*** (e.g., a friend or relative assisting the patient), if it concerns the patient's physical condition and is reasonably pertinent to treatment or diagnosis. (*Example:* P is unconscious after car accident; H, P's husband, brings her to hospital and says to ER doctor, "She was hit from the rear while on her bike." Admissible.)

☛ **Statements not in connection with treatment or diagnosis:** But where the statement about the speaker's physical condition is ***not*** made for the purpose of getting treatment or diagnosis, different (and more limiting) rules apply.

☞   Most important (and most often tested): The statement must be about the speaker's ***present*** (not past) physical condition. (*Example:* P says to W, his wife (a layperson), "Honey, I fell on the ice in front of D's house yesterday and it really hurt when it happened." Not admissible, because not a statement about P's *present* physical condition.)

☞   On the other hand, the statement can be made to a ***layperson***, i.e., one not connected with the giving of medical care or diagnosis. (*Example:* Same facts as prior example, but P says to wife W, "My back is still hurting from the fall yesterday." W can repeat the statement at trial.)

☞   Note that a statement about one's present physical condition may also come in as a statement of ***present sense impression***. (*Example:* P says over telephone, "Ouch, I just cut myself slicing bread.")

☛ For the two categories of "statement about physical condition" (for treatment/diagnosis or not), note that the declarant ***need not be unavailable***.

Statements about Declarant's Mental State

Statements about the declarant's ***present state of mind*** are sometimes admissible, sometimes not.

☛ When a declarant expresses *an intention or desire to do something,* the "present state of mind" exception usually applies, and the statement is admissible to prove that the declarant *in fact did that something*.

Example 1: Declarant's statement, "I'm going to call P and tell him to go ahead with the portrait" is admissible to prove that Declarant probably later accepted P's offer to paint Declarant's portrait.

Example 2: Declarant tells W, "I'm going to use my friend Ed's cabin this weekend." Admissible to prove that Declarant went to the cabin that weekend.

☞ Common scenario: Declarant's desire to commit suicide. (*Example:* "I have nothing to live for," admissible to prove that declarant probably committed suicide.)

☞ Watch out for cases where declarant mentions says that he or she plans to take an act *in conjunction with another person*. The statement will only be admissible to prove that the *other person* participated in the act, if there is *independent corroboration* that that participation occurred (and some courts won't let it in even in that event). (*Example:* Bonnie tells W, "Clyde and I plan to hold up the post office tomorrow." This will clearly be admissible to show that Bonnie held up the post office, but will be admissible to show that Clyde held up the post office only if there's some independent corroborative evidence that he did. Furthermore, some courts won't allow it against Clyde even with corroboration.)

☞ **Common application of this rule:** Murder victim says, "I'm going to meet with D." Not admissible to show D met with or murdered victim, unless there's corroboration that they met.

☛ **Past state of mind:** Statements about declarant's *past state of mind* are generally *inadmissible*. In other words, the declarant's statement must be about her *then-existing state of mind*, not her state of mind at some materially earlier moment. (*Example:* Defamation action. D newspaper offers testimony by W that Reporter told W, "When I wrote that piece on P two days ago, I believed every word of it." Not admissible, because Reporter's statement relates to his state of mind on a prior, not the present, occasion.)

☛ **Memory or belief:** Similarly, statements about declarant's *present memory or belief about past events* are generally *inadmissible to show the fact remembered or believed*. (*Example:* Victim says, "I believe that Dr. Shepard has poisoned me." Inadmissible, because although it's a statement about declarant's present belief, that belief relates to a past event.)

☞ But remember that there's an exception for *will* contests. (FRE 803(3), last clause.) (*Example:* Decedent tells W, "In the will I wrote last year, I left $10,000 to my son Mark." Admissible to show that at the time the will was written, Decedent intended to leave Mark the money.)

Excited Utterances

Whenever the declarant *blurts something out* at the *scene of an accident or crime*, the statement is probably admissible as an *"excited utterance."*

☛ Memorize the FRE test (803(2)): the exception applies to "a statement *relating to a startling event or condition*, made while the declarant was **under the stress of excitement that it caused**." Check for both elements: (1) **startling event** or condition; and (2) stress **caused by** the event or condition.

☛ Most frequently-tested: Make sure that the **amount of time** that has passed since the event is **short enough** that the declarant is **still under the stress**. Be skeptical of anything more than 1/2 hour or so, unless declarant was in shock, unconscious, or otherwise unable to reflect about the matter. (*Example:* A statement made by an accident victim the day after the accident, where the victim never went into shock or lost consciousness, will clearly not qualify.)

   ☞ But *some* time may pass between event and utterance — it's the *present sense impression* exception (see below), *not* the excited utterance exception, that requires true contemporaneity between event and statement.

☛ Frequently-tested: Even if the **identity of the declarant is unknown**, the statement is still **admissible**. (*Example:* P falls on steps. At the civil trial, W testifies for defense, "Just after P fell, I heard someone in the crowd say, 'She was taking the steps three at a time and tripped.'" Admissible even if the declarant's identity is not shown.)

Present Sense Impression

If you have a declarant **describing or explaining an event that's occurring at that very moment**, or that has **just** occurred, think of the **"present sense impression"** exception. A present sense impression must be **contemporaneous** with, or **immediately** following, the observation.

☛ Distinguish present sense impression from excited utterance:

   ☞ PSS is narrower, in the sense that very little time must elapse between event and statement. But it's broader, in the sense that PSS may relate to a **non-startling** and **non-stressful event**. So look for PSS especially where the event appears routine and non-startling at the time.

      Example: A witness to a car accident reports to a police officer, "A few minutes ago I saw. . . ." Not a PSS, because not contemporaneous. (Might be excited utterance, depending on how "shook up" the witness still was.)

      Example: Witness watches a car accident, and within 5 seconds after impact, says, "The red car didn't have its headlights on." PSS (and probably also excited utterance).

☛ Where declarant is making a statement about his **current physical condition**, especially about *pain* he's feeling, note that this is likely to be **both** PSS and "statement of physical condition."

Past Recollection Recorded

If a witness on the stand **cannot remember**, and there exists a writing written by the witness regarding the subject matter of the questioning, consider whether the **past recollection recorded** exception applies.

☛ Check for the following requirements: (1) the writer (or the source of the information) **had personal knowledge** of what he was writing; (2) the writing was made **shortly after the** *event*, so that it was fresh in the writer's or source's memory; (3) the writer or source can testify as to the *accuracy* of the writing; and (4) the writer/witness's recollection is *presently impaired*.

☛ Most-often tested: Did the writer have the required *first-hand knowledge* of the subject matter of the writing? If the writer is recording another person's declaration, the required knowledge will usually be missing if only the writer testifies.

 ☞ Common scenario: A police officer writes an accident report at the scene of an accident, and includes in it a statement by W, a witness. At trial, the officer cannot by himself read W's statement from his report, because the officer has no first-hand knowledge of the matters recited in the W's statement. (But the statement *can* be introduced if W testifies to having made it when his own memory was fresh, *and* the officer also testifies to writing it down accurately.)

Business Records

Whenever there's an attempt to admit a *writing* into evidence to prove that an event mentioned in the writing occurred, consider whether the document may be admitted as a *business record*.

☛ **Test for business record:** A writing is admissible as a business record if: (1) the writing was made *at or near the time* of an event, (2) by, or from information supplied by, a *person with knowledge*; (3) the writing was *kept in the course of a regularly conducted business activity*; and (4) it was the business' *regular practice to make the record* (i.e., the record was *"regularly kept"*), (5) all as shown by the testimony of a *qualified witness*. FRE 803(6).

☛ *Examples of business records:* An answering service's telephone message log; a patient's chart in a hospital; a business' invoice showing that a shipment was made.

 ☞ Many times the same document may be considered both a business and a public record. Don't forget to mention both options. (*Example:* A police report made at the scene of an accident, in a jurisdiction that defines "business" broadly to include "institutions" and non-profit organizations, as the FRE do.)

☛ **Document must be offered in evidence:** Do a threshold check to see if the business records exception is even plausible to apply in the circumstances. The fact that the substance of a witness's trial testimony has previously been recorded in a business record is irrelevant — unless the *file or record itself* is being *admitted into evidence*, the business records exception doesn't apply. (*Example:* Supervisor testifies at trial to details about a construction job, including the number of workers used and the number of hours spent. The facts indicate that Supervisor had previously recorded these facts in a notebook, as part of his office routine. The notebook is not sought to be introduced. Because the notebook isn't coming in, the fact that the matters on which Supervisor is testifying were recorded in a business record is irrelevant — Supervisor's testimony is admissible as his first-hand non-hearsay knowledge, without reference to the business records exception.)

☛ Look for a record that was made in the *regular course of business* and in conjunction with the company's primary business.

 ☞ Commonly tested: *Accident or investigative reports* made by a business in anticipation of litigation. If the report is not related to a business activity of the entity, then it is not a business record, even though it is done routinely. In other words, if the sole purpose of the accident report is to **prepare for litigation**, it's probably not a business record; but if it's done for "regular" business reasons (e.g., to prevent similar occurrences by changing the way the business operates), it may be a business record. (*Example:* After an on-campus rape, Prexy, President of the College, interviews the victim in order to help the police arrest the rapist. Prexy takes notes of the victim's statements, and puts the notes in a file. This is probably not a business record, because it's probably not sufficiently related to the college's regular business.)

☞ Confirm that the source of the material had **personal knowledge** of the items reported. By "source of the material," we don't necessarily mean the person who wrote the entries. *A* may recite matters to *B*, who enters them in the record; in that case, all that's required is that *A*, not *B*, have personal knowledge. (*Example: A* and *B* both work for Company. *A* inspects the contents of each shipment, and orally says to *B*, "The computer-generated invoice for this shipment is correct." *B* then writes on the invoice, "Shipment of these items confirmed." If *B* testifies at trial that the invoices were routinely marked this way based on oral statements by a person with knowledge, then a particular such invoice is admissible to show that the goods noted on it were in fact shipped; no testimony by *A* is needed.)

☞ **Foundation:** Check to see that there was a **foundation** laid for each business record. However, this foundation can be laid by anyone with personal knowledge of **the routine** (i.e., that the records were routinely kept in the ordinary course of the business, based on input from someone with personal knowledge, etc.), **not necessarily someone with personal knowledge of how the routine was applied in this particular instance.** Thus in the above example, even *C* — let's say, an office manager who did not personally make the entries — could lay the foundation by saying in essence "It was our company practice to have each shipment checked by someone, and then the checker or someone working with the checker noted the confirmation on the invoice." In fact, it wouldn't matter that *C* didn't know the identity of the person who had the knowledge, or the person who made the notation, in this particular invoice — it's enough that *C* has knowledge of how the routine *generally* worked.

☞ **Certification:** Also, keep in mind that this foundation need **not** be laid by **live testimony** — it can instead be laid by a **certification** (a document) from a person with relevant knowledge, who says in the certification that the record satisfies the business-records exception. Cite to FRE 902(11) (certified records of regularly conducted activity) on this point.

☞ **Business duty:** Check that the **source** of the knowledge had a **business duty** to make the report. If not, many (though not all) courts will keep the evidence out, perhaps on grounds of untrustworthiness.

☞ *Typical application:* **Accident report**, in which declarant is a **witness who does not work for the business** that is preparing the report. (*Example:* P slips and falls in Store. W, another shopper, says to Manager, "P was running when she fell." Manager quotes this statement in an "accident report" routinely kept by Store. Most courts won't allow this report to come in as a business record, because W was not an employee of the business, and thus had no business duty to supply the information; the fact that W is not under the business' control also may make it less likely that W's information is trustworthy.)

☞   However, even if the source did not have a business duty to make the report, the source's statement as recorded in the business record will be admissible if it independently falls within *some other hearsay exception*. (*Example:* Same facts as above, but it's *P*, not *L*, who says to Manager, "I was running when I fell." Manager's report will be admissible against P, because the report was kept as a business record [assuming that it was kept for regular business reasons and not in anticipation of litigation], and P's own statement contained within the report is an admission when used against P.)

☛ Remember that *"business"* is defined very *broadly* in FRE 803(6) to include not just businesses but also "organizations" (implicitly including non-profits), "occupations," and "callings."

☛ **Trustworthiness:** In any business records issue, always check (and in an essay, discuss) the additional requirement of *trustworthiness*. Quote FRE 803(6)(E): the exception does not apply if the opponent shows that "the source of information or the method or circumstances of preparation indicate a lack of trustworthiness."

☞   Pay special attention to trustworthiness where an *accident report* is involved — if the business making the report is likely to be a defendant in litigation, the desire to avoid liability probably makes the report untrustworthy.

☞   Lack of trustworthiness can also be indicated by a lack of *detail* about *where the information came from*. (*Example:* On a death certificate, the cause of death reads, "Rung of ladder broke, and victim fell on head." If there's no indication on the certificate of where the information came from, the certificate is probably too untrustworthy to be admitted as a business record.)

☞   Pay special attention to trustworthiness where a *computer printout* is involved. Include in your answer (if essay) the special requirements that testimony include a description of: the equipment, how the computer was programmed and how errors in programming are detected and corrected, how data is entered, how errors in data are caught and corrected, and how unauthorized access to program or data files is prevented.

☞   In all of these issues involving trustworthiness, be sure to point out that under FRE 803(6)(E), the *burden is on the opponent* to show a probable *lack* of trustworthiness — in other words, there is a rebuttable presumption that the record *is* trustworthy.

☛ **Nonoccurrence:** Remember that *nonoccurrence of an event* may be proven by *lack of a record*, if it was the regular practice of the business to record all such matters. (*Example:* Libel suit against D newspaper, in a state which requires P to show he first asked for a retraction. D's office manager testifies that it's the routine practice of the paper to carefully keep in a single file all demands for retraction, and that he has searched the file for any demand by P, and found none. Admissible as a business record to show no retraction demand was made by P.)

☛ **Multiple hearsay:** Be alert to *multiple hearsay* problems, which must be analyzed layer by layer. If the business record *quotes a statement made by someone outside of the business*, and the record is offered to show the truth of that statement, the statement must itself fall within a hearsay exception. (*Example:* An operator of an answering service keeps a "Telephone Log" of all messages received. An entry in it reads, "May 3, Mr. D called P, said he accepted P's offer to paint D's portrait for $4,000." In P's contract suit against D, the log can be offered by P, but only after a multiple-hearsay analysis. The log comes in as a business record, to show that D's statement was made. D's statement itself comes in as an admission.)

☞ But where the business record quotes a statement by one working *in* the business, no multiple hearsay problem exists — the business records exception covers everything. (*Example:* A and B both work for Company. A tells B, "The shipment on order 256 was complete; I checked." B writes on the invoice, "Shipment complete." Because A worked in the business, the invoice can come in as a business record to prove the shipment was complete, and no independent hearsay analysis of A's oral statement is needed.)

Public Records

Whenever a document is prepared by a ***governmental body***, be alert to the possibility that the document may be admissible as a ***public record***. (FRE 803(8)).

Look for the public records exception in three main contexts:

❏ A government agency makes a report about its ***own activities***. (*Example:* To prove a police department tapped his phone, D could introduce an internal report prepared by the department saying, "We tapped D's phone.")

❏ A government official makes a written record of ***observations he made in the line of duty***, if his job required him to make those observations. (*Example:* In P's civil suit against D for a car crash, P could introduce a police report in which Officer says, "I saw the accident; D ran a red light.")

☞ *No criminal use:* This "observations made in the line of duty" exception does not allow the ***government*** to use the report ***against D in a criminal case***. (*Example:* Officer spots someone running away after a burglary, and writes in his report, "The burglar was a 6'2" hispanic male." In a criminal case against D for the burglary, this report can't be introduced against D. But it *can* be used *by* D to show that D doesn't fit the description.)

❏ Government ***conducts an investigation***, and makes ***factual findings*** in that investigation. The factual findings can be introduced. (*Example:* The National Transportation Safety Board investigates the crash of an airplane, and finds pilot error. In a civil suit against the airline, this report is admissible as a public record to show airline negligence.)

☞ *No criminal use:* Again, this exception ***can't be used by the government against D*** in a criminal case. (*Example:* The FBI investigates a bank robbery, and concludes in a report, "Devon did it." This report can't be introduced against Devon at his criminal trial, though it could introduced *by* Devon as a public record, if he so desired.)

☛ Be alert to the possibility that the document is a non-qualifying public record yet falls within ***some other hearsay exception***. Courts are split about what to do where the document satisfies a non-public-records hearsay exception (e.g., business records, or past recollection recorded) and is also a public record that's inadmissible under the public-records provision.

☞   In the most common case raising this issue, a ***police report*** about a crime might be an investigative report (a type of public record) and a business record. Here, the rule preventing the public record from being introduced against a criminal defendant will prevail, preventing the business-records use.

Learned Treatises

Where a published reference work is sought to be admitted for the truth of matters stated in it, think of the "learned treatise" exception (FRE 803(18)). Most frequently tested issues:

☛ The treatise can't be "free-standing" — it must come in as an ***adjunct*** to testimony by an ***expert*** witness. (It can only come in if it's ***"called to the attention"*** of an expert witness on ***cross***, or ***relied on*** by an expert on ***direct***.)

☛ Make sure that the treatise is not entered into evidence ***as an exhibit*** — all that may happen is that the publication's ***contents*** are ***read*** into the record.

☛ Make sure that the treatise is shown to be a ***reliable authority***. There are three ways to do this: by the witness herself, by another expert, or by judicial notice.

☞   When the treatise is used on cross, don't be sidetracked by the fact that the ***witness didn't rely*** on the treatise — as long as some other expert says that it's a reliable authority, or the judge takes judicial notice that it is, that's enough to allow it to be read. (*Example:* On direct, Expert 1 states that "Causes of Cancer" is a reliable authority. Now, Expert 2 may be cross-examined with passages from the book, even if Expert 2 says the book isn't authoritative, and/or denies having relied on it; these passages can be substantive as well as impeaching evidence.)

☛ The exception applies only to scholarly works. Thus it typically doesn't apply to articles in popular magazines or in general newspapers.

Commercial publications

☛ "Published compilations" can be used, if relied upon by the public for the type of information in question. (FRE 803(17). ***"Lists," "directories"*** and ***"market quotations"*** are examples. (*Example:* D is charged with burglary. He asserts the alibi defense that he was watching a particular movie on cable tv at the time. The tv listings page from the local cable guide may be introduced to prove that the movie wasn't playing on any channel at the time in question.)

Ancient documents

☛ Under the FRE, a document in existence for ***20 years*** or more can be admitted as a hearsay exception (the "ancient documents" exception), if its authenticity is established. (*Example:* The issue is whether a deed issued 15 years ago was made while the grantor, Bill, was of sound mind. An affidavit by Bill's brother Dave, signed at about the same time, states that Dave thinks Bill is insane for enumerated reasons. The affidavit is not admissible as an ancient document, because it's too new; but if it were 22 years old, it could be introduced as an ancient document, to prove that at that time Bill was insane.)

THE "DECLARANT UNAVAILABLE" EXCEPTIONS

The remaining exceptions require that the declarant be *"unavailable."*

Here are examples of fact patterns where the witness will be considered to be unavailable:

❏ W is *dead*;

❏ W deliberately *avoids service*;

❏ W does not respond to a *subpoena*;

❏ W takes the stand, but *refuses to testify*. (Most often, W takes the 5th Amendment.) It doesn't matter whether W's refusal is lawful (i.e., a privilege in fact applies) or wrongful (i.e., W can be held in contempt).

❏ W claims a *lack of memory* as to the declarant's statement.

Former Testimony

Where there is past testimony that one party wishes to offer at the present trial, but the testifier is unavailable, consider the hearsay exception for *former testimony*.

☛ Remember that the former testimony must have been given at a *"hearing."* (FRE 804(b)(1)). A "hearing" is in essence a proceeding in which the testifier testifies *under oath*, and is subject to *cross-examination*.

   ☞ *Examples that qualify:*

      A *preliminary examination* in a criminal case.

      A *deposition*.

      A *previous trial* concerning a related or similar charge.

   Examples that don't qualify:

      A sworn *affidavit*. (This is not a "hearing" and isn't subject to cross-examination.)

      A signed *transcript* of a *confession or interrogation* in front of the police or the prosecutor. (Same shortcomings as affidavit.)

☛ Also remember that the party against whom the former testimony is being offered must have had the *"opportunity and similar motive"* to "develop" the testimony (usually by *cross-examining the witness*) at the time it was given. (FRE 804(b)(1)).

   ☞ *Common "distractor":* Profs. will often try to fool you by saying in the fact pattern that no cross-examination took place in the earlier proceeding. That's irrelevant — as long as the party against whom the testimony is now sought to be introduced had an *opportunity* and *incentive* to cross-examine, the fact he didn't *take* that opportunity doesn't block the former testimony exception from applying. (*Example:* Peter is injured when a Twig-model car he owns, made by Carco, explodes. Peter brings a civil suit against Carco in Alaska state court. In that suit, Peter calls Expert to testify that the Twig was defectively designed. Carco doesn't cross-examine Expert. Later, Paula sues Carco when her Twig explodes. Expert is now unavailable. Paula may put Expert's testimony at the Peter-vs-Carco trial into evidence as substantive proof that the Twig is defectively designed. Since Carco had a similar motive to cross-examine

Expert in the Peter trial as it would have today if Expert were giving live testimony, it doesn't matter that Carco didn't in fact conduct any cross.)

Dying Declarations

When the declarant is **badly injured** or **very sick** at the time of the declaration, consider whether her statement may be admitted as a dying declaration.

☛ Most important element to look for: that the statement concerned the **cause or circumstances of declarant's impending death.**

    ☞ *Example where this element is not satisfied:* Duane is charged with murdering Victor. Duane wants to put into evidence a statement made by Edward to Walter, in which Edward said, "Now that I'm about to die of AIDS, I wanted to get something off my chest — it was me, not Duane, who killed Victor." (Edward in fact died soon thereafter.) Not admissible as a dying declaration, because the point for which the statement is sought to be admitted relates to who killed Victor, not to the cause or circumstances of Edward's death.

    ☞ *Example where this element is satisfied:* Valerie, believing she will soon die of gunshot wounds, says, "Dexter shot me." If Valerie dies (or is otherwise unavailable at Dexter's trial), admissible against Dexter to show that Dexter shot her.

☛ There is no requirement that the declarant actually die (let alone that she die from the thing she thought she would die of). But she must be unavailable.

☛ The declarant must believe that she will die **imminently**. Thus if declarant believes that she has successfully escaped, say, a murder attempt, the exception doesn't apply.

☛ Remember that the FRE allow for the exception in **criminal homicide** prosecutions (but no other kinds of criminal cases) as well as in **civil** cases. (FRE 804(b)(2)).

Declarations Against Interest

Whenever the declarant makes a statement that, at the time made, seems **damaging to the declarant**, consider whether it's a declaration against interest.

☛ Look for the declarant to be either a **non-party**, or a party who wants to **use his own statement**. (If the declarant is the party **against whom** the statement is to be used, you can avoid fulfilling the requirements of a declaration against interest — unavailability, against interest when made, and personal knowledge — by treating the statement as an admission.)

☛ Make sure that the statement was against the declarant's **pecuniary or penal interest** when made. (But remember that at common law, only statements against pecuniary interest, *not* those exposing the declarant to criminal liability, count.)

    ☞ Common fact pattern: A *passenger* in a car makes a statement to a police officer at the scene of a crime or accident, and the statement is incriminating to (or against the financial interest of) the *driver* but *not the passenger*.

    Examples: (1) Car accident; Passenger tells police, "We should have had our lights on." (2) Car accident; Passenger tells bystander, "We were coming back from a wedding at which we had both been drinking." In each case, Passenger's statement is against the driver's pecuniary and penal interest, but not against Passenger's own interest, because a passenger isn't responsible for putting the car's lights on or not being drunk in the vehicle. Therefore, neither statement qualifies as a declaration against interest.

☞ Make sure that the declarant *knew*, at the time of the statement, that it was against her interest. (Hindsight doesn't count.)

☛ Confirm that the ***declarant is unavailable***. This is an easy one to forget, because unlike many of the other "declarant unavailable" exceptions (e.g., dying declaration), there's nothing in the core declaration-against-interest scenario to jog your mind into focusing on this requirement.

☛ In an essay, mention whether it's a declaration against pecuniary interest or against penal interest (or both).

☞ Most frequently-tested: A statement that would subject the declarant to ***criminal liability***. (Note in your answer that at common-law, exposure to criminal liability doesn't suffice, but that under FRE 804(b)(3) it does.)

Example 1: P sues Insurance Co. for failing to pay off on insurance claim; Insurance Co. defends on grounds that it cancelled policy for non-payment, and sent P the statutorily-required notice doing so. P offers testimony by Neighbor that Mailman, who delivered all mail to P's neighborhood during the time in question (and who is now in prison in another state) told Neighbor shortly after the time of alleged cancellation, "I just threw away a lot of the mail recently instead of delivering it, because my back hurt." Admissible, because the statement could have led to Mailman's prosecution for destruction of U.S. mail.

Example 2: Suit against a ladder manufacturer for personal injuries suffered by P when P fell from a ladder. The manufacturer may present testimony by W, who says, "X [now unavailable] told me that the fall happened because he, X, kicked the ladder out from under P." Admissible, because it was against X's pecuniary interest when made (since it exposed X to a civil suit by P), as well as against X's penal interest (prosecution for battery).

☛ **Use by defendant:** In criminal prosecutions where the ***defendant*** wants to introduce the out-of-court statement, beware the special rule that kicks in when the declarant ***inculpates himself*** by the same statement that ***exculpates the defendant*** — here, the declaration-against-interest exception applies only if there are *"corroborating circumstances"* that *"clearly indicate* [the statement's] *trustworthiness."* (FRE 804(b)(3)(B).) (*Example:* Murder trial of Dexter, for killing Valerie. Dexter produces testimony of Officer, a police officer, who says, "Zeke [now dead] confessed to me that he killed Valerie." Unless there's some independent evidence indicating that Zeke in fact killed Valerie, Officer's testimony is not admissible as a declaration-against-interest.)

☛ **Use by prosecution:** In criminal prosecutions where the ***prosecution*** wants to use the statement, check to see if the declarant had a ***self-serving motive*** that conflicted with the supposedly against-interest aspects. If so, the statement ***won't*** be admissible.

Key scenario: Declarant *"confesses"* after being caught red-handed. During the course of the confession, he ***implicates D***, against whom the confession is now sought to be used. (In this fact pattern, Declarant is "unavailable" at D's trial, usually because Declarant pleads the Fifth.) If Declarant was trying to *minimize his own culpability* (e.g., "D was the ringleader, and I was just the errand boy"), or was trying to *"curry favor"* with the authorities by implicating D, you should conclude that the declaration wasn't really against Declarant's interest when made, and should therefore not be admitted under the against-interest rule.

☞ **Confrontation Clause:** Also, in any question falling into this Key Scenario (Declarant gives police a confession implicating D, then is unavailable at trial), remember that the statement would almost certainly be blocked by D's *Confrontation Clause* rights under the federal constitution. Cite *Crawford v. Washington, infra*, p. 364 and *Davis v. Washington, infra*, p. 367. As long as Declarant's confession was "testimonial" (and if he made it in response to police interrogation, it would be), it can't be used against D whom it also implicates, unless Declarant takes the stand and is available for cross by D.

☞ **Collateral statements:** Finally, remember that the *precise statement itself* must be "against interest" — it's not enough that the statement is *"collateral to"* an against-interest statement. So even if parts of Declarant's confession are clearly against his interest, other parts that aren't against his interest (e.g., parts where he implicates someone else) can't come in as being collateral to the against-interest parts. Cite *Williamson v. U.S.* on this point.

☛ **Near death:** If the declarant is *near death* at the time of the declaration, question whether the statement is truly against his interests. (*Example:* Same facts as earlier example [Zeke confesses to crime for which Dexter is now charged.] Now, assume that Zeke, at the time of his confession, knew he was dying of a bullet wound. He probably wasn't very worried about criminal liability, so the court may well refuse to admit the statement, on the grounds that it doesn't have the special guarantee of truthfulness that serves as the basis for the against-interest exception.)

☞ Where the statement is against pecuniary interest, however, consider the possibility that the declarant, though dying, had an interest in *preserving his estate* for inheritance by his next-of-kin. In that case, the impending death would not be enough to remove the declarant's pecuniary interest.

PRIOR STATEMENTS BY TESTIFYING WITNESSES

Prior Inconsistent Statements

Remember that under the FRE (but not at common law), a prior inconsistent statement by a trial witness is sometimes admissible as substantive evidence.

☛ Remember the requirements for a prior inconsistent statement to be substantively admissible: (1) the declarant must *testify* and be available for cross; (2) the prior statement must have been made *under oath* at a *trial, hearing, "other proceeding"* or *deposition*.

Example: In a multiple-car collision case, W testifies for P that D went through a red light. D may contradict W's testimony by reading into the record W's statement at a deposition taken in the case, in which W said that the light was yellow when D went through it. This statement is admissible substantively, to prove that the light was yellow (as well as admissible to impeach W).

☞ Note in your answer that the FRE classify admissible prior statements as ***nonhearsay***, not as hearsay admissible because of an exception.

☞ Don't confuse this exception with the *"former testimony"* exception. Here, the statement must be in ***conflict*** with the current testimony. On the other hand, there's ***no requirement that the prior statement have been subject to cross examination.***

Example: A prior inconsistent statement from a witness's testimony at a ***grand jury hearing*** is admissible against the defendant, even though that defendant had no lawyer present to cross-examine the witness. In contrast, the statement would not be admissible under the "former testimony" exception because no cross was possible.

☞ Make sure the ***declarant*** is ***presently testifying.*** If the prior inconsistent statement is offered to contradict a prior out-of-court declaration rather than the declarant's live testimony, the exception doesn't apply.

Example: Murder prosecution of D for shooting V. The prosecution puts on W1, who says, "One day before V died of his gunshot wounds, he was pretty sure he'd die, and he said to me 'D did this to me.' " [This is admitted as a dying declaration.] Now, the defense offers W2, V's friend, who says, "After the shooting, when V thought he'd recover, he said to me in his hospital room, 'X did this to me.' " W2's testimony is not admissible as a prior inconsistent statement because it's not being offered to contradict V's live at-trial testimony. (Also, it doesn't qualify because V wasn't under oath at a proceeding when he made the statement to W2.) However, W2's testimony *is* admissible to *impeach W1*.

☞ Distinguish between use of a prior inconsistent statement for ***impeachment*** purposes and use for ***substantive*** purposes. What we're talking about here is substantive use. (But don't forget that if you determine that the statement is substantively admissible, then it's automatically also available for impeachment.)

☞ If the statement was not given under oath at a formal proceeding, but was made by (and is sought to be used against) a ***party***, consider whether it's admissible as an ***admission***.

Prior Consistent Statement

Prior consistent statements are rarely tested. When they are, remember the FRE approach: the consistent statement is admissible only to rebut an express or implied charge that the witness has been ***improperly influenced***, or has recently ***fabricated*** his story. Note that the prior consistent statement must have been made ***before*** the influence or fabrication came into existence.

Prior Identification

Remember that prior statements of ***identification*** are fairly easy to admit. Under FRE 801(d)(1)(C), a statement that "identifies a person as someone the declarant perceived earlier" is nonhearsay if the declarant testifies at trial and is available for cross.

☞ So the typical scenario involves a trial witness who testifies that ***at some earlier point in time***, she identified D as the perpetrator. (*Example:* W testifies at trial, "After the rape, I picked D out at a lineup as the person who raped me." Admissible.)

☞ **Common scenario:** W is asked at trial to identify the defendant as the perpetrator of the crime charged. She says she can't, because his appearance is now different. The prosecution then asks W to repeat the previous identification that took place after the crime. (*Example:* W says at trial, "I can't now ID the defendant as the man who raped me, because the defendant has a beard covering his face, and the man who raped me didn't, and I can't tell if the two are the same." The prosecution then shows that W picked a person out of a lineup conducted after the rape, and that the person picked was in fact D. Admissible.)

Residual ("Catchall") Exception

In any hearsay problem where you don't find any exception that applies, consider whether the *residual ("catchall") exception* (FRE 807) applies.

☞ **Most important:** The two most important things to watch for in analyzing the catchall are:

   ☞ The statement must have "*circumstantial guarantees of trustworthiness.*"

   ☞ The statement must be *"more probative"* on the point for which it is offered than any other reasonably available evidence. Therefore, be most on the look-out for the catchall when the *declarant is unavailable* (though unavailability is not a strict requirement).

☞ **Grand jury testimony against D:** Most likely scenario for use of the catchall: The prosecution wants to use a person's *grand jury testimony* against a criminal *defendant*. (This can't come in under the former testimony exception, because the defendant wasn't present during the grand jury testimony.) Usually this happens where the testimony is from someone who refuses to testify at trial.

   ☞ **Witness was intimidated:** If the reason the witness refuses to testify is because he was *intimidated by D*, then the answer is easy: point out that a separate Federal Rule, 804(b)(6), makes the statement admissible because the declarant's unavailability was procured by the defendant's intentional wrongdoing. (And, by the way, note that under 804(b)(6), you *don't* have to consider whether the declaration has any *guarantees of trustworthiness* — even a completely *untrustworthy* declaration gets *automatically admitted* if the declarant is unavailable because of the defendant's intentional wrongdoing.)

   ☞ **Confrontation Clause:** Also, in any scenario where W's grand jury testimony is sought to be used by the prosecution against D in D's criminal trial, note that D's rights under the *Confrontation Clause* of the Sixth Amendment probably prevent this use if W is not available to be cross-examined about the statement by D at D's trial. See *Crawford v. Washington* (*infra*, p. 364), saying that any out-of-court "testimonial" statement by W (including grand jury testimony) can't be admitted against D in a criminal trial if W doesn't take the stand.

☞ **Near miss:** Also, allude to the "near miss" problem, if the facts just miss qualifying for one of the traditional hearsay exceptions. Say that most courts don't hold the "near miss" against the proponent, and allow the catchall to be used despite the near-miss if the required "circumstantial guarantees of trustworthiness," etc., are present.

CHAPTER 7

CHAPTER 7

CONFRONTATION AND COMPULSORY PROCESS

ChapterScope

This chapter covers two clauses of the Sixth Amendment, each of which may render unconstitutional certain evidence rules in criminal trials.

- **Confrontation Clause:** A criminal defendant is guaranteed the right to *confront opposing witnesses.* Most importantly, this means that any out-of-court "testimonial statement" by W can't be used against D in a criminal trial unless W is available to be cross-examined by D.

  - ❏ The use of one co-defendant's *out-of-court confession* (given under police interrogation) against another, where the confessor is not available for cross-examination at trial, is one of the scenarios most likely to violate the Confrontation Clause.

- **Compulsory Process Clause:** The Compulsory Process clause on its face guarantees a criminal defendant the right to subpoena witnesses for his defense. However, it's been interpreted a bit more broadly than that: any rule of evidence or procedure that *unfairly restricts* a criminal defendant's ability to *put on a defense* might be found to violate the Clause. (*Example:* An evidence rule that prevents one accomplice from testifying *on behalf of* another, but allows one accomplice to testify *against* the other, violates the Clause.)

I. INTRODUCTION

A. Constitutional limits: In most contexts, there are no meaningful federal constitutional limits on the rules of evidence — the states are free to admit or exclude whatever evidence they wish, subject only to the requirement that they not violate a party's right to a fair trial, as guaranteed by the Fourteenth Amendment's Due Process Clause. In *criminal* trials, however, evidentiary rules that *disadvantage the defendant* may run afoul of two quite specific constitutional provisions, both part of the Sixth Amendment: the Confrontation Clause and the Compulsory Process Clause.

1. Confrontation Clause: The Confrontation Clause, which guarantees a criminal defendant the right "to be confronted with the witnesses against him," to some extent "constitutionalizes" the hearsay rule. Thus if a state were to completely abolish the rule against hearsay, at least some types of out-of-court declarations could still not be introduced against a criminal defendant.

   a. Testimonial statements: For instance, where the prosecution tries to take an out-of-court "*testimonial* statement" by W (e.g., *grand jury testimony*) and use it against D, the statement won't be admissible against D if W isn't available at trial for cross by D, even if a traditional hearsay exception (e.g., for declarations against interest) applies.

b. **Joint trial:**   Also, the Confrontation Clause poses problems where two co-defendants are *tried jointly*. An item of evidence that is completely admissible against one of the defendants (e.g., his own voluntary confession) may violate the other defendant's Confrontation Clause rights even if that evidence is never formally admitted against him.

c. **Exclusionary tool:**   The Confrontation Clause is mainly an *exclusionary* tool — when applicable, it operates mainly to allow the defendant to keep out certain types of damaging evidence (though occasionally it may entitle him to cross-examine a witness on a point that would otherwise be off-limits, or to produce extrinsic evidence to impeach a witness).

2. **Compulsory Process Clause:**   The Compulsory Process Clause, by contrast, is an *inclusionary* tool, i.e., one that may allow the defendant to gain admission of otherwise-inadmissible evidence. The clause (which guarantees the defendant's right to "have compulsory process for obtaining Witnesses in his favor") has been interpreted not only to mean that the defendant may subpoena witnesses, but also that he may have the right to ask questions, offer documents, and offer testimony, even though these would normally be inadmissible under the jurisdiction's rules of evidence.

II. CONFRONTATION CLAUSE — INTRODUCTION

A. **History:**   At the very least, the drafters of the Confrontation Clause intended to assure a criminal defendant's right to *be present* at his trial, to *learn* what evidence is being introduced against him, and to *question* those who give live testimony. Probably the drafters also intended to exclude some types of hearsay evidence. For instance, they probably wished to prevent abuses like the trial of Sir Walter Raleigh, who was convicted principally based on the out-of-court confession (later recanted) of an alleged co-conspirator, who was not produced for live testimony or cross-examination at Raleigh's trial.

1. **Contrasting views:**   A few scholars — most notably Wigmore — have contended that the Confrontation Clause *only* guarantees the right to be present and to cross-examine *live witnesses*, and that the clause should *never* be interpreted to require exclusion of evidence because of its hearsay nature.

2. **Modern view:**   But a majority of the Supreme Court has *never accepted* this limited view. Today, the precise scope of the Confrontation Clause remains somewhat blurry. But at least a couple of general principles may be stated:

❑ Hearsay statements that are *"testimonial"* in nature may not be admitted, because of the Confrontation Clause, unless the accused gets some chance to *cross-examine* the declarant (either at the time the out-of-court statement is first made, or at the accused's later trial). See *Crawford v. Washington, infra*, p. 364.

Example: For instance, the alleged co-conspirator's confession in the Raleigh case would certainly be inadmissible today on Confrontation Clause grounds. That's because: (1) the confession was clearly "testimonial" (intended for use at a later trial, or likely to be so used); (2) Raleigh had no chance to cross-examine the co-conspirator at the time of the confession; and (3) Raleigh had no chance to cross-examine the conspirator at Raleigh's own trial. This would be so even if the judge believed that the confession was reliable.

❏ Hearsay statements that are *not "testimonial"* (i.e., not intended for use at a later trial, and not reasonably foreseeable to the speaker as being the sort of thing that would be used at trial) *do not need to undergo Confrontation Clause scrutiny at all.*

> **Example:** An excited utterance will normally not be "testimonial." If the particular excited utterance is indeed found not to be testimonial (i.e., not made with an intent that it be used in an investigation or prosecution), the Confrontation Clause will not block it from admission, whether the declarant is made available for cross-examination or not. See *infra*, p. 368.

❏ *Forensic reports* (e.g., a *lab report* on how much alcohol D's blood contained) will usually *be testimonial*, and will therefore usually be admissible to prove the truth of what they assert only if someone *involved in the preparation of the report* is available for cross-examination at trial. See *infra*, p. 382.

3. **Application to states:** The Confrontation Clause applies to *state* trials as well as federal trials. *Pointer v. Texas*, 380 U.S. 400 (1965).

B. **Declarant produced at trial:** A literal reading of the Confrontation Clause might suggest that no out-of-court declaration could ever be used against a criminal defendant unless the defendant had been given a right of *cross-examination at the time of the statement.* But the Supreme Court has *not* taken such an extreme view. So long as the declarant is *available at trial* to be cross-examined about his earlier declaration, the fact that the defendant did not cross-examine him at the time of the statement (or even have the opportunity to do so) will not by itself mean that the statement is barred by the Confrontation Clause. And that seems to be true even if the declaration is "testimonial" in nature.

> **Example:** Again consider the co-conspirator's confession in the Raleigh case. Suppose that the confessor was called as a witness at Raleigh's trial, and was willing to testify (and be cross-examined by Raleigh). The Confrontation Clause would not block the confession from being admitted against Raleigh — the fact Raleigh could cross-examine the declarant (the confessed co-conspirator) now, at trial, would be enough to overcome any Confrontation Clause problem stemming from the fact that Raleigh didn't get to cross-examine the confessor at the time of the confession.

C. **Preference for live testimony:** The Confrontation Clause clearly reflects the drafters' *preference for live testimony* in lieu of out-of-court declarations wherever possible. This preference, of course, does not mean that out-of-court declarations will never be admissible against a criminal defendant. But it does mean that all other things being equal, an out-of-court declaration is more likely to be found violative of the Confrontation Clause if the same evidence could be furnished by live testimony from an available witness, than where this is not the case.

1. **Observation of demeanor:** A key reason for the Confrontation Clause's preference for live testimony is that only where there is live testimony does the jury have a chance to observe and weigh the *demeanor* of the witness. Even if the prior out-of-court declaration was subjected to cross-examination, and even if a transcript was made of it, the criminal jury is deprived of the opportunity to conclude, for instance, that the declarant's nervous

mannerisms (e.g., shifting in his seat, failing to look at the jury or examiner, etc.) make his testimony suspect. See, e.g., *Barber v. Page*, 390 U.S. 719 (1968) ("The right to confrontation is basically a trial right. It includes both the opportunity to cross-examine and the occasion for the jury to weigh the demeanor of the witness.")

III. CONFRONTATION CLAUSE — THE MODERN APPROACH

A. **Modern cases:** Let us look in detail now at how the Supreme Court has radically altered the meaning of the Confrontation Clause beginning with a key 2004 case, *Crawford v. Washington*.

B. **The old approach (*Ohio v. Roberts*):** The case that established the now-abandoned "old" approach to the handling of hearsay under the Confrontation Clause is ***Ohio v. Roberts***, 448 U.S. 56 (1980). There, the Supreme Court established a ***two-pronged approach*** for when hearsay may be admitted in the face of a Confrontation Clause problem.

    1. **Two-pronged approach:** The Court held in *Roberts* that the Confrontation Clause imposed ***two separate requirements,*** each of which had to be satisfied before hearsay may be admitted against an accused:

        ❏ First, "in the usual case," the prosecution had to either ***produce the declarant at trial*** so that she could be ***cross-examined***, or demonstrate the declarant's "unavailability." This prong applies, the Court said, even if the accused had had a prior opportunity to cross-examine the declarant.

        ❏ Second, if the first prong was satisfied (i.e., the witness was shown to be unavailable), the hearsay would be admitted only if it contained ***"indicia of reliability."*** In the case of a ***"firmly rooted hearsay exception,"*** reliability would be ***inferred***. But in the case of hearsay that does not fall within a firmly-rooted exception, then there had to be ***"particularized guarantees of trustworthiness"*** arising out of the **specific facts surrounding the statement.**

    2. **Significance:** So *Roberts* applied a ***"reliability"*** test for whether the Confrontation Clause applied to a particular piece of hearsay evidence. If the declarant was available but not produced at trial for cross-examination, the evidence was ***admissible if it was "reliable"*** (evidenced either by falling within a firmly-rooted hearsay exception or by involving particular facts indicating reliability), and ***inadmissible otherwise***. Thus the sole value protected by the Confrontation Clause, in the *Roberts* view, was the defendant's interest in ***not having unreliable hearsay admitted against him*** in the absence of a chance to cross-examine the declarant.

    3. **Overruling by *Crawford* and *Davis*:** *Roberts* remained the most important word on the meaning of the Confrontation Clause for nearly 25 years. But then, a series of decisions – beginning with one in 2004 and the other in 2006 – essentially overruled *Roberts* entirely. Here's a very brief summary of what these first two cases hold:

        ❏ The 2004 decision, *Crawford v. Washington*, holds that where an out-of-court declaration is ***"testimonial,"*** no matter how "reliable" the declaration is the Confrontation Clause ***prohibits the use*** of the declaration at trial unless the declarant is ***made avail-***

able for cross-examination.

❑ The 2006 decision, *Davis v. Washington*, purports to define *what declarations are "testimonial."* At least in the case of a police interrogation, a testimonial statement is one where "the primary purpose of the interrogation is to *establish or prove past events potentially relevant to later criminal prosecution.*"

❑ *Davis* also establishes that where a declaration is *non-testimonial*, the statement can be admitted *without any Confrontation Clause review at all.*

C. ***Crawford v. Washington***: The 2004 decision in ***Crawford v. Washington***, 541 U.S. 36 (2004) established that where the out-of-court declaration is *"testimonial"* in nature, *no matter how "reliable" the declaration is*, its admission will be *blocked* by the Confrontation Clause unless the declarant is made *available for cross-examination* either at trial or at the time the declaration was made.

1. **Facts:** D was charged with assaulting and attempting to murder V, during the course of a fight the two had. The episode began when D came to believe that V had tried to rape D's wife, Sylvia. D and Sylvia went to V's apartment, and D ended up stabbing V. D and Sylvia both gave statements to the police about the fight. D said that he had acted in self-defense, because he had seen V "goin' for somethin' before, right before everything happened." Sylvia, however, told police that she did not see anything in V's hands before D attacked V.

2. **Statement against penal interest:** At D's trial, the prosecution could not require Sylvia to testify, because of the adverse-spousal-testimony privilege. (See *infra*, p. 449.) Instead, it offered Sylvia's police statement as evidence that the stabbing was not in self-defense. The prosecution argued that because Sylvia admitted that she had led D to V's apartment, and had thus facilitated the assault, her entire statement was admissible under the hearsay exception for statements against penal interest. The trial judge agreed, the statement was admitted, and D was convicted. D argued that the use of this out-of-court declaration violated his Confrontation Clause rights.

3. ***Roberts* criticized:** In an opinion by Justice Scalia, in whose rationale six other Justices joined, the Supreme Court agreed with D. In doing so, the Court took the occasion to revisit its entire Confrontation Clause jurisprudence, and to criticize the rationale behind *Roberts*.

   a. **Combatting civil-law mode of criminal procedure:** The Court began by reviewing the meaning of the right of confrontation under English law prior to the Sixth Amendment's passage in 1791. (This was important because the Sixth Amendment Confrontation Clause effectively carried over whatever rights of confrontation existed under English and American common law at the time the Sixth Amendment was enacted.) The Court noted that in the 16th and 17th centuries, justices of the peace and other officials had the right to examine suspects and witnesses in private before trial; courts could then use transcripts or results of these examinations against an accused at his later trial, with the accused having no right to cross-examine the examinee. The use of private-inquiry testimony from Sir Walter Raleigh's alleged co-conspirator against Raleigh at his criminal trial was the most notorious example of this use of uncross-examinable material against an accused. But by 1791, the Court concluded, English common law and procedure had established that unless the accused had had the right to cross-examine the maker of the out-of-court statement before the trial, the statement *could not be used in evidence unless the maker was produced at trial.* In the colonies prior to 1791, a similar rule existed, the Court said.

b. **Main purpose of Sixth Amendment :** Therefore, the Court concluded, the "principal evil" at which the Confrontation Clause was directed was the "use of *ex parte* examinations as evidence against the accused." The text of the Confrontation Clause — with its reference to the right to be confronted "with the witnesses against" the suspect — showed that the focus of the Sixth Amendment was on statements by "witnesses," in other words, by "those who 'bear testimony.'"

c. **Testimonial verses nontestimonial statements:** This brought the Court to make a core distinction that it had rarely made before in Confrontation Clause cases: a distinction between out-of-court statements that were *"testimonial"* and those that were not. "An accuser who makes a *formal statement to government officers* bears *testimony* in a sense that a person who makes a *casual remark* to an acquaintance does not." Therefore, testimonial statements are to be *scrutinized* under the Confrontation Clause *far more closely* than nontestimonial ones are.

d. **Statements to police officers:** The Court then briefly described some examples of testimonial statements. *Ex parte* statements (i.e., statements without the defendant present) made at a preliminary hearing were one example. Statements "taken by police officers in the course of interrogations" — like Sylvia's statement here — were another example of a testimonial statement "under even a narrow standard." Police interrogations, the Court said, "bear a *striking resemblance* to *examinations by justices of the peace in England.* The statements are not *sworn* testimony, but the absence of oath was not dispositive [in English law]."

e. **Modern cases reviewed for results:** The Court then reviewed modern American cases concerning when out-of-court testimony of statements could be admitted against an accused. The Court concluded that these modern cases, at least in their *results*, had remained faithful to the understanding of the framers of the Confrontation Clause: *"testimonial statements* of witnesses absent from trial have been admitted only where the declarant is unavailable, and *only where the defendant has had a prior opportunity to cross-examine."*

f. **Modern cases reviewed for rationales:** On the other hand, the Court concluded, the *rationale* behind modern cases — especially *Roberts* — was *inconsistent* with the understanding of the Sixth Amendment's framers. *Roberts* had conditioned the admissibility of all hearsay evidence on whether it fell within a "firmly rooted hearsay exception" or at least bore "particularized guarantees of trustworthiness." In the case of testimonial statements, the Court believed that the framers of the Sixth Amendment *did not mean to "leave the Sixth Amendment's protection to the vagaries of the rules of evidence, much less to amorphous notions of 'reliability'."* Admitting out-of-court statements merely because they were deemed reliable by a judge was "fundamentally at odds with the right of confrontation." The Confrontation Clause "commands, not that evidence be reliable, but that reliability be *assessed in a particular manner*: by *testing in the crucible of cross-examination.*"

g. **Application of new approach to present facts:** The facts of the present case illustrated to the Court the precise failings of *Roberts*. Sylvia had made her statement *while in police custody*, and while she was herself a *potential suspect*; indeed, she was told that whether she would be released depended on "how the investigation continues." Furthermore, she had responded to leading questions from the police. The various reviewing courts in the state-court system had disagreed about whether her statement was "reliable" and why. The case was thus "a self-contained demonstration of *Roberts*' *unpredictable and inconsistent application.*"

h. **New standard:** Finally, the Court articulated its *new standard* for dealing with testimonial statements: in the case of such evidence, "The Sixth Amendment demands what the common law required: *unavailability and a prior opportunity for cross-examination.* ... Where testimonial statements are at issue, the only indicium of reliability sufficient to satisfy constitutional demands is the one the Constitution actually prescribes: *confrontation.*" Because Sylvia was unavailable at trial, and because D had had no previous opportunity to cross-examine her about her statement inculpating him, the statement was *inadmissible without any consideration of whether the surrounding circumstances made it "reliable" or not.*

  i. **What is testimonial:** The Court also noted that it was not spelling out a comprehensive definition of "testimonial" in *Crawford*. It did, however, say that "whatever else the term covers, it applies at a *minimum* to *prior testimony at a preliminary hearing*, before a *grand jury*, or at a *former trial*; and to *police interrogation.*" These were "the modern practices with closest kinship to the abuses at which the Confrontation Clause was directed." (As we'll see shortly below, the court has since given a much more comprehensive definition of "testimonial," in later cases including *Davis v Washington*.)

D. **The meaning of "testimonial":** *Crawford* left a lot of confusion about the boundary line between out-of-court statements that would be deemed "testimonial" and those deemed non-testimonial. Since then, in a series of cases the Court has tried to articulate more precisely where the boundary line falls.

1. *Davis v. Washington*: The first — and still most important — case in which the Court attempted to define "testimonial" was *Davis v. Washington*, 126 S.Ct. 2266 (2006). There, the Court articulated a rule for distinguishing between testimonial and non-testimonial declarations, at least in those situations in which the declaration occurs as the result of an *official interrogation*:

❏ Declarations made in the course of an official interrogation will be *testimonial* if and only if "the *primary purpose* of the interrogation is to *establish or prove past events potentially relevant to later criminal prosecution,*" as is the purpose of the typical after-the-fact *crime-scene interview* of a victim.

❏ By contrast, statements *won't* be testimonial if the primary purpose of the interrogation is "to enable police assistance to meet an *ongoing emergency*," as in the typical *call to 911*.

a. **Two joined cases:** The opinion delivered by the Court under the name *Davis v. Washington* was actually the Court's review of two unrelated lower-court decisions, both of which involved declarations by victims of domestic violence who did not testify at the criminal trial of their assailant. One of the cases (which we'll refer to as the "*Davis* case") involved the admissibility of the victim's emergency call to 911. The other one was a companion case, *Hammon v. Indiana* (which we'll refer to as the "*Hammon* case"); that case involved the admissibility of the victim's statement to the police when she was interviewed at the crime scene shortly after the attack, but when she no longer felt herself to be in danger. The Supreme Court concluded that the tape of the 911 call in the *Davis* case could be introduced without Confrontation Clause issues because it was non-testimonial, but that the crime-scene statements in the *Hammon* case were testimonial and therefore were inadmissible due to the declarant's unavailability for cross-examination.

b. **The *Davis* case (911 tape):** Let's first look at the facts and holding of the *Davis* portion of the case.

   i. **Facts of Davis case:** In the Davis case, the victim, McCottry, frantically called 911 to report that someone (initially, she didn't say who) was "jumpin' on me again" and "usin' his fists." The operator asked, "Do you know his last name?"; McCottry supplied his last name (Davis), and then in response to further questions told the operator Davis' first name and middle initial. Under further questioning by the operator, McCottry disclosed that Davis had just left in a car, explained the purpose of Davis' visit (to "get his stuff"), and described the context of the assault. The operator then told McCottry that the police were on their way; two officers arrived soon thereafter. The entire call was taped.

   ii. **Use of tape at trial:** Davis was tried for violating a domestic no-contact order. McCottry did not appear as a witness. The officers who had responded to the 911 call testified that they observed what appeared to be fresh injuries on McCottry's person, but they did not testify about what caused those injuries. The prosecution's only proof about causation was to play a portion of the 911 tape — apparently mainly the part in which McCottry identified Davis as her attacker — over Davis' Confrontation Clause objection. The jury convicted. The Washington Supreme Court held that because the attacker-identification part of the tape was not testimonial under *Crawford*, admission of that part had not violated Davis' confrontation clause rights.

   iii. **Decision affirmed by Supreme Court:** In an opinion by Scalia, the Supreme Court ***unanimously*** agreed with the Washington Supreme Court holding: the part of the 911 tape in which McCottry identified Davis as her attacker was ***not "testimonial,"*** and therefore admission of that part of the tape ***did not violate*** Davis' Confrontation Clause rights even though he had never had an opportunity to cross-examine McCottry.

      (1) **Rationale:** Scalia pointed to several factors that made it clear that the attacker-identification portion of the 911 call was not testimonial. As to each factor, he contrasted the facts of Davis with those in the after-the-fact witness-interrogation in *Crawford* (where, of course, the Court had found the answers to be testimonial):

❑ Here, McCottry was "speaking about events *as they were actually happening*, rather than 'describ[ing] *past* events'." In *Crawford*, by contrast, the declarant (Sylvia Crawford) had been interviewed hours after the events she was describing.

❑ Here, McCottry was "facing an ongoing *emergency*," and seeking "help against bona fide physical threat." Sylvia Crawford had not been facing such an ongoing emergency.

❑ Here, the questions asked by the 911 operator and answered by McCottry were "necessary to be able to resolve the present emergency, rather than simply to learn (as in *Crawford*) what had happened in the past." This was true, for instance, of the operator's key question about the assailant's identity: the answer would enable the dispatched officers to know whether they would be facing a violent felon.

❑ Finally, here the "level of *formality*" was strikingly *lower* than it had been in *Crawford*. Whereas Sylvia Crawford had been calmly answering questions at the station house, McCottry was giving "frantic answers" over the phone, in what seemed to the 911 operator to be neither a tranquil nor a safe environment.

(2) Summary: Scalia summarized McCottry's statements this way: "[T]he circumstances of McCottry's interrogation objectively indicate its primary purpose was to enable police assistance to *meet an ongoing emergency.* She simply was not acting as a *witness*; she was not *testifying*. [Emphasis in original.] What she said was not a 'weaker substitute for live testimony' at trial ... like ... Sylvia Crawford's statement in *Crawford*. In [cases like *Crawford*, finding the out-of-court statements to be testimonial], the ex-parte actors and the evidentiary products of the ex parte communication *aligned perfectly with their courtroom analogs.* McCottry's emergency statement does not. No 'witness's goes into court to proclaim an emergency and seek help."

c. **The *Hammon* case (crime-scene interview):** But in the *Hammon* portion of the case, the Supreme Court reached the *opposite* conclusion: that the crime-scene interrogation there had yielded *testimonial responses*, which under the Confrontation Clause therefore *could not be admitted* if the defendant had no chance to cross-examine the declarant.

i. **Facts of *Hammon*:** The facts of the *Hammon* case were somewhat like those of *Crawford*: an after-the-fact interrogation of the victim/declarant, with an investigative rather than emergency focus.

Amy and Hershel Hammon were a married couple. Late one night police received a call about a domestic disturbance taking place at the Hammon home. When officers arrived, they found Amy alone on the porch; she assured them that "nothing was the matter." The officers went inside the house, and found some evidence of violence (shattered glass on the floor from a broken space heater). One officer separated Hershel from Amy so that the other could again ask Amy, without Hershel's being present, what had happened. This time, Amy told the officer that Hershel had assaulted her. The officer asked Amy to write out a battery affidavit; she did so by handwriting a statement describing the assault (e.g., that Hershel "shoved me down on the floor [and] hit me in the chest and threw me down.")

ii. **Use at trial:** Hershel was charged with domestic battery. Amy did not testify at trial (she was subpoenaed by the prosecution but apparently didn't show up). After the officer who had interrogated Amy gave testimony authenticating the affidavit, it was admitted (over Hershel's Confrontation Clause objection) as a ***present sense impression*** (see *supra*, p. 244). Also, the officer was permitted to testify in detail about what Amy had said to him orally before signing the affidavit (e.g., "She informed me that Mr. Hammon had pushed her onto the ground [and] had shoved her head into the broken glass of the heater..."); the trial court reasoned that these statements were admissible as ***excited utterances*** (*supra*, p. 242). The Indiana Supreme Court affirmed.

iii. **Supreme Court finds violation:** But by an 8-1 vote on this point (all but Justice Thomas), the Supreme Court concluded that both Amy's oral statements and her affidavit ***were "testimonial"*** under *Crawford*, so their admission ***violated Hershel's Confrontation Clause rights*** due to Amy's unavailability for cross.

(1) **Rationale:** Scalia asserted that the Hammon facts were "not much different from the statements we found to be testimonial in *Crawford*," because:

❏ The interrogation was "part of an ***investigation into possibly criminal past conduct***" (thereby satisfying the *Davis* portion's "establish or prove past events potentially relevant to later criminal prosecution" requirement);

❏ There was "***no emergency in progress***";

❏ The officer who was asking the questions was not seeking to determine (as had been the case in the *Davis* case) "'what is happening,' but rather, '***what happened***'."

In sum, the primary (if not sole) purpose of the interrogation was to ***"investigate a possible crime,"*** and the fruits of such an interrogation were therefore inevitably testimonial.

(2) **Domestic-violence argument:** Indiana had argued in the *Hammon* case that the Court should allow greater "flexibility" in the use of out-of-court testimonial-type evidence in domestic violence cases, because of assailants' widespread intimidation and coercion of victims in such cases to make sure they don't testify. But Scalia rejected this call, in a two-part answer: (1) "We may not ... vitiate constitutional guarantees when they have the effect of allowing the guilty to go free"; but (2) under the forfeiture doctrine embodied in FRE 804(b)(6) (see *supra*, p. 304), if the defendant in a domestic violence case in fact intimidates or coerces the victim not to give trial testimony, the defendant will ***forfeit*** his confrontation rights.

iv. **Thomas dissent:** Thomas was the only justice who disagreed with the outcome in the *Hammon* case. In a dissent from the result in *Hammon*, he argued that the only kinds of out-of-court statements that should be deemed testimonial — and thus subject to Confrontation Clause scrutiny — are those that have "some degree of **solemnity**." So he would (like all other members of the Court) recognize the applicability of the Confrontation Clause to "formalized testimonial materials" like affidavits, depositions, prior testimony, and "confessions, when extracted by police in a formal manner." But in the case of crime-scene questioning like that in *Hammon* — non-custodial, non-Mirandized sessions that were not a "formalized dialog" — he would not regard the statements as being testimonial, and would thus admit them without reference to the Confrontation Clause.

E. **The significance of an "emergency" (*Michigan v. Bryant*):** The two *Davis* fact patterns (*Davis* itself and *Hammon*) illustrate the significance of *whether there is a pending emergency* in the determination of whether the declaration is testimonial. In the *Davis* portion of the case, where the declaration came in a 911 call about a crime in progress, the emergency nature of the call contributed heavily to the Court's conclusion that the caller's statements were *not* testimonial. By contrast, in the *Hammon* portion, the fact that there was *no longer any emergency* in progress was a key factor in the Court's conclusion that the statements *were* testimonial.

A post-*Davis* case illustrates once again that the presence or absence of an emergency is likely to make a critical difference in whether the declaration is considered testimonial. The case is ***Michigan v. Bryant***, 131 S. Ct. 1143 (2011).

1. **Facts:** *Bryant* presented the classic situation of a *shooting victim* who *tells the police the name of his assailant* and the circumstances of the shooting, then *dies*. The issue was whether this statement could be introduced against the assailant. That issue turned on whether the victim's statement was to be considered "testimonial."

    a. **Report of a shooting:** Late one night, Detroit police officers responded to a radio dispatch that a man had been shot. At the scene, they found the victim, Covington, lying on the ground in a gas station parking lot. Covington had a gunshot wound to his abdomen, appeared to be in great pain, and spoke with difficulty. The police asked him a number of questions, including "what had happened, who had shot him, and where the shooting occurred." Covington responded that "Rick" had shot him about half an hour before. Covington said that he had had a conversation with Rick (who turned out to be the defendant, Richard Bryant) through the back door of Rick's house; when Covington turned to leave after the conversation, he was shot through the door, then drove himself to the gas station, where the police found him.[1]

    b. **End of conversation:** Covington's conversation with the police lasted for about 10 or 15 minutes, then ended when emergency medical services arrived. Covington was taken to the hospital and died shortly thereafter.

    c. **Investigation:** Immediately after the conversation, the police who had spoken with Covington left the gas station, called for backup, and went to Bryant's house. They didn't find Bryant, but they found blood and a bullet on the back porch, and an apparent bullet hole in the back door.

---

1. Covington apparently knew that Bryant was a drug dealer. See Scalia's dissent. There was evidence, not referred to in the *Bryant* decision, that Covington had bought drugs from Bryant in the past.

d. Trial testimony: At Bryant's trial, several of the officers who had spoken with Covington testified about what he had told them. The jury convicted Bryant of second-degree murder.

e. Michigan court finds a violation: The Michigan Supreme Court concluded that the introduction of Covington's statements violated Bryant's Confrontation Clause rights. The court reasoned that (1) the police behavior did not suggest that they perceived an ongoing emergency at the gas station; and (2) Covington's primary purpose in making his statements was to tell the police about past facts (e.g., who shot him), making his statements "testimonial."

2. Majority applies "emergency" rationale: By a 6-2 vote,[2] the Court *reversed* the Michigan ruling. The majority opinion, by Justice Sotomayor, concluded that Covington's statements were ***non-testimonial***, because the ***primary purpose*** of the participants in the interrogation (the police and Covington) was to respond to an ***ongoing emergency***. Therefore the admission of Covington's statements to the police officers did not violate Bryant's Confrontation Clause rights.

a. Meaning of "ongoing emergency": *Davis* had established that where police questioning is primarily done for the purpose of responding to an ongoing emergency, the answers will typically not be testimonial. Both fact patterns in *Davis* had involved a particular type of emergency: a domestic violence dispute, where whatever danger there was consisted of the danger that the assailant posed to the victim/declarant. But in *Bryant*, the case did not involve domestic violence, the victim had already fled, and there was little danger that the assailant would hurt him in the future. Instead, the Court was confronting for the first time a situation in which there seemed to have been an ongoing emergency that "extends ***beyond an initial victim*** to a ***potential threat to the responding police and the public at large***."

i. Primary purpose was to combat emergency: Sotomayor repeated *Davis*'s point that the ***"primary purpose"*** of the interrogation is what counts in determining whether the declarant's statements are testimonial. Where the "primary purpose" is to ***respond to an ongoing emergency***, that purpose "is not to create a record for trial," so the response is nontestmonial and is thus "not within the scope" of the Confrontation Clause. If the primary purpose *is* to create a trial record, the resulting declaration is testimonial, and under *Crawford* may not be introduced unless the declarant is available for cross-examination at some point. So the issue in *Bryant* was whether the "primary purpose" of the interrogation was to deal with this ongoing extended emergency (i.e., the danger to the responding police or the public at large), or was instead to create a record for trial.

ii. Relevance of reliability and hearsay exceptions: Sotomayor also dropped an intriguing hint that if the declaration is ***highly reliable*** — and ***corresponds to a traditional hearsay exception*** — this may make the statement less likely to be considered "testimonial." When there is an ongoing emergency, she said, the participants are likely to be focused on ending the threatening situation, not on prov-

---

2. Justice Kagan did not participate.

ing past events for trial purposes. "Because the *prospect of fabrication* in statements given for the primary purpose of resolving [an] emergency is presumably *significantly diminished*, the Confrontation Clause does not require such statements to be subject to the crucible of cross-examination." This logic, she said, is "not unlike that justifying the *excited utterance exception* in hearsay law ... Excited utterances are *considered reliable* because the declarant, in the excitement, presumably cannot form a falsehood[.]"

(1) Other hearsay exceptions: Sotomayor then listed in a footnote a number of *other hearsay exceptions* that "similarly rest on the belief that certain statements are, by their nature, *made for a purpose other than use in a prosecution* and therefore should not be barred by hearsay prohibitions." She cited business records as an example. She seemed to be saying that where a statement falls within one of these many exceptions found to guarantee reliability, the statement is less likely to be testimonial, making it less likely that the Confrontation Clause applies.[3]

b. Factors to consider: Sotomayor then took up the issue of how the court is to determine the "primary purpose" of the statements. Several major principles and factors apply, she said:

[1] **Objective test:** The test is *objective, not subjective*. In other words, "the relevant inquiry is not the subjective or actual purpose of the individuals involved in a particular encounter, but rather the purpose that *reasonable participants would have had*, as ascertained from the individuals' statements and actions in the circumstances in which the encounter occurred."

[2] **"Ongoing emergency" important:** The existence of an *"ongoing emergency"* is "relevant," because an emergency "focuses participants on something other than 'proving past events potentially relevant to later criminal prosecution.'" Sotomayor implied that the existence of an ongoing emergency makes it *much more likely* that the participants' primary purpose was something other than the making of a record to be used at trial.

[3] **Danger to police or public:** Where, as here, the threat is not just to the declarant/victim but also to the *police* or the *public at large*, the inquiry about whether the threat is ongoing "cannot narrowly focus on whether the threat solely to the first victim has been neutralized because *the threat to the first responders and public may continue*."

[4] **Type of weapon:** The duration and scope of an emergency will likely depend on the *type of weapon* involved. Thus in *Hammon*, the assailant (Hershel Hammon) was armed only with his fists, so that removing the victim to a separate room was enough to end the emergency; but if Hershel had had a gun,

---

3. If that's the case, then *Bryant* represents a stunning pivot back towards the supposedly-abandoned *Ohio v. Roberts* approach, under which the statement's reliability, and the fact that it qualified for a traditional hearsay exception, was enough to prevent the statement from being covered by the Confrontation Clause.

removing the victim to a different room might not have been enough to end the emergency.

[5] **Medical condition of declarant:** Similarly, the ***medical condition*** of the declarant will often be relevant. For instance, a badly injured victim might be incapable of forming any purpose at all, let alone a testimonial one.

[6] **Level of formality:** Finally, the existence of an ongoing emergency, while an important factor in the "primary purpose" analysis, is not the only factor. For instance, the degree of ***formality*** in the encounter is another significant factor. The presence of formality "suggests the absence of an emergency." By contrast, the present encounter's ***informality*** indicated that the interrogation was focused on resolving an emergency, not gathering facts to be used in a prosecution. Here, "the questioning ... occurred in an ***exposed, public area*** ... and in a ***disorganized fashion***," making it distinguishable from, say, the formal station-house interrogation in *Crawford* that was found to be testimonial.

c. **Consider both declarant and interrogator:** The central question in all interrogation scenarios is whether the "primary purpose" is testimonial or not. But *whose* primary purpose counts? The most important part of the *Bryant* majority opinion is probably its answer to that question. What counts is the "primary purpose of the *interrogation*," and the statements and actions of "***both*** the declarant ***and interrogators*** provide objective evidence" of the investigation's purpose. Therefore, courts making the "primary purpose" assessment are entitled to "consult[] all relevant information, including the statements and actions *of interrogators.*"

   i. **Interrogators' motive counts:** Sotomayor acknowledged that both the interrogators and the declarant might have ***mixed motives***. And, of course, the motive(s) of the declarant might be different than the motive(s) of the interrogator. This "both parties' motives are to be considered" section of the opinion is quite confusing. But it seems to allow for the possibility that the purpose of the "*interrogation*" (the central issue) might be found to be non-testimonial when the *interrogators*' primary purpose is to deal with an ongoing emergency, even if the declarant has (due to, say, severe injuries) no purpose, and perhaps ***even if the declarant's principal (or sole) purpose is to lay the groundwork for a later prosecution.*** As we'll see shortly below, when we consider how the *Bryant* Court applied its new rules to the facts, the police's purpose indeed seems to have dominated the Court's decision making.

d. **Application of test to facts:** Sotomayor's opinion then ***applied*** these new rules to the facts of the case. She concluded that the overall purpose of the "interrogation" was the ***nontestimonial one*** of dealing with a public emergency, not the testimonial one of preparing a record for later use in Bryant's trial. To get to that conclusion, she went through the various factors (discussed above) that are to be considered in making the testimonial/nontestimonial distinction. Here is a sampling of her reasoning:

[1] **Significance of declarant's injuries:** The ***severity of Covington's injuries*** — taken together with his constant questions about when emergency medical services would arrive and his obvious pain and difficulty in talking — lowered the likeli-

hood that his statements should be found testimonial: "We cannot say that a person in Covington's situation would have had a 'primary purpose' to establish or prove past events potentially relevant to later criminal prosecution."[4]

[2] **Ongoing emergency:** The police were justified in regarding the emergency as ***ongoing***. The police did not know why, where, or when the shooting had occurred. The police's questions — "what had happened, who had shot [Covington], and where the shooting occurred" — were "the exact type of questions necessary to allow the police to '***assess the situation***, the ***threat to their own safety***, and possible danger to the potential victim' (citing *Davis*), and ***to the public***[.]" And nothing in Covington's answers would have indicated that the emergency had ended. For instance, Covington did not know the location of the shooter, and said nothing to foreclose the possibility that the shooter might arrive on the scene and shoot at Covington again.

[3] **Informality:** The ***informality of the questioning*** also pointed towards the conclusion that the interrogators' primary purpose was to deal with an ongoing emergency. "The situation was fluid and somewhat confused: the officers arrived at different times; apparently each, upon arrival, asked Covington 'what happened?'; and ... they did not conduct a structured interrogation."

[4] **Summary:** Thus the overall circumstances of the encounter, coupled with the statements and actions of both Covington and the police, "objectively indicate"[5] that "the 'primary purpose of the interrogation' was 'to enable police assistance to meet an ongoing emergency.'" Consequently, Covington's identification and description of the shooter and the location of the shooting were not testimonial hearsay, and the Confrontation Clause did not bar those statement from being admitted against Bryant.

3. **Scalia's dissent:** Justice Scalia wrote an angry dissent, in which he was joined by Justice Ginsburg. This was the first time that Scalia found himself in dissent in the line of confrontation cases that started with *Crawford*.

a. **"Emergency" story "transparently false":** Scalia began by attacking the majority's basic conclusion that the primary purpose of those involved in the interrogation here was to deal with an ongoing emergency. "Today's tale — a story of five officers conducting successive examinations of a dying man with the primary purpose, not of obtaining and preserving his testimony regarding his killer, but of protecting him, them, and others from a murderer somewhere on the loose — is ***so transparently false*** that professing to believe it demeans this institution."

---

4. The Court's "we cannot say..." phrasing suggests that the ***burden is now on the defendant*** to make an affirmative showing that the declarant's primary purpose was to prove past events for purposes of later criminal prosecution, not on the prosecution to prove the opposite. So in a case — like *Bryant* itself — where the evidence of the declarant's intent is ***ambiguous***, apparently the defendant ***loses***, and the statement comes in as non-testimony.

5. Remember, the Court was applying an "objective" test for "primary purpose" (see *supra*, p. 373): the issue is what *reasonable actors* in the position of the interrogators and the declarant would likely be intending, not what the actual participants intended.

b. **Declarant's perspective counts:** Scalia disagreed with the majority's conclusion that both the investigators' and the declarant's intention matter when determining the "primary purpose" of the interrogation. For Scalia, "the ***declarant's intent is what counts.***"

   i. **Application:** Applying this "declarant's purpose" standard made this "an ***absurdly easy case***" for Scalia. Five different officers in sequence asked the same questions to Covington, including who shot him, where did it happen, how tall was the shooter, how much did he weigh, and what chain of events led to the shooting. Since Covington knew that the shooting was the work of a drug dealer, not a spree killer who might endanger others, and since he knew that the encounter had ended six blocks away and 25 minutes earlier, he knew that his answers "had little value except to ensure the arrest and eventual prosecution of Richard Bryant." Thus the primary purpose of his statements was obviously a testimonial one.

   ii. **"Malleable" approach:** Scalia worried that the majority's version of the primary purpose test would be highly ***manipulable*** by police and judges to achieve the desired outcome.

   (1) **The "mixed motives" problem:** Both the interrogators and the declarant often have ***mixed motives*** for their questions and statements. Therefore, courts would now have discretion "to sort through two sets of mixed motives to determine the primary purpose of an interrogation." Therefore, "if the defendant 'deserves' to go to jail, then a court can focus on ***whatever perspective is necessary to declare damning hearsay non-testimonial.*** And when all else fails, a court can ***mix-and-match perspectives*** [of the declarant and the interrogators] to ***reach its desired outcome***." This ***"malleable approach"*** transforms the guarantee of confrontation into "no guarantee at all."

   iii. **Reliability inquiry:** Scalia was especially critical of the majority's announcement that in deciding whether a statement is testimonial, the court should look to "***standard rules of hearsay**, designed to **identify some statements as reliable***." For Scalia, this was an unfortunate return to the "unworkable standard" of *Ohio v. Roberts*, under which an out-of-court statement was admissible if it "falls within a firmly rooted hearsay exception" or otherwise "bears adequate indicia of reliability." Scalia asserted that "reliability tells us *nothing* [emphasis in original] about whether a statement is testimonial." And a focus on reliability would give trial judges discretion to chip away at the right being protected by the Confrontation Clause. Judges cannot "be trusted to assess the reliability of uncross-examined testimony in politically charged trials or trials implicating threats to national security."

4. **Criticism of majority:** The majority approach in *Bryant* has been widely criticized. The most frequent criticism echoes Scalia's, that the test for primary purpose is so ***malleable*** that the court (or perhaps the police) can make the case come out however they want. As one commentator says, "One of my concerns is that police officers will quickly learn that they can get statements ***characterized as non-testimonial*** if they testify, in effect, 'I came up to the scene and didn't know what was happening. My principal concern was securing the public safety. What this person told me was very important for that purpose.' " Fried-

man, The Confrontation Blog, *www.confrontationright.blogspot.com/2011/03/preliminary-thoughts-on-bryant-decision.html*, accessed on Feb. 13, 2013.

F. Interrogations by persons not working for law enforcement (*Ohio v. Clark*): All of the cases we've examined so far in the modern *Crawford* line — *Crawford* itself, *Davis v. Washington*, *Hammon v. Indiana* and *Michigan v. Bryant* — involved out-of-court statements made in response to interrogation, where the questions were asked by ***law enforcement personnel.***[6] Let's now consider out-of-court statements made in response to questions asked by persons who are ***not*** working on behalf of law enforcement: does this fact automatically prevent the statement from being "testimonial"? Based on the only post-*Crawford* Supreme Court case to involve questioning by non-law-enforcement personnel, the short answer is that (1) the response is ***not automatically*** rendered "non-testimonial"; but (2) the fact that the questioner isn't part of law enforcement certainly tends to make it ***less likely*** that the declarant's ***"primary purpose"*** will be found to have been a testimonial one.

The case in question was ***Ohio v. Clark***, 135 S.Ct. 2173 (2015), where the declarant was a ***three-year-old boy*** who told his ***preschool teachers*** that he had been abused by his mother's boyfriend. The court held (unanimously) that this statement was ***not testimonial***, thereby preventing the Confrontation Clause from applying, and making the statement admissible against the boyfriend.

1. **Facts of *Clark*:** In *Clark*, L.P., a three-year-old boy, lived in Cleveland with his mother and the mother's boyfriend, Clark (whom we'll refer to as "D"). When D dropped L.P. off at preschool one day, his teachers noticed that he had bloodshot eyes, red marks on his face, and bruises on his upper body. When the teachers asked him, "Who did this?" L.P. answered that D did it. The teachers called a child-abuse hotline, which triggered an investigation that led to D's prosecution for assault, domestic abuse and child endangerment.

   a. **Ohio statute on competence:** Under an Ohio evidence rule, children younger than 10 are incompetent to testify if they "appear incapable of receiving just impressions of the facts and transactions respecting which they are examined, or of relating them truly." The trial judge found that under this standard, L.P. was incompetent to testify. Since L.P. couldn't testify in court, L.P.'s out-of-court statement could only be admitted if the Confrontation Clause didn't apply.[7]

   b. **L.P.'s statements are admitted:** After finding L.P. to be incompetent to testify, the judge allowed L.P.'s out-of-court statements to his teachers to be admitted against D even though the statements were hearsay. The judge did this pursuant to a different Ohio evidence rule that allowed the admission of reliable hearsay statements made by child abuse victims.

---

6. In *Davis*, the statement was made by the victim to a 911 operator, but the operator's function was to dispatch the police.

7. Remember, if L.P. had been available to be cross-examined at trial about the out-of-court statement, admission of that statement could not have been a Confrontation Clause violation, because the availability of cross-examination would have given D the very right of "confrontation" that the Clause confers. See *supra*, p. 362.

c. Confrontation Clause argument rejected, and D is convicted: D argued that the admission of L.P.'s statements against him violated his Confrontation Clause rights. The trial judge rejected this argument, holding that the statements were ***not testimonial,*** and were therefore not covered by the Confrontation Clause. D was convicted and appealed. After an intermediate appellate court in Ohio reversed his conviction — by accepting D's Confrontation Clause argument — the case came to the Supreme Court.

2. **Holding:** In an opinion by Justice Alito, the Court ***unanimously*** reversed, holding that the trial court had gotten it right: L.P.'s statements were indeed ***non-testimonial***; therefore, the Confrontation Clause could not possibly apply to them.

3. **"Primary purpose" test applied:** Alito's opinion summarized the court's modern Confrontation Clause cases, beginning with *Crawford*. Those decisions, he said, made the distinction between testimonial and non-testimonial statements key, because "a statement ***cannot fall within the Confrontation Clause unless its primary purpose was testimonial.***" As he summarized the case law, "the ***primary purpose test*** is a ***necessary, but not always sufficient, condition*** for the exclusion of out-of court statements under the Confrontation Clause."[8]

4. **No automatic bar to statements made to persons other than police:** Alito then noted that *Clark* raised a question that the Court had previously avoided answering, "whether statements to ***persons other than law enforcement officers*** are subject to the Confrontation Clause." Speaking for a unanimous court, Alito in effect answered "yes": the Court "decline[s] to adopt a ***categorical rule*** excluding [such statements] from the Sixth Amendment's reach." The Court was rejecting such a categorical rule "[b]ecause at least *some* statements to individuals who are not law enforcement officers could conceivably raise confrontation concerns[.]" So if the primary purpose of a statement made to a person who was not a law enforcement officer was nonetheless testimonial, the statement would be covered by the Confrontation Clause, and thus normally[9] rendered inadmissible if the declarant was unavailable to testify.

5. **Meaning of "testimonial":** Alito reviewed how post-*Crawford* decisions had ***defined "testimonial."*** In *Davis v. Washington* (*supra*, p. 367), the Court had said that a statement would be non-testimonial if it was "not procured with a ***primary purpose of creating an out-of-court substitute for trial testimony.***" And *Hammon* (*supra*, p. 370) had articulated a similar — though not identical — definition: a statement made in response to an interrogation would not be testimonial unless "the primary purpose of the interrogation is to ***establish or prove past events potentially relevant to later criminal prosecution.***"

---

8. Here's what Alito meant by the "not always sufficient" language: even an out-of-court statement whose primary purpose was testimonial might not be excludible under the Confrontation Clause, because the Clause "does not prohibit the introduction of out-of-court statements that would have been admissible in a criminal case at the time of the founding." This aspect of the decision is covered *infra*, p. 367.

9. "Normally" because of the situation mentioned in the prior footnote, that of "out of-court statements that would have been admissible in a criminal case at the time of the founding" (a category that so far seems to include only dying declarations); see *infra*, p. 380.

6. **Statement here was not testimonial:** Alito then focused on the statements at issue here, L.P.'s statements to his preschool teachers. He phrased his conclusion this way: "[c]onsidering all the relevant circumstances here, L.P.'s statements clearly were not made with the ***primary purpose*** of ***creating evidence for Clark's prosecution.***"

   a. **Two factors:** Alito pointed to two factors that made it unlikely that L.P.'s statements had a primary purpose of creating evidence to be used in a later prosecution of D: (1) the statements were made to ***non-law-enforcement personnel in an emergency situation***; and (2) the declarant was a ***very young child.*** We'll analyze these factors one at a time, in Pars. (b) and (c) below.

   b. **Statement made to one interested in safety, not prosecution:** First, Alito found it highly significant that L.P.'s statements occurred in the context of an ***ongoing emergency that had to do with L.P.'s safety,*** not with a possible prosecution. When the teachers asked L.P. how he had been hurt and by whom, they ***feared ongoing child-abuse*** — their main concern was that if they released L.P. to his guardian at the end of the day, they might be entrusting him to the very person who had abused him. Thus the "primary purpose" of the conversation, Alito said, was to ***protect L.P.***, not to ***"gather evidence*** for Clark's prosecution."

      i. **Rule of thumb:** In fact, Alito articulated a rule of thumb that is likely to prove important in future cases: "Statements made to someone who is ***not principally charged with uncovering and prosecuting criminal behavior*** are ***significantly less likely to be testimonial*** than statements given to law enforcement officers." So the fact that the statements here were made to teachers rather than police officers — without more — made it very unlikely that the statements had a primary purpose of creating evidence to be used in a prosecution (the only primary purpose that can trigger the Confrontation Clause).

   c. **Extreme youth:** A second major factor, Alito said, was L.P.'s ***extreme youth*** (remember, he was just three years old), which made it very unlikely that his statements satisfied the primary-purpose test.

      i. **Rule of thumb:** Again, Alito set forth a rule of thumb: "Statements by ***very young children*** will ***rarely, if ever,*** implicate the Confrontation Clause." Only a conversation whose primary purpose was to "gather evidence for [a] prosecution" could be testimonial. And, Alito wrote, "it is extremely unlikely that a 3-year-old child in L.P.'s position would ***intend his statements to be a substitute for trial testimony.***" Rather, "a young child in these circumstances would simply want the abuse to end, would want to protect other victims, or would have ***no discernible purpose at all.***"

7. **Mandatory duty to report:** Lastly, Alito disposed of one other issue in the case. D had pointed out that under an Ohio ***"mandatory reporting"*** statute, L.P.'s preschool teachers were ***required*** to report suspected child abuse to authorities. D argued that the statute had in effect converted the teachers' questioning of L.P. into the equivalent of law-enforcement questioning of a witness. But Alito ***rejected*** this argument: "The teachers' pressing concern was to protect L.P. and remove him from harm's way [and] they undoubtedly ***would have acted with the same purpose*** whether or not they had a state-law duty to

report abuse." Therefore, the existence of the mandatory reporting statute did not turn L.P.'s statements into "testimonial" ones.

8. **Primary-purpose as necessary but not always sufficient for Clause to apply:** *Clark* doesn't make new law as to the function of the primary-purpose test. But Alito's opinion contains a crisp statement of existing law as to how the test does and doesn't apply in Confrontation Clause situations. As Alito put it, "the primary purpose test is a ***necessary, but not always sufficient, condition*** for the exclusion of out-of court statements under the Confrontation Clause[.]" Let's examine how both the "necessary" and the "not sufficient" branches of this proposition work:

   a. **"Necessary":**   For a statement to be excludible by virtue of the Confrontation Clause, that statement ***must*** have had a primary purpose that was "testimonial," i.e., made in order to "establish or prove ***past events potentially relevant to later criminal prosecution***[.]" (*Hammon, supra,* p. 370.) So satisfaction of the primary purpose test is always ***"necessary"*** (required) for the Confrontation Clause to bar the statement from evidence.

   b. **Not always "sufficient":** On the other hand, the fact that an out-of-court statement has a primary purpose that is testimonial is ***"not sufficient"*** to guarantee that the statement will be barred by the Confrontation Clause. That's because, as Alito put it in *Clark,* "We have recognized that the Confrontation Clause does not prohibit the introduction of out of-court statements that ***would have been admissible in a criminal case at the time of the founding.***"

      i. **Dying declarations:** So far, the only type of out-of-court declaration that the Court has identified as not being barred by the Confrontation Clause even if the declaration is found to be testimonial — i.e., the one type of statement for which testimonial status is *not sufficient* to trigger the Clause — is the ***dying declaration.*** The Court has confirmed that at the time the Constitution (including the Confrontation Clause) was adopted, the common-law right to confront witnesses did not apply to bar the introduction of dying declarations. See *Gilles v. California,* 544 U.S. 353 (2008).

         Example: Vic lies dying of a gunshot wound. Wit, a uniformed on-duty police officer who happens to be passing by, tries to stanch the bleeding with a tourniquet. While Wit is doing this, he asks Vic, "Who shot you?" Vic answers, "D did it. He's always wanted me dead, and now he's about to get his wish. Promise me you'll bring him to justice." Vic then dies. At D's murder trial, the prosecution offers Wit's testimony about what Vic told him, offered to prove that D really did the shooting. D objects on Confrontation Clause grounds, asserting that the Clause applies because the primary purpose of Vic's "D shot me" statement was to "establish or prove past events potentially relevant to later criminal prosecution[.]"

         D's objection will be overruled. It's true that Vic's statement was "testimonial," since Vic's primary purpose in making it was clearly to help Wit get a conviction. But the statement meets the hearsay-exception requirements for dying declarations (see *supra,* p. 290), which were admissible in criminal prosecutions at the time the Constitution was adopted in 1788. Therefore, the Confrontation

Clause does not apply, and the dying declaration is admissible even though Vic is not available to be cross-examined.

9. **Significance of *Clark*:** *Clark* does not make any significant new law. But it helps solidify a couple of propositions about when a statement is "testimonial," and thus capable of triggering the Confrontation Clause:

   a. **Statements made to non-law-enforcement person:** Statements made to people who are ***not associated with law enforcement*** are not ***automatically*** deemed to be non-testimonial. But for a statement to be testimonial (and thus eligible to be covered by the confrontation clause), the statement must have a "primary purpose" of creating an "out-of-court substitute for trial testimony[.]" And, *Clark* tells us, statements to "someone who is ***not principally charged with uncovering and prosecuting criminal behavior"*** are ***"significantly less likely to be testimonial*** than statements given to law enforcement officers."

   b. **Statements made by young children:** Similarly, statements made by ***young children*** are quite unlikely to be testimonial. To quote the majority opinion, "Statements by very young children [e.g., the 3-year-old L.P. in *Clark*] will rarely, if ever, implicate the Confrontation Clause."

      i. **Adolescents:** But the fact that the declarant is not yet an "adult" does not by itself make her statement less likely to be testimonial. ***Adolescents***, for instance, can easily make testimonial statements.

         Example: Suppose that on the approximate facts of *Clark*, the victim, V, was a 13-year-old boy who, when asked by a teacher about bruises on his face, said that they came from being beaten by D, his mother's boyfriend. There's a good chance that V would be found to have known enough about child abuse as a potential crime, and about how criminal prosecutions work, that V's statement would be found to have had the primary purpose of "establish[ing] or prov[ing] past events potentially relevant to later criminal prosecution" (the definition of "testimonial" given in *Hammon, supra,* p. 370). If so, D would have been entitled to have the statement excluded on Confrontation Clause grounds. Cf. R. Friedman, The Confrontation Blog, http://confrontationright.blogspot.com, June 19, 2015, accessed on Nov. 7, 2017: "If we took a case very similar to *Clark* but made the victim [a] 13-year-old ... I think the case would have looked very different."

10. **Statements made to health-care providers:** One scenario involving statements made to non-law-enforcement personnel arises frequently: statements made by ***victims of sexual assault, domestic violence***, and the like to ***health-care providers, such as rape counselors and forensic nurses.*** As long as the focus of the interaction between the health-care provider and the victim is on ensuring that the victim ***remains safe*** and ***gets appropriate treatment,*** the court is likely to hold that the victim's answer to questions like, "Who did this to you?" was non-testimonial, and thus beyond the reach of the Confrontation Clause.

    Example: J.M., a young mother who has recently sustained bruises all over her body and is in great pain, is taken by paramedics to the emergency room of a hospital. At the emergency room, a Forensic Nurse begins her examination of J.M. by asking her what happened to her. J.M. answers that she was struck repeatedly with a belt by her boyfriend Ward. The Forensic Nurse continues the examination to rule out internal injuries, enters an order that J.M. be listed as a "no information" patient in the hospital's record system (so that no one, especially Ward, can learn her whereabouts), discharges J.M. to her parents' home instead of the home J.M. shares with Ward, and refers J.M. to two domestic-violence support organizations. Ward is charged with various felonies arising out of the attack. J.M. fails to cooperate with the prosecution or to appear at scheduled depositions. At trial, with J.M. absent, the prosecution offers J.M.'s statement to the Forensic Nurse implicating Ward. Ward claims that the statement is a testimonial one, and is therefore inadmissible by virtue of the Confrontation Clause. The trial judge disagrees, allows the statement into evidence, and finds Ward guilty.

Held (on appeal), for the prosecution. *Clark* and other Supreme Court cases establish that a statement is testimonial only if "in light of all the circumstances, viewed objectively, the 'primary purpose' of the conversation was to 'creat[e] an out-of-court substitute for trial testimony'." Here, J.M.'s statements to the Forensic Nurse "served the primary purpose of medical treatment." That treatment included making sure that the hospital records would not disclose J.M.'s whereabouts to her attacker, ensuring that J.M. would be discharged to a safe location, and referring J.M. to appropriate sources of domestic-violence counseling. All of these medically-relevant steps could not have been taken without the Nurse's first having determined that J.M. had been attacked by her domestic partner rather than by, say, a stranger. Since J.M's statement was non-testimonial, it was not covered by the Confrontation Clause, and was therefore properly admitted against Ward. *Ward v. Indiana*, 50 N.E.3d 752 (Ind. 2016).

G. Forensic reports: So far, all of the cases we have examined starting with *Crawford* have involved "*interrogations*," in which someone — usually but not always a member of law enforcement — asks questions to which the declarant, generally a crime victim, gives answers. But the Confrontation Clause has to deal with a second, quite different, arena: *forensic reports*, in which an expert, often affiliated with law enforcement, makes a statement (usually written) about *what a piece of evidence shows.* In these forensic-report situations, the Confrontation Clause question is, must the *person who prepared the report* be available for cross-examination at trial, if the report is to be accepted as evidence of facts that it asserts?

In general, the Court's answer has been *"yes"*: assuming that the forensic report is offered to prove the truth of some statement in it, the preparer of the report — or at least someone with first-hand knowledge of any testing described in the report — *must appear at the trial* and be subject to cross-examination. This can be seen from a trio of Supreme Court decisions that began in 2009.

1. **Lab reports by law-enforcement personnel (*Melendez-Diaz*):** The first of these cases was *Melendez-Diaz v. Massachusetts*, 129 S.Ct. 2527 (2009). There, the Court held that *laboratory reports* by created by or for law enforcement personnel will ordinarily be *"testimonial"* under *Crawford* and *Davis*. Therefore, such a report cannot be introduced to prove the truth of matters asserted in it, unless a *person involved in producing the report is made available* for cross-examination at trial.

a. **Facts:** In *Melendez-Diaz*, D was charged with cocaine trafficking under Massachusetts state law. To prove that the substance seized by the police from D was cocaine, the prosecution offered into evidence ***"certificates of analysis"*** stating that the tests conducted by the state police laboratory on the substance confirmed that it was cocaine. The analysts who prepared the certificates signed them and had them notarized. Such notarized certificates were admissible under state law to serve as prima facie evidence of the composition of the substance being analyzed. The prosecution did not make the analysts themselves available at trial.

b. **Majority finds reports to be "testimonial":** In an opinion by Justice Scalia (the author of *Crawford* and *Davis*), a five-member majority of the Court held that the certificates ***were "testimonial statements" under Crawford.*** Therefore, the analysts who prepared them were "witnesses" for Confrontation Clause purposes. Since the prosecution neither produced the analysts for cross-examination at trial nor showed that they were unavailable, admission of the certificates violated D's Confrontation Clause rights.

   i. **Rationale:** The majority reasoned that these certificates of analysis contained the ***precise testimony*** that the authors (the analysts) would be expected to provide if they were called as witnesses at trial. Furthermore, under state law the very ***purpose*** of the certificates was to serve as evidence of the composition of the substance in question, so the analysts who prepared them must have been aware of their evidentiary purpose. Therefore, the analysts were witnesses "against" D, the statements were "testimonial" under *Crawford*, and their use triggered D's Confrontation Clause rights.

      (1) **Consequence:** Therefore, the majority said, if the prosecution wanted to use the certificates as evidence, it had to either produce the analysts for cross-examination at trial, or else show both that (1) the analysts were unavailable to testify at trial and (2) the defendant had been given a ***chance to cross-examine them*** before trial.

c. **Dissent:** The four ***dissenters***, in an opinion by Kennedy (joined by Roberts, Breyer and Alito), argued that *Crawford* and *Davis* did not and should not cover forensic analysts. The dissenters believed that those two cases should be limited to testimony by an ***"ordinary" witness***, i.e., an individual "who witnesses (that is, ***perceives***) an ***event*** that gives him or her ***personal knowledge of some aspect of the defendant's guilt***." The dissenters believed that the right of confrontation did not apply to "laboratory analysts who conduct routine scientific tests."

   i. **Warning:** Justice Kennedy warned that under the majority's approach, prosecutors would often face ***large practical difficulties*** in presenting live testimony by the analyst who prepared the lab report: the analyst might be ill, out of the country, prevented from appearing because of bad weather, or required to testify at another defendant's trial asserting the same right. The result, he predicted, would be that the defendant would "go free on a technicality," giving a "windfall to defendants" without providing "any perceptible benefit" to society.

2. **"Surrogate testimony" won't suffice (*Bullcoming*):** *Melendez-Diaz* made it clear that when a forensic report is used for testimonial purposes (such as the analyst certificates i that case, which were found to be the equivalent of testimony that the seized substance was cocaine), the report must be accompanied by a live witness who can be cross-examined about the report. But *Melendez-Diaz* did not deal with *which witnesses* must be called in connection with such a report. Obviously, testimony by the person who *actually did the analysis* whose results are recited in the report would suffice. But what if that person is not available? Can someone *other than the preparer* of the report — a *"surrogate witness,"* so to speak — appear in court, so as to meet the demands of the Confrontation Clause?

The second case in the Court's recent trio of forensic-report cases suggests that the answer will usually be *"no."* At least where the surrogate witness is not intimately familiar with the particular work reflected in the report, that witness's testimony is *not sufficient* to satisfy the Confrontation Clause, even. if the witness is familiar with the general methods used by the person who actually prepared the report. The case so holding is *Bullcoming v. New Mexico*, 131 S.Ct. 2705 (2011).

a. **Facts:** In *Bullcoming*, D (Donald Bullcoming) was arrested in New Mexico for drunk driving. When he refused to take a breathalyzer test, police got a warrant to test his blood for its blood alcohol content (BAC). They sent the sample to the New Mexico Scientific Laboratory Division (SLD), where Caylor, a forensic analyst, used a gas chromatograph machine to test the sample's BAC. Caylor prepared a report stating that the test showed that D had a BAC of .21, enough to support a charge of aggravated DWI.

    i. **Substitute witness used:** At D's trial, the prosecution did not present Caylor as a witness, saying that he had recently been put on unpaid leave for a reason not revealed. Instead, the prosecution proposed to introduce Caylor's report as a *business record*, pursuant to the sponsoring testimony of Razatos, a different scientist in the SLD who had not observed Caylor's work or reviewed his analysis. D's counsel objected on Confrontation Clause grounds, but the trial court overruled the objection and admitted Caylor's report as a business record. D was convicted.

    ii. **State court affirms:** The New Mexico Supreme Court affirmed the conviction. That court conceded that the report was "testimonial," and that it therefore could not be admitted without a sponsoring witness who could be cross-examined about it. But the court said that *Razatos' testimony sufficed*: Razatos had sufficient knowledge about the operation of the gas chromatograph that his availability for cross-examination about how the test was done was sufficient to satisfy D's Confrontation Clause rights.

b. **Reversed by 5-4 vote:** By a 5-4 vote, the Supreme Court reversed, holding that Razatos' testimony was *not sufficient* to satisfy D's right of confrontation. The majority opinion, by Justice Ginsburg, said that *"surrogate testimony"* of the kind that Razatos presented did not meet Confrontation Clause standards because it "could not convey *what Caylor* [the certifying analyst] *knew or observed* about the events his certification concerned, i.e., the *particular test and testing process* he employed."

Furthermore, this surrogate testimony could not "expose any *lapses or lies* on the certifying analyst's part."

    i.   **Unpaid leave:** For Ginsburg, it was especially significant that Razatos had no knowledge of the *reason Caylor had been placed on unpaid leave*. If it was Caylor rather than Razatos on the stand, D's counsel "could have asked questions designed to reveal whether incompetence, evasiveness, or dishonesty accounted for Caylor's removal from his workstation."

c. **Sotomayor's concurrence:** Justice Sotomayor concurred in part (and in the result). Since the case was decided by 5-4, her vote was necessary to the outcome. She stressed that the Court was *not deciding* the significance of several factors which if present might produce a *different outcome* in other forensic-report cases. Since these factors may be present in future cases, her comments are worth mentioning:

    [1] **Medical reports:** Some reports, although forensic in nature, might be admissible for an *alternate primary purpose* that would prevent them from being found to be "testimonial," Sotomayor said. For instance, a *medical report* done principally for the purpose of giving a crime victim *treatment* would be admissible, because its primary purpose would not be testimonial.

    [2] **Personal connection by witness:** If the witness at trial — even though she did not prepare the forensic report — had had some "*personal*, albeit limited, *connection*" to the test at issue, that might be enough to permit the witness to meet the requirements of the Confrontation Clause. For instance, the result might be different if "a *supervisor* who *observed an analyst* conducting a test testified about the results or a report about such results." Similarly, a person who *reviewed the report* might be adequate. This issues weren't posed here, Sotomayor said, because it was clear that Razatos had had no involvement at all in the test and report.

    [3] **Independent opinion:** If the trial witness was *not* asking that the *report be put in evidence*, but was merely giving his *independent opinion of the facts, based on the report's conclusions*, that testimony might pass muster. (This turned out to be a prescient observation, since that's exactly what a plurality deemed to have happened in the next case in the forensic-reports trio, *Williams*, discussed *infra*.)

    [4] **Machine-generated reports:** Finally, Sotomayor said, there might not be a confrontation problem if the state introduced "*only machine-generated results*, such as a printout from a gas chromatograph." Here, the Caylor report that was being introduced contained Caylor's own statements covering such matters as the procedures used in handling the blood sample. It was possible, Sotomayor observed, that the standalone introduction of the machine's output would not pose Confrontation Clause problems.

d. **Dissent:** The same four justices who had *dissented* in *Melendez-Diaz* also dissented in *Bullcoming*. Justice Kennedy (joined by Roberts, Breyer and Alito) argued that Caylor's testimony was not necessary to meet the demands of the Confrontation Clause, because he made no sworn statement in his report, making the case different from *Melendez-Diaz*.

    i.   **"Chain of custody" rationale:** Kennedy reasoned that Caylor's role as certifying analyst here was "no greater than that of ***anyone else in the chain of custody***." The information in the report was "the result of a scientific process comprising ***multiple participants' acts***, each with its own evidentiary significance." That being the case, requiring the state to "call the technician who filled out a form and recorded the results of a test is a ***hollow formality***." The defense had many ways to attack the reliability of the test (e.g., the right to call Caylor itself, or the right to call other expert witnesses to explain that such a test is not always reliable).

    ii. **Disruption of criminal procedures:** By insisting on live testimony from one of the multiple participants in the testing process, Kennedy said, the majority was "extending and confirming *Melendez-Diaz*'s ***vast potential to disrupt criminal procedures***." More generally, by applying *Crawford* to laboratory reports, the Court was making an "interpretation of the word ***'witness'*** at odds with its meaning elsewhere in the Constitution." Even if *Melendez-Diaz* was to remain in force (which Kennedy thought it shouldn't), the Court ought to at least not extend it so as to "bar the ***reliable, commonsense evidentiary framework*** the state sought to follow in this case."

3. **Report comes in without testimony of preparer (*Williams v. Illinois*):** Finally, in the last case of the trio on forensic reports and the Confrontation Clause to be decided by the Court to date, the prosecution ***won one*** — some of the substance of a forensic report was found to have been ***properly presented*** to the trier of fact, without testimony by anyone who was involved in the preparation of the report. ***Williams v. Illinois***, 132 S.Ct. 2221 (2012). However, in *Williams*, no opinion captured a majority of the Court, and it is impossible to state a single rationale that explains why the prosecution won.

    a. **Facts:** *Williams* was a DNA-matching case. L.J. was sexually assaulted in Chicago, and the Illinois state police lab (ISP) sent vaginal swabs taken from her to a private out-of-state DNA lab, Cellmark. Cellmark prepared a DNA profile apparently based on those swabs, and returned the profile to the ISP. Sandra Lambatos, a forensic specialist at the ISP, then searched Illinois' own state-wide DNA database, and discovered that the Cellmark profile matched a sample that the Illinois database had for D (Sandy Williams), which D had given pursuant to an unrelated charge. At the time Lambatos did the search, D was not yet under suspicion for L.J.'s rape. Once suspicion focused on D because of the match, he was put in a lineup and identified by L.J. as her assailant.

    i. **Trial:** D's trial was a bench trial, i.e., before a judge sitting without a jury. No one from Cellmark testified about preparation of the DNA profile from the vaginal swabs. One ISP employee testified about preparing the swabs for DNA testing before they were sent to Cellmark. Another ISP worker testified about having prepared the DNA sample known to have come from D and entering it into the Illinois database. Then, Lambatos took the stand as an expert witness in forensic DNA analysis.

      (1) Lambatos' testimony: Lambatos testified from shipping manifests and other records that the ISP had sent the vaginal swabs to Cellmark, and had received a profile back from Cellmark. She then testified that it was commonly accepted practice for one DNA expert to rely on the records of another DNA expert. Therefore, she said, she relied on the Cellmark profile as being a correct profile of the DNA found in the vaginal swabs. She then stated her expert opinion that there was a match between the Cellmark sample and the sample known to be from D found in the Illinois database. On cross, Lambatos acknowledged that she did not conduct or observe any of the testing on the vaginal swabs by Cellmark; she relied on Cellmark to produce a reliable DNA profile.

(2) Trial judge's reponse: D's counsel objected, on Confrontation grounds, to Lambatos' testimony relying on the Cellmark report, since the report had not been put in evidence and Lambatos had no personal knowledge of how the report was prepared. But the prosecution argued that under Illinois evidence law (which matches the FRE on this point), an expert is allowed to disclose the ***facts on which her opinion is based***, even if the expert is not competent to testify to those underlying facts. The trial judge agreed that Lambatos' reliance on the report was allowable even though the report never came into evidence. The judge then found D guilty.

ii. Affirmed by state supreme court: The Illinois Supreme Court affirmed, on the grounds that when Lambatos referred to the Cellmark report during her testimony, she did so "for the limited purpose of ***explaining the basis for***" her expert opinion, ***not*** for the purpose of ***showing the truth*** of the matter asserted in the report. Therefore, there was no confrontation problem.

b. Supreme Court affirms: By yet another a 5-4 vote, the Supreme Court agreed that D's confrontation rights had ***not been violated*** by the trial judge's handling of the Cellmark report. But no five judges agreed on the rationale, with four offering two distinct rationales, and a fifth offering a completely different third rationale.

i. Alito's plurality opinion: Writing for a four-justice ***plurality*** (Roberts, Kennedy, Breyer and himself), Justice Alito gave two rationales in support of the conclusion that the use of the Cellmark report here did not violate D's confrontation rights.

(1) Basis for expert's opinion: First, he said, the Illinois Supreme Court's rationale was correct: when Lambatos summarized the findings of the Cellmark report, she was not offering those findings for the ***truth of what they asserted***, but merely to explain the ***"basis for"*** her own conclusion that the two DNA profiles matched. Thus when she mentioned that Cellmark had generated its DNA profile from the vaginal swabs of the victim, she did not mean to assert that it was *really true* that Cellmark had generated that DNA profile from the swabs (she didn't claim to have personal knowledge of whether this was true); she was merely saying that her own expert conclusion (that the DNA profile known to be D's matched the DNA from the swabs) was based on the *premise* that the Cellmark profile was generated from those swabs. Since only testimonial statements offered to prove the truth of the matter asserted can violate the Confrontation Clause, the fact that what was at issue here was a "premise not offered for its truth" meant that no violation occurred.[10]

(2) No "targeting" purpose: As a second rationale, Alito reasoned that even if the Cellmark report *had* been admitted for its truth, there would have been no Confrontation Clause violation because the report did not have "the primary purpose of ***accusing a targeted individual of engaging in criminal conduct***." Alito asserted that in all of the Court's prior *Crawford*-line decisions, use of an out-of-court statement violated the confrontation right only if the statement "had the primary purpose of ***accusing a targeted individual***." Here by contrast, the primary purpose of the report was not to "accus[e] a targeted individual," but to "***catch a dangerous rapist who was still at large***." Thus Alito seemed to be adding a never-before-articulated requirement to the "primary purpose" test: an out-of-court statement could be testimonial, and thus violative of the Confrontation Clause, only if the statement's primary purpose was not just to be testimonial, but to "***accuse a targeted individual.***"

    ii. **Fifth vote from Thomas:** Justice Thomas did not join the reasoning behind *either* of the plurality's rationales — indeed, he expressly agreed with the dissent's view that both of these rationales were "flawed." But by concurring in the result, he supplied the fifth vote needed for the holding that the Confrontation Clause was not violated. He did this based on a rationale that he had frequently articulated, but that no other member of the Court had ever supported: that only statements having a certain "formality and solemnity" (like affidavits and hearing testimony) could violate the Confrontation Clause, and that the Cellmark report here did not have those formal attributes, apparently because the report did not contain any certification or oath.

  c. **Dissent:** Justice Kagan *dissented*, joined by Justices Scalia, Ginsburg, and Sotomayor.

    i. **False report:** She began by relating an example of the type of horrific fact-finding error that might occur if a person in D's position was not permitted to cross-examine the maker of a forensic report. In the "Kocak" case in California some years before, the same lab that was involved here, Cellmark, had prepared a report saying that the DNA sample found on a rape victim's bloody sweatshirt matched a control sample known to be the defendant's DNA. The analyst who prepared the report testified that the lab had identified this match. But the analyst then realized to her horror that the lab had confused the defendant's DNA control sample with the *victim's* control sample, and that the report was saying merely that the blood-based DNA on the sweatshirt matched the victim's DNA. Kagan noted that had the prosecutor in the Kocak case merely asked someone not connected with the lab to present the lab's findings — with the defendant having no opportunity to cross-examine the report's maker — the error probably would not have come to light. Therefore, it is vital, Kagan said, that the preparer of a forensic report be in court and subject to cross-examination.

---

10. Alito seemed to feel that with respect to this "not offered for its truth" rationale, it was very significant that the factfinder was a *judge*, not a jury. While a *jury* might have been misled into believing that Lambatos was asserting that the Cellmark report really was produced from the vaginal swabs, no trial judge would have made that mistake, he said.

ii. **"Not for truth" rationale rejected:** Kagan also rejected the plurality's rationale that Lambatos had not offered the Cellmark report *for its truth*. Lambatos' conclusion was completely *dependent on the truth of the report* — to determine the validity of Lambatos' conclusion, the factfinder (here, the judge) *had to assess the truth* of the out-of-court statement (the report). Specifically, Lambatos' assertion that there was a "match" between the DNA on the victim's vaginal swabs and D's control DNA sample was meaningful only if Cellmark had in fact prepared its profile from the vaginal swabs. So the factfinder could assess Lambatos' testimony as relevant (i.e., as showing a "match" tying the vaginal swabs to D) only by finding that Cellmark had in fact prepared its profile from the swabs rather than from some other source (e.g., from a sample known to have come from D). Lambatos thus was exactly like the expert in *Bullcoming* (Razatos), who testified to the truth of someone's else's report without any first-hand knowledge — Lambatos' testimony was the very sort of surrogate testimony that had been rejected in *Bullcoming*.

(1) **Other tests rejected:** Finally, Kagan rejected both the plurality's new "targeted individual" variant of the primary-purpose test and Thomas's solemnity-based test. With respect to the former, none of the Court's cases had ever suggested that to be testimonial, the statement must be "meant to accuse a *previously identified* individual." And there was no reason for such a requirement; true, the lack of a targeted individual made it less likely that the lab was pursuing a *personal vendetta*. But the bigger reliability problem — and the most likely subject of cross-examination — would come from "careless or incompetent work," as to which the lack of a targeted individual "makes not a whit of difference."

d. **Confusing effect of *Williams*:** So *Williams* leaves Confrontation Clause doctrine in a more confused state than it was before. The only proposition of law and fact on which five justices could agree was that the Cellmark report could *not* be admitted on the rationale that it was offered only to show the basis for the testifying expert's opinion, not for its own truth. And yet, the report ended up admissible because of a combination of four votes from the plurality, plus a fifth vote from Thomas that was based on an entirely different rationale.

i. **Effect:** For future cases, it sounds as though the only way a statement in a laboratory report offered for its truth can come in without firsthand testimony about how it was produced will be if the report happens to satisfy *two quite independent requirements:*

[1] Under the four *Williams*-plurality justices' newly-tweaked primary-purpose test, by which a statement that does not *accuse a targeted individual* is non-testimonial, the lab report in question must not accuse any such person; plus

(ii) Under Thomas' completely different one-justice view that a report that *lacks "solemnity"* can never be testimonial, the lab report in question must lack solemnity.

There should not be many reports that happen to satisfy both of these requirements simultaneously.   Therefore, there shouldn't be many lab reports that are admissible without firsthand "sponsoring" testimony.

IV. CONFRONTATION CLAUSE — AN ATTEMPTED SYNTHESIS

A. **An attempted synthesis:**   Let's now try to synthesize what all of these *Crawford*-line cases mean. Some aspects of post-*Crawford* Confrontation Clause doctrine are pretty well solidified by now, but others are muddled. Since the critical distinction is whether the out-of-court statement is "testimonial" or non-testimonial, we'll first review that distinction. We'll then attempt to summarize separately the rules for handling testimonial and non-testimonial statements.

B. **The main rule:** The main rule about the Confrontation Clause is this: If the out-of-court statement is *"testimonial,"* it *may not be admitted against the accused* — in the absence of the declarant's presence and availability for cross-examination at trial — unless *two separate requirements are met*:

❏ First, the declarant must be *"unavailable" to testify at trial*; and

❏ Second, the accused must have had *a prior opportunity* to *cross-examine the declarant* about the statement.

By contrast, if the statement is *not testimonial*, then its admission *cannot violate the defendant's confrontation rights.* See *infra*, p. 396.

C. **Distinguishing testimonial and non-testimonial statements:** Here's a summary of the Court's present thinking about when a statement is or isn't testimonial.

1. **Listing of "testimonial" statements:**   At a minimum, the following types of statements *will* be considered testimonial under *Crawford* and *Davis v. Washington*:

❏ *prior testimony* at a *preliminary hearing*;

❏ *prior testimony* before a *grand jury*;

❏ testimony at a *former trial* (whether of the present defendant or of someone else);

❏ an *affidavit* issued as part of a law-enforcement proceeding;

❏ statements made in *forensic laboratory reports* created to help solve or prosecute a crime;

❏ perhaps most significantly, *statements made during the course of police interrogations,* including interviews by police at *crime scenes,* as long as the focus of the interrogation is on *investigating a completed crime*, not on *managing an ongoing emergency.*

2. **More detailed discussion:** Here is a more detailed discussion of the three most important situations in which the testimonial/non-testimonial distinction has to be made: (1) *interrogations* by law enforcement; (2) informal statements made to persons who are *not part of law enforcement*; and (3) statements made in *forensic* reports.

a. Interrogations by law enforcement: The most common situation in which the testimonial/non-testimonial distinction has to be made is when the out-of-court statement occurs during the course of an *"interrogation"* of a witness or victim *by law enforcement officers*. Here (as well as in the non-law-enforcement scenario), the Court follows a *"primary purpose"* approach:

❏ **Prove past events:** The statement will be testimonial if and only if "the *primary purpose* of the interrogation is to *establish or prove past events potentially relevant to later criminal prosecution."* (*Davis*) So the typical after-the-fact *crime-scene interview* of a victim will be testimonial.

❏ **Some other purpose:** By contrast, statements *won't* be testimonial if the primary purpose of the interrogation is to achieve some objective other than proving past events for potential prosecution. Most importantly, if the purpose of the interrogation is "to enable police assistance to meet an *ongoing emergency,*" the statement will not be testimonial (and can be admitted without worrying about the Confrontation Clause). Much of our discussion below therefore focuses on distinguishing between statements whose primary purpose is to establish past events for a later prosecution, and statements whose primary purpose is to help the authorities deal with an ongoing emergency.

Here are some factors that influence a court's decision about whether the primary purpose of the interrogation is to make a record for prosecution, or to deal with an ongoing emergency:

i. Emergency danger to police or public: An *ongoing emergency* does not necessarily have to consist of an ongoing danger to the initial *victim*. In some circumstances, the danger can extend to *"the responding police and the public at large."* (*Michigan v. Bryant*). For instance, if declarant is a shooting victim, and the police reasonably believe that the shooter is still at large and poses a danger to themselves or the public, this can qualify as an ongoing emergency (making the declaration non-testimonial) even if it's clear to all that the declarant-victim is himself still in danger. (*Bryant*).

ii. Purpose of interrogators and victim: In determining the primary purpose, what counts is the "primary purpose of the *interrogation*," and the statements and actions of *both* the declarant *and interrogators* are to be considered in determining the "investigation's" purpose. (*Bryant*) Therefore, if the *police* think that they are dealing with an ongoing emergency, apparently that will be enough to cause the declarant's statements to be non-testimonial even if the *declarant* believes that he is himself in no further danger. (That's what seems to have happened in *Bryant*)

iii. Objective test: In determining the primary purpose of the investigation, the test is an *"objective,"* not "subjective" one. That is, the issue is not the subjective or actual purpose of the individuals involved in a particular encounter, but rather "the purpose that *reasonable participants would have had*, as ascertained from the individuals' statements and actions in the circumstances in which the encounter occurred." (*Bryant*)

iv. **Other factors:**   In determining the primary purpose of the interrogation (e.g., to deal with an ongoing emergency, versus to record facts for a later prosecution), the Court has singled out several factors as being potentially significant:

❑ **Type of weapon:** The *type of weapon* involved may make a difference. If the wrongdoer used only his *fists*, then separating him from the victim may be enough to end the emergency (as in *Hammon*), making it more likely that the purpose of the ensuing interrogation is testimonial (to make a trial record). But if the wrongdoer used a *gun* and is now on the loose, the emergency is less likely to be over than in the fists-only situation (making the declarations less likely to be testimonial).

❑ **Medical condition of declarant:** The *medical condition of the declarant* may make a difference. For instance, a badly injured victim might be incapable of forming *any purpose at all*, let alone a testimonial one. (And if such a victim makes a statement without *any* purpose, the statement won't be testimonial, because an affirmative purpose to make a factual record to be used for prosecution — not merely the absence of a purpose to achieve some other objective — seems to be required for a triggering of confrontation rights.)

❑ **Level of formality:** The degree of *formality* in the encounter will often be suggestive of the encounter's primary purpose. Thus if the encounter is *highly informal* (e.g., in public, and/or carried out in a disorganized fashion), this makes it more likely to be for the purpose of dealing with an emergency, not for the purpose of developing facts for trial. Conversely, a station-house interrogation, conducted in an organized fashion (as in *Crawford*), suggests a purpose of making a trial record, making the statement more likely to be testimonial.

❑ **Falls into hearsay exception:** If the declaration *fits within a traditional hearsay exception* (and is thus presumptively *reliable*), it's apparently more likely to be found non-testimonial. So for instance, if the declaration is an *excited utterance* — and perhaps even if it's, say, a *co-conspirator's statement* made in the furtherance of the conspiracy, or a *business record* created in the ordinary course of the business's operation — such a statement is not only more reliable but less likely to have been made primarily for use in a prosecution, making it less likely to be found testimonial. (*Bryant*)

b. **Statements to non-law-enforcement agents:** If the declarant's statement is *not* made to a law enforcement agent, it's *less likely to be found to be testimonial* than in the law-enforcement-interrogation scenario. The Supreme Court has decided only one case that was clearly of this type, *Ohio v. Clark* (where the Court unanimously agreed that the 3-year-old abuse victim's statement to his preschool teachers about the cause of his injuries was not testimonial).

i. **Statement to caregiver:** If the statement is made by a crime victim to a non-law-enforcement *caregiver* in order to get *medical or other treatment* made necessary by the crime, the statement is *unlikely* to be found to be testimonial.

(1) Statement to preschool teacher: *Ohio v. Clark* falls into this category: when 3-year-old L.P. arrived at preschool with bruises and told his teachers that his mother's boyfriend had done this, the Court found that the teachers were motivated primarily by caring for L.P., making the conversation non-testimonial.

(2) Medical service providers: The same result — a finding of non-testimoniality — is likely where a crime victim's statement is made to a provider of *medical services.*

Example: Suppose a victim of *sexual assault or domestic violence* goes to the hospital for medical treatment, and is interviewed by a *forensic nurse* or a *psychologist.* The caregiver asks, "What happened?" The victim names her attacker and describes the attack. As long as the information is found to be relevant to *treatment* and/or to *protecting the victim from further harm* — for instance, by making sure she is not discharged to the care of her attacker, or by giving her an appropriate referral for psychological counseling — the victim's statement will almost certainly be found to be non-testimonial, and thus admissible against the assailant without triggering the Confrontation Clause. See, e.g., *Ward v. Indiana, supra,* p. 382.

ii. Statement to friend or family member: Now, suppose the statement is made by a crime victim to a *friend or family member.* Here, it's certainly possible that the statement may be held to be testimonial.

Example: V, a 35-year-old woman, tells her friend, "If I should ever be found dead in my bed of an apparent heart attack, don't believe it — tell the police that my husband Dave has probably had me poisoned for the insurance money." V is soon thereafter found dead, Dave is prosecuted for her murder, and the prosecution offers V's statement against him. Since V seems to have made the statement for purposes of seeing to it that Dave would be prosecuted for murder if V died, V's statement would almost certainly be found to have been testimonial, and would therefore trigger Dave's Confrontation Clause right to have it excluded.

(1) Unlikely to be found testimonial: However, it's relatively *rare* for a statement to a friend or family member to be found to be testimonial, as it would in the above example — that's because a person speaking to a friend or family member will rarely have the primary purpose of creating a substitute for in-court testimony. One writer concludes that in the post-*Crawford* cases in which declarants' statements to friends or family members have been categorized by lower courts, only about 5% of declarations have been found to be testimonial.[11]

iii. Statement to 911 operator: Finally, suppose the declaration is made to a *911 operator.* Here, too, the trend is towards finding the statement to be non-testimo-

---

11. See Keenan, *Confronting Crawford v. Washington in the Lower Courts,* 122 Yale LJ 782 at 814, reporting that of approximately 300 randomly-chosen reported cases in which the court had to characterize a declaration as testimonial or not, 74 of the cases involved a declaration made to a private citizen; the court classified the declaration as testimonial in only four of the 74.

nial. Thus in one study, only about 20% of declarations to such operators were found to have been testimonial.[12]

c. **Statements in forensic reports:** Our final category of declarations is statements made in ***laboratory and other forensic reports***. The cocaine-identification report in *Melendez-Diaz* (*supra*, p. 382), the blood-alcohol-content report in *Bullcoming* (p. 384), and the DNA profile made from vaginal swabs in *Williams v. Illinois* (p. 386) are the three illustrations of this category that have come before the Supreme Court.

   i. **Always "testimonial":** In general, it's been clear in these cases that the report, if offered for the truth of the factual matters contained in it, was "testimonial." That is, forensic reports are virtually *always* prepared in connection with a crime (even if a suspect has not yet been identified), and the report is virtually always intended to be usable in an eventual prosecution. So the main issue in these forensic-report cases has generally *not* been "Were the factual statements in the report 'testimonial'?"

   ii. **Three main issues:** Rather, the three main disputed issues in these forensic-report cases have been: (1) Was the report ***offered for the truth*** of the matter asserted in it?; (2) If the answer to (1) is yes, must there be a ***witness present*** in court to "sponsor" the report?; and (3) if the answer to (2) is yes, what must be that witness's ***degree of involvement*** in (or at least familiarity with) the underlying testing and the making of the report? Let's try to summarize the Court's holdings on these three questions, in paragraphs (iii), (iv) and (v) below.

   iii. **"Truth of the matter asserted":** The Confrontation Clause applies only when at least one statement in the forensic report is being offered to establish ***the truth of the matter asserted in the statement***. So, for instance, if a majority of the Court is convinced that the relevant statement was being offered solely for its non-truth purposes, there would be no Confrontation Clause issue at all. But although the prosecution has sometimes tried to convince the Court that such a non-truth purpose was present (as in *Williams v. Illinois*), no majority of the Court has ever agreed in a given case.

      (1) **Basis of expert's opinion:** Most dramatically, in *Williams*, five justices indicated that they will generally be skeptical of attempts by a testifying expert to describe factual statements in the forensic report of another (non-testifying) expert, and to assert that these statements are being offered merely as the non-evidentiary ***"basis for"*** the ***testifying expert's opinion***. See *supra*, p. 389.

   iv. **Must there be a sponsoring witness?:** As to the next issue — must there be a ***live witness*** to "sponsor" the forensic report — the answer will almost always be ***"yes."*** It's theoretically possible that a forensic report might be so completely the product solely of a ***machine*** running without human intervention or interpretation,

---

12. Keenan, previous footnote, at 814: only eight out of 38 such calls were found testimonial. (Courts will sometimes differ as to whether a 911 call should be treated as being to law-enforcement or not — if the call is routed to the police dispatcher, it's reasonable to view the operator as being an agent of law enforcement. But the "primary purpose" testimony should be applied the same way whether the operator is treated as a member of law enforcement or not.)

that the report itself could be found to be "self-authenticating" and thus not in need of live sponsoring testimony.[13] But there will be few if any such self-authenticating lab reports; much more typical will be the report from the gas chromatograph machine in *Bullcoming*, where a human was found to be required to appear in court to testify about how the machine works, how its settings were adjusted, how its results were interpreted, etc.

v. **Type of witness required:** So the final issue is, given that a live witness is required, what ***involvement*** or ***knowledge*** must that witness have concerning the underlying testing and the preparation of the report reciting the test results? We don't have a full answer to this question yet, but we have some partial answers that rule out some important possibilities.

(1) **No "surrogate" testimony:** In general, ***"surrogate witnesses"*** will ***not suffice***. That is, a live witness who ***neither participated in the testing*** nor ***reviewed*** the report of the testing will not be sufficient, even if the witness knows the general way in which the equipment in question works.

Example: In *Bullcoming*, recall that the live witness (Razatos) knew how a gas chromatograph is used in the New Mexico Police lab to produce a blood alcohol content report. But since Razatos wasn't the one who did the test, or even reviewed the report of the test, his testimony was not enough to meet the requirements of the Confrontation Clause, according to five justices.

(2) **Observer of test:** It remains possible that someone who is not the operator of the testing equipment, but who ***observes*** the testing being done, may suffice as the live witness. A majority of the Court seems to require a witness with detailed "first hand knowledge" about how the testing was done. But there is no reason to believe that this requires actual operation of the machinery and/or actual writing of the report.

(3) **Reviewer:** It may even be possible that a witness who does not observe the testing, but carefully ***reviews the resulting report***, and who has detailed knowledge of how this type of testing is generally done, may suffice. For instance, the ***supervisor of a department*** might be permitted to testify that she reviewed the equipment operator's report, and reasonably believes that it was done in a particular manner, thus entitling the supervisor to present the report for its truth value.

(4) **Thomas as wildcard:** Keep in mind that Justice Thomas' unique view — that only statements of considerable ***"solemnity"*** will trigger the Confrontation Clause — may make it easier for a forensic report to be admitted without violating the clause. That's how the one forensic report that a majority of the Court allowed to be used without live testimony by its maker (the DNA profile in *Williams*) passed muster. Four members of the Court (the four who dissented in *Bullcoming* and who made up the plurality in *Williams*) would allow

---

13. Justice Sotomayor, in *Bullcoming*, mentioned this theoretical possibility, but no other member of the Court has commented on it.

surrogate testimony generally; and Thomas would allow any report that isn't very formal. This combination might produce, as it did in *Williams*, five votes to allow in a forensic report that's both informal in the sense that it does not certify anything or have other indicia of formality, and that's supported by testimony from someone who didn't see or review the test but knows how the equipment works.

   vi. Summary: So in summary, a forensic report that's prepared by a human, and that "certifies" that tests have reached a particular conclusion, will have to be accompanied by *live testimony* from either the person who prepared it, or at the very least from a person who is very familiar with the circumstances under which the testing and report-writing were done.

D. Present law on "non-testimonial" statements: Now, let us turn to statements that, under *Crawford*, are *"non-testimonial."*

1. **Significance:** Taking *Crawford, Davis* and *Ohio v. Clark* together, it's clear that the *Confrontation Clause plays no role where a non-testimonial statement is concerned.* Therefore, as a Confrontation Clause matter, the statement can come into evidence regardless of whether it falls within a *firmly-rooted* hearsay exception, and regardless of whether it contains *particularized guarantees of trustworthiness*.

   Example: Suppose that X and W are old friends, who have committed various crimes together and who trust each other. One day, while the two are having a casual conversation, X says to W, "You know that murder of V last year — well, D and I were the doers." (X is not intending to supply "evidence" against D – he's just gossiping.) Later, in a prosecution of D for the murder, the prosecution would like to offer W's testimony about what X told him. X refuses to repeat the remark at D's trial, pleading the Fifth Amendment.

   The remark is *non-testimonial,* since X was not speaking as part of a formal proceeding or a police investigation, and had no reason to believe that the remark would or might be a substitute for in-court testimony in a criminal proceeding. Therefore, this non-testimonial declaration *doesn't get Confrontation Clause analysis at all*, and there is no constitutional barrier to its use against D. Thus as a matter of the constitutional right of confrontation (as opposed to the rules of evidence), it doesn't matter whether X's remark fits some traditional hearsay exception or not (something that *would* have mattered in the pre-*Crawford* regime of *Ohio v. Roberts*).

V.   CONFRONTATION: SOME SPECIAL ISSUES

A. **Four special topics:**   Let's now examine four special topics concerning the Confrontation Clause:

   [1] Where the confrontation right applies to an out-of-court declaration, what type of procedures will satisfy the requirement that the declarant be *"subject to cross-examination"* concerning the statement?

   [2] Are there circumstances in which the defendant, by his actions, can *forfeit* his right of

confrontation?

[3] What are the special problems posed when two or more defendants are *tried simultaneously*, and one has made a *confession* implicating the other(s)?

[4] What restrictions can the government put on the defendant's right to *cross-examine* a witness in *special situations* (e.g., where the witness is a victim of *sexual abuse* or *child abuse*)?

B. **What constitutes "subject to cross-examination":** If the out-of-court declaration is "testimonial" for purposes of *Crawford*, recall that it will be admissible at trial only if the declarant is *subject to cross-examination by the accused*. What does "subject to cross-examination" mean? There are actually two different times at which the declarant may be found to have been subject to cross-examination by the accused: (a) *at the time of the declaration*; and (b) *at the time of the accused's trial*. Let's consider each.

1. **Cross at time of declaration:** With respect to cross-examination at the time of the declaration,[14] we again have two scenarios to worry about: (a) where the accused's lawyer *actually conducted* a meaningful cross-examination of the accused; and (b) where the accused's lawyer had the *opportunity* to conduct a meaningful cross, but did *not use* that opportunity.

   a. **Actual conducting of meaningful cross:** First, let's suppose that the accused's lawyer *actually conducted a meaningful cross-examination* of the declarant at the time of the declaration, in circumstances reasonably approximating a criminal trial (e.g., the declared was under oath; the accused's lawyer was competent; the accused already had been charged with, or knew that he was likely to be charged with, the same offense as he ultimately stands trial for; the declaration occurred at a judicial proceeding; and a transcript was made). If these trial-like conditions are satisfied, it seems pretty clear that this cross-examination on behalf of the accused meets the demands of the Confrontation Clause. Therefore, the fact that the declarant is unavailable at the accused's later trial *won't matter*. The key case establishing this is *California v. Green*, 399 U.S. 149 (1970), the facts and holding of which are set out in the following example.

      Example: At D's preliminary hearing on marijuana-sale charges, the declarant (Porter) testifies that D asked Porter to receive marijuana from D and re-sell it. After Porter gives this testimony, D's lawyer extensively cross-examines him. Then, at D's subsequent trial, Porter becomes evasive, claiming to be unable to say whether his preliminary-hearing testimony was fact or fantasy. The prosecutor reads excerpts from Porter's preliminary-hearing testimony into the record, and D is convicted. D asserts that this reading violated his Confrontation Clause rights.

      Held, conviction upheld. D had the opportunity to cross-examine Porter at the time of the preliminary hearing, and did so "under circumstances closely approximating those that surround the typical trial" (e.g., at proceedings before a "judicial

---

14. The scenarios that raise this "cross at the time of the declaration" question will generally be ones involving formal proceedings at which the target of the proceeding was allowed to be present: *preliminary hearings* and *previous trials*.

tribunal," equipped to provide a "judicial record of the hearings," with D represented by counsel, indeed the same counsel as represented him at the later trial). Therefore, the demands of the Confrontation Clause are satisfied, even if Porter is viewed as having been unavailable for confrontation at a later trial. *California v. Green, supra.* (Nothing in *Crawford* changes this result.)

b. Mere unused "opportunity" to cross-examine: But what if the accused merely has an *"opportunity"* to conduct such a cross-examination of the declarant at the time of the declaration, and *does not take advantage* of that opportunity? Here, it is less clear whether the declaration can be used at the accused's later trial without Confrontation Clause problems, if the declarant is unavailable at that trial. We simply don't know the answer yet.

2. Cross at time of trial: Now, let's suppose that the accused did not cross-examine (or even have an opportunity to cross-examine) the declarant at the time the declaration was made. It is clear that some types of opportunities to cross-examine the declarant *at trial* will satisfy the Confrontation Clause, but that in other scenarios, even if the declarant is in some sense "present," the accused may be found to have no meaningful opportunity to cross-examine. In all of the following scenarios, we refer to the declarant as "W" (because she is in some sense a "witness" at trial).

a. Declarant present at trial and testifies fully: First, assume that W is presented as a witness at trial, and testifies fully, both on direct by the prosecution and on cross by the accused. Here, it is clear that the Confrontation Clause is satisfied, so that there is no difficulty with introducing W's prior out-of-court not-previously-cross-examined statements. See *Crawford*: "The Clause does not bar admission of a statement so long as the declarant is present at trial to defend or explain it."

> **Example:** On the basic fact pattern of *Crawford*, assume that Sylvia and D were not married (so that there was no marital privilege preventing Sylvia's testimony), and that Sylvia took the stand at D's trial. Assume further that Sylvia asserted, both on direct and on cross from D, that the statement she gave to the police was accurate. It's clear that there is no Confrontation Clause problem with the prosecution's using Sylvia's statements to the police inculpating D, even though D had no opportunity to cross-examine her at the time those statements were made — Sylvia's full availability for cross-examination at trial is by itself enough to satisfy the requirements of the Confrontation Clause.

b. Declarant appears at trial but is evasive: Now, what if W claims that he *cannot recall* the underlying event? Here, D could argue that his Confrontation Clause rights are violated by use of W's prior statement, because D cannot effectively cross-examine W about that prior statement.

i. W is honest: Where circumstances indicate that W is *honest* in stating that he cannot remember the underlying event, the defendant's Confrontation Clause argument will probably always *fail*.

ii. W is lying: If the circumstances indicate that W is *lying* when he says he can't recollect the underlying event, D may have a slightly better chance of establishing a Confrontation Clause violation. For instance, if he can show that the prosecution is cooperating with the witness in a subterfuge to get the prior statement admitted without risk of cross-examination concerning its specifics, a court ought to find that D's confrontation rights have been violated.

   c. **W pleads a privilege:** Now, suppose that W takes the stand, but then pleads the Fifth Amendment privilege against self-incrimination (see *infra*, p. 437), or some other privilege, so that D gets no meaningful chance to ask W about W's prior statement. Here, it seems clear that for Confrontation Clause purposes, W is *"unavailable"* for cross examination. Therefore, unless D had a meaningful opportunity for cross-examination at some prior time (e.g., at the time the statement was made), the statement cannot be admitted against D.

   d. **Identification of person:** Suppose that W's prior statement is one *identifying the defendant* as the perpetrator of the crime (e.g., by picking him out of a police lineup). Assuming that W is available at trial to explain, and be cross-examined about, this prior identification, D's Confrontation Clause challenge to the out-of- court and identification is very unlikely to succeed, even after *Crawford*.

C. **D's forfeiture of rights by making the witness unavailable:** Suppose the defendant *causes the declarant to be unavailable*, for instance by *killing* her. Does this amount to a *forfeiture* by the defendant of his Confrontation Clause right? The answer is, *yes*, but *only if the defendant acted for the purpose of procuring the declarant's unavailability*. See *Giles v. California*, 128 S.Ct. 2678 (2008), also discussed *supra*, p. 279.

   1. **Ordinary murder case:** So in an ordinary murder case – ordinary in the sense that D killed V for some purpose *other than* preventing V from testifying against D – the fact that D killed V will *not* be deemed to be a forfeiture by D of his Confrontation Clause rights. (For instance, in *Bryant v. Michigan*, *supra*, p. 371, the controversy over the admissibility of the shooting victim's statement was necessary because there was no evidence that D had killed the victim in order to prevent him from testifying.) Therefore, the prosecution will still be blocked by the Confrontation Clause from introducing testimonial-type statements made by V before a typical murderous act (e.g., a statement by V to police investigators about a threat of violence D made to V three months previously, and not motivated by any potential testimony by V against D).

   2. **D acts to avoid V's testimony:** But if the prosecution can show that D procured the declarant's unavailability *for the purpose of avoiding the declarant's trial testimony* (e.g., by killing her), then D will be deemed to have forfeited his Confrontation Clause rights. See the example on p. 279 (D kills V to prevent V from testifying against him at an upcoming trial; V's prior statements about the crime are admissible notwithstanding D's Confrontation Clause rights).

D. **Special problem of multi-party confessions and joint trials (*Bruton*):** A major function of the Confrontation Clause has been to limit the prosecution's ability to introduce *confessions by accomplices and co-defendants*. As far as the Confrontation Clause is concerned, a confession will always be admissible against the *confessor* (since the confessor has no right to cross-examine himself). The Confrontation Clause issue is whether the confession can be introduced against a person other than the confessor (e.g., an *accomplice* or *co-conspirator*) if the confession implicates that other person, and the confessor does not testify at the other person's trial. Let's consider several scenarios involving *A*'s confession that implicates *B*, offered against *B*.

1. **Non-testimonial remark:**   First, consider a ***non-testimonial remark*** that implicates both the speaker (call him X) and D. The prior example on p. 396 — X makes a casual remark to his old friend-in-crime W, implicating X and D — is illustrative.

    The fact that the remark is non-testimonial means that there is **no Confrontation Clause problem** with having W repeat the remark at D's trial, even if X won't take the stand to be cross-examined. That's so because *Davis v. Washington* makes it clear that under *Crawford*, non-testimonial remarks are automatically freed from Confrontation Clause scrutiny.

2. **True testimonial "confessions":**   Next, let's consider true "confessions," i.e., self-inculpatory statements made by the declarant while in ***custody*** or ***in response to police interrogation.*** Here, the statement is clearly testimonial (since *Crawford* and *Davis* make it clear that statements made in response to police interrogations are testimonial). This means that if confessor X does not take the stand at D's trial, the confession **cannot be used against D** even though it falls within the declaration-against-interest hearsay exception and even though the confession may have all the circumstantial guarantees of trustworthiness in the world.

    > **Example:** X is in custody for a burglary. During interrogation, the police ask X whether he had anything to do with the murder one year earlier of V. X says — at time when he has no apparent motive to curry favor with the police — "As a matter of fact, D and I did that murder together." The prosecution charges D alone with the murder (having reached a deal with X to charge and try him separately). The prosecution calls X as a witness, but X pleads the Fifth Amendment and refuses to confirm the confession. The prosecution would like to show the jury a videotape of X's confession, including the portion implicating D.

    > X's confession is clearly testimonial, because it was given in response to police interrogation. Therefore, *Crawford* and *Davis* mean that X's confession cannot be admitted against D, unless X is made available for cross-examination about it (which the facts say is not the case, due to X's pleading of the Fifth Amendment). And this is true even though if the confession is believed by the judge to contain circumstantial guarantees of trustworthiness.

    a. **Joint trials:**   Finally, let's consider a variant on the above "X implicates himself and D" confession scenario. Suppose that the prosecution ***tries X (the confessor) and D jointly.*** Here, even before *Crawford*, the Supreme Court has so mistrusted the use of uncross-examined confessions against persons other than the confessor that the Court has held that even a stringent ***limiting instruction*** will not solve the problem. In ***Bruton v. U.S.***, 391 U.S. 123 (1968), the Court held that if D1 confesses in a way that implicates himself and D2, D1's confession can't be used at their joint trial unless D1 takes the stand, and that's true even if the jury is ***instructed to regard the confession only as evidence against D1.***

    > **Example:** D1 and D2 are jointly tried for robbery. D1 has orally confessed to police that he and D2 committed the crime together. At the joint trial, D1's confession is admitted only against him, and the judge tells the jury that it is not to consider the con-

fession as evidence against D2. D1 never takes the stand, so D2 never gets to cross-examine him about his confession. D2 is convicted, and appeals on Confrontation Clause grounds.

Held, for D2: despite the judge's limiting instruction, and despite the fact that D1's confession is, technically, only evidence against D1 and not D2, D2's Confrontation Clause rights have been violated **merely by the jury's hearing of D1's confession**. That's because the jury could not be expected to follow the judge's limiting instruction. *Bruton v. U.S.*, *supra*.

i. The "two jury" technique: One way around the problem of *Bruton* is to use **two juries** when co-conspirators are being tried. The trial court empanels a separate jury for each defendant. Then, D1 is allowed to withdraw his jury during presentation of evidence that D2 confessed and implicated D1. This saves the necessity of conducting two entirely separate trials.

E. Right to confront testifying witnesses: As we have seen from the above discussion, the Confrontation Clause's usual function is to allow a defendant to exclude a hearsay statement. There is another function that the Clause serves, however: it guarantees certain **procedures** at trial. In particular, it guarantees that the accused may be **present** at the trial, and that he may **test the testimony** of live witnesses by **cross-examining** them.

1. W's refusal to answer: For instance, if W gives testimony against D as part of the prosecution's direct case, and then wilfully refuses to answer the defense's questions on cross-examination, the Confrontation Clause generally requires that W's direct testimony be **stricken** at D's request. L&S, p. 605.

2. Restrictions on cross-examination: Difficult questions can arise when the trial judge or the state has a sound **policy reason** for **restricting certain lines of cross-examination**.

a. Rules of relevance: State rules of evidence, as applied by the trial judge, may constitutionally limit cross-examination to relevant matters, and may prevent the defense from unduly repetitive or argumentative questioning or the harassment of witnesses. L&S, p. 606. However, if the judge takes an unduly restrictive view of what should be allowed on cross-examination, this may violate the defendant's Confrontation Clause rights. *Id.*

b. Witness's name or residence: A conflict between the confrontation rights of the accused and the rights of witnesses is posed when the state's evidence rules (or the trial judge in his own discretion) prevent the defense from asking a prosecution witness his **true name** or **true address**. This often happens where there is reason to believe that the defendant (especially an organized crime member) may use the information to **threaten or even murder the witness.** So far, the Supreme Court has not dealt with this conflict, but lower courts have held that it is **not unconstitutional** to prohibit the asking of such questions where there is reason to fear that the information may indeed endanger the witness.

c. Rape shield laws: Similarly, the defendant's Confrontation Clause rights may be impaired by so-called **rape shield** laws, which limit a rape defendant's right to cross-examine the victim about her prior sexual conduct. For instance, if a state passed a shield law that flatly prohibited any inquiry into the victim's past sexual conduct, no matter how relevant such conduct was to the defendant's defense, a Confrontation Clause violation might well result.

Example: D denies having had intercourse with V at all. The prosecution produces evidence that V contracted gonorrhea, and that D had the disease prior to the episode. A shield law that prevents D from showing that V had had intercourse with X shortly before the alleged D-V encounter, and that X had gonorrhea, would probably violate D's Confrontation Clause rights.

By contrast, there is probably no Confrontation Clause violation from a shield law where the prosecution shows that D and V were strangers, and that D had sex with V in a parking lot. In this situation, D almost certainly does not have a Confrontation Clause right to inquire into V's past promiscuity in order to show consent. Here the direct evidence of consent is so small, and the link between past promiscuity and present consent so attenuated, that no constitutional Confrontation interest of D is really being impaired. See L&S, p. 639.

i.   **Federal Rule:** FRE 412 (the federal rape shield provision) largely avoids the Confrontation Clause problem by expressly allowing any evidence of the victim's past sexual behavior if it is "constitutionally required to be admitted." See FRE 412(b)(1); see also *supra*, pp. 44-47.

3.   **Right to be face-to-face with W:**   There is an additional aspect to the defendant's Confrontation Clause right: the defendant has the right to be *within the view* of witnesses testifying against him at trial. The Clause "guarantees the defendant a *face-to-face meeting* with witnesses. . . ." *Coy v. Iowa*, 487 U.S. 1012 (1988). However, this guarantee is not absolute — it may be outweighed by a showing that the particular witness needs special protection.

a.   **Child-abuse cases:**   The defendant's right to be face-to-face with his accusers is most often relevant in *child-abuse* cases. Many states have procedures whereby the child victim is permitted to give trial testimony without having to look at the defendant. (For instance, in *Coy, supra*, a screen was placed between the witness stand and the defendant, so that the child victims could not see the defendant while testifying, although he could see them.) *Coy* establishes that the state may not make a blanket declaration that in certain broad categories of cases (e.g., child-abuse cases), the defendant's right to be face-to-face with his accusers is outweighed by the state's interest in protecting witnesses. Only if there is an *individualized* finding that the particular witness in question needs special protection, may the defendant be deprived of his right to be viewed by the witness. (No such individualized findings existed in *Coy* itself.)

b.   **Individualized findings made:**   A post-*Coy* case shows that in some circumstances a court will in fact properly find that a particular witness needs special protection, so that the defendant's right to be faced by the witness can be taken from him. In *Maryland v. Craig*, 110 S.Ct. 3157 (1990), the trial judge in a state sexual assault case found that each of two child witnesses, if she were required to testify in front of D in open court, would suffer serious emotional distress that would prevent her from reasonably communicating. Therefore, the judge approved the taking of each child's testimony in a separate room, at which only the witness, prosecutor and defense counsel were present; the child's testimony was simultaneously displayed to the courtroom via ***closed-circuit TV.*** This arrangement preserved D's right to cross-examine the witness and to make objections (via an electronic link with defense counsel), but prevented the witnesses from seeing D. The Supreme Court held that this procedure did ***not*** deprive the defendant of his Confrontation Clause rights.

    i. Rationale: In *Craig*, the individualized findings — that these ***particular*** child witnesses, not child witnesses in general, needed special protection — were held to be sufficient to validate the procedure. (The majority cautioned that there must be a finding that it is the ***presence of the defendant***, not the mere prospect of giving testimony in court, that would cause the trauma to the child witness.)

VI. COMPULSORY PROCESS

A. General meaning: A criminal defendant's ability to present an effective defense is buttressed by a second Sixth Amendment clause, the Compulsory Process Clause. That clause provides, "[I]n all criminal prosecutions, the accused shall enjoy the right . . . to have ***compulsory process*** for ***obtaining witnesses*** in his favor."

    1. Interpretation: The Clause thus on its face gives the defendant the right to ***subpoena*** defense witnesses; a witness who fails to honor the subpoena may be imprisoned by the trial judge for contempt of court. But the Clause has been interpreted even more broadly, to entitle the defendant to ***obtain and present all evidence*** helpful to his defense.

B. State or federal rules restricting evidence: The main relevance of the Compulsory Process Clause to us here, however, is that it may render unconstitutional state or federal evidence rules that would ***restrict the defense's ability to present exculpatory evidence.*** Even a well-established rule of exclusion may run afoul of the Clause, if its effect is to prevent the defendant from presenting relevant and material evidence.

    1. Restrictive hearsay rule: A Supreme Court case illustrating compulsory process principles is *Chambers v. Mississippi*, 410 U.S. 284 (1973). The case was decided on Due Process rather than Compulsory Process Clause grounds, but the Court was clearly trying to protect the same values that are protected by the Compulsory Process Clause, namely, the defendant's right to present all relevant and material exculpatory evidence.

        a. Facts: D was charged with murdering V, a policeman, while both were in a crowd. Another man who was in the crowd, W, later gave a sworn confession to D's lawyers that he, not D, had shot V. But W later repudiated this confession. At D's trial, he was allowed to call W, and to read W's confession to the jury, but was not permitted to examine W as a hostile witness (because Mississippi, like many jurisdictions, still followed the common-law rule that a party who calls a witness "vouches for his credibility" and thus may not impeach him; see *supra*, p. 119). During cross-examination by the prosecution, W said that he had recanted this confession, and that he had made it only to gain part of a tort recovery. D then tried to present testimony of three witnesses to whom W had confessed at various times; the judge rejected this testimony as hearsay. (Again, Mississippi followed the common-law rule recognizing an exception for declarations against pecuniary interest but not an exception for statements against penal interest.)

b. Holding: The Supreme Court held that the combination of these two common-law rules — the rule against impeaching one's own witness and the standard hearsay rule — violated D's due process right to present a fair defense. The "no impeachment of own witness" rule was irrational as applied here, since W's interests were clearly adverse to D's (even though in his testimony W did not accuse D of the crime). Similarly, it was unreasonable for Mississippi to reject the hearsay testimony of those who observed W's confession, since there were numerous assurances that this testimony would be reliable: the confessions were sharply against W's penal interest, there were several confessions that corroborated each other, and each was made spontaneously to a close acquaintance shortly after the murder. In summary, D was prevented from developing critical and reliable evidence in support of his defense.

c. Significance: *Chambers* demonstrates that even ***traditional rules of evidence*** may violate the defendant's Compulsory Process rights, if they have the effect of preventing him from presenting important, and apparently reliable, evidence. L&S, p. 624. (In fact, even under the Federal Rules, testimony by the witnesses to W's confession would have been inadmissible, because although it was against W's penal interest, W was not unavailable, as required by FRE 804(b)(3)'s "statement against interest" exception. *Id.*)

2. **"Arbitrary or disproportionate" standard:**   The Supreme Court has articulated the standard for when rules excluding particular types of evidence will violate an accused's Compulsory Process rights: such rules will not abridge the accused's rights "so long as they are ***not 'arbitrary' or 'disproportionate*** to the purposes they are designed to serve.'" (Furthermore, this "arbitrary or disproportionate" standard will be violated only if the exclusion of evidence infringes upon a "weighty interest" of the accused. See *infra*, p. 405.) *U.S. v. Scheffer*, 523 U.S. 303 (1998).

  a. Polygraph results: The facts and holding of *Scheffer* illustrate that rules excluding evidence reasonably thought to be ***unreliable*** will not violate the defendant's Compulsory Process rights. The issue in *Scheffer* was whether the complete exclusion of ***polygraph evidence*** from court-martial trials — and thus the exclusion of evidence offered by D that he "passed" a polygraph — violated his rights. The Court noted that the scientific community remains "extremely polarized about the reliability of polygraph techniques." Therefore, the outright ban on such evidence in military trials was a "rational and proportional means of advancing the legitimate interest in barring unreliable evidence," so that it did not violate D's Sixth Amendment right to put on a defense.

C. Equality principle: The Supreme Court is especially likely to hold that a state rule of evidence violates the defendant's Compulsory Process rights if the rule in general ***favors the prosecution***. That is, there is probably a core value supported by the Compulsory Process Clause, the value of ***"equality in the right to produce evidence in court."*** L&S, p. 627.

  Example: D1 and D2 are charged with the rape and murder of a woman, and are tried separately. At D1's trial, W, a witness for the prosecution, testifies that D1 told him that D1 killed the woman after telling D2 to run an errand. At D2's trial, D2 calls W to give the same testimony, but it is excluded as inadmissible hearsay.

Held, exclusion of W's testimony in D2's trial violated D2's right to a fair trial, especially given that the prosecution thought that the testimony was reliable enough to be used against D1. "The hearsay rule may not be applied mechanistically to defeat the ends of justice." *Green v. Georgia*, 442 U.S. 95 (1979).

1. **Not the only principle:** However, "equality" between prosecution and defense is not the only value served by the Compulsory Process Clause. For instance, in *Chambers v. Mississippi, supra*, p. 403, both of the exclusionary evidence rules at issue there — the rule against impeaching one's own witness and the rule that statements against penal interest are not exceptions to the ban on hearsay — probably do not over the long run benefit prosecutors over defendants. Nonetheless, the impact of these rules *in that particular case* was so severe that D's right to present an effective defense was compromised.

D. **Only "weighty interests" are protected:** Even a somewhat arbitrary state rule of evidentiary exclusion will violate the Compulsory Process clause only if it infringes on a *"weighty interest"* of the accused. *U.S. v. Scheffer, supra*.

1. **Direct testimonial evidence preferred:** The Court seems to be more likely to hold that the defendant's interest in the evidence in question is sufficiently "weighty" when that evidence is *direct lay testimonial evidence about what happened* than, say, when the evidence is *scientific or other expert opinion of a circumstantial nature*.

    a. **Illustration from *Scheffer*:** Thus in *Scheffer* itself, the Court held that D's interest in introducing evidence that he had passed a polygraph showing his lack of criminal intent (intent to ingest an illegal drug) was insufficiently weighty, because D had already directly testified to his lack of intent, and the polygraph evidence would have merely been "expert testimony to bolster [D's] own credibility." By contrast, the *Scheffer* Court said, other cases in which the Compulsory Process clause had been found violated by the exclusion of evidence involved important *firsthand testimony*. For instance, in one case a statute that prevented co-defendants or co-participants in a crime from testifying for one another implicated a weighty interest, in that it denied the accused the right to put on the stand "a witness who was physically and mentally capable of *testifying to events that he had personally observed*."

E. **Due process:** A defendant's right to present all material and reliable evidence in his own defense is protected not only by the Compulsory Process Clause but also by the Fourteenth Amendment's general *Due Process* Clause. That is, if a state rule of evidence prevents the defendant from presenting material and reliable exculpatory evidence, the effect may be so great as to constitute a violation of a defendant's right to a fair trial. Indeed, where a rule of evidence is overall neutral as between prosecutor and defense, but is highly unfair in its application in the particular case, the Supreme Court seems to prefer to decide the case on due process rather than compulsory process grounds — this is what happened in *Chambers, supra*, p. 403. L&S, pp. 628-29.

Quiz Yourself on
CONFRONTATION AND COMPULSORY PROCESS *(Entire Chapter)*

91. The state calls Harry Houdini as a key witness at a criminal trial. Just as the prosecutor finishes his questioning, Houdini's appendix bursts and he dies. What should the trial judge do with respect to Houdini's direct testimony, and why? _____

92. Pretty Boy is on trial for conspiracy to distribute cocaine. The prosecution has a recording of a telephone conversation between Scarface and a person who is (unbeknownst to Scarface or Pretty Boy) a government informant. In the phone conversation, Scarface tells the informant how Pretty Boy plans to distribute cocaine to the informant. (At the time, Scarface is assisting the distribution scheme.) Scarface refuses to testify on Fifth Amendment grounds. The prosecution offers the tape under the hearsay exception for a co-conspirator's statement. Pretty Boy objects, claiming his rights under the Confrontation Clause would be violated by allowing the tape into evidence. How do you rule? _____

93. Velma, a 24-year-old woman, arrives at the emergency room of Hospital with bruises all over her body. Frieda, a forensic nurse, examines Velma, and begins by asking her, "What happened to you?" Velma replies, "My husband Dolph beat me with his fists and a belt." Frieda's main purpose in asking the question is to ascertain what type of less-visible injuries she should check Velma for; Frieda also wants to be sure that when she discharges Velma she can help Velma find a place where she will be safe from whomever inflicted the injuries. After admitting Velma to Hospital overnight, Frieda discharges her the next morning, while making sure that a nearby shelter for abused women has a spot for her. Frieda also contacts the local police department, as a statute requires her to do in cases of suspected domestic violence. A few days later, Regina, a police officer in the department's domestic violence squad, visits Velma at the shelter, and explains that she, Regina, is investigating whether the person who inflicted the bruises on Velma should be prosecuted. Regina asks Velma to describe how she got her injuries. Velma repeats the same details as she told Frieda. Dolph is charged with assault and domestic violence. Velma declines to cooperate with the prosecution, and disregards a prosecution subpoena to appear at Dolph's trial. At the trial, the prosecution offers in evidence Velma's out-of-court statements made to Frieda and Omar. Dolph objects to both statements on Confrontation Clause grounds.

   (a) As to Velma's statement to Frieda, should the court sustain Dolph's Confrontation Clause objection? _____ **(b)** As to Velma's statement to Regina, should the court sustain Dolph's Confrontation Clause objection? _____

94. Bart is arrested for drunk driving. Because the arresting officer's breathalyzer is broken, Bart is taken to police headquarters. He consents to having a blood sample taken from him, which is sent to a police lab. A technician, Ted, uses a gas chromatograph to analyze the sample's blood alcohol content (BAC). The machine reports that the BAC of the sample is .12%, above the minimum for DUI. Ted then fills out a form in which he states, "The sample labelled 'Bart' was shown by the chromatograph to have a BAC = .12%." Ted then signs a certification at the bottom of the form, saying that it "is true to the best of my knowledge and belief." Bart is charged with DUI. In court, the prosecution presents testimony by Tilda, another technician in the lab, who is familiar with how the lab uses gas chromatographs, describes the process for the jury, and offers the report in evidence. Under cross-examination by Bart's counsel, Tilda acknowledges that she did not personally watch Ted do the test on the sample, or otherwise review his work. However, she testifies that "I have worked alongside Ted for years, and know that he performs every gas chromatograph test carefully and accurately." Bart's lawyer objects to the introduction of the report into evidence on Confrontation Clause grounds. How should the court rule? _____

95. While Bugs Bunny is under surveillance near the Statue of Liberty, he is stopped on suspicion of planning to blow up the Statue, based on an informant's tip that Bugs and friends are planning an explosion for two months hence, on the anniversary of 9/11. He is taken to a New York City police station, and questioned about his plans. After polite questioning (no torture) by Officer Krupke, Bugs says, "Well, I was just casing the Statue to give advice to my friend Donald Duck about how to blow it up; Donald was going to arrange the explosion." Donald is later arrested in Queens, New York, and brought to trial for conspiring with Bugs to blow up the Statue. (Bugs is not put on trial.) At Donald's trial, the prosecution puts Bugs on the stand to ask him about the conspiracy, but Bugs pleads the Fifth. The prosecution then puts on Officer Krupke, who offers to describe how Bugs gave the statement implicating Donald. The prosecution asserts that the statement is admissible under the declaration-against-interest hearsay exception. Donald asserts that it's barred by the Confrontation Clause. Who wins? _____

96. Butthead is arrested and kept in custody on armed robbery charges. While in custody, he gives a confession implicating both himself and his friend Beavis. Now, Beavis and Butthead are both defendants in a joint trial on the armed robbery charges. Butthead declines to take the stand. The prosecution offers Butthead's confession, and agrees that the judge should issue a limiting instruction to the jury that the confession is admissible only against Butthead, not against Beavis. Should the judge admit the confession on this basis? _____

Answers

91. Strike the testimony, because the defense was deprived of its right to **cross-examine** Houdini. The defendant in a criminal trial has a right under the Sixth Amendment to **confront** witnesses against him. This right consists mainly of the right to cross-examine. Even where (as here) the unavailability of the witness for cross was not due to the fault of the calling party, the confrontation clause dictates that the direct evidence not be used against the defendant. The same result would occur if Houdini pleaded the Fifth Amendment instead of answering questions on cross. (In fact, if the court believes that the direct testimony was so critical and influential that an instruction to strike will not be sufficient to undo its effect, the court should order a mistrial.)

92. Objection overruled. Before we get to the Confrontation Clause argument, let's review how the case would be analyzed under the common law and the FRE. A *co-conspirator's statement* (if made *during* and in *furtherance* of the conspiracy) is an exception to the hearsay rule at common law and an exclusion from the hearsay rule under FRE 801(d)(2).

Crawford v. Washington (U.S. 2004) and *Davis v. Washington* (U.S. 2006) hold that "non-testimonial" out-of-court statements don't have to undergo Confrontation Clause analysis at all. (This was a change from the holding in the earlier case of *Ohio v. Roberts*.) Scarface's statement was clearly "non-testimonial" — since he did not even know he was speaking to an informant, he was not making a statement that he thought would be used in conjunction with some sort of law enforcement proceeding. Therefore, under *Crawford* and *Davis*, Scarface's out-of-court declaration cannot be a Confrontation Clause violation.

93. (a) No, because the Confrontation Clause does not apply to Velma's statement to Frieda. An out-of-court statement cannot fall within the Confrontation Clause unless the statement's *primary purpose* was *"testimonial." Ohio v. Clark* (2015). And a statement will be testimonial only if it was "procured with a primary purpose of creating an out-of-court substitute for trial testimony." *Washington v. Davis.* Here, the statement was made to Frieda, a nurse, who was someone "not principally charged with uncovering and prosecuting criminal behavior" (*Clark*); statements to such persons are "significantly less likely to be testimonial than statements given to law enforcement officers." (*Id.*) Like the statement made by a 3-year-old in *Clark* to his preschool teachers about the source of his injuries, Velma's statement to Frieda was made primarily for the purpose of helping Frieda to get Velma correct medical attention, and to keep Velma safe from her attacker. Therefore, Velma's statement to Frieda, like the child's statement in *Clark,* is almost certain to be found to be non-testimonial. Consequently, Velma's statement cannot trigger Doph's Confrontation Clause rights, and will therefore be admissible against him. Cf. *Ward v. Indiana* (2016), from which the facts of this question are loosely drawn.

(b) Yes, because her statement to Regina was testimonial. Where an out-of-court declaration *is* testimonial, and the declarant is not available for cross-examination by the defendant, the declaration's use by the prosecution will normally violate the defendant's Confrontation Clause rights. (And that's true, by the way, even if the declaration is covered by a well-established hearsay exception, though Velma's statement to Officer Regina here does not seem to fall within any such exception.) Velma's statement to Regina is almost certain to be found to be testimonial: Velma made her declaration to Regina after learning that Regina was investigating whether the facts merited a prosecution of Velma's attacker. Therefore, a court would almost certainly conclude that the declaration was "procured with a primary purpose of creating an out-of-court substitute for trial testimony" (*Davis'* test for testimoniality, cited in *Clark*), and/or was given in response to an interrogation whose primary purpose was "to establish or prove past events potentially relevant to later criminal prosecution" (the test for testimoniality in *Hammon v. Indiana*, also cited in *Clark*). Once the court determines that Velma's statement to Regina was testimonial, then unless the statement falls within a hearsay exception that was recognized as an exception to a criminal defendant's common-law right of confrontation at the time the Constitution was adopted in 1789 — a category that so far includes *only* dying declarations — the defendant's Confrontation Clause right requires that the statement be excluded from use against him. Since Velma's statement was testimonial and was not a dying declaration, Doph's Confrontation Clause right requires that it be excluded from being introduced against him, given that Velma is not available for cross-examination by Doph's lawyer.

94. **Objection sustained.** The facts here are on all fours with *Bullcoming v. New Mexico* (U.S. 2011). By a 5-4 vote there, the Supreme Court held that the testimony by the tester's colleague — even one who was familiar with the particular type of forensic test in question — was not sufficient to satisfy the Confrontation Clause's requirement that a "testimonial" out-of-court statement in a forensic report, if offered for its truth, must be supported by the testimony of someone who was personally involved in the preparation of the report. For instance, because Ted wasn't present for cross, Bart's counsel had no chance to quiz him about whether he might have made a mistake on the test in question, whether the sample might have been mis-labeled, whether Ted had a history of making mistakes in such tests, etc. Therefore, under the logic of the majority in *Bullcoming*, the presence of Tilda as an alternative witness was not sufficient to give Bart a fair opportunity to use the tools of cross-examination to show that the report might have been erroneous, and introduction of the report would violate Bart's Confrontation Clause rights.

95. **Donald.** Under *Crawford v. Washington* (U.S. 2004), declarations against interest that are ***"testimonial,"*** when used against an accused, violate the accused's Sixth Amendment Confrontation Clause rights, unless the declarant is subject to cross-examination on behalf of the accused either at the time of the declaration or at the accused's later trial. *Crawford* indicates that where police conduct an interrogation whose focus is on crime-detection rather than dealing with an ongoing emergency, the responses of the person being interrogated will almost always be found to be "testimonial." Therefore, the prosecution can't use Bugs' statement implicating Donald against Donald unless Bugs was made available for cross by Donald either at the time the statement was made (which he wasn't) or at Donald's trial. Since Bugs has pleaded the Fifth, he's not deemed subject to cross by Donald. Therefore, it would violate Donald's

EXAM TIPS ON CONFRONTATION AND COMPULSORY PROCESS

Confrontation Clause rights for the statement to be admitted against him.

96. No (and it's reversible error as to Beavis if she does). Even with a limiting instruction, the jury is likely to consider the confession as substantive evidence against Beavis, not just against Butthead. Therefore, before D1's confession may be introduced against D2, D1 must take the stand and be meaningfully available for cross-examination. Since Butthead refuses to take the stand (a refusal that's within his rights because of the Fifth Amendment, even if Beavis tries to require him to testify), the confession can't come in at all, on account of Beavis' Sixth Amendment right to confront witnesses against him. *Bruton v. U.S.*

The post-*Bruton* case of *Crawford v. Washington* reinforces this conclusion — *Crawford* says that one defendant's testimonial statement implicating himself and another can't be admitted against the latter, if the confessor doesn't take the stand. Here, Butthead's confession under interrogation is "testimonial" (virtually all statements made in response to non-emergency police interrogation are, *Crawford* says), so under *Crawford* using this confession against Beavis would violate Beavis' Confrontation Clause rights, unless Butthead is made available to be cross-examined by Beavis' lawyer.

Therefore, the typical solution in situations like this is to have ***separate trials*** (or at least ***separate juries***); then, only the jury hearing the case against Butthead would hear Butthead's confession.

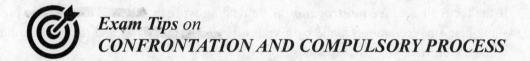

Exam Tips on
CONFRONTATION AND COMPULSORY PROCESS

Whenever your question involves a criminal prosecution, and evidence is being introduced against the defendant, check for the possibility of a Confrontation Clause problem.

Most commonly, you'll have to decide whether the use of ***hearsay*** presents a Confrontation Clause problem. If so, do the following analysis:

☛ First, check to see whether the out-of-court declaration is ***"testimonial."*** (The main types of "testimonial" declarations are ones made ***at preliminary hearings***, ***grand jury hearings***, ***prior trials***, and above all, ones made in ***police interrogations*** and ***forensic reports***.)

    ☞ For the declaration to be "testimonial," it must be "made for the ***primary purpose*** of ***creating evidence*** for [a person's] ***prosecution***." [*Ohio v. Clark*]

    ☞ If the out-of-court declaration ***is testimonial***, say that the Confrontation Clause blocks it from being used against the accused unless the declarant is made available for cross by the accused either at the time the statement is made or at the accused's trial. [Cite to *Crawford v. Wash.* and *Davis v. Wash.* on this point.]

Example: Several hours after the fatal shooting of V by persons unknown, X is questioned by the police about the shooting. X says, "I didn't shoot V, but I did lend my gun to D knowing that D wanted to shoot V, and I then watched as D did the shooting." At D's murder trial, X pleads the Fifth. The prosecution then offers (as a declaration against interest) testimony by Ollie, the police detective who interviewed X, about what X said concerning the shooting. Because X's statement during interrogation was "testimonial" (i.e., it was made as part of a police investigation into past criminality, not, say, to deal with a present emergency) it can't come in against D unless X is made available for cross by D. Since X has pleaded the Fifth, he's not available for cross. Therefore, the Confrontation Clause blocks X's statement from being used against D.

☞ But if the criminal defendant *intentionally caused* the declarant to become unavailable (e.g., by killing him), and the defendant did so for the *purpose of preventing testimony* by the declarant, keep in mind that it *doesn't matter* whether the out-of-court declaration is deemed testimonial, because the defendant will be deemed to have *forfeited* any Confrontation Clause rights he may otherwise have had. [Cite *Giles v. California* on this point.]

☞ If the out-of-court declaration is *not testimonial,* say that under *Crawford* and *Davis,* *no Confrontation Clause scrutiny* needs to be done *at all.*

Example: V calls a 911 operator, and says, "Send the police — my boyfriend Bob is beating me up." V doesn't take the stand at Bob's trial for battery. The recording is admissible as an excited utterance without any Confrontation Clause analysis, because under *Davis* it's non-testimonial (i.e., it's focused on getting emergency help, not on aiding the authorities in investigating past events or in prosecuting crimes).

☞ If the focus of a *police interrogation* is on dealing with an *ongoing emergency*, presume that any declaration made by a victim is *non-testimonial*, and thus admissible without Confrontation Clause issues.

Example: Immediately after V is wounded in the stomach by D in a knife fight, O, a police officer, sees V and says, "Don't you need medical help?" V responds, "Yeah, D knifed me; for God's sake, call an ambulance." V then dies. Since the primary intent of V and O in the conversation was to deal with an ongoing emergency (getting help for V), not making a case for later prosecution, V's statement is not testimonial, and can be introduced without Confrontation Clause issues. [Cite to *Mich. v. Bryant.*]

☞ If the declaration is made to a person who is *not part of law enforcement*, start with the *presumption* that the statement is *not testimonial* — it will be rare that a statement to a "civilian" (e.g., a *teacher* or *medical provider*) will be deemed testimonial.

Example: In Hospital's Emergency Room, V tells the doctor, Doc, "I got these bruises earlier tonight when my husband, H, beat me." This is not testimonial (since in speaking V wasn't mainly motivated by a purpose of creating evidence for a prosecution of H). Therefore, H has no Confrontation Clause right to block Doc from repeating V's statement as part of the state's case in a prosecution of H if V doesn't testify.

☛ **Confession implicating someone else, used during joint trial:** Special variation to watch for: *A* and *B* are tried together, and *A*'s confession implicating himself and *B* is used. If the same jury hears *A*'s confession implicating *B* (and *A* doesn't take the stand), then *B*'s Confrontation Clause rights are violated even if the prosecution only purports to be offering the confession against *A*. [Cite to *Bruton v. U.S.*]

CHAPTER 8

PRIVILEGES

ChapterScope

Privileges exempt a witness from testifying about a particular subject matter. The recognition of privileges encourages the maintenance of certain relationships which society deems important. Key concepts are:

■ The **FRE don't specify** what privileges should be recognized in federal courts. Instead:

❏ In **federal-question** cases, **each individual court decides**, based on general **"common law"** principles, what privileges to recognize, and how to draw the boundaries of those privileges;

❏ In **diversity** cases, the federal court must apply the privilege law of the **state whose substantive law applies** (usually, the state where the federal court sits).

■ The most commonly-recognized privileges are as follows:

❏ **Attorney-client:** A client has a right **not to disclose** (and the right to prevent his lawyer from disclosing) any **confidential communication** between the two of them relating to the professional relationship.

❏ The privilege does **not** apply where the confidence relates to the commission of a **future crime or fraud**.

❏ **Physician-patient:** Most states grant a physician-patient privilege, under which the patient has the right to refuse to disclose (and the right to prevent the physician from disclosing) a **confidential communication** made by the client to a physician for the purpose of **obtaining treatment or diagnosis**.

❏ **Psychotherapist:** Virtually all states (even those not recognizing a general physician-patient privilege) recognize a privilege for confidences made by a patient to a **psychotherapist** (psychiatrist or psychologist).

❏ **Self-incrimination:** Every person has the privilege not to "testify against herself."

❏ There are actually two sub-privileges:

❏ **Witness:** First, a **witness** (i.e., any person giving testimony, other than a defendant testifying at her own criminal trial) may refuse to answer any question put to her, on the grounds that it may tend to incriminate her. (But the witness must **take the stand**, then assert the privilege question-by-question.)

❏ **Accused:** Second, the **accused** in a criminal trial **need not take the stand at all**.

❏ **Immunity:** If a witness is given **immunity** from prosecution, she can no longer assert the privilege. The immunity may either be **"transactional"** (protects W against any prosecution for the transaction about which she testifies) or **"use"** (merely protects W against direct or indirect use by the prosecution of the immunized testimony, in a subsequent prosecution).

❑   **Marital privileges:** There are two types of *marital privilege* (some jurisdictions only recognize one):

❑   **Adverse testimony privilege:** The *"adverse testimony"* privilege means that a currently-married person may not be compelled to testify against his spouse (regardless of the subject-matter of the testimony) in the spouse's criminal trial. In federal courts, the *witness-spouse* is the *holder* of the privilege, and chooses whether or not to testify. In some state courts, the accused spouse may assert the privilege and prevent the witness-spouse from testifying even if the latter wants to. The spouses must *still be married* at the time of the testimony.

❑   **Confidential communications:** The *"confidential communications"* privilege prevents the disclosure of *confidential communications* made by one spouse to the other during the marriage. This privilege may be *asserted by either spouse*. It applies even if the spouses are *now divorced* (so long as they were married when the communication occurred).

I.   PRIVILEGES GENERALLY

A.   **Introduction:** A privilege is the *right of an individual not to disclose information about a particular event*. L&S, p. 645. The best-known privileges are the privilege against self-incrimination, and the privileges for confidences exchanged between husband and wife, attorney and client, physician and patient, and clergyman and penitent.

1.   **Rationale:**   All of the exclusionary evidence rules we have considered so far are motivated by society's interest in having *more accurate adjudication*. Hearsay evidence, for instance, is generally excluded because it is thought to be unreliable and, therefore, not helpful to the truth-seeking process. The rationale behind the privilege rules, by contrast, is not a truth-seeking rationale at all. Giving a person the right to withhold information that is relevant (and probably highly reliable) does not aid the accuracy of verdicts; "rather than facilitating the illumination of truth, [privileges] shut out the light." McC, p. 100.

2.   **Other values:**   Instead, the privilege rules promote broader social goals that have little, if anything, to do with truth-seeking. There are two main interests promoted by the privilege rules: (1) the encouragement of certain *professional advisory relationships*; and (2) the maintenance of certain *zones of privacy*.

a.   **Professional relationships:**   Three of the most important generally-recognized privileges — attorney-client, physician-patient, and clergyman-penitent — are designed to facilitate *professional advisory relationships.* Each involves a non-professional who seeks advice about a difficult technical subject from a person whose profession it is to give that advice. Confidences exchanged pursuant to that relationship are protected because society has made the judgment that without such protection against disclosure, many people would not use these professionals, and those who did would find their utility severely reduced.

Example: Suppose that client-lawyer confidences were not privileged against disclosure. Suppose also that Mary has been involved in an automobile accident with another driver. She thinks she may have a valid claim of her own, but she also worries that the other driver may have a valid claim against her. Without the safety net of a ban on the disclosure of lawyer-client confidences, Mary may decide not to go to a lawyer at all, on the theory that the disclosures she makes about the accident are likely to come back to hurt her (in the event of a suit by the other driver against her, at which suit Mary's lawyer could be forced to testify about confidences by Mary that would be damaging to her defense). In that event, justice may be ill-served, since Mary will never find out that she has a meritorious claim (if that is indeed the case).

Alternatively, Mary may consult a lawyer but conceal those facts about the accident that she thinks put her in a bad light. Here, too, justice may be ill-served, since the lawyer may give inaccurate advice (e.g., by telling Mary to bring a suit that, had he known the facts, he would have told her was meritless).

b. Privacy: Two of the other major privileges — the spousal privilege and the privilege against self-incrimination — are motivated mainly by *privacy* concerns. Especially in today's times, when government and "big business" appear to have limitless capacity to gather information about the individual, most people feel that the individual needs a "zone of privacy" which cannot be penetrated.

3. **Usually not constitutionally-based:** Most privileges are *not constitutionally-based*. (The privilege against self-incrimination is the only exception.) Therefore, each state is free to establish whatever privileges it wishes, and to define the contours of those privileges as it wishes. See *infra*, p. 414.

4. **List of major privileges:** Here is a list of the major privileges, which we will be considering one at a time in this chapter:

   a. The *attorney-client* privilege;

   b. The *physician-patient* privilege;

   c. The *clergyman-penitent* privilege;

   d. The *spousal* (i.e., husband and wife) privilege;

   e. The privilege against *self-incrimination*;

   f. The *government secrets* privilege (including the privilege against disclosing the identity of *informants*); and

   g. A miscellaneous group of occasionally-recognized privileges (journalist-source, parent-child, business trade secrets, and accountant-client).

5. **Groupings:** These privileges fall into three main categories: (1) "Professional counseling"; (2) "Zone of privacy"; and (3) "Institutional."

   a. **Professional counseling:** The commonly-recognized *"professional counseling"* privileges, which protect confidential communications given in the course of a professional relationship, are: lawyer-client, physician-patient, and clergyman-penitent. Additionally, the accountant-client privilege, recognized in a few jurisdictions, falls within this category.

b. **"Zone of privacy":** As noted, two major privileges reflect the need for a *"zone of privacy"* around certain key human relationships or around the individual: the spousal privilege and the privilege against self-incrimination. Additionally, the parent-child privilege (recognized in a few states) falls within this class.

c. **"Institutional":** Finally, several privileges can be thought of as being *"institutional,"* in the sense that they are motivated by the need to protect some of society's major institutions rather than to protect the individual who asserts them. The "government secrets" privilege (including the government's right not disclose the identities of confidential informants in criminal cases) is motivated by the need to protect the institution of government. Similarly, those jurisdictions that have recognized a journalist-source privilege have done so not so much to protect the journalist as to protect the institution of the free press, thought to be of key importance to society.

B. **Where applicable:** Where a privilege not to disclose certain information exists, that privilege applies *regardless of the proceeding*. That is, if W is privileged not to disclose fact or communication A, he will be protected against having to disclose A in a trial (whether by judge or jury), administrative hearing, deposition or other discovery proceeding, or any other proceeding. L&S, p. 650.

C. **Who may assert:** The privilege belongs to the *person whose interest or relationship is intended to be fostered by that privilege.* Therefore, he is the *only one* who may assert it. McC, pp. 101-102.

1. **Significance:** The practical significance of this rule is that if P and D are the only parties to a lawsuit, and W is the person whom the privilege protects, the choice whether to assert or waive the privilege belongs solely to W, not to either of the litigants.

> **Example:** D is charged with murder. X is a co-defendant who is being separately tried. The prosecution calls L, X's lawyer, to testify about statements X has made to L that implicate D in the crime. The privilege to prevent L from disclosing these statements belongs *solely to X*. Therefore, it is solely up to him whether to assert the privilege or waive it. If X waives the privilege, D is powerless to stop L's testimony on attorney-client privilege grounds. (The testimony may violate D's Sixth Amendment Confrontation Clause rights, if X is not available for cross-examination at the trial — see *supra*, p. 362 — but this has nothing to do with privilege law.)

2. **Complete discretion of trial judge:** Where the owner of the privilege is not a litigant, and one of the parties objects to evidence on the grounds that that non-litigant's privilege would be violated, the judge may use his discretion to exclude the evidence on the grounds that the absent owner of the privilege would want it that way. However, if the judge lets the evidence in anyway, the party who opposed the evidence may, in most jurisdictions, *not complain on appeal*, since the privilege was not his in the first place. McC, pp. 102-103.

D. **Sources of privileges:** As noted, privileges (except for that against self-incrimination) are not constitutionally mandated. Therefore, each state, and the federal system, is free to develop whatever privileges it wants. It may do so by statute, by "common law" development (i.e., case law), or both.

1. **State development:** All states recognize, in some form, the husband-wife and attorney-client privileges. McC, p. 109. Most states do so by statute. McC, p. 107. Additionally, all recognize a privilege for certain government information. McC, p. 109. All but ten recognize some kind of physician-patient privilege. McC, p. 131. All but three have a clergyman-penitent privilege. McC, p. 109. After that, coverage drops off rapidly: journalist-source, parent-child, and accountant-client are all recognized only by a minority of jurisdictions.

    a. **No Federal Rules:** The proposed Federal Rules on privilege were never enacted (see *infra*, p. 416). Therefore, in the privilege area, states have been left without the simple alternative that they have had in other evidence areas of simply enacting the Federal Rules. However, some states have enacted the proposed-but-never-enacted Federal Rules on privileges; others have enacted the similar (but not identical) Revised Uniform Rules of Evidence privilege provisions, drafted in 1974.

2. **Federal courts:** The Federal Rules of Evidence, as originally proposed, approved by the Supreme Court, and presented to Congress, would have completely codified the federal law of privilege into nine non-constitutional privileges (required reports, attorney-client, psychotherapist-patient, husband-wife, clergyman-communicant, political vote, trade secrets, secrets of state and other official information, and identity of informer; Proposed Federal Rules 502-510). But this package was so controversial that *Congress rejected it.*

    a. **Actual treatment:** Instead of enacting specific rules of privilege, Congress enacted a single general rule describing what the *source of privilege law* in the federal courts should be. That rule, FRE 501, provides:

        > "**Privilege in General**
        >
        > The *common law* — as interpreted by *United States courts* in the light of reason and experience — governs a claim of *privilege unless* any of the following provides otherwise:
        >
        > - the United States *Constitution*;
        >
        > - a *federal statute*; or
        >
        > - rules prescribed by the Supreme Court.
        >
        > But in a *civil case*, *state law governs* privilege regarding a *claim or defense for which state law supplies the rule of decision.*"

    b. **Meaning:** FRE 501 sets up a two-part system of privilege law in the federal courts:

        i. **Diversity cases:** In civil cases where "state law supplies the rule of decision," state law of privilege applies. The main significance of this provision is that in *diversity cases*, the federal court must usually *follow state law of privilege.*

        ii. **Federal question cases:** In criminal cases, and in civil "federal question" cases, the federal courts are free to *use their own judgment* — they are not bound by the privilege law of the state in which they sit. In making this *"federal common law"* of privilege for federal question cases, the federal courts often look to the Proposed Federal Rules of Evidence (PFRE 502-510), though they are not bound by these provisions. We, too, will often be considering the Proposed Federal Rules as we go through the various privileges.

c. **Rule 502 on attorney-client privilege waivers:** Apart from FRE 501, there is only one other Federal Rule dealing with privileges, Rule 502. That rule doesn't set forth any actual privilege; it merely prescribes when an otherwise-applicable ***attorney-client privilege*** will be deemed ***waived***. Rule 502 is discussed *infra*, p. 421.

II. THE ATTORNEY-CLIENT PRIVILEGE

A. **Introduction:** The essence of the attorney-client privilege is that a client has the ***right not to disclose*** (and the right to prevent his lawyer from disclosing) ***any confidential communication between the two of them relating to the professional relationship.***

1. **Proposed Federal Rule:** The Proposed Federal Rule of Evidence on the attorney-client privilege, like the rest of the specific privilege rules, was never enacted. However, because PFRE 503 codifies the prevailing common-law approach in most respects, it is worth reproducing here:

"(a) **Definitions.** As used in this rule:

(1) A *"client"* is a person, public officer, or corporation, association, or other organization or entity, either public or private, who is rendered professional legal services by a lawyer, or who consults a lawyer with a view to obtaining professional legal services from him.

(2) A *"lawyer"* is a person authorized, or reasonably believed by the client to be authorized, to practice law in any state or nation.

(3) A *"representative of the lawyer"* is one employed to assist the lawyer in the rendition of professional legal services.

(4) A communication is *"confidential"* if not intended to be disclosed to third persons other than those to whom disclosure is in furtherance of the rendition of professional legal services to the client or those reasonably necessary for the transmission of the communication.

(b) **General rule of privilege.** A client has a privilege to ***refuse to disclose*** and to prevent any other person from disclosing ***confidential communications*** made for the ***purpose of facilitating the rendition of professional legal services to the client***, (1) between himself or his representative and his lawyer or his lawyer's representative, or (2) between his lawyer and the lawyer's representative, or (3) by him or his lawyer to a lawyer representing another in a matter of common interest, or (4) between representatives of the client or between the client and a representative of the client, or (5) between lawyers representing the client.

(c) **Who may claim the privilege.** The privilege may be ***claimed by the client***, his guardian or conservator, the personal representative of a deceased client, or the successor, trustee, or similar representative of a corporation, association, or other organization, whether or not in existence. The person who was the ***lawyer*** at the time of the communication ***may claim the privilege but only on behalf of the client***. His authority to do so is presumed in the absence of evidence to the contrary.

(d) **Exceptions.** There is ***no*** privilege under this rule:

(1) *Furtherance of crime or fraud.* If the services of the lawyer were sought or obtained to enable or aid anyone to **commit or plan to commit what the client knew or reasonably should have known to be a crime or fraud**; or

(2) *Claimants through same deceased client.* As to a communication relevant to an issue between parties who claim through the same deceased client, regardless of whether the claims are by testate or intestate succession or by inter vivos transaction; or

(3) *Breach of duty by lawyer or client.* As to a communication relevant to an issue of **breach of duty by the lawyer** to his client or by the client to his lawyer; or

(4) *Document attested by lawyer.* As to a communication relevant to an issue concerning an attested document to which the lawyer is an attesting witness; or

(5) *Joint clients.* As to a communication relevant to matter of common interest between two or more clients if the communication was made by any of them to a lawyer retained or consulted **in common**, when offered in an action **between any of the clients**."

2. **State approach:** The attorney-client privilege exists in **every state**. In most states, the privilege is controlled by statute. M, p. 180. Some, but probably not most, are modeled on the Proposed Federal Rule quoted above.

3. **Summary of requirements:** The provisions of the attorney-client privilege are intricate, and are discussed in detail below. Here, as a starting point, are some of the key aspects of the privilege, as it applies in most states:

a. **"Client":** The "client" can be a *corporation* as well as an individual;

b. **Belongs to client:** The privilege belongs to the *client*, not to the lawyer or any third persons. The lawyer may assert it, but only if he is acting on behalf of the client in doing so.

c. **Professional relationship:** The privilege applies only to communications "made for the purpose of facilitating the rendition of *professional legal services* to the client." For instance, if the lawyer is giving business advice, or advice as a friend, the privilege does not apply.

d. **Confidential:** The privilege applies only to communications which are intended to be *"confidential."* Thus, if the client discloses the content of the communication to a third person not associated with the lawyer-client relationship (e.g., a friend), the privilege will be lost.

e. **Fact of employment and client's identity:** The fact that the lawyer-client relationship *exists*, and the *identity* of the client, are normally *not* privileged. Only the substance of the confidences exchanged between them is privileged. (But there are exceptions; see *infra*, p. 422.)

f. **Physical evidence:** Normally, the privilege does not permit the lawyer to conceal *physical evidence* or documents given to him by the client (other than documents written for the purpose of communicating from client to lawyer).

g. Crime or fraud exception: The privilege does not apply where the confidence relates to the commission of a *future crime* or *fraud*.

We consider most of these aspects individually below.

B. The professional relationship: The privilege applies only in the context of a professional lawyer-client relationship. As PFRE 503(b) puts it, the privilege applies only to communications "made for the purpose of facilitating the rendition of *professional legal services* to the client. . . ."

1. **No retainer needed:** The required lawyer-client privilege can exist even though the client *does not pay a fee.* For instance, if the client receives a *free initial consultation* from the lawyer, the privilege applies even though, at the end of the consultation, either the client or the lawyer decides that the lawyer should not handle the case. McC, p. 124.

2. **Non-legal advice:** But the mere fact that the person giving the advice is a lawyer is not enough — the relationship must involve the giving of *legal* advice. "When lawyers are consulted as *family friends*, *business advisors*, or political consultants, the privilege is inapplicable." L&S, pp. 659-60.

3. **Reasonable belief:** Suppose the "lawyer" being consulted is in fact a charlatan who has never been admitted to the bar. So long as the client *reasonably believes* that the person he is talking to is a lawyer, this is all that is required. McC, p. 124. Similarly, so long as the lawyer is admitted (or believed by the client to be admitted) in *any* state, the fact that he is not (and is known by the client not to be) admitted in the state where the advice takes place is irrelevant. *Id.*

4. **Client holds the privilege:** The privilege *belongs to the client*, not to the lawyer or anyone else. (See the discussion of who may claim a privilege, *supra*, p. 414, in the context of privileges generally.)

   a. Waiver by client: Like any privilege, the attorney-client privilege may be *waived* by the client's words or actions. For instance, if the client *discloses* to a third person (e.g., a friend) the substance of what he told the lawyer, this will be considered a waiver, and the privilege will no longer apply. McC, p. 130.

   i. Waiver by lawyer acting on behalf of client: The privilege can also be waived by virtue of a *disclosure made by the attorney*, if the attorney is acting on the client's behalf. But disclosure by the attorney will *only* cause a waiver if under principles of agency law, the attorney is deemed to have been acting on behalf of the client. So, for instance, if the client *objects* to the disclosure and the attorney does it anyway, the disclosure will not constitute a waiver of the client's privilege. M&K, §5.28, pp. 385-86. For more about waiver, see *infra*, p. 420.

C. Confidential communications: Only *"confidential"* communications are protected by the privilege. A disclosure is "confidential" if the client intends that it not be disclosed to persons other than the lawyer and those working with the lawyer. The client need not expressly state that he wants the communication to be held confidential; it is enough if, under the circumstances, he could reasonably assume that there would not be disclosure to others. McC, p. 128.

1. **Client-to-lawyer:** Most importantly, disclosures by the *client to the lawyer* are protected if they are intended to be confidential.

a. **Non-verbal communication:** When the client communicates orally or in writing to the lawyer, this is obviously covered. But what if the communication is *non-verbal?* For instance, suppose that the client rolls up his sleeve to show a scar. This should be treated as a confidential (and therefore protected) communication, since it was intended as a disclosure, and was intended to remain secret.

b. **Lawyer's observation:** However, where the lawyer makes an observation that *third parties* could also have made, this will not be a confidential communication.

   Example: Shortly after Wife is found dead with stab wounds, Husband visits Lawyer to seek advice. Lawyer notices scratch marks on Husband's hands and face. Since these scratch marks could be viewed by anyone who happens to see Husband at that time, Lawyer's observations will not be protected by the attorney-client privilege, and he can be forced to testify about seeing them. (But if Husband had covered them with a bandage, and then removed the bandage to show them to Lawyer, Lawyer could not be forced to testify that he saw the scratches underneath the bandages, though he could be forced to testify that he saw the bandages.) L&S, p. 660.

c. **Mental state:** When a criminal defendant asserts an insanity defense, the prosecutor may try to question the lawyer about the client's mental state around the time of the crime. Courts are split on whether the lawyer can be forced to testify in this situation. The better view seems to be that the lawyer should not be forced to testify, since his conclusions about the client's mental state in all probability derive from their conversations about privileged matters. *Id.*

2. **Lawyer-to-client statements:** The privilege also applies to statements made *by the lawyer* to the client. McC, p. 125.

3. **Information involving third parties:** Suppose the communication is not between client and lawyer, but between client and some *third party*. Whether the privilege applies depends on whether the third party is *assisting the lawyer* in rendering legal services.

a. **Representative of lawyer:** Thus if the third party is assisting the lawyer, this party is in essence a *representative* of the lawyer, and communications involving him are treated the same way as if he were himself a lawyer. For instance, if an *expert* is retained by the lawyer to help investigate the case and to give tactical advice, any communication between the client and the expert will be privileged.

   Example: P brings a personal injury action against D, claiming that he has suffered a brain concussion and other medical injuries. At the request of P's lawyers, X, a physician, gives P a psychiatric and neurological examination. D attempts to force X to testify about the examination. No physician-patient privilege applies in the case, so X claims that he was acting as a representative of P's lawyers, and that the attorney-client privilege applies.

   Held, the attorney-client privilege applies. X was acting as P's lawyer's agent in examining P. (Had X been giving P medical treatment, the privilege would not apply; but the examination here was solely for purposes of conducting the litigation.) *City and County of San Francisco v. Superior Court*, 231 P.2d 26 (Cal. 1951).

b. Not assisting lawyer: But where the third person is *not* assisting the lawyer, there is no privilege for communications between that third person and the lawyer or client, even if these communications relate to the lawyer's providing of legal services. McC, p. 125.

Example: D is charged with murder. L, D's lawyer, while investigating the case to prepare D's defense, interviews X. X tells L, "I saw D near the scene of the murder moments before it happened." Because X is not acting as L's agent at the time he makes the statement to L, the statement is not privileged. Therefore, L can be required to testify about the statement. (However, the work-product immunity rule, discussed briefly *infra*, p. 431, may protect L from having to disclose the substance of X's oral statement. But that rule is quite distinct from the attorney-client privilege, which does not apply here.)

i. Lead generated by client: Suppose that, on the facts of the above example, the only way that L ever knew to interview X was because D told him that X might have some information. In this instance, D can make a strong argument that L's interview with X is a direct by-product of the earlier privileged communication between D and L, and that the interview should therefore also be privileged. D might well prevail with this argument — just as he might prevail if he had told L where the body was buried, and the prosecution then tried to force L to testify about how and where he found the body. (As to this discovery-of-evidence situation, see discussion, *infra*, p. 425.)

4. Tangible evidence and documents: Suppose the lawyer receives *tangible evidence* or *documents* from his client. May he be forced to disclose the existence of these items, or how he came into their possession? Generally, the attorney-client privilege adds nothing to the situation: if the client would have been required to disclose or turn over the items had they remained in his possession (e.g., because they are evidence in a criminal case), the lawyer must do the same. But the lawyer may be privileged to withhold information about how he came to possess the item. The matter is discussed more extensively *infra*, p. 425.

5. Miscellaneous issues: Here are some miscellaneous issues concerning whether a communication is "confidential" and thus privileged:

a. Waiver: The attorney-client privilege can be *waived*. Most importantly, if the client *voluntarily discloses* the communication — or consents to its being disclosed by someone else, such as her attorney — the disclosure will act as a waiver.

i. Presence of third persons: One form of waiver-by-disclosure will occur when the client permits a *third person to be present* when the communication takes place, if that person's presence does not advance to legal representation.

Example: If the communication takes place on a crowded elevator, where it is overheard by third persons, this setting will indicate that the client could not reasonably have expected confidentiality. Similarly, if the client, following the conference with the lawyer, tells a friend all about the conference, this is likely to be held to be an implied waiver of confidentiality.

(1) Clerks or relatives: However, if the third party's presence is ***reasonably helpful*** to the conference, that presence will not destroy the confidentiality. Thus if the lawyer's ***secretary*** or ***clerk*** is present, this will make no difference. Similarly, if the client's friend or relative attends the meeting in order to help (e.g., the friend interprets for the client, who cannot speak English very well), this too will not waive the privilege. McC, p. 128.

(2) Inadvertent eavesdropping: If the client and lawyer take reasonable precautions to protect confidentiality, the fact that, unbeknownst to them, ***eavesdropping*** occurs will not cause the privilege to be waived, under modern decisions.

ii. **Inadvertent disclosure:** Disclosures of privilege information sometimes occur ***inadvertently***. FRE 502 (added in 2008) says that for purposes of federal-court litigation, an inadvertent disclosure does ***not*** operate as a waiver as long as the privilege-holder "took ***reasonable steps*** to ***prevent*** [the] disclosure" before it happened, and then "***promptly took reasonable steps*** to ***rectify*** the error" after it occurred. Rule 502(b), (c).

(1) Electronic disclosure: This rule making it easier for a party to escape waiver when there is inadvertent disclosure is especially important in the modern age of ***electronic discovery***. Rule 502 means that if a party is required in a litigation to produce thousands of documents, the party no longer needs to worry that the inadvertent inclusion of a protected document in a large pile of documents being produced will cause the privilege to be waived in that or later litigations. And that, in turn, means that the party no longer has to painstakingly ***review each individual document*** for possible attorney-client privilege before producing the set to the other side. See ACN to Rule 502.

iii. **Multiple clients:** Where ***multiple clients*** (either with separate counsel or sharing the same counsel) are present during an otherwise-confidential disclosure, special issues arise. See *infra*, p. 430.

b. **Identity, fact of retention:** Only communications ***relating to the provision of legal services*** are protected. Thus the client's identity, or the fact that the lawyer has been retained, usually are not protected. (This is discussed further *infra*, p. 422.) Similarly, communications from lawyer to client about ***ministerial*** matters are probably not protected.

Example: D, who is free on bail pending trial, does not appear at trial. In support of its case for bail jumping, the prosecution demands that D's lawyer, L, testify about whether he told D the time and place of the trial. L refuses to give this information on the grounds of attorney-client privilege.

Held, the privilege does not apply. Communication between lawyer and client about the trial date does not involve "the subject matter of defendant's legal problem. . . . Such communications are non-legal in nature. Counsel is simply performing a notice function." *U.S. v. Woodruff*, 383 F.Supp. 696 (E.D.Pa. 1974).

c. **Underlying fact:** It is the ***communication*** that is privileged, ***not*** the ***underlying facts*** that are communicated. Therefore, the client can be required to disclose the underlying fact even though he has communicated it to his lawyer.

Example: P, a pedestrian injured in a collision with D's car, brings a personal injury action against D. In preparing for trial, P tells L, a lawyer, that she (P) was crossing the street against the light at the time of the accident. L may not be required to testify or otherwise disclose the fact that P has made this statement (since this is a privileged communication). However, P may be called to the stand and required to testify about whether the light was green, even though that fact was the subject of a communication from her to her lawyer. (But P cannot be required to say whether she told this to the lawyer.) See W&B, Par. 503(b)[03].

D. Fact of employment; client's identity: Sometimes a client will want to keep secret the ***mere existence*** of the attorney-client relationship, including the client's identity, address, fee arrangements, and other information about the terms of the lawyer's employment.

1. **General rule:** The general rule is that the ***fact*** that the attorney has been hired, and the ***identity*** of the client, are ***not*** privileged. McC, p. 127.

2. **Exceptions:** But at least some courts have recognized exceptions to this general rule of non-privilege:

    a. **Anonymous restitution:** For instance, where the client wishes to make ***anonymous restitution*** of some sort, courts have sometimes allowed him to do so through his lawyer.

    Example: Two taxpayers have their lawyer mail the IRS a check for delinquent taxes, without revealing the taxpayers' identities. (The taxpayers are afraid of a criminal investigation, and decide that if one occurs, they will be in better shape if they can show that they have already paid the taxes, albeit anonymously. They realize that if they give the IRS their names, the very investigation they fear will be made more likely.) The IRS responds by demanding that the lawyer disclose the taxpayers' identities.

    Held, the identities are protected by the attorney-client privilege and need not be released. *Baird v. Koerner*, 279 F.2d 623 (9th Cir. 1960).

    i. **Criticism:** Cases like *Baird*, allowing the attorney to handle payments on behalf of an anonymous client, are criticized on the grounds that this approach allows the client to do with impunity through a lawyer what he could not do directly or through some other kind of agent. For instance, the taxpayers in *Baird* would not have been able to send the money into the IRS directly without disclosing their identities; why should they be able to "launder" their payment by use of a lawyer?

    b. **"Missing link":** Courts also sometimes allow the identity of the client to remain secret where so much other information is already public that disclosure of the client's identity would have the effective result of disclosing a privileged communication, or violating the client's privilege against self-incrimination.

E. Physical evidence and documents: Suppose the client turns over to the lawyer ***physical evidence*** or ***documents***. Is the fact that the lawyer now has these items in his possession privileged? Can he be required to disclose not only that he has them, but how he got them? These and related issues are probably the most difficult ones in all of attorney-client privilege law. Courts are frequently in disagreement on how to resolve these issues.

Example: D, charged with murder, hands a gun to L, his lawyer. L has reason to believe that the gun was the murder weapon. (1) May L keep silent and decline to turn the gun over to the prosecution, on the grounds that he obtained it through his client's exercise of the attorney-client privilege? (2) If L must or does turn the gun over, can he refuse to say how he got it or what D told him about it, on privilege grounds? The issues are complicated, and courts may disagree on some aspects.

1. **Can't assist in ongoing fraud:** We must begin by keeping in mind the overarching principle that the attorney-client privilege does not apply where the lawyer's assistance is sought to enable the client to *commit a future crime or fraud*. (See *infra*, p. 428.)

2. **Concealment of evidence:** All states have statutes prohibiting the intentional concealment or destruction of *evidence* in pending proceedings. Therefore, the lawyer who helps his client conceal or destroy evidence is a co-conspirator to a *new crime*, and their actions and discussions together concerning the concealment or destruction are therefore *not privileged*.

   a. **Contraband and crime fruits or instrumentalities:** This rule is especially clear where the item is *contraband*, *stolen money*, or a *fruit* or *instrumentality* of crime. In this situation, the nature of the item, and the illegality of possessing or concealing it, are so clear that the courts will not hesitate to hold the attorney-client privilege inapplicable. See, e.g., *In re Ryder*, 263 F.Supp. 360 (E.D.Va. 1967) (lawyer's concealment of gun used in, and cash taken during course of, bank robbery, not within privilege).

   b. **Destruction advice to client:** Similarly, the lawyer may not *advise his client* to *destroy* contraband, stolen goods, or other clear evidence of crime. If he does give such advice, the giving of that advice is not privileged.

      Example: Client telephones his lawyer, and confesses to just having murdered his ex-wife. Lawyer asks, "Did you get rid of the weapon?" Client says, "No, I still got the weapon." Lawyer says, "Get rid of the weapon and sit tight and don't talk to anyone, and I will fly down in the morning." Unbeknownst to them, a telephone company operator has been eavesdropping on the call. Client, charged with murder, claims that this conversation may not be disclosed because it comes within the attorney-client privilege.

      Held, the privilege does not apply to this conversation. The rule making the privilege inapplicable to advice on how to commit a crime "must extend to one who, having committed a crime, seeks or takes counsel as to how he shall escape arrest and punishment, such as advice regarding the destruction or disposition of the murder weapon or of the body following a murder." Lawyer's advice here was "not in the legitimate course of professional employment in making or preparing a defense at law." *Clark v. State*, 261 S.W.2d 339 (Crim.App.Tex. 1953) (the eavesdropping aspect of which is discussed *supra*, p. 414).

   c. **Ambiguous evidence:** Suppose that the lawyer receives, or learns about, a tangible item that is not contraband, stolen money, or some other fruit or instrumentality of a known crime. For instance, the item may be one which would be *evidence in a civil suit*; or it may be a "neutral" item (i.e., not a fruit or instrumentality of crime) that would nonetheless be admissible in a criminal prosecution that has not yet commenced but is likely. In this situation, the outcome is less clear; most courts, however, would nonetheless apply the general rule that so long as the item is likely to be evidence in a civil or criminal case, the lawyer may not conceal it or advise his client to conceal it, and if he does so, his conduct is not privileged.

Example: Client is the defendant in a messy divorce case, in which Client's fidelity to his wife will be a material issue. Client asserts that he has always been faithful. During one of his conferences with Lawyer, Client leaves on the desk a ring inscribed (with a recent date), "To Client, with all my lust and love. [signed] Alice." Client's wife is not named Alice. May Lawyer keep the ring and conceal its existence during the suit? Most courts would probably say "no," since the item is relevant evidence in the pending suit. (But Lawyer may probably turn it over to Client with an admonition that it may have to be produced as part of discovery. See *infra*.)

3. **Attorney's choices:**   If the client comes to the lawyer with a tangible item that is clear evidence, what the lawyer may not do, as noted, is to conceal or advise the client to conceal it. The lawyer does, however, have several choices:

    a. **Decline to take:**   The wisest may well be for him to *decline to take possession of the evidence* at all, leaving it with the client. He should advise the client against destroying the evidence. (If he has reason to believe that the client will not listen to this advice, it is not clear what his obligations are. This issue is discussed further *infra*, p. 425.)

        i. **Lawyer's obligation:**   If the lawyer follows this course, declining to take possession of the item, does he then have any obligation to *notify the prosecution* that the evidence exists? L&S (p. 679) suggest that so long as the client has not left the item with the lawyer, and has taken it away at the conclusion of their meeting, the lawyer has no obligation of disclosure.

    b. **Hold for reasonable time:**   Alternatively, the lawyer may take the evidence for a *reasonable time*. This is especially true if evaluation of the item's value as evidence depends on some kind of *inspection* or *testing*. For instance, if the client is charged with murder by shooting, and the item is a gun that the lawyer suspects (but does not know) to be the murder weapon, the lawyer may keep the gun for long enough to have ballistics tests performed on it to determine whether it is the murder weapon.

        i. **After reasonable inspection:**   Once the lawyer has held the item for the period of reasonable inspection or testing, he may normally *return the item* to the client. If he does so, he must certainly advise the client that destruction or concealment of evidence is a crime. (But if he believes the client will destroy or conceal it, he probably cannot return it. See *infra*.)

        ii. **Stolen property:**   If the lawyer knows that the property has been *stolen*, he has an obligation to *return it* to its *rightful owner* once the time for reasonable inspection has passed. If the lawyer does not do this, he is a receiver of stolen goods, and is thus participating in an ongoing crime, so that the privilege does not apply.

c. **Turn over to prosecution:** If the lawyer believes that the client will ***destroy or conceal*** the evidence, most courts would probably require the lawyer to ***turn the item over*** to the other side (usually the prosecution).

4. **Evidence of source:** Suppose that the other side does discover the evidence (whether through its own efforts or because the lawyer discloses and/or returns it). Can the lawyer be forced to testify about his ***source***, i.e., that he got it from the client, or discovered it on the basis of information supplied by the client? The answer depends in part on whether the lawyer ever actually had possession of the item.

   a. **No possession:** First, consider the situation in which the lawyer never really gets custody of the item. For instance, he may merely have learned from the client that the item exists; or, the client may have shown it to him during their meeting, then taken it away. In this situation, the lawyer probably does ***not*** have to disclose what he has learned about the item — he has not participated in the concealment of evidence (assuming that he has not encouraged the client to conceal or destroy the item). L&S, p. 679.

   b. **Custody:** If, however, the lawyer has taken possession of the item, courts are in dispute.

      i. **Need not disclose source:** Some courts have held that the lawyer ***need not disclose*** (or at least testify about) his source, even though he may be obligated to turn the item over to the prosecution.

      ii. **Better view:** However, other courts have held that the lawyer may be forced not only to turn over the evidence to the prosecution, but also to ***disclose its source*** at trial. This is probably the better view in most situations, since the contrary approach — allowing the lawyer to refuse to testify about how he got the item — lets the client "launder the evidence." That is, under the contrary approach, the client is able to "remove [the evidence] from her possession and place it in the hands of the government without having the government connect it up with its source." Salzburg, 66 Iowa L. Rev. 811, 838 (1981).

      Example: D, charged with murdering and robbing X, meets with Lawyer while in jail. D tells Lawyer that he saw a wallet near X's body after the crime, picked it up, tried to burn it, and threw it into the garbage behind his (D's) house. Lawyer sends an investigator to find the wallet from the garbage. Lawyer then turns the wallet over to the police, tells them that he believes the wallet belonged to X, but refuses to say how he came into possession of it.

      Held, Lawyer must reveal how he got the wallet. Had Lawyer left the wallet in its original position and condition (so that the police could have found it in D's trash can), Lawyer would have no obligation to disclose the fact that he knew its whereabouts. But once he chose to remove or alter it, he necessarily deprived the prosecution of its opportunity to observe the evidence in its original condition or location. Once this happened, the original location and condition of the evidence "loses the protection of the privilege," and Lawyer must disclose that location and condition. A contrary rule would "permit the defense in effect to 'destroy' critical information; it is as if . . . the wallet in this case bore a tag bearing the words 'located in the trash can by [D's] residence,' and the defense, by taking the wallet, destroyed this tag." Allowing the lawyer to refuse to disclose how and where he found the evidence "might encourage defense counsel to race the police to seize critical evidence." *People v. Meredith*, 631 P.2d 46 (Cal. 1981).

5. **Information from third parties:** The above discussion of physical evidence that comes into the attorney's possession assumes that the attorney got possession directly from the client, or that at least he learned where to find the item directly or indirectly from the client. If the lawyer discovers the item through an entirely ***independent investigation***, or it is given to him by a ***third person*** who is not working for the lawyer, remember that the attorney-client privilege ***simply does not apply***.

6. **Writings:** Sometimes the tangible item received by the lawyer will be a ***document***; for instance, a letter, receipt, or other writing. The lawyer's obligation to turn over that document is likely to depend on whether the document was ***prepared by the client***.

   a. **Not prepared by client:** If the document was not prepared by the client, the document is no different from any other kind of tangible evidence, and the rules discussed extensively above apply.

      Example: D is charged with murdering and robbing X in X's apartment. D denies ever having been to the apartment. D gives Lawyer a receipt showing X's purchase of a stereo system. This receipt is no different from the stereo system itself — it is stolen property and Lawyer must turn it over to the police.

   b. **Self-incrimination:** But if the writing was ***prepared by the client***, the client might be protected from having to disclose it by his privilege against self-incrimination (see *infra*, p. 437). If so, the lawyer ***stands in the client's shoes***, and need not disclose it either.

      i. **Work product immunity:** Where the item sought to be disclosed is a document, you should also keep in mind the ***work product immunity*** doctrine. This doctrine (discussed *infra*, p. 431) prevents certain documents prepared by or on behalf of attorneys, in connection with a pending litigation, from being the subject of a discovery order.

F. **Corporate clients:** Up until now, our discussion of attorney-client privilege has assumed that the client is an ***individual***. To what extent does the privilege also protect clients that are ***corporations***? The short answer is that corporations ***are*** protected by the privilege. However, several of the ways in which corporations differ from individuals raise special problems when determining what is privileged: (1) for the privilege to apply at all, the client must be the corporation, yet the communication necessarily comes from an individual employee of the corporation, who is not speaking to "his" lawyer; (2) the lawyer may be an "in-house" lawyer, i.e., an employee of the very corporation he is representing; and (3) lawyers, especially in-house lawyers, often give business advice, and often receive a broad range of corporate reports and records that go far beyond the typical communications between an individual and his lawyer.

   1. **Corporations have privilege:** It is clear that, at least in the abstract, a corporation may take advantage of the attorney-client privilege. See, e.g., *Upjohn v. U.S.*, 449 U.S. 383

(1981) (discussed more extensively below), implicitly recognizing that corporations are protected by the privilege.

2. **Who may communicate:** When the client is an individual, it is very clear that the communications must come from or to the client in order for the privilege to apply. Yet, in the corporate setting, the "client" is the corporation, and the corporation as such cannot communicate — only its employees can do so. It has never been clear whether statements by or to even low-level, non-managerial employees will be deemed to be by (or to) the corporation.

   a. **"Control group" test:** Prior to 1981, a major approach was the *"control group"* test. By this test, only if the employee who dealt with the corporation's lawyer was a member of the corporate "control group" (i.e., one who is "in a position to control or . . . to take a substantial part in a decision about any action which the corporation may take upon the advice of the attorney") could the communication be deemed to be between lawyer and client, because only in that situation did the employee "personify" the corporation. (The quoted language is from *City of Philadelphia v. Westinghouse Electric Corp.*, 210 F.Supp. 483 (E.D.Pa. 1962), in which the test was first articulated.)

   b. **Supreme Court's *Upjohn* case:** In 1981, the Supreme Court rejected the "control group" test, in *Upjohn v. U.S.*, 449 U.S. 383 (1981). Unfortunately for students, the Court did not say what the correct standard is, merely that the control group test is not it.

      i. **Facts:** In *Upjohn*, the corporation learned that officials of one of its subsidiaries had made possibly illegal payments to foreign government officials in order to get business. The corporation thereupon sent a questionnaire to all of its foreign managers above a certain rank, asking for detailed information about such payments. The letter was signed by the Chairman of the company, and told the recipients that the answers would be treated as "highly confidential"; responses were to be sent to the company's General Counsel. The IRS learned of the questionnaires, and attempted to obtain them via subpoena. The company argued that the responses were protected by the attorney-client privilege (and also by the work product immunity doctrine).

      ii. **Privilege claim upheld:** The Court held that the lower court was wrong in using the "control group" test (under which the questionnaire responses would not be privileged because the foreign managers were not of sufficiently high rank to "personify" the corporation). Use of the control group test, the Court held, would frustrate the purposes of the attorney-client privilege because it would discourage the communication of relevant information by the corporation's employees to attorneys seeking to render legal advice to the client corporation. Often, quite low-level employees will have the information that the lawyers need, and the fact that these employees are not part of the control group is irrelevant. Similarly, it will often be low-level employees who need to carry out the lawyer's advice. (The Court also held that, to the extent that some of the foreign managers responded orally instead of by written questionnaire, the lawyer's notes and recollections of the conversations were protected by work product immunity; see *infra*, p. 431.)

c. **Who may communicate:**   *Upjohn* leaves it unclear whether absolutely every employee will be deemed to be speaking "for" the corporation, so that the privilege applies. For instance, it is not clear whether the privilege would apply if a low-level employee, completely on his own, called one of the company's in-house lawyers to ask a question relating to company business. It is possible that only communications authorized by a member of management will be deemed to be sufficiently "on behalf of" the corporation so as to make the privilege apply.

3. **Must concern employee's employment:**   The mere fact that one party to the communication is an employee is **not** sufficient — the communication must relate to the employee's *performance of corporate duties*.

    Example: Driver, an employee of Bus Company, happens to see an accident involving one of Bus Company's buses on his way to work one morning. If Driver tells the company's lawyer the details of what he saw, this communication will *not* be privileged, because Driver was not acting on company business at the time he witnessed the accident. W&B, Par. 503(b)[04].

4. **Reports and other routine communications:**   The communication must be ***primarily*** for the purpose of obtaining ***legal services***. Thus, if the communication is a ***routine report*** generated in the ordinary course of the corporation's business, and happens to be received by one of the corporation's attorneys, the privilege will not apply. For instance, accident reports, personnel records, and financial documents are all items which may be circulated to the company's lawyers, but which are not privileged because they are not created primarily for the purpose of obtaining legal services.

5. **Confidentiality:**   The privilege will apply only if the communication is treated ***confidentially***. This does not mean that no one but the originator of the communication and the lawyer may learn of it. But it does mean that the corporation must handle the communication on a ***"need to know"*** basis — disclosure should be limited to "those persons who, because of the structure of the corporation, must know of the communication in order to ensure that the attorney is obtaining both full and accurate information." 69 Mich. L. Rev. 360 (1970).

G. **Exceptions to the privilege:**   We briefly consider now several exceptions to the attorney-client privilege, situations in which the privilege is deemed not to exist even though the standard requirements discussed above are met.

1. **Crime or fraud:**   When the client asks for help in defending against charges of a crime or wrong that he has already committed, the privilege of course applies — assisting even avowed criminals in preparing their defense is one of the functions of the privilege. But when the client asks for assistance in carrying out or defending against ***future crimes*** or wrongs, the privilege does ***not*** apply. The privilege's main goal — promoting justice — would be undermined if it could be used as a "cloak or shield for the perpetration of a crime or fraudulent wrongdoing." *U.S. v. Gordon-Nikkar*, 518 F.2d 972 (5th Cir. 1975).

    Example: Client says to Lawyer, "If X and I were to rob the First National Bank, and X were then to get caught and give a confession saying that I was with him on the job, could the police use that confession against me?" Circumstances subsequently make it clear that at the time of this conversation, Client has not yet pulled the bank job, but he does so thereafter. Even though this conversation clearly relates to the obtaining of legal services, it is not privileged, because it really seeks the lawyer's help in carrying out a future crime. Therefore, at Client's trial, Lawyer could be forced to testify about the conversation.

a. Cover-up of past crime: The dividing line between seeking advice about past crimes or wrongs (privileged) and seeking such advice about future crimes or wrongs (not privileged) is usually clear. But, one situation can cause trouble: where the client seeks advice about how to ***avoid discovery*** of his ***prior wrongdoing***. Here, the rule is as discussed above (*supra*, p. 423) in the treatment of physical evidence: if the discussions relate to the fraudulent concealment or destruction of evidence, or other obstruction of justice, the communications involve perpetration of a ***new future crime or fraud,*** and are thus ***unprivileged.*** See, e.g., *In re Ryder, supra*, p. 423 (holding unprivileged the lawyer's concealment of a weapon and money associated with a past bank robbery).

b. Knowledge: The "crime or fraud" exception applies only where the client ***knew*** or should reasonably have known that his contemplated act would be wrongful. W&B, Par. 503(d)(1)[01]. Thus, if the lawyer tells the client that his proposed action is legal, and the client's belief in this advice is reasonable, the privilege applies even though the lawyer was wrong. See PFRE 503(d)(1).

c. *In camera* examination: When one party asserts the privilege, but the opponent argues that the communication falls within the future-crime-or-fraud exception, how should the court ***determine*** whether the privilege applies? If the court examines the communication, some of the value of the privilege is lost. But without an examination of the communication itself, it will be hard — sometimes impossible — to determine whether a crime or fraud was in fact being planned. In cases arising under the Federal Rules, the trial judge is now authorized to conduct an ***in camera examination*** of the communication to determine its admissibility. The Supreme Court so held in *U.S. v. Zolin*, 491 U.S. 554 (1989).

i. Rationale: The Court in *Zolin* reasoned that "the costs of imposing an absolute bar to consideration of the communications in camera . . . are intolerably high." There are simply too many abuses of the privilege which could never be demonstrated except by considering the communication itself.

ii. Threshold showing: On the other hand, the Court held in *Zolin*, the party asserting the crime-or-fraud exception must make a ***threshold showing*** before the *in camera* examination may be made: that party must show "a factual basis adequate to support a ***good faith belief*** by a ***reasonable person***" that *in camera* review of the materials may reveal evidence establishing the crime-or-fraud exception. This will prevent "fishing expeditions." (Thus in *Zolin* itself, this threshold showing was satisfied by lawfully-obtained, unprivileged, partial transcripts of the lawyer-client conversation, suggesting that an *in camera* examination of the full tapes of the conversation might well reveal evidence that the crime-fraud exception applied.)

2. **Through same deceased client:**   In general, the privilege *survives* the *death* of the client. But there is one exception, which almost swallows this whole rule: if the suit is a *will contest* or other case in which the issue is who receives the deceased client's property, the privilege does *not* apply. See, e.g., PFRE 503(d)(2) (no privilege where issue is "between parties who claim through the same deceased client, regardless of whether the claims are by testate or intestate succession or by *inter vivos* transaction").

> **Example:** Client dies, leaving an ostensibly valid will that gives his entire estate to Son and that completely disinherits Daughter. Daughter sues to have the will declared invalid on the grounds that Client was incompetent when he made it. Son may call Lawyer (who prepared the will) to testify as to the conversations between Client and Lawyer leading up to the will, to show that Client was in control of his faculties. Daughter may also call Lawyer to testify as to these Client-Lawyer communications.

3. **Attorney-client dispute:**   If the lawyer and client become involved in a *dispute* between themselves concerning the services provided by the lawyer, the privilege does *not* apply to their dispute. For instance, if the lawyer sues the client for a fee, the lawyer may testify as to communications between them that would otherwise be privileged. The lawyer may similarly disclose otherwise-privileged confidences as part of his defense of a malpractice action brought by the client. McC, p. 129; PFRE 503(d)(3).

4. **Joint clients:**   The privilege may be inapplicable to a dispute between *multiple clients* who were originally on the same side of a transaction.

   a. **Same lawyer:**   If two clients *retain a single lawyer*, and a dispute later breaks out between the two, the privilege does *not* apply. This is true whether or not the other client was privy to the communication in question. See discussion of PFRE 503(d)(5).

      i. **Insurer-insured:**   This principle has been applied to disputes between an insured and his insurance company.

      > **Example:** Driver is sued by Passenger for injuries arising out of an automobile accident. Insurer, who insures Driver, hires Lawyer for the case. Driver makes confidential communications to Lawyer. Later, Driver and Insurer have a dispute about the policy limits. In that dispute, most courts would probably hold that Insurer may compel Lawyer to testify about otherwise-privileged communications between Driver and Lawyer, since Lawyer represented both Driver and Insurer. W&B, Par. 503(b)[07].

   b. **Different lawyers:**   Now suppose that the two clients retain *separate lawyers*. If both lawyers and both clients meet together to discuss common legal issues, the privilege *applies*, even in the event of a later dispute between clients. That is, the privilege exists in the "multiple client, multiple lawyer" setting but not the "multiple client, one lawyer" setting, a result some have criticized as being anomalous.

   c. **Action vs. the world:**   If the eventual lawsuit is between the multiple clients and *some third party*, the privilege *applies*, whether there was one lawyer or more.

H. **Other constraints and ethical issues:**   So far, we have focused strictly on the attorney-client privilege. However, there are several other bodies of law which may be relevant to a situation in which the attorney-client privilege is invoked. These include: (1) the Code of Professional

Responsibility and related ethical constraints upon lawyers; (2) the work product immunity doctrine; and (3) in criminal cases, the Sixth Amendment right to counsel. We will touch very briefly upon these as they relate to situations where the attorney-client privilege is at issue.

1. **Code of Professional Responsibility:** Virtually all states have adopted either the American Bar Association's 1969 Code of Professional Responsibility (CPR) or the ABA's 1983 Model Rules of Professional Conduct (MRPC). We will refer to these two sets of rules, collectively, as "professional ethics."

   a. **Confidentiality:** Professional ethics give the lawyer a right and duty not to *disclose confidential information*. In one sense this right/duty is broader than the attorney-client evidentiary privilege. For instance, MRPC 1.6(a) imposes on the lawyer the duty not to disclose any "information relating to representation of a client."

      i. **Covers nonprivileged information:** This ethical duty of confidentiality covers much information that is not covered by the attorney-client evidentiary privilege. For instance, if the lawyer learns information about the client *from a third party* who is not affiliated with the lawyer, the lawyer is required by professional ethics not to disclose that information, even though it is not covered by the evidentiary attorney-client privilege (see *supra*, p. 426). Similarly, if the client gives information both to the lawyer and to other persons (thus destroying the confidentiality required for the evidentiary privilege; see *supra*, p. 420), this is nonetheless information which, as a matter of professional ethics, the lawyer may not divulge.

      ii. **Not applicable where disclosure required by law:** Conversely, however, in a *litigation* context (either discovery or at trial), the professional ethics rules against disclosure must *give way* if the communication is not privileged.

         Example: Lawyer, defending Client on a murder charge, learns from Client's ex-wife that, prior to the killing, Client owned a gun much like the one used in the killing. This knowledge is not covered by the attorney-client privilege, since it comes from a person other than the Client. However, professional ethics prevent Lawyer from disclosing this fact to, say, his best friend. But if the prosecution, at trial, calls Lawyer to testify about his conversation with the ex-wife, Lawyer must do so — the evidentiary rule that there is no privilege takes precedence over the professional ethics obligation not to disclose. However, the attorney should wait until the court has *ordered* him to disclose the information before doing so.

2. **Work product immunity:** The doctrine of *work product immunity* prevents the attorney from being required to disclose certain information that he obtains *while preparing for a lawsuit*. Most states have followed the approach laid down by Federal Rule of Civil Procedure 26(b)(3).

   a. **Qualified protection:** Under FRCP 26(b)(3), a party may obtain discovery of a document that was "prepared in anticipation of litigation or for trial" by the other party or that party's lawyer "only upon a showing that the party seeking discovery has *substantial need* of the materials in the preparation of his case and that he is unable without undue hardship to obtain the substantial equivalent of the materials by other means." This form of the work product immunity supplies *"qualified"* immunity (i.e., immunity that is capable of being overridden).

Example: Recall the questionnaires filled out by the foreign managers in the *Upjohn* case, and returned to Upjohn's general counsel. Assume for the moment that these questionnaire responses had been held by the Supreme Court not to be privileged (perhaps because they were disclosed to too many other non-lawyer employees within the corporation, thus waiving confidentiality). Because these documents were prepared in anticipation of possible litigation, the IRS could obtain discovery of them, under FRCP 26(b)(3), only by showing that it had a "substantial need of the materials" to prepare its case, and couldn't get the substantial equivalent without "undue hardship." Because the managers are spread all over the earth, the IRS might be able to make such a showing of need, in which case it could get discovery of the questionnaires. Thus the questionnaires would only be subject to a "qualified" work product immunity.

b. **Absolute immunity for "mental impressions, conclusions, etc.":** Some materials are so much the product of the *lawyer's own thinking,* that they receive what is essentially an *absolute* work product immunity. The last sentence of FRCP 26(b)(3) states that "in ordering discovery of such materials when the required showing has been made, the court shall protect against disclosure of the *mental impressions, conclusions, opinions*, or *legal theories* of an attorney or other representative of a party concerning the litigation." Probably there is no showing of need that will be enough to compel disclosure of this kind of material, although the Supreme Court explicitly declined to decide this issue in *Upjohn* (or since).

Example: Recall that Upjohn's general counsel also conducted oral interviews of some managers, and made notes of what they were saying and his conclusions from what they were saying. The Supreme Court in *Upjohn* held that this information received more than the basic "qualified" privilege, and that the IRS had not shown sufficiently compelling need for this information. (The Court declined to hold that such information could *never* be compelled to be disclosed, but it did say that the showing of need by the IRS was not even close to enough.)

c. **Significance:** The important point to remember is that the work product immunity doctrine provides a *second, independent basis* for a lawyer's refusal to disclose certain documents during the trial preparation phase. Even though the document could be admissible at trial if the other side obtained it, the lawyer can refuse to give it over in discovery. (If the other side happens to get it anyhow, perhaps first from some non-lawyer source, the document then can be admitted at trial if the attorney-client privilege does not apply. If the attorney-client privilege *does* apply, the work product immunity rule never springs into action, because discovery is only allowed of "unprivileged" material; see FRCP 26(b)(1).)

d. **Waiver:** A party can *waive* the work product immunity just as she can waive the attorney-client privilege. And basically the same rules governing when waiver occurs apply to the work product immunity scenario. Therefore, the client's *voluntary disclosure* of the substance of the work product to a third-party unconnected with the representation will constitute a waiver.

    i. **Inadvertent disclosure not a waiver:** However, FRE 502 comes to the assistance of the party who *inadvertently* discloses work product materials, just as it helps a party who inadvertent discloses attorney-client-privileged material. As long as the client and her lawyer take *reasonable steps to guard against* such inadvertent disclosure, and to *remedy* it when it occurs, the disclosure will not be treated as a waiver. (See *supra*, p. 421, for a discussion of FRE 502 in the attorney-client-privilege context.)

III. PHYSICIAN-PATIENT PRIVILEGE; PSYCHOTHERAPIST-PATIENT PRIVILEGE

A. Generally: All but ten states have by statute enacted some form of *physician-patient* privilege. McC, p. 142. In general, these statutes give a patient a privilege against the disclosure of: (1) *confidential communications* (2) made to a *physician* (including *psychiatrist*) (3) if made for the purpose of obtaining *treatment*, or diagnosis looking toward treatment.

    1. History: There is *no* common-law physician-patient privilege analogous to the attorney-client privilege. Thus, in those ten states that have not enacted a statute granting the privilege, the privilege does not exist.

    2. Rationale: The rationale for the physician-patient privilege is similar to that often given for the attorney-client privilege: unless the patient can rely upon confidentiality, she will not disclose all relevant matter (including embarrassing private details about health and bodily condition), and will thus not receive the best diagnosis and treatment. *Id.*

        a. Criticism: However, the analogy to the attorney-client privilege is probably flawed. When a client discusses a particular matter with a lawyer, the possibility of litigation, and thus disclosure, is much on his mind, and the existence of the privilege is likely to make a real difference in his willingness to disclose details. When a patient consults a doctor, on the other hand, the patient is probably worried about getting cured, and is likely to be totally unconcerned about possible disclosure in court (indeed, the patient probably doesn't even know whether a statutory privilege exists). Therefore, it is hard to see how the privilege really has the effect of encouraging confidential disclosures that would not otherwise be made. *Id.*

        b. Constitutional underpinning: A second rationale for the privilege has begun to emerge: some aspects of the physician-patient privilege may be protected against government-compelled disclosure by virtue of the federal *Constitution's* implied *right of privacy*. The Supreme Court has not yet spoken directly on this subject, but it has recognized a right of privacy concerning a number of highly personal areas (e.g., those relating to the decision whether to have a child). Several lower courts have held that governmentally-compelled disclosure of confidences between patient and doctor may in some instances violate that right.

    3. Psychotherapist-patient: Nearly all states, and some federal courts, now recognize a separate *psychotherapist-patient privilege*. This privilege is discussed *infra*, p. 435.

B. Special issues: Here is a brief discussion of some of the special issues that arise in construing statutes granting a physician-patient privilege:

1. **Relationship:**   Under most statutes, the privilege applies only where the patient is consulting a ***physician***, and is doing so with a purpose of obtaining ***treatment***, or a ***diagnosis*** that will lead to treatment.

    a. **Other professionals:**   Thus under most statutes, disclosures to other health professionals, such as dentists, druggists, or social workers, will ***not*** be covered. McC, p. 143. (But if the state has a separate psychologist-patient privilege, the definition of "psychologist" may be broad enough to include social workers, family counselors, and the like.)

    b. **Consulted for litigation:**   The requirement that the consultation be for treatment, or diagnosis leading to treatment, means that some other kinds of common consultations are ***not covered*** by the statute. For instance, if the ***court appoints*** a physician to make a physical or mental examination of the party, or if the party hires a doctor to review his condition for the sole purpose of testifying as an ***expert witness*** on the party's behalf at trial, the privilege will not apply. McC, p. 143.

2. **Confidentiality:**   Most, but not all, statutes have been interpreted to include a requirement that the disclosure be intended by the patient to be ***confidential.*** (Recall that a similar requirement of confidentiality applies to the common-law attorney-client privilege; see *supra*, p. 418.) McC, pp. 144-145. Thus if the patient later discloses to, say, a friend the substance of the communication to the doctor, the privilege would not apply in these states.

    a. **Public records:**   State and municipal laws often impose upon the physician the duty to ***report*** certain types of health information (e.g., gunshot wounds and venereal disease) to the authorities. Generally, the privilege statutes have been held not to bar the physician from complying with the public recording statute. When the physician is required to report a particular piece of information to authorities under such a statute, he will generally be held to be required to disclose it to the ***court*** as well — that is, most physician-patient privilege statutes have been interpreted not to apply to material required to be reported to health or other public officials. McC, p. 145.

3. **Who holds privilege:**   The privilege belongs to the ***patient, not the doctor***.

    a. **Physician's records*:***   For instance, courts generally refuse to recognize any right on the part of a physician to decline to ***disclose his records***, where there is no evidence that the patient in question is asserting any privilege. (The physician may attempt to exercise the privilege on the part of the patient, in which case it is generally up to the judge's discretion whether to accept this exercise without evidence of the patient's actual wishes. But if the patient waives the privilege, the doctor then has no right to refuse to disclose the information.)

4. **Waiver:**   The physician-patient privilege, like any privilege, may be ***waived*** by its holder.

    a. **Patient-litigant exception:**   Probably the majority of physician-patient privilege cases are ones in which the patient is a ***party*** and his physical or mental condition is in issue. (For instance, he may be the plaintiff in a tort suit in which his physical condition is at issue, or he may be the decedent insured under a life insurance policy as to which the cause of death makes a difference.) Nearly all physician-patient statutes have some kind of *exception* for the *"patient-litigant"* situation, under which a patient-litigant who *puts his medical condition in issue* is deemed to have in effect *waived* the privilege.

   i. California statute: For instance, California's statute removes the privilege for any communication relating to "an issue concerning the condition of the patient if such issue has been tendered by: (a) the patient; (b) any party claiming through or under the patient; (c) any party claiming as a beneficiary of the patient through a contract to which the patient is or was a party; or (d) the plaintiff in an action . . . for damages for the injury or death of the patient." Cal. Evid. Code, §996. Thus, if P claims to have suffered paralysis as the result of D's negligence, D may require P's physician to disclose any communications between P and the doctor relating to the alleged paralysis, under the California statute.

   ii. Insurance suit: Similarly, where the suit is against an *insurance* company under a life insurance policy, medical information concerning the *cause of death* is not privileged, under California's and nearly all other statutes.

   iii. What constitutes "putting in issue": It will not always be clear when a patient-litigant has put his mental or physical condition "in issue." The mere fact of bringing suit is not enough to justify compelling the plaintiff to disclose all facts of his personal medical history.

   Example: Suppose that P suffers what is indisputably a broken leg which he alleges to be the result of D's negligence. Suppose further that D believes that P is a chronic liar, and that the broken leg has nothing to do with D's conduct. Even though D has good reason to believe that P has a history of lying, and that that history might be disclosed in the records of P's psychiatrist, these psychiatric records will probably not be required to be disclosed over P's objection — P has not placed his mental condition in issue merely by bringing suit for physical injuries.

   iv. Limited waiver: Furthermore, the fact that the patient-litigant has implicitly waived some aspect of the privilege merely by bringing the suit (or by disclosing partial information) does not mean that *all* aspects of medical condition are covered by the waiver. In general, the courts construe the waiver as *narrowly* as they can, consonant with the need to protect the right of the other party (generally the defendant) to present his case.

5. "Public safety": Another exception to the privilege, recognized by some courts in recent years, might be called the *"public safety"* exception. If a physician (usually a psychiatrist) believes that his patient may be *dangerous* to others, many states allow him to disregard the patient's privilege and give a *warning* to the authorities or to any person he identifies as a likely *victim*. This topic is discussed more fully as part of the treatment of the psychotherapist-patient privilege, *infra*, p. 435.

C. Psychotherapist-patient: A *"psychotherapist-patient"* privilege evolved from the physician-patient privilege, and has now attained the status of a *separate privilege* in most jurisdictions.

1. **Present status:** The psychotherapist-patient privilege is actually now *more widely accepted* than the physician-patient privilege:

    a. **State-court treatment:** *All but one* of the states now recognize some form of the psychotherapist-patient privilege. *Doe v. Diamond*, 964 F.2d 1325 (2d Cir. 1992).

    b. **Federal treatment:** In federal-court suits based on federal claims, the Supreme Court has *recognized* the psychotherapist-patient privilege. See *Jaffe v. Redmond*, 518 U.S. 1 (1996). In *Jaffe*, the Court said that the privilege "serves the public interest by *facilitating the provision of appropriate treatment* for individuals suffering the effects of a mental or emotional problem." If the privilege were not recognized, confidential conversations between psychotherapists and their patients "would surely be *chilled*." And recognizing the privilege would not cause a significant *loss of evidence*, because without the privilege patients would not make many litigation-relevant statements (e.g., admissions by a party to litigation) anyway.

        i.   **Extended to social workers:** In fact, in *Jaffe* the Court extended the federal-court privilege to cover conversations between patients and licensed *social workers*. Thus in *Jaffe* itself, D was a police officer being sued on a federal civil-rights claim by the family of a man she killed in the line of duty. The Court's decision protected post-shooting conversations that D had with a social worker employed by her employer.

2. **Rationale:** The case for recognizing a psychotherapist-patient privilege is at least as strong as that for recognizing a general physician-patient privilege, if not stronger. When a patient consults a physician for a physical ailment, much of what the physician needs to know can be determined by visual examination and testing, as to which the patient's need to make "full disclosure" is not necessarily all-important. But the utility of psychotherapy rests almost entirely on complete and candid *disclosure* by the patient of highly personal, and perhaps embarrassing, details. Furthermore, there are many individuals who might commit *crimes* or other anti-social acts (e.g., sexual assaults) if they don't get treatment from a mental-health professional. Thus many courts (including the Supreme Court in *Jaffe, supra*) and legislatures have reasoned that society needs to give people an *incentive* to induce them to consult a therapist; a privilege for confidences is such an incentive.

3. **Psychologists:** In most states, and in most federal courts that recognize the psychotherapist privilege, the privilege extends to both medical doctors and *psychologists*.

4. **Mental or emotional condition:** The privilege extends only to communications made for the purpose of obtaining treatment or diagnosis of the patient's *mental or emotional condition*. M&K §5.35, p. 413. This "mental or emotional condition" limitation means that *marriage counseling* is probably *covered* (because of its heavy emotional content) but *vocational* and *educational counseling* usually are not. *Id.*

5. **Qualified privilege:** The privilege is a *qualified* one. Most importantly, it may be overridden where needed to protect a *criminal defendant's* right of *confrontation* (see *supra*, p. 361). Thus where there is some evidence that a key *prosecution witness* suffers from a mental or emotional condition that might case doubt on his credibility, the court is likely to override the privilege by allowing the defendant to review the witness's psychiatric records and to present evidence on the subject at trial. See *Doe, supra*, for an illustration.

6. Waiver: The same general rules regarding *waiver* apply to the psychotherapist-patient privilege as to the physician-patient privilege (*supra*, p. 434). For instance, if the patient's mental condition is at issue in a suit in which the patient is a party, the "patient-litigant" exception applies to render the privilege inapplicable.

   a. "Public safety": If a therapist reasonably believes that his patient may be *dangerous* to others, many states allow him to disregard the patient's privilege and give a *warning* to the authorities or to any person he identifies as a likely *victim*.

   i. Danger itself nullifies privilege: Some states (most notably California) go further, and hold that where a communication from patient to therapist reasonably leads the therapist to believe the patient may be dangerous, the mere *existence* of that reasonably-perceived danger — and not the therapist's giving of a warning — is enough to render the communication unprivileged. In these states, if a patient makes threats in speaking to a therapist (whether the threats are directed at the therapist or at third persons), the therapist and patient won't be able to block law enforcement officials from learning about the communication and using it as evidence.

   Example: The Ds (Erik and Lyle Menendez) are charged with murdering their wealthy parents. The prosecution seeks tapes and notes made by a psychotherapist, Dr. Oziel, of his sessions with the Ds after the murder. In two sessions (Oct. 31 and Nov. 2), the Ds made threats to harm Dr. Oziel. The Ds claim that the notes and tapes of these (as well as other) sessions are protected by the therapist-patient privilege.

   Held (on appeal), for the prosecution. Under the Cal. Evid. Code's "dangerous patient" exception (§1024), as soon as a communication indicates the existence of a danger to the therapist or another person, and the need for disclosure to prevent that danger, that communication is no longer privileged. The Oct. 31 and Nov. 2 sessions qualified, because of the threats the Ds made directly to Dr. Oziel. Therefore, regardless of whether Dr. Oziel ever in fact disclosed the communications to anyone else, they are no longer privileged, and the prosecution may have them and use them at trial. *Menendez v. Superior Court*, 834 P.2d 786 (Cal. 1992).

   ii. Tort liability: Some courts allow the *victim* of violence by a patient to sue the patient's therapist if the patient communicated to the therapist an intent to harm the victim, and the therapist unreasonably failed to warn the victim. The classic case is *Tarasoff v. Regents of University of California*, 551 P.2d 334 (Cal. 1976).

IV. THE PRIVILEGE AGAINST SELF-INCRIMINATION

   A. Introduction: We turn now to the privilege against self-incrimination. At the outset, two important things about this privilege, in contrast to the other ones discussed above, should be noted: (1) it is the only privilege that is explicitly required by the federal *Constitution*; and (2) it is, and has always been, a very *controversial* privilege, one which large segments of the population would prefer to see abolished or at least drastically curtailed.

1. **History:** A detailed treatment of the historical development of the privilege against self-incrimination is beyond the scope of this outline. See generally McC, pp. 161-166. In brief, the privilege developed as a response by the English Parliament and common-law courts to abuses by ecclesiastical and political courts. During the Fifteenth through Seventeenth Centuries, two courts in particular — the notorious Star Chamber and High Commission — forced those accused of religious or political crimes to testify under oath, to undergo rigorous questioning, and often to be physically tortured.

2. **Two branches:** The privilege has two distinct branches:

   a. **Witness:** The first provides that a *witness* (defined here as any person giving testimony other than a defendant testifying at his own criminal trial) may refuse to answer any question put to him on the grounds that it may tend to incriminate him. But the witness must *take the stand*, listen to each question, and assert the privilege question-by-question.

   b. **Accused:** The second branch provides that the *accused* in a criminal trial *need not take the stand at all*. That is, the accused gets complete immunity from even being questioned, let alone being forced to answer.

3. **Constitutional language:** The privilege derives, as noted, from the U.S. Constitution. The Fifth Amendment provides that *"no person . . . shall be compelled in any criminal case to be a witness against himself. . . ."*

   a. **Protects witnesses also:** This language, on its face, looks as though it applies only to a defendant in a criminal proceeding. However, since 1892 the Supreme Court has interpreted the provision as also applying to persons other than criminal defendants, that is, to witnesses in grand jury proceedings, congressional investigations, other people's criminal trials, etc.

4. **Applied to states:** Until 1964, the Fifth Amendment privilege was *not binding on the states*. But in that year, the Supreme Court held in *Malloy v. Hogan*, 378 U.S. 1, that the Fourteenth Amendment's Due Process Clause incorporates the Fifth Amendment's privilege against self-incrimination. Since the Fourteenth Amendment binds the states, they must honor the Fifth Amendment privilege.

   a. **Emphasis on federal privilege:** Because the Fifth Amendment is now binding on the states as a result of *Malloy*, our discussion below of the privilege focuses exclusively on the Fifth Amendment. Bear in mind, however, that nearly all *state constitutions* contain a privilege against self-incrimination, and state courts are free to interpret these state constitutional provisions in a way that creates a broader privilege than what exists under the Fifth Amendment.

B. **General rules:** We consider now the general parameters of the privilege, including four issues: (1) Who may assert the privilege? (2) In what kinds of proceedings does it apply? (3) To what types of information does it apply? and (4) How may it be invoked?

1. **Who may assert:** The privilege is a *"personal"* one.

   a. **May not assert another's privilege:** This means, first of all, that a person may not assert *another's* privilege.

Example: D is on trial for robbery. The prosecution presents testimony by X, an unindicted co-conspirator, in which X says that he and D did the robbery together. D may not exclude this testimony by arguing that it violates X's privilege against self-incrimination — since it is X who is testifying, only he may assert (or, as in this case, waive) his privilege against self-incrimination.

b. **Business organization:** The "personal" nature of the privilege also means that *business organizations* do *not* have the privilege.

   i. **Corporations, partnerships, and associations:** Thus neither *corporations, partnerships*, nor labor unions may claim the privilege.

   ii. **Sole proprietorship:** But where a person does business as a *sole proprietorship*, he may assert the privilege. In other words, it is not the fact of doing business that removes the privilege, it is the use of an "artificial organization" (e.g., a corporation or partnership) that causes the privilege not to apply. See *U.S. v. Doe*, 465 U.S. 605 (1984), implicitly recognizing that a person does not forfeit protection he would otherwise have merely by doing business as a sole proprietor.

c. **Use by agent:** The rules just discussed mean that an *agent* of a corporation or other artificial entity may not claim the privilege on the entity's behalf. But suppose the agent claims that answering questions about the entity's affairs will incriminate *him* personally, or that producing the business' records will do so.

   i. **Records:** The individual may *not* refuse to produce the entity's *records*. One who associates himself with a corporation or other artificial business entity is deemed to give up the right to assert the privilege, with respect to the entity's business records. McC, pp. 187-188.

   ii. **Pre-existing documents:** In any event, a person who attempts to use the privilege to avoid surrendering business records faces a second problem: since the documents are pre-existing and were generally kept voluntarily, the documents themselves are not "compelled" and the privilege does not apply to them. See *infra*, p. 444. (However, the *act of production* is compelled, and if that act would be incriminating, there may be a privilege to refuse to do so. See *infra*, p. 444.)

   iii. **Answering questions:** The agent of the corporation or partnership may also probably be required to *identify* the records he has produced, even though that identification may incriminate him (e.g., by showing that he probably had at least some knowledge of their contents).

   iv. **Personal business documents:** Keep in mind that even the rule making the privilege inapplicable to production of a business entity's documents applies only to documents that properly belong to the *organization* rather than to the individual. For instance, even a person who works for a corporation could probably assert the privilege not to produce his personal *pocket calendar*, despite the fact that it contained information about work done for the company, if the employee bought it, maintained it, and only he had access to it. McC, p. 192.

2. **Proceedings where applicable:** In what *kinds of proceedings* does the privilege apply? It of course applies when asserted by the defendant in a criminal trial. But it also applies

when asserted by a *witness* who is not currently on trial. It does not matter *what kind of proceeding* is involved.

a. Various contexts: Some of the contexts in which a person may assert the privilege are:

   i. When he is a witness in a *grand jury investigation* (regardless of whether he is the "target" of the investigation);

   ii. When he is a witness in *another person's criminal trial*;

   iii. When he is a party or a witness in a *civil* proceeding;

   iv. When he is a party or a witness in pre-trial *discovery* proceedings (e.g., he is a party or non-party whose deposition is being taken in a civil suit);

   v. When he is being *questioned by the police*, regardless of whether the questioning takes place in "custody."

   See generally McC, p. 205.

b. Different manner of invoking: Remember that the privilege applies quite differently when the person asserting it is a defendant in a criminal trial than in all other situations — the criminal defendant may refuse to undergo questioning at all (by refusing to take the witness stand); all other persons asserting the privilege must take the stand, listen to the question, and then assert the privilege. This distinction is discussed more extensively *infra*, p. 441.

c. Confessions: The relationship between the privilege against self-incrimination and *confessions* that take place in police custody is a complicated one, usually covered extensively in Criminal Procedure courses. For present purposes, all you need to keep in mind is this: under *Miranda v. Arizona*, 384 U.S. 436 (1966), the police must, prior to custodial interrogation of a suspect, warn him that he has a right to remain silent, that any statement he does make may be used as evidence against him, and that he has the right to the presence of an attorney during questioning. If the police do not follow these rules, any statement made by the suspect is not admissible. The decision relied essentially on a Fifth Amendment rationale — that a custodial interrogation is inherently coercive, and that without these procedural safeguards, therefore, no confession can truly be regarded as being the product of the suspect's free will.

3. Information must be "testimonial": Not all activity that might incriminate a person is protected — only "testimonial" activity is covered by the privilege. This limitation essentially means that only products of an individual's *thoughts* are covered by the privilege. L&S, p. 757. Or, as the notion is sometimes put, the activity must be *"communicative."*

a. Samples: Thus taking a *blood sample* from an individual does not violate his Fifth Amendment rights, because a blood sample is not evidence of a "testimonial or communicative nature." *Schmerber v. California*, 384 U.S. 757 (1966). Similarly, the suspect may be required to give *fingerprints*, *handwriting samples*, or even to *speak* so that his voice may be compared with a previously intercepted conversation. (The speaking is not "testimonial," because, even though it involves the speaking of words, its effect is not to communicate the suspect's thoughts, merely to give a sample of one of his physical characteristics, namely his voice.) Similarly, a suspect may be required to appear in a *lineup* for identification.

    b. Gestures and other non-verbal but testimonial acts: Conversely, some *non-verbal* actions are nonetheless communicative, and, therefore, covered by the privilege. For instance, a person's gesture (e.g., nodding or shaking his head in response to a question) is clearly testimonial. Similarly, other actions may have an implicit communicative dimension. For instance, if the state demands that a person produce certain *records*, his doing so contains an implicit communication that "these are the records you asked for," as well as "I had these records in my possession or was able to get them." For this reason, the privilege may sometimes be used to prevent compulsory production of documents; this subject is discussed further *infra*, p. 444.

4. Testimony must be "compulsory": The communication must be not only "testimonial" but also *"compulsory."*

    a. Voluntarily-written documents: The main impact of this requirement of compulsion is that where a person voluntarily puts information in *written form,* the document is *not privileged* even though it is incriminating and testimonial. (But the person may have a privilege against *producing* the document for the government; see *infra*, p. 444.)

5. Must be incriminatory: The response must have a tendency to *incriminate* the person.

    a. Ridicule or disgrace: The possibility that answering a question may subject a person to *ridicule*, *disgrace*, or other non-criminal sanctions, is *not sufficient*. L&S, p. 756.

    b. No possibility of criminal prosecution: Similarly, the privilege does not apply if there are *procedural reasons* why the witness could not be prosecuted. For instance, if the statute of limitations has run, or the witness has already been either convicted or acquitted, or the witness has been granted immunity (see *infra*, p. 447), the privilege will not apply because there is no possibility of subsequent prosecution.

C. Procedure for invoking: The procedure for claiming the privilege varies depending on whether the person asserting it is doing so as a criminal defendant.

1. Criminal defendant: When the assertion is made by the defendant in a criminal trial, he may invoke the privilege by *declining to testify*, and declining even to be questioned.

    Example: D is on trial for murder. The prosecutor knows that D is guilty as sin, and knows that if he could just get D on the witness stand, D would, by his demeanor and his refusal to answer questions, signal his guilt to the jury. However, D's privilege against self-incrimination means that he *need not take the witness stand at all*, so that he will not even have to listen to the prosecution's questions, let alone respond to them. (If D does take the witness stand in his own defense, he will be deemed to have waived his privilege with respect to at least some questions on cross-examination; see *infra*, p. 443.)

    a. Suspect in custody: A similar right to *refuse all cooperation* is given to a *suspect* who is in *police custody* — under *Miranda*, the accused has the right to refuse to speak to the police at all. That is, he is not required to listen to question after question, and each time to respond "I refuse to answer on the grounds that it may tend to incriminate me."

2. **Non-defendant witness:** But where the privilege is being claimed by a *witness*, i.e., a person other than the defendant in a criminal trial, the rule allowing total non-cooperation does *not* apply. The witness must take the stand, be sworn, listen to the question, and then assert the privilege.

   a. **Grand jury or other investigative body:** Suppose that a person is already a suspect at the time he is called before a *grand jury*, congressional committee, or other investigative body. May he claim to be a "defendant" and thus decline to take the witness stand at all? The answer is *"no"* — even though the investigation may have focused on that person, he must still take the stand, be sworn, listen to the questions, and then assert the privilege. L&S, p. 759. (But the suspect at a *preliminary hearing* probably does have the right to refuse even to be subjected to questioning. McC, p. 192.)

   b. **Court must decide:** When the privilege is asserted by a criminal defendant, he himself is the sole determiner of his right to claim the privilege — no judge may rule on whether his taking the stand would tend to incriminate him. But this is not true of witnesses other than criminal defendants — such a witness must assert the privilege, but it is up to the *court* to decide whether there is some basis for his assertion.

      i. **"Incriminatory" response:** Recall that the basic notion behind the privilege is that it is a right not to incriminate oneself. Therefore, the privilege may only be invoked where the response might be *"incriminatory."*

      ii. **Link in chain:** However, the requirement of an "incriminatory" response has been very loosely interpreted by the courts. The response need not be one which, by itself, would support a conviction. It is enough that the response would *"furnish a link in the chain of evidence* needed to prosecute. . . ." *Hoffman v. U.S.*, 341 U.S. 479 (1951).

      iii. **Burden of proof:** Furthermore, courts realize that if the witness is required to "prove" that the response might be incriminatory, the witness will be forced to divulge some or all of the very information that is privileged. Therefore, if there is no evidence either way on the issue of whether the response would really be incriminatory, the privilege must be allowed. As the Supreme Court put it in *Hoffman, supra*, the court may only deny the claim of privilege if it is " '*perfectly clear*, from a careful consideration of all the circumstances in the case, that the witness is mistaken, and that the answer[s] *cannot possibly* have such tendency' to incriminate." (Emphasis in original.)

      iv. **Burden of proof shifted:** Thus it is the party who seeks the testimony who bears the *burden of proving* that responding to the questions cannot possibly tend to incriminate the witness. As a practical matter, the person seeking the testimony (generally the government) generally cannot make this showing — it is very hard to prove a negative — so the "assertion of the privilege is usually sufficient to forestall further questioning." L&S, p. 757.

D. Waiver: When a person takes the stand and gives some testimony, to what extent has she *waived* her right to then assert the privilege in response to further questions? The answer depends in significant part on whether the person is a criminal defendant or an ordinary witness — the criminal defendant forfeits a major part of the Fifth Amendment privilege just by taking the stand at all, whereas an ordinary witness does not.

1. **Criminal defendant:** The defendant in a criminal trial, as noted, has the privilege not to take the witness stand at all. If he does take the stand and testifies in his own defense, he has *waived a significant portion* of his Fifth Amendment privilege.

   a. **Cross-examination regarding direct testimony:** At the very least, all courts agree that he has waived the privilege with respect to those questions that are *necessary for an effective cross-examination*. L&S, p. 759. As the Supreme Court has put it, the accused has waived the privilege at least with respect to matters "reasonably related to the subject matter of [the] direct examination." *McGautha v. California*, 402 U.S. 183 (1971).

2. **Witness:** In contrast to a criminal defendant, an ordinary witness does not have the right to decline to take the witness stand at all. As noted, the ordinary witness must take the stand, be sworn, listen to the question(s), and plead the Fifth Amendment. Therefore, it would be unfair to hold that the witness, by merely taking the stand and answering truly non-incriminatory questions (which he is compelled to answer) has waived the privilege with respect to incriminatory ones.

   a. **Disclosure of details:** On the other hand, if the witness makes a general and incriminatory statement about a matter, he may not then refuse to answer *follow-up questions eliciting the details*, at least where the details would not add significantly to the incrimination.

   b. **Perjury:** One setting in which a waiver will generally be found *not* to have occurred is where the witness gives non-incriminating testimony relating to a matter under questioning by one party, and his story is then forcefully *challenged on cross-examination* by the other party. If the witness realizes that truthful answers to the cross-examination questions will make it clear that the witness lied on direct, the possibility that the witness will open himself up to perjury charges by answering on cross will be sufficient to justify assertion of the privilege.

   c. **Other proceedings:** If the witness does waive the privilege, this waiver is effective *throughout the proceeding* in which it occurs, but *not* for *subsequent* proceedings. Thus it would apply to later appearances in the same trial. But a waiver during *grand jury* proceedings would not prevent the witness from asserting the privilege when called as a witness at a subsequent trial on the indictment returned by the grand jury. McC, p. 215.

   d. **Use of waived testimony:** If a witness has the right to assert the privilege, but declines to do so and answers the questions, the answers may be *used against the witness* in a later criminal proceeding.

E. Documentary evidence: The government sometimes issues a subpoena for the *production of documents*; this is called a subpoena *duces tecum*. To understand how compliance with such a subpoena might cause the recipient of the subpoena to be forced to incriminate himself, we must first distinguish between: (1) the *contents* of the subpoenaed documents; and (2) the *act of complying with the subpoena* for those documents, i.e., the act of handing the documents over to the government.

> **Example:** The IRS suspects Taxpayer of tax fraud. It issues a subpoena *duces tecum* to him, ordering him to produce all of his personal financial records for the last three years. To understand how Taxpayer's Fifth Amendment rights may be implicated, we must look at first, the self-incrimination interest he may have with respect to the documents themselves, and second, the interest he may have in resisting production of those documents.

1. **Contents:** The *contents* of the subpoenaed documents will virtually never be protected by the Fifth Amendment. Even though Taxpayer, in our above example, created the documents himself, and even though those documents may incriminate Taxpayer, his claim that government use of those documents to convict him would violate his Fifth Amendment rights fails for one simple reason: he was not *compelled* to create the documents in the first place. That is, at the time he created these documents, he did so voluntarily, not pursuant to any governmental order.

   a. **Private documents:** A few courts have held that some papers are *so private* that, even though their author was not compelled to write them, the Fifth Amendment protects their author from having them used against him. However, the majority view now seems to be that there are *no "privacy" aspects to the Fifth Amendment at all*, so that if the document was created voluntarily, it may be used against its author no matter how private it is (putting aside the issue of whether the author may be compelled to turn the document over to the government, an issue discussed immediately below).

2. **Production:** A person's act of *producing* the documents in response to a subpoena, by contrast, may indeed constitute implicit compelled self-incrimination. For instance, if Taxpayer hands documents over in response to the IRS's subpoena in our above tax fraud hypothetical, he is implicitly saying three things that may be incriminating: (1) that the records exist; (2) that the records were within his possession or control; and (3) that taxpayer believes that these are indeed what the government has asked for, i.e., his personal financial records for the last three years. At the very least, this implicit "testimony" by Taxpayer might be later used by the IRS to *authenticate* the records in a criminal prosecution of Taxpayer; it may prevent Taxpayer from claiming these are not his records, or that he had no idea what was in them.

   a. **Status of law:** May the recipient of the subpoena, therefore, refuse to produce the documents because of the risk of this implicit incriminating "testimony"? The law in this area is unclear. However, it seems that if the court concludes that there is indeed a risk of implicit authentication or other incrimination from the act of production, the court must relieve the person of the obligation to produce the records.

      i. ***Doe* case:** The Supreme Court upheld this kind of "implied authentication" claim in *U.S. v. Doe*, 465 U.S. 605 (1984). The sole proprietor of several businesses argued that if he were to produce the subpoenaed business records (including telephone records), he would be implicitly admitting that the records existed, that they were in his possession, and that they were genuine. The Court upheld a lower court finding that these allegations were "sufficient to establish a *valid claim of the privilege. . . .*" The Court indicated that the government could then *rebut* this claim by producing evidence that possession, existence, and authentication could later be proved by means *independent* of the proprietor's implied authentication. However, the government had not made such a showing, so the claim of privilege stood. (But the Court stressed that the documents themselves were not privileged; if the government could get them by some other means, it would be able to introduce them against the proprietor at trial, since he was not compelled to create them in the first place.)

3. **The "required records" exception:** In our highly regulated economy, many records are *required* by the government to be kept, especially the records of businesses in closely-regulated industries. A person who keeps such *"required records"* could plausibly argue that, if they are incriminating and he is forced to turn them over to the government, his Fifth Amendment rights have been violated.

   a. **The "required records" doctrine:** But this is, in general, a *losing argument.* The Supreme Court has held that no violation of the Fifth Amendment occurs where: (1) the law requiring the keeping and turning over of the records is "essentially regulatory"; (2) the records are of a kind which the regulated party has customarily kept; and (3) the records are analogous to "public documents." The rule making the Fifth Amendment inapplicable to such records has come to be known as the *"required records"* exception.

   b. **Penal statutes:** But if the statute is essentially *penal* rather than regulatory, the "required records" exception will not apply. Thus the Court has held that individuals may not be required to register or pay an occupational tax as required by federal wagering tax statutes, nor be required to register a regulated firearm under another federal statute. See, e.g., *Grosso v. U.S.*, 390 U.S. 62 (1968) (the wagering tax and firearm registration provisions are not "essentially regulatory"; rather, they are directed at a narrow group suspected of criminal activities, and do not involve records that the individual would otherwise customarily keep).

   c. **Production:** If the documents do fall within the "public records" exception, the person required to have filed them has *no* Fifth Amendment privilege concerning them: not only may he not argue that their content is privileged, but he also may not refuse to *produce them* on the theory that doing so would amount to an implied authentication (see *supra*, p. 444). McC, p. 219.

F. **Inferences and comment:** When a criminal defendant or ordinary witness pleads the Fifth Amendment, the public's reaction is likely to be, "He must have something to hide" or "He must be guilty." Of course, people's tendency to react in this way limits the usefulness of the privilege itself. While no procedural safeguards can completely remove this natural human reaction, the Supreme Court has held that two procedural safeguards are *constitutionally required* to protect the usefulness of the privilege: (1) neither the judge nor participants may make an *adverse comment* on a criminal defendant's failure to testify; and (2) the criminal defendant is entitled to have the jury *instructed* that his failure to testify is not to be held against him.

1. **"No comment" rule:** Neither the judge nor the prosecution may encourage the jury to draw an *inference of guilt* from a criminal defendant's failure to testify. The Supreme Court so held in *Griffin v. California*, 380 U.S. 609 (1965).

   a. **Arguments by prosecution:** The requirement that the prosecution not comment on the defendant's silence is not always easy to apply. Probably the key distinction is between talking about what the "defendant" has done and what the "defense" has done: if the prosecution says, "The defendant has not seen fit to explain away this evidence, and if anyone should know, he should," there is clearly a violation of the *Griffin* no-comment rule. But if the prosecutor points out that certain evidence has been left uncontradicted "by the defense," this will usually be permissible. McC, pp. 194-195. However, even comments about what "the defense" has not done may violate *Griffin* if the facts are such that the jury would reasonably conclude that only the defendant himself could have controverted the evidence, by taking the stand. *Id.*

2. **Right to instruction:** The criminal defendant has an affirmative right to have the judge *instruct the jury* that they are not to draw any adverse inference from the defendant's failure to testify. *Carter v. Kentucky*, 450 U.S. 288 (1981). The jury may make a negative inference from the defendant's silence anyway, but the judge has the obligation, upon request, to use the "unique power of the jury instruction" to reduce such inferences to a minimum.

3. **Silence at other proceedings:** Suppose the criminal defendant has remained silent at *prior proceedings*. May this silence be commented upon at the later criminal trial? In some kinds of situations, the prior silence may not be commented upon.

   a. *Doyle:* One situation in which the defendant's prior silence may *not* be commented upon at the later criminal trial is where the defendant has exercised his *Miranda* right to remain silent during a *custodial police interrogation*. In *Doyle v. Ohio*, 426 U.S. 610 (1976), the defendant remained silent under police questioning, and then claimed at trial that he had been framed. On cross-examination, the prosecutor impeached D's credibility by asking, in effect, "Why didn't you speak up and tell that story to the police?" The Court held that because the defendant had had an affirmative constitutional (*Miranda*) right to remain silent under police questioning, his due process rights would be violated if the prosecution were allowed to capitalize at trial upon this exercise of a constitutionally-protected privilege.

   b. **Other silence not protected:** But the defendant's prior silence in some other contexts may be commented upon.

      i. **Pre-arrest silence:** For instance, the defendant's *pre-arrest silence* may be commented upon. That is, if the defendant has not been placed in custody, the fact that he has not voluntarily gone to the police to tell them his story may be commented upon to impeach his trial testimony. Thus in *Jenkins v. Anderson*, 447 U.S. 231 (1980), D defended against a murder charge by claiming self-defense. On cross-examination, the prosecutor brought out the fact that D had left the scene of the crime, and during the two weeks between the crime and his arrest, did not go to the police to tell them his story. Since this pre-arrest silence was not induced by governmental action (unlike the defendant's silence in *Doyle*, which was induced by the *Miranda* warnings the police gave him), the prosecution's comments were not "fundamentally unfair."

    ii. Defendant does not take stand: In *Jenkins, supra,* the defendant took the stand, and the prosecutor used his pre-arrest silence to impeach his credibility. *Jenkins* does not make clear what happens if the defendant does *not* take the stand, and the prosecution comments (perhaps in summation) on the defendant's pre-arrest silence. It seems likely that so long as the defendant's failure to tell his story to the police was not induced by governmental action (e.g., the giving of *Miranda* warnings), that silence may be commented upon even when the defendant does not take the stand.

    iii. Grand jury: Suppose the defendant is called to testify before a **grand jury** or at a **preliminary hearing**, but asserts his Fifth Amendment right to remain silent. The logic of *Jenkins* indicates that the prosecution should *not* be allowed to comment on this silence at the defendant's later criminal trial — in this situation, the defendant's silence stems from the exercise of a clear constitutional privilege, and should thus not be able to be commented upon any more than the silence of the defendant who asserted his *Miranda* rights in *Doyle.*

4. Civil suits: When the suit is a *civil* one, there is apparently no rule against commenting upon a party's failure to testify or a witness's assertion of a Fifth Amendment privilege.

    a. Party: Thus if a party fails to testify at a civil proceeding, the other party may ask the trier of fact to draw an adverse inference from this failure. This is probably true even if the non-testifying party has failed to do so because he is afraid of incriminating himself.

    b. Silence by non-party witnesses: Similarly, a **non-party witness's** assertion of the Fifth Amendment may probably be commented upon.

G. Immunity: The Fifth Amendment privilege applies only where the person asserting it faces some danger of having his testimony used against him in a criminal prosecution. (See *supra,* p. 441.) Therefore, one way to nullify a person's Fifth Amendment privilege is to grant him *immunity* from prosecution.

1. "Transactional" vs. "use" immunity: There are two types of immunity that may be granted: *transactional* immunity and *use* immunity.

    a. Transactional immunity: Transactional immunity protects the witness against any prosecution for the transactions about which he has testified. For instance, if a witness testifies under a grant of transactional immunity to having robbed the First National Bank on April 14, 1994, he cannot be prosecuted for that robbery — even if the prosecution does not directly or indirectly make use of his testimony in the prosecution.

    b. Use immunity: Use immunity, by contrast, is much narrower — it merely protects against the direct or indirect use of the testimony in a subsequent prosecution. Thus if the witness testifies under a grant of use immunity that he robbed the First National Bank on April 14, 1994, the prosecution may not use that testimony as part of the prosecution, but it may nonetheless prosecute him for the robbery if it can prove its case without making any use whatsoever of his testimony.

2. Use immunity sufficient: For years, it was thought that a person's Fifth Amendment privilege would be nullified only by the grant of transactional, not use, immunity. But in *Kastigar v. U.S.*, 406 U.S. 441 (1972), the Supreme Court held that ***use immunity is sufficient*** to nullify the witness's Fifth Amendment privilege.

    a. Burden on prosecution: However, the witness must indeed be protected against even ***indirect*** use of his testimony. The burden of proving that there has been no use is placed upon the prosecution at the subsequent trial. The prosecution must prove that it did not use the testimony to obtain ***leads*** to information or witnesses, focus the subsequent investigation, interpret the independently-derived evidence, plan cross-examination, or in any other way.

        i. Don't use transcript: As a practical matter, the only way the prosecutor will be able to bear this burden is if he has ***not witnessed*** the testimony, nor read a transcript of it. For instance, in the Iran-Contra affair, Special Prosecutor Walsh instructed his entire staff not to watch or read the testimony of potential defendants before congressional committees investigating the affair.

3. Procedural issues: Here are a few procedural aspects of immunity:

    a. By statute: Prosecutors normally do not have inherent authority to grant immunity. Instead, prosecutorial authority to grant immunity is generally conferred by ***statute***; the statute describes the situations in which immunity may be granted, and the scope (use versus transactional) of that immunity. Immunity from federal prosecution is covered by a single statute (the Witness Immunity Act, 18 U.S.C. §§6001-6005), which allows only use immunity. Many states, however, retain transactional immunity.

    b. Procedure for granting: The prosecution must initially decide that immunity is justified. It must then ***apply to the court*** for the grant; the court generally has the right to refuse the request if the grant would not be in the public interest. McC, p. 221.

    c. Perjury not covered: A grant of immunity generally does not immunize the witness from use of his immunized testimony as part of a subsequent ***perjury*** prosecution. Thus if the witness gives immunized testimony that is false, that testimony may be introduced against him at a subsequent perjury prosecution.

    d. Other jurisdictions: If immunity is granted by jurisdiction A, can jurisdiction B nonetheless use the immunized testimony in a subsequent prosecution? The answer seems to be "no." Thus if a state grants immunity, the federal government may not use the immunized testimony (or its fruits) in a subsequent federal prosecution. *Cf. Murphy v. Waterfront Commission of New York Harbor*, 378 U.S. 52 (1964). Conversely, if a witness is given federal immunity, the supremacy clause of the U.S. Constitution should prevent use of that testimony in a subsequent state prosecution. L&S, p. 757. Finally, if one state gives immunity, other states should be barred from using that testimony in their own prosecutions. *Id.* The latter result could be based on due process or self-incrimination grounds.

4. Defense witness immunity: Suppose that a criminal defendant would like to be able to offer what he thinks will be the favorable testimony of a witness, W, but that W refuses to testify on self-incrimination grounds. May the defense require the prosecution to grant use immunity to W so that the defense will get the benefit of his testimony? Such a grant is known as *"defense witness immunity."* Since immunity is normally granted at the wishes of the prosecution, for government purposes, it can be argued that fair play requires that defense witness immunity be awarded under at least some circumstances.

   a. General rule: However, the vast majority of courts that have considered the issue have *refused to grant* defense witness immunity.

V.   THE MARITAL PRIVILEGES

A. Two privileges: Two distinct privileges protect the marital relationship in most states: (1) the privilege against adverse spousal testimony; and (2) the privilege protecting confidential communications.

   1. Nature of the two provisions: Although the two privileges overlap to some extent, there are significant differences between them. Here is a "thumbnail sketch" of the two:

   a. Adverse testimony: The *adverse testimony* privilege (sometimes called the *"spousal immunity"*) gives a spouse *complete* protection from *adverse testimony* by the other spouse. Thus if Husband is on trial for a crime, this privilege protects Husband from having Wife take the witness stand to testify against him, regardless of the subject matter of her testimony.

   b. Confidential communication: The *confidential communications* privilege protects only against the disclosure of confidential communications made by one spouse to the other during the marriage. For instance, if Husband tells Wife during their marriage, "I just shot X," Wife cannot be forced to disclose this communication at Husband's subsequent trial. However, if Wife *witnessed* Husband kill X, most states would probably hold the confidential communications privilege inapplicable, so that Wife could be forced to tell what she saw.

   2. Rationale: Both privileges have historically been justified on the grounds that they *promote marital harmony*. The adverse testimony privilege is said to do so on the theory that requiring one spouse to testify against the other will tend to break up the marriage. The confidential communications privilege arguably promotes marital harmony by encouraging the exchange of confidences between spouses.

   3. Distinctions: In many situations, both privileges will apply. However, there are a number of situations in which only one will apply. Here are some of the situations in which one but not the other will apply:

   a. End of marriage: The adverse testimony privilege applies only if the parties are still married *at the time of the trial*. The confidential communications privilege, by contrast, applies so long as the parties were married at the time of the communication, even if the marriage has *subsequently ended*.

   Example: H and W are married. H tells W, "I've just shot X." Before H is tried for the crime, he and W are divorced. H cannot assert the adverse testimony privilege at trial, because he and W are no longer married. He may, however, assert the confidential communications privilege to prevent W from testifying about the statement H made to her.

b. **Pre-marital communication:** Conversely, if the communication took place *before* the parties were married, the confidential communication privilege will not apply. But if the parties to the conversation have married by the time of trial, the adverse testimony privilege will apply. Thus, "individuals are allowed to and, indeed, have married to prevent testimony against them." L&S, p. 721. (But see Proposed FRE 505(c)(2), never enacted, which would have made the adverse testimony privilege inapplicable to "matters occurring prior the marriage.")

c. **Civil vs. criminal:** The adverse testimony privilege is usually allowed only in *criminal* cases. The confidential communications privilege, by contrast, is available in civil as well as criminal cases. L&S, p. 722.

d. **Party vs. non-party:** The adverse testimony privilege may be invoked only by *a party*. The confidential communications privilege, by contrast, may be invoked by a non-party *witness*. *Id.*

e. **Acts:** The adverse testimony privilege will prevent the non-party spouse from testifying even as to *acts* committed by his/her spouse; by contrast, the confidential communications privilege will generally not bar such testimony, since it applies only to communications.

Example: W watches H shoot X to death in a public park. The adverse testimony privilege will prevent the prosecution from calling on W to describe what she has seen. The confidential communications privilege will not (since even those states giving a loose reading to the requirement of a "communication" will hold that a shooting that takes place in a public park is not intended to be "confidential" and is thus not covered by the privilege).

4. **Variety of state statutes:** States vary as to whether both or just one of the privileges apply:

a. **Adverse testimony:** Only a slight majority of states recognize the adverse testimony privilege. 98 Harv. L. Rev. 1567 (1985).

b. **Confidential communications:** By contrast, *virtually all states recognize the confidential communications privilege* (including those that recognize the adverse testimony privilege). McC, p. 113.

c. **Federal Rule:** In federal courts, *both* privileges are recognized. The confidential communications privilege is deemed part of the common law and thus generally applicable under FRE 501 (see discussion *supra*, p. 415); it is generally held to belong to the spouse who *makes* the communication. 98 Harv. L. Rev. 1571-72. The adverse testimony privilege belongs only to the *testifying spouse*, as the result of the Supreme Court's holding in *Trammel v. U.S.*, discussed *infra*.

B. **Adverse testimony privilege:** Here are some of the details of the adverse testimony privilege:

1. **Who holds:** Courts and statutes are not in agreement about *who holds* the adverse testimony privilege.

    a. **Federal practice:** In federal cases, the adverse testimony privilege belongs to the *testifying spouse*, not the party spouse. That is, the defendant in a federal criminal trial may not block his or her spouse's testimony; only the witness-spouse may assert or waive the right. The Supreme Court so concluded in *Trammel v. U.S.*, 445 U.S. 40 (1980).

        i. **Rationale:** The Court in *Trammel* concluded that the main rationale for the adverse testimony privilege — preventing marital discord — does not justify giving the defendant spouse the right to block the voluntary testimony of the witness spouse. The Court reasoned that if one spouse is willing to testify against the other, "their relationship is almost certainly in disrepair; there is probably little in the way of marital harmony for the privilege to preserve." There is a strong countervailing interest, the Court noted, in making available to the trier of fact all relevant information.

        ii. **Application to facts:** The facts of *Trammel* illustrate how the adverse testimony privilege is used, and limited, in federal criminal cases. W, D's wife, was arrested for narcotics smuggling during a routine airport customs search. In return for not being prosecuted, she agreed to cooperate with the government in its case against D. She then testified in detail about the roles she and D played in a heroin distribution conspiracy. Since the Court held in *Trammel* that only the witness-spouse could assert the adverse testimony privilege, D was out of luck. Furthermore, although the federal courts recognized the independent privilege for confidential marital communications (see *infra*, p. 452), that privilege was inapplicable to most of W's testimony, since she was describing her and her husband's actions, not their confidential communications to each other.

        iii. **Criticism:** Some commentators have criticized the Court's decision in *Trammel* to vest the privilege solely in the testifying spouse. L&S (pp. 720-21) assert that the opinion "ignores the role that the government may play in setting one spouse against the other," and gives the government "strong incentives to break up those marriages it can." For instance, on the facts of *Trammel* itself, the rule giving the privilege exclusively to W gave the federal prosecutors strong incentive to use whatever pressure they could (including the threat of criminal prosecution) to induce W to testify against D; the marriage was unlikely to have survived the resulting testimony. By contrast, the marriage would have had a better chance of surviving had the privilege been found to belong to D — the prosecution would probably not have bothered trying to convince W to testify, since it would have known that D could then block the testimony.

    b. **States:** Those thirty or so states that recognize the adverse testimony privilege vary about whom the privilege belongs to. Fourteen allow the party to prevent his/her spouse from giving adverse testimony; another four treat the non-party spouse as being "incompetent" to testify. The remaining states follow the federal approach of vesting the privilege in the witness spouse. 98 Harv. L. Rev. 1567.

2. **Criminal vs. civil:**   Most jurisdictions, including the federal courts, limit the adverse testimony privilege to *criminal* cases. 98 Harv. L. Rev. 1570. States vary as to whether the privilege applies in grand jury proceedings; the privilege does apply in *federal* grand jury proceedings. *Id.*, n. 55.

3. **"Testimony" required:**   The privilege applies only to *"testimony"* by the spouse. Thus the spouse may be required to give non-testimonial evidence such as a handwriting sample or a fingerprint. *Id.*

    a. **Out-of-court statements:**   However, the privilege is often held to apply to *out-of-court statements* by the spouse, not just in-court testimony.

        Example: W tells X that she has just watched her husband, H shoot Joe Smith. Many states, and the federal courts, will hold the adverse testimony privilege applicable to prevent X from repeating W's statement in court (even if that statement satisfies some hearsay exception).

4. **Divorce:**   As noted, the witness and the defendant must be married *at the time of the testimony* for the privilege to apply. Thus, a defendant has no privilege to keep his *ex-spouse* off the stand. (But conversely, in most states he may prevent his current spouse from testifying against him, even as to matters that occurred before the marriage. However, courts will not apply the privilege if they find the marriage is a "sham," and some exclude pre-marital events. See, e.g., Proposed FRE 505(c)(2), never enacted by Congress, which excludes pre-marital events.)

5. **Crime or tort against spouse or children:** The adverse testimony privilege does *not* apply where one spouse is charged with a *crime or tort against the other spouse*, or against the *minor child* of either. M&K §5.31, p. 406.

C. **Confidential communications:**   We turn now to the second privilege, that for *confidential communications* between spouses.

1. **Where applied:**   This privilege is much more widely recognized than that for adverse spousal testimony: virtually every state recognizes it.

    a. **Federal:**   In federal courts, nothing in the Federal Rules explicitly grants the privilege. In fact, the Rules as drafted explicitly declined to give the privilege, instead giving a narrowly-tailored adverse testimony privilege (see *supra*, p. 450). However, because Congress deleted all of the proposed privilege rules, the confidential communications privilege remains *applicable in federal courts* because of FRE 501's statement that "[t]he *common law* — as interpreted by United States courts in the light of reason and experience — governs a claim of privilege[.]" Since federal courts prior to the enactment of the Federal Rules of Evidence had always recognized the confidential communications privilege as a common-law matter, that privilege has been carried forward under the Rules.

2. **Who holds:**   As with the adverse testimony privilege, there is disagreement about *who holds* the confidential communications privilege.

    a. **Traditional view:**   The traditional common law view, probably accepted by the majority of states, is that *either spouse* may assert the privilege. But some critics have argued that only the spouse who ***made the communication*** should be protected, since the purpose of the privilege is to foster confidences between spouses. 98 Harv. L. Rev. 1571.

   b. Federal: There is no clear rule in federal cases. Most federal courts give the privilege only to the spouse who made the communication. *Id.* at 1571-72.

3. "Communication" required: Only ***"communications"*** are privileged. An oral or written statement obviously is covered. Most courts also include ***gestures***. McC, p. 114.

4. Confidentiality: The communications privilege applies only where the communication is ***"confidential."***

   a. Presence of third persons: Thus the ***presence of a third person*** at the time the communication was made will generally show that it was not intended to be confidential. This is true even where the third person is a ***child*** of the couple, if the child is old enough to understand what is said. L&S, p. 722.

5. Marital status: The parties to the communication must be ***married at the time of the communication***. If this requirement is met, it does not matter that the parties have gotten divorced between the time of the communication and the time of the trial. Most courts apply the privilege even where the spouses are ***legally separated*** at the time of the communication. McC, p. 115.

6. Exceptions: The states have carved out various ***exceptions*** to the communications privilege. Here are some common ones:

   a. Crime against other spouse: Prosecution for crimes ***committed by one spouse against the other*** or against the children of either. McC, p. 117.

   b. Suit between spouses: Suits by ***one spouse against the other***. The most common illustration is a ***divorce*** suit.

   c. Justification: A criminal prosecution in which disclosure of the communication would justify the accused spouse's action or reduce the severity of his offense. (E.g., W tells H that V has raped her; H kills V. Most states would hold the privilege inapplicable to W's statement, since it would show that H committed manslaughter rather than murder.) This exception is important where the non-defendant spouse would otherwise assert the privilege over the defendant's objection.

   d. Facilitating crime: Communications made for the purpose of ***planning*** or ***committing*** a crime, or helping someone else do so. (E.g., H brings home loot from a robbery and asks W to help him hide it; since H is seeking W's help in committing an additional crime — possession of stolen goods — many states would find the privilege inapplicable to H's statement.)

VI. MISCELLANEOUS PRIVILEGES

  A. Priest-penitent privilege: The ***priest-penitent*** privilege probably did not exist at common law. McC, p. 109. However, all states except West Virginia now have statutes granting some form of privilege for confidential communications between a clergyman and penitent. 98 Harv. L. Rev. 1556.

1. **Federal practice:** A privilege for clergymen-penitent confidences was included in the Proposed Federal Rules of Evidence privilege provisions, but was deleted by Congress together with all of the other specific privileges. See PFRE 506. However, a federal court in a federal question case would probably recognize some form of the privilege as a matter of common-law interpretation, under FRE 501 (see *supra*, p. 415).

2. **Scope of privilege:** In most states, the privilege covers all confidential communications made by a person to a clergyman in his professional character as *spiritual advisor*.

B. **Journalist's privilege:** The most dramatically growing privilege in recent years has been the privilege given to *journalists* to decline to divulge the *identities* of their confidential *news sources*.

1. **Rationale:** Reporters have forcefully argued that they must be able to promise confidentiality to their sources, and that those sources will *"dry up"* if their identities may be subject to compulsory disclosure. McC, p. 109. Since the use of confidential sources lets reporters be more effective, and since more effective reporting is in the public's interest, journalists contend that the grant of at least a limited privilege is socially desirable. Journalists are most concerned about disclosure of the identity of their sources, but are also concerned about being forced to disclose the *contents* of the communications when those contents are intended as "background" information rather than for publication (especially where the information would itself identify the source). L&S, p. 767.

2. **Statutes:** The journalist-source privilege has evolved mostly by the enactment of state statutes. A little over half the states have enacted *"shield laws"* that give journalists various degrees of protection against being forced by legal process to testify about their confidential sources. 98 Harv. L. Rev. 1602, n. 57. Even the narrow statutes generally protect the journalist from having to disclose the identity of his sources; some give him protection against forced disclosure of his notes and records about what he has learned from the source. *Id.*

3. **Constitutional argument:** Reporters have frequently argued that a privilege against compelled disclosure of sources is not only socially desirable but *constitutionally required*. They contend that since the First Amendment protects freedom of the press, compulsory disclosure of sources interferes with proper functioning of the press and thus violates the First Amendment.

   a. **Claim rejected in *Branzburg*:** The Supreme Court *rejected* such a constitutionally-based journalist source privilege in *Branzburg v. Hayes*, 408 U.S. 665 (1972). However, because the vote was 5-4, and the critical vote was supplied by Justice Powell's somewhat equivocal concurrence, *Branzburg* does not eliminate the possibility that in some situations, forcing a journalist to reveal his sources might violate the First Amendment.

   b. **Present law:** Post-*Branzburg* decisions by the lower federal courts have, indeed, often recognized a constitutionally-based journalist's privilege, sometimes on First Amendment grounds. 98 Harv. L. Rev. 1603-04. For instance, if the information being sought is not very central to the case of the litigant who is seeking it, or can be gotten from other sources, post-*Branzburg* courts have often given the journalist a privilege to refuse to disclose the information.

    c. **Common-law basis:** Some federal courts have recognized a qualified journalist source privilege on *common-law*, rather than constitutional, grounds. L&S, p. 782. They have relied on FRE 501, which requires federal courts in criminal cases and federal question civil cases to apply to questions of privilege "[t]he common law — as interpreted … in the light of reason and experience[.]"

4. Conflict between privilege and defendant's rights: Suppose that it is a criminal defendant who seeks information, including identification of sources, from a journalist. In this situation, any privilege the journalist has (whether from a state shield statute, from the Constitution or from the common law) may *conflict* with the defendant's Sixth Amendment right to *compulsory process* and to *confront witnesses* against him.

    a. *Farber* **case:** At least one court has held that where such a conflict exists, the journalist's privilege must *give way* to the defendant's Sixth Amendment rights. *Matter of Farber*, 394 A.2d 330 (N.J. 1978).

        i. **Facts:** Farber, a New York Times reporter, investigated a series of unsolved hospital deaths, and then wrote a series of articles that led to the prosecution of one Dr. Jascalevich for murder. The defense subpoenaed Farber's records of his investigation, but Farber asserted both the First Amendment and New Jersey's broadly worded shield law in refusing to comply. (He went to jail on contempt charges rather than comply.)

        ii. **Holding:** The New Jersey Supreme Court conceded that Farber's refusal was covered by the New Jersey shield law. But the information sought was so central to Jascalevich's defense, and so completely unavailable from other sources, that granting a privilege to Farber would amount to denying Jascalevich his federal and state constitutional right to have "compulsory process for obtaining witnesses in his favor."

        iii. **Procedure:** Therefore, the court held, if Jascalevich could convince the trial judge that there was a reasonable probability that the information sought was material and relevant, and not obtainable by other means, the judge should inspect the materials *in camera*. The trial judge would then decide which information was so vital and otherwise unavailable that it should be turned over to the defense.

C. Government information: Litigants will often need information that is in the *possession of the government.* This may be the case both where the government is a party to the litigation (e.g., a criminal prosecution in which the accused, to prepare his defense, needs information from law enforcement files) and where it is not a party (e.g., a routine civil suit between two private litigants, as to which government-held information is relevant). Yet government will often have a strong countervailing interest in not disclosing the material.

1. Organization of discussion: A number of distinct privileges for government-held information have evolved. Our discussion below first focuses on general problems of "government secrets," with distinct treatment for: (1) military and state secrets; (2) Executive-branch deliberations (including Presidential privilege); and (3) law enforcement investigative files. Then, we give a separate and more detailed treatment to the problem of government informants.

2. **Government secrets generally:** When a litigant has a legitimate need for secret information held by the government, courts generally apply a ***balancing test*** to determine whether to treat the information as privileged or require it to be disclosed: the litigant's need for the information is balanced against society's (i.e., the government's) need to keep the information secret. However, the way this balancing test gets applied varies depending on the context; in one instance (military and state secrets), the privilege is usually held to be absolute so that there is no balancing at all.

3. **Military and diplomatic secrets:** An ***absolute privilege*** exists as to ***military*** and ***diplomatic*** secrets. No matter how badly a litigant needs a document or other information held by the government, the government is privileged not to disclose it if it can show a reasonable chance that without the privilege, a secret relating to ***national defense*** or international relations would be disclosed.

    a. **Federal Rules:** This "absolute privilege" approach is followed by the Proposed Federal Rule of Evidence on the subject (which was, of course, dropped by Congress with all the other specific privilege rules). PFRE 509 grants an ***absolute privilege*** to a "secret of state," defined as a "governmental secret relating to the national defense or the international relations of the United States." While PFRE 509 is not binding on the federal courts, they are likely to consider it in interpreting the "common law" in criminal and federal question civil cases; see FRE 501 (*supra*, p. 415).

4. **Other government information:** Two other types of government information are generally given a ***qualified*** privilege, one which will apply only where the damage to the public welfare from disclosure outweighs the litigant's need for the information. These two areas are: (1) internal governmental policy-making deliberations; and (2) law enforcement investigatory files.

    a. **Internal deliberations and policy making:** When government officials, especially members of the ***Executive Branch***, make policy decisions, they need to be able to discuss the various options candidly with each other. To encourage such candor in the exchange of views, a privilege has generally been recognized for intragovernmental opinions and recommendations concerning ***policies to be adopted.***

        i. **Factual reports not covered:** But the privilege applies only to opinions and policy deliberations, not to ***factual reports***. For instance, in *Reynolds, supra*, the Air Force's report investigating the crash of the military plane would not fall within the privilege, since it did not involve policy deliberations, and merely reported facts.

        ii. **Presidential privilege:** This privilege for intragovernmental deliberations is probably based on the common law, not the Constitution. But one subset of it does seem to have a constitutional dimension: deliberations between the ***President*** and his advisors are protected by a qualified privilege that derives from the constitutional principle of ***separation of powers***. In *U.S. v. Nixon*, 418 U.S. 683 (1974), the Supreme Court seemed to hold that President Nixon's claim of executive privilege concerning his deliberations with his top advisors was supported by constitutional separation-of-powers principles. But, the Court held, the privilege was not absolute: it must yield to a "demonstrated, specific need for evidence in a pending criminal trial."

b. **Law enforcement investigatory files:** A similar qualified privilege is recognized for *investigative files* compiled by *law enforcement* agencies. For instance, a criminal defendant has no general right to make the government turn over to him the files it compiled in investigating and preparing the case (though under criminal discovery rules he may have the right to certain items, such as statements by witnesses and the results of scientific tests). See PFRE 509(a)(2)(B).

c. **Effect of Freedom of Information Act:** When information is held by the *federal* government, the *Freedom of Information Act* (FOIA) may come into play. FOIA makes most kinds of governmental information available to any citizen (even a non-litigant) upon request. If particular information would be available under FOIA, a court is very unlikely to recognize a claim of privilege to prevent it from being introduced into evidence at a proceeding. (But FOIA has special exemptions that match most of the government-secrets privileges; for instance, law enforcement investigatory files and military secrets are specifically exempted from FOIA.)

5. **Consequences of upholding claim:** What happens when the court upholds the government's claim of privilege? The answer depends on whether the government is a party to the suit:

a. **Government not a party:** When the government is *not* a party, its successful privilege claim merely makes the evidence *unavailable*, just as if a witness had died. There are no other consequences from the claim of privilege. McC, p. 154.

b. **Government a party:** But where the government *is* a party, it may have to *pay a price* for its assertion of privilege.

i. **Prosecution:** Most dramatically, if the case is a *criminal* prosecution brought by the same government unit that is asserting the privilege, and the court concludes that the material would be materially helpful to the defense, the court will generally offer the government a *choice*: it must either disclose the material or *dismiss the prosecution*. *Id.*

ii. **Civil plaintiff:** Similarly, if the government is a plaintiff in a civil action, it may have to choose between releasing the material or having its claim dismissed. *Id.*

iii. **Government is defendant:** Where the government is a *defendant* in a civil action brought by a private litigant, the government usually will *not* be put to this painful choice. Instead, the government will usually be allowed to have its cake and eat it too — it can decline to release the material, yet assert a defense which might be disproved by release of the material. For instance, where the government is sued under the Federal Tort Claims Act, the government can claim that it was non-negligent, yet at the same time refuse to release privileged materials which, if they were released, might show governmental negligence.

6. **Government informers:** The government has a special privilege to decline to disclose the *identity* of *informants* who give it information about crimes. McC, pp. 155-156.

   a. **Rationale:** Use of informants is necessary for the prosecution of many types of crimes, especially so-called "victimless" ones (e.g., narcotics crimes). Yet if an informant could not rely on the government's ability to keep his identity secret, this kind of information might dry up — even with the privilege, many an informant has been murdered or tortured when his identity became known to those he implicated in crime.

   b. **Protects identity only:** Most courts have held that the government informant privilege protects only the *identity* of the informant, not the substance of the *information* that he gives to the government. However, if the content would effectively reveal the informant's identity, the content, too, is privileged.

   c. **Qualified privilege:** The privilege is not an absolute one. Most importantly, if disclosure of the informant's identity is likely to be of material assistance to a criminal defendant in preparing his *defense*, the government must disclose that identity, or drop the case. *Roviaro v. U.S.*, 353 U.S. 53 (1957).

      i. **Witness:** Furthermore, if the government calls the informant as a *witness*, it must disclose his identity. See PFRE 510(c)(1). For instance, the government may not put an informant on the stand wearing a mask to conceal his identity.

7. **Required reports and returns:** There is one last category of government-held information that may in some circumstances be privileged. Many statutes require individuals to make *reports* to, or file *returns* with, government agencies. *Traffic accident* reports and *tax returns* are two examples. The government has *no* general privilege to decline to disclose such reports. However, if the statute that imposes the duty to report also includes a provision prohibiting the government from disclosing the information, then courts will generally *honor* that specific statutory prohibition, treating it as a privilege. McC, p. 156.

   a. **Rationale:** Often, such specific statutory privileges for a given kind of report are motivated by the theory that the state's promise of confidentiality is needed to *encourage* private citizens to make the report. For instance, state statutes requiring doctors to report cases of *venereal disease* to public health officials generally include such a confidentiality provision on the theory that without one, doctors will often not comply.

D. **Trade secrets:** Some courts have recognized a privilege for *trade secrets*. A trade secret may be a secret process, information about the marketplace, or any other knowledge which a business has that aids it in competing. There are several common situations where the trade secret privilege may be invoked: (1) *antitrust* actions in which the government or a private litigant tries to force the defendant to disclose information about the defendant's marketplace position that would show that the defendant is a monopoly; (2) patent or unfair competition suits in which the plaintiff tries to get the defendant to disclose secret information about a device or process that is the subject of the suit; and (3) tort and breach-of-warranty suits in which the plaintiff, usually an individual, tries to get the defendant to give detailed manufacturing information about a product that is claimed to be defective and/or dangerous.

1. **Qualified privilege:** Most courts have treated the trade secrets privilege as being *qualified* rather than absolute. That is, the holder's need to keep business information from

leaking out into competitors' hands is weighed against the litigant's need to develop information for his case. Thus PFRE 508 (never enacted) grants the privilege, but only "if the allowance of the privilege will not tend to conceal fraud or otherwise work injustice."

2. **Protective order:** If the judge does partly override the privilege because of a litigant's great need for the material, he may issue a ***protective order*** limiting the use to which the information may be put. For instance, the litigant receiving the information may be ordered not to disclose it to anyone else. See the last sentence of PFRE 508, and the Advisory Committee's Note thereto.

E. **Exclusionary rule:** Before we leave the subject of privileges, we mention in passing one rule that is sometimes thought of as a privilege. This is the rule, formulated by the Supreme Court, that evidence obtained in violation of the Constitution (usually the Fourth Amendment) may not be admitted in a criminal prosecution of the person whose rights were violated. This so-called "exclusionary rule" is not really a rule of privilege, however, since privilege rules prevent the acquisition of evidence as well as its use at trial, whereas the exclusionary rule prevents only use at trial. L&S, p. 766. In any event, treatment of the exclusionary rule is beyond the scope of this outline, since the subject is usually covered in Criminal Procedure courses. See *Emanuel on Criminal Procedure*.

Quiz Yourself on
PRIVILEGES *(Entire Chapter)*

97. Charles Kiting visits Attorney Myles Crooked and says, "I'm planning on bilking millions of innocent people out of their life savings in a fraudulent real estate investment scheme and I need your help in setting it up." Crooked agrees, and they set to work. When Kiting is subsequently tried for fraud, Crooked is called as a witness by the state. Kiting objects to his testimony, claiming attorney/client privilege. How do you rule? _____

98. Pinnocchio drives a truck for the Geppetto Wood Chipper Company, owned by Gino Geppeto. He hits a car driven by Jim N.E. Cricket. Cricket sues Geppetto. Geppetto and Pinnocchio meet with a lawyer, John E. Corkran, to discuss their case. Corkran calls in his paralegal to take notes on the case. At trial, Cricket calls Pinnocchio to testify to admissions Geppetto may have made during the conference with Corkran and his paralegal. Geppetto objects, citing attorney/client privilege. How do you rule? _____

99. Lizzie Borden runs in to the legal offices of Dewey, Cheatham and Howe, brandishing an axe dripping blood. When one of the women in the waiting room screams, Attorney Dewey runs out, and Borden tells him (in front of the screaming woman): "I've just murdered my parents! Will you defend me?" Dewey does so. At her trial, prosecutor calls the woman from the waiting room to testify to Borden's statement. Borden objects, claiming attorney/client privilege. How do you rule? _____

100. Popeye sues Bluto for battery. Bluto calls Dr. Seahag as a witness. The defense asks Seahag about comments made to her by Olive Oyl, concerning Olive Oyl's obtaining medical treatment from Dr. Seahag. Can Popeye's attorney object on the grounds of doctor/patient privilege? _____

101. Peter Pan is knocked unconscious in a barroom brawl. He is rushed to the Emergency Room, where he is examined and treated by Dr. Feelgood. As Feelgood is examining Peter, a packet of angel dust falls from Peter's pocket. At Peter's trial for possession of a controlled substance, the prosecutor calls Feelgood to testify as to what he saw in the emergency room. Peter objects, claiming doctor/patient privilege. How do you rule? _____

102. Beethoven is called as a witness by the plaintiff in a civil suit for battery. When Beethoven is asked whether he was at the scene of the incident, he refuses to answer, invoking his Fifth Amendment privilege against self-incrimination. Plaintiff moves that Beethoven be ordered to answer. The judge believes that there is no chance that the answer itself will incriminate Beethoven, and only a relatively small chance (perhaps 5-10%) that if Beethoven is forced to answer, the answer will lead prosecutors to other material incriminating him. How should the judge rule on Beethoven's Fifth? _____

103. Bonnie and Clyde successfully rob a series of banks. After accumulating an adequate amount of cash, they settle down and marry. At Clyde's subsequent federal trial for one of the bank robberies, the prosecution seeks to introduce Bonnie's testimony as to conversations she and Clyde had at the time of the robbery. Bonnie is willing to testify, because she's been told it will help her get a lighter sentence when she is tried later. Clyde objects. Which, if either, of the marital privileges applies? _____

104. Mickey is on trial in federal court for conspiring with Donald to defraud Goofy. At Mickey's trial, the prosecutor calls Mickey's wife Minnie to the stand to testify as to a conversation between Mickey and Donald that she heard while married to Mickey. Mickey objects, citing the spousal testimony privilege. Can Minnie testify anyway, if she wants to? _____

105. Rebby Hensable is charged with beating his eight-year-old daughter. The prosecution offers testimony by Hensable's wife's that Hensable did, in fact, hit his daughter. Hensable objects, on the grounds of the spousal testimony privilege. Can Mrs. Hensable testify over her husband's objections? _____

————————————

Answers

97. **Objection overruled**. Where legal services are sought in connection with ***planning or committing a future crime or fraud*** (as opposed to defending against prosecution for an already-committed crime or fraud), there is no attorney/client privilege.

98. **Objection sustained**, even though others were present. It's true that the attorney-client privilege does not apply if the communication isn't "confidential," and that the presence of persons other than the attorney and the client will usually prevent confidentiality from existing. However, where the "others" are people ***reasonably necessary to the professional consultation*** — e.g., a business associate, joint client, parent, or spouse — the communication will still be considered confidential.

RELATED ISSUE: Say Geppetto lost the case, and cross-claimed against Pinnocchio for indemnity to cover amounts recovered by Cricket. If Pinnocchio called the paralegal to testify as to Geppetto's admissions in the conference, the testimony *would* be admissible — because the attorney/client privilege isn't applicable to joint consultations with an attorney if the later suit is between those who conferred. (Note, however, that the communication would still be privileged as to a *third party* — it's just not applicable as between those conferring.)

99. **Objection overruled**. To be privileged a communication must be ***confidential.*** Thus, the presence of a third party (the screaming woman) destroyed the privilege here. (Note that although there was no formal attorney/client relationship established before the statement was made, preliminary discussions are covered by the privilege. Thus if Lizzie and Dewey had been alone when they had this preliminary discussion, the privilege would have applied.)

100. No. A third party isn't entitled to assert the privilege, because the privilege exists solely for the *patient's* benefit. Since Olive Oyl (the patient) isn't a party to the case, she's not present to assert it herself; however, *Seahag* could assert it on her behalf, which is what usually happens.

101. Objection overruled. Where the information the doctor receives covers something non-medical, or the facts are those a layperson could observe, they will be considered outside the scope of the privilege.

102. [Yes, we concocted this whole question just to make that pun. Sorry.] **The judge should allow Beethoven to remain silent**. First, a person may assert the Fifth even where the response would not by itself support a conviction — it's enough that the response could "furnish a *link in the chain of evidence* needed to prosecute." *Hoffman v. U.S.* Second, the witness need not prove that the answer might furnish such a link; rather, the burden goes the other way: only if the court finds it "*perfectly clear* . . . that the answer *cannot possibly have such tendency*" to incriminate, may the court disallow the Fifth Amendment plea. *Id.* So where, as here, the court concludes that there is a real (but small) chance of incrimination, the plea must be honored.

103. Neither. Bonnie and Clyde weren't married at the time of the conversations, so the *marital confidences* privilege doesn't apply. As to the *spousal testimony* privilege, in federal courts this privilege is vested solely in the testifying spouse (cf. *Trammel v. U.S.*). Therefore, since Bonnie's willing to testify, Clyde can't assert the privilege; this is true even though Bonnie may have been in a sense "coerced" to testify by the threat of heavier punishment if she didn't.

RELATED ISSUE: Suppose Bonnie and Clyde had been married when the robberies and the communications took place, but are now divorced. The marital confidences privilege would apply because the communications took place during the marriage; divorce doesn't destroy the privilege. But the spousal testimony privilege couldn't be invoked (even if Bonnie wanted to invoke it), because it is only applicable if the witness and the defendant are married at the time of the testimony.

104. Yes — the choice is entirely hers. In federal criminal trials (as well as in some state courts), a spouse *may* testify against the other spouse *regardless* of whether the other spouse consents, since the privilege to testify belongs to the *witness-spouse* only. *Trammel v. U.S.* (Note that if Minnie wished to testify as to *things Mickey told her in confidence* while they were married, she would probably be prevented from doing so if *Mickey* objected, since all courts who recognize the marital confidence privilege agree that the spouse who made the communication can assert the privilege.)

105. Yes. The spousal testimony privilege doesn't apply where one spouse is charged with a *crime against the other spouse or their children.* (The marital confidences privilege doesn't apply either, in this situation.)

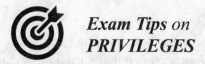

Exam Tips on
PRIVILEGES

Usually, it's not hard to spot whether a fact pattern poses an issue of privilege — the pattern will probably tell you that the witness refuses to testify, and often it will tell you the asserted grounds. The problem thus is almost entirely one of determining whether the particular privilege applies.

Here's what to look for:

General

When a fact pattern contains an issue regarding a privilege:

☞ Know the controlling rule of law. Each state, of course, sets up its own rules of privilege. In the federal courts, the *FRE do not contain specific privilege rules*; therefore: (1) for civil *diversity* cases, the federal court uses the *state* law on privilege; and (2) in *criminal* cases, and in *"federal question"* civil cases, the court uses its *own judgment*, i.e., "federal common law."

☞ Watch for *eavesdroppers*, a commonly-tested scenario. The modern rule is that the presence of an easvesdropper does *not* destroy the privilege of a confidential communication, if and only if the eavesdropping *wasn't reasonably to be anticipated*. (*Example:* During a recess of a criminal trial, D tells his wife, "I should have known that X would spill his guts." A reporter who is sitting behind D hears the statement and testifies to it. D should probably have anticipated the possible presence of a reporter; if so, he'll lose the spousal privilege and the reporter's testimony will be allowed.)

Attorney-Client

When an attorney is being asked to divulge information about a party to a lawsuit, consider whether the attorney-client privilege applies.

☞ First, look for an *attorney-client relationship*. The client must have been *seeking professional legal advice* when communicating with the attorney. (*Example:* Suit by P against D for breach of an oral contract in which P is to paint D's portrait. P produces testimony that D said to his attorney-wife W, "Since oral agreements are valid, I'm going to call P and tell him to go ahead with my portrait." Since P wasn't attempting to procure legal advice from W when he made the statement, the attorney-client privilege doesn't apply.)

    ☞ Remember that the attorney *doesn't have to be paid or retained* in order for the privilege to apply, as long as an attorney-client relationship (i.e., an attempt to get professional legal advice) existed at the time of the communication. (*Example:* P wants to bring a product liability action against D, a drug manufacturer, for liver damage he says D's pills caused. P initially consults attorney X about his claim, and tells X that his liver was malfunctioning even before he took the pills. X declines to represent P. The privilege still applies.)

☞ Make sure the evidence is a *"confidential communication."* Look for a disclosure by the client and an intent that the disclosure remain secret.

    ☞ Trick question: A communication may be protected even though it is nonverbal. However, a lawyer's *observation of a client's physical appearance* that third parties could also have made is not covered. (*Example:* D is the driver of a car in which his attorney, L, is a passenger. The car crashes, injuring P, a pedestrian. In a civil suit by P against D, D is not represented by L. P calls L to testify, and asks, "Didn't D appear to be drunk just before the accident?" L's answer can't be blocked by the attorney-client privilege, because the answer doesn't involve any communication between L and D, merely L's observations of D's physical appearance.)

☞ **Previously-prepared documents** that a client gives to an attorney are **not** a communication. (*Example:* P sues D, a car manufacturer, for defective design of the Thunderwheel. P subpoenas from D records of tests that D performed on the Thunderwheel before the accident occurred. D objects on the grounds that D has given these records to its lawyer, thereby subjecting them to attorney-client privilege. D will lose — only materials prepared for the purpose of communicating with a lawyer can be protected under the attorney-client privilege. [Nor are the documents protected by attorney work-product, since they weren't prepared in anticipation of litigation.])

☛ Confirm that the privilege hasn't been **waived.** Look for the presence of **third parties** — if a third party is present whose presence wasn't reasonably necessary, the privilege will be lost. (*Example:* D makes the communication to L, his lawyer, in front of a cab driver who has nothing to do with the litigation or the conference. The privilege is lost.)

☞ But if the third party's presence is **reasonably necessary** to the conference, then the privilege isn't waived. (*Examples:* Employees of Client; guardian of Client; investigators; joint clients.)

Example: Pedestrian is injured by a truck driven by Driver and owned by Driver's boss Employer. Driver and Employer attend a conference with Lawyer, who represents Employer, and Investigator, who has been retained by Lawyer to help defend the anticipated suit. In the civil trial of Pedestrian's suit against Driver and Employer, Pedestrian attempts to compel Driver to testify about admissions Driver made at this meeting. Driver won't have to testify — all communications at the meeting are privileged even though Employer and Investigator were present, since their presence was reasonably necessary.

☞ But if the meeting involves **joint clients** who later are asserting **claims against each other**, the privilege doesn't apply to evidence about those claims. (*Example:* Same facts as prior example. Now, Owner makes a cross-claim against Driver as part of Pedestrian's suit. Owner can testify to admissions made by Driver in the meeting with Lawyer — this testimony will be admissible only as to the Owner-vs.-Driver claim. Same result if Owner sued Driver in a later suit separate from Pedestrian's suit.)

☞ If the privileged material is **inadvertently disclosed** to a third-party, remember that FRE 502 says that **no waiver** occurs, as long as the disclosing party took **reasonable steps** (though unsuccessful) to avoid such disclosures beforehand, and then took reasonable steps to **remedy** the mistaken disclosure after it occurred.

☛ Other instances where the privilege doesn't apply:

☞ Claim by **lawyer against client**, or vice versa. (*Example:* If Client sues Lawyer for malpractice, either may put on evidence about communications between them.)

☞ Furtherance of **crime or fraud**. (*Example:* Product liability suit by P against D for making pills that damaged P's left main coronary artery. D subpoenas Lawyer, whom P originally consulted but who would not take the suit, and asks, "Didn't P tell you he had a defective left main coronary artery before he began taking our pills?" D cannot block the question, because any such admission by P would have indicated that P was hoping to persuade Lawyer to participate in a fraud, by bringing a fraudulent claim.)

Physician-Patient

When a doctor is being asked to divulge information about a party to a lawsuit, consider whether the *physician-patient* privilege applies.

☛ Remember that the communication must be *related to treatment* of a condition, or to diagnosis that is expected to lead to treatment. (*Example:* D is on trial for drug possession. The prosecution calls W, an M.D., who testifies that he gave D a physical exam, and that during the exam D stated that he, D, was a drug addict and asked W if W would like to buy drugs. These statements by D will not be privileged, because they don't relate to the diagnosis or treatment of a condition.)

☞ If the communication is done solely to permit the M.D. to serve as an *expert witness* in litigation (i.e., no treatment is contemplated), most states hold that the privilege does *not* apply.

☛ Also, the privilege doesn't apply where the patient has *placed her physical condition in issue*. Common scenario: A personal injury suit.

Example: P sues D, a cosmetics company, for injuries she claims she suffered where her leg became infected as a result of using a hair remover made by D. D calls Doc, who testifies that when he examined P's leg injury, P told him she had infected it by falling on a rusty pitchfork. Not privileged, because P's suit has placed her physical condition in issue.

☛ Remember that the majority rule is that the privilege *can't be used in criminal proceedings.*

☛ Remember that the privilege is *held* exclusively by the *patient*. So the doctor can't assert the privilege if the patient doesn't want to, and if the patient is a litigant the other party can't assert the privilege either.

☞ Common scenario: The defendant objects to testimony by the plaintiff's doctor. (*Example:* Personal injury suit. W, an MD, testifies for P that she examined P, and that P described pain she was feeling in her lower back. D objects on grounds of patient-physician privilege. Objection overruled: only the patient can assert the privilege. [Also, observe that there's no hearsay problem, because there's a hearsay except for statements of physical condition made to a doctor for treatment or diagnosis.])

☛ Remember that the privilege also applies, in virtually every state, to confidential communications between a patient and a *psychotherapist* (including non-M.D. *psychologist*).

Self-Incrimination

Whenever someone refuses to answer a question, consider whether the Fifth Amendment privilege against *self-incrimination* may be invoked.

☛ If the witness is *someone other than a criminal defendant*, make sure that the witness has *taken the stand and been asked a question.* (A criminal defendant may, in his own case, refuse to take the stand at all, but anyone else must take the stand before claiming the privilege.) (*Example:* Murder trial of D. The prosecution subpoenas W, who the prosecution thinks was present at the scene of the crime. W may not refuse to appear in court, or to take the stand, on Fifth Amendment grounds. She must take the stand and be asked questions; only then may she plead the Fifth.)

☞ The privilege may be invoked at a ***civil proceeding***, if the witness reasonably believes that the answer might tend to incriminate her for purposes of some later theoretically-possible prosecution. (*Example:* W, a witness in a civil case involving a car crash, testifies to witnessing the crash. D's lawyer asks her, "Weren't you actually robbing a store in Carson City on the day this accident occurred?" W may plead the Fifth, even though she has never been charged with the robbery — it's enough that W's answer might possibly be used against her in a later prosecution for the robbery.)

☞ If W does plead the Fifth, the trial judge has discretion to order any earlier testimony by W in the matter ***stricken from the record***, on the grounds that W's plea has deprived the party opposing W from ***meaningfully cross-examining*** W.

☛ Also, point out in your answer that ***no comment*** may be made upon a criminal defendant's ***refusal to testify*** on his own behalf.

☛ Make sure the evidence is ***testimonial and compulsory***. Common traps (where the evidence does *not* violate the Fifth Amendment):

☞ The evidence consists of testimony of a witness regarding an ***admission*** made by the defendant. The privilege never applies to *A*'s repetition in court of an out-of-court statement made by *B*. (Example: D's trial for murdering V. The prosecution puts on W, who testifies, "D said to me, 'I killed V.' " D cannot raise any Fifth Amendment claim against this testimony.)

☞ The evidence consists of testimony of a witness based on her ***observations of the defendant.***

☞ The evidence consists of an ***audiotape*** or ***videotape*** of the defendant, that was recorded without his knowledge, while he talked to a non-law-enforcement person; since the defendant isn't "compelled" to give the evidence, the Fifth Amendment doesn't apply. (*Example:* The police secretly videotape D telling his friend, "Sure I did it, but they'll never catch me." There's no Fifth Amend. privilege, because D's statement wasn't compulsory.)

☛ Remember that it's unnecessary for the person invoking the privilege to ***show how*** the statement might be incriminating. In a criminal case, D has the absolute right to claim the privilege without any showing at all. A witness who is not a criminal defendant may invoke the privilege unless it's virtually impossible to conceive of circumstances in which the answer called for would be incriminating.

☛ Determine what kind of immunity, if any, has been granted. Be sure to distinguish between ***use*** immunity and ***transactional*** immunity. Typically, you'll be told which of the types has been granted, and you'll have to figure out the consequences of that grant.

☞ When a witness is given immunity (either type), she is ***no longer entitled to claim*** the Fifth Amendment, and must give the testimony or be held in contempt.

☞ **Use immunity:** Use immunity prevents the *use* of a person's testimony or its fruits in a subsequent *criminal proceeding* against that person.

    ☞ Use immunity prevents *even the indirect use* of the testimony. Thus any kind of *"fruit"* that is *in any way derived* from the testimony is blocked. (*Example:* Mayor, the Mayor of Gotham, is subpoenaed by a grand jury investigating municipal bribery. After being given use immunity, she testifies that Commish, Gotham's Building Commissioner, has frequently taken bribes and shared them with her. Both Mayor and Commish are indicted for taking bribes. The only evidence against Commish is Mayor's grand jury testimony. Commish pleads guilty in return for promising to testify against Mayor. This testimony will be barred by the grant of use immunity to Mayor — because Mayor's testimony was the only evidence against Commish, his plea bargain and testimony against Mayor are the indirect fruits of Mayor's immunized testimony, and therefore may not be used against Mayor.)

    ☞ Remember that use immunity *doesn't protect against prosecution*, just against use of the immunized testimony. So if the government can go forward without any direct or indirect use of that testimony, the prosecution is allowed. (*Example:* Based on descriptions obtained from bank employees, D is arrested for robbing X Bank. D is subsequently picked out of a line-up by a bank employee, and is charged with armed robbery in state court. He is then subpoenaed by a federal grand jury investigating robberies of certain federal banks. After being granted use immunity, D admits his participation in robbing X Bank. D may still be tried in state court if the only evidence presented is the testimony of the bank employees who picked him out of the lineup, because that testimony did not derive in any way from D's immunized testimony.)

    ☞ Watch for instances where use immunity *doesn't* render evidence inadmissible:

    For instance, the prosecution is not barred from using the immunized testimony against *someone other than the witness.* (*Example:* Sidekick is given use immunity, then asked in a grand jury proceeding about crimes that he carried out for his employer, Boss. Sidekick implicates Boss in various crimes. Boss is now prosecuted for those crimes. The grant of use immunity to Sidekick doesn't prevent Sidekick's grand jury testimony from being used against Boss, because the grand of use immunity only protects the witness (Sidekick), not anyone else.)

☞ **Transactional immunity:** Transactional immunity *prevents criminal prosecution* for the *entire transaction(s)* about which the person has testified, even if the prosecution doesn't make use of the immunized testimony. So it's broader (better for the witness) than use immunity.

    ☞ Common trap: Look for a subsequent *civil suit* — the immunized testimony *can* be used in the civil suit (since the immunity only applies to *criminal prosecutions*). (*Example:* D, a member of a professional crime organization, is offered transactional immunity in return for testifying against other members of the organization. He so testifies, and during the course of his testimony admits having killed V. V's wife then brings an action for damages resulting from the wrongful death of V. This action may proceed, and may in fact make use of D's immunized testimony. [Same result if the immunity was use rather than transactional.])

Marital Communications / Spousal Immunity

When a spouse is asked to testify, consider whether the privilege for ***confidential marital communications*** and/or the ***adverse testimony privilege*** (spousal immunity) applies.

☛ *Distinguish:* The privilege for confidential marital communications only prevents disclosure of confidential ***communications*** made by one spouse to the other during the marriage. The adverse-testimony privilege (or principle of "spousal immunity") gives a criminal complete protection from adverse testimony — whether it relates to a communication or not — by his or her spouse.

☞ Sometimes both privileges will apply, but often only one will. (*Example:* Suppose Wife sees Husband kill V. If the jurisdiction recognizes the adverse testimony privilege, that privilege will apply, so that Wife can't be forced by the prosecution to testify to what she saw. But the confidential communications privilege won't apply on these facts, since there's no communication, merely observation.)

☛ **Confidential communications:** For the privilege for confidential marital communications:

☞ Look for a ***communication***. Gestures are usually covered; a few courts also cover acts that are not intended to communicate, but that take place in private.

☞ The spouse's physical appearance generally isn't a communication, so it can't be covered. (*Example:* In a rape prosecution, D's wife testifies that D returned home on the night in question with scratches on his arm. The testimony doesn't violate the confid. commun. privilege, because there was no "communication," merely an observation of something physical. [But if the testimony was that D intentionally pulled up his sleeve to *show* his wife his scratches, this gesture might be found to be communicative and thus covered.])

☞ Make sure that the communication was intended to be ***confidential***. This is the most frequently-tested aspect.

☞ Thus, look out for the presence of third persons. If a third person's presence is known to the speaking spouse, there's no intent to keep the communication confidential, and thus no privilege. (*Example:* H makes the disclosure to W at dinner, with the butler present. No privilege.)

☞ Where the defendant spouse objects, but the testifying spouse seems willing to testify (even if it's because she's being threatened with being prosecuted herself), flag the issue of, ***"Whose privilege is it?"*** Courts are split; some say it can be asserted by ***either***, but others that it can be asserted only by the spouse who ***made the communication*** (who will usually, but not always, be the defendant if it's a criminal trial).

☞ Remember that the communication must have been made ***during the marriage.*** But the parties' ***present marital status doesn't matter.*** (*Example:* Even if H and W are now divorced, H can prevent the prosecution from using W's testimony against H about something H said when they were married.)

☞ The privilege applies to ***both criminal and civil suits*** (but not to a suit between the spouses, e.g. a divorce suit).

☛ **Adverse testimony / spousal immunity:** In analyzing whether the adverse testimony privilege (spousal immunity) applies, look to these factors:

☞ The ***nature of the proceeding.*** Most states limit the spousal immunity to ***criminal cases.***

☞ ***Who holds*** the privilege. In federal cases, the privilege belongs to the testifying spouse, not the party spouse. [*Trammel v. U.S.*] (*Example:* Prosecution of H. W cuts a deal to testify against H in return for not being prosecuted herself. H can't block W's testimony, because the privilege belongs to the testifying spouse, not the litigant spouse.)

☞ The parties' ***marital status.*** It doesn't matter whether they were married when the act or communication occurred; all that's required is that they be married now. (*Example:* W can refuse to testify against H as to something H told her before they were married.)

☞ Remember that this privilege covers ***all testimony*** by the spouse, even testimony ***not involving any communication.*** (*Example:* In a jurisdiction where the privilege exists, W may refuse to testify about whether she saw scratch marks on H after he allegedly raped V.)

☞ Remember that all federal courts recognize the privilege (though as noted only the testifying spouse may assert it), but only a slight majority of states recognize it.

CHAPTER 9

REAL AND DEMONSTRATIVE EVIDENCE, INCLUDING WRITINGS

ChapterScope

This chapter focuses on two main things: (1) the requirement that physical evidence (mainly documents) be "authenticated" and (2) the Best Evidence rule. The chapter also discusses the use of particular types of tangible evidence, including pictorial evidence, computer print-outs, diagrams, summaries, views, demonstrations and experiments. The key concepts are:

- ■ **Authentication:** Before a tangible item may be introduced into evidence, the item must be *"authenticated."* That is, there must be a showing that *the item is what its proponent claims it to be.* (*Example:* Before a letter purportedly signed by D may be introduced against him, there must be enough of a showing that the letter was written by D, to justify a reasonable jury in finding that the letter was indeed written by him.)

  - ❏ **Real evidence:** If the object is *"real"* evidence (i.e., the object is claimed to have been involved in some underlying event at issue in the litigation), authentication means showing that the object is *the one that was involved.* (*Example:* If a knife is to be admitted as the murder weapon in a stabbing case, there must be a showing that the knife was in fact used in the killing.)

    - ❏ **Chain of custody:** If real evidence is being offered, a *"chain of custody"* must usually be established for that item. That is, for each person who handled the item, there must be a showing of *what that person did with it*.

  - ❏ **Demonstrative:** If the evidence is *"demonstrative,"* authentication usually means showing that the object *fairly represents or illustrates* what it is claimed to represent or illustrate.

- ■ **Best Evidence Rule:** The Best Evidence Rule (B.E.R.) states that when the terms of a writing are being proven, generally the *original writing must be produced* unless it is shown to be unavailable.

I. INTRODUCTION

A. Real and demonstrative evidence: So far, we have focused almost exclusively upon "testimonial" evidence. That is, we have concentrated on evidence consisting of testimony by a live witness in which the witness makes assertions about facts — with such evidence, the jury does not have a first-hand sense impression of the ultimate fact, and must rely on the witness's own observation, memory, and narration. In this chapter, we consider evidence that the trier of fact can *perceive first-hand*, without a witness as intermediary.

1. **Consequence of distinction:** The most important consequence of this distinction is that testimonial evidence always requires the trier of fact to assess the *credibility* of the wit-

ness, whereas the kind of evidence considered in this chapter — "real" and "demonstrative" evidence — may be evaluated without considerations of credibility. (However, often the real or demonstrative evidence will need to be "sponsored" by a live witness, whose credibility is important in determining whether the evidence is what its proponent says it is.)

Example 1: The issue is whether D acted reasonably when he shot V in response to V's brandishing a knife at him. W testifies that he witnessed the event, and that V's knife was a large, lethal-looking switchblade. This is testimonial evidence, and the jury can only decide the nature of the knife (and therefore the nature of the threat apparently posed by it) by evaluating W's credibility (including his ability to perceive accurately, remember what he saw, and describe it accurately).

Example 2: Same facts. Now, however, the prosecution produces the actual knife brandished by V. Here, the jury perceives first-hand this "real" evidence, and is therefore able to see for itself that the knife is really an obviously-fake plastic prop, not a dangerous switchblade. No judgment of credibility is needed for the jury to evaluate this evidence (except the credibility of the "sponsoring" witness produced by the prosecution, who states that the knife produced by the prosecution is indeed the one brandished by V).

2. **"Real" distinguished from "demonstrative" evidence:** We consider two distinct types of evidence in this chapter: ***"real"*** and ***"demonstrative"*** evidence.

a. **"Real":** As we will use the term, "real" evidence is a tangible object that ***played some actual role*** in the matter that gave rise to the litigation. L&S, p. 988.

Example: The knife in Example 2, above, is "real," since it is the very knife that was used in the altercation that forms the basis for the lawsuit.

i. **Other examples:** Other examples of "real" evidence would be: (1) the actual ransom demand letter written by D to V, introduced by the prosecution in a kidnapping prosecution of D; (2) a wiretap recording of D soliciting a bribe from an undercover operator, introduced in the bribery prosecution of D; and (3) an automatic photo taken by equipment at a bank, showing D cashing a check, introduced in a forgery prosecution of D. In each of these three instances, the object is the very one used in the underlying controversy.

b. **"Demonstrative":** "Demonstrative" evidence, by contrast, is tangible evidence that merely ***illustrates*** a matter of importance in the litigation. L&S, p. 988. Common types of demonstrative evidence include maps, diagrams, models, summaries, and other materials created especially for the litigation.

Example: Same facts as Examples 1 and 2 on p. 470, *supra*. The prosecution is unable to recover the knife allegedly brandished by V. From circumstantial evidence, the prosecution is convinced that what was really waved was an obviously-fake Halloween knife. The prosecution buys such a knife from a costume store, and has the knife marked as People's Exhibit 1 for Identification. It then presents a witness to the original event, W, who testifies that this Exhibit closely resembles the "knife" actually used by V. Exhibit 1 is "demonstrative" evidence, rather than "real" evidence, because it is not the very knife used in the underlying event, and merely illustrates some point of interest (namely, the type of knife used by V).

c. **Note on terminology:** Some courts and commentators use the term "demonstrative" more broadly, to refer to ***all*** kinds of tangible evidence (i.e., to refer to both what we are calling "real" as well as what we are calling "demonstrative"). This is the usage made by McCormick, for instance; see McC, p. 390.

d. **Significance of distinction:** The distinction between "real" and "demonstrative" evidence is important because it helps determine the standards that the evidence must meet to be admissible. In particular, the ***"foundation"*** that must be laid for real evidence is generally somewhat different from that needed for demonstrative evidence.

    i. **Foundation for real evidence:** For real evidence, the required foundation relates to proving that the evidence is indeed the object used in the underlying event. Thus suppose that in a prosecution for selling heroin to an undercover agent, the state presents white powder that it says was sold by D to the agent; the foundation consists of evidence tending to prove that this powder was indeed the powder sold by D to the agent.

    ii. **Demonstrative evidence:** The foundation for demonstrative evidence, by contrast, does not involve showing that the object was the one used in the underlying event. Rather, the foundation generally involves showing that the demonstrative object ***fairly represents*** or illustrates what it is alleged to illustrate. For instance, where a drawing is presented to illustrate the relative positions of the protagonists and witnesses to a killing, the foundation will normally consist of testimony by one or more eyewitnesses or investigators stating that the drawing does indeed fairly represent the positions of those present at the event.

3. **General rule for real and demonstrative evidence:** In the broad sense, the standards for admitting real and demonstrative evidence are no different than for admitting testimonial evidence. Tangible evidence (whether real or demonstrative) will be admitted if: (1) it is ***relevant***, in the sense that it makes some consequential and contested proposition of fact more or less likely, or aids the jury in understanding some issue (see *supra*, p. 11); unless (2) its ***probative value*** is ***outweighed*** by prejudice, confusion, delay, or other ***countervailing consideration*** (see *supra*, p. 15).

a. **What chapter is about:** Therefore, most of this chapter is not about the broad requirements for admissibility of tangible objects. Rather, it is concerned with three main questions: (1) What foundation must be laid before the object may be introduced (especially, what ***"authentication"*** must be supplied)?; (2) When do the especially dramatic properties of real and demonstrative evidence — including the fact that the jury perceives such evidence directly, rather than through impressions derived from an intermediary's testimony — make the evidence ***so prejudicial***, confusing, or so much more important-seeming than it really is, that it should be excluded even though relevant and properly-authenticated?; and (3) In the case of writings and other recorded communications, when is the proponent required to offer the ***"original"*** rather than a mere "copy"?

B. Direct vs. circumstantial: When analyzing real evidence, it is often useful to distinguish between "direct" and "circumstantial" evidence. A given tangible object can be direct proof of some facts, and circumstantial proof of other facts.

>   **Example:** Suppose that the real evidence in question is a three-year-old child, and the child's appearance. If the case is a personal injury action in which the claim is that the child's face has been disfigured by loss of an eye, the child's face, when shown to the jury, is direct evidence of the loss of an eye. If, by contrast, the suit is a paternity proceeding, the child's face (and its similarity or dissimilarity to the face of the defendant who is alleged to be the father) is merely circumstantial evidence that he and the defendant are related.

>   **1. Significance:** Why is the distinction between direct and circumstantial real evidence significant? Direct evidence, when properly authenticated, will almost always be admitted unless admission would involve substantial prejudice or other strong countervailing consideration. When circumstantial evidence is offered, by contrast, the trial judge generally has **broader discretion** to conclude that waste of time, confusion, or mild prejudice outweigh the item's probative value. McC, p. 392.

>>   **a. Appearance of person:** For example, where the **physical appearance** of a person is sought to be introduced for circumstantial purposes, courts will often conclude that the inference sought to be established is so weak, and the possibility of prejudicing one side or confusing the jury so great, that the evidence should be suppressed.

>>   **Example:** In **paternity proceedings**, the plaintiff will often attempt to display the baby or child to the jury, to establish that there is a **resemblance** to the defendant. While courts traditionally have allowed such evidence, the modern trend seems to be to hold that the possibility of prejudice to the defendant is great, and that a lay jury cannot properly determine whether the degree of resemblance is enough to make it more probable than it would otherwise be that a father-child relationship exists.

II. AUTHENTICATION

A. Authentication generally: All real and demonstrative evidence must be **"authenticated"** before it is admitted. That is, it must be shown to be **"genuine."** What does it mean for a tangible object to be "genuine"? In general, it means that the object must be **what its proponent claims it to be**. See FRE 901(a).

1. Real evidence: Where the object is **real** evidence, authentication normally consists of showing that the object is **the** object that was involved in the underlying event.

>   **Examples:** (1) Proof that this object is the gun that was actually used by the defendant in robbing the bank; (2) Proof that this document is the contract actually signed by plaintiff and defendant; (3) Proof that this tape accurately reproduces a conversation in which D tried to bribe a public official.

2. Demonstrative: Where the evidence is **demonstrative,** authentication basically involves a showing that the object **fairly represents or illustrates** what it is claimed to represent or illustrate.

Examples: (1) Proof that this diagram really shows the position of the parties and witnesses at the time of the murder; (2) Proof that this experiment on brake failures in a car accurately reproduced the conditions existing when P's car malfunctioned; (3) Proof that this summary of evidence already introduced at the trial accurately reflects that evidence.

3. **No assumption of authenticity:** The key rule of authentication is that, with few exceptions, an object offered in evidence will *not be presumed to be authentic*. That is, the proponent bears the burden of establishing that the object is what he says it is; he may not merely offer the object and put his adversary to the burden of showing that the object is not genuine.

4. **Applies to all evidence:** Historically, the requirement of authentication has generally applied only to writings and other tangible evidence. However, modern courts recognize that *all* evidence must be authenticated, including conversations and other *intangible evidence.* This approach is codified in the Federal Rules — FRE 901(a) implicitly applies to all evidence, and at least some of the illustrative authentication methods given in 901(b) cover intangible evidence (e.g., 901(b)(6), which deals with "telephone conversations").

5. **Relevance:** The requirement of authentication is a special case of the requirement that all evidence be *relevant*. For instance, suppose that in a murder prosecution, the prosecution offers into evidence a gun. Without a showing that the gun has at least some connection to the crime (e.g., that it was found at the scene), the gun is simply irrelevant — it does not make any proposition of fact more or less probable than it would be without the gun. Thus, the requirement of authentication is a requirement that there be "a logical nexus between the evidence and the point on which it is offered." L&S, p. 997.

B. **Methods of authentication:** As we noted above, authentication consists of showing that an item of evidence *is what the proponent claims it is*. Techniques for doing this vary depending on whether the evidence is real, demonstrable, a writing, etc.

1. **Real evidence:** Recall that we used the term "real" evidence to describe an object that played some actual role in the events leading up to the lawsuit. Authenticating an item of real evidence consists of showing that the item really *is* the item that was actually used in the underlying transaction (e.g., that the gun being presented at trial really was the gun used to kill the victim). There are two general methods of authenticating an item of real evidence:

a. **Ready identifiability:** The first method is sometimes called *"ready identifiability"* or "unique identifiability." If the item has a *unique*, *one-of-a-kind* characteristic, this method can be used. The sponsoring witness merely testifies that the object he originally saw has a specified unique characteristic, and that the item shown to him in court bears that same unique identifier. This testimony is all that is needed for identification of the object, i.e., for authenticating it. Imwinkelried, p. 66.

Example: D is charged with stabbing V to death. W is a police officer who inspected the crime scene shortly after the killing occurred. After W testifies about beginning the inspection of the crime scene, the following testimony would authenticate the knife as the murder weapon:

Prosecutor: What did you do during this inspection?

Witness: I looked for any evidence of what had killed the deceased.

Prosecutor: What did you find?

Witness: I found a knife next to the body, which was a pearl-handled switchblade about ten inches long, coated with a sticky red substance.

Prosecutor: What did you do then?

Witness: In the case of a comparatively inexpensive object like this one, I mark it for identification by scratching my initials and the date into the handle.

Prosecutor: I show you People's Exhibit No. 1 for identification. What is it?

Witness: It's the knife I found.

Prosecutor: How can you tell that that's what it is?

Witness: As I said, I marked my initials and the date on the handle. They're right there.

Prosecutor: Has the Exhibit changed since you found it?

Witness: No, it seems to be in the same condition I found it.

Prosecutor: Your honor, I now offer People's Exhibit No. 1 for identification into evidence as People's Exhibit No. 1.

Court: It will be received.

See Imwinkelried, pp. 67-68.

b. **Chain of custody:** The second method for authenticating real evidence is by showing its **"chain of custody."** This method is used when one of the elements for ready identifiability is absent. For instance, the object may not have any uniquely identifying characteristic, or the witness may not previously have observed that unique identifier, or the key issue may not be the identification of the object itself but rather, its chemical composition or other condition. The chain of custody method of authentication requires that every "link" in the chain of custody — every person who has handled or possessed the object since it was first recognized as being relevant to the case — must explain what he did with it.

Example: D is charged with selling cocaine to an undercover agent. Before the prosecution may introduce a bag of white substance as being the cocaine sold by D, it would need to call the undercover agent, the person to whom he turned over the bag, the chemist who performed the test, the person to whom the chemist gave the drug, and anyone else who had custody of the drug up until the appearance of the packet in court. Each witness would testify how he handled the item (e.g., "I put the glassine envelope into a large gray envelope, which I sealed and marked with the name of the case and the date, and placed it in the police safe used for evidence"). Each witness would also be asked: (1) whether the condition of the object appears to be the same as when he or she had custody of it; and (2) whether anyone else had access to the evidence during the time the witness had custody (e.g., **Q:** Did anyone else have the combination to the lock on the property storage safe? **A:** Only the head of the property storage section and myself).

    i. Prevention of tampering: A key reason for the elaborate chain-of-custody method is to prevent (or at least discourage) *tampering* with evidence. The chain-of-custody method will need to be used most often by the prosecution in a criminal case, probably the situation in which innocent and not-so-innocent switching of evidence is most likely. The chain-of-custody method is discussed further *infra*, p. 488.

2. Demonstrative evidence: Where the evidence is "demonstrative" (i.e., used merely to *illustrate* some fact or evidence in the case), the function of authentication is quite different. Here, the object is authenticated not by showing that it is one that was actually used in the underlying events (since it was not), but rather, by showing that it *fairly represents* some aspect of the case.

    Example: In a complicated multi-defendant bank-robbery case, the prosecution offers into evidence a diagram showing the positions of the witnesses, victims, and defendants during the robbery. This diagram will have to be authenticated by a sponsoring witness who can testify that it fairly represents the actual positions of those involved. In this case, that will have to be someone who personally witnessed the robbery (rather than, for instance, the person who drew the diagram).

3. Writing: Special techniques exist for authenticating a *writing* or other recorded communication. These are discussed in detail beginning *infra*, p. 477.

4. Federal Rules: The Federal Rules state a simple principle of authentication. FRE 901(a) provides that "To satisfy the requirement of authenticating or identifying an item of evidence, the proponent must *produce evidence sufficient to support a finding that the item is what the proponent claims it is*." This general principle controls *all* authentications and identifications, including those involving real evidence, demonstrative evidence, writings, and even intangible events (e.g., telephone conversations).

    a. Illustrations: The Federal Rules do not purport to give detailed standards for authenticating each of the many special types of evidence. Instead, FRE 901(b) gives 10 examples of authentication that satisfy 901(a)'s general provision:

      "(b) Examples. The following are examples only — not a complete list — of evidence that satisfies the requirement [of authentication]:

        (1) *Testimony of a Witness with Knowledge. **Testimony*** that an item *is what it is claimed to be.*

        (2) *Nonexpert Opinion About Handwriting.* A **nonexpert's opinion** that *handwriting* is *genuine*, based on a *familiarity* with it that was *not acquired for the current litigation*.

        (3) *Comparison by an Expert Witness or the Trier of Fact.* A **comparison** with an **authenticated specimen** by an **expert witness or the trier of fact.**

        (4) *Distinctive Characteristics and the Like.* The **appearance**, contents, substance, internal patterns, or other **distinctive characteristics** of the item, taken together with all the **circumstances**.

(5) *Opinion About a Voice.* An **opinion identifying a person's voice** — whether **heard firsthand or through mechanical or electronic transmission or recording** — based on hearing the voice **at any time under circumstances that connect it with the alleged speaker.**

(6) *Evidence About a Telephone Conversation.* For a **telephone conversation**, evidence that a call was **made to the number assigned at the time to**:

(A) a **particular person**, if circumstances, including **self-identification**, **show that the person answering was the one called**; or

(B) a **particular business**, if the call was **made to a business** and the **call related to business reasonably transacted over the telephone.**

(7) *Evidence About Public Records.* Evidence that:

(A) a document was **recorded or filed in a public office** as authorized by law; or

(B) a purported public record or statement is **from the office where items of this kind are kept.**

(8) *Evidence About Ancient Documents or Data Compilations.* For a **document or data compilation**, evidence that it:

(A) is **in a condition that creates no suspicion** about its authenticity;

(B) was in a **place** where, if authentic, it would likely be; and

(C) is **at least 20 years old** when offered.

(9) *Evidence About a Process or System.* Evidence **describing a process or system** and showing that it **produces an accurate result.**

(10) *Methods Provided by a Statute or Rule.* Any method of authentication or identification **allowed by a federal statute or a rule** prescribed by the Supreme Court."

i.   Discussed elsewhere: Most of these illustrative types of authentication are discussed at various places below. See, e.g., the treatment of handwriting (*infra*, p. 478), voice identification in telephone conversations (*infra*, p. 479), public records (*infra*, p. 483), ancient documents (*infra*, p. 482), and processes or systems (*infra*, p. 502).

b. Testimony of witness with knowledge: Illustration (1) above (FRE 901(b)(1)) covers the most basic method of authentication: a witness may authenticate an item by giving "***testimony*** that [it] is what it is claimed to be."

Example: Recall the example on p. 473, *supra*, involving the knife found at the murder scene. W's testimony that this is the knife he found, and that he can recognize it because he carved his initials into it, is what 901(b)(1) refers to as "testimony that an item is what it is claimed to be."

5. Judge-jury allocation: In determining the authenticity of an item of evidence, both the judge and the jury play a role. It is not up to the judge to decide whether the item *is* what its proponent claims it to be; that job is for the jury. But it is up to the judge to decide whether there is *some evidence* from which a jury *could reasonably find* that the item is what it is claimed to be. This principle is reflected in the actual wording of FRE 901(a):

the requirement of authentication is satisfied by "evidence *sufficient to support a finding* that the item is what the proponent claims it is."

a. **Prima facie case:** In other words, the judge must admit the evidence "once a *prima facie case* has been made on the issue [of authenticity]. . . . [FRE 901(a)] requires only that the court admit evidence if sufficient proof has been introduced so that a *reasonable juror could find* in favor of authenticity or identification. The rest is up to the jury." W&B, Par. 901(a)[01]

b. **Conditional relevancy:** This rule about the role of the judge in determining matters of authenticity — that the judge merely makes a preliminary determination of whether a jury *could* reasonably find that the item is authentic — is an illustration of the principle of *"conditional relevance."* There are many other contexts in which the judge must similarly make a conditional determination of admissibility, subject to later proof of a fact to the satisfaction of the jury. See FRE 104(b). The topic is discussed more generally *infra*, p. 579.

c. **Right to challenge authenticity:** Because the judge is merely deciding whether there's a prima facie case for authenticity (i.e., whether a reasonable jury could find that the document is what its proponent claims it to be), it follows that even after the document is admitted, the opponent may *challenge the document's authenticity,* as well as the weight to be given to it.

C. **Authentication of writings and other recorded communications:** Most authentication problems arise with respect to *writings* and other *communications*. Special rules have developed to handle some recurring issues in this area.

1. **Authorship:** Usually, authentication of a writing will consist of showing *who its author is.*

2. **No presumption of authenticity:** The general requirement of authentication applies to writings and other communications every bit as much as it applies to non-assertive evidence like a knife or a bloodstained bedspread: there is *no presumption of authenticity*. Instead, the proponent bears the burden of making an affirmative showing that the writing or communication is authentic.

a. **Writing's own recital not sufficient:** Most dramatically, the requirement that documents be authenticated means that a writing's *own recital* regarding its authorship or source *will not be automatically believed.*

Example: D is being prosecuted for possessing a firearm while a convicted felon. To prove that D was previously convicted of robbery in Colorado, the prosecution offers various police documents recording an arrest and conviction of D; the documents bear the legend "Denver Police Dept." at the top. *Held*, the documents were not properly authenticated — testimony was needed to establish that these documents really did come from the Denver Police Department. *U.S. v. Dockins*, 986 F.2d 888 (5th Cir. 1993).

i. **Signature:** Similarly, the fact that a document bears a particular person's *signature* does not by itself authenticate the document as being written by that person.

3. **Direct testimony:**   A writing or communication may, of course, be authenticated by ***direct testimony*** that the document is what its proponent claims it to be.

    > **Example:** Consider the arrest-and-conviction record in *Dockins, supra*. The prosecutor could have authenticated the record by calling a member of the Denver Police Dept. to the stand, and asking him whether he recognized the document. That member could then have said something like, "These documents are exact copies of ones in my files." Alternatively, the prosecutor could have called a member of the FBI (the police agency that investigated the weapons charge), to testify "I requested from the Denver P.D. any documents about D's prior arrest and convictions, and they sent me back these documents." Either approach would have sufficed.

4. **Distinctive characteristics; circumstances:**   There is an increasing trend to allow a writing's ***distinctive characteristics***, and the ***circumstances*** surrounding it, to suffice for authentication. FRE 901(b)(4) allows use of "[t]he appearance, contents, substance, internal patterns, or other ***distinctive characteristics*** of the item, taken together with ***all the circumstances.***"

    > **Example:** In a complicated antitrust case, the Ps seek introduction of certain diaries by Mr. Yajima, an employee of one of the Ds, who is now dead. The Ps claim that the diaries are authentic accounts of what took place at the meetings of an industry trade group at which the Ds conspired in restraint of trade. *Held*, the plaintiffs have made a *prima facie* case for the diaries to be considered "authentic" (i.e., written by Mr. Yajima, and dealing with the meetings they purport to deal with). This conclusion is supported by a wide variety of internal and extrinsic clues, including: (1) a logo of D's corporate employer, found on the diaries; (2) testimony given by Mr. Yajima in a prior proceeding; (3) the fact that Yajima's employer produced the diaries during discovery, and referred to them in its interrogatory answers; and (4) the diaries' similarity to other documents that had previously been authenticated. *Zenith Radio Corp. v. Matsushita Electric Industrial Co., Ltd.*, 505 F.Supp. 1190 (E.D.Pa. 1980).

5. **Signature or other handwriting:**   Often, a document's author can be established by showing that it was ***signed*** or written in the hand of a particular person. One way to do this, of course, is by testimony of the witness that he actually observed the document being signed or written. But another common method is to have the witness ***identify*** the ***signature or handwriting*** on the document as belonging to a particular person.

    a. **Weak witness credentials will suffice:**   Courts do not require the witness to have any special abilities or training at handwriting analysis for this purpose. It will be sufficient if the witness has ***seen*** the writing of the person in question at some time previously (even if a decade ago).

    b. **Federal Rules:**   The Federal Rules recognize the general rule that non-experts may identify handwriting; FRE 901(b)(2) allows "[a] ***nonexpert's opinion*** that handwriting is genuine, based on a ***familiarity with it that was not acquired for the current litigation.***" Thus if W is not a handwriting expert, he may give testimony that X wrote the document in question if he has had occasion to see X's handwriting before the litigation began (e.g., because he has had correspondence with X). But he may not give such testimony based solely upon a study of handwriting specimens from X in preparation for his trial testimony.

    i. Expert testimony: If handwriting testimony is to be given based upon a study of ***specimens made in preparation for the testimony***, it ***must be given by an expert.*** In that event, the expert testimony must meet the ***scientific-reliability standards*** of FRE 702.

  c. Exemplars: Handwriting may also be proved by the use of ***exemplars***, i.e., specimens of the handwriting of the person claimed to be the author of the document in question.

    i. Jury may compare: Once the exemplar has been admitted, most courts hold that it is up to the jury to compare the exemplar with the offered writing, to conclude whether the latter was written by the same person. The jury can be helped to do this by expert testimony offered by the proponent, but such expert testimony is ***not required***. McC, p. 405.

6. Reply letters and telegrams: A ***letter*** or ***telegram*** can sometimes be authenticated by the circumstantial fact that it appears to be a ***reply*** to a prior communication, and the prior communication is proved. For instance, if P can prove that he wrote a letter to D on January 1, a letter that purports to have been written by D to P on January 15, and that alludes to the contents of the earlier P-to-D letter, will generally be held to be authenticated by these circumstantial facts.

  a. Proving first communication: But observe that for this technique to be used, the proponent must ***prove*** the first communication. If the first communication was in writing, probably the original must be produced, if available, because of the Best Evidence rule (see *infra*, p. 490). But oral testimony about the first letter will generally suffice if that letter has been lost or destroyed.

7. Telephone conversations: Recall that the requirement of authentication now is generally held to apply to intangible as well as tangible evidence. One illustration is that when the contents of a ***telephone conversation*** are sought to be proved, the proponent must authenticate the conversation by ***establishing the parties to it.***

  a. Incoming vs. outgoing: The methods for authenticating a phone conversation are different depending on whether the sponsoring witness initiated the call (what we'll call here an "outgoing call") or received the call (an "incoming call.")

  b. Outgoing calls: For "*outgoing* calls" (calls made ***by*** the sponsoring witness), FRE 901(b)(6) provides a specific procedure. 901(b)(6) says that

    "For a telephone conversation, [authentication may be made by] evidence that ***a call was made to the number assigned at the time to:***

      (A) ***a particular person***, if ***circumstances, including self-identification***, show that the ***person answering was the one called***; or

      (B) ***a particular business***, if the call was ***made to a business*** and the call ***related to***

business reasonably transacted over the telephone."

So the proponent can authenticate the outgoing phone call by showing that: (1) W made a call to the **number assigned by the phone company** to a particular person or business; and (2) the **circumstances** show that the person who talked on the other end **was in fact** the person the caller was trying to reach (or that the business called was the business the caller was trying to reach).

i.   Proof of "circumstances": How does the proponent show the "circumstances" demonstrating that the person on the other end was in fact the one the caller (the sponsoring witness) was trying to reach? There are two common ways:

❏   First, **self-identification** by the person on the other end will suffice. (901(b)(6)(A) expressly mentions "self-identification" as being enough.)

Example: A party (the proponent) wants to show that W called X, and that X then said a particular something. The proponent can do this by having W testify: (1) "I looked up X's number in the phone book, and called that number"; and (2) "When a person answered, I asked to speak to X. The voice on the other end said, 'This is X.' " W has now authenticated the conversation as having taken place between himself and X; therefore W can now describe what was said (assuming, of course, that the restrictions of the hearsay rule don't get in the way).

❏   Alternatively, the **witness/caller's identification of the voice** on the other end will suffice.

Example: Same basic facts as above example. W can, after saying he called X's listed phone number, testify: "I recognized the voice on the other end as being that of X, because I had talked to X in person and on the phone many times before, and his voice was very distinctive."

Note: The special method described in 901(b)(6) (based on proof that the other party's listed number was called) is **not the only way** to authenticate an outgoing conversation. The methods for authenticating *incoming* calls, described below, may also be used for outgoing calls. For instance, suppose the sponsoring witness called what he says was the callee's **unlisted** phone number, or called some place that was **not the callee's home or office** (but was a place where the caller had reason to believe the callee was at that moment). Under these circumstances, 901(b)(6) can't be used, because it doesn't fit — that section requires a showing that the number called was the number assigned to the callee by the phone company.

But authentication can nonetheless be achieved by any other method that establishes that the caller reached the callee. For instance, this could be done by having the caller testify, "I called the unlisted number at which I had previously reached X, and reached a person who said he was X and who *knew things* about the relationship between X and me that only X could have known." But probably, **self-identification** by the person on the other end of the line is ***not enough***, where there's no proof that the number called really belonged to X. M&K, §9.10, p. 1085.

ii. **Call to business:** If the outgoing call is made to a ***business***, 901(b)(6)(B) says that authentication can be made by showing that the call was made to the phone number listed for the business, and the conversation "related to business [that would be] ***reasonably transacted over the telephone***."

Example: W testifies that he called the number listed for XYZ Corp., spoke to an unidentified person there, and placed an order for 26 widgets made by XYZ. Since the placing of an order is the sort of business that would reasonably be done by a phone call, the conversation has been authenticated, even though W can't say which employee at XYZ took the call.

c. **Incoming calls:** For ***incoming*** calls (calls made ***to*** the witness), the FRE do not prescribe any specific means of authentication analogous to 901(b)(6). Nonetheless, the requirement of authentication means that there must be a showing that the caller was indeed the person that the proponent of the phone-call evidence claims him to have been.

i. **Self-identification not enough:** The most important principle concerning incoming calls is that ***self-authentication by the caller is not enough***, because of the risks that: (1) someone may ***impersonate*** the caller; or (2) the callee (who is the sponsoring witness) may ***fabricate*** the whole conversation. M&K §9.9, p. 1084.

Example: W wants to testify that he received a phone call from X, and that they discussed a certain topic. It's not enough for W to testify, "At 8:00 p.m. on the night of June 21, I received a call from someone who said he was X." W (or the proponent of W's testimony) will have to come up with some additional evidence that the caller really *was* X.

ii. **Common methods:** There are a number of forms this "additional evidence" (that is, evidence in addition to the caller's self-identification) that the caller was who he is claimed to be can take. Here are some:

❑ Most commonly, the callee, W, testifies that he ***recognized the voice*** of the caller as being X's voice, based on prior face-to-face or telephone conversations that W had had with X.

❑ Alternatively, the callee testifies that the call was ***in response*** to a communication between X and himself at an ***earlier time*** (e.g., "I sent an email to X asking her to call me, and I got a call from someone who said she was X and was responding to my email.").

❑ Or, the caller ***displays knowledge*** (e.g., a code name or code word) that only X would have had.

❑ Or, ***phone company records*** show that a call was made at the time in question to the callee's number, from the number assigned to X.

See M&K, §9.9, pp. 1083.

8. **Sound recordings:** Some courts have imposed especially tough authentication requirements where a *sound recording* is sought to be admitted, perhaps because they fear that such recordings are especially susceptible to tampering or distortion.

9. **Attesting witnesses:** Documents are often *attested to* or *subscribed to* by "witnesses." This is most commonly the case with *wills*. A special rule for authentication of such documents has evolved: at common law, before the document may be authenticated, at least one *attesting witness* must be called to the stand (unless all attesters are shown to be unavailable). McC, p. 404.

   a. **Federal Rule:** The Federal Rules cut back sharply on this common law requirement concerning attested-to documents. FRE 903 provides that "[a] subscribing witness's testimony is necessary to authenticate a writing only if required by the law of the jurisdiction that governs its validity." Thus so long as *state law* does not impose a requirement that a subscribing or attesting witness be called, no subscribing or attesting witness need be called in the federal proceeding. (But if the state whose law governs the validity of the document would require such testimony, as some states still require in the case of wills, the federal court must follow suit.)

      i. **Attestation not required:** FRE 903, like most state statutes today, drops the requirement of testimony by the subscribing witness in those situations where the document was not *required* by local law to be attested to, but the attestation took place anyway.

10. **Ancient documents:** A document that is very *old* generally carries with it some assurance of reliability by that fact alone. For instance, it is not likely that even a dishonest person would take the trouble to forge a document where the forgery does not bear fruit (in the sense of being used as evidence in a proceeding) until many years have passed. McC, pp. 405-406. Furthermore, direct authentication of an old document is often difficult; for instance, there are unlikely to be witnesses who can testify that they saw it executed. Therefore, special rules have been developed to make authentication of so-called *"ancient documents"* easier.

    a. **Common law:** At common law, a writing is automatically deemed authenticated as an ancient document if it meets three requirements:

       i. **Thirty years old:** It is at least *thirty years old*;

       ii. **Unsuspicious:** It is *unsuspicious* in appearance;

       iii. **"Produced from":** It has been "produced from" (i.e., found in) a place of custody *natural* for such a document.

       McC, p. 406.

    b. **Federal Rules:** The Federal Rules preserve and in fact broaden the special ancient-document authentication principles. FRE 901(b)(8) says that in the case of a "*document or data compilation*," authentication requirements are satisfied by evidence that the document or compilation:

       "**(A)** is in a *condition* that *creates no suspicion* about its authenticity;

       (B) was in a *place* where, if authentic, it would likely be; and

(C) is *at least 20 years old* when offered."

i. **Easier-to-use:** So FRE 901(b)(8) keeps the three basic common-law requirements, but broadens the common-law approach in that: (1) the document needs to be only *twenty years old*, not thirty; and (2) the exception covers not only "documents," but also *"data compilations"* in any form. This clearly includes *electronically stored data* (e.g., a file copied from a computer).

c. **Not guarantee of admissibility:** Keep in mind that a showing that a document meets the three requirements for an "ancient document" merely overcomes the "authentication" hurdle, and *does not automatically guarantee admissibility.* For instance, a document that meets these requirements may nonetheless be inadmissible for a particular purpose because it is *hearsay.* McC, p. 406.

i. **Distinguished from hearsay rule:** Also, be careful of the distinction between the ancient document rule that covers authenticity, discussed here, and the ancient document rule that is recognized in many jurisdictions as an exception to hearsay rule, discussed *supra*, p. 270.

ii. **FRE approach:** For example, the *Federal Rules* have quite different standards concerning the required minimum age of an ancient document, depending on whether the issue is authentication or the hearsay exception. As you can see from the text of FRE 901(b)(8)(C) quoted above, *authentication* of a document as ancient requires merely that the proponent produce evidence that the document "is *at least 20 years old* when offered." But FRE 803(16)'s *hearsay exception* for ancient documents is now (following a 2017 amendment) considerably *stricter* about document age: even though the document has been authenticated for non-hearsay use by a showing that it is at least 20 years old, the document will *not qualify* for the ancient document hearsay exception if it was not *"prepared before January 1, 1998."*[1]

D. **Self-authentication:** There are a few categories of documents that are deemed so likely to be what they seem to be that no testimony or other extrinsic evidence of their genuineness need be produced. Such documents are said to be *"self-authenticating."* The categories of self-authenticating documents vary from state to state, and are almost always set by statute rather than case law.

1. **State statutes:** Here are the kinds of documents most likely to be made self-authenticating by state statutes: (1) *deeds* and other instruments that are duly *notarized*; (2) *certified* copies of *public records* (e.g., a certified copy of a death certificate); and (3) books of *statutes* which appear to be printed by a government body (most commonly used to establish the laws of a *sister state* or *foreign country*). McC, p. 410.

---

1. For instance, consider the example on p. 271 involving the hardcopy "Phony Document" dated Dec. 15, 1999, and offered into evidence in a trial in 2021. A showing by D that the document is "at least 20 years old" would be enough to meet the age prong of FRE 901(b)(8)'s authenticity requirement if the document is offered for non-hearsay purposes (e.g., to prove that someone who received the document was on notice as to what the document says). But despite the document's greater-than-20-years age, the document would *not* qualify for the FRE 803(16) hearsay exception, since it was not prepared before January 1, 1998.

2. **Federal Rules:**   The Federal Rules establish a broad set of self-authenticating documents. These are listed in FRE 902. In addition to the common categories listed above, Rule 902 makes self-authenticating these additional major categories:

   a. **Official publications:**   Any "book, pamphlet, or other publication purporting to be issued by a public authority" (not just statutes); see FRE 902(5);

   b. **Newspapers and periodicals:**   "Printed material purporting to be a *newspaper* or *periodical*"; see FRE 902(6);

   c. **Trade inscriptions:**   "An inscription, *sign*, tag, or *label* purporting to have been affixed in the course of business and *indicating origin, ownership, or control*." See FRE 902(7).

      Example: In a personal injury action against Green Giant Co., P seeks to introduce a can of peas bearing the label "Green Giant Brand . . . Distributed by Green Giant Company[.]" At common law, P was unable to get the label into evidence because it was not self-authenticating, and there was no independent proof that Green Giant Co. really "wrote" the label and, therefore, distributed the peas. *Keegan v. Green Giant Co.*, 110 A.2d 599 (Me. 1954). But under the Federal Rules, the label (and consequently the can to which it was attached) would be admissible as a label "purporting to have been affixed in the course of business and indicating origin, ownership, or control."

   d. **Business records:**   "*Record[s] of regularly conducted activity* that would be admissible under Rule 803(6)" (i.e., business records). However, the record must be accompanied by a *certification* by a "custodian or other qualified person," stating that the record "meets the requirements of Rule 803(6)(A)-(C)].]" See FRE 902(11). (To review, those requirements are that "(A) the record was made at or near the time by — or from information transmitted by — someone with knowledge; (B) the record was kept in the course of a regularly conducted activity of a business, organization, occupation, or calling, whether or not for profit; [and] (C) making the record was a regular practice of that activity[.]")

      Example: P, a merchant, is suing D, a customer, for what P says is an unpaid bill. P wants to introduce a computer record showing that D was invoiced for the merchandise and also showing that D has never been credited with a payment for this invoice on P's books. Instead of presenting live testimony by, say, D's accounts receivable manager, W, that the record meets the three business-records-exception requirements listed above, D can instead submit a written certification by W stating that the record meets the three requirements.

   e. **Electronic records:**   Records and data *produced by a computer program,* or *copied* from a computer, if accompanied by an appropriate *certification*. Two self-authentication provisions to this effect, Rules 902(13) and 902(14), were added in 2017. Let's first summarize each, and then examine how each might be used.

      i. **Records "generated by an electronic system":**   First is the broader of the two provisions, Rule 902(13). Rule 902(13) allows for self-authentication of *records "generated by an electronic process or system* that produces an accurate result[.]"

Such computer-generated records can be authenticated by means of a "certification of a qualified person that complies with the certification requirements of Rule 902(11) or (12)" (i.e., the sections covering certification of domestic and foreign business records respectively). In other words, the ***output from a computer program*** need not be authenticated by live testimony; instead, the output can be authenticated by a certification of the same sort that FRE 902(11) says can be used to authenticate a domestic business record.

ii. **Data "copied from an electronic device or file":** Second is a much narrower provision, Rule 902(14). 902(14) covers only authentication of ***"copies"*** of electronically-stored data. More precisely, the provision allows for self-authentication of ***"data copied from an electronic device, storage medium, or file,*** if authenticated by a ***process of digital identification[.]"*** As with the broader 902(13) provision, 902(14) dispenses with the need for a live witness to authenticate copies of electronic files; instead, the proponent can offer a certification of the sort used for authentication of business records.

The difference between 902(13) and 902(14) is that in the latter situation — which will always involve a "copy" of electronically-stored data — the authentication-by-certification must explain how a ***"process of digital identification"*** has been used to verify that what is being asserted to be a copy of a data file really *is* an exact copy.

iii. **How each section is used:** Here is an explanation of how each of the two certification procedures might be used.

(1) **Records "generated by an electronic system":** The Rule 902(13) process is used to authenticate the ***"output"*** of a computer program or other electronic system. So whenever the running of a computer program or the operation of an electronic system produces any kind of ***log file*** or ***data file*** (whether in electronic format or hardcopy), the log file or data file will be admissible based on a certification of how the file was produced, with no live "sponsorship" testimony required.

Example 1 (original digital text messaging log): Assume that whenever a particular model of Android smart cellphone sends a text message, the Android operating system makes an entry in a "text messaging log file" on the phone's internal storage device stating the time, sender's and recipient's phone number, and message text. Donna and Dev are charged with the federal crime of conspiring to distribute narcotics, and the prosecution wants to introduce a text message that prosecutors say Donna sent to Dev from her Android phone on April 2 at 4:30 PM ("Meet me with the blow in the 7/11 parking lot at 6 PM today"). Assume that all analysis of the text messaging log file on Donna's phone is done by a forensic technician, Rose, who works in an FBI lab.

If Rule 902(13) didn't exist, the prosecution would have to call Rose to the stand at trial, and she would give live testimony describing how she examined

Donna's phone, located the log file, and saw that the file contained the "Meet me with ..." contents.

But Rule 902(13) lets the prosecution dispense with any live authentication testimony by Rose or anyone else. Instead, the prosecution can submit a written *certification* prepared by Rose describing how Android phones create a log file of text messages and the process by which Rose examined the log file and found the 4:30 entry, and describing the full text of the message. Thus the prosecution is spared the burden of presenting a live witness in court when in all probability the defense would not have disputed that the message in question was sent when, how, and by whom the prosecution claims it was.

(2) Data "copied from an electronic device or file": The much narrower 902(14) deals only with the authentication of *copies* of digital files. Its main use is to permit a proponent to do all of its preparation on a *digital copy*, rather than on the "original" data file, so that there is no risk of an alteration of the original.[2] But the certification under 902(14) contains a requirement not present in 902(13): that the authentication be made by *"a process of digital identification,"* i.e., a process for showing that the contents of the original computer file and the copy are *identical*.[3]

Example 2 (copy of digital text message log): Same basic facts as Example 1 above. Now, however, assume that the FBI makes a practice of never analyzing or manipulating the original data from a smart phone seized from a criminal suspect — rather, FBI personnel use a non-destructive method of producing a "clone" (an exact digital copy) of the phone's contents, and then do their analysis on the cloned copy. Assume that in this case, Quentin of the FBI lab uses cloning to create and place on a laptop an exact copy of all files on Donna's cellphone, including the text messaging log. Rose then does her analysis on the copy, and never possesses or sees the original phone.

Without Rule 902(14), prosecutors would need to call Quentin to the stand to authenticate the making of the cloned copy, thereby laying the foundation for Rose's live testimony or her 902(13) certificate as to the contents of the log file. But 902(14) lets the prosecution instead submit a *certification* by Quentin explaining how he cloned the phone's contents, and describing the process by which he ran a standard hashing algorithm (see the above footnote) to determine that the electronic contents of the original phone and the contents of the

---

2. There is some *overlap* between the 902(13) and 902(14), but the overlap runs mostly in one direction. "[T]he electronic information that is covered by Rule 902(14) could also for the most part (but not completely) be covered by Rule 902(13). [But] the overlap does not run very far the other way, however; records generated by an electronic system may well not be a 'copy' of anything." Authenticating Digital Evidence, 69 Baylor L. R. 1, 40-41 (2017).

3. As the Advisory Committee Note to the 2017 Amendment that added 902(14) explains, today the task of showing that the original and copy of an electronic file are identical is ordinarily done by use of a *"hash value,"* which the Note describes as a "sequence of characters [that] is produced by an algorithm based upon the digital contents of a drive, medium, or file." As the Note explains, "identical hash values for the original and copy reliably attest to the fact that they are exact duplicates."

clone were indeed identical. Then, the prosecution would offer Rose's 902(13) certification, and the contents of the text message would have been authenticated without the need for the prosecution to have called either Quentin or Rose. Cf. Authenticating Digital Evidence, 69 Baylor L. R. 1, 44-46 (2017).

3. **Attack on genuineness:** The fact that a document is "self-authenticating" does *not* mean that it is irrebuttably presumed to be genuine. Self-authentication merely means that the ***proponent does not have to produce extrinsic evidence of authenticity.*** The opponent is always free to come forward with evidence showing that the document is *not* genuine (e.g., that a document purporting to be executed by X, and certified by a notary to have been executed by X, really was not signed by X). McC, p. 410. Where this happens, the evidence will be received, but the trier of fact will be free to conclude that the document is not genuine and should therefore be disregarded. L&S, p. 995.

E. **Ways of avoiding authentication:** The process of authentication often wastes a lot of time, given how seldom a document is other than what it purports to be. Therefore, modern courts have developed several other ways in which the proponent of evidence may avoid the need to authenticate it. Two are worth noting here:

1. **Request for admission:** In the federal courts, and in many states, a party may serve upon his opponent a written ***request for admission*** of the genuineness of any relevant document described in the request. See Fed. R. Civ. Proc. 36; McC, p. 409. For instance, in a contract dispute P might submit a copy of the alleged contract to D, and request that D admit the document's authenticity. If D unreasonably refuses to make the admission, a statute usually makes him liable for P's expenses in proving authenticity.

2. **Stipulation:** Similarly, the parties may jointly *stipulate* to the genuineness of a particular document, object, or fact. This is especially likely to occur during a ***pretrial conference*** run by the judge. McC, p. 409. See Fed. R. Civ. Proc. 16.

III. OTHER FOUNDATION REQUIREMENTS AND OBJECTIONS

A. **Introduction:** A party who has authenticated an object or document has merely passed the first hurdle to getting it into evidence. Depending on the nature of the item, he must then overcome one or more additional hurdles: (1) in the case of "real" evidence, he may have to prove the "chain of custody"; (2) in the case of "demonstrative" evidence, he must show that the evidence is useful and fairly representative of the fact or thing it purports to illustrate; and (3) in either case, he must avoid a finding that the evidence is unduly prejudicial. We consider each of these obstacles in turn.

B. **Mere relevance not enough:** Recall that in our discussion of authentication, we said that the authentication requirement is really an aspect of relevance — if the gun, bedspread, etc. offered in evidence is not really the very one used in the underlying event, it is probably not relevant to the action. Yet the stringency of requirements for the admission of real evidence goes beyond what would be required if mere relevance were all that had to be shown.

> **Example:** Suppose that, in a drug prosecution of A, W, the police chemist, is shown a sample of white powder, and testifies, "I tested this substance and found it to be cocaine; because of a lack of labeling, I know that the substance was taken from either

A or B, but I'm not sure which." If admissibility turned solely upon logical relevance, the court would admit the sample, since the sample and the supporting testimony by W make it more likely (a 50% chance) that A really possessed cocaine, than would be the case in the absence of this evidence. Yet no judge would admit the sample, because of the prosecution's utter failure to trace the sample directly to A. See L&S, p. 997.

1. **Chain of custody:**   Therefore, a requirement has evolved that calls for the *"special handling"* of real evidence, a requirement motivated more by a concern for fairness and prevention of official misconduct than by mere concerns of logical relevance: the requirement that a *"chain of custody"* be proved where the item is *not uniquely identifiable.*

   a. **Criminal cases:**   Proof of a chain of custody is *always* required in criminal cases if the object is not uniquely identifiable. The chain is only occasionally required in civil cases. L&S, p. 998. The difference is probably that when the police or prosecution come into possession of an item of evidence, they are likely to *know* that the item will need to be admitted, and are institutionally capable of documenting the chain as it develops; a private person, by contrast, will often not know that the object will ever be needed as evidence, and would be substantially more burdened by having to account for each change in the custody of the item. L&S, p. 998.

   b. **Links:**   Proving the chain of custody usually requires that *each person* who had custody of the item after it came into police or prosecution hands must testify as to three things: (1) how and when he came into possession; (2) how he stored the object while he had possession (and who else had access to it during that time); and (3) how he disposed of it and to whom and when.

   c. **Break:**   A "break" in the chain of custody is not necessarily fatal. For instance, the fact that others may have had the opportunity for brief access to the object will almost never lead it to be excluded — thus, the fact that the gun allegedly used in the murder lay on police officer W's desk for ten minutes while he was out of the room (during which time someone could have switched weapons) will virtually never lead the court to exclude the item. Generally, the court will only require "reasonable care and a reasonable showing that there was no realistic opportunity for tampering. . . ." L&S, p. 999.

2. **Condition unchanged:**   Similarly, if the object's *condition* is important, the proponent will have to show that that condition has not substantially *changed* between the time the object was acquired and some later time (e.g., the time it was tested or the time it is being introduced into evidence). Here, the problem tends to be strictly one of relevance — if the change makes the object no longer relevant for the purposes for which the proponent offers it, it will be excluded.

C. **Demonstrative evidence:**   There are no "special handling" requirements for *demonstrative* evidence. For instance, the proponent of a map or model will almost never be required to prove its chain of custody, because it is irrelevant who has had possession of the document since its creation. Instead, other issues commonly arise concerning the admissibility of demonstrative evidence:

1. **"Essential" vs. merely useful:**   Opponents of an item of demonstrative evidence sometimes argue that it should not be admitted because it is not *"essential"* to the case. How-

ever, there is no requirement that evidence created for illustrative purposes be essential. L&S, p. 1000. All that is required is that the evidence be *useful* to the jury in understanding testimony or real evidence in the case. *Id.* If the illustrative material meets this requirement, it will almost always be admitted unless there is some countervailing consideration. *Id.*

2. **Not a fair representation:** The most telling objection to evidence prepared for illustrative purposes is that the item does *not fairly represent* what it is supposed to illustrate. The trial judge generally has a great deal of discretion (which will rarely be reversed on appeal) in determining whether the illustration is indeed a sufficiently fair representation that it should be admitted. McC, p. 393.

   Example: D, prosecuted for the murder of V, claims that V pulled a knife on him and that the killing was in self-defense. The original switchblade is never recovered, but the prosecution concedes that one was used. The prosecution procures, as a model, a different type of switchblade that is two-thirds the size of the type believed used by V, but of similar shape and material. If this illustrative knife is offered into evidence, the trial judge may well conclude that its differing scale makes it so likely to mislead the jury that it should be excluded.

D. **Undue prejudice:** Whether the evidence is real or demonstrative, it may, like any other evidence, be excluded on the grounds that it is likely to lead to *unfair prejudice* to the other side.

1. **Gruesome photos:** For instance, in a murder case, the defendant may object to admission of photos of the victim's body, on the grounds that this will unfairly inflame the jury against the defendant. Most such objections are unsuccessful, since the photo often shows the nature of the victim's injuries, something relevant to the case. But the court will generally weigh the probative value against the prejudicial effect, and if the latter is substantially greater than the former, the court may exclude certain photos. For instance, the court might exclude life-sized blowups in favor of smaller prints, or might exclude a photo taken after an autopsy (showing mutilation from the autopsy), requiring a pre-autopsy photo instead.

2. **"Day in the life" films:** Plaintiffs in personal injury actions often try to introduce so-called *"day in the life" films*, i.e., short films depicting the plaintiff's daily life since the accident, and demonstrating the impact that the injury has had on the plaintiff. Such films are generally admissible. However, the court may exclude a particular film as being unduly prejudicial to the defendant.

3. **Bodily demonstration:** An injured plaintiff in a personal injury action may seek to *demonstrate his injuries* before the jury (e.g., by displaying his prosthetic device). Although this is likely to cause some prejudice to the defendant, the mere illustration of the injury or prosthesis will generally be allowed. If the plaintiff attempts to *perform* some activity, however, the court is more likely to bar the demonstration on the grounds that it will be prejudicial (and perhaps misleading as well). For instance, suppose that P claims that he is unable to bend his injured arm more than 90 degrees; a demonstration in which P's doctor tries to manipulate the arm into a greater bend, likely to be accompanied by a grimace of pain or scream by P, may be excluded by the judge on the grounds of undue prejudice. McC, p. 397.

IV. THE "BEST EVIDENCE" RULE FOR RECORDED COMMUNICATIONS

A. Best Evidence rule generally: The Best Evidence rule might be better called the Original Document rule. The rule in its common-law formulation is as follows: ***"An original writing, recording, or photograph is required in order to prove its content unless these rules or a federal statute provides otherwise."*** McC, p. 412.

> **Example:** P claims that D has defrauded her by selling her, as new, a car that has really been driven over 7,000 miles. W (P's husband) testifies that shortly after the car was delivered, he discovered a sticker on the inside of the car door, showing the current mileage as 7,244.
>
> *Held* (on appeal), W's testimony about what the sticker said should not have been admitted, because the Best Evidence rule required that the contents of a writing (the sticker) must be proved by introducing the writing itself, not by oral testimony about what the writing said, unless it was shown that the original sticker could not be produced in evidence. Here, P made no showing that the sticker could not be detached and brought into the court. *Davenport v. Ourisman-Mandell Chevrolet, Inc.*, 195 A.2d 743 (D.C.Ct.App. 1963).

1. Requirements: Taking the Best Evidence rule apart, we see that it has three main components:

  a. Original document: The *original document* must be produced, rather than using a copy or oral testimony about the document;

  b. Prove terms of writing: The rule applies only where what is to be proved is the *terms* of a *writing* (or under the modern approach, an equivalent recorded communication such as an audio tape of a conversation); and

  c. Excuse: The rule does not apply if the original is *unavailable* because it has been destroyed, is in the possession of a third party, or cannot be conveniently obtained, and the unavailability is not due to the serious fault of the proponent.

2. Only writings and equivalents: Probably the most important thing to remember about the Best Evidence rule is that it applies *only to writings* (and, today, equivalent recorded communications). It does *not apply to evidence generally*.

> **Example:** Suppose that D, a karate expert, is charged with killing V by a direct blow to the neck. The prosecution asks the pathologist who did the autopsy to illustrate on a plastic skeleton where the injury occurred. If D objects to use of the skeleton on the theory that it is not the "Best Evidence" (which would be the actual bones of V), this objection will *not* be sustained, because the Best Evidence rule only applies where what is being proved is the contents of a writing or other recorded communication.

3. Rationale for rule: The purpose of the Best Evidence rule is to make sure that the *exact terms* of the writing are brought before the trier of fact. If the original is not used for proving the terms, there are several reasons to fear that the trier of fact may be misled about what the writing says: (1) *distortion* may inadvertently occur when a copy (especially a handwritten copy) of the writing is produced, or an oral account of its contents is given;

(2) *fraud* is easier where the original need not be produced; and (3) if the original need not be produced, the proponent has a better opportunity to mislead by taking a small portion of a larger document out of context. L&S, p. 1007.

4. **Federal Rules:** The Federal Rules in general carry forward the common-law Best Evidence rule, in some ways broadening it and in other ways narrowing it:

   a. **Statement of Rule:** The federal version of the Best Evidence rule is stated in FRE 1002: "To *prove the content of a writing, recording, or photograph*, the *original* writing, recording, or photograph is required, except as otherwise provided in these rules or by Act of Congress."

   b. **Broadened to include other recordations:** In one sense, the Federal Rules broaden the class of items covered by the Best Evidence rule. Some common-law courts included only conventional writings within the rule. But the Federal Rules cover any "writing, *recording*, or *photograph*" whose contents are sought to be proved. "Writings" and "recordings" are in turn defined in FRE 1001 as follows:

      "(a) A *"writing"* consists of letters, words, numbers, or their equivalent set down in any form.

      (b) A *"recording"* consists of letters, words, numbers, or their equivalent recorded in any manner."

      i. **Illustrations:** So under the Federal Rules, an *audio tape* of a conversation, or a *computer tape* of data, would be covered by the rule, and if available their contents could not be proved by, say, oral testimony. This aspect is discussed further *infra*, p. 492.

   c. **Duplicate:** But the Federal Rules also make it easier than it was at common law to satisfy the Best Evidence rule. Most notably, FRE 1003 provides that "A *duplicate* is admissible to the same extent as the original unless a *genuine question is raised* about the original's authenticity or the *circumstances make it unfair* to admit the duplicate."

      "Duplicate" is defined in FRE 1001(e) as "[A] counterpart produced by a mechanical, photographic, chemical, electronic, or other equivalent process or technique that *accurately reproduces the original.*"

      i. **Photocopies:** Most significantly, *photocopies* are included in the definition. Therefore, a party may offer a photocopy instead of the original without any showing that the original is unavailable, and it is up to the adversary to raise a "genuine question" as to the authenticity of the original or the unfairness of using the duplicate. In view of the reliability and mechanical nature of photocopying, the adversary will generally be unable to bear this burden, and the photocopy will be admitted. This aspect is discussed further *infra*, p. 496.

B. **What is a "writing" or other recorded communication:** It will not always be clear what constitutes a "writing" (or, under the modern approach, an equivalent recorded communication). Here are some of the special issues that arise:

1. **Short inscription:** An object may have an *inscription* on it. For instance, a watch may be inscribed, "To Joe From Maryjane, With Love, December 12, 1982." Does this inscrip-

tion turn the watch into a "writing," so that the "contents" of the inscription may only be proved by producing the watch itself? Courts have treated the inscription issue on a case-by-case basis: the Best Evidence rule is more likely to be held applicable if the inscription is complicated, if its precise (rather approximate) content is important to the litigation, or if it is easily produced. McC, p. 413.

2. **Photographic evidence:** Photographs, X-rays, and similar products of the photographic process are generally not offered to prove their contents, so the Best Evidence rule usually does not apply regardless of whether the item is deemed to be a "writing." But occasionally, a photograph, X-ray, movie, etc. is offered to prove its contents; in this situation, it is not clear whether the common-law approach would treat them as "writings." Probably the majority rule, and clearly the trend, is to broaden the meaning of "writing" to include such items within the rule.

> **Example:** P brings a personal injury action against D. To prove her damages, she calls as a witness W, a radiologist, who has taken X-rays of P's spine and studied them. W does not bring the X-rays with him, and seeks to testify about their content.
>
> *Held*, the X-rays are, for purposes of the Best Evidence rule, a "document," i.e., a "physical embodiment of information or ideas." Therefore, P may not prove the contents of the X-rays by having W testify about them; instead, the X-rays themselves must be introduced in evidence if available. *Sirico v. Cotto*, 324 N.Y.S.2d 483 (Civ. Ct. N.Y. City 1971).

a. **Federal Rules:** The Federal Rules explicitly expand the Best Evidence Rule to include all "photographs" whose contents are to be proved. FRE 1002. "Photographs" is defined in FRE 1001(c) to include "a photographic image or its equivalent stored in any form." So still photographs, X-rays, videotapes, movies and computerized motion files like .mp3s ought all to be "photographic images" covered by the Rule. (But remember that most times when such materials are introduced, it will not be for the purpose of "proving the contents" of the item. See *infra*, p. 494.)

3. **Sound recordings:** When a *sound recording* is introduced for the purpose of proving the recording's contents, the Rule applies even according to most common-law courts. Again, however, remember that this occurs only when the recording is offered for the purpose of proving its contents.

> **Example:** D is charged with kidnapping. The prosecution offers testimony by W, a policeman, that the voice on a ransom tape delivered to the victim's parents resembles the voice of D. Since by this testimony W is trying to prove the contents of the tape, the court will probably hold that the prosecution must produce and introduce into evidence the tape itself if it is available. (But if W had personally received a telephone demand for ransom, he could testify to the contents of the call, without producing a tape he made of the call contemporaneously; in this situation, the tape would be incidental, and he would be proving the contents of the call, not of the tape.) See McC, p. 413.

C. **What constitutes "proving the terms":** As noted frequently above, the Best Evidence rule applies only where what is sought to be proved are the ***"terms"*** or ***"contents"*** of the writing or other communication.

1. **Existence, execution, etc.:** This limitation means that if all that is proved is that a writing *exists*, was *executed*, or was *delivered*, the Best Evidence rule does not apply.

   Example: Prosecution of D for kidnapping. A prosecution witness, W, mentions that a ransom note was received, but does not testify as to the note's contents. This proof that the ransom note was delivered does not constitute proof of its terms, so that note need not be introduced in evidence. (But if W goes on to testify to the details of what the note said, the note would have to be produced.)

2. **Incidental record:** Frequently an event occurs which is *memorialized* or evidenced by a writing. In general, the fact that there happens to be a writing memorializing a transaction does *not* mean that the transaction can only be proved by introduction of the writing. In this situation, the writing is treated as an *incidental by-product* of the transaction. For instance, the earnings of a business may be proved without putting the books and records into evidence; similarly, the fact that a payment was made may be proved without producing a receipt, and the fact of marriage may be proved without producing the marriage certificate. McC, p. 414.

   Example: In a wrongful death action, P (the estate of the decedent) wants to prove the decedent's earnings. P puts on testimony by one of the other partners in a business in which P was a partner, concerning the earnings of the partnership and the decedent's share. D contends that the best evidence of these earnings is the partnership books and records, and that oral testimony as to the earnings must therefore be excluded.

   Held, P was not attempting to prove the contents of the books and records. Rather, P was attempting to prove the earnings of the partnership, and the books and records were merely incidental recordations of those earnings. Therefore, the partner's oral testimony should have been admitted. *Herzig v. Swift & Co.*, 146 F.2d 444 (2d Cir. 1945).

   Note: But remember that if the proponent *does* try to prove the contents of a writing that happens to record a fact, the Best Evidence rule applies. For instance, W in *Herzig* would not have been permitted to testify, "The books and records of the partnership show that P's share for last year would have been $30,000," without producing the books and records themselves — in this situation, the terms of the writing *are* being proved.

   a. **Transcript:** A person's prior *testimony* can generally be proved by an oral account of a witness who heard the testimony, *even if a transcript exists*. In this situation, courts generally reason that what is being proved is the prior oral testimony, and that the transcript is merely an incidental recordation whose contents are not being proved.

   Example: D is charged with perjuring himself in testimony before a congressional committee. The prosecution calls W, who was a lawyer for the committee, to testify about what D said under oath to the committee. D objects, arguing that the best evidence of what D said is contained in the available transcript, and that W must therefore not be permitted to give oral testimony about what D previously said.

   Held, the oral testimony is admissible. "Here there was no attempt to prove the contents of a writing; the issue was what [D] had said, not what the transcript contained." (But a dissent forcefully argued that the majority's approach "appl[ies] a meaningless formula and ignore[s] crystal-clear actualities. The transcript is, as a matter of simple indisputable fact, the best evidence. The principle and not the rule of law ought to be applied.") *Meyers v. U.S.*, 171 F.2d 800 (D.C.Cir. 1948).

    i. **Confessions:** But where a criminal defendant has made a ***confession*** that has been both heard by a person and reduced to a written transcript, many if not most courts would rule that the transcript, not the testimony of the person who heard the confession, must be introduced. McC, p. 415. There is no logical reason for treating this confession situation differently from general testimony of the sort involved in *Meyers*, *supra*; probably the difference stems from courts' strong desire to protect against false or misleading evidence of confessions.

  b. **Photos and other non-testimonial items:** Suppose that a ***photograph***, x-ray, audio recording, video tape, etc., has been made of an object or event. Is live testimony about the object or event allowed in lieu of introducing the photograph, etc.? In general, the answer is ***"yes,"*** since the photograph or other recordation is merely an ***incidental*** record, and its "contents" are therefore not really being proved.

    Example: Suppose Lee Harvey Oswald had been brought to trial on a charge of assassinating President Kennedy. The famous Zapruder film shows the President during the moments when the bullets were hitting him. Assume the prosecution offers the testimony of W, who was watching the President at the moment the bullets hit, about the President's movements at that moment. The prosecution would be permitted to use this oral evidence from W, and would not be required to introduce the film instead. The prosecution is not trying to prove that the film had certain contents; instead, the film is an incidental recording of an actual event, and it is the actual event that is being proved. Thus the fact that the film may in some sense be the "best evidence" of the President's motions at the moment of impact would be irrelevant, and the Best Evidence rule would not apply.

    i. **Proof of contents of photograph:** But contrast this with other situations in which the contents of the photograph, x-ray, etc., really *are* being proved. For instance, suppose a prosecution is brought for distributing or showing an ***obscene*** still photo or movie, or for selling a photograph that ***infringes a copyright***. In this situation, the contents of the photo or film really *are* what is being proved, and therefore the photo or film must be introduced rather than be described by oral testimony.

3. **Contract, deed, or other key document:** There are some transactions in which the role played by a document is so key that the document really ***embodies*** the transaction. In this case, the Best Evidence rule requires introduction of the document rather than mere testimony about it. For instance, if P brings a ***contract*** action against D, all courts hold that the written contract must be introduced, and that its contents cannot be proved by oral testimony, other documents referring to it, etc. One might argue that the contract is just the incidental written record of the intangible agreement between the parties, and that the written document should not be required any more than the books and records of account in *Herzig*, *supra*, p. 493. But courts have rarely if ever accepted this argument. Thus not only contracts, but also *deeds and judgments,* are always required to be produced. McC, p. 414.

D. Collateral writings: During testimony, a witness may refer to some writings which have only the most tangential connection to the litigation. Even though the contents of the writing are in some sense being "proved," courts do not require production of the original, on the theory that it is not worth the time and effort that this will take. This willingness to dispense with the Best Evidence rule if the document is of only tangential importance is known as the *"collateral writings"* exception.

> **Example:** W, who witnesses the arrest of his neighbor, D, testifies that he knows the arrest took place on the day after the killing of V. He tells the court that he knows this because he witnessed the arrest on the same day he read about the killing in the newspaper, and the newspaper article referred to the crime as having taken place "yesterday." Here, W is proving the contents of a writing (the article). Yet the writing is so tangentially related to the case that nearly all courts would dispense with the requirement that the article itself be produced, and would allow oral testimony about its contents under the "collateral writings" exception. See McC, p. 415.

1. Factors: Trial judges are given a great deal of discretion in determining what writings are sufficiently collateral as to fall within the exception. Factors that the court takes into account include: (1) the *"centrality* of the writing to the principal issues of the litigation"; (2) the *complexity* of the relevant features of the writing; and (3) the *"existence of genuine dispute"* about the writing's contents. McC, p. 415.

2. Federal Rule: The "collateral writings" exception is codified in FRE 1004(d). That provision dispenses with the need for the original writing if "the writing, recording, or photograph is not *closely related* to a *controlling issue.*"

E. Which is the "original": Recall that the Best Evidence rule requires that the "writing itself" be produced. That is, an *"original,"* rather than a "copy," must be produced.

1. Duplicate originals: In some situations there may be *"duplicate originals."* For instance, there may be multiple copies of a contract, each executed by all parties. Or, there may be multiple copies of a contract, each executed by one party, with a statement in the contract providing that "so long as each party has signed at least one copy of this contract, any copy signed by any party shall be deemed an original executed copy." In this situation, *any of these originals* will meet the requirement of the Best Evidence rule (but secondary evidence, such as testimony about what the contract said, would not be admissible unless *all* of the duplicate originals were shown to be unavailable). McC, p. 416.

2. Original destroyed: If the court focuses carefully on which of two documents is the one whose contents are being proved, and that document turns out to be unavailable, the queer result may be that oral testimony is allowed in lieu of presentation of the other, closely related, document.

F. Reproductions: Today, there exist many techniques for making a very accurate copy of an original document, most notably the photocopier. However, when the Best Evidence rule developed at common law, copying was done by hand, and was notoriously inaccurate. Therefore, the rules on whether and when a "copy" may be used in lieu of the original have been broadened in the last half-century or so.

1. **Photocopying and other modern techniques:** The main method of copying today is by *photocopying*, or its electronic-records analog, the "scanning" of a document. The right to use a photocopy or computer scan in lieu of the original varies from state to state:

   a. **Statutes:** Most states have a *statute*, modeled on the Uniform Photographic Copies of Business and Public Records as Evidence Act, by which regularly-kept photographic copies of business and public records are *admissible*, even if the original is available. Thus in such states, a party may introduce a photocopy without showing the unavailability of the original. L&S, p. 1009.

2. **Federal Rules:** The Federal Rules treat copies produced by *any reliable modern method* (including photocopying and scanning) as being "duplicates" that are *presumptively admissible.* This result is reached by the combination of FRE 1001(e) and 1003:

   a. **Special treatment for "duplicate":** FRE 1003 makes "duplicates" admissible even if the original is available, under ordinary circumstances: "A duplicate is admissible to the same extent as the original unless a *genuine question* is raised about the original's authenticity or the *circumstances make it unfair* to admit the duplicate."

   b. **"Duplicate" defined:** FRE 1001(e) defines "duplicate" to include all copies made by accurate reproduction techniques: "A 'duplicate' means a counterpart produced by a mechanical, photographic, chemical, electronic, or other equivalent process or technique that *accurately reproduces the original*."

   c. **Rationale:** The rationale behind this broad federal rule is that these modern reproduction methods are sufficiently accurate that the burden of proof should be placed upon the opponent to show inaccuracy, not upon the proponent to show accuracy.

   d. **Scope:** Here are some kinds of copies that would be presumptively admissible "duplicates" under the Federal Rules: photocopies, mimeograph copies, carbon copies, images of a document scanned into a computer and then printed out on paper, copies of an original video or audio tape made by a re-recording, etc.

      i. **Handwritten or typed copies not covered:** But copies produced *manually*, whether *typed* or *hand-written*, are *not* "duplicates" under the Federal Rules. FRE 1001(e), Advisory Committee's Note. These methods of reproduction are so prone to inadvertent error or fraud that the principles behind the Best Evidence rule dictate their exclusion if the original is available.

G. **Excuses for non-production:** Recall that the Best Evidence rule does not inflexibly bar the use of secondary evidence — it bars such evidence only if the original is available, or is unavailable due to the serious fault of the proponent. In other words, the basic rationale for the rule is that the best *obtainable* evidence must be used. McC, pp. 417-418. Therefore, there are several kinds of "excuses" for non-production of the document that will allow the proponent to use an otherwise-inadmissible copy of the document or oral testimony about the document:

1. **Loss or destruction:** If the proponent can show that the original has been *destroyed* or *lost* through no fault of the proponent, he may use a copy.

a. **Federal Rules:** The Federal Rules codify this "lost or destroyed" exception. FRE 1004(1) dispenses with the need for the original if if ***"all the originals are lost or destroyed,*** and ***not by the proponent acting in bad faith***[.]"

Example: P claims that the creators of the movie "The Empire Strikes Back" have infringed on P's copyright in certain science fiction creatures, called "Garthian Striders." P claims to have created the characters before 1980, the year in which the movie appeared. P seeks to introduce drawings made after 1980, which he says are "recreations" of the original characters. P claims there were pre-1980 drawings, but that he has not been able to find them. The defendants object, citing the Best Evidence Rule.

Held, for the defendants. The drawings were "writings" within the meaning of (what is now) FRE 1001(a), and are therefore subject to the Best Evidence Rule. Since (the trial judge found) P lost or destroyed the originals in bad faith, FRE 1004(a) renders the recreated drawings inadmissible. *Seiler v. Lucasfilm, Ltd.*, 797 F.2d 1504 (9th Cir. 1986).

2. **Inconvenience:** Some courts have recognized extreme ***inconvenience*** as an excuse for non-production of the original. For instance, "one does not have to uproot a tombstone to prove in court the inscriptions which it bears. . . ." W,M,A&B, p. 229.

3. **Possession by third person:** If the original is ***in the possession of a third person***, and cannot be obtained by either informal or formal efforts (e.g., a subpoena *duces tecum*), this will excuse non-production. McC, p. 418. FRE 1004(b) incorporates this exception: copies may be used if "an original ***cannot be obtained by any available judicial process***[.]"

4. **Original in opponent's possession:** The proponent is excused from producing the original if he can show that: (1) the original is in the hands of his ***adversary*** or under the latter's control; and (2) the proponent has ***notified him*** to produce it at the trial, and the adversary has ***failed*** to do so. McC, p. 419.

a. **Federal Rules:** The Federal Rules embody this exception in FRE 1004(c), which excuses the failure to produce the original if "the party against whom the original would be offered had ***control*** of the original; was at that time ***put on notice***, by pleadings or otherwise, that the original would be a subject of proof at the trial or hearing; and ***fails to produce it*** at the trial or hearing…."

   i. **Significance of notice:** The "notice" referred to in FRE 1004(c) does not have to be one that ***compels*** the adversary to supply the document — that's why a ***pleading*** can suffice, and a subpoena is not needed. The notice merely allows the proponent to force the adversary to ***choose:*** the adversary can supply the original, or she can waive her objection to use of a copy or oral testimony, but she must do one or the other.

5. **Public records:** ***Public records*** and ***public documents*** need not be produced in their original form, since the originals are generally required to be kept in a public depository (e.g., the originally-filed copy of a real estate deed must remain in the land records). Instead, a ***certified copy*** may be used. See, e.g., FRE 1005, allowing use of a certified copy to prove the contents of "an official record — or of a document that was recorded or filed in a public office as authorized by law[.]"

H. Summaries: If original writings are so ***voluminous*** that they cannot be conveniently be introduced into evidence and examined in court, most courts permit a ***summary*** to be introduced instead. McC, p. 414. This summary must be sponsored by a witness (usually an expert) who has reviewed the underlying writings and the summary, and who can testify that the summary is an accurate reflection of the underlying documents; often, the witness is the person who prepared the summary.

1. **Underlying originals:**   Before a summary may be used, courts generally require that the ***underlying documents be made available for examination*** by the opponent. Also, since the summary actually becomes ***evidence*** (in contrast to the "demonstrative" use of charts, see *infra*, p. 502, where the chart is non-evidence that merely helps the jury understand previously-admitted evidence), the proponent must at least in a general sense establish the ***admissibility*** of the ***underlying evidence***. For instance, a summary of documents would not be admissible if the underlying documents were inadmissible hearsay. McC, p. 414.

2. **Federal Rules:**   The Federal Rules allow liberal use of summaries. FRE 1006 provides that "The proponent may use a ***summary, chart, or calculation*** to prove the content of ***voluminous writings, recordings, or photographs*** that ***cannot be conveniently examined in court***. The proponent must make the originals or duplicates ***available for examination or copying, or both,*** by other parties at a ***reasonable time and place***. And the court may ***order the proponent to produce them in court***."

   a. **Recordings and photographs:**   Observe that FRE 1006 allows summaries not only of writings, but also of ***recordings*** and ***photographs***.

   b. **Sponsoring witness needed:**   The summary must be ***sponsored*** by a ***witness*** (often an expert) who testifies that he has prepared or reviewed the underlying writings and the summary, and that the ***summary accurately reflects the underlying documents.***

   c. **Documents become evidence:** When Rule 1006 is used, the ***underlying documents become evidence***, even though they are not individually presented in court.

   d. **"Absence of entries" does not qualify:**   Testimony that one or more items ***have not been found*** in voluminous records, despite a diligent search by a person with access to the records, does ***not*** qualify under FRE 1006's summary-of-voluminous-records exception. So such testimony will have to come in under the exception in 803(7) for absence of regularly-kept records (*supra*, p. 254) or not at all.

   Example: P sues D, its customer, for non-payment of five particular bills out of hundreds that P sent D over the years. W, P's office manager, testifies that P keeps records of all payments received from any customer, and that W searched the records covering all transactions between P and D and could not find any indication in them that D paid the five bills in question. W's testimony is not admissible under FRE 1006 as a "summary of voluminous records," because ***it is not a summary*** of all the P-D records, merely a statement attesting to the absence of specific entries. So her testimony will have to come in, if at all, via the FRE 803(7) hearsay exception for "Absence of a Record of a Regularly Conducted Activity" (the business-records exception), not FRE 1006.

I. **Admission by adversary:** Sometimes a party makes an *admission* about the terms of a writing. All courts allow at least some such admissions to be used by the other party as evidence of what the writing says, in lieu of producing the original. McC, p. 421.

    1. **Federal Rules:** The Federal Rules allow use of some but not all types of party admissions to prove the contents of a writing. FRE 1007 provides that "The proponent may prove the content of a *writing*, recording, or photograph by the *testimony, deposition, or written statement* of the *party against whom the evidence is offered*. The proponent need not account for the original."

        Example: P sues D for negligence arising out of an automobile accident. In a deposition, D is asked, "Didn't you write to P saying you were sorry you went through a red light?" D responds, "Yes, I wrote the letter, but I now realize that I didn't go through a red light." FRE 1007 allows P to introduce this deposition testimony (rather than the letter itself) to prove that D wrote the letter and that it contained a statement by D that he went through the red light.

        a. **Oral admissions don't qualify:** Note that FRE 1007 does *not* allow proof of an unsworn *oral admission* by a party to prove the contents of a writing. "Since one of the strong policies underlying the Best Evidence rule is obtaining an accurate version of the contents of writings and the other items covered by the rule, if all oral admissions sufficed to prove the contents of writings, accuracy would be jeopardized." S&R, p. 1076.

        b. **Not exclusive means:** Even though FRE 1007 does not apply to allow oral admissions to prove contents of a writing or other contents covered by the B.E.R., there may be other opportunities to use oral evidence of a party's admission to prove such contents. For instance, suppose on the facts of the above example that D conceded having written the letter to P not in sworn deposition testimony, but in a casual conversation to a friend, W. If P can show that the letter has been lost or destroyed without his fault (thus meeting the terms of FRE 1004(a)), P may prove the contents of the letter by having W testify at trial as to what D told him. The difference is that this type of proof under Rule 1004 requires the original's loss or destruction, whereas Rule 1007, if applicable, may be used *even if the original is perfectly available. Id.*

J. **Preferences among secondary evidence:** Recall that the purpose of the Best Evidence rule is to make sure that the best available evidence of a writing's contents is used. If the original is not available, so that some kind of secondary evidence (e.g., a copy or oral testimony) must be used, does the same rationale apply? That is, must the proponent use the *"next best evidence"* available? The courts are split.

    1. **Minority ("English") rule:** A *minority* of American courts have adopted the position taken by the English courts, that *"there are no degrees of substantive evidence."* McC, p. 420.

        a. **Rationale:** This minority approach has the advantage of *simplicity:* courts do not get dragged into disputes about whether one type of secondary evidence is indeed better than another.

2. **Majority rule:**   Most American courts, by contrast, *do* recognize "degrees of substantive evidence." McC, p. 420. These courts hold that when there is a choice between a written copy and oral testimony, the *written copy must be used*. This approach has the virtue of carrying forward the general rationale behind the Best Evidence rule, that of making sure that the best available evidence is used.

3. **Federal Rules:**   The Federal Rules adopt the *minority* approach, that *there are no degrees of substantive evidence.* Under this view, if there exists a handwritten copy of a document, as well as a witness who remembers reading the original, the proponent may offer the oral testimony even though the handwritten copy would almost certainly be "better" evidence than the testimony. See Advisory Committee's Note to FRE 1004, which states: "The rule recognizes no 'degrees' of secondary evidence."

K. **Judge-jury allocation:**   There are many factual issues that may need to be determined in order to apply the Best Evidence rule. Most are to be decided by the judge as "preliminary questions of fact" (see *infra*, p. 577). But some are so central to the major issues in the case that they must be decided by the *jury.*

1. **Federal Rules:**   The Federal Rules explicitly allocate the division of responsibility between judge and jury for Best Evidence rule issues. Most states would probably follow roughly the same allocation. FRE 1008 provides:

> "Ordinarily, the *court determines* whether the proponent has *fulfilled the factual conditions* for admitting other evidence of the content of a writing, recording, or photograph under Rule 1004 or 1005. But in a *jury trial*, the *jury* determines — in accordance with Rule 104(b) — any issue about whether:
>
> > (a) an *asserted writing*, recording, or photograph *ever existed*;
> >
> > (b) another one *produced at the trial* or hearing is the *original*; or
> >
> > (c) other *evidence of content accurately reflects the content*."

a. **Decided by judge:**   Thus a variety of preliminary questions in applying the Best Evidence rule are to be decided by the *judge*, not the jury. For instance, it is the judge who must decide such matters as: (1) whether a particular item of evidence is an "original"; (2) whether a particular item is a "duplicate" under FRE 1001, and therefore presumptively admissible under FRE 1003; (3) whether the original has been lost or destroyed (and if so, whether this occurred due to the proponent's bad faith), as provided in FRE 1004(a); and (4) whether the evidence relates to a "collateral matter" (in which case the Rule does not apply) or rather to a controlling issue (see FRE 1004(d)). See S&R, p. 1078.

V.   SPECIAL TYPES OF REAL AND DEMONSTRATIVE EVIDENCE

A. **Pictorial evidence (photographs, x-rays, and movies):**   Pictorial evidence — including still photographs, x-rays, movies, and video tapes — presents some special issues.

1. **Authentication of pictures:**   Most importantly, how does one *authenticate* such pictorial evidence? All courts recognize one method; most also now recognize a second.

a. **"Illustrative of what witness saw" method:** Traditionally, most photographic evidence is admitted on the theory that it is merely a "graphic portrayal of oral testimony." McC, p. 394. That is, a witness testifies to facts, and then says that the photograph, movie, etc., *accurately reflects what the witness saw.* If X and W see P stab D, and X happens to make a movie of the stabbing, the movie could be authenticated by W's testimony: "I saw P stab D, and this movie accurately reflects the stabbing as I saw it."

    i. **Not necessarily by taker:** Observe that this method of authentication does *not* require that the sponsoring testimony be by the person who *took* the photograph or movie, or even that the sponsoring witness know anything whatsoever about the conditions under which the photograph was taken. Thus in the above stabbing hypothetical, W could authenticate the movie as being an accurate portrayal of what he witnessed even if W was not aware that X was shooting the movie, has no idea who X is, has no idea the type of camera used, etc.

b. **"Silent witness" method:** Most modern decisions also recognize a *second method* of authenticating a photograph, movie, etc. Under this method, the photo is verified not by the testimony of any witness who has actually witnessed the scene or event portrayed, but rather from testimony about the *reliability of the process* by which the photo was produced. McC, p. 394. This is sometimes called the *"silent witness"* theory of admission, because once the process is shown to be reliable, the picture or movie "speaks for itself" as to its contents.

    i. **X-rays:** This is generally the basis on which *x-rays* are introduced, for instance. After all, an x-ray can never be authenticated by the testimony of a human being that he has witnessed the scene shown in the x-ray, and knows the x-ray to be an accurate depiction of that scene. Instead, the x-ray is authenticated by the following kind of testimony: "I, a radiologist, took this x-ray, by commonly used techniques of proven scientific validity, and I therefore believe that it accurately represents the bones of the patient's hand."

    ii. **Automatic devices:** This method is similarly used to authenticate photos taken by *automatic* devices. For instance, banks have automatic cameras which record each teller transaction. A photograph taken by such a camera could be introduced even without a witness to testify that he personally observed the transaction and that the photograph is a true representation; instead, testimony about how the automatic camera system works, and testimony showing that the particular photo was taken at the appropriate time or in connection with the appropriate transaction, would suffice.

    iii. **Foundation requirement:** When a photograph or movie taken by an automatic device is introduced, with no testimony by one who witnessed the scene or event, courts impose a fairly heavy *foundation* requirement: the proponent must show in some detail how the machine works, how it was employed in the particular application, and, perhaps, that there was no editing or tampering. L&S, p. 1026.

2. Movies: *Motion pictures* are now generally treated like photographs. That is, if a foundation is laid so that there is reason to believe that the motion picture accurately portrays what it purports to portray, the film will be admitted.

B. Computer print-outs: *Computer print-outs* present two special problems, one of authentication and one as to the Best Evidence rule:

1. Authentication: When a computer print-out is offered as evidence of the facts contained in the print-out (typically financial or numerical facts), the print-out must be *authenticated*. Generally this is done by a witness who can testify as to the methods used to input the data into the computer and the methods used to produce a print-out of that data, as well as testimony showing why the result that appears on the print-out is an accurate reflection of the original transactions being recorded.

   a. Federal Rules: Under the Federal Rules, this kind of authentication could come under FRE 901(b)(9), which allows authentication by "[e]vidence describing a *process or system* and showing that it produces an accurate result." Alternatively, the proponent offering a computer print-out could submit a *certification* under FRE 902(13), describing how the print-out was made and why it is reliable; see *supra*, p. 484.

2. Best Evidence rule: Where a computer print-out is offered to prove the facts recorded in the document, the opponent may raise a Best Evidence argument. First, he may contend that the record on the computer (e.g., the hard disk or other electronic copy of the file) is the "best evidence," not the print-out. Alternatively, he may argue that the original paper records of the transaction, not the computer records, are the "original" and thus the best evidence (e.g., that to prove that a check was received from a customer, the original is the check itself, not the computer entry showing receipt of the check).

   a. Unsuccessful: In general, such objections will be *unsuccessful.* For instance, in federal courts the proponent may make use of FRE 1001(d), which provides that "For electronically stored information, *'original' means any printout* — or other output readable by sight — if it accurately reflects the information." This at least means that the printout, if shown to reflect the computer's data accurately, is an "original" of the computer-stored data, so that the electronic version of the data need not be used.

C. Maps, models, diagrams, and summaries: Recall that "demonstrative" evidence, as we use the term here, consists of items that were not involved in the underlying event, but *illustrate* events or testimony. Common examples of such demonstrative evidence are *maps*, *models*, *diagrams*, and *summaries*.

1. Authentication: These items must, of course, be authenticated. Here, authentication generally consists of showing that the map, model, etc., is an *accurate representation* of what it purports to portray. In the case of a model of an allegedly defective truck, for instance, the witness would testify that the model is an accurate portrayal (at a small scale) of the truck actually involved in the crash.

2. Generally admissible: So long as the object is properly authenticated and would be helpful to the jury in understanding other evidence or testimony, the judge will generally admit it. Trial judges have a wide discretion to determine whether the value of such illustrative items is sufficient to justify their admission.

3. **Charts and summaries:** Increasingly, lawyers try to help the jury understand previously-admitted evidence or testimony by the use of *charts* or *summaries.* (This use of charts and summaries to help the jury understand previously-admitted evidence is different from the use of such items to summarize writings that are too voluminous to be individually admitted; as to the latter, see *supra*, p. 498.) So long as the judge feels that the chart or summary will be helpful to the jury, and not be misleading, he will generally admit it. But again, trial judges have broad discretion about whether to admit such charts and summaries, and that discretion will rarely be reversed on appeal.

4. **Evidentiary status:** The evidentiary status of a map, model, chart, etc., is often unclear. Whenever possible, courts will treat such items as being *incorporated into the witness's testimony*, and thus part of the record on appeal. For instance, the court might ask the witness to draw a diagram on a large piece of paper attached to an easel, rather than on a blackboard, so that the drawing can be made part of the record on appeal. Otherwise, the appellate court may have trouble understanding the witness's testimony.. McC, pp. 393-394.

D. **Views:** Some events cannot be fully explained to the jury by testimony or by tangible evidence that can be brought into the courtroom. Where this is the case, the jury and/or judge may journey outside the courtroom to visit and observe a particular place. This excursion is called a *"view."*

> **Example:** D is accused of stabbing V in front of 523 Main Street. W, the sole eyewitness, testifies that she was just turning onto Main Street from First Avenue when she saw the stabbing and saw D's face; she says that D then turned and ran, and she never got any closer to him. The stabbing took place after dark, but W says that the street lights were bright enough for her to be able to see D's face.
>
> At the request of D's lawyer, the trial judge might allow the jury to take a view of the crime scene. In particular, he might let them stand after dark at the corner of First and Main, to see whether the face of a person standing at 523 Main could be visible and identifiable from First and Main under the street lights.

1. **Discretion of judge:** In nearly all courts, it is within the trial judge's *discretion* whether to allow the jury to take a view (or, in a bench trial, whether to take a view himself). Some of the factors that the judge is likely to consider in reaching his decision are: (1) How important to the case is the information which would be gained from the view? (2) Can the information be gained instead from maps, photographs, diagrams, or other in-court evidence? and (3) Has the place or object to be viewed *changed its appearance* materially since the event? McC, p. 398.

2. **Presence of judge:** Must the judge be *present* at the view? The answer varies, depending mostly on whether the case is civil or criminal.

   a. **Civil:** In civil cases, the judge need normally *not* be present. Instead, "showers" are hired to chaperone the jurors to the site of the view. Counsel and the parties are usually allowed to attend, although the judge generally has discretion about this. McC, p. 398.

   b. **Criminal cases:** In criminal cases, by contrast, many states have statutes *requiring* the judge to be present at the view. This way, the jury will not be exposed to inadmissible hearsay during the view, and will not be permitted to carry out unauthorized experiments that might be unfair to the defendant.

  i.   Unauthorized view: In fact, if members of the jury take a view without the permission or presence of the trial judge in a criminal case, this will often be grounds for granting the defendant's motion for a new trial.

3.   **Defendant's right to be present:** Statutes usually provide that the criminal defendant has the right to be *present* at the view. Furthermore, the defendant's constitutional right of confrontation (see *supra*, p. 362) may well include the right to be present at a view (although this is less clear in states in which, as discussed *infra*, the view is deemed not to be evidence). McC, p. 398.

E.   Demonstrations and experiments: *Demonstrations* and *experiments* will generally be admissible, if the trial judge concludes that their relevance outweighs any prejudice, waste of time, confusion, etc., that might result.

1.   **Demonstrations:** The most frequent kind of demonstration in the courtroom is that in which an injured plaintiff *displays* the *body part* that has been injured. Courts nearly always permit a simple display of the injury, on the theory that its relevance is greater than any prejudice that might result.

  a.   Actions or manipulations: But if the injured plaintiff wants to go beyond a mere display of his injury, and wants to *perform actions* or undergo *manipulation* to show the practical impact of the injury, courts are more hesitant. See *supra*, p. 489.

  b.   Similarity of conditions: Courts insist that the demonstration be relevant, in the sense that the matters demonstrated are *similar* to the matter in issue.

2.   **Experiments:** A party will often want to make an *experiment* to determine whether an event is possible, or to determine the causes of a prior event. This experiment may take place either in court or out of court prior to trial.

  a.   In-court experiment: Where a party proposes an in-court experiment, the trial judge has the same broad discretion as in determining whether to allow a demonstration. The court will pay special attention to whether there is a sufficient *similarity of conditions* between the original event and the test. McC, p. 397. For instance, if P, who has been injured by a defective cigarette lighter, wants to use a copy of the same brand to show how a jet of flame can erupt, the trial judge will want to be sure that the lighter to be used in the experiment is indeed the same model, and has not been doctored.

  b.   Out-of-court experiment: In-court experiments have two big drawbacks from the proponent's point of view: (1) It is often very hard to assure similarity of conditions if the experiment must take place in the courtroom; and (2) Since there is no way to be sure how the experiment will turn out, the proponent risks embarrassment and damage to his case if the experiment does not go as planned. Therefore, most experiments are carried out *before the trial*, out of court. The evidence issue that arises is: May the results of the out-of-court experiment be communicated to the jury?

  i.   Generally admissible: Again, such experiments may be admissible as evidence "if their probative value is not substantially outweighed by the usual counterweights of prejudice, confusion of the issues, and time consumption." McC, p. 361. As with in-court experiments, similarity of conditions is especially important.

F. **Exhibits in the jury room:** When may the jury be given tangible exhibits to inspect *in the jury room*?

1. **Tangible evidence including writings:** In most states, the jury is *allowed* to take tangible exhibits (including writings) into the jury room, if the exhibit was admitted into evidence. Sometimes this is required by statute. If not required by statute, the trial judge usually has *discretion* about whether to allow it in a particular case. Lilly, p. 534.

2. **Substitute for testimony:** However, if the writing is in effect a *substitute for testimony*, the jury will usually *not* be allowed to inspect it in the jury room. This is the case, for instance, if the exhibit is a *deposition transcript* or a report that was admitted under the past recollection recorded doctrine (*supra*, p. 245). In this situation, there is a danger that if this "written testimony" is allowed in the jury room, the jury will give it more attention than it deserves, and more attention than live testimony. *Id.*

   a. **Confession:** In criminal cases, a transcript of the defendant's *confession* is usually allowed in the jury room, even though the confession is testimonial. McC, p. 399. Apparently, this exception is based on the theory that the confession is so central to the case that the risk of the jury's paying extra attention to it is worth running. *Id.*

Quiz Yourself on

REAL AND DEMONSTRATIVE EVIDENCE; WRITINGS *(Entire Chapter)*

106. Patrolman Pete testifies he stopped defendant, Shernott Home, and found a package of white powder on his person. He testifies that he turned the package over to the police lab. The prosecutor then seeks to introduce a package of cocaine into evidence, saying it's the package that was found on Home's person. The defense objects on the grounds that the package hasn't been authenticated. How should the judge rule? _____

107. In David's murder trial for the killing of Goliath, the prosecution seeks to enter the murder weapon, David's slingshot, into evidence. The prosecutor calls David's best friend, Sparky, to the stand, and asks if he recognizes the slingshot. Sparky responds, "Yup, that's David's, all right. It's got notches in the handle for every giant he's killed. I'd know it anywhere." Must the court now admit the slingshot into evidence? _____

108. Shortly after the *Titanic* sinks, surviving passengers sue its owners, the White Star line, for negligence. They seek to admit into evidence a letter bearing the signature of the ship's captain, Smith, which he appears to have written to his wife during the fateful trip. It reads: "Double my insurance, honey. If this baby's unsinkable, my name's Jones." The letter is written on paper bearing a "*Titanic*" letterhead and Smith's imprinted monogram. Will the letterhead and monogram alone authenticate the letter? _____

109. Howard Huge, eccentric billionaire, dies. In a will contest, Huge's maid testifies that she knows Huge's signature because she had often seen that signature on her weekly paychecks. She further testifies that the signature on the will in question is Huge's. Under the FRE, has the will been properly authenticated so as to permit its admission into evidence? _____

110. Jacques Coustodian, janitor for a Las Vegas restaurant, is cleaning the men's room one night when he finds, scrawled on the wall of one stall: "I, Howard Hughes, being of sound mind and body. . . ." followed by a disposition of Hughes' property, and a signature purporting to be Hughes'. At a trial determining the bathroom will's authenticity, Coustodian is called to the stand. He is given a paper containing a signature known to be Hughes' and asked if it matches the one he saw. He says it does. Assuming a non-witnessed will can be valid, has the bathroom will been authenticated? _____

111. A typewritten letter purportedly written by Michelangelo to Leonardo da Vinci is offered into evidence. The letter includes the sentence, "By the way, in answer to the question in your February 25 letter, I don't think La Giaconda would look good with a mustache. The mysterious smile is plenty. Can't wait to see the finished product." Leonardo was working on the painting in secret, and Michelangelo was one of the few to know about it. Could a jury determine the authenticity of the letter — i.e., that it was written by Michelangelo — on this statement alone? _____

112. Nosmo King once underwent hypnosis therapy in order to give up smoking. As a result, whenever he hears the word "cigarette," he barks like a dog. In a trial, Percy seeks to introduce into evidence his recollections of what he says was a telephone conversation between himself and Nosmo, in which Nosmo called him. The conversation allegedly included this snippet:

Percy: Excuse me while I light a cigarette.
Caller: Grr — Arf! Arf! Arf! Arf! Arf!

Percy says that the caller identified himself as Nosmo, but Percy also admits that he, Percy, had never before (or since) spoken to Nosmo, so he doesn't know for sure that the caller really *was* Nosmo. Can Percy's recollection and description of the caller's speech patterns be enough to authenticate the conversation as one involving Nosmo? _____

113. Georgy Porgy kisses the girls and makes them cry. At his subsequent trial on battery charges, Georgy's friend, Orgy, testifies that right before the incident, Georgy had sent him a letter (which Orgy says he still has), in which Georgy seemed intent to go on a kissing rampage. The letter itself is not introduced, even though it's available. Is Orgy's testimony admissible? _____

114. Pied Piper sues Mayor Hamelin for breach of contract. Piper claims he was never paid for his services in ridding Hamelin's property of rats. Hamelin testifies, "I paid the Piper $1,000 on April 1." On cross of Hamelin, Piper shows that before testifying, Hamelin consulted his check register to see whether it contained a record of such a payment (though Hamelin did not mention the register in his direct testimony). Must the register be produced, under the Best Evidence Rule? _____

115. The Pied Piper sues the Mayor of Hamelin for breach of contract. To prove the contract's terms, the Piper offers a photocopy of the contract into evidence, without explaining the whereabouts of the original. The Mayor objects, claiming the Best Evidence Rule requires that Piper produce the original contract. How do you rule, under the FRE? _____

116. The contents of a letter from Mata Hari to Banda are relevant in a trial in which Mata Hari is a party. Banda is not in the jurisdiction and has had no fixed address for a year, although the letter is believed by the litigants still to be in Banda's possession. Under the FRE, will oral testimony about the contents of the letter be admissible, notwithstanding the Best Evidence Rule? _____

117. Mike Angelo takes his statue of David to the Renny Sanz Art Gallery to be polished. The statue is destroyed through the Gallery's negligence. When Mike sues the Gallery, he calls an expert witness to determine the value of the statue. The witness, Vermi Celli, is a licensed art appraiser, and says so during his testimony. Will the Best Evidence Rule require that Vermi produce his license to prove his status? _____

118. Ophelia Butts has her appendix removed by Dr. Goren Guts. The next time she has an X-ray, she finds out that Dr. Guts accidentally left a pocket radio in her abdomen. In her malpractice suit, Butts doesn't produce the incriminating X-ray, but testifies that she saw the X-ray and that it had a clear outline of a pocket radio where her appendix used to be. Will her testimony be sufficient, or must she produce the X-ray? _____

119. In a close encounter of the third kind, a Martian lands in Tim O'Hara's back yard, destroying his vegetable patch. When Tim sues the Martian for damages, Tim offers a photograph taken after the landing, to show the extent of the damages. In order for the photograph to be admissible, must the photographer testify to the circumstances under which the photograph was taken? _____

120. In the trial for the murder of Jay Gatsby, the jury requests a view of the scene of the crime — Gatsby's swimming pool at his mansion in West Egg, Long Island. Must the judge grant the request? _____

121. Smog Monster is on trial for destroying downtown Tokyo. Godzilla is testifying for the prosecution. To aid his testimony, Godzilla uses a small, plaster model of the city, and squashes with his fist the replicas of the buildings Smog Monster destroyed in real life. Smog Monster's lawyer objects, claiming that the model requires authentication by the person who built it. Is he correct? (Assume that monsters from Japanese horror movies are competent to testify in the jurisdiction, and that American law applies.) _____

Answers

106. **Objection sustained**. Absent evidence about who possessed the package (and what they did to or with it) from the time it was turned over to the lab until its production at trial — what's called a **"chain of custody"** — the package hasn't been authenticated and isn't admissible. FRE 901(a). The reason is that without a chain of custody, we don't know that the package is the *same one* that was originally seized by Pete.

107. **Yes**. Once an item of physical evidence has been "authenticated," it's admissible if relevant. The requirement that each item of evidence be authenticated is satisfied by "evidence sufficient to support a finding that the item is what the proponent claims it is." FRE 901(a). Sparky's testimony here is certainly sufficient to support a finding that the item is indeed David's slingshot.

108. **No**. The rule accepted by most courts is that letterheads, monograms, and other self-identifying statements are **not** by themselves generally enough to establish that the person or business with whom they are associated is the author or owner of the object. This is generally true under both the common law and the FRE. FRE 902 does have specific exceptions for other kinds of self-authenticating documents, such as official publications, including pamphlets issued by a public authority and certified copies of public records (FRE 902(4)), newspaper and periodicals (902(6)), trade inscriptions and the like (e.g., tags or labels) (FRE 902(7)), and commercial paper (902(9)). (But affidavits are not self-authenticating.)

However, the circumstantial evidence surrounding the letter (e.g., that it was found in Smith's wife's papers, if it was), when added to the letterhead and monogram, probably *would* be enough to constitute authentication. See FRE 901(b)(4), giving as an example of authentication "The appearance, contents, substance, internal patterns, or other *distinctive characteristics* of the item, taken together with all the circumstances."

109. Yes. A non-expert can testify to the authenticity of handwriting as long as familiarity with the handwriting was not acquired for the purposes of the litigation. FRE 901(b)(2).

110. No, because Jacques has no personal knowledge of Hughes' signature. Only an expert, or the jury itself, can determine the authenticity of a signature by comparing writing samples. FRE 901(b)(3).

RELATED ISSUE: Had Jacques actually seen a document known to contain Hughes' signature somewhere prior to the litigation, he would have been competent to testify as to the bathroom signature's authenticity. FRE 901(b)(2).

111. Yes. Under the *"Reply doctrine,"* a letter's authorship can be authenticated on the grounds that it contains information that is *special knowledge known to the author and few others.* So here, it's highly unlikely that the letter was by one other than Michelangelo, because no one else (or almost no one else) would have known enough to make the reference to the subject's smile.

112. Yes. It's true that when a witness testifies to a call that he received, the caller's self-identification is not sufficient authentication, because of the dangers of impersonation by the caller and fabrication by the witness.

However, under FRE 901(b)(4), *a person may be identified by any distinctive characteristics that provide a clue to identity* — be it a manner of speech, a distinctive expression, unique information, or the like. Here, the caller's barking, together with his self-identification as Nosmo, would be sufficient to constitute authentication.

113. No. Orgy's testimony attempts to reveal the contents of the letter. (He's not just testifying that he received a letter from Georgy, he's testifying about what the letter said.) Therefore, *the Best Evidence Rule applies*, so that the letter itself, rather than merely Orgy's testimony about what it says, must be introduced. FRE 1002.

RATIONALE: Orgy's testimony is a recollection/interpretation of Georgy's actual words. Therefore, it's likely to be a less accurate source than the letter itself would be.

114. Yes, if Hamelin is testifying essentially *on the basis of what he learned from the register*. In that event, the writing will have to be produced, because Hamelin is only reciting what the writing says. Thus the register, and not Hamelin, is the basis of the evidence and the jury is entitled to it. This is true even though Hamelin didn't explicitly mention the register in his direct testimony.

RELATED ISSUE: Suppose Hamelin was testifying as to his *direct recollection* of the transaction (done without consulting any writing prior to testifying), but it also happened that the transaction was originally recorded in the check register. Now, Hamelin's testimony would *not* violate the Best Evidence Rule, because he would be testifying from first-hand knowledge, not from what he learned from a document. (Of course, there can be close questions, as where the witness is testifying from his own memory, but he confirmed that memory by checking the written document before testifying. In that situation, the B.E.R. *doesn't* apply — it applies only where the witness is essentially *reciting what the document says*.)

NOTE: Where the B.E.R. applies on the issue of whether a check was written, the Rule probably does not require that the *canceled check* be offered into evidence — the check register probably suffices. However, if the check register is introduced instead of the canceled check, the register may be viewed with distrust by the jury.

115. Objection overruled. Under FRE 1001(e), a photocopy of a document is called a *"duplicate"* of that document. Under FRE 1003, the ***duplicate is admissible to the same extent as the original***, unless there's a "genuine question" about the authenticity of the original or it would be "unfair" to admit the duplicate. Since what's being offered here is a photocopy, and there's no question (so far as the facts tell us) about the authenticity of the original contract, and there's no reason to believe use of the photocopy would be "unfair," the copy should be admitted notwithstanding the B.E.R.

By the way, only ***highly-accurate mechanical/electronic reproductions*** of the original can be "duplicates," under 1001(e). In addition to photocopies, examples would include carbon copies, microfilm, copies of sound recordings, and other techniques not involving human interpretation. Inexact types of copies (e.g., handwritten transcriptions) are ***not*** "duplicates," and thus are not admissible unless it is shown that the original is unavailable and its unavailability is not due to serious misconduct of the proponent.

116. **Yes**. Because the original ***can't be subpoenaed***, it's deemed to be "unavailable." FRE 1004(b). Thus, secondary evidence, like notes, copies, and oral testimony, will be admissible to determine the letter's contents.

RELATED ISSUE: The same rule applies if the original is lost or destroyed (through no bad faith of the proponent), or it's in the possession of an opponent who refuses to produce it in court, or the fact sought to be proved by the writing isn't material. FRE 1004(a), (c) and (d).

RELATED ISSUE: The same rule applies if the writing is in the possession of a person in the jurisdiction who has a legal right to withhold it (e.g., because it's ***privileged***).

117. **No**. Because Verni's license relates only to a ***collateral matter***, the Best Evidence Rule does not apply. Under FRE 1004(d), an original is not required where a writing, recording, or photograph is not closely related to a "controlling issue." McC §234.

118. **Since Ophelia is testifying from knowledge she gleaned from the X-ray and the X-ray is available, it will have to be produced**. X-rays are treated the same as writings and photographs for purposes of the Best Evidence Rule. FRE 1002.

119. **No** — this is not necessary, according to the majority rule. As long as *some* witness testifies, based on personal knowledge, that the photograph accurately and correctly represents the facts contained therein, the photograph will be admissible. Testimony by the *photographer* is not necessary; nor is testimony about the circumstances under which the photograph was taken.

120. **No**. The court has broad discretion in granting jury views. Views will be allowed only where counsel and all parties can be present, with strict safeguards so that the jury is not exposed to too much extraneous information. Also, the court will generally try to ensure that the conditions (e.g., time of day) are as nearly as possible identical to those that obtained when the crime was committed.

121. **No**. A witness may use models, photos, and maps to illustrate his testimony as long as he testifies from personal knowledge that the exhibit ***fairly represents what it is designed to represent***. Thus, there's no need for separate testimony from the photographer, model-builder, etc.

NOTE: The judge has discretion to *exclude* demonstrative evidence if he believes it will likely be misleading or useless.

Exam Tips on
REAL AND DEMONSTRATIVE EVIDENCE; WRITINGS

Whenever a piece of evidence (a tangible "thing" as opposed to the testimony of a witness) is offered into evidence, here's what to look for:

Authentication

Confirm that the item has been properly *authenticated*.

☛ Look for *self-authenticating documents* — these don't need any sponsoring witness. *Examples:*

 ☞ *Trade inscriptions* that seem to indicate origin, ownership or control. (*Example:* Product liability action, claiming that there was glass in a can of corn eaten by P. P offers the can, which bears the label "David Foods, Inc." P will have to show that the can is the one he ate from, but he won't have to show that the can was made by David Foods — the label is self-authenticating, to show that it was affixed by David Foods [though David Foods is allowed to rebut this showing.])

 ☞ *Certified copies* of *public records*. (*Example:* In suit against insurance company, P's estate can offer a certified copy of P's death certificate to show P is dead, without having to put on a sponsoring witness who testifies, "This is a copy of P's death certificate, which I know to have been copied from the county's files.")

  ☞ But most types of documents are *not* self-authenticating under the FRE. (*Example:* Personal or business *letterhead* is not self-authenticating, so a litigant can't simply introduce, unsponsored, a letter on letterhead for the purpose of establishing that the letter was written by the person or business whose letterhead it is.)

☛ If the item does not fall into one of the (comparatively few) categories of self-authenticating items, make sure there is a *sponsoring witness*, who testifies that the item is what its proponent claims it to be. Make sure that the sponsoring witness's testimony falls into one of the two following categories:

 ☞ Either the sponsoring witness has *personal knowledge* that the item is what the witness claims it is (e.g., "This is the knife that D used when he stabbed me — I recognize the distinctive carved pearl handle") or

 ☞ The sponsoring witness(es) testifies as to the *chain of custody* for the object. (*Example:* Officer testifies, "I seized the plastic bag with white stuff in it from D's pocket; I turned it over to the inventory clerk at the police evidence lab." Clerk testifies, "I marked the bag, then gave it to Lab Technician," and so forth.)

☛ Common issue: identification of *handwriting* on a document. Most common sub-issue: can a *nonexpert* make the identification? Remember the rule (FRE 901(b)(2)): nonexpert opinion on the genuineness of handwriting may be given if based upon "familiarity with it *not acquired for the current litigation.*" (*Example:* Contract suit. D denies signing the contract.

P calls W, who testifies that W and D were partners for years, during which time W got to know D's signature, and that the signature on the disputed contract appears to be D's. Admissible even though W is not a handwriting expert, because W acquired familiarity with D's handwriting or signature through means other than preparing for litigation.)

☞ Conversely, if W acquired her familiarity with the writing in preparation for the litigation (e.g., by comparing known samples of X's writing with the disputed samples), W must be a handwriting expert.

☞ Also, remember two other methods of authenticating handwriting: an *admission* by the writing, and a *comparison performed by the jury* between the disputed sample and a known sample.

☞ Remember the special rule for *wills*: Under FRE 903, no attesting witness needs to testify, unless local state law so requires. But some states still require at least one attesting witness to testify to the will's execution.

☞ When the item is a *photograph* or *film*:

☞ There's no requirement that a chain of custody be proven, only that a witness testify that the photo is a fair and accurate representation of what it purports to illustrate.

☞ *Trap:* A question mentions that a photo or videotape was *mislaid* for a period of time, or that *possession was transferred* from person to person (with no clear chain of custody proven). None of this matters.

☞ The *photographer doesn't have to testify*. (*Somebody* has to testify that the photo is a fair representation of what it purports to represent, but that somebody doesn't have to be the photographer.)

☞ The photograph *doesn't* have to be an *exact depiction* of the entire scene as it was. It just has to fairly and accurately represent the thing(s) in issue. (*Example:* In a car-crash suit, a photo is offered to show the streets and traffic-flow where the accident took place. The fact that the landscaping on the sidewalk is different in the photo than it was at the time of the accident is irrelevant, because this isn't in issue; therefore, the photo can come in.)

☞ A physical *drawing, chart* or *illustration* of a witness's testimony is admissible, if the witness testifies from personal knowledge that the drawing is a fair representation of what it purports to illustrate. (*Example:* W is asked about previous business dealings between two parties. He offers into evidence a chart he prepared after refreshing his recollection by looking at company files. He states that the chart reflects his personal knowledge. The chart will be admissible if the judge thinks it would help the jury and not be misleading. This is true even if the chart contains statements not explicitly made orally by W.)

☞ Where what's being offered is a *computer print-out*, the authentication must be by evidence: (1) *"describing a process or system"* used to produce the result, plus (2) evidence showing that it "produces an *accurate result*." FRE 901(9). (*Example:* If a computer print-out of account balances is offered by P to show that D owes P money, P must first: (1) describe how customer-balance information gets entered into the system; and (2) show that the system for data entry, and the computer program that manipulates the data, are accurate.)

☞ Where what's at issue is the *parties to a telephone conversation*, authentication is vital and often tricky. Distinguish between outgoing and incoming calls:

☞ For *outgoing calls* (calls made *by* the witness), authentication usually requires a showing that: (1) W made a call to the *number assigned by the phone company* to a particular person, *and* (2) the *circumstances* show that the person who talked *was in fact* the person the caller was trying to reach. FRE 901(b)(6).

☞ For requirement (2), the most common "circumstances" are:

❏ *Self-identification* by the person on the other end. (*Example:* P wants to testify that he called D, and that D said something. P can do this by showing that: (1) he called the number listed in the phone book for D; and (2) when someone answered, P asked, "Who's this?" and the person answered, "It's D.") *or*

❏ *Voice identification* by the witness/caller. (*Example:* In above Example, P could say, "I dialed D's number, and I recognized D's voice from prior conversations with him.")

☞ For *incoming calls* (calls made *to* the witness), there must be a showing that the caller *was in fact* the one who she seemed to be. Most common ways to do this:

❏ W testifies that he recognized the voice of the caller from having spoken to her previously; *or*

❏ The caller is shown to have had knowledge that only the caller had. (*Example:* P wants to show that the person who left a message on P's answering machine was D. If P testifies that the caller said, "I accept your offer to sell your house for $225,000," and P also testifies that the only person who knew that P wanted to sell at this price was D, the required authentication is made.)

Trap: To prove that the caller was X, it's *not enough* for W to testify that the caller said he was X — there must be *some additional evidence* that the caller really *was* X (e.g., that W recognized the voice, that the caller had special knowledge, etc.).

Best Evidence Rule

The Best Evidence Rule (B.E.R.) requires that the *original writing* must (if available) be produced when, and only when, the contents of a *writing* (or other document) are being proved.

☞ So the "best evidence" is *not* required when *something other than a writing's contents* is being proven. In other words, there's no general rule requiring that every fact be proven by the "best evidence" of that fact.

Example: The authenticity of D's signature on a letter is at issue. P's witness, W, testifies, "I knew D's signature 10 years ago, and this letter contains D's signature." D can't object that testimony by someone who's seen D's signature more recently is the "best evidence" of that signature's validity and must be offered instead.

☞ Common situation: a writing has a *legally operative effect.* Here, the B.E.R. is very likely to apply. *Examples:*

❑ Suit against insurer. D wants to show that it sent a notice of cancellation to P. D's testimony, "I sent a notice of cancellation" won't suffice; the notice must be produced if available.

❑ Prosecution of movie company for obscenity. Testimony about what the film shows won't suffice; the film itself must be produced. (Under the FRE, films and photos are covered by the B.E.R.)

❑ Libel suit. The allegedly libelous document must be produced; testimony about what the document said won't suffice.

☛ Look for situations where W's testimony *relies* almost entirely on *what a document says*. (Distinguish these situations — covered by the B.E.R. — from those in which W relies in significant part on W's own personal knowledge — not covered.)

Example: V's cause of death is at issue. W testifies, "I found a suicide note at the scene, in which V said, 'I have nothing more to live for.' " The note must be introduced if available, because W's testimony is addressed to the issue of what the note said.

Example: Whether D has a police record is at issue. W can't testify, "I consulted our records, and saw that D was arrested and convicted for shoplifting," unless the records are also introduced.

☛ *Very common trap:* The B.E.R. *isn't* triggered merely because a writing *happens to contain the same info* as that being proven. If W *independently* has the same personal knowledge of a fact as is reflected in a document, W's testimony can be used instead of the document. (*Example:* The issue is what costs P sustained in performing a contract. P may testify based on his own memory of those costs — even if the memory was "refreshed" by consulting business records. The fact that the records contain the same cost figures doesn't mean that the records must be introduced, because P is testifying to his own knowledge of the costs themselves, and the fact that those same costs are recorded somewhere is coincidental.)

☛ Remember that under the FRE, the B.E.R. applies not only to writings, but also to *photographs* and *recordings (video and audio)*. FRE 1002.

☞ *Common scenario:* X-rays. (But be careful: B.E.R. applies only where the *contents* of the X-ray are really what's being proved, not some independently-known medical condition that happens to be shown on the X-ray. *Example:* Issue is whether P had a fractured arm. If W says, "I took an X-ray, and it showed a fracture," the B.E.R. applies and the X-ray must be introduced. But if W says, "Based on a physical examination and the results of my reading of an X-ray, I concluded that P had a fracture," probably the B.E.R. doesn't apply.)

☛ Always check whether the *collateral writings exception* to the B.E.R. applies: If W's testimony relates to a minor issue in the case, then even if W is testifying about what a writing said, the B.E.R. *doesn't* apply. (*Example:* W is asked how he remembers the date of a meeting. He says, "I remember it was May 3rd, because the day of the meeting the newspaper announced my daughter's engagement, and I know that story ran on May 3rd." Even though W is testifying as to the contents of a writing (the newspaper story), the B.E.R. won't apply, because the issue is collateral: it relates only to W's credibility as to the date. Thus the article doesn't have to be introduced.)

☞   When the contents of a writing are being used for ***impeaching a witness's credibility***, it's usually collateral (and thus need not be produced under the B.E.R.). (*Example:* W testifies on behalf of D in a criminal assault case. The prosecution, to attack W's credibility, asks W, "Didn't you once file a false insurance claim?" Even though this question is an attempt to prove the contents of a document, the B.E.R. doesn't apply [and the claim form doesn't have to be produced by the prosecution] because the only issue to which the question relates is W's truthfulness, a collateral issue. [In fact, the claim form can't be introduced even if the prosecutor wants to, because of the rule barring "extrinsic evidence" on a collateral matter.])

☛ Remember that the B.E.R. only applies where the original is ***available*** (or its unavailability is due to the proponent's ***bad faith***). In many exam q's, you're told that the original is lost or destroyed without fault, so you automatically avoid a B.E.R. problem (though you should mention the B.E.R. issue anyway, if it's an essay question). Common scenario: the original is ***burned*** in a fire that's not the proponent's fault.

☛ If the B.E.R. *does* apply, remember that it's normally satisfied by the introduction of either the original or a true ***"duplicate"*** of the writing. FRE 1003. For instance, a ***photocopy*** is admissible, unless there's a "genuine question" about the original's authenticity, or admitting the copy would be unfair.

CHAPTER 10

OPINIONS, EXPERTS, AND SCIENTIFIC EVIDENCE

ChapterScope

This chapter discusses the rules regarding opinion testimony by both non-experts and experts. It also discusses the use of scientific evidence. Here are the key concepts:

■ **Lay opinions:** Ordinarily, *non-experts* may *not* testify to their *opinions*. However, a statement of opinion by a non-expert is admissible if:

(a) the opinion is rationally based on the *perception* of the witness; and

(b) the opinion will be helpful to a clear understanding of the witness's *testimony* or the determination of a *fact in issue*;

■ **Expert opinions:** "Expert testimony" is admissible if the testimony:

(a) involves *specialized knowledge* (e.g., scientific or technical knowledge);

(b) would help the trier of fact to *understand the evidence* or to determine a *fact in issue*;

(c) is based on *sufficient facts or data*; and

(d) is the product of *reliable principles and methods* that have been *reliably applied to the facts* of the case.

❏ **Source of expertise:** The expert must be *"qualified,"* but the qualifications may come from *either* *experience* or *formalized training*.

❏ **Basis for opinion:** The expert's opinion may be based on any of several types of underlying facts or data, including: (1) the expert's *first-hand knowledge*; (2) facts *told to her outside the trial*; and (3) a *hypothetical* posed to her during the trial.

❏ **Facts reasonably relied on:** The facts or data relied on by the expert *need not consist of admissible evidence*, so long as they are of a *type reasonably relied on* by experts in the particular field. (*Example:* W may rely on what A told him about what B said to A — even though this is inadmissible hearsay — as long as experts in W's field would so rely.)

I. FIRST-HAND KNOWLEDGE AND LAY OPINIONS

A. Generally: Courts have a preference for the best available evidence on any given point. The hearsay rule and the Best Evidence rule are illustrations of this preference. Two other rules arising from the preference for the best available evidence are the rule requiring that a witness have first-hand knowledge of the facts about which he testifies, and the rule purporting to forbid ordinary witnesses from expressing their opinions.

B. First-hand knowledge required: An ordinary (non-expert) witness must limit his testimony to facts of which he has *first-hand knowledge.* That is, if the witness testifies about a fact that could have been perceived by the senses, the witness must have perceived it himself, not learned of it from someone else. McC, p. 16.

> **Example:** W, a passenger in P's car, testifies that D drove through a red light. On cross-examination, W admits that he didn't actually see what color the light was when D drove through, and that he is relying on what P told him shortly after the two cars collided. Since W is not testifying from personal knowledge about the color of the light, his testimony on that subject will be stricken.

1. **Distinguished from hearsay:**   An objection to testimony on the grounds that it is not based on the witness's personal knowledge can sometimes be confused with an objection based on *hearsay.* The distinction is this: if the witness's statement on its face makes it clear that the witness is merely repeating what someone else said, the objection is to hearsay; if the witness purports to be stating matters which he personally observed, but he is actually repeating statements by others, the objection is to lack of first-hand knowledge. McC, p. 17. See *supra,* p. 204, for a more complete discussion of the distinction.

2. **Experts:**   *Experts* are generally not limited to testifying about facts of which they have personal knowledge. For instance, an expert will often be asked to give an opinion based upon hypothetical facts listed by the questioner, in which case the expert may state what inference he would make, even though he has no first-hand knowledge of the facts used in the hypothetical. (See *infra,* p. 527.)

3. **Federal Rules:**   The federal courts, like all state courts, prohibit lay witnesses from testifying on matters as to which they lack personal knowledge. FRE 602 provides:

> "A witness may testify to a matter only if evidence is introduced sufficient to support a finding that the witness has *personal knowledge* of the matter. Evidence to prove personal knowledge may consist of the witness's own testimony. This rule does not apply to a witness's *expert testimony* under Rule 703."

C. Lay opinions: It is often said that the witness must confine herself to reciting the "facts," and that she may not state her *"opinions"* or *"conclusions."* However, in contrast to the rule just described above requiring first-hand knowledge, the rule barring opinions has never really been strictly applied, and is today often largely abandoned.

1. **Traditional formulation:**   Traditionally, the courts have stated the rule against opinion testimony as if it were a black-letter prohibition to be strictly enforced: the witness must confine himself to stating the "facts," and may not state his opinions, conclusions, or inferences relating to those facts.

> **Example:** W, a bystander, testifies that when D hit P (a pedestrian) with his car, D was driving "very carelessly." Many courts traditionally (and some today) would strike this testimony, on the grounds that W was giving his opinion about D's conduct, rather than confining himself to stating the "facts."

2. **Rationale:**   The rationale behind the rule barring opinion testimony is that the process of *making inferences* from the underlying facts properly belongs to the *trier of fact*, not to the witness. Thus in our above example, W should confine himself to stating how fast D

was driving, what side of the street he was on, whether he stopped for the traffic light, etc. It is the jury, not W, who should then infer from these basic facts whether D was indeed "careless."

    a. Preference for specificity: To put it another way, the rule barring opinions and conclusions is really a rule preferring the ***most specific available evidence.*** Again using our above example, if W testifies merely that D drove "carelessly," the jury is being deprived of the most specific possible information about D's conduct (e.g., whether he ran a stop light, how fast he was going, etc.). Since W has knowledge of these more specific aspects, he should limit his testimony to these specifics.

3. Exception for "short-hand renditions": Courts have always recognized an exception to the rule against opinions where the "opinion" is really a ***"short-hand rendition."*** That is, if the witness has perceived a number of small facts that cannot each be easily stated, he will be permitted to summarize the collective facts with a "short-hand" formulation. McC, p. 18.

    Example: D is on trial for murder, and raises an insanity defense. W, his mother, testifies that he was "in such a terrible shape," and was "mentally and physically ill." The trial judge strikes these remarks as opinions.

    Held, W's statements should have been admitted. W was not capable of describing D's condition in facts more specific than this, and the jury understood what W meant. *State v. Garver,* 225 P.2d 771 (Ore. 1950).

    a. Other examples: Here are some other situations in which W will often be allowed to speak in a somewhat conclusory, short-hand manner: (1) The car "passed at high speed"; (2) X "looked like he was no more than thirty years old"; and (possibly) (3) "Z looked like he was drunk." In each of these situations, it is somewhat hard for W to articulate the precise underlying facts that have led him to the conclusion (though in the case of (3), W might have been able to say that Z wasn't able to walk straight, had slurred speech, smelled of liquor, etc.). Lilly, p. 108. In general, trial judges have a wide degree of ***discretion*** in determining when to allow in a witness's conclusion or opinion under the "short-hand rendition" exception.

4. Criticism of general rule: More generally, many courts and commentators have criticized the entire attempt to distinguish between opinions and facts and to allow only the latter. These critics argue that even what appears to be a statement of facts always contains some inference or conclusion. What is important, these critics say, is that the jury be given as many of the underlying facts as is feasible; the fact that the witness also includes his opinion or inference is rarely damaging.

5. Modern view: Reflecting these criticisms, modern courts are generally much more willing to allow witnesses to state their opinions than the traditional no-opinions rule would imply. Many, if not most, take the view that "opinions of laymen should be rejected only when they are superfluous in the sense that they will be of no value to the jury." McC, p. 18.

6. Federal Rules: The Federal Rules embody this liberal modern view. FRE 701 provides as follows:

> **"Rule 701. Opinion Testimony by Lay Witnesses**
>
> If a witness is not testifying as an expert, testimony in the form of an opinion is *limited* to one that is:
>
> **(a)** *rationally based* on the *witness's perception*;
>
> **(b)** *helpful* to clearly *understanding the witness's testimony* or to *determining a fact in issue*; and
>
> **(c)** *not based on scientific, technical, or other specialized knowledge* within the scope of Rule 702 [covering expert testimony]."

    a. Perception of witness: Thus FRE 701(a) merely codifies the universal requirement (see *supra*, p. 516) that the witness have first-hand knowledge of the matter.

    b. Helpful: FRE 701(b) allows much more liberal introduction of a witness's opinions than the traditional common-law formulation does. Even if the witness's testimony is quite clearly an opinion, the judge should *allow* it in if it will be *helpful to the jury* in its fact-finding.

7. Specifics still preferable: Under the modern and federal approach, as under the traditional common-law rule, *specific testimony* is still preferable. If the matter is an important one, and the judge feels that the witness could be more specific than he is being, he will often require the greater specificity. For instance, in a negligence action, if W testifies, "D was going very, very fast," the judge might well ask W to estimate more precisely the speed of the vehicle.

    a. Cross-examination: Furthermore, even if the witness's opinion or conclusory statement is allowed on direct testimony, the adversary always has the right, during *cross-examination*, to ferret out the specifics. Thus if W is allowed to testify on direct that "D seemed intoxicated," D's lawyer can ask on cross questions like, "Did you smell liquor on his breath?," "Did he enunciate his words clearly?" etc.

8. Expert opinions: The rule against opinions, even in its straight common-law version, applies only to *lay* opinions, not to the opinions of experts. Indeed, the principal function of expert testimony is to draw inferences and state opinions from the facts. The nature of expert testimony is discussed extensively *infra*, p. 520.

    a. No expert testimony in lay clothing: The FRE try to keep lay opinions and expert opinions separate from each other. FRE 701(c) says that opinion testimony by lay witnesses is limited to those opinions that are "not based on scientific, technical, or other specialized knowledge within the scope of Rule 702." This rule is an attempt to ensure that expert testimony that cannot meet the tough standards of FRE 702 (see *infra*, pp. 520-522) *does not come in the back door* via the ordinary-opinion provisions of Rule 701.

    Example: Suppose that at D's trial for drug trafficking, W, an investigator with the Drug Enforcement Agency, offers to testify that when D used certain words in conversations, he was using code words to refer to drug quantities and prices. The prosecutor knows that the court will probably not treat this testimony as meeting the tough requirements of FRE 702 for expert testimony, due to W's lack of detailed knowledge about how drug dealers do their communications. Therefore, the prosecutor instead characterizes W's testimony as being opinion testimony by a lay (non-expert) occurrence witness. If the court believes (as it probably will) that W's testimony is based upon "specialized knowledge" and properly falls under the expert-testimony rules, it must not allow the evidence in as Rule 701 lay testimony. Cf. *U.S. v. Figueroa-Lopez*, 125 F.3d 1241 (9th Cir. 1997).

D. Opinion on "ultimate issue": In any case, some issues are more important than others. Some are *"ultimate issues,"* in the sense that the trier's decision on these issues necessarily decides the outcome of the case. For instance, in a prosecution for speeding, the rate of speed of the vehicle is an "ultimate issue."

1. **Rule barring opinions on ultimate issues:** Even those courts that generally allow witnesses to state their opinions may impose a rule barring "opinions on ultimate issues." Courts adhering to this view often apply it not only to lay testimony, but to expert testimony as well. This prohibition is justified on the theory that if a witness is permitted to express his opinion on an ultimate fact in issue, this "usurps the function of the jury." McC, p. 19.

2. **Modern view:** But most courts today have *abandoned* the rule barring opinion testimony on ultimate issues. *Id.*

   a. **Federal:** The federal courts have done so as well. FRE 704(a) provides that "An opinion is *not objectionable* just because it *embraces an ultimate issue*."[1] Under this rule, both lay witnesses and experts may give their opinions or inferences on ultimate issues (provided that they satisfy the requirements of other Rules; for instance, if the witness is not an expert, his testimony must satisfy the three parts of FRE 701, *supra*, p. 517).

3. **Exceptions:** Even in courts following the modern and federal view allowing testimony on ultimate facts, some types of ultimate issues may *not* be the subject of opinions:

   a. **How case should be decided:** For instance, a witness will generally not be permitted to give an opinion that amounts to an assertion of *how the case should be decided*. Thus in a negligence action by P versus D, no witness (not even an expert on safety) should be permitted to testify that "D should be liable for damages," because the whole case is about whether D should indeed be found liable. McC, p. 19. Some courts might similarly prevent any witness from saying that "D was careless" in this situation.

   b. **Questions of law:** Witnesses will not be permitted to express their opinion as to *questions of law* (except foreign law). McC, p. 20. The reason is that in our system, the *trial judge* should be the sole source of instruction to the jury about what the law is.

      i. **Related facts:** But a law expert or law enforcement expert may help the jury understand *facts,* even if these facts are very closely related to a rule of law. For

---

1. But note that 704(b) then goes on to state a narrow exception: "In a *criminal case*, an expert witness must not state an opinion about whether the defendant did or did not have a *mental state or condition* that constitutes an *element of the crime* charged or of a *defense*. Those matters are for the *trier of fact alone*."

instance, in a criminal prosecution for an uncommon and complicated crime, experts will generally be permitted to explain to the jury the "*modus operandi*" of a particular crime — this is allowed on the theory that the expert is merely describing a factual pattern, not instructing the jury as to the legal definition of the crime.

    c. Legal criteria: Some courts prevent questions and answers that use a ***legal term*** or ***label*** that has not been defined for the jury. For instance, even under the liberal federal rules, a judge would not allow the question, "Did T have capacity to make a will?" since the phrase "capacity to make a will" is a legal rather than everyday term; instead, the questioner would have to ask, "Did T have sufficient mental capacity to know the nature and extent of his property and the natural objects of his bounty and to formulate a rational scheme of distribution?" or some similar formulation using non-legal terms. See Advisory Committee's Note to FRE 704.

II. EXPERT WITNESSES — GENERALLY

    A. Reasons for using experts: An expert witness is, in brief, one whose ***specialized knowledge*** will be helpful to the jury in deciding the case correctly. See FRE 702.

    1. Opinions: Most of the time, the way an expert witness helps the trier of fact is by furnishing an ***opinion*** about ***inferences that should be drawn*** from a set of complex facts that the trier would not otherwise be capable of interpreting easily and correctly. Often, the underlying facts are placed into evidence through witnesses other than the expert.

      Example: The prosecution wishes to prove that a bullet found in the body of V was fired from a gun recovered from D's apartment. Through the use of lay witnesses, the prosecution could introduce the bullet recovered from V's body, as well as a bullet fired on a test range from the gun in question. It could then present testimony by W, a ballistics expert, in which W points out to the jury the identical grooves and other firing marks made on the two bullets. W would then give his opinion that, from these identical marks, it can be inferred that the two bullets were fired from the same gun.

    a. Contrast to lay opinions: Recall that courts are generally not sympathetic to opinions by lay witnesses, on the theory that it should be up to the jury, not the witness, to make inferences from facts in evidence. But the rule regarding opinions by experts is exactly opposite: the main purpose of expert testimony is to have the expert draw an inference from facts that the jury is not capable of easily interpreting on its own. Thus, in our above example, the jury might be able to inspect the bullets and notice that the firing marks appear to be the same on the two bullets, but it would have no way of inferring from this similarity the likelihood that the two bullets were fired by the same gun.

    2. Statements of fact: While the giving of opinions and inferences is the main function of expert testimony, experts also frequently testify as to facts. Often, for instance, the expert will be called upon to state the ***general scientific principles*** of his specialty. For example, when, in the above example, W stated that no two guns produce exactly the same marks on bullets that they fire, he was stating a scientific fact, not an opinion (though when he went on to say that the markings on the two bullets were so nearly identical that they must have been fired from the same gun, he was giving what would probably be viewed as an opinion). Most of the difficulties with expert testimony — and the main focus of our discussion of experts here — concern the use of expert opinions.

B. When expert testimony allowed: The Federal Rule on expert testimony, Rule 702, was extensively revised in 2000. We'll concentrate on that Rule in our discussion of expert testimony.

Rule 702 imposes *five requirements* that expert testimony must meet in order to be admissible:

[1] The expert witness must have "scientific, technical, or other *specialized knowledge*" that will "*help the trier of fact to understand* the evidence or to determine a fact in issue";

[2] The witness must be *"qualified"* as an expert by virtue of "knowledge, skill, experience, training, or education";

[3] The testimony must be based upon *"sufficient facts or data"*;

[4] The testimony must be the product of *"reliable principles and methods"*; and

[5] The witness must have *applied* these principles and methods "*reliably* to the *facts of the case*.*"*

We'll discuss each of these requirements in the above order (though that's not quite the order in which they appear in FRE 702).

1. Specialized knowledge will be helpful: The first requirement of FRE 702 (given in 702(a)) is that it must be the case that "scientific, technical, or other *specialized knowledge*" will "*help the trier of fact to understand* the evidence or to determine a fact in issue." There are two basic ideas embedded in this single requirement:

❏ the expert's testimony must involve *"specialized knowledge"* (often but not always *"scientific"* or *"technical"* knowledge); and

❏ that specialized knowledge must be *helpful to the jury* on some aspect of the case.

a. Ordinary evidence: Courts are quickest to find the subject of expert testimony to be appropriate where it involves the interpretation of facts of a sort that lay persons are *not usually called upon to evaluate.* Thus testimony on such issues as whether two bullets were fired from the same gun, whether two fingerprints match or whether proper medical practice was followed, would all be appropriate subjects for expert testimony because a lay person is never called upon in real life to evaluate such evidence. By contrast, courts are much more reluctant to allow expert testimony (or scientific tests) to aid the jury in making the kinds of evaluations that juries, and lay people outside of a courtroom, customarily make. L&S, p. 167.

i. Eyewitness reliability: For instance, courts presume that lay jurors can intelligently evaluate the reliability of an *eyewitness identification* (e.g., "The man sitting at the defendant's table is the one who attacked me"). Therefore, judges will often refuse to allow an expert on human memory and perception to testify as to the frequent unreliability of such eyewitness identifications. This topic is discussed further *infra*, p. 545.

    ii. Credibility of witness: Similarly, most judges believe that lay jurors are capable of intelligently evaluating the ***truthfulness*** of witnesses, based on demeanor, content of testimony, etc. Therefore, judges will usually resist testimony by experts that purports to help the jury decide whether a particular witness is telling the truth. For instance, most courts have refused to allow the prosecution in rape cases to produce an expert to testify that V exhibits the symptoms of "rape trauma syndrome," and is thus probably telling the truth about whether the attack occurred. See *infra*, p. 546.

2. Qualifications: The second requirement of FRE 702, given in the Rule's first sentence, is that the witness be ***"qualified"*** as an expert by ***"knowledge, skill, experience, training, or education."*** In other words, the expert must have ***knowledge and/or skill in a particular area*** that distinguishes her from an ordinary person.

    a. Source of expertise: Notice that under this definition, the expertise may come from *either **education/training** or **experience***. Most experts derive their expertise from both of these factors, but ***either*** will suffice if it makes the witness more knowledgeable about a specialized field than a lay person would be.

    Example: D is charge with conspiracy to import marijuana. The prosecution offers testimony by W that the marijuana in question came from Colombia. W has no special training or education in identifying marijuana, but has smoked it over 1,000 times, has dealt in it 20 times, and has identified its origin on over 100 past occasions.

    Held (on appeal), the trial judge's decision treating W as an expert will not be overturned. FRE 702 provides that expertise may be obtained by experience as well as from formal training or education, and the prosecution showed that W had ample practical experience in marijuana identification. *U.S. v. Johnson*, 575 F.2d 1347 (5th Cir. 1978).

    b. Need for sub-specialist: Generally, a specialist in a particular field will be treated as an expert even though he is not a specialist in the particular ***sub-field*** or ***branch*** of that field. For instance, if a medical condition involves brain damage or kidney failure, a doctor would probably be found to be a *qualified expert even though he was a general practitioner* rather than a neurologist or nephrologist. See McC, pp. 21-22.

        i. Discretion of court: Keep in mind, however, that the ***trial judge*** has a great deal of ***discretion*** about whether to treat a witness as being an expert. Thus in a case involving intricate issues relating to the proper technique for open heart surgery, a court might well hold that a general practitioner M.D. who had never done an open heart operation did not have expertise that would be helpful to the jury. See L&S, p. 863.

3. Based upon *"sufficient facts or data"*: The third requirement is that the testimony be ***"based upon sufficient facts or data."*** (See 702(b).) This requirement, plus the two that follow, reflect an attempt by the Rule drafters to ***keep out unreliable testimony***, sometimes called "junk science."

    a. Meaning: The phrase "facts or data" seems to be designed to cover two types of things on which the expert might rely:

❑ First, the witness may be relying on the "*facts of the case*." Often, this reliance will occur by means of a *hypothetical question* based on the facts of the case, posed by the proponent's lawyer to the expert. The use of such hypothetical questions is discussed *infra*, p. 525.

❑ Second, the witness may be relying on the **reliable opinions of other experts**. See Advisory Comm. Note to 2000 Amendment to FRE 702.

Example: In a murder/rape case, Expert 1 testifies that in his opinion the procedures used to do a DNA test on semen found on the victim's body conformed with good practice for performing such tests. (Assume that the court accepts this testimony as being reliable.) Now, Expert 2 takes the stand. Expert 2 wants to testify that only one man in 200 million would have semen with the same DNA pattern as the test specimen, and that D's semen has that same pattern. Since Expert 1's opinion testimony was reliable, Expert 2 is justified in relying on that testimony — to establish that the DNA tests were properly performed — in forming her own opinion that the test shows that D is almost certainly the man who deposited the semen.

4. **Product of *"reliable principles and methods"*:** The fourth requirement in FRE 702 is that the testimony must be the *"product of reliable principles and methods."* (See 702(c).) In the case of "scientific" testimony, this requirement is essentially a requirement that the testimony be based on "good science."

   a. **Applies to non-scientific testimony:** But this requirement of reliable principles and methods applies not just to scientific testimony but to *other types of expert testimony based on technical knowledge.* For instance, the Advisory Committee Notes to the 2000 Amendments to Rule 702 give the following Example:

   Example: "When a law enforcement agent testifies regarding the use of code words in a drug transaction, the principle used by the agent is that participants in such transactions regularly use code words to conceal the nature of their activities. The method used by the agent is the application of extensive experience to analyze the meaning of conversations. So long as the principles and methods are reliable and applied reliably to the facts of the case, this type of testimony should be admitted." 2000 Adv. Comm. Notes to Rule 702, 11th Par.

5. **Reliable application to the facts of case:** Finally, Rule 702 requires that the expert *"reliably applied the principles and methods* [referred to in 702(c)] to the *facts of the case.*" (See 702(d).) This is just common sense: the most reliable of "principles" and "methods" won't lead to useful testimony unless the witness shows that she is applying those principles and methods to the actual facts of the case.

   Example: Same basic facts as above example. Suppose W, a DEA agent, testifies that drug dealers often speak in code words to defeat eavesdroppers, and that if a drug dealer uses the word "brick," the term usually refers to a kilo of marijuana. Unless there is some showing (either through W's own first-person testimony or otherwise) that D actually used the word "brick," W's testimony about what D meant should be rejected because the methodology W is describing does not "apply reliably to the facts of the case."

C. Role of trial judge: It is up to the *trial judge*, not the jury, to decide whether the proposed witness should be allowed to testify as an expert. That is, the trial judge decides whether the five requirements summarized above have been met.

1. **Discretion:** On all of these requirements, the trial judge has relatively *wide discretion* about whether to admit or exclude. Thus whichever way the trial judge decides, reversals on appeal are relatively rare. Lilly, p. 485.

D. Factual basis for expert's opinion: Occasionally, the expert is called upon merely to state general scientific or technical principles, leaving it to the jury to decide how to apply these principles to the facts the jury has heard. Generally, however, the expert testifies concerning the facts of the case, either by stating some fact himself (e.g., the pathologist who did an autopsy of V testifies, "I found a puncture wound through the carotid artery") or by stating an inference about facts that have come from some other source (e.g., "Based on the facts you have stated in your hypothetical, counselor, I would say that the cause of death was. . . .") There are a number of a different ways in which an expert can learn about the facts of the present controversy, each of which we will consider in turn.

1. **Personal knowledge:** The simplest situation occurs when the expert has *first-hand knowledge* of the facts. Where this happens, he may testify to his observations just as any non-expert would, and he may then go on to give his inferences from those facts. McC, p. 22.

   Example: A police ballistics officer might testify that he personally fired a gun found in D's apartment, retrieved the bullet, and noticed a high degree of similarity between the markings on that bullet and the markings on a bullet found in V's body. He could then go on to state that based on the high level of similarity, and based upon his knowledge of ballistics, he believes that it is overwhelmingly probable that both bullets were fired from the same gun.

2. **Observation of prior evidence:** The expert may gain information about the case by *listening to other witnesses* who testify before he does.

   a. **Use with hypothetical:** The expert cannot say that he "knows" a certain fact merely because a prior witness has testified to it. Instead, the way the prior testimony enters into the expert's testimony is by use of a *hypothetical question*: the questioner asks the expert to assume that the prior testimony is true, and then to give an inference or opinion.

   b. **Difficulties:** Courts freely accept expert opinions based on testimony by prior witnesses, where the prior testimony is *clear* and the prior witnesses agree with each other. But if the prior witnesses disagree, or give ambiguous testimony, the court will be less quick to allow the expert to give an opinion based on this prior testimony. At the least, the court will require the expert to state exactly which testimony, and which facts, he is assuming to be true.

      i. **Prior testimony is itself an opinion:** Also, if the prior testimony *is itself an opinion*, the court may refuse to allow the expert to rely on it, on the theory that "opinions based on opinions" should be excluded. (But under FRE 703, an expert may rely on any facts or data "[i]f experts in the particular field would reasonably rely on those kinds of facts or data in forming an opinion on the subject[.]" So if an expert might reasonably rely on another person's opinion in forming a conclusion, the expert's reliance on the prior opinion should be allowable under FRE 703.)

3. **Hypothetical questions:** A third source of information for the expert is the *hypothetical question* itself. That is, even if the expert knows virtually nothing about the facts of the particular case, he may be given factual assumptions in the form of a hypothetical question, and may then express his opinion about the conclusion to be drawn from these assumed facts. Hypothetical questions are discussed extensively *infra*, p. 527.

4. **Otherwise inadmissible evidence:** Each of the three sources of information listed above (personal knowledge, observation of prior evidence, and presentation of assumed facts through a hypothetical) typically consists of admissible evidence. But what if the expert's opinion is based upon "facts" that could *not* otherwise be *admitted* into evidence?

   a. **Traditional rule:** Traditionally, many courts have *refused* to allow an expert to give an opinion that is based in part upon "facts" that are not supported by admissible evidence. Indeed, some courts have gone so far as to say that each fact relied on by the expert must be supported by *evidence actually admitted* at the trial, not just theoretically admissible; these courts would, for instance, prevent a doctor from expressing a medical opinion based upon a presumably accurate hospital record that was not formally introduced at the trial, even though the record could have been introduced as a business record (*supra*, p. 256). Lilly, p. 487.

   b. **Modern and federal trend:** But the modern trend, as exemplified by the Federal Rules, *removes* entirely the requirement that the expert's opinion be based solely upon admissible evidence. Thus FRE 703 states:

   > "An expert may base an opinion on facts or data in the case that the expert has been made aware of or personally observed. If *experts in the particular field* would *reasonably rely on those kinds of facts or data* in forming an opinion on the subject, *they need not be admissible for the opinion to be admitted.*"

   i. **Hearsay:** Thus FRE 703 means that an expert may base an opinion upon clearly inadmissible *hearsay*, if the type of hearsay is one that would be reasonably relied upon by experts in that situation.

   Example: While D is traveling from Jamaica to Bermuda, she stops over in Miami, where customs officials search her luggage and find cocaine base concealed in her luggage carts. At D's trial for drug crimes, she asserts she was an innocent dupe who had no knowledge of the cocaine. The prosecution rebuts this defense by putting on the stand W, a DEA agent, who offers expert testimony that the cocaine base would have been worth $217,000 in Bermuda, and that an innocent dupe such as D claimed to be would never have been entrusted with drugs of such high value. W concedes that his opinion that the cocaine was worth $217,000 in Bermuda was based upon being told that figure by another DEA agent, who had in turn been told it by the Bermudan police. D objects to the evidence, on the grounds that it is based upon inadmissible hearsay statements made to W by out-of-court declarants.

Held, for the prosecution. It is true that W's opinion about the value of the drugs was based upon otherwise-inadmissible hearsay. But where the expert witness testifies that a particular source of information — in this case, statements by other law-enforcement officials regarding their area of expertise — is regularly relied upon by experts like the witness, the fact that the source constitutes otherwise-inadmissible hearsay is irrelevant. *U.S. v. Brown*, 299 F.3d 1252 (11th Cir. 1999).

ii. **Not reasonably relied on:** Conversely, if a reasonable expert would *not* reasonably rely on a fact or data, that fact or data may not be relied upon by the expert in giving his opinion, if the fact or data is not admissible.

Example: The Advisory Committee's Note to FRE 703 asserts that an "accidentologist" could not give an opinion about the point of impact in an automobile collision based on the statements of bystanders, since the "reasonably relied upon by experts in the particular field" requirement is not satisfied. (The Note does not state how the Advisory Committee knew this.)

c. **Disclosure to jury:** In courts, such as the federal courts, that allow an expert to base his opinion upon otherwise-inadmissible facts or data, may these underlying facts or data be *revealed* to the jury? FRE 703 was amended in 2000 to answer this question. A new sentence was added, which now reads: "[I]f the facts or data *would otherwise be inadmissible*, the *proponent* of the opinion *may disclose* them to the jury *only* if their *probative value* in helping the jury evaluate the opinion *substantially outweighs their prejudicial effect.*"

Example: Dan is on trial for murdering Vic, a death that occurred by stabbing. There are no eyewitnesses. The prosecution puts on the stand Wit, a pathologist, who offers to testify that in his opinion, the murderer was likely to be a left-handed person more than 6 feet tall. In point of fact, Wit's opinion is based not only upon the nature of the stab wounds on Vic's corpse, but also upon the fact that, as Wit was told, Vic phoned Wanda (Vic's wife) before dying, and said, "This tall left-handed guy just attacked me, but I think I'm gonna be ok." Dan is a tall left-hander.

Vic's out-of-court declaration is not admissible, because it's hearsay not within any exception. (It doesn't qualify for the dying declaration exception to the hearsay rule because Vic didn't think he was dying; see *supra*, p. 290.) Therefore, before the prosecution can have Wit tell the jury the text of the statement by Vic on which he relied, the prosecution will have to convince the trial judge that the probative value of this statement in enabling the jury to evaluate Wit's testimony outweighs any prejudicial effect. Probably the judge will not so conclude, in which case the statement will not be revealed to the jury. (But Vic's general testimony — stab wounds were probably caused by a tall left-hander — would still be admissible, as long as it met the general reliability test of FRE 702.)

5. **Mandatory disclosure to jury:** The converse question is whether and when the expert is *required* to disclose to the jury the factual basis for his opinion.

a. **Disclosure on direct:** The courts are split as to whether the expert must disclose during direct examination the factual basis for his opinion or conclusion. Some require the underlying facts to be brought out before the expert gives his opinion, some merely require that the underlying facts be disclosed at some point during the direct examination, and some do not require disclosure at all on direct (though in these courts the adversary always has the right to inquire on ***cross-examination*** as to the underlying facts and assumptions). L&S, p. 866.

b. **Federal Rules:** The Federal Rules do ***not*** impose any requirement that the expert disclose during direct examination the data and assumptions he is relying on. FRE 705 provides that "Unless the court orders otherwise, an expert ***may state an opinion —*** and give the reasons for it — ***without first testifying to the underlying facts or data.*** But the expert may be required to disclose those facts or data ***on cross-examination.***"

   i. **Rationale:** Recall that FRE 703 allows the expert to base his opinion upon otherwise inadmissible facts, if other experts in the field could reasonably rely on such evidence. That being the case, the drafters of the Rules reasoned, there is no need for a blanket rule requiring the expert to state the underlying facts he is relying on. (Those common-law jurisdictions that required such disclosure on direct were generally ones that would not allow opinions based on inadmissible evidence, so the requirement of disclosure of the underlying facts might give the court the chance to prevent the expert from giving his opinion if the underlying facts were inadmissible.)

   ii. **Court has discretion:** Observe, however, that the phrase "unless the court orders otherwise" in Rule 705 gives the court ***discretion,*** in a particular instance, to require that the expert disclose on direct his factual basis. And keep in mind that under the last sentence of 705, the adversary always has the right to ***cross-examine*** the expert about the underlying data on which his conclusion is based.

E. **The hypothetical question:** The ***hypothetical question*** is still probably the most common way of presenting the expert with facts about the case from which to draw a conclusion. Therefore, we examine the law concerning hypothetical questions in some detail.

1. **General technique:** When a direct examiner asks the expert a hypothetical question, he generally does so by presenting the relevant facts to the expert in a fairly lengthy and specific manner.

   Example: P is trying to prove that the lung cancer he suffers from was caused by cigarettes he smoked, manufactured by D. P offers the testimony of W, an expert in lung disease, who has never personally examined P or P's medical records. P's lawyer might ask the following hypothetical question: "Assume, doctor, that a person has smoked one pack of cigarettes per day for the last twenty years. Assume further that the patient has not had substantial occupational or other exposure to asbestos. Assume that the patient has had a cough and emphysema for the last fifteen years. Assume that the patient's parents did not suffer from cancer. Assume finally that the patient is diagnosed as having cancer of the left lung at the age of 47, and that there is no other sign of cancer in the patient's body. On these facts, doctor, what if anything can you tell us about the likely cause of the lung cancer?"

2. **Evidentiary basis required:** Most skirmishing about hypothetical questions involves the extent to which there must be an ***evidentiary basis*** for the assumptions listed in the

question. Thus, in terms of our example above, the issue is the extent to which there must be evidence in the record that the patient has really been diagnosed as having lung cancer, that the patient really smoked one pack of cigarettes a day, etc. There are a number of sub-issues:

a. **In record at time of question:**   First, must evidence of each of the assumed facts be *in the record* at the time the question is asked? Some courts impose such a requirement, but the modern, and probably majority, trend, is to hold that there is *not* such a requirement. That is, most courts allow the question if the questioner assures the court that supporting evidence will be introduced later in the case. McC, p. 23.

b. **Inadmissible evidence:**   Second, must the underlying evidence be *admissible* (even if not yet admitted)? In courts that follow the federal rule that otherwise inadmissible evidence may be relied on by an expert if similar experts reasonably rely on this type of information, the data that supports the hypothetical may fall into this otherwise-inadmissible category. *Id.*

   i. **Illustration:**   For instance, consider our lung cancer example above: Assume that P's medical records are not admitted into evidence, and that the only source for the assumption that P has had a persistent cough for 15 years is P's statement to a doctor, who entered this information into those medical records. Since doctors generally can reasonably rely upon information placed in medical records by other physicians who have examined the patient, information from those records can form the factual basis for the hypothetical (even if those records might be otherwise-inadmissible hearsay). McC, p. 23.

c. **Based on opinion of another:**   Third, may the hypothetical be based on *another witness's opinion?* Some cases, usually older ones, say "no".

   i. **Modern and federal approach:**   But the modern trend, as exemplified by FRE 703, is as noted that an expert opinion may be based upon any data reasonably relied on by similar experts. If an expert could reasonably rely on another person's opinion, under the federal approach presumably that other opinion could be part of a hypothetical question and answer.

d. **Far-fetched assumptions:**   However, even under the modern and federal approach, the factual assumptions made in the hypothetical question *cannot be totally far-fetched.* There must be some evidence at some point in the trial to support, either directly or by inference, each of the facts hypothesized in the question. "The opinion will be stricken if the jury cannot possibly find that its factual underpinnings are true." L&S, p. 868.

3. **Advantage of hypothetical:**   The main advantage of the hypothetical question is that the party calling the expert *need not pay* for the expert's time in becoming personally acquainted with the facts of the case. In our lung cancer example, for instance, the plaintiff might not have been able to afford the medical expert if he had been required to pay for the expert's time in examining P and studying P's medical records. Also, the hypothetical approach has the merit of telling the jury exactly what factual assumptions the expert is making in arriving at his opinion. *Id.*

    a. Criticism: However, most commentators and many courts heavily criticize the hypothetical question technique. The main criticism is that the questioner generally gives a highly partisan *slanting* in listing the facts, one which often amounts to an early summation of the case for the benefit of the jury. McC, pp. 25-26. A second criticism is that if the questioner conscientiously tries to include all of the material facts, the question can become so long — often dozens of pages of trial transcript — that the jury gets confused or loses attention.

4. Federal approach: The Federal Rules respond to these criticisms by attempting to reduce practitioners' reliance on the technique. The Rules do *not* forbid the use of hypotheticals. But they take several steps to make the need for hypothetical questions less pressing than at common law. The Rules do this mainly by the first sentence of FRE 705: "Unless the court orders otherwise, an expert may state an opinion — and give the reasons for it — *without first testifying to the underlying facts or data.*"

    a. Remains useful: Even under the liberal federal approach, a practitioner may occasionally find it wise to use the hypothetical technique. For instance, she may want to use a "super expert" who testifies about how general scientific principles would be applied to particular facts, but as to whom there is not enough time (or money) for him to familiarize himself directly with the facts. Also, in a case where the underlying facts are sharply disputed, the questioner may find it helpful to state just her version of the facts to form the basis of the expert's opinion. L&S, p. 869, n. 17.

F. Procedural issues: Here are some procedural issues that often arise in connection with expert testimony:

1. Cross-examination: Cross-examining an expert witness is likely to be more difficult than examining a lay witness. The expert is often a knowledgeable — sometimes almost "professional" — witness; also, he is likely to be fiercely loyal to the side that called him. Most importantly, he has spent his career mastering a particular technical specialty, and knows far more about it than the lawyer who must cross-examine him. Nonetheless, there are several ways in which experts can often be effectively cross-examined:

    a. Bias: The examiner can attempt to show that the witness is *biased*. Most frequently, the examiner will do this by showing that the witness is being *paid* by the side that called him. Similarly, the examiner may bring out the fact that the expert has testified in many similar cases in the past, and has always allied himself with the same side (e.g., the plaintiff in asbestos cases).

    b. Different assumptions: The examiner may probe the *factual data* on which the expert's opinion is based. He may then try to vary this underlying base, perhaps by alluding to other, conflicting evidence.

        i. Hypothetical: This technique is especially useful where the expert's opinion on direct was made in response to a hypothetical question; the cross-examiner can merely vary the facts of the hypothetical (e.g., "Would your conclusion that the plaintiff's lung cancer was caused by smoking be changed, doctor, if it were assumed that the plaintiff came in daily contact with asbestos during his job as shipbuilder over a thirty-year period?").

c. Learned treatises: The examiner will sometimes be able to use *treatises*, *articles*, or other professional texts written by other experts to impeach the witness. Normally, the examiner must first get the witness to acknowledge that the text in question is a *standard authority* in the field. In most jurisdictions, the examiner may then impeach the expert by reading a portion of the text that contradicts the expert's testimony, and thus implying that the jury should disregard the expert's view.

　　i. Reliance unnecessary: A few courts allow the examiner to read the text during cross-examination only if the expert admits that he *relied* on the text in his training or in forming his present opinion. Lilly, p. 492, n. 4. But most courts allow use of the treatise as impeaching evidence so long as the expert concedes that it is authoritative, regardless of whether the expert has read it or relied on it.

　　ii. Treatise as substantive evidence: Many courts that allow the treatise to be read from allow it only as *impeachment* evidence, not as substantive evidence proving the truth of the facts stated in the treatise. But the Federal Rules, and some state courts, have a hearsay exception for learned treatises, whereby the treatise's contents are admissible as substantive evidence as long as the contents are brought out during direct or cross-examination of the expert. See FRE 803(18), discussed *supra*, p. 269.

2. Court-appointed experts: When a lawyer retains an expert to testify on behalf of the client, the lawyer of course usually looks for a witness who will express an opinion clearly favorable to that party. In most instances, each party will present an expert favorable to that party, leading to the much-criticized "battle of the experts." The jury is likely to be confused more than enlightened by the conflicting expert testimony, especially where the field of expertise is highly technical and/or there is a lot of jargon. Many commentators have proposed that this unhelpful battle can be avoided by the use of a *court-appointed expert*. The theory is that such an expert would be *"neutral,"* and his non-partisan testimony would therefore be more useful to the jury.

a. Federal Rule: The Federal Rules facilitate the appointment of an expert by the court. FRE 706 (too long to be worth reproducing in full here) codifies a number of aspects of court appointment of experts, including:

　　i. Court chooses own: The court may ask the parties to submit their own nominations or to agree upon a selection, but the court may also make a selection of its *own*;

　　ii. Costs: In most civil cases, the court can order the *cost* of the expert to be borne by either or both parties as if these expenses were court costs. (In criminal cases a statute often provides that the government must pay);

　　iii. No compulsion: The rule does not allow the court to *compel* the expert to accept the appointment; the court may appoint only if the expert consents. (But the rule applies only where the expert will have to *specially prepare* for trial; if a person with expertise happens to have knowledge of the facts of a particular case — e.g., a treating physician — the expert may be subpoenaed like any other person with personal knowledge and required to testify, willingly or not. L&S, p. 708.)

    iv. Deposition: The expert's *deposition* may be taken by either party;

    v. Cross-examination: The expert may be called to testify at trial by either party (or by the court), and each party — including the party calling him — may *cross-examine* him;

    vi. Disclosure to jury: Under 706(d), the court has discretion to *disclose* to the jury the fact that the witness has been appointed by the court.

  b. Not often used: However, federal courts have been slow to make use of this power to appoint expert witnesses.

3. Discovery: One key to effectively cross-examining an expert is to have had adequate *pre-trial discovery* of that expert, including discovery of his findings and conclusions.

  a. Federal approach: In federal courts, a party may obtain reasonably broad pre-trial discovery of experts that the other side expects to call at trial. Federal Rule of Civil Procedure 26(b)(4)(A)(i) lets a party send interrogatories to his adversary requiring the latter to "identify each person whom the other party expects to call as an expert witness at trial, to state the subject matter on which the expert is expected to testify, and to state the substance of the facts and opinions to which the expert is expected to testify and a summary of the grounds for each opinion."

    i. Deposition: But a party may not *depose* the other party's expected trial witnesses without a court order, and even then will generally have to pay for that expert's time in pre*paring for and attending the deposition. FRCP 26(b)(4)(A)(ii); 26(b)(4)(B). (If the expert is *not* expected to be called at trial, the other side will only under "exceptional circumstances" be able to obtain discovery about the expert's opinions on facts known to him. FRCP 26(b)(4)(B).)

III. EXPERT WITNESSES — *DAUBERT*, FRE 702, AND THE EXCLUSION OF UNRELIABLE TESTIMONY

A. Special rule for scientific evidence: As we have seen (*supra*, p. 521), an expert's testimony must be helpful — and in some courts, necessary — to the jury's understanding of the case. This is basically a requirement of relevance. But since expert testimony involves specialized knowledge that the jury is not necessarily equipped to evaluate on its own, there is a large risk that the jury will give such testimony more weight than it deserves.

    Example: In a 1986 rape case, W, the prosecution's expert chemist, testifies that hair and blood deposited on the victim match D's hair and blood. D is convicted, despite a fairly strong alibi. Only when a DNA test on the samples is finally performed in 2001 does it become clear that D could not possibly have been the rapist, and he is released from prison. All indications are that the jury believed W's testimony, and refused to seriously consider any evidence (e.g., D's alibi, backed up by several witnesses) that pointed in the opposite direction. See *N.Y. Times*, May 8, 2001, p. A1.

1. Danger of "junk" expert testimony: Because juries are relatively poor at determining whether an expert's testimony is reliable, the courts have gradually taken on an ever-greater role in excluding unreliable expert testimony. In the federal courts, this role derives mainly from a 1993 Supreme Court decision, ***Daubert v. Merrell Dow Pharmaceuticals.*** The principle of *Daubert* — that expert testimony must be shown to be "valid" — has subsequently been embodied in amended FRE 702's three reliability requirements: that expert testimony be "based upon sufficient facts or data"; that such testimony be "the product of reliable principles and methods"; and that the witness have "reliably applied the principles and methods to the facts of the case."

2. ***Frye* case:**   Before we get to *Daubert* and the new FRE 702 that embodies it, we need to take a brief look at the doctrine *Daubert* replaced, the so-called "*Frye* standard." The *Frye* standard, which derives from *Frye v. U.S.*, 293 F. 1013 (D.C.Cir. 1923), held that only scientific evidence that was ***"generally accepted"*** could be admitted.

    a. **Application in *Frye* itself:** The court in *Frye* upheld a lower court's refusal to admit the results of a lie detector test offered by the defendant in a murder case. The appeals court reasoned, "[W]hile courts will go a long way in admitting expert testimony deduced from a well-recognized scientific principle or discovery, the thing from which the deduction is made must be ***sufficiently established to have gained general acceptance*** in the particular field in which it belongs." The polygraph was simply too new a technique to have attained such acceptance "among physiological and psychological authorities."

    b. **Generally prevailed:** Until the 1993 decision in *Daubert*, all federal courts, and most state courts, paid at least lip service to the *Frye* standard.

3. ***Daubert* rejects *Frye*:** But in 1993, the Supreme Court rejected the *Frye* standard and substituted a new ***"reliability"*** standard, in ***Daubert v. Merrell Dow Pharmaceuticals, Inc.***, 113 S.Ct. 2786 (1993). The ruling is binding on the federal courts, but not on the state courts (which therefore remain free to follow *Frye* if they wish).

    a. **Facts:** The Ps in *Daubert* were minors born with serious birth defects, who claimed that these were caused by Bendectin, a drug manufactured by D that their mothers took during pregnancy. The Ps tried to establish their case by using the testimony of 8 experts, who would have offered two main types of evidence that Bendectin had caused the Ps' injuries: (1) analyses of test-tube and animal studies finding a link between Bendectin and malformations; and (2) unpublished "reanalyses" of previously published epidemiological (human statistical) studies, with the reanalysis finding a link between Bendectin and birth defects even though each published study had not found such a link. The lower courts refused to allow the expert testimony, holding mainly that the only "generally accepted" method of showing a link between a substance and a human birth defect was the use of epidemiological studies, and that unpublished "reanalyses" of prior studies did not qualify.

    b. **Holding by Supreme Court:** The Supreme Court threw out the *Frye* "generally accepted" test entirely. Instead, the Court held, in an opinion by Justice Blackmun, that scientific evidence must now meet two requirements before it can be admitted in federal courts:

        ❏   the evidence must be shown to be ***"scientifically valid"***; and

❏ the evidence must *"fit"* at least one issue in the case, i.e., be ***relevant*** to the task at hand.

c. **Superseded by FRE:** The Court began by concluding that the *Frye* test had been superseded by the enactment of the FRE. FRE 702 as it stood at the time of Daubert set forth the grounds for admitting scientific evidence ("If scientific, technical or other specialized knowledge will assist the trier of fact to understand the evidence or to determine a fact in issue, a witness qualified as an expert by knowledge, skill, experience, training or education, may testify thereto in the form of an opinion or otherwise"), and did not impose any requirement of "general acceptance." Because the FRE were (and are still) generally liberal on questions of admissibility, and because the "generally accepted" rule of *Frye* was conspicuously absent from the text of the Rule governing scientific evidence, the Court concluded that the FRE superseded the *Frye* test.

d. **New "scientific knowledge" test:** Instead, the Court concluded that Rule 702 itself imposed the requirement that scientific evidence be shown to constitute ***"scientific knowledge."*** To constitute "scientific knowledge," the Court said (at various points in its opinion), the evidence must be ***"scientifically valid,"*** must be ***"derived by the scientific method,"*** must be ***"good science,"*** and must "rest on a ***reliable*** foundation." (This is all one "prong" — which we'll call here the ***"reliability" prong*** — of the Court's analysis.)

e. **"Relevancy" prong:** The Court added a ***second prong*** to the analysis: in addition to the reliability prong, the evidence must be ***"relevant,"*** i.e., ***"sufficiently tied to the facts of the case*** that it will aid the jury in resolving a factual dispute." This is an issue of ***"fit,"*** the Court said. Evidence might be scientifically valid, but be sought by the proponent to be used for a purpose for which the evidence does not fit; in that case, the evidence must be rejected.

   i. **Illustration:** The Court gave the following illustration of what it meant by this "relevancy" prong. Suppose an expert has studied the phases of the moon. That expert may then have "scientific knowledge" about whether a certain night was dark. If an issue in the case is whether there was moonlight on a certain night, the scientific knowledge is relevant to that issue (and thus is admissible under *Daubert* because it satisfies both the "reliability and "relevancy" prongs). But use of the same knowledge on the issue of whether an individual was unusually likely to have behaved irrationally on that night would not be allowed, because it does not "fit" the issue (unless there were independent scientific grounds to support a link between phase-of-moon and human behavior).

f. **Determining scientific reliability:** Since the new test for scientific evidence is that the evidence constitute "scientific knowledge" or be "scientifically valid" (as well be tied to the facts), most of the Supreme Court's opinion in *Daubert* was devoted to ***how courts can determine whether proffered evidence is indeed "scientific knowledge."*** The Court listed these factors as ones that lower courts should consider:

   i. whether the theory or technique has been or can be ***reliably tested***. (If so, it's more likely to be found to be "scientific knowledge.")

ii. whether the theory or technique has been subjected to ***peer review and publication***. (If so, it's more likely to pass muster, because "submission to the scrutiny of the scientific community is a component of 'good science,' in part because it increases the likelihood that substantive flaws in methodology will be detected.")

iii. the technique's "known or potential ***rate of error.***" Obviously, the more errors in individual applications of a technique or test (e.g., false matches in DNA testing), the less likely the test is to be "scientific knowledge."

iv. whether there are ***standards*** controlling the technique's operations, and whether those standards are well-maintained. For instance, if there is a ***professional organization*** that maintains standards for how the test should be performed, that's a plus.

v. whether the technique or test has become ***"generally accepted."*** Under *Frye*, this was the sole factor. Under *Daubert*, it remains an important, though no longer dispositive, factor.

vi. whether the technique grows naturally out of work that the testifying expert was conducting ***independently of the litigation***, or was instead developed specifically for the present litigation. (This factor was not articulated by the Supreme Court, but was relied on by the Ninth Circuit on remand in *Daubert*; it's likely that other courts will agree.) Clearly, techniques developed independently of litigation are more likely to be found to be "scientifically valid," if only because the technique and its proponents are less likely to be biased than where the technique is developed solely for use in the particular lawsuit.

Note: The Court made it clear that these are "non-exclusive" factors. So the lower courts remain free to consider other factors that go to whether particular scientific evidence is "reliable." The last factor listed above — independence from the litigation — is one such factor.

Note: None of the listed factors is ***necessary*** to a finding of reliability. So evidence satisfying some but not all factors (e.g., a technique that hasn't yet been subjected to peer review or general acceptance, but that is shown to be testable and to have a low error rate) may nonetheless be found "reliable."

g. **Partial dissent:** In a partial dissent, Justice Rehnquist criticized the majority for placing an undue burden on federal judges: "I do not doubt that Rule 702 confides to the judge some gatekeeping responsibility in deciding questions of the admissibility of proffered expert testimony. But I do not think it imposes on them either the obligation or the authority to become ***amateur scientists*** in order to perform that role."

h. **Result on remand:** The Supreme Court did not decide whether the expert testimony proffered in *Daubert* met the new standard. Instead, it remanded to the Ninth Circuit on that issue. The Ninth Circuit then concluded that the evidence did ***not*** meet the *Daubert* standard. *Daubert v. Merrell Dow Phamaceuticals*, 43 F.3d 1311 (9th Cir. 1995). The Court of Appeals reasoned that research that is performed ***specifically for purposes of the litigation*** (which was the case here) will not be found to be "scientifically valid" (and thus admissible under *Daubert*) unless either: (1) the research is "subjected to normal scientific scrutiny through **peer review** and **publication**"; or (2) the experts "explain precisely how they went about reaching their conclusions and **point to some objective source** — a learned treatise, the policy statement of a professional association, a published article in a reputable scientific journal or the like — to show that they have **followed the scientific method**, as it is practiced by (at least) a **recognized minority** of scientists in their field."

    i. Application of standard: Under this fairly tough standard, the evidence was inadmissible — it was unpublished, it was developed specially for the present litigation, and the methodology behind it was not supported by published articles or other objective sources.

4. Questions raised by *Daubert*: *Daubert* raised many questions. Here are some:

    a. Scope: What's the *scope* of *Daubert*, i.e., to what types of evidence does it apply? It clearly applies to traditional "hard" scientific evidence (e.g., DNA testing, spectrographic voice analysis, epidemiology, and the like). But does it apply to evidence from the ***"soft" sciences*** like psychology (e.g., the reliability of hypnotically-induced testimony)? And does it apply to ***technology*** and other bodies of "specialized knowledge" that are ***not "science"*** at all ? The answer to both questions is now known to be ***"yes"*** — in the post-*Daubert* case of *Kumho Tire Co. v. Carmichael*, 119 S.Ct. 1167 (1999), the Court held that the principles of *Daubert* apply to all expert testimony, whether based on "scientific" principles or not. (*Kumho Tire* is discussed further *infra*, p. 537.) And new FRE 702, which embodies the *Daubert* principles, similarly applies to all expert testimony.

    b. Preference for "independent" research: Will ***"independent"*** research (i.e., research not done in connection with the litigation) be easier to introduce? The Ninth Circuit's opinion on remand expressed a very strong ***preference*** for such research — essentially, independent research is ***presumed*** to be "scientifically valid," whereas research done expressly for the purpose of producing evidence for the present litigation must be made to jump through additional hoops (publication/peer review, or objective support in the literature). There's a good chance other courts will agree that litigation-specific research is to be scrutinized more harshly.

    c. State-court view: Will ***state courts*** — especially courts in states adopting some version of the FRE — apply *Daubert*? Some have already done so at the highest-state-court level (Iowa, Montana, So. Dakota and West Virginia) and in others, lower courts have followed the decision (e.g., Ill, Minn.). But a few courts have squarely rejected the decision (e.g., Arizona, Florida and Nebraska).

5. What difference *Daubert* makes: In those jurisdictions adopting *Daubert*, here are the most important consequences:

    a. No "head count": The trial judge's job is probably harder than under *Frye*. It's no longer enough for the judge to conduct a ***"head count,"*** and to allow the evidence if and only if a majority or substantial minority of experts in the field have accepted the technique or test. Instead, the judge must attempt to make her own assessment of the reliability of the test or technique; "general acceptance" is now merely one factor to be considered (with testability, error rate, controls, peer review, etc. also needing to be taken into account).

    i. **"General acceptance" still counts:** General acceptance remains a major — probably the single most important — factor. Techniques that *are* generally accepted within the relevant field will rarely be excluded under *Daubert*. Techniques that have not yet been generally accepted may sometimes pass muster (e.g., if they're **very new**, have recently been published, and the expert has excellent credentials), but often will not. Certainly if the technique has been around a long time, and has been dismissed as *un*reliable by the vast majority of experts in the field, the technique is unlikely to be found "reliable" even if it meets some of the other factors (e.g., it's been published and peer-reviewed, but negatively).

b. **New techniques:** *New or "novel" techniques* clearly have a **better chance** of getting into evidence than under *Frye*. If the new technique has a good scientific pedigree, the fact that it hasn't yet had a chance to get "generally accepted" is no longer fatal.

c. **Significant gatekeeper role:** *Daubert* doesn't really allow materially more scientific material into evidence than *Frye*. The judge remains very much a "gatekeeper" under FRE 702 (especially the version of FRE 702 enacted in 2000); "junk science" can and should still be kept out. It's just that the trial judge has more factors to use in deciding whether something is really true science rather than "junk science."

    i. **Criminal cases:** *Prosecutors* have remained very successful at getting in scientific evidence in criminal cases. DNA tests (see *infra*, p. 542) are the best example — *Daubert* has if anything increased the admissibility of DNA results.

    ii. **Plaintiffs' use:** By contrast, plaintiffs often continue to have trouble getting scientific evidence in, under *Daubert*. Especially in **toxic tort** cases, plaintiffs have always had a hard time getting their expert testimony about **causation** into evidence, and *Daubert* hasn't made their life any easier. See, e.g., the Ninth Circuit's decision on remand in *Daubert* itself (*supra*, p. 534), in which the plaintiffs' expert evidence that their injuries may have been caused by Bendectin was held inadmissible, and summary judgment granted to the defendant.

d. **Role of judge:** The judge's role under *Daubert* is **not** to determine whether the **results** of the test or technique are reliable (i.e., accurate), in the particular case at hand. Instead, the judge's job is merely to determine whether the **methodology used** is reliable. So in a DNA case, the judge should ask, "Were the test, and the ensuing probability calculations, performed in a scientific and reliable manner?" *not*, "Is the expert correct in concluding that there is a match?" or "Is it true that there's only a 1 in 100,000 chance that a randomly-chosen person would match the sample?"

    i. **Actual finding:** However, on this issue of whether the method was reliable, the judge makes the **actual finding**. In other words, she must conclude that the method actually *is* or *is not* reliable (probably by a preponderance of the evidence), and it's *not* enough for her to conclude merely that there's enough evidence of reliability to allow a "reasonable juror" to find reliability.

ii. Left to jury: Then, if the evidence is allowed in, it's up to the jury to find whether the *results* of the test or technique are accurate. Thus in a DNA case, if the judge lets in the expert evidence, it's up to the jury (as part of its overall fact-finding) to decide whether there really *is* a match between sample and suspect, and to decide how likely it is that such a match would occur by chance.

B. The extension of *Daubert* to non-scientific evidence (*Kumho Tire*): The principles of *Daubert* apply not just to *"scientific"* testimony but to *"all expert testimony."* That's the conclusion of an important post-*Daubert* Supreme Court case, *Kumho Tire Co., Ltd. v. Carmichael*, 119 S.Ct. 1167 (1999).

1. **Facts:** *Kumho Tire* involved a minivan accident that was caused by a tire blowout, which was in turn caused by a separation between the tire's tread and the tire's steel-belted interior. The plaintiff's tire expert, Dennis Carlson, proposed to testify that the separation was caused by a defect in the tire's design or manufacture. He reached this conclusion despite the fact that (as he conceded) the tire was at least five years old, had an unknown but substantial number of miles on it, had a tread that was worn down to nothing in some places, and had at least two inadequately-repaired punctures.

   a. **Basis for opinion:** Carlson's conclusion was based on the following reasoning: (1) if a tread separation is not caused by a type of tire use called "overdeflection" (underinflating the tire or overloading the car), then ordinarily it is caused by a tire defect; (2) if a tire has been subjected to enough overdeflection to cause a separation, the tire should reveal at least two out of a list of four physical symptoms; (3) Carlson's physical inspection of the particular tire did not show any of these four symptoms, at least to a sufficient degree. Therefore, he concluded, the separation was caused by a defect rather than by overdeflection.

   b. **Trial court rejects:** The trial judge rejected Carlson's proposed testimony, concluding that it was unreliable under *Daubert*.

   c. **Court of Appeals reverses:** The Court of Appeals reversed, holding that because Carlson's testimony relied on his experience rather than on "application of scientific principles," *Daubert* should not have been applied.

2. **Supreme Court upholds trial court:** But the Supreme Court found that the trial judge, not the Court of Appeals, was right. In so concluding, the Court made these pronouncements:

   a. ***Daubert* applies:** First, the *Daubert* framework — and the trial judge's duty to be a gatekeeper — applies to *all expert testimony* (i.e., to testimony involving "technical" or "other specialized" knowledge under FRE 702), not just to "scientific" testimony.

   b. ***Daubert* factors may be considered:** Second, the trial judge may — but need not — consider any given specific factor mentioned in *Daubert*. That is, it is up to the trial judge to determine whether a particular *Daubert* factor is or isn't sensible to consider in a particular context. "[W]e can neither rule out, nor rule in, for all cases and for all time the applicability of the factors mentioned in *Daubert*, nor can we do so now for subsets of cases categorized by category of expert or by kind of evidence. Too much depends upon the particular circumstances of the particular case at issue."

i.   **Illustration:** The court gave the following illustration of how a particular *Daubert* factor might not apply in a particular case: Suppose that a scientific witness propounds a theory that has never been the subject of peer review. If the particular application at issue has never interested any scientist, the absence of the *Daubert* "peer review" factor will be irrelevant.

c.   **Trial judge gets flexibility in procedure, not just outcome:** Finally, the trial judge is to be given substantial latitude in selecting what *procedure* to use in evaluating the expert's reliability. The abuse-of-discretion standard should be used in evaluating the judge's procedure — only in the relatively rare case in which the trial judge uses a clearly inappropriate procedure should the court of appeals reverse. And that same abuse-of-discretion standard should apply to the trial judge's substantive conclusion about whether the expert testimony was in fact reliable.

i.   **Application to facts of case:** Applying this abuse-of-discretion standard to the facts of *Kumho Tire* itself, the Court concluded that the trial court's decision should be upheld. The Court pointed to a number of reasons that may have justified the trial judge's doubts about Carlson's reliability. For instance, Carlson could not say from his visual inspection whether the tire had traveled less than 10,000 or more than 50,000 miles; yet he purported to be able to tell, from that same visual inspection, whether certain small physical clues did or did not demonstrate over-deflection. Similarly, there was no indication in the record that other experts in the industry used Carlson's two-factor test for determining the existence of overde-flection. All in all, the trial judge's conclusion that Carlson's testimony was not reliable was within that judge's "lawful discretion."

C.   **Present FRE 702:** In response to *Daubert*, FRE 702, dealing with expert testimony, was amended in 2000. That amendment kept all of the text that was previously part of FRE 702. But it added several conditions on the admission of expert testimony. Such testimony is to be allowed only if "(b) the testimony is *based on sufficient facts or data*; (c) the testimony is the *product of reliable principles and methods*; and (d) the expert has *reliably applied* the principles and methods to the *facts* of the case."

1.   **Three tests:** So the post-*Daubert* FRE 702 adds three requirements that expert testimony must meet, all of which help ensure that the expert's testimony is technically reliable.

2.   ***Daubert* factors not enumerated:** Notice that the text of present FRE 702 does not attempt to *list the factors mentioned by the Daubert Court* (e.g., whether the technique or theory has been subject to peer review and publication), or any other factors relied upon by post-*Daubert* courts. However, the Advisory Committee Notes to FRE 702 say that "all of these factors *remain relevant* to the determination of the reliability of expert testimony under the Rule as amended."

3.   **Not just scientific testimony:** Observe also that present FRE 702 applies not just to "scientific" expert testimony, but to all testimony that involves *"technical or other specialized"* knowledge." So, for example, testimony about how a particular industry operates (e.g., how drug dealers communicate in codes) might not involve "scientific" principles, but since it involves "technical knowledge," it would be subject to the present standards of

FRE 702. This new language in 702 derives from the Supreme Court's post-*Daubert* decision in *Kumho Tire, supra*, p. 537.

> **Example:** Suppose that D, a senior officer of XYZ Corp., is charged with trading in XYZ's stock based on material nonpublic information. Suppose further that D's defense is that the information in question was not "material." Since the definition of "material" information is, in essence, information that a reasonable investor would be likely to consider important, both sides might supply testimony from experts in financial journalism or financial analysis, to testify how investors respond to particular types of corporate information. Even though this testimony would not truly be "scientific," the testimony would be subject to the requirements of FRE 702, since the testimony involves "specialized knowledge."

4. **Experience alone may suffice:** It is clear that under present 702, just like old 702, a person may be an "expert" without any specialized education or training — in other words, *experience alone may suffice*. However, the Advisory Committee notes that in this instance, the expert "must explain how that experience leads to the conclusion reached, why that experience is a sufficient basis for the opinion, and how that experience is reliably applied to the facts. . . . The trial court's gatekeeping function *requires more than simply 'taking the expert's word for it.'* " Adv. Comm. Notes to 2000 Amendments to FRE 702.

5. **Not a matter of which conclusion the trial court believes:** The trial court, in exercising its gatekeeper function, is *not* permitted to exclude an opinion or conclusion merely because the trial court does not *believe* that conclusion. As the Advisory Committee notes, "[T]he emphasis in the amendment on 'sufficient facts or data' is not intended to authorize a trial court to exclude an expert's testimony on the grounds that the court believes one version of the facts and not the other." Thus there can often be situations in which dueling experts will propound conflicting theories or conclusions — as long as each expert's testimony meets the fairly minimal requirements of reliability, the trial court must *allow both to testify.*

IV. SCIENTIFIC EVIDENCE AND EXPERTISE — PARTICULAR TYPES

A. **Overview:** An analysis of the hundreds of types of scientific evidence is obviously beyond the scope of this outline. However, we touch briefly upon a few of the more important and controversial types of scientific evidence.

B. **Probabilities:** A branch of mathematics called *probability theory* helps calculate the probability that a certain event has occurred. Courts disagree about whether computations made by use of probability theory may be presented to the jury to help them conclude whether a particular event took place.

> **Example:** P is negligently knocked down by a blue bus. P is unable to directly identify the bus as belonging to D, one of two local bus companies. He can establish, however, that D owns 85 of the 100 blue buses in town. Courts are in dispute about whether P may present this fact — perhaps accompanied by testimony by a probabilities expert

— and then argue to the jury that this fact shows an 85% probability that the bus that hit him was owned by D.

1. **Foundation:** All courts agree that if probability evidence is to be introduced at all, a *proper foundation* for it must be laid. In particular, solid evidence of the numerator and denominator used to compute the probabilities must be presented to the jury.

   a. ***Collins* case:** Failure to comply with the foundation requirements was the main reason why probability evidence was rejected in the leading case on the subject, *People v. Collins*, 438 P.2d 33 (Cal. 1968).

      i. **Facts:** In *Collins*, D and his wife were charged with robbery. There were no complete eyewitness identifications of either D or his wife. However, the prosecution apparently produced at least some evidence of six facts about the robbers: (1) they had a partly yellow automobile; (2) the man had a mustache; (3) the girl had a ponytail; (4) the girl had blond hair; and (5) the man was a black man with a beard; and (6) the robbers were an interracial couple in a car. The prosecution then called a mathematics professor, who was instructed to assume certain probabilities for each of these events (e.g., 1/10 for partly yellow automobile, 1/4 for man with mustache, etc.). The mathematician then testified that the probability that any given couple would possess these six factors by chance was to be computed by using the "product rule" (i.e., one multiplies each probability by the next). Applying this rule, the professor concluded that there was only one chance in 12 million that any given couple would possess these six factors. The prosecutor then argued to the jury that the individual probabilities he had assigned were "conservative," and that the chance of any couple other than D and his wife having these same characteristics was probably more like "one in a billion." D and his wife were convicted.

      ii. **Holding:** The California Supreme Court reversed the conviction. The court seemed to rely most heavily on the fact that there was no evidence in the record relating to any of the six individual probability factors used by the prosecutor (e.g., that only 1 in 10 automobiles is partly yellow). The court was also troubled by two other considerations: (1) There was no showing that the factors were "independent" of each other, a requirement for the "product" method of computing probabilities. (For instance, once a man is assumed to have a mustache, the chance that he would also have a beard is much higher than if he does not have a mustache, and much higher than the 1/10th the prosecutor assumed.) (2) The jury would be tempted to "accord disproportionate weight" to the resulting figure, instead of concentrating on the critical issue: "Of the admittedly few such couples [having all six factors], which one, if any, was guilty of committing this robbery?" (The court attached an Appendix in which, using sophisticated mathematics, it demonstrated that there was about a 40% chance that at least one *other* couple in the Los Angeles area had the same characteristics.)

2. **Opposition to use:** The *Collins* court was clearly troubled by what it saw as the prosecutor's inaccurate, mathematically-unsound application of probability principles. But the court also seemed troubled by the basic idea of using probability to assess guilt. Many other courts and commentators have expressed similar misgivings about giving the jury

even mathematically-sound probability estimates, often on the theory that jurors will give such evidence more weight than it deserves, because of its scientific-seeming nature.

3. **Supporters:** But other commentators argue that probability proof, when wisely used, enhances the accuracy of fact-finding and is thus desirable.

4. **Modern trend:** The modern trend is probably towards ***increased acceptance*** of probability evidence, when a careful scientific and mathematical basis for it is laid.

   a. **Paternity testing:** Courts have been especially willing to accept such evidence in ***paternity*** cases. New "DNA testing" techniques (described further *infra*, p. 542) allow scientists to exclude a quite high percentage of the male population from being the possible father of any given child. Whereas older tests were generally allowed into evidence only if they ***excluded*** the possibility of the defendant's paternity, experts testifying about the results of DNA tests are often allowed to express not only the fact that the defendant is ***not*** excluded from paternity, but also the "probability" that he *is* the father.

      Example: Suppose that D is claimed to be the father of C. DNA tests may now be performed that, typically, will allow the geneticist to state, "Not only are C's genetic markers consistent with D being C's father, but only one in several thousand males of the same race as D would have markers consistent with being the father of C." Nearly all courts will allow the geneticist to phrase her findings in this way, and to testify further that there is thus a "percentage of exclusion" of, say, 2,999 out of 3,000.

      Some but probably not most courts would also permit the geneticist to say that there was a "99.9% chance" that D was the father. However, this latter probability estimate is misleading: it merely means that the genetic marker is 1,000 times more likely to be found in a person who is the real father than in one who is chosen at random, not that the jury is 99.9% likely to be correct if they determine that D is the father. For this reason, McC, p. 387, argues that "testimony as to the 'probability of paternity' as it typically is calculated, should not be allowed."

   b. **Other contexts:** Outside of paternity cases, courts have also increasing allowed statistical evidence.

      i. **Sexual assault and murder cases:** Thus courts now frequently allow serological and DNA tests in ***rape*** cases and ***murder*** cases, where the test sheds some light on the likelihood that the defendant is or is not the perpetrator.

         Example: Many courts now allow the results of so-called DNA "fingerprints" of the defendant's blood and his semen. (See *infra*, p. 542.) As with the paternity test described above, such DNA tests typically come into evidence with two components: (1) a statement by the tester that the DNA "fingerprint" of D is the same as the DNA found in the blood or semen left on or in the victim; and (2) a statement that only some small percentage of persons chosen at random from the population would have this same fingerprint. As with the results of paternity tests, courts are much more likely to admit this testimony about frequency of occurrence within the population than they are to allow additional testimony purporting to be the "probability that D is guilty."

C. DNA testing: In a few short years, **DNA tests** have become a powerful and well-accepted method of tying a blood, semen or tissue sample to a particular person.

1. **Nature of DNA testing:** The essence of DNA testing is that at particular places on each human chromosome, people have chunks of DNA called "Variable Number Tandem Repeats" (VNTRs). There is a lot of variation in the **length** of people's VNTR at a particular chromosomal location. A relatively straightforward lab test can give a reading for the length of a body-fluid sample's VNTR at each of a number of chromosomal locations. The set of lengths for the various VNTRs constitutes a "DNA profile" for the sample (and for the person who is the source of the sample).

2. **Probability:** As DNA profiles are commonly computed today, it is not true that "no two people can have the same one." However, testing laboratories keep **charts** of how frequently members of different races and ethnic groups have a particular VNTR length at a particular location. For instance, the FBI has computed VNTR lengths for a randomly-chosen sample of 225 of its caucasian agents. On the assumption that a person's VNTR length at one chromosomal position is independent of the length at another position, one can use the chart to compute the probability that a randomly-chosen person of the race or ethnic group shown in the chart would have a particular combination of VNTR lengths. If the suspect's DNA profile (his combination of VNTR lengths) matches that of the sample recovered from the scene of the crime, an expert can say how likely it is that a randomly-chosen person would have that same profile merely by chance. (A more detailed explanation is given in *U.S. v. Bonds*, 12 F.3d 540 (6th Cir. 1993).)

    > **Example:** To grossly simplify, suppose that the "caucasian chart" used by a particular DNA testing lab shows that for chromosome location 1, 10% of the caucasian population has a length of 2, that for location 2, 15% of the population has a length of 4, and that for location 3, 20% of the population has a length of 3. Assume that both the suspect and the blood sample taken from the victim's clothing have length-2 at location 1, length 4 at location 2, and length 3 at location 3. (In the jargon of DNA testing, there's a *"match"* between suspect and sample.) Assuming (as scientists commonly assume) that nature determines a person's length at one location independently of length at another location, we can multiple the percentages to compute what portion of the Caucasian population would have that same 2/4/3 set of lengths. Thus the expert multiplies 10% x 15% x 20%, for a product of .3%. The expert thus concludes (and is usually allowed to testify), "Only 3 out of every 1,000 randomly-chosen caucasians have this particular set of VNTR lengths."

    > In actuality, more than 3 positions are used, and the resulting probability of a random match is typically much smaller than 3/1000. See, e.g., *U.S. v. Davis*, 40 F.3d 1069 (10th Cir. 1994) (trial judge correctly allowed FBI expert to testify that there were two different DNA profiles found in blood recovered from a robbery scene, that these profiles matched those of D1 and D2, that only 1 in 30,000 randomly-selected blacks would match D1's profile and that only 1 in 600,000 would match D2's profile).

3. **Generally allowed:** Nearly all courts today **allow** the results of properly-performed DNA tests to be introduced, in both civil and criminal cases (and both by the prosecution and by the defense). The most common use is in criminal cases where introduced by the prosecu-

tion, to show that the defendant's DNA profile matches that of blood or other fluid found on the victim or at the crime scene, and to show that it's very unlikely that a randomly-chosen member of the racial group of which the defendant is a part would have that same profile by chance.

a. ***Daubert***: Courts that follow the *Daubert* standard (all federal courts, and many states — see *supra*, p. 532 and p. 535) have also generally concluded that *Daubert* **applies** to determining whether the particular DNA evidence is admissible. Thus these courts require the trial judge to conclude that the evidence is "scientifically reliable" before it may be admitted. (The second prong of *Daubert* — relevance — is rarely in issue in DNA cases.) See, e.g., *U.S. v. Bonds, supra.*

    i. **Two phases:** Courts generally apply *Daubert* to two different issues regarding DNA. First, the court determines whether DNA profiling is **generally** reliable; on this issue, virtually all courts now agree that it is (and in fact some courts take judicial notice of its reliability). The second, more-frequently contested, issue is whether the particular way the tests were performed **in the present case**, and the way the probability of a random match was computed, are reliable. Here, most courts again find that the test passes muster, but some judges have found that lab errors (e.g., allowing samples to degrade before testing) aren't sufficiently reliable; other courts have found that the prosecution's probability estimates are too low (e.g., because the lab's "chart" doesn't consider the particular ethnic group to which the defendant belongs, and there's some evidence that matches are more likely within a particular ethnic group than within a group that has only race in common).

D. Speed detection: The police commonly use two methods of **speed detection** to determine whether a motorist has been speeding.

1. **Radar:** Most commonly, the police use ***radar***. Like all scientific tests, radar cannot be used unless the court is satisfied both that the general theory behind it is sound and that the application of theory to fact in the particular case was reliable.

a. **General theory:** The basic theory behind the use of radar to measure the speed of moving objects is now so generally accepted that not only are both the *Frye* (*supra*, p. 532) and *Daubert* (*supra*, p. 532) tests virtually always found to be satisfied, but courts will usually take **judicial notice** of radar's theoretical reliability. (See *infra*, p. 587 for a discussion of judicial notice.) Therefore, the prosecution generally does not have to put in any expert evidence as to the general reliability of radar as a speed detection technique. McC, p. 366.

b. **Accuracy in particular case:** On the other hand, the accuracy of radar depends very much on how carefully it is used ***in the particular case.*** Courts vary in how they handle the possibility that the particular equipment or its use may have been inaccurate: some require the prosecution to make at least some showing that the equipment was accurate when used (e.g., proof that its accuracy was confirmed both shortly before and after the arrest); others merely give the defendant the right to challenge the accuracy, and treat any showing of inaccuracy as going merely to weight rather than admissibility.

E. Intoxication: Several scientific techniques for determining whether a person is ***intoxicated*** exist.

   1. Breathalyzer: The most important is the ***breathalyzer***, which measures the amount of alcohol in the breath, and then extrapolates this to estimate the amount in the blood stream. In most states, a statutory scheme makes breathalyzer results automatically admissible if a proper foundation is laid. (To lay the foundation, the prosecution must produce a witness — usually the person who administered the test — who can testify that the device was one covered by the statute, and was correctly used in the particular case.) Many states also have enacted ***statutory presumptions*** that flow from particular findings; for instance, a level of .05% or less of blood alcohol generally raises a rebuttable presumption that the defendant was not drunk, and a level of .10% or higher raises a rebuttable presumption that he was drunk. McC, p. 368.

F. Handwriting and other forensic document analysis: "Forensic document examiners" examine documents to determine such things as who wrote the document and when. A few courts have applied *Daubert* to the forensic-document field. These courts have varied in how strict they are about receiving expert document-analysis testimony. At least one has ***rejected*** expert testimony about the ***authorship of handwritten documents,*** on the grounds that the proponent (the prosecution) failed to show that handwriting analysis is sufficiently scientific to meet the standards of FRE 702. See *U.S. v. Saelee*, 162 F.Supp.2d 1097 (D. Alaska 2001).

G. Psychology and psychiatry: Expert scientific testimony is often offered on issues of ***psychology*** and ***psychiatry***. Most frequently, such evidence relates to the mental condition of a criminal defendant, but it can also be relevant to a wide variety of other contexts (e.g., the reliability of eyewitness testimony, the truthfulness of a sexual assault victim, etc.).

   1. Mental condition of defendant: Whenever the ***mental condition*** of a ***criminal defendant*** is at issue, one or both sides is likely to try to use expert testimony bearing on this condition, usually in the form of a psychiatrist's opinion. This happens most often where the defendant raises an ***insanity*** defense, in which case both the defense and prosecution are likely to offer expert psychiatric testimony.

      a. Battle of the experts: Traditionally, the use of psychiatric testimony in insanity cases has led to a confusing "battle of the experts" — the defendant's psychiatrist almost invariably recites his opinion that the defendant is insane by whatever legal test is applied in the jurisdiction, and the prosecution's expert psychiatrist asserts that he is sane by this test. Each expert's opinion is often phrased in conclusory terms, so that the effect is frequently to entrust to the experts, rather than to the jury, the duty of making the ultimate legal conclusion as to sanity.

      b. Judicial response: Courts have struggled to restrict psychiatric testimony on the defendant's mental condition to medical diagnosis, and to leave the drawing of legal conclusions for the jury.

      c. Amendment to Federal Rules: Fear that psychiatric testimony in insanity cases was usurping the role of the jury led Congress to amend the Federal Rules of Evidence. In the aftermath of John Hinkley's insanity acquittal when charged with attempting to assassinate President Reagan, Congress not only made the insanity defense more difficult to establish as a matter of substantive law (e.g., by shifting the burden of persuasion to the defendant), but also added a new subsection (b) to FRE 704.

i. **Text of 704(b):** FRE 704(a) continues to state the general rule that testimony (whether by an expert or lay witness) is not objectionable because it embraces an "ultimate issue" to be decided by the trier of fact. But 704(b), added in 1984, provides an important exception: "In a *criminal* case, an expert witness must not state an opinion about whether the *defendant* did or did not have a *mental state or condition* that constitutes an *element* of the crime charged or of a *defense*. Those matters are for the *trier of fact alone*."

ii. **Significance:** FRE 704(b) makes it somewhat more difficult for a defendant to successfully assert an insanity defense. The defendant cannot present an expert to testify as to his opinion that the defendant is insane. Presumably, the psychiatrist will also not be permitted to state that the defendant "was unable to appreciate the wrongfulness of his conduct, due to his mental disease" (now the substantive standard for insanity in federal cases). However, the expert will probably still be able to give a medical diagnosis of the defendant, and perhaps to discuss the symptoms that this diagnosed condition might produce.

Example: Murder case; insanity defense. The defense psychiatrist expert will probably be permitted to state that D is, in his opinion, a schizophrenic with low impulse control. He will probably be permitted to state the reasons that led him to this conclusion. He might be permitted to say that this condition may have contributed to the particular homicidal act charged. He will not, however, be permitted to say that D's condition prevented him from appreciating the wrongfulness of the killing — this will be held to be an ultimate legal issue, properly left to the jury.

iii. **Other conditions:** FRE 704(b) applies not only to insanity questions, but to any other "ultimate issue" relating to a criminal defendant's mental state. For instance, if D is charged with murder (so defined as to require proof of premeditation), neither the defense nor the prosecution psychiatrist expert will be permitted to express his opinion as to whether D premeditated, or was capable of premeditating, the killing. W&B, Par. 704[03].

2. **Reliability of eyewitness testimony:** Scientists have consistently shown, over many years, that *eyewitness identifications* are notoriously unreliable. Yet, juries are constantly required to reach verdicts based on such identifications, especially in criminal cases. Consequently, many defense lawyers have attempted to introduce expert testimony, usually by psychologists, to persuade the jury that eyewitness identifications in general, and especially identifications of the type involved in the present case, are less likely to be accurate than the jury might otherwise suppose.

a. **Traditional judicial resistance:** Traditionally, courts have been relatively *unwilling* to accept such psychological testimony about the weaknesses of human perception and memory. This unwillingness seems to stem mostly from judges' belief that lay persons have a basic ability to judge the reliability of identifications, and a reluctance to allow experts to help the jury do what it can do adequately without the expert.

b. **Increasing willingness:** But trial courts seem to be growing increasingly willing to allow expert testimony about the unreliability of eyewitness identifications, at least in situations where: (1) the expert confines herself to stating general principles, and does not purport to give an opinion about whether the witness in the particular case is accurate; and (2) the expert testimony relates to particular aspect of the case (e.g., the fact that the witness is identifying a person of another race), rather than being about the general fallibility of eyewitness identifications. L&S (p. 167) state that "an acknowledged expert in this area [told us] that about half the time her testimony is ***allowed*** [by the trial judge]."

     i. ***Daubert*:** The *Daubert* standard (*supra*, p. 531), applicable in all federal and some state courts, probably makes expert testimony about the unreliability of eyewitness id's more likely to be admitted. For instance, if the expert is able to describe experiments done under the scientific method demonstrating the relative unreliability of such id's, and shows that the experimental results have been published and subjected to peer review, the fact that the theory may not have been "generally accepted" (the sole issue where under *Frye*) won't be fatal.

c. **Appellate court:** However, if the trial judge excludes such testimony, it is very difficult for the defendant to convince the appeals court to reverse. That is, the decision to admit or exclude such testimony is generally held to be within the trial court's ***discretion***, and that discretion is very rarely found to be abused.

d. **Appellate case overturns exclusion:** For one of the very few (perhaps the only) appellate cases overturning a trial court's refusal to allow expert testimony on the reliability of eyewitness identifications, see *State v. Chapple*, 660 P.2d 1208 (Ariz. 1983).

3. **Lie detectors, truth serums, and hypnosis:** A number of other scientific techniques rely on psychology to determine the credibility of witnesses, or to help witnesses become more accurate. These include the ***lie detector***, ***truth serums***, and ***hypnosis.*** All of these are discussed *supra*, pp. 168-171.

4. **Rape trauma syndrome:** Another instance in which a party may try to introduce expert testimony bearing on the credibility of a witness concerns evidence of so-called ***"rape trauma syndrome."*** To rebut defense assertions that the rape victim is distorting or making up the episode, prosecutors sometimes try to introduce testimony by a psychologist or social worker that the victim exhibits the symptoms of rape trauma syndrome, and therefore probably actually experienced the events she claims to have experienced.

Quiz Yourself on

OPINIONS, EXPERTS AND SCIENTIFIC EVIDENCE *(Entire Chapter)*

122. Bart Luck is found dead in his study by his maid, Hazel. Cardinell Syn is arrested and tried for murdering Bart by filtering sodium cyanide into the study. Hazel testifies for the prosecution: "When I found him, there was a faint smell of almonds in the room." (The distinctive smell of sodium cyanide is often likened to the smell of almonds.) Defense counsel objects, claiming that Hazel isn't competent to offer her opinion on the presence of sodium cyanide and that expert testimony is needed. How do you rule? _____

123. Bluto's pit bull, Mittens, has bitten several children in the neighborhood, although no one has ever brought suit or notified the police. One day, Mittens bites Olive Oyl. Olive sues Bluto. Olive calls Wimpy, a neighbor, who testifies as to Mittens' past conduct and to the way in which Bluto supervised Mittens. During Wimpy's testimony, he says, "I sure wouldn't have let Mittens run around loose like Bluto did." Under the FRE, is this testimony admissible, if objected to? _____

124. At a trial, expert testimony concerning hieroglyphics is required. One party offers the testimony of Jean-Claude Champollion, who speaks several ancient languages and was the first to "crack" the Stone. However, Champollion, age 17, is completely lacking in academic credentials and has not published anything. Can he still qualify as an "expert"? _____

125. Claire Voyant is a recognized expert on ghosts. She is called to testify as an expert witness in a trial where an issue is whether the house of Mrs. Whatsit is haunted. Must Claire have personally examined the house in order to be able to testify as an expert? _____

126. Napoleon Bonaparte's nephew, Joseph, challenges Napoleon's will on the grounds of lack of testamentary capacity. A psychiatrist, Able Elba, is called as a witness. He has been shown Napoleon's psychiatric reports for the last five years of his life (the will was written two years before Napoleon died), and he has interviewed Napoleon's relatives and doctors. Napoleon's executor asks him: "Did Napoleon have the capacity to make a will?" Joseph objects. Assuming Elba is basing his opinion on a proper source, is the question permissible, under the FRE? _____

127. Mrs. Sprat is on trial for killing the local grocer. Mrs. Sprat pleads "not guilty," and relies to a large extent on the fact that the person who committed the crime weighed around 400 lbs. and Mrs. Sprat weighs only 125 lbs. at the time of trial, two months after the crime. Mrs. Sprat calls an expert witness, Dr. Sal Ulite, who testifies that it is medically impossible to lose 275 lbs. in two months. On cross-examination, the prosecutor asks: "Are you familiar with Dr. Di Uretic's treatise 'How to Lose Weight and Influence People'?" Dr. Ulite admits she is not, offhand, familiar with the text. Prosecutor continues: "How do you reconcile your opinion on weight loss with Dr. Uretic's opinion that 'Under careful supervision patients can safely lose 150 lbs. a month'?" Under the FRE, can the statement from Uretic's book be admitted as substantive evidence? _____

128. Same facts as prior question. Now, assume for purposes of this question that the judge holds that the quoted portion of Dr. Uretic's treatise was properly read to the jury as substantive evidence. May this portion of the treatise be admitted as an exhibit? _____

129. Evelyn Copralight is an expert in the exotic and bizarre field of fecology; that is, the science of determining a person's mental competence by examining his stool sample. At trial, the defense seeks to have Copralight testify as an expert to prove that defendant is mentally unbalanced judging from his stool sample. What's the best argument for not allowing Copralight's expert testimony? _____

130. Rodney Coaker is detained at Miami Airport on suspicion of drug smuggling. Agents don't find major quantifies of drugs in his luggage. However, they pass his clothing through a newly-designed "cocaine spectrometer," which supposedly can detect minuscule amounts of cocaine. The spectrometer reports that there are trace quantities of cocaine in Coaker's underwear. He is tried on federal cocaine-smuggling charges. At trial, the designer of the spectrometer testifies that the device is reliable, and that the results reported for Coaker's underwear indicate that cocaine must have come in contact with the underwear shortly before the test. The design of the cocaine spectrometer has never been made public or subjected to peer review; nor has the device so far become generally accepted as a method of drug testing. Do these facts mean that the court should bar the use of the spectrometer evidence? _____

Answers

122. Objection overruled. Lay opinion testimony is admissible for "sense impressions" within the everyday experience of ordinary people. Hazel's testimony to the "almond" smell is thus admissible. (But if she were to testify that she smelled the "smell of sodium cyanide," this statement probably wouldn't be admissible, unless she were shown to have a special knowledge or expertise in identifying the smell of that chemical.)

123. No, probably. Under FRE 701, non-expert testimony is limited to opinions or inferences that are (1) rationally based on the perception of the witness; (2) helpful to a *clear understanding* of the witness's testimony or to the determination of a *fact in issue*; and (3) not based on scientific, technical or specialized knowledge. Wimpy's statement about what Wimpy would have done – which is tantamount to a statement that in Wimpy's opinion Bluto was negligent – certainly doesn't seem to satisfy either branch of condition (2): it doesn't help the fact-finder understand the substance of Wimpy's testimony (exactly how Bluto kept Mittens), and it's hard to see what material fact it helps establish. Also, a court is less likely to allow lay opinion on an issue that is very closely identified with one of the "ultimate" issues in the case; whether Bluto was negligent is such an issue here.

124. Yes. Under FRE 702, although education or training certainly help to qualify an expert, his knowledge, skill, and experience alone can suffice. Thus, a convicted burglar could give expert testimony as to the use of crowbars, wires, etc. in burglary, or a marijuana user could give expert testimony that a particular sample of marijuana hails from Hawaii.

125. No. An expert may testify based on three types of information:

1. *Personal observation*; FRE 703;

2. Facts *presented to the expert at trial* (e.g., a hypothetical question); FRE 705; OR

3. Facts of which the expert "has been made aware," typically *outside the courtroom*; FRE 703. (This category is the one that applies here.)

In fact, the second-hand data relied upon need not even be *admissible*, if it's of a *type upon which experts in the field reasonably rely*. So if Claire has been given, prior to the trial, facts about the house (e.g., photos; sound recordings; depositions by people living in the house), and these items are ones that experts in the field of ghost-analysis customarily rely upon, that would be sufficient to allow her to testify.

126. No. Elba's expert opinion won't be helpful to the trier of fact, as required under FRE 702. The question of Napoleon's "testamentary capacity" would require a *legal* opinion, not a psychiatric opinion. Had the question been "Did Napoleon have the mental capacity to understand the nature and extent of his property, to know the natural objects of his bounty, and to formulate a rational scheme of distribution?" it would probably be permissible, because it would call for opinions that are (more or less) in the domain of psychiatry.

127. Yes, but only if the prosecution establishes that Uretic's book is a *reliable authority*. FRE 803(18). If it does so, the statement will be substantively admissible. This can be done through testimony of the witness being cross-examined, through direct testimony by another expert, or by the court's taking judicial notice of the fact. *Id.*

NOTE: There's an additional requirement (satisfied here) before a treatise can be used substantively: it must have either been "*called to the attention* of [the] expert witness on cross-examination" (which happened here), or "relied on by the expert on direct examination[.]" FRE 803(18). So if the prosecution had not mentioned the treatise while doing the cross of Dr. Ulite, it wouldn't have been entitled to put the treatise into evidence thereafter unless it came up with its own expert who relied on (not just confirmed the authoritativeness of) the treatise in forming her own opinion. So, for instance, the prosecution couldn't have simply read the treatise to the jury after dismissing Ulite from the stand.

COMMON LAW RULE: At common law, virtually all courts would have rejected the treatise as substantive evidence. Furthermore, many courts would have regarded the question as improper even if used just for impeachment, on the grounds that only treatises that the witness relied upon could be used to impeach him.

128. **No**. Even under the liberal FRE approach to treatise evidence, the treatise can't be admitted as an exhibit; it may only be read orally to the jury. FRE 803(18), last sent. The purpose of this limitation is mainly to prevent the treatise from being taken into the jury room (because it might have too much influence if it was).

129. **That fecology does not consist of "reliable principles and methods"**. FRE 702 allows expert testimony on scientific or other "specialized knowledge," but only if, among other things, the testimony is "the product of reliable principles and methods," which are "reliably applied ... to the facts of the case." (These requirements are based upon the Supreme Court's opinion in *Daubert v. Merrell Dow Pharmaceuticals*, requiring that the proponent of scientific evidence establish the evidence's "scientific validity.") Unless the defense can show that fecology consists of "reliable principles and methods" (which would be shown by factors such as error rate, peer review, etc.), the evidence must be excluded.

130. **Not necessarily**, though they would certainly be *factors* that would *tend* to induce the court to exclude the evidence. Under *Daubert v. Merrell Dow Pharmaceuticals*, federal courts may not admit evidence derived from use of a scientific technique unless that technique is shown to be "scientifically reliable," as well as applicable to an issue in the case. These principles are now reflected in FRE 702's requirement that expert testimony be "the product of reliable principles and methods," which are "reliably applied ... to the facts of the case." The fact that the technique has not yet been subjected to peer review, and the fact that it has not yet become generally accepted, are factors tending towards a finding of non-reliability, but these factors are not dispositive. If the sponsoring expert is extremely well-credentialed, if he testifies that he and others have extensively tested the machine, and if he reports a low error rate for the machine, these positive factors might be enough to overcome the two negative factors.

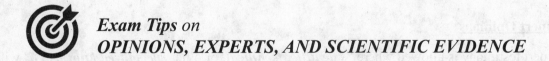

Exam Tips on OPINIONS, EXPERTS, AND SCIENTIFIC EVIDENCE

Lay opinions

☛ When a non-expert witness is testifying to what appears to be an opinion, examine two threshold issues before you apply the rules on opinions:

    ☞ First, make sure it really *is* an opinion, not some other form of evidence, such as reputation. (*Example:* If the examiner asks, "Isn't it correct that your dog is generally known to be gentle?" this question is really asking for reputation evidence, not opinion evidence.)

☞ Second, check that the statement is being *made in court*. The special rules on lay opinions apply only to in-court testimony, not to things said out-of-court (which may pose hearsay problems, but usually don't pose opinion problems). (*Example:* P wants to introduce a letter to P by W, in which W says, "In my opinion, D was travelling excessively fast before his car hit yours." This letter poses hearsay problems, but you don't need to worry about the opinion rules.)

☛ **Two requirements:** Remember that a non-expert witness may testify to an opinion if the opinion is both: (1) *rationally based on the perception* of the witness; and (2) *helpful* to a clear *understanding* of the witness's *testimony* or the *determination* of a *fact* in issue. FRE 701. Commonly-tested:

☞ Look for W's *sense impressions*, or W's perceptions of someone's or something's *appearance*, stated in terms of an opinion but based on *common everyday knowledge*. These are admissible when it *isn't reasonably practical* for W to state the *detailed underlying facts* that caused her to form her opinion. Examples:

❏ In a case where X's mental competence is in issue, W states that X's appearance changed over time from one of neatness and alertness to one of disorder and absentmindedness. That's admissible.

❏ In a case where D is alleged to have driven at excessive speed, W states, "I saw D's car come around the bend, and in my opinion, D was driving too fast for the road and weather conditions existing at the time." Admissible.

☛ **Common trap:** W didn't have had a *sufficient opportunity* to *perceive* the elements on which her opinion is based. *Examples:*

❏ If W hears a screeching sound made by one of the cars involved in an accident, but didn't see the car, W may not give an opinion as to the speed of the car.

❏ Where V is a pedestrian hit by a car, V can't testify, "I was hit by D, who was driving like drunken lunatic," if there's no evidence that V had an opportunity to observe D's behavior closely enough to form a rational opinion about whether D was in fact drunk.

☛ Remember that a non-expert may make a handwriting or voice identification (a form of opinion), if based on the witness's personal experience with the subject's voice or writing.

Expert Opinions

Expert testimony is allowed where "*scientific*, *technical*, or other *specialized knowledge*" will help the trier of fact either: (1) *understand the evidence*; or (2) *determine* a *fact* in issue. FRE 702.

☛ **Technical issue:** Look for a fact pattern where W is talking about some *technical issue* about which the ordinary person wouldn't have knowledge. That's your tip-off that you have to decide whether the requirements for expert testimony are met.

☛ **Foundation:** Make sure that a *foundation* has been laid, demonstrating the witness's expert *credentials*. The witness must be shown to possess some special technical expertise. This expertise may have been acquired by education, formal training, ***informal work experience*** ("on the job training"), or even amateur pursuit (a ***hobby***). (*Example:* A car mechanic can probably testify about what's likely to have caused a sudden brake failure, even though the mechanic has no formal training for diagnosing and fixing cars, just work experience.)

☞ **Stipulation:** Even though one party concedes (by offering a ***stipulation***) that the other's expert witness is qualified, the party offering the expert testimony is still permitted to ***continue questioning*** the witness about her qualifications. (The jurors determine ***how much weight*** to give an expert's testimony based on her qualifications, so the opponent of the witness can't, by offering to stipulate, take away the calling party's right to present these qualifications to the jury in detail.)

☞ Similarly, an expert may be ***impeached*** on cross by challenging her credentials, because this calls into question how much weight the jury should give to her testimony. (*Example:* The court permits W, a chemist, to testify as an expert witness. On cross, opposing counsel may ask W, "Isn't it true that you flunked two chemistry courses while you were in graduate school?")

☞ Examples of ***appropriate*** expert testimony:

❏ After a home is burglarized, a half-eaten piece of cheese is found in the kitchen. D is tried. W, a dentist, testifies that based on a comparison of impressions of D's teeth and a cast of the piece of cheese, in W's opinion the bite in the cheese was made by D. Admissible.

❏ After P's motorcycle is destroyed, its pre-accident value is in dispute. W, a motorcycle dealer, who never saw the bike but reviewed a picture of it and was told its make, model and year, testifies that in his opinion, such a motorcycle is customarily bought and sold on the used market for between $4,000 and $5,000. Admissible.

☞ Example of ***inappropriate*** expert testimony:

❏ W, a police officer, testifies that based on his 15 years of police experience, the skid marks made by D's car before an accident indicated that the car was travelling at 75 mph. Unless there's some evidence that W has particular expertise in interpreting skid marks (not just general expertise in police work), the testimony is inadmissible because the requisite foundation (showing of credentials) hasn't been laid.

☞ **Bases for expert opinion:** Opinion may be based on: (1) W's ***personal knowledge*** of the facts; (2) facts presented in the courtroom in the form of a ***hypothetical***; or (3) facts told to W outside the courtroom, and ***not in evidence***, as long as they are of a ***type reasonably relied upon*** by experts in the particular field. FRE 703.

☞ Most frequently-tested: An opinion based on ***material not in evidence***. Trap: The material relied on is ***inadmissible*** (usually hearsay); this ***doesn't matter***.

Example: W, an accident reconstruction specialist, testifies, on behalf of P, "Based in part on P's statement to me that she was going no more than 55 mph on a dry road when her brakes failed to work, I conclude that there must have been a manufacturing defect in the brakes." The fact that W's statement is based on inadmissible hearsay — P's out-of-court statement, in effect offered to prove that the accident happened the way P said it did — doesn't prevent W's testimony from being admissible. But P would have to show that accident reconstruction experts customarily rely on such oral accounts from accident survivors. (Also, P's lawyer would have to convince the judge that the probative value of introducing P's statement would outweigh its prejudicial value — otherwise, the statement itself could not be repeated by W to the jury, even though the opinion itself could still be admitted. See FRE 703.)

☞ Sometimes tested: use of a **hypothetical**. This is allowed, as long as the facts assumed in the hypothetical either have been or will be put **in evidence**. (*Example:* P claims whiplash. W, an orthopedist who has never treated or examined P, is called by P and asked, "If a person is sitting in the front seat of a stopped car that is hit from behind at 8 mph, is it possible for the person to sustain whiplash." W responds that it's possible. Admissible, if evidence that the impact occurred in this way has been or will be admitted.)

☛ *Trap:* Just because a highly-trained or highly-educated witness is testifying, don't assume that she's giving an opinion or that her opinion constitutes expert testimony. If she's testifying about matters she **personally observed**, and her testimony **doesn't** include opinions requiring **specialized knowledge**, the rules on expert testimony **don't apply**. (*Example:* P sues D bus company for whiplash. D claims no other passengers were injured. P calls W, an emergency-room doctor at the local hospital, who testifies that he treated 3 other passengers on that bus that day for what they said was neck pain. This isn't expert testimony, because it's a statement of W's personal knowledge of facts, and doesn't involve any opinion or inference requiring expertise.)

☛ **Ultimate issue:** Look for an opinion on an **ultimate issue of fact**. Mention that FRE 704(a) says that an otherwise-admissible opinion isn't deemed objectionable just because it embraces an ultimate issue of fact to be decided by the jury. (*Example:* If P claims that D exceeded the 60 mph speed limit and that negligence *per se* applies, W's testimony, "D looked like he was going over 60" is still admissible even though it covers the key factual issue in the case.)

☞ But W's opinion **can't** be posed in **conclusory legal terms**, because then W is treading on an area reserved to the judge and jury. *Examples:*

❏ Obscenity prosecution. Professor of film art testifies, for the prosecution, "In my opinion this film is 'obscene'." Inadmissible, because it's a legal, not factual, opinion.

❏ Psychiatrist testifies for the defense in a criminal case that "In my opinion, D didn't have malice aforethought when he shot V." Inadmissible, because it's a legal conclusion. (W should have restricted his testimony to a description of D's state of mind in non-legal terms, e.g., "D acted on a spur-of-the-moment impulse.")

Scientific Tests and Principles

When an expert's testimony concerns a scientific test or principle, check that the applicable test for reliability is satisfied. This topic is especially likely to be tested.

☛ **Federal cases:** For *federal* courts, apply the *Daubert*/FRE 702 standard, by which: (1) the testimony must **assist the trier of fact** to understand the evidence or determine a fact in issue; (2) the witness must be *"qualified"* as an expert by *"knowledge, skill, experience, training or education"*; (3) the testimony must be based upon *"sufficient facts or data"*; (4) the testimony must be the product of *"reliable principles and methods"*; and (5) the witness must have "*reliably applied* [these] principles and methods *to the facts* of the case."

☞　Pay special attention to factors (4) and (5) above (reliable principles/methods, applied reliably to the facts).

☞　As to factor (4), briefly cite some of the *factors* going to whether the testimony is the product of *"reliable principles and methods."* Here are the most important ones: (i) whether the test/principle can be *reliably tested*; (ii) whether it's been subject to *peer review* and *publication*; (iii) its *error rate*; (iv) whether it's *"generally accepted"* in the field, etc. (Note that "general acceptance" is still *a* factor under *Daubert*, even though no longer the *sole* factor.)

Example: Burglary prosecution; prosecutor says a piece of cheese left at scene has teeth marks that were made by D. Prosecution offers testimony by W, a dentist who's an expert on dental identification. Before W can testify to his ID of D, there'll have to be some showing that bite-mark identification is the product of "reliable principles and methods." If W testifies that there have been tests of the accuracy of such ID's, that the technique has been written up in peer-reviewed forensic journals, that it has a false-positive rate of less than, say, 1%, and that it's "generally accepted" by criminalists as a method of ID, this showing will be met. W will also have to show that he's applied the techniques of bite-mark ID to this particular bite mark in a "reliable" way (e.g., that he's compared the cheese with the dental records in a sufficiently precise way that his conclusion that there is a match is reliable).

☛ **State cases:** For *state* courts, mention that some have adopted *Daubert* but that some still use the *Frye* "generally accepted" standard (by which the test or principle can't come in unless its generally accepted by experts in the particular field).

☛ **Judicial notice:** If a test is very well established, the court may take *judicial notice* of its reliability instead of requiring proof of reliability. (*Example:* Probably lab tests for heroine and cocaine are now so well-established that the court may dispense with a showing of scientific reliability, and instead take judicial notice of reliability.)

☛ **Execution of test:** Regardless of the standard used, there'll still need to be a showing that the *particular way* in which the test was *carried out* was reliable.

Example: D is charged with drug smuggling, based in part on a showing that a trained dog sniffed D's luggage and signalled the presence of cocaine. Before this evidence is admissible to show that the luggage indeed contained cocaine, the prosecutor will have to show (in addition to the general reliability of dog-sniff drug IDs) that the particular dog was appropriately trained, that the handler was trained in how to interpret the dog's responses, and that standard procedures were followed in the particular case involving D.

☛ **Re-enactment:** Where the test is a re-enactment (to show that a certain result could or could not occur in certain conditions), the proponent of the re-enactment must show not only that the methodology is reliable but also that there was a ***substantial similarity*** between the original conditions and the test conditions.

Example: In a personal injury action against D (a motorcycle manufacturer), P claims that a fork on his motorcycle bent when he hit a bump, and that this bending caused him to lose control of the motorcycle and collide with a car. D's attorney offers into evidence a film showing a test on a motorcycle fork, showing the fork not bending while being subjected to 15,000 pounds of pressure. D will have to show identity of conditions between the original accident and the test (e.g., that the fork was the same, that the amount of pressure was the same, that the direction of the force was comparable, etc.).

CHAPTER 11

BURDENS OF PROOF, PRESUMPTIONS, AND OTHER PROCEDURAL ISSUES

ChapterScope

This chapter focuses on how burdens of proof and presumptions are applied. It also examines the roles of the judge and jury in determining issues of fact and law. The key concepts are:

- **Burden of production:** If P bears the *burden of production* with respect to issue *A*, this means that P has the obligation to *come forward with some evidence* that *A* exists.

  - **Consequence of failure to carry:** If a party does not satisfy this burden of production, the court will *decide the issue against him as a matter of law*, and *will not permit the jury to decide it.*

- **Burden of persuasion:** If P has the *burden of persuasion* on issue *A*, this means that if at the close of the evidence the jury *can't decide* whether *A* has been established with the relevant level of certainty, the jury must find against P on issue *A*.

  - **Measure of proof:** In civil cases, the requisite degree of certainty is usually by a *"preponderance of the evidence."* In criminal cases, the prosecution must prove all the elements beyond a reasonable doubt.

- **One shifts, other doesn't:** The burden of production as to an issue can, and often does, *shift* throughout the trial. The burden of persuasion, however, always *remains* on the party on whom it first rests.

- **Presumption:** A *"presumption"* establishes a relationship between a "basic" fact (call it "*B*") and a "presumed" fact ("*P*"). When we say that fact *P* can be presumed from fact *B*, we mean that *once B is established, P is established*, or at least rendered more likely.

  - **"Bursting bubble":** Under the FRE and in many state courts, a showing that *B* exists *causes the burden of production* on the issue of *P*/not-*P* to *shift* to the opponent of the presumption. But then, if the opponent shows some evidence of not-*P*, the presumption *disappears*, and doesn't influence the burden of persuasion. (This is the *"bursting bubble"* approach — once the opponent comes up with evidence of not-*P*, the presumption disappears from the case.)

- Judge-jury allocation as to admissibility of evidence:

  - **Issues of law:** The judge determines issues of law. Therefore, when the admissibility of evidence turns solely on an issue of law (e.g., whether the physician-patient privilege exists in the jurisdiction), the judge decides that issue.

  - **Issues of fact:** When an admissibility issue turns on a factual issue, that issue can be decided either by the judge or the jury, depending on the nature of the issue.

    - **Technical exclusionary rules:** Thus if an objection is based on a *technical exclusion-*

ary rule, any factual issue is decided by the *judge*. (*Example:* The judge decides whether something is *hearsay*.)

❑ **Conditional relevance:** But where the admissibility issue concerns *relevance*, the judge just *"pre-screens,"* with the final decision left to the jury. For instance, issues of *authentication* belong mainly to the *jury*. (*Example:* If one litigant claims that a document was sent by P to D, and the other party says the document is a forgery, the judge merely decides whether there's enough evidence of the document's authenticity that a reasonable jury could decide that it's authentic. Then, it's up to the jury to decide whether the document really *is* authentic.)

■ **"Harmless" error:** Appellate courts will only reverse if the error may have made a difference to the outcome. In other words, *"harmless errors"* (ones that couldn't have affected the outcome) aren't grounds for reversal on appeal.

■ **"Plain" error:** A party must normally make a *prompt objection* to inadmissible evidence, and if she doesn't, she'll be held to have *waived* the right to raise the error on appeal. But if the error is found to be a *"plain"* one (i.e., an egregious one), lack of objection *won't* waive the right to raise the issue on appeal.

I.   BURDENS OF PROOF

A. **Two burdens:**   Courts frequently refer to "the burden of proof." However, there are in reality two distinct burdens: (1) the burden of *production*; and (2) the burden of *persuasion*. In our discussion of each of these burdens, we will assume that plaintiff has both burdens with respect to an issue which we shall call A.

1. **Burden of production:**   When we say that P bears the burden of *production* with respect to issue A, we mean that P has the obligation to come forward with *some evidence* that A exists. This burden is sometimes referred to as the burden of *"going forward."*

   a. **Consequence of failure to carry burden:**   If a party does not satisfy this burden of production, the court will *decide the issue against him* as a matter of law. If A is part of P's *prima facie* case (e.g., a showing that the defendant was negligent in a negligence case), the consequence of P's failure to discharge his burden of production is that the judge will *direct a verdict* against P, without the case ever going to the jury. If A is not part of P's *prima facie* case, the court will direct the jury to *find against P* on issue A.

2. **Burden of persuasion:**   The burden of *persuasion* is quite different. When we say that P has the burden of persuasion on issue A, we mean that if at the close of the evidence the jury cannot decide whether A has been established with the relevant level of certainty (usually "preponderance of the evidence" in civil cases), the jury must find against P on issue A. The phrase *"risk of nonpersuasion"* is often used to describe this burden — if neither P nor D have persuaded the jury about whether A exists, to say that P bears the burden of persuasion or the risk of nonpersuasion means that he is the one who will lose on this issue.

3. **One burden shifts, other does not:** The burden of production as to issue A can, and often does, *shift* throughout the trial. The burden of persuasion, by contrast, always remains on the party on whom it first rests. The operation of both burdens can be better understood by use of the following drawing:

Figure 11-1

Adapted from Lilly, p.50

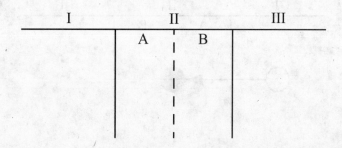

a. **Application of drawing:** Let's assume that P sues D in a negligence action, and that the only issue in dispute is whether D was in fact negligent. (That is, assume D concedes that P was harmed by D's act and that P was not contributorily negligent.) In all jurisdictions, negligence is part of P's *prima facie* case — that is, he has the burden of production as to it; also, in virtually every jurisdiction, P will have the burden of persuasion on the negligence issue. We will now add a "ball" to the drawing to show the location of the burden of production on the issue of D's negligence.

b. **Initial burden of production:** Since P bears the initial burden of producing evidence of negligence, at the start of the case the "ball" is in Zone I (literally, in P's court):

Figure 11-2

Initial burden of production on D

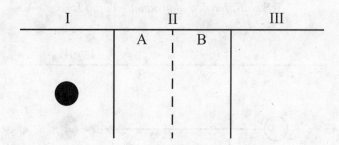

If P does not come up with enough evidence of D's negligence to allow a reasonable jury to find that D was negligent (i.e., P doesn't move the ball out of Zone I), at the conclusion of P's case, the judge will direct a verdict for D.

c. **Burden sustained:** Now, let's assume that P presents a witness, W, who testifies that he was in the car with D at the time of the accident, and that D was glancing at a blond model on a billboard by the side of the road rather than at the road when the accident occurred. Since this is evidence which, if believed by the jury, would allow a reasonable jury to find that D was negligent, P has moved the ball into at least Zone II.

Figure 11-3

P satisfies initial burden of production;
neither party bears it now

    i.   **Cross-examination:** Now, assume (as would almost certainly be the case) that D is able to cast some doubt on W's testimony by a reasonably effective cross-examination. If D does not come up with any other evidence of his non-negligence, the judge will probably conclude that the case remains in Zone II at the end of the evidence. If so, he will send the case to the jury on the issue of whether D was negligent — that is, he will let the jury decide this issue.

  d. **Shifting of burden:** Now, let's change our assumption about what P proved in his direct case — let's now assume that W testified about D's looking at the billboard, and that D chose not to cross-examine W. At the close of P's case, the judge would probably find that the ball was in Zone III — based solely on the evidence heard so far, a reasonable jury *must* find that D was negligent. Therefore by the close of P's case, *the burden of production has shifted* to D — if D were to rest without putting on a defense, D would lose.

Figure 11-4

P shifts burden of production onto D

  e. **Rebuttal evidence:** Finally, let us assume that D puts on rebuttal evidence of non-negligence, in the form of D's own testimony that he did not look at the billboard, and watched the road at all times. This testimony will probably be sufficient to move the ball back to Zone II. That is, the judge will probably conclude that a reasonable jury could believe either W or D. If so, the judge will let the case go to the jury.

Figure 11-5

*D satisfies initial burden of production;
neither party bears it now*

i.   **Incredible testimony:** Alternatively, if the judge finds that D's testimony is so totally unconvincing that no reasonable jury could believe it, he will conclude that D has not moved the ball back out of Zone III, in which case he will direct a verdict in favor of P at the close of D's case. (But judges will rarely take the case away from the jury based solely upon the judge's belief that a party's witnesses are not credible; therefore, the judge will probably let the case go to the jury, i.e., he will treat it as falling within Zone II.)

ii. **Back to Zone I:** It is even conceivable that D's case as to his own non-negligence will be so compelling that the ball will be moved all the way from Zone III back to Zone I. This might be the case, for instance, if D gave convincing evidence by another passenger in the car contradicting W's billboard story, plus impeached W's evidence by showing that W was not in the car at all at the time in question. In this event, at the close of the evidence the judge would direct a verdict in favor of D. However, such extreme swings in the burden of production are rare.

f. **Persuasion burden:** Now, let's consider the burden of ***persuasion:*** The burden of persuasion only matters (and is only measured) at the end of the case, when the issue is about to be considered by the jury. Assuming (as would be the case in almost every jurisdiction) that P has the burden of persuasion on the issue of D's negligence by a "preponderance of the evidence" (*infra*, p. 566), here's what would happen:

i.   **Significance of persuasion burden:** If the jury finds that the ball is in Zone IIA (non-negligence more probable than negligence), it will decide for D without the burden of persuasion's having any significance. If it finds that the ball is in Zone IIB (negligence more probable than non-negligence), it will decide for P, again without reference to the burden of persuasion. But if it finds that the ball is ***exactly on the dotted line*** that divides IIA from IIB (negligence exactly as probable as non-negligence), it will decide for D ***based on the burden of persuasion***.

ii. **Tie-breaker:** In other words, with respect to the usual civil issue (A or non-A) that is to be decided according to the preponderance of the evidence standard, the

only time the burden of persuasion makes a difference is when the jury finds A and non-A to be ***equally probable***.

Figure 11-6

*Only in this situation does the
burden of persuasion make a difference*

B. Allocating the burdens in civil cases: In civil cases, there is no simple formula for determining which side will bear the burden of production, or the burden of persuasion, as to a given issue. Here are some general guidelines:

1. **Usually on plaintiff:** On most civil issues, both the burden of production and the burden of persuasion are on the ***plaintiff.*** McC, p. 570. For instance, in a typical negligence case, the plaintiff bears both burdens — production and persuasion — with respect to showing the defendant's negligence, the plaintiff's harm, and the causal link between the two. (But the defendant bears both burdens with respect to comparative/contributory negligence, in most jurisdictions.)

2. **Pleading burden:** The burden of production and the burden of persuasion are both usually on the ***same party.*** Furthermore, this is usually the same party who has the burden of ***pleading*** on the issue. For instance, the plaintiff in a negligence case generally has the burden of pleading all three elements, as well as the burdens of production and persuasion as to those issues. Likewise, it is generally the defendant who bears the burden of pleading comparative/contributory negligence, as well as the burdens of production and persuasion.

3. **Substantive law:** The burdens are allocated by the jurisdiction's ***substantive law.*** That is, for every type of claim or defense, the jurisdiction has either a statutory or case-law precedent allocating the burdens. L&S, p. 794. The trial judge has little discretion about who bears the burdens, unless the issue happens to be one of first impression in the jurisdiction.

4. **Factors:** Courts and legislatures generally consider a number of factors in determining which party should bear the burdens on a given issue. Some of these factors are as follows:

   a. **Change of status quo:** The party who is attempting to ***change the status quo*** is more likely to have to bear the burdens. For instance, since the plaintiff in a negligence action is the one trying to change the status quo — trying to shift the financial loss from himself to the defendant — this is a reason for imposing most of the burdens on him.

   b. **Unusual event:** The party who is contending that the more ***unusual*** event has occurred will be more likely to have the burdens of proof. For instance, suppose P and D are in a business relationship, and P sues for services rendered; if D claims that the services were intended as a gift he will probably have the burden of proof, since services in a business context generally are not given gratuitously. McC, pp. 570-571. (But if P and D are father and son, are not in business together, and P sues D for services performed, it is P who will probably bear the burdens, since in a family situation services are generally performed without expectation of repayment. *Id.*)

   c. **Policy considerations:** Courts and legislatures often use the allocation of burdens as a means of pursuing *social policy*, including the *disfavoring* of certain defenses. This, more than anything else, probably accounts for most jurisdictions' decision to require the defendant to bear both burdens with respect to contributory negligence.

   d. **Peculiar knowledge of one party:** When knowledge of the facts required to prove a particular claim or defense lies *peculiarly within the knowledge* of one party, the burdens of proof are more likely to be placed on that party. For instance, a defendant in a contract action who claims that he has already paid for the goods or services generally bears the burdens of proving payment, on the theory that his records are a better source of information about the defense than are the plaintiff's. McC, p. 570. However, this "peculiarly within the knowledge of one party" doctrine is frequently *ignored*; for instance, a defendant must generally prove contributory negligence even though the facts surrounding the alleged negligence are probably better known to the plaintiff than to the defendant. *Id.*

5. **"Prima facie case":** The term *"prima facie case"* is often used to describe the collection of issues on which the plaintiff has the burden of *production*. W,M,A&B, p. 1181. According to the most common use of the term *"prima facie,"* the plaintiff has established a *prima facie* case for, say, negligence when he has produced enough evidence of defendant's negligence, his own harm, and a causal link, to permit the case to go to the jury.

C. **Allocation of burdens of proof in criminal cases:** The allocation of the burdens of proof in *criminal* cases is subject to constitutional (due process) limits.

   1. **Element distinguished from affirmative defense:** Before we can understand these constitutional limits on how the state may allocate the burdens of proof in a criminal case, we must first understand a key distinction which the Supreme Court has drawn between *"elements of the crime"* and *"affirmative defenses."*

      a. **Elements of the crime:** When the legislature defines a particular crime, those factors which the definition lists as part of the crime are the "elements" of that crime. For instance, if the state has defined murder to be the premeditated taking of another person's life, the two elements of the crime are: (1) the taking of another person's life; and (2) the mental state of premeditation.

      b. **Affirmative defense:** The state may choose to recognize certain factors as being *excuses* or *justifications* that prevent otherwise culpable conduct from being criminal, or that at least reduce the severity of the crime. These excuses and justifications are commonly made *"affirmative defenses,"* as distinguished from being elements of the crime. The state might, for instance, define murder in the simple way summarized in the prior paragraph, and then add a clause: "However, if the accused demonstrates that, at the time of the killing, he could not tell the difference between right and wrong, this shall constitute an affirmative defense."

    c. Significance: The key significance of the distinction is that the ***state has the burdens of production and persuasion with respect to all elements*** of the crime, whereas the ***defendant always has the burden of production***, and often the burden of persuasion, with respect to an ***affirmative defense***. (This distinction is explored further below, in connection with the discussion of constitutional limits on allocating burdens to the defendant.)

    d. Discretion: The state has a considerable amount of discretion in deciding whether to define a factor as being an element of the crime or, rather, an affirmative defense. For instance, a state could obviously choose to make absence of insanity an element of the crime of murder (in which case the prosecution would have the burden not only of producing evidence of sanity but of persuading the jury beyond a reasonable doubt that the defendant was sane), rather than making insanity an affirmative defense. The state is always free to make a given factor an element of the crime (since this works to the defendant's advantage).

        i. Limits on affirmative defenses: But there may be constitutional limits on the state's ability to make a factor an affirmative defense. For instance, the Supreme Court would probably hold that a state was violating the defendant's due process and Eighth Amendment rights if it authorized the death sentence for murder, and then defined murder as "the taking of another's life," while making absence of premeditation an affirmative defense as to which the defendant has the burdens of both production and persuasion.

        ii. Allowable affirmative defenses: It seems quite clear that the state may constitutionally make the following factors affirmative defenses, as to which the defendant bears the burden of both production and persuasion: ***insanity, self-defense, duress, voluntary intoxication,*** and ***extreme emotional disturbance.*** Most of these are discussed below in the context of burden of persuasion.

2. Elements of crime: If the state has made a factor an ***element of the crime***, the state must bear both the burden of ***production*** and ***persuasion*** with respect to that element. In fact, the Due Process Clause requires that the state not only bear the burden of persuasion on each element, but that it do so according to a ***"beyond a reasonable doubt"*** standard. The Supreme Court so held in *In re Winship*, 397 U.S. 358 (1970).

3. Allocation for affirmative defense: By contrast, the state has far more leeway with respect to allocating the burdens concerning an ***affirmative defense***:

4. Production burden: Apparently the state may impose on the defendant the ***burden of production*** on ***any affirmative defense***. McC, p. 593. Even if there is an overlap between conduct or a mental state the absence of which is an element of the crime, and conduct or a mental state which has been defined as an affirmative defense, the state may impose upon the defendant the burden of coming forward with at least some evidence in support of the affirmative defense.

    Example: Suppose the state defines murder to include only those killings in which the defendant acts "with premeditation and without fear for his own life or safety." Suppose further that the state defines self-defense as an affirmative defense. The state may constitutionally place the burden of production on D, in the sense that he must come forward with at least some evidence of self-defense before the jury will be given an instruction that self-defense can negate the crime. This is true even though the state has defined the crime in such a way that an aspect of the affirmative defense (fear for one's own safety) is also a factor the absence of which is an element of the crime. McC, p. 593.

5. **Burden of persuasion:** But the state is more limited when it comes to allocating the burden of *persuasion*. If the defense is a "true" affirmative defense, in the sense that it does not overlap with an element of the crime, the state may place upon the defendant the burden of persuasion by a preponderance of the evidence. But if there is a *substantial overlap* between an act or mental state needed to show an affirmative defense, and the absence of that act or mental state needed as an element of the crime, the *state* must bear the burden of persuasion (and, in fact, persuasion beyond a reasonable doubt). Determining when such an overlap exists can be difficult, as shown by a series of Supreme Court cases:

   a. **Heat of passion (*Mullaney*):** In *Mullaney v. Wilbur*, 421 U.S. 684 (1975), the Court held it unconstitutional for Maine to place on the defendant the burden of persuasion with respect to the affirmative defense of *"heat of passion."*

   b. **Extreme emotional disturbance (*Patterson*):** But one year after *Mullaney*, the Court held that a murder defendant *could* be constitutionally required to bear the burden of persuading the jury that he acted under *"extreme emotional disturbance."* *Patterson v. New York*, 432 U.S. 197 (1977). In *Patterson*, New York defined second degree murder to include the element of "intent to cause the death of another person," and made it an affirmative defense that the defendant "acted under the influence of extreme emotional disturbance for which there was a reasonable explanation or excuse." The Court concluded that the defendant, to succeed with the affirmative defense here, was *not required to negative any element of the crime*: a showing by the defendant that he acted under extreme emotional disturbance was not necessarily inconsistent with his having had the basic mental state for the crime (an intent to kill). (Three dissenters in *Patterson* contended that the defense of "extreme emotional disturbance" was a direct descendant of the "heat of passion" defense at issue in *Mullaney*, and that the prosecution should have the burden of persuasion on the emotional disturbance defense.)

   c. **Insanity:** So long as the state defines murder in such a way that sanity is not an element of the crime, the defendant may constitutionally be required to bear the burden of persuasion on *insanity*. *Leland v. Oregon*, 343 U.S. 790 (1952). (The *Patterson* Court indicated that it believed *Leland* was still good law.)

   d. **Self-defense:** The defendant can ordinarily be required to bear the persuasion burden with respect to the affirmative defense of *self-defense*.

   e. **Summary:** Following the string of cases ending in *Martin*, the state's right to assign the persuasion burden to the defendant on an affirmative defense is confused. However, some things seem clear:

    i. Great leeway: The state has substantial leeway to define affirmative defenses as it wishes, and to assign the burden of persuasion to the defendant as to those defenses. So long as there is not a ***virtual identity*** between the act or mental state defined as an element of the crime, and the act or mental state whose absence is an element of the affirmative defense, the state may define affirmative defenses as it wishes and impose on the defendant the persuasion burden as to those defenses.

    ii. Valid defenses: If the state is at all careful in defining the crimes and the defenses, it may impose upon the defendant the burden of persuasion concerning the common affirmative defenses of ***extreme emotional disturbance***, ***insanity***, and ***self-defense***; probably by careful drafting, the state can even make the defendant prove ***heat of passion*** (despite the fact that Maine, due to its clumsy drafting, failed to do this constitutionally in *Mullaney*).

D. Satisfying the burden of production: When a party bears the burden of production on an issue, ***how much evidence*** must he produce in order to discharge that burden? The answer varies depending on whether the case is civil or criminal.

    1. Civil case: In a civil case, the party bearing the burden of ***persuasion*** as to fact A will generally have to prove that A exists "by a preponderance of the evidence." (This preponderance-of-the-evidence test is discussed more extensively *infra*, p. 566.) If P has this persuasion burden concerning issue A, and also has the production burden on A, he will discharge his production burden if he comes forward with enough evidence ***so that a reasonable jury could conclude, by a preponderance of the evidence, that A exists***.

        a. Judge decides: It is the ***judge***, not the jury, who decides whether the party bearing the production burden has satisfied that burden. The judge's only function is to decide whether a reasonable jury could reach either conclusion — if not, he will take the case away from the jury in response to a motion for directed verdict.

        Example: Suppose that P, in a negligence case, has the burden both of persuasion and production as to D's negligence. (Assume there are no other issues in the case.) At the close of D's evidence, D moves for a directed verdict. The trial judge does ***not*** attempt to determine whether, in the judge's personal opinion, P has established D's negligence by a preponderance of the evidence. (That is the function of the jury.) Instead, he merely determines whether P has ***met his production burden***. To do this, the judge will ask himself, "Regardless of what I personally think about D's negligence, has P produced at least enough evidence so that a reasonable jury could find that D was negligent?" If the answer is "yes," the judge will deny (and if "no," the judge will grant) D's motion for a directed verdict. (Putting the matter in terms of our chart on p. 557, *supra*, the judge must decide whether the "ball" is in Zone I — in which case he must direct a verdict for D, or is rather in Zone II or III, in which case he will tell D to put on his case.)

        b. Single witness: A party will often be able to satisfy his burden of production by presenting just a ***single witness***, even though his adversary presents many more witnesses on the issue. Unless the single witness is patently unbelievable, the judge will ordinarily conclude that a reasonable jury might believe his testimony instead of the testimony of the greater number of witnesses on the other side, and will allow the case to go to the jury.

c. Disbelief of adversary's denials: But now, suppose that P, having the burden of proof on issue A, doesn't call any witnesses who testify to A, but does call his *adversary* (or witnesses favorable to the adversary), who testify to non-A. Suppose further that A cross-examines these witnesses, in a way that casts doubt on whether they are correct in asserting non-A. Has P, by this cross-examination, discharged his burden of producing some evidence of A? After all, P can claim that a reasonable jury might *disbelieve* the defense witness's assertions of non-A.

    i. Unsuccessful: Generally, P will be held *not* to have carried his production burden no matter how withering his cross-examination of D or D's witnesses. See, e.g., *Dyer v. MacDougall*, 201 F.2d 265 (2d Cir. 1952), so indicating. The reason is that if P were held to have carried his production burden here, then there is no situation in which D could ever successfully *appeal* the judge's *refusal to direct a verdict for him*. For, as the court pointed out in *Dyer*, no matter how overwhelming in the trial record was the evidence for the defendant who seeks a directed verdict, and no matter how non-existent the evidence for the plaintiff, an appeals court would still have to conclude that "a reasonable jury might have disbelieved all the witnesses, based on their demeanor, which we cannot evaluate on appeal. Therefore, the trial judge rightly sent the case to the jury." Therefore, to meet the production burden, a plaintiff must come up with *some affirmative evidence* for the proposition on which he bears the burden.

d. Burden on defendant: Recall that the production burden may *shift* during the trial. For instance, if P begins by having the burden of producing evidence of D's negligence, the evidence that P presents during his case may be so overwhelming that the production burden now shifts to D. (That is, in terms of our chart *supra*, p. 557, the ball shifts not just into Zone II, but all the way to Zone III, as shown in Drawing 11-4.) Now, unless D comes forward with some evidence that he was not negligent, at the close of D's case the judge will have to direct a verdict in *P's* favor (assuming there are no other issues in the case).

    i. Easy to satisfy: Here, however, D generally does not have the burden of producing direct evidence of his own non-negligence; he can probably carry his production burden by an effective *cross-examination* of P's witnesses, or by calling hostile witnesses in his own case and using leading questions to impeach their testimony. "Unless [D's] challenge to the plaintiff's case is incredible or does not dispute the central issues, the judge must let the case go to the jury." L&S, p. 795, n. 4.

2. Criminal case: In a *criminal* case, the prosecution bears the burden of persuasion on all issues. Furthermore, it must discharge this burden according to a "beyond a reasonable doubt" standard (see *infra*, p. 567). This tougher standard has an important effect on the burden of *production*.

a. Production burden on defendant: Recall that a criminal defendant will only be required to bear the production burden if the issue constitutes an *affirmative defense*. That is, when an issue is an element of the crime, it is the prosecution who will bear the production (as well as persuasion) burden. (See *supra*, p. 562.) If the defendant bears the production burden on a given affirmative defense — e.g., insanity or self-defense — the amount of evidence he must produce to get to the jury on that affirmative defense will generally ***depend on the persuasion burden.***

    i.   Illustration: For instance, if the legislature has said that a defendant must prove insanity by a preponderance of the evidence, then to meet the production burden the defendant must come forward with enough evidence of insanity so that a reasonable jury could conclude that the defendant was more likely insane than not. If he does not, the judge will instruct the jury that it must find the defendant to have been sane. If, by contrast, the legislature has said that although insanity is an affirmative defense, once properly raised the prosecution bears the burden of disproving it beyond a reasonable doubt (this is the practice in most states), then it is easier for the defendant to discharge his production burden. He must merely come forward with enough evidence of insanity so that a reasonable jury could have a reasonable doubt about his sanity.

    b.   Burden on prosecution: With respect to ***elements of the crime***, it is the prosecution which must (as a constitutional matter) bear the burden of production as well as persuasion — the prosecution has the burden of persuading the jury "beyond a reasonable doubt" as to each of these elements. The vast majority of courts have held that this tough standard ***also applies to the production burden***. That is, in order to even have the case go to the jury, the prosecution must come forward with enough evidence on each element that a reasonable jury could find that the element has been proved beyond a reasonable doubt. McC, p. 572. Under this majority view, if at the close of the prosecution's case the judge believes that a reasonable jury must have a doubt about one of the elements, he must direct a verdict of acquittal, ***even though he believes that it is more probable than not that the defendant committed the crime***.

E. Satisfying the burden of persuasion: We turn now to a different but related issue: What must a party do to satisfy the burden of ***persuasion*** on an issue? Again, the answer varies depending on whether the case is civil or criminal.

    1. Civil cases: In civil cases, a party who bears the burden of persuasion on an issue, A, must generally show that A exists "by a ***preponderance of the evidence***." This standard is usually interpreted to mean that the party bearing the persuasion burden must persuade the jury "that the existence of the contested fact is ***more probable than its non-existence***." McC, p. 575.

        a. Sheer statistics: There is an important practical exception to the principle that the civil burden of persuasion is carried by proof that the event is "more probable than not." Courts generally ***refuse*** to accept evidence that is ***purely statistical*** as sufficient to carry this burden, even though the evidence produces a likelihood of greater than 50%. Instead, courts generally require that the jury end up with an ***"actual belief"*** in the truth of the fact, not merely a probabilistic estimate of its truth. McC, p. 575.

        Example: Suppose that a jet plane "buzzes" Farmer's field, frightening a mule, which then kicks Farmer in the head. Farmer sues the Air Force, but the only evidence he can come up with that the plane belonged to the Air Force rather than to a civilian airline is that according to air traffic control records, 70% of the planes flying over Farmer's farm that day belonged to the Air Force.

Probably no court would find that Farmer had carried his burden of persuasion here, even though, on a purely statistical basis, there was a 70% chance that the offending plane belonged to the Air Force. Yet, had Farmer testified that he got just a fleeting glimpse of the plane, and he thought he identified a five-pointed star on the tail, the court would probably accept this as sufficient. In the latter situation, the trier could reasonably have an "actual belief" that the plane was an Air Force plane, rather than a mere statistical hunch. Yet, probably the traffic control records are a better predictor of whether the plane actually belonged to the Air Force than Farmer's weak testimony. See K&W, p. 767.

   b. **"Clear and convincing" standard:** For the vast bulk of civil issues, the party bearing the burden of persuasion must show the fact by a "preponderance of the evidence." But for a few types of issues, a stricter standard is used: the fact must be proved by ***"clear and convincing"*** evidence. Examples of claims requiring proof by clear and convincing evidence are: (1) suits to rescind a contract on account of ***fraud***; (2) suits on oral contracts to make a will; and (3) suits for the specific performance of an oral contract. McC, p. 575. In general, claims based on equity rather than law are more likely to be subject to this more stringent standard.

      i. **"Highly probable":** It has been argued that to meet the burden of persuading by "clear and convincing" evidence, the proponent must show that the fact is ***"highly probable."*** *Id.*

2. **Criminal cases ("beyond reasonable doubt"):** In criminal cases, the prosecution's burden of persuasion on all elements of the case means that these elements must be proved ***"beyond a reasonable doubt."*** This requirement is constitutionally mandated. Some jurisdictions do not attempt to define "reasonable doubt" for the jury, while others do. McC, p. 577.

   a. **Voluntariness of confession:** Suppose the prosecution wants to introduce a ***confession*** that it claims was given by the defendant, and the defendant asserts that the confession was ***involuntary***. There is no constitutional requirement that the prosecution prove the voluntariness of the confession beyond a reasonable doubt. Instead, the dictates of due process are satisfied so long as the trial judge determines that the confession was voluntary by a ***preponderance of the evidence***. *Lego v. Twomey*, 404 U.S. 477 (1972).

   b. **Sentencing facts:** In *sentencing* a defendant who has just been convicted of a crime, the judge will often need to take into account facts and allegations that were not elements of the crime, and thus not proved beyond a reasonable doubt by the mere fact of conviction. Proof of these facts relied on in sentencing probably does ***not*** have to be made beyond a reasonable doubt. However, some judges have required that such facts be established by a "clear and convincing evidence" standard.

II. PRESUMPTIONS

   A. **Presumptions generally:** The term "presumption" refers to a relationship between a "basic" fact (which we'll call B) and a "presumed" fact (which we'll call P). When we say that fact P can be presumed from fact B, we mean that once B is established, P is established or at least rendered more likely.

1. **Four meanings:**   However, the precise meaning of "presumption" is uncertain. When courts and legislatures say that P is to be presumed from B, they may mean any of at least four quite distinct things. In order from weakest to strongest link between P and B, these possibilities are as follows:

   a. **Permissible inference:**   The court or legislature may mean merely that once B is established (and in the absence of any direct proof about whether P does or does not exist), the jury *may* (but need not) conclude that P exists. This is the weakest link between B and P that is ever contemplated by the term "presumption." More commonly, this weak link is referred to as a *"permissible inference"* rather than a presumption.

   b. **Shifts production but not persuasion burden:**   The presumption may mean that if a party who has the burden of production on P establishes B, his adversary has the *burden of production* on non-P. That is, the existence of the presumption, according to this view, shifts the production burden to the person who does not benefit from the presumption. However, under this view, the burden of *persuasion* is *not shifted* — if the burden of persuasion on fact P would have been on a party in the absence of that presumption, that burden is still upon him even though he is the beneficiary of the presumption.

   c. **Shifts both production and persuasion burdens:**   Another view of presumptions is that once the beneficiary proves B, both the burden of production and the burden of *persuasion* shift to his adversary with respect to fact P. Under this view, if plaintiff would in the absence of a presumption have the burden both of production and persuasion as to P, once he establishes B it is up to defendant not only to produce some evidence of non-P, but to persuade the jury of P's non-existence.

   d. **Conclusive presumption:**   Finally, the term presumption may mean that once B is established, P is *conclusively (irrebuttably) presumed* to exist. Such a "conclusive presumption" really amounts to a *substantive rule of law*.

   Example: Suppose that the legislature enacts a statute providing that when a letter is shown to have been properly addressed and mailed, it shall be presumed to have been received by the addressee. Assume further that plaintiff is trying to prove that a letter he sent to defendant was received by defendant, that defendant denies having received the letter, and that in the absence of the presumption, plaintiff would have both the burden of producing evidence of defendant's receipt of the letter as well as the burden of persuading the jury, by a preponderance of the evidence, that defendant received the letter. Here is what would happen under each of the four above meanings of "presumption":

   Under definition (a) — permissive inference — even if P proved conclusively that he properly addressed and mailed the letter, and even if D came forward with no evidence at all that he never received it, the presumption's only result would be that the judge would instruct the jury, "If you find that plaintiff properly addressed and mailed the letter, you may, but need not, find that defendant received it."

Under definition (b) — shift of production but not persuasion burden — once P produced evidence of the basic fact (that he properly addressed and mailed the letter), this would be enough to shift to D the burden of coming forward with some evidence that he did not receive the letter. If D came forward with such evidence (e.g., his own testimony that he examines his mail every day, and knows that he did not receive the letter), this would probably be enough to discharge D's production burden. Since under this meaning of "presumption" the persuasion burden is not shifted, P would still have the burden of persuading the jury that D actually received the letter, and P would lose if the jury thought it was as likely that D did not receive the letter as that he did. (Probably the judge would not mention the presumption in instructing the jury, if the judge concluded that D had met his production burden by coming forward with some evidence of non-receipt.)

Under definition (c) — burden of persuasion, as well as production, shifted — once P produced evidence of proper addressing and mailing, D would not only have to produce some evidence of non-receipt, but would also now bear the burden of persuading the jury, by a preponderance of the evidence, that he never received the letter. If D came forward with some evidence of non-receipt (e.g., his testimony of non-receipt), the judge would then instruct the jury, "If you find that P properly addressed and mailed the letter, then you must find that D actually received it, unless you find it more probable than not that D never in fact received the letter." (The judge might also inform the jury of the presumption's existence.)

Under definition (d) — conclusive presumption — if P shows that the letter was properly addressed and mailed, the judge will conclude as a matter of law that D is deemed to have received the letter. The jury will not even get to decide this issue.

2. **Presumptions are rebuttable:** Most courts and commentators agree that only those relations between facts B and P summarized by definitions (b) and (c) are properly classified as presumptions in *civil* cases. That is, for a relationship to be a presumption in a civil case, it: (1) must at least shift the burden of *production* to the party opposing the presumption; and (2) must be *rebuttable*.

3. **Reasons for creating:** Presumptions may be created either by the legislature or by judges. Here are some of the many reasons why a judge or legislature might create a presumption:

   a. **Probability:** To reflect the judge's or legislature's belief that if the basic fact (B) is proved, it is so highly probable that the presumed fact (P) also exists that it is sensible and *time-saving* to assume the truth of P unless the adversary disproves it. McC, p. 581.

      Example: When a properly stamped and addressed letter is mailed, it is so probable that the addressee received it that it is sensible and time-saving to presume receipt unless the addressee shows otherwise.

   b. **Social and economic policy:** To carry out some *social* or *economic policy* by benefiting one contention over another.

Example: Statutes commonly create a presumption that when a woman gives birth to a child while married, the husband is presumed to be the father. This presumption furthers the social policy of not needlessly burdening children with the label of illegitimacy.

c. **Superior access to proof:** To counteract the opponent's *superior access* to proof.

Example: When a bailor turns goods over to a bailee in good condition, and they are returned in damaged condition, it is commonly presumed that the damage was due to the bailee's negligence. The bailee has better knowledge of what happened than the bailor, so it is only fair to shift to him the burden of showing what happened once the bailor demonstrates that the damage occurred while the goods were in bailee's custody.

B. **Effect of presumption in civil cases:** We turn now to a more detailed consideration of the effect of a presumption in a civil case. Our discussion focuses on what are usually thought of as "true" presumptions, i.e., definitions (b) and (c) above (presumption at least shifts the burden of production, and is rebuttable).

1. **Debate between Thayer and Morgan:** Probably the most famous intellectual disagreement in evidence history concerned the effects to be given to presumptions in civil cases.

   a. **Thayer ("bursting bubble") majority view:** Professor Thayer believed that presumptions should be given the effect of definition (b), that is, that they should shift the burden of production but not the burden of persuasion. Under the Thayer approach, once the opponent discharges his production burden by coming up with some evidence showing the non-existence of the presumed fact, the presumption *disappears from the case*, and the jury decides the issue as if the presumption had never existed. For this reason, the Thayer approach is often referred to as the *"bursting bubble"* approach. The Thayer approach has been adopted by a *majority* of jurisdictions.

   b. **Morgan (minority) view:** Professor Morgan argued that the Thayer approach gives too little weight to presumptions, and that a presumption should ordinarily be given the effect described in definition (c). That is, he contended that the presumption should shift not only the burden of production, but *also the burden of persuasion*, to the presumption's opponent. He contended that presumptions normally reflect well-reasoned and deeply held beliefs about policy or probability on the part of the legislature, and that these beliefs should not be disregarded merely because the opponent has managed to come up with just enough evidence of the non-existence of the presumed fact to take that issue to the jury. Nonetheless, only a minority of jurisdictions have adopted Professor Morgan's approach.

      i. **Partial adoption:** Some states have given a Thayer effect to some presumptions and a Morgan effect to others. For instance, the California Evidence Code divides presumptions into two categories: (1) Presumptions based on public policy place the burden of persuasion, not just production, on the presumption's opponent (a Morgan effect); but (2) Presumptions that do not implement any public policy other than facilitating correct adjudication do not shift the burden of persuasion (a bursting bubble or Thayer effect). See Cal. Evid. Code §600 et seq.

c. Chart: Observe that the Thayer and Morgan positions differ from each other only when the presumption's opponent comes up with evidence of the non-existence of the presumed fact. Table 11-1 on p. 572, *infra*, shows the effect of the presumption, under various states of the evidence, for both the Thayer and Morgan approaches.

2. Federal Rules: The choice between the "bursting bubble" and Morgan approaches is so difficult that when it came time to enact the Federal Rules, the Supreme Court and Congress disagreed. FRE 301, as originally approved by the Supreme Court, enacted the Morgan approach of having the presumption shift the burden of persuasion as well as production. But Congress rejected the Morgan approach, and by modifying FRE 301 instead enacted what is really the "bursting bubble" approach to presumptions:

> "In a *civil* case, unless a federal statute or these rules provide otherwise, the *party against whom a presumption is directed* has the *burden of producing evidence to rebut* the presumption. But this rule *does not shift the burden of persuasion, which remains on the party who had it originally.*"

a. Illustration: The workings of FRE 301 are illustrated by *Texas Dept. of Community Affairs v. Burdine*, 450 U.S. 248 (1981).

    i. Facts: P claimed that D, a public agency, had refused to promote her and had then fired her, because she was a woman. She sued under Title VII of the 1964 Civil Rights Act. Under prior decisions interpreting Title VII, the burdens of proof and the benefits of presumptions were distributed as follows: P had the burden of producing evidence that D intentionally discriminated against her. She also had the burden of persuading the trier of fact that such discrimination occurred. However, she had the benefit of a presumption: upon showing the basic fact (that she was qualified, that she was rejected, and that the position remained open for some time after the rejection, until it was filled by a male), she gained the benefit of a presumption that there had been unlawful discrimination against her.

    ii. Court of Appeals: The Court of Appeals had held that D should lose unless it came forward with evidence that would *persuade* the trier of fact that D had acted for lawful motives. In other words, the Court of Appeals held that the existence of the presumption shifted to D the burden of persuading the trier of fact as to D's motives.

    iii. Supreme Court: But the Supreme Court reversed. Although it referred to FRE 301 only in passing, it followed that Rule's approach to presumptions. As the Supreme Court held, the existence of the presumption affected only the initial burden of production, not the burden of persuasion — the burden of persuasion remained on P, not D. Therefore, D was not required to "persuade" the trier of fact that its motives were proper. Instead, D was required "only [to] produce admissible evidence which would allow the trier of fact rationally to conclude" that the presumed fact (improper motives by D) did not exist.

b. Instructions to jury: Under FRE 301, once the opponent of the presumption comes up with enough evidence of the presumed fact's non-existence that a jury could reasonably find that the presumed fact does not exist, the presumption clearly disappears

Table 11-1

Rebuttable Presumptions — Thayer/"Bursting Bubble" vs. Morgan

Presumption is that a properly addressed and mailed letter (basic fact) was received by the addressee (presumed fact). **B** is the beneficiary of the presumption and **O** is the opponent. Without the presumption, **B** would have the burden of persuasion (and production) that addressee received the letter. Presumption enters the case when **B** introduces some evidence of the proper addressing and mailing of the letter. This is the only issue in the case.

Type of presumption	O introduces:	The jury will be instructed that:
Thayer / "Bursting Bubble" (Burden of production, but not of persuasion, shifted to **O**)	No evidence of whether letter was either mailed properly (basic fact) or received (presumed fact)	If they find proper mailing, they must find receipt. [If reasonable jury must find proper mailing, judge will direct verdict for **B**.]
	Some evidence that letter was not properly mailed,* but no evidence regarding receipt	If they find proper mailing, they must find receipt.
	Some evidence that letter was never received (with or without evidence regarding proper mailing)	[No jury instruction requiring the jury to find receipt if they find mailing.] If **B** convinces jury by a preponderance of the evidence that letter was received, they shall decide for **B**; otherwise, they must decide for **O**. [In some states (and possibly under the Federal Rules), judge will tell jury that the presumption exists, but he will tell them that they may, not must, infer receipt from proper mailing.]
Morgan (Burden of persuasion, as well as production, shifted to **O**)	No evidence of whether letter was either mailed properly or received	[Same as for *Thayer*]
	Some evidence that letter was not properly mailed,* but no evidence regarding receipt	[Same as for *Thayer*]
	Some evidence that letter was never received (with or without evidence regarding proper mailing)	If they find proper mailing, they must find receipt (and thus decide for **B**), unless **O** convinces them by a preponderance of the evidence that letter was not received. [The jury thus learns of the presumption.]

* If **O**'s evidence of improper addressing or mailing is so convincing that no jury could reasonably find proper addressing and mailing, court will order the jury to find improper addressing or mailing, and presumption will not help **B**. This is true for *Morgan*-type presumption as well.

[Adapted from L&S, Table IX-1 (p.805)]

from the case in the sense that there is no effect on the burden of persuasion. This is a consequence of the fact that FRE 301 adopts the "bursting bubble" view. But it is not so clear whether the trial judge may ***tell the jury*** that a presumption exists. Apparently, the judge may tell the jury that it ***"may"*** infer the existence of the presumed fact from the basic fact, but the jury is not ***required*** to make this inference. Conference Report on R. 301; S&R, p. 86.

    c. **Criminal cases:** Observe that FRE 301 deals only with *civil* cases. Presumptions in *criminal* cases were to have been dealt with by FRE 303, but this Rule was not passed by Congress, which instead intended to deal with the subject in the complete recodification of federal criminal law which it was working on at the time. This recodification has not yet occurred. Therefore, presumptions in federal criminal cases are not governed by any general statute; the matter is left to case law, except that some particular federal statutes establish the effect of particular presumptions, and except that the constitution limits the use of presumptions against criminal defendants. These constitutional issues are discussed *infra*, p. 573.

3. **Constitutional questions:** Normally the use of presumptions in a civil case will not raise any *constitutional* issue.

C. **Effect in criminal cases:** In *criminal* cases, the main issues involving presumptions are ***constitutional***: To what extent may the state impose a presumption that operates to the defendant's detriment?

    1. **Terminology:** Before we can get into the constitutional issues, we must first revise our terminology. Recall that in the context of civil presumptions, we treated only "rebuttable presumptions" as being true presumptions — irrebuttable presumptions on the one hand, and permissive inferences on the other, were treated as being something other than presumptions. But in the criminal context, recent Supreme Court cases unfortunately use the term "presumption" to describe links between the basic and presumed facts that, in a civil context, would not be presumptions. The Supreme Court's terminology now seems to be as follows:

        a. **Permissive presumptions:** ***"Permissive"*** presumptions are those that never require the jury to do anything. A permissive presumption merely authorizes the judge to instruct the jury that it "may" infer the presumed fact if it finds the basic fact. (This is what, in the civil context, we referred to as a "permissive inference.")

        Example: The legislature, in defining the crime of stolen property, requires that the defendant be shown to have had knowledge that the property was stolen, but also provides that knowledge that the property was stolen may be inferred from the fact that it was stolen. If the judge merely instructs the jury, "If you find that the property was stolen, you may — but need not — infer that D knew it was stolen," this is a "permissive presumption."

        b. **Mandatory presumption:** Conversely, the Supreme Court now recognizes two types of ***"mandatory"*** presumptions (corresponding to the "bursting bubble" and Morgan presumptions in the civil context):

            i. **Burden of production only:** Some mandatory presumptions shift to the defendant the burden of producing some evidence on an issue, but do not shift the burden of persuasion. (This corresponds to the "bursting bubble," presumption on the civil side.)

    ii. Shift of persuasion burden: Alternatively, a mandatory presumption might also shift the burden of persuasion as well as production. (This corresponds to the Morgan view on the civil side.)

    iii. Affirmative defense: There is a very close practical relationship between a mandatory presumption and an ***affirmative defense***. An affirmative defense always has the effect of shifting to the defendant the burden of producing evidence on the defense; sometimes (but not always) it also has the effect of shifting the burden of persuasion to him (in which case it is comparable to a "bursting bubble" presumption). Yet, as we shall see, the Supreme Court has imposed greater constitutional limitations on the use of mandatory presumptions in criminal cases than on the use of affirmative defenses.

2. Constitutionality of affirmative defenses: Before we consider the constitutionality of presumptions, let's briefly recap the constitutional rules on ***affirmative defenses***: Recall that the state may treat any defense as an affirmative defense, and place both burden of production and persuasion on the defendant, so long as there is not a total overlap between the facts relevant to the affirmative defense and those relevant to an essential element to the offense. (See *supra*, pp. 563-564, especially the discussion of the *Mullaney* and *Patterson* cases.) Consequently, statutes treating self-defense, insanity, and extreme emotional distress as affirmative defenses, as to which the defendant bears the burdens both of production and persuasion, have been upheld against constitutional attack by the Court.

3. Presumptions: Now, we turn to the constitutionality of presumptions. A presumption's constitutionality in criminal cases depends heavily on whether the presumption is found to be "permissive" or "mandatory."

    a. Permissive: If the presumption is ***"permissive,"*** apparently all that is required is that the fact-finder could ***"rationally"*** have inferred the presumed fact from the basic fact.

    Example: In the case which gave rise to the Supreme Court's "permissive" versus "mandatory" terminology, a New York statute provided that the presence of a firearm in an automobile is (with certain exceptions) presumptive evidence of the weapon's illegal possession by all persons then occupying the vehicle. The three Ds (all adult males) were charged with illegal possession of guns that were found in the purse of a 16-year-old girl who was travelling with them in a car. The jury was told of the presumption, and told that "upon proof of the presence of the [guns], you may infer and draw a conclusion that [the prohibited weapons were] possessed by each of the defendants who occupied the automobile at the time when such instruments were found."

    By a 5-4 vote, the Supreme Court held that the presumption here did not violate the Ds' due process rights. The presumption here — as expressed to the jury — was "permissive," since the jury was told that it "need not be rebutted by affirmative proof. . . ." On all the facts in the record — including the fact that the guns were found in the handbag of a 16-year-old girl accompanied by three adult men — it was rational to infer from the presence of the guns in the car that they were possessed by the men.

County of Ulster v. Allen, 442 U.S. 140 (1979).

Note: The four dissenters in *Allen* contended that the presumption here was irrational — the mere fact that guns are found in a car cannot give rise to the rational inference that all occupants possessed the guns. Furthermore, the dissenters were not convinced that this was a truly "permissive" inference; they thought the jury might in fact not have relied on all the facts of the case or on logic, and may have relied solely on the presumption to find possession. The dissenters would have required that the presumed fact be "more likely than not" to flow from the basic fact, and that this determination be made abstractly, rather than by considering the particular facts of the case.

b. Mandatory: By contrast, if the presumption is found to be *"mandatory,"* it will be subjected to much more stringent constitutional scrutiny:

i. Shift of persuasion burden: If the presumption shifts the burden of *persuasion* to the defendant, it will normally be unconstitutional if the *presumed fact* is an *element of the crime*. The reason for this rule is that such a presumption runs afoul of the constitutional principle that the prosecution must prove each element of the crime beyond a reasonable doubt.

Example: In a murder case, D concedes having killed V, but contends that he did not do so "purposely or knowingly," so that he is not guilty of the crime of "deliberate homicide." The judge instructs the jury that "the law presumes that a person intends the ordinary consequences of his voluntary acts."

Held, this presumption violated D's due process rights. The presumption, as carried out in the judge's instruction, could have been interpreted by a reasonable jury as being "mandatory," and in fact as shifting to D the burden of persuasion on the issue of intent. For instance, the jury was not told that the presumption could be rebutted; furthermore, even if the jury understood that rebuttal was possible, it might have assumed that in the absence of rebuttal by D the mere fact of the slaying was enough to constitute proof of intent. An instruction that might be interpreted as shifting to D the burden of persuasion on any element of the crime is unconstitutional. *Sandstrom v. Montana*, 442 U.S. 510 (1979).

ii. Shift of production burden only: Where the presumption is "mandatory" but shifts only the burden of production, not the burden of persuasion, the presumption may be constitutionally valid. The Supreme Court in *Sandstrom* attached great importance to the fact that the burden of persuasion was shifted under the presumption there, and hinted that had the presumption merely shifted the burden of production and not of persuasion, the result might have been different.

iii. Beyond reasonable doubt: Even a mandatory presumption relating to an essential element of the crime (and even one which shifts the burden of persuasion to the defendant) would probably be constitutional if the prosecution showed that: (1) the presumed fact *flows from the basic fact beyond a reasonable doubt*; and (2) the basic fact is *true beyond a reasonable doubt.* McC, p. 598. But because there are very few presumptions that have this tight a link between basic fact and presumed fact, almost all presumptions used in criminal cases will have to be permissive ones.

4. **Reconciling affirmative defenses and presumptions:** It is hard to reconcile the Supreme Court's standard for evaluating affirmative defenses with its standard for evaluating mandatory presumptions. Consider two statutes, A and B. Under statute A, all possession of stolen property is made a crime, but the defendant is given an affirmative defense that he did not know the goods were stolen; he must establish this affirmative defense by a preponderance of the evidence. Under statute B, the crime is defined as the "knowing" possession of stolen property, and there is a presumption that a person who buys stolen property without making inquiries into the seller's title knows the goods to be stolen; the presumption may be rebutted, but in the absence of rebuttal evidence the presumption is binding on the jury. Statute A would probably be constitutional — under *Patterson* (*supra*, p. 563), D is not required to bear the burden of persuasion on any element of the crime (since guilty knowledge is not an element of the crime). Statute B, by contrast, is clearly unconstitutional under *Sandstrom* — it is a mandatory presumption, shifting the burden of persuasion on an element of the crime. Yet it is hard to see why statute B is less fair to defendants.

D. **Choice of law:** In federal cases (especially diversity cases), the well-known case of *Erie v. Tompkins*, 304 U.S. 54 (1938) requires that the federal courts use state substantive law if state law is the source of the right sued upon. *Erie* has always been applied to questions of burden of proof. Consequently, Congress, in enacting the Federal Rules, has decided that the federal courts should generally apply the state's law regarding **presumptions** (and the **effect** to be given to presumptions) in any case in which state substantive law has to be looked to.

1. **FRE 302:** Thus FRE 302 provides that "In a civil case, *state law governs the effect of a presumption* regarding a *claim or defense for which state law supplies the rule of decision.*"

> **Example:** P brings a diversity action against D, claiming that D was negligent in driving a car. Under *Erie v. Tompkins*, New Jersey law controls on the substantive issue of whether P has a claim for negligence, since the accident took place in New Jersey and the case is brought in New Jersey federal district court. A New Jersey statute establishes a rebuttable presumption that a person whose blood alcohol is more than .1% is legally drunk. New Jersey substantive law of negligence establishes the doctrine of negligence *per se*, by which violation of a statute (including the drunk driving statute) is *prima facie* evidence that the act that violated the statute is negligent. New Jersey law applies a Morgan approach to presumptions, so a presumption shifts to the opponent the burden of persuasion (as it would not under FRE 301).
>
> The federal court will have to follow New Jersey's approach to presumptions. That is, once P shows that D's blood alcohol level was higher than .1%, then even if D comes up with some other evidence that he was not drunk, the judge will have to instruct the jury that if it finds D's blood alcohol to have been higher than .1%, it must find D to have been drunk (and therefore, negligent under the negligence *per se* doctrine) unless D convinces the jury by a preponderance of the evidence that he was not drunk. In other words, the federal court must apply New Jersey's Morgan-style law of presumptions, rather than FRE 301's "bursting bubble" treatment.

III. JUDGE-JURY ALLOCATION

A. Introduction: We now examine the division of responsibility between the judge and the jury as it concerns decisions about the admissibility of evidence. In general, the judge decides issues of law, and the jury decides issues of fact. However, drawing this line is not always so easy. Furthermore, even where an issue is one of fact, and thus within the jury's province, the judge has a role to play (by instructing the jury, and perhaps by summarizing or commenting on the evidence).

B. Issues of law: All American courts follow the general principle that *issues of law* are to be decided by the *judge*, not the jury. Consequently, when the admission of a particular piece of evidence turns on an issue of law, it is up to the judge, not the jury, to decide whether the item should be admitted.

> **Example:** D calls P to the stand, and asks a question regarding statements made by P to L. P asserts that he need not answer because the communication was protected by the attorney-client privilege. D demonstrates that L, although he is a law school graduate, has not yet taken the bar exam in any state and is therefore not admitted anywhere. The resulting issue of law — whether the attorney-client privilege applies to a communication made to a law school graduate who is not yet admitted — will be decided solely by the judge. Therefore, it is the judge who will have sole control over whether P must answer. See L&S, p. 1056.

C. Issues of fact: The division of responsibility between judge and jury is more complicated when admissibility of a piece of evidence turns on an issue of *fact* rather than law.

1. Generally: In general, the roles of judge and jury turn on whether the objection to admission raises a technical exclusionary rule, or rather goes merely to relevance.

2. Competence: When an objection to admissibility is based on a *technical exclusionary rule* (e.g., hearsay), any factual question needed to decide that objection belongs solely to the *judge*. Thus when factual issues arise in connection with a *hearsay* objection, an objection based on *privilege*, an objection based on the alleged *incompetency* of the witness (e.g., a child), or most issues regarding the *Best Evidence* rule, the *judge must decide* the issue.

  a. Federal Rules: This rule is codified in FRE 104(a): "The *court must decide* any *preliminary question* about whether a *witness is qualified*, a *privilege exists*, or *evidence is admissible*."

  i. Rules of evidence not binding: FRE 104(a) then goes on to say, "In so deciding, the court is *not bound by evidence rules*, except those on privilege."

  > **Example:** Suppose that the judge has to decide whether V's out-of-court statement, "X shot me," is admissible under the "dying declaration" exception to the hearsay rule (see *supra*, p. 290). In determining this factual issue, the court could consider another out-of-court statement made by V just before to someone else, in which he said, "It seems like only a flesh wound" — the fact that this latter statement would not be admissible does not prevent the judge from considering it in determining whether the main statement qualifies as a dying declaration.

b. Some illustrations: Here are some illustrations of objections that would be treated as technical exclusionary ones, whose related factual issues will be decided by the judge:

Example 1: Whether a witness's notes were made when the matter in question was fresh in his mind, and thus qualify under the "past recollection recorded" exception to the hearsay rule (*supra*, p. 245).

Example 2: Whether H and W were really married at the time of a statement by H to W, so as to make the communication protected by the privilege for marital communications (*supra*, p. 452).

Example 3: Whether an original of a writing has really been lost (as alleged by the proponent), so as to give rise to an exception under the Best Evidence rule (*supra*, p. 490). (But see FRE 1008, discussed *supra*, p. 500, which provides that some factual issues related to the Best Evidence rule are to be given to the jury.)

c. Preponderance of the evidence: Most courts hold that the judge should decide such factual issues by a ***preponderance of the evidence*** standard. McC, p. 79.

Example: In a federal conspiracy case, the prosecution offers an out-of-court statement by an alleged co-conspirator. Under the co-conspirator's statement exception to the hearsay rule, a co-conspirator's statement is only admissible if it was made "during the course and in furtherance of the conspiracy." (FRE 801(d)(2)(E)). D asserts that the statement should only be admitted if the trial judge first concludes, beyond a reasonable doubt, that a conspiracy existed.

Held, for the prosecution. In federal cases, the issue of whether a conspiracy existed should be decided by a preponderance-of-the-evidence standard, not a "beyond-a-reasonable-doubt standard." (Also, the judge may consider the alleged statement itself in deciding whether the conspiracy has been proved by a preponderance of the evidence.) *Bourjaily v. U.S.*, 483 U.S. 171 (1987).

i. Voluntariness of confession: A ***confession*** may, of course, only be introduced against a criminal defendant if it was voluntarily made. In most states, it is solely up to the judge to determine whether the confession was voluntary. In such states, it is constitutional for the judge to decide this issue by a preponderance-of-the-evidence rather than a "beyond-a-reasonable-doubt" standard; *Lego v. Twomey*, 404 U.S. 477 (1972). (Other states follow a two-step rule, in which the judge will exclude the confession only if its involuntariness is very clear, and the jury gets an additional chance to disregard the confession if it finds it to be involuntary. McC, p. 276.)

3. Relevance: Now let us consider evidence to which the sole objection is that it is ***irrelevant***.

a. Ordinary relevance problem: Ordinarily, the judge may decide an objection based on relevance grounds without making any findings of fact. That is, if the proponent offers proof of fact *A*, and the opponent argues that the proof is irrelevant, the judge merely has to decide, "Does the proof tend to establish the existence of fact *A*?" and "Does establishment of fact *A* make some material issue in the case more (or less) likely than it would be without fact *A*?" The judge can answer both of these questions without making any findings of fact.

b. Conditional relevance: There are some pieces of proffered evidence, however, which are logically relevant *only if some other fact exists*. That is, evidence of fact *B* may be relevant only if fact *A* also exists. In this situation, evidence of fact *B* is said to be *"conditionally relevant,"* that is, conditioned upon fact *A*. This leads to the question, Who decides whether fact *A* has been established, the judge or the jury?

Example: P borrows D's car, and is injured when a tire blows out. D seeks to prove that as P drove away, D shouted, "The left tire's bad, so keep it under 55." (D claims that this statement made P assume the risk of the kind of accident that occurred.) P asserts that she never heard this warning, and points out that if she didn't, she cannot be held to have assumed the risk because she didn't know about it.

Evidence of fact *B* (that D made the warning) is not logically relevant unless fact *A* (that P heard the warning) is first established. The issue thus becomes, who should decide whether P heard the warning, judge or jury?

i. Jury decides: Nearly all courts, and the Federal Rules, hold that it is the *jury*, not the judge, who should decide such issues of conditional relevance. Thus it is the jury who would decide whether P heard D's warning.

ii. Role of judge: But the judge still has a role to play on the preliminary fact question. She must decide *whether a reasonable jury could find that the preliminary fact exists*: if the answer is "no," she will not allow the conditionally relevant evidence; if the answer is "yes," she will allow it (even if she believes that it is less likely than not that the preliminary fact exists). As FRE 104(b) puts it, "When the relevance of evidence depends on *whether a fact exists*, proof must be introduced *sufficient to support a finding* that the fact does exist. The court may admit the proposed evidence on the condition that the proof be introduced later."

Example: Let's return to our tire blowout example. Before D will be permitted to give detailed testimony about the warning he shouted to P, the judge will first decide whether a reasonable jury could conclude that P heard the warning (whatever its contents). If he concludes that a reasonable jury could not so find, he will prevent D from stating the contents of the warning. If he determines that a reasonable jury could find that P heard the warning, he will then allow D's testimony about the contents of the warning (even if he thinks that there is less than a 50-50 chance that P in fact heard the warning). If he decides to allow the jury to hear the testimony about the warning's contents, he might instruct the jury to consider those contents only if it first decides, by a preponderance of the evidence, that P heard the warning.

iii. Subject to "connecting up": Sometimes the proponent will want to show the conditionally relevant fact *before showing the preliminary fact*. To allow this, the judge will frequently admit the conditionally relevant evidence *"subject to connecting up,"* i.e., subject to the later introduction of evidence proving the preliminary fact. L&S, p. 1059, n. 4. For instance, in our tire blowout example the judge might allow the contents of D's warning to P to come in, subject to the later presentation of evidence that P in fact heard the warning. For this to happen, D's lawyer will have to assure the court that he will subsequently introduce evidence that P really heard the warning. If D does not come up with this evidence sometime in the case, the judge will order the testimony about the warning's contents to be ***stricken***. (In federal courts, the judge's authority to accept the conditionally relevant evidence in advance of proof of the preliminary fact is indicated by FRE 104(b)'s reference to admission of the former "on the condition that the proof be introduced later.")

    iv. Authentication: Questions of ***authenticity*** of documents or real evidence fall into this "conditionally relevant" category, and thus must be ***left to the jury*** (as long as the judge finds that there's enough evidence of authenticity that a reasonable jury could find that the item is what its proponent claims it to be). M&K §1.13, p. 49.

    Example: P claims that D has libelled P in a letter written by D to X. P offers a letter purporting to be from D to X, together with the testimony of W (X's widow) that W found the letter among X's effects after X died. So long as the judge thinks that there's enough evidence that the letter was written by D that a reasonable jury could *possibly* find that it was indeed written by D, the judge must, under FRE 104(b), let the document into evidence, even if the judge thinks that the letter was probably *not* written by D. It will now be up to the jury to decide (by a preponderance of the evidence) whether the letter really *was* written by D; if the jury concludes that it wasn't, then the jury will disregard the letter.

4. Presence of jury: When the judge has to decide a preliminary issue of fact, he will often receive evidence on that preliminary issue ***outside the presence of the jury***. Otherwise, the jury may hear prejudicial or privileged information that it will probably not be able to put out of its mind if the ultimate evidence is found inadmissible.

    a. Confessions: In fact, where the preliminary issue is whether a criminal defendant's ***confession*** was voluntary, the defendant probably has a ***constitutional right*** to have his evidence concerning the voluntariness of his confession heard outside the presence of the jury. In any event, in federal trials this is required by FRE 104(c):

        "(c) Conducting a Hearing So That the Jury Cannot Hear It. The court must conduct any hearing on a ***preliminary question*** so that the jury cannot hear it if:

            (1) the hearing involves the ***admissibility of a confession***;

            (2) a defendant in a criminal case is a witness and so requests; or

            (3) justice so requires."

D. Instructions: The subject of ***jury instructions*** is generally beyond the scope of this book. However, two kinds of instructions relate directly to evidence, and are worth discussing briefly:

1. Limiting instructions: First, when evidence has been admitted that should properly be considered only on some issues, the judge will on request give a ***limiting instruction***, which tells the jury for what issues the evidence can and cannot be considered.

Example: P, a golfer, is injured while riding a cart that he has rented from D, a golf course. P offers evidence that X, who had rented the cart before P did, had told D, "The brakes are bad." This evidence is not admissible to prove that brakes really were bad (since it is hearsay not within any exception), but is admissible to show that D was on notice of a possible defect. If the judge admits the evidence for this latter purpose, on P's request, the judge will issue a limiting instruction, telling the jury to consider the statement only on the issue of notice, not on the issue of whether the brakes really were bad. See Lilly, pp. 189-90.

    a. Confession of co-defendant: Limiting instructions are often of doubtful utility — the jury is usually unwilling or unable to refrain from using the evidence for the forbidden purpose. In one situation, a limiting instruction is ***constitutionally inadequate***: in a joint trial, the Confrontation Clause sometimes prevents one co-defendant's confession from being used against the other (see *supra*, p. 400), and the Supreme Court has held that a limiting instruction does not provide constitutionally sufficient protection. *Bruton v. U.S.*, 391 U.S. 123 (1968) (discussed *supra*, p. 400).

  2. Cautionary instruction: Another type of instruction relating to the evidence is the so-called *"cautionary instruction."* This is an instruction designed to alert the jury to the dubious value of a certain type of evidence. For instance, where the prosecution uses testimony by an accomplice against a criminal defendant, the judge may warn the jury to weigh carefully the significance to be attached to the accomplice's testimony, because of the latter's incentive to curry favor with the authorities. L&S, p. 1070.

E. Summary and comment: Depending on the jurisdiction, the judge may *summarize* the evidence, *comment* upon it, or both.

  1. Common-law rule: At common law, the judge could ***both*** summarize the evidence and comment on it. L&S, p. 1078.

  2. Federal Rule: Today, the federal courts and a minority of state courts preserve this power to both summarize and comment. *Id.*

  3. Majority rule: But in most states today, the judge may ***not comment*** on the evidence. This restriction is due to fears that if comment were allowed, the judge would in practice usurp the jury's role as fact-finder. *Id.* However, many of the states that forbid judicial comment allow, or even encourage, judicial summation. *Id.*

  4. Warning to the jury: Where the judge does comment on the evidence, she must also instruct the jurors that it is up to them to make the final decision as to the weight of the evidence and the credibility of the witnesses, and that they are in no way bound by her comments. *Id.*

F. Nonjury trials: Nearly everything we have said in this book so far assumes that the trial is to a jury. When the trial is a *"bench"* trial (i.e., one without a jury), the rationale behind many of the procedures and rules of exclusion changes: the trial judge is presumably better able to disregard inadmissible evidence whose contents he hears than would a lay jury; yet at the same time, he will often not be able to shield himself from hearing those contents as he would be able to shield the jury. (For instance, in a nonjury trial there is no analog to the practice of hearing an offer of proof outside the presence of the jury.)

1. **Same rules of evidence:**   Nonetheless, in general *all rules of evidence applicable to jury trials also apply to bench trials*. McC, p. 86. Most importantly, if an item of evidence would be inadmissible in a jury trial, it is inadmissible in a bench trial.

2. **Practical relaxation:**   On the other hand, appellate courts are understandably much more reluctant to reverse the trial court for an error of evidence law when a bench trial is involved. Therefore, appellate courts are generally *less strict in reviewing* evidentiary rulings made in a bench trial. *Id.*

   a. **"Sufficient competent evidence" rule:**   The most important way in which appellate courts do this is by applying the following rule: in a bench trial "the admission of incompetent evidence over objection will not ordinarily be a ground of reversal if there was *competent evidence* received *sufficient to support the findings*. The judge will be *presumed* to have *disregarded the inadmissible* and relied on the competent evidence." McC, p. 86.

   b. **Erroneous exclusion:**   But if the judge in a bench trial erroneously *excludes* evidence, the appellate court will *not* bend over backwards to uphold the verdict: the appellate court will reverse if the exclusion was "substantially harmful to the losing party." *Id.*

   c. **Provisional admission:**   These two contrasting appellate practices, turning on whether the mistake is to admit or to exclude evidence, have led many trial judges to protect themselves from reversal by the following tactic: When an item of evidence is objected to and the judge believes the evidentiary point is debatable, he will frequently *admit the evidence provisionally*, while telling the parties that he will reserve his evidentiary ruling until the evidence is all in. McC, p. 87. When the evidence is all in, he may not issue the ruling at all unless one or the other parties makes a motion to strike. If he does have to rule at the end of the case, he will err on the side of admitting rather than excluding debatable evidence. *Id.*

      i. **Criticism:**   This practice of reserving rulings until all evidence is in has the merit of saving time and of making sure that the appellate court has all available evidence in the record. But it is often criticized on the grounds that it reduces the importance of the exclusionary rules of evidence. *Id.*

IV. APPEALS AND THE "HARMLESS ERROR" DOCTRINE

A. **"Harmless error" generally:**   If an appellate court were to order a new trial every time it concluded that the trial judge had made an error in excluding or admitting a particular piece of evidence, the cost in judicial resources would be enormous. Therefore, appellate courts universally apply the *"harmless error"* standard: the verdict below will be reversed, or a new trial ordered, only if the appellate court believes that the error may have made a *difference to the outcome*; an error that is "harmless" (i.e., that probably did not affect the outcome) is disregarded.

1. **Federal Rules:**   The Federal Rules of Evidence obliquely impose the harmless error doctrine: FRE 103 begins by providing that "A party may claim error in a ruling to admit or exclude evidence only if the error affects a *substantial right* of the party[.]" Presumably, a

ruling admitting or excluding evidence only affects a party's "substantial right" if it may have affected the outcome. McC, p. 78.

2. **Different standards:**   How *likely* must it be that the error affected the outcome, for a new trial or reversal to be ordered on appeal? The answer depends on whether the defendant's constitutional rights have been violated:

   a. **Constitutional issue in criminal case:**   In a *criminal* case, where the error is the admission of evidence in violation of the defendant's *constitutional* rights, it is fairly easy for the defendant to convince the appellate court that the error was not "harmless." "[B]efore a federal constitutional error can be held harmless, the court must be able to declare a belief that it was harmless *beyond a reasonable doubt*." *Chapman v. California*, 386 U.S. 18 (1967).

   b. **Civil cases and non-constitutional criminal errors:**   In a *civil* case, and in a criminal case where the error does *not* affect the defendant's constitutional rights, it is harder for the appellant to avoid a finding of harmless error. Usually the error will be ignored as harmless unless the appellate court believes it *"more probable than not"* that the error affected the outcome.

B. **"Plain" error:**   Recall that a party's failure to respond promptly to the erroneous admission or exclusion of evidence may result in a *waiver* of that party's right to complain about the error on appeal. Thus the opponent's failure to object to the improper inclusion of evidence, or the proponent's failure to make a timely offer of proof in the face of an erroneous exclusion of evidence, will cause the error to be waived. But there is a key exception to this rule of waiver: if the appellate court concludes that the error was *"plain,"* it may treat the error as grounds for a new trial *even if no objection or offer of proof was made*.

1. **Civil cases:**   Reversals for plain error are *rare* in *civil* cases, perhaps because liberty and life are not involved. McC, p. 78.

2. **Criminal cases:**   In criminal cases, where by definition the error must have been to the defendant's detriment (since the prosecution cannot appeal an acquittal), courts are *more willing* to find plain error. McC, p. 78. This is especially likely to be the case if the defendant was represented by court-appointed counsel not of his own choosing. W&B, Par. 103[07].

3. **Standard:**   There is no precise standard for determining how prejudicial the error must be to be "plain." Most courts state or assume that the error must be more prejudicial to be "plain" than is required for an error that was pointed out at the trial level to avoid being "harmless."

   a. **Federal standard:**   In federal trials, the plain error doctrine is imposed by FRE 103(d): "A court may take notice of a *plain error affecting a substantial right*, even if *the claim of error was not properly preserved*."

C. **Sufficiency of evidence:**   Appellate courts serve another function when they review the evidence from the trial below: they will often need to determine whether there was *sufficient evidence* to support the decision of the trier of fact.

1. **Procedural context:**   The appellate court's duty to judge the sufficiency of the evidence can arise in a variety of procedural contexts. For instance, in a civil case a sufficiency

issue arises from the trial judge's handling of a motion for a directed verdict or a motion for judgment notwithstanding the verdict (j.n.o.v.) — if the judge directs the verdict or grants the j.n.o.v. motion, the party who didn't get to the jury or who lost the benefit of the jury verdict will raise the sufficiency issue; if the judge denies the motion, the movant will raise sufficiency. In a criminal case, it is always the defendant who argues that the evidence was insufficient to support the verdict (since if there is an acquittal, the prosecution cannot appeal). L&S, p. 852.

2. **Standard:**   In deciding whether the evidence was sufficient to support the fact-finder's decision, the appellate court does ***not*** attempt to determine how it would have decided the case. Its task is "only to determine whether the evidence was such that a ***reasonable trier of fact*** might have reached the decision below." *Id.* This determination in turn depends on whether the case is civil or criminal:

   a. **Civil:**   In a civil case, the appellate court's determination mirrors the "preponderance of the evidence" standard. Thus if the plaintiff wins at trial, the appellate court will ask itself: ***Could a reasonable jury have concluded that plaintiff proved all elements of his case by a preponderance of the evidence?*** In making this determination, the appellate court "gives the winning party the benefit of all doubts and assumes that the proof properly offered was accepted for all that it was worth, since the judge or jury might reasonably have given it the maximum possible weight." *Id.*

   b. **Criminal:**   In a criminal case, by contrast, the appellate court takes the "reasonable doubt" standard into account in determining sufficiency. Thus it will order a new trial (or, occasionally, dismiss the charge entirely) if it concludes that a ***reasonable jury could not have found the defendant guilty beyond a reasonable doubt*** (even if the appeals court finds the evidence sufficient to allow a jury to have found the defendant guilty "by a preponderance of the evidence").

   c. **Summary:**   In other words, the standard for review of sufficiency mirrors the standard of proof used at the trial level, except that the question is always whether the trier of fact could "reasonably" have decided the case as it did. *Id.*

   d. **Rare:**   In general, appellate courts ***rarely*** reverse the lower court outcome based on a conclusion that the evidence was not sufficient to support that outcome. L&S, p. 853.

Quiz Yourself on

BURDENS OF PROOF, PRESUMPTIONS AND OTHER PROCEDURAL ISSUES
(Entire Chapter)

131. In a contract dispute between Lincoln and Davis, Davis denies that he ever received a document Lincoln mailed to him. Lincoln produces evidence that the letter was properly addressed and mailed. Davis does not produce any evidence that he didn't receive the letter. The jurisdiction imposes a presumption that a properly addressed and mailed letter was received by the addressee. If the jury *believes* the letter was properly addressed and mailed, *must* it find that Davis received the letter? _____

132. Whether or not Judge Crater is still alive is at issue in a civil case. The jurisdiction applies a presumption that one who has not been seen or heard from for 7 years is dead. The party who seeks to prove his death shows that Crater hasn't been seen in seven years and that he hasn't contacted anyone in his family or any of his associates. The opponent offers no rebuttal. Will the judge now be "presumed" dead, under the FRE? _____

133. Jefferson sues Washington, claiming that Washington entered into a written contract with Jefferson under which Jefferson would ghost-write Washington's autobiography, "Father of My Country." The case is tried before a jury, operating under the FRE. Jefferson offers in evidence a document that purports to be signed by Washington, embodying the ghost-writing arrangement. Washington's lawyer attacks the document as a forgery. The trial judge believes that the document probably is a forgery, but he's not sure. Must the judge let the document into evidence? _____

134. Ayn Puty's leg is mangled and severed in an industrial accident. In a suit against her employer, Acme Iron Works, Ayn's lawyer seeks to admit the severed leg into evidence. Acme's lawyer doesn't object. Acme loses the case and appeals, objecting to admission of the leg. Under the FRE, since Acme didn't make a timely objection, is its right to appeal waived? _____

Answers

131. Yes. Once the "basic fact" (here, proper mailing) is proven , the burden of producing evidence disproving the "presumed fact" (here, receipt of the letter) is shifted to the party against whom the presumption operates (here, Davis). Therefore, since Davis didn't come up with any evidence that he didn't receive the letter, the jury must find that he received it.

RELATED ISSUE: However, this presumption, like most, is **rebuttable**. Thus if Davis can produce substantial rebuttal evidence to prove the letter did *not* arrive, the presumption will be destroyed. (The jury *could* still conclude that the letter was received, based on Lincoln's proof of proper mailing, but the jury wouldn't be *required* to so conclude.) Occasionally, the rebuttal evidence can be so compelling that it shifts the burden of production as to the presumed fact all the way back to the other party. (But there's probably no evidence Davis could come up with in this mailing situation that would cause this to happen, so the jury would probably remain free to find that Davis received the letter.)

132. Yes. Under FRE 301, the party against whom a presumption is directed has the **burden of going forward** with evidence to rebut the presumption. If he doesn't, the court will instruct the jury that if it believes the basic facts, it must presume the existence of the presumed fact. Here, since the basic facts necessary to establish the presumption (that Crater has unexpectedly been absent for seven years, and that no one who should have heard from him [e.g., his family and friends] has done so) were proven, the presumed fact, that Crater is dead, will be treated as established (in the absence of rebuttal).

133. Yes. The document is relevant if and only if it really was signed by Washington. Therefore, it falls under FRE 104(b), which states that "When the relevance of evidence depends on whether a fact exists, proof must be introduced **sufficient to support a finding** that the fact does exist. The court may admit the proposed evidence on the condition that the proof be introduced later." The fact that the judge isn't sure whether the document is genuine or not indicates that there's enough evidence to "support a finding" that it was signed by Washington. (In other words, there's enough evidence that a reasonable jury could find, by a preponderance of the evidence, that Washington signed it.) Consequently, under 104(b) the judge should admit the document, and leave it to the jury to decide whether Washington signed it. This question illustrates the general principle that questions of authenticity are left to the jury (as long as there is enough evidence of authenticity for a reasonable jury to decide either way).

134. No, probably. Under FRE 103(a), a party may claim error in a ruling to admit evidence "only if the error affects a substantial right of the party and: (1) [that] party, on the record: (A) timely objects or moves to strike; and (B) states the specific ground, unless it was apparent from the context[.]" However, 103(e) says that "[a] court may take notice of a ***plain error*** affecting a substantial right, even if the claim of error was not properly preserved." There's a good chance that the appellate court will rule that admitting a severed leg is so inherently prejudicial, and such an egregious mistake, that it amounted to "plain error." If so, Acme's appeal will be heard even though Acme did not make a timely objection.

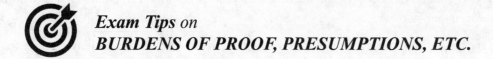

Exam Tips on
BURDENS OF PROOF, PRESUMPTIONS, ETC.

The material in this chapter is less-commonly tested than that in most of the other chapters.

☞ The single most frequently-tested issue is: what effect does a presumption have once the party not benefiting from it produces some substantial evidence of the non-existence of the presumed fact? Under FRE 301, the answer is: the presumption ***no longer has any effect;*** it's a "bubble" that has "burst" (for instance, it doesn't shift the burden of persuasion), and the jury ***can't be instructed*** about the presumption.

> *Example:* D in a contract case claims she notified P by letter that she was withdrawing from the contract (as she was permitted to do). D testifies that she put the letter in an envelope, with proper postage, addressed to P at his place of business (a P.O. box), and that she placed it in a U.S. mailbox. (This is enough to trigger the presumption that a properly-mailed letter was received by the addressee.) P testifies that he got his mail each day from a locked post office box, and that he never received any such letter. Because P has come forward with enough evidence of non-receipt of the letter to rebut the existence of the presumed fact (i.e., to allow a reasonable jury to conclude that P didn't get the letter): (1) the jury ***may not be told*** that it can "presume" that P got the letter; (2) the burden of persuasion remains on D (so if the jury thinks there's a 50-50 chance that P got the letter, P wins); and (3) the jury may still "infer" (just not "presume") from the fact of D's mailing that P received the notice.

CHAPTER 12

JUDICIAL NOTICE

ChapterScope

Judicial notice is the *recognition* by the court of the *truth of certain facts* without the introduction of *evidence* on those facts. Key concepts:

■ There are *two main types* of facts of which judicial notice can be taken:

❏ *"Adjudicative facts"* are those facts which relate to the particular event under litigation. The FRE's judicial-notice provisions concern only adjudicative facts, and most of your study of judicial notice will concern this type of fact.

❏ *"Legislative facts"* are more-general facts that do not concern the immediate parties, and that remain the same across a wide range of cases.

■ **Adjudicative facts:** There are two types of adjudicative facts of which a court may take judicial notice:

❏ **"General knowledge":** Facts that are *"generally known"* in the community. (*Example:* The fact that Chicago and Detroit are in different states, so that a trip from one to the other would be "interstate.")

❏ **"Certain verification":** Facts capable of *immediate verification* by consulting sources of *indisputable accuracy.* (*Example:* The fact that no two people share the same fingerprints, ascertainable from books on forensics.)

■ **Instructions to jury:** How the jury should be *instructed* about a judicially-noticed fact varies depending on whether the case is civil or criminal. Under the FRE:

❏ **Civil:** In *civil* cases, the trial judge instructs the jury that it *must* take the judicially-noticed fact as *conclusively* established.

❏ **Criminal:** But in *criminal* cases, the trial judge instructs the jury that it *may*, but *need not*, take the judicially-noticed fact as conclusively established.

I. JUDICIAL NOTICE GENERALLY

A. Function: Normally, a party who seeks to have the trier find that a fact exists must introduce evidence of that fact. However, our system provides a number of ways in which a party's obligation to produce evidence proving a fact may be relieved. Presumptions (*supra,* p. 567) are one such method. Another is the doctrine of *judicial notice*, whereby the *judge* accepts a fact as true even though no evidence to prove it has been offered. If the case is a civil one being tried to a jury, the judge, after taking judicial notice, will instruct the jury that it must find the fact.

Example: In a civil jury trial, P needs to establish that March 10, 1995 was a Tuesday. He can ask the judge to take judicial notice of this fact. Probably he will have to give the judge some assistance in verifying the fact (e.g., by showing the judge an almanac or calendar). But he will not have to introduce any evidence before the jury to establish this fact. Once the judge is convinced that March 10, 1995 was indeed a Tuesday, she will instruct the jury that they must treat that date as being a Tuesday in their deliberations. L&S, p. 838.

1. **Rationale:** The principal rationale for judicial notice is the *saving of time and money*. Litigants would have to spend more money proving their cases if they had to prove even incontrovertible facts; trials would be needlessly long.

2. **Correction after close of evidence or on appeal:** Another important function of the judicial notice doctrine is to allow a court to *correct a party's inadvertent failure* to provide evidence on a key, but indisputable, fact. For instance, if the losing party raises on appeal for the first time the argument that his adversary did not come up with evidence at trial of some indisputable fact necessary to the verdict, the appellate court may take judicial notice of that fact, thus saving the verdict below. Similarly, the trial court may, after the close of evidence at the trial, take judicial notice of a fact necessary to the verdict, rather than reopening the evidence for the party to supply that fact. See L&S, p. 842.

B. **Two types of facts:** The doctrine of judicial notice has evolved to recognize two distinct types of facts: (1) *"adjudicative"* facts; and (2) *"legislative"* facts.

1. **Adjudicative facts:** *Adjudicative* facts are those facts which relate to the *particular event*. "[T]hey help . . . explain who did what, when, where, how, and with what motive and intent." McC, p. 550.

2. **Legislative facts:** *Legislative* facts are "more general facts that do not concern the immediate parties." L&S, p. 838. They are facts which the judge considers as part of his law-making function. Any non-evidentiary fact which the judge considers in determining whether a statute is constitutional, how a statute should be interpreted, or how the common law should treat a particular issue, will be a legislative fact. For instance, a judge who is deciding whether the implied warranty of habitability should, as a common-law matter, be extended to apartment rentals, may take judicial notice of legislative facts concerning the nature of apartment rentals in big cities (e.g., that tenants generally are not capable of making structural repairs); see *Javins v. First National Realty Corp.*, discussed *infra*, p. 594.

3. **Significance of distinction:** The Federal Rules, and many states, recognize this distinction between adjudicative and legislative facts.

   a. **Main difference:** The main consequence of the distinction is that judicial notice of adjudicative facts is much more circumscribed: in most courts, the judge may take notice of an adjudicative fact only if the fact is *indisputable*, whereas he may take notice of a legislative fact much more liberally (in most situations, the fact merely needs to be more probable than not).

   b. **Covered by statute:** A second consequence is that judicial notice of adjudicative facts is more likely to be covered by a precise statute than is notice of legislative facts.

For instance, the federal rules deal only with adjudicative facts (in FRE 201), not with legislative facts.

C. Judicial notice of law: A third situation in which something may be established without the submission of formal evidence is so-called "judicial notice of *law*." This phrase refers to the doctrine that a party will in some situations not be required to "prove" what the law is by a formal submission of evidence; instead, the judge may research the relevant law himself, or the party may merely assist the judge's research (say, by submitting a non-evidentiary photocopy of the relevant provision). See *infra*, p. 595.

D. Federal Rules: The only Federal Rule dealing with judicial notice is FRE 201. FRE 201 deals only with notice of adjudicative facts; that is, it does not cover either notice of legislative facts or notice of law. FRE 201 largely mirrors the common-law treatment of judicial notice of adjudicative facts:

> **"Rule 201. Judicial Notice of Adjudicative Facts**
>
> **(a) Scope.** This rule governs judicial notice of an adjudicative fact only, not a legislative fact.
>
> **(b) Kinds of Facts That May Be Judicially Noticed.** The court may judicially notice a fact that is *not subject to reasonable dispute* because it:
>
> > (1) is *generally known* within the *trial court's territorial jurisdiction*; or
> >
> > (2) can be *accurately and readily determined* from *sources whose accuracy cannot reasonably be questioned.*
>
> **(c) Taking Notice.** The court:
>
> > (1) *may* take judicial notice *on its own*; or
> >
> > (2) *must* take judicial notice if a *party requests it* and the court is *supplied with the necessary information.*
>
> **(d) Timing.** The court may take judicial notice *at any stage* of the proceeding.
>
> **(e) Opportunity to Be Heard.** On timely request, a party is entitled to be heard on the propriety of taking judicial notice and the nature of the fact to be noticed. If the court takes judicial notice before notifying a party, the party, on request, is still entitled to be heard.
>
> **(f) Instructing the Jury.** In a *civil* case, the court *must instruct* the jury to *accept the noticed fact as conclusive.* In a *criminal* case, the court *must instruct* the jury that it *may or may not accept the noticed fact as conclusive.*"

II. ADJUDICATIVE FACTS

A. Definition: As noted, adjudicative facts are those specific facts relating to the particular parties in the action, and to their particular controversy. Examples would include: (1) whether a particular accident, which took place on March 10, 1980, took place on a Tuesday; (2) whether a particular street is part of the general business district of the town it is located in, where the issue is whether the speed limit is that for business districts; or (3) whether the local phone company is an interstate common carrier, for purposes of determining whether D has illegally intercepted communications on such a carrier. McC, p. 550.

1. **Application of doctrine:** Most modern cases hold that there are *two* different types of adjudicative facts that may be judicially noticed: (1) those that are *"generally known"* in the community; and (2) those that are "capable of *immediate* and *accurate verification*" by use of easily-available sources that are indisputably accurate. McC, pp. 551-553. Regardless of which category the fact falls into, the court will not take judicial notice of it unless it is convinced that that fact is virtually *indisputable*.

B. **Common knowledge:** The first of these categories — "common" or "general" knowledge in the community — gives rise to judicial notice only relatively rarely.

> **Example:** P sues D for personal injuries resulting from an automobile accident at the corner of Mission Street and Twenty-first Street in San Francisco. P contends that D was speeding at the time. The judge tells the jury that the statutory speed limit for any "business district" is 15 mph, and that a business district is one that is "mainly built up with structures devoted to business." No evidence is offered as to whether Mission Street at Twenty-first is a business district; however, the judge instructs the jury that this is so.
>
> *Held* (on appeal), the business character of Mission at Twenty-first Street is so well known, and so indisputable, that the trial court could correctly take judicial notice of it and, therefore, so instruct the jury. *Varcoe v. Lee*, 181 P. 223 (Cal. 1919).

1. **Judge's own knowledge insufficient:** Suppose the *judge himself* knows a fact to be so because of his past experiences. May he take judicial notice of that fact even though it is not "common knowledge"? The answer is *"no."* McC, p. 552.

C. **Certain verification:** Most adjudicative facts that are suitable for judicial notice are of the second category: facts capable of *immediate verification* by consulting sources of *indisputable accuracy*.

1. **History and geography:** For instance, facts of *history* and *geography* are often judicially noticed because they fall into this category. Thus the day of the week on which a certain date fell is judicially noticed because it can be verified in an indisputably accurate almanac; the boundaries of a city or state can be verified by consulting an indisputably accurate map, etc.

2. **Scientific tests and principles:** *Scientific principles*, including testing methods, are often subject to judicial notice of this type. Thus courts frequently take judicial notice of the general validity of such scientific methods as *blood tests* for paternity, *fingerprint* identifications, and *radar* tests for detecting speed.

   a. **Change over time:** Observe that the scientific principles of which a court may take judicial notice will *vary* with the passage of time, as new techniques become generally accepted. (See the discussion of various scientific methods *supra*, p. 539). Also, remember that judicial notice will only allow the court to assume the *general* reliability of a technique, not its correct application in a particular case; for instance, the trial judge in *Finkle*, even after taking judicial notice of VASCAR's general reliability, would still have insisted on a showing that the particular device used in that case had been correctly calibrated and correctly used.

3. **Court records:** Courts frequently take judicial notice of ***their own records*** of things that happened earlier in the litigation. McC, p. 555. For instance, if a case is re-tried, the judge might take judicial notice of the fact that a particular witness had not testified at the prior trial. Some, but not all, courts take judicial notice of court records in ***other cases*** from the ***same court***. *Id.* Most courts ***do not*** take judicial notice of court records from ***other courts***, though it is hard to see why. *Id.*

D. **Federal Rule 201:** Recall that FRE 201, the sole Federal Rule to deal with judicial notice, deals exclusively with adjudicative facts. In determining what facts are sufficiently indisputable, FRE 201 basically follows the common-law approach — the fact must be "not subject to ***reasonable dispute***," and may achieve this status in one of two ways: (1) by being "generally known" within the community; or (2) by being capable of being "accurately and readily determined from sources whose accuracy cannot reasonably be questioned."

E. **Jury's right to disregard:** When the judge takes judicial notice of an adjudicative fact, is that fact conclusively determined, or may the jury choose to find otherwise? In most courts, the answer varies depending on whether the case is civil or criminal:

1. **Civil:** In *civil* cases, most courts treat judicial notice as being ***conclusive*** on the issue. These courts, therefore, ***instruct the jury*** that they ***must*** treat the fact as being so. Courts are especially likely to make the judicial notice conclusive if they follow the majority view that judicial notice may be taken only of facts that are "indisputable." Thus FRE 201, after providing in section (b) that the noticed fact must be one that is "not subject to reasonable dispute," provides in section (f) that "In a civil case, the court ***must instruct*** the jury to ***accept the noticed fact as conclusive***."

2. **Criminal:** In a *criminal* case, courts generally hold that the noticed fact is ***not conclusive*** upon the jury. The reason for this difference from the civil context is that courts are afraid that to take away the jury's right to make their own determination of the fact would violate the defendant's ***constitutional right*** to a ***jury trial***.

> **Example:** D is charged with grand larceny, for the theft of a three-year-old automobile. The statute defines "grand larceny" to require that the property have a value of greater than $50. The prosecutor offers no evidence of the car's value. The trial judge charges the jury that it must treat the value of the property as being greater than $50. D is convicted.
>
> *Held* (on appeal) for D. The trial judge should not have told the jury that they were bound to treat the car as being worth more than $50. Even though the jury almost certainly would have assumed the car to be worth more than $50 as a matter of common sense, D had the right to have the jury make an actual determination of any element of the crime, under his state constitutional right to jury trial. "If a court can take one important element of an offense from the jury and determine the facts for them because such fact seems plain enough to him, then which element cannot be similarly taken away, and where would the process stop?" *State v. Lawrence*, 234 P.2d 600 (Utah 1951).

a. **Criticism:**   Remember that, in the vast majority of courts, judicial notice will only be taken of those facts that are truly "beyond dispute." As a dissent pointed out in *State v. Lawrence*, why should the jury be given a chance to contradict an indisputable fact? It is hard to see how the constitutional right to a jury trial includes a right to have a jury behave irrationally.

b. **Federal Rules:**   The Federal Rules follow the standard approach of not binding the jury in a criminal case. FRE 201(f) provides that "In a criminal case, the court must instruct the jury that it *may or may not accept* the noticed fact as conclusive."

c. **On appeal:**   One consequence of the rule that the jury is not bound to accept the judicially-noticed fact in a criminal case is that the prosecution's failure to supply evidence of an element of the crime *cannot be corrected on appeal*, even if the missing fact is one which would otherwise be the proper subject of judicial notice.

For instance, in *U.S. v. Jones*, 580 F.2d 219 (6th Cir. 1978), D was charged with illegally intercepting telephone conversations from an interstate common carrier. The prosecutor inadvertently failed to show that the telephone company in question provided interstate lines. Even though this fact may well have been appropriate for judicial notice at the trial level, the appellate court refused to take judicial notice of it — to do so would deprive D of his right, embodied in FRE 201(f), to have the jury disregard even a judicially noticed fact if it chooses to do so. Therefore, the court directed that D be acquitted.

F. **Procedure:**   We now take a brief look at some other procedural aspects of judicial notice:

1. **Advance notice to parties:**   Must the judge give *advance notice* to the parties that he plans to take judicial notice of a fact? Generally, the answer is *"no."* McC, p. 559.

    a. **Motion by party:**   In most situations, the question does not even arise — one party makes a motion asking the judge to take judicial notice of a fact, and this motion itself effectively gives advance notice to the other party.

    b. **On judge's own motion:**   However, virtually all courts also allow the judge to take judicial notice of a fact on his *own* initiative. In this situation, advance notice to the parties would enable the one who would be disadvantaged to explain why judicial notice would be inappropriate. Nonetheless, few if any courts require this to be done.

    c. **Right to argue under Federal Rules:**   The Federal Rules do not require the judge to give advance notice of his intent to take judicial notice. But FRE 201(e) does require the judge to give a party who so requests an opportunity "to be heard on the propriety of taking judicial notice and the nature of the fact to be noticed. If the court takes judicial notice before notifying a party, the party, on request, is still entitled to be heard." In other words, the judge may take judicial notice without giving the parties advance notice of his intent to do so; once he has taken the notice, however, the disadvantaged party may ask for a hearing, which must be granted.

2. **Contradictory evidence:**   Once the judge has judicially noticed a fact, may the disadvantaged party introduce *contradictory evidence* on that issue? The answer seems to depend on whether the taking of judicial notice is *conclusive* upon the jury, and thus probably depends in turn on whether the case is civil or criminal.

a. **Civil:**   If the case is civil, recall that most courts (and the Federal Rules) make the judicial notice conclusive upon the jury. In this situation, most courts have held that contradictory evidence is ***not admissible***. McC, p. 557. After all, judicial notice is only being allowed of facts that are deemed to be "indisputable," so little would be gained (and trial efficiency would be lost) if a party were to be permitted to try to rebut the irrebuttable. This seems to be true under the Federal Rules; see S&R, p. 60.

b. **Criminal:**   In criminal cases, recall that most courts do ***not*** make the judicially noticed fact conclusive upon the jury, mostly because of concerns about infringing the defendant's right to a jury trial. Most courts would probably also let the defendant introduce evidence to ***rebut*** the judicially noticed fact. Federal courts would probably follow this approach. S&R, p. 61.

3. **When taken:**   Most courts hold that judicial notice of an appropriate adjudicative fact may be taken ***at any time*** during the proceeding.

   a. **Before trial:**   For instance, notice may be taken ***before trial*** if the noticed fact relates to pre-trial proceedings. Thus a trial judge might take notice of a fact relating to ***jurisdiction*** even before the trial begins, if the defendant argues that the court has no jurisdiction over him or the subject matter.

   b. **On appeal:**   Similarly, in most states judicial notice may be taken even ***on appeal***. Thus at least in civil cases, if the trial judge has not taken judicial notice of a fact, the appellate court may do so on its own. McC, p. 560. (But most courts do not permit this in a criminal case tried to a jury; see *supra*, p. 592.)

   c. **Federal Rules:**   The Federal Rules apparently allow an appellate court to take judicial notice in a civil case; FRE 201(d) provides that "[t]he court may take judicial notice at any stage of the proceeding."

III. LEGISLATIVE FACTS

A. **Notice of legislative facts:**   Judges take constant notice of so-called *"legislative"* facts. The most important distinction between judicial notice of administrative facts and legislative facts is that whereas an adjudicative fact must be "indisputable" before it can be judicially noticed, this is not the case for a legislative fact. Most courts would probably say that the judge has the right to judicially notice any legislative fact so long as the judge ***believes it to be true***, even though it is not indisputable. L&S, p. 847.

1. **Types of legislative facts:**   Recall that a legislative fact is one that does not pertain directly to the particular parties and their controversy; rather, it is a more general fact that relates to whether a statute is constitutional, whether a common-law principle should be modified, how a statute should be interpreted, or some other aspect of a judge's law-making process.

   a. **Constitutionality:**   For instance, judges often have to consider a wide variety of legislative facts in determining the ***constitutionality*** of a statute.

      i. **Due process and equal protection:**   Thus in substantive due process cases, the judge will generally have to decide whether there is a rational relation between the objective sought by the legislature and the means it chose to achieve that objective. Similarly, consideration of non-evidentiary legislative facts will often be necessary to decide an equal protection challenge, especially one in which there is no special scrutiny and the court must thus decide whether there is a rational basis for the legislative classification.

   ii. Desegregation: Thus when the Supreme Court had to decide whether separate-but-equal segregated schools violated black children's equal protection rights, the Court relied on a large volume of non-evidentiary legislative facts about the effect of segregation on black children. For instance, the Court relied on non-evidentiary studies by psychologist Kenneth B. Clark showing the psychological impact of segregation. *Brown v. Board of Education*, 347 U.S. 483 (1954).

   b. Non-constitutional cases: In cases not involving the constitution, the judge will similarly often have to resort to legislative facts to interpret a statute, or to decide whether to extend or modify a common law principle. For instance, in the landmark case imposing an implied warranty of habitability for apartment rentals, the court relied on many legislative facts not introduced into evidence (e.g., that tenants have very little leverage to enforce demands for better housing, so that they are in a take-it-or-leave-it situation). *Javins v. First National Realty Corp.*, 428 F.2d 1071 (D.C.Cir. 1970).

B. Not usually codified: Unlike judicial notice of adjudicative facts, judicial notice of legislative facts is usually ***not handled by statute***. There are so many different contexts in which the need to take notice of legislative facts may arise that it is difficult or impossible to specify a single set of standards for when notice is appropriate. Instead, the judge is left pretty much on her own in deciding what facts should be taken notice of, and what the consequence of that notice should be.

   1. Federal Rules silent: Thus the Federal Rules are completely ***silent*** on the issue of judicial notice of legislative facts. S&R, p. 58. As in most state courts, the federal judge is left largely on his own (but under the supervision of the appellate court) in deciding what legislative facts to take notice of, and what procedures to follow in doing so.

C. Binding on jury even in criminal case: Recall that in criminal cases, judicial notice of an adjudicative fact is not binding on the jury. This rule does ***not*** apply to legislative facts: if the judge takes judicial notice of a legislative fact, this notice is ***binding on the jury*** even though the noticed fact operates to the detriment of the criminal defendant. Consequently, it will often be quite important to determine whether a particular fact is legislative or adjudicative.

   Example: The Ds are charged with illegally importing cocaine. The statute under which they are charged prohibits the importation of "cocoa leaves and any . . . derivative or preparation of cocoa leaves. . . ." The prosecution proves that the Ds imported cocaine hydrochloride, but does not introduce evidence to show that cocaine hydrochloride is a derivative of cocoa leaves. The trial judge instructs the jury that if it finds that what the Ds imported was cocaine hydrochloride, it must find that the substance was a proscribed cocoa leaf derivative. The Ds argue that the jury should have been permitted to disregard this factual conclusion.

Held (on appeal), the trial judge was correct in telling the jury that it must treat cocaine hydrochloride as being a cocoa leaf derivative. This fact was a legislative, not adjudicative, fact — legislative facts are "established truths, facts, or pronouncements that do not change from case to case but apply universally. . . ." and the question whether cocaine hydrochloride is a derivative of the cocoa leaf is a question of scientific fact applicable to all enforcement proceedings under federal drug laws. Since FRE 201 does not apply to legislative facts, Rule 201(f)'s provision that the jury is not bound in a criminal case is inapplicable. It was up to the judge, not the jury, to make this factual determination, since allowing juries to make that determination would produce the "preposterous" result that juries could make "conflicting findings on what constitutes controlled substances under federal law. . . ." *U.S. v. Gould*, 536 F.2d 216 (8th Cir. 1976).

IV. NOTICE OF LAW

A. Notice of law generally: Recall that under our system, questions of law are to be decided by the judge, not the jury. (*Supra*, p. 577.) This concept is often expressed by saying that the judge may take "judicial notice of law." Most importantly, this means that at least as to some types of law, when the judge determines what the law is he is *not restricted* to materials given to him by the parties; he may conduct his *own investigation*, into whatever materials he wishes, in determining what the law is. For instance, he is free to locate, read, and cite cases that he believes to be on point, even if neither party has called these cases to his attention.

1. **Restriction:** However, some types of law have historically been viewed as being so difficult to locate and verify that: (1) they must be "proved" by a party's formal submission of evidence; (2) they must be explicitly *pleaded*. Therefore, a judge's ability to take judicial notice of law (i.e., to dispense with the need for formal evidence or pleadings about what the law is) exists for some sources of law but not others.

B. Domestic law: Let us first consider *"domestic"* law, i.e., the law of the jurisdiction in which the court sits. A judge may always take *judicial notice* of domestic law; by corollary, a party need not "prove" domestic law. McC, pp. 562-563.

1. **State courts:** For a state court, "domestic" law is the *law of that state*, plus federal law (since federal law is controlling in every state). McC, p. 563. Thus a state judge has the right (and in fact the obligation) to take judicial notice of some controlling provision of federal law, even if neither party makes any showing of what that law is, or even calls it to the judge's attention.

   a. **Administrative regulations and municipal codes:** A state's own law, for judicial notice purposes, also includes *administrative regulations*, so long as these are published in a way that makes them readily accessible. L&S, p. 850. By contrast, *municipal ordinances* are usually *not* judicially noticeable, because they are often compiled in a haphazard way that makes them hard to research. McC, p. 563. Therefore, such ordinances must be proved.

2. **Federal courts:**   In federal courts, "domestic" law is usually held to include not only federal law, and not merely the law of the state where the federal court sits, but also the law of ***all states*** if relevant. *Id.*

C. **Laws of sister states:**   By contrast, the common-law rule has been that one state may ***not*** judicially notice the laws of a ***sister state***; instead, this must be "proved" by the submission of evidence as to what that sister state's law really is. M, p. 563. Thus if a case is being tried in state A and the law of state B is relevant (under conflict of laws principles), the party seeking to benefit from state B's law will probably literally have to introduce into evidence a certified copy of state B's statutes, court opinions, etc., if state A has not modified the common law's unwillingness to permit judicial notice of a sister state's law.

1. **Change by statute:**   However, most states have adopted the Uniform Judicial Notice of Foreign Law Act. L&S, p. 850. That Act allows the judge to take judicial notice of the law (whether statutory or common law) of every sister state.

D. **Law of other countries:**   The law of ***other countries*** may not be judicially noticed, according to most states. Therefore, a party must generally plead and prove such law. L&S, pp. 850-51.

1. **Federal Rules:**   But this is not the case in federal courts. Fed. R. Civ. Proc. 44.1 allows the federal judge to conduct his own research on an issue of foreign law, rather than limiting him to evidence supplied by a party. (But a party who intends to raise an issue concerning foreign law must nonetheless give notice of this fact in his pleadings, in contrast to the true "judicial notice of law" situation where no pleading concerning the law need be made.)

Quiz Yourself on

JUDICIAL NOTICE *(Entire Chapter)*

135. Juliet files a paternity suit against Romeo. Is the fact that the normal human gestation period is approximately 280 days a fact suitable for judicial notice? _____

136. Blair Wolf is on trial for a battery which allegedly took place after dark on April 1. Is the time at which the sun set on April 1 a fact suitable for judicial notice, assuming it's relevant? _____

137. Custer and Sitting Bull are involved in an automobile collision on April 1 at a bend on Little Big Horn Street. Custer sues Sitting Bull for negligence in crossing the double yellow line. Sitting Bull claims he was swerving to avoid a large tree which had fallen across his lane, which he couldn't see in time to stop. Sitting Bull asks the judge to take judicial notice of the fallen tree. In fact, the judge knows about the fallen tree because he lives on Little Big Horn Street. May the judge properly take judicial notice of the fallen tree? _____

138. Jeffrey Dahmhim is on trial for depriving a black man of his civil rights by eating him. Dahmhim takes the stand, and says, "I may be a member of the Ku Klux Klan, but I'm no racist." The prosecutor asks the judge to take judicial notice of the fact that the KKK is a white supremacist organization. The judge does so. (Assume that this is proper, as it probably would be.) Under the FRE, when the judge is giving the jury its instructions, may he tell it to accept as proven that the KKK is a white supremacist organization? _____

Answers

135. Yes. This is a *"notorious fact"* — one subject to common knowledge in the community. Thus, if either party asks the judge to take judicial notice of the fact, the judge *must* do so, under FRE 201(c)(2). In fact, the judge *may* take judicial notice of the gestation period even in the absence of such a request, under FRE 201(c)(1).

136. Yes. Although such a fact is not generally known, it's a *"manifest fact,"* i.e., one capable of verification through a readily accessible, undoubtedly accurate source — an almanac. Thus, it's suitable for judicial notice under FRE 201.

137. No. The judge's personal knowledge is irrelevant to judicial notice. The only facts that can be judicially noticed are *notorious facts* (subject to common knowledge in the community) and *manifest facts* (capable of verification through readily accessible, undoubtedly accurate sources). The condition of a roadway at a particular time *wouldn't* qualify, so its condition will have to be proven.

138. No. Under FRE 201(f) (2nd sent.), the judge in a *criminal* case must instruct the jury that it *may*, but *isn't required to*, accept as conclusive any fact judicially noticed. (The same rule applies at common law.) (Contrast this with *civil* cases, where the judge must instruct the jury to accept as *conclusive* any fact judicially noticed. FRE 201(f), 1st sent.)

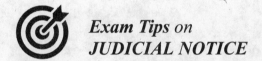

Exam Tips *on* JUDICIAL NOTICE

Questions on judicial notice are more common than you might expect, especially on multiple-choice exams (since the issue is very testable).

☛ A fact may be judicially noticed — so that proof of it isn't required — if either:

❑ It's *generally known* in the community. (*Example:* D is criminally charged with transporting toxic waste across state lines, by transporting waste from Detroit to Chicago without a license. If it's generally known in the community that Detroit and Chicago are in different states, then this fact may be judicially noticed.) *or*

❑ It's capable of *immediate and accurate verification* by use of easily-available sources that are *indisputably accurate*. Information that can be found in encyclopedias, almanacs, atlases, and the like typically qualify. (*Example:* W says that a certain event happened "on Father's Day of 2010." If a calendar would show that in 2010, Father's Day fell on June 17, the judge may take judicial notice of this fact.)

☛ Pay attention to the *procedural issues* surrounding judicial notice. In particular, watch for how the jury is instructed:

☞ In *civil* cases, the jury should be instructed that they *must accept as conclusive* any fact of which the judge has taken judicial notice. FRE 201(g)

☞ But in *criminal* cases, the judge must instruct the jury that it *may* — but is *not required to* — accept as conclusive any fact judicially noticed.

Also, keep in mind that the judge *must* take judicial notice of any fact that meets the requirements, if requested by a party and supplied with the required information. (Also, the judge *may* take judicial notice on her *own*, without a request from a litigant.) FRE 201(c) & (d).

MULTISTATE-STYLE EXAM QUESTIONS

Here are 30 multiple-choice questions, in a Multistate-Bar-Exam style. These questions are taken from *"The Finz Multistate Method,"* a compendium of 1100 questions in six of the Multistate subjects (*Contracts, Torts, Property, Evidence, Criminal Law* and *Constitutional Law*) written by the late Professor Steven Finz and published by Wolters Kluwer. To learn more about this book and other study aids, go to **www.WKLegaledu.com.**

1. Finney operated a chain of fast food restaurants which specialized in fried fish. Finney entered into a valid written contract with C-Foods, for the purchase of "six thousand pounds of frozen pinktail fish filets of frying quality," to be delivered by C-Foods over a period of six months. One week after C-Foods made its first delivery pursuant to the contract, however, Finney notified C-Foods that the product delivered was unacceptable because the filets delivered weighed only eight ounces each, and that they were cut from Grade B pinktail fish. Finney offered to return the unused portion of the delivery, and refused to make payment.

C-Foods subsequently brought an action against Finney for breach of contract. At the trial of that action C-Foods offered the testimony of Cooke. Cooke testified that he was the head chef at a leading hotel, and that he had been employed as a chef in fine restaurants for more than thirty years. He testified further that in that time he had purchased large quantities of fish on numerous occasions, and was familiar with the terminology used in the wholesale fish industry. Cooke stated that when the phrase "pinktail fish filets of frying quality" is used in the wholesale fish business, it means boneless pieces from six to nine ounces in weight and cut from Grade A or B pinktail fish. Upon proper objection by Finney's attorney, Cooke's testimony as to the meaning of the phrase should be

(A) admitted as evidence of trade terminology.

(B) admitted only if Cooke qualifies as an expert on the preparation of fried fish in fast food restaurants.

(C) excluded since it is an opinion.

(D) excluded unless the parties specifically agreed to be bound by the terminology of the wholesale fish industry.

Questions 2-3 are based on the following fact situation.

Dr. Withey was hired by the defense to examine the plaintiff in a tort case. At trial, Dr. Withey stated that during the course of the examination the plaintiff said, "My arm hurts so much, I don't see how I'll ever be able to go back to work."

2. Which of the following would be the defendant's strongest argument in support of a motion to strike the testimony?

(A) The plaintiff's statement was made in contemplation of litigation.

(B) The doctor was not examining the plaintiff for the purpose of treatment.

(C) The plaintiff's statement was self-serving.

(D) Evidence of the plaintiff's statement is more prejudicial than probative.

3. Dr. Withey then stated that during the course of the examination the plaintiff also said, "When I was struck by the car my right elbow struck the ground so hard that I heard a sound like a gunshot." If the defendant objects to this testimony, the court should

(A) sustain the objection, since the statement is hearsay.

(B) sustain the objection, since the examination was not performed for the purpose of diagnosis or treatment.

(C) overrule the objection, since the statement was part of a pertinent medical history.

(D) overrule the objection, since the statement described a former sense impression.

4. Fritz, a house painter, was charged with stealing three valuable figurines from the home of Valens while painting the interior of that home. At Fritz's trial, Valens testified that he first noticed that the figurines were missing about an hour after Fritz left his home. He stated that he looked Fritz's number up in the telephone book and properly dialed the number listed therein. Over objection by Fritz's attorney, Valens stated that a man answered the phone by saying, "Fritz speaking." Valens stated that he then said, "Fritz, where are the figurines?" and that the person at the other end of the line said, "'I'm sorry. I took them." The objection by Fritz's attorney should be

(A) sustained, unless independent evidence establishes that Fritz was the person to whom Valens was speaking.

(B) sustained, since Valens did not actually see the person to whom he was speaking.

(C) sustained, since the statement is hearsay.

(D) overruled.

5. After his vehicle collided with Pringle's on March 1, Dicton retained Addie, an attorney, to represent him in any possible litigation which might develop. Addie hired Vesto, a private investigator, to interview Pringle regarding the facts of the accident. On March 5, Vesto followed Pringle into a bar, sat next to him, and engaged him in conversation. During the conversation, Pringle described the accident which he had with Dicton, and said, "Just between you and me, I drank a six-pack of beer just before the accident happened. It's a good thing nobody smelled my breath." Eventually Pringle commenced a personal injury action against Dicton. At the trial of

the action, Pringle testified on direct examination that he had been driving at a slow rate of speed when Dicton's vehicle suddenly pulled out a driveway into his path.

On cross-examination, Dicton's attorney asked Pringle whether he had drunk alcohol during the hour prior to the accident. Pringle answered that he had not. Dicton's attorney then asked, "Didn't you tell an investigator from my office that you had consumed an entire six-pack of beer just before the accident?" If Pringle's attorney objects to the question, the court should

(A) sustain the objection, since Pringle's prior statement was not made under oath.

(B) sustain the objection, since it was unethical for Dicton's attorney to make contract with Pringle through an investigator.

(C) sustain the objection, since the statement is hearsay not within any exception to the hearsay rule.

(D) overrule the objection.

6. Postum was crossing the street on foot when she was struck by a Daxco delivery van driven by Currier, a Daxco employee in the process of making a delivery for Daxco. Following the accident, Currier was charged with reckless driving and pleaded not guilty. At the trial on the charge of reckless driving, Currier testified in his own defense. He stated that at the time of the accident, he had taken his eyes off the road to look for the address of the place to which he was supposed to make his delivery, and that as a result he never saw Postum before striking her.

Postum subsequently brought an action against Daxco for personal injuries resulting from Currier's negligence under the theory of respondeat superior. At the trial of *Postum v. Daxco,* Postum proved that Currier remained in Daxco's employ until Currier died from causes not related to the accident. Postum then offered a transcript of Currier's testimony at the reckless driving trial. Upon objection by Daxco's attorney, the transcript should be

(A) admitted under the prior testimony exception to the hearsay rule.

(B) admitted under the past recollection recorded exception to the hearsay rule.

(C) admitted as a vicarious admission under the official written statement exception to the hearsay rule.

(D) excluded as hearsay not within any exception to the hearsay rule.

7. Vason was found dead in his garage, hanging by the neck from a rope tied to a roof beam. His widow Alma brought an action against Vason's psychiatrist Si under the state's wrongful death statute. In her complaint, Alma alleged that Si was negligent in his treatment of Vason, whom he knew or should have known to be suicidal. In his answer, Si denied that he knew Vason to be suicidal, denied that he had treated him negligently, and denied that Vason's death was a suicide. At the trial of the wrongful death action, Nina, a nurse employed by Si, testified that the day before Vason's death, she heard Vason say to Si, "I think suicide is the only way out." Upon objection by Si's counsel, which of the following statements is most correct?

  I. The statement should be admitted for the purpose of establishing that Vason's death was a suicide.

  II. The statement should be admitted for the purpose of establishing that Si knew or should have known that Vason was suicidal.

(A) I only.

(B) II only.

(C) Both I and II.

(D) Neither I nor II.

8. Angel was insured by Innco Insurance Company under a policy which required Innco to pay the total value of any damage to Angel's motorcycle resulting from collision. After Angel's motorcycle was totally destroyed in a highway accident,

Angel submitted a claim to Innco as required by the terms of her policy. Innco offered only two thousand dollars, although Angel claimed that the motorcycle was worth twice that amount. Angel subsequently instituted an action against Innco for benefits under the policy. At the trial of Angel's action against Innco, which of the following is LEAST likely to be admitted as evidence of the motorcycle's value?

(A) Angel's testimony that it was worth four thousand dollars.

(B) Angel's testimony that two days before the accident she had received an offer of four thousand dollars from someone who wanted to purchase the motorcycle.

(C) The testimony of a used-motorcycle dealer who had never seen Angel's motorcycle, but who, after examining a photograph of it, stated that motorcycles like it were regularly bought and sold for prices ranging from three thousand five hundred to four thousand two hundred dollars.

(D) The testimony of an amateur motorcycle collector, who had bought and sold many motorcycles like Angel's, that two days before the accident he had looked at Angel's motorcycle because he was interested in buying it, and that in his opinion the motorcycle had been worth four thousand dollars.

Questions 9-10 are based on the following fact situation.

Lanham was the owner of a three-story professional building. The entire second floor of Lanham's building was rented to Dr. View, an optometrist. Persons visiting the office of Dr. View either rode in an elevator located inside the building or climbed a stairway which was fastened to the outside of the building and which led from the street level to the second floor only. Priller was a patient of Dr. View's. One day upon leaving Dr. View's office and descending the stairway on the outside of the building, Priller fell, sustaining serious injuries. She commenced an action against Lanham, alleging that the stairway was dangerous in that it was too steep, it lacked a handrail, and the stair treads were too narrow. Lanham denied that the stairway was dangerous. In addition, as an affirmative defense, he denied control over the stairway, asserting that it had been leased to Dr. View as part of the second-floor office.

9. At the trial, Priller called Walker, who had been employed by Lanham as building manager at the time of the accident, but who was presently unemployed. Walker testified that two days after the accident Lanham instructed him to install a handrail on the stairway, and to post a sign which read, "CAUTION: Steep and narrow stairway!" Lanham's attorney objected to the testimony and moved that it be stricken. Which of the following would be Priller's most effective argument in response to the objection and in opposition to the motion to strike?

(A) Walker is no longer in Lanham's employ.

(B) The testimony is relevant to establish that the stairway was dangerous.

(C) The testimony is relevant to establish that Lanham was aware that the stairway was dangerous.

(D) The testimony is relevant to establish that Lanham was in control of the stairway.

10. On cross-examination by Lanham's attorney, Walker testified that he had been employed by Lanham as building manager for a period of three years prior to the accident. He stated that the condition of the stairway was substantially the same during that period as it was on the day of Priller's accident, and that although many people used the stairway every day, Walker had never before heard of anyone falling while using it. Priller's attorney objected to this testimony. Should the court sustain Priller's objection?

(A) Yes, since evidence that no accident had occurred in the past is not relevant to the issues on trial.

(B) Yes, unless there is evidence that Walker

would have heard of such accidents had they occurred.

(C) No, if Lanham raised a defense of contributory negligence.

(D) No, since Walker was called as Priller's witness.

11. In an action by Pillow Products against Daphne, Pillow alleged that it had entered into a written contract with Daphne for the purchase of satin material which Pillow intended to use in manufacturing its products, and that Daphne failed to deliver the material as promised. At the trial, Legg testified that he worked in the Pillow Products legal department, and that he had negotiated the contract in question. He stated further that, although the original and all copies of the contract had been destroyed in an office fire, he knew the substance of its contents. When Pillow's attorney began to question Legg about the contents of the contract, Daphne objected. The trial court should

(A) sustain the objection, since Legg's testimony would violate the parol evidence rule.

(B) sustain the objection, since Legg's testimony would violate the best evidence rule.

(C) overrule the objection, since the absence of the original document has been explained.

(D) overrule the objection, since the Statute of Frauds is satisfied by the fact that a written memorandum of agreement was made.

12. Rider, an investigative reporter for the *Daily Globe,* wrote a series of articles exposing corruption in city government. In the articles, he said that "a building permit can be obtained for just about anything in this town if bribes are given to the right city officials." As a result of the series, a grand jury began investigating the allegations of corruption. When Rider was called to testify, however, he refused to divulge the sources of his information, claiming reportorial privilege. Rider was charged with contempt. While his prosecution on that charge was pending, the grand jury

continued with its investigation by causing the city's mayor, Mayo, to be served with a subpoena. When asked whether she knew of any city official accepting bribes for the issuance of building permits Mayo refused to answer, invoking her Fifth Amendment privilege against self-incrimination. After being granted use immunity, however, she testified that Coisms, the city's building commissioner, regularly accepted bribes for the issuance of permits, and that Coisms regularly shared the bribe money with Mayo. After Mayo's testimony, both Mayo and Coisms were indicted by the grand jury on charges of bribery. Because there was no other evidence against Mayo, prior to the trial, the prosecutor agreed to accept a plea to a lesser offense from Coisms if he would testify against Mayo. At Mayo's trial, if Mayo objects to the testimony of Coisms, the objection should be

(A) sustained, if the prosecutor had no evidence against Coisms other than Mayo's testimony.

(B) sustained, since a prosecutor may not bargain away the rights of one co-defendant in a deal with another.

(C) overruled, because the proceeding was instituted as a result of the statements made in the articles by Rider, not as a result of the testimony of Mayo at the grand jury hearing.

(D) overruled, if the testimony of Coisms was voluntary and not the result of coercion.

13. Pelton sued Transport Inc. for damage which resulted from a collision between Pelton's motorcycle and one of Transport's trucks. After receiving the summons, Thomas, the president and sole stockholder of Transport Inc., notified Lottie, the company attorney. Lottie said that she wanted to meet with Thomas and the driver of the truck. At Lottie's request, Thomas went to Lottie's office with Darla, who had been driving the truck at the time of the accident. While discussing the case with Lottie in the presence of Darla, Thomas said that on the day before the accident he was aware that the truck's brakes were not working properly, but that because of a heavy work load he postponed making the necessary repairs.

At the trial of Pelton's suit against Transport, Pelton attempted to have Darla testify to the statement which Thomas made to Lottie about the brakes. Transport's attorney objected on the ground of the attorney-client privilege. Should Darla be permitted to testify to Thomas's statement?

(A) Yes, because the attorney-client privilege does not apply to testimony by one who does not stand in a confidential relationship with the person against whom the evidence is offered.

(B) Yes, because it is presumed that a communication made in the presence of third persons is not confidential

(C) Yes, because communications made by or on behalf of corporations are not privileged.

(D) No.

14. At the trial of an automobile accident case, for the purpose of showing the relationship and directions of the streets involved, the plaintiff offered into evidence a photograph of the intersection where the accident occurred. The plaintiff testified that on the day of the accident the intersection looked exactly as depicted in the photograph, except that on the day of the accident some of the trees on the street had small Christmas ornaments on them. Upon objection, should the photograph be admitted in evidence?

(A) Yes, if the absence of Christmas tree ornaments did not prevent the photograph from being a fair representation of the intersection at the time of the accident.

(B) Yes, but only if the photograph was taken within a reasonable time following the accident.

(C) No, unless the photographer who made the photograph testifies to its authenticity.

(D) No, not under any circumstances.

15. Peterson was sitting in his car at a dead stop waiting for a traffic light to change color, when his

vehicle was struck in the rear by a car operated by Dodge, rendering Peterson unconscious. Police were called to the accident scene and as a result of their investigation Dodge was charged with "operating an unregistered vehicle," a misdemeanor. The following day, Dodge pleaded guilty to the charge and was sentenced to five days in jail.

Peterson subsequently asserted a claim for damages resulting from Dodge's negligence. Because of admissions which were made in the pleadings, a hearing was held on the sole questions of whether Dodge was negligent. At the hearing, a transcript of Dodge's conviction for operating an unregistered vehicle should be

(A) admitted.

(B) excluded, because it is not relevant to the question of negligence.

(C) excluded, because it was not the result of a trial.

(D) excluded, because it is hearsay, not within any exception.

16. A state statute provides that the owner of any motor vehicle operated on the public roads of the state is liable for damage resulting from the negligence of any person driving the vehicle with the owner's permission. Pavlov was injured when a vehicle operated by Dawson struck her while she was walking across the street. At the scene of the accident, Dawson apologized to Pavlov, saying, "I'm sorry. It isn't my car. I didn't know that the brakes were bad." Pavlov subsequently instituted an action against Oster for her damages, asserting that Oster owned the vehicle. She alleged that Oster was negligent in permitting the vehicle to be driven while he knew that the brakes were in need of repair, and that he was vicariously liable under the statute for the negligence of Dawson. Oster denied ownership of the vehicle. At the trial, Pavlov offered testimony by Mecco, a mechanic, that on the day after the accident Oster hired him to completely overhaul the brakes. Upon objection by Oster, the evidence is

(A) admissible, to show that Oster was the owner of the vehicle.

(B) admissible, to show that the brakes were in need of repair on the day of the accident.

(C) inadmissible, because the condition of the vehicle on any day other than that of the accident is irrelevant to show its condition at the time the accident occurred.

(D) inadmissible, under a policy which encourages safety precautions.

17. Keller had been a member of a professional crime organization for twenty years, and had participated in many crimes during that period of time. Because Keller's testimony was crucial to the district attorney's attempt to break the crime organization, he was offered immunity if he would testify against other members of the organization. He did so, and his testimony resulted in several convictions. Keller subsequently wrote and published a book entitled *Contract Killer,* in which he described in detail many of the crimes which he committed, including the shotgun murder of Vicuna. Following the publication of *Contract Killer,* Vicuna's wife commenced an action against Keller for damages resulting from the wrongful death of her husband. At the trial, a police officer who had been called to the scene of Vicuna's shooting testified that just before Vicuna died he heard him say, "I saw Keller pull the trigger on me." If Keller moves to strike the police officer's testimony, his motion should be

(A) granted, since a dying declaration is admissible only in a trial for criminal homicide.

(B) granted, if Keller received transactional immunity.

(C) denied, if Vicuna believed himself to be dying when he made the statement.

(D) denied, if the jurisdiction has a "dead man's statute."

Questions 18-19 are based on the following fact situation.

After the crash of Wing Airlines Flight 123, an

action for wrongful death was brought by the husband of a passenger killed in the crash. During the trial, the plaintiff called Weston, an employee of the State Aviation Agency which investigated the circumstances surrounding the crash.

18. Weston testified that during the course of his investigation he questioned a mechanic named Marshall on the day of the crash. He said that Marshall stated that he and a mechanic named Stevens had been assigned by the Wing Airlines airport supervisor to inspect Flight 123 before take-off, but that they did not inspect the plane as directed. If Weston's testimony is objected to, the judge should rule it admissible

   (A) if Weston testifies that Marshall claimed to be an employee of Wing.

   (B) only if independent evidence indicates that Marshall was employed by Wing at the time the statement was made.

   (C) only if independent evidence indicates that at the time the statement was made, Marshall was authorized to speak for Wing.

   (D) if Marshall is unavailable to testify.

19. Weston also read aloud from an investigation report which quoted an unidentified witness to the crash as stating that she heard an explosion several seconds before she saw the plane burst into flames. He testified that the report from which he was reading was one kept in the regular course of business by the State Aviation Agency, that the entry from which he was reading had been made by another investigator who worked for the Agency, that the investigator who made the entry was sworn to investigate airplane crashes and to keep honest and accurate records of the results of those investigations, and that the investigator who made the entry was now dead. Upon appropriate objection, the evidence should be ruled

   (A) admissible as a business record.

   (B) admissible as an official written statement.

   (C) admissible as past recollection recorded.

   (D) inadmissible as hearsay not within any exception.

Questions 20-21 are based on the following fact situation.

Kane's dog frequently dug holes in the lawn of Kane's neighbor Nixon, who had telephoned Kane to complain in a loud voice on several occasions. One day, after the dog dug up Nixon's prize rosebush, Nixon ran to Kane's house and banged on Kane's front door. When Kane opened the door, Nixon shouted, "You dirty son of a bitch." Kane struck him in the face with his fist, and closed the door. Nixon later sued Kane for battery, and Kane asserted the privilege of self-defense. At the trial Kane offered the testimony of a local shopkeeper who stated that he knew Nixon's reputation in the neighborhood, and that Nixon was known as "a bad actor who will fight at the drop of a hat." He also offered the testimony of the local parish priest who stated that he had known Kane for years, and that everyone in the community thought of him as a peaceable man who would never resort to violence except in self-protection.

20. If Nixon's attorney objects to the testimony of the shopkeeper, the objection should be

   (A) sustained, since evidence of Nixon's character is not relevant to his action for battery.

   (B) sustained, since Nixon is not the defendant.

   (C) overruled, since the testimony is relevant to Kane's assertion of the privilege of self-defense.

   (D) overruled, since Nixon placed his character in issue by bringing the lawsuit.

21. If Nixon's attorney objects to the testimony of the parish priest, the testimony should be

   (A) excluded, if it is offered as circumstantial evidence to prove that Kane did not strike Nixon without justification.

(B) excluded, unless the priest testified that his own opinion of Kane coincided with what the community thought about him.

(C) admitted, because Kane is the defendant.

(D) admitted, for the limited purpose of establishing Kane's state of mind at the time of the occurrence.

22. After receiving a tip, police officers stopped a car being driven by Davidson, and forced him to open the trunk. In it, the officers discovered a canvas bag containing seven pounds of cocaine. They seized the car and the cocaine as evidence, and placed Davidson under arrest. Without advising him of his rights to remain silent and to consult with an attorney, they questioned him about the cocaine. During the questioning, Davidson said, "I don't know anything about it. It isn't even my car."

Davidson was charged with illegal possession of a controlled substance. Subsequently, Davidson's motion to suppress the use of the cocaine as evidence was granted, and the charges against him were dismissed. Davidson thereupon commenced an appropriate proceeding against the police department for recovery of his automobile. On presentation of his direct case, Davidson testified that he owned the seized automobile, but had registered it to a friend for purposes of convenience. On cross-examination, the attorney representing the police department asked, "After your arrest, did you tell the arresting officers that it wasn't your car?"

If Davidson's attorney objects to this question, the objection should be

(A) sustained, because Davidson's interrogation was in violation of his *Miranda* rights.

(B) sustained, because Davidson's motion to suppress was granted.

(C) overruled, because the automobile in which the cocaine was transported is "fruit of the poisonous tree."

(D) overruled, because his denial that he owned the car was a prior inconsistent statement.

23. In the trial of a tort action in a United States District Court, if the substantive law of the state is being applied, which of the following statements is correct regarding confidential communications between psychotherapist and patient?

   I. The United States District Court MUST recognize the psychotherapist-patient privilege if it is recognized by the law of the state.

   II. The United States District Court MAY recognize the psychotherapist-patient privilege even if it is not recognized by the law of the state.

(A) I only.

(B) II only.

(C) I and II.

(D) Neither I nor II.

24. Derringer was charged with violating a federal law which prohibits the unlicensed transportation of specified toxic wastes across a state line. At his trial in a federal district court, the prosecution proved that Derringer had transported certain toxic wastes from Detroit, Michigan to Chicago, Illinois. The prosecuting attorney then moved that the court take judicial notice that it is impossible to travel between those two cities without crossing a state line. Upon proper objection by Derringer's attorney, the prosecution's motion should be

(A) granted, if it is generally known within the territorial jurisdiction of the court that it is impossible to travel from Detroit to Chicago without crossing a state line.

(B) granted, but only if the prosecution presents the court with a reputable map or other reference work indicating that a state line lies between the cities of Detroit and Chicago.

(C) denied, but only if Derringer's attorney demands an offer of proof for the record.

(D) denied, if the fact that Derringer traveled

across a state line concerns an ultimate issue of fact.

25. Draper was charged with the second degree murder of Valle under a statute which defined that crime as "the unlawful killing of a human being with malice aforethought, but without premeditation." Draper's attorney asserted a defense of insanity, and called Draper as a witness in his own behalf. After Draper testified on direct and cross-examination, his attorney called Dr. Wendell to the witness stand. Dr. Wendell stated that he was a psychiatrist, had practiced for thirty years, had treated thousands of patients with illnesses like Draper's, and had testified as an expert in hundreds of criminal homicide trials. He testified, "After listening to Draper's testimony, I am of the opinion that Draper did not have malice aforethought as our law defines it on the day of Valle's death." On cross-examination, Dr. Wendell admitted that he had never spoken to or seen Draper before, and that his opinion was based entirely on his observations of Draper's testimony.

Which of the following would be the prosecuting attorney's most effective argument in support of a motion to exclude Dr. Wendell's statement?

(A) Dr. Wendell's testimony embraces the ultimate issue.

(B) Dr. Wendell's opinions were based entirely upon courtroom observations.

(C) Dr. Wendell had insufficient opportunity to examine Draper.

(D) Whether Draper had "malice aforethought" is a question to be decided by the jury.

26. Dempsey was charged in a state court with third degree arson on the allegation that he set fire to his own house for the purpose of collecting benefits under a fire insurance policy. At his trial, Dempsey called Wrangler as a witness in his favor. On direct examination by Dempsey's attorney, Wrangler testified that at the time of the fire he and Dempsey were together at a baseball game fifty miles away from Dempsey's home.

On rebuttal the prosecuting attorney offered evidence that two years earlier Wrangler was released from custody after serving a five year sentence in a federal prison following his conviction for perjury. If Dempsey's attorney objects to the introduction of this evidence, the objection should be

(A) overruled, but only if Wrangler is given a subsequent opportunity to explain the conviction.

(B) overruled, because perjury is a crime involving dishonesty.

(C) sustained, because the conviction was not more than ten years old.

(D) sustained, unless the prosecuting attorney asked Wrangler on cross-examination whether he had ever been convicted of a crime.

27. At the trial of a personal injury action, Dr. Watson testified that she examined the plaintiff on the day of trial, and that at that time the plaintiff told her that she felt pain in her knee. On cross-examination, the defendant's attorney asked Dr. Watson whether she had ever met the plaintiff before the day of trial. Dr. Watson responded that she had not, and that her sole purpose in examining the plaintiff was to prepare for testifying at the trial. The defendant's attorney then moved to strike that portion of Dr. Watson's testimony which referred to the plaintiff's complaint of pain. In a jurisdiction which applies the common-law rule regarding confidential communications between patient and physician, should the defendant's motion be granted?

(A) Yes, because the examination was solely for the purpose of litigation.

(B) Yes, because the probative value of the statement is outweighed by the possibility of prejudice.

(C) Yes, because statements made to a physician are privileged.

(D) No, because the statement described what

the plaintiff was feeling at the time.

28. During the presentation of plaintiff's direct case in a personal injury action, the plaintiff's attorney called Dr. Wallace to the stand for the purpose of establishing that the plaintiff had sustained an injury to her epiglammis gland.

When the plaintiff's attorney began to question Dr. Wallace about her qualifications, the defendant's attorney conceded on the record and in the presence of the jury that Dr. Wallace was an expert on injuries of the epiglammis gland and objected to any further questions regarding the qualifications of Dr. Wallace. Should the plaintiff's attorney be permitted to continue questioning Dr. Wallace regarding her qualifications?

(A) No, because the qualifications of Dr. Wallace are no longer in issue.

(B) No, if the court is satisfied that Dr. Wallace qualifies as an expert on diseases and injuries of the epiglammis gland.

(C) Yes, because the court must determine for itself whether a witness qualifies as an expert, and cannot allow the matter to be determined by stipulation of the parties.

(D) Yes, because the jury may consider an expert's qualifications in determining her credibility.

Questions 29-30 are based on the following fact situation.

Handel, a federal officer, had been informed that a person arriving from Europe on a particular airline flight would be carrying cocaine in his baggage. Handel went to the airport and stood at the arrival gate with Findo, a dog which had been specially trained to recognize the scent of cocaine. When Dodd walked by carrying his bag, Findo began barking and scratching the floor in front of him with his right paw. Handel stopped Dodd and searched his bag. In it, he found a small brass statue with a false bottom. Upon removing the false bottom, Handel found one ounce of cocaine. Dodd, who was arrested and charged with the illegal importation of a controlled substance, claimed he had purchased the statue as a souvenir and was unaware that there was cocaine hidden it its base.

29. Assume for the purpose of this question only that Dodd's attorney moved for an order excluding the use of the cocaine as evidence at Dodd's trial. At a hearing on that motion, Handel testified that he was an expert dog trainer and handler, that he had personally trained Findo to signal by barking and scratching the floor in front of him with his right paw whenever he sniffed cocaine, that Findo had successfully found and signaled the presence of cocaine on several previous occasions, and that Findo had given the signal when Dodd walked away. If Dodd's attorney moves to exclude Handel's testimony regarding the way Findo acted when Dodd walked by, that testimony should be

(A) excluded, because the sounds and movements made by Findo are hearsay and not within any exception.

(B) excluded, unless Findo is dead or otherwise unavailable.

(C) admitted, but only if Findo's effectiveness is established by an in-court demonstration.

(D) admitted, because a proper foundation has been laid.

30. Assume for the purpose of this question only that at Dodd's trial the prosecution offers to prove that Dodd had been convicted fifteen years earlier of illegally importing cocaine by hiding it in the base of a brass statue. If Dodd's attorney objects, the court should rule that proof of Dodd's prior conviction is

(A) admissible, as evidence of habit.

(B) admissible, because it is evidence of a distinctive method of operation.

(C) inadmissible, because evidence of previous conduct by a defendant may not be used against him.

(D) inadmissible, because the prior conviction occurred more than ten years before the trial.

ANSWERS TO MULTISTATE-STYLE
EXAM QUESTIONS

1. **A**   Under both common law and the UCC, evidence of trade terminology is admissible for the purpose of establishing the meaning of a particular term in a contract between parties in the trade. Since the contract calls for the sale of fish at wholesale, evidence of trade terminology used in the wholesale fish industry is relevant to establish the meaning of the term in question.

Ordinarily, a witness is not permitted to testify to her opinion. A witness who qualifies as an expert in a particular field, however, may be permitted to testify to an opinion regarding her field of expertise. Since Cooke is not offering an opinion regarding the preparation of fried fish in fast food restaurants, he need not qualify as an expert in that particular field. **B** is, therefore, incorrect. **C** is incorrect because an expert may offer an opinion regarding her field of expertise. **D** is incorrect because even if parties have not specifically agreed to be bound by the terminology of a particular industry, that terminology may be relevant in determining the meaning of unexplained terms in a contract so long as both parties are likely to have been aware of the meaning of the trade terminology.

2. **D**   Hearsay is an out of court assertion offered for the purpose of proving the truth of the matter asserted. Thus, if the plaintiff's statement to Dr. Withey is being offered to prove that the plaintiff was experiencing pain in his arm, the statement would be hearsay. An exception to the hearsay rule, however, permits the admission of statements made as part of a medical history given in connection with a medical examination made for the purpose of treatment or diagnosis. Since Dr. Withey's examination was being made for the purpose of diagnosis, the patient's statement should be admissible. Under the FRE, the circumstances surrounding the medical examination in which a patient's statement was made go to the weight rather than to the admissibility of that statement. Thus the fact that the examination was not made for the purpose of treatment or that it was made in contemplation of litigation is not, alone, sufficient to prevent admission unless the prejudicial effect of the statement is likely to outweigh its probative value. While a court might not come to that conclusion, the argument in **D** is the only one listed which could possibly support the motion to strike.

A and **B** are incorrect because, unless the probative value is likely to be outweighed by the prejudicial effect, the fact that the examination was not being made for the purpose of treatment or that it was being made in contemplation of litigation would not be sufficient to result in its exclusion. **C** is incorrect because there is no rule which prevents the admission of self-serving statements.

3. **C**   Under FRE 803(4), statements purporting to describe the way in which a physical condition came about are admissible as part of a medical history if made for the purpose of diagnosis, and if pertinent to diagnosis. "Diagnosis" refers to the nature and origin of an injury. Even though Dr. Withey's examination was performed to enable her to testify, she was attempting to form a diagnosis. Since the sound made by the plaintiff's elbow striking the pavement might be pertinent to a determination of the nature and origin of plaintiff's injury, (i.e., diagnosis) the statement is admissible.

A is incorrect. A statement made as part of a medical history is admissible as an exception to the hearsay rule. **B** is incorrect because even though the examination was performed in contemplation of Dr. Withey's testimony, one of its purposes was to allow Dr. Withey to diagnose (i.e., determine the nature of) the plaintiff's injury. Although a witness might be permitted to testify to his own former sense impression, there is no exception to the hearsay rule for a witness's repetition of a declarant's former sense impression. **D** is, therefore, incorrect.

4. **D** Under the FRE, voice identification can be made by a witness who testifies that he properly dialed a number listed in the telephone book, and that circumstances including self-identification show that the person listed was the one who answered.

    A and **B** are, therefore, incorrect. Since Fritz's statement is contrary to his interests, it is an admission, which is not hearsay under the FRE and is admissible as an exception to the hearsay rule under common law. **C** is, therefore, incorrect.

5. **D** Since a person who makes statements which contradict each other might not be worthy of belief, a witness may be impeached on cross-examination by inquiry regarding prior inconsistent statements. See FRE 613.

    A is, therefore, incorrect. Although it may be unethical for an attorney to make contact directly with an adversary known to be represented by counsel, information obtained by such a contact is not necessarily inadmissible. In any event, **B** is incorrect because there is no reason to believe that Pringle was represented by counsel at the time of his conversation with Vesto, or, if he was, that Addie knew him to be. A statement of a party offered against that party is admissible as an admission. Under the FRE, an admission is not hearsay. (Under the common law, an admission is an exception to the hearsay rule.) **C** is, therefore, incorrect.

6. **C** Since an employer is vicariously liable for the negligence of an employee committed within the scope of employment, statements tending to establish that the accident resulted from Currier's negligence are relevant in Postum's action against Daxco. The evidence should, thus, be admitted unless excluded under the hearsay rule. Hearsay is an out of court statement offered to prove the truth of the matter asserted. These facts raise what is sometimes called a multiple level hearsay problem (i.e., a problem involving an out of court statement which contains another out of court statement). This is so because Currier's testimony at the reckless driving trial was not made during the negligence trial and so is an "out of court" statement, and because the evidence of his statement is contained in a transcript which was also not made as part of the negligence trial and so is an "out of court" statement. In order for multiple level hearsay (i.e., the transcript containing Currier's statement) to be admissible each level must be separately admissible. The first level of hearsay is the testimony by Currier at the reckless driving trial. Under the common law, statements by an employee are admissible against the employer only if the employee had the authority to make them. But FRE 801(d)(2)(D) requires only that the employee's statement concerned a matter within the scope of his employment, and was made while the employment relationship existed. Currier's statement is therefore a vicarious admission which is an exception to the hearsay rule at common law, and is not hearsay at all under the FRE. The second level of hearsay is the

transcript. Since it was made by a public official (the reporter), regarding matters in his own knowledge (that Currier made the admission), in the course of his public duties and at the time the matter recorded (Currier's statement) occurred, the transcript qualifies as an official written statement. **C** is, therefore, correct.

Under FRE 804(b)(1)(B), prior testimony is admissible as an exception to the hearsay rule only if the party against whom it is offered had an incentive and an opportunity to cross-examine when the testimony was first given. Since Doxco was not a party to the proceeding at which Currier's testimony was given, the testimony does not qualify for admission under this exception. **A** is, therefore, incorrect. The past recollection recorded exception requires that the record was made from the recorder's own knowledge and requires the recorder to authenticate the record in court. **B** is incorrect because Currier's statement was not authenticated or recorded by Currier. **D** is incorrect for the reasons stated above.

7. **C** Under FRE 803(3), statements of a declarant's then-existing state of mind are admissible as an exception to the hearsay rule. Since it is likely that a suicidal state of mind such as that indicated by Vason's statement to Si would continue until the following day, and since it is likely that a person with that state of mind would commit suicide, the fact that Vason was of a suicidal state of mind on the day before his death is relevant to the question of whether his death was a suicide. **I** is, therefore a correct statement. Hearsay is an out-of-court statement offered to prove the truth of the matter asserted in that statement. If Vason's statement to Si is offered for the purpose of establishing that Si knew or should have known that Vason was suicidal, it is not hearsay, since it is not offered to prove the truth of the matter asserted (i.e., that suicide is the only way out). **II** is, therefore, a correct statement.

8. **B** Since a statement as to the value of a chattel is a statement of opinion, and since lay opinions are not usually admissible, some qualification is necessary to demonstrate the competence of a person stating an opinion regarding the value of a chattel. Since an unaccepted offer to purchase a chattel suggests the offeror's opinion as to its value, an unaccepted offer to purchase is not usually admissible to establish the value of the subject chattel because the offeror is not necessarily an expert in the value of such chattels, and because even if the expert were an expert, his out of court statement as to its value would be hearsay. For this reason, evidence of an offer to purchase the motorcycle is probably inadmissible, and **B** is the correct answer.

In the belief that the owner of a chattel has some special knowledge about his property, courts usually allow a chattel's owner to give an opinion regarding its value. **A** is, therefore, likely to be admitted. In **C,** the motorcycle dealer would probably qualify as an expert on the value of motorcycles. An expert may testify to an opinion in response to a hypothetical question, even though he has no personal knowledge of the facts in a particular case. Thus, if the photograph can be shown to be a fair and accurate representation of the motorcycle immediately prior to the accident, the motorcycle dealer's opinion of its value may be admissible. **D** would be admissible since an expert's qualifications may be based on experience with the matter in issue, and the amateur motorcycle collector's previous purchases and sales might qualify him as such.

9. **D** Although evidence of subsequent repairs is inadmissible to establish that a condition

was dangerous or that the defendant was negligent, it may be admitted if relevant to some other issue. Since it is not likely that Lanham would have taken the action indicated if he were not in control of the stairway, the evidence may be admitted for the purpose of establishing control.

A is incorrect because it suggests that some rule of privilege prevents testimony by the defendant's employee, when no such rule exists. The admissibility of Walker's testimony does not, therefore, depend on his employment status. **B** and **C** are incorrect because of the rule of policy which prohibits evidence of subsequent repairs to establish fault.

10.   **B**   Testimony that a witness never heard of similar accidents in the past may be admitted as circumstantial evidence that the condition was not dangerous if a proper foundation is laid. This requires showing that the condition was substantially the same on the day of plaintiff's accident as it was during the period described by defendant, that there was sufficient traffic over the condition and sufficient time to provide an opportunity for such accidents to have occurred, and that the witness was likely to have heard of such accidents had they occurred. Since Walker testified that the stairs were in substantially the same condition throughout the period described, that many people used them every day for three years, and that he never heard of such an accident, the only element of the necessary foundation which is lacking is evidence that he probably would have heard of such an accident if it had occurred. His testimony is thus admissible if this can be shown, but is not admissible otherwise. **B** is, therefore, correct.

A is incorrect because the fact would tend to establish that the condition was not a dangerous one. Evidence of the non-occurrence of similar accidents in the past might tend to prove that the plaintiff did not use the care exercised by ordinary persons in encountering the situation. **C** is incorrect, however, because without evidence that Walker would have heard of such accidents had they occurred, the assertion of contributory negligence is not, alone, sufficient to make Walker's statement probative. **D** is incorrect because there is no rule which prevents a party from objecting to improper testimony elicited by cross-examination of its own witness.

11.   **C**   Under the best evidence rule, where the terms of a writing are in issue, the writing itself must be offered into evidence unless the writing is shown to be unavailable. FRE 1002. However, this rule does not apply if "all the originals are lost or destroyed, and not by the proponent acting in bad faith." FRE 1004(a). Since the original and all copies of the contract were destroyed in a fire, oral testimony as to its contents is admissible.

The parol evidence rule prohibits oral testimony of prior or contemporaneous agreements to alter the terms of a contract intended to be a complete integration of the parties, but does not prevent oral testimony regarding the contents of a written agreement. **A** is, therefore, incorrect. **B** is incorrect because the writing has been shown to be unavailable. The Statute of Frauds provides that certain contracts are unenforceable unless in writing, but does not relate to the evidence used to establish the existence of a contract. **D** is, therefore, incorrect.

12.   **A**   Although use immunity does not prevent prosecution relating to the transaction which was the subject of the testimony for which the immunity was granted, it does prevent

the subsequent use of that testimony *or its fruits. The "fruits" include all evidence gained as a direct or indirect result of the testimony.* If the prosecutor had no evidence against Cooms other than Mayo's testimony, then Cooms' testimony was one of the "fruits" of Mayo's, and should be excluded.

B is incorrect because it is based on a distorted view of the facts. By making a deal for the testimony of Cooms, the prosecutor has not bargained away any "rights" of Mayo. **C** is incorrect because the articles by Rider did not identify Cooms. Cooms's evidence must, therefore, be seen as one of the fruits of Mayo's testimony. **D** is incorrect because the use immunity granted Mayo makes Cooms' testimony inadmissible. The fact that it was given voluntarily and without coercion is not, alone, enough to make it admissible.

13. **D** A client is privileged to prevent another from disclosing the contents of a confidential communication with his attorney. Although the presence of third persons usually results in a finding that the communication was not intended to be confidential, this is not so if the presence of those persons was essential to the communications with the attorney. Darla's presence does not have that effect, since, as the driver of the truck, she was essential to the conference between Thomas and Lottie.

A is incorrect since, if the communication was confidential, the client's privilege applies to any attempt to disclose it. **B** is incorrect because Darla's presence was essential to the purpose of the conference. **C** is incorrect because corporations are entitled to the privilege, which clearly applies to communications between lawyers and high-ranking officers of the corporation.

14. **A** If relevant, a photograph or pictorial representation is admissible if a witness identifies it as a fair and accurate representation of what it purports to be. Since the directions and relationship of the streets which were the scene of an accident are relevant to the way in which the accident occurred, a photograph which fairly and accurately depicts them is admissible. Thus, even though the absence of Christmas tree ornaments in the photograph prevents it from showing all aspects of the accident scene exactly as they appeared on the day of the accident, it is admissible if it fairly and accurately represents the directions and relationship of the streets. Since the plaintiff testified that it does, the photograph should be admitted.

B is incorrect because a photograph which fairly and accurately represents what it purports to represent is admissible without regard to when it was taken. **C** is incorrect because the authentication of a photograph may be made by any competent witness who is familiar with what the photograph purports to represent, and need not be made by the photographer herself. **D** is incorrect for the reasons stated above.

15. **B** Evidence is relevant if it tends to prove or disprove a fact of consequence. Since the hearing is being held on the sole question of whether Dodge was driving negligently, the only facts of consequence relate to that question. Dodge was driving negligently if he was driving in a way in which the reasonable person would not. Since the fact that the vehicle was unregistered is not related to how it was being driven, the conviction for operating an unregistered vehicle is not relevant to the question of negligence.

A is, therefore, incorrect. An admission is a statement made by a party and offered against that party. **C** is incorrect because, if it is relevant, a guilty plea may be admissible as an admission. At common law, admissions fall under an exception to the hearsay rule. Under FRE 801(d)(2), an admission is not hearsay. Either way, **D** is incorrect.

16.   **A**   The law seeks to encourage safety precautions by prohibiting evidence of subsequent remedial measures from being used for the purpose of showing fault. See FRE 407. Such evidence may be admissible for other purposes, however. Here, Oster had denied ownership of the vehicle. Since it is unlikely that anyone other than the owner would arrange to have the brakes overhauled, the testimony of Mecco is relevant to establish Oster's ownership and should, therefore, be admitted.

          B is incorrect because of the above stated rule of policy. **C** is incorrect because the evidence is being used to establish that Oster was the owner of the vehicle, not to establish the condition of the brakes. **D** is incorrect since the evidence is admissible to establish ownership.

17.   **C**   Under FRE 804(b)(2), a statement is admissible as a dying declaration in a civil or homicide case if it was made by a person now unavailable, about the cause of his death, upon personal knowledge, and under a sense of immediately impending death. Since Vicuna is presently unavailable and said that he saw Keller shoot him, his statement is admissible if he made it with a sense of impending death.

          Although the common law made such statements admissible in cases of criminal homicide only, **A** is incorrect because FRE 804(b)(2) extends the exception to civil litigation as well. Transactional immunity prevents criminal prosecution, but does not prevent civil litigation. **B** is, therefore, incorrect. Where it exists, the effect of the "dead man's statute" is to exclude certain evidence, not to make it admissible. **D** is, therefore, incorrect.

18.   **B**   Hearsay is an out of court statement offered to prove the truth of the matter asserted in that statement. An admission is an out of court statement made by a party which is offered against that party. Under the common law, admissions are admissible as exceptions to the hearsay rule. Under FRE 801(d)(2), admissions are admissible because they are not hearsay. If an employee of a party makes a statement which is offered against the employer, the statement may be admissible as a vicarious admission of the employer if it was made while the employment relationship existed and concerned a matter within the scope of the declarant's employment. If Marshall was employed by Wing as a mechanic, his statement that he failed to inspect Flight 123 does concern a matter within the scope of his employment. It would not be admissible as a vicarious admission of Wing, however, unless it can be established that Marshall was so employed. If Marshall made an out of court statement that he was so employed, it would be hearsay if offered to prove his employment by Wing. For this reason, independent evidence of the employment relationship is required.

          A is, therefore, incorrect. Although the common law requires that the declarant be one authorized to speak for the party, **C** is incorrect because the FRE has abolished that requirement. **D** is incorrect because the unavailability of a declarant is not, alone, sufficient to make his out-of-court assertion admissible.

19. **D**   Hearsay is defined as an out-of-court assertion offered for the purpose of proving the truth of the matter asserted in the statement. FRE 801(c). Since there appears to be no reason for offering the statement of the unidentified witness except to prove the truth of the matter which asserts, it is hearsay. A business record may be admitted under an exception to the hearsay rule only if it was made by one who had personal knowledge of the information recorded or received it from an inherently reliable source. Since the investigator did not have personal knowledge and there is no indication that the witness interviewed by the deceased investigator was an inherently reliable source, **A** is incorrect. An official written statement may be admitted as an exception to the hearsay rule only as to information which the public official who recorded it knew of his own knowledge. Since the quote from the unidentified witness concerns information which the investigator did not know of his own knowledge, **B** is incorrect. Past recollection recorded is also admissible only if the record was made from the recorder's own knowledge and if the recorder is present in court to authenticate it. **C** is incorrect for these reasons, and because even if it were admissible, past recollection recorded can be read to the jury but not physically introduced into evidence.

20. **C**   Evidence is relevant if it tends to prove or disprove a fact of consequence. Relevant evidence is ordinarily admissible. Self-defense is a privilege to use force which the reasonable person in Kane's shoes would have considered necessary to prevent an attack upon himself. Evidence of Nixon's reputation for unprovoked violence is relevant because it tends to establish whether the reasonable person in Kane's shoes would have believed himself to be under attack.

       A and **B** are incorrect because the evidence is relevant to the reasonableness of Kane's fear. **D** is incorrect because the plaintiff's character is not related to the essential elements of a battery action.

21. **A**   Character evidence is not ordinarily admissible for the purpose of proving a person's conduct on a particular occasion. Thus, if evidence of Kane's character is offered to prove anything about his conduct on the occasion of the incident in question, it is not admissible.

       B is incorrect because a witness who testifies to a person's reputation is not required to know that person or to have any personal opinion about him. The "mercy" rule which permits a defendant to offer evidence of his own character as circumstantial evidence of his innocence applies only to criminal prosecutions. **C** is, therefore, incorrect. If the evidence were allowed for the purpose stated in **D**, it would be to prove that Kane did not strike Nixon without justification. **D** is, therefore, incorrect for the same reasons that make **A** correct.

22. **D**   The fact that a witness made prior statements which were inconsistent with his testimony indicates that he is not a credible witness, or at least that his testimony is not worthy of belief. Thus, for the purpose of impeachment, a witness may be cross-examined about prior inconsistent statements. Since Davidson's statement to the arresting officers was inconsistent with his statement on the witness stand, he may be cross-examined about it.

       The purpose of the exclusionary rule which prohibits the use of illegally obtained evidence or confessions is to remove police incentive for violating the constitutional rights of suspects. For this reason, statements obtained in violation of a prisoner's *Miranda* rights cannot be used against him in a criminal prosecution. Because use of such statements for impeachment in a civil proceeding is not ordinarily contemplated by the police, prohibiting such use is not likely to affect police conduct. For this reason, it has been held that statements obtained in violation of a prisoner's *Miranda* rights may be used for purposes of impeachment in civil proceedings. **A** is, therefore, incorrect. **B** is incorrect for two reasons: first, Davidson's motion was to suppress the use of the physical evidence, rather than the use of statements made during the interrogation; and, second, even an order suppressing the use of his statements in the criminal prosecution would not prevent their use in this civil proceeding. If statements are obtained from a prisoner in violation of his constitutional rights, the same policy which prohibits their use as evidence prohibits also the use of leads obtained as a result of those statements. This is the "fruit of the poisonous tree" doctrine. Although this doctrine may result in the exclusion of evidence, it never is used to justify the admission of evidence. **C** is, therefore, incorrect.

23. **A**   FRE 501 provides that in the trial of a civil proceeding in which state law provides the rule of decision, the rules of privilege shall be determined in accordance with state law. Thus, if a civil action is being tried in a federal court under the substantive law of a state, the federal court must apply the state law of privilege. If the state law recognizes a psychotherapist-patient privilege, the federal court must recognize it as well. **I** is, therefore, correct. If the state law does not recognize a psychotherapist-patient privilege, the federal law may not. **II** is, therefore, incorrect.

24. **A**   To save time and expense in proving facts which cannot reasonably be disputed, and to avoid the embarrassment which might result from a judicial finding which is contrary to well-known fact, a court may take judicial notice of certain facts without requiring evidence to establish them. Courts will take judicial notice of facts which are either generally known within the territorial jurisdiction of the trial court or capable of accurate and ready determination by resort to sources whose accuracy cannot reasonably be questioned. FRE 201(b). Thus, if it is generally known within the territorial jurisdiction of the court that it is impossible to travel from Detroit to Chicago without crossing a state line, the court may judicially notice that fact, making proof of it unnecessary.

Although the presentation of a map or other reputable reference would permit the court to take judicial notice, **B** is incorrect because this is not the only way; in the case of facts which are generally known, such references are not required. If the fact in question is one which qualifies for judicial notice, the objection of a party or the fact that it bears on an ultimate issue in the case will not prevent the court from judicially noticing it. **C** and **D** are, therefore, incorrect.

25. **D**   It is the jury's job to determine whether the evidence proves facts sufficient to satisfy the requirements of law as charged by the court. Expert opinion may be admitted to *assist* the trier of fact to understand the evidence or to determine a fact in issue, but it may not be stated in a way which would deprive the jury of its power to determine facts. Since the jury must decide whether Draper had malice aforethought, expert testimony regarding Draper's mental capacity would be admissible. Dr. Wendell's statement, however, did not express an opinion regarding Draper's mental condition, but rather his opinion whether Draper had malice aforethought.

Although the common law once prohibited expert testimony which "embraced the ultimate issue," **A** is incorrect because FRE 704(a) (and many states) have eliminated this restriction. The opinions of an expert may be based solely on courtroom observations (or may even be based on assumed facts contained in a hypothetical question). The fact that a testifying psychiatrist has never spoken to the subject or even seen him outside a courtroom may reflect on the weight (i.e., persuasive value) of his testimony, but not on its admissibility. **B** and **C** are, therefore, incorrect.

26. **B**   Under FRE 609(a), conviction for a crime punishable by imprisonment for one year or more or by death is admissible for the purpose of impeaching a witness. If either the conviction or the termination of incarceration occurred within the past ten years, the trial judge has discretion to exclude such a conviction only if it was not for a crime as to which dishonesty was an element that the prosecution was required to prove. Since Wrangler's perjury was punished by five years in prison, since his period of incarceration terminated within the past ten years, and since perjury is a crime defined to include dishonesty, the trial judge is without discretion to exclude evidence of Wrangler's conviction.

Although the common law requires confrontation prior to the use of certain evidence offered for the purpose of impeachment, **A** is incorrect because the FRE completely dispense with that requirement. FRE 609(b) provides that if more than ten years have elapsed since the conviction or termination of incarceration (whichever is *later*), the conviction is inadmissible unless the trial court finds that its probative value substantially outweighs its prejudicial effect. **C** is incorrect because if, as here, fewer than ten years elapsed, the conviction is admissible. Under the FRE, extrinsic evidence of prior inconsistent statements by a witness is admissible for the purpose of impeachment, but only if the witness is given a subsequent opportunity to explain the inconsistency. **D** is incorrect, however, because no such requirement exists regarding the use of convictions.

27. **D**   Under FRE 803(3), an assertion of the declarant's then-existing physical sensation is admissible as an exception to the hearsay rule. The common law makes a distinction which prohibits the admission of such statements if they were made in contemplation of litigation. The FRE does not make such a distinction, however, allowing the circumstances under which the statement was made to go to the weight rather than the admissibility of the evidence.

A and **B** are, therefore, incorrect. Where it is recognized, the physician-patient privilege may prevent the admission of testimony by a doctor regarding confidential communications with the patient over objection by the *patient*. **C** is incorrect because an objection based on the privilege would not be available to anyone but the patient.

28. **D**   Although the court decides whether evidence is admissible and whether a witness is competent to testify, it is for the jury to decide what weight to give testimony which the court has admitted. In doing so, the jury must determine how credible it finds a particular witness to be. If that witness is an expert testifying to her opinions, it would be impossible for the jury to make that determination without knowing the witness's qualifications. The concession by the defendant's attorney is not sufficient, since it is very

likely that the jury will hear contrary opinions given by other experts. To decide which of the experts it believes, the jury must be able to compare their qualifications. For this reason, the details of Dr. Wallace's qualifications remain an issue even though the defendant's attorney concedes that she is sufficiently qualified to testify to her opinions.

A and **B** are, therefore, incorrect. If all parties agree to a fact, a court may accept it as true without requiring further proof. Thus, if all parties agree that a particular witness qualifies as an expert, the court may, on the basis of that stipulation, dispense with the *requirement* of further proof (though it may not prevent the party offering the testimony of that witness from questioning her about her qualifications). **C** is, therefore, incorrect.

29.   **D**   Ordinarily, evidence of the behavior of a trained dog is admissible if a foundation is laid similar to the foundation required for any other kind of scientific evidence. This means that it must be shown that the dog was competent to do the job which it was doing and that its handler was competent to interpret the result. Since Handel was an expert dog trainer and handler, and since Findo successfully detected cocaine on several prior occasions, the proper foundation has been laid, and the evidence is admissible.

Hearsay is an out of court statement offered for the purpose of proving the truth of the matter asserted in that statement. Although our society tends to personify dogs, dogs are not persons and are not capable of making statements. For this reason, the behavior of a dog cannot be hearsay (Since a primary reason for the hearsay rule is that out of court declarants are not subject to cross examination and since a dog could not be cross examined in any event, it would not be logical to apply the hearsay rule to a dog's behavior.) **A** is therefore, incorrect. **B** is incorrect because, since the dog could not testify, its availability is irrelevant to the admissibility of its behavior. Although a court might permit demonstration of a scientific method, there is no requirement that it do so. **C** is, therefore, incorrect.

30.   **B**   In general, evidence of a person's past "crime [or] wrong" is "not admissible to prove a person's character in order to show that on a particular occasion the person acted in accordance with the character." FRE 404(b). Evidence of a crime or bad act is, however, admissible for "another purpose, such as proving ... *absence of mistake, or lack of accident.*" Here, evidence that Dodd previously smuggled cocaine using a brass statue with a false bottom tends to show that this time, it was as part of a standard "M.O.," not by "mistake" or "accident" (as he claims) that he arrived at customs with a brass statue with a false bottom containing cocaine. So **B** is correct.

FRE 406 permits evidence of habit to be used as circumstantial evidence that on a particular occasion the defendant's conduct was consistent with his habit. **A** is incorrect, however, because habit evidence requires a showing that the actor in question consistently acts in a particular way, and one prior experience is not sufficient to establish a habit. Although evidence of a defendant's previous conduct is inadmissible if offered against him for some purposes, it may be admissible if offered against him for others. **C** is thus incorrect because it is overinclusive. Evidence of a prior conviction is not usually admissible for the purpose of impeaching a witness if the conviction occurred more than ten years prior to the trial at which it is offered. **D** is incorrect, however, because Dodd's prior conviction is not being offered to impeach his credibility, but rather to establish a that his claim of ignorance is not true.

TABLE OF CASES

TABLE OF REFERENCES TO THE
FEDERAL RULES OF EVIDENCE

SUBJECT MATTER INDEX